COST ACCOUNTING

COST ACCOUNTING

Accumulation, Analysis, and Use

THIRD EDITION

MAURICE L. HIRSCH, Jr.
Southern Illinois University at Edwardsville

JOSEPH G. LOUDERBACK
Clemson University

COLLEGE DIVISION South-Western Publishing Co.
Cincinnati Ohio

AE64CA

This text was originally developed and produced by PWS-KENT Publishing Company. South-Western will market and sell this and future editions.

Sponsoring Editor: Mark Hubble
Production Editor: Elise S. Kaiser
Marketing Manager: Randy Haubner
Interior/Cover Designer: Julie D. Gecha
Manufacturing Coordinator: Marcia A. Locke
Cover Art: A silkscreen print "Dimensions" by Masaaki Noda. Used with the permission of the artist.

This book is printed on recycled, acid-free paper.

ISBN: 0-538-82174-4
International Student Edition ISBN: 0-534-97251-9

92 93 94 95 96 AB 10 9 8 7 6 5 4 3 2 1
Printed in the United States of America.

Library of Congress Cataloging-in-Publication Data

Hirsch, Maurice L.
Cost accounting : accumulation, analysis, and use / Maurice L. Hirsch, Jr., Joseph G. Louderback.—3rd ed.
p. cm.
Louderback's name appears first on the earlier edition.
Includes bibliographical references and index.
ISBN 0-538-82174-4 (hardcover)
1. Cost accounting. I. Louderback, Joseph G. II. Title.
HF5686.C8L595 1992
657'.42—dc20 91-25626
CIP

Preface

The third edition of *Cost Accounting: Accumulation, Analysis, and Use*, like the first and second, is designed for both one- and two-term courses. We have built on the strengths of the first two editions by introducing new topics and revising the order of the material. The book integrates some of the emerging topics of management and cost accounting with more traditional areas. Quantitative and behavioral material enhance much of the coverage and there is an increased emphasis on analytical thinking and writing throughout.

The material in the book assumes that students have a basic understanding of financial accounting and the journal entry/T-account framework. Students who have had a course in management accounting should be able to go through Chapters 2, 3, and 12 fairly quickly, although these chapters go beyond the typical coverage of basic management accounting courses. A knowledge of statistics is helpful for Chapters 3 and 12, but it is not a prerequisite.

The objectives of this edition are:

1. To present as much relevant material as possible in a clear, concise, interesting, and straightforward fashion. We want students to go well beyond knowing how to apply methods. We aim for students to gain an intuitive understanding of the issues so that they can make rational choices.
2. To introduce students to emerging areas in management and cost accounting. The last few years have seen a renewed interest in updating management and cost accounting practices to reflect changes in the manufacturing and competitive environments. Early on, we introduce topics such as activity-based costing and just-in-time inventory and incorporate them throughout the book.
3. To integrate quantitative techniques and behavioral dimensions where relevant throughout the book. We think that basic tools such as regression analysis and probability estimates should not be tacked on later.
4. To help students improve their analytical thinking and written communication skills through various assignments modeled on real-world

situations. In addition, review problems and many assignments stress the dynamic use of spreadsheet software to aid in analysis.

5. To provide a sequence of chapters that reflects the logical priority of the material. One manifestation of this objective is the early treatment of cost-volume-profit analysis, the analysis of cost behavior, and the distinction of costs used in management decision making from those used in financial accounting product costs. We think these topics should precede product costing for financial accounting because (***a***) they build a foundation upon which to base the remainder of the book and, (***b***) they give students a good perspective of the multiple uses of accounting data.
6. Most importantly, to motivate students to learn and to share our view that cost/management accounting is valuable, interesting, and challenging. With the changes in the marketplace and in the way goods are manufactured, we want to spur students to think about the choices they will make as managers.

NEW FEATURES

The third edition includes these new features:

1. A thorough introduction to and integration of developing areas such as activity-based costing, just-in-time inventory and management philosophy, and relevant nonfinancial information.
2. A new emphasis on analytical thinking and writing through the inclusion of Appendix B, Guidelines to Case and Memorandum Preparation, and specific problems in several chapters where students assume the role of an outside consultant writing to a member of management on various issues. Instructors can bring in outside cases from other sources and Appendix B will help students analyze them.
3. A revision of assignment material to incorporate new issues in management and cost accounting. In addition, spreadsheet templates are provided for several review problems and assignments. Templates are also available for most exhibits within chapters so that instructors can extend chapter examples.
4. A complete rewriting of all chapters, including new chapters and material. Chapter 4, Cost of Products: Two Needs, is a key chapter in this edition. It provides a transition from the introductory chapters to the following chapters that put cost accounting into practice.
5. Chapter 6 includes scrap, spoilage, and waste, rather than separating these topics as they were in the second edition.
6. There are several changes in the order of chapters from the second edition. Chapter 9 on variable costing now follows the chapters on

product costing. In addition, Chapters 10 and 11 on allocations (support departments and joint products) now come together. Finally, Chapter 12 on tactical decision making has been moved to precede Chapters 13 and 14 on capital budgeting. These changes should provide a more logical flow of material presentation.

7. Chapter 15 has been completely rewritten from the perspective of behavioral considerations of cost management rather than a focus only on the behavioral aspects of budgeting. This chapter is the basis for Chapters 16–19, which deal with several aspects of operational control.
8. Chapters 17–22 have been rewritten to reflect changes in the manufacturing and competitive environments. These changes have an impact on operational control, inventory management, and the use of learning curves.
9. We continue to move away from formulas and to stress basic understanding. This approach is evident throughout.

ORGANIZATION

As mentioned above, we have introduced a new chapter (Chapter 4) and have rearranged the order of the other chapters. While we have chosen an order that we think logical, flexibility exists for those who want to use other orders. As with earlier editions, after we introduce a topic (for example, regression) we incorporate it whenever appropriate in the balance of the book. However, an instructor can choose many paths for a one-term course or for two terms. Figure 1 on the next page shows the linking between chapters—information an instructor needs before assigning a subsequent chapter.

A course with a managerial emphasis might include Chapters 1–4, 12, 13, and 15–19. Two-term sequences could include the above chapters as a first term and add Chapters 5–11, 14, and 20–22 in the second term. Another two-course sequence could follow the chapter order of the book. Other one-term choices are available depending on the emphasis and the course level (junior, senior, graduate; first course, second course).

ASSIGNMENTS

We have expanded and improved the depth and breadth of assignments. We have provided a wide range of assignments, from simple and straightforward exercises that concentrate on a single fundamental principle to relatively unstructured cases and questions that require students to think logically and determine which principles are relevant to the analysis of a business problem and the application of specific methods. In addition, we have added several problems where students assume the role of a consultant and analyze situations to

Figure 1 Chapter Sequences

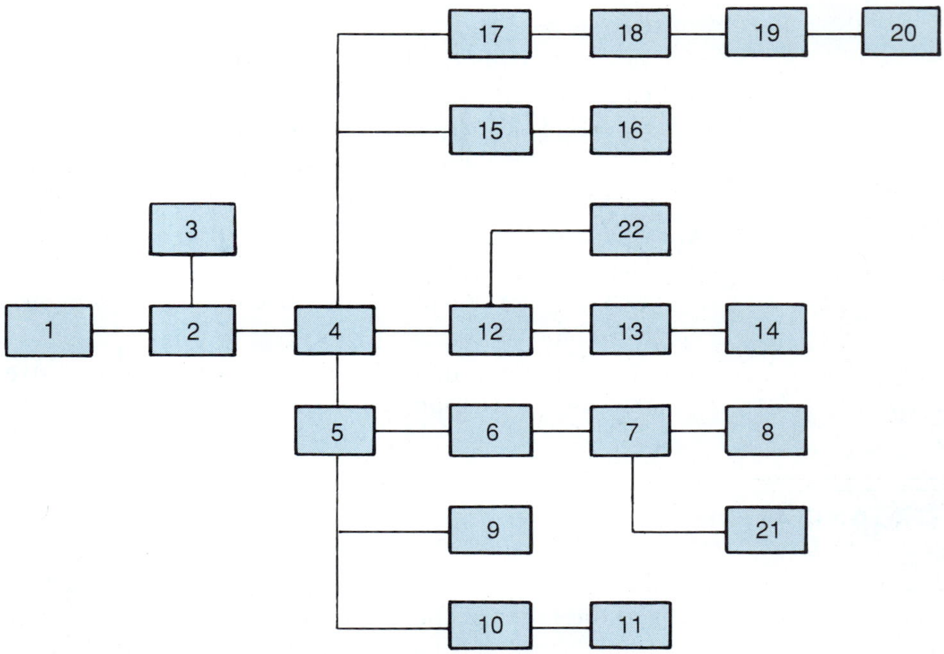

make recommendations to management. These assignments help students to improve their written communication skills and their analytical thinking ability. Our problems include comprehensive reviews of a chapter or sequence of chapters, as well as problems designed to reinforce specific points such as the irrelevance of historical costs to decisions. Many problems are based on material from CPA and CMA examinations.

SUPPLEMENTARY MATERIAL

The *Instructor's Manual* has detailed solutions with calculations to all assignments. Lotus 1-2-3.WK1 files are available for most chapter exhibits and review problems. In addition, many of the problems new to this edition have WK1 files available to adopters. All computer files require an IBM or compatible computer. The *Study Guide* by Donna Ulmer includes tutorial, review, and study aids. *Check Figures* are available in quantity at no charge to adopters. There is also a *Test Bank* available to adopters.

ACKNOWLEDGMENTS

Permission has been received from the Institute of Certified Management Accountants of the National Association of Accountants to use questions and/or unofficial answers from past CMA examinations. We also gratefully acknowledge the kind permission of the American Institute of Certified Public Accountants to use and adapt material from CPA examinations and the kind permission of the Institute of Internal Auditors to use material from CIA examinations.

We wish to thank the reviewers of the first two editions. We also thank the following reviewers for their helpful evaluation, criticism, and suggestions during the development of this edition: David E. Keys, *Northern Illinois University*; Lawrence M. Metzger, *Loyola University of Chicago*; Richard J. Murdoch, *Ohio State University*; and Kenneth P. Sinclair, *Lehigh University*.

Maurice L. Hirsch, Jr.
Joseph G. Louderback

Contents

Part II PRODUCT COSTING 141

Part I

COST ACCOUNTING FOR PLANNING AND DECISION MAKING

1

INTRODUCTION

Business people are awash in information. Recent decades have seen increases in the amount of information available and the rapidity with which it can be communicated. Computers, teleprocessing, and other technological innovations make it possible to develop more information than any manager can possibly use. The problem of information management, then, raises questions about what information to provide to managers. How often should particular kinds of information be given to managers? Which managers should receive which information? Does the form in which information is presented affect its use? How can we tell whether managers use information effectively? What does "using information effectively" mean?

INFORMATION AND ACCOUNTING

Accounting provides information to various users. Investors use financial accounting information to evaluate companies. Should an investor buy stock in a company? What are the expected dividends? How risky is it? Has management dealt with social issues affecting this company? The broad spectrum of information contained in an annual report is the basis for answering questions such as these.

Regulatory agencies also use financial information. Has a company followed Securities Exchange Commission rules for disclosure? Have appropriate Financial Accounting Standards Board and Accounting Principles Board pronouncements been followed?

Local, state, and federal taxing authorities also use information. Tax information often varies from financial accounting information. For example, while management uses straight-line depreciation for annual reports, it might use accelerated depreciation for tax purposes to get deductions earlier.

A third type of accounting information is used for internal auditing. Here, managers are concerned with the safety of the firm's assets and with good controls. For example, a restaurant manager is concerned about cash receipts and wants information that tells whether any employees have been dishonest. We can extend this internal auditing to areas such as inventory, where a manager wants to know how many cases of goods should be in inventory given opening inventory, current purchases, and current sales.

A fourth area of accounting deals with information for managerial decision making. Managers use managerial accounting information to plan and control company operations. Plans include products, prices, budgets, and equipment purchases. Controls include comparing plans with actual results and evaluating divisional or departmental performance.

These four functions are interrelated. The financial, tax, audit, and managerial functions use a common information base and a set of systems to coordinate information flow. Costs and benefits affect the complexity and sophistication of the accounting information system.

Although this book focuses on business firms, many techniques and concepts it discusses apply equally to not-for-profit entities such as governments, universities, churches, charities, and social groups. One important development of recent years is the application of cost accounting concepts and methods to managing nonbusiness entities.

The objectives of this book parallel the uses of management and cost accounting information. You should gain an understanding of the methods used to determine costs for financial reporting and income tax purposes as well as a perception that managers should look beyond these costs when making decisions. Most important, you should develop your analytical thinking and problem-solving skills—learn to think as an accountant. While some of the material is based on rules related to financial accounting, much of it concerns basic logical thinking: what is the problem at hand; what information do you need to address the problem; what solutions do you recommend, and how do you justify these conclusions? Finally, the problems faced by businesses and other economic organizations cannot be set out with their solutions: there are simply too many possible problems to allow a cookbook approach to cost accounting. The ability to use what you know in unfamiliar situations is the hallmark of a successful accountant—as it is for any successful person.

This ability cannot be stressed enough. Perhaps the toughest part of cost accounting is that there are few rules to follow to yield a unique answer. You often have to seek out relevant information and then decide how best to use that information to get your answer.

MANAGEMENT, ACCOUNTING, AND INFORMATION

To highlight the relationships among management, accounting, and information, we shall describe a real situation. The Laclede Electronics case raises questions that we shall consider throughout the book. As you read the case, try to identify the problems the people of Laclede faced and consider actions you might take to solve some of these problems.

Case Study: Laclede Electronics

Nancy Smith was a management consultant specializing in cost accounting systems and information flows. She had an MBA from a large midwestern university, was a CPA, and had extensive experience with computer hardware and software.

A month earlier, Smith had received a call from Bob Carver, vice president of finance for Laclede Electronics. Carver had described the company and had asked for help in setting up a cost accounting system and a system to aid in management decision making.

Laclede was one of two divisions of Montura Company. Its other division was King Manufacturing, which made parts for the automotive industry. Laclede had its headquarters in Kansas City and had three manufacturing plants located in Oklahoma, Arkansas, and Mississippi. Laclede's lines of business included government work (such as telecommunications equipment for military aircraft) and special order products for private industry (including equipment for the various telephone manufacturing companies that emerged after the breakup of AT&T). Laclede also made products for King division that were included in computer-aided monitoring systems for automobiles.

In meetings over the past few days, Carver had explained some of the problems to Smith and had asked her to outline an approach to solving them. Laclede had to account for its government work differently from its private-sector products. Government contracts usually were based on a cost plus formula. For example, if Laclede were building a communications switching system for a naval installation, the allowable costs included the actual materials used (mounting board, wiring, computer chips), the actual labor expended to manufacture and assemble the system, and some other costs that could not be directly associated with the product but were relevant nonetheless. These last costs are called **manufacturing overhead** and include a share of the plant manager's salary, the rent, and the property taxes and insurance on the plant and equipment. Manufacturing overhead also includes a share of costs of departments that support the manufacturing departments, such as security, finance, accounting, and personnel. Finally, overhead includes other costs such as maintenance supplies and labor and some general supplies that are related to production. Even though these costs are not part of the actual materials and labor used to make the assemblies, they rise in proportion to the amount of work in the plant. While the plant manager's salary is unaffected by changes in plant activity, costs such as maintenance change as manufacturing levels change.

Thus, to find the complete cost of an electronic assembly, Laclede's management must keep track of not only the direct material and labor costs, but also manufacturing overhead. For governmental work, these costs are the basis of the price the government pays. Typical contracts called for Laclede's cost plus 15 percent as the price of the job. Auditors from the General Services Administration came in regularly to ascertain whether Laclede's cost system complied with regulations.

The same elements of cost that were important in governmental work were important for private contracts. Estimated costs were used as bases for bidding on jobs. Actual costs associated with a contract end up as cost of goods sold and were compared with planned costs to see how profitable a particular contract had been.

Carver told Smith:

> Our growth has made the present accounting system inadequate. We used to be able to run our operations pretty much by eyeballing things because there was not much competition to worry about and our operations were pretty simple. Now our operations are much more sophisticated and complex. We have new departments for data processing, engineering, materials handling, and other support services. As overhead has risen, we have faced the problem of working it into our pricing as well as closely tracking costs that the government requires.
>
> We need better accounting information for a couple of reasons. First is the need to comply with government requirements as well as financial reporting requirements of the FASB and SEC. Second, and more important, we need better information for planning and controlling operations, evaluating the profitability of our products, and evaluating our managers. For example, firms in Brazil and Germany are actively competing in our markets. We need a better cost system so that we have a better idea of all the costs associated with certain products, product lines, and customers. We are also making some decisions that we never had to before, such as how to meet new concerns about quality and the environment. We are looking at whether we should make some components for our final assemblies or buy them from outside suppliers. We have heard quite a bit about the benefits of reducing our inventories and rearranging our work flows; what are the costs and benefits of these changes?
>
> We are in a changing world, trying to keep up with new technology and competition. We want to make sure that we have good information to see if we are pricing correctly, if we are meeting our cost goals, and whether this division is profitable.
>
> These are the matters that we hope you can help us with, and we do need help.

Laclede and Accounting Information

Laclede's problems are similar to those of most manufacturing companies and also similar in principle to those of service businesses and even to those of not-for-profit entities. Managers need information that yields acceptable financial reports (conforming to generally accepted accounting principles, tax law requirements, and pricing of governmental work) and helps them to plan and control their operations, make sound decisions, evaluate the performance of their subordinates, and, in general, run the business effectively and efficiently.

The remainder of this chapter introduces principles and concepts that we treat thoroughly in the rest of the book. The brief discussions that follow should make you aware of the ways that accountants approach problems and of the tools that accountants use. Again, we do not intend to settle anything in this chapter; we want you to become aware of the types of problems you will encounter in your work and the ways of approaching them.

Managerial Functions and Cost Classifications

Carver's statement to Smith mentioned several functions that managers perform and that, therefore, an accounting system must do to help those managers. You might have noticed that all of the items Carver mentioned have to do with analyzing costs. In fact, those items all indicate a need to determine what costs are relevant for a given purpose.

For instance, Carver mentioned that the company has to decide whether to make or buy components for its products. Clearly, the relative costs of making and buying are relevant to the decision. Yet not all costs are relevant; the salaries of office personnel, property taxes on the factory building, and many other costs can be ignored for that type of decision because they will not change whether a component is made or bought. It should also be clear, in evaluating the performance of, say, a plant manager, that costs incurred by the marketing department are irrelevant because the plant manager has nothing to do with them. These examples are simple cases of an important principle: the relevance of a cost depends on the purpose for which you are analyzing costs. A given cost, say, labor required to assemble a unit, can be relevant for one purpose and irrelevant for another.

The following table lists some managerial/accounting functions, or purposes, along with classifications of costs that are relevant to those functions.

Accounting/Managerial Functions or Purposes	*Relevant Costs*
Product costing	Material, labor, factory overhead; direct costs, indirect costs
Decision making	Differential costs
Planning	Variable costs, fixed costs
Control	Budgeted costs, actual costs
Performance evaluation	Controllable and separable revenues and costs; traceable and common costs

Other distinctions are also important. **Product costs** refer to the manufacturing costs associated with a product. These costs follow the product through the factory and eventually are part of cost of goods sold. Product costs are different than **period costs** such as costs of the marketing department or the salary of the company president. Period costs appear on the income statement as expenses of the period. We stated that differential costs are relevant to decision making. These are costs that will differ among different courses of action. **Sunk costs** are amounts already spent which, therefore, cannot be recovered. Sunk costs are *never* relevant to decisions.

Thus, Laclede's management can classify costs in different ways for different purposes. Different costs are relevant for different purposes.

PLANNING AND CONTROL

Different authors emphasize different aspects of managerial processes and use different terminology to describe managers' functions. Most agree that planning and control are two extremely important functions of managers. Planning involves setting goals and devising ways to meet them. Laclede's managers need to map out, among other things, its growth in profits and cash flow. Control involves determining whether things are going according to plan, and if not, what remedies might be applied. These concerns were reflected in Carver's complaint that information to enable corrective action was lacking.

Consider first the role of Montura's management. Montura has investments in both Laclede and King, and its managers need to know how those investments are working out. How do managers decide if an investment is working out satisfactorily? The answer depends on whether the investment is meeting expectations. (Of course, providing an adequate return is a necessary objective of any investment.)

When the managers of Montura established Laclede, they had some idea of the progress the division should have made by specific dates. For example, they might have believed that Laclede should be showing a profit by its third year of operations or that it should have revenues of $10 million in government work and $18 million in private work by the end of its fifth year. Plans might have included how much of Laclede's productive facilities to devote to making products for Montura's other division, King. Some ways need to be found to see if interdivisional transfers of goods are profitable to Montura. Perhaps management estimated a life cycle for Laclede from its embryonic stage in the late 1970s through an aging stage in the industry in, say, the late 1990s. This means that current objectives are related to where Laclede is in its life cycle.

In short, Montura's managers want to know whether Laclede is performing effectively and efficiently. Effectiveness is measured by whether Laclede is doing what is expected, producing the desired quantities of product, making expected inroads into new business areas, maintaining quality standards, and meeting delivery schedules. Efficiency is measured by the relationships of input to output. Is manufactured output produced at an acceptable cost? The questions of effectiveness and efficiency are separate. Laclede might turn out to be very efficient, but at such low sales volume that the division does not generate an adequate return on invested funds. It might be very effective in producing assemblies, but at so high a cost that new contracts are difficult to acquire.

Laclede's managers have similar considerations. They are concerned with whether their operations are doing as well as can be expected and where improvements might be made. The manager at the plant in Oklahoma wants to know if her costs are in line with costs on similar products at the Arkansas and Mississippi plants. These managers want much more detailed information about their individual areas of responsibility than do the managers at Montura, who are concerned primarily with overall results. For example, the manager of the Mississippi plant wants information about individual components of cost, such as the labor on a particular job, while managers at Montura are concerned less about the details of cost than about the profitability of the division as a whole.

Responsibility Accounting

Since the two operating divisions of Montura, Laclede and King, operate independently, some measures must be derived to ascertain how each is doing. Even within Laclede there is division of responsibility. The three plants have their own managements and need to be evaluated separately.

Responsibility accounting describes the concepts and techniques that underlie reporting on the performance of managers. The responsibility accounting system is based on Montura's and Laclede's organization and on the scope of each manager's responsibility. The responsibility accounting system should provide information about the factors that a manager can control. Managers should not be held responsible for factors beyond their control.

Consider the following example. Suppose management decides to make each plant's manager responsible for profits. Further, assume that a product in the Oklahoma plant needs some components that can be made in the Mississippi plant. If the Oklahoma plant must buy these components from the Mississippi plant, the Oklahoma manager becomes a captive customer of the other plant. If costs for these components go up because of inefficiency, the profits of the Oklahoma manager are adversely affected by factors outside of her control. One approach is to charge the Oklahoma plant the planned costs for the component, the cost that would be incurred if the other plant were to operate at a reasonably high level of efficiency. Another approach is to charge the Oklahoma plant the market price of the component, the price that the manager would have to pay to buy the component from independent manufacturers. We shall see that both of these alternatives have desirable and undesirable features.

The principle of controllability—that managers should be held responsible only for what they can control—is often very difficult to apply in practice. Thus it may be viewed more as an objective or goal of responsibility accounting than as a rule. We shall find that the principles of cost and managerial accounting are not ironclad and that a great deal of judgment and common sense is required. A later section of this chapter considers the problem of accounting and human behavior and offers some reasons for this situation.

Budgeting

Budgets are formal plans that detail a firm's objectives and the means by which to achieve them. The managers of Laclede should prepare budgets indicating their expectations about sales, production, production costs, other costs, and cash flows.

If a company does not have adequate budgets, it becomes impossible to judge whether it is performing according to expectations, since there are no real expectations. Moreover, a lack of formal budgets means that there is little or no control over the activities of the various plants. Is one plant expected to produce at a lower cost than another? Is it better to make certain products at one plant rather than another? Where should new capital equipment be placed? How much inventory should be carried at each plant? These are samples of questions that a budget should address.

There should be a budget for cash requirements—receipts and disbursements. Montura's management has invested cash in assets for Laclede. Expectations should be set at the corporate level about how much cash will be returned to Montura, and when to service outstanding loans and give a return to investors. Firms must carefully budget their cash flows, because running out of cash is a critical event: a firm earning profits but unable to pay its bills may be forced into bankruptcy or at least be seriously embarrassed. Such a firm could find it difficult to raise cash in the future, because banks and other financial institutions would be wary of lending it money. Laclede's managers need to be sensitive about projecting cash needs in periods of growth where disbursements for equipment, labor, material, and other costs may be made before revenues are collected.

Budgets are used to plan and to compare actual performance with plans. At periodic intervals, perhaps monthly or quarterly, managers compare actual results with budgets. Thus, budgeting provides feedback to managers and is also a tool for exercising control.

Analyzing Cost Behavior

Developing budgets requires knowledge of the patterns of behavior of costs—whether costs will change as activity changes or remain the same during wide ranges of activity. Consider Laclede's products. As the quantity of electronic assemblies increases, the costs of materials, labor, and some maintenance as well as some other items should also increase. However, some costs of operating the plant, such as depreciation and the salaries of the plant manager and clerks, probably will remain about the same no matter what the level of production.

Costs that change in response to changes in the level of activity (labor hours or production of finished assemblies, for example) are **variable costs**. Costs that remain about the same during wide ranges of activity are **fixed costs**. Figure 1–1 shows the behavior of both types of costs. The horizontal axis measures the level of activity, which is sometimes called the level of volume. That axis could be measured by sales of products in units, by sales in dollars, or by whatever other activity is important to the firm. Laclede probably would use labor hours or some measure of units of production as the measure of volume for its plants. Different costs might be associated with different measures of activity. For example, freight in may be associated with dollar volume of materials and components purchased, while some supplies and maintenance may be associated with the number of labor hours.

As later chapters show, determining patterns of cost behavior is often difficult. Its importance lies in providing a basis for planning and controlling costs. If the budget for production during one month at the Arkansas plant for a particular assembly is set for 1,000 units with a budgeted cost of $3 million, and if production actually turns out to be 910 units or 1,050 units, the $3 million budgeted cost figure should not be used to determine whether costs were or were not under control. Suppose that the managers of that plant determine that the variable cost of that particular assembly is $2,000, including the cost of materials, the cost of labor, and other costs that vary with the number of units produced. Further, the fixed costs of operating the plant, depreciation, salaries of personnel required whatever the level of production, and so on are budgeted at $1 million. Then, at a volume of 1,000 units, total budgeted costs

FIGURE 1–1 **Fixed and variable costs**

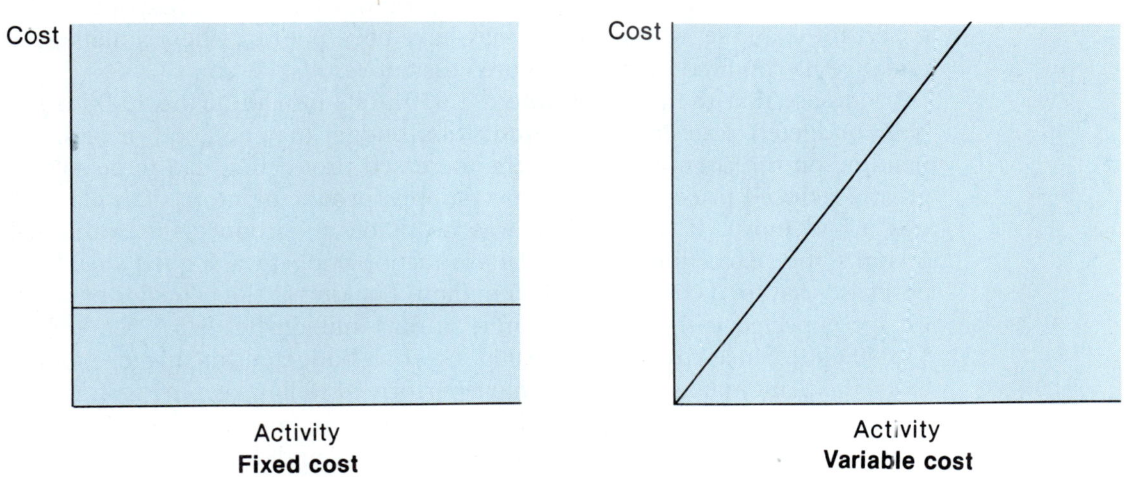

are \$3 million, consisting of \$2 million in variable costs (\$2,000 × 1,000) plus \$1 million of fixed costs.

At volumes other than 1,000 units, however, the managers should not expect costs of \$3 million. At lower levels of production, costs should be less than \$3 million; at higher levels, costs should be higher. The schedule below shows the costs that should be expected at three levels of volume.

	910 Units	*1,000 Units*	*1,050 Units*
Variable costs at \$2,000 per unit	\$1,820,000	\$2,000,000	\$2,100,000
Fixed costs	1,000,000	1,000,000	1,000,000
Total costs budgeted	\$2,820,000	\$3,000,000	\$3,100,000

The three budgeted levels of cost shown above are called **flexible budget allowances** for the production levels. A flexible budget allowance is simply a budgeted cost based on the actual output. The flexible budget allowance for any level of production can be expressed as the sum of fixed and variable costs expected at the level of volume achieved. For Laclede, the flexible budget allowance for any level of production of this assembly in the Arkansas plant can be expressed as the sum of fixed and variable costs expected at the level of volume achieved. In formula form,

$$\text{flexible budget allowance} = \$1{,}000{,}000 + (\$2{,}000 \times Q)$$

where

Q = the number of units produced.

The advantage of using a flexible budget allowance is that it enables the manager to compare actual costs with costs that should be incurred at the actual level of volume, rather than at the originally budgeted level of volume. The difference between a budgeted amount of cost and the actual amount of cost is called a **variance**. Variances are important when we analyze operations to see, for example, where control may have been poor or where a manager's initiative has pointed the way to more efficient results.

Suppose that the plant produced 1,050 units instead of the 1,000 originally budgeted. Exceeding the production budget may be good or bad, depending on the circumstances. If the increased production had to be sold at greatly reduced prices because of oversupply, producing more than planned was a bad move. If, however, it was profitable to produce the additional 50 units, then exceeding the original production budget was a good idea. Suppose also that total costs were \$3.05 million. Looking at the behavior of costs, we see expected costs for 1,050 units of \$3.1 million [(1,050 × \$2,000) + \$1,000,000]. Since costs were \$50,000 less than budgeted for this level of activity, the plant manager seems to have performed well in keeping costs down. Lacking a knowledge of the cost behavior patterns, someone looking at the difference between the actual cost of \$3.05 million and the original budget of \$3 million might have erroneously concluded that something was wrong with the operation.

The classification of costs by behavior is one way in which cost accounting differs from financial accounting. In published income statements, costs that are shown as expenses on the income statement are typically classified by object or function. An **object classification** simply denotes what the cost is for, such as salaries, utilities, depreciation, rent, and property taxes. A **functional classification** relates costs to the functional areas of the business, such as cost of goods sold (production), selling expenses, and general and administrative expenses. The functional classifications include various object classifications; some salaries appear as selling expenses, some as general and administrative expenses; depreciation on factory equipment appears in cost of goods sold, depreciation on office buildings as general and administrative expenses.

In cost accounting, object and functional classifications are usually secondary to other types of classification. Besides a behavioral classification, there are classifications by responsibility (which manager is responsible for controlling the cost) and by relevance to the intended use of the cost data. An example of the latter is in decision making, where some costs may be relevant for particular decisions but irrelevant for others.

TYPES OF MANUFACTURING

While cost and managerial accounting are relevant to all economic entities, the epitome of much of cost accounting is found in manufacturing companies. Manufacturing is now experiencing many exciting developments. Most of this book is devoted to manufacturing. We therefore now describe manufacturing, especially what is called *advanced manufacturing*. Covering manufacturing early will allow us to discuss aspects of new developments as they are relevant throughout the text.

Conventional Manufacturing

Conventional manufacturing has three principal varieties: process, job order, and repetitive (or mass production). **Process manufacturing** is the making of a single, homogeneous product in a more or less continuous process. Process manufacturers make products including foods such as frozen orange juice, flour, and some canned goods. The only difference in the output is the size of the container. Bulk chemicals are another example. Processing operations are usually efficient. The major problems in American industry have been associated with other types of manufacturing.

Job order manufacturing is the antithesis of process manufacturing. In its purest form it describes companies that manufacture to customer order and never make the same product twice. Construction companies are good examples. However, many job order companies make nearly the same products over and over, although each batch is different from the others. For example, printers make books that differ in size of page, number of pages, and number of copies in a press run. The books are similar, but each batch is different.

Repetitive manufacturers are the most common. They make relatively standard products, such as automobiles, and therefore make the same products over and over. However, because they make many products, not just one, they often do not have the smooth flow of a process manufacturing company. For instance, repetitive manufacturers must decide when to manufacture this product or that product, and in what quantities. They must schedule different products for production, not just run the same product constantly. Repetitive manufacturers, like job order manufacturers, also usually manufacture some parts and components as well as assembling them into the finished product.

Problems in Conventional Manufacturing In recent years unprecedented foreign competition has challenged much of American industry. Foreign companies now dominate many industries that American companies traditionally controlled. While there are many reasons for the drastic changes in the fortunes of American manufacturing, virtually all observers point to the strides that foreign companies have made in advanced manufacturing techniques as one reason. American manufacturers had things their own way for years after World War II. They dominated world markets and were able to sell virtually all they could make at reasonable prices. This favorable environment encouraged practices that once seemed reasonable but have come to hurt manufacturing in recent years. Quality was not as important as getting the product out of the factory door; many manufacturers allowed the practice of making extra products, components, and parts "just in case" some were defective, sales were better than expected, or just "not to run out." A result of this practice is high inventories of parts, components, goods in process, and finished product, which are costly to store and finance. To re-work defective products is also expensive.

Also, a tendency has existed to inspect for quality only after the product is finished, or perhaps at a few critical steps along the way. This practice means that much work was done on units that later had to be re-worked or scrapped. Companies incurred significant warranty costs for products that failed after delivery to the customer, an indication of poor quality. Overproduction also led to sales at prices much lower than normal, such as to discount stores and outlets that buy manufacturers' overruns. Such sales can hurt sales at regular prices.

Marketing has dominated manufacturing in some industries, proliferating products with special features. For example, think of the options available in American automobiles. Often, product design occurred without advice from manufacturing, so products became difficult to make. Some sloppiness was considered tolerable because American industry was strong enough to dominate the domestic market as well as many foreign markets.

The proliferation of products led to other troubles for many manufacturers. Multi-product companies must change over from making one product to making another. Such changeovers can be very costly. The cost might be measured by the wages of workers who set up for the change, which can occupy several hours. But the cost could also be much higher—the lost profit from sales that could not be made because production had to shut down during the changeover. One reason for frequent changeovers is rush orders that someone insists must be filled immediately. Interruptions of work disrupt flow, increase costs, and decrease quality.

Two related developments have upset the balance and dominance of American industry. Foreign companies not only have identified significant market niches where American companies were weak (such as small, fuel-efficient cars in the 1970s), but also have adopted up-to-date manufacturing methods. Foreign companies once seemed to target only high-volume products, but more recently they have entered specialty markets as well. As a result, American companies are exploring ways to update manufacturing plants and management philosophies to regain their competitive positions in the global marketplace.

Advanced Manufacturing

New manufacturing techniques are also called *advanced manufacturing technologies*, *the new manufacturing environment*, and *world class manufacturing*. With changes in manufacturing, there are changes in managerial accounting. The Institute of Management Accountants (IMA), the major professional organization of cost and managerial accountants, has sponsored a series of research projects under the name *Bold Step*, designed to explore the implications of new manufacturing methods, techniques, and strategies. *Management Accounting*, the journal of the IMA, and other publications abound with articles by academic and practicing accountants that analyze the effects of new manufacturing techniques and new management philosophies on accounting, suggesting ways that management accounting can help companies using new technologies, and describing specific approaches used by actual companies.

Perhaps the most familiar of the new manufacturing methods is *just-in-time* (JIT). *Flexible manufacturing systems* (FMS) is another, as is *computer-integrated manufacturing* (CIM). All share some characteristics.

One common description of JIT is that it is a philosophy of eliminating waste. Another is that it is a return to the basics of efficiency and quality. Yet another is that it is a "pull" environment dedicated to producing the right component at the right rather than the most convenient time. Specific features of JIT support these and other interpretations. An FMS is a manufacturing system in which managers have reduced changeover costs to nominal amounts and so have made possible rapid changeovers. A high form of its development is sometimes called *unit manufacturing*. Here, a single unit is produced at a time, instead of a batch of units, often to customer order. An important advantage of FMS is that they greatly reduce the response time between receiving and filling a customer's order.

In CIM, computers control most operations. CIM encompasses FMS and is often idealized as the perfect manufacturing environment. Very few true CIM installations are in service. It is not critical that you distinguish among features of JIT, FMS, and CIM. We shall discuss them together, concentrating on JIT because of its more widespread use.

Eliminating Waste JIT is most concerned with eliminating waste in all of its forms: materials, components, labor, and, perhaps most importantly, time. JIT helps develop smooth and rapid flows of products from the delivery of raw materials and purchased components to shipment to the customer. Toyota Motor Company developed JIT after World War II. Because Japan is crowded, the Japanese view waste as nearly criminal. One way to look for waste is to determine which manufacturing activities add value to products and which do not. JIT makes an important distinction between value adding and non-value adding activities and their associated costs. Non-value adding activities and costs are waste. For example, moving semi-finished products from one work station to another does not add value. Storing work in process between work stations is also non-value adding. Accordingly, work stations should be adjacent; as much work as possible should be done in a small cluster of machinery and workers to minimize movement of the product. These small clusters are often called *manufacturing cells*.

Manufacturing Cells Besides requiring less movement of product, JIT operations use less space than conventional operations because they do not need storage space for inventories or wide aisles for material-moving equipment. Figure 1–2 illustrates material and product flows in both a conventional operation and a JIT environment. The idea behind the conventional layout is to do all of the same kinds of work together, so that similar machines are placed together. In a manufacturing cell structure, the idea is to do as much work as possible on the products in as small a space as possible, so all of the machines needed for a particular product are together.

The cell structure requires that workers master several skills. They cannot learn only one machine or task as they often do in traditional manufacturing processes. In fact, in some JIT companies (for example, Harley Davidson, the motorcycle manufacturer), workers receive raises *only* by mastering new jobs. A sense of teamwork develops rather than a concentration on a single job or function. Flexibility is critical: workers must be able to shift from one kind of task (such as running a particular machine) to another and from making one product to another. JIT gives workers much more responsibility than they had under conventional manufacturing. This increase has resulted in higher morale and productivity. Workers are extremely important in JIT, working relatively independently and without close supervision. They have an important say in manufacturing methods and techniques. Managers listen to their suggestions.

Because workers also constantly inspect their work for quality, defective units rarely go beyond the point where they were spoiled, thus saving costs. All work done on a defective unit is wasted, as is the cost of re-working a unit if it is identified as defective before it is shipped. But perhaps most important is the cost of a unit failing after it reaches the customer. Warranty costs are one component, but the ill will created because of the failed product probably dwarfs all other costs. Think of people who will never buy a particular make of automobile because they once bought a lemon.

FIGURE 1–2 Material and Product Flows

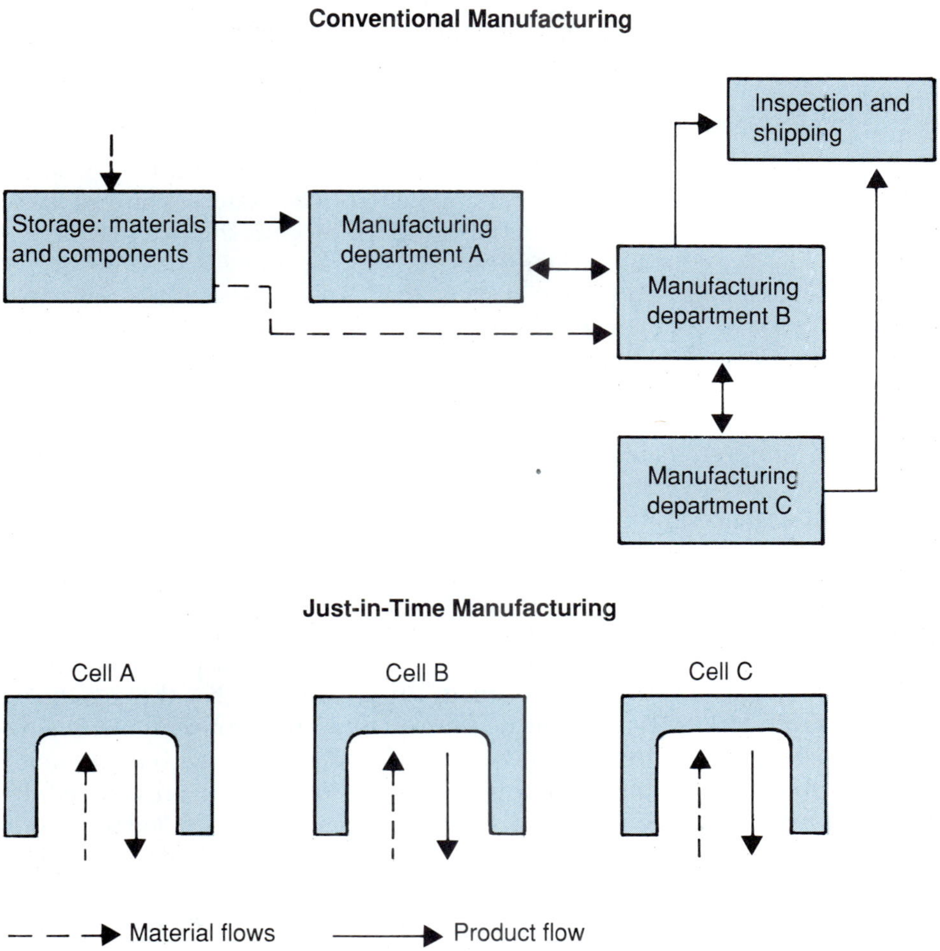

Reducing Lead Time **Lead time** or **cycle time** is the time it takes to make a product—from the arrival of raw materials and purchased components in the factory to shipping the finished unit to the customer. JIT operations continually try to reduce lead time. In conventional factories, lead time can be very long, as much as three to six months, even though the actual manufacturing time for a product might be a few days or less. Time is wasted because companies stock materials and components, make large batches of product, and interrupt production for rush orders. Thus, a component might sit in inventory for a month or more, then be used to make a product that sits in inventory for a month or so as it is worked on, then sits in finished goods inventory until it is shipped to a customer. The component could easily be around for several months, generating costs of insurance, storage, personal property taxes, the risk of theft or deterioration, and the cost of the money tied up.

JIT operations strive to make lead time and manufacturing time the same so that no time is wasted while the product is in the plant. This ideal is, of course, virtually impossible to achieve, but it serves as a goal against which to measure progress.[1] For example, in some JIT companies, suppliers' trucks drive into the plant and straight to the cell that needs the materials and components. These companies have no loading docks, just doors for the trucks to enter. Deliveries might arrive several times a day. The materials and components are processed immediately, and the finished product shipped that day or the next. This is no fantasy. Allen-Bradley works this way in one of its factories. The operation can take an order one day, produce any number of units (up to capacity) that same day, and ship the order the following day. The factory has some material on hand at the end of each day, but no finished or unfinished units; all product started is finished and shipped.[2]

Among the benefits of reducing lead time are greater customer satisfaction (have you ever waited two months for something you ordered?), lower costs (no storage space for inventory, no warehouses), and better matching of demand to production (no need to make large quantities of product to make sure you are well stocked; wait for an order before you make a unit).

Pull Versus Push JIT is often referred to as a "pull" operation, because the demand for products and components is pulled along rather than pushed. Loosely speaking, this means that as an order for a unit of product arrives, production begins on the components of the product so that those components wind up where they are needed just-in-time. In a conventional plant, problems with quality, interruptions, and other difficulties encourage managers to produce more components and finished products than are ordered. If there is a need for 20 components, a manager might order 25 "just-in-case" something goes wrong. This response makes perfect sense if quality is suspect and defects are discovered only at the end of the process. However, such a system causes high inventories and associated costs of storage, return on investment, spoilage, and handling. It also contributes to an attitude where waste, scrap, and reworking of defectives are thought to be normal, which does not encourage high quality.

One reason for long lead times is long changeover or set up times. High set up times encourage long production runs that are difficult to interrupt to make a few units of a previously underproduced product. Overruns are then sensible just in case some are defective or if demand is higher than expected.

---

[1] An indication of the importance of reducing cycle time and improving quality is that John F. Akers, Chairman of the Board of IBM, discussed both in his report to the 1989 annual meeting. Since the chairman's discussion is usually very general, including these matters indicates their high priority at IBM.

[2] Robert A. Howell and Stephen R. Soucy, "Cost Accounting in the New Manufacturing Environment," *Management Accounting*, August 1987, p. 45.

Overruns either pile up in inventory or are sold at reduced prices. Low-price clothing stores often state that they buy overruns. JIT operations do not permit such overruns; thus, it is important to reduce set up times, even to zero, which some companies have approached. Because set up time is non-value adding, it should always be a target for reduction.

FMS are also pull environments. The goal of FMS is to respond quickly to orders—to be flexible. If response time is short, there is no need to stock inventories of finished product. FMS are organized to reduce set up time so that manufacturers can respond more quickly to customer orders or market demand. In a mature FMS, production is by units, not by batches. Some apparel plants can make and ship an order of 10 pairs of Bermuda shorts of various sizes, colors, and patterns within 24 hours of receiving the order from a customer. FMS are partly a matter of technology, but also require careful adherence to quality control because FMS companies do not make overruns just in case some are defective.

Total Quality Control Advanced manufacturing emphasizes quality control throughout the process, back even to suppliers. Continuous improvement in manufacturing operations is a major goal. Quality is important because a worker who finds a defective component usually has the authority to shut down the entire operation until the cause of the defect is determined and cured. Advanced manufacturers design quality into products instead of simply inspecting them, requiring closer cooperation between design engineers and manufacturing people. Such cooperation was not common until recently. Advanced manufacturers also inspect work throughout the production process, rather than at the end. If a defective unit gets all the way through production, workers have wasted both time and materials. The relationship of quality to eliminating waste (and zero inventory) is that inventory hides defective work. If a company makes large batches of components, the defective component might remain hidden until much later, when it is put into the product. It is then too late to trace the defective part to an operation so that corrective action can be taken. In a JIT operation, a component goes immediately to the next step; defective components are found immediately.

JIT companies not only design quality into products, they also involve their suppliers in increasing quality. Many conventional companies perform costly inspections of shipments from suppliers, often using sophisticated statistical techniques to determine the percentage of defectives. JIT companies simply stop dealing with suppliers whose products are not of uniformly high quality. Once assured that a supplier is reliable, the JIT company stops inspecting its shipments. A side benefit is that JIT companies deal with fewer vendors than do conventional manufacturers, and thus save costs. The fewer vendors a company buys from, the fewer people needed in the purchasing function.

Workers also have much to do with quality. Workers constantly inspect their work and in most JIT operations can shut down an entire operation to correct a defect. The idea is to get it right the first time, not to crank out products with possible defects and inspect them later. The work in a JIT operation is not dull, routinized assembly work.

Benefits of JIT Better products at lower cost are two advantages of JIT. The commitment to quality, an absolute necessity in JIT, leads to products with better customer acceptance. (Why do you think U.S. automakers are continually advertising quality? Because in the late 1970s and early 1980s the Japanese had a corner on quality.) Because lead times are much shorter under JIT, companies get products to market much faster, which also increases sales.

Various costs decline for a number of reasons. The decline in defective products eliminates rework costs; the reduction of inventories eliminates costs such as storage, insurance, and financing. Continuous improvements in operations reduce costs as waste is reduced.

Increased morale of both workers and managers normally increases productivity. Workers and managers have a bigger stake in the company's success. They have more responsibility and more status. Recall that workers must master several skills and that they have the authority to shut down production.

In summary, JIT is characterized by:

1. products designed for manufacturability
2. relatively few, highly reliable vendors
3. relatively stable production
4. short cycle times, with small batches of production, quick set ups, and low set up cost
5. a pull environment, where parts and components are produced when needed, not pushed through and produced as convenient
6. multi-skilled workers who inspect their work and do much of the maintenance
7. a constant striving for improvement and reduction of waste in the form of non-value adding effort and cost
8. extremely low inventories, with no inventory at all as the ultimate objective.

PRODUCT COSTING

Any cost accounting system must provide information about unit costs of products. Inventory on the balance sheet and cost of goods sold on the income statement are affected by the way unit costs are determined. You are already familiar with first-in-first-out, last-in-first-out, and weighted average methods of accounting for inventory. These cost flow assumptions are also used in manufacturing operations. Other questions arise in manufacturing operations; the most fundamental is the costs to be included in determining inventory on the balance sheet. For financial reporting and tax purposes, virtually all manufacturing costs are included, but for some managerial purposes fixed costs of production are excluded from inventory. The financial reporting approach is called **absorption costing** (or sometimes **full costing**), while the other method is called **variable costing** or **direct costing**.

To illustrate, suppose that one of Laclede's plants produced a single product for an entire year with these results.

Units produced	5,000
Fixed production costs	$15,500,000
Variable production costs	$ 9,750,000

The per unit amount of inventory calculated under the two methods is shown below.

$$\text{cost per unit, absorption costing} = \$5{,}050 = \frac{\$15{,}500{,}000 + \$9{,}750{,}000}{5{,}000}$$

$$\text{cost per unit, direct costing} = \$1{,}950 = \frac{\$9{,}750{,}000}{5{,}000}$$

The $5,050 figure is used for financial reporting and tax accounting, and the $1,950 is used for some managerial purposes, especially decision making. In addition, for some decisions managers will include other, non-manufacturing variable costs, such as sales commissions. For other decisions they will include some fixed costs. The reasoning behind these different approaches will be discussed and illustrated in later chapters.

Other questions remain. We know that there are service departments at Laclede for data processing and personnel. In addition, if the plants also contain sales offices, then utilities, depreciation, and property taxes on the building relate to both production and selling. Determining how much of these costs to treat as manufacturing costs, and therefore as part of the cost of inventory, and how much to treat as selling expenses is not easy.

The same problem exists with services such as the computer department. This is a joint cost for the benefit of the central administration, the sales department, and the various plant departments. Government auditors are interested in how these costs are allocated between government and private business. Managers who are evaluated on profits or on costs are interested in how these costs are allocated to their operations.

DECISION MAKING

Making a decision means choosing one course of action from the available alternatives. Laclede's management made decisions about where to locate plants and what equipment to install in them. All decisions are future oriented. For this reason, a manager needs information about the future. In the strictest sense, however, information about the future cannot be obtained, because the future cannot be known with certainty. Therefore, all decisions involve some risk. It may turn out that the choice to build facilities for large military orders was a bad one, but no one will know that for some time.

One of the main jobs of the accountant is to develop information for decision making—that is, information about future revenues and costs. In some cases the information can be developed from historical data provided by the accounting system. If the manager of a plant is concerned with the level of future production costs, the accountant may be able to say that costs will be approximately $1 million plus $2,000 per unit produced, as described previously.

This formula for predicting costs is reasonable so long as the manager does not plan any changes in the production process and so long as there are no other changes (such as increases in wage rates) on the horizon.

In other cases the accounting system cannot be relied on to provide good predictions. The manager of the Mississippi plant may be considering a change in the production process and, therefore, has to know the likely effects on costs. The accountant will work with the plant manager and plant engineers to determine the probable effects on such factors as labor time. It might be that changing the process will reduce labor time by about 10 percent. The accountant estimates the consequent savings in costs and, together with the other managers, tries to determine whether the proposed change is worthwhile.

Accountants are staff personnel: they do not have the authority to make final decisions on such matters as changing production processes. However, operating managers want accountants not only to provide them with relevant information for a decision at hand, but also to be part of the decision-making process with their analyses and recommendations. Thus, accountants do exercise authority by expertise: their advice is often taken because they are the most knowledgeable managers in their own field. In some situations the accountant may have to expend considerable effort to persuade another manager to take a recommended course of action and may have to educate the other manager in the analysis and interpretation of cost information. We shall see in later chapters that determining what information is relevant for decision making is often a difficult task and that managers sometimes use information inappropriately. The accountant's choice of information, its presentation, and efforts in persuading managers to use information wisely can benefit the firm.

Accumulating relevant data and analysis, and coming to final recommendations involves using various models and techniques. Accountants draw on various models that deal with forecasting, with how to use limited resources most profitably, and with uncertainty. Access to microcomputers has increased our ability to analyze data and to use sophisticated models. Later chapters describe and illustrate the use of computers and statistical and mathematical models.

The increasing importance and status of managerial accountants was documented in an article on 3M. Managers at 3M regard divisional controllers as "business advisors and financial consultants who are part of the operating/decision-making team."[3] This attitude was not prevalent 20 years ago, when controllers and other management accountants were viewed by many operating managers as bean counters who existed only to harass them with trifling reports. A study by *Fortune* magazine found 3M to be the second-most admired corporation in America.

BEHAVIORAL CONSIDERATIONS

An important area of recent research in cost and managerial accounting is human behavior, especially the effects that various accounting techniques and practices can have on the performance of managers. The study of management from a behavioral standpoint is relatively new. Only in the past 20 or so years have management courses emphasized behavioral dimensions. Accountants now know that their work can affect managers' behavior favorably or unfavorably. We glimpsed the problem in the discussion of responsibility accounting, expand on it briefly here, and consider it in greater detail in later chapters.

This chapter has stressed the development of information for various purposes. It is commonly thought that information can be unbiased, neutral, and objective: that properly presented information will lead a manager to take the best action. This is just not so. *People* make decisions, evaluate subordinates, control operations. Quantitative information, which is the stock in trade of accounting, does not capture all the relevant factors and may influence managers to make unwise actions.

Consider this example. Managers are often evaluated on the basis of meeting a budget. A production manager who expects to exceed the flexible budget allowance may be tempted to take unwise actions. The manager could reduce costs, and thereby meet or more closely approach the budget by postponing expenditures for maintenance, employee training, quality control, and other items. Reducing these costs increases profits in the short term but could have serious adverse effects in the longer term.

COST CLASSIFICATIONS

We have seen that different costs are used for different purposes. The fixed versus variable cost distinction is important for planning and budgeting, while for responsibility accounting the critical consideration is whether the cost is

[3] Kathy Williams, "The Magic of 3M, Management Accounting Excellence," *Management Accounting*, February 1986, pp. 20–27.

controllable by a particular manager. Product costing using the absorption costing method requires calculating a fixed cost per unit, while variable costing does not.

In the remainder of the book we shall see that a single cost may be treated in several ways for different purposes: that a cost may be relevant for one purpose, irrelevant for another. Our attention will focus on the purposes for which the information is needed and on the development of information with its intended use in mind.

SUMMARY

Cost accounting information is used for many different purposes, and the type of information required for one use may not be the same as that required for others. The principal purpose of cost accounting is to provide information that managers can use to plan and control their operations, make decisions, and evaluate performance. Another important purpose is to provide information used for product costing for financial reporting and income taxation.

The topics of budgeting, analysis of cost behavior, and development of responsibility accounting systems were introduced, along with the very important topic of the behavioral considerations involved in developing and reporting accounting information.

REVIEW PROBLEM

Suppose that Laclede has just set up a production facility to handle a large order in the telecommunications field. This will be an ongoing product that will last at least two years in its present form. Managers have estimated that administrative costs will be $500,000 per year (central office costs, sales costs, and so on), plant fixed costs will be $2 million per year, and variable costs per unit will be $500.

1. What is the flexible budget for producing 10,000 units?
2. If 9,000 units were produced costing $6,600,000, was this above or below the budget for that amount? How much?
3. What is the absorption cost per unit if production is 10,000 units?
4. What is the direct cost per unit?
5. How are the administrative costs treated in financial statements?

ANSWERS TO REVIEW PROBLEM

1. The flexible budget for 10,000 units is $7,000,000, consisting of $2 million in manufacturing fixed costs and $5 million ($500 × 10,000 units) in variable costs.

2. Expected costs for 9,000 units would be \$6,500,000 (\$2 million fixed costs plus \$500 × 9,000 = \$4.5 million variable costs). Actual costs are \$100,000 over the flexible budget.
3. Absorption cost per unit can be derived from the flexible budget for 10,000 units; \$7 million divided by 10,000 units yields \$700 per unit.
4. Direct costs are the variable costs of \$500 per unit.
5. Note that the \$500,000 in administrative costs was not included in the determining of the production flexible budget or the cost per unit. These costs are period costs, not product costs, and would appear in an income statement in the section below the determination of gross profit.

ASSIGNMENTS

1–1 Relevant Costs Pierre Manufacturing has a single plant. Its managers are currently discussing whether to add additional space to the plant to add a product to their line. Special purpose machinery would have to be purchased to make this new product.

REQUIRED

What are the types of relevant costs that the managers should investigate to see if it is wise to add this new product?

1–2 Fixed and Variable Costs Managers of Halpen Hardware are deciding whether to open their store on Sunday. Current hours of operation are 9:00 A.M. to 9:00 P.M. Monday through Saturday. A recent lifting of restrictions on Sunday sales in the area has made the option of opening Sunday possible. Rent is \$5,000 per month, insurance \$3,000 per year; the store manager earns \$4,000 per month plus a bonus of 1 percent of sales; hourly workers are paid \$5.00 per hour (overtime pay if they work over 40 hours in a week); and utility costs (mostly electricity) are \$600 per month. On average, for every dollar of sales the cost of merchandise is \$0.35. It takes a minimum of four employees to run the store.

REQUIRED

1. How much profit or loss will the company earn if Sunday sales are \$1,000?
2. About how much in sales is necessary to make staying open from 10:00 A.M. to 5:00 P.M. on Sunday profitable?

1–3 Definitions Princess Hospital contracts with Messing Professional Services for doctors and nurses to staff its emergency room. Princess pays Messing \$5,000 per month for each doctor and \$25 per hour for each nurse. Of these fees, Messing keeps 20 percent and pays 80 percent to the doctors and nurses.

REQUIRED

1. What is the total cost to Princess Hospital per 8-hour shift per month if it has one doctor and three nurses for the emergency room?
2. How much will a nurse receive for working a 40-hour week?
3. What is the average cost per week to Princess for adding an additional doctor to the staff?

1–4 Definitions Marian Sun purchased a condominium in 1972 for $50,000. Since then, her family has grown and she is thinking about purchasing a bigger condominium in a different part of town. The price on the new condominium is $250,000, and real estate agents have estimated she will get $100,000 for her current property.

REQUIRED

1. In Sun's decision to buy a new condominium, how will her original purchase price of $50,000 affect the cost of a new place?
2. Ignoring taxes, what is the net amount she will pay for her new purchase?

1–5 Product and Period Costs For each cost below, state whether it is a period cost or a product cost and why.

1. wages paid to factory workers
2. sales manager's salary
3. research and development costs
4. factory maintenance costs
5. material components used in manufacturing
6. factory property taxes
7. depreciation on manufacturing equipment
8. computer costs
9. plant manager's salary
10. electricity for executive offices

1–6 Questions about Accounting The year has just begun, and you have enrolled in a course entitled Cost Accounting. Your roommate, who is not a business school student, asks you the following questions:

1. "Is this cost accounting course like the last accounting course you took? You did all sorts of debits and credits and things like that in the previous course. What makes this course different?"
2. "I was reading over your shoulder while you looked at Chapter 1 and saw something about behavioral considerations in accounting. I thought accounting was just numbers. What is this behavioral stuff, and how does it apply to accounting?"

REQUIRED

Please answer your roommate's questions.

1–7 Some Basic Questions

REQUIRED

Answer the following questions independently.

1. What are some major differences between a service industry (such as a public accounting firm) and a manufacturing industry (such as a manufacturer of automobile tires)? How would these two differ from or resemble a retailing establishment (such as a department store)?

2. What do you think are the differences between the following companies? Apex Ship Building Company manufactures luxury yachts to individual customers' specifications. Each boat is unique in design and finish. Broward Chemical Company, on the other hand, puts a single raw material (a petroleum derivative) through a single, continuous, and complex manufacturing process that, with the addition of certain other chemicals at various stages, yields ten different final products.

1–8 Managerial Information For many years Irving Flycatcher worked as an engineer in the rate department of Northern-Southern Power Company. Early in 19X1, Flycatcher and Sandy Newburglar, an attorney, opened a consulting business specializing in energy and other related matters. The two became partners in a new corporation called Energy Resource Associates.

Both Flycatcher and Newburglar had many talents besides consulting in the energy field. As an attorney, Newburglar wanted to do some regular corporate work for clients. Flycatcher had much experience in areas of accounting and engineering and could consult in those fields.

The usual procedure was that one of the principals in the company would bid a contract to a client for consulting services. Sometimes, when further expertise was needed, the company would hire outside personnel.

The new corporation had only the two principals as shareholders. The only information that needed to be generated external to the firm would be tax returns. Neither partner had experience in setting up an accounting and information system.

REQUIRED

Flycatcher and Newburglar have come to you for aid. First give them a description of the kind of business they are in. Then prepare a general discussion and outline of the type of information you think they will need to manage their new company. Consider what you would want to know if you were a partner in this business. What information would you need for planning and controlling? How would you organize costs?

1–9 Managerial Information On the advice of a friend, Conrad Archer was employed as a management consultant to Henderson Appliances, a retail store dealing in major appliances such as refrigerators, freezers, washers, dryers, and television sets. Roger Henderson, the sole proprietor, was prompted by various suppliers and by his bank to call Archer.

Henderson Appliances had been in business for about two years. Although Roger Henderson was an honest person, several problems had cropped up. Henderson recommended that Archer talk to one of Henderson's major suppliers as well as to his banker before visiting. Archer's interview with a major supplier yielded the following:

> I like Roger, and I think he is in a position to have a successful business. However, I just don't understand how he has stayed in business this long. When we have called him and asked him about paying a bill, he has always come through. However, on a recent personal visit when this issue came up, I found out that the way he generates cash is to sell some merchandise below cost. Thus, if he is buying a group of washing machines from me, he may dispose of some television sets at below what he paid for them.

An interview with Henderson's banker provided similar information:

> We are willing to stand behind Roger, but we are very concerned about his future. It is not uncommon that we have to hold twenty to thirty checks in the bank because there

> are not enough funds in Roger's account. Depending on the pressures Roger receives, he comes in and tells us the priority of paying checks as funds become available. In addition, I am concerned that Roger does not know how to differentiate between the direct costs of merchandise that he buys and the entire cost of doing business and earning a profit.

With this information, Mr. Archer met at some length with Roger Henderson. During the interview Henderson said:

> I know I need help. That is why I called you in. I hope that the information you got from one of my suppliers and my banker has been helpful. I really am confused as to how to run a business. I am not sure what information I need so that I can figure out what prices I should charge, what it costs me to do business, when I should order in new goods, and some way to know if I am making money.

REQUIRED

If you were Archer, what would you identify as the problems that Roger Henderson needs to address? What decisions does Henderson need to make on a daily, monthly, or yearly basis? What kind of information will he need to make these decisions?

1–10 Data and Information Fancy Pharmaceuticals Company produces two major lines, over-the-counter drugs and prescription drugs. The company has divided the production and sale of these two lines into separate divisions. Arthur Abraham, general manager of the prescription drug line, has been talking to one of his salespeople, Alice Carney. Carney discusses a recent contact she had with a customer:

> Arthur, we have a problem that we need to solve. I went into Ajax Drug Stores the other day and talked with Irving Ajax. We were discussing terms for our new contract. He is interested in adding both our prescription and our nonprescription line to his drugstore chain. We spent a long time talking about the FDA and how it defines the difference between prescription and nonprescription drugs. Irving is concerned over the recent trend in Washington to hold back drugs from the market too long. The FDA requires such a long testing program that Irving thinks it does not take care of the public. Of course, there is the other side that the FDA is really protecting the public by this rigorous program.
>
> Irving's credit seems to be very good. I have talked with the nonprescription division, and they are interested in his business. Most of his drugstores are in Peoria, but he has a few in Matoon. The Matoon market is very interesting with the decrease of the central business district and the addition of three new shopping malls on the outskirts of town. As I see it, we need to sign a contract with Ajax covering the next three years for a minimum amount of our full line of prescription drugs. I don't know what kind of arrangements the other division is making with Ajax. I just know it is interested in the account as well. If we don't make a deal now, Ajax may sign up with Trell Chemical instead. What should I do?

REQUIRED

What should Abraham's response be to Carney?

2

COST-VOLUME-PROFIT RELATIONSHIPS AND ANALYSIS

A key way that managers use information is in planning. They need information to answer questions about different courses of action regarding both recurring and nonrecurring problems including, for example, "What will our profits be if we sell 30,000 units? How would profits be affected if we reduced our selling prices and sold more units? Given current market conditions and the price our competitors charge, what must be our cost per unit in order to make a profit of $50,000?" Establishing cost-volume-profit relationships and analyzing these relationships can help managers answer such questions.

Cost-volume-profit analysis (CVP analysis) is a systematic method of examining the relationships among the variables that determine profits: revenues and costs.[1] Since it is a basic model of these relationships, CVP analysis simplifies real-world conditions that a firm faces. Like most models that are abstractions from reality, CVP analysis has a number of underlying assumptions and limitations that we discuss in this chapter. Despite these limitations, it is a powerful tool for managers to make better decisions.

[1] Cost-volume-profit analysis is also called *breakeven analysis*, *profit-volume analysis*, and *volume-cost-profit analysis*. All terms refer to the same relationships and basic techniques.

CVP analysis is the most fundamental tool in the accountant's repertoire because it provides straightforward ways to approach the problems implied by the questions posed in the paragraph above. Virtually all of management accounting depends to some extent on the relationship of costs, volume, and profits; the CVP framework is essential to the understanding of the value and the limitations of the management and cost accounting techniques that we discuss in this book.

In a traditional financial accounting income statement, expenses are categorized by function: cost of sales and sales, general, and administrative expenses, for example. When an income statement is presented in a CVP format for managerial decisions, expenses are classified by whether they go up (down) when volume rises (falls) or they stay the same when volume changes. Thus, rather than being labeled in a classification that relates to generally accepted accounting principles (GAAP), costs are shown based on how they behave relative to changes in volume. This is a major difference between CVP and financial accounting statements; the descriptive nature of CVP relationships helps managers to answer questions such as those in the first paragraph of the chapter, while financial accounting classification does not. We lay the foundation of this idea in this chapter and expand upon it in the next two chapters.

VOLUME AND COST BEHAVIOR

In basic CVP relationships, **volume** refers to some measure of profit-generating activity. Volume can be measured by sales in units, sales dollars, production in units, hours worked by employees, or any other activity that might be important. However, sales either in units or dollars is the most commonly used measure of volume, and we are concerned with these measures here. Other measures of volume will become important in Chapter 3 as we analyze the various ways of dealing with costs. In Chapter 4 we discuss other measures of activity based on events or transactions (such as setting up a machine or shipping an order) rather than on a volume-based measure. The main point of this discussion is to identify an activity that has a causal relationship with a cost or resource. This is a basis of what is now being called **activity-based costs**, but has always been at the heart of CVP analysis.

Our basic assumption is that all costs can be classified by their behavior, whether or not we can expect them to change in total in response to changes in volume. Costs that change with volume are called **variable costs**. Costs that remain constant in total over a fairly wide range of volume are called **fixed costs**. Consider this example:

Quadro Company sells high-quality mechanical pencils for $5 each. It buys them for $2.50 each and pays salespeople a 10 percent commission ($0.50) for each pencil sold. Both of these costs are variable, since each time a pencil is sold, costs increase by $3—a figure that includes the costs of the pencils and the commissions.[2] The firm also incurs about $10,000 per month for salaries, utilities, and rent. These costs will not change in total in response to changes in volume and therefore are fixed. However, when we call a cost fixed, we are not claiming that it cannot be changed. Salaries, for instance, could easily be changed by managerial decision since salaried employees could be hired, fired, or given raises. Thus, the term *fixed* means that a cost will not *automatically* change as volume changes. Finally, notice that variable costs are expressed as per unit amounts while fixed costs are expressed as total amounts per period, such as a month. Variable costs can be traced directly to the purchase and sale of pencils and change as volume changes. The fixed costs are a function of the entire operation and are not attributable to sales, but rather to the month regardless of whether volume is up or down.

The cost behavior of Quadro can be depicted graphically, as we do in the figures on page 32. Fixed costs remain constant regardless of sale volume, while total variable costs increase as volume increases, in this case, at a rate of $3 per unit. Remember that we have just begun and will introduce some refinements and discuss assumptions shortly.

Let us look now at the fundamental relationships of CVP analysis. Profit can be expressed as:[3]

$$\text{profit} = \text{sales} - \text{total costs}$$

Because we have classified costs as either fixed or variable with sales, we also have the following relationship:

$$\text{profit} = \text{sales} - \text{total variable costs} - \text{total fixed costs}$$

Sales are equal to selling price times unit volume, while total variable costs equal unit variable costs times unit volume. Using the familiar income statement format

$$\text{sales} - \text{total variable costs} - \text{total fixed costs} = \text{profit}$$

Thus, one can view the basic CVP relationship as an equation or as a columnar income statement. Both yield the same results and, once you know this basic relationship, answers to CVP questions come easily.

Suppose that Quadro's managers want to know what profit is likely to be if sales are 6,000 units per month. The income statement that follows uses the term **contribution margin**, a very important concept. Contribution margin is

---

[2] In financial accounting, the term *cost* relates to an expenditure; plant and equipment have a cost, as does inventory. The income statement shows *expenses*, costs that have expired in the earning of revenue. CVP analysis could also be termed *expense-volume-profit analysis* because it deals with expired costs—expenses. We are not concerned with the purchase of pencils by Quadro, but rather with the sales. We use the term *cost* because it is customary and, as later chapters show, its greater generality makes it a more accurate term than *expense*.

[3] Terms such as *income* and *income before taxes* are commonly used to denote profit. The term *net income* is normally reserved for income after taxes. We consider income taxes later in the chapter.

FIGURE 2–1 Cost-Volume Relationships

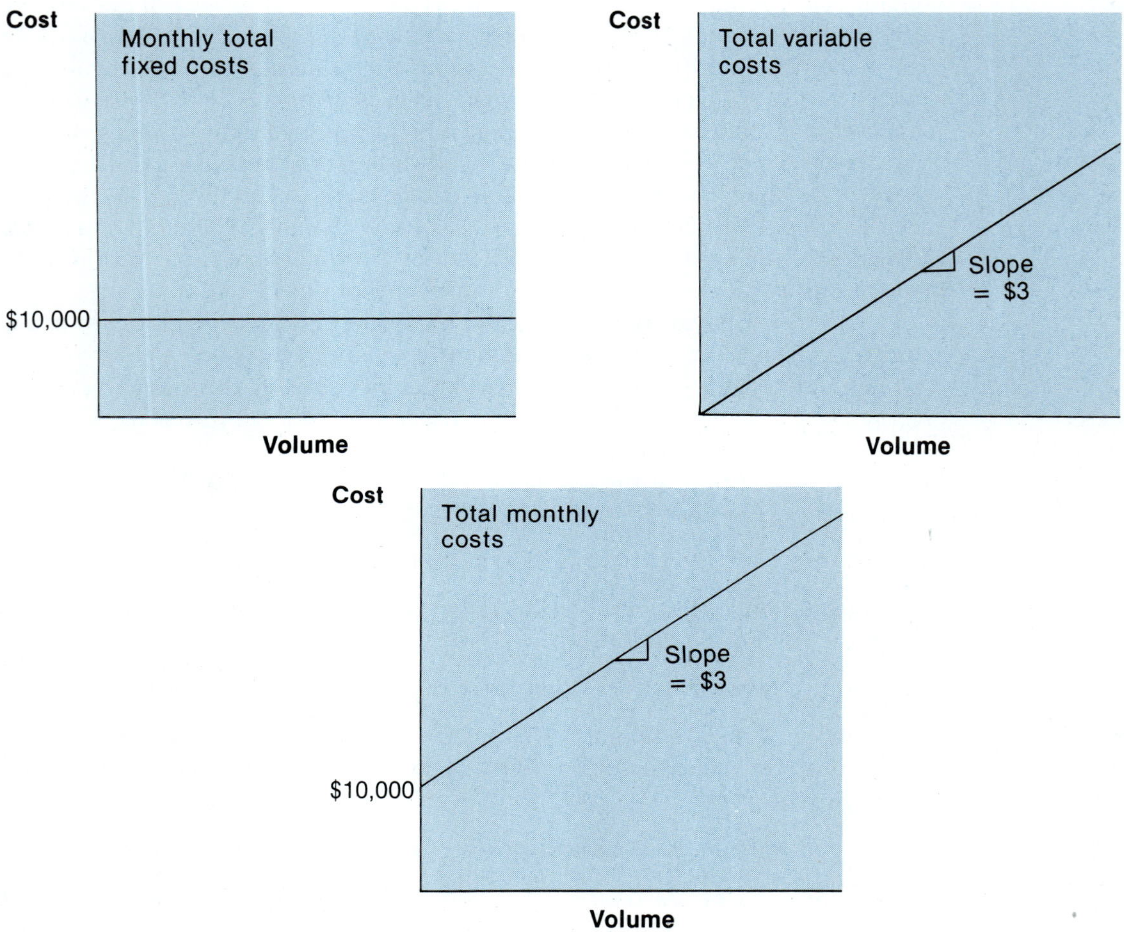

the difference between revenue and variable cost, either in total, as in the income statement below, or per unit. We shall see its importance as we proceed.

Sales, 6,000 × $5	$30,000
Variable costs, 6,000 × $3	18,000
Contribution margin	$12,000
Fixed costs	10,000
Profit	$ 2,000

In the following discussion, we shall use these symbols for brevity.

P = selling price per unit

V = variable costs per unit

F = fixed costs per period

Q = unit sales for period
Z = profit for period

We can now express profit as:

$Z =$	PQ	$- VQ$	$- F$
profit	sales dollars	total variable costs	total fixed costs

The above is not a formula or equation, but shorthand for our basic relationship. For Quadro, this relationship yields the same $2,000 profit shown above.

CONTRIBUTION MARGIN

The income statement above shows that Quadro Company would earn $12,000 in total contribution margin selling 6,000 units. It also earns a per unit contribution margin of $2, which is the $5 selling price minus the $3 per unit variable cost. Because Quadro earns $5 revenue per unit and incurs $3 variable cost to sell a unit, it has $2 per unit left to contribute to covering total fixed costs and earning profits.

We can also state the profit relationship in the following way:

$$Z = Q(P - V) - F$$

In this formulation, we simply multiply unit volume by per unit contribution margin $(P - V)$. We shall find a per unit contribution margin useful in making such analyses as determining the volume a company must earn to achieve a desired profit.

Cost-Volume-Profit Relationships

The following income statements for the Quadro Company illustrate some important CVP properties. The income statements reflect results at sales of 6,000 and 8,000 units.

QUADRO COMPANY
Income Statement

	6,000 Units		*8,000 Units*	
	Dollars	*Percentage of Sales*	*Dollars*	*Percentage of Sales*
Sales at $5 per unit	$30,000	100.00%	$40,000	100.00%
Variable costs at $3 per unit	18,000	60.00%	24,000	60.00%
Contribution margin, $2 per unit	12,000	40.00%	16,000	40.00%
Fixed costs	10,000	33.33%	10,000	25.00%
Income	$ 2,000	6.67%	$ 6,000	15.00%

We can determine sales, total variable costs, and total contribution margin by multiplying the appropriate per unit amount by the number of units sold. For example, you could determine that total contribution at 8,000 units is $16,000 by multiplying the $2 unit contribution margin by 8,000 units. Additionally, the percentages of variable costs to sales and of contribution margin to sales are constant at 60 percent and 40 percent, respectively. Variable cost per unit is 60 percent of the selling price ($3/$5), and total variable costs are 60 percent of sales. Similarly, contribution margin per unit is 40 percent of selling price ($2/$5), and total contribution margin is 40 percent of sales. The percentage relationships of fixed costs and of profits to sales do not remain constant. Fixed costs are constant in total and, therefore, decline as a percentage of sales as sales increase.

Relevant Range

CVP relationships cannot be expected to hold for all possible volumes. If Quadro Company managers expected to sell only a few units in a particular month, they would probably cut advertising costs, reduce office hours, and take other steps that would lower fixed costs from the $10,000 level. Similarly, if volume were expected to be 15,000 units, the firm would probably have to increase personnel and take other steps that would increase fixed costs.

Price and variable cost can also be affected by the range of volume. For example, at some level of volume Quadro might have to lower its prices or it might qualify for a quantity discount on materials. The basic CVP relationships are assumed to hold within a relevant range. The relevant range is self-defining: it is the range of volume where we can expect the CVP relationships to hold reasonably well.

The relevant range might be extremely wide for some firms, narrow for others. When we perform the various analyses already illustrated, we assume that the volume figures fall within the relevant range. If we have information to the contrary, we make necessary adjustments. For example, a firm can have one relevant range of about 4,000 to 10,000 units and another from 10,000 to 15,000. Managers must be aware of which range is appropriate for a current analysis so they can use costs and prices associated with that range.

The concept of relevant range also has a time dimension. CVP relationships cannot be expected to hold for long periods. We all know that prices change, material costs change, employees receive salary increases, and so on. The length of time that the relationships remain valid will differ according to the characteristics of the firm. Many authors suggest a year as the likely maximum. This period might be lowered depending on competitive activity, inflation, and other factors.

Review Problem

Using a spreadsheet, create income statements (showing dollars and percentages of sales) for 4,000, 6,000, 8,000, and 10,000 units. In creating your template, use a separate section for your basic data (price per unit, variable cost per unit, fixed costs, and number of units). Use cell addresses from the data section to link your income columns to these data. A solution appears below.

DATA SECTION								
Unit price	$5.00							
Unit variable cost	$3.00							
Fixed costs	$10,000							
Units	4,000		6,000		8,000		10,000	
SOLUTION SECTION								
				QUADRO COMPANY Income Statement				
Units	4,000		6,000		8,000		10,000	
	Dollars	%	Dollars	%	Dollars	%	Dollars	%
Sales	$20,000	100.00%	$30,000	100.00%	$40,000	100.00%	$50,000	100.00%
Variable costs	12,000	60.00%	18,000	60.00%	24,000	60.00%	30,000	60.00%
Contribution margin	8,000	40.00%	12,000	40.00%	16,000	40.00%	20,000	40.00%
Fixed costs	10,000	50.00%	10,000	33.33%	10,000	25.00%	10,000	20.00%
Profit(Loss)	($2,000)	-10.00%	$2,000	6.67%	$6,000	15.00%	$10,000	20.00%

It is a logical extension of the discussion above that 4,000 units produce a loss since [($5 − $3) × 4,000] is less than monthly fixed costs. Once the firm breaks even (profits equal zero at breakeven), profit as a percentage of sales increases. In addition, each 2,000 units adds $4,000 to profits: the contribution margin per unit times the unit increase.

These income statements also illustrate one of the major pitfalls of the use of financial accounting income statements: a tendency of some managers to look at fixed costs (or even profits) on a *per unit* basis. Since fixed costs are a function of time, not volume, such per unit costs can be misleading. Say that Quadro is currently selling 8,000 units. At that volume, fixed costs are $1.25 per unit ($10,000/8,000). If a manager used that figure when pricing (or predicting profits) at, say, 10,000 units, he would overestimate fixed costs since 10,000 × $1.25 = $12,500, 25 percent more than actual fixed costs of $10,000.

COST-VOLUME-PROFIT GRAPH

Figure 2–2 depicts the revenue and cost functions for the Quadro Company. The horizontal axis is measured in unit sales but could also be measured in dollar sales. A CPA firm or other firm that charges clients by the hour could use charged hours on the horizontal axis. Notice that the lines representing revenues and costs are solid within the relevant range of 4,000 through 12,000 units and dashed outside the range. We cannot assume that the behavior of revenues and costs outside the relevant range is the same as within the range. Some accountants prefer to draw lines only within the relevant range: the dashed lines are extended in Figure 2–2 to make it easier to see how the graph is constructed.

FIGURE 2–2 CVP Graph—Quadro Company

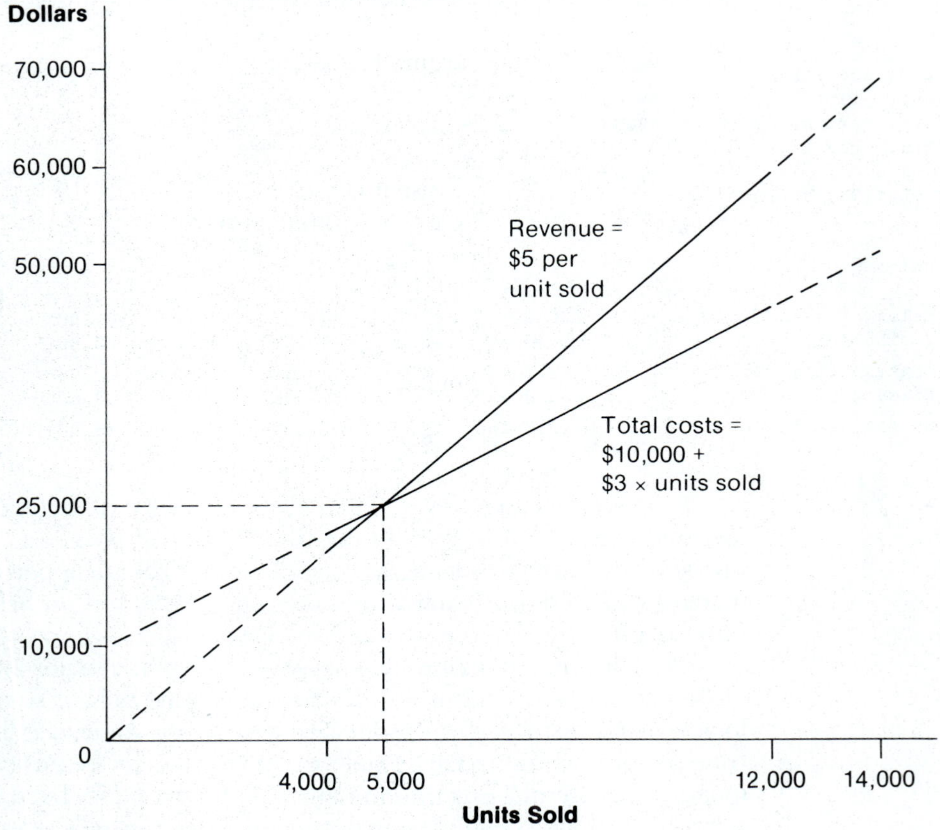

INTERPRETING THE COST-VOLUME-PROFIT GRAPH

The following points are important in viewing the graph. Total cost is a linear function (also called the *flexible budget*):

$$\text{total cost} = \text{fixed cost} + (\text{variable cost per unit} \times \text{volume})$$

or

$$TC = F + VQ$$

Total revenue is also linear, but there is a zero intercept:

$$\text{total revenue} = \text{price} \times \text{volume}$$
$$TR = PQ$$

Profit or loss is measured by the vertical distance between the total revenue line and the total cost line at any level of volume. Total variable cost is the vertical difference between the total cost line and the fixed cost line at any level of volume. Contribution margin is not as easy to visualize. It is the vertical distance between the total revenue line and total variable costs at any level of volume. We must determine total variable costs and subtract them from revenues to find contribution margin. Therefore, contribution margin cannot be read directly from the graph.

A graph is often helpful to visualize the effects of changes in volume from currently anticipated levels and to determine how rapidly profits fall if volume falls (or how rapidly they rise if volume rises). Working with the numerical values does not always give this information as clearly as a graph does.

The graphical approach may be especially helpful in assessing the probable effects of changes in the price-cost structure. For example, suppose that the managers of Quadro are considering paying salespeople straight salaries of $5,000 per month instead of the current $0.50 commission on each unit sold. The proposed change would increase fixed costs from $10,000 to $15,000 per month but would reduce variable cost per unit from $3 to $2.50. The contribution margin percentage would rise from 40 percent to 50 percent [($5 − $2.50)/$5].

Figure 2–3 depicts the new and existing relationships differently from Figure 2–2. In Figure 2–3, often called a profit graph, profit is shown as a single line, which makes it easier to read, especially if we want to graph more than one set of relationships. In a profit graph, the height of the line represents profit at the associated level of volume. Notice that the line depicting the existing relationships begins at a negative $10,000—fixed costs under existing conditions. The slope of that line is $2 per unit—contribution margin per unit under existing conditions. Under the proposed conditions, the line begins at a negative $15,000 and has a slope of $2.50 per unit—the fixed costs and the contribution margin per unit under the new plan.

The profit graph tells us that the breakeven point rises from 5,000 units to 6,000 units if we make the change, while profits would be the same under either set of conditions when volume is 10,000 units. The point where profit is equal under two sets of conditions is called the **indifference point** and can be useful information. In this case, the basic question is whether or not the managers of Quadro can reasonably expect volume to average more than 10,000 units. If so, the proposed scheme would be better than the existing one. However, by using the indifference point, we are assuming that volume would be the same under either scheme. It is possible that the motivational effects of changing the mode of compensation to salespeople could result in higher or lower sales than the company would achieve if it stuck with the existing structure. In some cases, however, it is reasonable to suppose that a change in the cost structure would not affect volume. For example, if the change involved manufacturing methods, there would be no reason to suspect that volume would change from what it would have been, provided the product's quality remained the same.

Later sections of this chapter outline ways of approaching such decisions. The graphical approach shows the probable effects of changes but does not indicate that a change should take place.

FIGURE 2–3 Profit Graph for Two Alternatives

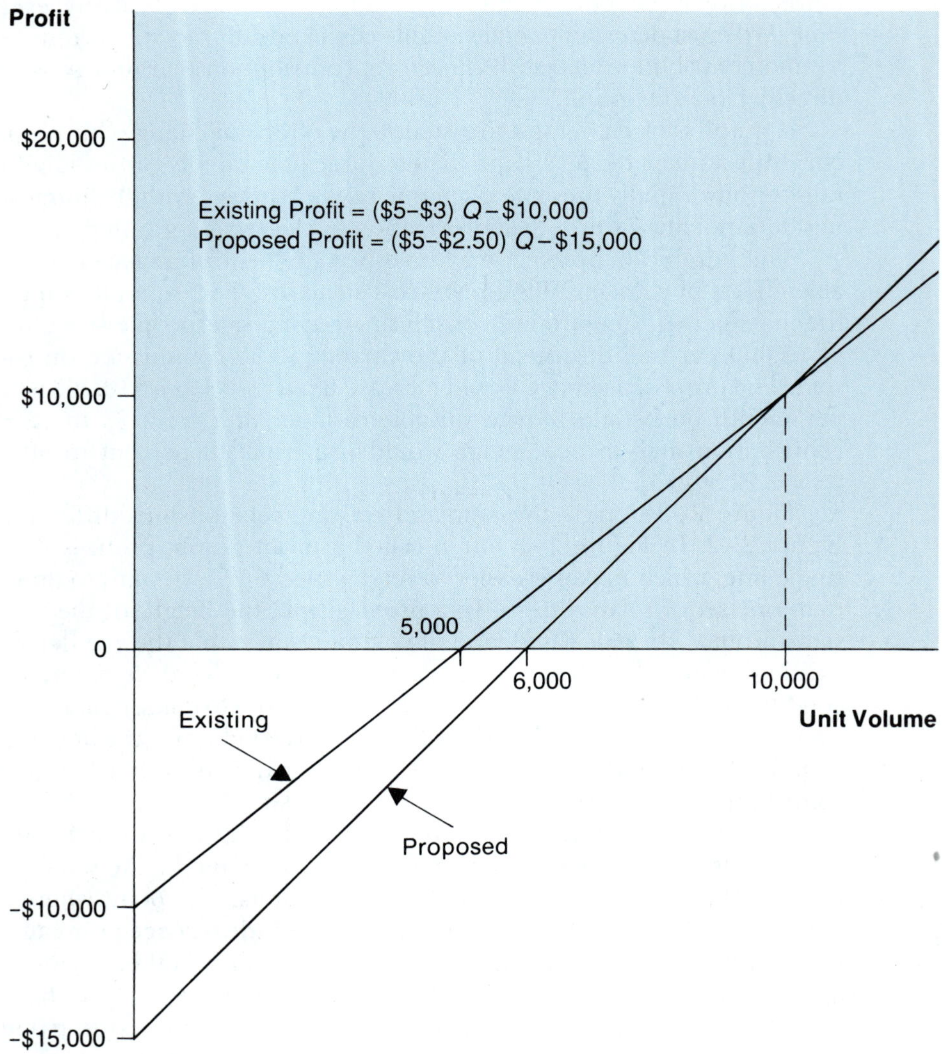

TARGET PROFITS

So far we have used CVP analysis to solve for profit at a projected volume; this analysis is used to solve for other variables as well. Sometimes managers will want to know the sales required to earn a particular profit that they have set as an objective. Such a profit is often called a **target profit**. At other times managers may wish to know the sales required to cover fixed costs without earning profit or showing loss. The level of sales required to show a zero profit is called the **breakeven point**. Breaking even is rarely an objective for a business, but is frequently an objective of a not-for-profit entity. The executive board of a student union might wish to break even, as might the directors of a not-for-profit nursery school. In a business context, managers want to know the breakeven point primarily to see how low volume would have to fall before the company would sustain losses, that is, to see how much a cushion or *margin of safety* the company has below its expected volume.

Target Profit and Volume

Virtually any type of analysis that uses CVP relationships can be executed in one of two ways: working with the basic profit relationship or using a columnar income statement format. Using the columnar format, we rely on the basic form of the contribution margin statement.

sales − variable costs = contribution margin − fixed costs = profit

Using the basic profit relationship, we can solve for the unit volume needed as follows:

$$Z = Q(P - V) - F$$
$$Q = (Z + F)/(P - V)$$

That is, the unit volume needed for a particular profit is the profit plus fixed costs, divided by the contribution margin per unit. In words:

unit sales required = (target profit + fixed costs)/(unit contribution margin)

Suppose that the managers of Quadro want to know the breakeven point, where profit equals zero. Using the formula above, the answer is 5,000 units.

unit sales required = ($0 + $10,000)/$2 = 5,000 units

Using the columnar format, with zero profit and $10,000 fixed costs, total contribution margin must be $10,000, which, divided by unit contribution margin, gives the required unit volume.

Contribution margin	$10,000/$2 = 5,000
Fixed costs	10,000
Profit	$ 0

So far, we have used CVP analysis to answer two questions:

1. Given price per unit, variable cost per unit, fixed costs, and volume, what are expected profits?
2. Given price per unit, variable cost per unit, and fixed costs, what volume must we sell to achieve a given target profit?

Both questions include one unknown; all other information is given (or assumed to hold true). In these and similar questions that follow, the columnar solution or the profit relationship equation is used. The only thing that changes is the single unknown variable for which to solve. Thus, in dealing with CVP analysis, a manager should focus only on the basic profit relationship; formulas or formats need not be memorized. The discussion below illustrates this point.

Contribution Margin Percentage

We said earlier that contribution margin as a percentage of sales remains constant as volume changes. For Quadro Company, the contribution margin percentage (or contribution margin ratio) is 40 percent (\$2/\$5). The ratio of variable cost to price is called the variable cost percentage or ratio, 60 percent here (\$3/\$5). Note that the contribution margin ratio is one minus the variable cost ratio.

The contribution margin percentage may be used instead of the per unit contribution margin in calculating profits and sales required to earn particular target profits. When the contribution margin percentage is used to solve for required volume, the required volume is expressed in sales dollars, rather than sales units.

The sales dollars needed to break even given a 40 percent contribution margin ratio are calculated by:

	Dollars	*Percent*
Sales		
Total variable costs		
Contribution margin	\$10,000	40%
Fixed costs	10,000	
Profit	\$ 0	

If fixed costs are \$10,000, then total contribution margin must also be \$10,000 at breakeven. With a 40 percent contribution margin ratio, a total contribution margin of \$10,000 requires \$25,000 (\$10,000/0.40) of sales. In formula,

$$\text{profit} = \text{total revenue} - \text{total variable costs} - \text{total fixed costs}$$

and

$$\text{contribution margin percentage} = \frac{\text{contribution margin}}{\text{total revenue}}$$

or

$$\frac{\text{unit contribution margin}}{\text{unit price}}$$

From the above, at breakeven:

$$\$0 = (\$5 - \$3)Q - \$10{,}000$$

and

$$Q = (\$0 + \$10{,}000)/\$2$$

If both sides are multiplied by \$5,

$$\$5Q = (\$5 \times \$10{,}000)/\$2 = \$25{,}000$$

This is the same as

$$PQ = \$10{,}000/0.40 = \$25{,}000$$

where

$$\text{CM\%} = \$2/\$5 = 0.40.$$

Note that both the columnar and equation formats result in the same final calculation.

The contribution margin ratio has a distinct advantage over the contribution margin per unit when the firm sells more than one product. A department store may sell articles ranging in contribution margin per unit from a few cents to hundreds of dollars. Similar differences in unit contribution margin would be found in many other types of firms. A clothing manufacturer might earn a $50 contribution margin on one type of sport coat, $38 on another. In the face of these different unit contribution margins we cannot work with a single per unit contribution margin for the firm as a whole. Under some conditions, though, we may be able to work with the contribution margin percentage.

First, if all products have the same contribution margin ratio, despite having different per unit amounts, we can perform all standard CVP analyses using the contribution margin percentage. If the ratio were 40 percent across all products, then each $100 in sales would produce $40 in contribution margin no matter which products were sold. It could be 10 units of one product, 15 units of another, and 5 units of a third, or any combination adding up to $100 in sales.

Second, if contribution margin ratios differ among individual products, but the products are generally sold in about the same relative percentages, the overall contribution margin ratio will be reasonably constant and can be used in CVP analysis. We illustrate this principle later.

OTHER ANALYSES

Managers are interested in many types of analysis besides the calculation of profits and the volume required to earn a specific target profit. Consider a few analyses that the managers of Quadro might want to make. One possible decision is whether the firm should increase its fixed costs to secure greater volume. Suppose that the sales manager of Quadro believed that an increase of advertising costs of $2,000 per month would increase sales by $3,000. Would the advertising costs be a wise investment? Nothing is said about the level of sales expected if the advertising campaign is not undertaken. It is not necessary to know this level, only to know that the expected increase in sales is $3,000. An increase in sales of $3,000 yields a contribution margin of $1,200 ($3,000 × 0.40). Thus, if only an additional $3,000 in sales could be expected, the campaign would result in $800 lower profits ($1,200 − $2,000).

Target Costs

In today's competitive world, selling prices are often set by the market. Therefore, in order to be profitable in the face of prices that others are setting, managers have to control costs. CVP analysis can be used to target both required variable costs and required fixed costs in order to earn a target profit. Assume that the market price for the pencils that Quadro sells drops to \$4.50. If fixed costs remain at \$10,000 per month and there is a sales commission of 10 percent (now \$0.45), what would variable costs per unit have to be in order to make \$6,000 at 8,000 units? Now our basic relationship is:

$$\begin{aligned} \$6{,}000 &= (\$4.50 - \$0.45 - V)8{,}000 - \$10{,}000 \\ 8{,}000V &= -\$6{,}000 - \$10{,}000 + \$36{,}000 - \$3{,}600 \\ \text{and } V &= \$2.05 \end{aligned}$$

Thus, holding everything else constant, if prices dropped \$0.50, variable selling costs would drop \$0.05 and the variable cost per pencil would have to drop by \$0.45 (\$2.50 − \$2.05) in order to retain the same profit. This makes sense since Quadro wants to retain a \$2 per unit contribution margin in order to earn the same profit at 8,000 units. Since the price went down \$0.50, then variable costs per unit must also go down \$0.50. This same type of analysis can be made regarding fixed costs by holding everything else at its original value and solving for the level of fixed costs that would allow the company to earn a specific target profit.

Target Return on Sales

Managers sometimes want to earn a profit that is a given percentage of sales. This ratio, income/sales, is called **return on sales** and is frequently used to measure profitability, as you may have learned in financial accounting or financial management courses. Sometimes a return on sales is viewed as a norm for firms in a particular industry. Some trade associations publish percentage income statements showing what the average firm earns as a percentage of its sales as well as showing various costs as percentages of sales. A manager might be interested in finding the volume required to earn the industry average return on sales, or perhaps to earn a percentage point or more higher.

Suppose the managers of Quadro Company believe that the firm should be able to earn a 15 percent return on sales. The target profit would then be stated as 15 percent of sales. Using the basic relationship for profit, we state profit as 15 percent of sales.

$$\begin{aligned} 0.15PQ &= Q(P - V) - F \\ 0.15(\$5)Q &= Q(\$5 - \$3) - \$10{,}000 \\ \$0.75Q &= \$2Q - \$10{,}000 \\ Q &= 8{,}000 \end{aligned}$$

The company needs to sell 8,000 units to earn a 15 percent return on sales. Sales would be \$40,000 (8,000 × \$5) and profit \$6,000 (\$2 contribution margin times 8,000 = \$16,000, less \$10,000 fixed costs), which is 15 percent of \$40,000.

We could also solve for sales dollars by using the contribution margin percentage as follows:

$$\begin{aligned} 0.15PQ &= 0.40PQ - \$10{,}000 \\ PQ &= \$40{,}000 \end{aligned}$$

A Pricing Decision

Suppose that the managers of Quadro are contemplating a change in the price of the product. They believe that sales will be 8,000 units and wish to know which price would yield a \$12,000 monthly profit. First, recall that the firm pays \$2.50 per unit for its product and that the remainder of the variable cost per unit is a 10 percent commission to salespeople. If the selling price changes, the commission per unit will change (as we showed above), but not the \$2.50 purchase price. Starting with the basic relationship,

$$(P - V)Q - F = \text{profit}$$

we substitute the values:

$$(P - \$2.50 - 0.10P)8{,}000 - \$10{,}000 = \$12{,}000$$

The term within the parentheses represents the selling price minus the \$2.50 purchase costs minus the commission, which will be 10 percent of the selling price.

$$\begin{aligned} 8{,}000P - \$20{,}000 - 800P - \$10{,}000 &= \$12{,}000 \\ 7{,}200P &= \$42{,}000 \\ P &= \$5.83 \end{aligned}$$

At a price of \$5.83 (rounded) the firm will earn \$12,000 monthly, provided that it can sell 8,000 units at that price. Pricing decisions are among the most common made by managers, especially in the consumer goods industries. Most firms have some discretion over prices, but rarely can they set whatever price they please and expect to achieve the same volume that a lower price would yield. We will examine the relationship between price and volume later in this chapter; for now we observe that if competitors of Quadro are selling similar products for \$4.80 or \$5.00, then Quadro will probably have trouble selling very many pencils at \$5.83 each. Prices set using CVP analysis must be reviewed for reasonableness in the light of the competitive conditions in the market. They cannot be too far out of line with the competition.

So far, managers of the Quadro Company have found critical values for unit sales, dollar sales, variable costs, and selling price. Each analysis has involved a particular arrangement of the basic CVP relationship, $Z = Q(P - V) - F$. In addition each problem has had only one unknown. Chapter 12 deals with decision-making problems with two or more unknowns.

Review Problem

Set up a spreadsheet for Quadro Company that will allow you to solve for unit sales, dollar sales, and selling price. Use the template QUADRO.WK1 provided with the text. A copy of the template is shown in Exhibit 2–1. Set up the template formulas so you can solve for various unknowns. Where appropriate, insert @IF statements to make the template flexible. Solve for the following:

1. Given all the original data, how many units must be sold to generate a target profit of \$8,000?

2. Given all the original data, what must total sales dollars be to generate profits of $10,000?
3. How many units must be sold to achieve a target return on sales of ten percent?

A sample @IF statement is shown in Exhibit 2–1. The solution and balance of relevant cell formulas are shown in Exhibit 2–2. The cell formulas will be useful in the discussion that follows.

EXHIBIT 2–1

```
 A       B          C          D          E          F          G        H
 2 QUADRO.WK1
 3
 4 DATA SECTION                        Original
 5                                       Value              Unknown=1
 6 Unit price                            $5.00
 7 Variable commission                  10.00%
 8 Commission per unit                   $0.50
 9 Other unit variable costs             $2.50
10 Total unit variable costs             $3.00
11 Fixed cost                          $10,000
12 Volume                                6,000                      1
13 Target profit ($ or %)                 0.00
14
15 SOLUTION SECTION
16                                     Dollars   Percent
17 Sales
18 Variable costs
19                                  -----------  ------
20 Contribution margin
21 Fixed costs
22                                  -----------  ------
23 Income
24
25                                    Computed
26                                      Value
27 Volume
28 Unit price
29 Unit variable cost
30 Contribution margin ratio
31
32
33
34
35

Sample @IF statement:

Cell E27:    @IF(G12=1,(E11+E13)/(E6-E10)), E12)
```

Note: this statement will have to be modified in order to solve Question 3 of the review problem.

EXHIBIT 2–2 Quadro Company—Review Problem Solutions

Direct solutions to the questions:

1. 9,000: ($8,000 + $10,000)/$2 = 9,000
2. $50,000: ($10,000 + $10,000)/0/40 = $50,000
3. 6,667: 0.10($5)$Q$ = ($5 − $3)$Q$ − $10,000 and Q = 6,667

```
Cell formulas for full sensitivity analysis:
                                          E
16                                  Dollars
17      Sales                       @IF(G6=1,(E13+E10*E27*E11),E6*E27)
18      Variable costs              @IF(G10=1,-(E13+E11-E6*E27),E10*E27)
19                                  ------------
20      Contribution margin         +E17-E18
21      Fixed costs                 @IF(G11=1,-(E13-E6*E27+E10*E27),E11)
22                                  ------------
23      Income                      +E20-E21

27                                  @IF(G12=1,@IF(E13<1,E11/(E6-E7*E6-E13*E6-E9),
                                     (E11+E13)/(E6-E10)),E12)
```

Risk and Return

Anyone prefers higher income to lower income, other things being equal. However, other things are usually not equal: if you wish to earn higher income (return), usually you must accept greater risk. If you wish to invest $10,000, you have many choices. You could buy government bonds or notes and earn a virtually certain return of perhaps 8 percent. You could buy a partnership share in an oil drilling expedition that might return 60 percent each year, but might lose your entire $10,000. Between these alternatives, you might buy common stocks of well-established firms with the expectation of earning perhaps a 15 percent return between dividends and stock appreciation. There is the possibility of loss if the stock prices fall, but you would almost certainly not lose your entire investment.

Managers face decisions involving risk and return daily. Usually it is riskier to concentrate on new products than on established ones, but it is also potentially more profitable. Increasing the degree of automation in a factory is potentially profitable, but also riskier because it adds fixed costs that cannot be avoided if volume does not live up to expectations. Even the amount of fixed costs might be uncertain at the time of purchase. For example, a wave soldering machine in an electronics company that was installed to achieve a certain level of quality was more than three times as expensive to operate than estimated. Basic CVP analysis is not set up to deal with risk, but it can be adapted to do so in several ways. One method is sensitivity analysis.

Sensitivity Analysis

Sensitivity analysis refers to a number of techniques that determine whether a particular factor in a decision is critical. In CVP context, if a relatively small change in a factor such as unit volume would cause a large change in profit, we could say that profit is sensitive to changes in volume and that volume is a critical factor. Sensitivity analysis finds much of its use in decision-making situations. Consider the two income statements below, which depict the expected annual results of two products, A and B. A firm's managers are considering which product to add to the line; they will not choose both.

	A		B	
	Dollar Volume	*Percent of Sales*	*Dollar Volume*	*Percent of Sales*
Sales	$800,000	100.0%	$1,000,000	100.0%
Variable costs	600,000	75.0%	300,000	30.0%
Contribution margin	$200,000	25.0%	$ 700,000	70.0%
Fixed costs	120,000		600,000	
Income	$ 80,000		$ 100,000	

The expected profits from Product B are $20,000 greater than those from Product A, given the volume, price, variable costs, and traceable fixed costs of each. If the managers of the firm were certain that the results would be as shown in these income statements, they would prefer Product B to Product A. However, the figures given are estimates that might or might not come true, and the managers should go further before deciding. They should determine how profits of each product would be affected by shortfalls.

One common test of sensitivity is the **margin of safety** (MOS). The MOS is the decline in sales that would bring the firm, or product, to breakeven. It may be expressed as a decline in units, dollars, or percentage. Product B has a higher contribution margin percentage than Product A. Thus, the income of Product B will be more sensitive to (will increase or decrease more rapidly in response to) changes in sales volume than will the income of Product A. Equal dollar changes in sales will produce greater income changes for Product B. The breakeven point and the MOS for each product are calculated below. We do not have unit data and, therefore, cannot calculate the MOS in units.

	A	B
Fixed costs	$120,000	$600,000
Divided by: Contribution margin percentage	25%	70%
Equals: Breakeven point in sales dollars	$480,000	$857,143
Margin of safety in dollars:		
$800,000 − $480,000	$320,000	
$1,000,000 − $857,143		$142,857
Margin of safety percentage:		
$320,000/$800,000	40%	
$142,857/$1,000,000		14.3%

Is Product B riskier than Product A because its margin of safety is lower? Not necessarily. A more complete evaluation would require a great deal more information about the probable ranges within which sales of the two products could be expected to fall. For example, if there are significant probabilities that volumes could be 20 to 25 percent below the expected levels, it would be reasonable to say that selecting Product B over Product A would mean that the firm had to take on more risk. At volumes 20 percent or so below expected levels, Product B would show losses while Product A would show profits.

The profits of Product B are more sensitive to changes in volume than those of Product A because the contribution margin percentage of Product B is higher than that of Product A. Therefore, equal dollar changes in sales volume will produce greater changes in profit for Product B on both the upside and the downside.

Sensitivity analysis can be applied to any of the critical variables: price, variable costs, fixed costs, and unit volume. A general procedure is to determine the change in profits that accompanies each specific change in one of the variables. In our example, any percentage change in sales volume would produce greater changes in profits for Product B than for Product A. However, volume and the variable cost percentages might be relatively certain and, therefore, the contribution margin percentages are in doubt. The reason could be that the cost of a component of each product is uncertain or that the amount of a sales commission may change from that used in determining the variable cost percentage.

Suppose that variable costs turn out to be higher than expected and that the managers are concerned about the potential effects on profits. Looking back at the original income projections, we see that equal percentage changes in variable costs, say 10 percent increases, would affect the profits of Product A more than the profits of Product B. A 10 percent increase in unit variable costs would cause a $60,000 decline in Product A's profits ($600,000 × 0.10) and a $30,000 decline in Product B's profits ($300,000 × 0.10).

The use of sensitivity analysis requires consideration of each specific situation. In our example, supposing that sales volume is the only factor that may be different from expected, we might be justified in saying that Product B represents better opportunities for higher profits than does Product A, but at a risk of having lower profits if expectations do not materialize. Managers who are conservative and inclined to avoid risk at the expense of sacrificing possibly higher profits might choose Product A. More venturesome managers might be more likely to choose Product B. The whole question of risk and return is extremely complex, and this book can only scratch the surface. An intuitive approach to the trade-off between risk and return is suggested by an anecdote concerning the late Bernard Baruch, a prominent Wall Street financier. A young man approached Baruch seeking advice on investing a newly inherited fortune. Baruch replied, "Young man, do you wish to eat well or sleep well?" That is, if you wish to eat well, you must take some risk in the hope of earning higher returns. If you wish to sleep well, you invest conservatively and accept lower, but more certain, returns.

Indifference Point

Earlier we discussed the **indifference point**, which provides one method of testing for sensitivity in terms of volume, selling price, or any other critical variable. To illustrate, assume that a firm has two possible ways to manufacture an essential component for a major product. One method requires a great deal of labor and little equipment; the other is highly automated and requires much less labor but a great deal of equipment, which would be leased from another firm. Data on the two alternatives are given below. Because revenue from the product is the same regardless of how the part is made, we need consider only costs.

	Labor-Intensive Process	*Automated Process*
Variable costs per unit	$12	$7
Annual fixed costs	$250,000	$800,000

We first determine the unit volume at which profits will be the same under either alternative. Because the selling price is the same either way, we need solve only for the volume where total costs will be the same. For the labor-intensive operation, total costs, $VQ + F$, are

$$TC = \$12Q + \$250{,}000$$

and for the automated process are

$$TC = \$7Q + \$800{,}000$$

The indifference point is the volume at which total costs are the same for both alternatives. Setting the two expressions equal to one another and solving for Q, we have

$$\begin{aligned} \$12Q + \$250{,}000 &= \$7Q + \$800{,}000 \\ \$5Q &= \$550{,}000 \\ Q &= 110{,}000 \end{aligned}$$

At unit volume of 110,000, total costs and profits will be equal under the two alternatives. Notice that the next to last step ($\$5Q = \$550{,}000$) simply expresses the differences in variable cost per unit and in total annual fixed costs. The calculation answers the question of how many times we must save $5 per unit in order to make up for an additional $550,000 in fixed costs.

Suppose now that volume is expected to be 120,000 units a year. The automated process would give $50,000 lower costs and higher profits than the labor-intensive process. Since each additional unit saves the firm $5, and since the total costs (and profits) are the same at 110,000 units, the additional 10,000 units over the indifference point will save a total of $50,000 ($5 × 10,000) in variable costs.

The decision to use the automated process is sensitive to changes in volume. A drop of more than 10,000 units, or 8.33 percent, from the expected volume would make the labor-intensive process the better alternative, all else being equal.

The indifference point may be expressed in terms of other variables. Perhaps the 120,000 volume figure is relatively certain, but the variable cost per unit under the automated process is uncertain. It might turn out to be more than \$7. We want to find out how high it could go without changing the decision to use the automated process. Since volume is known, we can express the equality of total costs under the two methods as

$$V(120{,}000) + \$800{,}000 = \$12(120{,}000) + \$250{,}000$$

where V is the variable cost per unit that will equate total costs under the two alternative processes. Solving for V, we find:

$$\begin{aligned} 120{,}000V + \$800{,}000 &= \$1{,}440{,}000 + \$250{,}000 \\ 120{,}000V &= \$890{,}000 \\ V &= \$7.417 \text{ (rounded)} \end{aligned}$$

That is, if variable costs under the automated process go over \$7.417, the better decision is to use the labor-intensive process. The \$0.417 increase in variable cost per unit over the estimated \$7 per unit is a bit less than 6 percent, which indicates that the decision is also sensitive to the estimate of variable cost per unit for the automated process.

Which process should be adopted? The indifference point and the sensitivity analysis we have explored so far are only two parts of such a decision. Choosing one alternative over the other might depend on more factors than numerical analysis. For example, in today's competitive world, the company might adopt the machine-intensive process although it is more expensive if its managers believe that in the long term volume would be affected by going with a process that might be perceived as "old technology." We discuss the interactions of variables (such as cost and volume) later in this chapter. With everything else equal, however, the choice depends on a manager's attitude toward risk and return. There is no best answer; the choices of individual managers would indicate whether they preferred lower expected profits accompanied by lower risk, or vice versa.

The use of the indifference point and sensitivity analysis has become more critical as companies adopt advanced manufacturing techniques and rearrange manufacturing flows to incorporate the principles of just-in-time (JIT), flexible manufacturing systems, manufacturing cells, and computer integrated manufacturing. Several factors are changing as managers investigate new options for manufacturing. First, laborers who had been paid hourly (a variable cost) might now be paid weekly. While they still might have an hourly rate, they are virtually guaranteed 40 hours of work each week; thus, labor becomes a fixed cost. In addition, computer integrated manufacturing, robotics, and new inventory philosophies might incorporate changes for which the company has no experience. Therefore, managers are unsure about the cost of new methods. These and other factors point to the need for sensitivity analysis when comparing alternative courses of action. Chapters 13 and 14 address this point again in a discussion of decisions on acquiring capital assets.

Spreadsheets and Sensitivity Analysis

We have already used spreadsheets in single-variable sensitivity analysis in the Quadro example. By setting up a spreadsheet with appropriate formulas derived from the basic profit relationship equation, we can find needed volume, target price, target variable cost, or target fixed cost to achieve a given level of profits (such as breakeven). This type of sensitivity analysis can include more than one variable.

In the discussion above, we illustrated how small changes in a single variable might have far-reaching effects on total profits. However, in some cases, even though most variables when looked at *one at a time* have little effect on income, small changes in a couple of variables together might make a big difference. Exhibit 2–3 shows data for Solitude Company including an income statement based on managers' original estimates of unit price, unit variable cost, period fixed costs, and volume. (A template of this exhibit is labeled EXH2–3.WK1.) Original estimates yield an income of $30,000, a 15 percent return on sales.

You should verify that *one-at-a-time* sensitivity analysis shows that income becomes zero if each of the variables is changed by the following percentages *while holding all other variables at their original values*.

EXHIBIT 2–3 Original Estimates—Solitude Company

DATA SECTION

	Original Estimate	Percent Change	Revised Estimate
Unit price	$20.00	0.00%	$20.00
Unit variable cost	$10.00	0.00%	$10.00
Period fixed costs	$70,000	0.00%	$70,000
Volume	10,000	0.00%	10,000

SOLUTION SECTION

Income Statement
Solitude Company

	Dollars	Percent of Sales
Sales	$200,000	100.00%
Total variable costs	100,000	50.00%
	---------	------
Contribution margin	100,000	50.00%
Fixed costs	70,000	35.00%
	---------	------
Income	$30,000	15.00%

(Template for this exhibit is available: EXH2-3.WK1)

Unit price	−15.00%
Unit variable cost	+30.00%
Fixed costs	+42.86%
Volume	−30.00%

Thus, a manager looking only at single-variable sensitivity analysis could conclude that only large changes in variables seriously decrease income. However, Exhibit 2–4 shows changes for all the variables with no change more than 8 percent. Profit is close to zero. (You can use EXH2–3.WK1 to experiment with changes in the variables and to duplicate Exhibit 2–4. Changes in the "Percent Change" column will be reflected in the rest of the spreadsheet.) While more sophisticated ways exist to perform sensitivity analysis that take into account distributional assumptions, using an electronic spreadsheet is a dynamic way to test various assumptions and estimates to see what happens if more than one variable changes at a time.

What Exhibits 2–3 and 2–4 illustrate in simple form can be expanded to include many variables. For example, a company recently was examining its options to expand into another city. A spreadsheet was constructed that included 50 variables. Not only could these variables interact with one another within a year, but they could also interact over time. The company built a three-year projection of income using these variables, and then undertook a

EXHIBIT 2–4 Revised Estimates—Solitude Company

DATA SECTION

	Original Estimate	Percent Change	Revised Estimate
Unit price	$20.00	-5.00%	$19.00
Unit variable cost	$10.00	7.00%	$10.70
Period fixed costs	$70,000	7.00%	$74,900
Volume	10,000	-8.00%	9,200

SOLUTION SECTION

Income Statement
Solitude Company

	Dollars	Percent of Sales
Sales	$174,800	100.00%
Total variable costs	98,440	56.32%
Contribution margin	76,360	43.68%
Fixed costs	74,900	42.85%
Income	$1,460	0.84%

Using EXH2-3.WK1, we made changes in the *"Percent Change"* column. Thus, for example, for unit price, −0.05 was inserted.

series of sensitivity analyses where several variables were changed, as in Exhibit 2–4, to see the effect of these changes over the entire time period.

ASSUMPTIONS OF CVP ANALYSIS

CVP analysis can be used to answer several types of questions and can help in decision making. We have also seen how it can be used when a manager is uncertain about some of the variables used in the analysis. Even so, can we really expect it to work in practice? What about inflation? Is it really likely that fixed costs will remain fixed and variable cost per unit will remain constant throughout the relevant range? In fact, is it realistic to say that all costs are either fixed or variable with sales?

In our discussion so far, we have mentioned several of the basic assumptions of CVP analysis. These include:

relevant range (considering both volume and time)

linearity of total costs ($TC = VQ + F$)

linearity of total revenue ($TR = PQ$)

single variable that affects costs: volume

variable cost per unit constant in the relevant range

unit price constant in the relevant range

fixed costs do not change in the relevant range

constant sales mix of multiple products

In addition, we will add another assumption in the discussion below, one that was implicit in our analysis so far:

production volume equals sales volume

The following sections discuss the assumptions of CVP analysis and what happens to the validity of the analysis if the assumptions are not met. We also discuss some ways in which the analysis can be changed to make it more consistent with the critical assumptions.

Conceptual Considerations

Figure 2–4 shows two types of revenue and cost functions. The solid curves are drawn as an economist might portray the operations of a firm, the dashed lines as accountants and other managers typically portray them. The dashed lines do not extend as far as the curves, consistent with the concept of relevant range. (Most accountants are aware of what is usually called the economist's model of the firm. Accountants and other managers use the linear model primarily for greater simplicity and because it is a good approximation of the behavior of revenues and costs within the relevant range.)

FIGURE 2–4 Linear and Curvilinear CVP Relationships

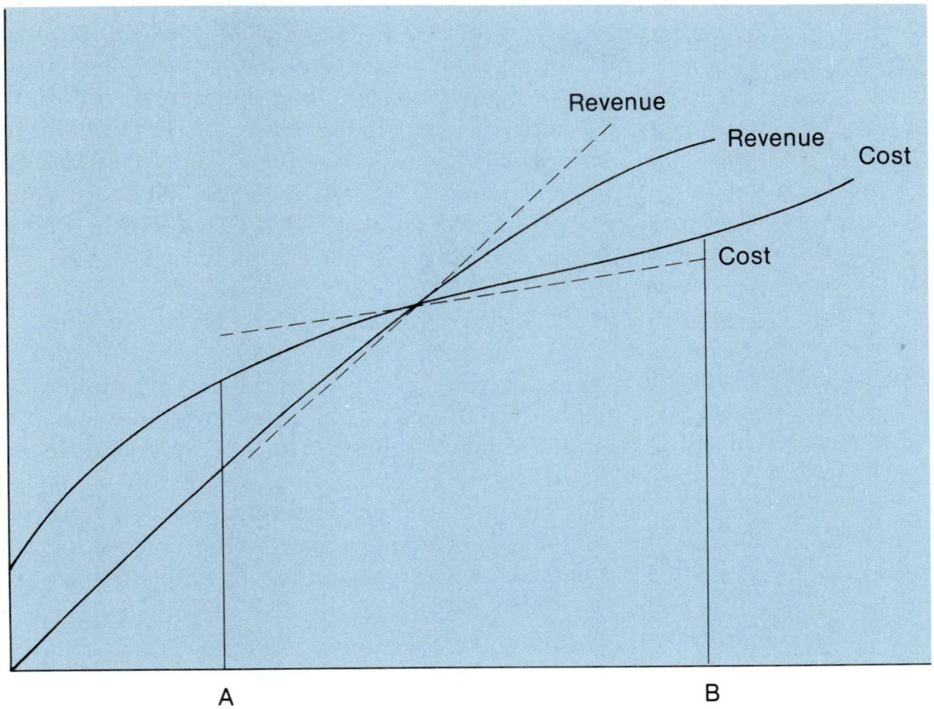

Basic economic theory provides explanations for the curvilinear behavior of the revenue and cost functions. Taking revenues first, the curve shows that total revenue rises not at a constant rate, but at a decreasing rate. This behavior results from the law of demand, which states that, other things being equal, the lower the price, the higher the quantity buyers will demand and vice versa. As a simple example, GM could not sell an unlimited number of cars at current prices. If GM reduced its prices, as it does with various rebate programs, the quantities demanded by customers should increase.

Notice the conditional statement above about other things being equal. Changes in taste, prices of competing goods, and other factors might make possible rising volume along with rising prices. The point is that the quantity demanded will be greater at lower prices than at higher prices if price is the only factor changing.

Now consider the cost curve. Notice that it rises rapidly to point *A*, then less rapidly to point *B*, then more rapidly again. The economic interpretation of this form of cost curve is that at both very low and very high levels of volume, operations are relatively less efficient than in the middle. Consider an automobile manufacturer with large amounts of fixed costs that will be incurred at zero volume, such as depreciation, property taxes, some salaries, and so on. If it operates at very low levels of volume, it must have supervisors, utilities, inspectors, and enough workers to keep the assembly line going. These workers will be relatively inefficient because they will frequently be idle waiting for cars to come along the line. Hence, the time they put in might allow for the production of many more cars than they actually produce. The plant will run at normal efficiency at a more reasonable level of volume. However, as production approaches the capacity of the plant, inefficiencies will rise. Overtime pay will be required at higher rates, less skilled workers will have to be hired, more maintenance will be needed because of heavy machine use, and other factors will contribute to more rapidly rising costs. Therefore, with a given set of resources and plant capacity, costs over the entire range of that capacity are reflected by the total cost curve in Figure 2–4.

We meet these theoretical problems with the use of linear CVP analysis by referring to the concept of the relevant range. We assume that linear revenue and cost functions are sufficiently accurate for planning and decision-making purposes within the relevant range. (In fact, we define the relevant range as that area over which linear relationships are reasonably good models.) If the firm is contemplating operations well outside its current relevant range, or if for some other reason it cannot use linear functions, it can still use CVP analysis: it is possible to formulate and work with curvilinear revenue and cost functions.

Practical Considerations

The most pertinent question from a practical point of view is whether *any* curves, linear or nonlinear, can reasonably describe the operations of a modern, complex firm. This question has several aspects.

Managerial Discretion We stated early in this chapter that fixed costs are not expected to be fixed absolutely, but that they do not automatically change in response to changes in volume. Managers can raise or lower some fixed costs, such as advertising, research and development, and some salaries and bonuses. However, costs such as depreciation and property taxes cannot be easily changed in the short term without changing the character of the business.

We assume in CVP analysis that fixed costs will remain constant in that managers will not be changing the levels of those costs over which they have discretion. If such changes are being considered, it is still simple to incorporate the probable effects of such changes into the analysis. In fact, one of the basic uses of CVP analysis is determining the probable effect of changes in key variables. Therefore, the fact that fixed costs might actually be altered by managerial action does not present serious problems for CVP analysis as the discussion of sensitivity analysis illustrated.

Measures of Volume We assume that all costs are either fixed or vary with sales. Some costs will probably vary with other measures of volume. Costs of the purchasing department may vary with frequency of purchasing rather than with sales volume. Costs of the credit department will probably vary with the number of new customers seeking credit, which in itself may not vary with sales. Maintenance costs might be affected by the number of times machines need to be set up to make a new component or product. In short, factors other than sales will cause changes in the level of costs; therefore, our assumption that all costs are fixed or variable is rarely correct, as is our assumption that variable costs change only with changes in sales volume. This notion lies at the heart of activity-based costs—finding the activity or transaction that causes a cost to change. We expand on this concept in Chapter 4.

The fact that some costs will vary with other measures raises two questions. First, are the amounts of such costs likely to be so large that they will harm our analysis? Second, if these costs are large, can we do anything about them insofar as CVP analysis is concerned? Production costs will vary more generally with units produced rather than with units sold. As we discuss in Chapter 3, even within production, costs might vary with several different measures of volume.

If some costs do vary with other measures, we may still be able to predict them; prediction is the critical problem. Chapter 3 discusses questions involved in estimating patterns of cost behavior; Chapter 4 expands on tracing costs to non-volume related measures.

Random Fluctuations Can we expect price and cost always to be the same per unit or per period? Probably not. Prices might change several times over a year as might parts of unit variable costs. Even fixed costs may change. Therefore, do we expect firms in the real world to be describable by a simple CVP graph or by a simple linear formula for either revenue or costs?

Selling prices, variable costs, and fixed costs are likely to fluctuate over short periods and within the relevant range. We recognize that the selling price might have to be lowered because of competition and that suppliers may raise their prices, thereby increasing unit variable costs. Fixed costs may well fluctuate; heating costs, for example, depend on the weather and cannot be predicted exactly. In short, the profits or the volumes required to earn profits or any other answers we get from CVP analysis are estimates, not perfect predictors of actual profits or costs.

Remember that CVP analysis is essentially hypothetical: it answers "what if" questions and requires estimates of the values that key variables will take on. The analysis is not precise. The real question is whether fluctuations in selling prices and cost will be large enough to make significant differences between predicted and actual results. We think that CVP analysis is sufficiently accurate to be of considerable use to managers. It is true that if the firm's selling prices and unit variable costs fluctuate widely over short periods (as is often the case with some agricultural products), then CVP analysis may not be very useful. However, firms facing chaotic situations are relatively rare. The relationships graphed in Figure 2–5 apply to most firms. The revenue and

FIGURE 2–5 Cost Band

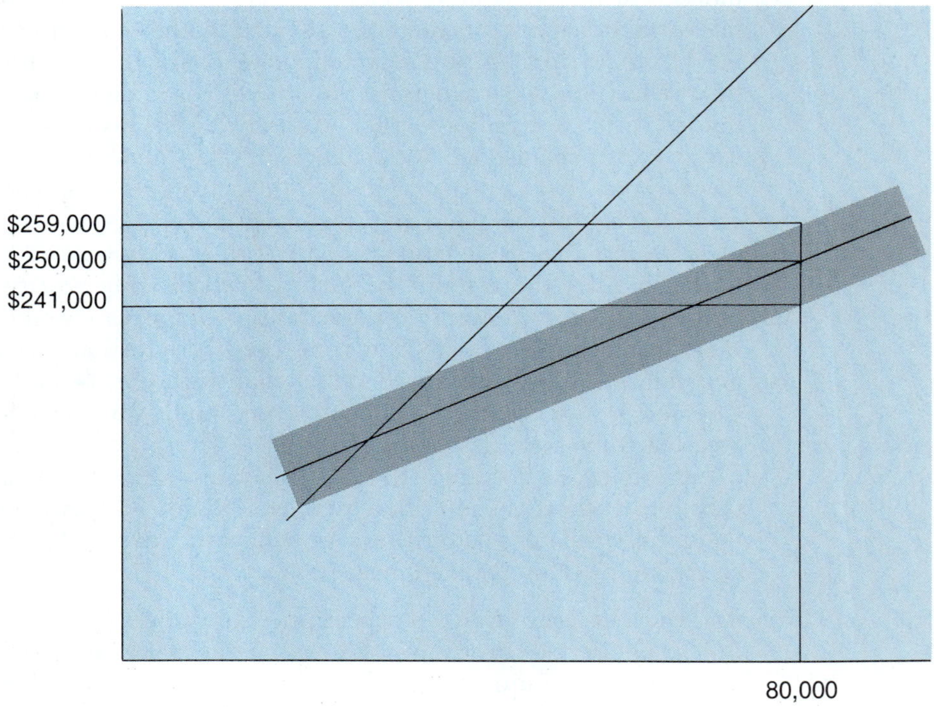

cost lines in the graph are bands. The single-point estimates that we make are really averages. We usually expect revenues and costs at particular levels of volume to vary somewhat. For example, Figure 2–5 shows the range of expected costs at a volume of 80,000 units. The $250,000 amount is the result of applying CVP analysis, with the $241,000 and $259,000 amounts representing the range of the estimate. That is, we expect that costs will be about $250,000, but we realize that they might be as high as $259,000 or as low as $241,000. A similar band could be constructed around the revenue line. Chapter 3 deals in depth with the questions raised by such estimates of the expected range of costs or revenues so that managers can develop a statistical range (confidence interval) around basic estimates.

The cost band in Figure 2–5 captures much of what we have said about practical considerations. The effects of managerial discretion over some costs, the response of some costs to measures other than sales, and random fluctuations widen the cost line. The basic cost-volume-profit model does not provide precise answers but gives general ideas about the behavior of revenues and costs.

Inventories Financial accounting practices and income tax law require that fixed production costs be included in the determination of inventory, rather than subtracted from contribution margin as we do in CVP analysis. As long as inventories remain about the same from beginning of period to end of period, the income calculated under the financial reporting and tax method will approximate that calculated by CVP techniques. If inventories change significantly, however, large differences will occur between the income computed under CVP analysis and that under financial or tax requirements. This subject is covered in detail in later chapters. We note now that the problem does not invalidate CVP analysis because internal reporting for managerial purposes does not have to conform to that used for financial or tax purposes.

Inflation The assumptions that costs will remain constant within the relevant range and the discussion about a reasonable range for costs are based on a moderate rate of inflation. With inflation of, say, about 4 percent a year, CVP analysis will yield reasonable results as we have discussed above. However, in an economy where inflation is severe, 100 percent, for example, then costs and prices are changing so rapidly that it is almost impossible for managers to establish the time dimension of the relevant range. While all costs change over time, if costs change so quickly that there is never a reasonable pause, managers are forced to add another variable into the basic relationship: inflation. This variable can be incorporated for individual cost elements (e.g., cost of materials versus the cost of labor) or on a broader basis by using an overall index (such as the Consumer Price Index or the Wholesale Price Index).

Review Problem

Revise the illustration in Exhibits 2–3 and 2–4 to include inflation. Assume that inflation affects unit price and unit variable costs to the same degree. Also assume that only 25 percent of fixed costs are affected by inflation since the other costs are fixed by long-term contracts (such as rent) or are due to depreciation, which is set at the time of the original purchase of an asset. First build in a 4 percent inflation factor for both price and costs. You can use the template EXH2–5.WK1 shown in Exhibit 2–5.

With both price and costs affected by the same inflation rate, since only 25 percent of fixed costs are subject to inflation, income rises with the 4 percent inflation factor. Now use the same changes used in Exhibit 2–4 and, in addition, change the inflation factor for costs to 6 percent while leaving the inflation adjustment for price at 4 percent. The results are shown in Exhibit 2–6. Thus, we can build in inflation when setting up sensitivity analysis. It might not be as simple as shown, however, since there are interrelationships among changes in unit price, unit variable costs, and fixed costs and the inflation rate. Thus, even with our original model, we can incorporate inflation implicitly in the original estimates and the percentage changes.

EXHIBIT 2–5 Effects of Inflation—Solitude Company

DATA SECTION

Inflation rate	Prices	4.00%			
	Costs	4.00%			

	Original Estimate	Percent Change	Revised Estimate	Percent Inflation Affected	Inflation Adjusted Estimate
Unit price	$20.00	0.00%	$20.00	100%	$20.80
Unit variable cost	$10.00	0.00%	$10.00	100%	$10.40
Period fixed costs	$70,000	0.00%	$70,000	25%	$70,700
Volume	10,000	0.00%	10,000	0%	10,000

SOLUTION SECTION

Income Statement
Solitude Company

	Dollars	Percent of Sales
Sales	$208,000	100.00%
Total variable costs	104,000	50.00%
Contribution margin	104,000	50.00%
Fixed costs	70,700	33.99%
Income	$33,300	16.01%

EXHIBIT 2–6 Effects of Inflation—Solitude Company

DATA SECTION

Inflation rate	Prices	4.00%			
	Costs	6.00%			

	Original Estimate	Percent Change	Revised Estimate	Percent Inflation Affected	Inflation Adjusted Estimate
Unit price	$20.00	-5.00%	$19.00	100%	$19.76
Unit variable cost	$10.00	7.00%	$10.70	100%	$11.34
Period fixed costs	$70,000	7.00%	$74,900	25%	$76,024
Volume	10,000	-8.00%	9,200		

SOLUTION SECTION

Income Statement
Solitude Company

	Dollars	Percent of Sales
Sales	$181,792	100.00%
Total variable costs	104,346	57.40%
Contribution margin	77,446	42.60%
Fixed costs	76,024	41.82%
Income	$1,422	0.78%

MULTIPLE PRODUCTS

Our examples to this point have been related to single products. Obviously, since many firms have several products, CVP must be adaptable to multiple products to be useful to many managers. We mentioned earlier that a multiple-product firm would not use a contribution margin per unit but an average contribution margin percentage. We also said that if we were to use the contribution margin percentage, either all products had to have about the same contribution margin percentage or the mix of sales of individual products had to be relatively constant (the constant sales mix assumption). The sales mix is the makeup of the relative proportions of products sold. Below is the calculation of a weighted average contribution margin percentage—a percentage that reflects the relative amounts of each product's sales. Data are:

	Products			
	A	*B*	*C*	*Total*
Percentage of dollar sales	40%	25%	35%	100%
Contribution margin percentage	30%	40%	50%	

The weighted average contribution margin percentage is calculated below.

	Products			
	A	*B*	*C*	*Total*
Sales mix percentage (percentage of dollar sales) × $1 =	40%	25%	35%	100%
Sales per $1 of total sales ×	$0.40	$0.25	$0.35	$1.00
Contribution margin percentage =	30%	40%	50%	
Contribution margin per dollar of total sales	$0.12	$0.10	$0.18	$0.395
Weighted average contribution margin percentage	39.50%			

Managers will use the 39.5 percent weighted average contribution margin percentage in making CVP analysis. Thus, we introduce another variable into our considerations: the weighted average contribution margin percentage.

The rationale for these calculations is that of each $1 in total sales, $0.40 comes from Product A; of that $0.40, 30 percent, or $0.12, becomes contribution margin. Hence for each $1 in total sales of all three products, Product A provides contribution margin of $0.12. Similar reasoning for the other two products shows that the firm gains a $0.395 contribution margin for each $1 in total sales, which is 39.5 percent. The calculations can be abbreviated so that we simply multiply the sales mix percentage for each product by its contribution margin percentage, then add the results to get the weighted average contribution margin percentage:

$$(40\% \times 30\%) + (25\% \times 40\%) + (35\% \times 50\%) = 39.5\%$$

Remember that this technique requires that the sales mix remain fairly constant. If the mix changes, say with higher percentages going to Product A and lower percentages to Product C, the weighted average contribution margin percentage would decline because Product A has a lower contribution margin percentage than does Product C.

When there are multiple products, managers are mostly limited to estimates and sensitivity analysis for the entire company. Since many fixed costs are common to all products (factory rent, managers' salaries, property taxes, for example), it may be impossible to get a meaningful breakeven for any single product. If, say, period fixed costs for the above example are $395,000, then the breakeven sales for the company are $1,000,000 ($395,000/0.395). If these costs are common to all products, we *cannot* find breakeven sales for Product A per se since the fixed costs are associated with *all* products.

SOME REFINEMENTS

When we consider the assumptions of CVP analysis, we can modify the basic analysis. The distinction between the level of fixed costs expected throughout the relevant range and the level expected at very low operation leads us to classify fixed costs as **avoidable** or **unavoidable**. Avoidable fixed costs can be eliminated by changing the operation, perhaps dropping one product from the firm's line or shutting down a regional sales office. This idea is expanded in Chapter 4. Decisions such as these receive extended treatment in Chapter 12.

Discretionary and Committed Costs

The question whether managers will change costs such as advertising, research and development, employee training, and other costs that may be changed relatively easily leads to another distinction: **discretionary costs** and **committed costs**. Discretionary costs are those that can be changed by management decision within short periods. They are also called *managed costs*, reflecting the ability of managers to alter them more or less at will. The existence of discretionary costs is the principal reason why some people prefer the term *nonvariable costs* to the term *fixed costs*. These costs do not change automatically and necessarily in response to changes in volume, but they do change, and perhaps frequently, as a result of management decisions.

Analyzing discretionary costs can sometimes present problems. For example, a discretionary cost may appear to be a variable cost because it is incurred at a constant rate of sales. Advertising may always be 5 percent of sales, or research and development 3 percent of sales, because of a management de-

FIGURE 2–6 Step-Variable Costs

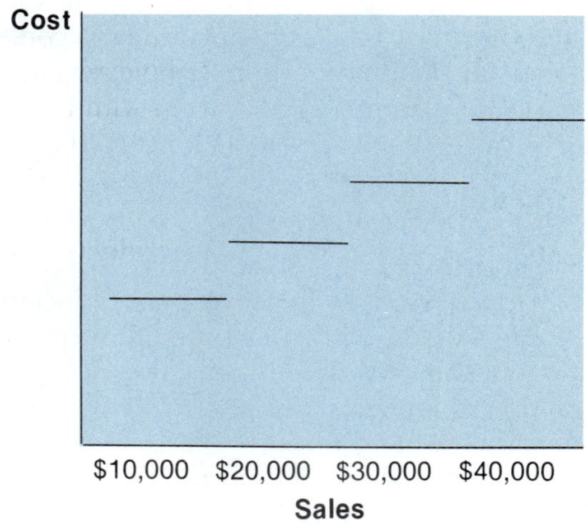

cision that the firm will base its expenditures for these items on the level of sales. Hence the costs will hold the same percentage relationships to sales at various levels of volume as the result of management decision, not because of an underlying economic relationship. The variable cost of goods sold or sales commissions will vary directly with sales because of economic relationships or contractual agreements.

In some sense, most fixed costs are discretionary over the long run. If a firm has ten engineers in its Plant Engineering Department, as long as the engineering function is necessary there must be at least one engineer; that is the unavoidable core, a true *fixed* cost. While the costs of the other nine engineers are fixed in the short run, employing them is a discretionary decision.[4]

Step-Variable Costs

One reason we do not expect costs to change in direct proportion to changes in volume is that some costs are incurred in large chunks, not continuously. For example, a firm may need an additional salaried salesperson for each $10,000 monthly increase in sales. The salary would then behave as shown in Figure 2–6, jumping from one level to the next as each $10,000 increment in sales is reached. These costs[5] are called **step-variable costs** because they vary with volume, but not in direct proportion.

[4]Some writers call the costs associated with the other nine engineers *long-run variable costs* since they are not core fixed costs and can be changed with conditions.

[5]Some writers call these costs *step-fixed* because they remain fixed over some range of volume, then jump to a higher level. We can call them *step-variable* because volume affects their levels.

Planning for step-variable costs essentially requires an estimate of the sales level and determination of the number of salaried people required. It is not a matter of multiplying volume by a unit variable cost. If such costs are a large proportion of total costs, planning becomes more tedious, but if they are a relatively small proportion, they may generally be treated as variable costs for firmwide planning.

INCOME TAXES IN CVP ANALYSIS

Our calculations so far have ignored income taxes. Introducing income taxes requires a straightforward modification of our basic profit relationship and CVP calculations. We are assuming that income taxes are assessed at a flat rate of pretax income. Tax law, however, is exceedingly complex and requires much more careful study. Yet for many corporations the flat-rate assumption does little harm to CVP calculations.

Basically all that is required to deal with income taxes and after-tax income is to recognize that after-tax income equals pretax income multiplied by one minus the tax rate. Thus, in solving for the unit volume required for a particular after-tax profit, divide the target after-tax profit by one minus the tax rate, which gives the pretax income required, and then solve in the usual way.

Suppose that Quadro Company, with its \$2 unit contribution margin and \$10,000 fixed costs, wanted an after-tax profit of \$12,000 per month. The company's tax rate is 40 percent.

$$\$12{,}000 = (\$2Q - \$10{,}000) \times (1 - 0.40)$$

$$Q = \frac{\dfrac{\$12{,}000}{1 - 0.40} + \$10{,}000}{\$2} = \frac{\$20{,}000 + \$10{,}000}{\$2} = 15{,}000 \text{ units}$$

Income taxes do not affect the breakeven point because at breakeven profits are zero both before and after taxes, since there are no income taxes at zero pretax profits.

SUMMARY

CVP analysis is used for planning and decision making. Basic to the analysis is the classification of cost by behavior: whether the cost varies with volume or remains constant through wide ranges of volume. The concept of contribution margin is critical to CVP analysis; it is used to find required volumes and to solve for other important unknowns in various situations.

CVP analysis rests on a number of assumptions and thus will not be literally true for all firms with volumes ranging from zero to high volumes. The analysis will often produce reasonable results that can be used within the relevant range. It can be used to answer questions such as the following: What is the price required to give us a particular target profit? Given current market conditions and prices, what must our variable cost per unit be to give us a particular target profit? How many units must we sell to justify an increase in fixed costs? Would it be desirable to reduce variable costs and increase fixed costs?

We have seen how spreadsheets help us to answer these questions and allow us to work with the basic CVP relationship and to expand our analysis to include changes in several variables at one time.

REVIEW PROBLEM

Anderson Company sells a single product for $20 per unit. Anderson pays $12 per unit for the product and pays a commission of ten percent of the selling price to salespeople. All sales are subject to commission. Fixed costs are $120,000. Do each of the following steps independently:[6]

1. Determine the breakeven point in units and in dollars.

2. Determine the volume in both units and dollars required to earn $40,000.

3. Anderson's managers believe that they can sell 25,000 units. What selling price is needed to give a $40,000 monthly profit? *Hint*: Remember that the commission on sales is a percentage of selling price.

4. What unit volume will yield a 6 percent return on sales?

5. Repeat parts 1 and 2 assuming a 40 percent income tax rate. The $40,000 target in part 2 is not the after-tax target.

6. Anderson's managers are considering a change in the commission structure. The change would reduce the commission to five percent of selling price and increase fixed costs to $150,000. At what unit volume would Anderson earn the same pretax profit under the existing structure and under the proposed one?

7. It turns out that Anderson actually sells three products. Data on these products appear below.

	A	B	C
Selling price	$10	$20	$30
Unit variable cost	4	12	15
Percentage of dollar sales	20%	50%	30%

[6]You may want to modify QUADRO.WK1 to help you answer these questions.

The unit variable costs include purchase cost and commissions. Determine the weighted average contribution margin percentage and the monthly sales required to earn a \$40,000 profit before taxes.

ANSWERS TO REVIEW PROBLEM

1. 20,000 units; \$400,000

$$\$120{,}000/(\$20 - \$12 - \$2) = 20{,}000$$

The 10 percent commission is \$2 per unit. The \$400,000 is either 20,000 × \$20, or, using the contribution margin percentage, 30% (\$6/\$20).

$$\frac{\$120{,}000}{0.30} = \$400{,}000$$

2. 26,667 units; \$533,333

$$\frac{\$120{,}000 + \$40{,}000}{\$6} = 26{,}667$$

\$533,333 is \$20 × 26,667, or \$160,000/0.30.

3. \$20.44 (rounded)

$$\begin{aligned} 25{,}000\,(P - \$12 - 0.10P) - \$120{,}000 &= \$40{,}000 \\ 25{,}000P - 2{,}500P &= \$460{,}000 \\ P &= \$20.444 \end{aligned}$$

4. 25,000 units

$$\frac{\$120{,}000}{0.30 - 0.06} = \$500{,}000, \text{ divided by } \$20 \text{ gives } 25{,}000 \text{ units}$$

5. There is no effect on the breakeven point because at zero pretax profit (breakeven), there are no taxes. For a \$40,000 after-tax profit at a 40 percent tax rate, you need \$66,667 pretax profit (\$40,000/0.60). Thus, (\$120,000 + \$66,667)/\$6 = 31,111 units.

6. 30,000 units

The easiest way to solve this part is to find the contribution margins under the two alternatives, set pretax profits equal, and solve for volume. The current contribution margin is \$6. Contribution margin after the reduction in commissions is \$7 per unit (the five percent commission is \$1 per unit, which makes total unit variable cost \$13). Profit is

Current		*Proposed*
$\$6Q - \$120{,}000$	=	$\$7Q - \$150{,}000$
$\$1Q$	=	\$30,000
Q	=	30,000

7. 47%; $340,425

	A	B	C
Percentage of dollar sales	20%	50%	30%
Contribution margin percentage	60%	40%	50%
Weighted contribution	12%	20%	15%

Weighted average contribution margin percentage is 47 percent (12% + 20% + 15%).

$$(\$120{,}000 + \$40{,}000)/0.47 = \$340{,}425$$

ASSIGNMENTS

2–1 Basic CVP Analysis The following data relate to Hobart Company, which sells a single product:

Price per unit	$ 20
Purchase cost per unit	11
Sales commissions, 10% of selling price	2
Monthly fixed costs	$80,000

REQUIRED

Answer each question independently of the others.

1. Determine the volume needed to earn $40,000 per month before taxes.
2. Determine the volume needed to earn $40,000 per month after taxes, when the tax rate is 40 percent.
3. Determine the selling price needed to earn $30,000 per month, pretax, at a volume of 15,000 units. Remember that commissions are 10 percent of selling price.
4. Suppose that the firm could increase the number of units sold by 2,000 per month (at the $20 price) if it increased fixed promotional expenses by $8,000 per month. By how much, and in what direction, would its pretax income change?
5. The firm's salespeople would like to change their compensation from a 10 percent commission to a 5 percent commission plus $20,000 per month in salary. They now receive only commissions. At what volume (at the $20 price) would the firm earn the same income under the proposed plan as the firm would earn under the existing plan?

2–2 CVP Graph The graph on the following page depicts the cost-volume-profit relationships for Byham Company, a wholesaler of dry goods. Volume is measured by a standard unit, which is a weighted average of selling prices and variable costs for all products that the firm sells.

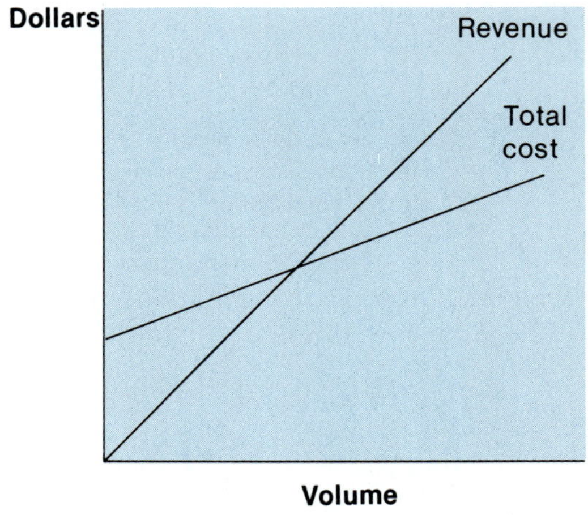

The president of the firm wants your advice about a number of matters. She suggests that you answer the following questions by stating what, if anything, would happen to the revenue line and the total cost line. (For example, an increase in selling prices would rotate the revenue line up, not affect the total cost line.)

REQUIRED

Treat each case independently of the others.

1. What would happen if the sales mix shifted toward higher percentages of products that have low selling prices and low variable costs?
2. The firm now pays salespeople a 10 percent commission. It will begin paying a 5 percent commission plus a flat monthly salary.
3. The firm will sell more units than previously expected.
4. Both selling prices and purchase costs will rise by 10 percent over all products.
5. Monthly rent will increase by $2,000.

2–3 Target Profits (AICPA) Kalik Company sells radios for $60. Variable expenses are $40 per unit, while fixed expenses total $30,000.

REQUIRED

1. Determine the number of radios that Kalik must sell to earn $70,000.
2. Determine the dollar sales that Kalik needs to break even.

2–4 Product Mix The Layton Department Store has three major departments: clothing, furniture, and appliances. Annual fixed costs are about $1,600,000. Data on the three departments appear below.

	Clothing	*Furniture*	*Appliances*
Sales mix, percentage in dollars	45%	30%	25%
Contribution margin percentage	40%	50%	55%

REQUIRED

1. Determine the dollar volume that will give a pretax profit of $300,000 at the sales mix given above.

2. During the coming year, variable costs of clothing are expected to increase by 10 percent, *not* 10 percentage points. What effect would this have on the firm's weighted average contribution margin percentage and volume required to earn $300,000 before taxes? You might wish to set up a hypothetical unit to trace the effects.

3. Using your results from part 2, determine the percentage increase in selling prices in the clothing department that would bring the weighted average contribution margin back to the original value that you used in part 1.

2–5 Basic CVP Analysis The Rhom Company sells a single product. Data relating to expected operations in 19X6 appear below.

Sales, 100,000 units at $8		$800,000
Variable costs:		
Purchase price of product	$300,000	
Commissions, 10% of sales	80,000	380,000
Contribution margin		420,000
Fixed costs		300,000
Profit before taxes		$120,000

The president of the firm has some questions for you. Each situation is independent of the others.

REQUIRED

1. What is the firm's breakeven point?
2. What unit sales would give a pretax profit of $180,000?
3. If the firm could sell 100,000 units and wanted a pretax profit of $180,000, what price would it have to charge? (Remember that commissions are a percentage of sales.)
4. If the purchase price of the product increased by 10 percent, what volume would be required to earn a $120,000 pretax profit?
5. What volume would give a 20 percent return on sales?
6. If the selling price of the product increased by 10 percent, what volume would give a pretax profit of $120,000?

2–6 CVP Relationships Fill in the blanks for each of the following independent situations. There are no income taxes.

	Unit Sales	*Selling Price*	*Unit Variable Cost*	*Total Fixed Costs*	*Profit*
1.	40,000	$10	$6	$____	$60,000
2.	____	6	2	40,000	20,000
3.	20,000	____	6	90,000	50,000
4.	30,000	12	____	70,000	50,000

2–7 CVP Relationships—Income Taxes Fill in the blanks for each of the following independent situations, assuming an income tax rate of 40 percent.

	Unit Sales	Selling Price	Unit Variable Cost	Total Fixed Costs	After-Tax Profit
1.	60,000	$10	$6	$ ____	$60,000
2.	____	8	5	40,000	30,000
3.	20,000	____	6	90,000	45,000
4.	30,000	12	____	90,000	72,000

2–8 Profit Graph As the chief staff accountant of Linington Industries, you must present reports to upper-level management. This afternoon you are to report on three products that the firm could introduce during the coming year. A marketing manager will discuss the prospects for unit sales volume for each product; your job is to show the cost-volume-profit relationships. You would like to make it easy for the assembled managers to see the relationships, so you plot them all on a single profit graph. The following data are supplied to you.

Product	Selling Price	Variable Cost per Unit	Annual Fixed Costs
X-1	$10	$6	$ 60,000
X-2	18	8	200,000
X-3	12	4	120,000

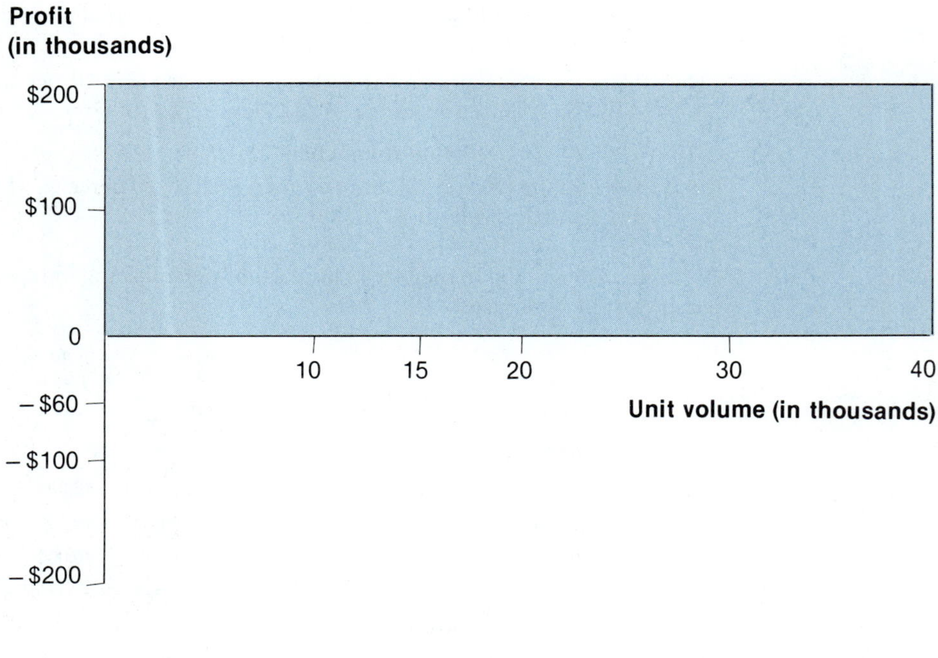

REQUIRED

Draw in the lines representing profit or loss for each product and comment on the results.

2–9 Breakeven Pricing The alumni of Waterford University are having a reunion. The committee in charge of the reunion has decided to hold a dinner dance at the Rockington Hotel. The following estimates of costs are available to the committee:

Rental of ballroom	$ 300
Orchestra	$1,500
Tickets, mailing, etc.	$ 600
Meal, per person	$ 12
Sales tax on meal	7% of price
Favors, programs, door prizes, per person	$ 2.50

The committee expects about 300 people to attend and wants the affair to break even.

REQUIRED

1. Determine the price per person that will accomplish the committee's objective.

2. One member of the committee wants to price the tickets at $20 per person. How many people would have to attend to reach the breakeven point?

2–10 Profit Planning (AICPA) Wilson Company prepared the following preliminary forecast concerning Product G for 19X2, assuming no expenditures for advertising:

Unit selling price	$10
Unit sales	100,000
Variable costs	$600,000
Fixed costs	$300,000

Based on a market study in December 19X1, Wilson estimated that it could increase the unit selling price by 15 percent and the unit sales by 10 percent if it spent $100,000 on advertising.

REQUIRED

If Wilson were to incorporate these changes into its 19X2 forecast, what should the income from Product G be?

2–11 CVP Relationships—Taxes Each of the following situations is independent of the others.

REQUIRED

Answer each question on the basis of the available information.

1. A firm in the 40 percent tax bracket with a contribution margin percentage of 30 percent had sales of $1,000,000 and income after taxes of $30,000. What were the firm's fixed costs and its income taxes?

2. A firm with a contribution margin of $2 per unit earned $50,000 before taxes and had fixed costs of $200,000. What were its unit sales?

3. A firm with sales of $2,000,000 and fixed costs of $600,000 earned $300,000 after taxes. The tax rate was 40 percent. What were its variable costs?

4. A firm showed a loss of $40,000 (ignoring taxes) on sales of $200,000. In the next period, it earned $10,000 before taxes on sales of $300,000. What was its contribution margin percentage? What were its fixed costs?

2–12 Use of Unit Costs The controller of Arvan Industries prepared the following income statement, based on expected volume of 100,000 units per month for the coming year.

Sales		$22
Variable costs	$14	
Fixed costs	6	20
Profit		$ 2

REQUIRED

1. Determine the monthly breakeven point.
2. Determine the unit volume needed to double the expected *total* monthly profit.
3. Determine the unit volume needed to double the expected *per unit* monthly profit.

2–13 Product Mix The Raffin Company makes three products. Data follow:

	Product 101	*Product 102*	*Product 103*
Selling price	$10	$20	$40
Variable costs	7	12	16

Total annual fixed costs are $840,000. The firm's experience has been that about 20 percent of dollar sales come from Product 101, 60 percent from 102, and 20 percent from 103.

REQUIRED

1. Compute the breakeven point in sales dollars. Determine the number of units of each product that would be sold at the breakeven point.
2. Suppose the firm expected to sell $2.5 million at the normal mix. Would it be wise to spend an additional $100,000 on advertising that would increase the mix of Product 103 to 30 percent while reducing the mix of Product 101 to 10 percent? Total sales would remain at $2.5 million.
3. Assume now that the mix is 20 percent, 60 percent, 20 percent in *unit* sales for Products 101, 102, and 103, respectively. What is the breakeven point in total units?
4. Suppose that the firm expects to sell 85,000 total units in the mix given in part 3. Would it pay to spend an additional $100,000 in advertising to shift the mix to 10 percent, 60 percent, and 30 percent for 101, 102, and 103, respectively? Total sales for the firm are still 85,000 units.

2–14 Fundamental Sensitivity Analysis Cliff Bryant, president of Bryant Company, has given you the following forecasted results for the company's only product:

Unit sales	30,000
Selling price	$20
Unit variable cost	$ 8
Total fixed costs	$300,000

REQUIRED

1. Bryant is concerned about the effects of changes in the variables. He says that any of them might change unfavorably by 10 percent. Determine which unfavorable 10 percent change would reduce expected profits the most. Consider one at a time; that is, hold all others constant at the expected amounts.
2. Bryant also knows that any of the variables could change in a favorable direction. Determine which 10 percent favorable change would increase expected profits the most. Again, do your analyses one at a time.

2–15 Profit Planning and Inflation The data below are from the 19X7 records of the Scagway Household Products Company. For 19X8, the managers of the firm expect purchase prices to rise by an average of 8 percent, selling prices by 6 percent, and physical volume by 10 percent. Operating expenses should rise 9 percent in all categories, except for commissions, which will remain at 10 percent of sales. The tax rate should be 40 percent in 19X8.

Revenue		$2,560,000
Cost of sales, all variable		1,820,000
Gross profit		740,000
Sales commissions, 10% of sales	$256,000	
Office salaries	198,000	
Rent	36,000	
Heat and light	17,300	
Miscellaneous	13,400	520,700
Profit before taxes		219,300
Income taxes at 40%		87,720
Net income		$ 131,580

REQUIRED

1. What should the firm's after-tax income be in 19X8?
2. What sales volume would give the firm the same income in 19X8 as it earned in 19X7, with the changes in costs and prices projected for 19X8?

2–16 Service Business Frank James's automobile repair business employs six full-time mechanics. James himself supervises, takes care of office and administrative work, and occasionally does repair work.

James charges customers for materials and labor. He charges 20 percent over his cost for materials and multiplies the wage rate of the mechanic by two in determining the labor charge. Late in 19X5 James developed the following estimates for 19X6, based on historical results and expected changes.

Payroll, mechanics	$103,500
Rent	7,500
Utilities	14,300
Insurance	6,500
Other overhead costs	16,600
Materials for repair work, cost	48,500

James estimates that about 85 percent of mechanic time is chargeable to customers, with the remainder being holiday pay, sick leave, vacations, and so on.

REQUIRED

Write a formal memorandum to management. Use a microcomputer and a word-processing program along with a spreadsheet program for supporting schedules. See Appendix B for guidelines for memoranda presentation.

Frank James has hired you as a consultant. Mr. James is an excellent mechanic, but knows little about accounting. Write a memorandum to Mr. James in which you show him:

a. what profit he should earn in 19X6
b. what multiple of labor he would have to charge (all other data remaining as originally given) to earn a $50,000 profit.

Make sure to include any other issues that you believe important in relation to Mr. James's desire to increase profits.

2–17 CVP Analysis, Changing Cost Structure Tripleweek Book Company publishes paperbacks, principally romantic novels. The firm has acquired the rights to *Echo Valley* by C. M. Jones. Although Jones's books have done well in the past, the president of Tripleweek is not confident about *Echo Valley* because the hardcover edition did not do particularly well.

The critical problem is the first press run. Tripleweek would normally order 200,000 copies from the printer, but the president thinks that it might be better to order 50,000 or 100,000. She has obtained the following prices from the printer.

	Press Run		
	50,000	*100,000*	*200,000*
Set up	$ 9,000	$ 9,000	$ 9,000
Paper and printing	50,000	92,000	170,000
Totals	$59,000	$101,000	$179,000

The reductions in per copy prices for paper and printing arise because the printer can get quantity discounts on the paper it buys for the book, and some of the savings are passed on to Tripleweek.

The price of the book on the newsstands will be $2.25, of which Tripleweek gets $1.50. Unsold copies are sent to discounters at $0.40 each. As a rule, Tripleweek loses sales that it cannot meet from the first run. Books such as *Echo Valley* generally sell for about 60 days and then fade away. It takes about 60 days to order and print a new press run, so Tripleweek either makes it on the first run or not at all.

REQUIRED

Use an electronic spreadsheet to solve the following:

1. For each press run, determine the number of copies that Tripleweek must sell at the regular price to break even.
2. Besides the breakeven points you have already calculated, what information can you give the president to assist her in making the decision?

2–18 Unit Costs and Pricing The controller of Farnum Company is responsible for recommending prices for the company's products. Each product is expected to provide a pretax profit of 20 percent of revenue. She has just received the following information about a proposed new product.

Expected annual unit volume	20,000
Estimated unit variable cost	$14
Estimated unit fixed costs at 20,000 units	$ 6

REQUIRED

1. What selling price will yield the desired profit?
2. The controller showed the analysis from part 1 to the marketing manager, who said that at that price the company could not expect to sell more than 18,000 units. What selling price would yield the desired profit at 18,000 units?
3. What would you expect the marketing manager to say when he sees the price you calculated in part 2?

2–19 Changes in Operations (AICPA) Pitt Company is considering a proposal to replace existing machinery used to manufacture Product A. The new machinery will increase fixed costs by $120,000 and reduce unit variable costs by 20 percent through savings in materials and labor. Before considering the change, Pitt had budgeted Product A's results as shown below.

Sales	$2,000,000
Variable costs	70% of sales
Fixed costs	$ 400,000

REQUIRED

Determine the increase or decrease in profit that should result from accepting the proposal.

2–20 CVP Analysis, Taxes Hobart Company makes a garden hose. Expected results for 19X9 appear below.

Sales 200,000 hoses at $4		$800,000
Cost of sales:		
Variable manufacturing costs	$300,000	
Fixed manufacturing costs	200,000	500,000
Gross margin		300,000
Selling and administrative expenses:		
Commissions, 5% of sales	$ 40,000	
Fixed S&A expenses	120,000	160,000
Income before taxes		140,000
Income taxes at 40%		56,000
Net income		$ 84,000

The treasurer of the firm has asked for your assistance in answering some questions about operations. Consider each independently of the others.

REQUIRED

1. How many units would the firm have to sell to earn an after-tax income of $120,000?
2. What is the firm's breakeven point?

3. What price per unit would the firm have to obtain selling 200,000 units to earn an after-tax profit of $100,000?
4. What volume would the firm have to obtain to earn a 15 percent after-tax return on sales?

2–21 CVP Analysis (AICPA) Daly Company has determined the number of units of Product Y that it must sell to break even. However, Daly would like to earn a 20 percent return on sales of Product Y.

REQUIRED

1. Explain how breakeven analysis can be used to determine the number of units of Product Y that Daly would have to sell to achieve its objective.
2. If the unit variable cost of Product Y were to increase as a percentage of selling price, how would that affect the number of units that Daly would have to sell to break even?
3. Identify the limitations of breakeven analysis in managerial planning.

2–22 Alternative Cost Structures Your boss, the president of Nevco, Inc., has informed you that he is considering the lease of a new machine. The lease is $12,000 per month and runs for one year. The machine should reduce labor and other variable costs by about $0.40 per unit. Volume of the product is currently about 50,000 units per month, and you expect it to remain there for the next year.

REQUIRED

1. Determine whether leasing the machine is wise.
2. Suppose that the firm could lease the machine for a five-year period at $10,000 per month. What advantages and disadvantages do you see to the five-year as opposed to the one-year lease?

2–23 Unit Costs The controller of Delpt Company has just handed you the following data relating to the company's budgeted operations for the coming year.

Selling price	$20
Unit cost	19
Unit profit	$1
Volume	40,000
Expected pretax profit	$40,000

The controller told you that she thought the information should be presented this way so that you could concentrate on the critical factors instead of having to wade through 10 or 15 different types of cost. She added that about $5 of the unit cost represented salaries, rent, depreciation, and utilities, and $14 was the purchase price of the one product that the firm sells.

The president of the firm then asked you the following questions. Answer each independently of the others.

REQUIRED

1. How many units must we sell to earn a $60,000 profit?
2. If we could sell 35,000 units, what price would we have to charge to earn a $35,000 profit?
3. Would we be better off reducing our price by $1 to increase our volume 10,000 units (from 40,000 to 50,000 units, and from $20 to $19 in price)?
4. How many units must we sell to earn a 10 percent return on sales?
5. How many units must we sell to show a unit profit of $2?

2–24 Product Mix Nelson Sporting Goods Company makes, among other things, golf balls of two types—the Z-flight and the Pro-flight. The managers of the firm have been looking for ways to improve profitability and have come up with three suggestions. If none of the suggestions is accepted, they expect the following results. Revenue and cost data are per dozen balls.

	Z-flight	*Pro-flight*
Suggested retail price	$14.00	$18.00
Net revenue to Nelson, 80% of retail	11.20	14.40
Variable manufacturing costs	4.10	4.80
Sales commissions at 10% of net	1.12	1.44
Total variable costs	5.22	6.24
Contribution margin	$ 5.98	$ 8.16
Expected sales, dozens of balls	80,000	48,000

Nelson sets retail prices, prints them on the packages, and charges retailers 80 percent of the suggested retail. Retailers stick fairly closely to the suggested retail price, although there is some discounting.

The three suggestions and their expected results are as follows:

1. Decrease the suggested retail price of Pro-flights by $1 per dozen. The manager who made this suggestion believes that total sales of both balls would go up by 10 percent and that the mix of Pro-flights would increase to about 70 percent of the sales of Z-flights.
2. Increase the suggested retail price of Z-flights by $1 per dozen. The manager who made this proposal thinks that total sales of both balls would remain the same, with a shift of 5,000 dozen from Z-flights to Pro-flights.
3. Spend $80,000 on advertising Pro-flights. The expectation is that sales of Pro-flights would increase by 20,000 dozen, with about 30 percent of that increase coming at the expense of sales of Z-flights.

REQUIRED

You are a consultant hired by Nelson. Write a memorandum to Nelson's management in which you evaluate each suggestion, make a recommendation about which suggestion Nelson should follow, and justify your recommendation. Make sure to discuss factors outside of specific problem information that are important to Nelson in this situation. See Appendix B for guidelines for memoranda presentation.

2–25 Selling Price (AICPA) Freeman, Inc., management has performed cost studies and projected the following annual costs based on a 40,000 unit volume.

	Total Annual Cost	*Percentage of Total Annual Cost That Is Variable*
Materials	$400,000	100%
Direct labor	360,000	75
Manufacturing overhead	300,000	40
Selling and administrative	200,000	25

REQUIRED

1. Compute Freeman's unit selling price that will yield a 10 percent return on sales at 40,000 units.
2. Assume that management sets a $30 selling price. Determine the dollar sales necessary to earn a 10 percent return on sales.

2–26 Committed and Discretionary Costs The Moss Company expects to bring out a new product in about three months. The product requires very close tolerances in the manufacturing process, and a computer is needed to ensure quality control. The managers of the firm expect the product to be successful, but they cannot be sure that it will be.

One question the managers must resolve is the lease of a computer to handle quality control. The particular computer needed can be leased in two ways:

1. A month-to-month lease at $3,000 per month.
2. A three-year lease at $2,400 per month.

The three-year lease cannot be canceled until it runs its course. If the product should prove unsuccessful, the firm will be stuck with the computer because it does not have alternative uses; it is specially designed for products like the one the firm will introduce.

REQUIRED

Discuss the factors you would want the managers to consider in reaching a decision.

2–27 Unit Costs and Prices PFR Company expects the following monthly results in 19X4:

	Total	*Per Unit*
Sales, 50,000 units × $10	$500,000	$10
Variable costs, 50,000 × $4	200,000	4
Contribution margin	300,000	6
Fixed costs	200,000	4
Profit	$100,000	$ 2

REQUIRED

Consider each part independently.

1. A manager suggests raising the price to $11.25. She estimates volume at 40,000 units at that price, with a $2.25 per unit profit, calculated as follows:

Price	$11.25
Variable costs	4.00
Contribution margin	7.25
Fixed costs $200,000/40,000	5.00
Profit	$ 2.25

Should PFR increase the price? Show why or why not.

2. Refer to the original data. A large chain store has offered to buy 30,000 units per month at $6.50 each. These units are in addition to the 50,000 at the $10 price. The controller estimates that accepting the order would increase fixed costs by $40,000 because PFR would be above its relevant range. Unit variable costs would remain at $4. He calculates the unit costs at 80,000 units at $7.00.

Variable cost	$4.00
Fixed costs, $240,000/80,000	3.00
Total unit cost	$7.00

The controller then said: "We would be accepting a price below our unit cost, which is senseless, so I recommend that we do not accept the offer." Determine whether the controller was correct.

3. Assume the same facts as in part 2 except that the price offered is $8.75 and fixed costs would increase by $150,000. The controller's analysis is:

Variable cost	$4.00
Fixed costs, $350,000/80,000	4.375
Total unit cost	$8.375

The controller recommends accepting the offer because the price exceeds the unit cost. Determine whether the controller is correct.

2–28 Changes in Cost Structure Levin Calculator Sales, a marketing company, is reevaluating how to compensate its retail sales personnel. Salespeople currently earn a 10 percent commission on sales and get a base salary of $10,000 each. A proposed incentive plan would lower base salary to $5,000 but would change the commission to 16 percent. There are six retail salespeople, and average sales are $50,000 per month in the retail outlet. Normal contribution margin is 40 percent (not considering sales costs), and fixed costs other than salaries of salespeople are $40,000 per year.

REQUIRED

1. How would the proposed change affect breakeven for Levin? Why?

2. At what level of sales would management be indifferent between these two plans?

2–29 Profit Planning (CMA) Early in 19X7, the controller of Davan Company prepared the following income statement for 19X6.

Sales	$900,000
Variable costs:	
Manufacturing	$315,000
Selling and administrative	180,000
Total variable costs	495,000
Contribution margin	405,000
Fixed costs:	
Manufacturing	$ 90,000
Selling	112,500
Administrative	45,000
Total fixed costs	247,500
Income before taxes	$157,500
Income taxes at 40%	63,000
Net income	$ 94,500

These results are from selling 1,800 tons of product. Capacity is 3,000 tons. Answer each part independently.

REQUIRED

1. Determine the breakeven point in tons of product.
2. If sales volume for the coming year were to be 2,100 tons, and all other factors would remain the same as they were in 19X6, what would net income be?
3. Davan is considering marketing its product in a new territory. It would have to pay a $25 per ton sales commission and spend $61,500 annually on advertising. How many tons would it have to sell in the new territory to maintain its current net income of $94,500?
4. Davan is considering replacing a highly labor-intensive process with some automatic machinery. The change would result in an additional $58,500 in annual fixed manufacturing costs and would reduce variable manufacturing costs by $25 per ton. Determine the breakeven point if the change is made.
5. The managers of Davan expect that they will have to reduce the selling price by 10 percent and that variable costs will increase by $40 per ton. Determine the volume in sales dollars that Davan would need to earn an after-tax profit of $94,500.

2–30 Cost Classification Carmen Company expects to produce 20,000 units of a particular product in the coming year. The product requires 2 pounds of a raw material called Z-gon, which the firm expects to buy at $3 per pound.

Recently the manager of the company that supplies Z-gon suggested that he would be willing to sell 40,000 pounds of Z-gon to Carmen at $2.75 per pound, provided that Carmen agreed to take 40,000 pounds, whether it could use it or not. The 40,000 pounds would be delivered in equal monthly amounts, which would suit Carmen because it generally makes the same quantity of product each month.

REQUIRED

Materials are generally considered a variable cost. If Carmen takes the offer, would the cost of materials still be variable? If not, what kind of cost would it be, committed or discretionary? What factors would the managers of Carmen want to consider before accepting the offer? Assume that if Carmen needed more than 40,000 pounds, it could acquire its additional needs at $3 per pound.

2–31 Special Order Pricing (AICPA) Wagner Company sells product A at $21 per unit. Its cost per unit based on full capacity of 200,000 units is as follows:

Materials, variable	$ 4
Direct labor, variable	5
Overhead, two-thirds fixed	6
Total	$15

Wagner has received an offer for 20,000 units from a foreign distributor. The only selling costs on the order are $3 per unit for shipping. Wagner has sufficient capacity to manufacture the additional units.

REQUIRED

Determine the minimum selling price that Wagner could accept for the special order.

2–32 Profit Improvement Jacob Fraher, owner and president of the Midland Manufacturing Company, was not happy with the results of the first quarter of 19X7. The income statement that distressed Fraher appears below.

Sales, 31,340 units		$385,482
Variable costs:		
Materials	$ 67,370	
Labor	78,590	
Manufacturing overhead	48,510	
Selling and administrative	21,780	216,250
Contribution margin		169,232
Fixed costs:		
Manufacturing	$103,450	
Selling and administrative	36,720	140,170
Income before taxes		$ 29,062

He had hoped that the firm would be able to show a pretax profit of $50,000 per quarter during the year. He called in Art Hamilton, his controller, and told him:

> I want you to determine what we need to do to earn $50,000 per quarter. Look at volume, selling price, variable cost, and fixed costs and come up with some way that we can improve the outlook.

REQUIRED

Design an electronic spreadsheet template to solve the following:

1. Determine the levels of volume, selling price, variable cost per unit (total only, not by individual component), and total fixed costs that would yield pretax profits of $50,000 per quarter. As you analyze each factor, hold all other factors constant at their existing levels. Also show the percentage change between the new value and the original value for each.
2. Repeat part 1, but find the levels (and percentage changes) that would cause the firm to break even.
3. Which variables seem more sensitive to change? Why?

2–33 CVP Analysis Paul Robertson is a tennis buff living in a medium-sized town in New England. The outdoor tennis season there generally runs from early April through mid-October. Robertson has conceived the idea of opening an indoor tennis club that would operate about 180 days each year. He has found a suitable building that he could rent for $20,000 per year on a two-year lease. He would need about $12,000 for equipment, including posts, nets, lockers, and office furnishings. The building could accommodate six courts, locker space, office space, and a lounge.

Robertson has developed the following estimates of operating costs, assuming that he would keep the club open from 10 A.M. to midnight, 180 days per year.

Rent	$20,000
Utilities	18,000
Salaries of attendants and office staff	42,400
Insurance	10,700
Miscellaneous, including $1,200 depreciation	7,600
Total	$98,700

In discussions with owners of similar clubs, Robertson has learned that a charge of $13 per court hour for the period from 10 A.M. to 7 P.M. is normal. From 7 P.M. to midnight, the usual charge is $9 per court hour. Thus, if four people played, they would each pay $3.25 or $2.25 per hour, depending on the time period.

REQUIRED

1. Suppose that Robertson could rent 80 percent of the available court time in both time periods. What profit would he earn?

2. Assume now that Robertson could rent 80 percent of the time from 7 P.M. to midnight. What percentage of the time would he have to rent from 10 A.M. to 7 P.M. to earn $50,000?

3. Suppose now that Robertson is confident of renting 80 percent of available time in both periods. He is considering a fixed-fee arrangement where he will offer a group of players an hour every week of the season (26 weeks); the fee will be $195 per group in the period from 7 P.M. to midnight, $285 in the period from 10 A.M. to 7 P.M. He believes that about 50 groups will take advantage of the deal for each time period (100 groups in all). He also believes that if the offer were not available, the takers would probably play about 20 hours during the season during the same period that they would select under the fixed-fee arrangement. Should he institute the fixed-fee arrangement?

4. Robertson knows that the building he is considering has been vacant for over a year, having been occupied by a manufacturing firm that went bankrupt. He believes that the building's owner would probably accept $17,000 per year rental on a five-year lease. What factors should he consider in deciding whether to pursue a five-year lease?

2–34 Profit Planning (CMA) Maxwell Company manufactures and sells a single product. Price and cost data follow.

Selling price per unit	$25.00
Unit variable costs:	
Materials	$11.00
Direct labor	5.00
Manufacturing overhead	2.50
Selling expenses	1.30
Total	$19.80
Annual fixed costs:	
Manufacturing overhead	$192,000
Selling and administrative	$276,000
Total	$468,000
Annual volume forecasted	3,000,000 units
Income tax rate	40%

REQUIRED

1. Determine the breakeven point.
2. Determine the number of units Maxwell would have to sell to earn $156,000 after taxes.
3. Maxwell's managers believe that direct labor rates could increase by 8 percent. If that happens, what will the breakeven point be?
4. If the direct labor rate does increase by 8 percent, by how much would Maxwell have to raise its selling price to maintain the same contribution margin per unit? By how much would it have to increase the selling price to maintain the same contribution margin ratio?

2–35 Converting an Income Statement Norbert Company's accountant prepared the following income statement for June 19X6, using the format that the company uses for statements to its banks and other interested outsiders.

Sales		$535,000
Cost of sales		242,000
Gross margin		293,000
Operating expenses:		
Commissions	$14,500	
Shipping	19,900	
Depreciation	45,400	
Salaries	85,300	
Other operating expenses	67,500	232,600
Income before taxes		$ 60,400

Wayne Norbert, the president of the company, would like you to recast the statement using a behavioral classification of costs. He and his accountant provide the following additional information:

1. Cost of sales includes $115,000 in fixed manufacturing costs.
2. Commissions and shipping are variable with sales.
3. Depreciation and salaries are substantially fixed, while other operating expenses include variable costs amounting to about $16,500.

REQUIRED

1. Prepare the income statement that Norbert wants.
2. After looking at your income statement, Norbert asks you to explain how it might suit his needs better than the other version. Tell him.

2–36 CVP Analysis for a Hospital (AICPA) Melford Hospital operates a general hospital but rents space and beds to separately owned entities providing specialized services such as pediatrics and psychiatrics. Melford charges each entity for common services, such as patients' meals and laundry, and for administrative services, such as billings and collections. Space and bed rentals are fixed amounts per year, based on the number of beds.

Melford charged the pediatrics service with the following costs for the year ended June 30, 19X7:

	Patient Days (variable)	*Bed Capacity (fixed)*
Dietary	$ 600,000	—
Janitorial	—	$ 70,000
Laundry	300,000	—
Laboratory	450,000	—
Pharmacy	350,000	—
Repairs and maintenance	—	30,000
General and administrative	—	1,300,000
Rent	—	1,500,000
Billings and collections	300,000	—
Totals	$2,000,000	$2,900,000

During the year ended June 30, 19X7, pediatrics charged patients an average of $300 per day, had a capacity of 60 beds, and had total revenue of $6,000,000. Pediatrics also employed the following personnel:

	Annual Salaries (each)
Supervising nurses	$25,000
Nurses	20,000
Aides	9,000

Melford requires that separately owned departments employ the following minimum numbers of personnel, based on patient days:

Annual Patient Days	*Aides*	*Nurses*	*Supervising Nurses*
Up to 21,900	20	10	4
21,901–26,000	26	13	4
26,001–29,200	30	15	4

Pediatrics always employs the minimum requirements in each category. These salaries are therefore fixed within ranges of annual patient days.

Pediatrics operated at 100 percent of capacity on 90 days in 19X7. It is estimated that during those 90 days, the demand for beds exceeded the capacity by about 20. Melford could make an additional 20 beds available for pediatrics during the year ending June 30, 19X8. The additional beds would increase pediatrics' fixed charges.

REQUIRED

1. Determine the breakeven point for pediatrics, expressed as the number of patient days, for the year ending June 30, 19X8, if it does not rent the additional 20 beds. Assume that revenue, cost per patient day, cost per bed, and salary rates will remain the same as they were in the previous year.
2. Assume that all data related to 19X7 will hold for 19X8, except that pediatrics will rent the additional 20 beds and therefore increase its per bed charges. Demand for beds will be the same in 19X8 as it was in 19X7. Determine the increase or decrease in profit for pediatrics that would accompany renting the additional beds.

2–37 Assumptions of CVP Analysis Some of your fellow students have found it difficult to understand some of the material and have asked you to help them. You agree to help and hear these questions:

1. "The question I have is about inflation," says one student. "I know that prices have been going up and will probably continue that way. I wonder how this is recognized in CVP analysis. After all, you know that you'll be paying higher salaries by year-end, paying more for materials and services, and probably charging more for your product."
2. An economics major took up the discussion. "My courses in economics have shown that companies cannot charge all they want to at all levels of volume. The law of demand states that as the price rises, the quantity demanded falls. Therefore, revenue lines are unrealistic: they should be curves."
3. The economics major continued: "Another point is that companies get what we call economies of scale. As the size of the plant increases, the operation becomes more efficient, with lower variable costs per unit. That is not reflected in the CVP graphs and equations either."
4. A student having trouble in financial accounting asked why the purchase price of a unit was a variable cost. "Suppose that you buy a unit for $6 and sell it for $10. In March you buy 2,000 and sell 1,000. The graph would show a contribution margin of $4,000. But your sales are $10,000 and your costs are $12,000."
5. A student who had worked in a factory the previous summer chimed in. "My problems are with fixed costs. What about when a firm hires supervisors for the factory, salespeople, or secretaries? Salaries should be fixed costs, but firms hire people and fire them too. Another point: costs such as advertising, research and development, employee training, and maintenance of buildings don't vary with sales, but management can set them at about any level it wants to and can change them on short notice. So how can they be fixed?"
6. "What bothers me is more fundamental," commented a student who worked in a department store. "I can see that businesspeople really can't predict what their revenues and costs are going to be. Suppliers of merchandise change their prices, and the store might not be able to change its prices because of competition The store sells a couple of thousand different items, and there is no way to do a chart for each one, even if you knew what costs and revenues would be. I just don't think it is possible to predict in the way the charts and equations imply that you can."

REQUIRED

Prepare responses to the questions and comments.

2–38 CVP and Profit Objectives (CMA) RayLok Incorporated has invented a secret process to freeze light intensity and manufactures a variety of products related to this process. Each product is independent of the others and is treated as a separate profit/loss division. Product (division) managers have a great deal of freedom to manage their divisions as they think best. Failure to produce target division income is dealt with severely; however, rewards for exceeding one's profit objective are, as one division manager described them, lavish.

The DimLok Division sells an add-on automotive accessory that automatically dims a vehicle's headlights by sensing a certain intensity of light coming from a specific direction. DimLok has had a new manager in each of the three previous years because the previous manager failed to reach RayLok's target profit. Don Barnes has just been promoted to manager and is studying ways to meet the current target profit for DimLok.

The two profit targets for DimLok for the coming year are $800,000 (20 percent return on the investment in the annual fixed costs of the division) plus an additional profit of $20 for each DimLok unit sold. Other constraints on division operations are presented below:

Production cannot exceed sales since RayLok's corporate advertising program stresses completely new product models each year, even though the "newness" of the models may be only cosmetic.

The DimLok selling price may not vary above the current selling price of $200 per unit but may vary as much as 10 percent below $200.

A division manager may elect to expand fixed production or selling facilities; however, the target objective that is related to fixed costs is increased by 20 percent of the cost of such expansion. Furthermore, a manager may not expand fixed facilities by more than 30 percent of existing fixed cost levels without approval from the Board of Directors.

Barnes is now examining data gathered by his staff to determine if DimLok can achieve its target profits of $800,000 and $20 per unit. A summary of these reports shows the following:

Last year's sales were 30,000 units at $200 per unit.

The present capacity of DimLok's manufacturing facility is 40,000 units per year, but capacity can be increased to 80,000 units per year by an increase in annual fixed costs of $1,000,000.

Present variable costs amount to $80 per unit, but if commitments are made for more than 60,000 units, DimLok's vendors are willing to offer raw material discounts amounting to $20 per unit, beginning with unit number 60,001.

Sales can be increased up to 100,000 units per year by committing large blocks of product to institutional buyers at a discounted unit price of $180. However, this discount would apply only to sales in excess of 40,000 units per year.

Barnes believes that these projections are reliable, and he is now trying to determine what DimLok must do to meet the profit objectives assigned by RayLok's Board of Directors.

REQUIRED

1. Calculate the dollar value of DimLok's present annual fixed costs.
2. Determine the number of units that DimLok must sell in order to achieve both profit objectives. Be sure to consider all constraints in determining your answer.
3. Without prejudice to your answer in part 2, assume Don Barnes decides to sell 40,000 units at $200 per unit and 24,000 units at $180 per unit. Prepare an income statement for DimLok showing whether or not Don Barnes' decision will achieve DimLok's profit objectives.

2–39 Marketing Decisions (CMA) Pittman Company manufactures telecommunications equipment. Pittman has always been production oriented and sells its products through agents. Agents are paid a commission of 15 percent of selling price. Below is the pro forma income statement from Pittman's profit plan for the coming fiscal year.

PITTMAN COMPANY
Pro Forma Income Statement
For the Year Ending June 30, 19X6
($000 omitted)

Sales		$16,000
Manufacturing costs:		
Variable	$7,200	
Fixed overhead	2,340	9,540
Gross profit		$ 6,460
Selling and administrative costs:		
Commissions	$2,400	
Fixed marketing costs	140	
Fixed administrative costs	1,780	4,320
Net operating income		$ 2,140
Less fixed interest cost		540
Income before income taxes		$ 1,600
Less income taxes (30%)		480
Net income		$ 1,120

After the profit plan was completed for the coming fiscal year, Pittman's sales agents demanded that the commissions be increased to 22.5 percent of the selling price. This demand was the latest in a series of actions that John Edgar, Pittman's president, believed had gone too far. He asked Maureen Elliott, the most sales-oriented officer in his production-oriented company, to estimate the cost to Pittman of employing its own sales force. Elliott's estimate of the additional annual cost to Pittman of employing its own sales force, exclusive of commissions, is presented below. Salespersons would receive a commission of 10 percent of selling price in addition to salary.

Estimated Annual Cost of
Employing a Company Sales Force
($000 omitted)

Salaries:	
Sales manager	$ 100
Salespersons	1,000
Travel and entertainment	400
Fixed marketing costs	900
	$2,400

REQUIRED

1. Calculate Pittman Company's estimated breakeven point in sales dollars for the fiscal year ending June 30, 19X6:
   a. if the events that are represented in the pro forma income statement take place
   b. if Pittman employs its own sales force.
2. If Pittman continues to sell through agents and pays the increased commission of 22.5 percent of selling price, determine the estimated volume in sales dollars for the fiscal year ending June 30, 19X6, that would be required to generate the same net income as projected in the pro forma income statement.
3. Determine the estimated volume in sales dollars that would result in equal net income for the fiscal year ending June 30, 19X6, regardless of whether Pittman Company continued to sell through agents and pays a commission of 22.5 percent of selling price or employs its own sales force.

2–40 Multiple Products SunSet Corp. makes two products. Prices and variable costs per unit as well as total fixed costs for the period are shown below. Variable manufacturing costs include material, labor, and variable overhead.

	Product 1	*Product 2*	
Units	13,000	200,000	
Price per unit	$60.00	$45.00	
Variable manufacturing costs per unit	30.00	25.00	
Variable selling costs per unit	3.00	2.00	
Fixed manufacturing costs			$1,500,000
Fixed selling/administrative costs			260,000

SunSet is subject to a 40 percent tax rate.

REQUIRED

1. Create a contribution margin income statement with columns for each product and the company as a whole.
2. What is each product's contribution margin percent? What is the weighted average contribution margin percent for the company?
3. What revenue would be needed in order to earn $1,800,000 after taxes?
4. Going to the original data, what do Product 1's unit variable manufacturing costs have to be to yield a 52 percent contribution margin for that product?
5. What are the strengths and weaknesses of the cost-volume-profit model in general and in light of today's manufacturing and competitive environment?

3

COST ANALYSIS AND FORECASTING

Chapter 2 briefly discussed some practical limitations of CVP analysis, including the likelihood that costs are not perfectly linear. In practice, we do not expect to find that all costs can easily be classified as fixed or as variable with sales. Some costs include both fixed and variable components. Such **mixed costs** are typified by items such as maintenance of machinery that will have some fixed component related to normal routine maintenance and some variable component related to the number of hours the machinery is used.

This chapter presents some techniques for analyzing cost behavior and determining the fixed and variable components of individual elements of cost. One question we shall consider is whether variable costs vary with sales or with some other measure of volume. We shall see that some costs vary with activities other than sales. When such costs exist, we must plan for them using the measure of activity with which they vary. We shall also consider the problem of the reliability of estimates of cost behavior—whether we can expect our predictions of costs to be sufficiently accurate to use in planning.

We can analyze costs with both simple and sophisticated quantitative models. Our emphasis is on the use of these techniques and interpreting results.

The purpose of analyzing costs is to plan future activities.[1] While our discussion focuses on cost forecasting as a tool for planning, the cost accountant

[1]A distinction can be made between cost estimation, a look back at what actually happened, and forecasting. We use the terms synonymously, referring to the use of all relevant data to provide estimates related to the future.

can use the techniques we discuss in noncost areas, as in helping the shipping department to minimize delivery times to customers.

OBJECTIVES OF ANALYZING COSTS

We need to understand cost behavior for several reasons. We must predict total costs to predict income. We need good estimates of variable cost to determine contribution margin, which is important in planning and making decisions. We also want to be able to predict costs so that we can compare budgeted and actual costs in exercising control. In particular we want to identify and understand **cost drivers**, the activities that cause particular costs to rise and fall.

Sales volume is an important cost driver, as we saw in Chapter 2. Other cost drivers include unit production, labor hours and machine hours used in production, number of customers, number of inventory items carried, and other drivers we shall encounter later. Labor hours drive such costs as fringe benefits, some manufacturing supplies, and small tools used by workers. Some cost drivers, such as the number of inventory items carried, are non-volume-related. The costs they drive do not relate to the total business of a company, but to *how* it does business. For instance, the more vendors a company uses, the more people it is likely to need in its purchasing department.

Understanding cost drivers helps managers to control costs by controlling activities. This control is particularly important with overhead costs, both manufacturing and non-manufacturing. For instance, a few years ago Hewlett-Packard, the highly successful electronics company, simplified its accounting system in one plant. The company had been collecting considerable information about direct labor, but stopped after it went to a highly mechanized manufacturing process. As the company stopped collecting detailed information about direct labor, it was able to cut out some 100,000 journal entries per month and thereby experienced ". . . significant savings in staff time and costs."[2]

The key to reducing costs is to reduce activities that drive costs but do not increase the value of the product—non-value adding activities, as they are called. Concentrating on the right cost drivers enables managers to effect significant cost reductions; concentrating on the wrong drivers gives disappointing results. Stories abound of companies that concentrated on reducing labor costs partly in the belief that overhead costs would also fall. Disappointment often followed. Some companies find that some costs rise when they add new products to their lines. Such costs, usually called set up costs, are driven by changeovers from manufacturing one product to manufacturing another.

[2] Rick Hunt, Linda Garrett, C. Mike Merz, "Direct Labor Not Always Relevant at H-P," *Management Accounting*, February 1985, pp. 58–62.

These costs can be substantial; they do not change when the volume of production changes, but when set ups change. Managers therefore try to reduce both the number of set ups and their costs. In advanced manufacturing environments employing flexible manufacturing techniques, as described in Chapter 1, set up costs are often close to zero. Therefore, a key objective in analyzing costs is to identify the cost drivers (activities) so that managers can both control the levels of those activities and forecast costs based on expected levels of activity. This is all part of *cost management*, which stresses managing and controlling costs by managing the activities that generate them.

COST ESTIMATION

Much of our information comes from accounting records. To determine the relevance of these data, we must answer some key questions. Is activity for the previous periods within the relevant range? Did prices change over the period? Is there a seasonal pattern of activity? Such questions need to be addressed even with the simplest approach.

Account Analysis

A simple yet effective method is *account analysis*. Accounting systems classify costs by *object*, what the cost is *for*, such as salaries, utilities, direct labor, and depreciation. In some cases we can determine the behavior of a cost from its name. This is especially true of fixed costs such as depreciation and advertising. Although account analysis can often tell you whether a cost is fixed or variable, it does not tell you how much the cost *should be*, only what it has been. Moreover, unless you also have information about the level of activity, you cannot determine variable cost per unit of activity. For example, materials are a variable manufacturing cost, but simply looking at the account gives no information about how much material cost is for a particular product. Account analysis is a good place to start and, perhaps, to end when checking whether the results obtained using other methods seem plausible.

Interviews

Interviewing is often effective in analyzing cost behavior. Managers can often tell you how their workloads are likely to change following some change in operations. For instance, a purchasing manager can probably determine whether she would need another clerk were the company to bring out a new product line that used all new components. The question here is what activities the unit does, what tasks it performs, and how those tasks are likely to be affected by changes in operations. The key to cost management is to reduce the activities so as to reduce the cost.

Technological (Engineering) Approach

The technological approach estimates cost behavior patterns from the technological features of operations. It is most applicable in manufacturing and has more limited applications in administrative functions such as the processing of forms. Industrial engineers are often able to determine that a particular product should require, for example, 3 pounds of a given material and 45 minutes of labor time and be able to make reasonable judgments about the behavior of some overhead costs, such as fuel, supplies, maintenance, and indirect labor. The estimates are based on the engineers' knowledge of the technological relationships among various types of machinery and of workers.

The principal advantage of this approach is that it does not rely on historical data. All other methods discussed in this chapter use historical data, which subjects them to the criticism that they include the inefficiencies of the past. If managers plan for costs based solely on historical results, they are ignoring an important question: *Should* the past be used as a guide to the future? The past *can* be used as a guide to the future, but doing so is not always wise. For example, if the workers of a firm have been producing three units of product per hour, the managers may plan on that level of efficiency in the future. But it may be possible to reduce the labor time by improving work methods so that output could rise to 3.5 units or so per hour.

Engineering estimates are also helpful in planning new production methods. If a new machine is to be installed, its operating costs and output are of considerable interest. Estimates of costs and output prepared by the firm's engineering staff might be the best available information.

We shall say more in Chapter 7 about engineering approaches to cost analysis. Such approaches entail difficulties: first, some costs may not be subject to the kind of direct analysis required; second, engineering estimates might give costs that are achievable only under ideal conditions, which few firms can expect. Managers who rely heavily on engineering estimates might be overly optimistic.

High-Low and Scatter Diagram Methods

Exhibit 3–1 shows data from the Robern Corporation, a manufacturer of horse trailers. The company produces two models—economy and deluxe—each able to carry two horses. The company wants to classify the behavior of its costs to set prices and make other decisions for the next year. Account classification has produced solid ideas of costs for metal, wood, electrical fixtures, and wiring. However, the managers are unsure of the behavior of electricity costs. Exhibit 3–1 shows weekly data. The economy model usually needs 100 welds, the deluxe model 125 welds. A scatter diagram for these costs is presented in Figure 3–1. The independent variable, the cost driver to be analyzed, is machine hours.

An inspection of the scatter diagram yields a visual check on the probable form of the cost behavior function. It seems likely that a straight line will be a good predictor of cost behavior. Looking at the scatter diagram is a good way

EXHIBIT 3–1 Data for Robern Electricity Costs

	Machine Time	*Power Costs*
	122	$1,103
	134	1,245
	156	1,249
	131	1,263
	109	1,121
	154	1,439
	165	1,441
	162	1,463
	99	1,009
	118	1,272
	112	1,141
	132	1,346
	137	1,363
	142	1,457
	136	1,189
	153	1,343
	103	1,050
	134	1,279
	172	1,463
	98	1,063
	127	1,278
	156	1,463
	176	1,310
	134	1,330
	139	1,427
	152	1,407
	103	1,197
	119	1,133
Mean	135	$1,280.1
Variance		$18,858

to get an intuitive feel for the validity of the results of finding the fixed and variable elements of cost. A scatter diagram is always a good tool in cost estimation.

In Chapter 2 we described total cost as being made up of fixed cost plus variable cost times the activity (usually volume). This is no more than the formula for a straight line, or $Y = A + BX$. If we know what costs are and we know the proper independent variable, then we can say that the total costs (the dependent variable) will change as the independent variable changes. Although it would be nice to *know* this relationship and have no worry about the uncertainty of our predictions, in reality we never know exactly what will happen in the future. We can use only a reasonable sample of the past as a basis to forecast the future cost relationship. Thus, our certainty as reflected in our description of total cost as $Y = A + BX$ is changed to $y' = a + bx$ (y' is called *y prime*), where y' is our estimate of total costs, a is an estimate of the fixed

FIGURE 3–1 Robern Electricity Costs

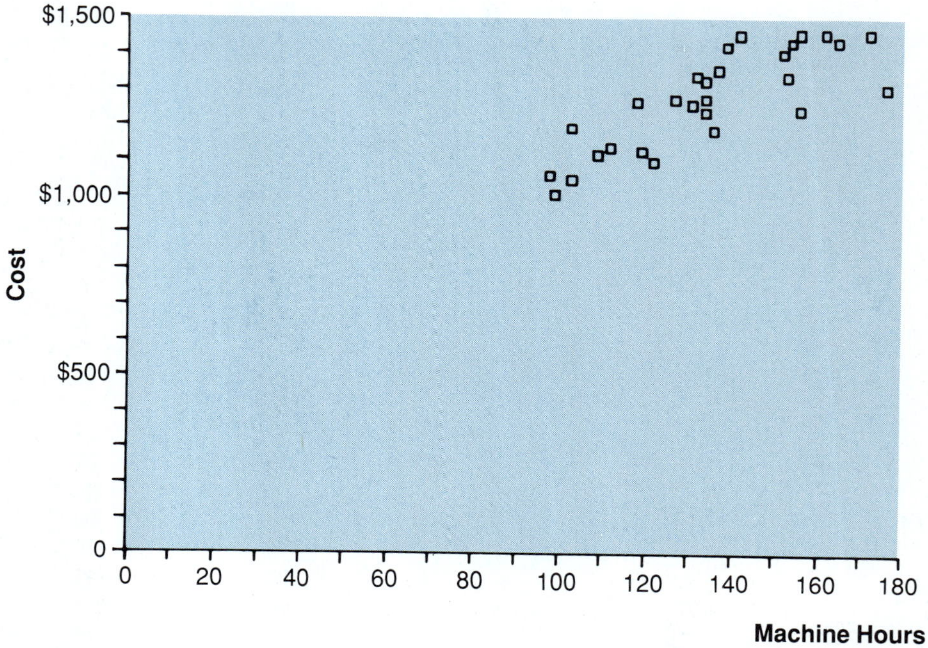

portion of total costs (more will be said about this later), and b is the estimate of the variable cost per unit of activity. Note again that all the elements of this relationship are estimates. We are estimating total costs based on the estimates of the fixed and variable elements of cost.

High-Low Cost Estimates

The scatter diagram, with information such as that in Exhibit 3–1, can be used to estimate the true cost function. In the **high-low method** you estimate the variable cost component by looking at the change in cost that occurs between the highest volume and the lowest volume of activity within the relevant range. If we divide that change in cost by the change in volume, we can get an estimate of variable cost.

The variable portion of cost is determined by:

$$\text{variable component of cost} = \frac{\text{cost at high volume} - \text{cost at low volume}}{\text{high volume} - \text{low volume}}$$

The high and low volumes should be within the relevant range. Applying the formula to Robern

$$\text{variable component of cost} = \frac{\$1{,}310 - \$1{,}063}{176 - 98}$$
$$= \$3.1666 \text{ rounded}$$

The fixed component is then found by using the relationship

$$\text{total cost} = \text{total fixed cost} + \text{total variable cost}$$

Total variable cost is the variable cost per unit of activity times total activity. So we can use total cost at either level of activity (high or low) to find the fixed component.

$$\begin{aligned}\text{fixed component} &= \text{total cost} - \text{total variable cost}\\ &= \$1{,}310 - \$3.1666 \times 176\\ &= \$753 \text{ thousand, rounded}\end{aligned}$$

Or, using the low volume,

$$\begin{aligned}\text{fixed component} &= \text{total cost} - \text{total variable cost}\\ &= \$1{,}063 - \$3.1666 \times 98\\ &= \$753 \text{ thousand, rounded}\end{aligned}$$

Note that we use the costs at the high and low volumes of activity, not necessarily the high cost and low cost. In fact, \$1,310 is not the highest cost, nor is \$1,063 the lowest. We use the high and low activities and their associated costs; we do not mix the observations of cost and activity. Figure 3–2 shows the line drawn on the scatter diagram.

As you can see, the line $y' = \$753 + (\$3.1666)(\text{number of hours})$ connects the highest volume and lowest volume costs. This statement shows the

FIGURE 3–2 Plot of High-Low Equation

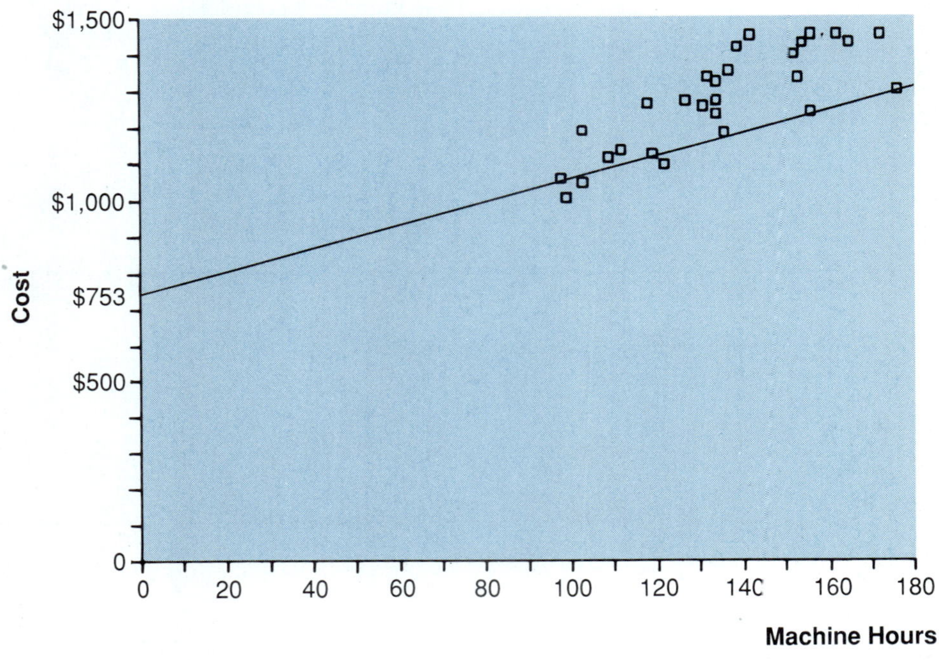

weakness of this method of cost estimation. Because the line is wedded to these two points, we can also get a cost formula that is a very poor predictor.

You can see from Figure 3–2 that the majority of the observations occur above the line. For this reason, managers would tend to underpredict costs. Moreover, the high-low method can produce some very poor results if the high and low observations are out of line with the others.

Visual Line Fitting

We can overcome the primary deficiency of the high-low method—its reliance on only two observations—by fitting a line visually to the plotted data. In Figure 3–3, we can compare the original high-low estimate with a visually fitted line. If you had a well-drawn plot on fine graph paper, you could take a ruler and move it around until you had a line that seemed best to you. Reading the graph gives you the $y' = \$580 + \$5.10x$ shown. In comparison to the line from our high-low estimate, the visually fit line has about the same number of observations falling on each side of it, and so it would be more likely to provide better estimates of costs.

To get the estimates of fixed and variable costs, first look at the point where the line hits the vertical axis. This is our intercept. We do not mean to imply that this figure is equivalent to total costs at zero volume; this is not true,

FIGURE 3–3 Visually Fitted Line

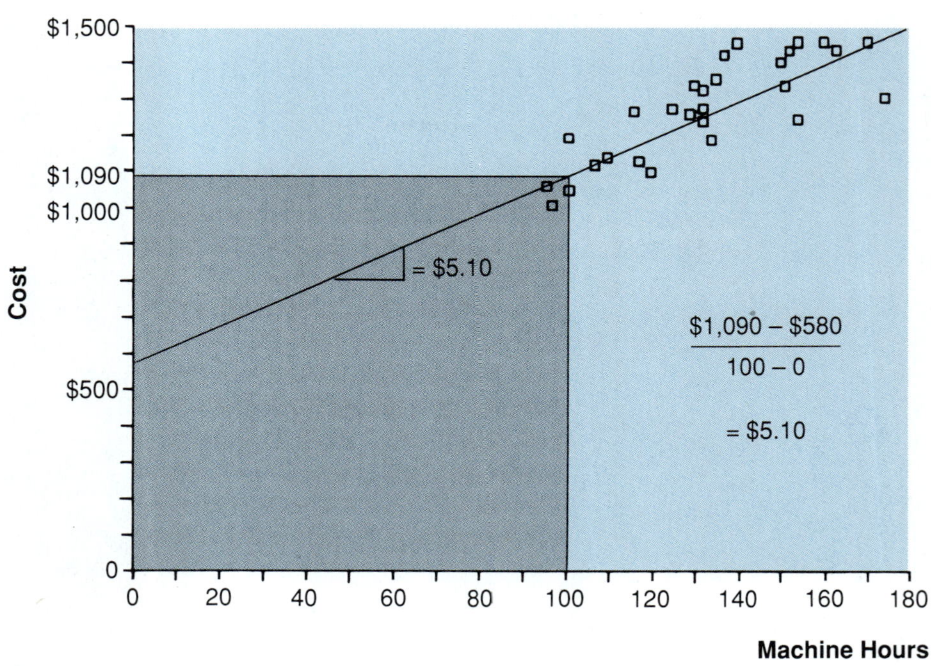

because zero is outside the relevant range. Once the intercept is determined, we can read the line to find our estimate of total costs at any level of volume. Total costs less fixed costs leaves total variable costs. Thus, variable cost per unit of activity can be found by dividing this number by the level of activity chosen.

STATISTICAL METHODS

The high-low method is faulty because it uses only two observations. The visual method is subjective. We need a mathematical technique that produces the best description of costs based on the sample observations.[3] In addition, we need ways to see how good this best line is. These techniques are called **regression** and **correlation** analysis.

Regression Analysis

Regression analysis describes the behavior of one variable based on that of another. The regression formula is $y' = a + bx$.

The data in Exhibit 3–1 are a sample of all possible data to describe electricity cost. Regression analysis uses data of this kind to estimate the true cost function by estimating the coefficients for the intercept (a) and the slope (b). Regression gives us ways to determine how good those estimates are.

Regression analysis is typically done by computer, for which many packages are available. Exhibit 3–2 shows Lotus 1-2-3 output for the regression line for our example. (See Appendix 3B for calculations.) The terminology differs slightly from ours, as it will in most commercial packages. You should be able to recognize some terms or figure out their meanings from the context. The term *constant* ($582.434) refers to the intercept—the estimate of fixed costs *within the relevant range*, not at zero activity. (Recall that our data are in thousands so that we must adjust the intercept, but not the slope.) The X coefficient (the appendix discusses why it says "X Coefficient(s)"), the slope or variable component, is $5.175057. We shall explain the remaining items.

The regression equation, then, is (rounding) $y' = \$582{,}434 + \$5.1751X$, where X = machine hours. This equation is very different from the high-low result of $\$753{,}000 + \$3.1666X$. The high-low equation will not give the same total cost predictions as the regression equation. In this example, the high-low equation understates the variable cost component, so that estimates of variable cost for products requiring significant amounts of machine time would be off, as would estimates of contribution margin for those products. Misstating contribution margin can cause serious problems in planning and decision making.

[3] *Best* has several definitions. In this context it indicates the mathematical superiority of this method over competing techniques.

EXHIBIT 3–2 Regression Results

	Regression Output:
Constant	582.4342
Std Err of Y Est	81.11969
R Squared	0.675985
No. of Observations	28
Degrees of Freedom	26
X Coefficient(s)	5.175057
Std Err of Coef.	0.702654

It does not matter whether variable cost is overstated or understated; any misstatement can be harmful in analyzing costs of products. Additionally, variable cost of contemplated new products would be misestimated using the high-low results. Figure 3–4 portrays the regression equation.

Measures of Goodness of Fit

The regression equation is the most precise of those developed so far. Also important is that regression analysis allows us to check for goodness of fit: How well does the equation fit the data and how good are our predictions likely to be? There are several important measures.

FIGURE 3–4 Plot of Regression Equation

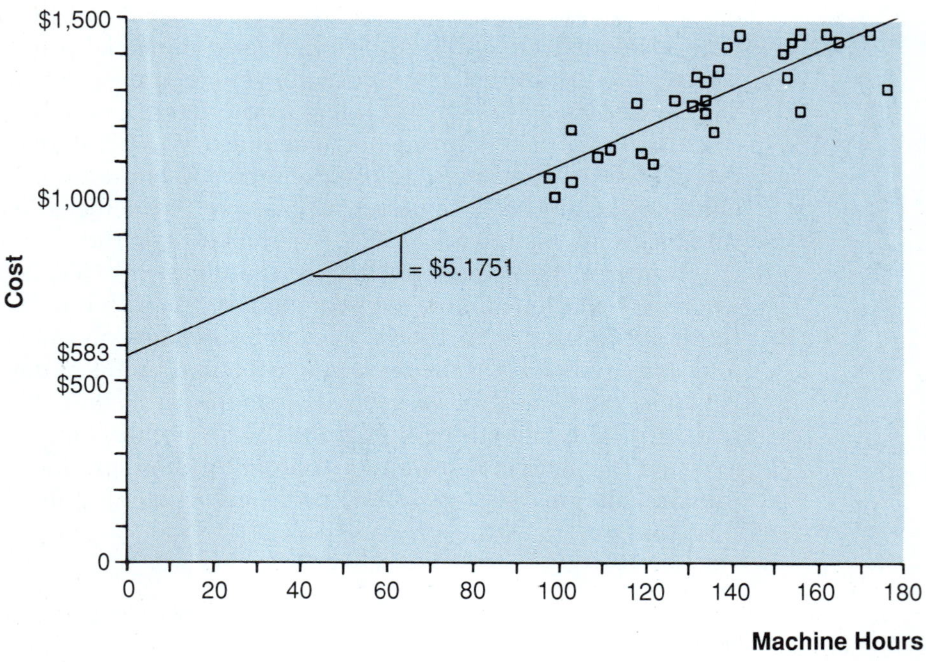

Standard Error of the Estimate The **standard error of the estimate** gives us an idea of how close to the actual results our predictions will be. For instance, at 120,000 hours we estimate total electricity cost at \$1,203,446 (\$582,434 + [\$5.1751 × 120,000]). But that is an expected value, an average. The actual result in any given case will almost certainly be different, but how different? Exhibit 3–2 shows the standard error of the estimate (Std Err of *Y* Est) to be \$81,119. It is calculated as:

$$S_e = \sqrt{\frac{\Sigma\,(y - y')^2}{n - 2}}$$

The squared deviations are divided by the number of observations less the two coefficients (a and b) that we are estimating. The $(n - 2)$ term is also called **degrees of freedom**, a term to be used later. The standard error of the estimate is quite similar to a standard deviation in normal probability analysis. It is a measure of the variability around the regression line.

The principal use of the standard error is to indicate how close we can expect our calculated costs (y') to come to the actual costs. We can calculate **confidence intervals**, bounds within which we can expect costs to be contained some specified percentage of the time. If we were dealing with a larger number of observations (say, 30 or more), we could use normal probability tables to calculate confidence intervals. When we have fewer observations, we generally use a Student t table (Table A–2 in Appendix A). In our example we have 28 observations and, therefore, 26 degrees of freedom as Exhibit 3–2 shows. A 95 percent confidence interval using Table A–2 is calculated by

$$y' \pm (t_{0.025})(S_e)$$

For example, we can say we are 95 percent confident that the *true cost* for electricity at 120,000 hours is

$$\$1{,}203{,}446 \pm (2.056)(\$81{,}119) \text{ or } \$1{,}036{,}665 \text{ to } \$1{,}370{,}226$$

Note that S_e is an average variance.[4] The denominator is lowered by the number of estimates that we are making. In simple linear regression, we are estimating two parameters, a and b, so the denominator is $(n - 2)$. The more parameters we estimate, the lower the denominator and the higher the standard error.

If all observations fell directly on the regression line, S_e would equal zero. This seems obvious, since there would be no deviations from the line and

[4] The standard error of the estimate is most properly used as a measure of variability around the entire regression line, as depicted in Figure 3–5. With a sufficiently large sample, it is possible to establish the kind of confidence intervals shown in this example. A more complete discussion of regression analysis includes the use of the standard error of the forecast, a measure that almost equals the standard error of the estimate at $\bar{x}$ but diverges as you move toward one end of the regression line or the other. It is sufficient in this discussion to treat the standard error of the estimate as a useful measure of variability and to ignore the more complex standard error of the forecast.

$\Sigma (y - y')^2 = 0$. The tighter the observations around the regression line, the lower the value of S_e. When the scatter diagram shows observations all over the chart, we can expect a high S_e, since we need a much bigger band to describe our estimate of true costs.

Correlation Analysis Like the standard error of the estimate, measures of correlation describe *goodness of fit.* There is a deviation between actual observations and the regression line. The deviations can be broken down as follows:

$(y - \bar{y})$ = total deviation from an average value of y
$(y' - \bar{y})$ = deviation from an average value of y described (explained) by the regression line
$(y - y')$ = unexplained deviation, also called *residual* or *error term*

The sum of the squared deviations, $\Sigma (y - y')^2$, measures how much of the change in y is *not* dependent on changes in x.

A measure of goodness of fit is obtained by calculating the **coefficient of determination** for the sample as

$$r^2 = 1 - \frac{\Sigma (y - y')^2}{\Sigma (y - \bar{y})^2}$$

which is also

$$r^2 = 1 - \frac{\text{unexplained variance}}{\text{total variance}}$$

See Appendix 3B for the calculation.

An explanation of our $r^2 = 0.676$ (from Exhibit 3–2) is that the regression line explains about 68 percent of the change in total electricity costs as the number of machine hours changes. Therefore, about 32 percent of the change in costs is the result of random events or other variables. Note that nothing is said about cause and effect. While it seems fairly obvious in this example that a cause-and-effect relationship exists, this is not always the case. Statisticians are always careful to state that regression and correlation analysis do not indicate causality, only association. This is fine, but accountants must plan and make decisions that require a belief in causality. Unless we are convinced that electricity costs are caused by machine hours, we have no reason to rely on the relationship in planning and decision making.

The meaning of the coefficient of determination might best be explained this way: without the regression equation, our best prediction of electricity costs is the mean. That is, if costs are not affected by changes in hours, the average cost is a reasonable estimate of future cost. However, in this case there is a large deviation of costs around the mean so that predictions using the mean will be far off most of the time. Using the regression equation to predict costs decreases the variation by about 68 percent, because 68 percent of the changes in electricity costs are associated with machine hours. Our predictions, then, will be about 68 percent better using the regression equation than using the mean.

The square root of the coefficient of determination is called the **correla-**

tion coefficient, (r). It takes its sign from the b regression coefficient. If the regression line perfectly explains y as x changes (x is a perfect predictor of y), r^2 (and r) will equal 1 for a positive relationship (or $r^2 = 1$, $r = -1$ for an inverse relationship). In such a case $\Sigma\,(y - y')^2 = \Sigma\,(y - \bar{y})^2 = 0$, since all observations fall on the regression line.

Figure 3–5 shows that at 122,000 hours, electricity cost is observed to be $1,103,000. Predicted cost is $1,213,796 while on average electric cost (regardless of activity level) is $1,280,100 (Exhibit 3–1). The term $(y - \bar{y}) =$ $177,143 is the deviation of the observation from the mean. Of this, $(y' - \bar{y}) =$ $66,347 is explained by the regression line. It is explained since $\bar{y}$ is constant and y' is known from the equation. Finally, the error or residual term $(y - y')$ $=$ $110,796 is considered a random, and unexplained, deviation from the regression line.[5] The ratio of the squared explained deviations over the squared total deviation yields r^2.

Standard Error of the Coefficient

Correlation analysis and the standard error of the regression equation give us an idea of how accurate our predictions are likely to be. We can fit a regression equation to almost any set of data, but if the spread of observations were nearly random, our predictions would be of little value. In the same vein, we are interested in knowing whether the regression coefficient, b, is a useful estimate of variable costs. First, if the observations are nearly random, then the coefficient will be close to zero, which indicates that changes in volume are not accompanied by significant changes in costs. If the coefficient is not significantly different from zero, in the statistical sense, we cannot rely on it for prediction.

If the variable portion of costs is zero, we are placed in the situation already discussed, in which it might be better to use average costs ($\bar{y}$) as our predictor, since if $b = 0$, volume has no effect on total costs. CVP analysis requires a good estimate of unit variable cost. So does decision making, as we will see in Chapter 12. Misestimates of variable cost can result in poor decisions as well as in errors in planning.

Therefore, we calculate the standard error of the b coefficient and test for significance. Exhibit 3–2 gives the standard error of the coefficient, S_b, as $0.702654.

Dividing b, the regression coefficient, by S_b, its standard error, gives a value called t. This t-value is used as we used the t table earlier in connection with the standard error of the estimate. Its critical values, which depend on degrees of freedom, are found in Table A–2 in Appendix A. In general, if t is greater than 2.0, we are willing to reject the hypothesis that the true value of b is zero. In other words, if t exceeds 2.0, we can be fairly confident that there is a slope to the regression line. With t greater than 2.0, and a reasonably large sample, there is roughly a 95 percent probability that the true value

[5] The error term is assumed to be normally distributed with a mean of zero.

FIGURE 3–5 Explained, Unexplained, and Total Variance

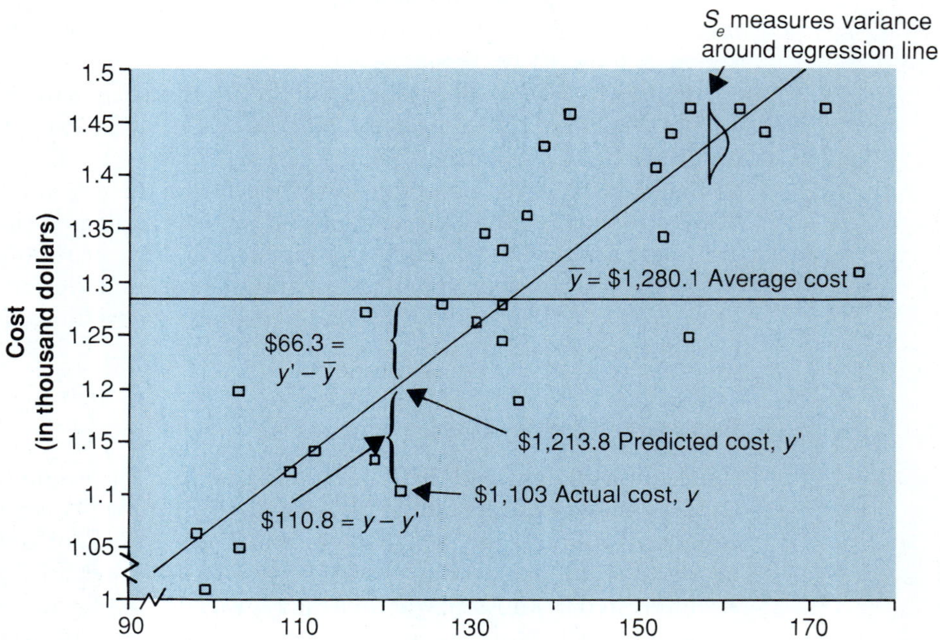

of b is greater than zero. For 26 degrees of freedom, the critical value for a 95 percent confidence level is 2.056. The t-value for our results is 7.365 ($5.175057/$0.702654), which is well above 2.056, indicating that there is near-zero probability that the true value of the coefficient is zero.

PROBLEMS IN COST ESTIMATION

Let us consider some difficulties in using regression analysis and scatter diagrams to estimate the fixed and variable components of costs. We deal first with some problems common to all methods of cost analysis, then proceed to specific questions of regression analysis.

Measurement Problems

We generally use accounting records to determine the values for use in regression or for plotting on a scatter diagram. In these records we would find, say, manufacturing overhead for each of a series of months and the number of units produced, direct labor hours or machine hours for each month as well. We are assuming that the volume (units or hours) and the cost (total overhead) relate to the same period. Although this is usually a reasonable assumption, it might not always hold.

For example, suppose the firm receives its utility bills at the end of each month and that the bills cover 30-day periods ending about the middle of each month. If the firm records each bill as a cost of the month in which it was received, the cost data for each month will contain some costs that applied to the last part of the preceding month and some that applied to the first part of the current month. Therefore, the accountant must use production data from the first half of the current month and the last half of the preceding month to determine the pattern of behavior of utility costs.

Leads and Lags It is not uncommon for costs to lag behind the associated activity. Maintenance costs are an example. We expect to find maintenance costs increasing as machinery is used more, but the increased costs might not appear in the same period as the heavier use of machinery, because the extra work will be done after the peak period of use is past (or before the peak as a preventative measure). Hence, we might find that maintenance costs have a variable component of, for example, \$0.22 per machine hour, but that the variable component shows up in the month after the hours are worked.

In such a case the equation for predicting costs could look as follows:

$$\begin{pmatrix}\text{total maintenance costs}\\ \text{in current month}\end{pmatrix} = \$XX + \left[\$0.YY \times \begin{pmatrix}\text{machine hours}\\ \text{in prior month}\end{pmatrix}\right]$$

Lead and lag relationships are more common in sales forecasting than in cost analysis.

Recording Problems For convenience, many firms record costs in such ways as to make the analysis of behavior difficult. One common example is the practice of recording the cost of some kinds of supplies (for example, wiping rags or small parts such as nuts and bolts) as they are purchased, not as they are used. Therefore, analysis could not reveal the pattern of behavior. Such costs are probably a relatively small proportion of total costs, so that no serious harm would be done.

A much more serious problem can arise because of the widespread practice of allocating some overhead costs to production departments. A firm might allocate fixed maintenance costs to production departments on the basis of the number of maintenance hours used. If accountants included these allocated costs in analyzing the cost structure of the production department, they could reach incorrect conclusions. If the objective is to determine the cost behavior pattern in a single production department, only those costs incurred within the department should be included. Allocated costs should be excluded from the analysis.

Economic Sense Authors of statistics books relate many instances of what is called *spurious correlation*, a high degree of correlation between two variables that do not seem related at all. Sales of the most expensive autos might be highly correlated with new housing starts, but the reason is likely to be that both variables are related to the general level of economic activity. When times are good, both expensive cars and houses sell well.

In analyzing costs, accountants must ask whether the independent variables being considered have some reasonable economic relationship to costs. Factory overhead costs might be closely related to the quantity of scrap produced, but to rely on that observed association for predicting costs might be unwise unless some reason for the association can be found.

Assumptions of Regression Analysis

Regression analysis makes several assumptions about the data; if any one of these assumptions is not met, problems can arise in using the regression equation and related measures such as the standard error. So long as we use simple regression analysis we can usually spot these potential problems by drawing a scatter diagram. It is always a good idea to draw a scatter diagram, even when using regression analysis. The following are some of the assumptions of concern.

Representativeness of Observations When applying regression analysis or any other technique that uses historical data, we are assuming that the observations come from a uniform population. That amounts to saying that we could not use cost data from 1970–1990 to estimate cost behavior in 1994 because prices have changed greatly and the production process was almost surely not the same during all that time. If the production process has changed, observations should be drawn only from periods after the change. Sometimes we can make adjustments. For example, if the price of electricity has been rising at a known rate, the accountant can adjust the observed cost figures so that they reflect the price currently in effect. Such adjustments, however, are not always possible.

The scatter diagram in Figure 3–6 shows that one unusual observation can have a pronounced effect on the regression line. The reason is that the least-squares criterion for fitting the line gives a great deal of weight to individual observations. An accountant looking at these observations might decide to throw out the **outlier** (the unusual observation). It could be caused by some unusual event such as a strike or a plant shutdown for vacation. We should not throw out observations just to get a nice fit of the regression line, but we are justified in omitting observations that are not representative of normal operating conditions. Thus, as well as omitting outliers, we might also eliminate observations well outside the expected range of activity, the relevant range.

Constant Variance Figure 3–7(a) shows the constant-variance assumption. An example of the violation of this assumption is given in Figure 3–7(b). Notice that the observations spread out as volume increases. We assume that the spread of the observations around the regression line is constant throughout the range of observations. When the assumption is met, we have **homoscedasticity**; when it is not met, we have **heteroscedasticity**.

FIGURE 3–6 Effect of Outlier Observation

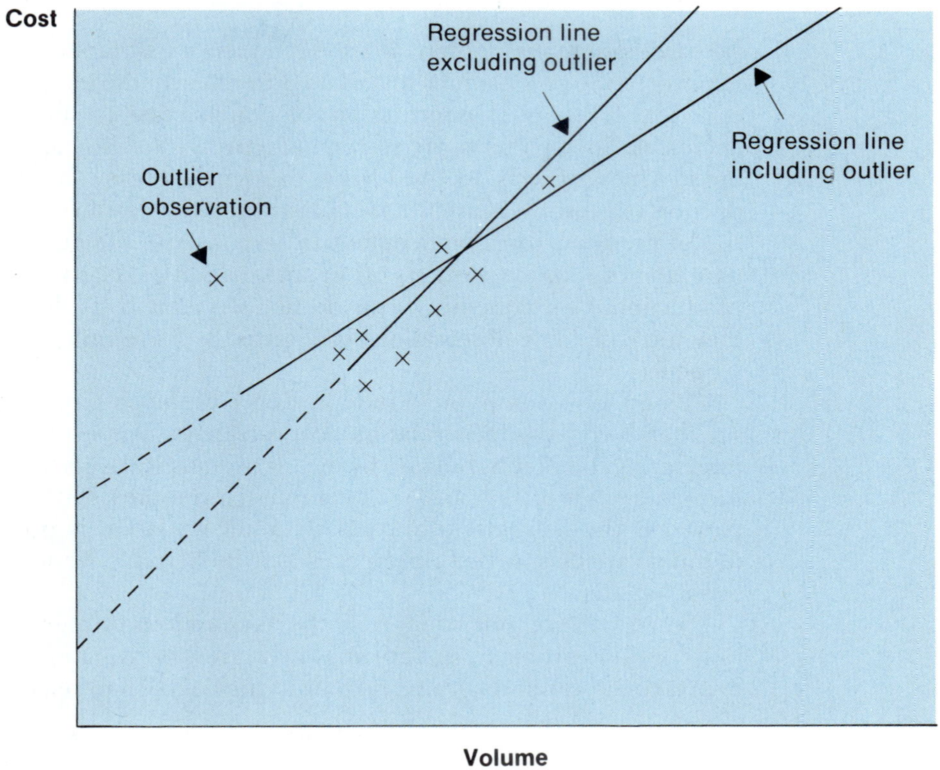

FIGURE 3–7 (a) Constant Variance (Homoscedasticity), (b) Nonconstant Variance (Heteroscedasticity)

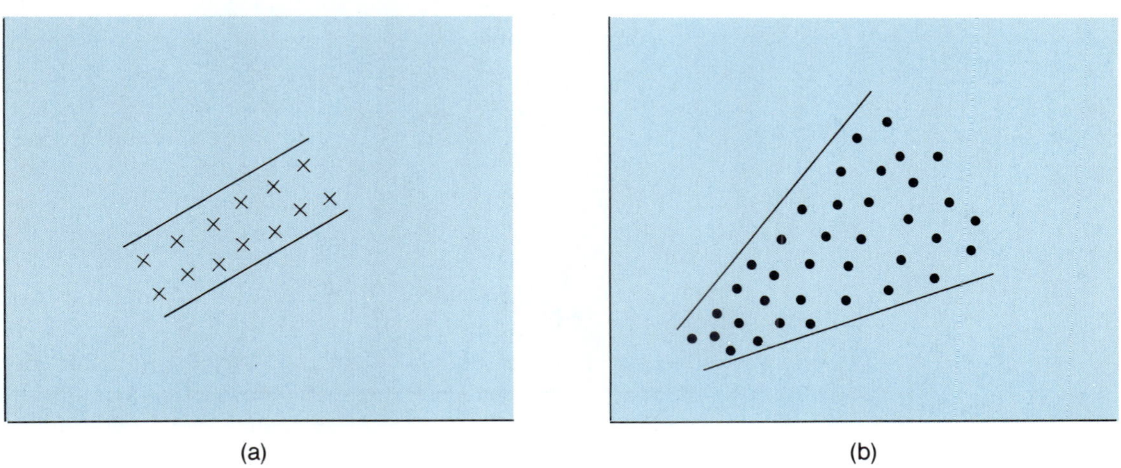

Heteroscedasticity may be the rule rather than the exception in cost data. It is reasonable to expect a higher degree of variability of costs at high levels of volume than at low levels.

Independence Stated loosely, the independence assumption requires that the *sequence* of the observations makes no difference in the levels of cost. However, costs may follow one pattern as production increases, a different pattern as it decreases. Such patterns are shown in Figure 3–8. The cause of the pattern is the stickiness of costs. As production rises, more workers are hired, but as production falls, workers are not laid off as rapidly. Most firms cannot adjust the size of the labor force immediately in response to changes in production volume; they do not lay workers off in anticipation of relatively small declines in production. Consequently, firms do not see their costs decline as rapidly as they increase. The observations in Figures 3–8 are numbered to show their sequence.

When the assumption of independence of the observations is not met, we say that there is **autocorrelation**. We can detect it not only by plotting and numbering the points, but also by means of statistical tests that are usually performed as part of the output of computer programs. One that is widely employed is the Durbin-Watson test. If autocorrelation is present, the use of dummy variables or first differences may be helpful. We will discuss dummy variables later.

Since violating one or more of the assumptions of regression analysis can cause serious problems in applying the regression equation, it is always good to prepare a scatter diagram and look at the data. Blind reliance on the results

FIGURE 3–8 Autocorrelation

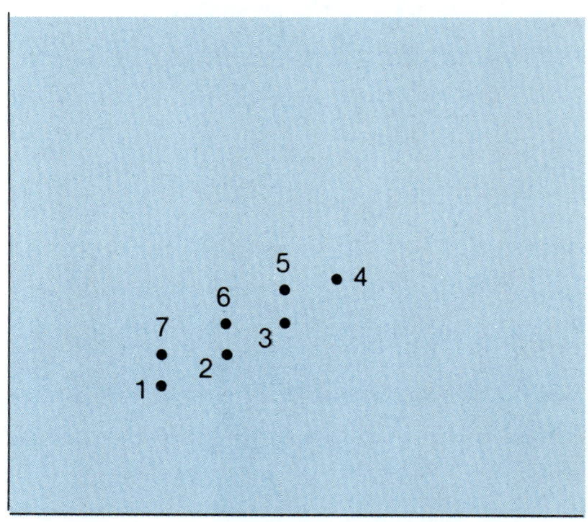

FIGURE 3–9 Alternative Cost Patterns: (a) The Economic Model, (b) Effect of Quantity Discounts

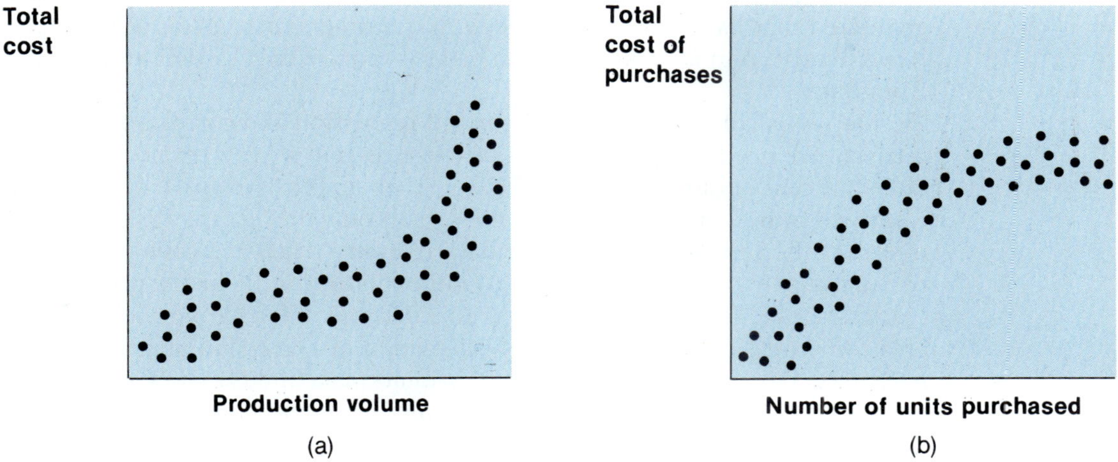

of a regression equation can prove costly: the technique should not be used in cookbook fashion.

Other Scatter Diagrams

The Robern example seems to indicate that the regression equation is a good estimator of cost behavior. The observations all seem to be in one volume range, and costs seem to move upward as volume increases. This is not always the case. As we have seen, the economic model of cost behavior cannot be described by a straight line. Other costs also can behave in a nonlinear fashion. Figure 3–9(a) shows a scatter diagram depicting the economic model. Figure 3–9(b) shows total cost where quantity discounts come into play as purchases increase.

COMPUTER OUTPUT FOR REGRESSION AND CORRELATION ANALYSIS

We have used various terms and shown some symbols in our discussion of regression and correlation analysis. Since so many computer programs are available, be aware of different words or symbols. For example, variable costs are called the slope or the regression coefficient and can be shown in various symbol forms other than b. Our discussion focused on r^2, the coefficient of determination. Some computer outputs list only r, the correlation coefficient, or they list both measures. We have consistently used y' for estimated cost. Some programs describe this as "Y ESTIMATED." In addition, since most computer programs are general purpose, various measures and numbers are generated that have not been included in our limited discussion of the topic. As with most computer output, you need to separate the relevant information from data.

Merely calculating the various parts of regression and correlation analysis is trivial. We need to understand these measures, but we rely on a computer to do 99 percent of our calculations. However, obtaining "the answers" from the computer or by working it out by hand is really only the beginning. We need to interpret the information. Are the data relevant? Have we come up with a useful estimate of costs? As a result of our analysis, can we better predict how cost changes with changes in the various drivers? We have not entered this area to become experts in the hand calculation of regression and correlation measures. We are dealing with the collection of data and the interpretation of the results to aid in decisions such as pricing or estimating CVP relationships or the like.

COST ACCOUNTING REQUIREMENTS FOR STATISTICAL ANALYSIS

We discussed several aspects of cost records in the section on account analysis. When we use regression techniques, we must investigate several important factors. Obviously the cost observations we use come directly from cost accounting records. Unless these records reflect costs recorded in a meaningful form, analysis is useless.

Specification of Observations and Variables

First, all factors that might affect the dependent variable should be identified at the outset. If you are investigating a sales forecast for the next year, you might identify factors such as prices, mix, inflation, introduction of new products, and limitation of some resources. If you are investigating manufacturing costs, you need to identify all the factors of production. Since we are going to rely on computers, our search for these factors can be thorough, but not so wild as to throw in factors on impulse.

Second, costs are accumulated over specified time periods (days, weeks, months). The period must be long enough so that current costs are matched with current production. For example, if data are entered only monthly in the cost system, daily observations are not possible. If a lag between costs and activity exists, it needs to be adjusted before data can be used. Thus, the cost time period must be long enough to permit this matching. However, cost periods cannot be too long. Because of averaging effects, yearly observations can mask the variability of costs.

Third, the Robern example shows a fairly large range of observations. But suppose that all observations were over a range of 120,000 to 125,000 hours. With this narrow a range the regression would not be too meaningful. Thus, observations must be over a reasonably broad range.

Fourth, there must be enough observations to have this statistical tool make sense. We are estimating a true cost function based on a sample group of observations. The more observations we have, the better our estimate. As noted earlier, with more than thirty observations we can gain greater confidence in our estimate.

Last, it may be difficult to get data needed for cost estimation. Many costs are common to various products in a department, plant, or company. Some cost records, too, may include errors. Are costs accurate? Is the independent variable accurate? If not, the regression, its coefficients, and standard errors might be misleading. The shorter the reporting period, the more devastating the effect of errors. This is especially true if production levels are random and do not have a steadily increasing (or decreasing) pattern.

Remember also that we are dealing with short-run variable costs—those which vary quickly with activity. Regression analysis with monthly observations probably will not catch step-variable costs, such as the costs of clerks in the purchasing function. These costs might increase over time as large jumps take place in the driver. In the purchasing function, drivers could include the number of different parts or components purchased and the number of vendors.

Cost Estimation and Human Behavior

Communicating relevant information is a key to managerial and cost accounting. As we add sophisticated models to our communication process, we can both help and hinder the information user's understanding. Unless the creators and users of information know the strengths and weaknesses of models such as regression and correlation analysis, the results from these newer quantitative techniques can be misinterpreted, unwisely rejected, or overly relied on.

In using a quantitative tool, an information preparer, such as an accountant, must know what a model will do and not do and how it works. Otherwise the results and their interpretation can be dangerous. Few managers actually type data for a regression analysis into a computer. Unless managers know the meaning of regression analysis, however, how are they going to use the output?

Even if the accountant understands a quantitative model, the results need to be explained in such a way that a well-informed user can understand them. Every profession uses jargon to explain things, but it can stand in the way of common understanding. Imagine the difference between the two conversations from which the following remarks were extracted:

BILL: I just regressed units and batches against chemical costs and came up with $y' = 2{,}000 + 0.94x_1 + 3.8x_2$ with $r^2 = 0.9578$ and b significant at 0.0001.

HARRY: I was investigating chemical costs and related how they change with the number of gallons we produce and the number of batches. What I found was a good relationship between these items and the fact that chemical costs equal about $2,000 per month plus 94 cents for each gallon we produce and plus $3.80 for each batch we start into production.

Bill relies on jargon to produce his message for the listener. If the listener has Bill's level of expertise, this form of communication might be adequate. Bill may be hiding behind the jargon, however; he may not be able to explain in everyday language what it all means. Harry understands and communicates better.

Computer printouts lead to another kind of information problem. We are all limited in the number of things we can deal with. If a computer printout includes all sorts of coefficients, t values, probabilities, standard errors, and so on, the user might have to cope with too much information. Therefore, it is the preparer's responsibility to produce an analysis that presents usable results in an understandable and reasonable format. This calls for editing, deciding what results to show and why, and selecting the form and format for presentation. Much research is being done in this area.

SUMMARY

The major effort of cost analysis is to find cost drivers to be able to predict costs, determine variable costs, and identify fruitful avenues for reducing costs. Costs do not always fit into fixed or variable classifications. Mixed costs contain both fixed and variable elements. Some costs vary with sales, some with production, others with the number of orders placed by customers, still others with the number of incoming shipments of parts. Identifying cost drivers is critical to cost management.

Scatter diagrams and regression analysis are both useful in analyzing cost behavior, but only regression gives formal measures of goodness of fit. Such measures enable accountants and other managers to evaluate cost drivers and to determine confidence intervals.

REVIEW PROBLEM

Counts Company hires temporary workers to process factory documents such as work orders, materials requisitions, and labor time tickets. The controller has collected the following data from the past 17 weeks.

Transactions Processed (hundreds)	Temporary Employee Costs
500	$4,580
350	3,790
675	5,520
585	5,880
425	3,350
472	3,720
520	4,510
460	3,750
390	3,910
680	6,070
765	6,020
640	5,290
350	3,290
440	3,410
390	4,050
620	5,380
660	5,640

Use Lotus 1-2-3 to do a regression analysis of the data. Template REVRP.WK1 on your diskette has the data. The following is the output from REVRP.WK1.

```
OUTPUT SECTION=========================================
                Regression Output:
        Constant                              828.8751199
        Std Err of Y Est                      408.09191453
        R Squared                             0.8482597678
        No. of Observations                             17
        Degrees of Freedom                              15
        X Coefficient(s)   7.1810270076
        Std Err of Coef. 0.7842000542
```

The interpretation might be as follows. There is a fixed component of \$829 within the relevant range. The variable component of cost is \$7.181 per 100 transactions. The fit of the equation is very good. The standard error of the estimate of \$408 indicates that about 68 percent of the costs are within \$408 of the regression line, 95 percent within \$816 (2 × \$408). Moreover, r^2 of 0.8483 indicates that nearly 85 percent of the variation in cost is associated with the number of transactions processed. Finally, the slope is clearly significant because the *t*-value is 9.157 (7.181/0.7842), which is well beyond the critical value of 2.0.

APPENDIX 3A: MULTIPLE REGRESSION AND CORRELATION ANALYSIS

The simple linear regression illustrated in the chapter uses a single variable to predict costs. The basic CVP model assumes that sales volume is the principal determinant of cost levels. Our example in the chapter used machine hours as the cost driver. However, in many cases, more than one activity drives costs. In such cases we can use **multiple regression analysis**. Multiple regression uses two or more independent variables to predict the level of the dependent variable.

Multiple Regression Using Two Independent Variables

A regression equation using two independent variables appears as follows:

$$y' = a + b_1x_1 + b_2x_2$$

where b_1 and b_2 are regression coefficients associated respectively with the two independent variables x_1 and x_2. Visually this relationship is shown by a plane (see Figure 3–10) rather than by a line.

As was the case in simple regression, a is the intercept where the plane touches the y axis. However, this analysis has two slopes. Therefore, b_1 and b_2 are not exactly analogous to the slope of a simple regression. The interpretation of b_1 and b_2 involves looking at one while holding the other constant. If you hold x_2 constant, b_1 is the change in y' as x_1 changes by one unit. Similarly, b_2 is the change in y' when x_2 changes by one unit while x_1 is held constant. This kind of analysis, where everything is held constant except one variable, is common to many accounting models. It is the basis of the "what if" sensitivity analysis in CVP relationships, and it will be the basis of variance analysis as discussed in Chapter 7.

The normal equations for three-variable regression analysis (see Appendix 3B) follow.

$$\begin{aligned}
\Sigma y &= na + b_1 \Sigma x_1 + b_2 \Sigma x_2 \\
\Sigma x_1y &= a \Sigma x_1 + b_1 \Sigma x_1^2 + b_2 \Sigma x_1x_2 \\
\Sigma x_2y &= a \Sigma x_2 + b_1 \Sigma x_1x_2 + b_2 \Sigma x_2^2
\end{aligned}$$

We will not go through a full illustration using these normal equations, since computers can do this task. As the number of independent variables expands, so does the number of equations, making hand calculation increasingly more difficult.

As our discussion shows, we have tried to approximate many functions with a line. This is the basis of CVP analysis, for example. However, since we are faced with the problems of possible nonlinear functions and the reality that many costs move with changes in more than one variable, multiple regres-

FIGURE 3–10 Multiple Regression with Two Independent Variables

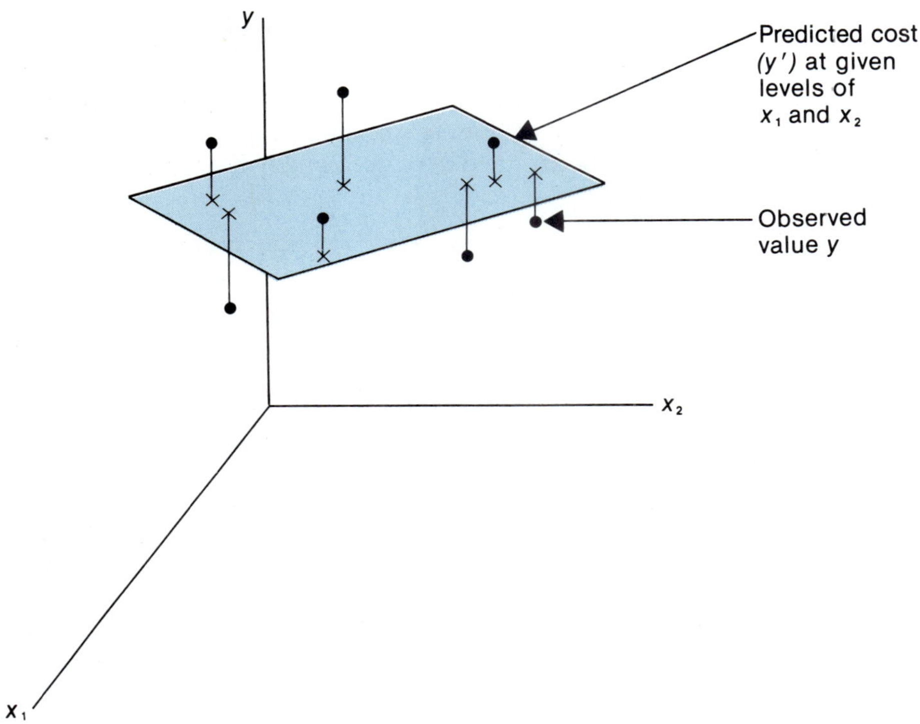

sion may give the decision maker a better predictive tool than simple linear regression.

Standard Error of the Estimate The standard error of the estimate is an extension of simple regression. The only difference is that we use $n - 3$ as the denominator (and as the degrees of freedom), since the analysis estimates three parameters (a, b_1, and b_2). We get the same result—the amount of variation in y that is unexplained by the regression plane. Therefore, the same kind of confidence intervals can be constructed as in the simple model.

For ease of explanation the discussion is limited to two independent variables. Multiple regression techniques can be used with scores of variables if it makes sense to do so.

Dummy Variables Sometimes a factor affecting costs is not entirely quantitative in nature. The winter season in a factory, for example, is such a variable. Therefore, a dummy variable of 1 if it is winter and 0 if it is not winter may be added as an independent variable to help explain cost. In essence, a dummy variable of the 0, 1 type changes the intercept. Assume that a multiple regression produces the following results:

$$y' = 82{,}367 + 14.5x_1 + 27{,}341x_2$$

where

$$y' = \text{total utility cost}$$
$$x_1 = \text{machine hours}$$
$$x_2 = 1 \text{ in winter, } 0 \text{ otherwise}$$

If it is winter, $y' = 109{,}708 + 14.5x_1$; in other seasons, $y' = 82{,}367 + 14.5x_1$.

Another use of dummy variables is in dealing with autocorrelation. The value 0 may be assigned to periods of rising production, 1 to periods of falling production.

Multiple Correlation Analysis With multiple regression there is more than one measure of correlation. R^2 is the coefficient of multiple determination and the ratio of the explained variance over the total variance. Also, there are coefficients of partial determination for each independent variable. Assume that a regression, as in simple regression, using two independent variables produces the following results:

$$y' = 12{,}500 + 167.9x_1 + 324x_2$$

and

$$R^2 = 0.895$$
$$r^2_{Y2\cdot1} = 0.505$$

$R^2 = 0.895$ means that the plane describes 89.5 percent of the variation of costs. The partial coefficient $r^2_{Y2\cdot1} = 0.505$ means that 50.5 percent of the variation of y is explained by x_1 when holding x_2 constant.

Multicollinearity

All the assumptions that underlie simple regression analysis apply to multiple regression analysis as well. Multiple regression analysis also may be harmed by **multicollinearity**, which occurs when two or more independent variables are correlated. For example, if a product requires twenty minutes of labor time and fifteen minutes of machine time, the two variables will be closely correlated. A multiple regression equation that used both labor time and machine time as independent variables would have multicollinearity.

The chief problem with multicollinearity is that the individual b values have no meaning: they cannot be considered the likely changes in cost arising from a one-unit change in that variable. The equation itself may be used for predicting total costs, but the coefficients cannot be used as estimates of variable cost of the particular factor. Multicollinearity can exist when the independent variables are either positively or negatively related. The example in the preceding paragraph showed positive correlation: the more labor time, the more machine time. Sometimes products can be made using either labor or machine time, where using more of the one means needing less of the other.

Multicollinearity can be found in a variety of ways. One method is to correlate the independent variables. A rule of thumb is that if two independent variables have a coefficient of determination greater than 0.80, multicollinearity exists. As a rule, the standard errors of the coefficients will be relatively large when multicollinearity exists, so that the t-values will be relatively low. If t-values for two or more independent variables are less than 2, and the coefficient of multiple determination is high, multicollinearity may be inferred.

Computer Techniques

With more and more sophisticated computer hardware and programming and with ease of access to such programming through time-sharing networks, even the small firm can benefit from these techniques. Since regression and correlation take so much calculation, computers are the only reasonable solution mode. In fact, with a technique called **stepwise multiple regression** we can have the computer search for the best two-variable, three-variable, four-variable . . . , n-variable model. Many models exist that look explicitly at seasonality and inflation. As these techniques are more widely used, the problem of estimation takes on a new dimension—interpretation and communication of output.

APPENDIX 3B: CALCULATIONS FOR EXAMPLE

This appendix gives the calculations for the regression equation and shows the calculations of the values used in the chapter to solve for the standard error of the estimate and coefficient of determination. Exhibit 3B–1 on page 114 is a Lotus 1-2-3 template showing the data and calculations. The values correspond to those in Exhibit 3–2 in the chapter.

We determine the intercept and slope, a and b using the normal equations.

$$\Sigma y = na + b\,\Sigma x$$
$$\Sigma xy = a\,\Sigma x + b\,\Sigma x^2$$

Using our data

$$35{,}844 = 28a + 3{,}775b$$
$$4{,}901{,}513 = 3{,}775a + 522{,}279b$$
$$b = \$5.1751$$
$$a = \$582.4 \text{ thousand}$$

ASSIGNMENTS

3–1 Simple High-Low (AICPA) The following relationships pertain to a year's budgeted activity for Smythe Company:

Direct labor hours	300,000	400,000
Total costs	$129,000	$154,000

REQUIRED

What are the budgeted fixed costs for the year?

EXHIBIT 3B–1 Calculations for Chapter Illustration

	X	Y	X^2	XY	Y_c	$(Y - Y_c)^2$	$(Y - Y_m)^{2*}$
	122	1,103	14,884	134,566	1,214	12,275	31,380
	134	1,245	17,956	166,830	1,276	954	1,235
	156	1,249	24,336	194,844	1,390	19,809	970
	131	1,263	17,161	165,453	1,260	7	294
	109	1,121	11,881	122,189	1,147	651	25,326
	154	1,439	23,716	221,606	1,379	3,553	25,236
	165	1,441	27,225	237,765	1,436	22	25,875
	162	1,463	26,244	237,006	1,421	1,781	33,437
	99	1,009	9,801	99,891	1,095	7,356	73,518
	118	1,272	13,924	150,096	1,193	6,227	66
	112	1,141	12,544	127,792	1,162	443	19,361
	132	1,346	17,424	177,672	1,266	6,474	4,337
	137	1,363	18,769	186,731	1,291	5,124	6,865
	142	1,457	20,164	206,894	1,317	19,518	31,278
	136	1,189	18,496	161,704	1,286	9,456	8,307
	153	1,343	23,409	205,479	1,374	975	3,951
	103	1,050	10,609	108,150	1,115	4,286	52,966
	134	1,279	17,956	171,386	1,276	10	1
	172	1,463	29,584	251,636	1,473	91	33,437
	98	1,063	9,604	104,174	1,090	707	47,151
	127	1,278	16,129	162,306	1,240	1,469	5
	156	1,463	24,336	228,228	1,390	5,367	33,437
	176	1,310	30,976	230,560	1,493	33,578	891
	134	1,330	17,956	178,220	1,276	2,928	2,486
	139	1,427	19,321	198,353	1,302	15,683	21,567
	152	1,407	23,104	213,864	1,369	1,441	16,093
	103	1,197	10,609	123,291	1,115	6,724	6,913
	119	1,133	14,161	134,827	1,198	4,260	21,651
Sum	3,775	35,844	522,279	4,901,513	35,844	171,167	528,033
Mean	135	1,280.1					

*Variance of Y, the square of each actual value of observation minus the mean of Y. Y_c is the calculated value of Y. $(Y - Y_m)$ is the difference between each value of Y and the mean of Y.

Calculations:

Standard error of estimate	81.1377	$\sqrt{171,167/26}$
R^2	0.6758	$1 - (171,167/528,033)$

There are slight differences between these values and those in Exhibit 3–2 given by rounding.

3–2 Estimating Fixed Cost (AICPA) Paine Corporation wishes to determine the fixed portion of its electricity expense (a semivariable expense) as measured against direct labor hours for the first three months of 19X4. Information for the first three months of 19X4 is as follows:

	Direct Labor Hours	Electricity Expense
January 19X4	34,000	$610
February 19X4	31,000	585
March 19X4	34,000	610

REQUIRED

What is the fixed portion of Paine's electricity expense rounded to the nearest dollar?

3–3 Basic High-Low (AICPA) This question is based on a company's maintenance expenses, which are to be analyzed to construct a flexible budget. Examination of past records disclosed the following costs and volume measures:

	Highest	Lowest
Cost per month	$39,200	$32,000
Machine hours	24,000	15,000

REQUIRED

1. Using the high-low method of analysis, calculate the estimated variable cost per machine hour.
2. Using the high-low technique, estimate the annual fixed cost for maintenance expenditures.

3–4 Use of Regression Results (CIA Adapted) For a simple regression analysis model that is used to allocate factory overhead, an internal auditor finds that the intersection of the line of best fit for the overhead allocation with the y axis is $5,000. The slope of the trend line is 0.20. The independent variable, factory wages, amounts to $900,000 for the month.

REQUIRED

What is the estimated amount of factory overhead to be allocated for the month?

3–5 Analyzing Cost Behavior As controller of Van Dine Enterprises, you are responsible for the training and development of members of your staff. You recently hired an accounting major from the state university and told her to spend a few days analyzing the cost structure in one of the firm's nearby plants. She has come back with the following questions.

1. "We use the units of production method of depreciation for some of our machinery and equipment. Does that make depreciation a variable cost?"
2. "We have a take-or-pay contract with one of our suppliers. We have to pay $600,000 per year for the material for any quantity up to 200,000 gallons. We pay $2.90 per gallon for anything over 200,000 gallons. We use 2 gallons for each unit of product and generally produce about 110,000 to 115,000 units per year. Is the $600,000 a fixed cost? Are variable costs zero until we get over 100,000 units of product, then $5.80?"

3. "Our union contract requires that we pay each worker who has five or more years of service for 35 hours per week even if they work less than that. About 20 percent of our workers have five years or more of service. Are their wages fixed or variable?"
4. "Our policy allows each product manager, who is responsible for sales and production of a product or product line, to spend an amount up to five percent of sales for advertising and promotion. Are these costs variable?"

REQUIRED

Answer the questions above.

3–6 Cost Analysis Managers of Oxnard Manufacturing Company had not paid much attention to cost behavior in the past because the firm had grown rapidly and been consistently profitable. It has become obvious to them recently, however, that the days of rapid growth are over and that more attention needs to be paid to planning and controlling costs. The firm's new controller made the following suggestion:

> I propose that we determine what costs should be at two levels of volume and interpolate between them. I suggest that we work with shutdown costs and costs at full capacity because it is relatively easy to determine what costs should be at those levels. In preliminary analysis, I have determined that our costs at shutdown should be about $94,500 per month, consisting of capacity-related costs such as depreciation and property taxes, minimum maintenance, and salaries of upper level management. We save supervisory costs and costs of some departments such as engineering, personnel, accounting, and data processing because we would lay off most of their employees. We also save on utilities, advertising, and most other similar costs. We have never shut down, but I am still confident about the $94,500. At the top end, we have a plant running full tilt 24 hours a day. I am not sure what costs we could expect at that level and would like to get together with some of you to see what we might plan on. Once we had the costs at those two levels, we could simply divide the difference in costs by 100 percent, which gives us the variable component of cost, expressed as dollars per percentage point of capacity used. We could use that figure to determine what our costs should be at levels of volume between shutdown and full capacity.

REQUIRED

Comment on the suggestion. How will the cost line developed using the proposed method be likely to differ from one developed using a scatter diagram of actual observation of costs?

3–7 Data Requirements and Regression Analysis You have asked your assistant to see what relationship, if any, seems to hold between total factory overhead cost and direct labor cost. After initial talks with various people and some independent checking, he has returned with the following:

1. All workers, direct and indirect, received a 12 percent pay increase six months ago.
2. Fuel is a large item of overhead. Its quantity is nearly the same each month, but the price has risen 2 to 3 percent each month from the beginning of the year.

3. Supplies, which range between 5 to 10 percent of total overhead cost, are recorded when purchased, rather than when used. The firm takes an inventory of supplies only at year-end.

REQUIRED

You wish to use at least fifteen months' data in the regression analysis. Write out a set of instructions for your assistant, stating what he should do, if anything, about each fact he has brought to your attention.

3–8 Preliminary Cost Classification The following is a partial list of accounts for Rhea Products Corporation.

Sales Expenses	*Occupancy Expenses*
601 Sales Supervisory Salaries	801 Supervisory Salaries
602 Commissions	802 Janitors and Security Guards
612 F.I.C.A. Tax Expense	810 Overtime Premium
616 Unemployment Insurance Expense	832 Janitorial Supplies
617 Newspaper Advertising	835 Repairs to Building
619 Convention Expense	842 Heat, Light, Air Conditioning
625 Association Dues	850 Depreciation—Building
634 Automobile Expense	860 Insurance—Building
641 Warranty Expense	

REQUIRED

1. You are to classify these accounts by analyzing account titles. Discuss each account as to whether it is a fixed, variable, or mixed cost. If it is variable or partially so, what should it vary with?
2. What are the problems associated with this kind of analysis?

3–9 Analyzing Cost Accounts Cunningham Corporation shows the following entries in its Maintenance account during June, 19X0:

1. maintenance labor: $3,000
2. parts: $5,500
3. tools and supplies: $7,650
4. rent: $500
5. bookkeeping: $600

Analysis of these entries shows that labor includes $300 of overtime pay, parts includes a $1,000 motor considered an unusual maintenance cost, tools and supplies includes a $5,650 drill press, and rent and bookkeeping are allocated expenses. Five hundred hours of labor were used. The overtime seemed linked to the major motor replacement.

REQUIRED

1. What are the relevent costs for CVP analysis that are useful for forecasting future costs? Why?
2. For July, labor was $2,100, parts $4,500, tools and supplies $1,500, rent $500, bookkeeping $600. Four hundred hours were worked, and there were no

overtime costs or extraordinary costs. Use these additional data to develop estimates of fixed and variable components of costs.

3–10 High-Low Forecasting Tabatha Phelps, president of Alpro Cat Food, shows you selected data for the cost of producing one of its products, Tuna Meowt cat snack food.

Date	Production	Cost
March 2	400 cans	$155
April 23	1,110	500
May 7	725	225
June 12	800	375
July 9	475	200
August 27	1,025	425
September 8	1,200	450
October 8	1,150	475
November 6	650	250

You have been asked to use these data to develop a cost-estimating formula based on the high-low method. Assume the data were selected at random from production reports.

REQUIRED

1. Plot the above data.
2. Compute a forecasting equation in the form of $y' = a + bx$, using the high-low method.
3. What would be the effect on your high-low estimate if data for March 2 show 400 cans produced for $125?
4. Using the estimate derived in part 2, what would you forecast for costs at a production of 900 cans?
5. Do you recommend using the high-low method in this case? Why or why not?

3–11 High-Low Forecasting Assume the following cost and production information for Apex Service Co.

Number of Service Calls	Cost	Number of Service Calls	Cost
100	$ 800	200	$1,800
125	900	225	1,900
150	1,000	250	2,000

REQUIRED

1. Compute a $y' = a + bx$ forecasting equation using the high-low method.
2. Is your answer to part 1 useful for forecasting? Why or why not? What improvements would you suggest?

3–12 Explaining Regression and Correlation (CMA Adapted) Regression analysis is a procedure used to measure the relationship of one variable with one or more other variables. Regression provides a rational statement rather than a causal statement with regard to the relationship. The basic formula for a regression equation is:

$$Y_i = \alpha + \beta_1 x_{i1} + \beta_2 x_{i2} + E_i$$

For a regression equation to provide meaningful information, it should comply with the basic criteria of goodness of fit and specification analysis. Specification analysis is determined by examining the population relationships for (1) linearity within a relevant range, (2) constant variance (homoscedasticity), (3) independence of observations (serial correlation), (4) normality, and (5) multicollinearity.

REQUIRED

1. Explain what is meant by the phrase "regression provides a rational statement rather than a causal statement."
2. Explain the meaning of each of the following symbols that appear in the basic formula for a regression equation:
   a. Y_i
   b. α
   c. β_1
   d. x_{i1}
   e. E_i
3. Identify the statistical factors that are used to test a regression equation for goodness of fit and, for each item identified, indicate whether a high or low value describes a "good" fit.
4. Explain what each of the following terms means with respect to regression analysis:
   a. linearity within a relevant range
   b. constant variance (homoscedasticity)
   c. serial correlation
   d. normality
   e. multicollinearity

3–13 Describing Regression Results The resident statistician of GRT Industries has given you the following regression results:

$$TC = \$325{,}432 + \$5.67D$$
$$r^2 = 0.65$$
$$S_e = \$36{,}759$$
$$S_b = \$1.35$$

where

TC = total cost

D = direct labor hours

REQUIRED

1. Determine the percentage of the variance of total cost that is associated with changes in direct labor hours.
2. There is a 95 percent probability that the "true" value of the b coefficient ($5.67) is between which two values (in dollars)?

3. A manager wants to know what S_e means and how he might use it in evaluating actions. Give him a brief informative answer.
4. The statistician told you that there are several assumptions underlying simple (one independent variable) regression analysis. Name two and describe each briefly. You might wish to use diagrams to illustrate your points.

3–14 Simple Regression Ballot Box Company is developing a new costing system. In reviewing data from the past several weeks, its accountant developed the following data:

Week	Maintenance Supply Costs	Maintenance Hours
1	$ 320	22.0
2	352	30.2
3	468	31.0
4	635	29.0
5	500	40.0
6	821	36.9
7	1,020	41.8
8	990	50.0
9	728	36.8
10	905	38.9

REQUIRED

1. Using regression analysis, calculate the intercept and slope.
2. Calculate the coefficient of determination, standard error of the estimate, and standard error of the slope.
3. Evaluate the results of the review for goodness of fit and usefulness.
4. Write a short memo that interprets the results of the review to management.

3–15 Basic Estimating Techniques A recent review of supply costs and production conducted at Hormutz Manufacturing Company shows the following:

Supply Costs	Production
$125	3,500 units
175	5,000
200	7,000
100	3,000
125	4,500
200	6,000
150	4,000

These data are weekly results from the last two months of production.

REQUIRED

1. Plot these data points.
2. Using the high-low method, find the intercept and slope.
3. Can you fit a line visually that is better than the one you calculated in part 2? Why is it better?

4. Calculate a regression line for these data. Also calculate r^2, S_e, and S_b. Explain the results of all of your calculations.

5. Recalculate the information asked for in part 4, disregarding the observations at 4,500 units and 7,000 units. Again, explain the results. Why would an accountant choose to disregard certain data points?

3–16 Interpreting Results (CMA Adapted) Alpha Company, which produces several products, is making plans for the introduction of a new product that will sell for $6 a unit. The following estimates have been made for manufacturing costs of 100,000 units to be produced the first year:

Direct materials	$50,000
Direct labor	$40,000 (labor rate is $4 an hour)

Overhead costs have not yet been estimated for the new product, but monthly data on total production and overhead cost for the past 24 months have been analyzed using simple linear regression. The following results were derived from regression and will provide the basis for overhead cost estimates for the new product.

Simple Regression Analysis Results ($y' = a + bx$)

dependent variable (y) = factory overhead costs
independent variable (x) = direct labor hours

Computed values	
y intercept	$40,000
Coefficient of independent variable	$2.10
Coefficient of correlation	0.953
Standard error of estimate	$2,840
Standard error of regression coefficient	0.42
Mean value of independent variable	$18,000
Coefficient of determination	0.908

REQUIRED

1. What percentage of the variation in overhead costs is explained by the independent variable?

2. Estimate the total overhead cost for an activity level of 20,000 direct labor hours.

3. Calculate a 95 percent confidence interval for the b value.

4. What is the expected contribution margin per unit to be earned during the first year on 100,000 units of the new product?

3–17 Interpreting Results (CMA Adapted) Armer Company is accumulating data to be used in preparing its annual profit plan for the coming year. The cost behavior pattern of maintenance costs must be determined. The accounting staff has suggested that linear regression be employed to derive an equation in the form of $y = a + bx$ for maintenance costs. Data regarding the maintenance hours and costs for last year and the results of the regression analysis are:

	Hours of Activity	Maintenance Costs
January	480	$ 4,200
February	320	3,000
March	400	3,600
April	300	2,820
May	500	4,350
June	310	2,960
July	320	3,030
August	520	4,470
September	490	4,260
October	470	4,050
November	350	3,300
December	340	3,160
Sum	4,800	$43,200
Average	400	3,600

Average cost per hour (43,200/4,800) = $9.00

a coefficient	684.65
b coefficient	7.2884
Standard error of the *a* coefficient	49.515
Standard error of the *b* coefficient	0.12126
Standard error of the estimate	34.469
r^2	0.99724
t value *a*	13.827
t value *b*	60.105

REQUIRED

1. If Armer Company uses the high-low method of analysis, what is the equation for the relationship between hours of activity and maintenance cost?
2. Based on the data derived from the regression analysis, if there were 420 maintenance hours in a month, at how much should maintenance costs be budgeted?
3. What is the coefficient of correlation for Armer's regression equation for the maintenance activities?
4. What is the percent of the total variance that can be explained by the regression equation?
5. What is the range of values for the marginal maintenance cost such that Armer can be 95 percent confident that the true value of the marginal maintenance cost will be within this range?
6. At 400 hours of activity, Armer management can be approximately two-thirds confident that maintenance costs will be in what range?

3–18 Selecting a Regression Barbara Vegas, the controller of Cunex Corp., is reviewing regression results from her staff. She is interested in predicting overhead costs for the upcoming period and has gathered the following data.

Month	Machine Hours	Overhead Costs	Units
1	3,300	$56,973	24,300
2	2,800	57,320	24,500
3	3,100	58,693	25,000
4	3,400	51,174	21,800
5	3,500	58,688	25,000
6	2,200	53,333	22,700
7	2,600	48,111	20,600
8	3,000	56,202	24,000
9	3,400	55,444	23,700
10	3,150	58,002	24,000
11	3,375	56,370	24,200
12	2,400	46,756	20,000
13	2,600	51,821	22,100
14	3,200	57,585	24,500
15	2,700	50,241	21,500
16	2,800	53,490	22,900
17	2,500	47,250	20,200
18	3,100	56,294	24,100
19	3,500	56,011	23,900
20	3,600	60,123	25,700

REQUIRED

Barbara Vegas has asked you, her assistant, to run some regressions using the above data and to analyze the results.

1. Run a regression using units as the single independent variable. Plot the data and the residuals.
2. Run a regression using machine hours as the single independent variable. Plot the data and the residuals.
3. Write a memorandum to Vegas in which you recommend which (if either) of the two regression results she should use to forecast overhead costs for the next year. Justify your choice. Your memorandum should be free of jargon and should address:
   a. whether the assumptions of simple linear regression seem valid in each regression; and
   b. whether you recommend the first regression, the second regression, or neither.

3–19 Explanation of Regression Results Manion Division of MICD Industries makes running and tennis shoes. Recently the marketing department asked you in your role as chief management accountant to help in their planning. They want to know if there is an association between shoe sales and the Consumer Price Index (CPI). After data gathering and computer input, you generated the following results based on monthly information:

```
INTERCEPT        2,121.3    STD. ERROR      40.43     T-VALUE    50.0
CPI              -3.002     STD. ERROR       1.58     T-VALUE     1.9
COEFF. OF DET.    .61       STD. ERROR EST.     906
```

REQUIRED

1. You hand these results to the marketing people, who say (this has been cleaned up to get a PG rating), "Good golly and gee whiz, what do all these things mean?" Carefully explain the results to the marketing folks. Realize that they have never seen regression results before, so do not use any jargon.

2. A joker in the bunch who had a course in managerial accounting in his MBA program remembers just enough to ask you to evaluate the results and to discuss the important underlying assumptions that you must make to use regression and correlation results and how these results can be used in light of these assumptions.

3. The CPI for next month is expected to be 304.5, but forecasters think it may be as high as 306 or as low as 303. Another member of the marketing group has studied some statistics and asks you to give a 95 percent confidence interval for next month's shoe sales, assuming a normal distribution. Justify your approach.

3–20 Simple Regression Analysis Febrile Company's consultants have just run a preliminary computer regression and correlation analysis on costs in the packaging department. The independent variable is number of packages, and the dependent variable is cost of packaging supplies. The computer output is shown below.

```
                         SIMPLE LINEAR REGRESSION

HOW MANY OBSERVATIONS DO YOU HAVE? 12

WHAT PERCENTAGE CONFIDENCE LEVEL DO YOU WANT--
  70, 80, 90, OR 95? 95

                                REGRESSION COEFFICIENT A               1090.05

                                REGRESSION COEFFICIENT B               8.85247

                                COEFFICIENT OF CORRELATION--R          .796266

                                COEFFICIENT OF DETERMINATION--R2       .63404

T-TEST OF CORRELATION%

R TIMES THE SQUARE ROOT OF N-2 DIVIDED BY THE SQUARE ROOT OF 1-R2
EQUALS 4.16237

CUMULATIVE T-DISTRIBUTION AT 97.5 PERCENT LEVEL FOR 10 DEGREES OF
FREEDOM EQUALS 2.225

SINCE 4.16237 EXCEEDS 2.225 THE OBSERVATIONS PROVIDE MORE THAN 95
PERCENT ASSURANCE THAT THE X AND Y VALUES ARE RELATED.
```

OBSERVED X VALUE	OBSERVED Y VALUE	Y VALUE ON REGRESSION LINE AT X	95 PC PREDICTION INTERVAL FOR PREDICTING Y AT X: LOWER LIMIT	UPPER LIMIT
132.25	2340	2260.79	1912.68	2608.9
96.75	1940	1946.52	1620.71	2272.34
100.5	1910	1979.72	1655.57	2303.88
120	2300	2152.34	1821.26	2483.43
110.1	2270	2064.7	1740.38	2389.03
110.5	1870	2068.25	1743.78	2392.71
108	1980	2046.11	1722.38	2369.85
105.5	1920	2023.98	1700.54	2347.43
100	1850	1975.3	1650.97	2299.62
127	2310	2214.31	1874.6	2554.02
96	1820	1939.89	1613.62	2266.15
54	1730	1568.08	1164.39	1971.78

REQUIRED

1. Write a memo to management explaining what simple linear regression is and what these results mean. Do not use jargon.
2. Plot the data. Does your interpretation of the results change? How?

3–21 Choice of Independent Variables You are currently estimating overhead costs in the production department. After research, you have identified three variables as potential predictors of cost. You have collected the following data for fifteen weeks:

Week	Overhead Costs	Production Volume #107	#110	#120
1	$12,899	22	25	63
2	9,266	64	96	37
3	7,153	30	62	30
4	11,000	50	0	47
5	11,900	31	77	58
6	8,415	52	7	34
7	10,672	52	85	43
8	12,128	34	43	57
9	8,003	57	53	31
10	10,888	28	51	51
11	10,414	30	59	47
12	10,500	55	54	45
13	11,732	55	16	52
14	7,751	25	68	34
15	12,870	54	45	60

REQUIRED

Choose the best variable or variables to predict overhead costs. Justify your choice. Where possible, check the assumptions of regression analysis.

3–22 Simple Regression—Communication and Analysis The data processing manager enters your office and says, "Well, I've been working on helping you guys in accounting forecast costs. I looked at one production department's costs and came up with a beauty of an analysis." He hands you the following:

```
LIST ALL DATA
? Y
VARIABLE    1         2
 OBS.
   1 73603.    9914.0
   2 27775.    9774.0
   3 14302.    4110.0
   4 69020.    8450.0
   5 45448.    8586.0
   6 8335.0    4383.0
   7 2850.0    209.00
   8 9208.0    6152.0
   9 75218.    9874.0
  10 74962.    369.00
WHICH VARS
? 1.2
SYMBOL
? *
```

REQUIRED

This assignment requires you to write a formal memorandum to management. Use a microcomputer and a word processing program and a spreadsheet program for supporting schedules. See Appendix B for guidelines for memoranda presentation.

You are a member of the accounting staff. Your boss, Tamara Yogore, is aware that the data processing manager has been working on new ways to estimate costs. She is very interested in the results of this first effort. However, she knows nothing about regression and correlation analysis and is adamant that you do not use jargon in any memos to her.

Write a memorandum to Yogore (with a copy to the data processing manager) in which you:

1. Carefully explain in simple terms what information has been generated.
2. Analyze the data that the data processing manager has given you. He says it is a beauty.

What questions do you have about the data, the analysis, or its underlying assumptions? Yogore does not have a copy of the printout you received. Carefully choose the content, form, and format of support schedules, exhibits, and graphs.

```
                                          SCATTER DIAGRAM
* . . . . . . . . . . . . . . . . . . . . . . . . . . . . . . . . . . . . . . . . . . . .
.                                           VARIABLE 1
.
.             782.34    13533.    26283.    39034.    51785.    64535.    77286.
.    10399.   + . . . . + . . . . + . . . . + . . . . + . . . . + . . . . +   10399.
.             .                                                           .
.             .                    *                                   ** .
.             .                                                           .
.             .                                                           .
.    8620.0   +                                *                          +   8620.0
.             .                                                     *     .
.             .                                                           .
.             .                                                           .
.             .                                                           .
.V   6840.8   +                                                           +   6840.8
.A            .                                                           .
.R            .   *                                                       .
.I            .                                                           .
.A            .                                                           .
.B   5061.5   +                                                           +   5061.5
.L            .                                                           .
.E            . *                                                         .
.             .       *                                                   .
.2            .                                                           .
.    3282.3   +                                                           +   3282.3
.             .                                                           .
.             .                                                           .
.             .                                                           .
.             .                                                           .
.    1503.0   +                                                           +   1503.0
.             .                                                           .
.             .                                                         * .
.             . *                                                         .
.             .                                                           .
.   -276.25   + . . . . + . . . . + . . . . + . . . . + . . . . + . . . . +   -276.25
.             782.34    13533.    26283.    39034.    51785.    64535.    77286.
.
.
.                                           VARIABLE 1
* . . . . . . . . . . . . . . . . . . . . . . . . . . . . . . . . . . . . . . . . . . . .

                                           INTERVAL
                                            SPACING     MINIMUM     MAXIMUM
          SCALING FOR VARIABLE 1   ---      2125.09     2850.00     75218.0
          SCALING FOR VARIABLE 2   ---      254.179     209.000     9914.00

   MORE
   ? N

                                              * * * * * * * * * *
      WANT TO EXIT FROM THE PACKAGE [YES OR NO]
      ? N
      WANT ADVANCED USER STATUS [YES OR NO]
      ? Y
```

```
SAME DATA
? Y
OUTPUT TO TERMINAL
? Y
TYPE CODE
? RE

                    * * * SIMPLE ONE-VARIABLE REGRESSION * * *
DEP. VAR.
? 2
IND. VAR.
? 1

INTERCEPT .................. 4225.01
REGRESSION COEFFICIENT ..... .488393E-01
STD. ERROR OF REG. COEF .... .395843E-01
COMPUTED T-VALUE ........... 1.23380
CORRELATION COEFFICIENT .... .399831
STANDARD ERROR OF ESTIMATE   3671.83

                    ANALYSIS OF VARIANCE FOR THE REGRESSION

   SOURCE OF VARIATION        D.F.     SUM OF SQ.      MEAN SQ.      F VALUE
ATTRIBUTABLE TO REGRESSION    1       .205238E+08    .205238E+08    1.5223
DEVIATION FROM REGRESSION     8       .107859E+09    .134823E+08
TOTAL                         9       .129382E+09
RESIDUAL TABLE
? Y
RESID. TO TEMP. FILE
? N

                          TABLE OF RESIDUALS

OBSERVATION    Y OBSERVED    Y ESTIMATED    RESIDUAL    RES. PCNT OF EST.
     1          9914.00       7819.72       2094.28         26.7820
     2          9774.00       5581.52       4192.48         75.1136
     3          4110.00       4923.51      -813.507        -16.5229
     4          8450.00       7595.89       854.106         11.2443
     5          8586.00       6444.65       2141.35         33.2267
     6          4383.00       4632.08      -249.084        -5.37735
     7          209.000       4364.20      -4155.20        -95.2110
     8          6152.00       4674.72       1477.28         31.6015
     9          9874.00       7898.60       1975.40         25.0095
    10          369.000       7886.10      -7517.10        -95.3209

TEST OF EXTREME RESIDUALS
  RATIO OF RANGES FOR THE SMALLEST RESIDUAL ............ .348079
  RATIO OF RANGES FOR THE LARGEST RESIDUAL ............. .245713
  CRITICAL VALUE OF THE RATIO AT ALPHA = .10 ........... .409000
MORE
? N

                        * * * * * * * * * *
WANT TO EXIT FROM THE PACKAGE [YES OR NO]
? Y
```

3–23 Explaining Results of Regression Analysis On your third day as assistant to the controller of ML Industries, the controller approaches you and says: "I have to go overseas tomorrow and I was supposed to give a talk to a group of our managers on regression analysis. Forbes over in the statistical analysis group gave me the output here [see below] to use for illustrative purposes. I want you to give the talk. We want people to start using statistics more than they do, and so it is important that you give them a good explanation of what the statistics tell them and how they can use them. I'll see you in three weeks."

REQUIRED

The output that the controller mentioned appears below. Develop clear and concise explanations of each piece of information in conformance with the controller's request. Both regression equations use samples of 35 monthly observations.

$$TOH = \$346{,}902 + \$6.142X;\ r^2 = 0.769;\ S_e = \$19{,}926;\ S_b = \$2.381$$

where

TOH = total factory overhead

X = direct labor hours

$$SGA = \$89{,}413 + \$1.27X_1 + \$0.827X_2;\ r^2 = 0.897;\ S_e = \$9{,}785;$$
$$S_b \text{ for } X_1 = \$0.814;\ S_b \text{ for } X_2 = \$0.675$$

where

SGA = total selling and administrative expenses

X_1 = dollar sales of Product 1, hundreds

X_2 = dollar sales of Product 2, hundreds

3–24 Regression Analysis and Inflation Sam Bozella, controller of Arway Industries, was discussing a problem with Richard Feister, president of the company. Bozella began:

> We have been using regression analysis to identify cost behavior patterns, but it has not given us the results we want. Part of the problem is that our costs have been rising rapidly over the last year. That is, the prices we pay for utilities, indirect labor, supervision, and other elements of cost are rising.
>
> I can see two ways to handle the problem. One is to use *constant dollars*. That way we multiply each month's costs by the ratio of the price level in the base period, say, at the end of last year, to the price level in the other months.
>
> The other way is to use *current dollars*. We would then multiply the costs in prior months by the ratio of the price level prevailing today to the price level that prevailed during the other month.
>
> Either way, we are simply restating costs in terms of a constant measuring rod. However, I am not sure which way we should go and what use we can make of the new results in planning for levels of cost in future months.

As an example, Bozella provided the following data:

Month	Actual Costs	Price Level	Constant-Dollar Restatement	Current-Dollar Restatement
December	$363,000	110	$363,000	$412,500
May	392,000	120	359,333	408,333
July	377,000	125	331,760	377,000

The constant-dollar restatement uses December as the base level. The costs of the other months are multiplied by the ratio of the price level in December (110) to the price level in the other month. The current-dollar restatement uses the ratio of the price level in the most recent month (July) to the price level in the other month.

REQUIRED

1. Suppose that the quantities of input factors such as utilities, indirect labor, supervision, and so on remain constant in relation to a measure of activity such as direct labor hours. Thus, if prices had not changed, a regression equation based on direct labor hours would have captured quite closely the behavior of costs. What effects do the monthly increase in price of input factors have on the regression results? Does the intercept change? the slope? the measures of goodness of fit?
2. Suppose that the firm adopts one of the methods illustrated above. Assuming that prices are expected to increase in the future, of what value is a regression equation using either constant dollars or current dollars in planning costs?

3–25 Assumptions of Multiple Regression Analysis The controller of Pergman Company has been trying to determine the labor cost of each of the company's four products. She has received information from the firm's industrial engineering staff and the following regression equation from the operations research department.

$$TC = \$456{,}000 + \underset{(\$0.67)}{\$0.87X_1} + \underset{(\$0.91)}{\$1.18X_2} - \underset{(\$0.88)}{\$0.65X_3} + \underset{(\$2.21)}{\$2.34X_4}$$

$$r^2 = 0.943; \quad S_e = \$14{,}823$$

Standard errors of the regression coefficients are in parentheses. TC is total labor cost, and X_1 through X_4 represent the quantities of each product made during the period.

REQUIRED

Comment on the usefulness of the equation.

3–26 Regression Analysis and Allocated Costs One of your jobs as the chief cost accountant of the Dale River plant of MCC, Inc., is to analyze the behavior of costs in various departments to provide information for planning and control. Your assistant, following your instructions, has just completed a regression analysis of the milling department. The data he used and the regression results appear below.

Month	Direct Labor Hours	Total Departmental Overhead Costs
January	12,300	$150,685
February	15,600	166,370
March	11,850	153,208
April	13,320	163,694
May	15,240	187,090
June	11,800	145,850

Results of the regression are:

$$\text{overhead cost} = \$61{,}586 + \$7.457DLH$$

$$r^2 = 0.719; \; S_e = \$8{,}848; \; S_b = \$2.332$$

Your assistant recently discovered, he adds, that the total overhead cost figures above include some general factory costs allocated to individual departments. During the period covered by these cost figures the monthly charge was $2.80 per direct labor hour.

REQUIRED

1. Without performing a new regression analysis, state what differences you expect to find between the results above and the results of a new regression analysis that exclude the allocated general factory costs. For example, do you expect the standard error of the estimate to rise, fall, or stay the same? What about the slope and intercept of the regression equation?
2. Eliminate the allocated costs and perform a new regression analysis, calculating all the measures given above.

3–27 Regression Results and Product Selection The managers of Barclay Products Company are considering two new products. The firm has made some of each to get some idea of the costs before putting one or both into full-scale production.

The results of regression analysis on each product prepared by a staff manager are:

	Wall Shelving	*File Box*
Monthly fixed production cost	$234,210	$186,452
Unit variable production cost	$ 8.52	$ 3.26
Standard error of estimate	$ 42,100	$ 29,543
Standard error of coefficient	$ 3.86	$ 1.18
r^2	.52	.59

The managers estimate volume for either product at about 30,000 units per month. The shelving will sell for $19 per unit, the file box for $12.

REQUIRED

Suppose that the firm can bring out only one product. Which one do you favor and why?

3–28 Evaluating Regression Equations (CMA Adapted) Elisko, Inc., is a major book distributor throughout the United States. Elisko's Shipping Department consists of a manager plus ten other permanent personnel—four supervisors and six loaders. The four supervisors and six loaders provide the minimum staff and frequently must be supplemented by additional workers, especially when the volume of shipments is heavy. Thus the number of people shipping orders frequently averages more than 30 per week, that is, ten permanent persons plus 20 temporary workers. The temporary workers are hired through a local agency.

Elisko must use temporary workers to maintain a minimum daily shipment rate of 95 percent of orders presented for shipping. The loss of efficiency from using temporary workers is minimal, and the $10.00 per hour cost of temporary workers is less than the $15.00 per hour for the loaders and $22.50 per hour for the supervisors on Elisko's permanent staff. The agency requires Elisko to use each temporary worker for at least four hours each day.

Jim Locter, Shipping Manager, schedules temporary help based on forecasted orders for the coming week. Supervisors serve as loaders until temporary help is needed. A supervisor stops loading when the ratio of loaders to supervisors reaches 7 : 1. Locter knows that he will need temporary help when the forecasted average daily orders exceed 300. Locter has frequently requested from two to four extra temporary workers per day to handle unexpected rush orders. If there was not enough work, he would dismiss the extra people at noon after four hours of work.

The agency has not been pleased with Locter's practice of overhiring and has notified Elisko that it is changing its policy. From now on, if a person is dismissed before an eight-hour assignment is completed, Elisko will still be charged for an eight-hour day plus mileage to the agency for reassignment. This policy will go into effect the following week.

Paula Brand, General Manager, called Jim Locter to her office when she received the notice from the agency. She told Locter, "Your staffing has to be better. This penalty could cost us up to \$300–\$500 per week in labor cost for which we receive no benefit. Why can't you schedule better?"

Locter replied, "I agree that the staffing should be better, but I can't do it accurately when there are rush orders. By being able to lay off people at noon, I have been able to adjust for the uncertain order schedule without cost to the company. Of course, the agency's new policy changes this."

Locter and Brand contacted Elisko's controller, Mitch Berg, regarding Locter's problem on how to estimate the number of people needed each week. Berg realized that Locter needed a quick solution until he could study the work flow. Berg suggested a regression analysis using the number of orders shipped as the independent variable and the number of workers (permanent plus temporary) as the dependent variable. Berg indicated that data for the past year were available and that the analysis could be done quickly on the accounting department's micro-computer.

Berg completed the two regression analyses that are presented below. The first regression was based on the data for the entire year. The second regression excluded the weeks when only the 10 permanent staffpersons were used; these weeks were unusual and appeared to be out of the relevant range.

Regression Equation

$$W = a + bS$$

where W = total workers (permanent plus temporary)

S = orders shipped

	Regression 1 (Daily data for 52 weeks)	*Regression 2 (Daily data for 38 weeks)*
a	5.062	0.489
b	0.023	0.028
Standard error (S_e) of the estimate for W	2.012	0.432
95% confidence for W	3.943	0.848
Coefficient of determination (r^2)	0.962	0.998
Standard error of coefficient (S_b)	0.0007	0.0002

Locter was not familiar with regression analysis and, therefore, was unsure how to implement this technique. He wondered which regression data he should employ.

When he recognized that the regression was based on actual orders shipped by week, Berg told him he could use the forecasted shipments for the week to determine the number of workers needed.

REQUIRED

1. Using Regression 1 based on data from a full year, calculate the number of temporary workers Jim Locter should plan to hire for a forecast indicating 1,200 shipments per day.
2. Which one of the two regressions appears to be better? Explain your answer.
3. Explain the circumstances under which Jim Locter can use the regression in planning for temporary workers.
4. Explain whether the regression analysis that Elisko, Inc., employed in this situation could be improved. If it cannot be improved, explain why.

3–29 Use of Computers for Regression The managers of Dallas Division of White Manufacturing have decided to use regression and correlation analysis to help establish cost patterns. One set of data for material costs on product U-101 appears below. All data are from the current year.

Units of Product	Material Cost
267	$10,625
324	14,886
137	5,146
235	9,960
183	7,941
372	15,762
416	18,200
361	15,133
209	8,019
158	6,214

REQUIRED

Generate regression and correlation analyses and a plot of the data; interpret the results.

3–30 Calculating and Interpreting Results The sales manager of Paul's Potato Chips is trying to estimate how many salespeople to hire to generate sales of $3,000,000 per month. Sales in recent months have varied between about $0.8 million and $2.0 million. Paul's is a relatively new company and is trying to establish itself with large supermarket and commercial users. Data for past sales show the following:

Month	Salespeople	Sales Volume (millions)
1	3	$0.8
2	5	1.3
3	7	1.5
4	8	1.7
5	10	1.9
6	11	2.0

REQUIRED

1. Use regression analysis to determine the intercept and slope of these data.
2. Explain your answers derived from part 1.
3. Can these data be used to predict the number of salespeople needed at a volume of $3 million? Why or why not?

3–31 Use of Regression Results (CMA) John Wood, a financial analyst for a major automobile corporation, has been monitoring the funds used in advertising campaigns and the funds used for automobile factory rebates. Financial data have been accumulated for the last 24 months along with customer sales (i.e., automobiles sold). Wood contends that there may be a relationship between the level of automobile sales and funds expended on advertising and/or factory rebates. If such a relationship can be determined, the company may be able to estimate sales demand based on various levels of funding commitments for one or both types of expenditures.

Regression equations and supporting statistical values were developed for the various relationships between variables and are presented below. The meanings of the notations used in the equations are as follows:

A = advertising funds in $100,000

R = funds for factory rebates in $1,000,000

D = customer sales demand (automobiles sold) in 10,000 units

The appropriate t-values for use in determining confidence intervals are as follows.

50% confidence	+0.69
95% confidence	+2.07

	Equation 1	Equation 2	Equation 3	Equation 4
Equation	$D = 2.455 + 0.188A$	$D = 2.491 + 0.44R$	$R = 6.052 + 0.005A$	$D = -0.184 + 0.186A + 0.437R$
Coefficient of correlation	0.643	0.560	0.014	0.838
Coefficient of determination	0.414	0.314	0.0002	0.703
Standard error of the estimate	1.325	1.434	2.202	0.922
Reliability of the coefficient of correlation at 5% and:				
22 degrees of freedom	0.404	0.404	0.404	
21 degrees of freedom				0.498

REQUIRED

1. The corporation is projecting advertising expenditures of $1,500,000 and factory rebate expenditures of $12,000,000 for the next period. Calculate expected customer demand in units using:
   a. Equation 1
   b. Equation 4
2. Assume that Equation 4 is employed to estimate a total customer demand of 104,160 automobiles for a period. Using a 50 percent confidence level, determine the range of automobile sales that could occur during the time period.

3. Select the regression equation that is most advantageous to predict customer sales demand and explain why it is best.
4. Explain the significance of Equation 3 and its value for the regression analysis evaluation.
5. Each of the regression equations includes a constant.
   a. Discuss the meaning of the constant term included in regression Equation 2.
   b. What is the significance of the negative value in regression Equation 4? Explain your answer.

3–32 Time Series Analysis (CMA) Glenall Company makes numerous small industrial items. In some cases the items are sold individually, but most are sold in combinations. The market for these products is extremely competitive. Recently, the company has been losing sales because of stock shortages. The product demand, production, and inventory history by month for the 19X3–19X4 fiscal year are reproduced below.

Month	*Sales Demand*	*Production*	*Ending Inventory*
July	9,400	10,000	5,600
August	10,200	10,000	5,400
September	10,200	10,000	5,200
October	15,300	12,000	1,900
November	15,600	12,000	0
December	15,800	16,000	200
January	18,300	16,000	0
February	19,300	18,500	0
March	19,600	19,500	0
April	15,900	19,500	3,600
May	16,200	16,000	3,400
June	17,200	16,000	2,200

All production schedules are planned by an ad hoc committee of production and sales personnel. On the fifth of every month, production is determined for the coming month. Demand is determined by actual sales and unfilled orders received since the fifth of the prior month. There are no back orders. Thus, sales that cannot be filled within 60 days of receipt are lost. Once production runs are determined, they cannot be easily changed without substantial set up, sequencing, and raw material carrying costs.

The production manager blames faulty demand forecasts for the current crisis, while the sales manager blames the production manager for not keeping enough safety stock on hand to satisfy customer demand. Company officials are not satisfied with the current forecasting method and have decided that a more sophisticated basis should be employed. Two models that have been proposed are a three-month moving average and a time series regression.

Amy Chew of Glenall's Planning Department was assigned to develop both models and was told that both models are to be based on historical data. She developed the moving average model to forecast demand for the coming month based on the actual sales demand for the prior three months as shown below.

$$D_t = \frac{\sum_{i=1}^{3} D_{t-i}}{3}$$

where

D_t = forecasted sales demand for coming month
D_{t-i} = actual sales demand for prior month i.

The model based on the time series analysis was developed through the use of the least-squares method. The demand was regressed on a trend with four seasonal components (i.e., each quarter of the year was considered a seasonal component). The fourth quarter seasonal factor was actually incorporated into the intercept term. The resulting model is reproduced below.

$$D_T = 11{,}100 + 488T + S_i$$

where

D_T = forecasted sales demand for month T
T = the month in the time series (e.g., July 19X3 = 1)
S = quarterly seasonal factor
i = applicable quarter; i = 1, 2, or 3
S_1 = seasonal factor for first quarter (July, August, September); value = −2,110
S_2 = seasonal factor for second quarter (October, November, December); value = +2,060
S_3 = seasonal factor for third quarter (January, February, March); value = +4,100
r^2 = 0.99
F statistic = 467

The seasonal factor to be used in the model depends upon the month for which the sales demand is being forecasted, that is, the forecast for January means the third quarter seasonal factor would be applicable.

REQUIRED

1. Forecast Glenall Company's sales demand for July 19X4 using:
   a. the moving average model
   b. the model based on the time series analysis
2. Compare and contrast, in general terms, the model based on the time series analysis with the moving average model with respect to:
   a. complexity
   b. applicability to Glenall Company
3. If past sales trends continue for Glenall Company, which of the two models will yield the more accurate forecast for future sales demand? Explain your answer.

3–33 Dealing with Nonlinear Data Jeff Appleton, controller of Sleep Products Division, was presented these data for one of the division's products.

Units	Costs
250	$123,177
100	28,648
200	77,857
400	600,307
300	208,274
350	338,606
150	47,305
325	273,945
375	456,720

REQUIRED

1. Plot these data.
2. Since the plot shows a curvilinear (exponential) pattern, Appleton decided to transform the data using logs to see whether a more nearly linear pattern would result.
   a. Using natural logs, transform the cost data.
   b. Plot the transformed data.
   c. Calculate appropriate regression and correlation statistics and interpret the results.

3–34 Multiple Regression Results (Appendix) Susan Zeller, marketing manager of Colday Manufacturing, has been looking at the way changes in advertising expenditures and sales price affect sales levels. Over the past few months Zeller has been experimenting with one of the company's products and has the following data:

Price	Advertising	Sales Volume
$ 6	$ 5,000	13,000
6	100	7,000
8	7,000	10,000
8	10,000	15,000
10	5,500	6,500
10	13,000	12,000
12	10,000	11,000
12	14,000	8,000

The results shown on pages 138–139 were obtained from a computer multiple regression package using SPSS. The first set of results shows a multiple regression using all variables. The second and third sets of results show simple regression.

REQUIRED

1. Interpret the results.
2. Is either price or advertising (or both) a good predictor of sales? Why or why not?

```
DEPENDENT VARIABLE..      SALES

MEAN RESPONSE     10312.50000     STD. DEV.     3011.14003

VARIABLE(S) ENTERED ON STEP NUMBER   1..   PRICE
                                           ADVER

MULTIPLE R               .76849    ANALYSIS OF VARIANCE DF          SUM OF SQUARES      MEAN SQUARE   F        SIGNIFICANCE
R SQUARE                 .59058    REGRESSION                 2.    37483586.97207   18741793.48603  3.60625           .10
ADJUSTED R SQUARE        .42682    RESIDUAL                   5.    25985163.02793    5197032.60559
STD. DEVIATION       2279.70011     COEFF OF VARIABILITY 22.1 PCT

--------------------- VARIABLES IN EQUATION ---------------------   ----------------- VARIABLES NOT IN EQUATION ------------
VARIABLE                  B     STD ERROR B         F           BETA              VARIABLE         PARTIAL   TOLERANCE          F
                                              SIGNIFICANCE  ELASTICITY                                                   SIGNIFICANCE
PRICE           -1326.0797      552.03969     5.7703034   -1.0527364
                                                   .061     -1.15731
ADVER            .74816474      .28736578     6.7783560    1.1409918
                                                   .048       .58584
(CONSTANT)       16205.787      3640.6931     19.813998
                                                   .007

                                   S U M M A R Y   T A B L E

STEP       VARIABLE            F TO         SIGNIFICANCE   MULTIPLE R   R SQUARE   R SQUARE   SIMPLE R   OVERALL F   SIGNIFICANCE
     ENTERED   REMOVED    ENTER OR REMOVE                                          CHANGE
 1   PRICE                    5.77030            .061          .18854     .03555     .03555    -.18854    3.60625          .107
     ADVER                    6.77836            .048          .76849     .59058     .55503     .34364

DEPENDENT VARIABLE..    SALES

MEAN RESPONSE     10312.50000     STD. DEV.     3011.14003

VARIABLE(S) ENTERED ON STEP NUMBER   1..   PRICE

MULTIPLE R               .18854    ANALYSIS OF VARIANCE DF          SUM OF SQUARES      MEAN SQUARE   F       SIGNIFICANCE
R SQUARE                 .03555     REGRESSION            1.         2256250.00000    2256250.00000  .22118           .65
ADJUSTED R SQUARE             0    RESIDUAL               6.        61212500.00000   10202083.33333
STD DEVIATION        3194.07003     COEFF OF VARIABILITY 31.0 PCT
```

```
------------------- VARIABLES IN THE EQUATION ---------------------   ----------- VARIABLES NOT IN THE EQUATION ------------
VARIABLE              B      STD ERROR B        F           BETA       VARIABLE     PARTIAL        TOLERANCE          F
                                           SIGNIFICANCE  ELASTICITY                                               SIGNIFICANCE
 PRICE         -237.50000     505.02681     .22115581    -.1895444
                                                 .655     -.20727
(CONSTANT)      12450.000     4683.4260     7.0666141
                                                 .038

DEPENDENT VARIABLE..      SALES

MEAN RESPONSE     10312.50000      STD. DEV.     3011.14003

VARIABLE(S) ENTERED ON STEP NUMBER   1..   ADVER

MULTIPLE R              .34364    ANALYSIS OF VARIANCE DF        SUM OF SQUARES     MEAN SQUARE  F       SIGNIFICANCE
R SQUARE                .11809     REGRESSION          1.        7495131.97338   7495131.97338  .80343           .40
ADJUSTED R SQUARE            0    RESIDUAL             6.       55973618.02662   9328936.33777
STD DEVIATION       3054.33075     COEFF OF VARIABILITY 29.6 PCT

------------------- VARIABLES IN THE EQUATION -------------------   ---------------- VARIABLES NOT IN THE EQUATION ------------
VARIABLE              B      STD ERROR B        F          BETA                VARIABLE    PARTIAL    TOLERANCE          F
                                          SIGNIFICANCE  ELASTICITY                                                  SIGNIFICANCE
 ADVER          .22533279     .25139163     .80342835    .3436447
                                                .405      .17644
 (CONSTANT)     8492.9377     2299.3403     13.642984
                                                .010
```

Part II

PRODUCT COSTING

4

COST OF PRODUCTS: TWO NEEDS

Determining costs of products and product lines, especially of manufactured products, occupies the next few chapters. It is important to have good estimates of the costs of products for two principal reasons. First, managers make many decisions about products and lines that should be based on appropriate cost information. Decisions such as pricing and whether to emphasize, phase out, or drop a product or product line are examples.

The second reason for determining product costs is to show appropriate values for inventory and cost of goods sold on the company's financial statements. Generally accepted accounting principles (GAAP) impose specific requirements for determining the costs of manufactured inventory and of goods sold during a period. These costs are also used for income tax purposes.

The costs relevant for financial reporting are not necessarily the same as those for managerial decisions. One important difference is that inventory and cost of sales for financial reporting are limited to manufacturing costs, while costs for managerial decisions also include selling and administrative costs. Determining costs of products for managerial decision making is not bound by GAAP.

PRODUCT COSTS FOR MANAGERIAL DECISION MAKING

Let us begin with the simplest case, a company that makes one product. All the company's costs relate to that product. For managerial decision-making purposes, such as pricing, the total costs of the company can be divided by production to get a reasonable estimate of unit cost. Included in unit cost is not only the cost to manufacture the product (material, labor, and factory overhead), but also costs for marketing, information processing, and general management. Note that for financial accounting purposes, we are interested in the costs of only material, labor, and factory overhead (product costs as opposed to period costs) to determine cost of goods sold during a period. For financial reporting, costs related to functions such as marketing are treated as period costs.

If the same company introduces a second product, determining unit cost is no longer a simple matter of dividing total costs by total production. With one product, all costs were traceable, or separable, to that single product. With the introduction of the second product, determining the cost of each product can become difficult.

For managers to determine the cost of each product, they must have reasonable estimates of the resources committed to and consumed by each product or service. At one end of the spectrum are costs that are **direct**, **separable**, or **traceable** to the product. Such costs relate to only one product; if the product were not made, the cost would disappear.[1] If materials or purchased parts costing $20 are used in manufacturing one product, this cost should clearly be included in the cost of that product.

At the other end of the spectrum are **common costs**, which relate to producing, selling, or managing more than one product or service. Such costs usually exist regardless of the particular products or services offered. Examples include rent on the factory building, the plant manager's salary, and depreciation on machinery used to make all products. It is impossible to determine how much, for instance, rent on the factory building was incurred to produce each product.

Direct Variable Manufacturing Costs

In the traditional model used for decades in management and cost accounting, accountants and operating managers classified materials and labor as both variable and direct.[2] A firm making automobile engines, for example, needs an

[1] Some costs will disappear immediately, including materials and other direct variable costs. Others may disappear over time, such as moving a full-time engineering position to half time or not filling jobs when they open.

[2] See H. Thomas Johnson and Robert S. Kaplan, *Relevance Lost: The Rise and Fall of Management Accounting* (Boston: Harvard Business School Press, 1987.)

engine block for each engine produced. Thus, the cost of parts such as the engine block is both variable (total costs change as production changes) and direct (used for that product on a one-to-one basis).[3] Labor might or might not be variable and/or direct. If laborers are hired only when there is work and paid an hourly or piece rate, and if there is a relatively constant relationship between labor effort and production (for example, that each engine usually requires 3.6 labor hours), then labor is both variable and direct.

Let us look at a process that generates several products, such as refining crude oil. Workers who feed crude oil into the refining process are not dealing with one product, because the refining process yields dozens of products from the raw material. Thus, while the costs of the laborers are direct to the entire process, they are not direct to any of the products.

Labor cost is not always variable. As manufacturing companies have become more machine intensive and paid workers salaries instead of hourly wages, their labor costs have become fixed. A company that does not lay off workers every time production falls has some fixed component in its labor cost.[4]

Common Manufacturing Costs

We said earlier that on the other end of the spectrum from direct costs are common costs of resources used for more than one product. As long as a multiproduct company operates a manufacturing plant, such costs as depreciation, property taxes, the salary of the plant manager, and utilities will exist regardless of the quantity of each product made in a given period.[5] For managerial decision making, common costs present a serious problem.

Clearly, common resources and their costs will not go away if a particular product or product line is dropped. Nevertheless, in some decisions such as pricing, managers must consider common costs to be sure that they are covered by revenues. If the total of all products' contribution margins does not cover total fixed costs (both direct and common), the company will not make a profit.

Direct Fixed Manufacturing Costs

Some manufacturing costs are direct or traceable to a product but are not variable. If salaried workers make only one product, their cost is fixed, but direct to that product. Other examples of direct fixed manufacturing costs include

[3] A single component such as an engine block can be used in more than one model of an automobile. However, its consumption (cost) will still be on a one-to-one basis.

[4] In practice, labor costs may be more complex. Workers are often kept on the job in the very short run if work fails to materialize. They might do routine maintenance or the like. Thus, labor may be variable in such a case. The idea is to discover the economic reality of a particular situation: will workers be paid for some period of time such as 40 hours regardless of the work they do? If so, then labor is fixed.

[5] While this statement is arguable, the general idea is correct. Some base costs are common on a broad scale.

the cost to set up a production line to make a particular product, engineering time used to plan and supervise the manufacture of a particular product or line, and salaries of supervisors whose responsibilities are limited to one product.

It should be relatively straightforward to trace such direct costs to the products that use the resources. If workers in a crew receive salaries of $1,200 per 40-hour week and spend eight hours to produce a batch of one product, then 8/40ths or $240 is direct and traceable to those products. If the crew produced 1,000 units during the eight-hour span, the labor cost per unit is $0.24 ($240 divided by 1,000 units). Other costs that are direct to the product might be associated with the product as a whole rather than with a particular production run. Suppose a company that produces automobile frames uses robotic machinery to weld pieces of the frame. The costs to maintain the efficiency and effectiveness of the robots are direct to the product as a whole, but not to any *specific* production run or unit. Managers might decide to estimate the life of a product (how long they expect to sell it in its present form) and the quantity to produce over the product's life, and then assign a portion of these costs based on these estimates. If a product is expected to have an economic life of three years and sell a total of 300,000 units in that period, total direct product costs would be divided by 300,000 and applied on a unit basis over the three-year period.[6]

Direct Non-manufacturing Costs

Most products have direct costs incurred by non-manufacturing departments. Sales commissions are a good example of direct, variable non-manufacturing costs. An example of a direct, fixed cost is the cost of sales and marketing managers whose responsibilities are limited to a single product. Other direct, fixed costs include salaries of people who provide customer service for a product line.[7] If the accounts receivable section of the accounting department employs one person who deals only with receivables for a single product line, again we find direct costs for that line. When managers are trying to determine what resources are consumed by a particular product line or model, these costs are as important to trace as manufacturing costs.

Companies acquire resources and use them for specific reasons. While some resources are common to all production or general management functions, it is nonetheless possible to trace some of their use to particular products by analyzing the activities that generate the needs for the resources and relating those activities to products.

---

[6] Managers are often faced with this problem: there is a direct cost associated with the entire product, but such a cost is common to units of product; a reasonable way must be found to divide such costs (allocate them) to units of product.

[7] Some customer service costs may be direct to a particular group of customers. While the discussion focuses on products and product lines, other ways exist to classify and assign direct costs.

Accuracy of Direct Costs

This is a good time to discuss the ideas of *accuracy* and *precision*. Too often people carry an answer to four decimal places (since it *looks* precise) but ignore the accuracy of the data used to determine the answer. Some authors argue that **accuracy** is being right to the first digit (e.g., is it in the 20 percent range or the 30 percent range?).[8] When managers try to determine why specific resources are used, they should concentrate on accuracy and not worry too much about precision. It is useful to be able to say that a programmer who writes instructions for robotic equipment and performs other functions in the data processing department spends 25 percent of her time on a particular product. Nothing is gained by saying that the programmer spends 24.6 percent or 26.2 percent of her time on that product.

PRODUCT COSTS FOR FINANCIAL ACCOUNTING

Managers who make decisions about products or product lines need accurate information about which costs are traceable (and to what) and which costs are common. The direct cost of a product in this context includes any and all costs that can be traced to it. There is no distinction between a product cost and a period cost. The focus is on traceability of costs.

In financial accounting, however, GAAP govern the valuation of inventories and cost of goods sold. The rules govern the calculation of *unit costs*. In this section, we discuss these rules and procedures and show how costs are reflected in the financial accounting system. Product costs for financial accounting are important not only for external financial statements, but also for determining income taxes. Such unit costs are not necessarily a subset of the cost of products for managerial decision making. For example, GAAP allow some traceable costs to be allocated as if they were common; thus, the methods that many companies use to determine unit costs for financial accounting purposes follow the rules but might be inaccurate.

Absorption Costing

Product costs used for financial accounting and tax accounting purposes include only manufacturing costs, not selling and administrative costs (unlike product costs for decision making). Financial accounting product costs include common manufacturing costs, in addition to direct manufacturing costs. The financial accounting cost of each product, then, includes its own direct manufacturing costs plus a share of common manufacturing costs. Thus, these product costs include the cost of material, labor, and factory overhead. *Direct*

[8] For example, see Robert Kaplan, "Accounting Critic Robert Kaplan," *INC.*, April 1988, p. 64.

materials are materials and components that become a part of the product. *Direct labor* consists of the wages paid to those who work directly on the product. *Factory (or manufacturing) overhead* consists of all manufacturing costs besides direct materials and direct labor.[9] Some examples are depreciation on factory buildings and equipment, utilities used in the factory, salaries of production supervisors and plant management, and costs of support departments such as the factory payroll department and the plant accounting department.

In some firms, an important element of manufacturing overhead is *indirect labor*, which consists of salaries and wages of non-supervisory people who do not work directly on the products, such as material handlers (who move materials and semi-finished products around the plant) and maintenance workers. The classification of direct versus indirect here is not the same as when managers accumulate costs of products for internal decision making. Direct material and direct labor are, with the exception noted above, "direct" in both the managerial and financial accounting sense. Traditionally, support costs such as materials handling and maintenance are considered indirect in a financial accounting context since such people are not directly working on products. Indeed, as our discussion has shown, such costs can be direct in the sense of traceable to a particular product or product line. This can be confusing to managers; there has been a tendency for managers to use financial accounting product costs (and the classification and allocation of costs used in such costs) as the equivalent of traceable costs. Using costs this way can lead to poor decisions. We discuss the major causes of such problems in Chapter 5.

In summary, *absorption costing* for financial accounting purposes includes all manufacturing costs (material, labor, manufacturing overhead) whether traceable or common, fixed or variable. Since some of these costs are common, managers must choose how to allocate them to specific products. In most cases, direct variable costs are attached to a product on a one-to-one assignment. Overhead is usually an indirect and/or common cost and is allocated (the usual term is *applied*) based on some activity. In the discussion that follows, we will assume that a company uses absorption costs and has many products.

MANUFACTURING INVENTORIES AND COST FLOWS

A merchandising firm, whether wholesale or retail, generally uses a single inventory account because it has only one type of inventory: goods held for resale. In contrast, manufacturers usually have three types of inventory: one for

[9] There is an exception when labor is not considered a direct cost. In some companies, labor is part of manufacturing overhead and assigned to units of production as are other overhead costs.

the materials and purchased components[10] they use, another for finished goods, and a third for goods in process, on which some but not all work has been done. This third account is needed because manufacturing is not instantaneous. It takes time to turn lumber into tables, cloth into pants and coats, wire into nails. Accordingly, a manufacturer has a more complicated record-keeping process than does a merchandiser.

The pattern of cost flows that we describe in the following pages applies to most cost accounting systems. Some companies' systems will vary, but the general form is as described. The basic financial accounting problem for manufacturing firms is to determine costs for units of product to be able to assign values to inventories and cost of goods sold. Figure 4–1 diagrams the basic pattern of cost flows.

Two other matters before we proceed: first, in this book we capitalize account titles when we are referring to the account itself, rather than to the physical products or costs involved. For example, the account *Cost of Goods Sold* includes the cost of goods sold during the period. The account *Materials Inventory* includes the cost of materials on hand. This practice should help clarify the difference between events and the recording of events.

Second, as you know, terminology varies considerably. In cost accounting, companies use different terms for the same account. To reflect the diversity in practice, we shall use different but synonymous terms to refer to accounts. For instance, *Materials*, *Inventory of Materials*, and *Stores* all designate an account that includes the cost of materials on hand, while *Accrued Wages*, *Wages Payable*, and *Accrued Payroll* represent an account that shows amounts owed to workers.

Cost Flows

All three types of manufacturing costs (materials, direct labor, and manufacturing overhead) flow through accounts in the same basic pattern—from recording the incurrence of costs (acquiring materials, labor, and overhead) to transferring costs to Work-in-Process Inventory to Finished Goods Inventory and to Cost of Goods Sold. This pattern of flows reflects the economic events that happen on the factory floor. As more and more work converts raw materials and purchased parts into finished goods, the accounting system shows increasing costs of products that should be accurate estimates of the costs of the products.

---

[10]The term "materials" covers at least two things: raw materials, such as crude oil or rolls of steel, and purchased parts or components. Raw materials must be fabricated to make them into a final product or a component of a final product. A company might buy all its component parts rather than fabricating any parts from scratch. "Materials" in most cases means one or both of these general categories. In addition, materials usually include items of significant and/or easily identifiable costs. Thus, for example, screws, nuts, bolts, and washers might be included in manufacturing overhead rather than materials.

FIGURE 4–1 General Flows of Costs

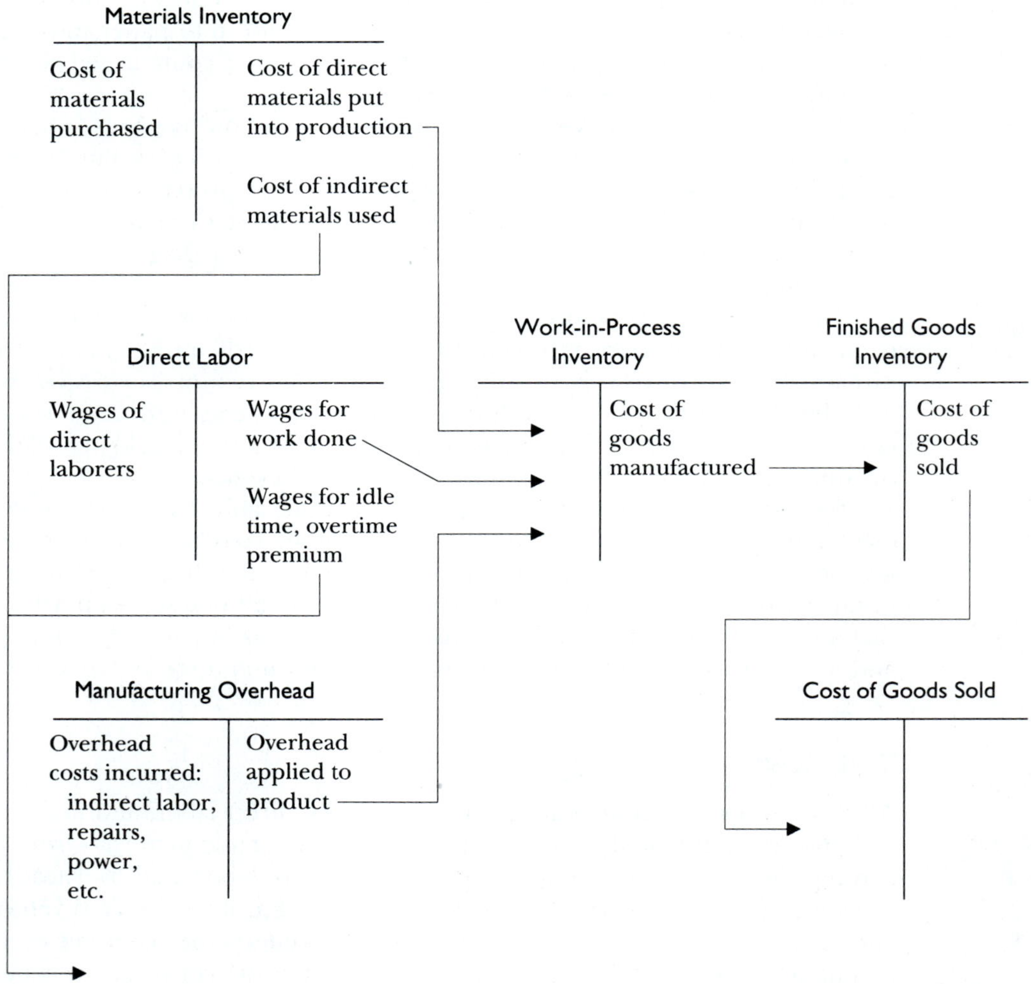

Costs are first collected in accounts that indicate their object classification, such as Direct Labor, Utilities, Depreciation, and Salaries. Overhead costs are then usually collected into a single Manufacturing Overhead account. The costs then flow from Materials, Direct Labor, and Manufacturing Overhead into Work in Process. The ending balance of Work in Process contains the cost of products that are unfinished at the end of a period. The costs of the inputs to the production process (materials, labor, and overhead) are debited to the Work-in-Process account, the cost of goods manufactured (completed) is credited to it, and its balance represents the cost of goods still in process.

Determining the costs to be transferred to Finished Goods Inventory and the ending balance of Work-in-Process Inventory can be the most difficult

EXHIBIT 4–1 Statement of Cost of Goods Manufactured and Sold for Year Ended December 31, 19X7—SLM Company (in thousands of dollars)

Direct materials:		
Inventory of direct materials, January 1	$ 879	
Purchases and freight in	3,456	
Cost of materials available for use	4,335	
Less: Inventory of direct materials, December 31	951	
Cost of direct materials used in production		$ 3,384
Direct labor		12,321
Factory overhead		16,344
Total manufacturing costs		32,049
Add: Work-in-process inventory, January 1		3,897
Less: Work-in-process inventory, December 31		4,065
Cost of goods manufactured		31,881
Add: Finished goods inventory, January 1		10,306
Less: Finished goods inventory, December 31		11,015
Cost of goods sold		$31,172

phase of the cost accounting cycle. Intricate problems might be encountered, as we shall see in later chapters.

The debit to Finished Goods Inventory and the credit to Work in Process reflect the cost of goods manufactured. This area can be difficult to determine; the problem is made more troublesome the more products a firm makes and the more complex its manufacturing environment.

The flows of costs through the various types of inventory accounts are summarized in the **statement of cost of goods manufactured and sold**. Usually, this statement is prepared only for internal use. It provides the backup detail for the single figure, cost of goods sold, that appears in the income statement in a published annual report. Exhibit 4–1 is an example. Despite its detail, this example is relatively straightforward, with three basic parts: (1) the determination of the cost of materials put into production; (2) an analysis of the work-in-process inventory, with its inputs of materials, labor, and overhead; and (3) an analysis of the finished goods inventory, culminating in the determination of cost of goods sold.

THE CHANGING ENVIRONMENT

Traditional cost accounting models, as explained in the last section, developed when direct labor was a significant part of total production costs and when many overhead costs were related to labor. In recent years, costs have shifted from labor to machinery. Developments in computer integrated manufacturing (CIM), robotics, and the rearranging of machinery into manufacturing cells have shifted more costs from labor to overhead. In many factories labor costs are less than five percent of total manufacturing costs.[11] In addition, because of both internal and external factors, companies have become more complex, putting resources into place that are related to activities other than labor or machine time.

In a labor-intensive manufacturing environment, many overhead costs vary with direct labor hours or cost. Many other overhead costs, while not variable with labor, are attributable to labor. Such costs as supervision, factory personnel, payroll, and some insurance depended on the number of laborers. Overhead costs, both fixed and variable, were applied to units of product based on how much direct labor (hours or dollars) was included in the product.

Because direct labor has become both relatively fixed and a small percentage of total manufacturing costs, an assumption of a cause-and-effect relationship between labor and overhead costs is often inapplicable. When overhead costs do not depend on direct labor, we need new ways to trace the use of resources to units of product.

In addition, product lines have become more complex. When Henry Ford introduced the Model T Ford, there was a saying that it was available in any color as long as you wanted black. Companies now make a variety of models with different features and options, some selling in high volume, some low. To have many products causes complexity, which increases overhead costs.

Let us compare simple and complex manufacturing environments: a company that makes relatively few, high-volume products compared with one that makes dozens of products, some high-volume, some low-volume. The more complex company must stock more parts and materials, and thus probably needs more people in the purchasing department and more storage space. The complex company needs more people to expedite orders and to schedule machinery. The complex company requires more machine set ups to change from one product or part to another, which requires more people and disrupts output. In short, product complexity requires more resources because there are more things to buy, store, track, make, and ship. Costs are unrelated to how many labor or machine hours are needed to make a product, but result from simply having that product.

Finally, the scope and nature of competition has changed. Foreign companies have introduced high-quality products at prices below those of U.S. manufacturers. Such competition makes it more important for companies to understand their product costs. When a company dominated its industry, a

---

[11] In their recent survey, Howell, et al (*Management Accounting in the New Manufacturing Environment*, Montvale, NJ: National Association of Accountants, 1987, p. 10) show that manufacturing costs are, on average, 53 percent materials, 15 percent direct labor, and 32 percent manufacturing overhead. Howell (in Robert Capettini and Donald Clancy, eds., *Cost Accounting, Robotics, and the New Manufacturing Environment*, Sarasota: American Accounting Association, 1987) says that direct labor should fall to less than 5 percent where there is computer integrated manufacturing. Also see P. Linnen, "No Inventory—No Cost Systems," *Hewlett-Packard Financial Notes*, September 1983, p. 1.

lack of understanding of costs might have caused little difficulty, but in a more competitive environment, such ignorance could be very serious. Therefore, with costs shifting from labor to computers and machinery, increased competition that has often redefined the marketplace, and complex product lines, many companies find that existing systems to show the cost of products or product costs are inadequate and lead their managers to make incorrect decisions.[12]

DIFFERENT SYSTEMS FOR DIFFERENT NEEDS

This chapter has discussed the determination of traceable costs to find costs of products for managerial decision making and to define product costs in a more restricted way for financial accounting reporting purposes. Management accountants have long hoped that one system could generate information useful for both purposes. In a simple setting (few products that use roughly the same kinds of resources), this goal is relatively easy to accomplish. However, as explained above, both the internal and the external environments of many companies are changing.

Managers had been tracing overhead costs to products using single measures such as direct labor because of the relationship between the use of labor and the incurring of overhead costs. In certain market conditions (variety of the product offered and/or competitive pressure), such simple measures seemed adequate even if manufacturing had changed. In the face of changes in both the internal and the external environments, however, the vast majority of companies still use a simple labor-driven cost accounting system for financial record keeping.[13]

Heretofore, operating managers have accepted accounting information as accurate, with some confusion between precision and accuracy. Numbers carried out to the penny (e.g., $1,221.88) must be accurate to many people. Although the internal and external worlds have changed, financial accounting has changed little insofar as cost accounting (valuing of inventories and cost of goods sold) is concerned. Managers have, unfortunately, used this financial accounting information as if it were the truly accurate cost-of-product information discussed earlier. An illustration later in this chapter shows how this acceptance can lead to poor decisions.

[12] Examples can be found in Kaplan, op. cit.; Robin Cooper and Robert S. Kaplan, "How Cost Accounting Distorts Product Costs," *Management Accounting* (April 1988), pp. 20–27; Mike Jeans, "Aligning Product Costing Techniques with Manufacturing Realities," *Journal of Cost Management for the Manufacturing Industry*, Fall 1988, pp. 49–50, and Michael W. Grady, "Is Your Cost Management System Meeting Your Needs?," *Journal of Cost Management for the Manufacturing Industry*, Summer 1988, pp. 11–15.

[13] For example, see Henry R. Schwartzbach, "The Image of Automation on Accounting for Indirect Costs," *Management Accounting*, December 1985, pp. 45–50.

We will take this perspective in this book: financial accounting is governed by standards and rules developed through various processes. One can argue about problems in financial accounting and how to solve them. This is not the function of this book; our concern is dealing with management accounting (providing relevant information for internal decision making) and cost accounting (providing information to support a company's financial recordkeeping system). While we discuss issues relating to both, we do not propose changes in the basic financial accounting model or how cost accounting information relates to it. That discussion is part of courses in financial accounting theory.

We believe that managers should differentiate between cost of products for managerial decisions and product costs for financial and tax accounting. We believe that, for now, two systems are needed for these different needs. In fact, in addition to the two needs regarding the cost of products, an accounting information system should address other needs. Thus, our general model is:

Regular Systems

1. *Cost of Products for Managerial Decision Making*. This system should provide accurate information on how each product or product line uses resources. The focus is on traceability; no differentiation is made between product costs and period costs, and between manufacturing and non-manufacturing costs and resources.
2. *Product Costs for Financial Accounting*. This system should follow prescribed procedures for financial accounting. Product costs include only manufacturing costs. While the same sense of direct/traceable costs should be maintained in this system as in the first system, there are more problems in this system because of the necessity of dividing common costs (e.g., fixed manufacturing overhead) among products and units of product.
3. *Operational Control*. There is a need for information besides unit-cost or product information. In a manufacturing operation, managers want to know if they are operating efficiently and effectively. Examples of operational control information include questions such as: How much material is being used? What are the measures of throughput in the manufacturing process? Are budgets being met?

Ad-Hoc Needs

Special Studies. Managers must, from time to time, perform special studies. For example, managers investigate whether existing equipment should be replaced, whether to introduce a new product or discontinue an old one, and how to determine a selling price for goods when there is idle capacity. Regular systems should provide much useful information for such special studies. Some additional information might have to be gathered as well. Although such studies are, by definition, different each time they are conducted, most companies do not need a series of systems to address these needs. Managers do not start every analysis from scratch; they might have a basic spreadsheet model they use in similar situations. Either no regular system is maintained for such special studies or the normal system does not routinely generate the information needed for special studies.

We have seen some of the basic information that goes into regular systems and special studies. Our discussion of cost-volume-profit analysis and forecasting in Chapters 2 and 3 included elements of information used for these four needs. Regression and correlation analysis allow managers to examine costs for relationships. When costs are variable or mixed, regression and correlation analysis provide useful information. The emphasis in cost-volume-profit analysis is on how costs behave: do they change with changes in volume or remain the same? Fixed costs are considered as a block, a lump sum that is a function of time and the general level of capacity. Fixed costs are often common to several products or lines.

In the next few chapters, we will develop the financial accounting/cost accounting product costing model. Even within the financial accounting framework, we want to make choices that reflect costs as accurately as possible. We will not ignore the needs of the management accounting/internal decision-oriented model, but will show how issues of one affect the other in both functional and dysfunctional ways. Later chapters will discuss aspects of operational control and special studies. These four information system models do not operate completely independently. Many times managers have concerns across the entire information system network of a company. These systems might all draw from a common database. We propose that the three regular systems be maintained as separate systems depending on the internal and external environments of a company.

BASIC PRODUCT COSTS

In this section, we illustrate product costs for financial accounting in a labor-oriented manufacturing environment and show the effects on these costs when labor is no longer the relevant measure of causality of overhead costs. In addition, we expand these illustrations to show cost of products for managerial decision making.

Labor-driven Manufacturing Environment

Sanibel Company makes two products, Product 1 and Product 2. Unit cost data appear in Exhibit 4–2.

Under absorption costing, each unit of product assumes some share of fixed manufacturing overhead. In this case, managers have determined that manufacturing overhead cost varies with direct labor hours (DLH); therefore, they think that DLH is a good base for assigning overhead to units of product. They believe, then, that DLH is the best base for applying fixed overhead.

Total annual fixed overhead is estimated as $800,000 and DLH as 100,000 hours. These estimates yield a fixed overhead application rate of $8.00 per

EXHIBIT 4–2 Sanibel Company—Unit Costs

Per unit:		*Product 1*		*Product 2*
Direct materials		$5.00		$6.00
Direct labor:				
Hours	0.3		0.5	
Rate per hour	$15.00			
Cost per unit		4.50		7.50
Variable overhead:				
Rate per hour	$9.00			
Cost per unit		2.70		4.50
Fixed overhead:				
Rate per hour[a]	$8.00			
Cost per unit		2.40		4.00
		$14.60		$22.00

[a]Where Overhead is applied based on direct labor hours (DLH)
Fixed Overhead

Annual fixed overhead	$800,000
Annual DLH	100,000
Fixed overhead/DLH	$8.00

DLH as shown. Fixed overhead per unit, then, is $8.00 times direct labor hours per unit (e.g., 0.3 hours for Product 1). The managers also believe that nearly all fixed overhead is common. Therefore, the production of one product versus the other has no effect on the use of specific company resources (people, machines, space, etc.).

To determine if their cost system is accurate, the managers of Sanibel asked the accounting staff to interview department managers for better estimates to relate resources to their uses. The study focused on *fixed* manufacturing overhead since managers had good evidence that variable overhead was related to direct labor hour use. Exhibit 4–3 shows the results of this study.

The interviews revealed that one person supervises each product line and a general manager supervises both product lines. The product supervisors each earn $25,000 per year and the general manager $50,000 per year. About 75 percent of total engineering time is spent on Product 1, the remaining 25 percent on Product 2. Material handling costs reflect the greater amount of work in process and finished goods of Product 2 carried. In addition, Product 2 uses more individual components than Product 1. Maintenance workers set up machinery between runs. An average production run is 5,000 units for each product (thus, at current production levels of 125,000 units for each product, both products need 25 set ups—125,000/5,000). Wages, tools, and other costs totaling $60,000 annually are used for set up functions. Other costs were deemed common to both products. Thus, rather than overhead being related only to labor, other activities have been identified that require resources. This identification yields **activity-based costs**. Activities such as

EXHIBIT 4–3 Sanibel Company—Schedule of Overhead

	Total	Product 1	Product 2	Set Ups	Common
Fixed Manufacturing Overhead:					
Supervision	$100,000	$ 25,000	$25,000		$ 50,000
Building occupancy	100,000				100,000
Depreciation	200,000				200,000
Engineering	80,000	60,000	20,000		0
Maintenance	170,000			$60,000	110,000
Material handling	150,000	15,000	45,000		90,000
Annual FOH	$800,000	$100,000	$90,000	$60,000	$550,000

Annual production was expected to be
Product 1: 125,000 units
Product 2: 125,000 units

number of set ups are **cost drivers**, activities that affect the use of resources (costs).

Sanibel now makes about 125,000 units of each product, requiring 37,500 hours for Product 1 (0.3 × 125,000) and 62,500 hours for Product 2 (0.5 × 125,000), a total of 100,000 labor hours, all that are available. Using the product costs reflected in Exhibit 4–2, we find that these production levels yield a total cost of $4,575,000 (125,000 units of Product 1 at $14.60 per unit and 125,000 units of Product 2 at $22.00 per unit). This cost can also be determined using a flexible budget allowance such as we prepared in Chapter 2.

Annual fixed costs	$ 800,000
Variable costs:[14]	
Product 1:	
125,000 at $12.20	1,525,000
Product 2:	
125,000 at $18.00	2,250,000
Total cost	$4,575,000

Total costs using unit-cost information in Exhibit 4–2 equal the flexible budget allowance for this level of production as long as the planned activity of 100,000 DLH is used. In Chapter 5 we discuss examples where production is over or under planned activity.

After the study performed by the accounting staff (Exhibit 4–3), corporate managers were curious about the effects that a more accurate tracing of costs might have on unit-cost information. Exhibit 4–4 shows new calculations of total costs, unit costs, and a comparison under the two costing systems.

There is no great difference between the systems. Why is this so? First, both systems have a large proportion of common fixed costs ($550,000 out of

[14]The sum of material, labor, and variable overhead costs per unit from Exhibit 4–2.

EXHIBIT 4–4 Sanibel Company—Comparison of Costing Methods

Traceable costing:

	Product 1	*Product 2*	
Production	125,000	125,000	
Variable cost/unit	$12.20	$18.00	from Exhibit 4–2
Total variable cost	$1,525,000	$2,250,000	
Direct overhead[a]			
Supervision	25,000	25,000	
Engineering	60,000	20,000	
Material handling	15,000	45,000	
Set ups[b]	30,000	30,000	
Common overhead, allocated[c]	206,250	343,750	
Total	$1,861,250	$2,713,750	$4,575,000
DLH-based Total[d]	1,825,000	2,750,000	4,575,000
$ change—total	36,250	(36,250)	
Cost per unit	$14.89	$21.71	
DLH-based $/unit	$14.60	$22.00	
Percent change	1.99%	−1.32%	

[a] Supervision, engineering, and material handling are assigned based on information in Exhibit 4–3.

[b] Set ups are based on production of runs of 5,000 units and set up costs of $60,000 per year.

[c] Common overhead is applied based on DLH:
$550,000 from Exhibit 4–3
100,000 annual DLH
$5.50 per DLH

[d] 125,000 units of Product 1 at $14.60 = $1,825,000.
125,000 units of Product 2 at $22.00 per unit = $2,750,000.

$800,000). Second, equal amounts of both products are manufactured. Finally, a large portion of variable costs (all of variable overhead) seems to be labor driven. Taking these factors into account, no substantial difference exists between the two methods or systems. While using a single rate of $8.00 per hour to apply fixed overhead might be less accurate than using costs based on the interviewing process, in this simple labor-driven company, no real harm is done.

Review Problem

In the example above, no significant difference existed between results obtained using either of the costing systems. What would happen if direct labor hours for Product 2 remained at 0.5 but dropped for Product 1? Construct an electronic spreadsheet template[15] that will allow you to see the effect of the

[15] A template is in the file SANIBEL.WK1 on the disk that accompanies this text. See the appendix to this chapter for instructions on the use of this template.

EXHIBIT 4–5 Sanibel Company—Solution to Review Problem

Sensitivity Analysis—DLH for Product 1

Product 1				Product 2			
DLH	DLH-Based Cost/Unit	Activity-Based Cost/Unit	Percent Difference	DLH	DLH-Based Cost/Unit	Activity-Based Cost/Unit	Percent Difference
0.3	$14.60	$14.89	1.99%	0.5	$22.00	$21.71	−1.32%
0.2	11.40	11.92	4.56%	0.5	22.00	21.57	−1.95%
0.1	8.20	8.95	9.15%	0.5	22.00	21.46	−2.45%
0.05	6.60	7.47	13.18%	0.5	22.00	21.42	−2.64%

Product 1 DLH	Units Produced: Product 1	Units Produced: Product 2	DLH Used
0.3	125,000	125,000	100,000
0.2	125,000	150,000	100,000
0.1	125,000	175,000	100,000
0.05	125,000	187,500	100,000

following DLH combinations on direct-labor-based costs and activity-based costs (i.e., costs determined through the interviews):

Product 1 DLH	Product 2 DLH
0.3	0.5
0.2	0.5
0.1	0.5
0.05	0.5

In constructing your worksheet, make sure to use all 100,000 direct labor hours. Keep production of Product 1 at 125,000 units and vary production of Product 2 so that all the time is used.[16] Remember that you will have to calculate both sets of unit costs (original and revised) with each set of times shown above. Use the base case (0.3 hours for Product 1) to check your spreadsheet against the information in Exhibits 4–2 and 4–4. The solution to this sensitivity analysis review problem appears in Exhibit 4–5.

As Exhibit 4–5 shows, costs for Product 1 rise when comparing the more accurate, activity-based costs to those derived through applying overhead on the basis of direct labor hours. Product 2 costs drop as Product 1 costs rise. A significant difference in unit costs now exists between the two systems. In the

[16] The template SANIBEL.WK1 does this automatically.

first example, both products had relatively equal direct labor hours. As the difference between the two products' use of labor widens, so does the difference in costs that the two cost systems give. Since the labor-hour-based system charges overhead costs based on DLH, Product 2 receives an increasing burden under this system compared to Product 1.

Returning to the first example, where Product 1 uses 0.3 hours per unit and Product 2 uses 0.5, even though one system more accurately traces costs to each product, Sanibel might not change systems. The difference between unit costs under the two systems is very small, less than 2 percent. However, if the company were to make other products or if Product 1 were to use less time (e.g., 0.05 hours per unit), not only would accuracy increase, but managers might also reach incorrect conclusions about the products if the original direct-labor-based system were used to apply all overhead.

Machine-driven Environment

With Sanibel Company's fairly simple manufacturing setting and large proportion of common manufacturing overhead, direct labor is both a variable cost and a reasonable independent variable (or *cost driver*) for overhead. Compare Sanibel with Lighthouse, Inc., which makes three products, one of which is in much greater demand than the others. Most of Lighthouse's manufacturing is computer operated. Workers attend computers while robots load and unload materials and products from machines. Labor cost is fixed because the union contract calls for a forty-hour week and two-weeks' notice to lay off anyone. Exhibit 4–6 shows basic data for Lighthouse, Inc., and unit costs when direct labor is used as the cost driver for overhead. As with Sanibel, under Lighthouse's current product costing system, all overhead is applied based on a plantwide rate of $100.81 overhead per labor hour: $25.81 for variable overhead and $75.00 for fixed overhead.

Lighthouse's change from labor-driven to machine-driven, computer-aided manufacturing occurred fairly recently. Its cost accounting system has not been revised. Thus, as Exhibit 4–6 shows, overhead costs are applied using direct labor hours. The estimates for both fixed and variable overhead are based on last year's experience and the presumption that DLH accurately measure how these costs are incurred.

The company president was concerned because the product prices that would yield reasonable profits were out of line with competitors' prices; some prices were substantially higher and others much lower than those of the competition. Both corporate and operating managers thought that production processes were as efficient and advanced as any in the industry. Therefore, the president asked the controller to investigate the accounting numbers to see if costs were accurate. The controller gathered information about materials, labor, and variable and fixed overhead. Studies began that included analysis of the data using linear regression and interviews similar to those in the Sanibel Company example. Exhibit 4–7 shows the results of these studies. In one significant change from the Sanibel example, the Lighthouse study revealed that

EXHIBIT 4–6 Lighthouse, Inc.

Unit Costs—Current Costing System
Direct Labor Based Application of Overhead

Per unit:		*Product 1*		*Product 2*		*Product 3*
Direct materials		$15.00		$20.00		$25.00
Direct labor						
Hours	0.1		0.2		1.0	
Rate per hour	$15.00					
Cost per unit		1.50		3.00		15.00
Variable overhead						
Rate per hour[a]	$25.81					
Cost per unit		2.58		5.16		25.81
Fixed overhead						
Rate per hour[b]	$75.00					
Cost per unit		7.50		15.00		75.00
		$26.58		$43.16		$140.81

Where overhead is applied based on direct labor hours (DLH).

[a]Variable Overhead

Last year's variable overhead	$516,200
Last year's DLH	20,000
Variable overhead/DLH	$25.81

[b]Fixed Overhead

Annual fixed overhead	$1,500,000
Annual DLH	20,000
Fixed overhead/DLH	$75.00

Current production (and sales) and total costs:

	Units	*Cost[c]*
Product 1	1,000	$26,581
Product 2	4,500	194,231
Product 3	19,000	2,675,438
		$2,896,250

[c]Unit costs are rounded to nearest cent; computed total costs are from unrounded figures. Using the rounded numbers, Products 1, 2, and 3, are, respectively, $26,581, $194,229, and $2,675,390 to total $2,896,200.

some fixed costs could be traced to each product and that variable overhead was related to *machine hours*. This analysis identifies the best cost driver for variable overhead and might change the base for applying common fixed overhead.

Both costing systems handle materials and labor the same. Although management has determined that labor cost is fixed, at least in the short term, it is reasonable to assign labor costs to products based on direct work. Overhead costs are assigned on the bases of both the results of regression/correlation

EXHIBIT 4–7 Lighthouse, Inc.—Proposed Costing System

	Product 1	*Product 2*	*Product 3*	*Total*
Production (units)	1,000	4,500	19,000	
Material and labor cost/unit	$16.50	$23.00	$40.00	
Variable overhead/unit[a]	$7.50	$7.50	$25.00	
Total variable cost	$24,000	$137,250	$1,235,000	$1,396,250
Traceable overhead[b]				
Supervision	5,000	5,000	25,000	$ 35,000
Depreciation	1,000	0	0	1,000
Engineering[c]	11,321	18,113	90,566	120,000
Maintenance	1,500	2,000	10,000	13,500
Material handling[c]	5,185	12,963	51,852	70,000
Common overhead[d]	18,312	82,406	1,159,782	1,260,500
Total	$66,318	$257,732	$2,572,200	$2,896,250
Cost per unit	$66.32	$57.27	$135.38	

[a]Variable overhead is based on regression information showing that variable overhead is highly correlated to machine hours with the regression coefficient of about $25/MH. Machine hours are:

Product 1: 0.3 hours per unit
Product 2: 0.3
Product 3: 1.0

[b]Total fixed overhead is $1,500,000 as shown in Exhibit 4–6. Traceable overhead is based on information gained through interviews with managers and through an analysis of accounting data. Traceable overhead is $239,500, leaving $1,260,500 in common fixed overhead.

[c]Common engineering and material handling costs are all supervisory personnel. Since such managers supervise staff who are directly assigned to certain products, these supervisory costs are assigned based on traceable percents in these two categories:

Engineering:

	Product 1	*Product 2*	*Product 3*	*Total*
Traceable	$2,500	$4,000	$20,000	$26,500
Percent	9.43%	15.09%	75.47%	100.00%
Allocation of supervisory cost	$8,821	$14,113	$70,566	$93,500
Total applied	$11,321	$18,113	$90,566	$120,000

Material Handling:

	Product 1	*Product 2*	*Product 3*	*Total*
Traceable	$2,000	$5,000	$20,000	$27,000
Percent	7.41%	18.52%	74.07%	100.00%
Allocation of supervisory cost	$3,185	$7,963	$31,852	$43,000
Total applied	$5,185	$12,963	$51,852	$70,000

[d]The balance of common overhead is applied based on machine hours (MH); $1,260,500/20,650 annual MH = $61.04 per MH where $1,260,500 = $1,500,000 total fixed overhead (Exhibit 4–6) less the sum of supervision, depreciation, engineering, maintenance, and material handling assigned above.

EXHIBIT 4–8 Lighthouse, Inc.—Comparison of Variable Overhead

	Product 1	*Product 2*	*Product 3*	*Total*
DLH-based	$2,581	$23,229	$490,390	$516,200
MH-based	7,500	33,750	475,000	516,250
Difference	($4,919)	($10,521)	$15,390	($50)

analysis (machine hours as the cost driver for variable overhead) and interviews and data analysis regarding direct and common fixed overhead. In addition, common engineering and material handling costs are allocated based on each product's share of traceable overhead in these departments.

The results are quite different from those in Exhibit 4–6. A comparison of the two follows:

	Product 1	*Product 2*	*Product 3*
Proposed system—total	$66,318	$257,732	$2,572,200
DLH-based system—total	26,581	194,231	2,675,438
$ change—total	39,737	63,500	(103,238)
Proposed cost/unit	$66.32	$57.27	$135.38
DLH-based cost/unit	$26.58	$43.16	$140.81
Percent change	149.49%	32.69%	−3.86%
$ change—per unit	$39.74	$14.11	($5.43)

First, we must determine if the new cost system is more accurate than the old. To use regression analysis to determine relationships between overhead costs and one or more independent variables is superior to management judgment alone.[17] As Exhibit 4–8 shows, a substantial difference exists in the amounts of variable overhead applied using direct labor hours compared with machine hours. There is also a difference when comparing how common fixed overhead is applied (a total of $1,500,000 using direct labor and $1,260,500 using machine hours), as you should verify.

Behavioral Problems

The interviewing that happened in both the Sanibel and Lighthouse examples is not as easy a method as might appear. Operating personnel are asked to state how their resources are being used. This question can be threatening. Managers might wonder how this information is *really* going to be used even if

[17] We assume in the Lighthouse, Inc., example that sufficient data could be obtained, that there were minimal problems with the data (i.e., with autocorrelation, for example), and that the measures coming from a regression and correlation analysis were good (i.e., strong r^2, significant t-test, etc.).

the accounting staff has told them of the cost study. If the head of engineering reports that a particular engineer spends all of her time on a certain product line, this information could imply that if the line were dropped, the engineer could lose her job. Because of such implications managers might not be candid.

Interviews might identify indirect links between costs and products or product lines. For example, certain costs in the maintenance department might first be associated with the set up function of converting machinery from making one component to making another. The next step, then, is to divide total set up costs by the number of set ups during a period (such as a year) and to assign set up costs to products based on the number of set ups each product requires.

Suppose in this example that there is reason to believe that the statistical measures used and the information gathered from the interviews are accurate. As shown above, a material difference exists between the costs the two systems give.[18] Products 1 and 2, small-order items, are shown to be much more expensive to produce than the existing cost system reflects. Product 3, a long-run product, is shown to be less expensive. This is not surprising. Producing more products rather than fewer (e.g., three versus one) can require more resources to track the products (orders, purchasing and handling of materials, scheduling machinery and people, and other functions). Under a system that allocates costs to products based on a single factor (such as direct labor hours), products that use more of this factor (e.g., Product 3 as compared to Product 1) will bear more overhead costs. When managers can determine better ways to assign costs to products, in many cases the costs of products such as Product 3 will fall and the costs of products with short production runs will rise.

Cost of Products for Managerial Decision Making

Managers basing decisions regarding pricing, retaining, or dropping a product (based on profitability) on information from the product costing system can make mistakes if overhead is inaccurately applied, as Exhibit 4–6 illustrates. If the managers at Lighthouse, Inc., based prices on estimates of market prices (what they expect their competitors to charge for like products), they could believe that Products 1 and 2 were extremely profitable while Product 3 was barely profitable or possibly unprofitable. Suppose they set the following prices:

Product 1	$110
Product 2	90
Product 3	160

[18] Often students state that a product is now more (less) expensive to produce when comparing two cost systems. The true cost has not changed. What has changed is our ability to approximate costs.

Under the existing system, indicated profits by product are:

	Product 1	Product 2	Product 3
Price	$110.00	$90.00	$160.00
Cost (Exhibit 4–6)	26.58	43.16	140.81
Indicated profit	$ 83.42	$46.84	$ 19.19
Profit as percentage of sales	76%	52%	12%

We now know that the costs in Exhibit 4–6 are much less accurate than those in Exhibit 4–7. In addition, as we discussed, the costs identified in Exhibits 4–6 and 4–7 relate only to product costs. In making decisions about pricing and profitability, it is important to identify all significant costs associated with a product or product line—both manufacturing *and* non-manufacturing. For these purposes, managers do not distinguish between period costs and product costs. The question, then, is which costs are associated with a product.

The president ordered the same kind of analysis of manufacturing costs to be conducted to consider other costs. The results of the study appear in Exhibit 4–9.

EXHIBIT 4–9 Lighthouse, Inc.—Cost of Products for Managerial Decision Making

	Product 1	Product 2	Product 3	Total
Direct manufacturing costs:				
Material	$15,000	$90,000	$475,000	$580,000
Labor	1,500	13,500	285,000	300,000
Variable overhead[a]	7,500	33,750	475,000	516,250
Fixed overhead[b]	24,006	38,076	177,418	239,500
Total	$48,006	$175,326	$1,412,418	$1,635,750
Direct sales and administrative costs[c]	2,500	4,000	30,000	36,500
Total direct costs	$50,506	$179,326	$1,442,418	$1,672,250
Units	1,000	4,500	19,000	
Direct cost/unit	$50.51	$39.85	$75.92	
Unallocated common costs:				
Manufacturing				$1,260,500
Sales and administrative[d]				400,000
				$1,660,500
Suggested prices/unit	$110.00	$90.00	$160.00	

[a] From machine-hour based variable overhead in Exhibit 4–8.

[b] Sum of traceable fixed costs from Exhibit 4–7.

[c] Results of new study of non-manufacturing costs.

[d] $436,500 in total sales and administrative costs less $36,500 in traceable costs.

Two differences exist between this exhibit and the preceding ones. First, both product and period costs that are related (traceable) to products are shown. Second, common costs are not allocated to products. Managers can see traceable/direct product profit margins (either in total or per unit). Since all other costs are believed to be common (i.e., they will not disappear or change if any one of the products is dropped), there is no reason to allocate these costs. As shown in Exhibit 4–9, prices can be based on a criterion such as a target percentage of product cost. In this case, the target is 220 percent of indicated cost.

An interesting incongruity is that many managers use product costs such as those in Exhibit 4–6 or 4–7 as one basis for prices when there is no market.[19] Thus, managers seem to want to allocate common manufacturing costs to units of product. However, they do not seem to trace non-manufacturing costs to products. If allocating common manufacturing costs is justified by the desire to have a full or complete product cost, it seems inconsistent to ignore other traceable costs just because they are *not* manufacturing costs. Thus, managers often ignore traceable sales and administrative costs while they include common manufacturing costs.[20] Much in the same way that pricing based on 220 percent of indicated cost is illustrated in Exhibit 4–9 with traceable costs as a base, managers seem to use product costs developed for financial accounting purposes as a basis for a mark-up procedure to come up with prices.

Review Problem

Using the data from the Lighthouse example and an electronic spreadsheet, create templates[21] showing income by product and in total based on (1) information in Exhibit 4–6 and (2) information in Exhibits 4–7 and 4–9. Each template should have four columns of figures—one for each product and one for the company as a whole. Hold product prices constant at $110, $90, and $160, respectively, and assume that the company sells all that it produces. Once you have created these two income statements (called *pro forma statements*), discuss how managers might interpret each. A suggested solution showing the completed income statements appears in Exhibits 4–10 and 4–11.

In the suggested solution to the review problem, the formats of the two income statements are markedly different. Exhibit 4–10 shows a traditional financial accounting–oriented income statement where costs are separated into product costs (cost of goods sold) and period costs (selling and administra-

[19] See, for example, Michael Cornick, William D. Cooper, and Susan B. Wilson, "How Do Companies Analyze Overhead Costs?" *Management Accounting*, June 1988, pp. 41–43.

[20] Managers do include these costs when calculating a unit price by marking up product costs by some percent. However, they ignore these costs in the sense that they do not, in many cases, explicitly trace them to a product as part of the decision-making process.

[21] Templates called LHEXIST.WK1 and LHPROP.WK1 are on the disk that accompanies this text.

EXHIBIT 4–10 Lighthouse, Inc.—Solution to Review Problem

Pro Forma Income Statement
Existing Cost System

	Product 1	Product 2	Product 3	Total
Revenue	$110,000	$405,000	$3,040,000	$3,555,000
Cost of goods sold	26,581	194,231	2,675,438	2,896,250
Gross profit	$83,419	$210,769	$364,562	$658,750
Selling and administrative costs*				436,500
Income before taxes				$222,250

*Based on information in Exhibit 4–9.

tive expenses). Common manufacturing costs are allocated to each product. Exhibit 4–11 focuses on direct costs as does Exhibit 4–9; no distinction is made between product costs and period costs. Common costs are not allocated to products. Note these differences before discussing what managers could interpret when reading each of these statements. For example, gross margin in Exhibit 4–10 is not the same as direct manufacturing margin or direct margin in Exhibit 4–11.

Bearing in mind these distinctions, let us analyze the two statements. Both income statements yield the same income before taxes. This is not surprising, given that total costs are the same for both systems; the question is where to assign costs. In the income statement using the existing cost system, Products 1

EXHIBIT 4–11 Lighthouse, Inc.—Solution to Review Problem

Pro Forma Income Statement
Proposed Cost System

	Product 1	Product 2	Product 3	Total
Revenue	$110,000	$405,000	$3,040,000	$3,555,000
Direct manufacturing costs	48,006	175,326	1,412,418	1,635,750
Direct manufacturing margin	$ 61,994	$229,674	$1,627,582	$1,919,250
Direct sales and administrative costs	2,500	4,000	30,000	36,500
Direct margin	$59,494	$225,674	$1,597,582	$1,882,750
Common costs				
Manufacturing				1,260,500
Sales and administrative				400,000
Income before taxes				$222,250

and 2 look very profitable. Gross profit as a percentage of sales for the three products is:

	Gross profit/sales	*= gross profit percent*
Product 1:	$83,419/$110,000	= 76 percent
Product 2:	$210,769/$405,000	= 52 percent
Product 3:	$364,562/$3,040,000	= 12 percent

As we discussed, Products 1 and 2 look very profitable under this costing system. A manager accepting these figures would want to stress these products. Product 3, by comparison, is doing only fair. It seems the company might be better off to produce only short-run products if the market does not improve for products such as Product 3.

However, this income statement provides managers with a distorted view of these products. Exhibit 4–11 illustrates that, given the market prices, all three seem to be earning about the same profit. Direct margin as a percentage of sales is:

	Direct margin/sales	*= direct margin percent*
Product 1:	$59,494/$110,000	= 54 percent
Product 2:	$225,674/$405,000	= 56 percent
Product 3:	$1,597,582/$3,040,000	= 53 percent

This last example is an illustration of the two systems: cost of products for managerial decision making and product costs for financial accounting. The review problem shows how managers can make better decisions if they (1) have an accounting system that accurately reflects cost traceability, and (2) if they look at all costs, not just manufacturing product costs.

SUMMARY

One function of management accountants is to provide information for the financial reporting system of a company: to value inventories of work in process and finished goods as well as cost of goods sold. Product costs that include materials, labor, and variable and fixed overhead are calculated as part of this process. Only manufacturing costs are included. Unit-cost information includes both traceable costs and an allocation of common costs; from a financial accounting point of view, the major criterion is whether a cost is a product cost or a period cost.

However, managers want additional information to decide, say, how much to charge for a product or whether to drop a product. The cost of products for managerial decision making includes any and all costs that are traceable to a product or product line. Common costs are identified as such and do not need to be allocated to units of product.

While it would seem that product costs for financial accounting are a subset of cost of products for managerial decision making, this might not be true. In many cases, financial accounting numbers are created using a simple measure, such as direct labor hours, to apply common overhead to units of product. This measure might be inaccurate given changes in the environment; however, many accounting systems have not kept up with changes in the manufacturing process.[22] In addition, managers seem to focus on financial accounting numbers as if manufacturing product costs (which include allocations of common costs) are the same as traceable cost of products. Thus, it is even more important to stress the decades-old idea of authors in cost and management accounting: managers should have different cost systems to meet different needs.

In particular, we propose three systems (product costs for financial accounting, cost of products for managerial decisions, and operational control) and a series of ad hoc systems for special studies. This chapter discussed the basics of product costs for financial accounting and cost of products for managerial decision making. Illustrations included cases where costs were not accurately traced to products; in such cases, poor data lead managers to make bad decisions.

In many cases, manufacturing is moving from a labor-machine combination to a computer-machine environment. Direct labor is decreasing as a part of the total cost of production. Manufacturers are making a complex array of products to fill many needs in the marketplace. Foreign competitors are challenging domestic manufacturers in product innovation, quality, service, and price. Accounting information should reflect the economic events taking place in a company and be used effectively as the basis for decisions by both managers and investors. These changes in the internal and external environment of many firms challenge accounting to keep up.

Given these changes and the speed at which things change, operating managers are increasingly asking accountants to take an active role not only in designing better information systems, but also as partners in the decision-making process. This need challenges the accounting profession to keep current and be better able to provide useful information to managers.

APPENDIX 4A: TEMPLATES FOR REVIEW PROBLEMS

Templates for review problems, SANIBEL.WK1, LHEXIST.WK1, and LHPROPOSE.WK1, are shown in Exhibits 4A–1, 4A–2, and 4A–3, which also provide explanations. The templates are designed to be used on any electronic spreadsheet package that recognizes .WK1 files.

[22] We know of no published evidence to suggest that independent auditors have criticized firms when there may be little or no association between overhead and a cost driver (such as direct labor hours) used to allocate overhead.

EXHIBIT 4A–1 SANIBEL.WK1

1	A	B	C	D	E	F	G	H
2	Hirsch and Louderback			COST ACCOUNTING, Third Edition				
3	Chapter 4			SANIBEL.WK1				
4								
5								
6	DATA SECTION							
7	Materials and labor per unit:							
8				Product 1		Product 2		
9	Direct Materials[a]			$5.00		$6.00		
10	Direct Labor[a]							
11	Hours		0.3		0.5			
12	Rate per hour		$15.00					
13	Cost per unit			$4.50		$7.50		
14							Total	
15	Unit and hour information:			Product 1		Product 2	Hours	
16	Units produced[b]			125,000		125,000	100,000	
17	Labor hours available (budgeted)						100,000	
18	Units per batch			5,000		5,000		
19								
20	Fixed manufacturing overhead[c]:							
21				Total	Product 1	Product 2	Set ups	Common
22	Supervision			$100,000	$25,000	$25,000		$50,000
23	Building occupancy			100,000				100,000
24	Depreciation			200,000				200,000
25	Engineering			80,000	60,000	20,000		0
26	Maintenance			170,000			60,000	110,000
27	Material handling			150,000	15,000	45,000		90,000
28				--------	--------	--------	--------	--------
29	Annual fixed overhead			$800,000	$100,000	$90,000	$60,000	$550,000
30								
31	Variable manufacturing overhead[a]:				Rate per hour		$9.00	
32								
33	SOLUTION SECTION							
34	1. Labor-based overhead[d]							
35				Product 1		Product 2		
36	Direct materials							
37	Direct labor							
38	Variable overhead							
39	Fixed overhead							
40				-----------		-----------		
41	Cost per unit			$0.00		$0.00		
42								
43	2. Activity-based overhead[e]							
44				Product 1		Product 2	Total	
45	Units produced							
46	Number of setups[f]							
47								
48	Direct materials							
49	Direct labor							

(continued)

(EXHIBIT 4A–1 continued)

Variable overhead		
Direct fixed overhead		
Supervision		
Engineering		
Material handling		
Setups		
Common overhead, allocated		
	-----------	-----------
Total costs of production	$0	$0
Cost per unit		
3. Comparison of costing methods - cost per unit:		
Activity-based	$0.00	$0.00
Labor-based	0.00	0.00
	-----------	-----------
Difference	$0.00	$0.00
Percent change	0.00%	0.00%

[a] Figures from Exhibit 4–2.

[b] When you change the number of labor hours for Product 1, the template will automatically change the number of units of Product 2 to make sure that 100,000 labor hours are used.

[c] Figures from Exhibit 4–3.

[d] All these figures should be per unit.

[e] While the direct labor-based costs are presented in a per unit framework, the activity-based costs are shown first in total and then divided into per unit figures.

[f] With 125,000 units each of Product 1 and Product 2, there will be a total of 50 set ups (250,000 units/5,000 units per batch). As the labor hours for Product 1 decrease, the number of units of Product 2 increases (see note 2 above). Thus, the number of set ups for Product 2 will change as will the total number of set ups. This will change how set up costs are assigned to each product since average cost per set up will fall as total units (and batches) increase.

You will be presented with a problem when labor for Product 1 is 0.05 hours per unit. This will cause 187,500 units of Product 2 to be manufactured, resulting in an uneven number as far as batches are concerned. The solution in Exhibit 4–5 treats this as a half batch. You might want to treat the last 2,500 units as a full batch regarding set up costs.

When using the templates provided (or when setting up your own templates), keep all raw data in the DATA SECTION. Thus, all cells in the SOLUTION SECTION should contain formulas tied to appropriate cells in either the DATA SECTION or the SOLUTION SECTION. This linking will allow you to change data at the top of the template and have the worksheet automatically adjust the entire solution. For example, in solving the review problem for Sanibel, once you have entered all the template formulas, you have to change only the labor time for Product 1 from 0.3 to 0.2 and the whole numerical analysis shown in the SOLUTION SECTION will automatically change.

SANIBEL.WK1

The top portion of the worksheet (DATA SECTION) consists of information from Exhibits 4–2 and 4–3. The order and presentation are different, but the content is the same. Also included is a mechanism to adjust the number of

EXHIBIT 4A–2 **LHEXIST.WK1**

```
1   A         B            C        D           E           F          G          H          I          J
2 Hirsch and Louderback        COST ACCOUNTING, Third Edition
3 Chapter 4                    LHEXIST.WK1
4
5
6 DATA SECTION[a]
7                              Product 1               Product 2              Product 3
8 Suggested prices/unit[b]        $110.00                 $90.00                $160.00
9 Units produced                    1,000                  4,500                 19,000
10
11 Direct Materials/unit           $15.00                 $20.00                 $25.00
12
13 Direct Labor
14  Labor hours per unit              0.1                    0.2                      1
15  Rate per hour       $15.00
16
17                                                                                                    Total
18 Labor hour information:       Product 1               Product 2              Product 3             Hours
19  Labor hours used                  100                    900                 19,000              20,000
20  Labor hours available
21    (budgeted)                                                                                     20,000
22
23
24 Variable manufacturing overhead:                                       $25.81 per direct labor hour
25 Fixed manufacturing overhead:                                    $1,500,000
26 Selling and administrative costs[a]:                               $436,500
27
28 SOLUTION SECTION
29                              Product 1               Product 2              Product 3
30 Product Cost (per unit):
31  Materials
32  Labor
33  Variable Overhead
34  Fixed Overhead
35                             -----------             -----------            ---------
36 Total
37
38                                          Pro Forma Income Statement
39                                            Existing Cost System
40
41                              Product 1               Product 2              Product 3            Total
42 Revenue
43 Costs of Goods Sold
44                             -----------             -----------            ---------            -----------
45 Gross Profit
46 Selling and
47  Administrative Expenses
48                                                                                                  -----------
49 Income Before Taxes
```

[a] Materials, labor, and overhead cost information comes from Exhibit 4–6.

[b] Product prices from p. 164.

[c] Sales and administrative-cost information is shown in Exhibit 4–9.

EXHIBIT 4A–3 LHPROPOSE.WK1

```
1    A        B          C          D            E           F          G            H           I           J
2  Hirsch and Louderback      COST ACCOUNTING, Third Edition
3  Chapter 4                  LHPROPOSE.WK1
4
5
6  DATA SECTION
7                             Product 1               Product 2             Product 3
8  Suggested prices/unit[a]    $110.00                  $90.00               $160.00
9  Units produced                1,000                   4,500                19,000
10
11 Direct Materials/unit        $15.00                  $20.00                $25.00
12
13 Direct Labor
14  Labor hours per unit           0.1                     0.2                     1
15  Rate per hour      $15.00
16                                                                                                  Total
17 Machine hour information[b]:  Product 1               Product 2             Product 3              Hours
18  Machine hours per unit         0.3                     0.3                     1
19  Machine hours used             300                   1,350                19,000                 20,650
20  Machine hours available
21    (budgeted)                                                                                     20,650
22
23 Variable manufacturing overhead[b]:     Rate per machine hour     $25.00
24
25 Fixed manufacturing overhead[c]:
26  Traceable Overhead         Product 1               Product 2             Product 3             Total
27    Supervision               $5,000                  $5,000               $25,000                $35,000
28    Depreciation               1,000                       0                     0                  1,000
29    Engineering               11,321                  18,113                90,566                120,000
30    Maintenance                1,500                   2,000                10,000                 13,500
31    Material Handling          5,185                  12,963                51,852                 70,000
32                         -----------             -----------           -----------            -----------
33      Total                  $24,006                 $38,076              $177,418               $239,500
34
35 Direct selling and
36  Administrative costs[d]     $2,500                  $4,000               $30,000                $36,500
37
38 Unallocated common costs[e]
39  Manufacturing overhead                                                                       $1,260,500
40  Sales and administrative costs                                                                  400,000
41
42
43   A        B          C          D            E           F          G            H           I           J
44 SOLUTION SECTION
45
46                            Product 1               Product 2             Product 3
47 Product Cost (per unit):
48  Materials
49  Labor
50  Variable Overhead
51  Fixed Overhead
52                         -----------             -----------           -----------
53 Total
54
55
```

(continued)

(EXHIBIT 4A–3 continued)

56		Pro Forma Income Statement			
57		Proposed Cost System			
58					
59		Product 1	Product 2	Product 3	Total
60	Revenue				
61	Direct Manufacturing Costs				
62		-----------	-----------	-----------	-----------
63	Direct Manufacturing Margin				
64	Direct Sales and				
65	Administrative Costs				
66		-----------	-----------	-----------	-----------
67	Direct Margin				
68					
69	Common Costs				
70	Manufacturing				
71	Sales and Administrative				
72		-----------	-----------	-----------	-----------
73	Income Before Taxes				

Where

[a] Product prices come from p. 164.

[b] Exhibit 4–7, Note a, shows machine hour and variable overhead information.

[c] Fixed manufacturing overhead costs under the proposed system are shown in Exhibit 4–7.

[d] Direct sales and administrative costs are shown in Exhibit 4–9.

[e] Unallocated common costs are shown in Exhibit 4–9.

units of Product 2 as you change the hours per unit for Product 1. This mechanism is in place to use all 100,000 labor hours given any labor time you specify for either product.

The SOLUTION SECTION has three sections. Section 1 is designed like Exhibit 4–2; you should put *unit cost* information in this section, using formulas that link it to the data section. Section 2 is designed like Exhibit 4–4, based on *total costs* in the main. Note that this section includes a line for units produced and for the number of set ups. As the total number of units changes, the number of set ups will change, and so will the average cost per set up. Finally, section 3 provides the dollar difference and the percent difference between the two cost systems.

LHEXIST.WK1 and LHPROPOSE.WK1

Basic data are given for each costing system. In addition, the solution sections of the templates reflect the two ways managers can view costs. LHEXIST.WK1 shows a traditional income statement format, while LHPROPOSE.WK1 shows a management decision-making orientation. Link cells in the solution section with appropriate data at the top of each template to create each income statement. Exhibits 4–10 and 4–11 show an abbreviated set of results for you to check against your results.

ASSIGNMENTS

4–1 Different Accounting Systems This chapter discussed different management accounting systems for different purposes. When addressing the following, use references from the text, class discussion, and outside readings.

REQUIRED

1. Explain the idea of product costing for financial accounting, cost of products for managerial decision making, and operational control systems. Be complete and use examples.
2. When would it be most appropriate for a company to have the separate cost systems you explained above? How would such a company be different from a company that did not need separate systems?

4–2 Cost Systems: Different Companies Marian Manufacturing produces four standard products in long runs. Each run uses roughly the same machinery and support departments. There are eight production departments and three support departments. The difference in the products is in the quality, the type of raw materials, and the assembly time each requires.

Beryl, Inc., manufactures several products, both standard and special order. Production runs range from 1,000 to 100,000 units. There are four production departments and five support departments in the plant. Different products use different amounts of time in each production department. Some products require specific support from, say, engineering and data processing.

At a recent meeting of a local manufacturing group, the presidents of these two companies approached you with the same concerns. They have been reading articles in trade magazines about the need for different cost systems for different purposes. Each has only one cost system—a job costing system using a predetermined plantwide overhead rate.

REQUIRED

If you were hired as a management consultant to each of these companies, what would you tell each president about the need to have more than one cost system? What would you recommend about how the system(s) should be designed?

4–3 Proposal for New Product (CMA Adapted) Garwin Company is a regional manufacturer of wood frame windows and has been in business for twenty-seven years. Demand for its products has been, and continues to be, very good. Management believes, however, that it has failed to take advantage of demand in the related metal and plastic frame window market as well as complementary markets.

The Product Development Group, a committee of upper management that cuts across organizational lines, has been created to propose and develop new products for Garwin. Management wants to take advantage of its expertise in the window frame business rather than diversify into different or unrelated product areas. Thus, only new products that would expand or be complementary to Garwin's current product line would be considered. The Product Development Group will be required to develop and submit a proposal for any new products that it recommends.

Greg Morton has been appointed to serve on the committee. Morton declared, "I've never been involved in a product introduction proposal. I think this is going to be interesting, but I'm not sure if I understand what developing a product introduction proposal entails."

REQUIRED

For the Product Development Group's proposal for a new product to be complete, it should address all aspects that Garwin Company needs to consider.

1. Identify and explain the major issues that Greg Morton should expect to address in the proposal.
2. For each issue identified, explain what data should be included as support for the product addition.

4–4 Product Profitability (AICPA Adapted) The officers of Bradshaw Company are reviewing the profitability of the company's four products and the potential effects of several proposals for varying the product mix. The following is an excerpt from the income statement and other data:

	Totals	*Product P*	*Product Q*	*Product R*	*Product S*
Sales	$62,600	$10,000	$18,000	$12,600	$22,000
Cost of goods sold	44,274	4,750	7,056	13,968	18,500
Gross profit	$18,326	$ 5,250	$10,944	$(1,368)	$ 3,500
Operating expenses	12,012	1,990	2,976	2,826	4,220
Income before income taxes	$ 6,314	$ 3,260	$ 7,968	$(4,194)	$ (720)
Units sold		1,000	1,200	1,800	2,000
Sales price per unit		$ 10.00	$ 15.00	$ 7.00	$ 11.00
Variable cost of goods sold per unit		$ 2.50	$ 3.00	$ 6.50	$ 6.00
Variable operating expenses per unit		$ 1.17	$ 1.25	$ 1.00	$ 1.20

Consider each of the following proposals independently of the other. Consider only the product changes stated in each proposal; the activity of other products remains stable.

REQUIRED

1. What is the effect on income if Product R is discontinued?
2. What is the effect on income if Product R is discontinued and a consequent loss of customers causes a decrease of 200 units in sales of Q?
3. What is the effect on income if the sales price of Product R is increased to $8 with a decrease in the number of units sold to 1,500?

4–5 Product Profitability (AICPA Adapted) Use the facts presented in Assignment 4–4.

REQUIRED

1. The plant in which Product R is produced can be used to produce a new product, T. Total variable costs and expenses per unit of Product T are $8.05,

and 1,600 units can be sold at $9.50 each. What is the total effect on income if Product T is introduced and Product R is discontinued?

2. Part of the plant in which Product P is produced can easily be adapted to the production of Product S, but changes in quantities may make changes in sales prices advisable. What is the total effect on income if production of Product P is reduced to 500 units (to be sold at $12 each) and production of Product S is increased to 2,500 units (to be sold at $10.50 each)?

3. Production of Product P can be doubled by adding a second shift, but higher wages must be paid, which will increase the variable cost of goods sold to $3.50 for each additional unit. What is the total effect on income if the 1,000 additional units of Product P can be sold at $10 each?

4–6 Cost for Two Purposes Waffle Company's records include the following costs:

1. materials used for Model 23
2. salaries—plant management
3. data processing department
4. sales commissions—Model 23
5. supplies used to make Model 23
6. plant insurance—building and equipment
7. salaries—corporate officers
8. depreciation on machinery in Dept. 200
9. depreciation on plant building
10. labor in Dept. 200
11. set up costs
12. shipping department costs
13. depreciation in Dept. 205

Model 23 is manufactured in departments 200, 201, and 205. Department 200 is used exclusively for Model 23, while departments 201 and 205 produce parts for several products. Department 200 is fully automated, using the latest in robotics machinery, all numerically controlled. The maintenance department performs all equipment set ups.

REQUIRED

For each of the above:

1. Which costs are common, and which separable? Be clear to what a cost is separable (traceable) if it is traceable.
2. What costs qualify as financial accounting product costs and what would be classified as period costs?
3. What costs would be appropriate to include to calculate the direct margin of a product for managerial decision making?
4. Can you identify special problems with any of the above costs? If so, what are they and how do you propose to resolve them?

4–7 Allocation of Common Costs MWH Company had one product, X, and it then added Product Y. Data for the company both before and after adding Y are:

Product X only	
Total overhead	$400,000 (all traceable)
Units produced and sold	100,000
Direct labor hours	20,000
Machine hours	25,000

Products X and Y	*Product X*	*Product Y*	*Common Costs*
Total overhead	$370,000	$40,000	$50,000
Units produced and sold	100,000	20,000	
Direct labor hours	20,000	2,000	
Machine hours	25,000	18,000	
Transactions	2,000	1,400	

Overhead shown under each product is traceable to that product. While total overhead was $400,000 with only Product X, overhead totals $460,000 with both X and Y.

REQUIRED

1. When the company had only Product X, what was the appropriate way to assign overhead to Product X? What is the appropriate cost per unit for X?
2. With both products X and Y, the company has not only traceable overhead, but also common overhead ($50,000). Allocate common costs to products X and Y using:
   a. units
   b. direct labor hours
   c. machine hours
   d. transactions

   Show your allocation to X and to Y for each method of allocation. Also produce a cost per unit for each method that includes traceable costs and your allocation of common costs.
3. Why does the change in allocation methods affect Y more than X?
4. Which method of allocation is best (a) for financial accounting product costs, (b) for pricing decisions, and (c) to assess the profitability of a product? In each case, explain why your method is the best.
5. Is any method of allocating the common costs more accurate than any other method? Why?

4–8 Segmented Income Statements—Costs of Activities Claxton Industries makes three principal product lines: sporting goods, housewares, and hardware. The company has suffered reduced profitability in the past few quarters and the top managers have acted to improve the situation. The most recent quarterly income statement, segmented by product line, appears below. Common fixed costs were allocated to the lines based on relative sales or labor content.

CLAXTON INDUSTRIES
Income Statement
Second Quarter, 19X9
(in thousands of dollars)

	Total	Sporting Goods	Housewares	Hardware
Sales	$3,337.0	$650.0	$921.0	$1,766.0
Cost of sales	1,928.8	357.3	545.7	1,025.8
Gross margin	1,408.2	292.7	375.3	740.2
Operating expenses:				
Selling expenses	787.6	157.1	225.9	404.6
Administrative expenses	514.6	94.2	135.6	284.8
Total operating expenses	1,302.2	251.3	361.5	689.4
Income before taxes	$ 106.0	$ 41.4	$ 13.8	$ 50.8

The managers were still not happy with the 3.2 percent return on sales, but the $106 thousand pretax profit was a bit higher than the previous quarter's profit. The managers agreed that they should concentrate on sporting goods and hardware because their return on sales (ROS) were higher than that of housewares, so that additional sales of sporting goods and hardware would be more profitable. One manager wanted to ignore housewares because its ROS was only 1.5 percent. "If we only keep a cent and a half from a dollar's sales, why even bother with it?"

When asked to confirm the managers' judgments about relative profitabilities, the controller pointed out that some common costs were allocated to the product lines and that some distortions might result from those allocations. She had therefore asked her assistant to prepare an alternative income statement without making allocations. The assistant's analysis of Claxton's cost structure revealed the following, with dollars in thousands.

Variable costs, percentage of sales:			
Cost of sales	28.00%	32.00%	35.00%
Selling expenses	2.00%	1.50%	1.80%
Administrative expenses	0.90%	0.70%	2.00%
Direct fixed costs:			
Cost of sales	$158	$141	$197
Selling expenses	56	87	133
Administrative expenses	13	22	43

The assistant evaluated the costs by examining the activities that generate them. For example, she found that sporting goods required relatively more attention from manufacturing support personnel such as engineers than did hardware and so was assigned relatively higher direct fixed manufacturing costs. By the same token, hardware consumed considerably more administrative time than did sporting goods, giving it relatively more direct cost.

REQUIRED

1. Prepare a new segmented income statement using the assistant's findings.
2. Comment on the differences between your statement and the one above. For example, what decisions are easier or more difficult to make with your statement?

4–9 Segmented Income Statements, Activity Analysis Vic Kemp, executive vice president of Taylor, Inc., was examining the most recent monthly income statements, which were segmented by geographical area. Taylor, a distributor of products used by paper manufacturers, had begun operations in the western part of the United States 20 years previously and had expanded into the southern and eastern markets only a year ago. Taylor did not manufacture its products, but bought them for resale.

Because Taylor had a good reputation and strong product lines, it had done well in the new markets, or so Kemp thought. The company had relatively few people and other assets in the market areas. The bulk of expenses were incurred at the home offices in Corvallis, Oregon.

TAYLOR, INC.
Income Statement
October 19X9
(in thousands of dollars)

	Total	*Eastern*	*Southern*	*Western*
Sales	$2,896.0	$589.0	$752.0	$1,555.0
Cost of sales	1,231.9	200.3	300.8	730.9
Gross margin	1,664.1	388.7	451.2	824.2
Selling expenses:				
Salaries and commissions	754.2	156.2	192.6	405.4
Shipping and warehousing	187.3	43.2	67.1	77.0
Other selling expenses	84.5	12.1	27.6	44.8
Total selling expenses	1,026.0	211.5	287.3	527.2
Administrative expenses:				
Salaries	147.2	42.6	36.8	67.8
Building occupancy	61.7	22.7	26.5	12.5
Other	56.1	12.3	22.1	21.7
Total administrative expenses	265.0	77.6	85.4	102.0
Total operating expenses	1,291.0	289.1	372.7	629.2
Income before taxes	$ 373.1	$ 99.6	$ 78.5	$ 195.0

Kemp was happy with the results in the new territories, but at the same time mistrusted them, not really knowing how the statements were prepared. Kemp was also concerned that the push into the new territories had caused managers to neglect the western territory, which seemed to be slipping in profitability. He was concerned that the income statements did not give him the kind of information he needed to make judgments and decisions. He had asked the chief accountant for an explanation of the income statements, but to little avail. The chief accountant usually put him off by saying that it was very complicated and he did not have the time to explain every number.

Taylor's chief accountant had been allocating costs to the markets using a set of formulas based on relative sales volume in both unit and dollar terms. No one else quite knew how he prepared the statements. Kemp finally went to the controller and asked for a special study to get the information he needed. The controller had been concerned with the allocation methods for some time and collected the following information based on analyses of the activities in each territory.

Variable costs, percentage of sales:			
Cost of sales	34.00%	40.00%	47.00%
Selling expenses	14.00%	13.00%	16.00%
Administrative expenses	0.00%	0.00%	0.00%
Direct fixed costs:			
Cost of sales	$ 0	$ 0	$ 0
Selling expenses	152	155	207
Administrative expenses	9	12	19

The controller explained that she developed the information by analyzing the cost drivers, activities associated with each category. For instance, the eastern territory had relatively heavy direct fixed selling expenses, for several reasons. First, with more established competitors in that region, new customers were harder to cultivate. Second, shipping costs were higher because orders from the east were smaller than those from the other regions, thus losing economies of large shipments. Other reasons contributed to the differences between the activity-based direct costs and the costs as allocated in the income statement above.

REQUIRED

1. Prepare a segmented income statement using the contribution margin format. Work with totals only for selling expenses and administrative expenses. Ignore the individual components of those cost categories.
2. Tell Mr. Kemp how each territory is doing.

4–10 Cost of Products: Two Purposes Seneca Corp. began business last year, when it bought new equipment and constructed a building. Business has been good; the plant usually operates fairly close to capacity. Information relating to Seneca's two products and its operations are:

		Per Unit	
		Product 1	*Product 2*
Variable costs:			
Materials		$35.00	$50.00
Labor at $24.00 per hour		2.40	4.80
Commissions		5.00	7.50
Factory overhead		7.00	9.00
Fixed costs:			
Factory overhead			
Supervisors' salaries	$ 50,000		
Material handling	35,000		
Maintenance	40,000		
Building depreciation	20,000		
Equipment depreciation	30,000		
Property taxes	4,000		
Sales and administration:			
Management salaries	120,000		
Sales salaries	50,000		
Insurance	12,000		
Other	80,000		

(continued)

Other information:	*Product 1*	*Product 2*	*Common*
Units	50,000	5,000	
Components per unit	2	3	
Labor hours per unit	0.1	0.2	
Machine hours per unit	0.3	0.2	
Supervision	30%	20%	50%
Building space	60%	20%	20%
Equipment value	70%	20%	10%
Maintenance	50%	25%	25%
Sales salaries	40%	10%	50%
Insurance			
Plant			$10,000
Office			2,000

Seneca allocates common factory overhead using these bases:

Supervisors' salaries	Machine hours
Material handling	Components
Maintenance	Machine hours
Building depreciation	Percent of building use
Equipment depreciation	Percent of traceable depreciation
Property taxes	Percent of building and equipment depreciation
Insurance	Percent of equipment depreciation

REQUIRED

State all of your assumptions for the following:

1. Calculate the product cost per unit appropriate for financial reporting.

2. Calculate the cost of product per unit appropriate for managerial decisions.

3. Which costs would you use for the following purposes?
a. deciding which product to expand into a new market
b. deciding if one of the products should be dropped
c. comparing your prices to those of your competitors
Explain your choices.

4–11 Pricing Decisions (CMA Adapted) Hall Company specializes in packaging bulk drugs in standard dosages for local hospitals. The company has been in business since 19X8 and has been profitable since its second year of operation. Don Greenway, Director of Cost Accounting, installed a standard cost system after joining the company in 19Y2.

Wyant Memorial Hospital has asked Hall to bid on packaging of one million doses of medication at full cost plus a return on full cost of no more than 9 percent after income taxes. Wyant defines cost as including all variable costs of performing the service, a reasonable amount of nonvariable overhead, and reasonable administrative costs. The hospital will supply all packaging materials and ingredients. Wyant has indicated that any bid over $0.015 per dose will be rejected.

Greenway accumulated the following information prior to the preparation of the bid.

Direct labor	\$4.00/DLH
Variable overhead	\$3.00/DLH
Fixed overhead	\$5.00/DLH
Administrative costs	\$1,000 for the order
Production rate	1,000 doses/DLH

Hall Company is subject to an effective income tax rate of 40 percent.

REQUIRED

1. Calculate the minimum price per dose that Hall Company could bid for the Wyant Memorial Hospital job that would not reduce Hall's net income.
2. Calculate the bid price per dose using the full cost criterion and the maximum allowable return specified by Wyant Memorial Hospital.
3. Without prejudice to your answer to part 2, assume that the price per dose that Hall Company calculated using the cost plus criterion specified by Wyant Memorial Hospital is greater than the maximum bid of \$0.015 per dose allowed by Wyant. Discuss the factors that Hall Company would consider before deciding whether or not to submit a bid at the maximum price of \$0.015 per dose.
4. Discuss the factors that Wyant Memorial Hospital should have considered before deciding whether or not to employ cost plus pricing.

4–12 Plant Closing Decision (CMA Adapted) GianAuto Corporation manufactures automobiles, vans, and trucks. Among the various GianAuto plants around the United States is the Denver Cover Plant. Coverings made primarily of vinyl and upholstery fabric are sewn at the Denver Cover Plant to cover interior seating and other surfaces of GianAuto products.

Ted Vosilo is the Plant Manager for Denver Cover. The Denver Cover Plant was the first GianAuto plant in the region. As other area plants were opened, Vosilo, in recognition of his management ability, was given responsibility for managing them. Vosilo functions as a regional manager although the budget for him and his staff is charged to the Denver Cover Plant.

Vosilo has just received a report indicating that GianAuto could purchase the entire annual output of Denver Cover from outside suppliers for \$30 million. Vosilo was astonished at the low outside price because the budget for Denver Cover's operating costs for the coming year was set at \$52 million. Vosilo believes that GianAuto will have to close down operations at Denver Cover in order to realize the \$22 million in annual cost savings.

The budget for Denver Cover's operating costs for the coming year is presented on the next page. Additional facts regarding the plant's operations are:

Because of Denver Cover's commitment to use high quality fabrics in its products, the Purchasing Department was instructed to place blanket purchase orders with major suppliers to ensure the receipt of sufficient materials for the coming year. If these orders are canceled as a consequence of the plant closing, termination charges would amount to 15 percent of the cost of direct materials.

Approximately 700 plant employees will lose their jobs if the plant is closed, including direct laborers and supervisors as well as the plumbers, electricians, and other skilled workers classified as indirect plant workers. Some would be able to find new jobs while many others would have difficulty. All employees would have difficulty matching Denver Cover's base pay of $9.40 per hour, which is the highest in the area. A clause in Denver Cover's contract with the union may help some employees; the company must provide employment assistance to its former employees for twelve months after a plant closing. The estimated cost to administer this service would be $1 million for the year.

Some employees would probably elect early retirement because GianAuto has an excellent pension plan. In fact, $3 million of the 19X6 pension expense would continue whether Denver Cover is open or not.

Vosilo and his staff would not be affected by the closing of Denver Cover. They would still be responsible for administering three other area plants.

Denver Cover considers equipment depreciation to be a variable cost and uses the units-of-production method to depreciate its equipment; Denver Cover is the only GianAuto plant to use this depreciation method. However, Denver Cover uses the customary straight-line method to depreciate its building.

DENVER COVER PLANT
Budget For Operating Costs
For the Year Ending December 31, 19X6
($000 omitted)

Materials		$12,000
Labor:		
Direct	$13,000	
Supervision	3,000	
Indirect plant	4,000	20,000
Overhead:		
Depreciation—equipment	$ 5,000	
Depreciation—building	3,000	
Pension expense	4,000	
Plant manager and staff	2,000	
Corporate allocation	6,000	20,000
Total budgeted costs		$52,000

REQUIRED

1. Without regard to costs, identify the advantages to GianAuto Corporation of continuing to obtain covers from its Denver Cover Plant.
2. GianAuto Corporation plans to prepare a numerical analysis that will be used in deciding whether to close the Denver Cover Plant. Identify:
   a. the recurring annual budgeted costs that can be avoided by closing the plant
   b. the recurring annual budgeted costs that are not relevant to the decision; explain why they are not relevant.
   c. any nonrecurring costs that arise from the closing of the plant; explain how they affect the decision.
   d. any revenues or costs not mentioned that GianAuto should consider before making a decision.

4–13 Continuation of Problem 2–40 This problem builds on the facts of problem 2–40. Additional information for SunSet is as follows:

	Product 1	Product 2
Direct labor hours per unit	0.6	0.5
Machine hours per unit	1.0	0.75
Components per unit	2	3

REQUIRED

1. Create a financial accounting income statement with a column for each product and one for the company as a whole. Use direct labor hours to apply fixed overhead.
2. Calculate each product's return on sales percentage (before taxes) and the company's overall return on sales (before taxes).
3. In problem 2–40 you were asked to calculate the contribution margin percentage for each product and the weighted average contribution margin percentage for the company. Comment on the use of contribution margin percentages and return on sales percentages for managerial decisions. Which do you believe is more useful? Why?
4. A study of fixed costs reveals that certain costs are directly related to each product as follows:

	Product 1	Product 2	Common
Fixed manufacturing costs	$100,000	$400,000	$1,000,000
Fixed selling/administrative costs	30,000	30,000	200,000

Create a financial accounting income statement similar to that required in part 1 above. Choose direct labor hours, machine hours, or components as your basis for applying common fixed overhead.

5. Is the income statement in part 4 more accurate than the income statement in part 1? Why or why not? Explain fully.
6. Defend your choice of an application base for common fixed manufacturing overhead.

4–14 Continuation of Sanibel Review Problem The review problem for Sanibel (pages 158–160) shows that as the labor time for Product 1 goes down from 0.3 hours per unit to 0.05 hours per unit, the difference widens between a direct-labor-based cost system and an activity-based cost system.

REQUIRED

1. If you have not done so, use the template SANIBEL.WK1 to confirm the results in Exhibit 4–5. Common fixed overhead is allocated using direct labor hours. Any differences should be due to rounding.
2. Reset labor hours per unit to 0.3 for Product 1 and to 1.0 hours for Product 2. Repeat the process of part 1 by successively using 0.3, 0.2, 0.1, and 0.05 hours per unit for Product 1 while holding Product 2 at 1 hour per unit. Make sure

that 100,000 hours are used in total. (The template will do this automatically.) What conclusions can you draw regarding the effects of the two product costing systems on each of the products?

3. Reset labor hours per unit for Product 1 to 0.3 and for Product 2 to 0.5. Allocate common fixed overhead based on each product's share of traceable costs. Hold Product 2 labor time at 0.5 hours per unit but vary Product 1 labor time from 0.3 to 0.05. Are the results different than those obtained in part 1? Why?
4. What is the justification for using direct labor hours as the basis to allocate common fixed overhead in parts 1 and 2? What is the justification for using proportion of traceable fixed overhead as the basis to allocate common fixed overhead in part 3?
5. Is using an activity-based costing system more accurate than a direct-labor-based system in this case? Why or why not? Should the company switch to the activity-based costing system? Why?
6. Is using proportion of traceable fixed cost as an allocation base for common fixed overhead more accurate than using direct labor hours as a basis? Why or why not? If the company switches to an activity-based costing system, should it also change its allocation method for common fixed overhead to proportion of traceable fixed cost? Why?

4–15 Overhead Rates and Pricing Glenway Company manufactures pumping equipment. Some of its jobs require many components and parts that the firm must buy from outside suppliers, while others need a great deal of fabrication, milling, and other operations because the firm must make them to order.

The controller of the firm develops a plantwide overhead rate in advance of each year. Late in 19X4 she used the following data to develop the $3.275 rate to be used in 19X5:

	Estimates for 19X5	
Department	*Overhead*	*Direct Labor Hours*
Fabrication	$ 486,300	109,900
Grinding and milling	396,500	73,200
Assembly	285,200	173,500
Totals	$1,168,000	356,600

Rate per direct labor hour = $3.275 ($1,168,000/356,600)

The controller has instructed her staff to set prices at 120 percent of factory cost. The wage rates expected to prevail in 19X5 were $8.60 in the fabrication department, $6.40 in the grinding/milling department, and $5.20 in the assembly department.

During 19X5 the firm bid on many jobs, getting some and losing others. Data on two jobs appear below, reflecting expected costs.

	Job	
	A	B
Labor		
Fabrication	$ 37,840 (4,400 hours)	$ 15,480 (1,800 hours)
Grinding/milling	17,664 (2,760 hours)	4,736 (740 hours)
Assembly	5,096 (980 hours)	11,024 (2,120 hours)
Materials	63,400	137,500
Total labor and materials	$124,000	$168,740

REQUIRED

1. Determine the prices that Glenway would have bid for each job.
2. Suppose that a competitor has exactly the same departmental setup, cost structure, expectations about labor hours, and profit objective. The only difference is that the competitor uses departmental overhead rates to determine total factory costs. What would the competitor have bid for each job?
3. Besides applying overhead using departmental rates, what other things can management do to get more accurate costs for pricing?

5

PRODUCT COSTING: FINANCIAL ACCOUNTING

This chapter begins a sequence that deals primarily with product costs for financial accounting. Chapter 4 stated that the main concern of product costing for financial accounting is to determine unit manufacturing costs. Unit costs are needed to value inventories and to determine cost of goods sold for financial reporting and tax purposes. Therefore, much of what accountants do in this area is governed by GAAP (and, to a lesser extent, tax law). Within these rules, it is the accountant's role to determine unit cost; it is hoped that the method chosen will be as close to the economic reality of the situation (as accurate) as possible—a concern we discussed earlier.

We shall mostly be dealing with absorption costing. **Absorption costing** uses fixed manufacturing costs and variable manufacturing costs in determining unit costs. In Chapter 2 we argued that calculating unit fixed costs is unwise because fixed costs are not incurred per unit, but in total. However, absorption costing is required for financial reporting and income tax reporting. In addition, managers use unit fixed costs in some types of managerial planning and analysis.

PRODUCT COSTS AND PRICING

One common use of unit fixed costs is to set long-term prices, a practice we discussed as a problem in Chapter 4. Many companies use absorption costing data to set prices. Thus, managers use product costs for financial reporting (including both traceable and common manufacturing costs) as if they were equal to cost of products for managerial decision making (which might also include other non-manufacturing costs). Many managers believe that when a market price exists for a product, unit product costs can provide some measure of how competitive a firm is in the marketplace. If competitors offer products at this price, managers assume that such competitors are profitable; thus, managers believe their company can judge its efficiency by whether it makes a profit at the market price less the product cost. In the absence of market prices, absorption costing unit costs are used as a base to establish prices. Studies have shown that absorption costing unit costs are the most used basis for many pricing decisions.[1] As we have discussed, this practice often has serious pitfalls.

Many sales agreements provide for the price to be based on product cost. An agreement might specify the price as cost plus $20,000, or as 120 percent of cost. Both federal government and many private-sector contracts include such provisions. When prices are based on costs, it is important to know what is included and excluded from such costs. Hospitals, for example, are reimbursed for the traceable costs of providing a service plus some share of common costs. It is important that both the hospital and the reimbursing agency (for example, insurance carrier or governmental agency) agree on the cost reimbursement.

MANUFACTURING OPERATIONS

Chapter 4 discussed the normal flows of manufacturing costs. First, resources are acquired (direct material, direct labor, and various overhead resources). As these resources are consumed, their costs are transferred to a Work in Process account. As goods are finished, their costs are transferred from Work in Process to Finished Goods. Finally, as goods are sold, their costs move to the Cost of Goods Sold account. This process ties into basic notions from financial accounting: any manufacturing cost incurred during a period will be reflected as an asset (materials, work in process, or finished goods inventory) or as an expense (cost of goods sold) by the end of the period.

One objective of a manufacturing accounting system is to provide in

[1]This is true both for prices to outside customers and for internal transfers of goods as we will discuss in Chapter 18. Supporting studies include Robert G. Eccles, *The Transfer Pricing Problem: A Theory for Practice* (D. C. Heath and Company, 1985); and Daniel P. Keegan and Patrick D. Howard, "Transfer Pricing for Fun and Profit," Price Waterhouse *Review*, no. 3 (1986), pp. 37–45. Also see Chow et al., "A Compilation of Recent Surveys and Company-Specific Descriptions of Management Accounting Practices," *Journal of Accounting Education*, vol. 6 (1988): 183–207; and Bernard A. Coda and Barry G. King, "Manufacturing Decision-Making Tools," *Journal of Cost Management for the Manufacturing Industry*, Spring 1989, pp. 29–37.

numbers a picture of what is happening in the factory. The cost flows in Figure 4–1 on page 150 generally outline the way many manufacturing accounting cost systems represent actions from the purchasing of inputs to the final sale of products. All companies make certain choices so these records reflect their production methods. Although the general type of production varies along a continuum, we can model two distinct ideas that describe the ends of this spectrum. Consider two companies: Valentine Brick Company manufactures a single type of brick in a series of continuous processes. Each brick is identical to every other. York Machine Shop produces custom replacement parts for machinery. Each part is made to order and is unique. Parts vary in complexity; their prices range from $50 to $5,000.

These two firms are very different. Thus, their systems, designed to reflect product costs, must incorporate these differences. Valentine Brick Company makes a uniform product. It is neither necessary nor cost effective to know what *each* brick costs. It is accurate enough to calculate an average cost per brick produced during a period. Thus, average unit cost per brick could be calculated with a formula such as:

$$\text{cost per brick} = \frac{\text{total manufacturing costs for period}}{\text{total number of bricks made during period}}$$

This type of production employs a uniform process with a homogeneous product. The above formula typifies **process costing**, which we discuss in detail in Chapter 6. The essential elements of process costing are that it requires determining total manufacturing costs *for a period of time* and total unit production *for that same period of time*. Since every brick is more or less like every other brick, the managers of Valentine Brick do not need to know the specific cost of any one brick. Thus, the average unit cost derived from a formula such as the one above can be used to determine inventories and cost of goods sold.

At York Machine Shop, however, average costs are of no use to managers, because each job is different. Managers of this company need to know the cost of *each* job to see if a particular job was profitable (were costs as planned? was the price high enough?). Moreover, if York has any inventory at the end of a period, average costs do not reflect such inventory values. An average cost would probably exceed the selling price of some products (violating the lower of cost or market rule for inventory valuation) and be far below the actual cost of others. This type of manufacturing operation uses a **job order cost system**. Such a system accumulates costs by job, specific unit, or specific batch of units. Thus, York would keep track of the costs of each order, not just of the costs over a period of time.

Many companies fall in the middle of the process-job order continuum. Consultants in manufacturing accounting state that most manufacturing companies outside the chemical and petroleum fields use the job order concept. As we shall see, even these job order companies use some of the concepts that we will develop regarding processing costing. Thus, while we speak of these two systems as different, manufacturing accounting cost systems can include elements of both. With repetitive manufacturing, where the same product (or set of products) is made on an ongoing basis, the process is continuous in some ways, but can also be classified as a job order situation.

As an example of a firm that falls between pure job order and pure process costing, consider a furniture manufacturer with a diverse set of products, that produces 3,000 of the same desk during a month. Such a company could use average unit cost over that month to reflect the cost for each desk. Yet this company might think of those 3,000 desks as a single batch or as, say, 30 batches of 100 desks each. Even if the company uses a job order costing system, as we discuss in Chapter 6, if there is unfinished work on a batch at the end of a period the firm may use process costing ideas to establish unit costs. Thus, while we treat the procedures for job order costing differently than those of process costing, most systems that reflect product costs for financial accounting include elements of both concepts.

Finally, while we emphasize manufacturing operations, we also note that service operations use the same basic techniques. CPAs, consulting engineers, and lawyers use a form of job order costing because each needs information about the cost of work done for a particular client. Service firms can also use process costing for repetitive activities such as handling phone catalog orders, computer data entry, and scoring standardized tests.

JOB ORDER COSTING

The basic idea of job order costing is tracking the costs of each job. What constitutes a job varies from firm to firm. Each job may be a unique piece. In many cases a job is a batch of similar units, such as ten desks. In still other cases a job is a batch of dissimilar items ordered by the same customer. Thus, a dining room set consisting of a table, eight chairs, and a china cabinet could be considered a single job. This grouping creates no problem as long as the whole set is either in inventory or is sold.

General Pattern of Job Order Costing

A job order firm determines the cost of each unit or batch of units that it produces. Therefore, the costs of each job must be separated from other jobs. Any manufacturing resources used to produce the job, such as direct material or direct labor, are recorded for that job. This recording can be done using a manual job order cost sheet (to show the costs recorded for a job), by having a computer database for each job, or by many other means that keep the costs of each job distinct from other jobs. Appendix 5A shows samples of documents that might constitute such a system.

As costs are incurred, they are recorded in appropriate accounts. Thus, the cost of materials purchased is placed in the Materials Inventory account and direct labor cost in the Direct Labor account. Direct materials and direct labor costs are transferred from the Materials Inventory account and the Direct Labor account to Work-in-Process Inventory as costs are associated with each job. Manufacturing overhead costs, including both fixed and variable costs such as indirect materials and supplies, indirect labor, and depreciation on factory equipment, are first recorded in descriptive accounts according to the object of the expenditure. These include Indirect Labor, Depreciation on Equipment, and Utilities. These costs are later transferred to a single account called, for example, Factory Overhead, Manufacturing Overhead, or Factory Burden. Overhead costs might be divided into fixed and variable elements at this stage. Overhead accounts are clearing accounts; costs simply pass through them on their way to Work-in-Process Inventory.

While it is relatively easy to trace and record direct, variable costs to each product, it can be much harder to determine how much of direct fixed[2] and/or common variable and fixed costs to allocate to a job.[3] The allocation of manufacturing overhead, which usually contains common costs, is the subject of much discussion. As illustrated in Chapter 4, overhead is traced/allocated to individual jobs based on some factors (bases) such as pounds of material, number of set ups, direct labor hours, machine hours, or units of product, to name a few. When this *application of overhead* (assignment of overhead costs to product) occurs, the overhead account is credited and Work-in-Process Inventory is debited.[4]

The Work-in-Process Inventory account shows the total cost of all jobs not yet finished. Because its balance equals the sum of costs on the job order cost records of the unfinished jobs, it thereby functions as a control account (as does Accounts Receivable) because it is backed up by individual subsidiary records. When a job is finished, its cost as reflected in the job order cost records is credited to Work-in-Process Inventory and debited to Finished Goods Inventory.

Exhibit 5–1 shows a job order cost record for Job 327 of Imtract Company. Entries associated with this job are:

Date			
2–12	Work-in-Process Inventory	$ 820	
	Materials Inventory		$ 742
	Direct Labor		78
2–15	Work-in-Process Inventory	1,865	
	Materials Inventory		1,865

(continued)

[2]While any cost that is direct is traceable to a job, often financial accounting records do not provide an easy way to associate such costs with products.

[3]We will use the term *allocate* (or *allocation*) in a very specific way. If a cost cannot be traced to a product but some portion of that cost is assigned to the product, this is an *allocation*. On the other hand, if a one-to-one tracking of resource acquisition and use to a product occurs, this is not allocation; it is tracing or assigning based on a relationship.

[4]While there are alternate ways of doing this, this is the easiest to follow.

2–20	Work-in-Process Inventory	560	
	Direct Labor		560
2–28	Work-in-Process Inventory	412	
	Materials Inventory		412
2–28	Work-in-Process Inventory	2,150	
	Direct Labor		2,150
2–28	Work-in-Process Inventory	5,576	
	Factory Overhead		5,576
2–28	Finished Goods Inventory	11,383	
	Work-in-Process Inventory		11,383

We have shown briefly how costs of materials, direct labor, and manufacturing overhead flow into Work-in-Process Inventory and then to Finished Goods Inventory. When Job 327 is sold, a debit is made to Cost of Goods Sold and a corresponding credit is made to Finished Goods Inventory for $11,383. We shall now illustrate cost flows more comprehensively and delve further into the major problem of product costing—the application of manufacturing overhead to products.

EXHIBIT 5–1 Sample Job Order Cost Sheet

IMTRACT COMPANY
Job Order Cost Sheet

Customer : Wilkins Company
Description : 10 Casings, #1275
Date Started : 2–12
Date Finished : 3–14

Job Order Number: 327

Material Costs			*Labor Costs*			*Factory Overhead*		
Date	*Reference*	*Amt.*	*Date*	*Reference*	*Amt.*	*Date*	*Reference*	*Amt.*
2–12	M-361	$ 742	2–12	W-1486	$ 78	2–28	J-1011	$5,576
2–15	M-401	1,865	2–20	W-1520	560			
2–28	M-615	412	2–28	W-1606	2,150			
Totals		$3,019			$2,788			$5,576

Summary

Selling Price		$13,400
Costs:		
Materials	$3,019	
Direct labor	2,788	
Factory overhead	5,576	
Total costs		11,383
Gross profit		$ 2,017

EXHIBIT 5–2 Data for February, 19X9—Manners Company

	Jobs			
	J-5	*F-1*	*F-2*	*Total*
Direct materials used in February	$11,800	$ 9,600	$13,200	$34,600
Direct labor costs for February	9,500	14,500	5,800	29,800
February costs	21,300	24,100	19,000	64,400
Beginning inventory	6,500	0	0	6,500
Totals, excluding February overhead	$27,800	$24,100	$19,000	$70,900
Other February data:				
Direct labor hours worked	1,950	3,040	1,010	6,000
Machine hours used	80	150	70	300
Machine set ups	1	1	1	3

Illustration of Job Order Costing

Manners Company manufactures industrial instruments. These instruments usually contain some standard parts such as casings, dials, and sensing devices. They do, however, require special fabrication of nonstandard parts. Manners, therefore, uses job order costing. Each job is started when an order from a customer is received and approved. Workers analyze the specifications, requisition materials, and do the fabricating and assembly work. When finished, the instruments are sent to the finished goods storage area to be prepared for shipment.

At the beginning of February, 19X9, Manners had one job in Process (J-5) and no finished goods inventory. In February, Manners finished J-5 and started two others, F-1 and F-2. The company finished F-1 in February.

Exhibit 5–2 shows the amounts of direct labor and direct material used on each job in February as well as the cost of job J-5 carried over from the January, 19X9, balance sheet. We have the direct material and direct labor costs accumulated for each job; we still need to determine how to assign overhead to each job. The $6,500 beginning inventory value for job J-5 includes all manufacturing costs including overhead applied to that job in January.

Accounting for Overhead

For product costing, we must apply (assign) some portion of both variable and fixed manufacturing overhead to jobs. This information is necessary to determine inventory on the balance sheet and, in turn, for income. We must include both fixed and variable overhead in determining the costs of jobs. For planning and control, it is no problem to include traceable variable overhead as a cost of product because it is an incremental cost, like materials and labor, related to the product. Thus, if the traceable variable manufacturing overhead is $2.00 per direct labor hour and $40.00 per machine hour, an accountant would feel confident that each job should have overhead costs of $2.00 times direct labor hours used and $40.00 times machine hours used. Likewise, any traceable fixed overhead can be applied to a job and the resulting product costs will be accurate. For example, a company might have a clerk in finished goods whose job entirely consists of storing and filling orders for a single product. That person's salary, say $16,000, is traceable to that product and should be applied to it.

Problems do exist with the application of common overhead costs. Many overhead costs are not incremental to any particular job. An accountant cannot say that a particular job used $230 worth of heat, light, general plant salaries, and depreciation.

Bases for Applying Overhead As Chapter 4 illustrated, if a company made only one product, it could assign overhead to units of product simply by dividing total overhead by the number of units produced and applying that per unit amount to each unit. However, such a calculation is obviously inappropriate for a job order company because the units it makes are not uniform. It is absurd to assign the same amount of total overhead to producing a chair, a table, and a sofa if those products require different amounts of various overhead resources.

There are two levels of questions to ask when deciding how to apply overhead to units of product. First, what are the various overhead cost pools? Second, what is the causal relationship that determines how these cost pools are used?

Determining Cost Pools Companies require and use resources to perform various functions. Plant managers and their staffs do the general administration of the manufacturing facility. An engineering department might have personnel involved in plant layout, product design, and quality control. A maintenance department might set up machines between jobs and also repair machinery. An employee service department might deal with plant payroll, insurance claims, and the like. All are examples of manufacturing overhead cost pools. Thus, as a first step, a company divides its overhead into cost pools based on some general organization or function as illustrated above.

Determining an Activity Basis Resources are in place, it is hoped, because they benefit operations. As Chapter 4 illustrated, the next task is not only to understand why a set of resources exists, but also to determine a basis for assigning resource costs to product lines, products, and/or units of product. What are human and machine resources used for? Do they support direct labor; are they used in setups? We want to use a causal basis to apply overhead if one exists. With traceable costs, we can find these relationships by using regression and correlation analysis and interviewing various managers. If costs are common, there is no cause-and-effect relationship between the resource cost and its use by any particular job, product line, product, or unit of product. Finally, some traceable costs might be so small that it is not cost effective (nor will accuracy be increased) to assign them using a causal variable.

As a general rule, then, if a company has identified causal variables that reflect how resources are used, it should use that basis (*cost driver*) to apply manufacturing overhead to jobs, product lines, products, or units of product. Cost drivers include input factors (such as pounds of material, direct labor hours, or machine hours), particular activities (including number of set ups, components, or purchase orders), or outputs (units of product, a particular product, or product line). For common costs, management must find a reasonable way to allocate them. In many cases, managers choose the cost driver related to traceable costs in the same cost pool.

Finally, cost pools themselves can be subdivided based on various appropriate cost drivers. For example, if maintenance works on machine set ups and maintenance, the total maintenance cost pool may be divided into one subdivision for set ups (traceable to jobs, where the cost driver is number of set ups) and the other for maintenance (common to jobs and might be allocated using number of machine hours). Costs such as those for a single piece of maintenance equipment used in both functions and the general administration of the department might be divided pro rata into the two cost pools and allocated based on the cost driver of each pool.

Popular Cost Bases Chapter 4 included illustrations of the problems that can be encountered if incorrect bases are used to apply manufacturing overhead. Recently many authors (from academia, manufacturing, and public accounting)[5] have criticized the popularity of direct labor cost or direct labor hours as the single basis that many companies use to apply manufacturing overhead to units of product. As we have seen, a single basis is appropriate to use when it reflects how resources are used (and, therefore, how costs are incurred); however, once there is a differential use of significant resources, a single basis or cost driver is inadequate and can lead to inaccurate estimates of unit product costs. In addition, as labor cost becomes more fixed and a smaller proportion of total manufacturing costs, labor cost may lose its appeal as an application basis even in simple settings.

While the idea of traceable and common costs is not new to management and cost accounting, managers are taking a new interest in defining appropriate cost pools and cost drivers. The demise of the single, direct labor related basis for applying overhead is approaching.

Actual Costing

In the above example of the salary of the finished goods clerk, actual monthly salary would be divided to be assigned to units of product. This is an example of *actual costing*, where the actual costs incurred for each period (month,

[5] See Robin Cooper, "Does Your Company Need a New Cost System?" *Journal of Cost Management for the Manufacturing Industry*, Spring 1987, pp. 66–69; Robin Cooper and Robert S. Kaplan, "How Cost Accounting Distorts Product Costs," *Management Accounting*, April 1988, pp. 20–27; and similar articles.

quarter, year) are accumulated and assigned to units of product. In the case of manufacturing overhead, actual costs for the period are applied to units of product through the bases discussed above.

For example, assume that Manners Company had the following overhead for February:

Cost Pool	*Amount*	*Cost Driver*
Indirect labor and supplies	$ 4,000	direct labor hours
General plant	12,000	machine hours
Machine set ups	1,200	number of set ups

Combining this information with that from Exhibit 5–2, we have the following overhead application rates:

$4,000/6,000 direct labor hours	= $0.6667	per direct labor hour (DLH)
$12,000/300 machine hours	= $40.00	per machine hour (MH)
$1,200/3 set ups	= $400.00	per set up

Some of this overhead is traceable to particular jobs and other overhead is common. However, all must be applied to February jobs. Overhead charged to jobs is:

	Jobs			
	J-5	*F-1*	*F-2*	*Total*
Indirect labor and supplies:				
1,950, 3,040, and 1,010 DLH at $0.6667/DLH	$1,300	$2,027	$ 673	$ 4,000
General plant:				
80, 150, and 70 MH at $40/MH	3,200	6,000	2,800	12,000
Machine set ups:				
1 each at $400 per set up	400	400	400	1,200
Total overhead applied	$4,900	$8,427	$3,873	$17,200

The total costs of the three jobs appear below. Data are from Exhibit 5–2 and the overhead amounts just shown.

	Jobs			
	J-5	*F-1*	*F-2*	*Total*
Direct materials used in February	$11,800	$ 9,600	$13,200	$34,600
Direct labor costs for February	9,500	14,500	5,800	29,800
Applied February overhead	4,900	8,427	3,873	17,200
February costs	26,200	32,527	22,873	81,600
Beginning inventory	6,500	0	0	6,500
Totals	$32,700	$32,527	$22,873	$88,100

During February, the following occurred:

1. Job J-5 was finished. Thus, its cost of $32,700 (including costs incurred in January and costs incurred in February to finish the job) was first transferred to Finished Goods Inventory and then to Cost of Goods Sold.
2. Job F-1 was both started and finished in February. It was not shipped, however, and its cost of $32,527 is in Finished Goods Inventory at month's end.
3. Job F-2 was started during February but not finished. Work will have to be performed on this job in March. Thus, its cost of $22,873 will remain in Work-in-Process Inventory at the end of February.

As stated above, we have accounted for all costs incurred in February. They have ended up either on the balance sheet as inventories or in the income statement as part of cost of goods sold.

Actual costing has some serious drawbacks and is not widely used in medium-sized and large firms. We shall look at the reasons for this after we illustrate the more prevalent method of applying overhead costs, which is called *normal costing*, or *actual-normal costing*. It will be easier to see why actual costing is inferior after we see how normal costing works.

Normal Costing and Predetermined Overhead Rates

First, under normal costing (as in actual costing), product cost includes direct materials and direct labor at actual cost. In this respect, actual and normal costing yield the same results. The difference between the two methods is the treatment of manufacturing overhead.

The essence of normal costing is that it uses a *predetermined overhead rate* to assign overhead costs to jobs. A predetermined overhead rate is simply a rate calculated at the beginning of a period, usually a year, to determine the overhead cost included in each job worked on during the period. The basis used for application should be as discussed above: an input factor, activity,[6] or output that is causally related to the use of a resource. Thus, the selection of a basis for applying overhead is the same under both actual and normal costing. The only difference is that under normal costing the *rate* at which overhead is applied is determined in advance, not after the fact, as it is under actual costing.

Calculation of Predetermined Overhead Rate A predetermined overhead rate is calculated as follows for each cost pool and cost driver:

[6]The term *activity* is used by many managers to describe any or all three of the different cost-driver bases we have illustrated. Some writers refer to *transactions* as the generic word as well.

$$\text{predetermined overhead rate} = \frac{\text{total budgeted overhead cost}}{\text{total budgeted activity}}$$

where total budgeted activity is expressed as pounds of material, number of components, direct labor hours, machine hours, number of set ups, number of units, etc., as appropriate. Although a rate may be set for any length of time, a year is the most common period selected. As discussed above, when managers must allocate a common cost, the choice of an allocation basis becomes subjective, based on some criteria of reasonableness and equity.[7]

Such a general formulation of an overhead rate can include both fixed and variable costs. Say that Manners Company managers have analyzed overhead using regression analysis and determined the annual cost behavior pattern for indirect labor and supplies as \$20,000+ (\$0.50 × direct labor hours). The firm expects to work about 80,000 direct labor hours during the year and, therefore, sets the predetermined overhead rate at \$0.75 per direct labor hour (DLH), calculated as follows:

$$\begin{aligned}\text{predetermined overhead rate} &= \frac{\$20{,}000}{80{,}000\text{ DLH}} + \$0.50\text{ per DLH}\\ &= \$0.75\text{ per DLH}\end{aligned}$$

Likewise, predetermineed overhead rates can be calculated for the other two cost pools. Assume that set ups are performed by a person whose total annual salary is \$14,400, or \$1,200 per month. If the total number of set ups is estimated at 48 per year, then the predetermined rate per set up is \$300 (\$14,400/48). Finally, assume that annual general plant costs (virtually all fixed) are budgeted at \$150,000 and there are 3,000 estimated annual machine hours. This yields a \$50.00 per-machine-hour predetermined overhead application rate. Exhibit 5–3 shows the overhead application and total costs under normal costing.

Overapplied and Underapplied Overhead In February Manners Company incurred overhead costs of \$17,200, which was \$3,200 less than the \$20,400 overhead applied. When overhead incurred exceeds overhead applied under normal costing, overhead has been *underapplied*. Conversely, when overhead applied exceeds overhead incurred, overhead is *overapplied*. Rarely does overhead applied equal actual overhead in any given month or for an entire year.

A look at the formula for determining total normal applied overhead will provide insight. Total applied overhead is the predetermined overhead rate multiplied by actual activity:

$$\text{overhead applied} = \text{actual activity} \times \frac{\text{total budgeted overhead}}{\text{total budgeted activity}}$$

[7]Issues regarding such choices for allocations and when to exclude allocated costs from unit product costs are discussed in Chapters 4, 9, and 10.

EXHIBIT 5–3 Cost of Jobs—Manners Company

		J-5	F-1	F-2	Total
February costs:					
Direct materials, from Exhibit 5–2		$11,800	$ 9,600	$13,200	$34,600
Direct labor, from Exhibit 5–2		9,500	14,500	5,800	29,800
Overhead applied in February		5,763	10,080	4,557	20,400
Total costs for January		27,063	34,180	23,557	84,800
Plus costs in beginning inventory		6,500	0	0	6,500
Total accumulated costs		$33,563	$34,180	$23,557	$91,300
Overhead application, February					
Indirect labor and supplies:					
Direct labor hours		1,950	3,040	1,010	
Rate per DLH	$0.75	$1,463	$ 2,280	$ 757	$ 4,500
General plant:					
Machine hours		80	150	70	
Rate per MH	$50.00	$4,000	$ 7,500	$3,500	$15,000
Set up costs:					
Set ups		1	1	1	
Rate per set up	$300.00	$ 300	$ 300	$ 300	$ 900
Total overhead applied, February		$5,763	$10,080	$4,558	$20,400

Thus, if total budgeted activity equals total actual activity *and* total budgeted overhead equals total actual overhead, no overapplied or underapplied overhead will result. (It is also possible that differences would cancel out so there would be no under- or overapplication, but that is unlikely). However, it is not likely that accountants and other managers will make predictions right on the nose.

Consider the formula the Manners Company used for indirect labor and supplies: $20,000 + $0.50 per direct labor hour. For the year, the firm expects variable overhead costs for this cost pool to be $0.50 per direct labor hour. If this budgeted rate is also the actual rate, there will not be overapplied or underapplied *variable* overhead for this item, because total incurred variable overhead would be $0.50 multiplied by direct labor hours worked, and so would be the amount applied under normal costing. However, the same reasoning cannot be used for the fixed portion of this overhead cost; the firm does not expect to *incur* fixed indirect labor and supplies costs at $0.25 per hour, but expects it to *total* $20,000, regardless of the volume of activity. If the firm's expectations of cost and volume are realized, the average fixed overhead rate will be $0.25 per hour, but at any level of volume other than 80,000 direct labor hours, or cost different from $20,000, the average rate will differ from $0.25 per hour.

For example, consider the data below, which indicate the amounts of variable and fixed overhead *expected* to be incurred for this cost pool and to be applied at 75,000, 80,000, and 85,000 direct labor hours.

	75,000 hours	80,000 hours	85,000 hours
Variable overhead incurred at $0.50	$37,500	$40,000	$42,500
Variable overhead applied at $0.50	37,500	40,000	42,500
Over- or underapplied	0	0	0
Fixed overhead incurred	$20,000	$20,000	$20,000
Fixed overhead applied at $0.25	18,750	20,000	21,250
Over- or underapplied	($ 1,250)	0	$ 1,250

Overhead for an entire year can be overapplied or underapplied. We expect the same for each month, only more so because of conditions peculiar to individual months. First, even if budgeted volume for the year is achieved, it is unlikely that it will be spread evenly over all months. Most firms have seasonal patterns, with some busy and some slow months. Thus, during relatively slow months we would expect underapplied overhead, and during relatively busy months, overapplied overhead. Manners actually worked 6,000 direct labor hours in February, a bit below the average of 6,667 hours (80,000 hours/12 months).

Second, the fixed costs included in the budgeted annual amount will probably not be spread evenly over the year. Looking at some general overhead costs, heating bills will be higher than average during the winter; property taxes will be paid once per year; and heavy preventive maintenance programs might be carried out in one particular month. Various other factors will affect the pattern of monthly fixed costs, so these costs will probably not be level throughout the year. Manners has budgeted $20,000 for fixed overhead related to indirect labor and supplies for the year, an average of $1,667 per month ($20,000/12). Even if actual costs are about as budgeted, they will not be exactly $1,667 per month.

Some firms minimize the effects of uneven cost patterns by using accruals and deferrals. For example, you know from financial accounting that if an insurance premium is paid in January, it will be allocated on monthly income statements in equal amounts. The expense will appear evenly over the life of the policy. Similar action can occur with such costs as property taxes. If property taxes are paid in November, they might be accrued montly. Each month there is a debit to Overhead and a credit to Accrued Property Taxes. If accruals and deferrals are used, the result will be that monthly or quarterly overapplied and underapplied fixed overhead will relate primarily to activity, the denominator of the formula.

These two factors virtually guarantee that actual and applied overhead will differ. Fixed overhead often is the principal reason; actual variable overhead should be about the same as applied variable overhead if the budgeted variable overhead rate is reasonably close to the actual rate.

Managerial Analysis of Overhead

Complete analyses of variances between planned and actual results appear in Chapter 7. Here we make a few important points regarding overapplied and underapplied overhead.

In looking at overapplied or underapplied overhead, the manager should consider whether actual overhead was about the same as budgeted overhead for *the particular month*. We noted that some fixed costs are incurred unevenly. The firm's budgets are usually prepared by month and will reflect these patterns.[8] For example, the monthly budgets for overhead in the winter will reflect higher heating costs. If budgeted overhead cost for a month is about the same as the actual amount, the manager has some assurance that things are going more or less according to plan, even if a significant amount of overapplied or underapplied overhead occurs.

The second consideration is whether volume was about as expected for the month. The predetermined overhead rate is based on expected volume (activity) for the year, but the managers will probably have good ideas of expected monthly volumes as well. Therefore, if volume for a particular month is about as expected, though different from the monthly average, there is generally no cause for concern, despite overapplied or underapplied overhead.

Manners Company incurred overhead of $17,200 in February with the following breakdown of costs and activities:

	Costs	*Activity*
Indirect labor and supplies	$ 4,000	6,000 labor hours
General plant	12,000	300 machine hours
Set up costs	1,200	3 set ups
Total	$17,200	

General plant costs (virtually all fixed) are budgeted at $150,000 per year, or an average of $12,500 per month ($150,000/12). Suppose that budgeted fixed overhead for February was $14,000, higher than the $12,500 budgeted monthly average because of seasonal factors. Also suppose that the fixed portion of indirect labor and supplies costs is budgeted at $2,500 for February and the set up costs are expected to follow their average of $1,200 per month. Thus, the firm would expect overhead costs of $20,700 based on the following:

	Fixed		*Variable*		*Total*
Indirect labor and supplies	$ 2,500	+	($0.50 × 6,000)	=	$ 5,500
General plant	14,000				14,000
Set up costs	1,200				1,200
					$20,700

[8]Chapter 16 deals with cash budgets, where such details would appear.

Overhead, then, was somewhat less than expected ($17,200 versus $20,700), given activity in February and the budgeted fixed overhead in February.

The same kind of analysis can be made of the activities themselves. A comparison shows the following:

	Annual Activity	Monthly Average	Actual Activity	Difference
Indirect labor and supplies	80,000	6,667	6,000	−667 DLH
General plant	3,000	250	300	50 MH
Set ups	48	4	3	− 1

For each of these activities, the firm had some expectations for February. If managers had expected 7,000 direct labor hours, 350 machine hours, and 5 set ups (jobs), there might be some cause to worry because the shortfall might indicate that total demand for the firm's products for the year and, therefore, labor hours, machine hours, and set ups would be less than budgeted. However, if the expected activities were closer in aggregate to the actual activities for the month, then no concern is necessary.[9]

Actual Overhead Applications

Given that underapplied and overapplied overhead are inevitable consequences of the use of predetermined overhead rates, why not go ahead and use actual rates? We must consider the question in two parts, the first having to do with monthly or other interim-period results, the second having to do with an entire year.

If actual overhead costs were applied monthly, the rates would vary enormously for reasons that we have discussed, including fixed cost patterns and uneven activity in any of the measures a firm uses to set various overhead rates. Because job order firms often use costs for setting, or negotiating, prices, fluctuations in the overhead rates could cause confusion. If the rate per machine hour were to vary from $35 in January to $40 in February and to $55 in March, a manager trying to decide a price for a job to be done in April would be severely handicapped. Moreover, in months of relatively low activity the firm could show losses on jobs because of extremely high overhead rates.

Advocates of actual overhead costing might argue that it does cost more to operate a factory during cold months and that it does cost more per machine hour or direct labor to operate in months of low volume. Therefore, costs of jobs should reflect the changing conditions under which jobs are produced. Monthly variations in overhead rates are facts of life. The problem with this argument is that it focuses on short periods, rather than on a more reasonable period such as a year. Because the principal source of changes in actual overhead rates from month to month is fixed overhead costs, we can appeal to the

[9]We assume in this discussion that the three activities are somewhat dependent and will go up or down in relation to one another.

following examples to refute the actual-costing argument. Suppose that a manager decides to postpone working on a particular job from March to April because March has been fairly slow and the overhead rates will be fairly high, whereas April is expected to be busy and so the overhead rate will be low. Is work done the first week of April cheaper, as far as fixed overhead is concerned? Obviously not. The total work done in March and April combined would be the same whether the job was scheduled for March or April. Hence, to charge actual costs at fluctuating overhead rates per unit creates confusion and might encourage managers to behave unwisely.

Turning to the annual situation, most firms do end up applying actual overhead incurred to jobs worked on during the year as a whole. We shall illustrate this procedure shortly. However, even if firms convert from normal costing to actual costing for overhead, they still use a predetermined overhead during the year, rather than waiting until year-end to apply actual overhead to each job. The reason for doing so is that the predetermined rates should provide a reasonable estimate of the actual rates. The total amount of overapplied or underapplied overhead should not be too great at year-end unless unforeseen conditions upset the firm's plans.

During the year the firm's managers estimate costs and use them to set prices. They evaluate individual jobs to see whether they were profitable and, therefore, whether to accept similar jobs at similar prices in the future. These analyses cannot be put off until year-end; they must occur continually throughout the year. Predetermined rates are the best estimates of actual overhead rates for the year. Therefore, they are used to apply overhead costs to jobs during the year. If circumstances change, so that the budgeted overhead costs or activities or both are no longer expected, the predetermined rates might be changed to incorporate the new information. For example, if a firm receives a large order in May, it may revise its original estimates (budgets) of pounds of material, direct labor hours, machine hours, etc., as well as its overhead costs, and change the predetermined overhead rates to reflect the revised budgets.

Journal Entries and Accounts

Figure 4–1 on page 150 diagrams the general pattern of flows of costs. Companies acquire inputs (materials, direct labor, factory overhead), put these inputs into process, and as goods are completed, transfer the costs to Finished Goods Inventory. At the time of sale, the cost is transferred to Cost of Goods Sold.

This section provides journal entries and T-accounts that reflect the operations of Manners Company for February. Most of the data are from Exhibits 5–2 and 5–3. Other necessary data are added in the descriptions of each entry. The T-accounts summarizing the activities appear in Exhibit 5–4. The journal entries are numbered to provide easy reference to the T-accounts.

Purchase of Materials The firm bought materials costing $41,200 during February, all on account. The company had $6,300 in materials inventory at the beginning of the month.

EXHIBIT 5–4 Accounts for the Manners Company

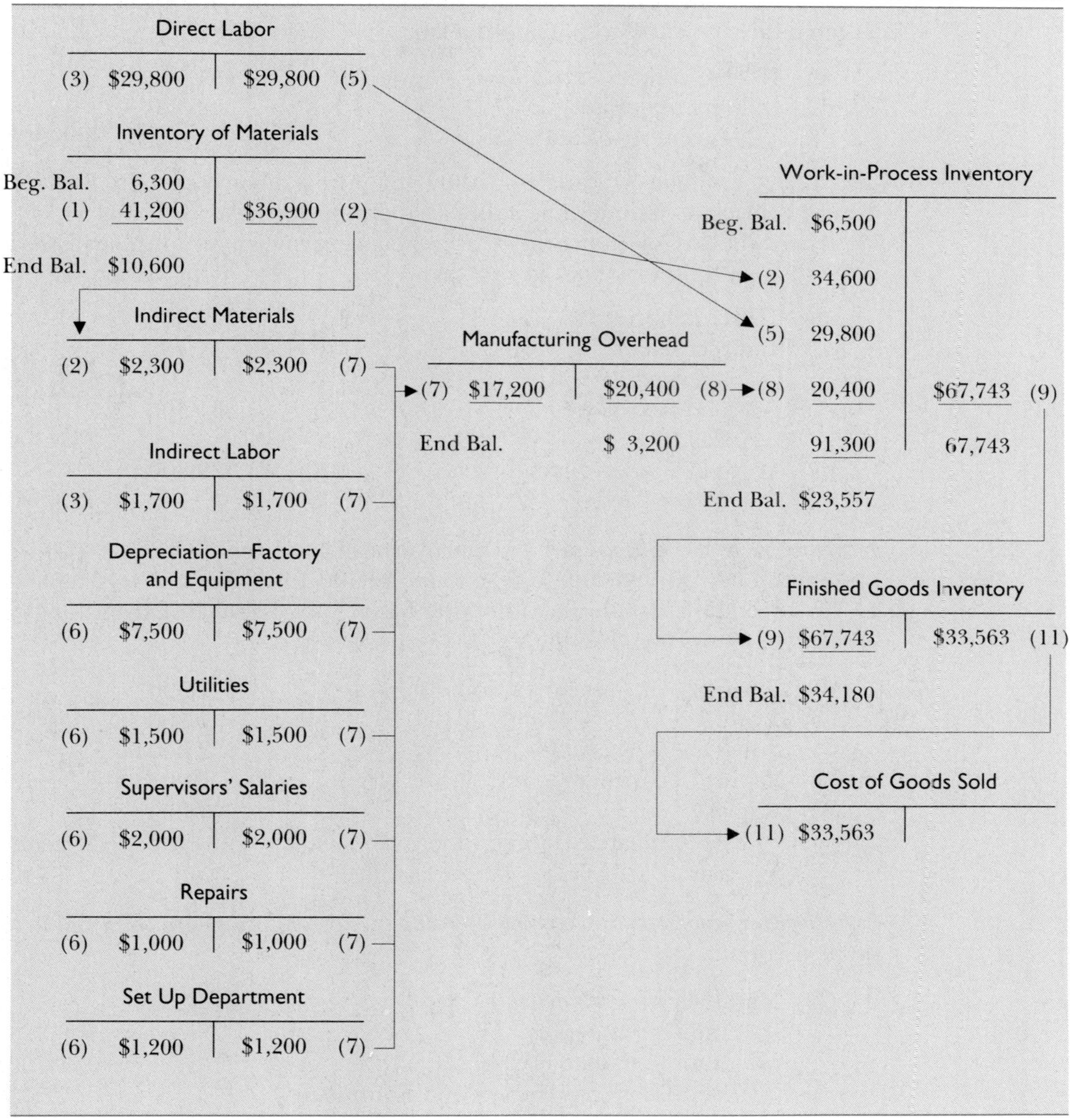

(1) Inventory of Materials	$41,200	
Accounts Payable		$41,200

When cash is paid, Accounts Payable is debited and cash credited.

Issue of Materials We know from Exhibits 5–2 and 5–3 that direct materials used during February cost $34,600. Assume that indirect materials (supplies, lubricants, abrasives, etc.) costing $2,300 were also issued. These indirect materials are part of overhead because they cannot be identified with any particular job or are too small to warrant tracking.

		Debit	Credit
(2)	Work-in-Process Inventory	$34,600	
	Indirect Materials	2,300	
	Inventory of Materials		$36,900

Labor Costs Exhibits 5–2 and 5–3 show that direct labor costs were $29,800 during February. Assume that indirect labor, an overhead cost, was $1,700. We record the payroll in two steps, accrual and payment. At this point, direct labor costs are put into Work in Process.

		Debit	Credit
(3)	Direct Labor	$29,800	
	Indirect Labor	1,700	
	Accrued Payroll		$31,500
(4)	Accrued Payroll	$31,500	
	Cash		$31,500
(5)	Work-in-Process Inventory	$29,800	
	Direct Labor		$29,800

Incurrence of Other Overhead Costs Actual overhead costs were $17,200. So far we have accounted for $4,000 of that total: $2,300 for indirect materials and $1,700 for indirect labor. The following figures are assumed. Except for depreciation, we assume that all the costs were paid in cash.

		Debit	Credit
(6)	Depreciation—Factory and Equipment	$ 7,500	
	Utilities	1,500	
	Supervisors' Salaries	2,000	
	Set up Department	1,200	
	Repairs	1,000	
	Accumulated Depreciation		$ 7,500
	Cash		5,700

Collecting Overhead Costs and Applying Overhead Overhead costs are collected in a single account.

		Debit	Credit
(7)	Manufacturing Overhead	$17,200	
	Indirect Materials		$ 2,300
	Indirect Labor		1,700
	Depreciation—Factory and Equipment		7,500
	Utilities		1,500
	Supervisors' Salaries		2,000
	Set up Department		1,200
	Repairs		1,000

The balance in Manufacturing Overhead is now $17,200. The entry in which to apply overhead at the various levels of activity and predetermined overhead rate (Exhibit 5–3) is:

(8) Work-in-Process Inventory	$20,400	
Manufacturing Overhead		$20,400

Completion of Jobs Jobs J-5 and F-1 were completed in February. The costs of these jobs (see Exhibit 5–3) must be transferred to Finished Goods in a total of $67,743 ($33,563 + $34,180).

(9) Finished Goods Inventory	$67,743	
Work-in-Process Inventory		$67,743

Sales Job J-5 was sold for $67,500 and F-1 remains on hand on February 28. Assume that the sale was for cash. Entry 11 records the cost of the job sold.

(10) Cash	$67,500	
Sales		$67,500
(11) Cost of Goods Sold	$33,563	
Finished Goods Inventory		$33,563

Selling and Administrative Expenses Finally, selling and administrative expenses for February, all paid in cash, were $22,300. For simplicity, we omit the detailed listing of individual expenses.

(12) Selling and Administrative Expenses	$22,300	
Cash		$22,300

We include entries 10 and 12, which are not concerned with manufacturing cost flows, to permit us to prepare the income statement shown in Exhibit 5–5.

Let us look closely at these entries. Entries 1, 3, 4, 6, and 12 are made more or less continuously throughout the period. They relate to purchasing materials, accruing and paying employees, recording overhead costs, and incurring and paying selling and administrative expenses. These activities are carried on continually during a period.

Entries 2, 5, 7, and 8 are made at the end of a period, such as a week or month, depending on how often the firm wants to update its records. These entries reclassify costs from their object categories to product costs—costs that are considered in the determination of inventory. Job order cost records might

EXHIBIT 5–5 Manners Company—Income Statement for February

Sales	$67,500
Cost of Sales (Job J-5)	33,563
Gross profit—normal	$33,937
Overapplied overhead	3,200
Gross profit	$37,137
Selling and administrative expenses	22,300
Income	$14,837

be more up to date than the Work-in-Process general ledger account during a given period, but at the end of the period both records should agree.

Trace the flows of costs through the accounts in Exhibit 5–4 to make sure that you understand them.

Disposition of Overapplied and Underapplied Overhead

At the end of a year, overapplied or underapplied overhead is disposed of in one of two ways. First, if the amount is relatively small, say less than 5 percent of total overhead, it might be included in cost of goods sold. Thus, if cost of goods sold including applied overhead were $2,355,500 and underapplied overhead were $2,500, the $2,500 would simply be added to cost of goods sold. In the same way, a small amount of overapplied overhead would be subtracted from cost of goods sold. Using this method, underapplied overhead is treated as a period cost, not as a product cost. Overapplied overhead is treated as a negative period cost.

Exhibit 5–5 shows overapplied overhead as an adjustment (negative expense), after gross profit calculated with normal cost of goods sold. This is a common treatment, especially for monthly income statements. An equivalent alternative is to show underapplied (or overapplied) overhead as part of cost of goods sold (income is the same with either treatment). Some accountants and managers prefer to see overapplied or underapplied overhead as a separate item, instead of buried in cost of goods sold, because it focuses attention on the effect on income.

If the amount of overapplied or underapplied overhead is relatively large, the usual procedure is to allocate it to Finished Goods Inventory, Work-in-Process Inventory, and Cost of Goods Sold in proportion to the amounts of *applied overhead* included in each of those categories. This procedure converts the firm to actual overhead costing. Exhibit 5–6 shows the procedure using Manners' data. Because there are three cost-pool-cost-driver combinations, each must be prorated separately. The details of this exhibit reveal that while both indirect labor and supplies and general plant were overapplied, set up costs were underapplied.

The principal reason to allocate overapplied or underapplied overhead and to go to an actual costing basis is that financial reporting requires that substantially all costs of manufacturing be included in the determination of inventory and cost of goods sold. If a firm has no inventories at the end of a year, all of its manufacturing costs including total actual overhead will show as an expense in the income statement, because they obviously cannot be included in inventory. Hence, the procedure shown in Exhibit 5–6 differs from a direct charge or credit to costs of goods sold only if there are relatively large inventories at year-end. Notice that the results in Exhibit 5–6 are the same as those obtained earlier when we used actual costing for Manners Company. This, of course, is what proration does—it converts normal costing to actual costing.

EXHIBIT 5–6 Manners Company—Proration of Overapplied Overhead

	Actual	*Normal*	*(Over)/ Underapplied*
Indirect labor and supplies	$ 4,000	$ 4,500	($ 500)
General plant	12,000	15,000	(3,000)
Set up costs	1,200	900	300
Total	$17,200	$20,400	($3,200)

Prorate over/underapplied overhead based on percentage of applied overhead in job to total applied overhead.

Amounts of applied overhead (Exhibit 5–3):

	Percentage of Total			
	J-5	*F-1*	*F-2*	*Total*
Indirect labor and supplies				
Applied overhead	$1,463	$2,280	$757	$4,500
Percent of total	32.50%	50.67%	16.83%	100.00%
General plant				
Applied overhead	$4,000	$7,500	$3,500	$15,000
Percent of total	26.67%	50.00%	23.33%	100.00%
Set up costs				
Applied overhead	$300	$300	$300	$900
Percent of total	33.33%	33.33%	33.33%	100.00%

Proration of overhead:

	J-5 Cost of Goods Sold	*F-1 Finished Goods*	*F-2 Work in Process*	*Total*
Proration:				
Normal cost	$33,563	$34,180	$23,557	$91,300
Prorated overapplied overhead (based on above percents)				
Indirect labor and supplies	(163)	(253)	(84)	(500)
General plant	(800)	(1,500)	(700)	(3,000)
Set up costs	100	100	100	300
Total costs including prorations	$32,700	$32,527	$22,873	$88,100
Actual cost	$32,700	$32,527	$22,873	$88,100

Where
proration of overhead is based on multiplying the percent of overhead costs applied to a job within a cost pool by the amount of over- or underapplied overhead in that pool. Thus, for indirect labor and supplies, Job J-5 received an allocation of 32.5 percent of ($500) of overapplied overhead.

A third treatment can be used at interim dates such as the ends of months or quarters: to show the amount of overapplied or underapplied overhead, respectively, as a current liability or current asset. Opinion 28 of the Accounting Principles Board recommends this treatment for interim reporting.[10] It is appropriate when the firm *expects* overapplied or underapplied overhead at the end of an interim period such as the first quarter or half of the year. An expected difference between applied and incurred overhead relates to either or both of the factors we have discussed—uneven incurrence of some fixed overhead items and uneven amounts of activity. For Manners Company, the income statement would not show the $3,200 overapplied overhead, thus lowering income by $3,200. Instead there would be a current liability of $3,200 on the February 28 balance sheet.

Departmental Overhead Rates

Manners Company used a single overhead rate for each cost pool. All labor hours and machine hours were assumed to contribute equally whether from fabrication, assembly, or some other department in the plant. (Set up costs seem limited to fabrication.) In the same way that cost pools and drivers are identified based on how resources are acquired and consumed, departmental differences can cause a subdivision of these pools and activity bases.

Many simple manufacturing accounting systems use a single plantwide rate based on a single cost driver. As we have discussed, this system is appropriate when resources are fairly homogeneous and the mix of products is simple. Even in this simple setting, at least two conditions encourage using departmental overhead rates. One is that different departments' overhead costs are associated with different measures of activity. The second condition is that even if overhead in all departments is related to the same activity, the *rates* might vary so much from department to department that a single rate might obscure important differences. Chapter 4 shows how this condition occurs when a single cost driver is used when multiple drivers are more appropriate. The above is an extension of that idea.

Review Problem

Exhibit 5–7 includes data for March, 19X9, for Manners Company. Based on these data,

1. Calculate job costs using actual costing for all jobs in March.
2. Calculate job costs using normal costing for all jobs in March.
3. Analyze overapplied and/or underapplied overhead to show how much is related to activity and how much is related to costs.

The results are shown in Exhibits 5–8, 5–9, and 5–10.

[10] Accounting Principles Board, *Opinion No. 28: Interim Financial Reporting* (New York: American Institute of Certified Public Accountants, 1973).

EXHIBIT 5–7 Review Problem (Data for March, 19X9— Manners Company)

	Jobs					
	F-2	*M-1*	*M-2*	*M-3*	*M-4*	*Total*
Direct materials used in March	$3,000	$14,000	$6,500	$7,000	$8,800	$39,300
Direct labor costs for March	1,800	12,000	5,000	4,000	11,200	34,000
Direct labor hours worked	375	2,500	1,100	1,100	1,925	7,000
Machine hours used	30	90	50	40	90	300
Machine set ups		1	1	1	1	4

Overhead incurred in March:

	Amount			
Cost Pool	*Fixed*	*Variable*	*Total*	*Cost Driver*
Indirect labor and supplies	$2,000	$3,500	$5,500	direct labor hours
General plant	15,000		15,000	machine hours
Machine set ups	1,200		1,200	number of set ups
			$21,700	

EXHIBIT 5–8 Review Problem (Manners Company— Actual Costing)

	Jobs					
	F-2	*M-1*	*M-2*	*M-3*	*M-4*	*Total*
Direct materials used in March	$3,000	$14,000	$6,500	$7,000	$8,800	$39,300
Direct labor costs for March	1,800	12,000	5,000	4,000	11,200	34,000
Actual overhead applied[a]						
Indirect labor and supplies	295	1,964	864	864	1,513	5,500
General plant	1,500	4,500	2,500	2,000	4,500	15,000
Set up costs	0	300	300	300	300	1,200
March costs	$6,595	$32,764	$15,164	$14,164	$26,313	$95,000
Beginning inventory[b]	22,873					22,873
Totals	$29,468	$32,764	$15,164	$14,164	$26,313	$117,873

Where

	Amount	*Activity*	*Application Rate*
[a]Indirect labor and supplies	$5,500	7,000	$0.7857 per labor hour
General plant	15,000	300	50.00 per machine hour
Set ups	1,200	4	300.00 per set up

[b]At actual costs (see Exhibit 5–6)

EXHIBIT 5–9 Review Problem (Manners Company— Normal Costing)

	Jobs					
	F-2	*M-1*	*M-2*	*M-3*	*M-4*	*Total*
Direct materials used in March	$3,000	$14,000	$6,500	$7,000	$8,800	$39,300
Direct labor costs for March	1,800	12,000	5,000	4,000	11,200	34,000
Normal overhead applied[a]						
Indirect labor and supplies	281	1,875	825	825	1,444	5,250
General plant	1,500	4,500	2,500	2,000	4,500	15,000
Set up costs	0	300	300	300	300	1,200
March costs	$6,581	$32,675	$15,125	$14,125	$26,244	$94,750
Beginning inventory[b]	22,873					22,873
Totals	$29,454	$32,675	$15,125	$14,125	$26,244	$117,623

Where

[a]Indirect labor and supplies applied at	$0.75 per labor hour
General factory applied at	$50.00 per machine hour
Set up costs applied at	$300.00 per set up

[b]At actual costs (see Exhibit 5–6)

The procedures for finding actual overhead rates are the same as for February. Earlier information shows the normal rates to use all during 19X9. The value of Job F-2 (in ending inventory from February) is shown at actual cost so that the answer in Exhibit 5–10 will not be clouded by activities or costs in February.

In March total overhead is underapplied by a total of $250. However, there is much offsetting of activity and cost, especially in general plant costs. Activity is higher than usual (50 hours) causing overapplication based on activity (50 times $50 per machine hour); costs were higher than a budget based on one-twelfth of total costs, causing underapplication based on costs. Higher activity in indirect labor and supplies and general factory costs leads to overapplication while higher costs in these same areas lead to underapplication. Combined (as in Exhibit 5–10), these two sources (activity and costs) yield a total of $250 underapplied. Exhibit 5–10 summarizes how the sources of overapplied and underapplied overhead can be traced. These sources have different meanings to managers, as we have discussed.

SOME REFINEMENTS AND ALTERNATIVES

Having looked at alternative ways of dealing with overapplied and underapplied overhead, we will now examine alternatives relating to other aspects of product costing.

EXHIBIT 5–10 Review Problem (Manners Company—Analysis of March Overhead)

Activity:

	Actual Activity	*Monthly Average*	*Difference*	
Indirect labor and supplies	7,000	6,667	333	DLH more than monthly average
General factory	300	250	50	MH more than monthly average
Set up costs	4	4	0	Set ups more than monthly average

Since activity for both indirect labor and supplies and for general factory overhead is more than the monthly average, overhead will be overapplied because of activity.

Costs:

	Actual Fixed	*Budgeted Fixed*	*Difference*	*Actual Variable*	*Budgeted Variable*	*Difference*	*Total Difference*
Indirect labor and supplies	$2,000	$1,667	$333	$3,500	$3,500	$0	$333 over budget
General factory	15,000	12,500	2,500				2,500 over budget
Set up costs	1,200	1,200	0				0

Since costs are over budget for indirect labor and supplies and for general factory overhead, overhead will be underapplied because actual costs exceeded budget.

Sources of overapplied and underapplied overhead:

	Activity	*Normal Rate*	*(Overapplied) Underapplied Overhead*
Activity sources			
Indirect labor and supplies	333	$0.25	($83)
General factory	50	$50.00	(2,500)
Set up costs	0	$300.00	0
Total (over)/underapplied overhead because of activity			($2,583)
Cost sources			
Indirect labor and supplies			$333
General factory			2,500
Set up costs			0
Total (over)/underapplied overhead because of cost			$2,833
Total underapplied overhead—March			$250

Check figures:

Actual March overhead	$21,700	Exhibits 5–7 and 5–8
Total applied overhead (normal costing)	21,450	Exhibit 5–9
Total underapplied overhead—March	$250	

Manufacturing Overhead Applied

Many firms use an account called Manufacturing Overhead Applied, which is credited for the amounts of overhead applied during a period. Manufacturing Overhead is debited for overhead costs incurred but not credited for amounts applied. The difference between the balances in these two accounts is the amount of overapplied or underapplied overhead. If Manners Company had used these two accounts in February, they would have appeared as follows at the end of February:

MANUFACTURING OVERHEAD		MANUFACTURING OVERHEAD APPLIED	
$17,200			$20,400

The difference between the two amounts is the overapplied overhead for February. At year-end, or whenever the accounts are to be closed, the balances in each account are offset by entries crediting Manufacturing Overhead and debiting Manufacturing Overhead Applied. If Manners had decided to close the overapplied overhead for February to cost of goods sold, it would have made this entry:

Manufacturing Overhead Applied	$20,400	
Manufacturing Overhead		$17,200
Cost of Goods Sold		3,200

Again, this refinement does not change the final results. Its purpose is to keep the major cost account for overhead directly related to actual costs. The balancing entry clearly shows that the $3,200 is overapplied overhead.

Review Problem

Assume that there was neither overapplied nor underapplied overhead for Manners Company in January. Also assume that the entry shown above was *not* made at the end of February; the company makes one entry for the quarter rather than monthly. What would the adjusting entry need to be at the end of March (quarterly adjustment for over- or underapplied overhead) if the total of overapplied or underapplied overhead were closed to cost of goods sold?

ANSWER TO REVIEW PROBLEM

February—overapplied overhead	$3,200	
March—underapplied overhead	−250	
Total adjustment	$2,950 overapplied	
Manufacturing Overhead Applied	$41,850	
Manufacturing Overhead		$38,900
Cost of Goods Sold		2,950

where actual and applied overhead figures are added over the two months (Exhibits 5–3, 5–7, and 5–9).

Labor and Overhead

We have seen that some labor costs such as indirect labor are considered overhead rather than direct labor. Direct labor costs charged to the Work-in-Process account are only those direct labor hours productively worked on specific jobs. Workers classified as direct laborers frequently will work more hours than they charge to individual jobs. If machines are being reset, or if materials have run out, or if some other temporary stoppage of work is experienced, direct laborers will be idle. The cost of idle time is often treated as an overhead cost.

If idle time is a necessary consequence of the production process and management decisions, it will be budgeted as overhead and included as an element of total overhead costs. For example, a firm might have a policy of providing a specified minimum number of hours for its work force. The policy might be based partly on the concern that frequent layoffs would result in skilled workers leaving the firm. It is reasonable to call such idle time a cost of the product produced and to include the costs as overhead.

When a firm does plan for and budget idle time, it will calculate its predetermined overhead rate based on the budgeted productive hours, rather than total budgeted hours. For example, if a firm expects total direct labor hours to be 100,000, with 5 percent idle time, it will use 95,000 hours in the denominator of a calculation where direct labor hours is the cost driver or chosen activity. It will also include 5 percent of expected direct labor cost as an overhead element.

However, if actual idle time is greater than budgeted, it might be considered an expense of the period on grounds that it does not contribute to the making of products and, therefore, should not be part of their cost. Thus, if idle time were caused by continual machine breakdowns, it may be considered an expense of the period and not part of overhead cost.

Overtime Premium

Overtime premium is the difference between the total wage rate paid for overtime work and the normal wage rate. A worker who normally receives $7 per hour receives $10.50 per hour working at time-and-a-half for overtime. Of that amount, $3.50 is the overtime premium. Overtime premium usually is considered an overhead cost, not part of direct labor cost. The reasoning is that overtime work is required because there is more work than can be done during normal working hours. This cost should be borne by all jobs, rather than just by the jobs worked on during the overtime period. For example, if Jobs A and B are worked on during a particular day, it really does not matter which was worked on during normal hours and which during overtime hours. If Job B is done during the overtime period, it should not be charged with the overtime premium, because the scheduling was likely arbitrary. To penalize Job B makes no economic sense.

The exception to the rule occurs if a rush order requires that the factory work overtime. Then, even if the rush order was worked on during normal hours, it might be charged with overtime premium because it was the cause of the overtime.

Departmental Accounts

Departmentalized job order firms might use separate accounts for direct labor and overhead costs for each department. They might have accounts such as Direct Labor—Assembly, Direct Labor—Fabrication, Depreciation—Assembly Department Equipment, and so on. Such accounts are helpful in analyzing overapplied or underapplied overhead by department when departmental rates are used for each cost pool. They are also helpful in controlling costs because they are identified with responsibility—the departmental cost accounts reflect the performance of the departmental manager.

The control aspect of departmental accounts can be achieved without using such accounts if labor and overhead costs are analyzed by department although recorded only in total. Many firms use what is called a *departmental cost sheet* or *departmental expense analysis*, which is essentially a supplementary record detailing costs by department. A manager who wishes to determine whether individual departments are staying within their established budgets uses these sheets.

Variable and Fixed Overhead Accounts

Planning, control, and decision making are enhanced by separating costs into fixed and variable components. Some firms use separate accounts for fixed and variable overhead. The basic procedures are the same, except that the individual overhead costs are gathered into one or the other account depending on their behavioral patterns. Two different rates are used to put overhead costs into Work in Process—a variable overhead rate and a fixed overhead rate. Each job has two entries associated with overhead. In the Manners Company example, for general plant costs the predetermined overhead rates were $0.25 per machine hour for fixed overhead and $0.50 per machine hour for variable overhead.

The advantage of using two overhead rates and accounts is that the managers might look at different jobs from the standpoint of contribution margin (or direct-cost-based margin) that they generate, rather than the so called profit, which includes allocated fixed costs. Decisions regarding pricing, accepting special orders, and subcontracting work are better made with information regarding cost behavior and traceability.

SUMMARY

Absorption costing, in which fixed manufacturing costs are assigned to units of product or specific jobs, is required for financial reporting and income tax accounting. Absorption costing is not compatible with cost-volume-profit analysis or with planning and control. It is useful and necessary in situations in which pricing depends on cost. However, since only manufacturing costs are included and other costs might be traceable to a product or job that are considered period costs in the financial accounting model, absorption costs may not be a true measure of the total costs of a product or job.

Firms that make unique products use job order costing, in which costs are accumulated by individual job. Direct materials and direct labor are charged to jobs as used. Manufacturing overhead is applied to jobs using predetermined rates based on the budgeted overhead for the period and on budgeted activity for that same period. Activity is defined by reference to an input factor, an output factor, or some other activity that best describes why resources were acquired and how they are used.

APPENDIX 5A: SOURCE DOCUMENTS IN JOB ORDER COSTING

This appendix describes and illustrates the procedures that underlie job order cost accounting systems. Chapter 5 stated that the basic document is the job order sheet, which details the costs of each job and serves as a subsidiary ledger to the Work-in-Process Inventory account. The principal documents that we will describe are the materials requisition and the work ticket, which are the references for the charges of materials and direct labor to individual jobs.

Because individual pieces of material and blocks of labor time must be charged to specific jobs, job order costing requires voluminous records. Therefore, job order systems are expensive to operate and subject to errors and deliberate deception. From a behavioral standpoint, any recording system that requires workers to specify the time spent on various tasks is open to deception. Consider a line manager in charge of three jobs, one of which is taking much more time than estimated, while the others are running well. She might be tempted to have workers charge some of their time spent on the problem job to the other jobs, so that the records would not draw attention to the slow-moving job.

Direct Materials

All materials, both direct and indirect, are generally stored in a central location. Workers needing materials for individual jobs go to the storeroom and pick up the required items. The issuance of materials is recorded on a requisition, such as the one shown in Figure 5A–1. Periodically the requisitions will be sorted by job and the job order sheets brought up to date. The sorted requisitions might be summarized on a worksheet called a Summary of Material Requisitions or Material Use Summary. This schedule would also serve to make the journal entry to record the issuance of materials.

FIGURE 5A–1 Materials Requisition Form and Material Use Summary

BINGHAM MANUFACTURING COMPANY

Material Requisition Requisition Number________

Date________ Department________ Job Number________

Quantity	Description	Cost	Total

Received by:______________ Approved:______________

Material Use Summary

Date	Requisition Number	Job Number	Description	Quantity	Cost

Direct Labor

Workers will fill out work tickets (also called job tickets, job time tickets, and time tickets) indicating the time spent on each job. Like material requisitions, these tickets will be summarized periodically and posted to the job order sheets, perhaps through the medium of a labor cost summary or labor cost recapitulation. Examples of these documents appear in Figure 5A–2.

In many job order firms, workers will indicate the time that they do *not* spend working on particular jobs. As it sometimes happens, there might not be enough work or workers must wait for materials or for machinists to set up

FIGURE 5A–2 Time Ticket and Direct Labor Summary

BINGHAM MANUFACTURING COMPANY

Time Ticket

Employee ______________ Hourly Rate ______________

Clock No. ______________ Date ______________

Department ______________ Job No. ______________

Operation ______________ Approved ______________

Time Started ______________

Time Finished ______________

Total Time ______________

Direct Labor Summary

Date	Ticket No.	Job No.	Department	Operation	Hours	Rate	Cost

or repair machinery. The total time worked on jobs, plus the idle time, should equal the total time for which workers are paid during a period. Making the reconciliation of the time tickets with the total hours that are paid should enable managers to determine whether all entries to the job order sheets have been made, although it will not prevent incorrect entries. For example, workers may charge the wrong job on their time tickets or a posting could be made to the wrong job order sheet. Again, the complexity and volume of job order records is one of the problems of that type of system. Therefore, management

FIGURE 5A–3 Summary of Cost Flows for Direct Materials and Direct Labor

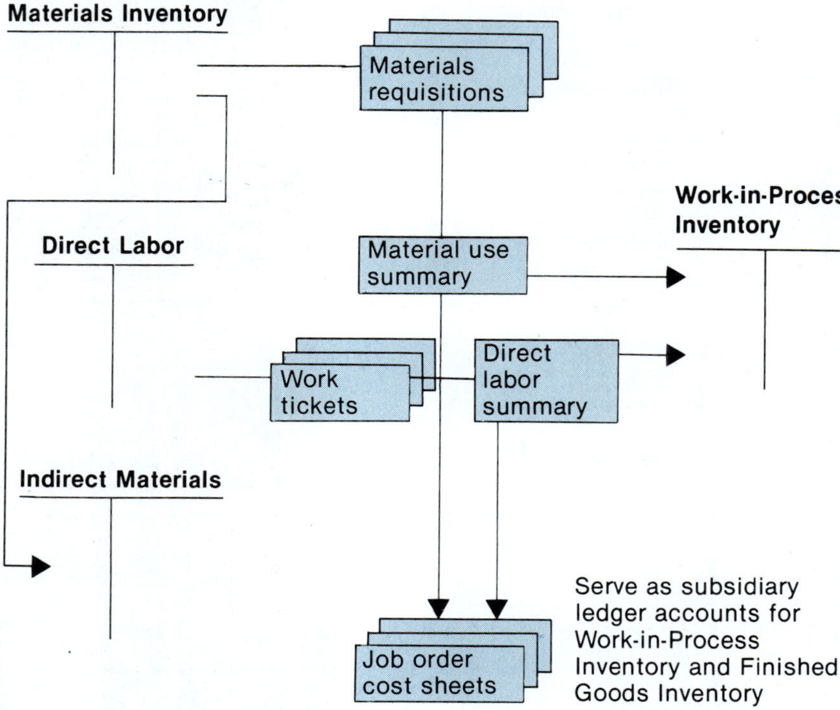

should ensure that there is a good internal auditing system so that records are accurate. Figure 5A–3 summarizes the cost flows and source documents for direct materials and direct labor.

ASSIGNMENTS

5–1 Actual Overhead Cost One of your classmates is puzzled at the use of predetermined overhead rates. Specifically, he askes you: "How is it possible to 'apply' overhead and still have correct figures? I learned in financial accounting that accounting is based on what has actually happened, so it seems to me that you should always use actual overhead costs."

REQUIRED

Answer your classmate's question.

5–2 Statement of Cost of Goods Manufactured and Sold Use the following information to prepare a statement of cost of goods manufactured and sold for the Cronin Company for the year ended June 30, 19X7. All data are in thousands of dollars.

Direct labor	$2,456
Purchases of materials	1,987
Inventory of materials, June 30, 19X7	171
Inventory of materials, July 1, 19X6	203
Inventory of finished goods, June 30, 19X7	451
Inventory of finished goods, July 1, 19X6	397
Factory overhead	3,124
Inventory of work in process, June 30, 19X7	96
Inventory of work in process, July 1, 19X6	102

5–3 Actual and Normal Costing For the question that follows, use language suitable to an average person who has not taken this course and, therefore, does not know any management or cost accounting terms or jargon to explain:

1. What is actual costing?
2. What is normal costing?
3. How are they the same?
4. How are they different?
5. What is the justification for each?

5–4 Basic Job Order Cost Flows The Nezperse Company makes a variety of industrial fittings to customer order and uses a job order costing system. The following information comes from the records of the firm.

	Materials	*Direct Labor*
Inventories at July 31, 19X6:		
Finished goods	$12,345	$21,541
Work in process	7,539	12,312
Cost put into process in August, 19X6	$70,634	$90,870
Inventories at August 31, 19X6:		
Finished goods	$11,235	$19,790
Work in process	4,560	11,290

The firm applies overhead at 150 percent of direct labor cost. Actual overhead for August was $128,978.

REQUIRED

1. Determine the total amounts of July 31 inventories of finished goods and work in process.
2. Determine ending inventories of finished goods and work in process.
3. Determine cost of goods sold for August, assuming that any overapplied or underapplied overhead is (a) deferred until year-end and so ignored in monthly income statements; (b) treated as an adjustment to cost of goods sold for the month; and (c) allocated to cost of sales and ending inventories based on the relative shares of overhead applied during the month. For part (c) assume that all beginning inventories of finished goods and work in process were sold during August.

5–5 Comparison of Actual and Normal Costing Boyett Company had the following activity in 19X7:

Sales	$980,000
Direct labor hours	24,000
Cost of materials used on jobs	$150,000
Direct labor cost at $10/hr	$240,000
Factory overhead costs	$276,000
Selling and administrative expenses	$160,000

Boyett had no beginning inventories. At year-end, jobs that were in ending inventories had the following:

Machine hours	2,800
Direct labor cost	$28,000
Material cost	$18,000

REQUIRED

1. Prepare an income statement for 19X7, assuming that Boyett uses actual costing and allocates overhead based on direct labor hours.
2. Prepare an income statement for 19X7, assuming that Boyett uses normal costing. The predetermined overhead rate is based on 25,000 expected machine hours and $275,000 budgeted overhead cost. Show any overapplied or underapplied overhead as an adjustment to normal cost of goods sold.

5–6 Activity-Based and Departmental Versus Plantwide Rates Robson Industries is a job order company with two production departments. Currently Robson uses a single plantwide overhead rate based on direct labor hours. Mr. Robson has asked you to show him how results would differ using departmental rates (still based on direct labor hours) and how they would differ if other bases were used to apply overhead instead of the current plantwide rate.

Expected results for 19X7 appear below.

	Department			
	Fabrication	*Assembly*	*Common*	*Total*
Factory overhead:				
Salaries, supplies, depreciation	$300,000	$100,000	$200,000	$ 600,000
Maintenance	40,000		50,000	90,000
Other	160,000	100,000	150,000	410,000
Total budgeted overhead	$500,000	$200,000	$400,000	$1,100,000
Activities:				
Total budgeted direct labor hours	40,000	50,000		
Total budgeted machine hours	60,000			
Total budgeted set ups	60			

About 75 percent of maintenance costs in fabrication relate to set ups. Fabrication overhead is traceable and is related to machine hours (MH).

Mr. Robson shows you the following data from a recent job. He asks you to illustrate various methods of dealing with overhead using this job as an example.

Job MC-1033:

	Costs	Activities
Materials	$22,000	
Direct labor		
Fabrication	$12,000	1,200 labor hours 2,000 machine hours 1 set up
Assembly	$7,400	740 labor hours

REQUIRED

You are a member of the accounting staff of this company and are to write a memo to Mr. Robson in which you:

1. Show in detail the costs of Job MC-1033 based on applying overhead using
   a. a single plantwide rate based on direct labor hours (DLH)
   b. separate departmental rates, each based on direct labor hours as well as applying common overhead based on a plantwide rate based on DLH
   c. various identified activity bases. Apply fabrication overhead (except for set up costs) based on machine hours (MH), set up costs based on number of set ups, and both assembly and common overhead based on DLH.

   Your schedules of costs should include supporting figures showing the various overhead rates per DLH, MH, and set up as appropriate.
2. Mr. Robson has asked you to analyze which of the three methods is most appropriate for his company. Your memorandum should include an analysis of each system, the strengths and weaknesses of each, and your recommendation based on your analysis. Use Appendix B as a guide.

5–7 Overhead Rates The following data are expected results for the Johnson Company, which manufactures plumbing supplies.

	Department I	Department II	Total
Budgeted overhead for 19X5	$220,000	$245,000	$465,000
Budgeted direct labor cost for 19X5	$ 55,000	$100,000	$155,000

During the year, the firm worked on a number of jobs. Data for two such jobs appear below.

	Job	
	K-65	M-42
Materials	$2,500	$3,800
Direct labor:		
Department I	6,000	2,000
Department II	1,000	8,000

REQUIRED

1. Compute the total cost of each job, assuming that the firm used a plantwide overhead rate that was predetermined using the budgeted data given above.

2. Compute the total cost of each job, assuming that the firm used departmental overhead rates, predetermined using the budgeted data given above.
3. Comment on the differences in your answers to parts 1 and 2. Is there any reason to favor one method or the other?

5–8 Relationships—Cost of Goods Manufactured and Sold Fill in the blanks of the following Statement of Cost of Goods Manufactured and Sold.

Direct Materials:		
Beginning inventory of materials	$ ____	
Purchases and freight in	3,269	
Ending inventory	185	
Cost of materials used in production		$ 3,277
Direct labor		6,325
Factory overhead		____
Total manufacturing costs		$12,423
Beginning inventory of work in process		1,210
Ending inventory of work in process		____
Cost of goods manufactured		12,356
Beginning inventory of finished goods		____
Ending inventory of finished goods		3,451
Cost of goods sold		$12,678

5–9 Straightforward Job Order Costing Alton Company manufactures various types of furniture. The following data relate to jobs worked on in August.

	Job Number		
	HG-11	*WS-14*	*CF-32*
Balance at August 1	$21,000	$ 0	$ 0
Materials added in August	12,400	9,850	4,670
August direct labor	12,800	13,200	21,700
August machine hours	1,920	1,980	3,250

The company applies overhead at $10 per machine hour. Actual overhead in August was $65,800. Job HG-11 was completed and sold for $115,500. Job WS-14 was completed but not shipped, and job CF-32 was incomplete.

REQUIRED

1. Determine the amount of overhead to be applied to each job.
2. Determine the total cost of each job.
3. Determine the ending inventories of work in process and of finished goods.
4. Determine the amount of overapplied or underapplied overhead.
5. Prepare an income statement for August. Selling and administrative expenses were $33,500. The company treats any overapplied or underapplied overhead as an adjustment to normal cost of sales.

5–10 Journal Entries and T-Accounts Using the information from Assignment 5–9, prepare journal entries and T-accounts to reflect August activity.

5–11 Activity-Based Costs Dwyer Company produces two products at its single plant in Wold, Missouri. Information from the accounting department about the two products includes the following for 19X9:

	Product 1	Product 2
Units	100,000	20,000
Price per unit	$150	$80
Material cost per unit	$ 25	$35
Labor (at $15 per hour)	0.4 hours	0.1 hours
Machine hours	0.6 hours	0.9 hours
Overhead	$3,246,000 total variable cost in 19X8	
	$5,200,000 fixed	
	42,000 labor hours worked in 19X8	
Selling and administrative expenses		
	$1,000,000 fixed plus $6 per unit variable	

Dwyer uses actual costing. Based on past experience, it uses direct labor hours as the basis for applying overhead to products. Its tax rate is 40 percent.

REQUIRED

1. Construct a traditional income statement with three columns: one for each product and one for the company as a whole. Selling and administrative expenses should be shown only in the company column, not by product.
2. During the end of 19X8, management decided to test whether direct labor hours were the best (and only) cost driver. After reviewing past records, they ran some simple linear regressions. Results are:

Regression 1:		Regression 2:		Regression 3:	
Plantwide Information		Cost Pool 1		Cost Pool 2	
Constant	$5,199,642	Constant	$5,000,243	Constant	$199,773
DLH	$0.0123	MH	$40.0121	DLH	$2.9979
r^2	0.23	r^2	0.87	r^2	0.81
s_b	$0.0111	s_b	$11.0678	s_b	$0.9837

where

DLH = direct labor hours; MH = machine hours

The same studies identified $75,000 in selling and administrative expenses that were attributable to Product 2. The analysis was based on the previous year since production and costs were the same as those expected this year. Management is deciding whether to use a single, plantwide rate based on direct labor hours or to use one rate for Cost Pool 1 and another rate for Cost Pool 2.

Is it reasonable to apply manufacturing overhead using direct labor hours as the single cost driver? Why or why not? If not, how would you apply manufacturing overhead? State your reasons clearly without using jargon.

3. Based on the decision you made in part 2 regarding applying overhead, construct an income statement with a column for each product and one for the company as a whole. Instead of a traditional income statement format, use a

contribution margin format. Do not allocate common costs to products; show them in the company column only. Round any information you use from the regressions above to the nearest thousand dollars for an intercept and the nearest dollar for a slope.

4. If managers based decisions on the traditional income statement you created in part 1, rather than the contribution margin type income statement in part 3, what problems might occur?

5–12 Actual Costing and Normal Costing The Rosen Company worked on three jobs in April of 19X6. Data on the jobs appear below.

	Job		
	97	98	99
Materials used	$12,500	$9,300	$25,300
Direct labor	11,900	8,500	13,600

The firm incurred factory overhead costs of $74,800.

REQUIRED

1. Determine the total cost of each job, assuming that the firm uses actual costing, allocating total incurred overhead to individual jobs based on the relative amounts of direct labor cost in each job.
2. Determine the total cost of each job, assuming that the firm uses normal costing, applying overhead cost to individual jobs at a predetermined rate of $2 per direct labor dollar.
3. Give two reasons why the overhead costs allocated to the jobs might have differed under parts 1 and 2.
4. Discuss the advantages and disadvantages of each of the two allocation methods used above.

5–13 Basic Entries Macon Enterprises has a job costing system based on actual costs. During January the following occurred:

1. Purchases of materials included 70,000 pounds of berium and 37,500 pounds of tedium for a total cost of $72,650. There was no beginning inventory of materials.
2. At the beginning of the month, work in process included two jobs totaling $14,000 in material and $23,000 in labor and overhead costs. During January $70,000 of new material was used along with $50,000 in direct labor, $26,000 in indirect labor and supplies, and $25,000 in fixed overhead. Ending inventory of work in process included $20,000 in material and $31,000 in labor and overhead.
3. There was no inventory of finished goods at either January 1 or January 31.

REQUIRED

Make the appropriate journal entries and T-accounts.

5–14 Basic Job Order Costing Richman Company makes components for special machinery used for bottling various liquids. Because each component differs in some respects from all others, the firm uses job order costing. The firm had the following jobs in process at March 31, 19X6. It applies overhead at $0.50 per material dollar, $1.50 per direct labor dollar, and $100 per set up, based on studies it had conducted to see the best relationships between costs and cost drivers. Each job requires one set up. There was no finished goods inventory in March.

Work in Process—March 31, 19X6:

	Job		
	3-12	*3-16*	*3-17*
Direct materials	$ 4,120	$ 3,875	$ 3,685
Direct labor	6,387	8,642	2,375
Overhead	11,741	15,001	5,505
Total costs	$22,248	$27,518	$11,565

During April, 19X6, the firm completed these three jobs and began several others. The materials and labor required to complete the jobs in process at March 31 were as follows (no additional set ups were required):

	Job		
	3-12	*3-16*	*3-17*
Direct materials	$1,820	$2,750	$6,140
Direct labor	1,530	1,956	5,110

The cost of all jobs *started and completed* in April (16 jobs) was:

Materials	$35,900
Direct labor	37,300
Applied overhead	75,510

At the end of April, the following jobs were in process:

	Job	
	4-13	*4-19*
Materials	$1,986	$6,945
Direct labor	2,890	8,985

Actual overhead incurred in April was:

April overhead	
Material related	$28,000
Labor related	89,000
Set ups	2,000
Total	$119,000

At April 30, jobs in the inventory of finished goods had these costs:

Costs of jobs in Finished Goods Inventory as of April 30:	
Materials	$13,996
Direct labor	6,228
Overhead	16,740
Total costs	$36,964

REQUIRED

Determine the ending inventory of work in process and cost of goods sold for April. Assume that overapplied or underapplied overhead is written off as an adjustment to cost of goods sold.

5–15 Normal Costing Relationships Fill in the blanks for each of the following independent cases. Assume normal costing with the predetermined overhead rate based on labor hours.

Predetermined Overhead Rate	*Total Budgeted Overhead*	*Total Budgeted Labor Hours*	*Total Actual Labor Hours*	*Overhead Applied*
___	$150,000	30,000	28,000	$ ___
$4	___	20,000	22,000	$ ___
___	$ 80,000	___	11,000	$ 88,000
$3	___	18,000	___	$ 45,000
$6	$120,000			$108,000

5–16 Journal Entries The Arcadia Company, a job order firm, began the month of October with the following balances:

Materials inventory	$22,435
Work-in-process inventory	67,492
Finished goods inventory	37,896

The following events occurred during October:

1. Materials purchases were $96,400.
2. Materials costing $91,200 were charged to jobs.
3. Direct labor incurred and charged to jobs was $241,360.
4. 5,500 machine hours were used on jobs.
5. The firm applied overhead to jobs as follows:

   material-related overhead: $1 per material dollar
   machine-hour-related overhead: $50 per machine hour

6. Actual overhead incurred was $347,500.

7. Jobs costing \$657,320 were completed and sent to finished goods storage.
8. Jobs costing \$622,480 were sold for \$987,600, all sales on credit.

REQUIRED

1. Prepare journal entries to record these events. The firm allows overapplied or underapplied overhead to accumulate in Factory Overhead until year-end (December 31). Do not write explanations for the entries.
2. Prepare T-accounts for the three inventory accounts and post the appropriate entries to them. Determine the ending balances in the inventory accounts.

5–17 Determine Material Costs (AICPA) Worrell Company uses job order costing, applying overhead at 90 percent of direct labor cost. The account for work-in-process inventory showed the following for March:

Beginning balance	\$ 12,000
Direct materials used	40,000
Direct labor used	30,000
Overhead applied	27,000
To finished goods	(100,000)

Job 232 is the only one in process at the end of March. It has applied overhead costs of \$2,250.

REQUIRED

Determine the direct material cost of Job 232 at the end of March.

5–18 Overhead Rates, Application, and Proration Hart Company manufactures pumping equipment. All pumps go through the fabrication and assembly departments, although different types spend different proportions of time in each department. The firm's cost accountant has developed the following equations for budgeting overhead for the coming year, 19X6:

$$\text{fabrication department overhead} = \$487{,}300 + \$9.62X_1$$
$$\text{assembly department overhead} = \$164{,}200 + \$4.21X_2$$

where

X_1 = machine hours in the fabrication department
X_2 = machine hours in the assembly department

Budgeted machine hours for 19X6 are 31,600 for fabrication and 17,650 for assembly.

At the end of 19X5 the firm had inventories of finished goods and work in process with \$45,225 in overhead from the fabrication department, \$22,105 from the assembly department.

During 19X6 the firm experienced the following:

	Fabrication	*Assembly*
Total machine hours	32,175	16,120
Machine hours on jobs:		
In ending inventory of finished goods	2,165	1,310
In ending inventory of work in process	1,720	880
Actual overhead costs	\$821,090	\$229,748

REQUIRED

1. Determine the overhead rates for the two departments, using the budgeted overhead costs and budgeted direct labor hours. Round to the nearest tenth of a cent.
2. Determine the amounts of applied overhead in each ending inventory and in cost of goods sold, and prorate each department's overapplied or underapplied overhead to the appropriate places. Determine the actual overhead costs in each ending inventory and in costs of goods sold.

5–19 Cost of Goods Manufactured (AICPA) Hamilton Company uses job order costing. It applies factory overhead at 150 percent of direct labor cost, writing off any overapplied or underapplied overhead to cost of sales at month-end. Job 101 was the only one in process at January 31. Its accumulated costs were

Direct materials	$4,000
Direct labor	2,000
Applied overhead	3,000
Total	$9,000

Hamilton started Jobs 102, 103, and 104 during February. It used $26,000 in direct materials and $20,000 in direct labor, and it incurred $32,000 in factory overhead. At February 29, the only job in process was 104, which had $2,800 in direct materials cost and $1,800 in direct labor.

REQUIRED

1. Determine cost of goods manufactured in February.
2. Determine the amount of overapplied or underapplied overhead for February.

5–20 Overhead Application (AICPA) Elliott Company manufactures tools to customer specifications. The following data pertain to Job 1501 for February.

Direct materials used	$4,200
Direct labor hours	300
Direct labor rate per hour	$ 8.00
Machine hours used	200
Predetermined overhead rate per machine hour	$15.00

REQUIRED

Determine the total cost recorded on Job 1501 in February.

5–21 Relationships The following fragmentary information is available from the records of the QL Company. All data relate to the year ended December 31, 19X8. The firm writes off any overapplied or underapplied overhead to cost of goods sold. The predetermined overhead rate is $2 per direct labor dollar.

Overhead incurred	$ ______
Overhead applied	$310,000
Beginning inventories:	
Materials	$ 88,000
Work in process	$110,000
Finished goods	$ ______

Ending inventories:	
Materials	$ 95,000
Work in process	$120,000
Finished goods	$104,000
Cost of goods sold, including $3,000 underapplied overhead	$644,000
Cost of goods manufactured, excluding any underapplied overhead	$ ____
Cost of materials put into process	$ ____
Purchases of materials	$207,000
Direct labor cost	$ ____

REQUIRED

Fill in the blanks, then check your work by preparing a statement of cost of goods manufactured and sold.

5–22 Dual Overhead Rates The controller of Pittston Industries, a job order manufacturing company, developed the following estimated overhead rates for the coming year:

Variable overhead rate	$7.20 per direct labor hour
Fixed overhead rate	5.60 per machine hour

The controller told the president that he wanted to apply variable and fixed overhead separately to give the firm's managers better information. The president said that she saw no benefits from the procedure and asked the controller why the current policy of using a single overhead rate based on labor hours should not be continued.

REQUIRED

Comment on the controller's proposal.

5–23 Overhead Application and Cost Control The Princeton Electronics Company makes a variety of equipment for industrial customers. The firm uses normal costing, applying overhead to individual jobs at a rate of $6 per direct labor hour. The variable component of the rate is $3.60. The fixed component of $2.40 is based on $288,000 annual budgeted fixed overhead and 120,000 annual budgeted direct labor hours. Fixed overhead is expected to fall evenly in each month of the year.

During the first three months of the year the firm's results were

	January	*February*	*March*
Actual variable overhead	$28,800	$34,000	$45,200
Actual fixed overhead	$22,000	$22,000	$26,000
Actual direct labor hours	8,000	10,000	12,000

REQUIRED

1. Determine the amounts of overapplied or underapplied overhead for each month.
2. Using the available information, comment on the causes of the overapplied or underapplied overhead. For example, were actual costs greater than budgeted

costs in any month? Was activity, expressed in direct labor hours, above or below normal levels in any month?

5–24 Updating Application Rates (CMA Adapted) Upton, Inc., manufactures a line of home furniture. The company's single manufacturing plant consists of the Cutting, Assembling, and Finishing Departments. Upton uses departmental rates for applying manufacturing overhead to production and maintains separate manufacturing overhead control and manufacturing overhead applied accounts for each of the production departments.

The following predetermined departmental manufacturing overhead rates were calculated for Upton's fiscal year ending May 31, 19X6.

Department	*Rate*
Cutting	$2.40 per machine hour
Assembly	5.00 per direct labor hour
Finishing	1.60 per direct labor dollar

Information regarding actual operations for Upton's plant for the six months ended November 30, 19X5, is presented below.

	Department		
	Cutting	*Assembly*	*Finishing*
Manufacturing overhead costs	$22,600	$56,800	$98,500
Machine hours	10,800	2,100	4,400
Direct labor hours	6,800	12,400	16,500
Direct labor dollars	$40,800	$62,000	$66,000

Based upon this experience and updated projections for the last six months of the fiscal year, Upton revised its operating budget. Projected data regarding manufacturing overhead and operating activity for each department for the six months ending May 31, 19X6, are presented below.

	Department		
	Cutting	*Assembly*	*Finishing*
Manufacturing overhead costs	$23,400	$57,500	$96,500
Machine hours	9,200	2,000	4,200
Direct labor hours	6,000	13,000	16,000
Direct labor dollars	$36,000	$65,000	$64,000

Diane Potter, Upton's Controller, plans to revise departmental manufacturing overhead applied accounts for each department through November 19X5 to recognize the revised application rates. The following analysis was prepared by Potter from general ledger account balances as of November 30, 19X5.
revised departmental application rates. She then plans to adjust the manufacturing overhead applied accounts for each department through November 19X5 to recognize the revised application rates. The following analysis was prepared by Potter from general ledger account balances as of November 30, 19X5.

Account	Direct Material	Direct Labor	Manufacturing Overhead	Account Balance
Work-in-process inventory	$ 53,000	$ 95,000	$ 12,000	$ 160,000
Finished goods	96,000	176,000	48,000	320,000
Cost of goods sold	336,000	604,000	180,000	1,120,000
	$485,000	$875,000	$240,000	$1,600,000

REQUIRED

1. Determine the balance of the manufacturing overhead applied accounts as of November 30, 19X5, before any revision for the:
   a. Cutting Department
   b. Assembly Department
   c. Finishing Department
2. Calculate the revised departmental manufacturing overhead rates that Upton, Inc., should use for the remainder of the fiscal year ending May 31, 19X6.
3. Prepare an analysis that shows how the manufacturing overhead applied account for each production department of Upton, Inc., should be adjusted as of November 30, 19X5, and prepare the adjusting entry to correct all general ledger accounts that are affected.

5–25 Actual Costing Barnes Company makes small measuring devices for industrial companies. Several of its products are relatively standard, including a pressure gauge, model YZ-361. The firm uses actual job order costing. At the end of each month a clerk divides total factory overhead incurred by total direct labor hours. He multiplies the overhead rate per labor hour by the number of hours on each job to determine overhead cost for the job.

The firm produced a lot of 50 units of YZ-361 in April, and another in July. The materials and labor for each 50-unit batch appear below.

	April Order	July Order
Materials	$680	$705
Direct labor at $8 per hour	760	736

Total factory overhead and direct labor hours were:

	April	July
Total factory overhead	$162,360	$152,440
Total direct labor hours	12,300	9,200

REQUIRED

1. Determine the total cost of each of the two batches of YZ-361.
2. Do the results of part 1 indicate that the firm was more or less efficient in April than in July? Why or why not? What other information would you need to give an opinion about efficiency?

5–26 Normal Costing Some results of the Barnes Company appeared in Assignment 5–25. Suppose now that the firm uses normal costing, with a predetermined overhead rate based on the following budgeted figures:

total annual budgeted overhead = $1,560,000 + $2.50 per direct labor hour
total budgeted direct labor hours = 120,000

The firm's chief cost accountant expects fixed overhead to be incurred about equally in each month, at $130,000. Direct labor hours fluctuate from month to month.

REQUIRED

1. Calculate the predetermined overhead rate from the data given above.
2. Determine the total costs of each of the two jobs described in Assignment 5–25.
3. Determine the amounts of overapplied or underapplied overhead for April and July.

5–27 Income Projections (CMA) Molid Company was founded by Mark Dalid three years ago. The company produces a modulation-demodulation unit (modem) for use with minicomputers and microcomputers. Business has expanded rapidly since the company's inception.

Bob Wells, the company's general accountant, prepared a budget for the fiscal year ending August 31, 19X6. The budget was based on the prior year's sales and production activity because Dalid believed that the sales growth experienced during the prior year would not continue at the same pace. The pro forma statements of income and cost of goods sold that were prepared as part of the budget process are presented below.

MOLID COMPANY
Pro Forma Statement of Income
For the Year Ending August 31, 19X6
($000 omitted)

Net sales		$31,248
Cost of goods sold		20,765
Gross profit		$10,483
Operating expenses:		
Marketing	$3,200	
General and administrative	2,200	5,400
Income from operations before income taxes		$ 5,083

MOLID COMPANY
Pro Forma Statement of Cost of Goods Sold
For the Year Ending August 31, 19X6
($000 omitted)

Direct materials:		
Materials inventory, 9/1/X5	$ 1,360	
Materials purchased	14,476	
Materials available for use	$15,836	
Materials inventory, 8/31/X6	1,628	
Direct materials consumed		$14,208

(continued)

Direct labor		1,134
Factory overhead		
Indirect materials	$ 1,421	
General factory overhead	3,240	4,661
Cost of goods manufactured		$20,003
Finished goods inventory, 9/1/X5		1,169
Cost of goods available for sale		$21,172
Finished goods inventory, 8/31/X6		407
Cost of goods sold		$20,765

On December 10, 19X5, Dalid and Wells met to discuss the first quarter operating results (i.e., results for the period September 1–November 30, 19X5). Wells believed that several changes should be made to the original budget assumptions that had been used to prepare the pro forma statements. Wells prepared the following notes that summarized the changes that did not become known until the first quarter results had been compiled. The following data was submitted to Dalid:

The estimated production in units for the fiscal year should be revised upward from 162,000 units to 170,000 units with the balance of production being scheduled in equal segments over the last nine months of the fiscal year. Actual first quarter production was 35,000 units.

The planned ending inventory for finished goods of 3,300 units at the end of the fiscal year remains unchanged. The finished goods inventory of 9,300 units as of September 1, 19X5, had dropped to 9,000 units by November 30, 19X5. The finished goods inventory at the end of the fiscal year will be valued at the average manufacturing cost for the year.

The direct labor rate will increase eight percent as of June 1, 19X6, as a consequence of a new labor agreement that was signed during the first quarter. When the original pro forma statements were prepared, the expected effective date for this new labor agreement had been September 1, 19X6.

Direct materials sufficient to produce 16,000 units were on hand at the beginning of the fiscal year. The plans for direct materials inventory to have the equivalent of 18,500 units of production at the end of the fiscal year remain unchanged. Direct materials inventory is valued on a first-in, first-out basis. Direct materials equivalent to 37,500 units of output were purchased for $3,300,000 during the first quarter of the fiscal year. Molid's suppliers have informed the company that direct material prices will increase five percent on March 1, 19X6. Direct materials needed for the rest of the fiscal year will be purchased evenly through the last nine months.

On the basis of historical data, indirect material cost is projected at ten percent of the cost of direct materials consumed.

One-half of general factory overhead and all of marketing and general and administrative expenses are considered fixed.

After an extended discussion, Dalid asked for new pro forma statements for the fiscal year ending August 31, 19X6.

REQUIRED

1. Based on the revised data presented by Bob Wells, calculate Molid Company's projected sales for the year ending August 31, 19X6, in:

a. number of units to be sold
b. dollar volume of net sales.

2. Prepare the pro forma statement of cost of goods sold for the year ending August 31, 19X6, that Mark Dalid requested.

5–28 Application of Overhead and Pricing Policy Winters Company makes industrial instruments and uses a job order costing system. Customers ask the firm to bid on machines of particular specifications, and Winters must be the lowest bidder to get the job. When the firm receives the specifications, an estimator develops an analysis of the material and labor requirements. He then applies overhead, based on direct labor hours, using the firm's predetermined rate. This analysis goes to the marketing manager, who sets a price, usually 125 percent of total expected production cost.

The firm has typically set its predetermined overhead rate based on direct labor hours at 80 percent of capacity. Capacity is about 400,000 hours per year. The president of the firm has told the controller that he should use 70 percent of capacity to set the rate for 19X6, arguing that, "We should absorb our overhead faster so that we can be more certain that we don't have a lot of underapplied overhead."

Budgeted overhead is $1.8 million fixed and about $1.80 variable with direct labor hours. The average wage rate is $10 per hour for direct laborers. The controller believes from prior experience that the cost of materials used is generally about 60 percent of direct labor cost. Selling and administrative expenses, virtually all fixed, are budgeted at $650,000. The firm has negligible inventories.

REQUIRED

1. Compute the predetermined overhead rate that the firm would use if it budgeted direct labor hours (a) at 80 percent of capacity and (b) at 70 percent of capacity.

2. Suppose that a particular job should take about 50 direct labor hours and that materials will be about 60 percent of labor cost. What would the price of the job be, using each of the two predetermined overhead rates that you calculated above and setting price at 125 percent of production cost?

3. Prepare income statements assuming (a) the firm uses 80 percent of capacity to set the overhead rate and also works at 80 percent of capacity, and (b) the firm sets the overhead rate using 70 percent of capacity and works at 70 percent of capacity. (Notice that there will be no overapplied or underapplied overhead, because actual hours will equal budgeted hours.) Assume the same relationships as in part 2.

4. Suppose that the firm will use 70 percent of capacity to set the predetermined overhead rate. How many hours must it actually work to earn the amount you calculated for 80 percent of capacity in part 3? Because there are no inventories, you can use volume-cost-profit analysis here.

5. Discuss the options for applying fixed overhead other than by direct labor hours. How should management decide a basis (or bases) for application?

6. What do you recommend?

5–29 Selecting Bases for Overhead Rates The managers of the Magill Furniture Company have been thinking about changing the bases that the firm uses to charge overhead to jobs. The firm currently uses a plantwide rate of $4 per direct labor hour but finds that it misapplies overhead by wide margins. One of the managers collected data from the past 24 months of operations and developed the following regression equations. Standard errors of the b coefficients are in parentheses. Y_t is total factory overhead; Y_1 and Y_2 are overhead in the fabrication and assembly departments, respectively; D_t, D_1, and D_2 are direct labor hours—total, fabrication, and assembly, respectively; and M_t, M_1, and M_2 are machine hours—total, fabrication, and assembly.

$$Y_t = \$789{,}542 + \underset{(\$0.97)}{\$1.27D_t}; \quad r^2 = 0.237; \quad S_e = \$203{,}245$$

$$Y_t = \$691{,}452 + \underset{(\$0.76)}{\$1.68M_t}; \quad r^2 = 0.452; \quad S_e = \$143{,}220$$

$$Y_1 = \$302{,}350 + \underset{(\$0.68)}{\$2.23D_1}; \quad r^2 = 0.593; \quad S_e = \$63{,}245$$

$$Y_1 = \$237{,}980 + \underset{(\$1.07)}{\$3.86M_1}; \quad r^2 = 0.708; \quad S_e = \$39{,}697$$

$$Y_2 = \$157{,}320 + \underset{(\$1.02)}{\$2.96D_2}; \quad r^2 = 0.672; \quad S_e = \$28{,}729$$

$$Y_2 = \$276{,}230 + \underset{(\$0.43)}{\$0.72M_2}; \quad r^2 = 0.302; \quad S_e = \$78{,}972$$

REQUIRED

Make recommendations to the managers regarding the overhead application rates.

5–30 Job Order Cost System (CMA Adapted) Constructo, Inc., is a manufacturer of furnishings for infants and children. The company uses a job order cost system and employs a full absorption accounting method for cost accumulation. Constructo's work-in-process inventory at April 30, 19X8 consisted of the following jobs.

Job No.	*Items*	*Units*	*Accumulated Cost*
CBS102	Cribs	20,000	$ 900,000
PLP086	Playpens	15,000	420,000
DRS114	Dressers	25,000	250,000
			$1,570,000

The company's finished goods inventory, which Constructo evaluates using the FIFO (first-in, first-out) method, consisted of five items.

Item	*Quantity and Unit Cost*	*Accumulated Cost*
Cribs	7,500 units @ $64 each	$ 480,000
Strollers	13,000 units @ $23 each	299,000
Carriages	11,200 units @ $102 each	1,142,400
Dressers	21,000 units @ $55 each	1,155,000
Playpens	19,400 units @ $35 each	679,000
		$3,755,400

Constructo applies factory overhead on the basis of direct labor hours. The company's factory overhead budget for the fiscal year ending May 31, 19X8, totals $4,500,000, and the company plans to expend 600,000 direct labor hours during this period. Through the first eleven months of the year, a total of 555,000 direct labor hours were worked, and total factory overhead amounted to $4,273,500.

At the end of April, the balance in Constructo's Materials Inventory account, which includes both raw materials and purchased parts, was $668,000. Additions to and requisitions from the materials inventory during the month of May included the following:

	Raw Materials	*Purchased Parts*
Additions	$242,000	$396,000
Requisitions:		
Job CBS102	51,000	104,000
Job PLP086	3,000	10,800
Job DRS114	124,000	87,000
Job STR077 (10,000 strollers)	62,000	81,000
Job CRG098 (5,000 carriages)	65,000	187,000

During May, Constructo's factory payroll consisted of:

Account	*Hours*	*Cost*
CBS102	12,000	$122,400
PLP086	4,400	43,200
DRS114	19,500	200,500
STR077	3,500	30,000
CRG098	14,000	138,000
Indirect	3,000	29,400
Supervision		57,600
		$621,100

Below are the jobs completed and the unit sales for May:

Job No.	*Items*	*Quantity Complete*
CBS102	Cribs	20,000
PLP086	Playpens	15,000
STR077	Strollers	10,000
CRG098	Carriages	5,000

Items	*Quantity Shipped*
Cribs	17,500
Playpens	21,000
Strollers	14,000
Dressers	18,000
Carriages	6,000

REQUIRED

1. Describe when it is appropriate for a company to use a job order cost system.
2. Calculate the dollar balance in Constructo's work-in-process inventory account as of May 31, 19X8.
3. Calculate the dollar amount related to the playpens in Constructo's finished goods inventory as of May 31, 19X8.

4. Explain the proper accounting treatment for overapplied or underapplied overhead balances when using a job order cost system.

5-31 CVP Analysis in a Job Order Firm Armand Forman operates a machine shop that does job order work for larger industrial firms. Forman has been trying to determine what profit he is likely to earn in 19X7 and has amassed the following data:

Expected material cost	$200,000
Expected direct labor hours	40,000
Direct labor wage rate, per hour	$ 9
Expected factory overhead at 40,000 labor hours	$400,000
Expected selling and administrative expenses	$120,000

Forman believes that factory overhead is about 60 percent fixed, 40 percent variable at the budgeted level of direct labor hours and that the variable portion changes closely with direct labor hours. Selling and administrative expenses appear to be virtually fixed. Forman plans to apply overhead to jobs at $10 per direct labor hour and to charge prices at 120 percent of factory cost (materials, direct labor, and *applied* overhead). He keeps minimal inventories.

REQUIRED

Answer each question independently.

1. What profit will Forman earn if all his predictions are correct?
2. What profit will he earn if he follows the pricing policy outlined above but is able to generate only 35,000 direct labor hours and $175,000 in material costs?
3. Based on the original assumptions, what markup over factory cost would give Forman a $100,000 profit?
4. Does the labor/material mix on Forman's jobs affect profitability? For example, would he earn the same profit on a job that required $2,000 in materials, $8,000 in direct labor, as he would on a job requiring $8,000 in materials, $2,000 in direct labor?

5-32 Overhead Rates and Profitability The following data relate to the March operations of Troy Foundry, Inc., which manufactures machinery.

	Department			
	Milling	Machining	Assembly	Total
Direct labor cost	$ 83,900	$225,000	$184,300	$493,200
Departmental overhead	230,400	379,600	147,600	757,600

The controller calculates an actual, plantwide overhead rate each month and uses that rate for costing jobs. He then reviews major jobs to see how profitable they were. The firm sets prices based on a gross profit objective of 20 percent of sales price. In working up prices, estimators use the most recent available overhead rate, which is usually the rate from the previous month.

After determining the March rate to be $1.5361 per labor dollar and costing out the jobs for the month, the controller analyzed profitability, working with the following two jobs.

	Job	
	M-12	*M-28*
Price	$163,000	$245,000
Materials	$ 17,100	$ 46,700
Direct labor:		
Milling	28,500	8,600
Machining	12,200	39,600
Assembly	4,800	17,300
Overhead at $1.5361 per labor dollar	69,893	100,615
Total costs	132,493	212,815
Gross profits	$ 30,507	$ 32,185

At the levels of operation in March, variable overhead as percentages of total departmental overhead were about 70, 75, and 20 percent in milling, machining, and assembly, respectively.

The controller noted that neither job showed the target gross profit and job M-28 was especially low.

REQUIRED

1. Calculate the contribution margin earned on each job.
2. Can you offer some reasons why jobs would not show the target gross profit under the system that the firm uses?
3. Would you make any suggestions to the controller? If so, what?

5–33 Job Order Costing, Service Business Grafton Associates is an engineering consulting firm employing forty professional engineers and ten office, clerical, and other support personnel. The firm treats each client as a job, preparing a cost sheet that records salaries, overhead, and expenses such as travel and lodging incurred by employees working in the field.

All employees fill out a weekly time report showing how much time they spent on a particular client's business and what expenses were incurred. The sheets also detail time spent on nonchargeable matters such as general administration or idle time between client engagements. The hourly cost of employee time is based on annual salary and a 2,000-hour working year, which is what the employees average. Phillip Grafton, the firm's owner, has instructed the clerks to apply overhead at the rate of 60 percent of salary cost.

Grafton has made the following estimates for the coming year, 19X6:

Salaries of professional staff	$1,188,000
Salaries of support personnel	121,000
Rent, utilities, and other costs not directly billable to clients	565,000

During the first week of January three employees worked on a job involving General Construction Company. Their time and expenses appear below.

Employee	*Hours on Client Business*	*Expenses*
Paul White	36	$360
Frederick DePrima	29	185
Ann Connor	22	0

White is a junior engineer earning \$23,500 per year. DePrima is a senior engineer earning \$38,200, and Connor a supervisor earning \$47,300. White's and DePrima's expenses related to travel they performed on behalf of the client.

Grafton bills clients for actual expenses (travel, etc.) and for twice the hourly salary cost of employees' work. He expects about 20 percent of the salaries of professional staff and 50 percent of salaries of support personnel to be nonchargeable and part of overhead. (The overhead of \$565,000 estimated for 19X6 does not include this salary cost. It is included in the salary figures for each category of employee given above.)

REQUIRED

1. Compute the cost of work done for General Corporation Company in the first week of January, using the firm's methods.
2. Determine the amount that Grafton will bill General.
3. Determine whether Grafton is likely to overapply or underapply overhead during 19X6.
4. What profit can Grafton expect for 19X6?
5. What overhead rate would Grafton have to use to fully apply overhead costs, including nonchargeable time?

5–34 Overhead Rates Warner Company makes three products in three departments. It bases its prices on costs, as the schedule below shows.

	Product		
	A	B	C
Direct materials	\$ 10.00	\$ 30.00	\$ 50.00
Direct labor at \$8/hr	40.00	48.00	88.00
Overhead at \$7.80/DLH	39.00	46.80	85.80
Total cost	89.00	124.80	223.80
Allowance for profit at 15% of cost	13.35	18.72	33.57
Selling price	\$102.35	\$143.52	\$257.37
Labor time required (hr/unit):			
Department I	0	4	2
Department II	1	0	6
Department III	4	2	3

The overhead rate of \$7.80 was based on total estimated overhead and total estimated direct labor hours. Data by department are

	Department		
	I	*II*	*III*
Variable overhead per DLH	\$ 7.10	\$ 4.10	\$ 2.80
Fixed overhead per year	\$300,000	\$280,000	\$171,000

The firm planned to produce 10,000 units of each product during the current year.

REQUIRED

1. Verify the \$7.80 overhead rate by determining total estimated direct labor hours and total estimated overhead costs.

2. Develop overhead rates for each department and redo the pricing analysis, using the departmental overhead rates to apply overhead. Are the differences between the prices you determine and the ones given above significant? Why?
3. What other suggestions do you have for developing a more accurate pricing analysis?

5–35 Overhead Rates Tom Kowalski was a Certified Public Accountant in practice in a suburb of Los Angeles. One day he received a telephone call from Arnold McEwen, the controller of Newhart Manufacturing Company. McEwen wanted to engage Kowalski to look at the firm's cost accounting system with a view to suggesting improvements. He said that a friend who was a controller at another company had recommended Kowalski. After further discussion, Kowalski accepted the job.

Kowalski spent several days familiarizing himself with the company's operations and accounting system. The firm had begun as a small machine shop doing specialty work for aircraft companies in southern California. It had grown steadily through branching out into various types of work but had kept its technological basis by concentrating on the basic metalworking operations of cutting, grinding, stamping, and machining. For example, the firm now makes such products as fireplace screens, lamp parts, grates, and metal components of other products.

Most products were made to customer specifications, although occasionally the firm's salespeople were able to persuade customers to accept one of the more standard products that the firm made more or less continually. These standard items accounted for about 30 percent of revenue, which currently totaled about $9 million annually.

The firm used a job order costing system. Each job was charged with actual material and direct labor costs. Overhead was applied to jobs on the basis of direct labor cost. A predetermined rate was developed quarterly. Toward the end of each quarter McEwen and Richard Winchell, the production manager, developed estimates of direct labor cost and factory overhead for the following quarter. The rate used in the next quarter was estimated overhead for the quarter divided by estimated directed labor cost. McEwen and Winchell usually developed the rate two or three weeks before the quarter began.

McEwen explained to Kowalski that the quarterly rate was used because there was some seasonality in operations and the managers liked to have cost data that were as current as possible.

The costs developed for each job were used for inventory valuation and for analyzing the profitability of individual jobs. Additionally, costs were the principal basis for pricing on nonstandard jobs. Salespeople could quote prices on standard work, but on nonstandard items a cost estimator worked up the costs. Winchell and Frank Stein, the sales manager, usually looked at the estimates for large jobs but not small ones (under $500). The general pricing rule was to charge 125 percent of total estimated cost, but this rule was sometimes broken. For example, customers often told salespeople what they thought a fair price was, based on bids from other firms or on work done by Newhart in the past. When the price determined by the formula was significantly different from the fair price suggested by the customer, Winchell and Stein usually made adjustments toward the fair price. These adjustments generally brought the quoted price to within 6 to 10 percent of the fair price.

Other times, Winchell and Stein concluded that a lower price than provided by the formula would be appropriate to get a foot in the door of a new customer. In a few cases they raised the price to discourage business that promised to be difficult or that was offered by a slow-paying customer.

Kowalski came to two major conclusions. He believed that departmental overhead rates should be used instead of the plantwide rate currently in effect. He also thought that the rates should be developed on an annual basis, not quarterly.

Kowalski used the firm's existing cost records to see whether his first proposal would be feasible. He found that he could trace over 70 percent of total overhead costs to individual departments. Such items as supervision were easily traced to specific departments, because supervisors worked only in one department. Similarly, depreciation on factory equipment, most supplies and indirect labor, and most maintenance were also clearly associated with individual departments.

Kowalski could not trace such costs as utilities, depreciation and property taxes on the factory building, and support services such as accounting, engineering, personnel, and general factory administration to individual departments. He decided to allocate these costs to departments on bases that seemed reasonable. He allocated costs related to the factory building on the basis of square feet in each department, costs related to personnel and general administration on the basis of direct labor cost in each department, and so on. He then prepared the analysis shown in Exhibit 5–11.

The response to Kowalski's proposals was generally unfavorable. No one favored the abandonment of the quarterly rate in favor of annual rates. Only two departmental supervisors favored the use of departmental rates over a single plantwide rate. The comments that appear below are typical of those that Kowalski received.

RICHARD WINCHELL, PRODUCTION MANAGER: I don't like either proposal. First, the idea of annual rates is bad. We can't budget that far in advance, and even if we could I wouldn't favor annual rates. We need up-to-date cost information for control and pricing. As we operate now, we know fairly soon whether the rate is correct or not. We generally have fairly substantial differences between the actual rate and predetermined rate, but if we did it annually we wouldn't know for a full year whether the rate or rates were correct.

Our costs change from quarter to quarter, and so does our labor. We have to reflect different conditions in our pricing policies. For example, our overhead in the winter is heavy because of heating, property taxes (paid in January), and preventive maintenance. You are telling us that we should lose money in the winter and try to make it up in the summer, which is crazy.

Second, the idea of departmental rates leaves me cold. It would involve much more work and would not give us better information. We run a plant, not a group of departments. We have to cover all costs, not just the costs you say are related to individual departments. What are we supposed to do if one department's business falls off? Shut it down? The plantwide rate recognizes that every department has to contribute to the total picture, not just to its own benefit.

FRANK STEIN, SALES MANAGER: I am opposed to the departmental rates for a couple of reasons. First, I've always thought allocating costs wasn't a good idea, and that is exactly what you propose when you throw in building depreciation, general administration, and so on. These costs aren't really associated with any department. If business falls off in, say, the grinding department, you won't lay off any payroll clerks, nor will you save the depreciation on building space that grinding occupies. Your allocations are arbitrary and do not reflect the true costs of the departments. We could play around with your methods of allocation and get different rates from the ones you developed. So why go through all of this business when all it will do is add to the costs of accounting and upset the departmental managers? I assume that you would start using the data for evaluating the performance of departmental supervisors, and the allocated costs in there would have nothing to do with whether they were operating efficiently or not.

EXHIBIT 5–11 Kowalski's Memorandum

I have two major recommendations: first, that the firm develop predetermined overhead rates by department, rather than plantwide; second, that these rates be developed annually, instead of quarterly. I have prepared the following material in support of my recommendations.

Effects of Departmental Rates

The following analysis is based on an average quarter's activities.

Department	*Direct Overhead Costs*	*Allocated Costs*	*Total Costs*	*Labor Costs*	*Overhead Rate*
Cutting	$ 73,400	$ 22,300	$ 95,700	$ 46,500	$2.058
Grinding	104,200	37,400	141,600	31,500	4.495
Stamping	98,400	34,200	132,600	21,700	6.111
Machining	67,900	28,600	96,500	40,700	2.371
Totals	$343,900	$122,500	$466,400	$140,400	

The plantwide rate would be $3.322 ($466,400/$140,400) per direct labor dollar.

As you can see, the plantwide rate does not reflect the true picture because it ignores differences among the departments. Adopting departmental rates would make for better pricing and analyses of profitability.

Annual Rates Versus Quarterly Rates

Quarterly rates (plantwide) in the past few quarters have ranged from $4.156 down to $2.978 because of differences in total labor costs and seasonal fluctuations in some elements of overhead. Accordingly, prices are set too high in some quarters, too low in others. Confusion results and both management and customers are misled. The year is the basic accounting period, and setting overhead rates annually in advance would further the objectives of making the data more relevant for decision making and control.

I welcome your comments. This memo is only a first step based on preliminary analysis. I shall prepare a more complete report after conferring with interested parties.

REQUIRED

Write a formal memorandum to management, using a microcomputer and a word processing program along with a spreadsheet program for supporting schedules. See Appendix B for guidelines for memoranda presentation.

In this situation, you are a consultant who has been hired by McEwen. Since there is a controversy regarding Kowalski's report, McEwen thought an independent voice might help. You are to address your memorandum to McEwen. Your task is to make recommendations regarding Kowalski's suggestions that the company move to departmental overhead rates established on an annual basis.

1. In your analysis and discussion, use the following two jobs as examples to illustrate the difference between plantwide and departmental overhead rates shown in Kowalski's memo. Each job requires $1,000 in materials.

Department	*Required Direct Labor Hours*	*Hourly Labor Rate*	*Total Labor Cost*
Job L-4757:			
Cutting	132	$5.50	$ 726.00
Grinding	43	5.20	223.60
Machining	38	6.80	258.40
Totals	213		$1,208.00
Job Q-1906:			
Cutting	35	5.50	$ 192.50
Grinding	29	5.20	150.80
Stamping	51	7.20	367.20
Machining	18	6.80	122.40
Totals	133		$ 832.90

Show what product costs would be using (a) a plantwide rate and (b) departmental rates.

2. Explain why there are differences in overhead costs between the two methods. Are these differences significant in this case?
3. Make sure you not only deal with Kowalski's proposals, but also respond directly to the criticisms of Winchell and Stein. If you can suggest improvements, do so.
4. Discuss how your analysis of Kowalski's suggestions would change if you learned that (a) factory overhead was nearly all fixed and (b) factory overhead was nearly all variable.

5–36 Overhead Application and Ethics (CMA Adapted) Tom Savin has recently been hired as a cost accountant by the Offset Press Company, a privately held company that produces a line of offset printing presses and lithograph machines. During his first few months on the job, Savin discovered that Offset has been underapplying factory overhead to the work-in-process account, while overstating expense through the general and administrative account. This practice has been going on since the start of the company, which is in its sixth year. The effect in each year has been favorable, having a material impact on the company's tax position. No internal audit function exists at Offset, and the external auditors have not yet discovered the underapplied factory overhead.

Before the sixth year audit, Savin pointed out the practice and its effect to Mary Brown, the corporate controller, and asked her to let him make the necessary adjustments. Brown directed him not to make the adjustments but to wait until the external auditors had completed their work and see what they uncovered.

The sixth year audit has now been completed, and the external auditors have once more failed to discover the underapplication of factory overhead. Savin again asked Brown if he could make the required adjustments and was again told not to make them. Savin, however, believes that the adjustments should be made and that the external auditors should be informed of the situation.

Since there are no established policies at Offset Press Company for resolving ethical conflicts, Savin is considering one of the following alternative courses of action.

1. Follow Brown's directive and do nothing further.
2. Attempt to convince Brown to make the proper adjustments and to advise the external auditors of her actions.
3. Tell the Audit Committee of the Board of Directors about the problem and give them the appropriate accounting data.

REQUIRED

1. For each of the alternative courses of action that Tom Savin is considering, explain whether or not the action is appropriate. Refer to specific standards of **Statements on Management Accounting Number 1C** (**SMA 1C**), "Standards of Ethical Conduct for Management Accountants," to support your answer.
2. Without prejudice to your answer in part 1, assume that Savin again approaches Brown to make the necessary adjustments and is unsuccessful. Describe the steps that Savin should take in proceeding to resolve this situation. Use **SMA 1C** to support your answer.

6

PRODUCT COSTING: FINANCIAL ACCOUNTING II

Firms use job order costing when they make more than one kind of product. With different products, which use different amounts of resources, the notion of a single unit cost for all products is meaningless. Firms that make the same product more or less continuously, however, can use some form of process costing. While job order costing captures information regarding a particular job (or batch) regardless of the time needed to produce it, process costing focuses on a time period. **Process costing** calculates the average unit cost of production over a period, usually a month. Some basic concepts involved in process costing are useful in job order costing, as we will discuss below. Process costing systems can be found in companies that produce bricks, flour, cement, sugar, some bulk chemicals, and other products for which the units are homogeneous.

This chapter begins with a simple case where a simple unit cost includes materials, labor, and overhead. From there we divide costs into pools as Chapters 4 and 5 illustrated; materials will be separated from labor and overhead and we will apply overhead based on direct labor. The next stage incorporates expanded cost pools and cost drivers. Finally, we incorporate the notion of spoilage and unit costs. The illustrations in this chapter apply equally to actual costing and normal costing. Chapter 5 described the difference between these methods; actual costing uses actual costs for all productive inputs, while normal costing uses actual material and direct labor costs but applies overhead based on predetermined rates.

DETERMINING PRODUCTION

To find unit cost for a product for a month, the numerator is cost and the denominator is unit production. The basic difficulties of process costing are determining the denominator in this basic formula and coupling these units with an appropriate numerator. In the discussion of job order costing, we noted in our illustrations that certain jobs are incomplete as a period starts (as reflected in beginning inventory of Work in Process); these jobs are normally completed in the next period. Costs associated with them are transferred to Finished Goods Inventory (and possibly to Cost of Goods Sold). Other jobs are both started and completed in one period. Again, the costs of these jobs are moved into Finished Goods Inventory and Cost of Goods Sold as appropriate. Finally, we showed that some jobs are started, but remain incomplete at the end of a period; the costs of these jobs end up in ending inventory of Work in Process.

Since we identify specific jobs and record costs for each job separately, it is not difficult in job order costing to know the value of beginning or ending inventories of Work in Process or the value of jobs that are complete and in Finished Goods (or that have been sold). With a single, homogeneous product, we are also concerned with goods in beginning and ending inventories of work in process and the costs of goods moved to Finished Goods; however, costs are not tracked by specific job, and we must find out how many units were produced to determine unit costs.

The problem arises with Work-in-Process Inventory and the units in work in process. Units in process at the beginning and at the end of a period are by definition less than complete. (Were they complete, they would be in finished goods inventory.) Thus, a company could have 2,000 units that are 40 percent complete or 11,000 units 75 percent complete or any combination of units and percentages of completion. To have a meaningful figure in the denominator of a cost-per-unit formula, we must express these partly completed units in a common form.

We accomplish this expression by using the concept of **equivalent unit production** or **equivalent production**. The meaning of equivalent production is clear from the following example. If a firm has 3,000 units on hand that are 40 percent complete, we can say that it has the equivalent of 1,200 complete units (3,000 × 40%). We are saying that the firm could have completed 1,200 units in the same time required to do 40 percent of the work on 3,000 units.[1] This is the essence of the equivalent production concept, but it is not always so easy to apply.

[1] While this work may not be technically feasible in all cases, the concept is appropriate in the context of finding equivalent units of production.

If all inputs for production (material, labor, various types of overhead) were used in direct relation to one another, few problems would occur. However, these inputs may be used unevenly. Thus, while all the materials for some products may have been issued, perhaps only half of the machine time needed to complete the units has been expended. Consider, for example, the manufacture of bricks. Bricks are made of clay and straw mixed together and formed into desired shapes and sizes and baked in kilns. Thus, when the bricks are ready for the kilns, they are complete so far as materials are concerned; no more materials and no more material costs are required. The bricks are incomplete only insofar as the costs associated with the kiln time required to finish them. Suppose that a firm had two million bricks ready for the kilns and that the labor and overhead costs associated with baking the bricks are 25 percent of the total labor and overhead cost. These bricks are 100 percent complete with respect to materials and 75 percent complete with respect to labor and overhead. As we shall see, we must therefore calculate unit costs separately for each cost factor. That is, in this example, we must calculate a cost per unit for materials and a separate cost per unit for direct labor and overhead costs. Different levels of completion lead to different equivalent units of production; thus, the denominator changes in calculating unit costs.

Taken together, labor and overhead costs are called **conversion costs**, the costs of converting materials into finished products. In a simple cost setting where overhead is a function of labor cost or labor hours, we can combine labor and overhead into one cost pool and one level of completion. If there were more cost pools (overhead was either not related to labor or related to more factors than labor) and products were at different stages of completion based on the cost drivers used for these pools, we would have to break conversion costs into more than one cost per unit; the denominators would be different for each cost pool.

Another factor in the determination of equivalent production is the work in process **cost flow assumption**, which is usually either weighted average or first-in-first-out (FIFO). The cost flow assumption primarily affects whether the beginning inventory of Work in Process is used in unit cost calculations. Each cost flow assumption requires us to look at a proper pairing of costs and equivalent production.

EQUIVALENT UNIT PRODUCTION

The first example of process costing is a factory that operates a single process, where all costs are incurred evenly (i.e., if a product is 50 percent complete for one input factor, it is 50 percent complete for all input factors). You recall from previous accounting courses that the weighted average inventory method for a merchandising company uses the form:

$$\text{unit cost} = \frac{(\text{cost of beginning inventory} + \text{dollar purchases})}{(\text{units in beginning inventory} + \text{units purchased})}$$

That is, the weighted average method combines current period purchases, both units and dollars, with the beginning inventory, both units and dollars. In process costing, that general relationship also holds, but with weighted average equivalent unit production substituted in the denominator and the current period production costs substituted for purchases in the numerator.

The FIFO method for determining unit cost for a merchandising company, provided that the company paid the same price for all units bought during a period, is:

$$\text{unit cost} = \frac{\text{dollar purchases}}{\text{units purchased}}$$

The FIFO method uses only current period activity in both units and cost. In process costing we substitute current period production costs for purchases in the numerator and FIFO equivalent unit production for units purchased in the denominator. We will see that FIFO equivalent unit production represents the work done in the current period. You should recognize that our process costing computations are essentially the same as those you already know.

We now turn to the specific computations for equivalent unit production. In this example, we work with only one cost factor or assume that the percentages of completion are the same for all input costs.

FIFO Equivalent Unit Production

FIFO equivalent unit production simply represents the production of equivalent full units during the current period. In this example, Polk Company had the following data for March:

Units in beginning inventory, 40% complete	10,000
Units put into production	115,000
Total units	125,000
Less: Units in ending inventory, 80% complete	15,000
Units completed	110,000
Cost of beginning inventory	$ 16,900
Current period costs	$318,600

To answer the question how much work was done in March, in terms of equivalent units, we could proceed in two ways. First, we look directly at that work. The company completed 110,000 units, of which 10,000 were already in process at the beginning of the month. Accordingly, it started and completed 100,000 units (110,000 − 10,000). (Alternatively, it put 115,000 units into process and had 15,000 units in ending inventory, which also gives 100,000 units started and completed.) The company also completed work on the 10,000 units in beginning inventory, doing 6,000 units of equivalent units of work in March, which is 10,000 multiplied by 60 percent. Because those units were 40 percent complete to begin with, 60 percent remained to be done this period. Finally, the company also did 12,000 equivalent units of work on the ending inventory, which is the 15,000 units in the ending inventory multiplied by 80 percent. Summarizing:

Units started and completed	100,000
Equivalent units of work to finish beginning inventory	6,000
Equivalent units of work to start ending inventory	12,000
FIFO equivalent unit production = work done in March	118,000

We can interpret the 118,000 equivalent units this way: given the amount of work actually done in March, Polk could have started and completed 118,000 units.

Equivalent Unit Production—Weighted Average

Weighted average equivalent unit production differs from FIFO equivalent production in only one respect. Because the weighted average method combines the beginning inventory with the current period work, we use the number of physical units in the beginning inventory, not the equivalent units. Thus, weighted average equivalent unit production is:

Units started and completed	100,000
Physical units in beginning inventory	10,000
Equivalent units in ending inventory	12,000
Weighted average equivalent unit production	122,000

Notice that the sum of the first two elements is 110,000, which is the number of units completed. Units completed include units from beginning inventory that were completed plus units started and completed during the period. With the weighted average method, we do not have to determine the number of units started and completed; we can simply add the number completed to the equivalent unit production in ending inventory, as shown below:

Units completed	110,000
Equivalent units in ending inventory	12,000
Weighted average equivalent unit production	122,000

In effect the 122,000 units represent the total available equivalent units (similar to units available for sale in a merchandising company). It is the 4,000 equivalent units in beginning inventory (10,000 × 40%) plus work done in the current period (FIFO equivalent unit production). We can see this by comparing the two computations:

	FIFO	Weighted Average
Units started and completed	100,000	100,000
Work done to complete beginning inventory	6,000	6,000
Work done to start ending inventory	12,000	12,000
FIFO equivalent unit production	118,000	118,000
Plus: equivalent units in beginning inventory		4,000
Weighted average equivalent unit production		122,000

While this schedule highlights the difference between the two methods, usually, it is simpler to make the computations in the following way:

Units completed	110,000
Equivalent unit production in ending inventory	12,000
Weighted average equivalent unit production	122,000
Less: Equivalent unit production in beginning inventory	4,000
FIFO equivalent unit production	118,000

We said previously that the difference between FIFO and weighted average is that weighted average adds the number of equivalent units in beginning inventory to FIFO equivalent unit production. Therefore, we can also see that FIFO subtracts that number from weighted average equivalent unit production.

While any of these techniques will work, it is important to understand the relationships. The FIFO method deals with current production (finishing beginning inventory, starting and completing units, and starting units that will become ending inventory of work in process) while the weighted average method does not distinguish when a unit was produced (last period or the current period) and deals with total production achieved (units completed, regardless of when they were started, plus units started that remain unfinished at the end of the period). One final point: if there is no beginning inventory, both methods will produce the same result, because their only difference lies in the treatment of the beginning inventory.

UNIT COSTS

As we mentioned earlier, FIFO uses only the costs of the current period, while weighted average uses those costs plus the cost of the beginning inventory. The unit cost calculations for each method, using the costs from page 250, are:

$$\begin{aligned}\text{FIFO unit cost} &= \text{current cost/FIFO equivalent unit production}\\ &= \$318{,}600/118{,}000\\ &= \$2.70\end{aligned}$$

$$\begin{aligned} \text{weighted average unit cost} &= \frac{(\text{current period cost} + \text{cost of beginning inventory})}{\text{weighted average equivalent unit production}} \\ &= (\$318{,}600 + \$16{,}900)/122{,}000 \\ &= \$2.75 \end{aligned}$$

We have completed the basics of equivalent unit production and unit cost computations. Next we will examine the determination of the cost of the ending inventory of Work in Process and the related transfer of cost from Work-in-Process Inventory to Finished Goods Inventory.

ENDING INVENTORY OF WORK IN PROCESS AND TRANSFERS TO FINISHED GOODS

Since the weighted average method does not differentiate between costs of work done in a prior period and current costs, the calculated unit cost can be used to value both the ending inventory of work in process and the units transferred to finished goods. The costs in ending inventory of Work-in-Process Inventory must reflect only the work performed to date on these unfinished goods. Thus the units in the calculation are equivalent units, not physical units—12,000 in our example, not 15,000. The ending inventory of work in process is $33,000, $2.75 per unit times 12,000 equivalent units in the ending inventory; the costs transferred to Finished Goods should be $302,500, 110,000 units completed times $2.75 per unit.

In journal entry form we have the following:

Work-in-Process Inventory	$318,600	
Various accounts		$318,600
To record costs incurred in current period		
Finished Goods Inventory	$302,500	
Work-in-Process Inventory		$302,500
To record transfer of units, 110,000 at $2.75		

The T-account for Work-in-Process Inventory appears as follows under the weighted average method:

WORK-IN-PROCESS INVENTORY

	Debit	Credit	
Beg. bal.	$ 16,900		
Current costs	318,600		
		$302,500	To Finished Goods
Totals	$335,500	$302,500	
End. bal.	$ 33,000		

The T-account illustrates again how the weighted average method works; beginning inventory costs and current costs are combined and divided by total production to get unit costs. The transfer to Finished Goods and the ending balance are all valued at this unit cost.

This is a good place to reinforce a basic relationship: *the costs of the beginning inventory plus current costs equal costs transferred to finished goods plus the cost of ending inventory*. This same relationship applies to the units themselves. *Units in beginning inventory plus current production equal units transferred out plus units in ending inventory*. In our example:

$$10{,}000 + 115{,}000 = 110{,}000 + 15{,}000$$

Let us turn our attention to the FIFO method. Here, unit costs are associated with current production. Costs of beginning inventory are kept separate and not included in the unit cost calculation. Remember that current work includes finishing the beginning inventory, starting and completing units, and starting some units that remain in ending inventory. Since ending inventory is associated with current production, it has a cost of $32,400 under FIFO, 12,000 equivalent units times the $2.70 FIFO unit cost. Using the basic relationship of costs stated above, if we know the value of ending inventory, we can trace back to the value of units transferred to Finished Goods: $335,500 − $32,400 = $303,100. Knowing that the total of costs associated with beginning inventory and current costs is $335,500 and that the value of ending inventory is $32,400 lets us easily solve for the value of units transferred.

We should make sure our calculations are correct and logical. The transfer of units to Finished Goods involves two types of units, those started and finished in March and those in beginning inventory. The unit cost in the beginning inventory is not necessarily the same as the one calculated for the current period FIFO cost for the units started and completed and for the work done to complete the beginning inventory. Remember also that we have held aside the costs associated with work done in the prior period and that these costs must be reflected when we transfer the units in beginning inventory to Finished Goods. A summary of the relevant figures follows:

Cost of beginning inventory (relates to 4,000 equivalent unit production)	$ 16,900
Cost to finish beginning inventory, 6,000 × $2.70	16,200
Cost to start and complete, 110,000 × $2.70	270,000
Total cost transferred	$303,100

With FIFO, the journal entry to reflect this is:

Finished Goods Inventory	$303,100	
Work-in-Process Inventory		$303,100

and the T-account would be:

WORK-IN-PROCESS INVENTORY

Beg. bal.	$ 16,900		
Current costs	318,600		
		$303,100	To Finished Goods
Totals	$335,500	$303,100	
End. bal.	$ 32,400		

COST OF PRODUCTION REPORT

Companies that use process costing typically reconcile costs using a **cost of production report**, which summarizes and accounts for the flow of physical units and of costs. The report is a formal statement of the basic relationship of units and of costs introduced above. The report for Polk appears below and reflects a FIFO inventory flow.

Cost of Production Report

Unit data:	
Beginning inventory	10,000
Units put into production	115,000
Total to be accounted for	125,000
Units completed and transferred	110,000
Ending inventory	15,000
Total accounted for	125,000
Cost data:	
Beginning inventory	$ 16,900
Current period costs	318,600
Total to be accounted for	$335,500
Transferred to Finished Goods Inventory	$303,100
Ending inventory	32,400
Total accounted for	$335,500

The cost section of the cost of production report is essentially a summary of Work-in-Process Inventory. The upper portion of the report shows the basic unit relationship; the lower portion shows the same relationship for costs. Both of these relationships are from financial accounting and provide checks on your work.

REVIEW PROBLEMS

In April, Polk had these results:

Units put into process	137,000
Units completed	132,000
Units in ending inventory, 90% complete	20,000
Cost incurred in April	$365,700

Use these data with the March inventory data to determine the following for both FIFO and weighted average and to prepare cost of production reports:

1. Equivalent unit production
2. Unit cost for April

3. Cost of the ending inventory of work in process
4. Cost of units transferred to finished goods

Use an electronic spreadsheet to solve these problems. Design a single spreadsheet template that can be used for both FIFO and weighted average. Answers appear in Exhibit 6–1.

Notice that the accounting for *physical* units is the same for both FIFO and weighted average (although the equivalent units of production are different).

EXHIBIT 6–1 Answers to Review Problems

Data section:		*Units*	*Percentage Complete*	*Equivalent Units*
Beginning inventory		15,000	80%	12,000
Units put into process		137,000		
Units completed		132,000		
Units in ending inventory		20,000	90%	18,000
Cost information:		*FIFO*	*Weighted Average*	
Beginning inventory		$32,400	$33,000	
Current period costs		$365,700	$365,700	
Total costs		$398,100	$398,700	
Solution section:				
1. Equivalent units of production				
Units completed			132,000	
Equivalent unit production (EUP) in ending inventory			18,000	
Weighted average EUP			150,000	
Less: Equivalent units in beginning inventory			12,000	
FIFO—EUP			138,000	
		FIFO	*Weighted Average*	
2. Unit costs				
Current period costs		$365,700	$365,700	
Costs of beginning inventory			33,000	
Total		$365,700	$398,700	
EUP		138,000	150,000	
Unit costs		$2.65	$2.658	
3. Ending inventory	18,000 units	$47,700	$47,844	

(continued)

(EXHIBIT 6–1 continued)

4. Transferred to Finished Goods Inventory			
Beginning inventory			
Beg. inv. costs		$32,400	
Costs to finish	3,000 units	7,950	
Started and completed	117,000 units	310,050	
		$350,400	
Transferred to Finished Goods	132,000 units		$350,856
5. Cost of production reports			

Unit data:	
Beginning inventory	15,000
Units put into production	137,000
Total to be accounted for	152,000
Units transferred to Finished Goods	132,000
Ending inventory	20,000
Total accounted for	152,000

	FIFO	*Weighted Average*
Beginning inventory	$32,400	$33,000
Current period cost	365,700	365,700
Total to be accounted for	$398,100	$398,700
Ending inventory	$47,700	$47,844
Transferred to Finished Goods	350,400	350,856
Total accounted for	$398,100	$398,700

Notice also that the costs to be accounted for differ because the beginning inventories are different under the two cost flow assumptions.

MATERIALS AND CONVERSION COSTS

Our previous example assumed either that Polk had only one element of cost or that the percentages of completion for all inputs were identical. As we mentioned earlier, it is more likely that materials costs will have a different percentage of completion than conversion costs (the sum of labor and overhead). Even within conversion costs (labor compared to various overhead cost pools) the percentages of completion might differ. Under either of these scenarios, it is necessary to track costs and equivalent unit production separately for each factor. No conceptual or practical difficulty is added by different percentages

EXHIBIT 6–2 Data for May—Cutting Department, Marvy Dolls, Inc.

	Unit Data	
Beginning inventory	20,000	
Units started in production	150,000	
Units completed	140,000	
Ending inventory	30,000	
Percentages of completion:	*Materials*	*Conversion Costs*
Beginning inventory	90%	70%
Ending inventory	80%	40%
Cost Data:		
Beginning inventory	$ 59,200	$106,200
Current period costs	613,200	897,000
Total costs	$672,400	$1,003,200

of completion. All we must do is apply the analyses described for each cost pool as we did for a single pool.

Exhibit 6–2 contains information about the Cutting Department of Marvy Dolls, Inc., an example that illustrates the separation of material costs from conversion costs. Not only are there different percentages of completion for materials and conversion costs, but there is also a separation of beginning inventory costs and current costs.

The calculations of equivalent unit production for each cost factor, unit cost for each factor, ending inventory, and costs transferred out for both weighted average and FIFO appear in Exhibit 6–3. Before you look at it, see if you can make these calculations yourself. As in earlier examples, the weighted average equivalent units of production consist of all work whether performed in May or in an earlier period. Different equivalent unit figures and unit costs are calculated for materials and for conversion costs. Ending inventory equals unit cost for each factor times equivalent units in ending inventory. Costs transferred out are units transferred times each unit cost for materials and conversion costs.

With FIFO, equivalent units for each factor are based on current production (May). While ending inventory is calculated the same way as weighted average, costs transferred out reflect the separation of costs related to beginning inventory (for both materials and conversion) and current costs. The only difference in the calculations in Exhibit 6–3 and those shown for Polk is that we must now make each calculation twice, once for materials and once for conversion costs. The journal entries and T-accounts shown are different from Polk's because we use separate Work-in-Process Inventory accounts for each

EXHIBIT 6–3 Calculations for May—Marvy Dolls, Inc.

Weighted Average	*Materials*	*Conversion Costs*
Units completed	140,000	140,000
EUP—ending inventory		
30,000 × 80%	24,000	
30,000 × 40%		12,000
Weighted average EUP	164,000	152,000
Unit costs:		
$672,400/164,000	$4.10	
$1,003,200/152,000		$6.60
Ending inventory:		
24,000 × $4.10	$98,400	
12,000 × $6.60		$79,200
Transferred out:		
140,000 × $4.10	574,000	
140,000 × $6.60		924,000
Total accounted for	$672,400	$1,003,200

FIFO	*Materials*	*Conversion Costs*
Weighted average EUP	164,000	152,000
Less: EUP in beginning inventory		
20,000 × 90%	18,000	
20,000 × 70%		14,000
EUP—FIFO	146,000	138,000
Unit costs:		
$613,200/146,000	$4.20	
$897,000/138,000		$6.50
Ending inventory:		
24,000 × $4.20	$100,800	
12,000 × $6.50		$78,000
Transferred out:		
Cost of beginning inventory	$59,200	$106,200
Complete beginning inventory		
2,000 × $4.20	8,400	
6,000 × $6.50		39,000
Started and completed		
120,000 × $4.20	504,000	
120,000 × $6.50		780,000
	$571,600	$925,200
Total accounted for	$672,400	$1,003,200

element of cost. (Many companies use one account for material costs, another for conversion costs. An overall Work-in-Process Inventory account might summarize the subsidiary accounts.) Maintaining separate accounts is not mandatory, but it is convenient and makes it easier to trace the flows of the costs. A cost of production report should also reconcile both material costs and conversion costs.

The journal entries, T-accounts, and a cost of production report for the weighted average method appear below.

Journal Entries

Work-in-Process Inventory—Materials	$613,200	
Materials Inventory		$613,200
to record cost of materials into process		
Work-in-Process Inventory—Conversion Costs	$897,000	
Various cost accounts		$897,000
to record conversion costs incurred		
Finished Goods Inventory	$1,498,000	
Work-in-Process Inventory—Materials		$574,000
Work-in-Process Inventory—Conversion Costs		924,000
to record cost of units transferred to finished goods inventory (Exhibit 6–3)		

WORK-IN-PROCESS INVENTORY—MATERIALS

Beg. bal.	$ 59,200		
Current costs	613,200	$574,000	To Finished Goods
Totals	$672,400	$574,000	
Ending inventory	$ 98,400		

WORK-IN-PROCESS INVENTORY—CONVERSION COSTS

Beg. bal.	$ 106,200		
Current costs	897,000	$924,000	To Finished Goods
Totals	$1,003,200	$924,000	
Ending inventory	$ 79,200		

FINISHED GOODS INVENTORY

From Work-in-Process Inventory	$1,498,000	

Cost of Production Report

Unit data:	
Beginning inventory	20,000
Started	150,000
To be accounted for	170,000
Ending inventory	30,000
Completed	140,000
Accounted for	170,000

Cost data:

	Total	*Materials*	*Conversion Costs*
Beginning inventory	$ 165,400	$ 59,200	$ 106,200
Current costs	1,510,200	613,200	897,000
To be accounted for	$1,675,600	$672,400	$1,003,200
Ending inventory	$ 177,600	$ 98,400	$ 79,200
Transferred out	1,498,000	574,000	924,000
Accounted for	$1,675,600	$672,400	$1,003,200

Note these points:

1. The journal entry transferring the cost of units completed to Finished Goods Inventory combines the material cost and the conversion cost of those units. Under weighted average, it is possible simply to add the unit costs for the elements and multiply that sum by the number of units completed. That is, $\$4.10 + \$6.60 = \$10.70$ and $\$10.70 \times 140{,}000 = \$1{,}498{,}000$. This process is not possible with FIFO.
2. The journal entries, T-accounts, and cost of production report are formal expressions of the calculations that determine ending inventory and transfers. Calculate equivalent unit production and unit costs to determine the ending inventory and transfers. If you make an error, it should show up in the T-account for Work-in-Process Inventory by not having the ending inventory you calculated (equivalent production in ending inventory times equivalent unit costs) and in the cost of production report by not having total costs accounted for that are equal to total costs to be accounted for. One reason for these reports is to cross-check units and costs.

ADDITIONAL COST POOLS

Multiple cost pools may have different percentages of completion. For example, if some operations within a department are labor driven, while others are related to machine time, there would be three pools: materials, labor, and machine. In addition, some overhead may be associated with materials.

As a review problem, assume that Marvy Dolls has three cost pools.[2] Some of Marvy's overhead is related to materials and some to machine use; none is related to labor. Instead of using conversion costs and information related to these costs as in Exhibit 6–2, they are now:

[2] The determination of the number of cost pools is based on the possibility that there will be different percentages of completion in these pools at the end of a period.

	Material-related costs	Labor	Machine-based overhead	Total
Percentages of completion:				
Beginning inventory	90%	70%	90%	
Ending inventory	80%	40%	50%	
Cost data:				
Beginning inventory	$ 27,800	$ 12,000	$ 66,400	$ 106,200
Current costs	292,000	103,500	501,500	897,000
Total	$319,800	$115,500	$567,900	$1,003,200

Notice that the totals for conversion costs have not changed, but particular cost pools have changed. Materials now include not only the cost of materials but also material-related overhead. Using these three cost pools and the new information above,

1. Calculate equivalent unit production for the machine-based overhead for both weighted average and FIFO.

2. Using the equivalent unit production in Exhibit 6–3 and the new calculations above, determine unit costs for material-related costs, labor, and machine-based overhead for both weighted average and FIFO.

3. Using only the FIFO unit costs, calculate the ending inventory value and the value of goods transferred out.

Answers appear in Exhibit 6–4.

As in the solution in Exhibit 6–3, nothing is new here. Instead of two cost pools, two equivalent units of production, and two unit costs, there are three of each. The procedure is exactly the same as when we showed one and two divisions of costs and percentages of completion.

EXHIBIT 6–4 Review Problem—Marvy Dolls, Inc.: Addition of Cost Pools

	Machine Time
1. Equivalent Units of Production:	
Units completed	140,000
EUP—ending inventory	
30,000 × 50%	15,000
Weighted average—EUP	155,000
Less: beginning inventory	
20,000 × 90%	18,000
FIFO—EUP	137,000

(continued)

(EXHIBIT 6–4 continued)

2. Weighted Average

	Beginning Inventory	Current Period	Total
Conversion costs:			
Labor	$12,000	$103,500	$115,500
Material-based overhead	27,800	292,000	319,800
Machine-based overhead	66,400	501,500	567,900
Total	$106,200	$897,000	$1,003,200

	Material-related costs	Labor	Machine-based overhead
Weighted average unit costs:			
Material costs	$672,400		
Material-based overhead	319,800		
Labor		$115,500	
Machine-based overhead			$567,900
Total	$992,200	$115,500	$567,900
Weighted average EUP	164,000	152,000	155,000
Unit costs	$6.05	$0.76	$3.66
FIFO unit costs:			
Material costs	$613,200		
Material-based overhead	292,000		
Labor		$103,500	
Machine-based overhead			$501,500
Total	$905,200	$103,500	$501,500
FIFO EUP	146,000	138,000	137,000
Unit costs	$6.20	$0.75	$3.66

3. Ending inventory:			
24,000 × $6.20	$148,800		
12,000 × $0.75		$9,000	
15,000 × $3.66			$54,909
Transferred out:			
Cost of beginning inventory	$87,000	$12,000	$66,400
Complete beginning inventory			
2,000 × $6.20	12,400		
6,000 × $0.75		4,500	
2,000 × $3.66			7,321
Started and completed			
120,000 × $6.20	744,000		
120,000 × $0.75		90,000	
120,000 × $3.66			439,270
	$843,400	$106,500	$512,991
Total accounted for	$992,200	$115,500	$567,900

MULTIPLE PROCESSES

Many process costing companies operate more than one process. In such cases, the company will typically maintain the Work-in-Process Inventory account for each process (or department, because a department is often the same as a process). Costs flow through the departmental accounts as do the products. As units leave a department, their costs also leave that department's Work-in-Process Inventory account and go to the account for the next department. The transferred costs are the cumulative costs—the total cost from all of the departments that have finished working on the units.

Let us illustrate the procedures by assuming that Marvy Dolls Cutting Department transfers dolls to the Sewing Department, which finishes the dolls and transfers them to finished goods. Data for the Sewing Department appear in Exhibit 6–5. Costs associated with the Cutting Department come from Exhibit 6–3.

Remember that any units transferred from the Cutting Department to the Sewing Department are complete with respect to the work of the Cutting Department; if they were unfinished, they would still be in process in the Cutting Department. In a sense, the Sewing Department is "buying" a component from the Cutting Department. For example, if a company made air conditioners and bought the fan component from another company, the costs associated with the fans would be the cost per unit from the supplier times the number of fans purchased. Obviously, the fans would be completed or the supplier would not have shipped them. The process is the same between de-

EXHIBIT 6–5 Data for May—Sewing Department, Marvy Dolls, Inc.

Unit Data:			
Beginning inventory		20,000	
Started in production (from Cutting Department)		140,000	
Completed		150,000	
Ending inventory		10,000	
Percentages of completion:	*Materials*	*Conversion Costs*	*Prior Department Costs*
Beginning inventory	60%	30%	100%
Ending inventory	75%	70%	100%
Cost Data:			
Beginning inventory	$ 5,406	$ 18,759	$ 214,480
Current period costs	57,909	483,955	1,498,000
Total costs	$63,315	$502,714	$1,712,480

partments. Nothing moves to the following department in a process flow until it is complete in the previous department.

The Sewing Department at Marvy Dolls adds materials to the cut dolls and performs conversion work. The important point with multiple processes is that there is a new account, Work-in-Process Inventory—Transferred-in Costs (or Prior Department Costs). This account contains the costs transferred in from the prior department. It is also necessary to calculate equivalent unit production for prior department costs, but as we stated above, this calculation should present no problem because all of the units are 100 percent complete with respect to prior department costs.[3] One additional point: to do the calculations for the transferred-in costs, we must select one of the cost flow assumptions from the Cutting Department. This is required because the debit to Work-in-Process Inventory—Prior Department Costs is the total of credits to the Work-in-Process Inventory accounts of the previous department, in this case, the Cutting Department. We shall use the weighted average method for the transfer—that is, suppose that the Cutting Department uses the weighted average method. However, we shall do the Sewing Department's calculations using both FIFO and weighted average. (It is possible, though unlikely, for different departments within a company to use different cost-flow assumptions.)

Notice that the $1,498,000 current period cost in the column for prior department cost is the total cost transferred out of the Cutting Department under the weighted average method (Exhibit 6–3). All other data are assumed. Exhibit 6–6 shows the unit cost calculations and dispositions. The transfer of prior department costs under FIFO is the number started and completed times the unit cost. No work is to be done on the beginning inventory as far as prior department costs are concerned because the prior department work has been done. With respect to prior department costs, equivalent units are the same as physical units because all units have 100 percent of their work done in prior departments.

COMPARISON OF METHODS

Unit cost calculations do not differ significantly under the two process costing methods unless there are large fluctuations in costs and relatively high inventories in relation to units completed. From a product costing standpoint, either method is acceptable for financial accounting. However, from a control standpoint, FIFO is preferable because it focuses attention on the current period costs. In addition, when current period unit costs are compared with those budgeted or with those of prior periods, only variable costs should be included.

[3] While some problems will state that the percentage of completion in beginning and/or ending inventories associated with previous department costs is 100 percent, this is implicit.

EXHIBIT 6–6 Sewing Department, Marvy Dolls, Inc.—May

Weighted Average	*Materials*	*Conversion Costs*	*Prior Dept. Costs*
Units completed	150,000	150,000	150,000
EUP—ending inventory			
10,000 × 75%	7,500		
10,000 × 70%		7,000	
10,000 × 100%			10,000
Weighted average EUP	157,500	157,000	160,000
Unit costs:			
$63,315/157,500	$0.402		
$502,714/157,000		$3.202	
$1,712,480/160,000			$10.703
Ending inventory:			
7,500 × $0.402	$ 3,015		
7,000 × $3.202		$ 22,414	
10,000 × $10.703			$ 107,030
Transferred out:			
150,000 × $0.402	60,300		
150,000 × $3.202		480,300	
150,000 × $10.703			1,605,450
Total costs	$63,315	$502,714	$1,712,480
FIFO			
EUP—weighted average	157,500	157,000	160,000
Less: EUP in beginning inventory:			
20,000 × 60%	12,000		
20,000 × 30%		6,000	
20,000 × 100%			20,000
Equivalent unit production—FIFO	145,500	151,000	140,000
Unit costs:			
$57,909/145,500	$0.398		
$483,955/151,000		$3.205	
$1,498,000/140,000			$10.70
Ending inventory:			
7,500 × $0.398	$ 2,985		
7,000 × $3.205		$ 22,435	
10,000 × $10.70			$ 107,000

(continued)

(EXHIBIT 6–6 continued)

FIFO	Materials	Conversion Costs	Prior Dept. Costs
Transferred out:			
Cost of beginning inventory	$ 5,406	$ 18,759	$ 214,480
Complete beginning inventory:			
8,000 × $0.398	3,184		
14,000 × $3.205		44,870	
0 × $10.70			0
Started and completed:			
130,000 × $0.398	51,740		
130,000 × $3.205		416,650	
130,000 × $10.70			1,391,000
Total transferred	60,330	$480,279	$1,605,480
Total costs	$63,315	$502,714	$1,712,480

FIFO equivalent production and current period costs should be used in analyzing cost behavior patterns with production as the independent variable. In using regression analysis or a scatter diagram in which the independent variable is units of production, the weighted average based production figures could give misleading results.

Since pricing is often based on long-run costs, companies that use product costs as a basis for pricing might see the weighted average method yielding a better basis. Even when other costs are added in an analysis of cost of products for pricing, weighted average variable costs might be useful. In addition, the weighted average method is very popular with firms using actual or normal costing, perhaps because it is simpler than FIFO. Even where FIFO is used, it tends to be modified as we have illustrated, rather than the strict FIFO, which requires each receiving department to keep separate track of units received from the sending department's beginning inventory and its current period production. Essentially, then, the choice is a matter of preference when a company uses actual or normal costing[4] and probably should be dictated by the cost of maintaining the system. By that criterion, the weighted average method would likely be the choice, but individual circumstances might encourage the use of FIFO.

[4]With standard costing, as we discuss in Chapters 7 and 8, firms use FIFO; weighted average is inappropriate in this case.

JOB ORDER COSTING AND EQUIVALENT PRODUCTION

In Chapter 5 we discussed the possibility that a company producing a diverse set of products and using a job order costing system might also use the concept of equivalent production to find unit costs for a period. Suppose that such a company works on batches of 1,000 units at a time. Production does not happen on all 1,000 units simultaneously; rather, management keeps track of costs based on batches of 1,000 units. Assume that at month end a batch is incomplete. The company can calculate equivalent unit production and equivalent unit costs for the work done during that period. Rather than waiting for the batch to be completed to get unit costs, that information might be important immediately for control, as discussed above. Thus, even if a company organizes its product costing system as job order, some of the basic parts of process costing can be used. Many companies that use job order costing also use process costing concepts to calculate unit costs.

LOST AND SPOILED UNITS

Few companies produce nothing but good units. Cracked bricks, warped pieces of lumber, and scratched chairs are produced with good units of these products. Input of 1,000 gallons might produce only 750 gallons of output. Some of these losses are normal and to be expected. Attempts to reduce them below a certain level might be more costly than allowing them to continue.[5]

Additional loss occurs when a firm puts more finished product into containers than the label states. For example, a maker of instant coffee may produce 4-ounce jars. It may set its machinery to be 98 percent sure that each jar contains at least 4 ounces. Given the available tolerances, the average weight of the coffee in a jar may be 4.08 ounces. Failure to have 4 ounces or more in a large percentage of its jars might bring the company fines and unfavorable publicity if government agencies detect the shortages; hence, the firm plays it safe and often overfills jars. The extra cost of coffee is more than offset, the managers believe, by the potential cost of underfilling.

The managerial problems of lost and spoiled units center on the question of the costs and benefits of reducing losses. Questions include: Are losses within acceptable ranges, given the techniques used? What does it cost us to lose units, and what would it cost to reduce the losses by specified amounts? In determining cost of product for managerial decision making, the principal question is whether the cost of lost or spoiled units should be included when looking at costs, say, as a basis for pricing. The principal question for product

[5] This has been a popular topic among engineers and production and operations managers.

costing for financial accounting centers on the definition of inventoriable costs; should the costs of lost and spoiled units be treated as expenses of the period or as part of the cost of good output? Note that the two concerns are similar; if a cost such as this is considered a period expense for financial accounting, that is the same as saying that it is unusual and should not be included in the cost of product for pricing purposes.

In the following discussion we use the term *spoilage* to refer to all types of such losses. This usage provides brevity and does no harm because the accounting for each type of loss is generally the same.

Normal and Abnormal Spoilage

Spoilage is classified into two types, normal and abnormal. **Normal spoilage** is the amount expected, given the firm's manufacturing techniques and assuming that the manufacturing process is under control. Thus, normal spoilage for one firm may be about four percent of good output, while for another firm in the same industry with more advanced equipment the rate might be about 0.5 percent. **Abnormal spoilage** is unexpected and is defined as total spoilage minus normal spoilage.

Throughout the discussion we shall speak of normal spoilage as a single number of units or single rate. From both conceptual and practical standpoints, however, normal spoilage should be viewed as a range, not as a point estimate. Even highly automated processes operating under near laboratory conditions will show differing amounts of spoilage in different periods, especially if the periods are short (say, days or weeks as opposed to months or quarters). The principles developed in Chapter 3 (regression analysis) are relevant to the determination of a range of normal spoilage.

When we speak of normal spoilage as, say, 200 units, we should interpret that figure as the midpoint of a range, say from 180 to 220 units. One important reason for the notion of a range of normal spoilage is that managers will be more likely to investigate abnormal versus normal spoilage. Failure to recognize that normal spoilage is a range may result in excessive investigation and, therefore, excessive costs.

Accounting for Spoilage

Accountants agree that normal spoilage costs should be allocated to the good output, because normal spoilage is by definition an inevitable consequence of the existing production process. Wide agreement also exists that the cost of abnormal spoilage should be expensed in the period incurred, not inventoried. The reasoning is that abnormal spoilage is not a necessary consequence of producing good output and is, therefore, not part of the cost of good products.

Accounting for Abnormal Spoilage In a process costing situation, whether actual or normal costing, determining spoilage costs requires calculating equivalent production including the abnormally spoiled units. This figure is used to determine a cost per unit as we have illustrated throughout this chapter. The number of units abnormally spoiled is multiplied by the cost per unit; the result is shown as an expense on the income statement.

You must often analyze the physical flow of units to determine how many were lost or spoiled. In some cases—for example, when losses are due to evaporation—you do not know the amount lost; you have to determine it from information about the beginning inventory, quantity put into process, quantity completed, and ending inventory.

To illustrate, assume the following facts about a manufacturing process. All materials are added at the beginning of the process.

Units in beginning inventory	1,000
Units put into process during the period	12,000
Units completed during the period	10,000
Units in ending inventory	2,000

We first reconcile the physical flow to determine how many units were lost or spoiled.

Units in beginning inventory	1,000
Units put into process	12,000
Units to be accounted for	13,000
Units completed	10,000
Units in ending inventory	2,000
Total	12,000
Units lost or spoiled (13,000 − 12,000)	1,000

A reconciliation like this is the first step in dealing with lost or spoiled units, unless you know the amount lost or spoiled. Note that the data used are not equivalent units; they are physical units, no matter what the percentage of completion. That is, you are trying to determine the number of *units* lost or spoiled; the determination of equivalent production follows this reconciliation. Exhibit 6–7 provides the data for an illustration.

A critical question in accounting for and managing spoilage is when it is *detected*, as opposed to when it occurs. That is, although spoilage might typically occur when units are halfway through the process, if it is not detected until the units are completed, workers will have done all the work on units that turn out to be spoiled. It is possible that materials would be added to the spoiled units as well because *the units are not known to be spoiled until they are finished*. This waste is one reason for inspecting units before they are finished and, more precisely, inspecting them after the stages in the process where spoilage is most likely to occur. Many manufacturing operations have immediate detection of spoilage through on-line measuring devices. For example, the placement, shape, and size of drilled holes can be monitored by a video camera connected to a computer; defective parts are automatically diverted off the production line. From an accounting perspective, the point at which spoilage is detected is important to determine how much cost was incurred to

EXHIBIT 6–7 Data for Illustration

Physical Flow			
Beginning inventory	1,000		
Units put into production	12,000		
Total to be accounted for	13,000		
Completed and transferred	10,000		
Ending Inventory	2,000		
Spoiled	1,000		
Total accounted for	13,000		
Percentages of Completion	*Materials*	*Conversion Costs*	
Beginning inventory	100%	70%	
Ending inventory	100%	60%	
Costs			*Total*
Beginning inventory	$ 1,760	$ 2,675	$ 4,435
Current period costs	24,240	33,925	58,165
Totals	$26,000	$36,600	$62,600

work on the spoiled units. In addition, because the units are worked on until found defective, we must include in their costs all of the costs incurred until detection.

The calculations of equivalent production and unit costs under the weighted average and FIFO methods are shown in Exhibit 6–8. Again, the only difference between these calculations and the ones you know is the inclusion of the abnormal spoilage in the unit cost calculations through its inclusion in equivalent production.

The unit costs in Exhibit 6–8 are now used to determine the amounts of cost transferred from Work-in-Process Inventory to Finished Goods Inventory (or to the next department) and the amounts of cost to be shown in the ending inventory of work in process, as well as the amount to be expensed as Abnormal Spoilage. Exhibit 6–9 shows the disposition of costs under the two cost flow assumptions, along with the appropriate calculations. Notice that the cost of spoiled units under both cost flow assumptions is simply the number of spoiled units multiplied by the cost per unit calculated in Exhibit 6–8.

Let us now review the procedure. *Essentially, you calculate the unit costs based on the equivalent production of all units, whether good or spoiled.* You are calculating a cost per unit, not a cost per good unit. You then use the unit costs in determining the amounts to be transferred to Finished Goods Inventory, left in Work-in-Process Inventory, and expensed as Spoiled Goods Expense or other descriptive title.

EXHIBIT 6–8 Unit Cost Calculations[a]

Equivalent Production	*Materials*	*Conversion Costs*
Units completed	10,000	10,000
Ending inventory (2,000 × 100%, 2,000 × 60%)	2,000	1,200
Spoiled units	1,000	1,000
Equivalent production—weighted average	13,000	12,200
Beginning inventory (1,000 × 100%, 1,000 × 70%)	1,000	700
Equivalent production—FIFO	12,000	11,500
Unit Costs—Weighted Average		
Beginning inventory costs plus current period costs	$26,000	$36,600
	÷	÷
Equivalent production—weighted average	13,000	12,200
Cost per unit	$2	$3
Unit Costs—FIFO		
Current period costs	$24,240	$33,925
	÷	÷
Equivalent production—FIFO	12,000	11,500
Cost per unit	$2.02	$2.95

[a]All data from Exhibit 6–7.

EXHIBIT 6–9 Disposition of Costs

Weighted Average		
Transferred to Finished Goods, $5 × 10,000		$50,000
Abnormal Spoilage Expense, $5 × 1,000		5,000
Ending inventory, ($2 × 2,000) + ($3 × 1,200)		7,600
Total accounted for		$62,600
FIFO		
Transferred to Finished Goods		
Materials, $1,760 + $2.02(10,000 − 1,000)	$19,940	
Conversion costs, $2,675 + $2.95(10,000 − 700)	30,110	$50,050
Abnormal Spoilage Expense, ($2.02 + $2.95) × 1,000		4,970
Ending inventory, ($2.02 × 2,000) + ($2.95 × 1,200)		7,580
Total accounted for		$62,600

Accounting for Normal Spoilage Two general methods are used to account for normal spoilage. One is to ignore the normally spoiled units in the calculations of unit cost by omitting them from computations of equivalent units. The other is to include normally spoiled units in these calculations, as we did with abnormally spoiled units. The cost of normally spoiled units is then computed the same way as the cost of abnormally spoiled units, and this cost is transferred to the next department or to Finished Goods. The first method, ignoring the spoilage, is simpler but does not allow the manager to see the cost of spoilage because it is not computed. It is useful to know the cost of spoilage when trying to limit spoilage and to see the economic consequence of spoiled units.

Let us use the data from Exhibit 6–7 again, but assume that all spoilage is considered normal. Exhibit 6–10 shows the unit costs using the first method—ignoring spoilage in the determination of equivalent production. Because we omit spoilage from equivalent production, the unit costs are higher than they were in Exhibit 6–8. The disposition of costs would be made in the usual fashion.

Again, this method is deficient because it obscures the quantity and cost of spoilage. The other method recognizes the cost of normal spoilage, treating it as part of the transfer to Finished Goods. To illustrate the second method, we change the assumption of spoilage to read that 800 units were normally

EXHIBIT 6–10 Unit Costs—Normal Spoilage Ignored

Equivalent Production (see Exhibit 6–8)	*Materials*	*Conversion Costs*
Units completed	10,000	10,000
Ending inventory, equivalent production	2,000	1,200
Equivalent production—weighted average	12,000	11,200
Beginning inventory, equivalent production	1,000	700
Equivalent production—FIFO	11,000	10,500
Unit Costs—Weighted Average (see Exhibit 6–8)		
Beginning inventory costs plus current period costs	$26,000	$36,600
	÷	÷
Equivalent production	12,000	11,200
Unit costs	$2.1667	$3.268
Unit Costs—FIFO		
Current period costs	$24,240	$33,925
	÷	÷
Equivalent production	11,000	10,500
Unit costs	$2.204	$3.231

spoiled, 200 abnormally spoiled. Making this change allows us to illustrate how we can treat both types of spoilage in the same situation.

Exhibit 6–11 presents the results. For comparison, we show summary results from Exhibit 6–9. The equivalent unit calculations are exactly the same as those in Exhibit 6–8. Both normally and abnormally spoiled units are included. The resulting unit costs are employed to determine the transfers to Finished Goods and to Abnormal Spoilage Expense. The only differences between Exhibits 6–11 and 6–9 are that part of the spoilage goes to Finished Goods in Exhibit 6–11 and part to Abnormal Spoilage Expense, whereas in Exhibit 6–9 it all goes to Abnormal Spoilage Expense. The ending inventories of work in process are the same in both exhibits.

Because the cost of normal spoilage goes to Finished Goods, we have to recalculate the unit costs of the transferred units. The 10,000 units completed have a per unit cost of $5.4026 in Finished Goods under FIFO, which is the total transfer of $54,026 divided by 10,000. The cost is $5.40 under weighted average ($54,000/10,000). Basically, the cost of normal spoilage is allocated to the good units transferred to Finished Goods. The units remaining in Work-in-Process Inventory receive no allocation because they are not yet inspected and we do not yet know how many will turn out to be spoiled.

EXHIBIT 6–11 Disposition of Costs:
800 Normally Spoiled Units, 200 Abnormally Spoiled Units

Weighted Average			*Results from Exhibit 6–9*
Transferred to Finished Goods:			
Good units, $5 × 10,000	$50,000		$50,000
Normal spoilage, $5 × 800	4,000		0
Total transferred to Finished Goods		$54,000	50,000
Ending Inventory, from Exhibit 6–9		7,600	7,600
Abnormal Spoilage Expense, $5 × 200		1,000	5,000
Total accounted for		$62,600	$62,600
FIFO			
Transferred to Finished Goods:			
Good units, from Exhibit 6–9	$50,050		$50,050
Normal spoilage, ($2.02 + $2.95) × 800	3,976		0
Total transferred to Finished Goods		$54,026	50,050
Ending Inventory, from Exhibit 6–9		7,580	7,580
Abnormal Spoilage Expense, ($2.02 + $2.95) × 200		994	4,970
Total accounted for		$62,600	$62,600

Spoilage Detected During Production

In our examples, the company detected spoilage at the end of the process, so that spoiled units had all material and conversion costs attached to them. Suppose now that the company detects spoilage when units are 40 percent through the process and, of course, removes them. Because all materials are added at the beginning of the process, equivalent unit production and unit costs for materials are not affected. However, equivalent units and, therefore, unit costs for conversion are affected. The company no longer does all of the conversion work on the units, but on only 40 percent of it. The following schedule shows the equivalent production and unit cost calculations for conversion costs with the new information. Assume that all spoilage is considered abnormal. The only difference between these calculations and those in Exhibit 6–8 is the equivalent production for spoiled units.

Units completed	10,000
Ending inventory, 2,000 × 60%	1,200
Spoiled units, 1,000 × 40%	400
Weighted average equivalent production	11,600
Beginning inventory	700
FIFO equivalent production	10,900

The unit costs are then

$$\text{FIFO} = \$33{,}925/10{,}900 = \$3.112$$
$$\text{Weighted average} = \$36{,}600/11{,}600 = \$3.155$$

The unit costs are higher than those in Exhibit 6–8 ($2.95 and $3.00) because while total costs are the same, equivalent units are lower here, which reflects less work done on the 1,000 spoiled units. The disposition of the costs appears below including the $2 and $2.02 unit costs for materials. Compare these with the disposition in Exhibit 6–9.

	Weighted Average	*FIFO*
To Finished Goods:		
10,000 × ($3.155 + $2.00)	$51,550	
Materials from Exhibit 6–9		$19,940
Conversion costs, $2,675 + $3.112 × (10,000 − 700)		31,617
Ending inventory of Work in Process:		
($3.155 × 1,200) + ($2.00 × 2,000)	7,786	
($3.112 × 1,200) + ($2.02 × 2,000)		7,774
Abnormal Spoilage Expense:		
($3.155 × 400) + ($2.00 × 1,000)	3,262	
($3.112 × 400) + ($2.02 × 1,000)		3,265
Total accounted for[6]	$62,598	$62,596

[6]The difference in the totals accounted for is from rounding unit costs to three decimal places.

SUMMARY

Firms that make the same product in more or less continuous processes use process costing. For such firms, the unit cost figure given by dividing costs by production is a reasonable figure because all units are more or less the same.

Process costing requires a cost flow assumption. Weighted average and FIFO are the principal assumptions used; each has advantages and disadvantages, and each requires different cost data and different data for equivalent production.

Job order companies can also use the notion of equivalent unit production to deal with unfinished batches at the end of a period. In addition, some losses and spoilage are inevitable in many manufacturing processes. When such losses or spoilage are within usual bounds (considered normal) the costs are appropriately considered part of the costs of producing good units. If such losses or spoilage are greater than normal, they are considered abnormal. From a financial accounting perspective, abnormal spoilage is considered a period expense since it is not a necessary cost of production. From a management accounting perspective, incremental costs of all spoilage are important in order to see the effects of both normal and abnormal spoilage.

ASSIGNMENTS

6–1 Equivalent Unit Calculations You have the following data available for two independent cases:

	a	*b*
Units in beginning work in process	5,000	10,000
Units completed	80,000	110,000
Units in ending work in process	6,000	12,000
Percentages complete:		
Beginning inventory	30%	60%
Ending inventory	70%	80%

REQUIRED

1. Determine equivalent unit production using the weighted average method.
2. Determine equivalent unit production using the FIFO method.

6–2 Unit Cost Calculations You now have available the following cost data for each case in assignment 6–1.

	a	*b*
Beginning inventory	$ 13,210	$ 6,620
Current period cost	496,200	238,560

REQUIRED

Use your results from assignment 6–1 and the data above to determine unit cost using both the weighted average and FIFO methods.

6–3 Inventories and Transfers This assignment is an extension of assignments 6–1 and 6–2.

REQUIRED

1. For each case, determine the ending inventory of work in process using the weighted average method and the FIFO method.
2. For each case, determine the cost of units transferred to Finished Goods Inventory using both weighted average and FIFO.

6–4 Basic Process Costing Marmat Company manufactures its one product from air, and so has only conversion costs. The company has only one process and uses the weighted average method. It began operations on January 1, 19X4 and had the following activity in January:

Units completed	100,000
Units in process at January 31, 40% complete	20,000
Conversion costs incurred in January	$216,000

REQUIRED

Determine equivalent unit production, unit cost, cost of the ending inventory of work in process, and the cost of units transferred to finished goods.

6–5 Basic Process Costing This is a continuation of assignment 6–4. In February, Marmat Company completed 120,000 units and had 30,000 units in ending work in process, 60 percent complete. February conversion costs were $270,000.

REQUIRED

1. Using the data above, as well as any relevant data from your solution to assignment 6–4, determine equivalent unit production, unit cost, cost of the ending Work-in-Process Inventory, and cost of units transferred to finished goods.
2. Prepare journal entries and T-accounts showing the flow of costs in February.

6–6 Basic Process Costing This assignment is an extension of assignment 6–5.

REQUIRED

Redo assignment 6–5, assuming that Marmat switches to the FIFO method for February.

6–7 Basic Process Costing The data below summarize the operations of Department 202 of Milton Manufacturing Company.

	Units	*Costs*
Beginning inventory	800	
Transferred-in costs, 100% complete		$ 1,000
Conversion costs, 70% complete		5,600
Transferred in during period	10,000	11,000
Transferred out	9,000	
Ending inventory, 60% complete for conversion costs	1,800	

Department 202 does not add materials to the product. Total conversion costs incurred during the period were $90,800.

REQUIRED

1. Using the weighted average method, determine the amounts of cost transferred to the next department and remaining in Department 202 Work-in-Process Inventory.
2. Repeat part 1, using FIFO.

6–8 Inventory and Transfers—FIFO (AICPA) The Cutting Department is the first stage of Mark Company's production process. Conversion costs for the department were 80 percent complete for the beginning inventory and 50 percent complete for the ending inventory. Mark uses the FIFO method. Other data appear below.

	Units	Conversion Costs
Beginning work-in-process inventory	25,000	$ 22,000
Units started and costs incurred during the period	135,000	$143,000
Units completed and sent to next department	100,000	

REQUIRED

1. Determine the conversion cost in the ending inventory of work in process.
2. Determine the amount of conversion cost transferred to the next department.

6–9 Cost Flow Relationships Each of the following cases is an independent situation. The data relate to conversion costs.

REQUIRED

Fill in the blanks, assuming the use of the weighted average method.

Case	Beginning Inventory	Current Period Costs Incurred	Costs Transferred Out	Ending Inventory	Equivalent Production	Unit Cost
a	$10,000	$210,000	$_____	$24,000	_____ units	$ 2
b	$_____	$ 64,000	$_____	$ 8,000	20,000 units	$ 4
c	$20,000	$_____	$ 90,000	$ 6,000	_____ units	$10
d	$40,000	$200,000	$180,000	$_____	15,000 units	$__

6–10 Miscellaneous Calculations (AICPA) Bronson Company had 6,000 units of work in process on January 1 that were 60 percent complete as to conversion costs. During January the company completed 20,000 units. At January 31 it had 8,000 units of work in process that were 40 percent complete as to conversion costs. Bronson uses the weighted average method.

REQUIRED

1. Determine the equivalent unit production as to conversion costs for January.
2. Determine the number of units started in January.

6–11 Cost Flow Relationships Each of the following cases is an independent situation. The data relate to conversion costs.

REQUIRED

Fill in the blanks, assuming the use of FIFO.

Case	Beginning Inventory	Current Period Costs Incurred	Costs Transferred Out	Ending Inventory	Equivalent Production	Unit Cost
a	$____	$ 93,000	$ 86,000	$12,000	____ units	$3
b	$21,000	$____	$____	$16,000	12,000 units	$8
c	$30,000	$120,000	$____	$20,000	10,000 units	$_
d	$10,000	$____	$100,000	$ 8,000	____ units	$4

6–12 Equivalent Production Brooks Chemical Company makes a product called tricide. Tricide goes through a mixing process in liquid form, then is dried under heat until it becomes powder. The yield rarely changes: each gallon put into the drying process yields 6 ounces of powdered tricide. The following information is available from the firm's records for the month of August.

	Mixing Department	Drying Department
Beginning inventory	18,000	114,300
Put into process	180,000	?
Ending inventory	26,000	81,200
Transferred out	?	?

Data for the mixing department are in gallons, for the drying department in ounces. All inventories are 100 percent complete for materials, 60 percent for conversion costs, at both July 31 and August 31.

REQUIRED

1. Determine weighted average equivalent production for both departments.
2. Repeat part 1, using FIFO.

6–13 Cost of Production Report (Weighted Average) This problem uses the weighted average equivalent production figures from assignment 6–12. Brooks Chemical Company showed the following figures for August, with the beginning inventory reflecting the use of the weighted average method.

	Mixing Department	
	Materials	Conversion Costs
Beginning inventory	$ 14,800	$ 22,400
Current period costs	146,300	379,800

REQUIRED

Prepare a cost of production report for the mixing department for August, using the weighted average method.

6–14 Second Department (AICPA Adapted) The wiring department is the second stage of Flem Company's production cycle. On May 1 the beginning work in process contained 25,000 units that were 60 percent complete as to conversion costs. During May the wiring department received 100,000 units from the first stage of the production cycle. On May 31 the ending work in process contained 20,000 units that were 80 percent complete as to conversion costs. The wiring department adds materials at the end of the process.

REQUIRED

1. Determine equivalent production for transferred-in costs, materials, and conversion costs, using the weighted average method.
2. Repeat part 1, using FIFO.

6–15 Process Costing and Decisions Mountainview Brick Company received an order for 300,000 bricks from a large construction company. The price was to be $1,000 per 1,000 bricks, and the customer would pay shipping costs. The usual selling price is $1,200 per 1,000, but Mountainview had excess capacity and accepted the order, even though it necessitated some overtime and expediting costs.

A member of the controller's staff made the following analysis before the firm accepted the order.

	Expected Results	
	Reject Order	*Accept Order*
Beginning inventory	$ 397,400	$ 397,400
Current period costs:		
Materials	$ 2,186,900	2,301,500
Conversion costs	3,765,000	3,984,700
Totals	$ 6,349,300	$ 6,683,600
Units completed	10,672,000	10,972,000
Equivalent units in ending inventory	886,400	886,400
Total equivalent production	11,558,400	11,858,400
Unit cost	$ 0.549	$ 0.564

Materials and conversion costs are generally about the same percentage complete. The staff member noted that the unit cost would rise somewhat but would still be less than the $1 selling price, and so the firm should accept the order. The actual results for the month turned out about as the staff member had predicted.

REQUIRED

Determine whether the firm should have accepted the order.

6–16 Process Costing—Second Department (AICPA) Lakeview Corporation is a manufacturer that uses the weighted average process costing method to account for costs of production. Lakeview manufactures a product that goes through three separate departments: Molding, Assembly, and Finishing. The following information was obtained for the Assembly Department for June 19X6.

Work in process, June 1—2,000 units composed of the following:

	Amount	Degree of Completion
Transferred-in from Molding	$32,000	100%
Costs added by Assembly Department:		
Direct materials	$20,000	100%
Direct labor	7,200	60%
Factory overhead applied	5,500	50%
Total added	$32,700	
Work in process, June 1	$64,700	

The following activity occurred during June. The Assembly Department received 10,000 units from the Molding Department at a cost of $160,000. The Assembly Department added $150,000 in costs, as follows:

Direct materials	$ 96,000
Direct labor	36,000
Factory overhead applied	18,000
Total	$150,000

Assembly completed 8,000 units and transferred them to the Finishing Department. At June 30, Assembly had 4,000 units in process, 90 percent complete as to materials, 70 percent as to direct labor, and 35 percent as to factory overhead applied.

REQUIRED

Prepare in good form a cost of production report for the Assembly Department for June. Show all calculations.

6–17 Process Costing—First Department Wynn Company operates a number of plants. One, the Kelton plant, makes a single product that goes through a mixing process and a drying process. The data below relate to the operations of the mixing department in January and February.

	January	February
Beginning inventory of work in process	0	600
Units put into process	12,400	13,100
Units completed and sent to drying	11,800	13,300
Ending inventory	600	400
Percentage completion of ending inventory:		
Materials	90%	50%
Conversion costs	60%	30%
Costs:		
Materials put into process	$258,640	$271,760
Conversion costs	526,860	569,770

REQUIRED

1. For both January and February, use the FIFO method to determine unit costs of production, transfer out to the drying department, and ending inventories. Round to the nearest dollar.
2. Repeat part 1 using the weighted average method.

6–18 Process Costing—Second Department This assignment is an extension of assignment 6–17. The product that the Kelton plant makes goes from the mixing department to the drying department. The drying department does not add materials. Data for the drying department for January and February appear below.

	January	*February*
Beginning inventory	0	1,000
Units transferred in	11,800	13,300
Units completed and sent to finished goods	10,800	13,800
Ending inventory	1,000	500
Percentage of completion of ending inventory:		
Transferred-in costs	100%	100%
Conversion costs	80%	70%
Conversion costs incurred	$212,750	$237,620

REQUIRED

1. Assume that the costs transferred in are the FIFO costs of the mixing department, from your solution to assignment 6–17. Determine the unit costs, transfers to finished goods, and ending inventories for the drying department for both months using FIFO. Round unit-cost calculations to four decimal places ($\frac{1}{100}$ of a cent).
2. Still assuming that the costs transferred into the drying department are the FIFO costs of the mixing department, repeat part 1 using the weighted average method for the drying department.

6–19 Journal Entries and T-Accounts This problem uses the data and solution to assignment 6–18.

REQUIRED

Using the FIFO method for both the mixing and drying departments, prepare the journal entries that affect the Work-in-Process accounts of both departments for January and February. Additionally, prepare T-accounts for the Work in Process of both departments.

6–20 Process Costing (FIFO)—Two Materials Reiner Company makes a single product. The firm heats a chemical called algon for about three hours, then adds another chemical called bygon and heats the mixture for an additional hour. Conversion costs are incurred evenly over the process. The firm uses process costing, even though it makes individual batches of the product. The firm has several vats for the heating and mixing and usually has a batch in each vat.

At January 1, 19X5, the firm had twenty batches in process. For fifteen of the batches the percentage of conversion was 40 percent, for the other five it was 90 percent. Material cost for the beginning inventory was $17,000 for algon and $6,000 for bygon, and conversion costs were $54,500. During January the firm completed 350 batches and at the end of the month had ten batches in process. All these batches were 80 percent complete for conversion.

Cost data for January were: algon put into process, $287,000; bygon put into process, $400,200; conversion costs, $1,820,000.

REQUIRED

1. Determine the unit costs of algon, bygon, and conversion for January, using FIFO.
2. Determine the cost of ending inventory of work in process and the cost transferred to finished goods.

6–21 Basic Process Costing Jardin Corporation uses process costing. Products are started in department 100. For December, beginning work-in-process inventory included 3,500 units that were 90 percent complete in materials and 70 percent complete for labor and other conversion costs. December 31 work-in-process inventory was 4,000 units 100 percent complete in materials and 50 percent complete in conversion costs. January 31 work-in-process inventory was 2,000 units 80 percent complete for materials and 60 percent complete in conversion costs. The firm put 32,000 units into production in December, 25,000 in January.

REQUIRED

1. Using both weighted average and FIFO, calculate equivalent units of production for department 100 for December and for January.
2. Assume that the following costs were recorded.

	Materials	*Conversion*
Work in process, 12/1	$ 111,037	$ 118,825
Current costs—December	$1,164,600	$1,459,350
—January	$ 873,300	$1,244,500

Determine the costs per equivalent unit in December and in January. (Use both weighted average and FIFO assumptions.)

3. Using FIFO, determine the inventories of work in process at December 31 and January 31 and the costs transferred out of department 100 in each of the two months.

6–22 Multiple Departments Orgostics, Inc. manufactures electronic circuit boards. Each board goes through department I, where it is etched and made ready for the components that will be put onto it. The components are assembled in sets in department II, which is mostly a matter of wiring purchased subassemblies. The final assembly is done in department III. In department III, two sets of components are put onto each board. The company uses weighted average process costing. All materials are put into process immediately in departments I and II. Department III does not add materials. Unit and cost data for the three departments for November appear below.

	Department I	*Department II*	*Department III*
Units completed	22,000	44,000	22,000
Units in ending inventory	4,000	6,000	1,000
Percentages complete	60%	80%	30%
Beginning inventory costs:			
Materials	$14,000	$ 34,000	$ 0
Conversion	10,900	16,500	16,400
Prior department costs	0	0	24,000
Current period costs:			
Materials	$90,000	$266,000	$ 0
Conversion	62,300	154,300	72,800
Prior department costs	0	0	?

REQUIRED

Determine the ending inventory for department III and the cost transferred to Finished Goods Inventory.

6–23 Change in Measure of Units Virgule Company makes shaving lotion in two departments, mixing and heating. The mixing department blends dry chemicals and transfers the resulting powder to the heating department, which adds water and heats the mixture. The finished lotion emerges from the heating department. The measure of output in the mixing department is pounds, in the heating department, gallons. Each pound put into process in the heating department results in 0.40 gallon of lotion. Data related to March, 19X0 are:

	Mixing Department	*Heating Department*
Beginning inventory	8,000 lb	4,000 gal
Put into production	74,000 lb	28,000 gal
Completed and transferred	70,000 lb	29,000 gal
Ending inventory	12,000 lb	3,000 gal
Costs		
Beginning inventory:		
Prior department costs	—	$20,200
Materials	$ 3,600	600
Conversion costs	12,000	1,800
Current period costs:		
Materials	33,300	4,200
Conversion costs	149,950	33,850

The ending inventory of the mixing department is complete for materials, 75 percent complete for conversion costs. The heating department ending inventory is complete for materials, two-thirds complete for conversion costs. The firm uses the weighted average inventory method.

REQUIRED

1. Determine the amount of cost transferred from the mixing department to the heating department.

2. Determine the amount of cost transferred from the heating department to finished goods and the ending inventory of work in process in the heating department.

6–24 Comprehensive Process Costing (AICPA Adapted) Ballinger Paper Company makes high-quality paper boxes. The box department performs two separate operations. One group of machines cuts and trims paper to the required dimensions. Another group of machines then folds and creases the paper, forming the boxes. All work in process consists of paper forms cut and trimmed, but not folded and creased. These forms are considered 50 percent complete as to conversion costs. The firm uses the weighted average method for all of its inventories. One square yard of paper yields four boxes.

Data relating to August, 19X4 appear below.

	Cost	*Quantity*
Materials (paper):		
Inventory at August 1	$ 82,000	400,000 sq yd
Purchases in August	326,000	1,300,000
Inventory at August 31	?	325,000
Box department:		
Beginning inventory of boxes in process:		
Material cost	$ 41,700	800,000 boxes cut and trimmed
Conversion cost	22,150	
Boxes completed and transferred to finished goods	?	6,000,000 boxes
Work in process at August 31	?	300,000 boxes
Finished goods:		
Beginning inventory	$ 46,400	400,000 boxes
Ending inventory	?	500,000 boxes

Conversion costs for August were $230,000.

REQUIRED

1. Determine the cost of materials put into production.
2. Determine the unit costs of boxes for August.
3. Determine the cost of boxes transferred to finished goods and the ending inventory of work in process.
4. Determine cost of goods sold and the ending inventory of finished goods.

6–25 Comprehensive Process Costing (AICPA Adapted) Data related to the August operations of Ballinger Paper Company appear in assignment 6–24. Let us assume that the firm uses FIFO for work-in-process inventory and continues to use weighted average for materials and finished goods.

REQUIRED

Redo parts 2, 3, and 4 from assignment 6–24 using FIFO. Your answer to part 1 remains valid for the new situation.

6–26 Process Costing and Decisions Williams Company operates a plant that weaves cotton. The plant also dyes and waterproofs some of the fabric. The plant currently sells about 40 percent of its output of 2 million square yards after weaving. It dyes the rest and waterproofs half of what it dyes. For technical reasons, it cannot waterproof undyed fabric.

The plant accumulates material and direct labor cost by department (weaving, dyeing, waterproofing) and applies overhead based on a single plantwide rate of $3.55 per direct labor dollar. The statement of gross margin below reflects a typical month's operations, in thousands of dollars.

	Total	*Woven Fabric*	*Dyed Fabric*	*Waterproofed Fabric*
Sales	$1,925.1	$ 640.2	$582.3	$702.6
Cost of sales	1,581.0	496.8	479.5	604.7
Gross margin	$ 344.1	$ 143.4	$102.8	$ 97.9
Gross margin percentages	17.9%	22.4%	17.7%	13.9%
Cost of sales calculations:				
Materials		$ 806.0	$ 58.3	$ 42.4
Prior department costs		0.0	745.1	479.5
Direct labor		95.8	34.2	18.2
Overhead at $3.55 per labor dollar		340.1	121.4	64.6
Totals		1,241.9	$959.0	604.7
Transferred to next department		745.1	479.5	0.0
Cost of sales		$ 496.8	$479.5	$604.7

Thus, the cost of sales for woven fabric is 40 percent of the total costs of the weaving department because the firm sells 40 percent of woven fabric and transfers 60 percent to the dyeing department. (Inventories are negligible.)

Some of the managers have expressed concern about the waterproofing operation because of its low gross margin percentage. They have also questioned whether the dyeing operation is sufficiently profitable. The demand for the firm's products exceeds production capacity. The firm accepts orders for the three different products and schedules production accordingly, within the constraint that it cannot weave more than 2 million square yards per month. Although demand is high, competition is strong, and the firm could not raise prices on any product without suffering a considerable drop in demand.

In analyzing the operations, the controller developed the following information about manufacturing overhead in each department. He had been critical of the practice of applying overhead on a plantwide basis, but he had not pushed for departmental rates because the other managers were not amenable to the change.

	Weaving	*Dyeing*	*Waterproofing*
Monthly fixed overhead (thousands)	$343.5	$52.4	$44.1
Variable per labor dollar	$ 0.60	$ 0.65	$ 0.35

REQUIRED

Analyze the situation and make whatever recommendations you think wise, supporting them with appropriate calculations and stating your assumptions.

6–27 Basic Spoilage, Three Alternatives Farnsworth Company makes machine parts. One department specializes in a small gear used in precision instruments. The gears are ground to small tolerances and are inspected at the end of the process. Spoiled gears must be thrown out. During March the department showed the following results:

Good gears completed	10,000
Spoiled gears	2,000
Ending inventory of work in process	3,000

Conversion costs in the beginning inventory and incurred during March totaled $81,420. The ending work-in-process inventory was 60 percent complete for conversion costs. We ignore materials to reduce calculations. The firm uses the weighted average method.

REQUIRED

Determine unit conversion costs, ending work-in-process inventory, and transfers to finished goods, under each of the following assumptions:

1. Spoilage is ignored.
2. Spoilage is considered normal, and its cost is computed.
3. Spoilage is considered abnormal.

6–28 Normal Spoilage, Comparison of Methods "I don't see why you go through all those calculations of spoiled units when it all comes out the same." Your boss made that comment to you as you were calculating the unit cost for the current period, as shown below. He went on: "Why don't you just ignore the spoiled units and calculate unit costs based on good output? It would work out the same, wouldn't it?"

Your firm uses the weighted average method and detects spoilage at the end of the process. Your calculations are:

	Materials	*Conversion Costs*
Units completed (good)	100,000	100,000
Ending inventories, 100% and 60% complete	20,000	12,000
Spoiled units (all normal)	10,000	10,000
Equivalent production	130,000	122,000
Total costs from beginning inventory and incurred during the period	$1,300,000	$1,830,000
Unit costs	$ 10	$ 15
Costs transferred to Finished Goods:		
Good units	$1,000,000	$1,500,000
Normal spoilage	100,000	150,000
Total	$1,100,000	$1,650,000
Ending Work-in-Process Inventory	$ 200,000	$ 180,000

REQUIRED

1. Calculate unit costs, amounts transferred to Finished Goods, and ending Work-in-Process Inventory as your boss has suggested.
2. Comment on the differences between your calculations in part 1 and those in the problem.

6–29 Abnormal Spoilage (FIFO) Crittendon Company makes a single product. Data for August appear below.

Unit data:		
Beginning inventory, work in process		1,200
Started in production		8,000
Completed, sent to finished goods		8,500
Ending inventory, work in process		500
	Materials	*Conversion Costs*
Percentages complete:		
Beginning inventory	100%	70%
Ending inventory	100%	40%
Cost data:		
Beginning inventory	$ 4,120	$ 9,980
Current period costs	33,600	112,840

All spoilage is considered abnormal, and its cost is expensed on the income statement for the month. Spoilage is detected at the end of the process. The firm uses FIFO.

REQUIRED

1. Determine the number of units spoiled in August.
2. Determine the cost of spoiled goods, costs transferred from Work in Process to Finished Goods, and cost of ending inventory of work in process.

6–30 Abnormal Spoilage (Weighted Average)

REQUIRED

Repeat assignment 6–29 using the weighted average method.

6–31 Spoilage, Normal and Abnormal (FIFO) Barnett Company makes a single product. Data for March appear below.

Unit data:	
Beginning inventory, work in process	2,000
Started in production	13,000
Completed, sent to finished goods	13,000
Ending inventory, work in process	1,200
Units spoiled	800

Cost data:

	Materials	*Conversion Costs*
Beginning inventory	$ 79,000	$ 91,080
Current period costs	611,000	1,172,160

Normal spoilage is 500 units. All inventories were 100 percent complete for materials and 60 percent for conversion costs. All spoilage is detected at the end of the process. The firm uses FIFO.

REQUIRED

Determine the costs of normal spoilage, abnormal spoilage, ending Work-in-Process Inventory, and transfers to Finished Goods. Be sure that you account for all costs, beginning inventory, and current period costs.

6–32 Tracing Normal Spoilage Argon Company produces a single type of fountain pen in a single process. The firm experiences normal spoilage of 5 percent of good output, detected at the end of the process. During the process, materials and conversion costs are continuous, so that we need consider only total costs. Additionally, all of the production costs are variable. The firm began April with no work-in-process inventory, completed 200,000 good units during the month, spoiled 10,000, and had 21,000 units 40 percent complete at the end of the month. Total production costs were $2,184,000.

REQUIRED

1. Determine the firm's equivalent production, considering normal spoilage.
2. Determine the cost of the ending work-in-process inventory and the cost transferred to Finished Goods.
3. Given that normal spoilage is 5 percent of good output, and assuming that April costs are under control, what is the unit cost per *good* unit? Does this unit cost correspond to the costs transferred to finished goods from your answer to item 2?
4. How many of the units in ending work-in-process inventory should turn out to be spoiled? Does the cost per good unit that you computed in part 3 correspond to the unit cost of the ending Work-in-Process Inventory, considering that work in process is only 40 percent complete?

6–33 Final Department (CMA) JC Company puts its single product through three departments, molding, assembly, and finishing. Data for the finishing department for May are:

Work-in-process inventory, May 1	1,400
Units transferred in from assembly	14,000
Units spoiled	700
Units transferred to finished goods inventory	11,200

	Materials	*Transferred In*	*Conversion*
Costs:			
Beginning inventory	$ 1,350	$ 6,500	$ 4,200
Current period	14,050	70,500	35,700

The finishing department adds materials at the start of the process. The beginning work-in-process inventory was 70 percent complete for conversion; the ending inventory was 40 percent complete. All spoiled units go through the entire process before detection. Normal spoilage is 560 units.

JC uses the weighted average method.

REQUIRED

1. Determine the cost of the ending inventory of work in process.

2. Determine the cost transferred to finished goods inventory.
3. Determine the cost of abnormal spoilage.

6–34 Lost Units, Comparison of Methods Norwalk Chemical Company manufactures a number of products in different plants. The Eastbourne Plant makes polycoat, which is used in the making of furniture waxes. The controller of the plant has been ignoring spoilage, which takes place in the form of evaporation. The plant engineers usually determine whether or not the amount of evaporation is within normal limits and take corrective action if it is not. In any case, the controller considers all evaporation to be normal and simply does not count it in determining unit costs.

The controller recently attended a seminar where a speaker argued that it was wise to calculate the cost of spoilage because it gave managers more information than they would otherwise have. The controller decided to try it using the previous month's data, but was unsure how to proceed. The data appear below.

Inventory at beginning of month, gallons		14,000
Gallons put into production		120,000
Gallons completed and sent to finished goods		102,000
Gallons in ending inventory		20,000
Gallons lost in processing		12,000
Cost of beginning inventory:		
Materials	$ 29,900	
Conversion costs	51,300	
Current period costs:		
Materials	239,500	
Conversion costs	732,600	

Inventories were complete with respect to materials at the beginning and ending of the month. The beginning inventory was 60 percent complete for conversion costs, and the ending inventory was 40 percent complete. The firm uses FIFO. The plant engineers believe that the losses take place very near the end of the production process, largely because of overheating.

REQUIRED

1. Calculate the unit costs of production, both materials and conversion costs, ignoring the lost units, as the controller has been doing.
2. Calculate the unit costs of production, both materials and conversion costs, including the lost units.
3. Looking at the results in parts 1 and 2, do you see any advantage to using one method or the other?

6–35 Spoilage and Process Costing Eatright Manufacturing presents the following information for February 19X7.

Beginning inventory—work in process:	
Materials	$ 27,850
Conversion costs	$ 40,800
(1600 units 75% complete for materials and 60% complete in conversion costs)	

Ending inventory—work in process:	
(2000 units 50% complete in materials and 40% complete in conversion costs)	
Units put into production during February	13,600
Units completed during February	12,000
Current production costs:	
Materials	$290,000
Conversion costs	$525,000

Assume that spoilage occurs and is identified on average when units are 50 percent complete both for materials and conversion costs.

REQUIRED

1. How many units were spoiled? What does this translate to in equivalent units?
2. If Eatright uses weighted average and accounts for this spoilage as abnormal, what is the value of ending inventory—work in process for February?
3. If Eatright uses FIFO and accounts for this spoilage as normal and ignores it, what costs are transferred to finished goods?
4. If the company followed the procedure in part 2, what would be the journal entry to record the month-end events?

6–36 Abnormal Spoilage, Two Departments (AICPA Adapted) The Dexter Production Company makes a single product, using a machining process and a finishing process. Company records for June 19X4 showed the following.

	Machining Department	*Finishing Department*
Units in process, June 1	0	0
Units transferred from prior department	0	60,000
Units started in production	80,000	0
Units completed and transferred out	60,000	50,000
Units in process, June 30	20,000	8,000
Percentages of completion of June 30 work-in-process inventories:		
Materials	100%	100%
Conversion costs	60%	70%

Spoiled units have no salvage value and are 50 percent complete with respect to materials and conversion costs. The firm's policy is to charge all spoilage to expense because all spoilage is considered abnormal.

Cost records showed the following for June:

	Machining Department	*Finishing Department*
Materials	$240,000	$ 88,500
Conversion costs	216,000	164,140

REQUIRED

1. For the machining department, determine the cost of ending inventory and of units transferred to the finishing department.
2. For the finishing department, determine the cost of ending inventory, the cost of units transferred to finished goods inventory, and the cost of abnormal spoilage.

6–37 Process Costing (CMA) West Corporation manufactures a product called Aggregate in its California plant. Materials are put into process at the beginning of the process. It transfers Aggregate to its Utah plant, where Aggregate is used to make other products. In manufacturing Aggregate, there is about 12 percent to 16 percent spoilage, all of which occurs at the end of the process. Such spoilage is considered normal. West includes spoilage in calculating equivalent unit production. The unit of measure of Aggregate is a pound. The following data relate to November:

Beginning work-in-process inventory	4,000, 75% complete
Ending work-in-process inventory	3,000, $\frac{1}{3}$ complete
Pounds put into process	16,000
Pounds completed	15,000

Costs:	*Beginning Inventory*	*Current Period*
Materials	$22,800	$ 81,600
Conversion	46,670	196,690

West uses the weighted average method of accounting for in-process inventories.

REQUIRED

1. Determine equivalent unit production for each cost factor.
2. Determine the ending inventory of work in process and the cost transferred out of the California plant.

7

STANDARD COSTS AND VARIANCES

This chapter builds on the principles of flexible budgets and extends their use to the development of standard costs. We pay particular attention to manufacturing firms. The chapter delves into the ways that managers set performance standards, how they use these standards for control and performance evaluation, and what problems they encounter in using standards, especially behavioral problems. We also discuss the use of standards in advanced manufacturing environments.

Among other things, managers are concerned with effectiveness and efficiency. Effectiveness relates to whether a job is done (did we manufacture the 10,000 units we needed?) and efficiency to the relationship of inputs to outputs (did it cost us more than it should have to produce the units?). In this chapter, our concern is primarily with measures of efficiency. We describe techniques for analyzing how well managers have controlled the acquisition and use of resources in producing a given quantity of output.

FLEXIBLE BUDGETS

Companies prepare budgets before the period being budgeted. Such budgets reflect *planned* levels of activity. However, for evaluating performance and assessing whether control was adequate, we need a budget based on the *actual* level of activity. Chapter 1 described a flexible budget allowance as the amount of cost that should be incurred given the *actual* level of activity. At the end of a period we need a flexible budget allowance against which to compare actual results. Suppose we have the following budget formula for monthly utility costs as well as other data.

Budgeted monthly utility cost	= $22,500 + $2.40 × units produced
Budgeted units for March	18,000
Actual units for March	19,400
Actual utility cost for March	$68,800

With these data we can easily determine that budgeted utility cost for March, *before the month began*, was $65,700. That is, before March began, we expected to spend $65,700 on utilities, given that we expected to make 18,000 units.

$$\text{Budgeted cost for March} = \$22{,}500 + (\$2.40 \times 18{,}000) = \$65{,}700$$

Does this mean that we overspent on utilities because the actual cost, $68,800, was greater than the original budget of $65,700? If you said no, you are correct. We cannot evaluate the actual cost against the original budgeted cost because the original budget assumed 18,000 units and we actually made 19,400 units. We need a flexible budget allowance that reflects 19,400 units. Therefore, we should make the following comparison, and determine that we spent less than expected on utilities given that we produced 19,400 units.

	Flexible Budget for Actual Units	*Actual Cost*	*Variance*
Utility cost	$69,060 $22,500 + ($2.40 × 19,400)	$68,800	$260 favorable

The original budget of $65,700 is no longer relevant for determining whether we used utilities efficiently. Of course, whether we should have produced 19,400 units instead of the original budget of 18,000 is another question. It might well be that a manager overproduced to keep workers busy. We shall see later that unwise use of budgets and standards can lead managers to take actions that harm the company. If the extra units simply pile up in a warehouse, the manager was wrong to increase output, but our principal concern here is whether the manager operated efficiently given the actual output achieved.

In this chapter we extend the idea of flexible budget allowances to the development and use of standard costs. Standard costs are per unit expressions of flexible budget allowances for *variable costs*. A flexible budget allowance for a fixed cost is the same regardless of the level of activity. We use standard costs to evaluate the efficiency with which we produced some number of units of product. Notice also that we could develop a flexible budget allowance based on inputs such as direct labor hours or machine hours; we shall do this later in analyzing variances.

A standard cost is the cost of a unit of product that the company expects to incur. We shall deal with ways to develop standards later in the chapter.

A standard cost consists of a standard price, or rate, and a standard quantity of an input factor such as materials, components, or direct labor. A standard price, or rate, is the expected cost of *a unit of the input factor*, such as $12 per gallon of material, $8 per hour of direct labor, or $6 variable overhead per machine hour. The standard quantity is the amount of the input factor that should be used to make a unit of product: three pounds of material, four direct labor hours, 0.05 machine hours. Thus, if a unit of product should require four direct labor hours and the standard labor rate is $8 per hour, the standard direct labor cost is $32 (4 hours at $8). These two factors (price and quantity) are the keys to independent analyses of the differences between planned and actual total costs. These differences are called **variances**, with one related to the price paid for the input factor, the other related to the quantity of the input factor used.

VARIANCES FROM PLANS

If a company uses materials that are more costly than planned, or if actual labor hours exceed the standard quantity, then costs are affected unfavorably. While managers are interested in aggregate measures of how they are doing in relation to plans, they are also interested in how each element of production separately affects costs (and, therefore, profits).

1. A **variance** occurs when the actual cost of inputs (material, labor, overhead) differs from standard costs. If profits are higher because of a variance, this is **favorable**; if profits are lower, this is **unfavorable**.
2. Managers want to *look at each cost element individually*: one variance at a time.

It is important to understand what we mean by a variance. We will compare standards with actual performance. A variance is a dollar reflection of the differences. This comparison does not reveal *why* a variance or series of variances has occurred; it identifies amounts but does *not* establish a *cause-and-effect* relationship. Chapter 21 deals with investigating variances to determine their causes. Later discussion in this chapter shows the importance of causality as it relates to the responsibilities of various managers.

PRODUCTION STANDARDS

Standards can be developed for each product a company manufactures. It is easier to develop standards for a product made continually (such as a certain model of an automobile) than for a special product (like the space shuttle). A company need not make only one product to use standard costs, but the products must be relatively standard—made roughly the same way, with the same operations. A processing firm of the type Chapter 6 describes obviously could use standard costs because its product is made the same way all of the time (unless it changes its technology or processing methods, in which case it could revise its standards). A job order company could use standard costs if it used standard operations on some of its products/components and made roughly the same kinds again and again. It would not benefit a job order company to establish standards unless it repeated the manufacture of products/components because the cost of establishing standards for one-time jobs would exceed the benefits.

Perhaps the most common use of standard costs is in **repetitive manufacturing**, where a company makes the same products over and over, but makes more than one. Automobile companies are a good example. Not all companies can successfully use standard costs. For example, a firm making individual, unique products may not be able to develop standards for production.

Advantages of Standard Costs

Chapter 1 referred to the following formula as a **flexible budget**:

$$\text{total cost} = \text{fixed cost} + (\text{variable cost})(\text{quantity})$$

If a budget is a plan for the next period, we can specify the assumptions that make up the budget. Production standards, then, are a list of usual (expected) production costs broken down by materials, labor costs, and overhead costs. They are what a product *should* cost to manufacture. Managers do not expect actual results in the future to exactly match these standards, but they use standard costs as a reference for comparison and control.

Control Standards represent what costs should be. When actual results differ from these standards, management can analyze the variances and evaluate performance as well as decide what actions should be taken. This is the *control* aspect of standards and variances.

Standards and variances also help to focus on the responsibilities of managers. For example, different managers are often responsible for acquiring and using resources, with purchasing managers acquiring materials and components and manufacturing managers using them to make products.

Pricing Standard costs are helpful in pricing decisions. Since standards are expected costs, they are a logical basis for prices.

For example, Universe Press prints magazines. Assume that a new customer asks management for a quotation on a 96-page magazine, specifying the grade and weight of paper, the trim size (such as $8\frac{1}{8} \times 10\frac{7}{8}$ inches), and the way in which colors are to be printed (such as a four-color front and back cover and only black and white for the rest of the magazine). The estimating department can go to a set of standards for that type of magazine and use them to establish what it will cost in paper, ink, labor, overhead, and so on to produce the magazine. These costs can be marked up to yield Universe a reasonable profit and then submitted to the prospective client.

Product Costing Another advantage of standard costs is that they can be used for product costing. Inventories are carried at standard cost, not actual cost, which reduces bookkeeping efforts and expense. Variances are placed into separate accounts, and are either treated as a period expense or prorated between inventories and cost of goods sold. This subject is covered in detail in the next chapter.

Developing Cost Standards

Standards from Historical Records A good first step in establishing standard costs is to analyze past records. Past data can be used to predict future costs if operating conditions are fairly constant between past and future time periods. If a new plant has been operating for only a year, these data may not be representative, since the bugs may not all be worked out of the equipment and personnel may still be learning how to operate the equipment efficiently and effectively.

Universe Press, for example, has been in business for many years and has used its current type of printing equipment for the past five years. A review of past records can reveal a clear pattern of costs. This review points to two distinct types of costs: start-up (or makeready) costs and running costs. Start-up costs are the costs of cleaning up a press from the last job, removing the printing plates from that job, mounting new printing plates, threading a new roll of paper through the press, and getting ready to run. Past records show that the more color the job requires and the more expensive the grade of paper, the longer (and more costly) the makeready. Standards can be developed as shown in Exhibit 7–1.

Standard running costs include standards for wage rates, running speed, paper and ink costs, and paper use. The wage rates, crew size, and crew makeup are set by union contract. Shorter running jobs usually entail a greater cost per unit than longer jobs. The presses cannot get up to high-speed operation with short jobs, and expected waste is higher.

Records are used here to establish standards in labor hours to be used and paper to be consumed. Current prices are applied to these standards to get the standard cost of production.

The principal difficulty with using historical data to establish standards is

EXHIBIT 7–1 Standard Makeready Costs

Clean up from old job and mount new plate	0.5 hour per each 8 pages
Add for each additional color	0.25 hour per each 8 pages
Add for coated paper	0.5 hour per job
Standard crew costs	$47.50 per hour
Standard overhead	$40.00 per labor hour
Plus standard paper and ink costs for the equivalent of 200 copies as expected start-up waste	

that inefficiencies may be built into the standards. Past operations may have been inefficient because of inadequate supervision, poor methods, or other factors. Standards based on past performance can perpetuate inefficiency.

Engineered Standards An alternative to using historical data is the engineering approach, which was discussed in Chapter 3 in connection with cost estimation. Basically, engineers develop standards for materials, direct labor, and variable overhead by studying the product and the production process. Time and motion studies or computer simulations reveal the labor time required for each operation in the production process. Material requirements are estimated on the basis of such factors as the expected normal waste from, for example, cutting circular pieces out of rectangular metal sheets. Variable overhead is estimated on the basis of factors such as fringe benefits for laborers and power requirements for machinery.

Engineered standards are especially useful for new products. Because the firm has no experience with these products, historical records are of no value except as they can be related to the operations needed to make the new products. For example, if a new product is expected to require a grinding operation similar to one used for an existing product, managers might be confident that the grinding time for the new product will be about the same as that for the existing product.

One problem with engineered standards is that they may be too tight, failing to allow for the behavior of workers. The mechanistic approach to management pioneered by Taylor and others in the early 1900s has fallen into disfavor because it fails to accommodate the attitudes and desires of workers, considering them to be adjuncts to machinery. The range of behavioral problems associated with the setting of standards is discussed later in this chapter.

Many companies produce in batches. For them, it is necessary to specify a lot size to develop standard costs. Very often, the larger the lot size, the lower the average cost of a unit. However, the larger the lot size, the higher the inventory. Because there are costs of having inventory (storage, deterioration, the opportunity cost of the money tied up in the inventory), the decision about lot size cannot hinge only on production costs. Many companies use a standard lot size in developing standard costs, which is the number they usually make in a batch. They might adjust the standards if they should manufacture a greater or lesser number.

ILLUSTRATION OF STANDARD COSTS

Mencento, Inc., a manufacturer of chemicals, uses standard costs to aid in planning and control. For one of its major products, engineers, production managers, and cost accountants have agreed on the standards shown in Exhibit 7–2, which also shows actual results for July.

In real life, there would almost certainly be several materials or components and direct labor of several grades from several departments. We use a single material and a single type of direct labor to focus on the general con-

EXHIBIT 7–2 Data for Illustration

Standard Costs:	
Materials: 2 pounds at $0.50 per pound	$1.00
Direct labor: 0.25 hours at $12 per hour	3.00
Variable overhead at $2 per direct labor hour	0.50
Fixed overhead at $3 per direct labor hour	0.75
Total standard cost	$5.25

Standard fixed overhead is based on budgeted fixed overhead of $90,000 per month and normal activity of 30,000 direct labor hours per month.

Actual Results:	
Production	100,000 units
Materials purchased: 150,000 pounds at $0.55	$ 82,500
Materials used	220,000 pounds
Direct labor: 26,000 hours at $11.80 per hour	$306,800
Variable overhead	$ 54,600
Fixed overhead	$ 93,000

cepts and keep the calculations to a minimum. For the same reason, we use only one basis to apply overhead. As previous chapters have noted, many companies apply overhead using several bases. Measures of activity other than labor hours could be used for determining the overhead rate or rates. Chapter 4 illustrated ways to select the measure of activity. There are, of course, many elements of costs included in both variable overhead and fixed overhead. These matters simply add to the calculations; they do not introduce any conceptual problems.

The fixed overhead calculation needs some explanation: the variable overhead per direct labor hour was most likely developed at least partly through regression analysis or other technique discussed in Chapter 3. From that analysis also came an estimate of fixed overhead. The estimated fixed and variable components serve as bases to develop budgeted rates: the estimates are not automatically used as budgets. Once the budgeted amounts, both fixed and variable, are developed, the calculation of the standard fixed overhead rate follows the same procedure used in Chapter 5 to calculate a predetermined overhead rate: divide total budgeted fixed overhead by the relevant measure of activity. Then the standard fixed overhead per unit of product is the rate per unit of activity times the units of activity required for the particular product.

VARIANCES

We begin the illustration of variance analysis with direct labor costs. There are few differences in calculating any of the variances, so when you understand the basic principles, you should be able to apply them to any cost. Recall that the most basic principle of variance analysis is to analyze one factor at a time, usually rate (price), or quantity (use, efficiency). All other factors should be held constant.

Labor Variances

What should Mencento's direct labor have been, *given that it produced 100,000 units*? The basis for determining total standard cost is the *actual output*. We are generally concerned with efficiency—the relationship of input to output, so we want to know how much it should have cost to produce 100,000 units. The total standard direct labor cost for 100,000 units is $300,000, 100,000 × $3 standard cost per unit. Or we could say that the company should have used 25,000 direct labor hours (100,000 × 0.25) to make 100,000 units, and, with a $12 standard rate per hour, we get the same $300,000. The 25,000 hours calculated above is often called **standard hours allowed**. Standard hours allowed is the number of hours of direct labor that should have been used to achieve actual output. Sometimes it is handy to use standard hours allowed in your calculations. The calculations, standard cost per unit of product times units produced and standard rate per labor hour times standard hours allowed, are equivalent. Because workers actually earned $306,800 working 26,000 hours, there is a total labor variance of $6,800 ($306,800 − $300,000), and it is unfavorable.

We want to separate the $6,800 total variance into two components: (1) the difference related to labor rate; and (2) the difference due to labor quantity. A rate variance answers the question: given the *quantity of inputs acquired* (direct labor in this case), did the company pay more or less than it should have, more or less than standard? The difference between actual total cost and the cost that should have been incurred *given the quantity of input acquired*, is the rate variance.

An efficiency variance, or quantity variance, answers the question: *given the output achieved* (100,000 units in this case), did we incur more or less cost than we should have, *holding the input price constant*? Many terms are used to describe these variances. Rate variances are sometimes called *price*, *budget*, or *spending variances*. Quantity variances are sometimes called *use* or *efficiency variances*. The particular term you use is insignificant as long as you know which kind of variance is being referred to. The schedule below shows how to analyze the total variance into its constituents.

Actual Labor Cost	*Actual Labor Hours at Standard Rate*	*Standard Cost*
26,000 hours × $11.80	26,000 hours × $12	100,000 units × 0.25 hours × $12
$306,800	$312,000	$300,000

$5,200 favorable	$12,000 unfavorable
Labor Rate Variance	Labor Efficiency Variance

The middle term is a flexible budget, as is total standard cost. The middle term is a flexible budget based on input—direct labor hours, while total standard cost is a flexible budget based on output—units of production.

Notice that the middle term shows the actual hours multiplied by the standard rate. Compare the middle term with actual cost. The only difference is in the rates, \$11.80 to \$12.00. They both use 26,000 hours—actual hours worked. Therefore, the \$5,200 difference relates solely to the \$0.20 per hour difference in rates. Given 26,000 hours of labor (inputs used), costs should have been \$312,000, but were \$306,800. Because actual cost is less than the cost that would have been incurred had Mencento paid the standard rate for the actual hours worked, the variance is favorable. Intuitively, you would rather pay \$11.80 than \$12.00, other things being equal.

Similarly, compare the middle term with the standard cost. The only difference is the number of hours—actual hours in the middle term, standard hours in the standard cost. Given the output achieved (100,000 units), the company worked 1,000 hours more than standard (26,000 − 25,000), so that at a standard rate of \$12 per hour, the use or efficiency variance is \$12,000. We use the standard rate here because as we go from the standard cost of \$300,000 to the middle term, we want to allow only hours to vary, not both hours and rate. This variance is unfavorable, because we used more hours than the standard allowed for 100,000 units. Remember that we want to allow one factor to change while holding all others constant.

An alternative calculation is to work with the differences. The labor rate variance is:

$$\begin{aligned}\text{labor rate variance} &= (\text{actual rate} - \text{standard rate}) \times \text{actual hours}\\ &= (\$11.80 - \$12.00) \times 26{,}000 \text{ hours}\\ &= \$5{,}200 \text{ favorable}\end{aligned}$$

The labor efficiency variance is:

$$\begin{aligned}\text{labor efficiency variance} &= (\text{actual hours} - \text{standard hours allowed})\\ &\quad \times \text{standard rate}\\ &= (26{,}000 - 25{,}000) \times \$12\\ &= \$12{,}000 \text{ unfavorable}\end{aligned}$$

Figure 7–1 shows the variances graphically. Expected costs are represented by the shaded rectangle *ACFD*. This is expected labor use of 25,000 hours given the output of 100,000 units, times the standard wage rate of \$12 or \$300,000 total standard cost. Actual costs are represented by the rectangle *ABHG* and are 26,000 actual hours at \$11.80 actual rate per hour, or a total of \$306,800. Thus, the total labor variance is \$6,800 unfavorable, since actual costs exceed standard costs by that amount. The labor rate variance is depicted by the rectangle *BCIH*: it is the \$0.20 per hour (\$12 − \$11.80) above standard wages times the actual 26,000 hours used.

The rectangle *EFIH* is part of the labor rate variance. This is the usual way of calculating variances, but you should be aware that *EFIH* is actually the interaction of the rate and use variances. That is, it could be argued that the rate variance should be based on standard hours, not actual hours. If we calculated the rate variance as $SQ(AP - SP)$, then the difference between the total variance and the sum of the rate and use variances is the interaction variance.

FIGURE 7–1 Labor Variances—Mencento Company

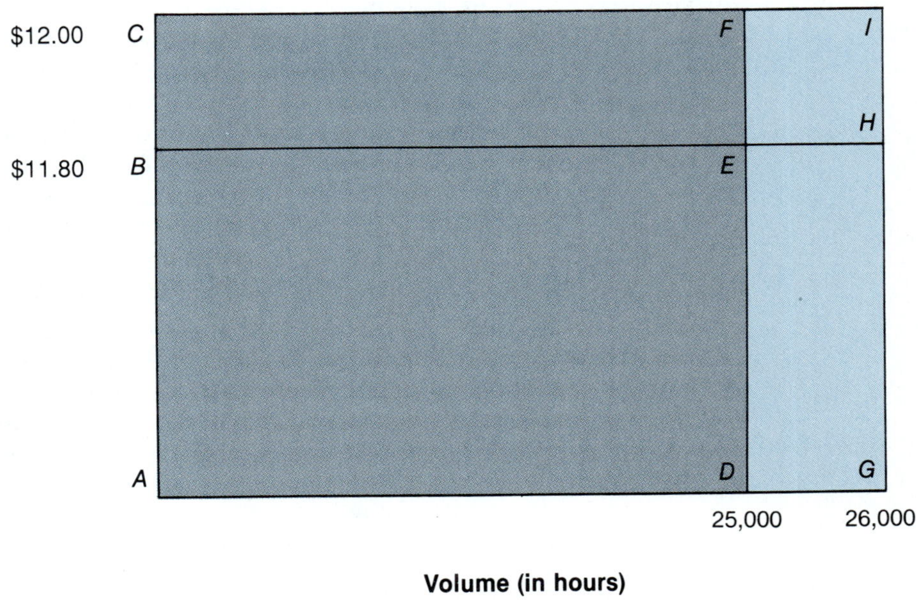

In summary, the following analyses can be made:

Traditional Standard Cost Variances

Rate	$AQ(AP - SP)$ = 26,000($11.80 − $12.00) =	$ 5,200F
Efficiency	$(AQ - SQ)SP$ = (26,000 − 25,000)$12 =	12,000U
Total variance		$ 6,800U

Three-way Analysis of Standard Cost Variances

Rate	$SQ(AP - SP)$ = 25,000($11.80 − $12.00) =	$ 5,000F
Efficiency	$(AQ - SQ)SP$ = (26,000 − 25,000)$12 =	12,000U
Interaction	$(AQ - SQ) \times (AP - SP)$ = (26,000 − 25,000) × ($11.80 − $12.00) =	200F
Total variance		$ 6,800U

AQ = actual quantity used
SQ = standard quantity for output achieved
SP = standard price per unit
AP = actual price per unit

The two basic labor variances are likely to be the responsibilities of two managers. The production manager is responsible for labor use, but probably not for the labor rate. As a practical matter, labor rates are typically set by contract. Labor rate variances arise because workers are assigned to jobs with different standard pay rates, new workers are hired at non-contract rates, or the standards are out of date.

The quantity of labor acquired is generally assumed to be the same as the quantity used. Exceptions do occur; for example, a company that suffers significant amounts of idle time because of product changeovers might distinguish between labor acquired and labor used in productive work. In fact, in some companies a good portion of the direct labor efficiency standard is really an idle time variance; instead of working inefficiently, workers are idle.

A behavioral problem can arise with labor efficiency variances when idle time is included in the actual hours figure. Idle time does not indicate labor inefficiency; rather it is a sign that production scheduling or some other function has failed. However, if supervisors are evaluated partly on the size and direction of the variance, they will try to minimize it. Including idle time in the time used to determine the efficiency variance encourages supervisors to have idle workers make units and components just to reduce the efficiency variance. Of course, making more units and components is costly in additional storage space, financing, insurance, taxes, and other costs. We have mentioned throughout this book that manufacturers are trying to reduce inventories through just-in-time and other modern techniques.

Materials Variances

Materials variances are, with one exception, calculated the same as labor variances. The exception relates to a difference between the two factors: materials can be stored and labor cannot. Therefore, with materials a difference can exist between the quantity acquired and the quantity used. The question is when to calculate the material price variance—at the time of acquisition, or at the time of use. Most accountants favor the date of acquisition, which is when the economic effect of the variance arises. Once you have paid, as Mencento did, $0.55 per pound (Exhibit 7–2), there is no way to change it. Additionally, because one of the uses of variance analysis is as feedback to managers, the more quickly the information is determined, the better. Both of these factors argue for calculating the price variance at the time of purchase of the materials or components. Using the Mencento data from Exhibit 7–2, we develop the following materials variances.

Actual Material Cost	*Actual Purchases at Standard Price*
150,000 lbs. × $0.55	150,000 lbs. × $0.50
$82,500	$75,000
$7,500 unfavorable	
Material Price Variance	

The variance is unfavorable because the actual $0.55 per pound price exceeded the $0.50 standard price. Material price variances are the responsibility of purchasing managers, but it should not automatically be assumed that a favorable variance is good. A purchasing manager could buy inferior materials, thereby generating a favorable price variance. Using these materials might result in higher waste, more labor time, and lower product quality. The result might be that the savings in material costs are dwarfed by higher costs elsewhere. We return to this question—interdependence of variances—later in the chapter.

We can also calculate the variance using the difference in prices.

$$\begin{aligned}\text{Material price variance} &= (\text{actual price} - \text{standard price}) \\ &\quad \times \text{actual purchases} \\ &= (\$0.55 - \$0.50) \times 150{,}000 \text{ lbs.} \\ &= \$7{,}500 \text{ unfavorable}\end{aligned}$$

The material use variance is calculated exactly the same as the labor use variance. Of course, we need materials used, not materials purchased, to make the calculation.

Actual Material Use at Standard Price	*Standard Cost*
220,000 lbs. × \$0.50	100,000 units × 2 lbs. × \$0.50
\$110,000	\$100,000
\$10,000 unfavorable Material Use Variance	

The variance is unfavorable because Mencento used 20,000 more pounds than standard. Mencento obviously had materials in inventory at the beginning of the period, because its use exceeded its purchases. Again, we can use the differences to calculate the variance,

$$\begin{aligned}\text{material use variance} &= (\text{actual use} - \text{standard use}) \times \text{standard price} \\ &= (220{,}000 - 200{,}000) \times \$0.50 \\ &= \$10{,}000 \text{ unfavorable}\end{aligned}$$

Variable Overhead Variances

The calculation of variable overhead variances parallels that of direct labor. In fact, some of the same numbers are used if variable overhead is related to direct labor. The total standard variable overhead cost is, of course, the per unit standard cost multiplied by the number of units produced. If variable overhead is related to direct labor, then total standard cost is also standard direct labor hours allowed times the variable overhead rate per direct labor hour. If other measures of activity are used, then total standard variable overhead is the standard number of units of the input factor (e.g., machine hours) for the output achieved times the variable overhead rate per unit of that factor. Budgeted variable overhead cost for actual activity at the standard rate, the middle term, is calculated the same as for direct labor. What we have termed a price or rate variance is called a **variable overhead budget variance** or **spending variance**. In our example,

Actual Variable Overhead Cost		*Actual Labor Hours at Standard Variable Overhead Rate*		*Standard Variable Overhead Cost*
		26,000 hours × $2		100,000 units × 0.25 hours × $2
$54,600		$52,000		$50,000
	$2,600 unfavorable Variable Overhead Budget Variance		$2,000 unfavorable Variable Overhead Efficiency Variance	

Both variances are unfavorable. Actual cost exceeds the budget based on actual activity of 26,000 labor hours, making the budget variance unfavorable. Actual activity exceeds standard activity of 25,000 direct labor hours making the efficiency variance unfavorable.

These variances are calculated the same as the direct labor variances, but their interpretations are different. Although the variable overhead budget variance is calculated the same as the direct labor rate variance, it is not necessarily related to a difference in rates. It can result from a difference between the actual and standard rates for items of variable overhead, such as fringe benefits, supplies, and power. However, it can also result from using more or less of a variable overhead element. For example, suppose that one component of variable overhead is power, which costs $0.02 per KWH and standard use is five KWHs per labor hour. A change in either the cost per KWH or in the use per direct labor hour will show up in the variable overhead budget variance. That is, the budget variance can include cost differences related to efficient or inefficient use of the variable overhead factor.

Similarly, the variable overhead efficiency variance relates not to the efficient or inefficient use of variable overhead (such as KWH of power), but to use of the factor to which variable overhead is related. In this case, the variable overhead efficiency variance results from the inefficient use of direct labor. If variable overhead were related to machine hours, the variable overhead efficiency variance would relate to the use of machine time. Note that the calculation of the variable overhead efficiency variance is exactly the same as for the direct labor efficiency variance except that the variable overhead rate is used, not the labor rate. Thus, the cost of using more labor than standard this period was not just the direct labor efficiency variance, but also the variable overhead efficiency variance. This makes sense: the more labor (or machine) time used, the higher the costs associated with labor (or machine) time. These costs include overhead that varies with labor (or machine) time.

Like the labor and material variances, variable overhead variances can be calculated using the differences between standards and actuals. This kind of calculation is misleading with the budget variance, because it is not a rate variance like the labor rate and material price variances. We can make the same kind of calculation, but there is no need to calculate the actual variable overhead rate.

$$\begin{aligned}
\text{variable overhead budget variance} &= (\text{actual rate} - \text{standard rate}) \\
&\quad \times \text{actual use} \\
&= (\text{actual rate} \times \text{actual use}) - \\
&\quad (\text{standard rate} \times \text{standard use}) \\
&= \$54{,}600 - (\$2 \times 26{,}000) \\
&= \$2{,}600 \text{ unfavorable} \\
\text{variable overhead efficiency variance} &= (\text{actual activity} - \text{standard activity}) \\
&\quad \times \text{standard rate} \\
&= (26{,}000 - 25{,}000) \times \$2 \\
&= \$2{,}000 \text{ unfavorable}
\end{aligned}$$

Fixed Overhead Variances

Fixed overhead variances are different from variable overhead variances. First, the fixed overhead budget variance is simply the difference between actual fixed overhead and budgeted fixed overhead. That is, there is no flexible budget for fixed overhead because, as long as we stay in the relevant range, budgeted fixed overhead does not depend on activity. Second, the other fixed overhead variance is called the *volume variance*, the *idle capacity variance*, the *denominator variance*, or the *application variance*. This variance is different from all of the others we have seen. It is the difference between budgeted fixed overhead and *applied fixed overhead*. Applied fixed overhead is standard fixed overhead per unit multiplied by units produced. It is calculated exactly the same as total standard cost for materials, direct labor, or variable overhead. However, it does not have the same meaning. Total standard variable cost is an economically significant number—the cost that you *should* incur given actual production. Applied fixed overhead is *not* the cost that you should *incur*: budgeted fixed overhead is. Applied fixed overhead is simply a result of using standard costs and has little or no economic significance. In fact, it can be a source of dysfunctional behavior, as we discuss later.

The three-column analysis appears below.

Actual Fixed Overhead		*Budgeted Fixed Overhead*		*Applied Fixed Overhead*
				100,000 units × $0.75
$93,000		$90,000		$75,000
	$3,000 unfavorable		$15,000 unfavorable	
	Budget Variance		Volume Variance	

Notice that the volume variance would be zero if the company had used 100,000 units to set the standard fixed cost. The fixed overhead rate per unit would then have been $0.90, so that producing 100,000 units would have resulted in applying $90,000 of fixed overhead. Thus, the volume variance arises solely because the level of activity used to set the standard fixed cost differs from the actual level of activity. (Note that if the company had produced 120,000 units there would have been no volume variance. Applied fixed overhead cost would then have been $90,000 [120,000 × $0.75].)

COMBINED OVERHEAD VARIANCES

Accountants do not always separate actual fixed overhead from actual variable overhead. They might know only actual total overhead, not its components, because many overhead costs are mixed costs. Separating the fixed and variable components is either not possible or not feasible. For instance, suppose that power is a mixed cost with a variable component of $0.50 per machine hour and a monthly fixed component of $40,000. The variable component relates to operating machinery, the fixed component to heat, light, and general needs that do not depend on activity. If the company has only one meter and gets only one bill, it cannot determine how much was used to operate machinery (the variable component) and how much went for heat, light, and other general purposes (the fixed component). The company cannot determine actual variable overhead and actual fixed overhead separately. (A company could install separate meters to determine actual fixed and actual variable overhead, but it might cost more to do so than the additional information is worth. It is never wise to buy more information than you can economically use.)

When we do not know actual variable and fixed overhead separately, we cannot calculate the fixed and variable overhead budget variances separately, but can calculate only a combined budget variance. We can also calculate the variable overhead efficiency variance and the fixed overhead volume, or application, variance. Some companies calculate only two variances: the application variance and what is termed the *controllable variance*, which is the combined budget variance and the variable overhead efficiency variance.

The two-way variance appears below for our example data.

Actual Overhead		*Budgeted Overhead for 100,000 Units*		*Applied Overhead*
		$90,000 + ($0.50 × 100,000)		($0.75 + $0.50) × 100,000
$147,600		$140,000		$125,000
	$7,600 U Controllable Variance		$15,000 U Application Variance	

The two-way analysis has little to recommend it because it obscures budget and efficiency variances. Recall that the variable overhead efficiency variance is not related to variable overhead, but to the activity: direct labor hours, machine hours, or whatever drives variable overhead. In evaluating the significance of variances, then, it is wise to look at the variable overhead efficiency variance in the context of its driver. Budget variances, however, require examining the cost elements: supplies, indirect labor, power, etc.

The three-way variance calculation makes much more sense than the two-way because it separates the combined budget variance from the variable overhead efficiency variance. Notice that we need only know that total actual overhead is \$147,600, not that it consists of \$54,600 variable and \$93,000 fixed, as we know from before.

Actual Overhead	*Budgeted Overhead for 26,000 Hours*	*Budgeted Overhead for 100,000 Units*	*Applied Overhead*
	\$90,000 + (\$2 × 26,000)	\$90,000 + (\$0.50 × 100,000)	(\$0.75 + \$0.50) × 100,000
\$147,600	\$142,000	\$140,000	\$125,000
\$5,600 U Budget Variance	\$2,000 U Efficiency Variance	\$15,000 U Application Variance	

The \$5,600 total budget variance agrees with the totals computed earlier, \$2,600 unfavorable variable overhead budget variance and \$3,000 unfavorable fixed overhead budget variance. The \$2,000 unfavorable variable overhead efficiency variance was also calculated earlier, as was the \$15,000 unfavorable application variance. Note carefully that the application variance still relates solely to fixed overhead. The \$0.50 × 100,000 units for variable overhead budgeted for actual output is also used in determining applied variable overhead. In fact, it *is* applied variable overhead. The difference between total budgeted overhead based on output and applied overhead lies in the fixed overhead alone. Again, the application variance has limited economic significance. It arises because the level of activity used to set the standard fixed cost is not the same as actual activity. We covered this point in Chapter 5.

INDEPENDENCE OF VARIANCES

Calculating variances is the first step toward providing information for control and evaluating performance. We pointed out as early as Chapter 1 that control requires giving managers information about *their* operations. Variances reveal sources (materials price, labor efficiency), not causes (workers slowed down in response to firing of popular supervisor and material quality fell, making labor time longer and wasting more material).

We calculate separate variances, which suggests that the variances are independent of one another. That is often not the case, as we mentioned earlier in connection with buying lower quality materials (giving a favorable material price variance) that held workers up (giving unfavorable labor and variable overhead efficiency variances) and resulted in more waste (giving an unfavorable material use variance). A particular action might cause several variances, favorable or unfavorable, either in the same or a different department. Calculating variances is an early step in exercising control and we must be careful not to misuse them. Before taking any action based on variances, managers should investigate their causes.

Standard Costs and Product Life Cycle

It is important to use any managerial tool to its best advantage. Some work well in certain circumstances, poorly in others. One factor affecting how well standard costs are likely to work is the life cycle stage of the product. Most products begin their lives with rapid sales growth, then mature and have stable sales, and finally decline.

Standard costs and variance analysis work best for mature, stable products such as clothing (except for high fashion clothing). They are less valuable for products in growth stages, particularly in the very early stages of a product's life, such as compact disk players. In the mature stage of product life, cost control is one of the principal competitive weapons. Low costs allow a company to weather poor periods and to earn reasonable returns. Price competition pervades mature markets, so low costs are essential to maintaining margins.

Products in growth stages, however, are often highly differentiated and have rapidly changing technology. They compete on style or function, but not on price. To use standard costs for rapidly growing and evolving products strikes many managers as nit-picking because increasing volume and achieving high market share are the critical success factors. Margins tend to be high, so that being a low-cost producer contributes little to overall profitability.

This is not to say that standard costs have no place with growing products, but that they should not be emphasized at the expense of gaining volume and a secure share of the market.

OTHER VARIANCES

The discussion so far has covered variable production cost variances and fixed production cost variances. Other production variances can be developed and it is possible to set standards in other areas. For example, the sales department may have standards for advertising. These standards may encompass not only a budgeted dollar amount for the period, but also a plan of mix between radio, TV, and the newspapers. At the end of the period, sales management can evaluate performance using the same kind of variance analysis we have used to look at production results.

If a standard changes so that the standard cost is out of date, we can calculate a change-of-standards variance. For example, if material costs have changed, it is important to know what portion of a material price variance was caused by change of standards and what was from another source (like buying below the level that qualifies for a quantity discount).

Companies that change standards during the year (as do many companies that use advanced manufacturing techniques) calculate a variance based on the difference between the standards. This is sometimes called a *frozen to current variance*.[1]

[1] Roger K. Doost and Evans Pappas, "Frozen-To-Current Cost Variance," *Management Accounting* (March 1988), pp. 41–43.

An example of this variance follows, using materials only for brevity.

Original standard, 2.9 gallons at $4	$11.60
Current (revised) standard 2.6 gallons at $4	10.40
Actual results, 10,000 units produced, 27,000 gallons used	

Actual Cost		Revised Standard		Original Standard
27,000 gals × $4		10,000 units × 2.6 gals × $4		10,000 units × 2.9 gals × $4
$108,000		$104,000		$116,000
	$4,000 U		$12,000 F	
	Material use variance		Frozen to current variance	

Why do this? Because accountants want to compare actual annual profit with the originally budgeted profit. To do so, they isolate differences that arise because of changed standards, which are quite different from efficiency or rate variances. If the company shown above had not changed its standard, it would have calculated an $8,000 favorable use variance, but that would have been a poor motivational tool because in fact the company did not meet the standard that was based on the most current information.

After-the-Fact Variances

Some authors have suggested the need for after-the-fact variances, calculated after adjustments are made to standards to reflect different operating conditions. Consider the following example. Corbett Printing Company is a job order shop with two different printing presses, a webfed press used for long jobs and a sheetfed press used for short jobs. Assume that the sheetfed press is fully scheduled for the coming month and another short job is received. If there is available time on the webfed press, the job can be run on it, but at a cost of higher material use and makeready time. Conventional variance analysis would show unfavorable variances on the job. However, standards should be adjusted to reflect the scheduling problem to see whether the job was run efficiently on the wrong press. This is the idea of after-the-fact variances.

Behavioral Considerations in Standard Setting

Our discussion of standard costs has centered on the mechanics of establishing such information. Since calculations and analyses of variances are conducted at least in part to help evaluate managerial performance, we must also investigate the human behavioral aspects involved when standards are set. Much of the discussion that follows applies also to the area of budgeting and will be extended in Chapters 15 and 16.

The Conflict

Standards can be used as an aid to planning in such areas as purchasing materials, scheduling workers, estimating cash flow needs, and pricing. For many reasons it is important to know expected sales levels and the flexible budget for expected output. A firm also needs to be competitive. Thus, the expectations included in budgets and standards are based on the most efficient way to produce a given quality of product. Variances can be a key to adaptive and corrective action, thereby saving future costs. A conflict can arise between the objectives of planning, controlling, and earning a satisfactory profit and the other budgeting objectives of motivating personnel to achieve these ends.

Motivation Budgets and standards are useless exercises in pencil pushing and computer number crunching unless they are viewed as a set of reasonable goals that managers are willing to try to attain. Each of us has personal, job-oriented goals: monetary rewards, promotion, peer approval, and job responsibility. We have mentioned a few company goals in planning, controlling, and profitability. Ideally a manager should be motivated to act in harmony with and agreement to company goals. Many authors use the term *goal congruence* to denote this sharing of common goals. However, we are interested not just in agreeing with company goals but in *acting* to achieve them.

A Model for Motivation Some writers have proposed a model to coordinate research and analysis in the area of budgets and motivation.[2] In essence, this model says that motivation is caused by:

1. intrinsic (internal or personally satisfying) rewards from goal-directed behavior—that is, engaging in the activity itself
2. intrinsic rewards associated with successful performance of a task
3. various extrinsic (external or managerially administered) rewards associated with the accomplishment of company goals

The second and third factors are weighted by the probability of achieving a work goal with goal-directed behavior. The third factor also is weighted by the probabilities that goal accomplishment will lead to certain external rewards.

Intrinsic rewards include personal pleasure derived from doing a job. A salesperson may enjoy extensive traveling, and this enjoyment motivates him to make efforts to achieve company goals. An actress enjoys the experience of being on stage regardless of other compensation from box office receipts or favorable reviews. Intrinsic rewards are positive emotions that we feel as we behave in an organizational-goal-directed manner congruent with personal goals.

In contrast, **extrinsic rewards** come from others. They include salary, promotion, level of authority and responsibility, approval of peers and supervisors, and public recognition of achievement.

Probability of Success This model weights these various rewards by the probability that goal-directed behavior will result in goal accomplishment. Here is where standard setting can come into play. A striving by management for

[2]The model, called expectancy theory, is based on the work of V. H. Vroom, *Work and Motivation* (New York: John Wiley & Sons, 1964) and is extended by L. W. Porter and E. E. Lawler III, *Managerial Attitudes and Performance* (Homewood, Ill.: Richard D. Irwin, Inc., 1968).

greater and greater efficiency can lead to lower and lower standard costs. This would reduce the probability that a budget would be met, and, under the model, would reduce motivation. Conversely, more lenient standards may be more motivating, but they could run counter to the goal of maximizing efficiency.

In some cases standards can influence workers, supervisors, and managers to perform in dysfunctional ways. We mentioned earlier that a purchasing manager could be motivated to buy inferior materials and components at low prices, thereby sacrificing quality. Purchasing managers might also buy large quantities, which is a serious mistake in a just-in-time company, to get a lower price. Workers might produce more than ordered to avoid an unfavorable labor use variance. (A worker might have orders to produce only 100 units in a day, when, say, 120 is the standard. That will generate an unfavorable use variance.) Supervisors and managers might overproduce to absorb more overhead and reduce idle capacity variances. Other abuses are possible as well, as we described earlier—unwisely manufacturing product and components to reduce labor efficiency variances. Accountants must be much more careful about the behavioral implications of performance reporting than they have in the past.[3]

Tight and Loose Standards

The term commonly used to describe the continuum of standard setting levels is **tight** to **loose**. The basic conflict we mentioned at the outset occurs when standards are too tight or too loose.

When standards are tight, it is highly probable that they will be missed more often than met. Variances are deviations from standard. They do not reflect how loose or tight the standard was. They imply inefficient operations rather than ineffective standards. Therefore, it is possible that variance reports can be used as pressure devices, unfairly associating an unfavorable variance with poor managerial performance. However, it may be that tight standards are motivating *because* they are more difficult to achieve. They may be a useful challenge (intrinsic reward) to a manager motivated by a need for achievement, in whom accomplishment produces a strong feeling of pride and self-reward. Loose standards may be so easy to attain that a manager is not motivated to beat or even meet them.

As is easily seen, there is a trade-off between tightness and looseness. Each situation must be evaluated in light of the production process, the product, and the behaviors of people in determining an answer to the level of tightness chosen. Many companies try to set tight but currently attainable standards.

Currently attainable performance reflects good performance under nor-

---

[3] An excellent description of problems with performance measures appears in James Brimson, "CAM-I Cost Accounting Systems Project," in Robert Capettini and Donald K. Clancy, *Cost Accounting, Robotics, and the New Manufacturing Environment* (Sarasota, FL: American Accounting Association, 1987), p. 5.31.

mal working conditions. It allows for recurring problems such as fatigue, but is not lax. Performance requirements are high but attainable if everything goes reasonably well.

Participation

The subject of participation will be dealt with more fully in the chapters on budgeting. It is useful to discuss the basic issues here, however, since they apply to standard setting as well. Put simply, participation involves the question of *who* sets standards. If upper management alone sets standards with advice from engineering and accounting, there is no participation by those responsible for meeting the standards. Full participation would mean that all operating personnel from line managers on up are an active part of the negotiating process leading to whatever standard is adopted.

Actual participation usually falls between these two extremes. In addition, real input of lower level personnel into a final decision may happen less in reality than on paper. A firm may purport to involve all its managers in standard setting, while in fact upper management rarely takes much advice in reaching a decision.

Like tightness, the degree of participation established depends on both production and human considerations. Participation can be intrinsically rewarding and can enhance the probabilities of success and reward. If operating employees believe that their participation really influences standards, the process reduces their feeling of helplessness to influence their work environment. As employees learn to attribute success (in negotiating standards) to their own personal efforts, the probability increases that they will become more achievement oriented. If they participate and their advice is at least partly accepted, they might be more likely to strive to meet the standards.

One manifestation of participation is the work circle or quality circle. In both, workers meet regularly, sometimes with supervisors, to discuss ways to do their jobs better. Obviously, for such circles to help, the workers must trust management and be highly motivated to do their jobs well. Tom Peters, author of several books on management, had a television series that provided instructive examples. A worker at a Harley-Davidson plant explained how she suggested a redesign of a fender light, making it easier to install and less likely to break. Other examples of successful participation of workers appear in the recent accounting literature.

PROBLEMS WITH VARIANCES AND STANDARDS

With any calculation, whether net income, a CVP relationship, or a linear programming solution, the results are only as good as the information used. The same holds true of variances. If standards are ill formed or out of date, variances have low information content.

Inflation and Standard Costs

Standard costs include both price and quantity components. In an inflationary economy, standard prices might require continual adjustment. Labor rates are usually fairly predictable because of long-term union contracts, but there might be increases every six months or so related to increases in the Consumer Price Index. Even if a company does not have union employees, wages reflect some combination of federal minimum wages and union wages paid by competitive firms.

Predictability of Material Prices

There is a predictability problem with material costs. Most contracts for materials are entered into to assure the purchaser a supply of materials and the supplier a more predictable production level. Prices are set at the beginning of the contract but can be changed as time passes. Thus, as a paper manufacturer experiences rising costs of labor, materials, and overhead, it may increase prices under the terms of its contracts with printers. It is important that the standard price be adjusted for this increase, or a spurious material price variance will occur. In addition, material use variances will be understated, since the standard price will be too low. On the other hand, holding standard price constant even though prices have risen can be defended on the grounds that the price variance is a good indicator to management regarding underlying cost changes over the year. Managers must decide whether changing the standard price or holding it constant will yield more useful information.

STANDARDS IN NEW MANUFACTURING ENVIRONMENTS

Throughout this book we have commented on differences between traditional and modern manufacturing. Modern manufacturers rely much more on automation and correspondingly much less on direct labor than do traditional companies. While modern manufacturers use standard costs, they frequently ignore some variances. For instance, the direct labor efficiency variance is often ignored by companies that use just-in-time and other modern methods. For such companies, that variance can actually be dangerous because it encourages the build-up of inventory to keep workers busy; idle workers mean unfavorable labor efficiency variances, and low production means unfavorable overhead efficiency and volume variances. Additionally, reporting labor efficiency variances detracts from the main objective of rapid, smooth throughput of high-quality products. An even more obvious example is the material price variance, which we discussed earlier. We said then that a favorable material price variance could be the result of buying substandard materials or components, resulting in increased waste, lowered labor efficiency, and a poorer quality product.

This does not mean that modern manufacturers ignore productivity—quite the contrary! But they do not use as much traditional variance analysis. Some managers have the capacity to monitor efficiency through computer links to the production process, thus generating real-time variances. Such managers have no need for accounting reports that are old when they are received. By the time they receive a report, they could have fixed the problem. Chapter 19 discusses productivity measures in advanced environments.

Some companies use actual costs from the most recent month or averages of the past few months (called *rolling averages*) as the basis for analyzing performance. Because of the enormous emphasis on improving productivity in JIT and other techniques, many managers believe that setting standards simply leads to employees trying to meet them, but not seeking continual improvement. It seems reasonable, however, to use the previous actuals as the standard to determine variances from the previous actuals. In any environment, it is desirable to know whether improvement (or deterioration) resulted from price changes or from changes in operating efficiency.

SUMMARY

Standard costs assist managers in planning, control, and decision making. Standard costs are used by many types of manufacturers that use standard operations: process, repetitive, and job order. Variance calculations isolate the sources but not the causes of differences between actual and standard performance. Further investigation is usually needed to determine why a particular variance occurred.

Standard costs have two elements: a standard quantity of an input factor (materials, labor, overhead) and a standard price for a unit of the input factor (gallon of material, hour of labor, hour of machine time). Variances are calculated to determine how much each element (price and quantity) of a factor contributed to the difference between standard and actual results. This separation begins the identification of responsibility because different managers are usually responsible for prices of inputs and use of inputs. However, variances are not always independent; one manager, acting to minimize a variance, might cause variances in other departments. Therefore, we cannot conclude that a variance indicates poor performance by the nominally responsible manager.

Setting standards is a behavioral problem. The level of performance can be from tight to loose, with currently attainable performance perhaps the most common. Participation in setting standards often helps in achieving good performance.

REVIEW PROBLEM

To review overhead variances, look at the data below for Olympics Company. Answer the following questions:

1. What is standard variable overhead per unit? Standard fixed overhead per unit? Total standard overhead per unit?
2. What is the flexible budget for overhead?
3. Calculate the various levels of overhead variances (1-way, 2-way, 3-way, and 4-way).

Olympics Company—Overhead Data

Budgeted overhead:	\$150,000 per year fixed overhead
	\$3 per DLH variable overhead
Standard labor:	$\frac{1}{3}$ hour per unit
Application basis:	100,000 units
Actual results:	90,000 units produced
	31,000 labor hours used
	\$94,550 variable overhead
	\$147,000 fixed overhead

ANSWERS TO REVIEW PROBLEM

1. Standard variable overhead per unit: $\frac{1}{3}$ hour × \$3 = \$1
   Standard fixed overhead per unit: \$150,000/100,000 = \$1.50
   Total standard overhead per unit: \$1 + \$1.50 = \$2.50
2. Flexible budget: \$150,000 + \$3 DLH
3. One-way variance: actual − standard
   (\$147,000 + \$94,550) − (90,000 × \$2.50) = \$16,550U

   Two-way variance:
   Controllable: actual − flexible budget at standard hours
   \$241,550 − [\$150,000 + (\$3 × 30,000)] = \$1,550 U
   Application: flexible budget at standard hours − applied
   [\$150,000 + (\$3 × 30,000)] − (90,000 × \$2.50) = \$15,000U

   Three-way variance:
   Efficiency: $(AQ - SQ)SP$
   [31,000 − (90,000 × $\frac{1}{3}$)] \$3 = \$3,000U
   Spending: actual − flexible budget at actual hours
   \$241,550 − [\$150,000 + (\$3 × 31,000)] = (\$1,450)F
   Application: \$15,000U

Four-way variance:

Efficiency:	\$3,000U
VOH Spending:	actual − budget = \$94,550 − (\$3 × 31,000) = \$1,550U
VOH Budget:	actual − budget = \$147,000 − \$150,000 = (\$3,000)F
Application:	\$15,000U

APPENDIX 7A: PRODUCTION MIX AND YIELD VARIANCES

Many products require more than one material and type of labor. In some cases, types of materials (or types of labor) are interchangeable. Materials are interchangeable if one can be substituted for another without significantly altering the final product. The recipe for a bottled salad dressing can be changed, say by using more vinegar and less oil. Managers try to reduce costs, consistent with maintaining quality, and to substitute less-costly ingredients is one way.

Labor is interchangeable if one type can be substituted for another. For example, workers who can perform any of three operations are interchangeable. When inputs are interchangeable, it is possible, and often helpful, to break down the efficiency variance into two components—mix and yield. This analysis recognizes that two factors affect cost—the total amount of materials (or labor) used (yield) and the mix of the inputs (shift to more expensive or to less expensive inputs). If materials (or labor) are not interchangeable, it is best to analyze each one separately as illustrated for single inputs.

Illustration

Mencento Chemical makes a single product. Exhibit 7A–1, a breakdown of material standards, shows that there are three materials used in its production. Assume these materials are interchangeable. Actual results for materials are:

Materials Used
99,000 lb Doubleyew
44,000 lb Ex
77,000 lb Wye
220,000 lb

Current Production
100,000 units

EXHIBIT 7A–1 Standard Costs—Mencento Company

Direct materials:	1 lb Doubleyew	at \$0.45/lb	\$0.45
	½ lb Ex	at \$0.80/lb	0.40
	½ lb Wye	at \$0.30/lb	0.15
			\$1.00

We will omit materials purchased and concentrate on materials used. As in our previous analyses, a logical reading of the data will help us grasp the significance of variances.

When we compare the standard cost data in Exhibit 7A–1 with actual results, two things seem evident. (1) The mix of materials was supposed to be 50 percent Doubleyew, 25 percent Ex, and 25 percent Wye, while actual results show 45, 20, and 35 percent, respectively. Wye (with a standard cost of \$0.30 per pound) has been substituted for more expensive Doubleyew and Ex. Therefore, we should have a favorable mix variance. (2) Although 100,000 total units were produced, instead of using 200,000 pounds of the various material inputs at their planned mix, the production process used 220,000 pounds. Thus, there should be an unfavorable quantity variance (or yield variance).

Material Mix and Yield Variances

As with all our analyses, we will examine one variance at a time.

Material	*AQ/Input SP/Input Actual Input Mix*	*AQ in Total SP/Input Standard Input Mix*	*SQ in Total SP/Input Standard Input Mix*
Doubleyew	(99,000 lb)(\$0.45)	($\frac{1}{2}$)(220,000 lb)(\$0.45)	(1 lb)(100,000)(\$0.45)
Ex	+ (44,000 lb)(\$0.80)	+ ($\frac{1}{4}$)(220,000 lb)(\$0.80)	+ ($\frac{1}{2}$ lb)(100,000)(\$0.80)
Wye	+ (77,000 lb)(\$0.30)	+ ($\frac{1}{4}$)(220,000 lb)(\$0.30)	+ ($\frac{1}{2}$ lb)(100,000)(\$0.30)
	\$102,850	\$110,000	\$100,000

Mix variance (\$7,150)F

Yield variance \$10,000U

Comparing the Variances

The single product, single input example yielded a \$10,000 unfavorable efficiency variance. This new multiproduct, multi-input example reveals the additional material mix components.

Why It Is a Yield Variance

The term **yield variance** comes from the fact that if 220,000 pounds of materials are put into the process, we expect 220,000 pounds of output (110,000 units). However, the process *yielded* only 100,000 units. Thus, we have an unfavorable yield of 10,000 units at a cost of $1 per unit or $10,000 unfavorable.

Linear Programming and Variances

Linear programming is often used to obtain the optimal mix of raw materials. In Chapter 12 a horse feed problem is presented with an objective function and constraints as follows:

$$\text{Min } \$0.30 \text{ corn} + \$0.50 \text{ oats} + \$0.45 \text{ barley}$$

subject to

$$\text{corn} \leq 0.5 \quad \text{(maximum corn desired)}$$
$$\text{corn} + \text{oats} + \text{barley} = 1 \quad \text{(combination equals 1 lb)}$$
$$0.15 \text{ corn} + 0.2 \text{ oats} + 0.1 \text{ barley} \geq 0.14 \text{ (protein required)}$$
$$0.1 \text{ corn} + 0.25 \text{ oats} + 0.35 \text{ barley} \geq 0.25 \text{ (roughage required)}$$

The optimal solution calls for the following grains and cost for each pound for feed:

Material	*Percent*	*Price*		*Price per Pound*
Corn	0.30	$0.30	=	$0.0900
Oats	0.25	0.50	=	0.1250
Barley	0.45	0.45	=	0.2025
				$0.4175

If managers used a linear program to aid in their feed mix decisions, they probably will use the mix suggested in the optimal solution. However, what happens if the price of one of the grains changes so that had the managers known of that change before formulating a large production run they would have changed the mix based on the new prices? For example, if oats dropped in price from $0.50 to $0.38, a new optimal solution calls for 100 percent oats and no corn or barley. This yields a new optimal (and standard) cost of $0.38 per pound.

If a normal price variance was calculated based on the prior standard costs, the following calculation would be made:

Material	*AQ/Input AP/Input Actual Input Mix*	*AQ/Input SP/Input Actual Input Mix*
Corn	0.30 × $0.30	0.30 × $0.30
Oats	0.25 × $0.38	0.25 × $0.50
Barley	0.45 × $0.45	0.45 × $0.45
	$0.3875	$0.4175

Normal price variance = $0.03F

This favorable variance reflects the $0.03 per pound that was saved from the lowering of the price of oats. However, by not predicting the change in grain prices and by staying with the old optimal mix, there is an opportunity cost variance of $0.0075 per pound as the difference between the actual cost of $0.3875 and the new optimal cost of $0.38 per pound. This kind of analysis can be worked into the notion of price, mix, and yield variances since managers are dealing with fully substitutable raw materials.

ASSIGNMENTS

7–1 Material Variances Treat each of the following as independent cases. Calculate the material price and the material use variances.

1. One thousand pounds of material were purchased for $3,600, and 900 pounds were used to produce 4,700 units. Standard materials are 0.2 pound per unit at $3.50 per pound.
2. A company used 4,300 gallons of Y with a total standard cost of $1,720 to yield 8,000 units of product. The company purchased 3,000 gallons of Y that period at $0.45 per gallon. Standards call for 0.5 gallon per unit of finished product.
3. Standards call for 3 pounds of material per gallon of finished product. Materials have a standard cost of $6 per pound; 10,000 units were produced, and 31,000 pounds of material were purchased (at $181,350) and used.

7–2 Basic Variance Computations Standard costs for one of Parker Mill's sweatshirts appear below.

Material: 2 pounds of yarn at $4 per pound	$ 8.00
Labor: 0.20 hours of labor at $9 per hour	1.80
Variable overhead: $8 per labor hour	1.60
Fixed overhead: $7 per labor hour	1.40
Total standard cost	$12.80

Standard fixed overhead is based on 18,000 standard hours and $126,000 budgeted fixed overhead per month.

Actual results in March were:

Production	100,000 sweatshirts
Materials purchased	190,000 pounds for $790,000
Materials used	202,000 pounds
Direct labor	21,000 hours; $180,100
Variable overhead	$166,500
Fixed overhead	$125,400

REQUIRED

Compute all variances.

7–3 Material Price Variance (AICPA) Durable Company installs shingle roofs on houses. The standard material cost for a type R house is $1,250, based on 1,000 units at a cost of $1.25 each. During April, Durable installed roofs on 20 type R houses, using 22,000 units of material at a cost of $1.20 per unit, at a total cost of $26,400.

REQUIRED

What is Durable's material price variance for April?

7–4 Material Use Variance (AICPA Adapted) Buckler Company manufactures vinyl top desks. The standard materials cost for the vinyl used per model S desk is $27.00, based on 12 square feet of vinyl at a cost of $2.25 per square foot. A production run of 1,000 desks in March resulted in the use of 12,600 square feet of vinyl at a cost of $2.00 per square foot, a total cost of $25,200.

REQUIRED

What is the material use variance resulting from the March production run?

7–5 Developing Standard Costs Jackson-Roberts makes a single product and has developed the following standards:

Materials	3 lb
Labor	0.75 hr

Materials cost $5 per pound, and labor rates are $15 per hour. Overhead is based on $1,500,000 in annual fixed costs and $40 per direct labor hour variable costs. Overhead is applied per direct labor hour based on production of 400,000 units per year.

REQUIRED

1. What is the standard cost per unit for material?
2. What is the standard cost per unit for labor?
3. What is the flexible budget allowance for overhead for producing 400,000 units?
4. What is the standard cost per DLH for overhead?
5. What is the standard cost per unit for overhead?

7–6 Basic Standard Costs and Variances Hogan Company manufactures garden statues. Each requires 20 pounds of material and two labor hours. The standard price of materials is $2 per pound. The standard direct labor rate is $8 per hour; the standard variable overhead rate is $6 per direct labor hour; and the standard fixed overhead rate is $10 per direct labor hour. The fixed overhead rate is based on monthly budgeted fixed costs of $25,000 and 2,500 standard direct labor hours.

During November, Hogan manufactured 1,000 units. It bought 25,000 pounds of material for $48,600 and used 20,500 pounds. Hogan paid direct laborers $15,800 for 1,900 hours, and incurred $12,500 in variable overhead and $24,200 in fixed overhead.

REQUIRED

1. Determine the standard cost of a statue.
2. Determine all variances.

7–7 Comprehensive Variance Analysis Bollman & Hutchins makes various personal care products. Standard costs per case for Renegade after-shave lotion follow. Mixing is an automated process. Direct labor relates to other operations in manufacturing the lotion.

Materials	44 gallons of base at $0.20 per gallon
	1 gallon of fragrance at $5.50
Direct labor	0.50 hours at $12 per hour
Variable overhead	$5 per mixing hour
Fixed overhead	$11 per mixing hour, based on 2,500 mixing hours at normal capacity
Standard mixing hours are 2.20 per case.	

Bollman & Hutchins produced 1,200 cases of Renegade during February and had these results:

Mixing hours	2,530
Material purchases	58,000 gallons of base at $0.22, none of fragrance
Material used	58,200 gallons of base, 1,280 of fragrance
Direct labor	585 hours, $6,770
Variable overhead	$12,900
Fixed overhead	$25,600

REQUIRED

Compute the standard cost of a case of Renegade and the variances for February.

7–8 Standards, Machine-Hour Base Compton Products operates a highly automated factory and therefore uses machine hours to set standard overhead costs. Each unit requires two pounds of material costing $4 per pound and 10 minutes of machine time. The standard variable overhead rate is $15 per machine-hour, the standard fixed rate $24, based on $84,000 budgeted fixed overhead and 3,500 standard machine hours. Compton does not classify any workers as direct laborers; rather, all factory workers are classified as indirect labor, which is a variable overhead account.

During June, Compton made 24,000 units using 3,920 machine-hours. Variable overhead costs were $56,300, fixed overhead $82,200. Purchases of materials were 54,000 pounds for $213,000 and 47,000 pounds were used.

REQUIRED

1. Compute the standard variable cost of a unit of product.
2. Compute the variances for June.

7–9 Relationships Each of the following situations is independent. The only element of cost being considered is direct labor.

REQUIRED

Fill in the blanks.

	Actual Labor Costs	Units Produced	Actual Hours Worked	Standard Hours for Production Achieved	Standard Hours per Unit	Standard Rate per Hour	Rate Variance	Use Variance
a.	____	2,000	5,600	6,000	___	$ 3	$ 300U	____
b.	$82,600	____	8,300	____	0.5	$10	____	$1,000U
c.	____	8,000	____	____	2	$ 8	$1,600U	$ 400U
d.	$24,500	____	____	6,000	3	___	$ 300F	$ 800U

7–10 Basic Variance Computations Carney Company makes a single product, and 19X6 results showed the following:

Units produced	21,000
Direct labor hours worked	70,000
Rate paid to direct laborers	$ 3.20
Materials purchased	50,000 lb ($102,500)
Materials used in production	46,000 lb
Variable overhead incurred	$150,000

Standards for this product were as follows:

Material, 2 lb at $2.05	$ 4.10
Direct labor, 3 hr at $3.25	9.75
Variable overhead, $2/DLH	6.00
Total standard variable cost per unit	$19.85

REQUIRED

Calculate all the variable cost variances.

7–11 Labor and Variable Overhead Variances Calculate labor rate, labor efficiency, variable overhead spending, and variable overhead efficiency variances for each of the following independent cases. In all cases overhead is applied per direct labor hour.

1. Standards call for 100 units per hour, and 8,000 units were produced using 75 hours. Standard wages are $20 per hour, and standard variable overhead is $15 per hour. Actual labor and variable overhead were $1,500 and $1,275, respectively.
2. The standard cost card for Product A-100 includes the following information:

	Cost per 1,000 Units
Direct labor: 2 hr at $17/hr	$34
Variable overhead at $10/DLH	20

Direct labor was $14,940 at an average of $18 per hour, and 400,000 units were produced. Variable overhead was $7,885.

3. Use the same standard costs as in part 2. For work in process, there were 10,000 units 75 percent complete in beginning inventory, 8,000 units 50 percent

complete in ending inventory, and 430,000 units were transferred to Finished Goods. A total of 810 hours was used at a cost of $14,175 for direct labor and $8,100 for variable overhead.

7–12 Actual Versus Standard A report prepared for management of Kueker Products shows the following results for one of its products for October 19X9:

Sales (9,200 units)	$386,400
Standard cost of sales	294,400
Standard gross margin	$ 92,000
Less:	
Variable cost production variances:	
Material price	$ 10,000F
Material use	5,000U
Labor rate	945U
Labor efficiency	3,600U
Adjusted margin	$ 92,455

Production was 12,000 units. All variances are shown as adjustments to cost of sales at the end of each period. Standards for this product are:

Materials	2 lb at $8.50/lb
Labor	0.5 hr at $12
Overhead is applied at $18/DLH	

During October, 43,000 pounds of material were purchased.

REQUIRED

1. Calculate the following:
   a. actual material price (on purchases)
   b. actual material used
   c. actual labor rate per hour
   d. actual labor hours used

2. In this case, management has placed all the variances on the report as period costs. Would the adjusted margin be higher, lower, or the same if the production variances had been treated as product costs?

7–13 Variances—Multiple Choice (AICPA) The data below relate to the month of April, 19X6, for Marilyn, Inc., which uses a standard cost system:

Actual total direct labor	$43,400
Actual hours used	14,000
Standard hours allowed for good output	15,000
Direct labor rate variance—debit	$ 1,400
Actual total overhead	$32,000
Budgeted fixed costs	$ 9,000
Normal activity in hours	12,000
Total overhead application rate per standard direct labor hour	$2.25

Marilyn uses a two-way analysis of overhead variances: budget (controllable) and volume.

REQUIRED

Select the *best* answer for each question.

1. What was Marilyn's direct labor usage (efficiency) variance for April 19X6?
   a. $3,000 favorable
   b. $3,000 unfavorable
   c. $3,200 favorable
   d. $3,200 unfavorable

2. What was Marilyn's budget (controllable) variance for April 19X6?
   a. $500 favorable
   b. $500 unfavorable
   c. $2,250 favorable
   d. $2,250 unfavorable

3. What was Marilyn's volume variance for April 19X6?
   a. $500 favorable
   b. $500 unfavorable
   c. $2,250 favorable
   d. $2,250 unfavorable

7–14 Variance Calculation (continuation of Assignment 7–5) During May, 40,000 units were produced using 132,000 pounds of material and 29,000 labor hours were worked at a cost of $435,000. Budgeted fixed overhead for May is $125,000 and actual fixed and variable overhead totaled $1,237,000 for the month.

REQUIRED

Calculate material use, labor rate and efficiency, and overhead budget, efficiency, and application variances.

7–15 Responsibility for Variances Using the information in assignments 7–5 and 7–14, comment on the variances you calculated. Explain possible reasons for these variances.

7–16 Fixed Overhead Variances Calculate fixed overhead spending and application (volume) variances for each of the following independent cases.

1. Fixed overhead is budgeted at $125,000 for March. Overhead is applied at $1.25 per direct labor hour. Standards call for 2 hours per unit. Actual fixed overhead for March was $120,000, and 45,000 units were produced.

2. Assume the same facts as in part 1, except that 97,000 hours were used to produce the 45,000 units.

3. Fixed overhead is applied at $2 per machine hour based on 13,000 machine hours per month. Actual fixed overhead in May was $30,000, and 75,000 units using 14,000 standard machine hours were produced.

7–17 Overhead Variances (AICPA) Universal Company uses a standard cost system and prepared the following budget at normal capacity for the month of January:

Direct labor hours	24,000
Variable factory overhead	$48,000
Fixed factory overhead	$108,000
Total factory overhead per DLH	$6.50

Actual data for January were as follows:

Direct labor hours worked	22,000
Total factory overhead	$147,000
Standard DLH allowed for capacity attained	21,000

REQUIRED

Using the two-way analysis of overhead variances, what is the budget (controllable) variance for January?

7–18 Three-Way Analysis of Overhead George Company has the following flexible budget for monthly overhead costs:

$$\$60,000 + \$4/\text{DLH}$$

Overhead is applied at $7/DLH. Standards call for 2 units per hour.

1. During January, 39,000 units were produced using 21,000 hours. Total overhead cost was $145,000.
2. During February, $147,000 in overhead was applied. Actual overhead was $142,000 for 22,000 hours.
3. In March, 42,000 units were produced using 19,500 hours and $143,000 in total overhead.

REQUIRED

Calculate overhead spending, efficiency, and application variances for January, for February, and for March.

7–19 Spending Variances (AICPA) The following information is available from Tyro Company:

Actual factory overhead	$15,000
Fixed overhead expenses, actual	$7,200
Fixed overhead expenses, budgeted	$7,000
Actual hours	3,500
Standard hours	3,800
Variable overhead rate per DLH	$2.50

REQUIRED

Assuming that Tyro uses a three-way analysis of overhead variances, what is the spending variance?

7–20 Spending Variance (AICPA) Under the three-variance method for analyzing factory overhead, which of the following is used in the computation of the spending variance?

	Budget Allowance Based on Actual Hours	*Budget Allowance Based on Standard Hours*
1.	Yes	No
2.	Yes	Yes
3.	No	Yes
4.	No	No

7–21 Relationships You are presented with the following data:

Materials purchased	$68,000 (42,000 lb)
Materials used	32,000 lb
Actual labor cost	$69,000 (31,500 hr)
Actual variable overhead	$36,000
Standard labor cost per unit	______
Standard material cost per unit	$ 45
Standard variable overhead cost per unit	______
Material price variance	$ 5,000U
Material use variance	______F or U
Labor rate variance	$ 6,000U
Labor efficiency variance	$ 3,000U
Variable overhead spending variance	______F or U
Variance overhead efficiency variance	______F or U
Standard labor rate	______
Standard direct labor hours per unit	30
Variable overhead rate per DLH	$ 1.15

REQUIRED

Fill in the blanks.

7–22 Production Variances Pilcher Products has the following production standards for a model PF-14 plastic tub used for farming applications:

Materials—plastic, 2.25 lb at $3/lb
—metal reinforcement rings, 3 at $0.25 each
Labor: 0.04 hr per tub
Labor rates: $14/hr

Overhead is applied at $30 per labor hour, consisting of $13 in variable costs and $17 in fixed costs. Budgeted annual volume of 100,000 tubs was used in determining fixed costs per unit.

Actual results for April 19X0 showed that 18,000 tubs were made using 700 labor hours at a cost of $10,000. During the month, 39,300 pounds of plastic were used, while 63,000 pounds were purchased for $195,300. There were no beginning inventories of plastic. A total of 54,000 rings were used, and 20,000 rings were purchased at $0.23 each. Variable overhead amounted to $9,600, while fixed overhead was $6,000.

REQUIRED

Set up a template to solve parts 1 through 4.

1. How many standard hours of labor are required to produce 18,000 tubs?

2. How many standard pounds of plastic are required to produce 18,000 tubs?

3. What is the expected cost *per tub* for overhead?

4. Calculate the following variances:
   a. material price, material use
   b. labor rate, labor efficiency
   c. overhead spending, efficiency, and application

5. Redo part 4 using your template and the following data for May, 19X0:

Tubs manufactured	8,000
Direct labor	$ 4,900 (335 hours)
Plastic purchases	0
Plastic used	20,000 pounds
Rings purchased	25,000 ($6,250)
Rings used	24,500
Variable overhead	$ 4,200
Fixed overhead	$ 6,000

6. Explain possible causes of the material and labor variances.

7–23 Overhead Variances The following data apply to June 19X8, production of Sabre Company:

Overhead incurred	$20,000
Direct labor hours	400

The firm uses an overhead rate of $48, based on 5,500 direct labor hours per year. At 5,500 hours, 37.5 percent of total budgeted overhead is variable. Of the overhead incurred during June, 60 percent was fixed.

The controller reported the following to the president. "Our fixed overhead variances totaled zero, and variable cost variances were $250 favorable even with an $800 unfavorable spending variance. The performance is partly due to our working only 400 hours, instead of the normal $458\frac{1}{3}$."

REQUIRED

1. Determine the fixed overhead budget and application variances and the variable overhead spending and efficiency variances.
2. Does the method of calculation used by the controller give good information? Why or why not?

7–24 Departmental and Plantwide Overhead ICC, Inc., budgets overhead based on departmental rates for departmental overhead and a plantwide rate for common costs. The bases for these rates are as follows:

Fabricating:	
Annual fixed overhead	$9,600,000
Variable overhead	$25/DLH
Assembly:	
Annual fixed overhead	$12,000,000
Variable overhead	$35/DLH
Common costs:	
Annual fixed overhead	$1,600,000

Overhead application is based on 800,000 labor hours a year for *each* department.

REQUIRED

Answer each of the following independently.

1. If a product has a standard of 3 hours in Fabricating and 2 hours in Assembly, what is the total standard fixed overhead per unit for that product?

2. Budgeted fixed overhead in January is $800,000 for Fabricating, $1,000,000 for Assembly, and $150,000 in common factory overhead. During January, the following occurred:

	Actual Hours	Standard Hours for Actual Output
Fabricating	75,000	74,000
Assembly	65,000	67,000

Overhead in January was as follows:

Fabricating	$2,625,000
Assembly	$3,317,000
Common	$ 150,000

Calculate overhead budget, efficiency, and application variances.

7–25 Variances—Job Order Ladle Company makes various products to special order. During November, it started work on 1,000 model CH-11 circuit boards. During the month it shipped 800 boards, and the remaining 200 boards were 100 percent complete for materials and 75 percent complete for conversion. Standards for this model are:

	Per Unit
Material:	
Board, 1 at $50	$ 50
Electronic chips, 10 at $20	200
Labor, 0.5 hr at $18	9
Overhead, $100/DLH	50
Standard cost per unit	$309

During November, 1,050 boards and 10,100 chips were transferred from the storeroom to the assembling department where CH-11 boards are made. All were used in making this order. Job cost sheets and payroll records show that 618 hours were used on this order during November at a cost of $10,506. Overhead is mostly fixed.

REQUIRED

1. Calculate all the variances you can that relate to this order.
2. What variances could you not calculate? What information do you need to calculate them?

7–26 Variances (CMA) Edney Company employs a standard absorption system for product costing. The standard cost of its product is as follows:

Raw materials	$14.50
Direct labor, 2 DLH at $8	16.00
Manufacturing overhead, 2 DLH at $11	22.00
Total standard cost	$52.50

The manufacturing overhead rate is based on normal annual activity of 600,000 direct labor hours. Edney planned to produce 25,000 units each month during 19X3. The budgeted manufacturing overhead for 19X3 is as follows:

Variable	$3,600,000
Fixed	3,000,000
	$6,600,000

During November of 19X3, Edney Company produced 26,000 units. Edney used 53,500 direct labor hours in November at a cost of $433,350. Actual manufacturing overhead for the month was $260,000 fixed and $315,000 variable. The total manufacturing overhead applied during November was $572,000.

REQUIRED

1. The variable manufacturing overhead spending variance for November is
   a. $9,000 unfavorable
   b. $4,000 unfavorable
   c. $11,350 unfavorable
   d. $9,000 favorable
   e. $6,000 favorable

2. The variable manufacturing overhead efficiency variance for November is
   a. $3,000 unfavorable
   b. $9,000 unfavorable
   c. $1,000 favorable
   d. $12,000 unfavorable
   e. $0

3. The fixed manufacturing overhead spending (budget) variance for November is
   a. $10,000 favorable
   b. $10,000 unfavorable
   c. $6,000 favorable
   d. $4,000 unfavorable
   e. $0

4. The fixed manufacturing overhead volume variance for November is
   a. $10,000 favorable
   b. $10,000 unfavorable
   c. $3,000 unfavorable
   d. $22,000 favorable
   e. $0

5. The total variance related to efficiency of the manufacturing operation for November is
   a. $9,000 unfavorable
   b. $12,000 unfavorable
   c. $21,000 unfavorable
   d. $11,000 unfavorable
   e. $25,000 unfavorable

7–27 Variance Calculation (AICPA) At the beginning of 19X4, Beal Company adopted the following standards:

	Input	*Total*
Direct materials	3 lb at $2.50 per lb	$ 7.50
Direct labor	5 hr at $7.50 per hr	37.50
Factory overhead:		
Variable	$3.00/DLH	15.00
Fixed	$4.00/DLH	20.00
Standard cost per unit		$80.00

Normal volume per month is 40,000 standard labor hours. Beal's January 19X4 budget was based on normal volume. During January Beal produced 7,800 units, with records indicating the following:

Direct materials purchased	25,000 lb at $2.60
Direct materials used	23,100 lb
Direct labor	40,100 hr at $7.30
Factory overhead	$300,000

REQUIRED

1. Prepare a schedule of budgeted production costs for January 19X4, based on actual production of 7,800 units.
2. For the month of January 1984, compute the following variances, indicating whether each is favorable or unfavorable:
   a. direct materials price variance, based on purchases
   b. direct materials usage variance
   c. direct labor rate variance
   d. direct labor efficiency variance
   e. factory overhead spending variance
   f. variable factory overhead efficiency variance
   g. factory overhead volume variance

7–28 Change of Standards Variances Krell Company manufactures machine tools that sometimes require design changes to make them suit customers better. Krell does not now change its standards when it changes designs because the controller wants to reconcile each year's actual results with the original budget. Changing standards during the year, she argues, would make it very difficult to do so. The production managers have been pushing for changes in standards that reflect design changes because their performance is unfairly measured.

One production manager has suggested changing the standards but then reconciling actual results to the original standard as well as to the new standard. This, he argues, simply requires dividing efficiency variances into two parts, one capturing the effects of changes in standards, the other reflecting efficiency in meeting the new standard of the revised design. The total efficiency variance is the difference between actual inputs at standard prices and the *original* standard inputs at standard prices.

The following data are representative of the kinds of changes that Krell makes.

	Original	*Redesigned*
Materials:		
6 feet at $3 per foot	$18.00	
8 feet at $3 per foot		$24.00
Direct labor:		
0.65 hours at $10 per hour	6.50	
0.58 hours at $10 per hour		5.80
Variable overhead at $7 per DLH	4.55	4.06
Totals	$29.05	$33.86

Production of the tool was 2,000 units, requiring 15,700 feet of material and 1,190 direct labor hours.

REQUIRED

1. Determine the material, direct labor, and variable overhead efficiency variables, ignoring the redesign.
2. For each variance, determine how much resulted from the design change and how much from efficient or inefficient use of input factors.

7–29 Standards and Variances, Two Products Trotter Company makes two types of cleaner that go through the same processes. The company does not keep records on the material and machine time used in making each type, only for the two as a whole. The company does not classify workers as direct laborers because the operations are almost fully automated. Standard cost data follow, per case.

	Household	*Industrial*
Machine time, minutes	20	30
Materials:		
6 pounds at $1 per pound	$ 6.00	
7 pounds at $1 per pound		$ 7.00
Variable overhead at $15 per machine hour	5.00	7.50
Fixed overhead at $18 per machine hour	6.00	9.00
Total standard costs	$17.00	$23.50

Fixed overhead is based on practical capacity of 10,000 monthly machine hours and $180,000 budgeted fixed overhead per month.

During March, the company had the following results.

Production	12,000 Household, 10,000 industrial
Machine hours	9,150
Material purchases	150,000 pounds at $0.97 per pound
Material used	147,800 pounds
Variable overhead	$148,500
Fixed overhead	$182,600

REQUIRED

1. Compute all variances for March.
2. Can you compute variances for each model? If not, why not? Explain why you might want to trace costs and variances to the individual detergents.

7–30 Use of Standard Costs (CMA Adapted) Standard cost accounting systems are generally considered among the best features of modern management accounting. Standard cost systems are employed widely, and managers depend on such systems for a variety of functions.

Portfolio management is a powerful concept that is important in finance and marketing. The marketing application of the concept is to develop and manage a balanced portfolio of products. Market share and market growth can be used to classify products for portfolio purposes, and the product classifications are often extended to the organizational units that make the product. The market share/growth classifications can be depicted in the following manner.

		MARKET SHARE	
		High	*Low*
MARKET GROWTH RATE	*High*	Rising Star	Question Mark
	Low	Cash Cow	Dog

Question marks are products that show high-growth rates but have relatively small market shares, such as new products that are similar to their competitors. Rising stars are high-growth, high-market-share products that tend to mature into cash cows. Cash cows are slow-growing established products that can be "milked" for cash to help the question marks and introduce new products. The dogs are low-growth, low-market-share items that are candidates for elimination or segmentation.

Understanding where a product falls within this market share/growth structure is important when applying a standard cost system.

REQUIRED

1. Discuss the major advantages of using a standard cost accounting system.
2. Describe the kinds of information that are useful in setting standards and the conditions that must be present to support the use of standard costing.
3. Discuss the applicability or non-applicability of using standard costing for a product classified as a
   a. cash cow
   b. question mark

7–31 Unit Costs and Total Costs Robert Grierson, production manager of Biltmore Industries, was disturbed at the results below. Budgeted production was 90,000 units, and actual production was 100,000 units.

	Budget for 90,000 Units	*Actual for 100,000 Units*
Materials	$ 288,000	$ 341,800
Direct labor	679,500	773,800
Variable overhead	339,750	391,300
Fixed overhead	850,000	860,700
Total costs	$2,157,250	$2,367,600
Cost per unit	$23.969	$23.676

Purchases of materials were about equal to use and were at five percent over standard prices. Labor rates were two percent over standard.

Grierson tells you that the five percent material price variance and two percent labor rate variance were the source of the unfavorable results, offering the following calculations to support his case.

Adjust budgeted costs to 100,000 units ($2,157,250 × 100/90)	$2,396,944
Materials price variance ($288,000 × 100/90 × .05)	16,000
Labor rate variance ($679,500 × 100/90 × .02)	15,100
Total allowable costs	$2,428,044

"Look, these guys who prepare the reports can't hold me to a budget for 90,000 units when I put out 100,000. Besides, they charged me with variances that I am not responsible for, so I actually came in way under budget. Even with the stupid way they made up the report, you can see that my unit cost was below budget, but I should look even better."

REQUIRED

Grierson is responsible for material and labor use and for all overhead costs. Determine whether his claim of good cost control is correct by calculating the variances for which he is responsible.

7–32 Standards and Idle Time Woodson Textiles manufactures sailcloth in its Petzel Mill. The standard labor cost per 100 yards of cloth is $16.00, which is two standard labor hours at $8.00 per hour. Orders were slow in March and the mill turned out only 1,400,000 yards, well below the usual volume. Workers were paid for 31,000 hours. The company guarantees a 40-hour workweek to employees with five years of service. About 3,200 of the 31,000 hours were idle time, when eligible employees were paid, but had no work.

REQUIRED

1. Calculate the labor efficiency variance using the 31,000 hours actually worked.
2. Can you conclude from your answer to part 1 that the work force was inefficient in August? Why or why not? What do you recommend?

7–33 Multiple Products Borgan Company manufactures three models of school desks. The standard material cost is $0.80 per pound; standard labor rate is $10.00 per hour; standard variable overhead rate is $3.00 per direct labor hour; and standard fixed overhead rate is $4.00 per direct labor hour. The standard fixed overhead rate is based on $600,000 monthly budgeted fixed overhead and 150,000 standard direct labor hours. The standard quantities of each cost factor for each model appear below.

	Model 1	*Model 2*	*Model 3*
Materials, pounds	24	20	14
Direct labor hours	5	4	2

Actual results for March were:

Production:	
Model 1	12,000
Model 2	16,000
Model 3	14,000

Materials purchased	1,400,000 pounds at $0.82
Materials used	822,000 pounds
Direct labor	151,000 hours for $1,512,160
Variable overhead	$451,300
Fixed overhead	$597,500

REQUIRED

Determine all variances. You need not determine the individual standard costs for the products.

7–34 Comprehensive Problem (CMA Adapted) Cain Company has an automated production process; consequently, machine hours are used to describe production activity. The company uses a full absorption costing system.

The annual profit plan for the coming fiscal year is finalized in April of each year. The profit plan for the fiscal year ending May 31, 19X2, called for 6,000 units to be produced requiring 30,000 machine hours. The full absorption costing rate for the 19X1–19X2 fiscal year was determined using 6,000 units of planned production.

Cain develops flexible budgets for different levels of activity for use in evaluating performance. A total of 6,200 units were actually produced during the 19X1–19X2 fiscal year and required 32,000 machine hours. The schedule below compares Cain Company's actual costs for the 19X1–19X2 fiscal year with the profit plan and the budgeted costs for two different activity levels.

CAIN COMPANY
Manufacturing Cost Report
for the Fiscal Year Ended May 31, 19X2
(in thousands of dollars)

		Flexible Budgets for		
Item	*Profit Plan (6,000 units)*	*31,000 Machine Hours*	*32,000 Machine Hours*	*Actual Costs*
Direct material:				
G27 aluminum	$ 252.0	$ 260.4	$ 268.8	$ 270.0
M14 steel alloy	78.0	80.6	83.2	83.0
Direct labor:				
Assembler	273.0	282.1	291.2	287.0
Grinder	234.0	241.8	249.6	250.0
Manufacturing overhead:				
Maintenance	24.0	24.8	25.6	25.0
Supplies	129.0	133.3	137.6	130.0
Supervision	80.0	82.0	84.0	81.0
Inspector	144.0	147.0	150.0	147.0
Insurance	50.0	50.0	50.0	50.0
Depreciation	200.0	200.0	200.0	200.0
Total cost	$1,464.0	$1,502.0	$1,540.0	$1,523.0

REQUIRED

1. What are the budgeted machine hours to produce one unit of product?

2. What is the actual cost of material for one unit of product?
3. What is the cost of material that should be processed per machine hour?
4. What is the budgeted direct labor cost for each unit produced?
5. What is the budgeted variable manufacturing overhead rate per machine hour?
6. Cain Company calculates spending, efficiency, and volume variances when analyzing manufacturing overhead costs. What is the manufacturing overhead spending variance for the year?
7. What is the manufacturing overhead volume variance for the current year?
8. Using the flexible budget formula, determine the total budgeted manufacturing cost (in thousands of dollars) for output of 6,050 units.

7–35 Standards—Job Costing (CMA Adapted) Justin Company recently installed a standard cost system to simplify its factory bookkeeping and to aid in cost control. The company makes standard items for inventory, but because its line includes many products, each is manufactured periodically under a production order. Before the installation of the system, job order cost sheets were maintained for each production order. Since the introduction of the standard cost system, the job order cost sheets have not been kept.

The fabricating department is managed by a general supervisor who has overall responsibility for scheduling, performance, and cost control. The department consists of four machine/work centers. Each work center is staffed by a four-person work group or team, and the centers are aided by a twelve-person support group. Departmental practice is to assign a job to one team and expect the team to perform most of the work necessary to complete the job, including acquiring materials and supplies from the stores department, machining, and assembling. The departmental practice has been practical and satisfactory in the past and is readily accepted by the employees.

Information regarding production cost standards, production, and actual costs for the fabricating department in the month of March follows.

Unit Standard Cost

	Part		
	A7A	C6D	C7A
Material	$2.00	$ 3.00	$1.50
Direct labor	1.50	2.00	1.00
Overhead (per direct labor dollar):			
Variable	3.00	4.00	2.00
Fixed	0.75	1.00	0.50
	$7.25	$10.00	$5.00

The departmental standard overhead rates are applied to the products as a percentage of direct labor dollars. The labor base was chosen because nearly all variable overhead costs are caused by labor activity. The departmental overhead rates were calculated at the beginning of the year as follows:

Departmental Overhead Rates

	Variable (including indirect labor)	*Fixed*
Estimated annual cost	$360,000	$ 90,000
Estimated annual department direct labor dollars	$180,000	$180,000
Overhead rate	200%	50%

Analysis of the Fabricating Department Account for March

Charges:		
Materials		
Job no. 307-11	$ 5,200	
Job no. 307-12	2,900	
Job no. 307-14	9,400	$17,500
Labor charges		
Job no. 307-11	$ 4,000	
Job no. 307-12	2,100	
Job no. 307-14	6,200	
Indirect labor	12,200	24,500
Variable overhead costs (e.g., supplies, electricity, etc.)		18,800
Fixed overhead costs (e.g., supervisor's salary, depreciation, property tax and insurance, etc.)		7,000
Total charges to department for March		$67,800
Credits:		
Completed jobs		
Job no. 307-11, 2000 units part A7A at $7.25	$14,500	
Job no. 307-12, 1000 units part C6D at $10	10,000	
Job no. 307-14, 6000 units part C7A at $5	30,000	$54,500
Variances transferred to the factory variance account:		
Materials[a]	$ 1,500	
Direct labor[b]	1,300	
Variable overhead	9,000	
Fixed overhead	1,500	13,300
Total credits		$67,800

[a]Material price variances are isolated at acquisition and charged to the Stores Department.

[b]All direct labor was paid at the standard wage rate during March.

REQUIRED

1. Justin Company assumes that its efforts to control costs in the fabricating department would be aided if variances were calculated by jobs. Management

intends to add this analysis next month. Calculate all the variances by job that might contribute to cost control under this assumption.

2. Do you agree with the company's plan to calculate job variances in addition to the currently calculated departmental variances? Explain your answer.

7–36 Variances and Standard Setting Saric Corporation used a regression and correlation program to help calculate overhead standards in the assembly department. Based on this analysis, Saric set overhead standards at $3,500 per month plus $3.50 per direct labor hour. During November 34,000 units were assembled. Overhead costs were $125,000, and 36,000 actual labor hours were used. Standards call for 1 hour per unit. Overhead is applied at $4 per DLH.

REQUIRED

Write a formal memorandum to management, using a microcomputer and a word processing program along with a spreadsheet program for supporting schedules. See Appendix B for guidelines for memoranda presentation.

You are a consultant hired by management. Your task is to write a memorandum to production management to discuss efficiency during November. As part of your memorandum:

1. Calculate and explain the overhead budget, and efficiency and application variances. Your explanation should include what information these variances give to the production managers.
2. Management has used the following regression and correlation analysis for establishing standards:

Intercept	$3,367.50
Regression coefficient	$ 3.43875
Correlation coefficient	0.947
Standard error of the estimate	$5,047.43
Standard error of the regression coefficient	$ 0.6926
Number of observations	25

Using this additional information, evaluate the variances calculated above. In your memorandum, avoid jargon. In addition, make sure to explain why regression was a good basis for setting standards. Your analysis should include any other factors that would be useful to the production managers planning and controlling overhead in this situation.

7–37 Interpretation of Variances Scorum Company uses standard costs for all input factors. Two components of variable overhead appear below.

Cost Factor	*Standard Quantity per Direct Labor Hour*	*Standard Rate per Direct Labor Hour*
Indirect labor	0.10 hr	$1.20
Fuel	0.40 gal	0.36

These costs are expressed in terms of standard labor hours following the general practice of relating variable overhead to an input factor like direct labor hours or machine hours. Expressed per unit of finished product for one of the firm's many products, the costs are

Cost Factor	Price per Unit of Cost Factor	Quantity per Unit of Product	Standard Cost per Unit of Product
Indirect labor	$12/hour	0.20	$2.40
Fuel	$0.90/gal	0.80	0.72

A unit of product requires two standard labor hours, so that the standards per direct labor hour are half of the standards for a unit of finished product. In March the firm made 1,000 units of the product using 2,050 direct labor hours. Actual indirect labor cost was $2,376 for 198 hours, and actual fuel cost was $765 for 850 gallons bought and used. The usual approach to computing variances gives the following:

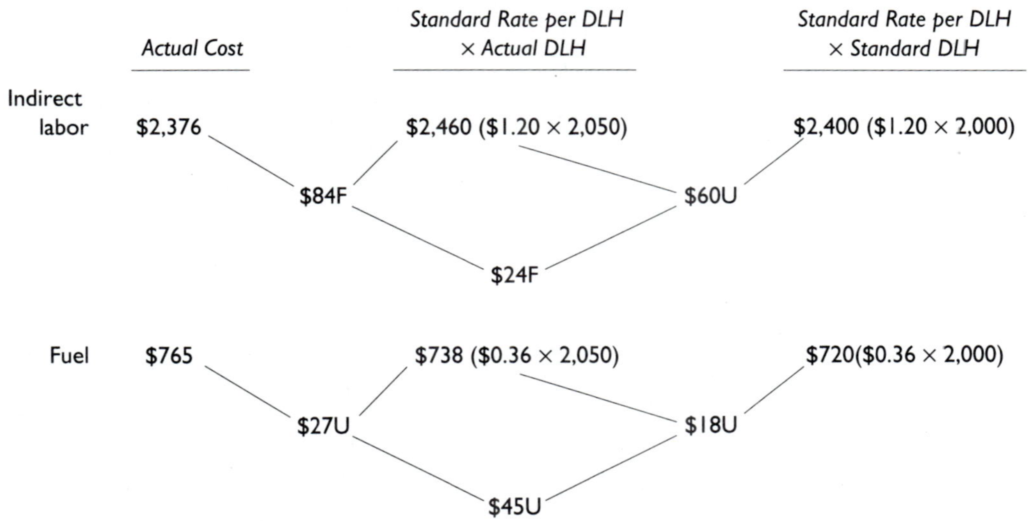

REQUIRED

Comment on the variances calculated above. Do they accurately reflect what they should? What changes do you recommend?

7–38 Variances: Good Output; Causes (CMA) Felton Company manufactures a complete line of radios. Because many models have plastic cases, the company has its own molding department for producing the cases. The month of April was devoted to the production of cases for one of the portable radios—Model SX76.

The molding department has two operations—molding and trimming. There is no interaction of labor in these two operations. The standard labor cost for producing ten plastic cases for Model SX76 is as follows:

Molders	0.50 hr at $6 =	$3
Trimmers	0.25 hr at $4 =	1
		$4

During April, 70,000 plastic cases were produced in the molding department. However, 10 percent of these cases (7,000) had to be discarded because they were found defective at final inspection. The purchasing department had changed to a new plastic supplier to take advantage of a lower price for comparable plastic. The new plastic turned out to be a lower quality and resulted in the rejection of completed cases.

Direct labor hours worked and direct labor costs charged to the molding department are shown below.

Direct Labor Charged to the Molding Department

Molders	3,800 hr at $6.25 =	$23,750
Trimmers	1,600 hr at $4.15 =	6,640
Total labor charges		$30,390

As a result of poor scheduling by the production scheduling department, the line manager of the molding department had to shift molders to the trimming operation for 200 hours during April. The company paid the molding workers their regular hourly rate even though they were performing a lower rated task. There was no significant loss of efficiency caused by the shift. In addition, the line manager of the department indicated that 75 hours and 35 hours of idle time occurred in the molding and trimming operations, respectively, as a result of unexpected machinery repairs required during the month.

REQUIRED

1. The monthly report that compares actual costs with standard cost of output for the month of April shows the following labor variance for the molding department:

Actual labor costs for April	$30,390
Standard labor cost of output (63,000 × $4/10)	25,200
Unfavorable labor variance	$ 5,190

This variance is significantly higher than normal, and management wants an explanation. Prepare a detailed analysis of the unfavorable labor variance for the molding department, showing the variance resulting from

a. labor rates
b. labor substitution
c. material substitution
d. operating efficiency
e. idle time

2. The line manager of the molding department is concerned with the large variances charged to the department. She feels that the variances due to labor substitution and change in raw materials should not be charged to the department. Does the line manager have a valid argument? Briefly justify your position.

7–39 Labor Mix and Yield Variances (CMA) (Appendix) Landeau Manufacturing Company has a process cost accounting system. An analysis that compares the actual results with both a monthly plan and a flexible budget is prepared monthly. The standard direct labor rates used in the flexible budget are established each year when the annual plan is formulated and held constant all year.

The standard direct labor rates in effect for the fiscal year ending June 30, 19X8, and the standard hours allowed for the output for the month of April are shown below:

	Standard Direct Labor Rate per Hour	Standard Direct Labor Hours Allowed for Output
Labor class III	$8	500
Labor class II	$7	500
Labor class I	$5	500

The wage rates for each labor class increased on January 1, 19X8, under the terms of a new union contract negotiated in December 19X7. The standard wage rates were not revised to reflect the new contract.

The actual direct labor hours worked and the actual direct labor rates per hour experienced for the month of April were:

	Actual Direct Labor Rate per Hour	Actual Direct Labor Hours
Labor class III	$8.50	550
Labor class II	$7.50	650
Labor class I	$5.40	375

REQUIRED

1. Calculate the dollar amount of the total direct labor variance for the month of April for the Landeau Manufacturing Company and analyze the total variance into the following components:
   a. direct labor rate variance
   b. direct labor mix variance
   c. direct labor performance (efficiency) variance
2. Discuss the advantages and disadvantages of a standard cost system in which the standard direct labor rates per hour are not changed during the year to reflect such events as a new labor contract.

7–40 Mix and Yield Variances (CMA) (Appendix) Energy Products Company produces a gasoline additive, Gas Gain. This product increases engine efficiency and improves gasoline mileage by creating a more complete burn in the combustion process.

Careful controls are required during the production process to ensure that the proper mix of input chemicals is achieved and that evaporation is controlled. If the controls are not effective, there can be loss of output and efficiency.

The standard cost of producing a 500-liter batch of Gas Gain is $135. The standard materials mix and related standard cost of each chemical used in a 500-liter batch are:

Chemical	*Standard Input Quantity in Liters*	*Standard Cost per Liter*	*Total Cost*
Echol	200	$0.200	$ 40.00
Protex	100	0.425	42.50
Benz	250	0.150	37.50
CT-40	50	0.300	15.00
	600		$135.00

The quantities of chemicals purchased and used during the current production period are shown in the schedule below. A total of 140 batches of Gas Gain was manufactured during the current production period. Energy Products determines its cost and chemical usage variations at the end of each production period.

Chemical	*Quantity Purchased in Liters*	*Total Purchase Price*	*Quantity Used in Liters*
Echol	25,000	$ 5,365	26,600
Protex	13,000	6,240	12,880
Benz	40,000	5,840	37,800
CT-40	7,500	2,220	7,140
Total	85,500	$19,665	84,420

REQUIRED

1. Calculate the purchase price variances by chemical for Energy Products Company.

2. Calculate the total material use variance related to Gas Gain for Energy Products Company and then analyze this total usage variance into the following two components:

a. total mix variance

b. total yield variance

7–41 Developing Standard Costs (CMA Adapted) ColdKing Company is a small producer of fruit-flavored frozen desserts. For many years, ColdKing's products have had strong regional sales on the basis of brand recognition: However, other companies have begun marketing similar products in the area, and price competition has become increasingly important. John Wakefield, the company's controller, is planning to implement a standard cost system and has gathered considerable information from his co-workers on production and material requirements for ColdKing's products. Wakefield believes that the use of standard costing will allow ColdKing to improve cost control and make better pricing decisions.

ColdKing's most popular product is raspberry sherbet. The sherbet is produced in ten-gallon batches, and each batch requires six quarts of good raspberries. The fresh raspberries are sorted by hand before entering the production process. Because of imperfections in the raspberries and normal spoilage, one quart of berries is discarded for every four quarts of acceptable berries. Three minutes is the standard direct labor time for sorting required to obtain one quart of acceptable raspberries. The acceptable raspberries are blended with the other ingredients; blending requires 12 minutes of direct labor time per batch. After blending, the sherbet is packaged in quart containers. Wakefield has gathered the following pricing information.

ColdKing purchases raspberries for $.80 per quart. All other ingredients cost a total of $.45 per gallon.

Direct labor is paid at the rate of $9.00 per hour.

The total cost of material and labor required to package the sherbet is $.38 per quart.

REQUIRED

1. Develop the standard cost for the direct cost components of a ten-gallon batch of raspberry sherbet. The standard cost should identify the
   a. standard quantity
   b. standard rate
   c. standard cost per batch

   for each direct cost component of a batch of raspberry sherbet.
2. As part of the implementation of a standard cost system at ColdKing, John Wakefield plans to train those responsible for maintaining the standards in the use of variance analysis. Wakefield is particularly concerned with the causes of unfavorable variances.
   a. Discuss the possible causes of unfavorable material price variances and identify the individual(s) who should be held responsible for these variances.
   b. Discuss the possible causes of unfavorable labor efficiency variances and identify the individual(s) who should be held responsible for these variances.

7–42 Standards and Behavior (CMA Adapted) CenPointe Device, Inc., is a manufacturer of continuous fluid metering devices for use in laboratories, chemical and pharmaceutical manufacturing operations, and nuclear power plants. The company was able to distinguish itself from its competition by the high precision and extended reliability records of its equipment. In the last few years, however, foreign competition had made inroads into CenPointe's market by offering better prices and delivery times as well as high quality products. CenPointe responded to this intensified competition by retooling its manufacturing operations to achieve lower production costs, to improve quality, and to shorten delivery times. This allowed the company to sell at a more competitive price and emphasize very short delivery time, even for equipment designed specifically for a new application.

The company is organized along functional lines. Manufacturing operations are the responsibility of the Vice-President of Production. Mary Rafferty, Director of Manufacturing Operations, reports to the Vice-President of Production, and all Production Supervisors of CenPointe's product lines report to her. Josh Gibson, Director of Quality Control, also reports to the Vice-President of Production, and he supervises the quality control personnel working on each product line.

The Production Supervisors of each product line have, in the past, received a listing of the orders to be filled during the month and measured their performance by how many orders they were able to fill. High quality was always stressed, and the Production Supervisors cooperated even if it meant some unfilled or reworked orders at the end of the month. The Production Supervisors were proud of their work.

The production data received from the floor was primarily used for accounting, financial reports, product pricing, and materials purchasing. Management reports went only to top management and the Quality Control Director for scrap performance.

To improve its competitive edge, CenPointe decided to develop a productivity measure for its manufacturing operations. For each product line, the company established goals for the quantity of material used in production, the amount of scrap, and the number of good units completed. The performance for each month was to be presented and discussed at a monthly meeting that included Rafferty, Gibson, all Production Supervisors, and a representative from the Accounting Department. The Production Supervisors' initial reaction to this system was positive because they saw an opportunity to participate and make suggestions.

Four months after the productivity measuring system and monthly meetings were implemented, the following conversation took place among three Production Supervisors, Roger Grier, Dana Berch, and Neil Bass.

> GRIER: "I really dislike these monthly meetings. The accounting people present data on last month's production that we have never seen before and Rafferty expects us to have answers."
>
> BERCH: "It's like an ambush by the enemy. When the accounting people have finished with us, Gibson hits us with his data."
>
> GRIER: "Where do the standards for material cost usage come from anyway?"
>
> BERCH: "I'm not sure. I think the Bill of Materials has something to do with it."
>
> GRIER: "But the data they present is in dollars and the Bill of Materials is in units. And how does the scrap rate data Gibson hits us with affect the accounting data?"
>
> BERCH: "I don't know."
>
> GRIER: "Let's talk to Rafferty about how all this information is assembled."
>
> BERCH: "Do you really want to talk about anything to the boss right now after she just criticized us in the meeting?"
>
> GRIER: "But she criticizes us every month. All the departments are always at least 20 percent below the financial standards. In fact, I consider it a good month when my department performs at 75 percent of standard."
>
> BERCH: "Let's just forget it. At next month's meeting, we can look amazed at the results again, apologize, and say that we will do better next month. That's what we have been doing for the last four months."
>
> GRIER: "I'm tired of looking bad at every monthly meeting. I'm going to find a way to look good at next month's meeting. Here comes Neil. I wonder what he thinks."
>
> BASS: "After the meeting, Rafferty gave me the production schedule requirements for my department for the rest of the month. I told her the schedule far exceeded the capability of my department. She told me that she was sure that I could find a way to meet the schedule. I told her that the product specifications had not yet been received from Quality Control for many of the orders that the Sales Department had committed to ship before the end of the month. She just smiled and walked away."

REQUIRED

1. Based on the conversation among the three Production Supervisors of CenPointe Device, Inc., discuss the likely motivation and behavior during the coming months of
 a. the Production Supervisors
 b. the employees of the Production Supervisors

2. Based upon the conversation among the three Production Supervisors of CenPointe Device, Inc.,
   a. Identify and explain the weaknesses of CenPointes' productivity measurement system and monthly meetings.
   b. Present a recommendation for correcting each identified weakness.

8

STANDARD COSTING

Chapter 7 developed variances relating to purchasing and production. We established basic relationships to compare planned performance with actual results. This chapter relies on that discussion and shows how firms use standard costs and variances in product costing.

Standard costing is the use of standard costs in product costing, in the cost accounting cycle from Materials Inventory through Work-in-Process Inventory to Finished Goods Inventory and, finally, to Cost of Goods Sold. In standard costing systems, inventories of materials, work in process, and finished goods are kept at standard cost, not actual or normal cost. Standard costing can be used by process-oriented firms such as those mentioned in Chapter 6 and also by job order firms that produce the same basic products over and over. A furniture manufacturer that produces only a few basic models could use standard costing. Standard costing is the usual basis for computer inventory accounting systems. Most large firms, and many small ones, use standard costing because it offers several advantages.

ADVANTAGES OF STANDARD COSTING

First, using standard costs in the accounts ties the planning and control aspects of standard costs into the accounting system. Firms that use actual or normal costing for product costing purposes and calculate variances only to judge production efficiency divorce the managerial aspects of standards from the accounting system. Second, the calculations required under standard costing are somewhat less cumbersome than those under actual or normal costing.

Third, standard costing is much the best choice for repetitive manufacturers. Consider a firm that makes 1,000 or so different products in the same factory. The products may differ in size, like panes of glass, or qualitatively, like different models of automobiles. In the automobile assembly plant, keeping track of costs for each individual car is prohibitively costly. Yet the plant could not use process costing, because the cars differ in so many important respects that no single denominator could be used to determine a cost-per-car figure. Standard costing is cheaper and more informative than actual or normal costing.

Finally, many larger firms are adopting complex inventory accounting and production scheduling computer software. It is virtually impossible to install these systems using actual costs. Thus, all of these major systems are based on standard inputs and standard costs. At the end of a period, the company simply counts the number of each model, multiplies the quantity of each model by its standard cost, and sums the results. The grand total is the inventory valuation. This procedure applies also to work in process, where the standard cost to the point of completion is used. Thus, an automobile at a particular point on the production line has a standard cost to that point.

RECORDING STANDARD COSTS

Standard costing parallels actual and normal costing so far as the basic flows of costs are concerned. Flows from Materials Inventory, Direct Labor, and Factory Overhead accounts through Work-in-Process Inventory to Finished Goods Inventory to Cost of Goods Sold are essentially the same under all costing methods. Standard costing involves transfers at standard cost, or at least at standard prices of input factors. The transfers depend on the way the system is operated.

An Overview of Standard Costing

First, we develop a basic overview of the two most common standard costing systems, the *after-production* and the *during-production* methods. Then we illustrate the same steps we did in Chapter 5: recording the costs incurred and moving costs to Work-in-Process Inventory, to Finished Goods Inventory, and to Cost of Goods Sold.

In the *after-production* method all costs put into Work-in-Process Inventory, taken out to Finished Goods Inventory, and finally moved to Cost of Goods Sold are at standard. Thus, the amount debited to Work-in-Process Inventory for materials is the standard cost of materials for the number of units produced, the direct labor cost put into Work-in-Process Inventory is the standard direct labor cost for the number of units produced, and so also with factory overhead. Such a system can be used if the entries in the accounting system are made after production for a period is known. That is, to know the standard labor cost (material cost, overhead cost) of units produced, you must, of course, know actual production.

Entries under this standard costing system are made periodically: weekly, monthly, or whenever the production for a period is known. Figure 8–1 illustrates the flows. Under this system the inventories are all carried at standard, and variances are, therefore, treated as period expenses. Later in the chapter we discuss how to dispose of variances.

If entries are made before production is known, they cannot reflect standard costs, but they can reflect standard prices. Thus, entries to Work-in-Process Inventory can reflect the actual quantity of materials, labor, and overhead put into process, but at standard prices per pound and rates per hour, not the actual costs. This type of standard costing system essentially does for materials and labor what normal costing does for overhead, since it applies them at standard, or predetermined rates, but with actual quantities.

FIGURE 8–1 Inventory Flow and Standard Costs: After-Production Method

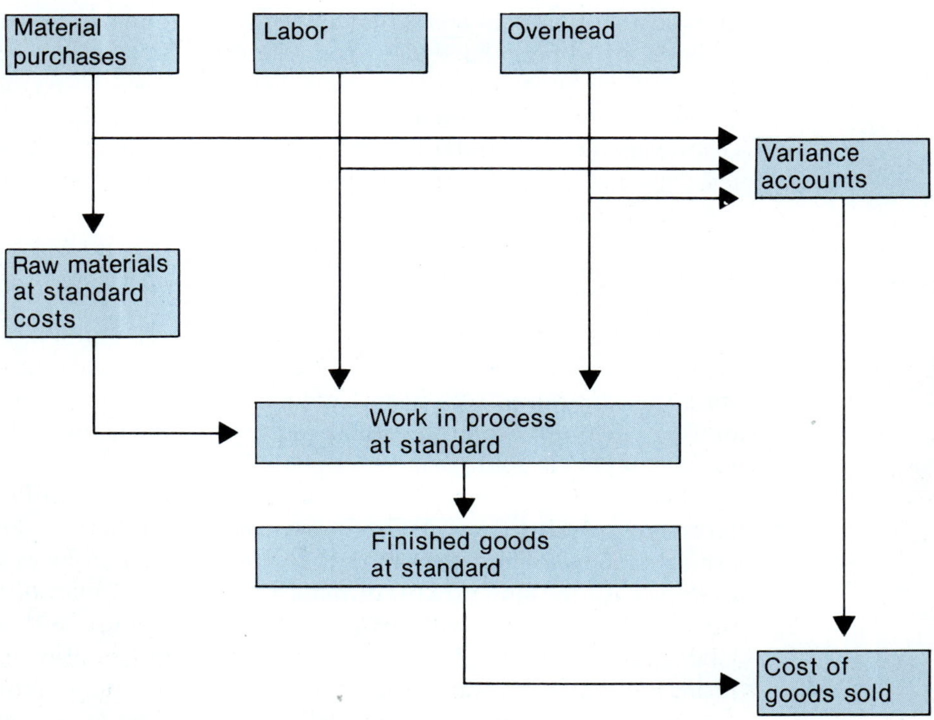

Illustration of Standard Costing

We begin with a simplified illustration, then consider some less straightforward matters. Exhibit 8–1 shows data for a product of Barton Mills, which operates a process-like factory. The exhibit also contains operating results for July, 19X6.

We must first find FIFO equivalent-unit production (EUP). Chapter 6 pointed out that FIFO is the better cost flow assumption for control purposes because it calculates EUP as the work done in the current period, where the weighted-average method mixes current period work and costs with those of previous periods. Because you are already familiar with variance calculations, we simply show the variances along with equivalent unit production in Exhibit 8–2. You might wish to verify the variance calculations as a review problem.

We are now ready to prepare journal entries and develop T-accounts. Remember that we are using the after-production method, which assumes that we know production before we make the entries.

Material purchases: Record materials inventory at standard price to isolate the price variance.

EXHIBIT 8–1 Standard Cost and Operating Results

Standard cost:

Materials, 4 yards at $2	$ 8.00
Direct labor, 0.60 hours at $11	6.60
Variable overhead at $5 per DLH	3.00
Fixed overhead at $8 per DLH	4.80
Total standard cost	$22.40

Fixed overhead is based on $400,000 monthly budgeted overhead and 50,000 monthly standard direct labor hours.

Operating results, July:

Units completed	80,000
Units in ending work-in-process, 30% complete	20,000
Units in beginning work-in-process, 40% complete	10,000
Units sold at $40	75,000
Material purchases, 250,000 yards	$488,000
Material use	330,000 yards
Direct labor, 47,800 hours	$530,000
Variable overhead	$248,000
Fixed overhead	$404,000

There were 500 units in the inventory of finished goods at standard cost of $11,200 ($22.40 × 500). There were 100,000 yards of material in beginning inventory at $2 per yard.

EXHIBIT 8–2 Equivalent Unit Production and Variances

Equivalent unit production:		
Units completed		80,000
EUP in ending work in process, 30% complete		6,000
EUP in beginning work in process, 40% complete		4,000
Less:		
FIFO EUP		82,000
Variances:		
Material price variance	$12,000 F	$488,000 − $2 × 250,000
Material use variance	4,000 U	(330,000 − 328,000) × $2
Direct labor rate variance	4,200 U	$530,000 − $11 × 47,800
Direct labor efficiency variance	15,400 F	(47,800 − 49,200) × $11
Variable overhead budget variance	9,000 U	$248,000 − 47,800 × $5
Variable overhead efficiency variance	7,000 F	(47,800 − 49,200) × $5
Fixed overhead budget variance	4,000 U	$404,000 − $400,000
Fixed overhead application variance	6,400 U	$400,000 − 82,000 × $4.80
Total	$ 6,800 F	

		Debit	Credit
1.	Materials Inventory (250,000 pounds × $2)	$500,000	
	Material Price Variance		12,000
	Cash or Accounts Payable		$488,000

Material use: Record standard cost of materials for actual output, isolating the use variance.

		Debit	Credit
2.	Work-in-Process Inventory (82,000 × $8)	$656,000	
	Material Use Variance	4,000	
	Materials Inventory (330,000 × $2)		$660,000

Labor: Record payroll at standard rate and actual hours, isolating the rate variance, then enter into work in process at standard cost for 82,000 equivalent units.

		Debit	Credit
3a.	Direct Labor (47,800 × $11)	$525,800	
	Direct Labor Rate Variance	4,200	
	Cash or Accrued Payroll		$530,000
3b.	Work-in-Process Inventory (82,000 × $6.60)	$541,200	
	Direct Labor Efficiency Variance		$ 15,400
	Direct Labor		525,800

Overhead: Record overhead recognizing the spending variances, then put into work in process at standard cost.

		Debit	Credit
4a.	Variable Manufacturing Overhead (47,800 × $5)	$239,000	
	Variable Overhead Spending Variance	9,000	
	Various Credits, Cash, Accrued Expenses		$248,000

		Debit	Credit
	Fixed Manufacturing Overhead (budget)	$400,000	
	Fixed Overhead Budget Variance	4,000	
	Various Credits, Cash, Accumulated Depreciation		$404,000
4b.	Work-in-Process Inventory (82,000 × $3)	$246,000	
	Variable Overhead Efficiency Variance		7,000
	Variable Manufacturing Overhead		$239,000
	Work-in-Process Inventory (82,000 × $4.80)	$393,600	
	Fixed Overhead Application Variance	6,400	
	Fixed Manufacturing Overhead		$400,000

Completion of goods: As goods are completed, we remove their costs from Work-in-Process Inventory and move them to Finished Goods Inventory.

		Debit	Credit
5.	Finished Goods Inventory (80,000 × $22.40)	$1,792,000	
	Work-in-Process Inventory		$1,792,000

Sales: As goods are sold we move their costs from Finished Goods Inventory to Cost of Goods Sold.

		Debit	Credit
6.	Cost of Goods Sold (75,000 × $22.40)	$1,680,000	
	Finished Goods Inventory		$1,680,000

The T-accounts for each type of inventory and for Cost of Goods Sold appear in Exhibit 8–3. Materials Inventory shows the standard price of the

EXHIBIT 8–3 T-Accounts

Work-in-Process Inventory

	Debit	Credit	
Beg Bal	$ 89,600		
(2)	656,000		
(3b)	541,200		
(4b)	246,000		
(4b)	393,600	$1,792,000	(5)
	$1,926,400	$1,792,000	
End Bal	$134,400		

Finished Goods Inventory

	Debit	Credit	
Beg Bal	$ 11,200		
(5)	1,792,000	1,680,000	(6)
	1,803,200	1,680,000	
End Bal	$123,200		

Materials Inventory

	Debit	Credit	
Beg Bal	$200,000		
(1)	500,000	$660,000	(2)
	$700,000	$660,000	
Bal.	$40,000		

Cost of Goods Sold

	Debit	Credit
(6)	$1,680,000	

20,000 pounds in the ending inventory, which is the 100,000 yards in beginning inventory plus the 250,000 yards purchased less 330,000 yards used.

The variance accounts now contain the variances for the period, as we have already calculated. What is the disposition of the variances? As with misapplied overhead, there are several alternatives. We can show variances on the income statement as adjustments to cost of goods sold (or gross margin). We can also prorate them among the inventory accounts and cost of sales. Prorating variances converts standard costing to actual costing. We must prorate variances if they are material *and* if ending inventories are significant. Generally accepted accounting principles permit the use of standard costs for financial reporting purposes as long as the financial statement results of using them do not differ materially from the results under actual costing. There will be little difference between the results if either inventories or variances are small. Appendix 8A covers proration of variances.

Variances on the Income Statement

When a company includes variances on its income statement distributed to outsiders, it usually lumps them in with standard cost of sales. Internal income statements usually have variances shown separately to draw attention to them. An example appears below, using an assumed selling price of $40 per unit. The variances here are shown by cost factor, but not by type of variance. Some managers might prefer to see all variances separately enumerated; others might be content with a single total figure.

Sales (75,000 × $40)		$3,000,000
Standard cost of sales	$1,680,000	
Materials variances	8,000 F	
Labor variances	11,200 F	
Overhead variances	12,400 U	
Cost of sales		1,673,200
Gross profit		$1,326,800

An alternative is to show standard gross profit, the difference between sales and standard cost of sales. The variances then show up as adjustments to gross profit. The advantage of the alternative is that it makes it easier to calculate the percentage of standard gross profit to sales, a number helpful to many managers. It is still possible to make the calculation using the format above as 44 percent ([$3,000,000 − $1,680,000]/$3,000,000), but it requires an extra step.

Showing variances as expenses (or if favorable, as negative expenses) relies on the view that standards represent what costs should be and that deviations from those costs (variances) are not inventoriable because they are abnormal. Recall that to be an asset, a cost must have future value to the entity. It is arguable that variances, because they represent deviations from what costs should be, are not of future value and should therefore be expensed.

Prorating Variances

From a control and managerial accountability standpoint, classifying all variances as expenses seems most appropriate. However, financial reporting and tax accounting generally require the use of actual costing. In developing financial statements for those purposes, therefore, variances must be prorated to inventories and cost of sales.

The variances in our example were not material and, therefore, could reasonably be written off as adjustments to cost of sales. However, if variances for a full year are material, they must be allocated to inventories and cost of sales. *Accounting Research Bulletin 43* requires that standard costs, to be acceptable for financial reporting purposes, be "adjusted at reasonable intervals to reflect current conditions so that at the balance-sheet date standard costs reasonably approximate costs computed under one of the recognized bases."[1] The recognized bases are FIFO, LIFO, and weighted-average cost flows.

We cover the calculations involved in prorating variances in Appendix 8A. However, the result of proration yields cost of goods sold and ending inventory balances exactly as if actual costing had been used to record all transactions.

Variances and Control

The purpose of identifying variances is to begin to investigate why results differed from plans by looking at various areas of responsibility. Accordingly, it is logical from a control and responsibility accounting perspective to show any variance as an adjustment to income. This is exactly what happens when the variances appear as an expense in the income statement above.

MULTIPLE PRODUCTS AND OVERHEAD BASES

Our basic example used a single product, with one material and one production department. Most companies are not so simple. Nonetheless, the principles of standard costing for more complicated companies are identical to those for simple companies.

Multiple Overhead Rates

In a single-product plant, all overhead relates to one product, no matter whether it is associated with labor time, material use, the number of vendors, or number of transactions. In a multi-product factory, overhead is driven by

[1]Committee on Accounting Procedure, *Accounting Research Bulletin No. 43, Restatement and Revision of Accounting Research Bulletins* (New York: American Institute of Certified Public Accountants, 1953), p. 17.

several activities and relates to many, or all, of the products. It is important to apply overhead based on the appropriate drivers. Calculating overhead rates in a multi-product situation is therefore done differently from how it is done in a single-product plant. In a multi-product setting, it is important to determine the appropriate overhead rates per unit of the activities that drive costs. These rates are then used in developing standard costs. Consider the following example.

Activity	*Overhead Cost Pool*	*Amount of Activity*	*Rate*
Machine time	$2,500,000	500,000 hours	$5.00 per hour
Number of personnel	$ 300,000	800 people	$375.00 per person
Number of vendors	$ 500,000	500 vendors	$1,000.00 per vendor

A particular product might then have the following standards. The product requires seven people and uses parts supplied by four vendors. The per-unit standards for personnel and vendors are based on 1,000 units of this product.

Materials, 8 components at $4	$32.00
Direct labor, 0.60 hours at $12	7.20
Machine time, 0.20 hours at $5	1.00
Personnel, 7 people at $375 divided by 1,000	2.625
Vendors, 4 vendors at $1,000 divided by 1,000	4.000
Total standard cost	$46.825

The company can calculate overhead variances for each cost pool separately. Remember from Chapter 7 that many advanced manufacturers use rolling averages instead of standards because they believe that using standards violates the principle of seeking continuous improvement.

Changeover (Set Up) Costs

Many multi-product companies establish normal or standard amounts to produce in a batch or production run. If it is costly to change over from making one product to another, the normal batch size will be relatively large. Changeover costs consist of direct or indirect labor and other overhead items, depending on how the changeover is done and what resources must be used. (For example, it might be necessary to destroy some material in setting up a machine for a particular product.) The less costly the changeover, the smaller the batch size. A JIT company that also employs flexible manufacturing has driven its changeover costs to near zero, so the optimal batch size is one unit. However, not all companies can reduce their costs this way.

Changeover costs are part of the standard cost, which must be based on the standard-size production run or batch. If the company consistently makes too small batches, it has unfavorable variances for changeover costs. If it makes too large batches, its changeover costs show favorable variances.

PRODUCT COSTING IN ADVANCED MANUFACTURING ENVIRONMENTS

Most advanced manufacturers carry insignificant inventories of work-in-process inventory; those that fully utilize flexible manufacturing carry almost no finished goods. With no significant inventories, product costing is unnecessary because all costs relate to products sold. Thus, all costs for a period can flow straight to Cost of Goods Sold. However, many advanced manufacturers have inventories large enough to be accounted for, so product costing is still a concern. Moreover, virtually all companies need product-cost records for auditing, tax compliance, and managerial purposes.

When inventories are relatively small, companies can use a technique called **backflushing**, or **backflush costing**. Backflushing is simple and requires relatively few entries during a period. There is no effort to keep the Work-in-Process Inventory and Finished Goods Inventory accounts at their "correct" balances. Companies typically maintain two inventory accounts—one for finished goods, the other for both materials and work in process. The following example shows one way to record events using a backflush system. Data for the example appear below.

There were no beginning inventories.

Materials and components purchased and put into process	$500,000
Labor and overhead costs incurred	$360,000
Units completed	80,000
Units sold	70,000

Material purchases are recorded in the following manner.

Materials and In-Process Inventory	$500,000	
Cash or Accounts Payable		$500,000

Because materials are put into process almost immediately, there is no need for separate accounts for materials and work in process. The combined inventory account will be closed at the end of the period.

Conversion Costs	$360,000	
Cash, Accounts Payable, Accumulated Depreciation		$360,000
To collect labor and overhead costs in a single account.		

Because advanced manufacturing companies have relatively little direct labor, they do not need detailed labor reporting. These first two entries are made throughout the month as events require.

At month-end it remains to determine unit cost and clear out the inventory accounts. The average cost of production was $10.75 ([$500,000 + $360,000]/80,000). Ending finished goods inventory of 10,000 units then has a cost of $107,500 ($10.75 × 10,000) and cost of sales the remaining $752,500 ($10.75 × 70,000).

At the end of a period, or perhaps when units are sold, an entry of the following type is made.

Cost of Sales	$752,500	
Finished Goods Inventory	107,500	
Materials and In-Process Inventory		$500,000
Conversion Costs		360,000

The recording could also be done using standard costs, but as we have already mentioned, JIT companies typically use actual, not standard, costs. However, it makes sense to use standard costs if several products are made because otherwise actual costs must be allocated among the products, then among the units. Such allocations are very shaky, so standard costs make a good deal of sense.

Other patterns are possible. Some companies charge all costs to Finished Goods Inventory as units are completed, then to Cost of Sales only at month-end.

COMPARISON OF ACTUAL, NORMAL, AND STANDARD COSTING

We can compare cost accounting systems along several dimensions. First, a product-costing system must use actual, normal, or standard costs. Second, the nature of the manufacturing operation tends to separate cost systems into job order, process, and repetitive manufacturing, based on how costs are accumulated. All three types of companies can use actual or normal costs. Any company that makes relatively standard products can use standard costing. (Most job order systems do not use standard costs because of the major differences among their products.)

The critical difference between standard costing and actual and normal costing is that the latter two are based on *inputs* and standard costing is based on *outputs*. That is, under standard costing the unit of product carries its standard cost wherever it goes (inventory or cost of sales). Under actual and normal costing, the cost of a unit depends on the inputs used to manufacture that unit. Under normal costing, overhead is applied to product, as it is under standard costing. However under normal costing the total amount of overhead applied depends on the amount of the input factor (direct labor hours, machine hours, etc.), while under standard costing it depends on the number of units produced.

Yet, with all these possibilities, the only real differences among the various methods and systems lie in the valuation of inventories. That is, total manufacturing costs, both fixed and variable, incurred in a particular period are given: costs incurred are costs incurred no matter what the cost system, so the choice of a cost system does not change actual costs.[2] The different techniques are simply ways of assigning costs to cost of goods sold and to inventories. If a company has no inventories, all of the various approaches will give the same amount of income on the income statement because all costs will be expensed.

STANDARD JOB ORDER COSTING

As we mentioned briefly earlier, job order firms can use standard costing if there is sufficient repetition in their products or in operations common to most products. For example, if a firm makes 40 to 50 different optical instruments that contain several standard components, such as lenses and frames, and that require similar operations, such as drilling, grinding, and chamfering, it might be able to use standard costing.

Individual jobs are charged with the standard cost of direct materials and direct labor, standard quantities times standard prices, and Work-in-Process Inventory consists of the standard cost of work done on each job to date. For example, suppose that the standard cost card for a particular optical instrument calls for grinding of one edge to take a half-hour. If the standard labor rate is $8 per hour, each grinding has a standard cost of $4. The worker marks the job ticket with the number of edges ground during the time worked on the job. The clerk determines the total standard hours allowed for grinding all the pieces.

ALTERNATIVE COST FLOW PATTERNS

In some cases accounting entries are made before production is known. It is then impossible to debit Work-in-Process Inventory at standard prices times standard quantities because standard quantities depend on production. Firms that make entries to Work-in-Process Inventory as the period progresses, and without knowing total production, use standard prices and actual quantities for direct labor and materials. They apply overhead at the end of the period, based on actual production. Transfers from Work-in-Process Inventory to Finished Goods Inventory and, ultimately, to Cost of Goods Sold are made at standard cost per unit times the number of units involved. This method is called *during production*.

The basic difference between the flows under the two possibilities is that the material use variance and direct labor efficiency variance go into Work-in-

[2] Note that managers might behave differently under different costing systems such that costs might be different. We are assuming that all activities are the same regardless of the costing system.

Process Inventory because actual quantities, not standard quantities, are used to make the debits to the account. At the end of the period these amounts are transferred out of Work-in-Process Inventory and it, as well as the other inventory accounts, appears at standard cost per unit times the number of equivalent units in process.

Because overhead usually is applied at the end of the period when production is known, the entries for overhead appear like those used in the illustration. In practice many variations are possible, but the essence of standard costing is that inventories are shown at standard, with variances isolated in separate accounts. Because variances are shown in accounts, instead of simply being computed, they become part of the basic accounting records. The value is that the accounting records then support and tie into the information needed for planning and control.

The entries below illustrate an alternative where actual quantities of materials, direct labor, and overhead at standard prices are put into Work-in-Process Inventory, then the efficiency variances are removed at the end of the period. The illustration uses the earlier example. We omit explanations of entries that do not change.

1.	Materials Inventory (250,000 pounds × $2)	$500,000	
	Material Price Variance		12,000
	Cash or Accounts Payable		$488,000
2.	Work-in-Process Inventory	$660,000	
	Materials Inventory (330,000 × $2)		$660,000
Put actual quantity of materials at standard price into process.			
3a.	Direct Labor (47,800 × $11)	$525,800	
	Direct Labor Rate Variance	4,200	
	Cash or Accrued Payroll		$530,000
3b.	Work-in-Process Inventory	$525,800	
	Direct Labor		$525,800
Put actual quantity of direct labor at standard rate into process.			
4a.	Variable Manufacturing Overhead (47,800 × $5)	$239,000	
	Variable Overhead Spending Variance	9,000	
	Various Credits, Cash, Accrued Expenses		$248,000
	Fixed Manufacturing Overhead (budget)	$400,000	
	Fixed Overhead Budget Variance	4,000	
	Various Credits, Cash, Accumulated Depreciation		$404,000
4b.	Work-in-Process Inventory	$239,000	
	Variable Manufacturing Overhead		$239,000
	Work-in-Process Inventory	$400,000	
	Fixed Manufacturing Overhead		$400,000
To put overhead into process at budgeted cost.			

		Debit	Credit
5.	Finished Goods Inventory (80,000 × $22.40)	$1,792,000	
	Work-in-Process Inventory		$1,792,000
6.	Cost of Goods Sold (75,000 × $22.40)	$1,680,000	
	Finished Goods Inventory		$1,680,000

The following entry is made when production is known. It simply isolates the remaining variances and corrects the Work-in-Process Inventory account.

		Debit	Credit
7.	Work-in-Process Inventory	$12,000	
	Material Use Variance	4,000	
	Fixed Overhead Application Variance	6,400	
	Direct Labor Efficiency Variance		$15,400
	Variable Overhead Efficiency Variance		7,000

Work in Process appears as follows.

WORK-IN-PROCESS INVENTORY

	Debit	Credit	
Beg Bal	$ 89,600		
(2)	660,000		
(3b)	525,800		
(4b)	239,000		
(4b)	400,000		
(7)	12,000	$1,792,000	(5)
	$1,926,400	$1,792,000	
End Bal	$134,400		

The balance is the same as in Exhibit 8–3 (page 351). Again, the critical point is not the way that entries are made or the point at which variances are recognized (although the earlier they are recognized the better), but that the inventory accounts show the standard costs of the goods on hand at the end of the period. During the period you can make entries in almost any way as long as you preserve enough information to determine the correct adjustment at the end of the period.

COMPUTER-BASED STANDARD COSTING SYSTEMS

A whole new set of terms has been created by software vendors and manufacturers for large, computer-based inventory accounting systems that use standard costing. A synonym in many cases for total standard costs is **total rolled-up cost**, which means the summation of all the input costs to get unit cost. If standard costs were established at the beginning of the year and, say, material prices have changed since then, a firm may leave the standard cost static but update the rolled-up cost.

Finally, we have identified four major inputs (materials, direct labor, variable overhead, and fixed overhead). Some computer-based systems (as well as some manual systems) designate these as **cost buckets**. These cost buckets also may break down material into freight-in and material cost and direct labor into set up labor and running labor.

SUMMARY

Standard costing is using standard costs and variances in a company's product costing system. We have shown the entries needed for such a system. Some companies use a standard costing system and assign all variances to the income statement made up for planning and evaluation purposes. However, to create both financial and tax reports, management must prorate significant variances between various inventories and cost of goods sold and, in essence, create actual costing statements. The examples in this chapter illustrate basic standard costing systems. Each company, based on its history, current needs, size, and cost-benefit trade-offs, will establish its own specific standard costing system.

REVIEW PROBLEM

Nimmer Company uses standard costing. It developed the following standards per unit of its one product. Because Nimmer is highly automated, it uses machine time to apply overhead and has no direct labor.

Materials, 3 gallons at $1.00 per gallon	$ 3
Variable overhead 0.50 machine hours at $12	6
Fixed overhead at $18 per machine hour*	9
Total standard cost	$18

*Based on budgeted fixed overhead of $450,000 and normal capacity of 25,000 standard machine hours ($450,000/25,000 = $18 per hour), or 25,000 units.

Actual results and variances appear below. There were no beginning inventories.

Actual results:
Production, 42,000 units, sales 40,000 units at $40
Material purchases, 140,000 gallons at $0.95, $133,000
Material use, 130,000 gallons
Machine hours, 22,000
Variable overhead, $251,000
Fixed overhead, $461,000
Variances:
Materials Variances
Price variance, $7,000 unfavorable [140,000 gallons × ($0.10 − $0.095)]
Use variance, $4,000 unfavorable [130,000 − (42,000 × 3)] × $1.00
Variable Overhead Variances
Budget variance, $13,000 favorable [$251,000 − (22,000 × $12)]

Efficiency variance, $12,000 unfavorable [22,000 hours − (42,000 × 0.50)] × $12
Fixed Overhead Variances
Budget variance, $11,000 unfavorable ($461,000 − $450,000)
Volume variance, $72,000 unfavorable [(25,000 − 21,000) × $18]

REQUIRED

1. Prepare journal entries to record the events assuming the after-production method.
2. Prepare T-accounts for Work-in-Process Inventory and Finished Goods Inventory.

ANSWER TO REVIEW PROBLEM

		Debit	Credit
1.	Materials Inventory (140,000 × $1.00)	$140,000	
	Material Price Variance	7,000	
	Cash or Accounts Payable		$133,000
2.	Work-in-Process Inventory (126,000 × $1.00)	$126,000	
	Material Use Variance	4,000	
	Materials Inventory		$130,000
3a.	Variable Manufacturing Overhead (22,000 × $12)	$264,000	
	Variable Overhead Budget Variance		$ 13,000
	Various credits		251,000
3b.	Work-in-Process Inventory (42,000 × $6)	$252,000	
	Variable Overhead Efficiency Variance	12,000	
	Variable Manufacturing Overhead		$264,000
4a.	Fixed Manufacturing Overhead	$450,000	
	Fixed Overhead Budget Variance	11,000	
	Various credits		$461,000
4b.	Work-in-Process Inventory (42,000 × $9)	$378,000	
	Fixed Overhead Volume Variance	72,000	
	Fixed Manufacturing Overhead		$450,000
5.	Finished Goods Inventory (42,000 × $18)	$756,000	
	Work-in-Process Inventory		$756,000
6.	Cost of Goods Sold (40,000 × $18)	$720,000	
	Finished Goods Inventory		$720,000

WORK-IN-PROCESS INVENTORY

	Debit		Credit
(2)	$126,000	(5)	$756,000
(3b)	252,000		
(4b)	378,000		
	756,000		756,000
Bal.	$0		

FINISHED GOODS INVENTORY

	Debit	Credit	
(5)	$756,000	$720,000	(6)
Bal.	$ 36,000		

Note that the $36,000 balance in Finished Goods Inventory is 2,000 unsold units at $18.

APPENDIX 8A: VARIANCE PRORATION

As we discussed in the chapter, to adjust financial accounting and tax accounting statements to reflect actual costs as required when there are variances that are material, we can either (1) redo all entries using actual costing or (2) prorate the standard cost variances. The result is the same either way. We will illustrate proration with an example in which there is no beginning inventory. We will discuss later how beginning inventories complicate the procedure.

As a general rule, each type of variance (materials, direct labor, overhead) is allocated (prorated) to each ending inventory and to cost of sales on the basis of the relative amounts of standard cost *for that factor* in each account. Data for an example appear in Exhibit 8A–1. To save time and concentrate on the problem at hand, we have presented the data assuming that all variances have been calculated. Familiarize yourself with the data first, making sure that you see how the figures for standard costs in the ending inventories and cost of sales were developed.

Because all conversion cost variances are prorated the same way, there is no need to break them down into individual items. However, the material price and use variances usually must be treated separately from the conversion cost variances because of different equivalent productions and ending inventories of work in process. Additionally, the material price variance is allocated separately because it relates to all ending inventories and to cost of sales. The other variances relate only to ending inventories of work in process and finished goods and to cost of sales.

EXHIBIT 8A–1 Data for Illustration

	Standard Cost of Materials	*Standard Conversion Costs*	*Total Standard Costs*
Sales	$200,000	$480,000	$680,000
Ending inventory of finished goods	100,000	240,000	340,000
Work in process:			
Materials	60,000		
Conversion costs		80,000	
Total work in process			140,000

Additionally, there were no beginning inventories and the ending inventory of materials has a standard cost of $50,000.

Variances	
Material price variance	$20,000 U
Material use variance	10,000 F
Conversion cost variances	80,000 U

Material Price Variance

There are several ways to allocate the material price variance. Some accountants allocate it to each of the ending inventories, cost of sales, and material use variance. Others ignore the material use variance in allocating the material price variance because they believe that the increase in accuracy is not worth the additional effort. The schedule below shows the allocation of the material price variance.

Account	*Standard Cost*	*Percentage of Total*	*Allocation of Material Price Variance*
Materials Inventory	$ 50,000	12.5%	$ 2,500
Work-in-Process Inventory	60,000	15	3,000
Finished Goods Inventory	100,000	25	5,000
Cost of Sales	200,000	50	10,000
Material Use Variance	(10,000)	(2.5)	(500)
Totals	$400,000	100.0%	$20,000

Notice that the allocation to the material use variance is negative because the material use variance was favorable. Essentially, this allocation recognizes that less material than the standard quantity was required to produce the units. The resulting allocation of the material use variance, augmented by the share of the material price variance, gives the same result as actual costing. The reason is that the standard costs of materials in the ending inventories of work in process and finished goods and in cost of sales reflect standard quantities of material, not actual quantities.

Material Use Variance and Conversion Cost Variances

The schedules below show the allocations of the material use variance and of the conversion cost variances based on the relative amounts of standard cost in each account. This part of the allocation should present no problems: the procedures are similar to other allocations that we have dealt with.

Material Use Variance

Account	*Standard Cost*	*Percentage of Total*	*Allocation of Material Use Variance*
Work-in-Process Inventory	$ 60,000	16.67%	$ 1,750
Finished Goods Inventory	100,000	27.78	2,917
Cost of Sales	200,000	55.55	5,833
Total	$360,000	100.00%	$10,500

Notice that the total amount of material use variance allocated is $10,500, which is the original $10,000 favorable variance plus the favorable allocation from the material price variance. In journal entry terms, the unfavorable material price variance is a credit to Material Use Variance, debits to the other accounts.

Conversion Cost Variances

Account	*Standard Cost*	*Percentage of Total*	*Allocation of Conversion Cost Variances*
Work-in-Process Inventory	$ 80,000	10%	$ 8,000
Finished Goods Inventory	240,000	30	24,000
Cost of Sales	480,000	60	48,000
Total	$800,000	100.00%	$80,000

Finally, the schedule below summarizes the prorations and shows the inventory valuations that would be used for financial reporting purposes.

Account	*Standard Cost*	*Unfavorable Material Price Variance*	*Favorable Material Use Variance*	*Unfavorable Conversion Cost Variances*	*Actual Cost*
Materials Inventory	$ 50,000	$ 2,500			$ 52,500
Work-in-Process Inventory	140,000	3,000	($1,750)	$ 8,000	149,250
Finished Goods Inventory	340,000	5,000	(2,917)	24,000	366,083
Cost of Sales	680,000	10,000	(5,833)	48,000	732,167
Total					$1,300,000

Standard costs in Exhibit 8A–1 total $1,210,000 ($680,000 + $340,000 + $140,000 + $50,000). Net variances are $90,000U ($20,000U − $10,000F + $80,000U). Thus, total actual costs are $1,300,000, which checks out with our total above.

At year-end the company makes the following journal entry.

Materials Inventory	$ 2,500	
Work-in-Process Inventory	9,250	
Finished Goods Inventory	26,083	
Cost of Goods Sold	52,167	
Material Use Variance	10,000	
Material Price Variance		$20,000
Labor and Overhead Variances		80,000

The labor and overhead variances would be detailed.

Why prorate variances? Why not just go back and do actual costing? A single-product company could probably just as well do actual process costing calculations, but a multi-product company cannot divide total production costs by total production to determine a unit cost. Moreover, a multi-product company would have to allocate each type of cost (materials, labor, overhead) to each product, then to units of the products. This allocation is likely to be much more involved than simply prorating the variances. A company with computerized records can easily determine the amounts of standard cost in each inventory account and in cost of sales. Once these values are determined, proration is relatively straightforward.

Proration with Beginning Inventories

When a firm has beginning inventories, the proration of variances cannot be done in the straightforward fashion illustrated above. When there are no beginning inventories, there is no need to adopt a cost flow assumption such as FIFO or weighted average. A cost flow assumption must be adopted when beginning inventories are present. FIFO is the best cost flow assumption for control purposes, because it isolates variances of current period work. Therefore, it is reasonable to adopt it for prorating variances as well. Using FIFO, we assume that all beginning inventories of finished goods were sold first, that all beginning inventories of work in process were completed first and sold after the beginning inventory of finished goods, and that all beginning inventories of materials were put into production before any materials purchased in the current period.

There are two difficult items to deal with when there are beginning inventories. First, using the FIFO cost flow, we must identify which materials *bought this period* have been *used this period* in our proration of the material use variance.

Second, if variances were prorated in previous periods, beginning inventories include some period variances. These variances (under FIFO) go directly to Cost of Goods Sold as long as the beginning inventories were less than the amount used (materials) or sold (work in process, finished goods) during the period, which is usually reasonable to expect.

Summary of Appendix 8A

Prorating variances allows us to adjust standard cost balances of inventories and cost of goods sold to actual cost. We have shown an example of proration; many computer-based accounting systems automatically do this adjustment. Thus, while it is important to understand the basic concept of proration, you may never actually have to do the calculations by hand.

ASSIGNMENTS

8–1 Analysis of Records (AICPA Adapted) Bovar Company began to manufacture a new mechanical device called the Dandy on May 1, 19X6. The firm also introduced a standard cost system at that date. Standard costs per unit of Dandy are

Raw materials, 6 lb at $1/lb	$ 6.00
Direct labor, 1 hr at $4/hr	4.00
Overhead, 75% of direct labor cost	3.00
	$13.00

The following data come from Bovar's records for May 19X6:

Unit production of Dandy	4,000
Unit sales of Dandy	2,500

	Debit	Credit
Sales		$50,000
Purchases of raw materials, 26,000 lb	$27,300	
Material price variance	1,300	
Material quantity variance	1,000	
Direct labor rate variance	760	
Direct labor efficiency variance		800
Manufacturing overhead total variance	500	

The amount shown for the material price variance applies to material purchased in May.

REQUIRED

Compute each of the following items for Bovar, showing computations in good form.

1. standard quantity of raw materials allowed, in pounds
2. actual quantity of raw materials used, in pounds
3. standard direct labor hours allowed
4. actual direct labor hours
5. actual direct labor rate
6. actual total overhead

8–2 Basic Entries and Variances—Materials Wild Horse Products makes a single product. Standards call for 2 pounds of materials at $15 per pound. During November, 40,000 pounds of materials were purchased for $620,000. Beginning inventory of work in process consisted of 2,000 units, 58,000 units were started in November, and 1,500 units were in ending inventory. During the month, 110,200 pounds of material were issued to the shop floor from materials inventory. Materials are introduced at the beginning of the production process. All inventories are carried at standard cost.

REQUIRED

1. Calculate the standard cost per unit for materials.
2. Calculate the material purchase price variance.
3. What is the entry to reflect inventory purchases?
4. Calculate the equivalent units of production for materials.
5. Calculate the material use variance.
6. What is the entry to reflect inventory use?

8–3 Basic Entries and Variances—Labor (continuation of Assignment 8–2) Labor standards are $\frac{1}{2}$ hour at $25 per hour. During November, 34,740 hours of labor were worked at a cost of $868,500. Beginning inventory of work in process was 60 percent complete insofar as conversion, and ending inventory was 40 percent complete.

REQUIRED

1. Calculate the standard cost per unit for labor.
2. Calculate the equivalent units of production for conversion costs.
3. Calculate the labor rate and the labor efficiency variances.
4. Show the entry to reflect incurring of labor costs.
5. Show the entry to reflect use of labor in production.

8–4 Basic Entries and Variances—Overhead (continuation of Assignments 8–2 and 8–3) Wild Horse expects annual fixed factory overhead to be $1,500,000, variable overhead to be $15/DLH, and 450,000 labor hours are used as the basis for standard overhead. November budgeted fixed factory overhead is $100,000. Actual overhead totaled $660,840 in November.

REQUIRED

1. Calculate the fixed overhead rate per direct labor hour.
2. Calculate the total standard overhead per unit.
3. What is the entry to reflect incurring overhead costs?
4. Calculate the overhead spending, efficiency, and application variances.
5. What is the entry to reflect use of overhead in production?

8–5 Basic Entries—Completed and Sold Products (continuation of Assignments 8–2, 8–3, and 8–4)

REQUIRED

1. Make the entry to reflect moving completed goods from the shop floor to the finished goods warehouse.
2. If 60,000 units were sold at $80 each, what are the entries that reflect the sales of these products?
3. Summarize all the variances calculated in the last three problems. Discuss ways of dealing with these variances at the end of November.

8–6 Standard Job Order Costing (AICPA) Milner Manufacturing Company uses a job order costing system and standard costs. One of its products has standard costs as follows:

Materials, 20 yd at $0.90/yd	$18
Direct labor, 4 hr at $6/hr	24
Total factory overhead, applied at five-sixths of direct labor cost (variable overhead is $15, fixed is $5)	20
Variable selling, general, and administrative expenses	12
Fixed selling, general, and administrative expenses	7
Total unit cost	$81

The standards are set based on normal activity of 2,400 direct labor hours. Actual activity for the month of October, 19X5, was as follows:

Materials purchased, 18,000 yd at $0.92/yd	$16,560
Materials used, 9,500 yd	
Direct labor, 2,100 hr at $6.10/hr	12,810
Total factory overhead, 500 units actually produced	11,100

REQUIRED

1. Compute total fixed factory overhead based on normal activity.

2. Prepare a schedule computing the following variances for the month of October 19X5:
a. materials price variance
b. materials use variance
c. labor rate variance
d. labor use (efficiency) variance
e. controllable (budget or spending) overhead variance
f. volume (capacity) overhead variance
Indicate whether each variance is favorable or unfavorable.

8–7 Standard Job Order Costing WEM, Inc., uses standard costing for its several products. Since products are made to order in batches, WEM uses job order costing. The estimating department developed the following standards for model ACA.

Standard Cost per 100

Material, 20 lbs at $10/lb	$200
Direct labor, 0.40 hr at $30/hr	12
Overhead at $350/DLH	140
Total	$352

During February, 20,000 units were produced. The following facts pertain to these units:

1. WEM used 4,250 pounds of materials.

2. WEM used 84 hours of labor at the union rate of $30 per direct labor hour.

3. The 20,000 units of model ACA were sold for $55 each.

4. Variances are closed to Cost of Goods Sold at the end of each month. Overhead is applied on a plantwide rate based on a flexible budget of $250,000 + $20/DLH per month.

REQUIRED

Record journal entries reflecting the above events. Record all variances you can.

8–8 Variances and Entries (CMA Adapted) Dash Company adopted a standard cost system several years ago. The standard costs for the prime costs of its single product are as follows:

Material: 8 kilograms at $5.00 per kilogram	$40.00
Labor: 6 hours at $8.20/hr	$49.20

The following operating data were taken from the records for November:

In process beginning inventory—none

In process ending inventory—800 units, 75 percent complete as to labor; material is issued at the beginning of processing

Units completed—5,600 units

Budgeted output—6,000 units

Purchases of materials—50,000 kilograms

Total actual labor costs—$300,760

Actual hours of labor—36,500 hours

Material use variance—$1,500 unfavorable

Total material variance—$750 unfavorable

REQUIRED

1. What is the labor rate variance for November?

2. What is the labor efficiency variance for November?

3. Determine the actual kilograms of material used in the production process during November.

4. What is the actual price paid per kilogram of material during November?

5. What is the total amount of material and labor cost transferred to the Finished Goods Inventory account for November?

6. What is the total amount of material and labor cost in the ending balance of Work-in-Process Inventory at the end of November?

8–9 Overhead Activity Enterprise, Ltd., has projected fixed overhead per month in various operating ranges as follows:

Shutdown of facilities	$ 35,000
Normal activity	160,000
Practical capacity	180,000

Management thinks that direct labor hours are a good way to apply overhead. Practical capacity of the plant is 120,000 direct labor hours, while normal activity is 80,000 hours.

During March, 85,000 labor hours were used for current production. Jeff Market, a staff accountant, has calculated the following variances for March. Actual overhead was $165,000.

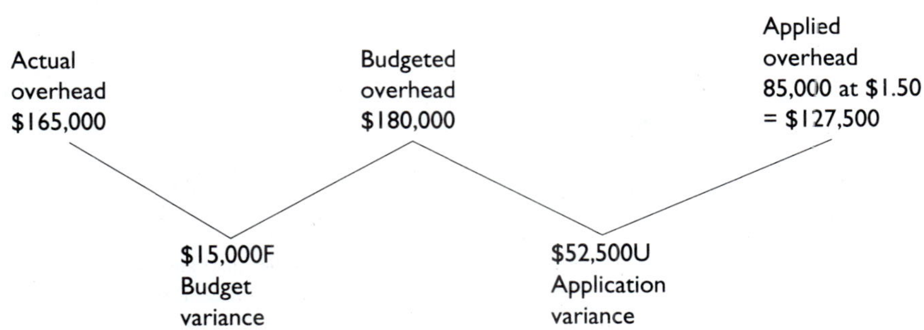

Market had some comments on his report, including the following: "It looks as if we controlled costs well in March with that favorable budget variance. Obviously, however, we will have to increase production during the year to wipe out the activity variance like we experienced in March."

REQUIRED

Comment on Market's analysis and comments. Suggest any improvements you believe would help management.

8–10 Basic Journal Entries Glow Corporation uses standard costing and isolates variances as soon as possible. The following data apply to activity in February 19X2, for its single product:

1. Glow purchased 2,087 pounds of a chemical named Aksarben for $118,959.
2. It used 3,200 hours of direct labor at a cost of $22,000, which includes $1,200 in overtime premium.
3. There were 2,000 units in beginning inventory of work in process 100 percent complete in materials and 80 percent complete in conversion costs.
4. Glow completed 10,000 units and sent them to the warehouse. The firm sold 12,000 units, which equaled budget. Revenue was $856,800. There was no ending inventory of work in process.
5. Glow used 13,800 feet of steel in production and 2,250 pounds of Aksarben.
6. Other factory overhead was $59,280 during February. Budgeted overhead, virtually all fixed, was $60,480. The firm does not use separate rates for fixed and variable overhead.

Standards for the product include

Aksarben	$52 per pound; $\frac{1}{4}$ pound per unit
Steel	$15 per foot; $1\frac{1}{2}$ feet per unit
Labor	$6.50 per hour; 0.4 hour per unit
Overhead	$18 per direct labor hour, based on 3,360 standard labor hours
Sales price	$68 per unit

REQUIRED

1. Record all the above events, isolating variances as soon as possible. All ending inventories are carried at standard. Variances are put into cost of goods sold at the end of each quarter.
2. Prepare a T-account for work in process to verify that ending inventory is zero.

8–11 Standard Job Order Costing TRF Company manufactures equipment used by bottling plants. TRF has specialized in several types of machinery for which it has developed standard costs. The company typically works on only a few large jobs at a time. TRF sets its overhead rate using the following data.

Budgeted monthly fixed overhead	$191,000
Budgeted variable overhead rate per machine hour	$2.65
Monthly machine hours used to set standard overhead rate	14,000

The data below relate to February. There were no beginning inventories.

	Jobs	
	DV-112	LY-625
Standards:		
Machine hours	6,400	8,200
Costs:		
Direct materials	$45,200	$57,800
Direct labor cost	$15,100	14,700
Actual data:		
Machine hours	6,620	8,090
Costs:		
Direct materials	$43,400	$59,780
Direct labor cost	$13,750	16,220

Actual overhead cost for February was $230,712. Both jobs were finished during February. Job DV-112 was sold, Job LY-625 remained in finished goods inventory. TRF bought no materials in February and paid its direct laborers at the standard rate. TRF makes journal entries at the end of each month, so it puts costs into process at standard.

REQUIRED

1. Compute the standard overhead rate per machine hour to the nearest penny.
2. Make the journal entries necessary to record activity for February.

8–12 Process Costing—Actual and Standard Barry-Davis Company uses actual FIFO process costing. However, Jane Barry, president, has proposed that standard process costing be used. November data for one product, weeding formula 1121, are:

November—Actual Costs

Beginning inventory—work in process	3,000 gal
	$ 6,500 material (80% complete)
	$17,350 labor and overhead (50% complete)
Current costs	$21,890 material (2,067 lb used)
	$98,875 labor and overhead (2,860 hr)
Transferred to finished goods	9,600 gal
Ending inventory—work in process	1,000 gal (75% complete materials; 40% complete labor and overhead)

Current costs include $24,000 in fixed overhead, $40,040 in labor, and $34,835 in variable overhead.

REQUIRED

1. Using FIFO actual costing, calculate equivalent units of production, equivalent unit costs, and the value of ending inventory—work in process.
2. Barry has asked the accounting department and manufacturing department to develop standards for various products. Standards for weeding formula 1121 are shown below.

100 Gallons—Weeding Formula 1121

Material, 25 lb at $11.20/lb	$ 280
Labor, 32 hr at $14.375/hr	460
Variable overhead at 90% of labor dollars	414
Fixed overhead at $8.625/DLH	276
	$1,430

Fixed overhead is budgeted at $25,000 per month and normal activity is 8,000 gallons.

a. What are equivalent units of production under FIFO standard costing?
b. What are the equivalent unit costs?
c. What is the value of ending inventory?
d. Calculate all variances.

8–13 Standards and Variances Throwbridge Company buys copper wire in 0.05-in. diameter and draws it through dies to stretch it. The smaller wire is used in many electronic components. As a rule, two or more drawings are necessary to bring the wire to the desired diameter. Data on three of the firm's best-selling diameters appear below, representing operations at normal levels of efficiency.

	Diameter		
	0.025 in.	*0.010 in.*	*0.008 in.*
Feet of 0.05-in. stock per foot of product	0.51	0.215	0.182
Number of drawings	2	3	3
Time for drawings, total hours per 1,000 ft of product	0.80	1.30	1.50

There is considerable waste in the process. The stretching and drawing time depends partly on the diameter to which the firm is aiming, so that the total drawing time is not linear with respect to the number of drawings.

Standard prices and rates are as follows:

Copper stock, 0.05 in.	$ 0.18/ft
Direct labor	12.50/hr
Variable overhead	6.25/DLH
Fixed overhead, based on 12,000 normal hours per month	15.00/DLH

During March the firm experienced the following results:

Purchases of copper stock, 3,680,000 ft	$647,300
Stock used	3,527,400 ft
Direct labor, 12,700 hr	$157,280
Overhead	$268,660
Production:	
0.025 in.	4,155,000 ft
0.010 in.	3,817,000 ft
0.008 in.	2,710,000 ft

REQUIRED

1. Develop standard costs for each of the three diameters of wire. Make the standards for 1,000-foot batches.
2. Calculate variances for March. For overhead, calculate a total budget variance and an application variance. The firm cannot determine the fixed and variable portions of actual overhead costs.

8–14 Journal Entries—Two Alternatives The following data apply to December production for Ree United, Inc.

1. Purchases were 4,300 pounds of plastic for \$9,725. A total of 2,560 pounds was used in production.
2. Conversion costs were labor—1,200 hr, \$7,896; overhead—\$1,836 variable, \$2,550 fixed.
3. Beginning inventory consisted of 100 units 50 percent complete for all costs. Ending inventory was 325 units 80 percent complete for all costs. Four hundred units were transferred to finished goods and sold for \$29,000.
4. Standards for the sole product are

Material, 4 lb at \$2.25/lb	\$ 9.00
Labor, 2 hr at \$6.50/hr	13.00
Overhead at \$3.50/DLH[a]	7.00
	\$29.00

[a]Based on \$2,400 fixed cost, 1,200 expected labor hours, and \$1.50 per DLH variable overhead.

5. All variances are treated as an adjustment to cost of goods sold.

REQUIRED

1. Record these transactions using a FIFO standard costing system where variances are identified as a part of work-in-process entries.
2. Record these transactions, assuming a FIFO standard costing system whose variances are identified at the end of the period after actual costs have been entered into work in process.

8–15 Standard Costing—Journal Entries Wapello Corporation makes a single product. Its standard costs are as follows:

Materials, 2 lb at \$4.50	\$ 9
Direct labor, 3 hr at \$5	15
Variable overhead, \$7 per DLH	21
Fixed overhead, based on normal capacity of 50,000 units	10
	\$55

At the beginning of 19X2 there were no inventories. During 19X2 the following events occurred:

1. Material purchases were 120,000 pounds for \$511,000.
2. Direct labor was \$790,750 for 151,000 hours worked.

3. Variable overhead incurred was $1,046,000.
4. Fixed overhead was $490,000.
5. Wapello used 95,000 pounds of materials.
6. Wapello produced 48,000 units. There were no unfinished goods at the end of 19X2.
7. Sales were 45,000 units at $120 each.

REQUIRED

1. Prepare journal entries to record these events. Isolate variances as early as possible. Assume that production managers are responsible for all variances except material price and labor rate.
2. Calculate ending inventory and cost of goods sold, assuming:
   a. standard process costing
   b. actual process costing

8–16 Proration of Variances (Appendix)

REQUIRED

Given the results you obtained in assignment 8–15 on Wapello Corporation, prorate the variances to appropriate inventories and cost of goods sold. Show all work. Allocate part of the material price variance to the material quantity variance in the proration procedure.

8–17 Standard Costs, Prices, and Profitability The managers of the Davis Plastics Company have argued for some time the merits of standard costs. The firm uses a standard costing system, with overhead allocated to products based on their relative machine times. At a recent meeting, one of the managers said that the standard costs got in the way of good pricing decisions because of the fixed costs included in the standard. Another manager pointed out that the factory required equipment, supervision, and other inputs that led to the incurrence of fixed costs and that incorporating the fixed costs into the standards was a rational way to allow for them.

One of the managers put the following data on a blackboard:

	#762	#456	#206
Selling price	$20	$15	$30
Variable costs	8	4	14
Fixed costs[a]	4	2	8
Total costs	12	6	22
Profit	$ 8	$ 9	$ 8
Machine hours required	1	½	2

[a]Fixed costs are allocated at $4 per machine hour. The firm has 10,000 machine hours per month available.

The manager commented that the pricing was pretty good, but not perfect. He said that the firm should raise the prices of #762 and #206 by $1 to make them equally profitable with #456. The manager who had said that standard costs got in the way of good pricing responded that the firm was operating at capacity and could sell all of any product that it wanted to, and he did not think that just raising those prices by $1 would do the trick. He asserted that the firm should receive an adequate profit from the machine hours it used but that the standard amount per hour was not a good reflection of that adequate profit.

REQUIRED

Determine the prices that the firm should charge for #762 and #206 to make them equally profitable as #456. Assume that the firm can sell all its output of any product at the prices you determine and that it is limited in machine-hour capacity.

8–18 Practical Capacity and Normal Activity The controller of the Charleston Manufacturing Company developed the following estimates of total factory overhead costs.

	Volume	
	80,000 Direct Labor Hours	100,000 Direct Labor Hours
Variable overhead at $6.50	$ 520,000	$ 650,000
Fixed overhead	855,000	904,000
Totals	$1,375,000	$1,554,000

Fixed overhead is higher at practical capacity of 100,000 direct labor hours because of increased requirements for supervisory personnel, higher utility costs, and the like. The controller had given some thought to using practical capacity as the basis for applying overhead, but she realized that it could create a problem. Specifically, she wondered how to compute the overhead budget variance and overhead volume variance. She expected actual volume to be about 80,000 direct labor hours.

REQUIRED

1. Calculate the fixed overhead application rate, using the cost and volume at practical capacity.
2. Assuming that actual direct labor hours are 81,000 and that actual fixed overhead is $886,400, calculate the fixed overhead budget variance and volume variance.
3. Comment on the results of part 2 and make a recommendation.

8–19 Comparison of Methods The president of Bolton Industries wants to know the differences among actual, normal, and standard costing. He gives you the following data for Bolton Industries, which makes a single product. There were no inventories at the beginning of 19X2.

	19X2	19X3
Sales in units at $10 each	10,000	8,000
Production in units	12,000	10,000
Materials and labor	$25,000	$19,000
Manufacturing overhead	$30,600	$31,000
Selling and administrative costs	$15,000	$15,000

REQUIRED

1. Prepare income statements for the two years using actual FIFO costing.

2. Prepare income statements for the two years using normal costing and assuming that the firm uses 11,000 units to set the normal overhead rate and sets budgeted manufacturing overhead using the formula, total manufacturing overhead = $22,000 + $0.80 × units produced. The firm uses this formula, and 11,000 units, in both years. Any overapplied or underapplied overhead is an adjustment to cost of sales.
3. Prepare income statements for both years using standard costing. The overhead standard is the same as given in part 2. The standard materials and labor cost, combined, is $2 per unit. Show variances as adjustments to standard cost of sales, separately identified to the extent that you determine particular variances.

8–20 Comprehensive Review of Chapters 6, 7, and 8 During March, 19X3, Northland division of Blann, Inc. had the following events regarding its sole product at the Jennings plant.

March 3	Purchased 40,000 lb of metal for $138,300
March 14	Paid wages for 4,000 hr worked in first part of March: $26,144
March 17	Paid various indirect labor costs and indirect expenses of $12,250 (all variable), all applying to March production
March 22	Purchased 10,000 lb of metal for $32,000
March 24	Paid various fixed costs of March equaling $6,500
March 30	Paid for materials purchased on March 3
March 31	Paid the balance of wages for March: 5,200 hr, $33,987
March 31	Paid various indirect labor costs and indirect expenses of $16,000 (all variable), all applying to March production

Inventories as of March 1, 19X3, were

Material—metal, 5,000 lb	$17,500
Work in Process, 1,000 units (100% complete in materials, 50% in conversion costs)	$8,145
Finished Goods, 2,500 units	$24,625

Standard costs called for the following:

Materials, 2 lb of metal at $3.20	$6.40
Labor, $\frac{1}{3}$ hr at $6.45	2.15
Overhead, $3.75 per DLH	1.25
	$9.80

Overhead includes $8,000 in budgeted fixed costs per month at a denominator activity of 10,000 hours.

Inventories as of March 31, 19X3, were:

Materials	3,500 lb
Work in Process	1,500 units (100% complete in materials and 50% in conversion costs)
Finished Goods	1,000 units

During March, 26,250 units were sold. Northland used standard process costing. Entries are made as events occur. At month-end entries are made to the Work-in-Process account at standard costs. Material price variances and labor rate variances are identified when costs are incurred. At month end all variances under $1,000 are charged to Cost of Goods Sold, while all other variances are prorated as appropriate to Materials, Work in Process, Finished Goods, and Cost of Goods Sold.

REQUIRED

1. Prepare proper journal entries to record the events of March. Post your entries to appropriate T-accounts. Use a single account for overhead incurred and applied.
2. Assume that Northland prepares its statements using normal costing with fixed overhead applied on the basis of the information given in the problem. What is the amount of underapplied or overapplied overhead? If this amount differs from the total fixed overhead variance calculated in part 1, explain the difference.

8–21 Proration of Variances (Appendix) Use the information developed for part 1 of assignment 8–20.

REQUIRED

1. Prorate variances as appropriate. Remember that there are beginning inventories.
2. Record journal entries to adjust accounts based on the proration of variances in part 1. Post these to your T-accounts.

8–22 Normal Costing and Standard Costing The following information pertains to Rubia Corporation, a manufacturer of a single product.

Overhead is applied using two bases: machine hours (MH) and pounds of material. Machine hours are used to apply both fixed overhead and the portion of variable overhead that seems associated with machine hours. Pounds of material are used only to apply variable overhead associated with the handling of material.

Budget information:			
Annual fixed overhead			$9,000,000
Annual machine hours			50,000 hr
Annual use of materials			200,000 lb
Variable overhead per machine hour			$60/MH
Variable overhead per pound of materials			$ 5/lb.
Standard cost per unit:			
Materials	2 lbs. @ $25/lb.	$ 50.00	
Labor	$\frac{1}{4}$ hr. @ $20/hr.	5.00	
Overhead	$\frac{1}{2}$ MH @ $240/MH	120.00	
	2 lbs. @ $5/lb	10.00	
Total standard cost per unit		$185.00	
Actual results—June, 19X9:			
Actual production		8,000 units	
Actual fixed overhead		$925,000	
Actual variable overhead			
machine-hour related		$220,400	
material related		$ 99,000	
Actual machine hours		3,800 hr	
Actual material use		16,500 lb	

There were no beginning inventories in June. Budgeted fixed overhead in June was $900,000.

REQUIRED

1. If the company uses normal costing and applies overhead based on annual budgeted figures, what is the amount of overhead that would be applied in June?
2. What is the over- or underapplied overhead in June assuming the company uses normal costing?
3. If the company uses standard costing, what is the amount of overhead that would be applied in June?
4. Calculate as many standard cost overhead variances as possible given the information. Clearly label them as favorable (F) or unfavorable (U).
5. Clearly state why the answer you calculated in part 2 (over- or underapplied overhead for June) does not equal the sum of all the overhead variances you calculated in part 4. You do *not* have to use figures. Rather, address the *reason(s)* why this difference occurs instead of tracing the numbers themselves.
6. The difference between actual overhead and normal overhead (under- or overapplied overhead) can be explained by looking at both numerator and denominator reasons. This problem has a little twist that makes this explanation a bit tricky. Show numerically the cause of the under- or overapplied overhead in June. Do not plug in any numbers.

8–23 Backflush Costing Timmins Company has completed the transition to just-in-time manufacturing and is attempting to simplify its recordkeeping. The controller has given you the following data for January and asked for the simplest, most direct way to record the events.

Beginning inventories	none
Units finished	100,000
Units sold	90,000
Materials purchased and used	$410,000
Direct labor and manufacturing overhead	$350,000

There was no ending inventory of materials or of work in process.

REQUIRED

Determine ending inventory and cost of goods sold.

8–24 Backflush Costing, Journal Entries (continuation of Assignment 8–23)

REQUIRED

Prepare journal entries for Timmins Company's January activity.

8–25 Prorating Variances (Appendix) Jambalaya Corporation uses standard process costing. For February 19X3 actual results were:

Beginning inventory—work in process (100% complete in material, 50% complete in conversion costs)	2,000 units
Ending inventory—work in process (100% complete in material, $66\frac{2}{3}$% complete in conversion costs)	1,500 units
Goods completed during February	8,000 units

Ending inventory—finished goods	1,000 units
Sales	7,000 units
Materials—ending inventory	5,000 lb

There were no beginning inventories in Materials or Finished Goods. The following costs were incurred in February.

Materials purchased (36,000 lb)	$342,000
Labor (23,000 hr)	$276,000
Overhead	$580,000

Standard costs are

Materials, 4 lb at $10/lb	$ 40
Labor, 3 hr at $12/hr	36
Overhead, $25/labor hour	75
	$151

There were no variances in January.

REQUIRED

1. Calculate material, labor, and overhead variances. (Remember: this is process costing.)
2. Prorate all variances to Materials Inventory, Work in Process, Finished Goods, and Cost of Goods Sold. (Ignore prorating first to Materials Use Variance.)
3. Calculate the actual values for inventories and the actual values for cost of sales by adjusting standard costs by the amounts prorated in part 2.
4. Verify the actual costs calculated in part 3 by calculating FIFO process costing actual values for ending inventories and Cost of Sales. (Use T-accounts.)

8–26 Proration of Variances—Financial Statements (CMA Adapted) (Appendix) Nanron Company uses a standard process cost system. All inventories are carried at standard during the year. The inventories and cost of goods sold are adjusted for all variances considered material in amount at the end of the fiscal year for financial statement purposes. All products are considered to flow through the manufacturing process to finished goods and ultimate sale in a first-in, first-out pattern.

The standard cost of one of Nanron's products manufactured in the Dixion Plant, unchanged from the prior year, follows.

Raw materials	$2
Direct labor (0.5 DLH at $8)	4
Manufacturing overhead	3
Total standard cost	$9

Because of the nature of the product and the manufacturing process, there is no work-in-process inventory of this product.

The schedule appearing below reports the manufacturing and sales activity measured at standard cost for the current fiscal year.

	Units	Dollars
Product manufactured	95,000	$855,000
Beginning finished goods inventory	15,000	135,000
Goods available for sale	110,000	$990,000
Ending finished goods inventory	19,000	171,000
Cost of goods sold	91,000	$819,000

The balance of the Finished Goods Inventory, $140,800, reported on the balance sheet at the beginning of the year included a $5,800 adjustment for variances from standard cost. There were unfavorable variances for labor for the current fiscal year consisting of a wage rate variance of $32,000 and a labor efficiency variance of $20,000 (2,500 hr at $8). There were no other variances from standard cost this year.

REQUIRED

1. Management has decided that the $52,000 labor variances are material. Prorate these variances as appropriate to cost of goods sold and finished goods inventory. Determine the full amount to be shown at year end for these two accounts.
2. What is the effect on the proration process of a beginning or ending inventory of work in process?

8–27 Proration—Adjusting Cost of Goods Sold (Appendix) (AICPA) Longhorn Manufacturing Corporation produces only one product, Bevo, and accounts for the production of Bevo using a standard cost system.

At the end of each year, Longhorn prorates all variances among the various inventories and cost of sales. Because Longhorn prices its inventories on the first-in, first-out basis and all the beginning inventories are used during the year, the variances allocated to the ending inventories are immediately charged to cost of sales at the beginning of the following year. This allows only the current year's variances to be recorded in the variance accounts in any given year.

Following are the standards for the production of one unit of Bevo: 3 units of item A at $1 per unit; 1 unit of item B at $0.50 per unit; 4 units of item C at $0.30 per unit; and 20 minutes of direct labor at $4.50 per hour. Separate variance accounts are maintained for each type of raw material and for direct labor. Raw material purchases are recorded initially at standard. Manufacturing overhead is applied at $9 per actual direct labor hour and is not related to the standard cost system. There was no overapplied or underapplied manufacturing overhead at December 31, 19X2.

After proration of the variances, the various inventories at December 31, 19X2, were priced as indicated in the material appearing below.

Raw Material:

Item	Number of Units	Unit Cost	Amount
A	15,000	$1.10	$16,500
B	4,000	0.52	2,080
C	20,000	0.32	6,400
			$24,980

Work in Process: 9,000 units of Bevo were 100 percent complete as to material items A and B, 50 percent complete in item C, and 30 percent complete as to labor. The breakdown of this inventory is as follows:

Item	Amount
A	$28,600
B	4,940
C	6,240
Direct labor	6,175
	45,955
Overhead	11,700
	$57,655

Finished Goods: 4,800 units of Bevo composed and valued as follows:

Item	Amount
A	$15,180
B	2,704
C	6,368
Direct labor	8,540
	32,792
Overhead	16,200
	$48,992

Following is a schedule of raw materials purchased and direct labor incurred for the year ended December 31, 19X3. Unit cost of each item of raw material and direct labor cost per hour remained constant throughout the year.

Purchases:

Item	Number of Units or Hours	Unit Cost	Amount
A	290,000	$1.15	$333,500
B	101,000	0.55	55,550
C	367,000	0.35	128,450
Direct labor	34,100	4.60	156,860

During the year ended December 31, 19X3, Longhorn sold 90,000 units of Bevo and had ending physical inventories as follows:

Raw Materials:

Item	Number of Units
A	28,300
B	2,100
C	28,900

Work in Process: 7,500 units of Bevo, which were 100 percent complete as to items A and B, 50 percent complete as to item C, and 20 percent complete as to labor, as follows:

Item	Number of Units or Hours
A	22,900
B	8,300
C	15,800
Direct labor	800

Finished Goods: 5,100 units of Bevo, as follows:

Item	Number of Units or Hours
A	15,600
B	6,300
C	21,700
Direct labor	2,050

There was no overapplied or underapplied manufacturing overhead at December 31, 19X3.

REQUIRED

Answer each of the following questions. Supporting computations should be prepared in good form.

1. What was the charge or credit to cost of sales at the beginning of 19X3 for the variances in the December 31, 19X2, inventories?
2. What was the total charge or credit to the three material price variance accounts for items A, B, and C for the year ended December 31, 19X3?
3. What was the total charge or credit to the three material quantity variance accounts for items A, B, and C for the year ended December 31, 19X3?
4. What was the total charge or credit to the direct labor rate variance account for the year ended December 31, 19X3?
5. What was the total charge or credit to the direct labor efficiency variance account for the year ended December 31, 19X3?

8–28 Normal Costing and Standard Costing Tunnel Company of Love, New Jersey, is run by Bruce and Marian Tunnel. The company makes a single product and currently uses actual costing. Marian Tunnel, who is in charge of the financial and accounting end of the business, is investigating the impact on internal and external statements of using either normal or standard costing. The public accounting firm of I. M. N. Fire has prepared partial income statements under each of the three methods as follows:

Partial Income Statements

	Actual	*Normal*	*Standard*
Revenue	$7,200,000	$7,200,000	$7,200,000
BI–WIP	51,125	51,125	51,125
Materials	890,000	890,000	?
Direct labor	167,600	167,600	?
Variable overhead	794,000	794,000	?
Fixed overhead	2,900,000	?	?
Less: EI–WIP	(138,294)		
Cost of Goods Sold	$4,664,431	?	?
Over/Underapplied Overhead		?	?
Standard cost variances[a]			?
Adjusted CGS			
Gross Profit	$2,535,569	?	?

[a]Include only variable cost variances here. Fixed cost variances should be included in the row "Over/Underapplied Overhead."

The following are additional facts:

1. 40,000 units were sold at $180 per unit.
2. All inventories are carried at FIFO costs.
3. Beginning inventories are as follows:

Materials	30,000 pounds	$300,000
Work in Process	1,000 units	
	100% complete materials	$ 20,000
	30% complete conversion	$ 31,125
Finished Goods	0 units	

4. During the period the following occurred:
   a. 60,000 pounds of materials were purchased for $660,000.
   b. 83,000 pounds of materials were used.
   c. 10,475 labor hours were used costing $167,600.
   d. 19,850 machine hours were used.
   e. 40,000 units were completed.
   f. 2,000 units remained in Ending Inventory—Work in Process—100 percent complete for materials and 50 percent complete for conversion costs.
   g. Equivalent units of production for the period are:
      Materials 41,000 units
      Conversion 40,700 units
   h. Factory overhead incurred was $2,900,000 fixed and $794,000 variable.
5. If the company were to use normal costing, Tunnel has decided to use machine hours to apply overhead. Fixed overhead is expected to be $3,000,000 per period and 18,750 machine hours will be the expected activity.
6. If the company were to use standard costing, the following costs would be used:

		Per Unit
Materials	2 pounds at $10/pound	$ 20.00
Direct labor	$\frac{1}{4}$ hour at $15/hour	3.75
Variable overhead	$\frac{1}{2}$ machine hour at $40/hour	20.00
Fixed overhead	$\frac{1}{2}$ machine hour at $160/hour	80.00
		$123.75

7. Any under/overapplied overhead or net standard cost variance is closed out to the income statement as an adjustment to cost of goods sold.

REQUIRED

1. Calculate all the standard cost variances (variable and fixed) that you can.
2. What are the amounts that should be shown for Materials, Direct Labor, Variable Overhead, and Fixed Overhead for the standard cost income statement?
3. How much fixed overhead should be applied under normal costing? What is over- or underapplied overhead for the period?
4. What are the values of Ending Inventory—Work in Process for
   a. normal costing
   b. standard costing
5. Fill in the remaining blanks in the normal costing and in the standard costing income statements.
6. Show in numbers and explain in words
   a. why actual costing gross profit differs from normal costing gross profit
   b. why actual costing gross profit differs from standard costing gross profit.

8–29 Standard Costing System John Moroney, controller of Garden Products Corporation, had returned to his office after attending a seminar on standard costing. He was enthusiastic about putting into practice some of the ideas he had gained. He called on Anthony Hobson, the firm's president, to discuss his ideas and received the go-ahead to develop a proposal for adopting a standard costing system. Hobson cautioned Moroney that upper-level managers would have to be convinced of the value of the system before he would order it put in place.

Moroney spent several days going through his notes and other materials he had gathered, refining his ideas about how the system should work at Garden Products. Eventually he wrote the material below to clarify his thoughts and give the other managers the opportunity to see what he had in mind.

> We currently use an actual-normal job order cost system. We charge actual materials and labor to each job and apply overhead based on a predetermined rate developed annually. Most of our production is standard (about 95 percent by dollar volume), and we have good data on the material and labor quantities needed for each model of lawnmower, tiller, snowblower, and so on.
>
> We presently initiate production based on our estimates of demand in the coming months. Stan Phillips, production manager, writes up production orders and assigns a number to each batch. Copies of the order go to the departmental supervisors and to my office. One of my clerks blanks up a job order cost sheet putting in the product number, quantity, and a few other items. The supervisors schedule the job and assign workers. The workers obtain the necessary materials from the storeroom, filling out materials requisitions. A copy of the requisition comes to my office, where a clerk uses it to

update our inventory records. Another clerk determines the FIFO cost of the materials issued and posts it to the job order cost sheet. The form is then filed.

Monthly, clerks go through the files of material requisitions and compare them with the Material Inventory accounts and a list of jobs in process. If there are discrepancies, someone goes down to investigate. We don't have many problems here, just a few lost requisitions each month. The physical inventory that we take once a year usually comes pretty close to our perpetual records.

Workers use time slips to indicate how much time they spend on each job and how much nonproductive time they have, such as waiting for materials and setting up machinery. My clerks receive these slips, sort them by job every day, and post them to the cost sheet after getting the worker's pay rate from the book we keep. The slips then go to another section where clerks use them to prepare the payroll records. They also check to see that the times on the slips for each worker correspond to the times on their clock cards. When a worker has overtime, the cost entered on the cost sheets is at regular time, with the overtime premium being debited to an account that is included in factory overhead.

When production notifies us that a job is complete, we apply overhead to the job order cost sheet, then move the sheet to the file for finished goods. When we are notified that part of the job has been sold, we note that on the cost sheet and also make an entry to debit Cost of Sales and credit Finished Goods Inventory. When the entire job has been sold, we put the cost sheet into the file of sold jobs, noting the price on the sheet. Tony Hobson uses the sheets to analyze the profitability of various models.

Once a month, we apply overhead to all jobs still in process, based on direct labor cost. Each department has a different rate, so we also keep track of the department that each worker is in on the cost sheets. Monthly, we reconcile the cost sheets with the general ledger totals for Work in Process and Finished Goods. We have to make sure that all direct labor costs have been accounted for either on jobs or in accounts such as Idle Time and Vacation Pay.

My proposal is that we develop standard costs for each of our models, or at least for the high-volume items. We will then keep track of the number of units of each model made each month, but not of the costs of individual batches. When my office is notified that a batch is completed, one of my clerks will debit Finished Goods Inventory and credit Work-in-Process Inventory for the standard cost of the completed units. Similarly, we will debit Cost of Sales and credit Finished Goods Inventory when we are notified of a sale.

We will still use the materials requisition slips to control inventory and update the perpetual records. But we will debit Work-in-Process Inventory for the standard prices times the actual quantities of materials issued, which will save a good deal of work over finding the actual FIFO prices. Incoming materials will be debited to Materials Inventory at standard prices, so that we will identify and isolate material price variances at the time of purchase.

We will no longer need the detailed time slips from each worker every day. Instead, we will simply debit Work-in-Process Inventory for actual labor costs each week, using the clock cards for determining payroll.

Once a month we will determine the total standard cost of all work done by looking at the Work-in-Process Inventory and transfers to Finished Goods. There will be more work involved here, because we have to determine how far along each job was in order to get the standard cost of the work done to that point. Once we do that, we will remove variances from Work-in-Process Inventory, putting them into individual variance accounts, so that month-end Work-in-Process Inventory will show standard costs.

Our procedures on overhead will be about the same as now. The principal difference is that we will apply overhead once a month based on the standard labor cost for the month, not the actual labor cost. We will not apply overhead to individual jobs, however, which will give a substantial saving in clerical time.

In general, I do not anticipate significant labor rate variances. Our work force is pretty stable, and we usually make sure that each hourly employee gets at least 40 hours per week. If we use a standard rate for each department based on the current average hourly wage in the department, the variance will be minimal even though the rates vary considerably among workers.

In addition to the savings in clerical work, we will have better information for planning and control. We will be able to see which departmental supervisors are keeping costs in line and which are going over. We can tell that now only in very crude terms.

Moroney showed his proposal to various managers. Virtually all had some comments. On the plus side, a number of managers stated that any reduction in bookkeeping was desirable so long as it did not lessen the quality of the information they received. Moroney summarized the comments under the following headings in order to be able to discuss each point that the managers brought up.

Need for Actual Costs. A few people argued that it would be a mistake to abandon the actual costing system because they would not be able to spot changes in costs of specific models. The costs of individual jobs, and therefore of specific models, would be smeared, and no one would be able to see unfavorable trends so long as total costs for all models were in line with standards.

Responsibility for Variances. Several managers, notably the supervisor of the assembly department, argued that variances in one department were not necessarily its fault. The supervisor of the assembly department told of a recent incident where a batch of mowers came to her with improperly lined-up bolt holes. One of the workers had to redrill to make the holes line up. Such extra time in the department would show up on her performance report but is the fault of another department. She also felt that work would get sloppy because of pressure to meet the standards.

Fineness of Standards. Several managers said that they could understand developing standard times for all of the operations in a given department as a whole, but not for each of the multitude of operations. Yet if output were to be measured accurately, it would be necessary to break down each operation and develop a standard for it. Without such breakdowns it would be impossible to evaluate partially completed work. Developing such breakdowns would be costly and subject to a great deal of inaccuracy. It would also cause problems, because workers would be held responsible for each operation, not for the overall task.

REQUIRED

Write a formal memorandum to management, using a microcomputer and a word processing program with a spreadsheet program for supporting schedules. See Appendix B for guidelines for memoranda presentation.

You have been hired by Anthony Hobson as an outside consultant. Write Hobson a memorandum in which you:

1. Discuss the pros and cons of Moroney's proposed system. Make it clear whether you support or oppose Moroney's suggestions. In addition, comment on the reservations expressed by the managers.
2. Discuss whether you would come to a different recommendation based on whether month-end Work-in-Process inventory is very large.

As with other reports, make sure that you have included a discussion of all relevant issues that are important, given the facts.

8–30 Job Order Costing—Journal Entries Use the facts developed in assignment 8–6 for Milner Manufacturing Company.

REQUIRED

1. Record the events of October 19X5 in a standard costing system.
2. How would you calculate an application variance if there was an ending inventory in work in process? Assume that the 500 units consist of 400 that were started and completed this period and 200 that were 50 percent complete in all cost elements.

8–31 Responsibility for Standards (CMA Adapted) Associated Media Graphics (AMG) is a rapidly expanding company involved in the mass reproduction of instructional materials. Ralph Boston, owner and manager of AMG, has made a concentrated effort to provide a quality product at a fair price with delivery on the promised due date. Expanding sales have been attributed to this philosophy. Boston is finding it increasingly difficult to supervise the operations of AMG personally and is beginning to institute an organizational structure to facilitate management control.

One recent change was the designation of operating departments as cost centers, with control over departmental operations transferred from Boston to each departmental manager. However, quality control still reports directly to Boston, as do the finance and accounting functions. A materials manager was hired to purchase all raw materials and to oversee the inventory handling (receiving, storage, etc.) and recordkeeping functions. The materials manager also is responsible for maintaining an adequate inventory based on planned production levels.

The loss of personal control over the operations of AMG caused Boston to look for a method of efficiently evaluating performance. Dave Cress, a new cost accountant, proposed the use of a standard cost system. Variances for material, labor, and manufacturing overhead could then be calculated and reported directly to Boston.

REQUIRED

1. Assume that AMG will implement a standard cost system and establish standards for materials, labor, and manufacturing overhead. For each of these cost components, identify and discuss:
   - *a.* who should be involved in setting the standards
   - *b.* the factors that should be considered in establishing the standards
2. Describe the basis for assignment of responsibility under a standard cost system.

9

VARIABLE COSTING: MANAGERIAL ACCOUNTING FOR PLANNING AND DECISION MAKING

Chapter 4 introduced the ideas of *cost of products* for managerial decision making and *product costs* for financial accounting. In Chapter 2 we saw that a contribution margin income statement helps to focus managers' attention on relevant costs for decision making. This chapter introduces variable costing, a technique that managers can use to prepare income statements in a cost-volume-profit format and thereby avoid some of the problems inherent in an absorption costing income statement.[1]

As you know, product costs for financial accounting include both fixed and variable manufacturing costs; we use absorption, or full, costs. **Variable cost-**

[1] In the past, this method has been called *direct costing*. However, since we define direct costs in a particular way in Chapter 4, we use *variable costing* in this chapter.

ing excludes fixed manufacturing costs from the calculation of product costs and the valuing of inventory; instead, fixed costs are expensed in the period they are incurred. Except in Chapter 2, in our previous discussion of cost of products for managerial decisions, we did not dwell on income statements or balance sheets. The focus was on particular decisions such as pricing or seeing how profitable a product is. Variable costing combines elements of a financial accounting structure with a management accounting philosophy. While we will construct income statements using a contribution margin format and will value inventories excluding fixed manufacturing costs, we will do so to evaluate how managers and segments are doing and to tie in our notions of cost-volume-profit analysis with those in the sections on product costing in the preceding chapters.

Because variable costing stresses contribution margin and shows total fixed costs as expenses, it is more compatible with managerial analyses than is absorption costing. For example, cost-volume-profit analyses cannot readily be made using absorption costing. It is possible to develop contribution margin information from an absorption costing system by isolating fixed and variable costs. Moreover, income determined under absorption costing is affected not only by sales, but also by production. Under variable costing, income is strictly a function of sales and is unaffected by production. This is a significant advantage of variable costing, as we shall see shortly.

Although variable costing is not acceptable for financial reporting and tax purposes, it may be used for internal reporting. Generally accepted accounting principles and tax laws do not govern internal reporting, although they can influence it. Firms can use variable costing for internal purposes and switch to absorption costing for financial reporting and income tax accounting. Variable costing can be used by job order firms and processing firms. It can be used with actual, normal, or standard costing.

Until now we have considered costing systems in two basic ways. A system is job order or process depending on whether costs are accumulated by individual unit or batch of units, or by department for each period. A system is actual, normal, or standard depending on whether unit costs contained actual costs for all inputs, actual labor and materials with a predetermined overhead rate, or standard costs for all inputs. We now have a third type of classification: whether the system includes fixed costs in the determination of inventory cost per unit for internal reporting purposes.

All product costing systems must include a selection from each of these three dimensions.

Production Method	*Type of Costs*	*Treatment of Fixed Costs*
Job order	Actual	Absorption
Process	Normal	Variable
	Standard	

Thus, a system can be actual variable process costing, normal absorption job order costing, and so forth.

ABSORPTION COSTING, INCOME, AND PRODUCTION

Exhibit 9–1 summarizes the operations of the Coulson Company for a two-month period. The firm uses standard absorption costing and writes off application variances as an expense on the income statement each month. The income statements given in Exhibit 9–1 conform to the firm's policies. In this illustration we assume that there are no variances from standard variable costs and no fixed cost budget variances.

The statements in Exhibit 9–1 show an interesting result when comparing April to March: sales increased from 9,000 to 10,000 units but income fell from $24,000 to $16,000. This seems counterintuitive because if the cost structure remains constant income should rise with increased sales. Note that production was higher in March than in April, 12,000 units versus 9,000 units. Fixed production costs were $40,000 both months and are applied at $4 per unit. However, with production of 12,000 in March and sales of 9,000, a good portion of fixed costs was deferred in ending inventory. Of the $40,000 in fixed costs, we shall see that 75 percent (9,000/12,000) is in cost of sales while the other 25 percent is in ending inventory. In April, the situation is reversed; sales are 10,000 units while production is only 9,000 units. As we shall see, April's income statement includes fixed costs in excess of the $40,000 incurred in the period.

Using the contribution margin format, income statements using standard variable costing appear in Exhibit 9–2. These income statements incorporate the basic information from Exhibit 9–1 but restate it using a variable costing format. Comparing Exhibits 9–1 and 9–2, we can see that both methods exclude selling and administrative expenses from inventory. These costs are expensed on the income statement in the period incurred. Using language from financial accounting, selling and administrative costs are *period costs*, not *product costs*. Second, under absorption costing, some or all of both fixed and variable manufacturing costs are considered to be product costs. In this example, all standard manufacturing costs are treated as product costs, with variances treated as expenses of the period. Variances could also be prorated to inventories and cost of sales as illustrated in Chapter 8. Then all manufacturing costs would be treated as product costs, because prorating variances essentially converts standard costing to actual costing. Under variable costing, the only costs considered to be product costs are variable manufacturing costs, with fixed manufacturing costs treated as period costs. The treatment of fixed manufacturing costs gives rise to the differences in incomes under the two methods.

Variable costing uses the basic income relationship we developed in Chapter 2. With variable cost per unit and total fixed costs held constant, income

EXHIBIT 9–1 Operating Data and Income Statements—Coulson Company

Unit Data

	March	April
Beginning inventory	0	3,000
Production	12,000	9,000
Total available	12,000	12,000
Sales	9,000	10,000
Ending inventory	3,000	2,000

Cost and Price Data

	March	April
Sales at $15 per unit	$135,000	$150,000
Variable production costs at $6	72,000	54,000
Variable selling costs at $1	9,000	10,000
Fixed production costs	40,000	40,000
Fixed selling and administrative expenses	20,000	20,000

Standard cost of goods sold is $10; $6 variable plus $4 fixed based on $40,000 monthly budgeted fixed production costs and 10,000 units normal activity.

Income Statements

	March	April
Sales	$135,000	$150,000
Beginning inventory	0	30,000
Current period production costs:		
Variable at $6 per unit	72,000	54,000
Fixed, applied at $4 per unit	48,000	36,000
Totals	120,000	120,000
Ending inventory at $10 per unit	30,000	20,000
Standard cost of sales at $10 per unit	90,000	100,000
Application variance[a]	8,000F	4,000U
Actual cost of sales	82,000	104,000
Gross margin	53,000	46,000
Selling and administrative expenses	29,000	30,000
Income	$ 24,000	$ 16,000

[a](10,000 − 12,000) × $4 = $8,000F; (10,000 − 9,000) × $4 = $4,000U.

rises or falls solely due to changes in sales. Thus, in March, variable costing income is given by

$$\text{sales} - \text{variable costs} - \text{fixed costs} = \text{income}$$
$$(9{,}000 \times \$15) - (9{,}000 \times \$7) - \$60{,}000 = \$12{,}000$$

EXHIBIT 9–2 Income Statements, Variable Costing—Coulson Company

		March		April
Sales		$135,000		$150,000
Beginning inventory	0		$18,000	
Variable production costs	$72,000		54,000	
Total available for sale	72,000		72,000	
Ending inventory at $6/unit	18,000		12,000	
Variable cost of sales		54,000		60,000
Variable gross margin		81,000		90,000
Variable selling expenses		9,000		10,000
Contribution margin		72,000		80,000
Fixed costs:				
Production	$40,000		$40,000	
Selling and administrative	20,000	60,000	20,000	60,000
Income		$ 12,000		$ 20,000

Notice that production data are not required, only sales and cost data. Notice also that *what we subtract from sales is not total variable costs incurred, but variable cost per unit multiplied by unit sales*. Variable costing does recognize inventories: some variable manufacturing costs are deferred in inventory. However, all fixed manufacturing costs are expensed.

We pointed out earlier that absorption costing income is affected by the level of production as well as the level of sales. Exhibit 9–3 shows how the level of production influences income under absorption costing. The level of production determines how much fixed manufacturing cost is deferred in inventory. When production exceeds sales (inventory increases), then the amount of fixed cost expensed through cost of sales and application variances is less than the amount incurred during the period. When sales exceed production (inventory decreases), the reverse is true. When sales equal production, the amount of fixed costs expensed equals the amount incurred, and absorption costing income will then equal variable costing income. (A review problem coming up shortly illustrates this point.)[2]

Under standard costing, the difference in income between variable and absorption costing can be calculated simply by using the following formula:

[2]There are some exceptions to these general statements. The stated relationships hold so long as unit costs are the same in both inventories.

EXHIBIT 9–3. Reconciliation of Absorption Costing and Variable Costing Incomes—Coulson Company

Flows of Fixed Production Costs—Absorption Costing	*March*	*April*
Fixed production costs in beginning inventory	0	$12,000
Fixed production costs incurred during period	$40,000	40,000
Total	40,000	52,000
Fixed production costs in ending inventory[a]	12,000	8,000
Fixed production costs expensed during period[b]	$28,000	$44,000
Flows of Fixed Production Costs—Variable Costing		
Fixed production costs expensed during period	$40,000	$40,000
Differences, equal differences in incomes for periods	($12,000)	$ 4,000

[a] Inventories: end of March, 3,000 units at $4 standard fixed cost = $12,000; end of April, 2,000 units at $4 = $8,000.

[b] These figures may also be found by taking the amount of standard fixed costs included in cost of goods sold for each month plus the unfavorable application variance or minus the favorable application variance for the month. In March, fixed production costs, at standard, in cost of sales were $36,000 (9,000 × $4) and the application variance was $8,000 favorable, giving the $28,000 total fixed production costs expensed in March.

$$\text{income under absorption costing} - \text{income under variable costing} = \begin{pmatrix}\text{change in inventory}\\ \text{in units}\end{pmatrix} \times \begin{pmatrix}\text{standard fixed}\\ \text{cost per unit}\end{pmatrix}$$

If inventory in units decreases, then variable costing income is greater than absorption costing income. This formula also presupposes that the standard fixed cost per unit figure used for the beginning inventory is the same as the one used for the ending inventory. Applying the formula for March and April gives

$$\text{March} = (3{,}000 \times \$4) = \$12{,}000$$
$$\text{April} = (-1{,}000 \times \$4) = -\$4{,}000$$

This reconciliation highlights an important and often overlooked point: differences in incomes under different costing methods relate solely to differences in the costs of inventories. The different formats and titles used under absorption costing and variable costing have nothing to do with the differences in incomes. The different formats and titles relate to the different things that the income statements concentrate on: absorption costing concentrates on the functional classifications of cost (production, selling, and administrative), while variable costing concentrates on the behavior of costs (variable and fixed).

The schedule below shows income statements for April under the two methods, using a crude format. The point of the schedule is to show that inventories are the reason for the differences in incomes.

	Absorption Costing	*Variable Costing*
Sales	$150,000	$150,000
Beginning inventory	$ 30,000	$ 18,000
Total production costs	94,000	94,000
Total	124,000	112,000
Ending inventory	20,000	12,000
Production costs expensed	104,000	100,000
Margin	46,000	50,000
Selling and administrative expenses	30,000	30,000
Income	$ 16,000	$ 20,000

Again, these income statements are in poor form and appear only to highlight the importance of inventories. Every number on each of the two statements is the same with the exception of those relating to inventories and, of course, those that depend on inventories such as production costs expensed and margin.

REVIEW PROBLEM: COULSON COMPANY

A template called COULSON.WK1 as shown in Exhibit 9–4 is on the disk accompanying this text. Use this template to construct a single month's income under both absorption and variable costing. Complete the template using first March's data and compare your results to Exhibits 9–1 and 9–2. Repeat this process using data from April. (Note that the format has been set up to accommodate both types of income statements but is not as distinct as Exhibits 9–1 and 9–2.) Finally, in May Coulson produced and sold 10,000 units. The cost structure remained the same as in the previous months (variable cost per unit and total fixed costs). Insert the new production and sales figures in your template and compare your results to those in Exhibit 9–5.

Exhibit 9–5 shows that when production and sales are equal, incomes under the two methods will be the same. This is true as long as standard (or normal) costing is used and the fixed cost per unit does not change from the prior period to the current period. Both methods will give the same total incomes over the life of a firm, since at both the beginning and end of its life a firm has no inventory. However, at any time during the firm's life when it does have inventory, cumulative income under absorption costing will be higher than cumulative income under variable costing. Over a period of time (such as a year or five years), if its inventories and cost structure remain relatively

EXHIBIT 9–4 Coulson.WK1

```
1       B         C         D         E         F         G         H
2
3
4
5   DATA SECTION
6                                             Month:           March
7   Unit data
8    Beginning inventory                                           0 units
9    Production                                               12,000
10   Sales                                                     9,000
11   Ending inventory                                          3,000
12
13  Cost and price data
14   Sales price per unit                                     $15.00
15   Variable production costs per unit                        $6.00
16   Variable selling costs per unit                           $1.00
17   Fixed production costs                                  $40,000
18   Fixed selling and administrative expenses               $20,000
19   Normal activity                                          10,000 units
20
21   Fixed manufacturing costs per unit                        $4.00
22
23  SOLUTION SECTION
24                                              Absorption  Variable
25                                                 Costing   Costing
26  Sales
27                                               ---------  ---------
28  Cost of sales
29   Beginning inventory
30   Production costs
31    Variable
32    Fixed
33                                               ---------  ---------
34   Total available
35   Less: ending inventory
36                                               ---------  ---------
37   Cost of goods sold
38                                               ---------  ---------
39  Standard margin
40  Application variance
41                                               ---------  ---------
42  Actual margin
43  Selling and administrative
44      expenses
45   Variable
46   Fixed
47  Fixed production costs
48                                               ---------  ---------
49  Income                                              $0         $0
50
51  Reconciliation:
52   Standard fixed cost per unit
53   Change in inventory
54   Difference in income
```

EXHIBIT 9–5 Coulson Company—May

B C D E	F	G H	
DATA SECTION			
	Month:	May	
Unit data			
Beginning inventory		2,000	units
Production		10,000	
Sales		10,000	
Ending inventory		2,000	
Cost and price data			
Sales price per unit		$15.00	
Variable production costs per unit		$6.00	
Variable selling costs per unit		$1.00	
Fixed production costs		$40,000	
Fixed selling and administrative expenses		$20,000	
Normal activity		10,000	units
Fixed manufacturing costs per unit		$4.00	
SOLUTION SECTION			
	Absorption Costing	Variable Costing	
Sales	$150,000	$150,000	
	---------	---------	
Cost of sales			
Beginning inventory	20,000	12,000	
Production costs			
Variable	60,000	60,000	
Fixed	40,000		
	---------	---------	
Total available	120,000	72,000	
Less: ending inventory	20,000	12,000	
	---------	---------	
Cost of goods sold	100,000	60,000	
	---------	---------	
Standard margin	50,000	90,000	
Application variance	0		
	---------	---------	
Actual margin	50,000	90,000	
Selling and administrative expenses			
Variable	10,000	10,000	
Fixed	20,000	20,000	
Fixed production costs		40,000	
	---------	---------	
Income	$20,000	$20,000	
Reconciliation:			
Standard fixed cost per unit	$4.00		
Change in inventory	0		
Difference in income	$0		

stable, incomes under the two methods for that period will be about the same. If fixed costs rise over time, the difference between absorption and variable costing inventories and incomes will widen, even if the physical amount of inventory remains reasonably constant.

ACTUAL COSTING RESULTS

The choice between variable costing and absorption costing concerns only the treatment of fixed costs as period costs or as product costs. Under either method, a company could use actual, normal, or standard costing (as well as job order or process costing). Again, the difference between incomes under any alternative methods depends solely on the differences in inventories. If Coulson were to use actual costing, its income statements would show inventories at actual cost and there would be no variances.

During October the firm had the following results. There was no beginning inventory.

Production		12,000 units
Sales at $15 per unit		9,000 units
Variable production costs	$73,500	
Fixed production costs	$39,500	
Total selling and administrative expenses	$29,000	

An income statement using actual absorption costing appears in Exhibit 9–6, along with a statement using actual variable costing. The results above show the same production and sales as in March of the original example (refer to Exhibit 9–1). The difference is that in October there are production cost variances netting $1,000 unfavorable (variable cost variances and fixed overhead budget variance).

TERMINOLOGY: DIRECT COSTING AND VARIABLE COSTING

Many accountants and businesspeople use the term *direct costing* to refer to what we have been calling variable costing. In Chapter 4 we defined *direct costs* as those that are traceable to a product, whether the costs are variable or fixed. In the terms of that chapter, we are assuming herein that all variable costs are traceable (or direct) to products. While some fixed costs may be traceable, we are focusing on cost behavior (variable costs versus fixed costs) rather than on direct versus common costs. Thus, it is important to refer to the method in this chapter as variable costing so that we are consistent with the definitions we have established earlier.

EXHIBIT 9–6 Income Statements for October—Coulson Company

Variable Costing

	Actual costing
Sales, 9,000 × $15	$135,000
Variable cost of sales:	
Production costs	73,500
Ending inventory	18,375[a]
Variable cost of sales	55,125
Variable gross margin	79,875
Variable selling and administrative costs	9,000
Contribution margin	70,875
Fixed production costs	39,500
Fixed selling and administrative expenses	20,000
Total fixed costs	59,500
Income	$11,375

Absorption Costing

	Actual Costing
Sales, 9,000 × $15	$135,000
Production costs:	
Fixed	39,500
Variable	73,500
Total available for sale	113,000
Ending inventory	28,250[b]
Cost of sales	84,750
Gross margin	50,250
Selling and administrative expenses	29,000
Income	$21,250

[a] $73,500/12,000 = $6.125 × 3,000 = $18,375.
[b] $113,000/12,000 = $9.4167 × 3,000 = $28,250.

EVALUATION OF METHODS

When we compare variable costing to absorption costing, we go back to our division of product costs for financial reporting versus cost of products for managerial decision making. In addition, the evaluation of variable costing is affected by changes in the manufacturing environment as well as by efforts in using the traceable margin reports we saw in Chapter 4.

Internal Reporting: Absorption Costing

Absorption costing has been the basis for internal reporting in many companies. While managers who prefer absorption costing do not deny the importance of contribution margin and the related concepts of cost behavior for planning and some decision making, they also point out that unless managers are aware of fixed costs (specifically fixed costs per unit), they might incorrectly price products. In the end, fixed costs must be covered to make a profit.

Managers agree that tactical decisions should be based on incremental costs (both variable and fixed costs) and revenue changes. However, if pricing were only to include incremental costs (traceable costs), then common costs would be ignored and the company might become unprofitable over the long term. Incremental revenues and costs might be useful for isolated tactical decisions but they are inappropriate for ongoing, normal decisions.

A proponent of absorption costing would go on to point out that all costs are variable in the long run. Commitments in fixed assets and staffing levels may be adjusted over time so that capacity may be set at any desired level, given time to adjust. Many fixed costs are a function of long-term commitments, and for the most part these are the costs that can get firms into trouble. Variable costs are short-term commitments—hours of labor time, kilograms of materials, and so on. These commitments do not have the same potential for plunging the firm into bankruptcy as do the long-term commitments represented by fixed costs. Accordingly, managers should always bear in mind the possible consequences of fixed costs, and the best way for them to do so is to use absorption costing. This argument is heavily behavioral, focusing on the possible unfavorable effects of managers' failing to consider fixed costs.

Another argument advanced by proponents of absorption costing is that variable costing does not necessarily provide information about incremental costs. Fixed costs may change if the level of production moves from one relevant range to another. Step-variable (or step-fixed) costs such as supervision change with changes in the level of activity. Therefore, to limit product costs to those that are strictly variable is to misstate the actual cost behavior of the firm.

Finally, it may be argued that absorption costing data should be used to set equitable prices. We saw in earlier chapters that some firms set prices based on the variable costs of production plus allowances for fixed production costs, selling and administrative expenses, and a profit margin.[3] Pricing formulas such as variable cost plus 15 percent for overhead and 10 percent for profit are not uncommon. Using variable costing data to set prices might be unfair if different products use different amounts of fixed assets and, therefore, different amounts of fixed cost. For example, if a firm sets prices at 250 percent of

[3]Chapters 2, 4, 5, and 6 made this point.

variable cost, it might, the argument goes, be charging some customers too little and some too much. Products that require substantial investment in fixed assets should be priced higher than those that do not, so that they bear a fair share of the costs associated with the higher investment.

Internal Reporting: Variable Costing

Proponents of variable costing argue that it does not downplay the importance of fixed costs: it shows them clearly on the income statement as a single figure (or as several figures), highlighting their impact on profits. They argue that the *total* fixed costs are important, not per unit amounts that can change with changes in volume under actual costing. Even under normal and standard costing, the total fixed costs applied to product on a per unit basis might not equal total incurred costs. With absorption costing, fixed costs show up in cost of sales and application variances, which makes it difficult to determine their overall impact.

Advocates of variable costing also point out that absorption costing does not provide full costs, since it does not unitize selling, general, and administrative expenses, which could be high in relation to manufacturing costs. Thus, managers who consider per unit fixed production costs in pricing decisions are not including all the costs that must be covered to earn a profit.

Advocates of variable costing argue that prices should be set to recover fixed costs and provide a profit. They do not think that unitizing fixed costs is useful in such decisions. Consider a multiproduct firm. Fixed costs will be allocated to product lines and then to units of product. Suppose that a particular product shows a loss on an absorption costing basis but does have a positive incremental profit (contribution margin less avoidable fixed costs). A manager might be tempted to raise the price of the product to make it pay its way. The economic law of demand states that as prices rise, the quantity demanded falls, and vice versa. We might then expect to see a decline in volume of the product. The decline might more than offset the increased price, so that incremental profit drops. The decline would also trigger reallocation of fixed costs, which would affect the apparent profitability of other products. If the absorption cost results after the price increase were worse than before, the manager might raise the price again or consider dropping the product, either of which could be very unwise decisions.

Prices can be set using variable costing data and total fixed costs. Again, no one argues that fixed costs are unimportant, only that they should not be expressed as per unit amounts.

A final argument is that variable costing is better for evaluating the effects of decisions. Most firms will perform postaudits of decisions, especially major ones. Managers will determine whether the decision worked out as expected and, if not, what adaptive and corrective actions need to be undertaken and what lessons can be learned for making future decisions. A manager who has determined a product mix using linear programming would be able to evaluate the results of this decision and determine whether things went according to plan using variable costing. It would be more difficult to do so using absorption costing.

Consider the simple situation depicted in the partial income statements below. The firm uses standard absorption costing, and one of its managers is considering a special order of 10,000 units at $12 each. The order will not affect sales at regular prices, and because variable costs are $5 per unit, the manager believes that the sale would be wise. Because inventory is high, the order would be filled from inventory.

	Without Special Order	*With Special Order*
Sales:		
80,000 at $20	$1,600,000	
80,000 at $20, 10,000 at $12		$1,720,000
Standard cost of sales at $13[a]	1,040,000	1,170,000
Standard gross margin	$ 560,000	$ 550,000

[a]Standard variable cost is $5, standard fixed cost $8 based on $800,000 budgeted fixed manufacturing costs and 100,000 units normal activity. Production for the period is 100,000 units, so there is no application variance.

These results suggest that the firm would lose money on the special order. The problem arises because the fixed costs of $80,000 on 10,000 units are shown as additional cost of sales under standard absorption costing. If the sale is not made, these costs will remain in inventory. Thus, the effects of the sale are a $70,000 increase in contribution margin [($12 − $5) × 10,000] and an $80,000 charge for fixed costs, giving the $10,000 reduction shown above. Variable costing income statements would show a $70,000 increase in contribution margin and profit. Accepting the order would be wise despite the effects on the absorption costing income statements. This type of analysis is covered in Chapter 12, and we illustrate it here to integrate our discussion of relevant costs with our discussion of variable costing.

The Changing Manufacturing Environment

In a labor-intensive manufacturing environment where labor is a variable cost, variable costs per unit are a significant portion of total unit costs. This is especially true because in such a setting a good deal of overhead is likely to vary with labor. As labor cost becomes fixed (a function of time instead of production) and as the manufacturing process becomes more machine-intensive and computer controlled, materials and material-related variable overhead might be the only variable production costs. These variable costs might be only 20 percent of total manufacturing costs. This puts a whole new light on variable costing.

In Chapter 4 we discussed creating accounting reports that focused on traceable costs and that in the best cases would not include any allocated common costs. Thus, costs would be traced to a business segment (such as the plant), a production process, a product or product line, a batch, or a unit of product. If, say, a cost were traceable to a production process but was common to units of product, it would not be allocated to the units. In a sense, this idea of activity-based costs is grounded on the notion of the contribution margin format income statement and variable costing. In variable costing, fixed costs are not allocated to units of product. In the extreme case that fixed costs are common to all units, then the notion of activity-based costing and variable costing income statements would be the same.

In an environment where fixed costs comprise up to 80 percent of total manufacturing costs, it makes even less sense to allocate them to units to get a fully absorbed unit product cost. One prime foundation of variable costing is that fixed costs are related to the period and not to units of product. As fixed costs rise as a proportion of total manufacturing costs, this principle makes even more sense.

External Reporting

Generally accepted accounting principles require the use of absorption costing for financial reporting. The major theoretical underpinning of this position seems to be the matching concept. In addition, all costs incurred end up on either the income statement or the balance sheet at the end of a period. The basic question is whether the cost has future value at the end of a period. If it does, it is an asset; if it does not, it is an expense of the period. Advocates of absorption costing believe that all the costs of production begin as assets. Material, labor (direct and indirect), and factory overhead are all costs incurred to produce finished goods. These goods have future value to the firm; the cost of the goods is not an expense until the goods are sold (the value is realized). Thus, since all the costs of production are incurred to create finished goods with potential future value to the company, it is not correct to treat some production costs (fixed costs) as expenses of the period.

While some discussion has occurred regarding the use of variable costing for external reporting, variable costing has not been permitted for financial reporting. However, there are valid arguments in favor of allowing its use for external reports. We have seen that production as well as sales affect income. Thus, a manager can manipulate income (raise it artificially) in the short run by increasing production even while sales are steady or falling.[4] Other arguments focus on the information/decision making aspect; if variable costing is a good managerial decision making tool, why would it be any less useful for external decision makers?

---

[4]Recent articles in *The Wall Street Journal* have pointed to income manipulation by MiniScribe.

Perhaps the most compelling argument for the use of variable costing for financial reporting centers on the definition of an asset.[5] Most accountants agree that an asset is an economic resource, something that provides future benefits to the firm. Inventory is an asset because it can be sold and, therefore, is a source of future cash inflows. However, a firm can produce more inventory, so that we might think of the future benefits of existing inventory as the costs that we avoid in not having to produce so much in the future. Fixed manufacturing costs do not reduce, or obviate, to use Professor Green's term, the need to incur costs in the future. Variable manufacturing costs incurred now do obviate the need to incur such costs in the future. Thus, fixed manufacturing costs do not comply with the meaning of an asset in the sense described and should not be included in inventory cost.[6]

Tax Considerations

We noted that variable costing is not acceptable for income tax accounting. However, firms may use normal costing with practical capacity as the basis for allocating fixed production costs to units of product for tax purposes.[7] The application variance may be expensed, but other variances (variable cost variances, fixed cost budget variances) generally must be prorated among inventories and cost of sales. Because the use of practical capacity gives the lowest possible fixed cost per unit figure, results will be closest to those of variable costing. Hence, using practical capacity and expensing application variances will reduce taxable income in periods of rising inventories or increase taxable income when inventories fall, in comparison to actual costing or normal costing using a lower basis for determining fixed cost per unit.

It should not be difficult to see why the Internal Revenue Service would not allow variable costing. In most years, inventories will rise because most firms grow. Even if physical inventories do not rise, the dollar value of inventories is likely to rise because prices rise. In such periods, tax payments would be lower if firms used variable costing than if they used absorption costing.

---

[5]The argument described here leans heavily on an exposition by Professor David Green, Jr., in "A Moral to the Direct Costing Controversy?" *The Journal of Business*, 33:3 (July 1960), 218–226.

[6]Professors George H. Sorter and Charles T. Horngren developed a method called relevant costing. Under their criteria, fixed costs could be included in inventory if they obviated the need to incur costs in the future, or reduced the future requirements. Thus, if variable costs were to increase or if expected sales were greater than current productive capacity, the fixed costs of the current period would obviate the need to incur the higher future variable costs or would provide benefits in the form of units of product that the firm would not be able to produce in the future. Under such circumstances, they would allow fixed costs to be included in inventory. See "Asset Recognition and Economic Attributes: The Relevant Costing Approach," *The Accounting Review* (July 1962), pp. 391–399.

[7]Regulation 1.471-11 (1975).

BEHAVIORAL CONSIDERATIONS

Throughout this book we stress that behavioral considerations are an important part of management and cost accounting. Our discussion in Chapter 4 included behavioral effects of changing competitive and manufacturing conditions. Chapters 7 and 8 emphasize the importance of behaviorally sound reporting, identifying variances by responsibility, and considering the effects of performance in one area affecting the performance in others. Because managers might be evaluated at least partially on their performance against standards, they are sensitive about the setting of standards and reporting of variances. If they think that standards have been set unfairly, they might be tempted to undermine the system or manipulate data to look better.

Income is one of the most common measurements of segment and managerial performance. Most firms prepare income statements by product, product line, geographical area, or some other segmented basis. If a manager is going to be evaluated based on these income statements, and perhaps receive a bonus based on income, it would be better if the manager thinks that the income statement is fair. Even if the income statement is thought to be fair, it still might lead managers to make incorrect decisions. With this in mind, let us consider the potential problems in evaluation and decision making that absorption costing and variable costing statements pose.

Both production and sales affect absorption costing. Thus, managers who fail to consider the effect of both elements can come to incorrect conclusions. Looking at the March results for the Coulson Company (page 391), a manager might conclude that sales of 9,000 units yield earnings of about $24,000 and might make plans based on that conclusion. That would be a mistake; Coulson earns only $24,000 selling 9,000 units if it makes 12,000 units, which it certainly cannot do over a long period. This same mistake could occur in looking at a single product or a product line.

Even if managers understand the effects on income of both production and sales, there is the issue of equity: will a manager think that the income numbers that either method generates are fair? If not, what will be the result? If a manager is evaluated on income and sales are not going up, income can be manipulated by increasing production. Thus, by increasing or decreasing production, a manager has the potential of meeting budgeted goals at least partially by changing production.

This possible abuse is the basis for several instructive examples, one of which appears as a problem at the end of this chapter.[8] Such manipulation can easily be discovered if it takes place over several years. If inventory levels increase beyond the usual amounts expected to meet future sales, we would be inclined to investigate, and we might expect to see that production has been too high to be economically justifiable.

Whether or not poor decisions are made by managers using one type of

[8] Also see Sorter and Horngren, *op. cit.*, for an example of the problem.

EXHIBIT 9–7 Product Line Income Statement, 19X5— Crawford Company (in thousands of dollars)

	Total	*Valves*	*Fittings*	*Pipe*
Sales	$2,345	$978	$648	$719
Variable production costs	1,035	453	313	269
Variable selling expenses	97	38	16	43
Total variable costs	1,132	491	329	312
Contribution margin	1,213	487	319	407
Avoidable fixed costs	456	204	109	143
Incremental profit	757	$283	$210	$264
Common and unavoidable fixed costs	684			
Income before taxes	$ 73			

information as opposed to another is important. It is also important to note that if managers see counterintuitive results such as falling income with rising sales, they might become distrustful of the system. If that occurs, they might ignore the information produced by the accounting system. They will almost certainly not improve performance if they distrust the accounting system.

The effects of production on income may be especially severe in segmented reporting. Chapter 4 dealt with the idea of traceable versus common costs and alternative forms of reporting segment performance where common costs are not allocated to products, product lines, or segments. This same idea holds in the use of variable costing with traceable fixed costs assigned to the appropriate segment and common fixed costs not allocated. An example of such a format is given in Exhibit 9–7. This income statement shows both variable costs and incremental fixed costs associated with each product. Because it uses the variable costing approach, it avoids the problems of the effects of production on income, while it highlights the fixed costs that could be expected to change if the product were dropped. A variation of this format appears in Chapter 19, where it is called tiered contribution analysis.

This type of income statement is compatible with the principle of controllability in management reporting. It highlights costs that are controllable in the short term, both variable and avoidable fixed costs. It shows unavoidable costs, including costs joint or common to the various segments, in one place, distinguishing them from the controllable costs.

FLOWS OF COSTS IN VARIABLE COSTING SYSTEMS

Firms that use variable costing for internal reporting could keep their cost accounting systems on either a variable costing or an absorption costing basis. Either way, they will have to make adjustments. If they keep the system using variable costing, they will have to adjust to absorption costing for financial reporting and tax purposes. If they keep the system on an absorption costing basis, they must adjust to develop variable costing information.

The basic flows of costs under a variable costing system are the same as under an absorption costing system, save that fixed production costs are not carried through Work-in-Process Inventory, Finished Goods Inventory, and Cost of Goods Sold. At year end, or whenever external financial statements are to be issued, the firm will allocate fixed manufacturing overhead to inventories and cost of sales. The procedure is much the same as that used to prorate variances in going from standard costing to actual costing. The following illustration shows the process.

Illustration: Cornwall Manufacturing Company

The Cornwall Manufacturing Company allocates fixed manufacturing overhead according to the relative amounts of variable manufacturing overhead in the various categories. An analysis of 19X7 data reveal:

Variable manufacturing overhead included in:		*Percentage of total*
Cost of Sales	$3,720,000	74.7
Ending Work-in-Process Inventory	272,000	5.5
Ending Finished Goods Inventory	986,000	19.8
Total	$4,978,000	100.0%
Total fixed manufacturing overhead		$9,874,000
Allocation of fixed overhead:		
To Cost of Sales	$7,375,800 ($9,874,000 × 74.7%)	
To Work-in-Process Inventory	543,070 ($9,874,000 × 5.5%)	
To Finished Goods Inventory	1,955,050 ($9,874,000 × 19.8%)	
Total	$9,874,000	

These allocations do not have to be reflected in the accounts. They could simply be made as worksheet adjustments so that the accounts would continue to show variable costs.

Determining Variable Costs

Many costs need to be estimated. While we might be sure that, say, property taxes are fixed, we might not know the fixed and variable portions of many other costs. This is one of the reasons proposed for the use of regression models in planning. However, even with sophisticated mathematical models to aid in CVP analyses and standard cost setting, the manager is still left with estimates. It is unusual to find perfect correlation between costs and volume. Rarely do actual costs equal standard costs. Finally, not only are standard costs estimates of expected total costs per unit, but the division of fixed and variable costs (especially in overhead) is an estimate. Even under actual costing or normal costing the estimate of the fixed and variable portions of mixed costs exists. Absorption costing minimizes the effect of this estimate, since fixed as well as variable costs are included in the inventory flow. Because variable costing treats fixed production costs as a period expense, firms using variable costing can experience more pronounced errors if estimates prove to be unreliable.

SUMMARY

Variable costing is a product costing alternative that is consistent with cost-volume-profit analysis. Variable costing treats fixed production costs as period costs, in contrast to absorption costing, where fixed production costs are inventoried. The two methods give differing income statement results when sales and production differ. Variable costing income is lower than absorption costing income when production is greater than sales, and vice versa. Variable costing is an alternative for internal reporting only. It is not acceptable for financial reporting or income tax accounting.

Variable costing also overcomes some objections to absorption costing, including some behavioral problems. Income, a common measurement for evaluation and decision making, is affected only by sales. Fixed cost per unit, an elusive figure at best, is eliminated under variable costing. Managers are apt to make better decisions and to feel that statements reflecting the performance of their segment are fairly represented.

Because of changes in the internal and external complexity of business, managers want cost and management accounting systems to reflect traceability and separability. Variable costing is in concert with such efforts.

REVIEW PROBLEM

Essington Company uses standard absorption costing with a standard fixed manufacturing cost of $3.00 per unit, based on normal activity of 250,000 units and $750,000 budgeted fixed manufacturing costs. Other data for 19X6 appear below.

Standard variable manufacturing cost, per unit	$6.00
Unit sales	240,000
Selling price	$15.00
Unit production	260,000
Total variable manufacturing costs	$1,560,000
Total fixed manufacturing costs	$750,000
Total fixed selling, general, and administrative costs	$800,000

REQUIRED[9]

1. Prepare an income statement for 19X6.
2. Prepare an income statement for 19X6 using variable costing.

[9] You might adapt the template COULSON.WK1 to fit this problem.

ANSWERS TO REVIEW PROBLEM

ESSINGTON COMPANY
Income Statements for 19X6

	Absorption Costing
Sales, 240,000 × $15	$3,600,000
Standard cost of sales, 240,000 × $9	2,160,000
Standard gross margin, 240,000 × $6	1,440,000
Volume variance, favorable	30,000
Actual gross margin	1,470,000
Selling, general, and administrative expenses	800,000
Profit	$ 670,000

Volume variance = (260,000 − 250,000) × $3

		Variable Costing
Sales, 240,000 × $15		$3,600,000
Standard variable cost of sales, 240,000 × $6		1,440,000
Standard contribution margin, 240,000 × $9		2,160,000
Fixed costs:		
Manufacturing	$750,000	
Selling, general, and administrative	800,000	1,550,000
Profit		$ 610,000

Note that the ending inventory is 20,000 units higher than the beginning inventory because production of 260,000 was 20,000 units higher than sales of 240,000. At $3 per unit, absorption costing income is $60,000 higher than variable costing income.

ASSIGNMENTS

9–1 Rationale for Variable Costing (AICPA Adapted) Grisp Company, a manufacturer with heavy investments in plant and equipment, uses absorption costing for both internal and external reporting. Its management is considering using variable costing for internal purposes only.

REQUIRED

1. What is the rationale for using variable costing for internal reporting?
2. Assuming that the quantity of ending inventory is higher than the quantity of beginning inventory, would income using variable costing be different from income using absorption costing? If so, specify whether it would be higher or lower and discuss the rationale for your answer.

9–2 Variable Costing and Direct Costing Much of the discussion in this chapter and others such as Chapter 4 has been concerned with product costs and product costing for financial accounting as cost of products for managerial decision making.

REQUIRED

1. In non-technical terms, define absorption costing and variable costing.
2. For what traditional reasons do managers prefer to use fully absorbed cost of products for managerial decisions?
3. For what traditional reasons do managers prefer to use variable cost of products for managerial decisions?
4. What is the difference between variable costing and direct or traceable costing? Why might the notion of direct costs be more appropriate to use in managerial reporting rather than variable costs especially given the new manufacturing and/or competitive environment?

9–3 Directness of Fixed Costs An argument advanced by some advocates of variable costing is that fixed costs are not directly associable with units of product and should therefore not be inventoried. One can also argue that some fixed costs can be associated with changes in the level of production and consequently are direct to small batches of production.

For example, suppose that a firm needs one line supervisor for each ten direct laborers and that each laborer makes 1,000 units of product per month. It is possible to argue that the salaries of line supervisors are direct to each 10,000 units of product, perhaps even variable because they will change in fairly close proportion to changes in output.

REQUIRED

Discuss whether costs such as the line supervisor's salaries discussed above can be considered inventoriable under variable costing.

9–4 Basic Variable Costing and Absorption Costing The data below are operating results for the Blanchard Company for 19X6, 19X7, and 19X8.

	19X6	*19X7*	*19X8*
Beginning inventory	0	2,000	2,000
Production	12,000	12,000	8,000
Sales in units, price $20/unit	10,000	12,000	10,000
Ending inventory	2,000	2,000	0

Variable production costs were $8 per unit each year, and fixed production costs were $60,000 each year. Selling and administrative expenses, all fixed, were $40,000 each year.

REQUIRED

1. Prepare income statements for each year using variable costing.
2. Prepare income statements for each year using absorption costing, with 10,000 units used to set a standard fixed cost of $6 per unit. Application variances are to be charged to the income statement as a gain or loss.
3. Prepare income statements for each year, using actual absorption costing and FIFO.

9–5 Relationships

REQUIRED

Treat each of the following cases independently.

1. A firm had income of $100,000 using absorption costing with a fixed overhead rate of $10 per unit. Inventory at the end of the period was 2,000 units

lower than at the beginning of the period. What was income under variable costing?

2. A firm had income of $100,000 under variable costing and $80,000 under absorption costing with a fixed overhead rate of $5 per unit. What was the difference between sales and production?

3. A firm had $60,000 income using variable costing and $100,000 using absorption costing with a fixed overhead rate of $2 per unit. What was the difference between the beginning and ending inventories, in units?

9–6 Basic Variable Costing and Absorption Costing The data below relate to the one product of Eastern Company.

Selling price		$12
Production costs, per unit:		
Variable	$5.50	
Fixed	3.50	
Selling and administrative costs, per unit:		
Variable	0.50	
Fixed	1.50	

The unit costs are based on normal volume of 8,000 units per month. During June the firm produced 7,500 units and sold 7,000. During July it produced 8,500 and sold 9,000.

REQUIRED

Prepare income statements for June and July using (a) absorption costing and (b) variable costing. Treat any application variances as adjustments to gross margin.

9–7 Standard Costing Arno Company makes two models of its only product, a sophisticated trap for rodents. Data relating to each model appear below.

	Regular Model	*Deluxe Model*
Standard material cost	$10	$20
Standard labor cost	5	8

All overhead is fixed and the firm uses budgeted direct labor cost for the coming year, 19X6, as the basis for determining standard cost. During 19X6 the managers expect to make 4,000 units of each model, for total direct labor cost of $52,000. Budgeted overhead is $104,000. There were no beginning inventories.

Operations for the year showed the following results:

		Regular	*Deluxe*
Production		4,200	3,600
Sales		4,000	3,200
Selling prices		$40	$70
Costs:			
Materials	$108,000		
Direct labor	54,000		
Overhead	98,000		
Selling and general, all fixed	35,000		

REQUIRED

1. Prepare an income statement using standard absorption costing. Identify all variances separately to the extent that you have the necessary information.
2. Prepare an income statement using standard variable costing.

9–8 Standard Process Costing Exco Company makes a single product. Standard cost data follow.

Materials, 3 gal at $2	$ 6
Direct labor, $\frac{1}{2}$ hr at $8/hr	4
Variable overhead at $6 per labor hour	3
Fixed overhead at $10 per labor hour	5
Total standard cost	$18

Annual budgeted fixed overhead is $500,000. There were no inventories at the beginning of 19X6. The firm's transactions during the year were:

1. Material purchases were 330,000 gallons at $1.90.
2. Material use was 304,000 gallons.
3. Direct laborers worked 47,500 hours at $8 per hour.
4. Variable overhead was $285,000.
5. Fixed overhead was $512,000.
6. The firm completed 97,000 units and sold 90,000 at $25 each. Work in process at year end was 3,000 units complete as to materials, 60 percent complete as to labor and overhead.
7. Selling and administrative expenses were $450,000.

REQUIRED

1. Determine ending inventories at standard cost, Materials, Work in Process, and Finished Goods.
2. Prepare an income statement using standard absorption costing, identifying all variances separately.
3. Without preparing a new income statement, determine what income would have been if the firm had used standard variable costing.

9–9 All Fixed Costs Whatley Company manufactures its one product from sewage, which it acquires free of charge from a nearby city. The production process is automated, with no human beings in the plant. All manufacturing costs are fixed at $1,100,000 annually. Selling and administrative expenses are also fixed at $600,000 per year. The company sells its product for $10 per unit. The plant has the capacity to produce 240,000 units annually. Activity over the past several years appears below.

	19X3	19X4	19X5
Units produced	240,000	220,000	200,000
Units sold	200,000	220,000	240,000

REQUIRED

1. Determine income in each year using absorption costing, with 220,000 units used to set the standard fixed manufacturing cost.

2. Determine income in each year using variable costing.
3. Comment on the differences between your results in parts 1 and 2.

9–10 Income Statements (AICPA Adapted) Bicent Company makes a single product. Cost data are, per unit:

Direct material (all variable)	$30.00
Direct labor (all variable)	19.00
Manufacturing overhead:	
Variable	6.00
Fixed, based on 10,000 units per month	5.00
Selling, general, and administrative:	
Variable	4.00
Fixed, based on 10,000 units per month	2.80

The product sells for $80 per unit. The following data reflect estimates for June 19X7 in units.

Beginning inventory	2,000
Production	9,000
Available for sale	11,000
Sales	7,500
Ending inventory	3,500

REQUIRED

1. Prepare an income statement for June, assuming the use of absorption costing with any application variance charged or credited to cost of goods sold.
2. Prepare an income statement for June, using variable costing.

9–11 Analyzing Income Roberta Company uses standard absorption costing for this internal reporting. Standards for the single product it makes are:

Standard cost per unit:			
Materials	2 lb	$30 per lb	$ 60.00
Labor	0.5 DLH	$20 per DLH	10.00
Variable overhead	0.6 MH	$30 per MH	18.00
Fixed overhead	0.6 MH	$80 per MH	48.00
Total cost per unit			$136.00

Where: DLH = direct labor hours

MH = machine hours

Annual fixed overhead = $80,000,000 (incurred evenly)

Annual machine hours = 1,000,000

During May, 19X9, the following occurred:

Units in beginning inventory	20,000
Units produced	150,000
Units sold	160,000
Sales price per unit	$200.00

Actual inputs (May):		
Materials purchased and used	290,000 lb	$8,845,000
Direct labor	73,000 DLH	$1,606,000
Variable overhead	89,000 MH	$2,670,000
Fixed overhead		$6,600,000

There was no balance in either the Materials Inventory or the Work-in-Process Inventory at the beginning or the end of the month.

Based on the above information, the following income statement was presented to management:

	Standard Absorption Costing
Sales	$32,000,000
Cost of production:	
Materials	$ 9,000,000
Direct labor	1,500,000
Variable overhead	2,700,000
Fixed overhead	7,200,000
Total cost of production	$20,400,000
Plus: Beginning inventory	2,720,000
Cost of Goods Available for Sale	$23,120,000
Less: Ending inventory	1,360,000
Cost of Goods Sold	$21,760,000
Variances:	
Material purchase price	145,000
Material use	(300,000)
Labor rate	146,000
Labor efficiency	(40,000)
Variable overhead spending	0
Variable overhead efficiency	(30,000)
Fixed overhead budget	(66,667)
Fixed overhead application	(533,333)
Total variances	(679,000)
Adjusted Cost of Goods Sold	$21,081,000
Gross profit	$10,919,000
Sales, General, Administrative Expenses:	
Variable	320,000
Fixed	1,499,000
Income before taxes	$ 9,100,000
Taxes at 40 percent	3,640,000
Net income	$ 5,460,000

REQUIRED

1. Using information in the above income statement, has management chosen to
a. make temporary entries to "hide" variances?
b. prorate variances as appropriate?
c. expense all variances this period?
Justify your answer.

2. If standard variable costing had been used, would income have been higher than, lower than, or the same as $5,460,000? Why? *(Note: you should* not *calculate new income for this part. Just say whether it would be higher, lower, or the same, and why.)*

3. If actual variable costing had been used, what is the new net income that would be shown? *Do not work up a new income statement for this part.* Instead, use the original net income and adjust it. Show each adjustment separately. You may assume that beginning inventory is valued at $1,760,000. *(Hint: remember that you are adjusting net income after taxes.)*

9–12 Standard Costs (continuation of Assignment 8–22) In addition to the information presented in that problem, Rubia sold 7,000 units at $250 per unit in July, 19X9. Selling and Administrative expenses were $100,000 plus 5 percent of sales. Other actual results from July are:

Materials purchased	20,000 pounds for $480,000
Direct labor	2,200 hours for $44,000

REQUIRED

1. Calculate material and labor variances.
2. Ignoring taxes, prepare an income statement using standard absorption costing. Assume that all variances (from this problem and those calculated in assignment 8–22) are put into Cost of Goods Sold. Show details or supporting schedules as appropriate.
3. Without creating a new income statement, if standard variable costing had been used, what would be the income before taxes? Demonstrate what income would be and *explain* why the difference (if any) occurs.

9–13 Effect of Production Wechter Company has the following information regarding budgeted operations in 19X0:

Beginning inventory	40,000 units
Production during the year	350,000 units
Sales during the year	370,000 units
Selling price	$10/unit
Variable manufacturing costs	$ 6/unit
Variable selling expenses	$ 1/unit sold
Fixed manufacturing overhead (based on annual production of 325,000 units)	$91,000 per year
Fixed selling and administrative expenses	$50,000 per year

Any over- or underapplied overhead is written off at the end of each year.

REQUIRED

1. Prepare a pro forma variable costing income statement for 19X0.
2. What is the effect on absorption costing income of an increase of production from 350,000 to 370,000 units? What is the effect on variable costing income of this same change?
3. By how much will variable costing income differ from absorption costing income based on the facts in part 2?

4. Going back to the original facts, what is the effect on absorption costing income if production is 400,000 units and sales are 360,000 units?

5. What are the proposed strengths and weakness of both absorption and of variable costing? How does the shift to a more fixed-cost manufacturing environment affect these arguments?

9–14 Relationships George Company produces a single product. Prices and costs have remained stable over the last several years. Overhead is applied on a per unit basis. During 19X0, production was 7,500 units greater than sales. George uses standard absorption costing for both financial and managerial accounting purposes; its income statements for 19X0 and 19X1 follow.

	19X0	19X1
Sales at $75	$1,125,000	$1,500,000
Cost of Goods Sold:		
Materials	90,000	120,000
Direct Labor	180,000	240,000
Variable Overhead	150,000	200,000
Applied Fixed Overhead	390,000	520,000
Standard Cost of Sales	$ 810,000	$1,080,000
Variances:		
Variable cost variances	25,000	10,000
Fixed cost budget variance	5,000	(12,000)
Fixed cost application variance	(260,000)	65,000
Adjusted Cost of Sales	$ 580,000	$1,143,000
Gross profit	$ 545,000	$ 357,000
Selling and Administrative expenses	262,500	300,000
Income before taxes	$ 282,500	$ 57,000

All variances are shown as an expense in the period they are incurred.

REQUIRED

1. What are variable costs per unit for Selling and Administrative expenses? What is the fixed portion of Selling and Administrative expenses?
2. If standard fixed overhead is applied on a per unit basis,
   a. What is the fixed overhead rate per unit?
   b. How many units were used as the denominator activity to determine the fixed overhead application rate?
3. How many units were sold in 19X1? How many units were produced in 19X1?
4. Prepare variable costing income statements for both 19X0 and 19X1.
5. Explain the difference between absorption income and variable income for each year.

9–15 Replacement Costs The controller and sales manager of B&M Enterprises were arguing about the desirability of selling some inventory to a large chain store. The price was to be $60 per unit, which was well below the usual $85 price. In support of his position, the sales manager offered the following data regarding the product. The cost figures are from operations of the previous month.

	Unit Costs
Materials	$12
Direct labor	25
Variable overhead, $0.80 per direct labor dollar	20
Total variable cost	$57

The sales manager said that accepting the offer would increase the firm's income by $3 for each unit sold. The controller, he declared, had advocated the use of variable costing precisely because it provided information that would be useful in making decisions such as the present one.

The controller opposed the sale. She stated that, although variable costing had advantages over absorption costing, it was not a cure-all. She pointed out that labor costs had risen by 10 percent since the units on hand were made and that the variable overhead rate per direct labor dollar had stayed at $0.80 because much of variable overhead was fringe benefits and other costs that were related to labor cost, not to labor time. She went on to say that the firm should always consider the cost to replace units, not the historical cost, because replacement cost was a measure of opportunity cost.

REQUIRED

Determine whether the firm should make the sale to the chain store. Support your position with appropriate calculations and make your assumptions explicit.

9–16 Variable Costing and Income Taxes

REQUIRED

1. What would happen if variable costing were made acceptable for income tax purposes? Comment from the standpoint of the federal government.
2. How would your response change given the new manufacturing and competitive environment?

9–17 Variable and Absorption Costing Standards The following data relate to the operations of Cramer Company for 19X5 and 19X6. There were no inventories at the beginning of 19X5.

	19X5	19X6
Production, in units	10,000	8,000
Sales, in units, at $10 per unit	$70,000	$90,000
Variable production costs incurred	30,000	24,000
Fixed production costs incurred	20,000	20,000
Selling and administrative expenses	15,000	15,000

Standard variable production cost is $3 per unit; budgeted fixed production costs are $20,000 per year.

REQUIRED

1. Prepare income statements for the two years, using variable costing.
2. Suppose that the firm uses 8,000 units to set its standard fixed cost for determining absorption costing inventories and income for tax purposes and financial reporting. Prepare income statements for the two years, using standard absorption costing. Treat any application variance as an adjustment to stan-

dard gross profit, so that actual gross profit is standard gross profit plus or minus any application variance.

9–18 Direct and Absorption Costing (AICPA) Gordon Company began operations on January 1. During the year, it made 100,000 units of product and sold 80,000 units at $10 per unit. Cost data follow.

	Fixed Costs	*Variable Costs*
Raw materials	—	$2.00 per unit produced
Direct labor	—	$1.25 per unit produced
Factory overhead	$120,000	$0.75 per unit produced
Selling and administrative expenses	$ 70,000	$1.00 per unit sold

Gordon uses an actual costing system.

REQUIRED

1. Determine Gordon's ending inventory of finished goods under both absorption costing and variable costing.
2. Prepare an income statement using variable costing.
3. Prepare an income statement using absorption costing.

9–19 "How's That Again?" The president of your firm is considering the use of standard absorption costing. She has asked you to develop a few examples to illustrate the effects on income of various events. You develop the following basic data:

Selling price per unit	$ 50
Standard variable production cost per unit	10
Annual budgeted fixed production costs	300,000
Standard fixed cost per unit, based on 10,000 units at normal activity	30

You assume, for simplicity, that selling and administrative expenses are zero. You then prepare the following income statement, assuming a beginning inventory of 1,000 units and production and sales of 10,000 units.

Sales	$500,000
Beginning inventory	40,000
Variable production costs	100,000
Applied fixed production costs	300,000
Ending inventory	(40,000)
Standard cost of sales	400,000
Standard gross margin	100,000
Application variance	0
Actual gross margin	$100,000

REQUIRED

The president asks you to redo the income statement to show the effects of each of the following events. Consider each event independently, and prepare five new income statements. In each case where production changes from the original 10,000 units, assume that actual production costs equal budgeted production costs for the new level of production.

1. Production increases to 10,001 units; sales remain at 10,000 units.
2. Production increases to 10,001 units; sales increase to 10,001 units.
3. Sales increase to 10,001 units; production remains at 10,000 units.
4. Sales decrease to 9,999 units; production increases to 10,001 units.
5. Sales increase to 10,001 units; production decreases to 9,999 units.

9–20 Analysis of Income Statements The president of the Myoko Company, a small manufacturer of automotive parts, has asked for your assistance in analyzing the firm's recent income statements.

	July	*August*	*September*
Sales	$232,417	$296,385	$247,811
Cost of sales	156,220	240,499	176,049
Gross margin	76,197	55,886	71,762
Selling and administrative costs	53,120	56,215	54,267
Profit before taxes (loss)	$ 23,077	($329)	$ 17,495

"Profits don't seem to be responding to increases in sales. I just don't understand what's going on," says the president. "My production supervisor tells me that his costs are under control, with fixed costs running at about $86,000 per month and variable costs averaging about 40 percent of selling price for all our products. Selling and administrative expenses seem to be running about as budgeted, too, so I don't see where the problem lies. I have some other data that you might like to see." He then gives you the following information.

Inventories:	
June 30	$ 97,320
July 31	188,415
August 31	106,434
September 30	88,712

The firm uses actual absorption costing for inventories.

REQUIRED

Prepare an explanation for the president.

9–21 Pricing Dispute You have been serving as the chair of a local charitable drive. You asked the manager of the Wheaton Bakery to donate loaves of its rye bread for door prizes. The manager agreed to give you the bread at cost, which he stated was 43¢ per loaf. Knowing that the retail price of a loaf is 74¢, you decided to investigate further. The manager of the bakery provided the following information.

Retail price per loaf		$0.74
Wholesale price to Wheaton		$0.43
Cost to manufacture and sell:		
Ingredients	$0.18	
Direct labor	0.08	
Overhead, manufacturing	0.14	
Overhead, selling and administrative	0.03	
Total cost		$0.43
Profit		$0.10

Both manufacturing and selling/administrative overhead are largely fixed and based on expected operations, at about 85 percent of capacity.

REQUIRED

Prepare a letter to the manager of the Wheaton Bakery explaining what you believe is a fair price and why.

9–22 Costing Methods—Income Statements (AICPA) Indiana Corporation began operations on January 1. Indiana uses an actual costing system. During the year, it made 100,000 units of product and sold 90,000 units at $9 per unit. Cost data follow.

	Fixed Costs	*Variable Costs*
Raw materials	—	$1.75 per unit produced
Direct labor	—	$1.25 per unit produced
Factory overhead	$100,000	$0.50 per unit produced
Selling and administrative expenses	$ 70,000	$0.60 per unit sold

REQUIRED

1. Prepare an income statement using absorption costing.
2. Prepare an income statement using variable costing.
3. Determine how much Indiana's operating income using variable costing would have increased if it had sold 91,000 units and still produced 100,000.
4. Redo part 3 assuming that Indiana used absorption costing.

9–23 Inventories and Income Statements (AICPA) Keller Corporation introduced a new product this year. Data for the year are:

Units produced	12,500
Units sold	10,000
Unit selling price	$15
Unit variable manufacturing cost	$ 8
Unit variable selling and administrative expenses	$ 3
Total fixed manufacturing costs	$25,000
Total fixed selling and administrative expenses	$15,000

REQUIRED

1. Determine Keller's ending inventory using variable costing.
2. Determine Keller's ending inventory using actual absorption costing.
3. Determine the total amount of variable costs charged to expense for the year if Keller uses variable costing.
4. Determine the total amount of fixed costs charged to expense if Keller uses absorption costing.
5. Prepare income statements for Keller using both absorption costing and variable costing.

9–24 Product Costing and Profitability The manager of Greg Division of General Products Company presented the following report to the president of the firm.

Income Statements—Greg Division

	March	April	May
Sales at $50 per unit	$1,000,000	$1,200,000	$1,380,000
Standard cost of sales	750,000	900,000	1,035,000
Standard gross profit	250,000	300,000	345,000
Production cost variances	30,000F	40,000F	55,000F
Actual gross profit	280,000	340,000	400,000
Selling and administrative costs	350,000	380,000	380,000
Income (loss)	($70,000)	($40,000)	$ 20,000

"We really have it going now," the manager said. "We had to spend a good bit on promotion, as evidenced by the increases in S&A expenses, but we are now out of the woods and should be able to keep sales at the May level from here on out." On questioning, the manager told the president that the production cost variances related to fixed costs. He explained: "We use a $10 per unit standard fixed production cost, and the variances arise because our production exceeds our normal activity of 30,000 units, which is the basis for determining the standard cost."

REQUIRED

1. Determine the standard variable cost per unit.
2. Determine production in each of the three months.
3. Is the division manager's optimism justified? Why or why not?

9–25 Analysis of Performance The president of Dorwaldt Company was not happy with the results for July and August, the first two months of the firm's fiscal year. She knew that income in those months should be less than the average budgeted monthly income of $40,000, because sales in the summer were slower than in the winter. Average budgeted monthly sales were $300,000.

Income Statements—Dorwaldt Company

	August	July
Sales	$200,000	$210,000
Standard cost of sales	120,000	126,000
Standard gross margin	80,000	84,000
Manufacturing variances, unfavorable	20,000	22,000
Actual gross margin	60,000	62,000
Selling and administrative expenses	80,000	80,000
Loss before taxes	($20,000)	($18,000)

The president asked the controller what was going wrong and heard that nothing was: sales were on target based on the monthly budgeted amounts for each month, and all costs were incurred as expected. The controller explained that output was relatively low, which accounted for the losses. Variable production costs were about 30 percent of sales dollars. Unit standard fixed costs were based on expected volume for the year.

REQUIRED

1. Determine the firm's breakeven point (monthly), assuming that production equals sales.

2. Is the controller correct in saying that the unfavorable application variances are the reason for the losses? Show why or why not.

9–26 Explaining Differences in Incomes Operating results for 19X5 and 19X6 for the Ulseth Company appear below. There were no inventories at the beginning of 19X5. All costs represent both actual and budgeted amounts.

	19X5	*19X6*
Sales at $10 per unit	$200,000	$190,000
Unit production	25,000	18,000
Production costs:		
Variable at $3 per unit	$ 75,000	$ 54,000
Fixed	$ 50,000	$ 50,000
Selling and administrative costs	$ 40,000	$ 40,000

REQUIRED

1. Prepare an income statement under variable costing for each year.
2. Prepare an income statement for each year under absorption costing, assuming that the firm uses 20,000 units as the basis for absorbing fixed overhead. Treat any application (volume) variances as adjustments to standard cost of sales.
3. Prepare a formal reconciliation of incomes under the two methods for each year.

9–27 Variable Costing Vernon Allbright, president of Vincent Products, has just been to a seminar on variable costing. He tells you:

> I am excited about the possibilities of using variable costing for planning. I think we can make better tactical decisions and can see better how everybody is doing under such a system. I am worried, though, that it will be costly keeping two separate sets of books, since we'll continue to need full costing information for our shareholders and the IRS. Is there anything we can do short of having duplicate systems to allow us to use variable costing while retaining the necessary parts of absorption costing?

With that, Allbright hands you the following income statement for 19X9. Vincent uses FIFO.

Income Statement, 19X9—Vincent Products

Sales (115,000 units)		$6,545,000
Cost of Sales:		
Beginning inventory	$ 418,500	
Current production	4,567,500	
Goods available for sale	4,986,000	
Less: Ending inventory	207,600	
Cost of Goods Sold		4,778,400
Gross Profit		1,766,600
Less: Sales Expenses		625,000
General Expenses		450,000
Interest		190,000
Income Before Taxes		$ 501,600

Beginning inventory of finished goods consisted of 10,000 units ($12 in materials, $19.85 in other costs, and $10 in fixed costs per unit). Current production included 110,000 units transferred to finished goods. In addition, there was no beginning inventory of work in process, but an ending inventory of 4,000 units 100 percent complete for materials and 75 percent complete in conversion costs. Current production costs consist of $12 per unit in materials, $10.26 in labor, $9.26 in variable overhead, and $10 in fixed costs. Fixed overhead incurred in 19X9 was $1,130,000.

REQUIRED

Assume Vincent's books were kept using variable costing, but management wants an absorption costing income statement and balance sheet. Considering Work in Process, Finished Goods, Cost of Goods Sold, and any other relevant accounts, show the entries to adjust the accounts from variable to absorption costing to have proper financial statements. Allocate fixed overhead on the basis of total variable conversion costs.

9–28 Actual Versus Standard: Variable and Absorption Costing Mayme Company presents the following data for 19X3:

	Actual
Beginning Inventory (units)	0
Production (units)	100,000
Sales (units), at $30	90,000
Costs for production of 100,000 units:	
Direct Materials	$350,000
Direct Labor	$610,000
Variable Overhead	$400,000
Fixed Overhead	$110,000
Selling, general, and administrative expenses	$250,000

REQUIRED

1. Prepare income statements for 19X3, using:
   a. actual absorption costing
   b. actual variable costing
2. Standard costs for the product appear below.

Standard Cost per Unit

Direct materials, 2 lb at $1.50/lb	$ 3.00
Direct labor, 1 hr at $6.25/hr	6.25
Variable overhead: $4.10/DLH	4.10
Fixed overhead[a]	1.25
Total	$14.60

[a]Fixed Overhead is based on $112,500 per year and 90,000 units of production.

Prepare income statements for 19X3, using:
a. standard absorption costing
b. standard variable costing
You may show one variance for each cost element. Show all variances as adjustments to cost of goods sold.

3. By doing parts 1a, 1b, 2a, and 2b, you have come up with four income figures. Explain the differences.

4. If production had been 90,000 units instead of 100,000 units, how would that have affected the four income numbers? (Do not do new statements to answer this question.)

9–29 Product Costing and Decisions The controller of Harding Products, Inc., was considering whether or not to accept an offer from Lacy Stores, a large chain of retailers. Lacy had offered to buy goods for $650,000, which was about $250,000 below the normal selling prices. Harding was overstocked and would fill the order from inventory. The controller prepared two pro forma income statements for the current year, one assuming that the firm accepted the order, the other assuming that it did not.

	Do Not Accept	*Accept*
Sales	$9,320,000	$9,970,000
Standard cost of sales	6,617,000	7,256,000
Standard gross margin	2,703,000	2,714,000
Manufacturing variances, unfavorable	67,000	67,000
Actual gross margin	2,636,000	2,647,000
Selling and administrative expenses	2,104,000	2,120,000
Income before taxes	$ 532,000	$ 527,000

The controller was surprised at the results. He knew that the sale would cause some increase in selling and administrative expenses, and his estimate of a $16,000 rise seemed reasonable. Standard cost of sales was about 71 percent of normal selling prices on all products, so the increase there also seemed right.

In discussing the decision with you, his new assistant, the controller stated that standard variable cost of sales was about 45 percent of normal selling prices for all products and that the manufacturing variances consisted largely of an application variance (about $55,000), the remainder being variable cost variances. Finally, he said that the beginning inventory at standard cost was about $456,000. The ending inventory would be about $1,330,000 if the firm did not accept the offer.

REQUIRED

Determine whether or not the firm should accept the offer.

9–30 Multiple Products Morton Manufacturing Company makes a wide variety of products. The firm uses standard costing—absorption costing for tax purposes, variable costing for internal reporting. The following information pertains to 19X9.

Beginning inventory at standard cost (6,500 standard hours):	
Absorption costing	$ 312,000
Variable costing	$ 195,000
Standard labor hours for 19X9 production	45,000 hr
Standard variable production cost for output achieved	$1,350,000
Budgeted fixed production cost	$ 900,000
Normal activity in standard labor hours, used to set per unit standard fixed costs	50,000 hr
Variable cost variances and fixed cost budget variance	$ 30,000U
Selling and administrative expenses	$ 850,000
Sales	$3,200,000

The number of units sold corresponds to about 41,000 standard labor hours. The material content of each product is about the same as the labor content. You may assume that all variable production costs may be expressed in terms of labor hours. Standard costs in 19X8 were the same as in 19X9.

REQUIRED

Prepare income statements for 19X9, using:

1. absorption costing
2. variable costing

9–31 Costing Methods, Decisions, and Analysis of Results Jay Dixon, president of QBM Company, had expected the month of May to show a turnaround. The firm had been barely breaking even in recent months, and toward the end of April, Dixon had ordered an across-the-board cut in prices of about 10 percent and an increase in advertising and promotional expenses of about $30,000 per month. Early sales reports in May showed that unit volume was up by about 25 percent, and Dixon was therefore shocked at the May income statement.

Income Statements—QBM Company
(in thousands)

	May	*April*
Sales	$2,251	$1,994
Cost of sales	2,076	1,496
Gross margin	175	498
Selling and administrative expenses	528	497
Income (loss) before taxes	($353)	$ 1

Ray Stout, QBM's controller, was also at a loss to explain the results. He told Dixon that costs were incurred as budgeted in both April and May. There were small shifts in the product mix from April to May, but because standard cost of sales was about 75 percent of selling price for all products (before the price reduction), that factor could not be important. Stout did say that production was well below normal in May. The firm had built up excess inventories in the early part of the year but had worked them down to normal in May.

In April, sales had approximately equaled production, and the level of activity in April was about the level used to set the standard fixed cost for each product. Monthly fixed production costs were about $800,000, and selling and administrative expenses were virtually all fixed. The firm writes off any variances to cost of sales during the month.

Dixon was convinced that he had made good decisions on prices and promotion, but the May results did not bear him out. He did not want to see any more months like May. He did expect that volume would hold at the May level if he kept prices and promotional expenses at their current levels.

REQUIRED

You are an outside consultant hired by Mr. Dixon. Write Dixon a memorandum in which you analyze the situation and recommend whether he should keep prices and promotion at their current levels or go back to the former levels. See Appendix B for guidelines for memorandum preparation.

9–32 Absorption Costing in Production Planning Corts Company produces two products, basic widgets and deluxe widgets. Several of its managers had been arguing for some time about the wisdom of the firm's policy with respect to fixed overhead costs. The firm used the practical capacity in each of its two departments—stamping and assembly—to determine figures for fixed cost per hour. These figures were used to set the standard costs of the two products. The schedule below shows the most recent results.

	Basic Widgets	*Deluxe Widgets*
Selling price	\$25	\$35
Variable costs	15	22
Contribution margin	10	13
Fixed costs	7	6
Profit per unit	\$ 3	\$ 7

The fixed costs were based on the hourly rates for fixed overhead in the two departments and the hours required to make each unit. Monthly fixed overhead was \$5,000 in stamping, \$18,000 in assembly, with available hours of 10,000 and 9,000, respectively, giving rates of \$0.50 and \$2. Basic widgets required 2 hours of stamping time, 3 hours of assembly. Deluxe widgets need 4 hours of stamping and 2 hours of assembly.

Demand for both products exceeds capacity. During the most recent month the firm produced and sold 2,500 deluxe widgets and no basic widgets. This resulted in an unfavorable application variance of \$8,000, which caused the managers a good deal of concern.

REQUIRED

You are an outside consultant hired by Darlene Corts, president. Write Corts a memorandum in which you develop and present your analysis of the optimal production plan for the firm. See Appendix B for guidelines.

9–33 Unit Costs and Pricing Policies Calgary Machine Works makes tools and dies for industrial companies. The firm has recently adopted a new pricing policy that calls for pricing all products by the following formula:

$$\text{price} = \frac{\begin{pmatrix}\text{variable}\\ \text{manufacturing cost}\end{pmatrix} + \begin{pmatrix}\text{applied fixed}\\ \text{manufacturing cost}\end{pmatrix}}{0.70}$$

Applied fixed manufacturing cost is calculated at \$8 per machine hour used for the product. This figure is based on budgeted fixed manufacturing costs of \$1,200,000 and budgeted machine hours of 150,000. Dividing the total manufacturing cost by 70 percent provides an allowance for selling and administrative expenses and for profit. Selling and administrative expenses are budgeted at \$745,000 fixed plus \$0.08 per sales dollar.

In general, variable manufacturing costs average \$10 per machine hour, but that average does not apply to every product. Inventories are negligible.

REQUIRED

1. Determine the profits that the firm would earn at the following levels of machine hours:
   a. 140,000
   b. 150,000
   c. 160,000
2. Suppose that the firm has 160,000 machine hours available and more demand than it can satisfy. Its managers also believe that the profit calculated in part 1c above is a satisfactory target. However, they wonder whether the pricing formula will yield that profit if the mix of products changes so that variable manufacturing costs per machine hour change. Determine whether the policy would work if variable manufacturing costs dropped to an average of $8 per machine hour.
3. Can you develop a formula that would yield the target profit no matter what variable manufacturing costs become? Assume that the firm can get all the business it can handle at 160,000 machine hours. Remember that the firm makes many different products, and you are developing a formula that should apply to any given product.

9–34 Conversion of Income Statement (CMA) The vice president for sales of Huber Corporation has received the following income statement for November. The statement uses direct costing, which Huber has just adopted for internal reporting purposes.

HUBER CORPORATION
Income Statement for November
(in thousands of dollars)

Sales		$2,400
Less: Standard variable cost of sales		1,200
Manufacturing margin		1,200
Less:		
Fixed manufacturing costs at budget	$600	
Fixed manufacturing cost spending variance	0	600
Gross margin		600
Less: Fixed selling and administrative costs		400
Income before taxes		$ 200

The controller attached the following notes to the income statement: The unit selling price averaged $24, and standard unit manufacturing costs were

Variable costs	$12
Fixed costs	4
Total	$16

The unit rate for fixed manufacturing costs is based on normal production of 150,000 units. Production in November was 45,000 units greater than sales. The November ending inventory was 80,000 units.

REQUIRED

1. The vice president for sales is concerned about the income statement, wondering what it would look like if prepared using absorption costing. Redo the income statement using absorption costing.
2. Reconcile the incomes under direct costing and absorption costing.
3. Tell the vice president of sales what features of direct costing should be useful to her.

9–35 Costing Methods and Profitability Analysis The sales manager of the Jamestown Furniture Company was attempting to analyze the profitability of three models of chairs. The three models accounted for about 35 percent of the firm's total revenues. All three models were manufactured in the Vahalia plant, one of four plants that Jamestown Furniture operated. At the request of the sales manager, a staff member had developed the income statement below from the previous year's operations. Dollar figures are in thousands.

The sales manager was distressed by the figures. She had thought that the Aragon line was profitable and had planned to increase advertising expenditures aimed specifically at increasing its sales. In consultation with the firm's chief cost accountant, she learned that variable factory overhead was about 60 percent of direct labor cost and that variable selling and administrative expenses were about 8 percent of sales revenue, principally for commissions.

She also received the following estimates of fixed costs that were directly associated with each model and could be avoided if the line were dropped. Costs are in thousands of dollars.

		Model		
	Total	*Aragon*	*Balway*	*Dorham*
Unit sales and production	22,780	6,540	11,800	4,440
Revenue	$2,808.3	$1,013.7	$1,062.0	$732.6
Materials and components	526.4	164.8	139.2	222.4
Direct labor	469.8	206.7	180.5	82.6
Factory overhead, 200% of direct labor	939.6	413.4	361.0	165.2
Selling and administrative expenses at 25% of revenue	702.1	253.4	265.5	183.2
Total costs	2,637.9	1,038.3	946.2	653.4
Profit (loss)	$ 170.4	($24.6)	$ 115.8	$ 79.2
Direct fixed factory overhead	$121.4	$46.5	$39.8	$35.1
Direct fixed selling and administrative costs	85.0	36.2	27.5	21.3
Total direct fixed costs	$206.4	$82.7	$67.3	$56.4

REQUIRED

Prepare an income statement for the year using the format shown in Exhibit 9–7. Compare this income statement with the one above from the standpoint of the uses that managers might make of the two statements.

9–36 Variable Costing and Profit Planning (CMA) Jack Stern is a successful investor whose specialty is revitalizing failed businesses. His goal is to maximize profits within the limits of careful use of external financing, which usually means limiting growth rates and foregoing some potential profit. Stern believes this is the key to his success and that unlimited growth can easily lead to fatal financing problems. Stern is once again set to test his approach.

Five years ago, Robert West perfected a technique for joining the edges of laminated plastic parts so that the edges of subsurface layers were not visible. Since subsurface layers are a different color than the surface layer, West's edges greatly improved the appearance of the finished product. West then designed equipment that permitted large volume production of the edges. West's product was unique, and sales and production levels grew rapidly. Rapid growth, however, soon exceeded West's management ability and his ability to obtain financing. A few months ago, West's firm closed, leaving a regional bank holding the plant, equipment, and some inventory.

Stern believes that the product has sales and profit potential and has offered the bank $400,000 in cash plus assumption of the loan for the plant, equipment, and inventory. The bank was only too happy to accept Stern's offer.

Stern has established Edge Company and contributed to it the acquired assets and $450,000 in cash. Edge Company's Statement of Financial Position at the start of business is presented below.

EDGE COMPANY INC.
Statement of Financial Position
as of January 1, 19X7
($000 omitted)

Assets:	
Cash	$ 450
Accounts receivable	0
Inventory	100
Plant and equipment	2,000
Total assets	$2,550
Liabilities and Equities:	
Accounts payable	$ 0
Current portion of long-term debt	90
Long-term debt	1,610
Common stock (no par value)	850
Retained earnings	0
Total liabilities and equities	$2,550

To implement his goal of making conservative use of external financing, Stern has established the following financial objectives:

Paying no dividends, thus keeping all cash generated within the company

Issuing no additional capital stock

Incurring no new long-term debt while servicing current interest and $90,000 of principal annually on the existing bank loan

Keeping the cash balance at no less than $50,000

Taking advantage of supplier credit but not allowing accounts payable to exceed $100,000

The bank's loan officer had commented that West was unable to control costs and working capital, and Stern agreed. He plans to hold variable costs at 75 percent of sales. Even though the existing plant and equipment have a capacity of $12,000,000 in annual sales, Stern's plan is to budget a lump-sum of $500,000 per year for fixed costs, including both depreciation and interest. Depreciation of plant and equipment is $100,000 per year.

In making his plans, Stern has used 20 percent as the average income tax rate applicable to Edge Company. Because some of the firms he acquires have been in income tax trouble, Stern makes a point of keeping tax payments current and aims to finish each year with no tax liability on the books.

Customers for products of this kind are notoriously slow payers; however, Stern is confident that accounts receivable can be kept at 15 percent of annual sales. He also believes that inventories can be maintained at 20 percent of annual variable costs.

Some of West's former sales people have been rehired, and they feel that Edge Company's first year sales could easily reach $5,000,000. But, Stern believes that managing growth is the most important part of the plan, and he plans to limit first year sales to $2,100,000.

REQUIRED

1. Determine whether Jack Stern's financial objectives can be achieved by preparing a pro forma income statement in a variable costing format for the Edge Company for the year ending December 31, 19X7 and a pro forma statement of financial position for Edge Company as of December 31, 19X7. Assume that Jack Stern's projections occur and sales are limited to $2,100,000.
2. Without prejudice to part 1 above, assume that the following results from the company's first fiscal year ending December 31, 19X7 occurred, and that Jack Stern's financial objectives were met.

   Sales: $2,000,000

   Net income: $0

   Cash balance at December 31, 19X7: $60,000

   Accounts payable at December 31, 19X7: $100,000

   Net working capital at December 31, 19X7: $470,000

   Compute the maximum amount by which Edge Company could increase dollar sales in its second year (ending December 31, 19X8) and still achieve Jack Stern's financial objectives.

9–37 Analyzing Income (CMA) Daniels Tool & Die Corporation has been in existence for a little over three years; its sales have been increasing each year as it builds a reputation. The company manufactures dies to its customers' specifications; as a consequence, a job order cost system is employed. Factory overhead is applied to the jobs based on hours, utilizing the absorption (full) costing method. Overapplied or underapplied overhead is treated as an adjustment to cost of goods sold. The company's Income Statements for the last two years are presented on the next page.

Daniels used the same predetermined overhead rate in applying overhead to production orders in both 19X6 and 19X7. The rate was based on the following estimates.

Fixed factory overhead	$25,000
Variable factory overhead	$155,000
Hours	25,000
Direct labor costs	$150,000

In 19X6 and 19X7, actual hours expended were 20,000 and 23,000, respectively. Raw materials put into production were $292,000 in 19X6 and $370,000 in 19X7. Actual fixed overhead was $37,400 for 19X7 and $42,300 for 19X6, and the planned direct labor rate was the direct labor rate achieved.

For both years, all of the reported administrative costs were fixed, while the variable portion of the reported selling expenses result from a commission of five percent of sales revenue.

DANIELS TOOL & DIE CORPORATION
19X6–19X7 Comparative Income Statements

	19X6	19X7
Sales	$840,000	$1,015,000
Cost of goods sold:		
Finished goods, 1/1	25,000	18,000
Cost of goods manufactured	548,000	657,600
Total available	$573,000	$ 675,600
Finished goods, 12/31	18,000	14,000
Cost of goods sold before overhead adjustment	$555,000	$ 661,600
Underapplied factory overhead	36,000	14,400
Cost of goods sold	$591,000	$ 676,000
Gross profit	$249,000	$ 339,000
Selling expenses	82,000	95,000
Administrative expenses	70,000	75,000
Total operating expenses	152,000	170,000
Operating income	$ 97,000	$ 169,000

DANIELS TOOL & DIE CORPORATION
Inventory Balances

	1/1/X6	12/31/X6	12/31/X7
Raw material	$22,000	$30,000	$10,000
Work in process			
Costs	$40,000	$48,000	$64,000
Direct labor hours	1,335	1,600	2,100
Finished goods			
Costs	$25,000	$18,000	$14,000
Direct labor hours	1,450	1,050	820

REQUIRED

1. For the year ended December 31, 19X7, prepare a revised Income Statement for Daniels Tool & Die Corporation utilizing the variable costing method. Be sure to include the contribution margin on your statement.
2. Prepare a numerical reconciliation of the difference in operating income between Daniels Tool & Die Corporation's 19X7 Income Statement prepared on the basis of absorption costing and the revised 19X7 Income Statement prepared on the basis of variable costing.
3. Describe both the advantages and disadvantages of using variable costing.

10

ALLOCATIONS—SUPPORT DEPARTMENTS

Throughout the discussion of product costs for financial accounting that began in Chapter 4, we stressed that both direct and indirect costs are associated with production. All these costs must eventually be associated with units of product to value ending inventories and cost of goods sold. Direct costs are usually associated with operating departments where manufacturing takes place. Indirect costs might be overhead of an operating department or might be associated with departments that support manufacturing, such as engineering, maintenance, plant payroll and benefits, computer services, and janitorial services. None of these departments actually manufactures goods, but they provide services to the operating departments.

Sometimes a cause-and-effect relationship exists between a cost driver and a cost of the support department (cost pool). For example, if the engineering department has a person who works solely on one product, the entire cost of that engineer should be associated with that product. When there is a causal relationship, the main job for managers is to identify the proper cost drivers for a cost pool and use these drivers to assign costs to segments, product lines, or units of product. The difficulty of this task may vary. Chapters 3 and 4 showed how both statistical methods and interviews can be used to help determine relationships.

In many cases, however, support department costs are common to many products and cannot be assigned using a causal cost driver. In such cases, managers must allocate these common costs to become part of the product cost for financial accounting. We reserve the use of the word *allocate* to the division of common costs among different cost objectives. Allocation is used in a more general way by many authors and managers. Any assignment of costs, whether traceable or common, is called allocation by many. However, when we use the term *allocation*, we mean the assignment of common costs only.

The subject of this chapter is the allocation of support department costs as well as a discussion of cost drivers compared to activities used to allocate common costs. Whether costs can be attributed because of a causal relationship or are allocated, all support department costs are divided among units of production to become part of the fully absorbed product cost.

Besides valuing ending inventories and cost of goods sold, there are often other reasons for allocating support department costs. In Chapter 18 on transfer pricing we shall discuss how goods or services provided by one department or segment of a company are priced to other departments within the company. Allocations can be used to determine the cost of a service in order to set such a price. However, as we discussed in Chapter 4, using allocated costs as a measure of "true" costs in a pricing or profitability evaluation can be dangerous.

We shall use the terms *service department* and *support department* to encompass many cost pools, some of which are not really departments at all. For example, depreciation on the plant building is not a department, but represents a service—shelter for manufacturing and other operations.

Most of our discussion to this point has been concerned with **final assignment** of costs; in Chapters 5 and 6 our discussion of how to assign overhead to units of product gave overhead for an operating department. In this chapter we deal with **intermediate assignment/allocation**, the allocation of support department costs to operating departments. The final assignment of costs to units of product follows the intermediate assignment or allocation. The process is shown in Figure 10–1.

The process outlined in Figure 10–1 relates to product costing by business firms and to a great many other situations. Many of the prices that we pay are based on allocated costs, as we shall see shortly. First, we will consider some of the theoretical bases for allocation and one of the principal counterarguments.

ALLOCATIONS: THEORETICAL JUSTIFICATION

The Matching Principle

The theoretical justification for cost allocation comes from the principles of financial accounting, especially the matching principle. The essence of the **matching principle** is that costs should be reported as expenses in the period when they cease to have future benefits. Thus, the cost of merchandise is reported as an expense when the merchandise is sold, because the revenue received from the sale constitutes the benefit. When the benefits of a particular cost are not so directly traceable to particular revenues, the cost is often allo-

FIGURE 10–1 Cost Allocation Process

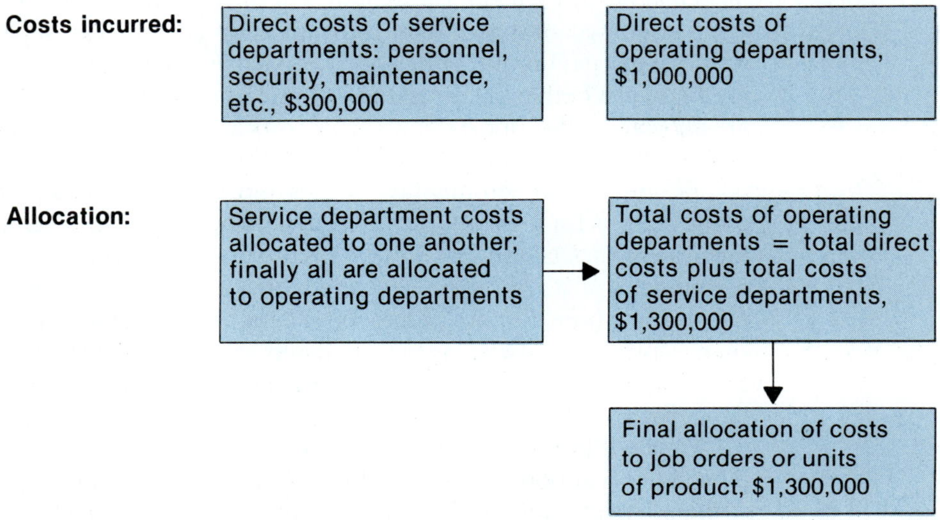

Example: Depreciation on building would be allocated to service departments as well as to operating departments. The amounts allocated to service departments would in turn be allocated to operating departments as part of the cost of a service center.

cated over the periods assumed to be benefited in a rational and systematic manner. Thus, depreciation is the allocation of a cost over an estimated useful economic life—the period over which the firm will benefit from owning the asset.

In a manufacturing situation, the notion that all costs of production should be treated as assets (costs that will provide benefits in the future) has long been recognized, and it forms the basis of the most prominent allocation that accountants make—the allocation of common production costs to units of output. The idea is that all production costs are incurred to produce the firm's output, and so each unit of product receives some benefits from these costs. It follows that each unit of output should be charged with some of the costs. The line of reasoning is sometimes called *costs attach* to denote the position that individual units of product pick up costs as they proceed through manufacturing processes.

Additionally, in the long run the fixed production costs become variable; that is, the firm can build a plant of any size, and it must renew the commitments that cause fixed costs. There is no doubt that fixed production costs and the costs of service departments such as maintenance, engineering, general factory administration, and factory accounting are necessary for the production of the firm's products.

In general, most accountants would accept the position that the costs mentioned above are joint to individual units of product. The costs are required for the firm to produce its products during a period, but they are not specifically traceable to specific units. This is where those who do not accept the allocation of joint costs part company with those who do.

Arbitrariness of Allocations

Whenever we have joint (or common) costs, there is no single perfectly defensible way to assign them. Without a cause-and-effect relationship, managers must find a way of allocating that is *equitable* or *reasonable*. Thus, there are many different ways to allocate a common cost—each considered equitable and reasonable. There is no objective way to choose from among these methods.

In Chapter 11 we discuss the problem of joint product costs. In this case, two or more products are produced using common resources and, therefore, costs. As you shall see, when managers decide how to allocate the common costs to the various products manufactured, there is no way to say that the results are the true costs of each product. At best they are a fair representation of costs. However, another manager might choose a different method of allocation that will result in different unit costs that are also considered equitable.

When a one-to-one relationship exists between a cost pool and a cost objective, there is no allocation problem. If we know that an engineer's time is associated with a particular product, we assign her costs to that product. We would all agree that such an assignment is correct and that there is no alternative way. When there is a many-to-one relationship, the same holds true. Multiple regression may identify several cost drivers that can be used to assign a particular cost pool. Neither one-to-one nor many-to-one relationships require allocation.

However, when we have a one-to-many situation, allocation is required. In this case, we have a cost that must be divided among many cost objectives and there is no causal or statistical relationship to make this division. The division of such a cost, then, is what we mean by *allocation*.[1] Accordingly, allocations of common costs are arbitrary, because we can make them in different ways and no one can win an argument about which method is correct. Nevertheless, accountants must allocate for product costing purposes. There are also some practical reasons for allocating.

---

[1] Arthur L. Thomas has written extensively on the problems of allocations. See "The Allocation Problem in Financial Accounting Theory," *Studies in Accounting Research*, No. 3, Sarasota: American Accounting Association, 1969, and "The Allocation Problem: Part Two," *Studies in Accounting Research*, No. 9, Sarasota: American Accounting Association, 1974.

Managerial Reasons for Allocating

While managers must allocate for product costing purposes, there are also practical reasons. Allocations influence behavior and can, therefore, be useful in achieving objectives. The Portables Group of Tektronix Company provides an interesting case.[2] The Group had been allocating overhead based on direct labor. Engineers and management had driven direct labor down to less than 7 percent of total manufacturing cost, nearly 3 percent on new products. Since overhead costs were high and rising, the overhead rate per direct labor hour was extremely high. Even though direct labor cost was low, the high overhead cost allocated using direct labor made the total labor and labor-related cost so high that it still appeared desirable to continue reducing direct labor. An internal study showed that roughly half of overhead costs related to materials and components. Costs such as purchasing, receiving, inspecting, storage, and recordkeeping were significant. Without an overhead charge on these items, design engineers had no incentive to standardize and reduce components; hence there was a proliferation of components. In fact, engineers were designing in more parts because they could often reduce direct labor.

The Group began to allocate its material-related overhead based on both the number of component parts carried and their annual use. It first determined an average cost per part by taking material-related overhead and dividing it by the total number of different parts (components) used. Each cost per part was divided by the total number of that part used in a year. Say that the cost per part was determined to be $1,000 per year. For a component where 10,000 parts were used annually, this is only $0.10 per unit. However, when only two parts are used, the cost is $500 per unit for that component. Thus, the system made it very expensive to use new components. This encouraged engineers to concentrate on reducing and standardizing parts rather than reducing direct labor. The unit costs should influence designers both to reduce the number of parts in a machine and to use standard, high-volume parts where possible. The managers believe the Group has achieved, and will continue to achieve, significant cost reductions.

Respondents to a study of practices of allocating indirect corporate costs to divisions of companies gave several reasons for making allocations that are relevant here as well as to divisions (which we will consider in Chapter 17).[3] About 90 percent of the companies allocated corporate costs to remind managers that these costs exist and must be covered by operations. About 46 percent said that allocating costs would stimulate managers to whom the allocations were made to pressure the providing managers to control their costs. Finally, 23 percent said that they allocated corporate indirect costs to encourage use of the services. Although these responses were to questions about al-

[2] John W. Jonez and Michael A. Wright, "Material Burdening," *Management Accounting*, August 1987, pp. 27–31.

[3] James M. Fremgen and Shu S. Liao, *The Allocation of Corporate Indirect Costs* (New York, National Association of Accountants, 1981).

locating corporate costs to divisions, the rationale seems applicable to service departments.

The reasons given above are behavioral; the main question in allocating is behavioral. Chapter 9 showed how allocating fixed costs to units of product could result in poor decisions. Yet allocating, or not allocating, can influence the behavior of managers and therefore can be helpful in accomplishing specific purposes. Additionally, allocations pervade modern life and affect our taxes and the prices that we pay, as the next section discusses.

ECONOMIC AND SOCIAL EFFECTS OF ALLOCATIONS

Cost plus pricing, which many business firms use, is one economic consequence of allocations: the prices charged for various products are affected by the allocations. The prices that the federal government pays for goods produced by private firms, especially defense contractors, often include cost allocations as provided under various standards of the Cost Accounting Standards Board. Other examples exist throughout a wide range of entities.

Hospitals are reimbursed under Medicaid and various insurance plans such as Blue Cross according to formulas that include the allocation of indirect costs. Hospitals allocate the costs of service departments such as admissions, medical records, laundry, and maintenance to the departments that provide patient services (surgery, pediatrics, maternity, etc.). In turn, these costs will be allocated to patient-days. State and local governments, universities, community service agencies, and others receive grants-in-aid from the federal government. Sometimes these grants allow for the inclusion of indirect costs in the reimbursement.[4] For example, part of the costs of operating the mayor's office, the central administrative services department, and the personnel department of a city will be charged to a grant that provides assistance to the aged or to juvenile authorities. Selecting one allocation method over another may result in significantly different reimbursements. The allocations have important economic consequences to the entities.

The rates that we pay for electricity, natural gas, and telephone service generally are determined by state utility commissions. Again, allocations are critical. For example, electric utilities (and other utilities) have high fixed operating costs, with fuel being the only significant variable cost. Utilities serve several classes of customers: residences, small businesses, light industry, heavy industry, streetlighting, and so on. The huge fixed investment in generating equipment is used to serve all customers. The investment is often allocated to

[4] See, for example, *A Guide for Non-Profit Institutions: Cost Principles and Procedures for Establishing Indirect Cost and Other Rates for Grants and Contracts with the Department of Health, Education, and Welfare* (Washington: U.S. Department of Health, Education, and Welfare, August 1974). This department is now called Health and Human Services.

various customer classes; then the fixed costs are similarly allocated and variable costs added to the fixed costs for each class. Total costs are subtracted from revenues from each class to obtain an income figure. The income figure for each class is divided by the allocated investment to get a rate of return by customer class. These rates of return are used by the utility management, public service commissions, and interested lobbying groups (household users, industrial users, and so on) to see whether each class is paying its fair share. Requests for increases in rates are advocated and disputed against this background.

The allocation question in rate setting and elsewhere has often been viewed as a cost accounting question, with the emphasis on determining the accuracy of an allocation scheme. However, because all allocations are arbitrary, because there is no such thing as the true cost of, say, providing electricity to homes as compared to businesses, the issues are better addressed from the standpoint of welfare economics and social policy. No one argues that customers should pay only the direct costs of service: someone must pay for the generating capacity, administrative overhead, interest on debt, and so on. What one can say is that we might all be better off if the arbitrariness of allocations and the fact that true costs usually do not exist were acknowledged, so that we could avoid wasting time and effort in arguing about justifying one allocation method versus another.

One final example: corporations pay income taxes to states and cities as well as to the federal government. A firm that operates in several states must allocate some of its costs to the business it does in each state to avoid multiple taxation. Multiple taxation arises if the firm earned, say, a total of \$100,000 and paid income taxes on \$60,000 of income in each of two states because it did not allocate all its costs between the business done in the two states. Obviously, firms would prefer to allocate more cost to business done in states with high tax rates, less to that done in states with low rates. State taxing authorities will sometimes attempt to disallow such allocations, so that multiple taxation may be unavoidable.

In summary, cost allocation is necessary for many purposes. This does not make it any less arbitrary; we must live with it. Some allocations are more reasonable and equitable than others, at least in the sense that those affected (such as utility customers) can agree that one set of allocations is better than another.

TERMINOLOGY

Let us review and expand the terminology introduced in Chapter 4 in the context of allocating support department costs. A cost objective or cost object is the recipient of an allocation, as when an operating department receives a share of support department costs or when a division receives a share of general corporate costs.

A **cost pool** is an amount to be allocated. The costs of a service or support department (such as data processing) that are to be allocated to operating departments constitute such a cost pool. In a different context, the general and administrative expenses of a city might form a cost pool that will be allocated to programs such as public safety, recreation, education, and economic development. Cost pools are developed in many ways and might contain all, or only a part of, the costs of a service department. For example, as we will discuss, the only costs of a maintenance department that wind up being allocated to operating departments might be budgeted costs rather than actual costs. In addition, some costs that are not allowable under reimbursement contracts, such as fund-raising costs of a hospital, might be excluded. Finally, costs that are directly associated (traceable) with a cost objective are so assigned and not allocated.

An **allocation base** is the measure of activity used to make the allocations. This is contrasted to the use of the term *cost driver*, which implies causal relationship. As you can see, measures of activity such as direct labor hours, machine hours, number of set ups, and so on can be used as allocation bases or as cost drivers depending on whether costs are traceable or common. The selection of an allocation base is given a great deal of attention, sometimes much more than it deserves. As we saw earlier, the allocation of costs may confuse rather than enlighten and rarely produces valuable information for planning, control, and decision making. In many cases it makes little difference what allocation base is used, but in others, such as those mentioned at the beginning of the chapter, it can make a significant economic difference to companies, public agencies, and consumers.

Indirect Costs

An allocation is essentially the distribution of indirect costs to cost objects. The contrast is that direct cost can be specifically traced to a cost object, while an **indirect cost** cannot be directly traced to the cost object of current attention. Any cost is direct to *some* cost object, but that cost object might not be the one of interest. For example, the salary of the vice president for production is direct (traceable) to the manufacturing function considered as a whole, but it is indirect (common) with regard to individual factories, departments within factories, and units of product. Costs that are directly associated with a relevant cost object need not be allocated.

Similar costs for different firms might be direct to a production department in one firm, indirect in another. A firm in which maintenance workers are employed by production departments would show their wages as direct to the departments. A firm that has a separate maintenance department would consider the wages as direct to the maintenance department, but indirect to the production departments. Hard-and-fast rules tend to be of little use in accounting in general and in cost accounting in particular. In both firms mentioned above, however, maintenance costs would be indirect to units of product and would have to be allocated to those units.

Cost Objectives

The selection of cost objectives is usually a straightforward process no matter what the entity. For a manufacturer, the ultimate cost objectives are units of product. For a hospital, they are the basic patient services rendered by maternity, medical, surgical, and pediatrics departments. For a defense contractor, they are individual projects or jobs, such as a particular batch of airplanes. Cost objectives might be intermediate or final (ultimate). An **intermediate cost objective** is one to which allocations will be made and from which other allocations will be made.

An example of an intermediate cost objective is a service department such as a computer center. Costs for depreciation on the building and a share of the costs of the personnel department are allocated to the computer center. These costs, as well as the direct costs of operating the center, are then assigned and allocated to other departments. Thus, allocated costs can pass through intermediate cost objectives en route to their final destinations. The full cost developed for a unit of product can include many levels of cost allocation. The complexities in cases such as utility cost allocations to various customer classes become enormous.

Cost Pools

Developing Cost Pools A cost pool might consist of the costs in a single account or in a group of accounts to be allocated using the same basis. Thus, depreciation on a building might be a separate cost pool, or the pool might consist of depreciation as well as other costs. Property taxes, heat and light, building maintenance, and janitorial service might be included along with depreciation in a single cost pool, because they could all reasonably be allocated using the same base such as relative amounts of space occupied.

Cost pools frequently consist of costs incurred by a particular department, especially a support department. Many illustrations of the cost allocation process are drawn from service departments. Additionally, service departments sometimes bring up interesting problems in cost determination and estimation as well as allocation, as we shall see in this chapter.

The amounts in cost pools can be affected by intermediate allocations. Two techniques that we describe later require that costs be allocated from one service department to another. For example, some of the costs of the personnel department can be allocated to the maintenance department and then allocated to various production departments.

Costs Included in Pools Often the costs included in pools are actual, incurred costs, but there are exceptions. Some costs are not allowable under reimbursement contracts and must therefore be excluded. Certain costs of defense contractors are not allowable under regulations of federal government procurement agencies. The effect of excluding costs from pools is that the ultimate allocations to cost objects will be lower than if the costs were allowable. The determination of allowability is a matter between the parties to a contract.

Another instance of excluding costs occurs when only budgeted or standard costs are allocated, while variances are not. The practice of allocating only budgeted or standard costs is wise, because it insulates the operating manager from the inefficiencies of service departments. For example, suppose the maintenance department of a large firm incurs costs of $245,000 during a particular month. The flexible budget allowance for the amount of work done is $228,000. Allocating the $228,000 to the operating departments that used maintenance services makes more sense than allocating the $245,000 because the operating managers are not responsible for the efficiency or inefficiency of the maintenance department. The head of the maintenance department is responsible for the $17,000 variance, and the operating managers should not be penalized (or rewarded) for inefficiencies (or efficiencies) of the maintenance department.

Finally, as Chapter 4 illustrated, traceable costs are assigned directly and removed from the cost pool. Thus, if a support department had total costs of $300,000 and $100,000 were directly traceable, only $200,000 is included in the cost pool to allocate.

Allocation Bases

When costs are traceable, managers should use the cost driver that has a cause and effect with these costs to assign them. Pronouncements of the Cost Accounting Standards Board stress the use of a base that reflects a cause-and-effect relationship or one based on benefits received.[5] The benefits-received criterion as outlined in the CASB Standards is similar to the cause-and-effect criterion. Both require the accountant to look at the activities of the support departments (or, more generally, the cost pools) and of the cost objectives (specific government contracts, for example) to determine how the support department benefits are distributed. However, when we allocate costs, we are saying that there is no clear cut cause-and-effect relationship between an activity and a cost objective. We are reduced to choosing an allocation base that is equitable and reasonable as discussed above.

Bases Commonly Used Some commonly used allocation bases appear below. Some seem perfectly reasonable, others tenuous. To argue that, for example, it makes more sense to allocate building depreciation on the basis of cubic footage occupied rather than square footage is often wasting time and effort. (The argument would run that because some departments, especially production departments, occupy space with very high ceilings to accommodate equipment, they should be charged more than departments that occupy space with ceilings of normal height.) One important point is that allocations must be made and, therefore, that some base must be used.

[5] Cost Accounting Standards Board, Standard No. 403, *Allocation of Home Office Expenses to Segments*, and Standard No. 418, *Allocation of Direct and Indirect Costs*.

Common Bases for Allocation

Cost	*Possible Bases*
Personnel	Number of employees, hours worked, dollar payroll
Data processing	Computer time used
Central purchasing	Number of purchase orders, dollar volume of orders
Telephone	Number of calls, number of telephones
Employee fringe benefits	Dollar payroll, hours worked

Dual Allocation Bases Firms might use two allocation bases—one for variable costs, one for fixed costs. The reasoning is that variable costs can be associated with the current use of a service, whereas fixed costs provide the capacity to render the service. For example, having $220,000 in maintenance equipment does not provide services, but it provides the capacity to provide services that could not be provided without it. When a firm develops the capacity to provide services to its operating departments, it does so with some consideration of the expected long-run use of these services. Because the managers of the operating departments often participate in the decision to develop a particular amount of capacity, it is reasonable to allocate the fixed costs in proportion to their expected long-run use. An example showing how the dual allocation bases work appears below.

Costs of Maintenance Department

Variable	$ 30,000
Fixed	$ 80,000
Total	$110,000

	Operating Departments	
	Fabrication	*Assembly*
Percentage of maintenance service used	30%	70%
Expected long-run average use	40%	60%
Allocations:		
Variable costs, 30%, 70%	$ 9,000	$21,000
Fixed costs, 40%, 60%	32,000	48,000
Total ($110,000 allocated)	$41,000	$69,000

ALLOCATION METHODS FOR SUPPORT DEPARTMENT COSTS

Three general methods are used to allocate support department costs to operating departments. They vary from a simple, direct method to one using reciprocal allocations. While the more complex methods may seem more accurate than the less complex methods, this is not necessarily the case. Since we are allocating (dividing common costs among various cost objectives), accuracy is not the issue. A case can be made, however, that the more complex methods are more equitable and reasonable, but this is a subjective evaluation.

There are times that managers might choose to allocate costs using some of the methods illustrated in this chapter despite some indication of a cause-and-effect relationship. The cost of finding out such a relationship to get more accurate information might outweigh the benefit. We assume that managers will trace costs where it is economically beneficial and will allocate other costs.

The simplest method is the direct method where all costs of a support department are allocated to the operating departments in one procedure. These allocations use the relative shares that each operating department bears to the allocation base. If a service department supports other service departments, no consideration is given to this fact under the direct method. The **step-down** (or **step**) **method** allocates service department costs both to operating departments and to other service departments by proceeding in steps allocating each support department's costs one at a time until all service department costs have been allocated to operating departments. This method gives some recognition to the support that service departments give to other service departments (called *reciprocal services*) but not full recognition. Finally, the **reciprocal method** uses simultaneous equations or matrix operations to give full recognition to reciprocal services. This method is often cited as the ideal.

When causality exists, the reciprocal method is the only correct method to use. While our main focus is on allocation, the reciprocal method can be used not only to allocate common variable costs (or ones that cannot be easily traced to cost objectives) but also as a way of assigning traceable variable support department costs to operating departments.

The first step in applying any method is to determine the amounts in the cost pools and the percentages of service that each service department provides to other departments. The latter determination requires us to select allocation bases for each service department and to find the relative shares of the service that other departments use. Each of the three methods requires somewhat different calculations of these relative shares. We shall illustrate each method using the data in Exhibit 10–1. In all cases, our objective is to allocate *all* of the costs of the service departments to the operating departments.

Notice that no percentages are shown in the cells representing the work done by a service department for itself. For example, no value is entered in the space showing personnel services for the personnel department. If we simply added up the total number of people working in all departments, we would obviously find that some people work in personnel. Similarly, the building services department probably occupies and maintains space, which is the basis used to allocate its costs. We ignore the percentages of work done by departments for themselves—that is, self-service costs. Doing so has both theoretical and practical merit. Thus, there could be 110 employees, of whom ten are in the personnel department, so that the total used to determine the percentages would be 100.

EXHIBIT 10–1 Data for Illustration

Percentages of Service:

	Service Performed For					
	Service Departments			*Operating Departments*		
Service Performed By	*Personnel*	*Plant Administration*	*Building Services*	*Molding*	*Extruding*	*Totals*
Personnel	—	20%	10%	20%	50%	100%
Plant administration	20%	—	—	50%	30%	100%
Building services	15%	10%	—	50%	25%	100%
Direct costs of departments—before allocation	$30,000	$210,000	$80,000	$680,000	$800,000	$1,800,000
Statistical Bases						
Personnel: number of employees[a]	—	20	10	20	50	100
Plant administration: managerial estimates of relative efforts spent on each department, no statistical estimates						
Building services: square footage occupied	3,000	2,000	—	10,000	5,000	20,000

[a]Self-service omitted; see text.

Direct Method

The direct method requires that we determine solely the percentages of service that the operating departments consume, and it ignores those consumed by other service departments. Exhibit 10–1 presents all the percentages of use, so that we must restate the percentages related to the operating departments to allocate all of the service departments' costs. The calculations for the allocations are given, along with the results, in Exhibit 10–2.

The final results—$873,154 total overhead for the molding department, $926,846 for the extruding department—are used to determine the actual overhead rates for the two departments if the firm used actual costing. If the firm used normal costing, these figures are the amounts of actual overhead used to determine overapplied or underapplied overhead. Additionally, the calculations made in Exhibit 10–2 could be done before the period, using budgeted data. The total overhead figures are then used in setting predetermined overhead rates for the two operating departments.

EXHIBIT 10–2 Cost Allocations—Direct Method

	Personnel	Plant Administration	Building Services	Molding	Extruding	Total
Overhead costs before allocation	$30,000	$210,000	$80,000	$680,000	$800,000	$1,800,000
Personnel, 20/70, 50/70[a]	(30,000)			8,571	21,429	
Plant administration, 50%/80%, 30%/80%[a]		(210,000)		131,250	78,750	
Building services, 10,000/15,000, 5,000/15,000[a]			(80,000)	53,333	26,667	
Total				$873,154	$926,846	$1,800,000

[a]The ratios used to determine the allocations are based on the operating departments' relative shares of the use of the service. Thus, for the personnel department, of the 70 employees in the two operating departments, 20 are in molding, 50 in extruding. Plant administration devotes 50 percent of its efforts to the molding department, 30 percent to extruding, for a total of 80 percent.

Step-Down Method

The step-down or simply the step method gives partial recognition to the services that one service department performs for other service departments. The method has a number of variations, but it usually requires as many steps as there are service departments. In our example there will be three steps. In some cases, especially with local governments, step-downs may be done in just two or three steps no matter how many service departments.

To apply the step-down method, begin by allocating the costs of one service department to the other departments that it supports, both service and operating. Then select another service department and allocate its costs, continuing this process until all service department costs have been allocated to the operating departments. Two points must be kept in mind. First, the costs that end up being allocated include not only those incurred by a service department, but also any costs allocated *to* it from other service departments. For example, if service department A incurred costs of $40,000 and has been allocated an additional $5,000 from one or more other service departments, allocate the $45,000 total when department A costs are allocated to other departments. Second, once you have allocated the costs of a particular service department, you do not reallocate any costs back to it. These points should be clear after we go through the example.

A question that arises when the step-down method is used is the order in which the departments will be selected. Should we begin with personnel, with plant administration, or with building services? There are three general rules. One is to select the sequence based on the number of other departments, both service and operating, that the service departments support. Thus, if service department A provides support to two operating departments and one other service department, its costs will be allocated before those of service department B, which supports only one operating department and one service department.

Another criterion is to select departments according to the percentages of their service that go to other service departments. The service departments are ranked in descending order according to these percentages. Thus, if 30 percent of department A's services were consumed by other service departments, and 20 percent of department B's services were consumed by other service departments, the costs of department A would be allocated before those of department B. The rationale is that the costs of the support departments serving other support departments should be allocated first to recognize reciprocal services best.

A third criterion for selecting departments is to take them in descending order of the dollar amounts of their costs before allocation. These last two criteria are often used as tie breakers with the first criterion when two or more service departments support the same number of operating and service departments.

There is a good reason for determining some order of allocation since the step method aims to recognize the services of support departments for other support departments. However, since we are allocating costs, the choice among criteria is based on equity and reasonableness rather than on one criterion being better than another. In many cases no significant difference in allocations is caused by the order of allocating; however, in some situations the order does have a material effect. Therefore, because managers will make a subjective (arbitrary) choice of which allocation method to use and, if using the step method, another arbitrary choice of the order of allocation, they should not place too much value on the resulting allocations when determining cost, deciding on prices, or evaluating profitability. However, some criterion must be used to proceed with the step-down method.

We now use the data from Exhibit 10–1 to allocate the service department costs using the step-down method. We shall use the criterion that departments be selected in descending order of the percentage of their services used by other service departments. Thus, the order is personnel, building services, and plant administration. The results are given in Exhibit 10–3.

As you look at the exhibit, keep the following points in mind. First, once you have allocated the costs of a department, you do not allocate any more costs *to* it. For example, the services provided *to* personnel by the other service departments are ignored, because personnel costs are the first to be allocated. Second, the costs cumulate. The costs allocated from building services include not only its directly incurred costs, but also costs allocated to it from personnel. Similarly, the costs allocated from plant administration include its incurred costs plus the allocations from the other two service departments. Finally, be sure you understand the determination of the percentages used to make the allocations. In each case, they are the percentages from Exhibit 10–1 divided by the total of the percentages of each department to which allocations will be made. This step is easy to check. Make sure that the costs allocated *to* the other

EXHIBIT 10–3 Cost Allocations—Step-Down Method

	Personnel	Building Services	Plant Administration	Molding	Extruding	Total
Overhead costs before allocation	$30,000	$80,000	$210,000	$680,000	$800,000	$1,800,000
Personnel, 20%, 10%, 20%, 50%[a]	(30,000)	3,000	6,000	6,000	15,000	
Building services, 10%/85%, 50%/85%, 25%/85%[a]		(83,000)	9,765	48,824	24,411	
Plant administration, 50%/80%, 30%/80%[a]			(225,765)	141,103	84,662	
Total				$875,927	$924,073	$1,800,000

[a]Percentages: Personnel, from Exhibit 10–1; building services, from Exhibit 10–1, 10 percent to plant administration, 50 percent to molding, 25 percent to extruding, total 85 percent; plant administration, from Exhibit 10–1, 50 percent to molding, 30 percent to extruding.

departments equal the costs allocated *from* the department you are currently handling.

Notice especially that the relative percentages *change* as we move to a different department. For example, plant administration provides 80 percent of its services to operating departments, but because its costs are allocated last, they are all allocated to the operating departments in the operating departments' relative shares of the 80 percent (50%/80% and 30%/80%).

The step-down method improves on the direct method because it at least partially considers reciprocal services. For example, the services that the personnel department provides to the other service departments are considered in the first allocation, but the service that other departments provide to the personnel department is never considered.

Reciprocal Method

The reciprocal method fully considers all reciprocal services, thereby overcoming one problem of the direct and step-down methods. Two techniques can be used: simultaneous equations and matrix inversion. Matrix inversion is a linear algebra technique that has certain advantages over the use of simultaneous equations. It is illustrated below and in Appendix 10A.

In setting up an equation to determine how to allocate the costs of each department we are essentially determining the total costs of the department including the costs of the services provided to them by other service departments. We use the following notation:

P = total costs of the personnel department
A = total costs of the plant administration department
B = total costs of the building services department

These total cost figures include not only the direct costs of operating the departments (for example, the \$30,000 incurred by the personnel department), but also the costs allocable to them from the other service departments. To solve for these total costs, we solve the following equations:

$$(10\text{–}1)\quad P = \$30{,}000 + 0.20A + 0.15B \text{ (personnel)}$$
$$(10\text{–}2)\quad A = \$210{,}000 + 0.20P + 0.10B \text{ (plant administration)}$$
$$(10\text{–}3)\quad B = \$80{,}000 + 0.10P \text{ (building services)}$$

The terms in each of these equations correspond to the *columns* in Exhibit 10–1. The logic of setting up the equations this way requires some discussion. Take the personnel department, which *receives* 20 percent of the services performed by plant administration and 15 percent of those performed by building services. Thus, the total cost to run the personnel department is not just its \$30,000 direct cost, but also 20 percent of plant administration cost and 15 percent of building services cost.

However, both plant administration and building services use the services of the personnel department, and so on. Accordingly, we must solve for the total costs of all departments simultaneously. We have three equations and three unknowns. Solving the three equations simultaneously can be done in various ways. In this case one relatively straightforward method is to substitute the equations for A and B into the equation for P. This substitution gives

$$(10\text{–}1a)\quad P = \$30{,}000 + 0.20[\overbrace{\$210{,}000 + 0.20P + 0.10(\$80{,}000 + 0.10P)}^{\text{equation for } A}] + 0.15(\overbrace{\$80{,}000 + 0.10P}^{\text{equation for } B})$$

Multiplying the terms in parentheses by the coefficients gives

$$(10\text{–}1b)\quad P = \$30{,}000 + \$42{,}000 + 0.04P + \$1{,}600 + 0.002P + \$12{,}000 + 0.015P$$

Collecting terms gives

$$(10\text{–}1c)\quad 0.943P = \$85{,}600 \qquad P = \$90{,}774.13$$

We now solve for A and B, using the value for P. Beginning with B, we have

$$(10\text{–}3a)\quad \begin{aligned} B &= \$80{,}000 + 0.10P \\ &= \$80{,}000 + 9{,}077.41 \\ &= \$89{,}077.41 \end{aligned}$$

Solving for A:

$$(10\text{–}2a)\quad \begin{aligned} A &= \$210{,}000 + 0.20P + 0.10B \\ &= \$210{,}000 + \$18{,}154.83 + \$8{,}907.74 \\ &= \$237{,}062.57 \end{aligned}$$

EXHIBIT 10–4 Final Cost Allocations—Reciprocal Method

	Combined Service Departments	*Molding*	*Extruding*	*Total*
Costs before allocation	$320,000	$680,000	$800,000	$1,800,000
Allocations (to nearest dollar):				
Personnel				
($90,774 × 0.20)		18,155		
($90,774 × 0.50)			45,387	
Plant administration				
($237,063 × 0.50)		118,531		
($237,063 × 0.30)			71,119	
Building services				
($89,077 × 0.50)		44,539		
($89,077 × 0.25)			22,269	
Total		$861,225	$938,775	$1,800,000

As we noted before, each of these costs exceeds the direct costs of each department. The personnel department total cost of $90,774 is more than three times its direct costs of $30,000.

When we allocate these costs to the operating departments, we must use the percentages originally given in Exhibit 10–1 without adjusting them. Since 30 percent of the personnel department costs have already been allocated to service departments, we allocate 20 percent of the personnel department's costs of $90,774 to the molding department and the remaining 50 percent to the extruding department. The allocations are given in Exhibit 10–4. Note that this procedure results in the correct total of $1,800,000 in overhead costs (both direct and allocated) shown for the operating departments.

Exhibit 10–4 provides complete data for the allocation of costs to the operating departments. Exhibit 10–5 shows the full reciprocal allocation to support and operating departments, and illustrates how to use matrix algebra with reciprocal allocations. An explanation of this method is included in Appendix 10A. Besides exploring the use of the matrix method, use Exhibit 10–5 as a way to verify that the results in Exhibit 10–4 are correct. Each entry is the final service department cost figure multiplied by the percentages in Exhibit 10–1, which are reproduced in Exhibit 10–5.

Evaluation of Methods

Let us stress that these three methods are used to allocate common service department costs to operating departments. Thus, we are saying that there is no way we can assign these costs based on a causal relationship. One of these methods, the reciprocal method, however, is used for variable service depart-

EXHIBIT 10–5 Intermediate and Final Cost Allocations—Reciprocal Method (Matrix Approach)

1. Set up equations that reflect original costs and percentages.

$$\begin{aligned} P &= \$30{,}000 \qquad\qquad\quad + 0.20A + 0.15B \\ A &= \$210{,}000 + 0.20P \qquad\qquad + 0.10B \\ B &= \$80{,}000 \;\; + 0.10P \end{aligned}$$

2. Rearrange equations to equal original cost.

$$\begin{aligned} P - 0.20A - 0.15B &= \$\ 30{,}000 \\ -0.20P + A - 0.10B &= \$210{,}000 \\ -0.10P + B &= \$\ 80{,}000 \end{aligned}$$

3. Put into matrix form (see Appendix 10A).

$$\underset{A}{\begin{bmatrix} 1 & -0.20 & -0.15 \\ -0.20 & 1 & -0.10 \\ -0.10 & 0.00 & 1 \end{bmatrix}} \underset{x}{\begin{bmatrix} P \\ A \\ B \end{bmatrix}} = \underset{b}{\begin{bmatrix} \$\ 30{,}000 \\ 210{,}000 \\ 80{,}000 \end{bmatrix}}$$

4. Find inverse of matrix A and multiply by matrix b.[a]

$$\underset{A^{-1}}{\begin{bmatrix} 1.0604 & 0.2121 & 0.1803 \\ 0.2227 & 1.0445 & 0.1379 \\ 0.1060 & 0.0212 & 1.0180 \end{bmatrix}} \underset{b}{\begin{bmatrix} \$\ 30{,}000 \\ 210{,}000 \\ 80{,}000 \end{bmatrix}} = \underset{x}{\begin{bmatrix} \$\ 90{,}774 \\ 237{,}063 \\ 89{,}077 \end{bmatrix}}$$

5. Use the percentages in Exhibit 10–1 and the solution above (or that found by using simultaneous equations) and allocate costs to the support and to the operating departments.

	Personnel	*Plant Administration*	*Building Services*	*Molding*	*Extruding*	*Total*
Costs before allocation	$30,000	$210,000	$80,000	$680,000	$800,000	$1,800,000
Allocations:						
Personnel	(90,774)	18,155	9,077	18,155	45,387	
Plant administration	47,413	(237,063)		118,531	71,119	
Building services	13,361	8,908	(89,077)	44,539	22,269	
Total	0	0	0	$861,225	$938,775	$1,800,000

		Work Done for					
Work Done By	*Cost*	*Personnel*	*Plant Administration*	*Building Services*	*Molding*	*Extruding*	*Total*
Personnel	$ 90,774	—	0.20	0.10	0.20	0.50	1.00
Plant administration	237,063	0.20	—	—	0.50	0.30	1.00
Building services	89,077	0.15	0.10	—	0.50	0.25	1.00

[a] Matrix inversion and multiplication are easily performed using an electronic spreadsheet.

ment costs when there is a traceable relationship for these costs among the support and operating departments. This topic will be covered later. If we are discussing how to allocate common fixed costs, then, the choice among the methods is usually inconsequential so long as the allocations are not used for reimbursement, pricing, and other decision making purposes.

As earlier chapters have pointed out, allocating fixed costs is undesirable for planning, control, and decision making. If fixed costs are allocated by any of the methods described and if managers use those allocated costs for managerial purposes, they will be committing a serious error. If the allocated fixed costs are used only for product costing purposes, any of the methods can be used without providing misleading information. The same comment applies to selecting bases for allocation and to grouping departmental costs into cost pools. As long as we are considering only fixed costs, there is no correct method of allocating these costs for managerial purposes. Throughout this book we have discussed the theoretical issues leading to this conclusion.

In general, then, the criteria to be used for selecting an allocation method depend on whether traceable costs are included in the cost pools. If not, then the basic criterion is the cost to the firm of using one method rather than another. The direct method is the easiest to apply and, therefore, the cheapest, but the use of computers makes it relatively easy and cheap to employ the reciprocal method. The step-down method may not be costly to use, but the decisions required on the sequence in which departments are selected make its use sometimes seem arbitrary. Of course, any allocation of common costs is arbitrary, but if the method is consistently applied, there may be less irritation to managers than if it is changed at frequent intervals.

SERVICE DEPARTMENTS WITH VARIABLE COSTS

A special problem exists when support departments have variable costs and provide service to other support departments. The true variable cost to operate such departments includes not only the direct variable costs, but also a portion of the variable costs from the supporting departments. In this case, we are not dealing with allocation but with a cause-and-effect relationship. The reciprocal method determines the true variable costs and reflects the interdependence of the service and operating departments. This matter is best addressed by an example using information from Exhibit 10–6.

Illustration: Thornton Company

The data in Exhibit 10–6 describe the operations of Thornton Company during a typical month. Maintenance and power are service departments, while fabrication and assembly are operating departments. All cost data are for variable costs only.

The $9 and $2 variable cost per unit figures could be used for planning,

EXHIBIT 10–6 Thornton Company

Units of Work and Percentages:

Work Done By	Work Done For: Maintenance	Power	Fabrication	Assembly	Total
Maintenance, in hours	0	100 (10%)	700 (70%)	200 (20%)	1,000 (100%)
Power, in kilowatt hours	400 (20%)	0	1,200 (60%)	400 (20%)	2,000 (100%)

Technological Requirements:

Each hour of maintenance requires the use of 0.40 kwh of power (400/1,000), since the 1,000 hours of maintenance work required the consumption of 400 kwh. By the same reasoning, each kilowatt hour of power requires 0.05 hour of maintenance (100/2,000).

Cost Data:

	Direct Variable Cost per Unit	Total for Period
Maintenance	\$9/hr	\$9,000
Power	\$2/kwh	\$4,000

control, and decision making if not for the reciprocal relationships. That is, if maintenance and power were not dependent on one another, increasing maintenance by one hour would increase maintenance cost by \$9. However, if we increase maintenance, we must also increase power, which in turn increases maintenance, and so on. Therefore, the variable cost figures required for planning must be determined by solving simultaneous equations to determine the total costs of the two departments.

Proceeding as before, we set up equations for each department's cost:

$$M = \$9{,}000 + 0.20P \qquad (10\text{–}4)$$

$$P = \$4{,}000 + 0.10M \qquad (10\text{–}5)$$

where M = total costs of the maintenance department
P = total costs of the power department

Substituting the equation for P into the equation for M:

$$\begin{aligned} M &= \$9{,}000 + 0.20(\$4{,}000 + 0.10M) \\ 0.98M &= \$9{,}800 \\ M &= \$10{,}000 \end{aligned} \qquad (10\text{–}4a)$$

Solving for P,

$$\begin{aligned} P &= \$4{,}000 + 0.10(\$10{,}000) \\ P &= \$5{,}000 \end{aligned} \qquad (10\text{–}5a)$$

Dividing these adjusted total costs by the outputs of each department gives new variable cost per unit figures, which we shall call **adjusted variable costs**:

$$\text{maintenance} = \$10(\$10{,}000/1{,}000)$$
$$\text{power} = \$2.50(\$5{,}000/2{,}000)$$

These adjusted variable costs are the relevant ones for planning and decision making, as we now illustrate.[6]

Illustration: External Versus Internal Purchase

Suppose the firm could buy its power from an outside company for $2.50/kwh. If our calculations of the adjusted variable costs are correct, the firm should incur the same total direct costs of $13,000 ($9,000 + $4,000) for the two activities. If power is bought outside, the firm no longer needs the services that the maintenance department provides to the power department. Therefore, total maintenance time will be 900 hours (700 for fabrication, 200 for assembly) at the current level of activity of the operating departments. The total power requirements will be 1,600 kwh for the operating departments, plus 0.40 kwh per hour of maintenance. (See the technological requirements section of Exhibit 10–6.) In equation form, letting K = required number of kilowatt hours of power,

$$K = 1{,}600 + 0.40(900)$$
$$K = 1{,}960$$

The total direct variable cost is then $13,000, as shown below:

Maintenance, 900 × $9	$ 8,100
Power (bought from outside source), 1,960 × $2.50	4,900
Total	$13,000

If power is bought internally, the adjusted variable costs of $10 and $2.50 for maintenance hours and kilowatt hours of power are relevant to any decision in which the activity of one department is to be increased, so long as the technological relationships (0.40 kwh per hour of maintenance and 0.05 hour of maintenance per kilowatt hour of power) are expected to hold.

The allocations of the service department costs to the operating departments are also relevant for planning and decision making. These allocations

---

[6] Alternatively, we could solve directly for the variable costs using the following equations:

$$V_M = \$9 + 0.40V_P, \quad V_P = \$2 + 0.05V_M$$

where V_M is the variable cost per hour of maintenance and V_P is the variable cost per kilowatt hour of power. (Each hour of maintenance requires 0.40 kwh. Each kilowatt hour requires 0.05 hr of maintenance.) Replacing the equation for power with the equation for maintenance, we get:

$$V_M = \$9 + 0.40(\$2 + 0.05V_M)$$
$$0.98V_M = \$9.80$$
$$V_M = \$10$$
$$V_P = \$2.50$$

are given below. Figures come from Exhibit 10–6 and from the new, total variable costs calculated above.

	Fabrication	Assembly
Maintenance:		
700 × \$10	\$ 7,000	
200 × \$10		\$2,000
Power:		
1200 × \$2.50	3,000	
400 × \$2.50		1,000
Totals	\$10,000	\$3,000

Suppose that the managers use the \$9 and \$2 figures for planning. Suppose further that the manager of one operating department is considering a change in operations that will increase maintenance requirements by 100 hours per month but save \$950 in other costs. If he uses the \$9 variable cost, he will make the change, because there will be a \$50 monthly saving [\$950 – (100 × \$9)]. But if maintenance requirements in an operating department increase by 100 hours, power requirements of the maintenance department increase. In turn, because maintenance serves power, maintenance requirements will increase further. We can show that the actual cost increase will be \$1,000 (100 × \$10), using the following equations:

$$M' = 100 + 0.05P' \quad (10\text{–}6)$$
$$P' = 0.40M' \quad (10\text{–}7)$$

where M' = the total increase in maintenance hours
P' = the total increase in kilowatt hours of power

The relationships of 0.40 kwh per hour of maintenance and 0.05 hour of maintenance per kilowatt hour were given above. Solving by substituting (10–6) into (10–7) gives:

$$M' = 100 + 0.05(0.40M')$$
$$0.98M' = 100$$
$$M' = 102.04 \text{ (rounded)}$$
$$P' = 40.82 \text{ (rounded)}$$

Using the direct variable costs of \$9 and \$2 gives a total cost increase of \$1,000 [(102.04 × \$9) + (40.82 × \$2)], which is the same result we would get using the \$10 adjusted variable cost for maintenance.

BEHAVIORAL CONSIDERATIONS OF ALLOCATIONS

Earlier chapters stressed the principle of controllability—that managers should be held responsible only for what they can control. Managers cannot control allocated common costs, and so these costs should not be shown on a manager's performance reports. There is no reason that costs allocated for product costing purposes must appear on performance reports. It is possible, then, to allocate for product costing but not for control and performance evaluation.

Some accountants and other managers take the position that managers who receive services (benefit from the activities of service departments) should bear some of the cost of those services. They argue that cost allocations are therefore appropriate for performance reporting. The question is whether the costs that are allocated to operating departments are a reasonable reflection of the benefits that managers receive from the service departments.

Capacity and Current Use

In most cases, fixed assets are put into place based on capacity needs. For example, a mainframe computer purchase analysis would include the long-term capacity needs for that equipment. In any particular year, use might be at or under the capacity of the equipment. While it is important to separate traceable and common costs, for the many reasons we have outlined, the idea of fixed capacity costs versus variable operating costs exemplifies what can happen if both costs are treated as if they were common. In such a case, each department's share of support department costs depends on the use of other departments. This is in contrast to charging a department only for costs based on its use of a service. An example clarifies this point.

Monthly service department costs are \$100,000 + \$5/hour.

	Operating Departments	
	Molding	*Finishing*
Use of service, January	1,000 hr	2,000 hr
February	1,000	1,000

If allocations were made on the basis of relative use, January would show:

	Molding	*Finishing*
Variable Costs	\$ 5,000	\$10,000
Fixed Costs	33,333	66,667
Total	\$38,333	\$76,667

And February would show:

Variable Costs	\$ 5,000	\$ 5,000
Fixed Costs	50,000	50,000
Total	\$55,000	\$55,000

The molding department received a higher allocation in February than in January solely because of the increased allocation of fixed costs under the relative share allocation base. If traceable variable costs had been assigned based on current use and fixed costs allocated based on capacity requirements over the long run, the only change in the costs shown for the operating departments from month to month would be the result of using more or fewer hours, and it would be shown solely in how variable costs were assigned.

Whenever an allocation scheme involves the allocation of fixed costs on the basis of actual relative use of the service, managers will find that their allocations differ because of the actions of other managers. This situation is undesirable. Managers might postpone using the service for fear that the allocation will be high in a particular month, even though it might be desirable to use it. For example, postponing of maintenance services may be detrimental to the department and the firm in the long run but might be commonplace because managers wish to keep down their allocated costs.

An additional way to avoid behavioral problems in allocating costs is to allocate standard or budgeted costs, rather than actual costs, as discussed earlier in this chapter (pages 440–441). The use of standard or budgeted costs for allocations does not penalize (reward) the operating manager for inefficiencies (efficiencies) of the service departments. Variances between actual and standard or budgeted costs are left with the service department as far as performance evaluation is concerned, although they may be allocated to products through operating departments for product costing purposes.

Transfer Prices

Some firms do not use cost allocations for performance evaluation. Instead they use **transfer prices**, which are preset charges for goods or services provided by one segment of the firm to another. Instead of allocating some dollar amounts based on the costs of the service departments, the providing department charges the consuming department for the services. The price might be based on the market price that the segment would have to pay to obtain the service, and such prices might add up to a great deal more than the cost of running the service department.

Transfer prices are discussed in detail in Chapter 18. They are especially prevalent in decentralized companies where operating divisions deal with one another as well as with outside firms. We are interested here in how transfer prices can help us with the problems of allocating actual, budgeted, or standard costs.

Transfer prices can be valuable from a behavioral standpoint, especially if they approximate market prices. A manager who buys a service from another department in the firm might feel better about it knowing that it would cost about the same to buy the service outside. In some firms, managers who believe they can get the service cheaper outside are permitted to do so. So if the computer center charges $80 per hour for computing time, and time on a similar machine costs $70 from an outside firm, managers can buy the service outside.

A 1987 study provides an excellent description of the use of the concept of artificial profit centers. Weyerhauser Company uses a "charge-back" system to encourage control of corporate overhead costs. These costs are incurred principally for the benefit of operating units such as Weyerhauser's paper and forest products companies.[7]

Weyerhauser requires corporate service departments to charge all of their costs to users of their services. For example, the Financial Services Department charges for services such as general accounting, salaries payroll, accounts payable, and accounts receivable. The bases vary depending on the type of activity; for instance, charges for accounts receivable are based on invoice volume, weighted for special requirements that require hand processing, and the number of customers. General Accounting charges are based on separate rates for three types of employee: analytical, clerical, and systems. Preparing reports and employee assistance incur charges. Users are free to acquire the services from corporate departments or outside.

One result of the charge-back system is that service department managers have become profit conscious. The Information Services Department was once essentially a mainframe operation. Users were able to get equivalent service cheaper from outsiders or microcomputers, resulting in a loss of business for the department. The department then began to reduce costs and to seek outside business to make up the deficiency.

Weyerhauser managers see several benefits for this technique, which is similar to artificial profit centers. By paying for services, operating managers ratify the decisions of service department managers: if the services are not worthwhile, the service department will not charge back all of its costs. Thus, service departments must act as if the operating departments are customers; they cannot simply do what they wish because they will not be paid for unwanted services. A greater spirit of teamwork among line and staff departments also exists because they must cooperate in determining what services to provide and at what cost.

So long as transfer prices approximate market prices, they satisfy the criterion that managers should be charged for the services from which they receive benefits. Moreover, the use of transfer prices rather than allocated costs entails that managers who do not use the service do not pay for it. Transfer prices are charged only for services used, whereas allocations are frequently based on other criteria, so that even if managers make little or no actual use of a service, they receive allocations of its costs.

Another important advantage of transfer prices over cost allocations is that they can be used to encourage or discourage the use of various services. By setting the transfer price of, say, maintenance time very low, upper level managers encourage department managers to use the service more than they otherwise would. If regular maintenance is highly desirable, the low transfer price will have a favorable behavioral impact. If managers begin to overuse a

---

[7] H. Thomas Johnson and Dennis A. Loewe, "How Weyerhauser Manages Corporate Overhead Costs," *Management Accounting*, August 1987, pp. 20–26.

service because of a low transfer price, upper level management may raise the price to discourage increases in use. This kind of flexibility is not available with cost allocations.

Finally, it is important to note that product costing requires cost allocation and that transfer prices generally are not appropriate in that context. Transfer pricing is used for motivation and performance measurement, but usually not explicitly for product costing or income tax accounting. The reason is that financial reporting is based on the cost principle, and transfer prices do not necessarily approximate costs.

SUMMARY

Cost allocations are the assignment of common costs to various cost objects. Such allocations are necessary to establish full product costs for financial reporting. In addition, at other times fully absorbed costs are needed or useful in pricing various goods and services. Accountants are interested in allocations since they are necessary at times. However, the essence of the renewed interest in more accurate cost of products is the elimination of as many allocations as possible. Including allocated costs might cause managers to make decisions that are not consistent with economic reality.

Several methods are commonly used to allocate service department costs to operating departments. The direct method fails to consider the services that departments provide each other, while the step-down method partially recognizes them. The reciprocal method fully recognizes services performed by one department for another. It is especially valuable when service department costs are variable; in this case, the method is the attribution of costs with a cause-and-effect relationship rather than an allocation.

Cost allocations can affect the behavior of managers. Upper level management may decide to use transfer prices for services, rather than allocating costs. Transfer prices can be used to encourage or discourage the use of services as upper level managers desire.

REVIEW PROBLEM

Tarragon Manufacturing Company has two production departments and three service departments. Data appear below.

	Service Provided To				
Service Provided By	*Personnel*	*Power*	*Administration*	*Machining*	*Assembly*
Personnel	0%	5%	10%	40%	45%
Power	5%	0%	10%	50%	35%
Administration	10%	10%	0%	60%	20%
Direct costs	$500	$1,200	$900	$4,000	$3,500

REQUIRED

1. Allocate the service department costs and find the total costs of the operating departments using the direct method. Allocate to the nearest dollar.
2. Repeat part 1 using the step method in the following sequence: administration, personnel, power.

ANSWERS TO REVIEW PROBLEM

1.

	Machining	*Assembly*	*Total*
Personnel (40/85, 45/85)	$ 235	$ 265	$ 500
Power (50/85, 35/85)	706	494	1,200
Administration (60/80, 20/80)	675	225	900
Total	$1,616	$ 984	$ 2,600
Direct costs	4,000	3,500	7,500
Total costs	$5,616	$4,484	$10,100

2.

	Administration	*Personnel*	*Power*	*Machining*	*Assembly*	*Total*
Direct costs	$900	$500	$1,200	$4,000	$3,500	$10,100
Administration (10%, 10%, 60%, 20%)	(900)	90	90	540	180	
Personnel (5/90, 40/90, 445/90)		(590)	33	262	295	
Power (50/85, 35/85)			(1,323)	778	545	
Total				$5,580	$4,520	$10,100

APPENDIX 10A: MATRIX SOLUTIONS

Matrix algebra techniques provided significant advantages over the use of simultaneous equations in solving problems of cost allocation and, in the case of variable support department costs, of determining adjusted variable costs. Electronic spreadsheet programs make the actual matrix manipulation simple. We will use the problem on pages 452–454 to show both the manual way to set up and use matrices and how to employ electronic spreadsheets. In the following we employ a more general notation than we used in the chapter.

S_1 = costs of the maintenance department
S_2 = costs of the power department

The first step in setting up the problem for matrix solution is to rearrange the original equations:

$$S_1 = \$9{,}000 + 0.20S_2$$
$$S_2 = \$4{,}000 + 0.10S_1$$

to read

$$\begin{aligned} S_1 - 0.20S_2 &= \$9{,}000 \\ -0.10S_1 + \qquad S_2 &= \$4{,}000 \end{aligned}$$

That is, S_1 and S_2 appear in the same columns. In matrix algebra, the equations above are solved using the following format. The coefficients of S_1 and S_2 form a matrix, A, the values for S_1 and S_2 (the solution) form a column vector, x, and the direct costs of the departments form another column vector, b. In matrix notation:

$$\overset{A}{\begin{bmatrix} 1 & -0.20 \\ -0.10 & 1 \end{bmatrix}} \overset{x}{\begin{bmatrix} S_1 \\ S_2 \end{bmatrix}} = \overset{b}{\begin{bmatrix} \$9{,}000 \\ \$4{,}000 \end{bmatrix}}$$

That is, the vector x multiplied by the matrix A gives the vector b. To solve, we multiply both sides of the equation by A^{-1}, the inverse of the matrix A:

$$A^{-1}Ax = A^{-1}b$$

The inverse of a matrix multiplied by the original matrix gives an identity matrix, I, which has ones along the main diagonal (upper left through lower right) and zeros elsewhere. Therefore $A^{-1}A$ is $\left[\begin{smallmatrix} 1 & 0 \\ 0 & 1 \end{smallmatrix}\right]$ in this case. Multiplying a vector by the identity matrix leaves the vector unchanged, so that $Ix = x$. Therefore $A^{-1}b = x$.

Determining the inverse of a matrix can be time consuming. However, when the matrix to be inverted is 2×2 (2 rows, 2 columns) with ones along the main diagonal, as is our matrix A, the procedure is simple and quick. It will not work for a 2×2 matrix without ones on the main diagonal.

Step 1. Subtract from 1 the product of the off-diagonal elements (upper right element multiplied by lower left element). In our example, the result is 0.98 $[1 - (-0.20 \times -0.10)]$.

Step 2. Change the signs of the off-diagonal elements and divide all elements by the result from step 1. The result is the inverse:

$$\overset{A^{-1}}{\begin{bmatrix} 1/0.98 & 0.20/0.98 \\ 0.10/0.98 & 1/0.98 \end{bmatrix}}$$

which equals

$$\overset{A^{-1}}{\begin{bmatrix} 1.0204 & 0.2041 \\ 0.1020 & 1.0204 \end{bmatrix}}$$

We can now solve for the vector x using matrix multiplication.[8]

[8] S_1 = \$10,000 from $(1.204 \times \$9{,}000) + (0.2041 \times \$4{,}000)$.
S_2 = \$5,000 from $(0.1020 \times \$9{,}000) + (1.204 \times \$4{,}000)$.

$$\overset{A^{-1}}{\begin{bmatrix} 1.0204 & 0.2041 \\ 0.1020 & 1.0204 \end{bmatrix}} \overset{b}{\begin{bmatrix} \$9{,}000 \\ \$4{,}000 \end{bmatrix}} = \overset{x}{\begin{bmatrix} \$10{,}000 \\ \$\ 5{,}000 \end{bmatrix}}$$

The allocations to the operating departments are simply the adjusted costs multiplied by the percentages of each service consumed by each operating department:

$$\begin{aligned} \text{fabrication} &= \$10{,}000 = (\$10{,}000 \times 70\%) + (\$5{,}000 \times 60\%) \\ \text{assembly} &= \$3{,}000 = (\$10{,}000 \times 20\%) + (\$5{,}000 \times 20\%) \end{aligned}$$

Once you have determined the A and b matrices, you can employ an electronic spreadsheet to solve the matrix inverse (A^{-1}) and then multiply A^{-1} by b to get x. Working with a 2×2 matrix is relatively straightforward. If there were, say, 6 service departments, finding the inverse by hand is difficult to say the least. Consult the instructions for the electronic spreadsheet program you are using to see how to do matrix inversion and matrix multiplication. Use the example in Exhibit 10–5 to check yourself on how to set up proper matrices and use programs for inversion and multiplication.

The elements on the main diagonal of A^{-1} have special significance. Divided into the corresponding elements of x, they give the savings in cost that would come from eliminating the department. Thus, they give the maximum amount that the firm could pay to obtain the service outside without reducing profits. This assumes that the level of operations would remain the same. For S_2, which we showed in the chapter had incremental costs of \$4,900 (page 453), we obtain

$$\$5{,}000/1.0204 = \$4{,}900$$

and for S_1

$$\$10{,}000/1.0204 = \$9{,}800$$

In applying this technique, remember that the corresponding elements must be used. In the 2×2 case, both elements on the main diagonal are the same. The 1.0204 we used above for S_2 is the lower right element. Thus, the element to use is the one in the same row as the cost you are considering. When the matrix is 3×3 or greater, the same values will probably not show all along the main diagonal.

Let us consider our example from a different standpoint. So far we have worked with percentages of service provided to other departments and with total units of service provided. These data, from Exhibit 10–6, may come from observation of the results for a period or from planning prior to a period. In the latter case, the percentages and totals would have to be derived from unit data regarding the operating departments' requirements for services as well as the service departments' requirements for services. The data in Exhibit 10A–1 relate to the technological requirements of a single unit of product. We use P_1 to refer to the fabrication department, P_2 for the assembly department.

EXHIBIT 10A–1 Technological Requirements

Units of Product

Two hours in each operating department.

Operating Department Requirements

Requirements per hour of time in operating department:

	P_1	P_2
S_1	0.35	0.10
S_2	0.60	0.20

Service Department Requirements

From Exhibit 10–6:

		Consuming Department	
		S_1	S_2
Providing	S_1	0	0.05
Department	S_2	0.40	0

Our first objective is to determine the amounts of service required from S_1 and S_2 to make a single unit of product. The direct requirements of service to the operating departments are simply the requirements in Exhibit 10A–1 multiplied by the hours of operating time required to make a unit of product. The reciprocal service department requirements also come from Exhibit 10A–1. Letting S_1' = units of service department 1, S_2' = units of service department 2, P_1 and P_2 = the times in operating departments 1 and 2 per unit of product, we have

$$S_1' = 0.35P_1 + 0.10P_2 + 0.05S_2'$$
$$S_2' = 0.60P_1 + 0.20P_2 + 0.40S_1'$$

Because both P_1 and P_2 are 2 hours per unit of product, we have

$$S_1' = 0.90 + 0.05S_2' \qquad [0.90 = (0.35)(2) + (0.10)(2)]$$
$$S_2' = 1.60 + 0.40S_1' \qquad [1.60 = (0.60)(2) + (0.20)(2)]$$

Restating in matrix form:

$$\overset{B}{\begin{bmatrix} 1 & -0.05 \\ -0.40 & 1 \end{bmatrix}} \overset{x}{\begin{bmatrix} S_1' \\ S_2' \end{bmatrix}} = \overset{b}{\begin{bmatrix} 0.90 \\ 1.60 \end{bmatrix}}$$

Solving by finding B^{-1} and multiplying by b:

$$\overset{B^{-1}}{\begin{bmatrix} 1.0204 & 0.051 \\ 0.4082 & 1.0204 \end{bmatrix}} \overset{b}{\begin{bmatrix} 0.90 \\ 1.60 \end{bmatrix}} = \overset{x}{\begin{bmatrix} 1 \\ 2 \end{bmatrix}}$$

This result means that one unit of S_1 and two units of S_2 are needed to make one unit of product. These values include the reciprocal requirements of $0.05S_1$ per unit of S_2 and $0.40S_2$ per unit of S_1. The total service department variable cost per unit of product is \$13. That amount can be obtained by multiplying the final values of x given above by the direct variable costs of \$9 and \$2 [(1 × \$9) + (2 × \$2)] or by multiplying the final variable costs of \$10 and \$2.50 by the b vector [(0.90 × \$10) + (1.60 × \$2.50)]. The difference between this solution technique and the one shown earlier lies in the statement of the problem. Here, we dealt directly with the technological coefficients required; earlier we dealt with percentages of service. The earlier method can be used only when the results for a period are known, so that one can determine the percentages of reciprocal service.

The matrix inverse may also be used to determine the total requirements of the service departments at any level of activity. The values for the b vector are simply the requirements for service department work at the expected level of output ($0.90S_1$ and $1.60S_2$ per unit of product) multiplied by the inverse.

It may seem a waste of time to invert a 2 × 2 matrix rather than simply to solve two simultaneous equations. However, as noted before, the matrix inverse gives some information that the other method of solution does not. Additionally, in realistic situations (say, 8 to 20 service departments), solving by matrix inversion is more efficient and is the method used by many computer programs. A large system of simultaneous equations may take hours to solve by hand, but milliseconds by computer.

ASSIGNMENTS

10–1 Service and Administrative Costs (CMA Adapted) An organization's service and administrative costs can be substantial, and some or all of these costs are usually allocated to cost objects. Thus, the allocation of service and administrative costs can have a significant impact on product cost and pricing, asset valuation, and segment profitability.

The National Association of Accountants has issued **Statement on Management Accounting (SMA) Number 4B**, "Allocation of Service and Administrative Costs," to help management accountants deal with the problems associated with the allocation of service and administrative costs. This statement identifies three general types of cost construction or allocation objectives: full cost, responsibility cost, and differential cost. When service and administrative costs are allocated to cost objects, some allocation base must be selected. **SMA Number 4B** identifies four criteria in selecting a specific allocation base—benefit, cause, fairness, and ability to bear the costs.

REQUIRED

1. What are service and administrative costs?
2. When service and administrative costs are allocated, the costs are first grouped into homogeneous pools and then allocated to cost objects according to some allocation base.
   a. Explain "homogeneous pools" and "cost objects."
   b. Compare and contrast the benefit and cause criteria for selecting an allocation base.
   c. Explain the "ability to bear costs" criterion for selecting an allocation base and discuss why this criterion has limited use.
3. Organizations that follow a full cost construction would allocate service and administrative costs to applicable cost objects.
   a. Explain "full cost."
   b. Identify circumstances under which the full cost construction is appropriate.
4. When an organization follows a responsibility cost construction, service and administrative costs are not usually allocated. However, there may be situations when the allocation of such costs would be appropriate.
   a. Identify the situations under responsibility cost construction when the allocation of service and administrative costs is acceptable.
   b. Discuss the reasons why service and administrative costs should not be allocated to responsibility cost centers.
   c. If service and administrative costs are allocated to responsibility centers, explain how the costs should be reported.

10–2 Allocating Travel Costs Jim Brodsky is a senior accounting major at State University who is inverviewing for a job. His home is in the same city as the university. He has been invited to make office visits to two firms over the Christmas vacation. Barton & Co. wants him to visit its Cleveland office, while Thurston, McIlvaine would like him to visit its Detroit office. From Jim's home, the round-trip air fare to Cleveland is $240 and to Detroit is $350. Jim can get a round-trip ticket to go to both cities on the same trip for $440.

REQUIRED

Make a recommendation as to how Barton & Co. and Thurston, McIlvaine should split the air fare.

10–3 Cost Allocation Galco Industries allocates indirect costs to departments and product lines using direct labor hours as the basis. The allocations for 19X5 are based on 400,000 direct labor hours and $1,910,000 indirect costs. Data related to one product line, cleaners, and to all others as a group, for 19X5 follow.

	Totals	*Cleaners*	*All Others*
Direct labor hours	400,000	50,000	350,000

REQUIRED

Allocate the indirect costs to cleaners and to the others using direct labor hours as the basis.

10–4 Multiple Activity Bases (continuation of Assignment 10–3) The managers of Galco are convinced that they need several bases to reflect the activities that drive their indirect costs. After careful study, the controller developed the following information regarding cost pools and activities that drive the pools.

Cost Driver	Amount of Activity	Amount of Related Indirect Costs
Labor hours	400,000 hours	$1,580,000
Recordkeeping	150,000 entries	180,000
Number of parts	4,000 parts	150,000
Total indirect costs		$1,910,000

Data related to one product line, cleaners, and to all others as a group, for 19X5 follow.

	Totals	Cleaners	All Others
Direct labor hours	400,000	50,000	350,000
Record-keeping entries	150,000	6,000	144,000
Number of parts	4,000	100	3,900

REQUIRED

1. Assign each group of costs separately to cleaners and to the group of others using the separate bases.
2. The company sells 30,000 cases of cleaners annually. Its direct costs are $16.50 per unit. Calculate the total per case costs using your results from this assignment and the previous assignment. Comment on the difference.

10–5 Importance of Cost Allocations Several years ago, a syndicated columnist wrote about a case that the federal government was developing against one of the largest firms in the United States. The columnist made the following points, attributed to inside sources from the federal government:

1. The company used "a bit of bookkeeping sleight-of-hand" that resulted in placing the "entire burden of its research and development costs, both foreign and domestic, on its United States operations." The U.S. operations included sales to the federal government.
2. The company also allocated "an overly generous amount for selling and marketing expenses which, by rights, should have been allocated to its non-governmental domestic operations."
3. The result was that the company was able to "boost the price of products sold to the government." The firm's "allegedly inflated costs" made it appear that it was earning less than it actually was.

The column included the terms *price gouging*, *profit hype*, and *excess profits*.

REQUIRED

Comment on the issues involved in cost plus pricing and on the implications of the statements given above.

10–6 Basic Cost Allocation Barner Company makes several products in a single factory that has two operating departments and three service departments. The controller is developing overhead rates for the operating departments and has asked for your assistance. Budgeted data for the coming year appear follow. "S" means service department.

	Square Feet	*Employees*	*Total Direct Overhead Costs Before Allocation*
Fabrication	900	40	$265,000
Assembly	2,000	80	420,000
Building Services (S)	100	20	165,000
Personnel (S)	200	20	90,000
Administration (S)	900	30	320,000

The controller believes that the correct bases for allocation are: Building Services, square footage; Personnel and Administration, employees.

REQUIRED

1. Allocate the service department costs using the direct method. Determine the total costs that the controller will use to set the overhead rates for each operating department.
2. Allocate the service department costs using the step-down method. The sequence you should follow is the percentage of service given to other service departments. (Begin with the service department that provides the greatest percentage of its services to other service departments.)

10–7 Step-Down Allocation The controller of Plainview Manufacturing Company has prepared the following information related to operations for 19X6.

	Operating Departments		
	Milling	*Refining*	*Finishing*
Direct labor hours	141,000	235,000	162,000
Direct labor cost	$1,385,000	$2,416,000	$1,586,000
Direct overhead	$2,740,000	$1,934,200	$1,017,000

Using various allocation bases, the controller developed the following estimates of percentages of service department effort devoted to other departments.

	Service Departments		
Percentages of Effort to Other Departments	*Personnel*	*Administration*	*Engineering*
Personnel	0%	5%	0%
Administration	10	0	8
Engineering	8	11	0
Milling	17	21	38
Refining	41	35	34
Finishing	24	28	20
Service department costs	$165,000	$486,000	$292,000

REQUIRED

Allocate the service department costs, using the step-down method. Begin with the department that performs the largest percentage of service for other service departments. Determine the total overhead rates per labor hour for each operating department after all allocations.

10–8 Reciprocal Method During February Cronin Company experienced the following results.

Percentage of Work Performed For	Service Department		
	Maintenance	*Engineering*	*Administration*
Maintenance	0%	10%	15%
Engineering	5%	0%	10%
Administration	5%	0%	0%
Milling	60%	40%	45%
Machining	30%	50%	30%
Totals	100%	100%	100%

The service department direct costs were: maintenance, \$60,000; engineering, \$90,000; administration, \$200,000.

REQUIRED

Assign the service department costs to the operating departments, using the reciprocal method.

10–9 Allocating Fixed Costs Managers of the operating departments of Morton Company have been unhappy with the allocation of power costs. Several years ago the firm built its own generating unit, which now supplies all the power the plant needs. The costs of generating power are allocated to the operating departments based on their relative use, which has created some problems, because the allocation to each department depends on the use it makes of power and also on the use that other departments make.

Variable costs of generating power are about \$0.03 per kilowatt hour, and monthly fixed costs are about \$320,000. The generating plant has monthly capacity of 500,000 kwh, and the operating departments have the following use:

	Department		
	Foundry	*Machining*	*Coating*
Average monthly use	200,000 kwh	180,000 kwh	80,000 kwh
Maximum monthly use	230,000	190,000	120,000

The controller has been thinking of using the average or maximum monthly needs as the basis for allocating the fixed portion of power costs, with variable costs assigned on the basis of actual use. The peak loads in each department do not occur in the same months, so the 500,000-kwh capacity is sufficient.

REQUIRED

1. Determine the amount of monthly fixed cost that would be allocated to each operating department, using their average requirements as the basis.

2. Determine the amount of monthly fixed cost that would be allocated to each department, using the maximum requirements as the basis.
3. Which basis, average or maximum, would you recommend? What are the arguments for and against your choice?

10–10 Charges for Joint Services Bill Cameron, a tax accountant with Culbertson & Co., was assigned to research a particularly complicated and relatively rare problem for a client. When Cameron was about halfway through the research, Ms. Culbertson informed him that another client had a similar problem and asked him to extend the scope of his efforts. Cameron spent 100 hours on the project, about 80 of which related to the original problem, 20 to the extension. Cameron estimated that the second client's problem would have required about 60 hours had he not done the work on the original problem. Cameron's hourly rate is $40.

REQUIRED

Suggest a fair allocation of charges to the two clients.

10–11 Variable Service Department Costs The Rock Ridge Plant of York Steel Company is located in a remote area near a major source of iron ore. There are also several coal mines nearby, which are also owned by York. The plant has its own electrical generating equipment, which uses some of the coal.

The plant requires 250,000 tons of coal and 10,000,000 kilowatt hours of electricity for the steelmaking process. Additionally, each 100 kwh of electricity require 1 ton of coal, and mining 1 ton of coal uses about 10 kwh. The variable cost to produce a kilowatt hour, apart from the cost of coal, is $0.10, and the variable cost to mine a ton of coal, apart from the cost of electricity, is about $8.

REQUIRED

1. Determine the total annual requirements of coal and electricity for the steelmaking process.
2. Determine the total variable cost per ton of coal and per kilowatt hour of electricity.

10–12 Service Department Allocations (AICPA) Hartwell Company distributes service department overhead costs directly to producing departments without allocation to the other service departments. Information for January appears below.

	Maintenance	*Utilities*
Overhead costs incurred	$18,700	$9,000
Services provided to:		
Maintenance department	—	10%
Utilities department	20%	—
Producing department A	40%	30%
Producing department B	40%	60%

REQUIRED

1. Determine the amounts of service department costs that Hartwell would allocate to each producing department.
2. Repeat part 1 assuming that Hartwell elects to use the step-down method, first allocating the costs of the utilities department.

3. Write the equations necessary to allocate the service department costs using the reciprocal method and determine the amounts of service department cost allocated to each producing department.

4. Is any of these methods more accurate than any other? What conditions would have to exist to support your answer?

10–13 Reciprocal Attribution (AICPA Adapted) 4N Company has two service departments (designated below as S_1 and S_2) and three production departments (designated as P_1, P_2, and P_3). The schedule below shows overhead directly attributable to each department, along with the percentages of service that each service department performs for other departments.

Service Department	Percentages to Be Allocated to Departments: S_1	S_2	P_1	P_2	P_3
S_1	0	10%	20%	40%	30%
S_2	20%	0	50	10	20
Overhead before allocation	$98,000	$117,600	$1,400,000	$2,100,000	$640,000

The firm uses the reciprocal method to assign costs.

REQUIRED

Determine the amounts of cost attributed to each production department.

10–14 Allocations and Behavior Clifford Electronics operates a single plant. Clifford allocates indirect costs to departments and then to product lines based on their direct labor content. Each department concentrates on one product line. The cost of an average unit of one of its major lines, made in Department Z, appears below. The data relate to a recent month when the company made 50,000 units of the product line.

Materials and components	$ 90
Direct labor at $12 per hour	24
Indirect costs at 500% of direct labor	120
Total cost	$234

The indirect cost rate of 500 percent of direct labor cost is based on actual total indirect costs divided by the $2,000,000 total company-wide labor cost for the most recent month. Because of the high combined labor and indirect costs, the department manager urged the Design Engineering Department to work on reducing the labor time in the product. The engineers did a great deal of redesigning that resulted in a 25 percent reduction in labor time over a six month period, largely by using more costly parts and components that required less time to assemble. The department manager was then surprised to see the following analysis for the sixth month of the program, when production was 50,000 units.

Materials and components	$ 95
Direct labor at $12	18
Indirect costs at 650% of direct labor	117
Total cost	$230

The manager was aghast and could not understand why such a concentrated effort had shown so little payoff. The manager of engineering was also distressed. The most disappointing aspect was the sharp increase in the indirect cost rate. The manager decided to determine its cause. He learned that total labor hours for the company decreased about 10 percent over the six month period because other departments were also trying to reduce labor costs.

REQUIRED

1. Determine total indirect costs allocated to the product line in each month.
2. What reasons might exist for the disappointing results?

10–15 Allocations and Behavior (continuation of Assignment 10–14) The controller of Clifford Electronics was well aware of the problems created by its use of direct labor to allocate all indirect costs. She did considerable analysis and developed the following plant-wide pools of average monthly indirect costs, as they related to particular cost drivers.

Activity	*Amount of Activity*	*Amount of Related Indirect Costs*
Labor cost	$ 3,480,000	$ 9,880,000
Recordkeeping	2,400,000 entries	840,000
Materials	$48,000,000 cost of materials	11,350,000
Engineering hours	4,000 hours	770,000
Total indirect costs		$22,840,000

The controller noted that using direct labor cost to allocate the indirect costs gave a rate of about 650 percent, as Department Z experienced in a previous month. That is, $22,840,000/$3,480,000 = 656 percent. She wanted to see how the assignment of costs would change using these four bases instead of just direct labor. She collected the following data for the line described in the preceding assignment.

Labor cost	$ 900,000
Recordkeeping	400,000 entries
Cost of materials used	$4,750,000
Engineering hours	300 hours

REQUIRED

1. Calculate the rate per unit of activity for each group of indirect costs.
2. Use the rates calculated in part 1 to determine the assignment of indirect costs to Department Z's product line separately using the four bases. Determine the unit cost of the average product in Department Z's line using the new allocations.
3. Comment on the differences between this scheme and one that uses only direct labor cost.

10–16 Cost Accounting Standards Board Allocation Method Cost Accounting Standard No. 403, *Allocation of Home Office Expenses to Segments*, sets up an allocation scheme for home office expenses that cannot be allocated to segments (departments, plants, divisions) on some basis of benefits or causality. The method works in the following way.

You determine the percentages that each segment has to the total of each of (1) total payroll, (2) operating revenues, and (3) tangible capital assets plus inventories. These percentages are then added together and divided by 3 to get an unweighted average. The segment then receives an allocation equal to the total cost to be allocated multiplied by the unweighted average percentage.

For example, if a plant has 20 percent of total firm payroll, 15 percent of revenues, and 30 percent of tangible capital assets plus inventories, its share of the "residual," or leftover home office expenses, will be 21.667 percent, calculated as 65% (20% + 15% + 30%) divided by 3.

Note that the expenses allocated in the manner described are residual expenses, those that cannot be reasonably allocated in some other fashion. The Board stated that such expenses should be relatively low and should consist primarily of such items as the expenses associated with "the chief executive, the chief financial officer, and any staff which are not identifiable with specific activities of segments."

The General Militronics Corp. home office had the following 19X6 expenses:

Data processing	$2,500,000
Central purchasing	800,000
General corporate staff and officers	940,000

Data related to the firm's three divisions are (in millions).

Division	Operating Revenue	Payroll	Material Purchases	Tangible Capital Assets Plus Inventories	Data Processing Transactions
Instruments	$26.4	$14.2	$ 8.6	$19.0	2,700
Vehicles	55.0	22.1	19.6	28.0	4,500
Armament	17.3	6.3	7.8	9.5	800

REQUIRED

Allocate the three home office expenses in conformity with the CASB Standard.

10–17 Matrix Solution (Appendix) You instructed your assistant to develop a matrix solution to your cost attribution problem. Because he had not worked with the reciprocal method, you wrote out the following equations and told him to use a computer program that solves matrix problems.

$$S_1 = \$120{,}000 + 0.20S_2 + 0.15S_3$$
$$S_2 = \$176{,}000 + 0.05S_1 + 0.25S_3$$
$$S_3 = \$103{,}000 + 0.20S_1 + 0.15S_2$$

where S_1, S_2, and S_3 represent the costs of the service departments.

REQUIRED

1. Set up the equations in matrix form.
2. Find the inverse of the matrix using Lotus 1-2-3 or a similar program.
3. Determine the final amounts of costs of each service department.
4. Suppose that all the service department costs are variable. Determine the amount that the firm could save if it were able to eliminate each of the departments.

10–18 Fairness of Cost Allocations Mr. Able employed a landscaper who came to his house each Monday to mow the lawn, trim the hedges, and do other work. Able paid $20 per week for the service. One day Mr. Baker, who lived next door to Able, asked the landscaper how much he would charge to do his lawn work. The landscaper said that he would do it for $17 per week if he had to come on a day other than Monday. However, he told both Able and Baker that he would do both of their yards for $30 in total if he could do them on the same day. That would save him a trip.

Able and Baker agreed to accept the offer to do both yards for $30 per week. They were unsure how much each should pay and came to you for advice.

REQUIRED

List a few fair ways that Able and Baker could split the $30 cost.

10–19 Cost Allocations—Revenue Base Sweeten Company has three managers, each in charge of a separate product line. The firm's practice is to allocate joint costs to the product lines using revenue as the base. The firm had the following results in two recent months, in thousands:

		Product Line		
		Suits	*Sweaters*	*Accessories*
June Results:				
Revenues		$400	$200	$300
Direct costs (variable and separable fixed costs)		180	90	120
Product margin		$220	$110	$180
Total joint costs	$450			
July Results:				
Revenues		$400	$300	$300
Direct costs		180	160	120
Product margin		$220	$140	$180
Total joint costs	$450			

The manager of the sweater line conducted a promotional campaign in July and also lowered selling prices to increase the product margin.

REQUIRED

1. Allocate the joint costs to product lines for June and July and determine the income figure for each line in each month.
2. Comment on the practice of using revenue as the allocation basis.

10–20 Joint Costs and Pricing The Town of Nacandaga is in a resort area. About 3,000 of the 10,000 houses in the town are owned by people who occupy them only during the summer season, which runs for about four months.

The town water company supplies virtually every house in the town. The charge for water has always been a flat rate per 1,000 gallons: it is currently $3.50/1,000. Recently some of the year-round residents have begun to complain that the summer residents do not carry a fair share of the costs of the water company. The town does not have a minimum monthly charge, so that the summer residents pay only during the time that they occupy their houses and use water.

The town controller has developed the following information:

Variable cost of water	$0.20 per 1,000 gal
Annual fixed costs	$2,500,000
Annual consumption	780,000,000 gal

The water company is expected to break even each year, not to show a profit.

REQUIRED

Devise a pricing method that you consider fair and equitable. State the reasoning that you used in developing the method.

10–21 Dual Allocation Rates Brinson Company operates its own electric power plant. In the past, the controller has allocated the costs of generating power to the users (other departments of the firm) based on their relative actual use each month. One result has been widely fluctuating allocations, in part caused by the high fixed costs of the plant and the wide variations in monthly use. The controller has decided to try a different scheme, assigning variable costs based on actual use and fixed costs based on expected long-term use. Data that the controller has developed appear below.

Variable cost per kilowatt hour		$0.40
Monthly fixed costs	$1,500,000	
Expected long-term use:		
Department I		20%
Department II		40%
Department III		40%
Use during a recent month:		
Department I		60,000 kwh
Department II		90,000 kwh
Department III		100,000 kwh

REQUIRED

1. Determine the total costs of the electric power department for the month described and assign the costs to the departments, using the relative actual use basis.
2. Assign the costs to the departments, using the controller's proposed method.
3. Which basis seems better to you? Why?

10–22 Allocations and Behavior[9] Resnick Company has just installed a Wide Area Telephone Service (WATS) line that costs $1,200 per month, but there is no charge for each individual call. Because only one call at a time can be made, people frequently have to wait to use the line. Only a few people in the company are permitted to use the regular long-distance service if the WATS line is busy. Before the WATS line was installed, Resnick's monthly long-distance bill averaged $2,400.

When it came time to decide how to allocate the $1,200 among departments (production, marketing, personnel, etc.) there was considerable disagreement. Some argued that because there was no variable cost per call, there should be no allocation at

[9] Jerold L. Zimmerman, "The Costs and Benefits of Cost Allocations," *The Accounting Review*, 54:3 (July 1979), pp. 504–521, analyzes the effects of a similar example.

all. Others felt that the $1,200 should be allocated based on the expected long-term use of the service. Still others argued that the cost should be allocated based on actual use each month.

Actual use averages about 120 hours per month (about 75% of total working hours in a month).

REQUIRED

1. Discuss the issues involved, especially the likely behavioral consequences of different allocation (or nonallocation) schemes. Make a recommendation.
2. Suppose now that the telephone company charged $400 per month plus $0.20 per minute to use the WATS line. How, if at all, would your recommendation change?
3. Finally, suppose that the company acquired a toll-free number for incoming calls (800 number) instead of a WATS line. The line permits customers to call in for free, but does not allow outgoing calls. Because the line serves all of the company's product lines, there is the question whether, and how, to allocate the cost to product lines. Discuss the issues and make a recommendation.

10–23 Cost Allocation and Pricing for Not-for-Profit Entity The city of Anderson is about to begin charging for its trash collection service. Previously, the city had financed the service from general revenues, but the Anderson City Council has decided that the customers should pay for the service. The city manager has developed the following information from various records:

Total annual tons collected		10,000
Number of customers:		
Business	1,000	
Residential	11,000	
Total annual costs:		
Salaries and wages		$350,000
Gas, oil, maintenance on trucks		160,000
Depreciation, insurance on trucks		20,000
Total costs		$530,000

The city collects trash from each business twice a week (Mondays and Thursdays). It collects trash from each residential customer once a week and makes all these collections on Tuesdays, Wednesdays, and Fridays. About 60 percent of the total amount of trash is collected from businesses. The trucks drive about 200,000 total miles per year. Because businesses are concentrated closer together than residences, only about 10 percent of the mileage relates to business collections. The city manager believes that all costs are essentially fixed, with the exception of the gas, oil, and maintenance of the trucks, which varies with the number of miles that they drive.

The city council wants the operation to recover costs but not to show any appreciable profit or loss.

REQUIRED

You have been hired by the City Council as a consultant. Use the guidelines for memorandum preparation in Appendix B and write a memorandum to the City Council in which you:

1. Show the price per week that customers would pay if the charge were based on the number of collections.

2. Show the price per week that each class (business and residential) would pay if the charge were based on the amount of trash collected for each class.
3. Show the price per week that each class would pay if the charge were based on two factors: (a) a charge for miles driven to collect each class's trash and (b) a charge based on the amount of trash collected. The first part of the charge should recover the variable costs; the second part should cover the fixed costs.
4. Finally, develop a proposal for setting prices that you think is fair to both classes. Provide an adequate rationale for your proposal.

10–24 Variable Service Department Costs During March the following results occurred in the operations of the Kimball Company:

Service Performed By	Percentage of Service Performed For				
	Power	Engineering	Foundry	Grinding	Total
Power	0	20%	30%	50%	100%
Engineering	25%	0	60%	15%	100%

The variable costs of the service departments are: power, $30,000; engineering, $50,000. The total quantities for the service departments are: power, 200,000 kwh; engineering, 4,000 hours.

REQUIRED

1. Determine the total variable costs of each service department and the "adjusted variable cost" per unit of service for each service department.
2. Determine the amounts of variable service department costs attributed to each production department.
3. Show that if the firm buys power from an outside supplier at the variable cost per kilowatt hour that you calculated in part 1, it will show the same total variable costs for power and engineering that it now does ($80,000). Remember that the firm will not need to provide engineering services to obtain power and that its power requirements will be lowered because the engineering department will need less power.

10–25 Homogeneity of Cost Pools The Cost Accounting Standards Board requires that government contractors accumulate indirect costs in homogeneous pools and allocate the costs in the pools to the final cost objectives "in reasonable proportion to the beneficial or causal relationship of the pooled costs to cost objectives. . . ." (See *Cost Accounting Standard No. 418*.) The following data relate to a firm that has a single contract with a governmental agency, contract A:

	Fabrication Department	Assembly Department	Totals
Labor cost at $8/hr	$2,400,000	$4,000,000	$6,400,000
Indirect costs	$4,800,000	$2,000,000	$6,800,000
Indirect cost rate per labor dollar	$2	$0.50	$1.0625
Labor cost on contract A	$100,000	$800,000	$900,000

REQUIRED

1. Allocate the indirect costs to contract A, using the plant-wide rate.
2. Allocate the indirect costs to contract A, using the departmental rates.

10–26 Multiple Bases (CMA Adapted) Herbert Manufacturing Company uses a job order accounting system. Overhead consists primarily of supervision, employee benefits, maintenance costs, property taxes, and depreciation and is applied on the basis of actual direct labor hours required for each product.

During October, Herbert added a new product line, furniture for fast-food restaurants, to its line of custom restaurant furniture. Management has been analyzing the results for January through September and comparing them to the results for October. These results are indicated below (in thousands):

HERBERT MANUFACTURING COMPANY

	Fast-Food Furniture	Custom Furniture	Consolidated
Nine months, year to date, 19X8:			
Gross Sales	—	$8,100	$8,100
Direct Material	—	$2,025	$2,025
Direct Labor:			
Forming	—	758	758
Finishing	—	1,314	1,314
Assembly	—	558	558
Overhead	—	1,779	1,779
Cost of Sales	—	$6,434	$6,434
Gross Profit	—	$1,666	$1,666
Gross Profit Percentage	—	20.6%	20.6%
October, 19X8:			
Gross Sales	$400	$ 900	$1,300
Direct Material	$200	$ 225	$ 425
Direct Labor:			
Forming	17	$ 82	99
Finishing	40	142	182
Assembly	33	60	93
Overhead	60	180	240
Cost of Sales	$350	$ 689	$1,039
Gross Profit	$ 50	$ 211	$ 261
Gross Profit Percentage	12.5%	23.4%	20.1%

Management has been discussing whether allocation of overhead based on direct labor hours continues to be appropriate. The accounting manager has suggested that supervision and employee benefits should be allocated on direct labor hours but that the balance of the costs seem more machine related and should be assigned based on machine hours.

The actual direct labor hours and machine hours for October are

	Fast-Food Furniture	Custom Furniture
Machine Hours:		
Forming	660	10,700
Finishing	660	7,780
	1,320	18,480
Direct Labor Hours:		
Forming	1,900	9,300
Finishing	3,350	12,000
Assembly	4,750	8,700
	10,000	30,000

Supervision and employee benefits totaled $108,000 in October, and the balance of the overhead items totaled $132,000.

REQUIRED

1. Reassign October overhead according to the accounting manager's recommendation.
2. Based on your results in part 1, recalculate gross profits and gross profit percentages for October. What conclusions can you draw from this analysis?

10–27 Cost Assignment Formulas in Budget Appropriations The vice president for administration of NMC Company recently issued the following directives regarding the staffing of the firm's personnel department and general administration department.

> The authorized size of the personnel department is to be determined as follows: The department shall have 50 employees for every 1,000 production workers and 20 employees for every 1,000 nonproduction employees. Employees of the personnel department shall count as nonproduction employees for the purpose of this calculation.
>
> The authorized size of the general administration department shall be 100 employees for every 1,000 production workers and 60 employees for every 1,000 nonproduction employees. However, the employees of the general administration department shall *not* be counted for the purpose of this calculation.

This states that the size of the personnel department depends in part on itself, because its employees are counted in determining its authorized size. However, the size of the general administration department is not affected by its own size, but only by the sizes of the other departments.

REQUIRED

1. Assume that the firm has 100,000 production workers. Determine the authorized size of the personnel department and of the general administration department.
2. Assume that the costs of operating the personnel department are $100,000, those of the general administration department $200,000. Further, assume that the firm has 50,000 workers in each of two production departments, I and II. Use the reciprocal method to assign the costs of the two service departments. The basis for the assignments is the number of employees in each service department serving the other departments. Remember that the

personnel department has employees who serve itself, and you should ignore them in determining the percentages.

10–28 Revenue Centers and Reimbursements The administrator of Burrows Hospital has been grappling with some problems associated with reimbursements under a medical insurance plan. Although the hospital can charge patients whatever rates it chooses, its reimbursements under the plan, for patients covered by it, are limited by the following formula:

$$\text{total annual reimbursement} = \text{total annual cost} \times \frac{\text{charges to covered patients}}{\text{total charges to patients}}$$

The total annual cost figure is the annual cost of each revenue center. The hospital currently treats the following departments as revenue centers: medical/surgical, outpatient emergency room. The total annual cost figure includes costs allocated from non-revenue centers such as admissions, dietary, administration, and building depreciation.

The administrator has developed the following information about the medical/surgical department, in thousands of dollars:

	Total	*Medical*	*Surgical*
Total annual costs	$300,000	$100,000	$200,000
Total patient charges	400,000	120,000	280,000
Charges to covered patients	80,000	60,000	20,000

The hospital now considers medical/surgical to be a single department. The figures above for each of the types of service are the ones that would be used if the department were separated into two revenue centers.

REQUIRED

1. Calculate the reimbursement that the hospital would receive if it treated the medical and surgical services as a single revenue center (the present practice).
2. Calculate the reimbursement when each service is treated as a separate revenue center.

10–29 Assignment of Costs (CMA) Bonn Company recently reorganized its computer and data processing activities. The small installations located within the accounting departments at its plants and subsidiaries have been replaced with a single data processing department at corporate headquarters responsible for the operations of a newly acquired large-scale computer system. The new department has been in operation for two years and has been producing reliable and timely data for the past twelve months.

Because the department has focused its activities on converting applications to the new system and producing reports for the plant and subsidiary managements, little attention has been devoted to the costs of the department. Now that the department's activities are operating relatively smoothly, company management has requested that the departmental manager recommend a cost accumulation system to facilitate cost control and the development of suitable rates to charge users for service.

For the past two years, the departmental costs have been recorded in one account. The costs have then been allocated to user departments on the basis of computer time used. The schedule below reports the costs and charging rate for 19X5.

DATA PROCESSING DEPARTMENT
Costs for the Year Ended December 31, 19X5

(1) Salaries and benefits	$ 622,600
(2) Supplies	40,000
(3) Equipment maintenance contract	15,000
(4) Insurance	25,000
(5) Heat and air conditioning	36,000
(6) Electricity	50,000
(7) Equipment and furniture depreciation	285,400
(8) Building improvements depreciation	10,000
(9) Building occupancy and security	39,300
(10) Corporate administrative charges	52,700
Total costs	$1,176,000
Computer hours for user processing[a]	2,750
Hourly rate ($1,176,000 ÷ 2,750)	$ 428

[a] Use of available computer hours:

Testing and debugging programs	250
Set up of jobs	500
Processing jobs	2,750
Down time for maintenance	750
Idle time	742
	4,992

The department manager recommends that the department costs be accumulated by five activity centers within the department: Systems Analysis, Programming, Data Preparation, Computer Operations (processing), and Administration. He then suggests that the costs of the Administration activity should be assigned to the other four activity centers before a separate rate for charging users is developed for each of the first four activities.

After reviewing the details of the accounts, the manager made the following observations regarding the charges to the several subsidiary accounts within the department:

1. Salaries and benefits—records the salary and benefit costs of all employees in the department.
2. Supplies—records punch card costs, paper costs for printers, and a small amount for miscellaneous other costs.
3. Equipment maintenance contracts—records charges for maintenance contracts; all equipment is covered by maintenance contracts.
4. Insurance—records cost of insurance covering the equipment and the furniture.
5. Heat and air conditioning—records a charge from the corporate heating and air-conditioning department estimated to be the incremental costs to meet the special needs of the computer department.
6. Electricity—records the charge for electricity based on a separate meter within the department.
7. Equipment and furniture depreciation—records the depreciation charges for all owned equipment and furniture within the department.

8. Building improvements—records the amortization charges for the building changes required to provide proper environmental control and electrical service for the computer equipment.
9. Building occupancy and security—records the computer department's share of the depreciation, maintenance, heat, and security costs of the building; these costs are allocated to the department on the basis of square feet occupied.
10. Corporate administrative charges—records the computer department's share of the corporate administrative costs. They are allocated to the department on the basis of number of employees in the department.

REQUIRED

1. For each of the ten cost items, state whether or not it should be distributed to the five activity centers, and for each cost item that should be distributed, recommend the basis on which it should be distributed. Justify your conclusion in each case.
2. Assume the costs of the Computer Operations (processing) activity will be charged to the user departments on the basis of computer hours. Using the analysis of computer utilization shown as a footnote to the department cost schedule presented in the problem, determine the total number of hours that should be employed to determine the charging rate for Computer Operations (processing). Justify your answer.

10–30 Alternative Allocations and Attributions (AICPA) Thrift-Shops, Inc., operates three food stores in a state that recently enacted legislation permitting municipalities within the state to levy an income tax on corporations operating within their respective municipalities. The legislation establishes a uniform tax rate that the municipalities may levy, and regulations that provide that the tax is to be computed on income derived within the taxing municipality after a reasonable and consistent allocation of general overhead expenses. General overhead expenses have not been allocated to individual stores previously and include warehouse, general office, advertising, and delivery expenses.

Each of the municipalities in which Thrift-Shops, Inc., operates a store has levied the corporate income tax as provided by state legislation, and management is considering two plans for allocating general overhead expenses to the stores. The 19X9 operating results before general overhead and taxes for each store were as follows:

	STORE			
	Ashville	*Burns*	*Clinton*	*Total*
Sales, net	$416,000	$353,600	$270,400	$1,040,000
Less cost of sales	215,700	183,300	140,200	539,200
Gross margin	200,300	170,300	130,200	500,800
Less local operating expenses:				
Fixed	60,800	48,750	50,200	159,750
Variable	54,700	64,220	27,448	146,368
Total	115,500	112,970	77,648	306,118
Income before general overhead and taxes	$ 84,800	$ 57,330	$ 52,552	$ 194,682

General overhead expenses in 19X9 were as follows:

Warehousing and delivery expenses:		
Warehouse depreciation	$20,000	
Warehouse operations	30,000	
Delivery expenses	40,000	$ 90,000
Central office expenses:		
Advertising	18,000	
Central office salaries	37,000	
Other central office expenses	28,000	83,000
Total general overhead		$173,000

One-fifth of the warehouse space is used to house the central office and depreciation on this space is included in other central office expenses. Warehouse operating expenses vary with quantity of merchandise sold.

Delivery expenses vary with distance and number of deliveries. The distances from the warehouse to each store and the number of deliveries made in 19X9 were as follows:

Store	*Miles*	*Number of Deliveries*
Ashville	120	140
Burns	200	64
Clinton	100	104

All advertising is prepared by the central office and is distributed in the areas in which stores are located.

As each store was opened, the fixed portion of central office salaries increased $7,000 and other central office expenses increased $2,500. Basic fixed central office salaries amount to $10,000 and basic fixed other central office expenses amount to $12,000. The remainder of central office salaries and the remainder of other central office expenses vary with sales.

REQUIRED

1. For each of the following plans for assigning general overhead expenses, compute the income of each store that would be subject to the municipal levy on corporation income:
   Plan 1. Allocate all general overhead expenses on the basis of sales volume.
   Plan 2. First, allocate central office salaries and other central office expenses evenly to warehouse operations and each store. Second, allocate the resulting warehouse operations expenses, warehouse depreciation, and advertising to each store on the basis of sales volume. Third, allocate delivery expenses to each store on the basis of delivery miles times number of deliveries.
2. The managers of the firm believe that they can expand sales by $50,000 in any one of the three stores, but not more than one. Expanding would increase fixed operating expenses of the store by $7,500 and require ten additional deliveries from the warehouse. Determine which store the company should expand.

11

ALLOCATION: JOINT PRODUCTS

The allocation problem has many aspects. We have seen problems associated with allocation of overhead and with allocation of support department costs. In this chapter we deal with allocation of common costs when a single manufacturing process yields more than one product. When an oil refiner processes crude oil, several products may emerge, including gasoline, diesel, motor oil, jet fuel, and so on. In some cases adjustments can be made to control the amount of, say, gasoline versus jet fuel in a batch. The refiner cannot, however, produce a gallon of gasoline from a gallon of crude petroleum. In other processes, the output of various products is fairly mixed and managers have little discretion over product mix.

When manufacturing yields two or more products from a single process, they are *joint products* and the process giving rise to them is a *joint process*. The term *joint products* is often reserved for products with significant value and the term *by-products* is used for productions with little (or even negative) value. As might be expected, the costs associated with a joint process are called *joint costs*.

Usually one or more raw materials enter the joint process, and later the joint products appear as separate entities. The point at which the joint products appear is called the **split-off point**; it is only at split-off that the joint products become individually identifiable.

Some joint products are sold just as they come out from split-off, others require further processing to make them saleable, and some can be sold either at split-off or after additional processing. We are usually concerned with this last type in decision making involving joint products. An example is a meat packer, who can sell hides or process them into tanned leather.

Some outputs of a joint process have little or no value. Metal shavings may be collected and sold, but the revenue from selling them is usually inconsequential. In a technical sense, metal shavings, sawdust, and other such materials that are a normal result of a production process are joint products. Since the term *joint product* usually is limited to products with relatively high value, the terms *by-product*, *scrap*, and *waste* are used to refer to outputs of little or no value. The differences among these outputs are terminological to a great extent. Different people will use different terms to refer to the same thing. Let us look briefly at the distinctions in the use of the terms.

Waste is a term usually reserved for material that has no value, or negative value, because it must be disposed of at some cost. Waste presents no accounting problems. It is neither inventoried nor sold. In just-in-time inventory systems, general plant philosophy is to eliminate waste. A considerable amount of management time is spent investigating waste and making sure that the process is adjusted to drive waste to zero. Just-in-time inventory is discussed in this light in Chapters 20 and 21 on inventory practices and variance investigation.

By-product may denote anything that results from a production process. We speak of smoke as an undesirable by-product of burning coal. In accounting, the term usually is reserved for a joint product that has some value, but relatively little in relation to the one or more other joint products. The joint products of relatively high value are often called **main products** to distinguish them from the relatively low-value by-products.

Scrap is also a joint output if it emerges as a normal consequence of the production process. The difference between scrap and by-products is not always clear, and one firm might call something scrap that another calls a by-product. As a rule, scrap is the leftover part of raw materials, whereas by-products are different from the material that went into the process. Metal shavings and sawdust usually would be considered scrap. Distillates from chemical processes usually would be considered by-products. The term *scrap* usually is limited to material that has some use. It may be sold or reprocessed.

When a product is processed beyond its split-off point, it is considered a by-product, not scrap. However, the mere fact that a product is not processed further does not mean that it will be considered scrap. The criterion noted before, that by-products are different from the material that went into the production process, generally controls the classification. Both scrap and by-products require accounting treatment because they are sold or reprocessed. In some cases the same accounting treatment could be used for either one. As we shall see later, by-products that are processed beyond split-off require special treatment.

This chapter deals with two principal concerns: (1) the accounting treatment of joint products, by-products, and scrap and (2) the managerial considerations that these types of products present, especially how far to process joint products beyond split-off.

PREVALENCE OF JOINT PRODUCTS

We cited earlier a few examples of joint products, but it might be helpful to list more to show how common they are and therefore how widespread the problem is for accountants.

Virtually all meat and leather products are joint. Steaks, roasts, hamburger, and hides come from cattle; pork chops, ham, and pigskin from hogs. Most basic wood products are joint. Planks and boards of various sizes, studs, sheets of veneer, and chips used for composition board all come from logs. In most cases a specific log will yield several products (pieces of different sizes), so all are joint.

Many plastics result from joint processes, as do chemicals and gases. The list could go on, but the point should be clear: joint products are everywhere. In fact, the more difficult economic times of recent years have stimulated the search for new uses of joint products, especially by-products or scrap that once were discarded. Recycling heat generated by computers to reduce fuel requirements is one example.

DECISION MAKING WITH JOINT PRODUCTS

Firms that make joint products face two basic decisions: (1) whether to sell joint products at the split-off point or process them further and (2) whether to operate the joint processes at all.[1] In the first type of decision the joint costs are irrelevant because they are sunk. The joint products have been produced (or the firm plans to produce them), and the only decision is whether to sell them at split-off or process them further. In the second type of decision the *avoidable* costs of operating the joint process (for example, the cost of materials and direct labor) are relevant.

We introduced the concepts of relevant costs for decisions in Chapter 2 in our discussion of cost-volume-profit relationships and the decisions that managers can make based on these relationships. Chapter 12 expands this discussion. Dealing with decisions about whether to sell a joint product at split-off or to process it further links these chapters. Thus, this first section deals with relevant costs for managerial decision making.

[1] The following discussion applies also to by-products (which are joint products), but for brevity we shall use the term *joint products*.

ILLUSTRATION: WALTON CHEMICAL'S JOINT PRODUCTS

Walton Chemical Company produces three joint products, 101, 102, and 103. The data in Exhibit 11–1 reflect the average monthly results. In this analysis, we concentrate on production values, ignoring when a product is sold. Thus, we use the term *sales value* in the exhibit instead of *sales*. Sales value is total current output valued at current selling prices. Figure 11–1 diagrams current operations and choices open to management. Note that Product 101 has no value at split-off. In other words, if it is to be sold at all, it will only be after further processing. However, with the other two products, managers can sell them at split-off or process them further and then sell them. Another decision that managers must also make is whether to operate the joint process at all.

We first examine the decision whether to process joint products beyond the split-off point. If the additional revenue from further processing is greater than the additional cost of that processing, it is wise to process further rather than selling at split-off. The schedule on page 486 shows that 101 and 102 should be processed beyond split-off, while 103 should be sold at split-off. It is important to point out that only avoidable costs of further processing, those costs that are incremental if further processing is done, should be used in the analyses. Notice that even though Product 101 cannot be sold at split-off, we still evaluate the decision to process it further. If the avoidable costs of further processing exceeded the sales value of Product 101 after further processing, and if the firm could simply junk it at the split-off point with no cost, the firm would be better off dumping it at split-off. The schedule shows the gain or loss of processing beyond split-off.

EXHIBIT 11–1 Data for Walton Chemical Company

	Joint Products		
	101	*102*	*103*
Monthly output (lb)	40,000	20,000	20,000
Sales value at split-off	0	$ 30,000	$105,000
Sales value after further processing	$40,000	$100,000	$150,000
Avoidable costs of further processing	$18,000	$ 40,000	$ 57,000
Joint process—monthly costs:			
Avoidable	$80,000		
Unavoidable[a]	$20,000		

[a]Consists of fixed costs such as allocated costs and depreciation on equipment

FIGURE 11–1 Walton Chemical Company

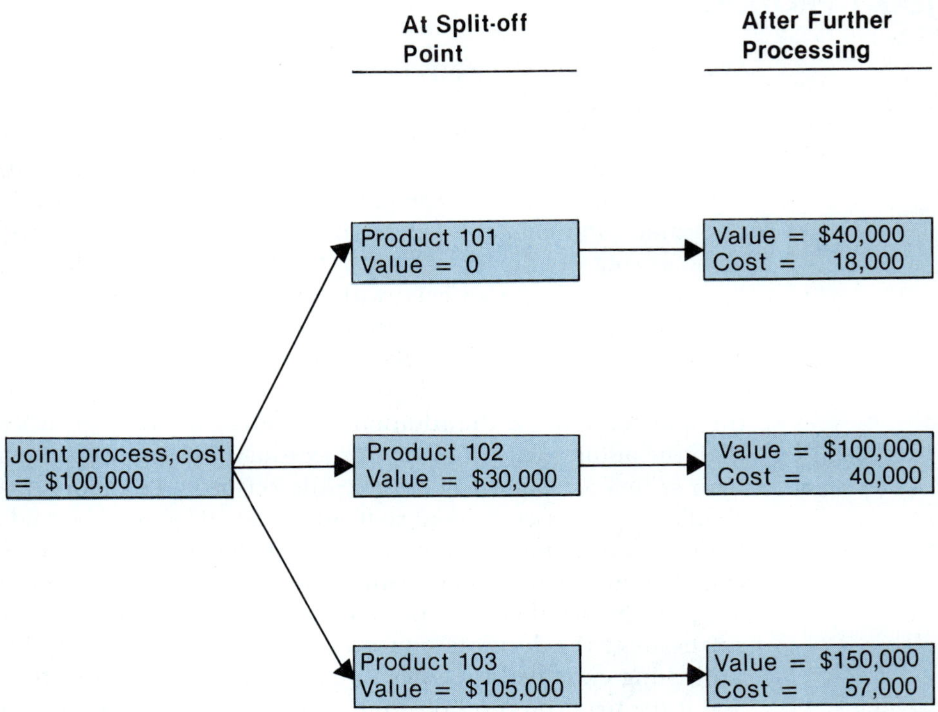

	101	*102*	*103*
Sales value after further processing	$40,000	$100,000	$150,000
Sales value at split-off	0	30,000	105,000
Incremental revenue from further processing	40,000	70,000	45,000
Incremental costs of further processing	18,000	40,000	57,000
Net gain (loss) from further processing	$22,000	$ 30,000	($ 12,000)

As we can see from the schedule, Products 101 and 102 should be processed beyond split-off (additional revenue exceeds incremental costs) and Product 103 should be sold at split-off (at a net savings of $12,000 above selling it after further processing). This analysis can also be viewed from the perspective of additional margin gained by further processing less the sales value that would be foregone if the product were not sold at split-off.[2]

	101	*102*	*103*
Sales value after further processing	$40,000	$100,000	$150,000
Avoidable costs of further processing	18,000	40,000	57,000
Margin from further processing	$22,000	$ 60,000	$ 93,000
Less: Sales value at split-off point	0	30,000	105,000
Net gain (loss) from further processing	$22,000	$ 30,000	($ 12,000)

This analysis uses only costs that would change if different decisions are made. Thus, if a cost of further processing is unavoidable, it is not relevant since it will be the same whether a product is sold at split-off or later. Similarly, the costs of the joint process itself are common to all the joint products. Therefore, they will not change depending on the timing of when products are sold. However, such costs are relevant to another decision: should the joint process be operated at all? Shutdown is a viable option. In determining whether or not to operate a joint process, the relevant data are the margins achievable from making the best decisions about the further processing of joint products, and the avoidable costs of operating the joint process.

The schedule below shows the total margin obtainable from selling each joint product at its most advantageous point. Because the total margin is greater than the avoidable costs of operating the joint process, the firm should continue to operate it.

	Total	*101*	*102*	*103*
Revenue	$245,000	$40,000	$100,000	$105,000
Avoidable costs of further processing	58,000	18,000	40,000	0
Product margin	$187,000	22,000	60,000	105,000
Avoidable costs of joint process	80,000			
Advantage to operating joint process	$107,000			

[2]This concept is called *opportunity cost* and will be further developed in Chapter 12.

You should now see why we must deal with the further processing decision before the decision whether to operate the joint process. We cannot make the latter decision until we know the total incremental margin available from making the best decisions on further processing.

Multiple Split-off Points

Some products that can go through processing beyond split-off themselves yield additional joint products. Each of the new joint products might be saleable at split-off or might be processed further. While this complication requires that we make more calculations, it is not in principle any different from the basic case. Suppose, for instance, that Walton's Product 102 could take either of the following paths after its split-off. Path A is the original case, where incurring $40,000 in further processing costs yields a new product with a sales value of $100,000. In path B, the product is processed into 102X and 102Y, which have split-off values as shown and can each be further processed as shown.

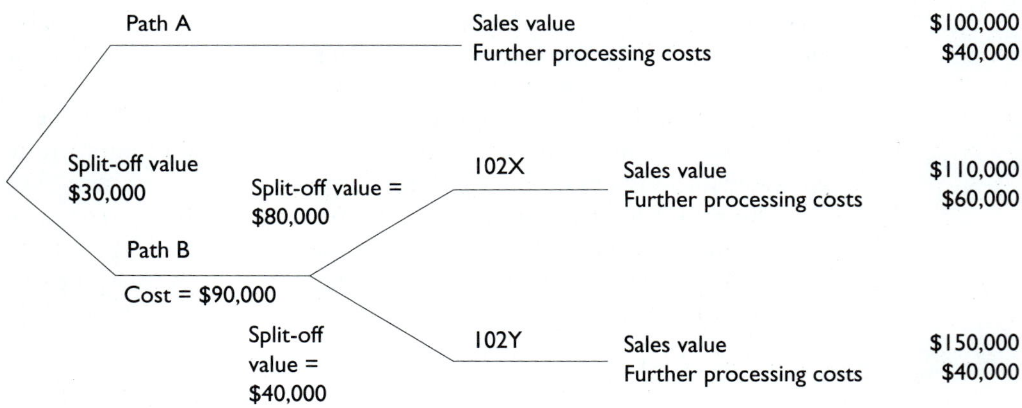

Thus, by spending $90,000, Walton can obtain 102X and 102Y, with respective split-off values of $80,000 and $40,000. Then 102X can be further processed for $60,000, giving a product with a sales value of $110,000. Similarly, 102Y could be further processed at cost of $40,000 to yield a product with a sales value of $150,000.

Generally, it is easiest to work backward, deciding at each stage whether further processing or sale at split-off would be better, until you have reached the initial split-off point. First, we see that 102X should not be processed further because we would spend $60,000 to earn $110,000, but we can sell it at its split-off point for $80,000. Product 102Y should be processed further, because the incremental revenue exceeds the incremental cost. The schedule below shows these results.

	102X	102Y
Sales value after further processing	$110,000	$150,000
Avoidable costs of further processing	60,000	40,000
Margin from further processing	50,000	110,000
Sales value at split-off	80,000	40,000
Advantage (disadvantage) of further processing	($30,000)	$ 70,000

Note that we do not include the $90,000 cost to follow path B by processing 102. All we have done so far is determine the best decisions for 102X and 102Y, not whether to follow path B. Now we can analyze path B. The schedule below shows that following path B benefits the company by $100,000, which is greater than the $60,000 benefit of following path A.

	Total	102X	102Y
Revenue	$230,000	$80,000	$150,000
Further processing costs	40,000	0	40,000
Margins	190,000	80,000	110,000
Cost to obtain 102X and 102Y	90,000		
Net benefit	$100,000		

The $100,000 exceeds both the $60,000 from path A and the original split-off value of $30,000, which means that the company is $40,000 better off following path B than path A. Notice that the $90,000 cost to process 102 into 102X and 102Y was included only in the analysis of the path as a whole, not in the decisions relating to 102X and 102Y (sell them at their split-off points or process them further). This, of course, is because that cost is irrelevant to determining what to do with the new joint products, but relevant in deciding whether to take path B.

ALLOCATING JOINT COSTS TO JOINT PRODUCTS

In the discussion above, we concentrated on costs for managerial decision making. Much like the discussion in Chapter 4, the relevant costs used were those that were separable to the decisions at hand. However, when we shift our focus to product costs for financial accounting, we are now faced with an allocation problem similar to those explored in Chapters 4 and 5: besides separable costs associated with each product, some portion of the joint costs of production must be assigned to each unit produced.

The major constraint on the selection of an allocation method for the joint costs is that the inventory valuation should not exceed the net realizable value of the product—its expected selling price less costs to complete and sell. From the standpoint of financial reporting and income tax accounting, this requirement is virtually the only one that need be satisfied. You may recall from financial accounting that net realizable value is the ceiling on the market value of inventory in the application of the lower of cost or market rule.

As we discussed in earlier chapters, the allocations made for financial reporting and income tax purposes are of no value for managerial purposes. Misleading information can result from such allocations, and they should be ignored by managers. About all that we can ask of an allocation method for internal managerial purposes is that it does not impede making good decisions. In general, the two methods that we shall discuss will not be harmful in the sense that managers would make the wrong decisions.

Bases used to allocate joint costs to joint products fall into two general categories: physical measures such as pounds, gallons, and square feet; and value measures such as selling price and net realizable value. The use of physical measures is unwise, because it may easily result in showing book losses for products that are in fact profitable in that they contribute to the covering of joint costs and earning of profits, and it may also result in inventory valuations that violate the lower of cost or market rule by showing products at amounts greater than their net realizable values.

To illustrate, assume that Walton Company (Exhibit 11–1) had no beginning inventories and sold 30,000 pounds of Product 101 of the 40,000 pounds produced. The total selling price was $30,000, three-fourths of the total sales value of $40,000 for the 40,000 pounds.

Physical Measures

Walton could allocate joint costs based on relative weight. If it did, 50 percent would go to Product 101 [40,000/(40,000 + 20,000 + 20,000)]. An income statement for Product 101 would show the following results:

Sales		$30,000
Production costs:		
Additional, beyond split-off	$18,000	
Joint $100,000 × 50%	50,000	
Total	68,000	
Ending inventory, 25%	17,000	
Cost of goods sold		51,000
Loss		($21,000)

Using this base for allocation results in showing a loss on Product 101, whereas the product contributes to the covering of joint costs and earning of income. Additionally, the $17,000 inventory figure is greater than the sales value of $10,000 ($40,000 total sales value less $30,000 sales) and is therefore unsuitable for financial reporting purposes. Unless physical measures closely parallel values of joint products, their use may give misleading results, and therefore they should be avoided.

Relative Sales Value Method

As its name suggests, the relative sales value method allocates joint costs based on the products' relative sales values. Generally these should be the sales values at whatever point the products are sold, rather than their split-off values. In our example, we would have the following allocations:

	Total	*101*	*102*	*103*
Sales	$245,000	$40,000	$100,000	$105,000
Percentages of total		16.3%	40.8%	42.9%
Joint costs allocated	$100,000	$16,300	$40,800	$42,900

This method offers a slight improvement over physical measure methods but can still give results that violate the lower of cost or market rule. In our example, all products' total costs are less than their sales values, but that need not be true. For instance, if the further processing costs of Product 101 increased to any more than $23,700, the relative sales value method would show total costs in excess of $40,000. (With further processing costs of $23,700 and allocated joint costs of $16,300, total costs are $40,000, which equals sales value.)

Net Realizable Value Method

One of the most commonly advocated methods for allocating joint costs is the net realizable value method, under which the allocations are made in accordance with the net realizable values of the products. The **net realizable value** (NRV) of a joint product that can be sold at the split-off point is simply its selling price at split-off less any expected selling costs. If the product has no market at split-off, its net realizable value is its selling price after further processing minus the costs of further processing and any selling costs expected. In either case, the basis for the allocation is the total net realizable value of the quantity produced during the period, not the actual sales for the period.

Please note that if the product has any value at split-off, it is that value, less any expected selling costs if the product is sold at split-off, that we use for the NRV. It does not matter whether we actually sell it at split-off or process it further.

The net realizable values of Walton Company's products are shown below, with all data from Exhibit 11–1.

	Total	*101*	*102*	*103*
Sales value at split-off	$135,000	—	$30,000	$105,000
Sales value after further processing minus costs of further processing	22,000	$22,000		—
Net realizable value	$157,000	$22,000	$30,000	$105,000
Percentage of total	100%	14%	19%	67%

Using these data, we obtain the allocations of the joint costs of $100,000 as well as the total inventoriable costs of each product. Only production costs, separable and joint, are included in the inventory valuation. If we had expected selling costs for one or more of the products, we would not include them in inventory, although they would be used to determine the net realizable values.

	Total	*101*	*102*	*103*
Allocated joint costs	$100,000	$14,000	$19,000	$67,000
Additional processing costs	58,000	18,000	40,000	—
Total costs	$158,000	$32,000	$59,000	$67,000
Pounds of output (Exhibit 11–1)		40,000	20,000	20,000
Cost per pound		$0.80	$2.95	$3.35

The net realizable value method has two important results as long as the total net realizable value for all the joint products exceeds the total production costs.[3] First, all products will appear profitable on the income statement; second, the inventory valuations on the balance sheet will be less than net realizable values, thereby conforming to the lower of cost or market rule.

Constant Gross Margin Rate Method

An alternative to the net realizable value method is the constant gross margin rate method. This method results in all joint products' showing the same percentage rate of gross margin; in other words, it assumes that each product contributes an equal percentage amount per dollar of sales. This method works backward from gross margin to joint cost allocations. (1) You first find the overall rate of gross margin (gross margin/sales value) assuming that the optimal decisions have been made for the individual joint products. (2) You then multiply this rate by the sales value of each product and subtract the result from the sales value, giving the total cost of each product. The further processing costs and selling costs (if any) are then subtracted from the total cost figures to give the joint cost allocations. Using our example:

Step 1.

	Total	*101*	*102*	*103*
Sales value—best decisions	$245,000	$40,000	$100,000	$105,000
Further processing costs	(58,000)	18,000	40,000	0
Joint costs	(100,000)			
Gross margin	$ 87,000			
Gross margin rate, 35.51%	$87,000/$245,000			

[3]Technically, we must also assume that all joint products have either positive split-off values or sales values after further processing in excess of further processing costs. Products that violate these conditions usually would not be considered main products, but rather by-products. Addi-

The gross margin rate is applied to the individual products so that each has the same gross margin (35.51 percent in the example). First the gross margin of each product is calculated. Then, total costs are backed out given sales and the gross margin. Separable costs are subtracted from total costs so that what is left over is the allocation of joint costs. As a check, total joint cost allocations are compared with the amount of joint costs to be allocated. The calculations are:

Step 2.

	101	*102*	*103*
Sales value	$40,000	$100,000	$105,000
Gross margin at 35.51%	$14,204	35,510	37,286
Total costs	25,796	64,490	67,714
Less: Additional processing costs	18,000	40,000	0
Allocated joint costs	$ 7,796	$ 24,490	$ 67,714
Total allocation equals $100,000			

The constant gross margin rate method has some of the same properties as the net realizable value method: all products will show profits and will be valued for inventory determination at less than net realizable value. The net realizable value method is used more in practice, but the constant gross margin rate method has an advantage if managers do pay attention to the full costs of the joint products. The advantage is that the constant gross margin rate method will give income statements by product, and for the entire group of joint products, that show the same gross margin rate no matter how much of the output is sold and how much remains in inventory. The net realizable value method will not necessarily do this. The constant gross margin rate method is not widely used.

Other than following the rule that inventory cannot be valued above net realizable value, the only guidelines in this allocation discussion are reason and equity—much like the discussion about allocation of common overhead costs in Chapter 4. If the method that managers choose is reasonable and does not violate the rule regarding inventory valuation, then there is no theoretical basis for choosing one method over another. However, as the following review problem illustrates, managers may differ in what they consider reasonable.

Review Problem

CQ Company manufactures three products (Products A, B, and C) from a single joint process. Exhibit 11–2 shows data for this company. Using the template shown in Exhibit 11–2,

tionally, we can sometimes get inventory values exceeding net realizable value if the joint costs exceed the total split-off values.

EXHIBIT 11–2 CQ Company (CQ.WK1)

```
1     B        C        D        E        F        G        H        I
2  CQ.WK1   CQ Company - Joint Product Cost Allocation: Three Methods
3
4  DATA SECTION
5
6  Products                                       A        B        C    Total
7  Sales value at split-off                 $50,000   $5,000  $70,000 $125,000
8  Sales value after further processing      80,000   60,000  100,000
9  Costs of further processing               20,000   50,000   25,000
10 Common costs for joint process                                       100,000
11
12 SOLUTION SECTION
13 Best decision
14 (1=split-off), 0=further processing)
15 Best margin
16 Common costs
17                                                                     ---------
18 Margin for joint process as a whole                                        0
19
20 RELATIVE SALES VALUE:
21  Sales value at best option
22  Percentages of total
23  Joint costs allocated
24
25 Product profitability:
26  Revenue
27  Separable costs
28  Allocated joint costs
29                                         -------  -------  -------  -------
30  Income                                       0        0        0        0
31  Gross margin percentage
32
33 NET REALIZABLE VALUE:
34  Net realizable value
35  Percentage of total
36  Joint costs allocated
37
38 Product profitability:
39  Revenue
40  Separable costs
41  Allocated joint costs
42                                         -------  -------  -------  -------
43  Income                                       0        0        0        0
44  Gross margin percentage
45
46 CONSTANT GROSS MARGIN RATE:
47
48 Sales value - best decision
49 Further processing costs
50 Joint costs
```

(continued)

(EXHIBIT 11–2 continued)

```
51                                                                    ---------
52 Gross margin                                                              $0
53 Gross margin rate
54
55 Sales value
56 Gross margin at        0.00%
57                                       -------  -------  -------
58 Total costs                                 0        0        0
59 less: additional processing costs
60                                       -------  -------  -------
61 Allocated joint costs                       0        0        0        0
62
63 Product profitability:
64  Revenue
65  Separable costs
66  Allocated joint costs
67                                       -------  -------  -------  -------
68  Income                                     0        0        0        0
69  Gross margin percentage
```

1. Allocate joint process costs to each product using
   a. relative sales value method
   b. relative net realizable value method
   c. constant gross margin rate method

2. Show income by product and for the company as a whole. Assume that all products made are sold (i.e., there is no inventory problem, just valuing cost of sales). The completed template (CQ.WK1) is shown in Exhibit 11–3.

It is interesting that while Product B has a positive separable margin ($10,000 after further processing), it does not have a positive income using the relative sales value method. In addition, to achieve the overall gross margin rate of 18.75 percent, Product B receives a *negative* allocation of common costs. Managers may have differing views on which of these methods seem reasonable or equitable. They consider issues of whether a product with a positive separable margin should be allocated costs so that its profits are negative and whether it is reasonable to have negative allocations of joint costs.

ACCOUNTING FOR BY-PRODUCTS AND SCRAP

Several methods may be used to account for by-products, but scrap is usually accounted for in only one way in actual and normal costing systems. We will consider standard costing systems in a later section. Recall from earlier discussion that the difference between scrap and by-product may be hazy. The

EXHIBIT 11–3 CQ Company (CQ.WK1 completed)

1	B C D E	F	G	H	I
2	CQ Company: CQ.WK1 Completed				
3					
4	DATA SECTION				
5					
6	Products	A	B	C	Total
7	Sales value at split-off	$50,000	$5,000	$70,000	$125,000
8	Sales value after further processing	80,000	60,000	100,000	
9	Costs of further processing	20,000	50,000	25,000	
10	Common costs for joint process				100,000
11					
12	SOLUTION SECTION				
13	Best decision				
14	(1=split-off, 0=further processing)	0	0	0	
15	Best margin	$60,000	$10,000	$75,000	$145,000
16					100,000
17					---------
18	Margin for joint process as a whole				45,000
19					
20	RELATIVE SALES VALUE:				
21	Sales value at best option	$80,000	$60,000	$100,000	$240,000
22	Percentages of total	33.33%	25.00%	41.67%	100.00%
23	Joint costs allocated	33,333	25,000	41,667	100,000
24					
25	Product profitability:				
26	Revenue	$80,000	$60,000	$100,000	$240,000
27	Separable costs	20,000	50,000	25,000	95,000
28	Allocated joint costs	33,333	25,000	41,667	100,000
29		-------	-------	-------	-------
30	Income	26,667	(15,000)	33,333	45,000
31	Gross margin percentage	33.33%	-25.00%	33.33%	18.75%
32					
33	NET REALIZABLE VALUE:				
34	Net realizable value	$50,000	$5,000	$70,000	$125,000
35	Percentage of total	40.00%	4.00%	56.00%	100.00%
36	Joint costs allocated	40,000	4,000	56,000	100,000
37					
38	Product profitability:				
39	Revenue	$80,000	$60,000	$100,000	$240,000
40	Separable costs	20,000	50,000	25,000	95,000
41	Allocated joint costs	40,000	4,000	56,000	100,000
42		-------	-------	-------	-------
43	Income	20,000	6,000	19,000	45,000
44	Gross margin percentage	25.00%	10.00%	19.00%	18.75%
45					
46	CONSTANT GROSS MARGIN RATE:				
47					
48	Sales value - best decision	$80,000	$60,000	$100,000	$240,000
49	Further processing costs	20,000	50,000	25,000	95,000
50	Joint costs				100,000

(continued)

(EXHIBIT 11–3 continued)

Gross margin				$45,000
Gross margin rate				18.75%
Sales value	$80,000	$60,000	$100,000	
Gross margin at 18.75%	15,000	11,250	18,750	
	-------	-------	-------	
Total costs	65,000	48,750	81,250	
less: additional processing costs	20,000	50,000	25,000	
	-------	-------	-------	
Allocated joint costs	45,000	(1,250)	56,250	100,000
Product profitability:				
Revenue	$80,000	$60,000	$100,000	$240,000
Separable costs	20,000	50,000	25,000	95,000
Allocated joint costs	45,000	(1,250)	56,250	100,000
	-------	-------	-------	-------
Income	15,000	11,250	18,750	45,000
Gross margin percentage	18.75%	18.75%	18.75%	18.75%

names given to different outputs are not of great importance. In fact, the first method we describe in this section can be used for both by-products and scrap.

Other Income Method

The simplest method of accounting for by-products and scrap is to ignore them for inventory determination, simply crediting Other Income, Miscellaneous Income, or Income from Sales of By-Products (or Scrap) when they are sold. This method predominates in accounting for scrap. It is also used for by-products that are not processed beyond the split-off point and are of so little value that leaving them out of inventory would have an imperceptible effect on the firm's financial statements.

Sometimes the credit is to Cost of Goods Sold, which has the same effect on income as does crediting one of the accounts mentioned above (reducing an expense account has the same effect on income as increasing a revenue account). While not strictly accurate, this procedure does no harm if the amounts are small.

The firm may keep records of the physical quantities of an item for control purposes, but the only effect on the financial statements would occur in the period of sale (an increase in income). The main product, or products, would be allocated all of the costs of production. Thus, the only journal entry required would be at the time of sale and would appear as follows:

Cash (or Accounts Receivable)	xxxx	
Income from Sale of Scrap (or By-Product)		xxxx

Net Realizable Value Method

By-products are frequently inventoried at net realizable value, especially if they require processing beyond split-off. If a by-product requires processing past split-off, the costs beyond split-off should be inventoried, and so the other income method is inappropriate. Suppose that a by-product is expected to sell for $400. Before it can be sold, it must be separately processed at a cost of $120. At the time of sale the firm expects to incur selling costs of $20 for sales commissions. The net realizable value is $260 ($400 − $120 − $20). At the time of split-off the following journal entry would be made:

Inventory of By-Product	$260	
Work-in-Process Inventory		$260

When the additional processing has been done, the entry is:

Inventory of By-Product	$120	
Cash, etc.		$120

And at the time of sale, assuming the sale is for cash and commissions are accrued:

Cash	$400	
Inventory of By-Product		$380
Accrued Commissions		20

Under the net realizable value method no profit or loss is recognized on the by-product as long as expectations are correct. If the selling price or selling costs turn out to be different from expectations, a gain or loss would be recognized at the time of sale. For example, if the selling price had been $415, a $15 gain would be recognized.

Essentially, the net realizable value method reduces the cost of the main product or products. The credit to Work-in-Process Inventory in the first entry above results in $260 less cost to be charged to the main product and therefore $260 more profit when the main product is sold. Thus, if the costs of the process that generated the by-product totaled $24,000, the main product(s) would be charged $23,740 ($24,000 − $260), reducing inventory valuations and reducing the subsequent cost of goods sold.

The net realizable value method of accounting for by-products is not the same as the net realizable value method of allocating joint costs to joint products. The use of the same term to refer to two different methods is unfortunate, but widespread. The net realizable value method of accounting for by-products *values* them at their net realizable values. The net realizable value method of allocating joint costs to joint products *uses* the net realizable values to determine the amounts of joint cost to be allocated to each joint product.

The net realizable value method is sometimes criticized because it can result in premature recognition of profit. The inventory of a by-product is shown at market value (less additional expected costs), which results in all of its profit being recognized on sales of the main product. The premature recognition of profit would occur if at the end of a period all of the main product had been sold and the by-product remained in inventory. In that case, showing the inventory of by-product at net realizable value leaves no profit to be recognized on the sale of the by-product in the next period.

So long as the amounts involved are not material, we may safely ignore the problem of premature profit recognition. If the amounts are material, some accountants would modify the method by reducing the amount allocated to the by-product by a normal profit. Thus, if a normal profit on sales of $400 were assumed to be $30, the first entry given above would show a debit to Inventory of By-Product of $230 ($260 − $30). A profit of $30 would then be shown at the time of sale. The entry could appear as:

Cash	$400	
Inventory of By-Product ($230 + $120)		$350
Accrued Commissions		20
Income from Sales of By-Product		30

In this modification of the net realizable value method, the weak point is the *normal* profit. Because a by-product is a joint output, along with the main product or products, there is really no such thing as its *cost*, just as there is no such thing as *the* cost of a joint product. Consequently, any allocation that gives inventory costs conforming to the lower of cost or market rule is at least defensible for financial reporting. In fact, if a normal profit is defined as the overall gross margin expected multiplied by the sales value, this method produces the same results as the constant gross margin rate method would, treating the by-product as a joint product.

SUMMARY

Joint products and by-products abound in manufacturing and refining processes. Costs incurred up to the split-off point are joint to all of the products and must be allocated to the joint outputs for product costing purposes. These allocations can create problems in analyzing the profitability of individual products. The allocated joint costs are irrelevant to decisions about whether to process the products beyond the split-off point. For planning and control purposes, the major objective is to make the allocations in such a way that they do not interfere with decision making.

The net realizable value method of allocating joint costs, as well as the constant gross margin method, will ordinarily satisfy the objective of allocating in a way that will not interfere with decision making.

Accounting for by-products, which are joint products of relatively low value, varies greatly in practice. Because of the relatively low value of by-products, the choice of a method is largely governed by the cost of operating the accounting system.

REVIEW PROBLEM

Colco Company produces three joint products. Data for a typical month appear below.

	Biart	Triart	Quadart
Tons produced	20	50	10
Selling price per ton at split-off	$500	$0	$20
Selling price after further processing	$650	$980	—
Variable costs of further processing, per ton	$220	$180	—

Monthly joint processing costs are $24,000.

REQUIRED

1. Determine whether Colco should process Biart beyond split-off.
2. Colco treats Quadart as a by-product, offsetting its net realizable value against the cost of the joint process. Use the net realizable value method to allocate the joint costs. Determine the unit cost of each product.
3. Suppose that Colco began a month with no inventories, produced the quantities shown above, and sold 90 percent of the output of each product. Prepare an income statement for the month, down to gross margin.
4. Suppose now that Colco could separate Biart into two new products, Bi-A and Bi-B. The output of Bi-A would be 14 tons per month, of Bi-B 6 tons. The cost of the process would be $250 per ton of Biart. Bi-A could be sold for $700 per ton, Bi-B for $600 per ton after it went through additional refining that would cost $150 per ton. Determine whether it would be profitable to proceed with the further processing of Biart.

ANSWERS TO REVIEW PROBLEM

1. No, because it costs $220 to increase revenue by $150 per ton ($650 − $500).
2. Quadart's cost is its $20 net realizable value.

	Biart	Triart	Quadart
Tons produced	20	50	10
Net realizable value per ton	$500	$800	$20
Total net realizable value	$10,000	$40,000	$200
Percentage of main products:			
$10,000/($10,000 + $40,000)	20%		
$40,000/($10,000 + $40,000)		80%	

(continued)

Joint costs	$24,000		
Minus net realizable value of Quadart	200		
To be allocated	$23,800		
Allocations:			
$23,800 × 20%		$ 4,760	
$23,800 × 80%			$19,040
Further processing costs		0	9,000
Total product costs		$ 4,760	$28,040
Divided by quantities		20	50
Cost per ton		$238.00	$560.80

3.

	Total	*Biart*	*Triart*	*Quadart*
Sales (18, 45, and 9 tons)	$53,280	$9,000	$44,100	$180
Cost of sales ($238, $560.80, $20)	29,700	4,284	25,236	180
Gross margin	$23,580	$4,716	$18,864	$ 0

4. The proposal is unwise.

	Bi-A	*Bi-B*	*Total*
Revenue:			
14 × $700	$9,800		
6 × $600		$3,600	$13,400
Further processing costs:			
Biart, 20 × $250			(5,000)
Bi-B, 6 × $150			(900)
Net			$ 7,500
Net realizable value of Biart at split-off			10,000
Disadvantage of proposal			($ 2,500)

ASSIGNMENTS

11–1 Allocation or Attribution? In plain language explain:

1. allocation

2. attribution

3. Is the use of the relative net present value method, the relative sales value method, and/or constant gross margin rate method a way to allocate or to attribute costs? Justify your answer in terms of your response to parts 1 and 2 above.

11–2 Accuracy in Division of Joint Costs Daryl Company uses the net realizable value method to divide its joint production costs among its various products. The president of Daryl has asked you to write a memo in which you discuss whether this method leads to accurate costs. If you believe there is a more accurate method, suggest it.

REQUIRED

You are a consultant to management. Using the guidelines in Appendix B, write a memorandum to the president in which you respond to these questions.

11–3 Basic Joint Cost Allocation The following data relate to the operations of the MLL Company for April. The firm produces three joint products, all of which require additional processing beyond the split-off point. There were no beginning inventories.

	Product		
	100	101	102
Production in gallons	18,000	12,000	10,000
Sales	14,000	12,000	8,000
Ending inventory	4,000	0	2,000
Selling price per gallon	$ 2	$ 4	$ 10
April sales	$28,000	$48,000	$80,000
Costs of additional processing	$ 9,000	$ 9,600	$15,000

Total joint processing costs were $60,000. The ending inventories have been through all processing and are ready for sale.

REQUIRED

1. Allocate the joint costs using the net realizable value method and prepare a statement of gross margin for April, by product.
2. Repeat part 1, using the constant gross margin rate method to allocate the joint costs.

11–4 Processing Decisions LMC Company produces two chemicals in a joint process. Both X-on and Y-on emerge in quantities of 5,000 pounds from each 10,000-pound batch of raw materials. X-on sells for $10 per pound, Y-on for $2 per pound. Neither product receives processing beyond split-off. One of your staff has prepared the following analysis, which, she says, shows that the firm would do better to dump the Y-on.

	X-on	Y-on
Revenue per batch	$50,000	$10,000
Material costs	(10,000)	(10,000)
Labor and overhead	(8,000)	(8,000)
Profit (loss) per batch	$32,000	($ 8,000)

The labor and overhead are variable with the number of batches processed. The raw material costs $2 per pound.

REQUIRED

1. Determine the profit that the firm would earn per batch if it dumped Y-on at split-off.

2. Suppose the firm could process Y-on into another product it could sell for $5 per pound. Additional processing would have variable costs of $1 per pound and monthly incremental fixed costs of $20,000. The firm processes three batches per month. Should it process Y-on beyond split-off?

11–5 By-Product Costing Marquette Company makes three chemicals in a joint process. March data appear below. There were no beginning inventories. The firm sells product Y-16 at split-off, the others after further processing.

	Product		
	X-202	Y-16	Y-18
Pounds produced	48,000	4,000	6,000
Selling price at split-off, per pound	$1.65	$0.70	—
Additional processing costs, beyond split-off, per pound	0.20	—	0.08
Selling price after further processing, per pound	2.25	—	0.97
Selling costs per pound	0.08	0.02	0.04

Monthly joint costs are $78,000. The firm regards product X-202 as its main product, the others as by-products. At the end of March 1,200 pounds of Y-18 were on hand that had not been processed beyond split-off. There were 500 pounds of Y-16 on hand. All X-202 was sold. The firm inventories Y-18 at its net realizable value and uses the other income method of accounting for Y-16.

REQUIRED

1. Determine inventory at March 31.
2. Prepare an income statement for March.
3. Suppose that the 1,200 pounds of Y-18 on hand at March 31 had gone through the additional processing and were ready for sale. What differences would there have been in your answers to parts 1 and 2? Do not make new calculations; just describe the differences.

11–6 Allocations and Decisions Your assistant enters your office and proclaims that you made a costly mistake in recommending that Product 106 be processed beyond its split-off point. He shows you the following analysis.

	Product 106	
	Sold at Split-off	Sold after Further Processing
Revenue	$34,400	$61,800
Costs:		
Further processing		21,100
Joint	17,315	28,502
Gross profit	$17,085	$12,198

Total joint costs were $151,000, and the total sales value of joint products at split-off was $300,000, including the $34,400 for Product 106. All products except 106 were sold at split-off. Total sales value was then $327,400, with product 106 sold after further processing, and that figure was used to make the allocation of $28,502.

REQUIRED

1. Verify the calculations of allocated joint costs, as you were told the assistant performed them.
2. Determine whether you made an error in recommending that product 106 be processed beyond split-off. If you did not err, prepare a suitable explanation for your assistant.

11–7 NRV Allocation (AICPA) Grafton Company makes joint products A and B in Department One from a process that also yields by-product W. Product A and by-product W are sold after separation, while product B must be further processed in Department Two. The cost assigned to by-product W is its market value less $0.40 per pound for delivery expenses. Data for July appear below.

Product	Production in Pounds	Sales Price per Pound
A	2,000	$4.50
B	4,000	9.00
W	500	1.50

Joint cost in Department One	$18,000
Cost to process product B in Department Two	$10,000

REQUIRED

1. For purposes of allocating joint costs using the net realizable value method, what is the net realizable value of product B?
2. What is the joint cost in Department One that will be allocated to the joint products?

11–8 NRV Allocations (AICPA) Stowe, Inc., produces two joint products, PEL and VEL. Joint production costs for March were $15,000. Further processing costs were $8,000 for 800 units of PEL and $12,000 for 400 units of VEL. Neither product can be sold at split-off. PEL sells for $25 per unit, VEL for $50. Stowe uses the net realizable value method for allocating joint costs.

REQUIRED

Determine the joint costs allocated to each product in March.

11–9 Main Products and By-Products—Comparison of Methods The following data relate to the operations of the Foster Company in July, 19X6. There were no beginning inventories.

	Product	
	X-con	Z-con
Pounds produced	10,000	2,000
Selling price per pound	$12.00	$3.00
Selling costs per pound sold, all variable	$ 2.50	$0.50
Pounds sold	8,000	1,500

Both products arise from a joint process. The joint costs for July were $50,000.

REQUIRED

1. Prepare an income statement for July, with separate columns for each product, assuming that the two products are both treated as main products and that joint costs are allocated using the net realizable value method.
2. Prepare an income statement for July, assuming that Z-con is treated as a by-product and is inventoried at net realizable value, with its inventory valuation used to offset the costs of X-con.

11–10 Basic Joint Product Decisions Flagston Chemical Company makes two joint products, X-1 and Y-1. Each can be sold at split-off or processed further. Results expected to continue over the next few months appear below.

	X-1	*Y-1*
Selling price per pound, at split-off	$12	$18
Per pound variable cost of further processing	4	7
Selling price per pound, after processing	18	30

REQUIRED

1. Determine which, if either, product(s) Flagston should sell at split-off.
2. Suppose that monthly output is 10,000 pounds of both X-1 and Y-1 and that in addition to the variable cost of further processing, there are $40,000 of avoidable fixed costs that Flagston must incur to process either product further, $80,000 to process both. Which product(s), if either, should Flagston process further?
3. Assuming the $40,000 avoidable fixed cost to process each product further, at what selling price at the split-off point should Flagston change its decision for each product? That is, how high could the price of a product being processed further go before Flagston would sell it at split-off, and how low could the price of a product being sold at split-off go before Flagston should process it further?

11–11 Processing Decision Zeeco Company manufactures a number of chemical products, mostly industrial solvents. The processes used to make the major products generate joint products of lesser value. The firm maintains a large research and development staff to examine ways to make better use of the joint products.

The firm presently makes 400,000 gallons of X-diampyl per month, which is all that it can sell. The process also generates about 0.5 gallon of a chemical called chlorogen for each gallon of X-diampyl. Chlorogen sells for $0.40 per gallon.

Recently, a chemist in R&D developed a way to make chlorogen into two new products, X-chloro and Y-chloro. Preliminary investigations indicate that these products would bring $0.44 and $0.90 per gallon, respectively. Each 1,000-gallon batch of chlorogen would require about $30 in other ingredients and would yield about 390 gallons of X-chloro and 440 gallons of Y-chloro, with the rest lost to evaporation. Labor costs would be about $40 per batch. The firm's standard overhead rate is $2.40 per direct labor dollar, including a fixed component of about $1.50. The process would not add to the firm's fixed costs.

REQUIRED

1. Determine whether the firm should process chlorogen beyond split-off.
2. Suppose that further processing would add $15,200 to monthly fixed costs, required for additional supervision and other costs not considered in part 1. Would your recommendation be the same as it was in part 1?

11–12 Multiple Split-off Points Corcoran Chemical Company operates a plant that has three departments. In department I, a raw material costing $60 per ton is processed into Algon and Betagon. Department II processes Algon into Trigon and Zygon, while department III processes Betagon into Betaplus. The plant can handle 800 tons of raw material per month. Yields of products, along with other data, appear below.

Department I: 1,200 pounds of Algon and 600 pounds of Betagon per ton of raw material
Department II: 0.60 pound Trigon and 0.25 pound of Zygon per pound of Algon
Department III: 0.90 pound Betaplus per pound of Betagon

All losses are from evaporation and cannot be reduced with the existing techniques for processing. Cost data by department are

Department	*Unavoidable Monthly Fixed Costs*	*Avoidable Monthly Fixed Costs*	*Variable Cost per Hour of Processing*
I	$20,000	$55,000	$12
II	11,000	37,000	14
III	9,000	17,000	9

The unavoidable fixed costs consist of depreciation and allocated costs such as rent.

Processing times are as follows: department I, 2 hours per ton of raw material; department II, 2 hours per 1,000 pounds of Algon; department III, $\frac{1}{2}$ hour per 1,000 pounds of Betagon.

Prices and variable selling costs are:

	Algon	*Betagon*	*Trigon*	*Zygon*	*Betaplus*
Price per pound	$0.12	$0.10	$0.34	$0.20	$0.14
Selling expense per pound	0.02	0.01	0.04	0.04	0.01

REQUIRED

1. Determine the firm's optimal processing decisions and the profit it will earn by making those decisions.
2. Determine the price of Betaplus at which the firm would be indifferent between selling Betagon and processing it into Betaplus. Assume that unit selling expenses would remain as given.
3. Suppose that some new machinery could be leased for $12,000 per month. The machinery would enable the firm to increase the yield of Algon to 1,300 pounds per ton of raw material. The yield of Betagon would remain at 600 pounds. Would it be financially advantageous to acquire the new machinery if all other cost and revenue data remained the same?

11–13 Processing Decision Walker Pork Company makes a number of pork products and processes the hides into tanned leather for sale to other firms. The assistant controller has developed the following income statement for a typical month, which she believes shows that the firm should stop tanning the hides and sell them after they come off the animals. The price per hide would be $6 without tanning.

	Meat	*Hides*	*Total*
Sales (10,000 hogs processed)	$840,000	$120,000	$960,000
Cost of hogs	437,500	62,500	500,000
Processing costs:			
Separation of hide and meat	131,250	18,750	150,000
Separate processing	220,000	23,000	243,000
Total costs	$788,750	$104,250	$893,000
Profit	$ 51,250	$ 15,750	$ 67,000

The separate processing costs are all incremental. About 70 percent of the costs of separating the hides and meat are incremental.

REQUIRED

Analyze the assistant controller's proposal.

11–14 Joint Cost Allocation Quanto Company makes three joint products. It allocates joint costs to each product using the net realizable value method. It also uses FIFO. Data for April 19X7 appear below.

	Product		
	896	*451*	*341*
Units in beginning inventory	2,000	0	6,000
Units produced during April	25,000	46,000	20,000
Units in ending inventory	4,000	8,000	0
Units sold	23,000	38,000	26,000
Cost of beginning inventory	$7,800	$0	$60,600
Selling price at split-off	$3	$0	$7
Selling price after further processing	$9	$12	$15
Selling expenses per unit, at split-off and after additional processing	$0.40	$0.20	$0.80
Additional processing costs for April	$30,000	$120,000	$80,000
Total joint costs = $600,000			

All products were processed beyond the split-off point. Selling expenses are incurred when the products are sold.

REQUIRED

Prepare an income statement for April with necessary supporting schedules.

11–15 Joint Costs—Selling at Split-off Byron Gumbo, controller of Rice Manufacturing, Inc., has been looking over the costs of making the company's two main products, Filé and Flambe. To make these two products, a common raw material is used in a joint process to produce Filé powder and Flambe cake. Further work is required to bring both products to a finished stage of Filé liquid concentrate and Flambe pellets. The standard costs for the joint process are as follows.

Standard Costs to Produce 1 lb Semiprocessed Filé Powder and ½ lb Semiprocessed Flambe Cake	
Raw materials, 2 gal at $25	$ 50
Direct labor, 15 hr at $12	180
Variable overhead at $15/DLH	225
Fixed overhead[a]	80
Standard joint cost	$535

[a]Based on $1,600,000 per year and 40,000 gallons (standard use) of raw material.

During 19X4, Rice plans to produce 20,000 pounds of Filé powder and 10,000 pounds of Flambe cake. Flambe cake cannot be sold as an intermediate product and must be processed into pellet form at a cost of $500,000 for the planned production. Flambe pellets sell for $300 per pound. There is a market for both Filé powder and liquid concentrate. The semifinished product can be sold for $350 per pound, while the liquid concentrate sells for $800 per gallon. It takes 2 pounds of powder to produce 1 gallon of concentrate. Further processing costs are $120,000 for each 1,000 gallons.

REQUIRED

Should Gumbo sell Filé at split-off?

11–16 Joint Products and CVP Analysis Marcot Company processes a raw material into three joint products. Data relating to a single batch appear below.

	Joint Products		
	X-10	Y-15	Z-30
Gallons per batch of material	40	120	30
Selling price at split-off, per gallon	$1	$3	$ 7
Additional processing costs, variable per gallon	$3	$2	$ 5
Selling price after further processing, per gallon	$5	$7	$11

Monthly fixed costs, all unavoidable, are $110,000. The raw material cost per batch is $180, and direct labor and variable overhead associated with each batch are $60.

REQUIRED

1. How many batches must the firm process to earn $40,000 each month?
2. Suppose that the firm could increase the output of Z-30 by 10 gallons per batch if it used a new raw material that costs $210. Direct labor and variable overhead would remain constant, as would the yields of the other joint products. Would it be to the firm's advantage to use the new material?
3. Assume that the firm is using the old material. If the price of Z-30 after further processing increased to $14, how many batches would the firm have to produce to earn a $40,000 monthly profit?

11–17 Make or Buy Decision Thorson Company manufactures a number of products. Among them are three chemicals that arise from a single raw material put through a single process. Data on these products for a typical month appear below.

The firm processes product 101 beyond split-off at a cost of $100,000 and sells 102 and 103 at split-off. The joint costs of $600,000 are allocated using the net realizable value method. Of the $600,000, about $100,000 is unavoidable cost such as depreciation.

The firm currently buys a chemical outside for $8 per gallon and uses it in a product made in another department. The manager in charge of that product has discovered that he could use product 102 in place of the chemical he now buys, provided that he put 102 through some additional processing. The additional processing would cost $1.50 per gallon variable, and incremental fixed costs would be about $15,000 per month. He would need 20,000 gallons of 102 per month.

		Product		
	Total	*101*	*102*	*103*
Output in gallons	100,000	60,000	30,000	10,000
Revenue	$1,100,000	$720,000	$180,000	$200,000
Cost of sales	700,000	472,000	108,000	120,000
Gross margin	$ 400,000	$248,000	$ 72,000	$ 80,000

Looking at the data above, the manager made the following calculation to show that it would be better for the firm to process 102 and stop buying the chemical outside.

Processing cost of product 102, $108,000/30,000	$3.60
Variable processing cost	1.50
Fixed processing cost per unit, $15,000/20,000	0.75
Total unit cost	$5.85

"That's less than the $8 we now pay, so it should be a good deal to use 20,000 gallons inside," was the conclusion.

REQUIRED

Determine whether the manager is correct.

11–18 Relationships (AICPA Adapted) Bensom Company makes three joint products. The following data are available from operations from August, in thousands of dollars:

	Product			
	N	O	P	*Total*
Sales value at split-off	$__	$__	$50	$200
Allocated joint costs	$ 48	$__	$__	$120
Sales value if processed further	$110	$90	$60	$260
Additional costs, if product processed beyond split-off	$ 18	$14	$12	$ 44

The firm allocates joint costs using the relative sales values at split-off. It also made the best decisions about selling at split-off or processing further.

REQUIRED

1. Fill in the blanks above.
2. Determine the gross profit that the firm earned. There were no inventories at either the beginning or end of August.

11–19 Further Processing Decision (CMA Adapted) Cum-Clean Corporation manufactures a variety of cleaning compounds and solutions for household and industrial use. Although most are processed independently, a few are related.

Grit-337 is a coarse cleaning powder with industrial uses. It costs $1.60 per pound to make and sells for $2.00 per pound. A small portion of Grit-337 is used with several other ingredients to make a silver polish that sells for $4.00 per jar. This additional processing requires $\frac{1}{4}$ pound of Grit-337 per jar of polish. The additional processing costs to make the polish are $2.50 per jar. There are also variable selling costs of $0.30 per jar. If the company were to stop making the polish, it could avoid fixed costs of $5,600 per year.

REQUIRED

Determine the number of jars of polish the company must sell to justify further processing of Grit-337.

11–20 Joint Products and By-Products (CMA) Multiproduct Corporation is a chemical manufacturer that produces two main products (Pepco-1 and Repke-3) and a by-product (SE-5) from a joint process. If Multiproduct had the proper facilities, it could process SE-5 further into a main product. The ratio of output quantities to input quantity of direct material used in the joint process remains consistent with the processing conditions and activity level.

Multiproduct currently uses the physical method of allocating joint costs to the main products. The FIFO inventory method is used to value the main products. The by-product is inventoried at its net realizable value, and the net realizable value of the by-product is used to reduce the joint production costs before the joint costs are allocated to the main products.

Jim Simpson, Multiproduct's controller, wants to implement the relative sales value method of joint cost allocation. He believes that inventoriable costs should be based on each product's ability to contribute to the recovery of joint production costs. The net realizable value of the by-product would be treated in the same manner as with the physical method.

Data regarding Multiproduct's operations for November 1986 are presented below. The joint cost of production amounted to $2,640,000 for November, 19X6.

	Main Products		By-Product
	Pepco-1	Repke-3	SE-5
Finished goods inventory in gallons on November 1, 19X6	20,000	40,000	10,000
November sales in gallons	800,000	700,000	200,000
November production in gallons	900,000	720,000	240,000
Sales value per gallon at split-off point	$2.00	$1.50	$.55*
Additional processing costs after split-off	$1,800,000	$720,000	
Final sales value per gallon	$5.00	$4.00	

*Disposal and selling costs of $.05 per gallon will be incurred to sell the by-product.

REQUIRED

1. Describe the relative sales value method and explain how it accomplishes Jim Simpson's objective.
2. Assuming Multiproduct Corporation adopts the relative sales value method for internal reporting purposes,
   a. calculate how the joint production cost for November, 19X6 would be allocated
   b. determine the dollar values of the finished goods inventories for Pepco-1, Repke-3, and SE-5 as of November 30, 19X6
3. Multiproduct Corporation plans to expand its production facilities to enable the further processing of SE-5 into a main product. Discuss how the allocation of the joint production costs under the relative sales value method would change when SE-5 becomes a main product.

11–21 Joint Products—Variable Proportions Tyndall Company produces three bulk chemicals in a joint process. The process and raw materials allow the firm to vary, within limits, the proportions of each product that emerge from a single batch. Information about the percentages of each product that can be produced, and about other characteristics of each product, appears below. The firm can process 100,000 pounds of raw materials per month, yielding 100,000 pounds of the three joint products.

	Output—Range of Percentages				
Product	*High*	*Low*	*Price at Split-off*	*Price After Further Processing*	*Cost per Pound of Further Processing*
Nalgon	30%	20%	$3.20	$3.80	$0.40
Norphyll	40	30	2.50	3.10	0.80
Kryton	50	20	1.80	3.70	0.70

REQUIRED

Develop a production plan for the firm, including the quantities of each product that it should make and the disposition of each product (sell at split-off or process further).

11–22 Negative Net Realizable Value Blackman Company runs a joint process that produces two saleable products and a toxic waste. Data for a typical month are as follows:

	Saleable Products		
	CZ-60	*MR-42*	*Waste*
Quantity produced, in pounds	60,000	35,000	5,000
Selling price at split-off	$10/lb	$8/lb	0

Monthly joint costs are $550,000. The firm currently pays an outside contractor $20,000 a month to haul the waste to a safe dump.

REQUIRED

1. For product costing for financial accounting purposes, how would you treat the $20,000 paid to haul away the waste? As an expense? As part of the cost of producing the saleable products? Why?

2. Suppose that the firm could process the waste into a saleable product at a cost of $24,000 per month. The new product would sell for $2 per pound. Would it be advantageous for the firm to do the processing?
3. Assume that your answer to part 2 was that it would benefit the firm to process the waste. For product costing purposes, how would you allocate costs to each product?

11–23 Joint Cost Allocations (AICPA) Crowley Company produces joint products A and B from a process that also yields by-product Y. The by-product requires additional processing before it can be sold. Crowley uses the net realizable value method of accounting for the by-product. Data related to January's activity appear below. Total joint costs were $40,000.

Product	Unit Production	Market Value	Costs after Split-off
A	800	$44,000	$4,500
B	700	32,000	3,500
Y	500	4,000	1,000

REQUIRED

Determine the amount of joint cost to be allocated to each of the joint products.

11–24 Variable Proportions—Calculus Braton Chemical Company makes two chemicals, beon and zeon, in a joint process. The process takes 10,000 gallons of raw material and heats it under pressure to yield the joint products. The output of the process depends on the running time: the longer it runs, the more zeon and the less beon. However, evaporation occurs and increases rapidly as the time increases. The equations below give the quantities of beon and zeon, expressed as functions of the number of hours each batch stays in the process.

$$Q_b = 10{,}000 - Q_z - 100H^2$$
$$Q_z = 1{,}000H$$

Where Q_b = number of gallons of beon
Q_z = number of gallons of zeon
H = number of hours the process runs for each batch

The last term in the first equation, $-100H^2$, represents evaporation. Thus, the total yield is always less than 10,000 gallons.

Beon sells for $10 per gallon, zeon for $20. The cost of the raw material is $65,000 per 10,000 gallons. The variable cost to operate the process is $500 per hour.

REQUIRED

Determine the optimal time for operating the process, the quantities of each product that the firm will make, and the gross profit at the optimal mix.

11–25 Joint Cost Allocations—Gross Margins (CMA) Doe Corporation grows, processes, cans, and sells three main pineapple products—sliced, crushed, and juice. The Cutting Department removes the outside skin, which is processed into animal feed. The skin and resulting feed are treated as a by-product.

The Cutting Department also cores and trims the pineapples for slicing. The three main products (sliced, crushed, and juice) and the by-product are identifiable after the Cutting Department has finished its work. The trimmed pineapples go to the Slicing Department, which slices and cans them. Some additional juice is produced here, which is packed in the cans with the slices. The pieces trimmed in the Cutting Department go to the Crushing Department. Again, some juice is generated here and packed in cans with the crushed pineapple.

The core and other material left over from the Cutting Department are pulverized into liquid in the Juicing Department. About 8 percent of good output of juice is lost from evaporation as the juice is heated.

Doe uses the net realizable value method for both the main products and by-product. Doe processed 270,000 pounds of pineapple in May. Other data for May appear below.

Department	*Costs Incurred*	*Percentage of Product by Weight Transferred to Departments*	*Selling Price per Pound of Final Product*
Cutting	$60,000	—	none
Slicing	4,700	35%	$0.60
Crushing	10,580	28%	0.55
Juicing	3,250	27%	0.30
Animal feed	700	10%	0.10
Total	$79,230	100%	

REQUIRED

1. Determine the number of pounds of pineapple that result as output for slices, crushed, juice, and animal feed.
2. Determine the net realizable values of each of the four products.
3. Allocate the Cutting Department cost to each product.
4. Determine the gross margin on each product, assuming all output is sold.
5. Discuss the significance of the gross margin figures to planning and control.

11–26 Cost Allocations and Gross Profit (AICPA) Warfield Company manufactures products C, D, and E from a joint process. It allocates joint costs using relative sales values at the split-off point. Data for one month appear below.

	C	*D*	*E*	*Total*
Units produced	6,000	4,000	2,000	12,000
Joint costs allocated	$ 72,000	?	?	$120,000
Sales value at split-off	?	?	$30,000	$200,000
Additional costs to process further	$ 14,000	$10,000	$ 6,000	$ 30,000
Sales value if processed further	$140,000	$60,000	$40,000	$240,000

REQUIRED

1. Determine the joint costs allocated to product D.

2. Assume that Warfield further processed the 2,000 units of product E and sold them. Determine the gross profit earned on product E for the month.

11–27 Comprehensive Joint Products Problem Steger Chemical Company buys a single raw material for $0.10 per pound. The material is put through a process from which three products emerge. The processing is done in batches of 1,000 pounds of material and requires 10 labor hours per batch. The joint process has associated fixed costs of $2,200 per month, of which $1,200 is avoidable. The output of a 1,000-pound batch is as follows:

Product	*Quantity in Pounds*	*Selling Price per Pound*
Algex	300	$0.90
Gamex	200	1.80
Deltex	400	0.75
Waste	100	0

Each of the three usable products can be put through further processing. Algex can be made into two new products, Nonex and Querex. The variable cost to process a 100-pound batch of Algex is $40 for labor and overhead. Fixed costs associated with the process are $12,000 per month, of which $4,800 is avoidable. The output per 100 pounds of Algex is:

Product	*Quantity in Pounds*	*Selling Price per Pound*
Nonex	45	$3
Querex	40	2
Waste	15	0

Gamex can be processed further and sold for $1.90 per pound. The additional processing requires one labor hour per 100 pounds.

Deltex can be refined and sold for $1.20 per pound. The additional refining requires three-fourths of a labor hour per 100 pounds put into the refining process. Evaporation during the process takes 10 percent of the quantity put into the process. The refining process also has incremental, avoidable fixed costs of $2,200 per month.

For all processes, the cost per hour of labor time is $20, which includes labor and variable overhead. The firm can process 10 tons of raw material per month and can sell all of any product it makes. Selling and administrative expenses are $1,600 per month.

REQUIRED

Answer each question independently of the others, unless otherwise stated.

1. Determine the firm's best production plan. Which products should be sold at split-off, and which processed further?
2. Prepare an income statement for a month, based on your answer to part 1.
3. The selling prices of some of the products might change in the next few months. The president of the firm is concerned about the possibilities and the potential effects on the firm's operations. Specifically, the president asks you the following questions.

a. At what price per pound for Querex would the firm earn the same profit processing Algex into Nonex and Querex as it would selling Algex at split-off?

b. At what price per pound for Gamex, after further processing, would the firm earn the same profit processing it further as it would selling it at split-off?

4. The firm has the opportunity to rent equipment for $2,000 per month. Using the equipment would enable the firm to increase its capacity to 12 tons of raw material per month. No other costs would be affected. All additional output of any product could be sold at the prices given. Determine the effect on the firm's monthly profit if the equipment is rented.

5. The president of the firm has learned of a new process, which could be used to make a new product called Postex. Each 100-pound batch of Postex requires 50 pounds of Nonex and 50 pounds of Gamex (as it emerges from the joint process). Postex could be sold for $4 per pound. The combining process would require two labor hours per 100-pound batch. Additional fixed costs of $800 per month would also have to be incurred. Determine the effect on monthly profit of making Postex.

6. Another new process is also available. In this process the firm would combine Algex and Gamex (after Gamex has been further processed) into Zentex. A 100-pound batch of Zentex requires 50 pounds of each of the other products and three labor hours. Additional fixed costs would be $1,500 per month. Zentex can be sold for $2.50 per pound. Determine the effect on the firm's monthly profit of making Zentex.

11–28 Adding a Department (CMA Adapted) The management of Bay Company is considering a proposal to install a third production department within its existing factory building. With the company's present production set up, raw material is passed through department I to produce materials A and B in equal proportions. Material A is then passed through department II to yield product C. Material B is presently being sold "as is" at a price of $20.25 per pound. Product C has a selling price of $100 per pound.

The per pound standard costs currently being used by the Bay Company are as follows:

	Department I (Materials A and B)	*Department II (Product C)*	*(Material B)*
Prior department costs	—	$53.03	$13.47
Direct material	$20.00	—	—
Direct labor	7.00	12.00	—
Variable overhead	3.00	5.00	—
Fixed overhead:			
Attributable	2.25	2.25	—
Allocated ($\frac{2}{3}$, $\frac{1}{3}$)	1.00	1.00	—
	$33.25	$73.28	$13.47

These standard costs were developed by using an estimated production volume of 200,000 pounds of raw material as the standard volume. The company assigns department I costs to materials A and B in proportion to their net sales values at the point of separation, computed by deducting subsequent standard production costs from sales prices. The $300,000 of common fixed overhead costs are allocated to the two producing departments on the basis of the space used by the departments.

The proposed department III would be used to process material B into product D. It is expected that any quantity of product D can be sold for $30 per pound. Standard costs per pound as proposed, developed by using 200,000 pounds of raw material as the standard volume, are shown below.

Department D would occupy space that is not currently used, and there are no foreseeable alternative uses for the space. The firm's managers expect sales and production levels to continue at their present levels. They also expect selling prices to hold at their present levels.

	Department I (Materials A and B)	*Department II (Product C)*	*Department III (Product D)*
Prior department costs	—	$52.80	$13.20
Direct material	$20.00	—	—
Direct labor	7.00	12.00	5.50
Variable overhead	3.00	5.00	2.00
Fixed overhead:			
Attributable	2.25	2.25	1.75
Allocated ($\frac{1}{2}$, $\frac{1}{4}$, $\frac{1}{4}$)	0.75	0.75	0.75
	$33.00	$72.80	$23.20

REQUIRED

1. Determine whether the firm should make product D.
2. Suppose that the managers expect the price of product D to be $30 per pound about 75 percent of the time, $25 about 25 percent of the time. Other prices are expected to remain constant. The attributable overhead of department III is unavoidable once the department is set up, but the firm can avoid the variable costs of producing product D if it sells material B at split-off. Should the firm install department III under these conditions?

11–29 Determine Joint Costs, Constant Gross Margin (AICPA Adapted) O'Conner Company manufactures products J and K in a joint process. During a recent month the firm produced 4,000 units of product J, which had a value at the split-off point of $15,000. Processing product J would have given revenue of $20,000. The additional processing costs would have been $3,000. For product K, 2,000 units were produced having a sales value at split-off of $10,000. Processing product K further would have yielded revenues of $12,000 and additional processing costs of $1,000.

The firm used the relative sales values of the products at the split-off point to allocate the joint costs. Product J received $9,000 of allocated joint costs.

REQUIRED

1. Determine the total joint costs for the month.
2. What would have been the allocations of joint costs if the firm had used the constant gross margin rate method and had made the best decisions regarding each product (sell at split-off or process further)?

11–30 Processing Decisions Wilkinson Company manufactures a variety of furniture, all from wood. The firm operates several integrated factories, each with its own sawmill for cutting timber into pieces of desired sizes, and with other departments that make the finished products. The factories sometimes sell cut lumber, rather than convert it into finished goods, especially when they cannot operate the finishing departments at full capacity. Because the output from the sawmill is rough-cut, the lumber department must do additional work before it sells the lumber. Sales of lumber are usually about 7 to 8 percent of total physical output of the sawmill.

In March of 19X6 the general manager of the Marathon Plant, which specialized in pine furniture, received the following income statement, with dollars in thousands. The Marathon Plant operated three departments: lumber, office furniture, and home furniture.

			Furniture	
	Total	*Lumber*	*Office*	*Home*
Sales	$743.2	$96.5	$369.3	$277.4
Materials and sawmill costs	334.4	43.4	166.2	124.8
Added materials	11.9	0.0	7.6	4.3
Direct labor	126.7	6.2	77.3	43.2
Overhead	163.3	21.2	91.1	51.0
Cost of sales	636.3	70.8	342.2	223.3
Gross margin	106.9	25.7	27.1	54.1
Selling/administrative expenses	87.8	11.4	43.6	32.8
Profit (loss)	$ 19.1	$14.3	($ 16.5)	$ 21.3
Percentage of sawmill output	100.0%	18.8%	47.2%	$ 34.0%

From consultations with the controller, the manager knew:

1. The materials and sawmill costs were allocated to operations on the basis of relative sales dollars. These costs were about 80 percent variable at the present level of operations, which was nearly full capacity for the sawmill.

2. Added materials (hardware and other nonwood items) and direct labor were variable.

3. Variable manufacturing overhead was about 60 percent of direct labor across all departments. Fixed overhead was about 80 percent avoidable across all departments.

4. The controller allocated selling and administrative expenses on the basis of sales because the only variable component was a 5 percent commission on all products (including lumber), so that total expenses depended only on sales volume.

5. The home furniture department was operating at capacity, but the office furniture department was at 70 percent capacity. The manager expected this situation to continue. Severe competition in the office furniture business had resulted in drops in prices and an oversupply on the market. Demand for lumber was strong.

The general manager was disturbed by the results for the office furniture department but was unsure what to do.

REQUIRED

Analyze the situation and make a recommendation based on the available information. State clearly any assumptions that you must make. List items of information that you would want to better ground your recommendation.

11–31 Qualities of Products "As I see it, we ought to cost the B-grade wood based on its selling price and let the A-grade wood take the major burden." Tom Norton, the sales manager of Bainbridge Wood Products, was speaking to Sandy Charles, the controller, about wood that had blemishes, knots, and other defects that made it less desirable than A-grade wood. All wood went through the same processes. After being cut and sanded, it was inspected and classified as A-grade or B-grade. The company used strict inspection procedures to classify its wood. Wood that passed the tests and became grade A was sold to furniture makers for use on exposed surfaces, where appearance was important. The B-grade wood was sold for use in unexposed areas of furniture. The price of A-grade wood was relatively stable, but that of B-grade fluctuated considerably. Bainbridge often had difficulty selling B-grade wood, and Norton was trying to persuade Charles to accept an offer from Batesville Furniture for large quantities of B-grade wood over the next year.

Charles was not excited about the offer and produced the schedule below to justify the position.

	Cost per 1,000 Board Feet
Purchase price	$65.00
Direct labor	12.45
Overhead	18.65
Total	$96.10

About 80 percent of the overhead is fixed.

"Look," she said, "we cannot sell B-grade wood at $86, as you want to, and make any money. It all comes from the same tree, goes through the same processes, costs us the same. I hope you won't take offense, Tom, but I really think that your salespeople just don't want to get out and sell the B-grade wood because it's harder to sell. Moreover, about 35 percent of our output is B-grade, so we cannot let it go at below cost prices."

Norton then pressed his suggestion that costs be assigned based on value. "Why don't we recognize that we really have a by-product here and assign costs in some way that reflects the relative values of the grades? Then we wouldn't be trying to get uncompetitive prices for the B-grade wood and watching it pile up in the yard. We can usually get $140 a thousand for A-grade wood, but the B-grade market is usually between $80 and $105." "Tom," replied Charles, "cost is cost and price is price. We can't change our costs every time prices change. All of that wood has the same cost."

REQUIRED

1. Suppose that Bainbridge processes about 10 million board feet per month. Show how the costs would be allocated to the A-grade and B-grade wood, treating the B-grade wood as a main product and using the $86 per thousand price as its net realizable value.
2. Repeat part 1 assuming that Bainbridge treats the B-grade wood as a by-product and costs it at its net realizable value.
3. Make a recommendation and support it.

12

TACTICAL DECISION MAKING

Managers use accounting data extensively in making decisions. They use other data as well (market and manufacturing data, for example), but cost and price data, supplied by the accounting system, are important in most decisions. This chapter treats decisions variously called **tactical**, **short-term**, or **operating**. Such decisions usually run their course within a year or less. In fact, some people classify short-term decisions as those whose effects will not last more than one year. Thus, short-term decisions do not involve acquiring new plant assets or making significant capital expenditures. Long-term decisions, called capital budgeting decisions, are covered in Chapters 13 and 14.

We use the term *tactical* to describe short-term decisions because they are not *strategic decisions*. Strategic decisions set the course for a company or other organization for a long period. Strategic decisions include entering or not entering new markets, and developing or not developing particular types of products. Short-term decisions are *operating*, not financial. They do not involve deciding, for example, whether to issue stock or debt. They involve the day-to-day operations of the organization.

William T. Morris says:

> It is sometimes helpful to think of decision-making behavior as characterized along a continuum from random decision making at one extreme, through inspirational decision making, to systematic behavior at the other extreme. By random behavior we might mean decisions with no detectable pattern, order, logic, or consistency. Random decisions are those which we, as observers, find impossible to model, to explain, or to predict. Inspirational decisions are those which feel "good" or "right" to the decision maker himself, but to the observer

> the explanation of the choice seems highly oversimplified, leaving out most of the obvious considerations present in the situation and placing excessive weight on one or two factors. Systematic deciding implies that the decision maker and the observer can fully see the logic, the pattern, the process that explains choices. Systematic behavior has a sort of consistency, predictability, and clarity that indicates the decision maker knows what he is doing when he decides.
>
> There is a strong belief, and considerable evidence to support the belief, that systematic decision making increases the probability of achieving a good outcome. There is evidence that almost any systematic method of deciding, even though highly simplified, is better than none.[1]

The tactical decisions that we consider in this chapter are solved by systematic means but usually are nonrecurring. (The *type* of decision can recur, but specific decisions are unique.) Routine problems need to be solved only once; then procedures can be set up to handle them when they recur. For example, once a product pricing formula and the appropriate costs to use in it have been established, all that needs to be done is to update the information, rather than rethink the process, each time a product needs to be priced.

A good decision is consistent with the objectives of the decision maker and the information available. Making a good decision does not necessarily lead to a good result: the future may bring events, favorable and unfavorable, that could not have been predicted. This does not mean that a poor decision was made. If a manager used available information well, then the decision was good *at the time*.

The objectives of the manager might lead to selecting an action that is not the most profitable. That is, the action that the manager expects to give the best economic results might require doing something that conflicts with company policy or be inconsistent with one of the company's strategies. For instance, it might be wise in the *short-term* to use excess capacity to manufacture products of less-than-usual quality for a chain store to be sold under the chain's brand name. But if one strategy is to concentrate on high-priced, high-quality products, the deal with the chain is inconsistent and managers should reject it (or rethink the strategy).

Additionally, we deal for the most part with the quantifiable aspects of decisions. Most decisions have nonquantifiable aspects, which can sometimes be overriding. For example, it might be cheaper for a company to buy a component than to make it. Managers might decide to make it because they are not sure that the outside supplier will meet delivery schedules, produce a component of acceptable quality, or make technological improvements. As Chapters 13 and 14 discuss, managers base many strategic decisions on qualitative issues such as competitive advantage, reliability of suppliers, and customer satisfaction.

---

[1] William T. Morris, *Decision Analysis* (Columbus, OH: Grid, Inc., 1977) p. 1.

RELEVANT INFORMATION

Tactical (or short-term) decisions have an immediate rather than long-term economic impact. Such decisions can usually be quickly reversed. For example, if a price is set too high, it can be lowered. These types of decisions are different from long-term decisions (like capital budgeting) and strategic decisions. Capital budgeting decisions deal with projects that will stretch over a span of at least one year and require a large commitment of resources. Strategic decisions involve the future direction of a company. What organizational structure should it have? What are the goals and objectives for the next five years? As you might expect, it is sometimes difficult to distinguish decisions that have only an immediate effect from those with more lasting effects. Because it can be difficult to determine where short-term effects end, we shall use the term *tactical* rather than *short term*.

Some of the common decisions we investigate in this chapter have longer term implications. In some cases, the best short-term decision is also best for the long-term. For instance, a company might profitably buy parts rather than manufacture them. However, a few years later it might find itself in difficulty if the major supplier goes out of business, reduces the quality of the parts, or raises prices. To develop the internal capacity to manufacture the parts could take a while. Sometimes a series of short-term decisions turns into a long-term decision. A manufacturer with excess capacity might contract to work for other companies. As it accepts more and more work, it could fill its plant with such work and need to make capital expenditures simply to keep up with its regular business. This is an example of creeping into a long-term decision through a series of short-term decisions.

Thus, this discussion of relevant information is the basic framework for all decisions, whether strategic, long term, or tactical. When there are longer term effects, however, a manager usually must extend the analysis to consider the time value of money. We discuss this subject in Chapters 13 and 14.

The Criterion of Relevance

Information is **relevant** if it relates to revenues and costs that will differ among the alternative courses of action being considered. For example, the material on cost behavior in Chapters 2 and 3 explains that variable costs change in total as volume changes, fixed costs remain constant. Therefore, if a manager is deciding how many units to produce next month, fixed costs are irrelevant, since they will not change unless volume moves outside the relevant range.

Relevant revenues and costs are often called incremental or differential. Revenues and costs are **incremental** (or **differential**) if they are expected to differ under different courses of action. The concepts of relevant/irrelevant revenues and costs must be applied case by case. A particular cost might be relevant to one decision, irrelevant to another. For instance, the cost of automobile insurance is relevant to a decision to buy one model of car versus another, if those cars call for different insurance premiums. Once you own a car, however, the insurance premium is irrelevant in deciding whether to drive the car on a particular 100-mile trip. Likewise, some of the incremental costs of buying and driving a new automobile are the purchase price and operating costs. Once you have bought the car, though, the purchase price is no longer incremental of operations. The purchase price is no longer relevant to decisions involving how much you will drive the car. You cannot change the purchase price. In the parlance of decision making, the purchase price is a **sunk cost**. A sunk cost is one already incurred and, therefore, cannot be changed.

Sunk costs are irrelevant for decision making. As we shall see in Chapters 13 and 14, however, the historical cost of an asset may be relevant because it will affect taxes through gains or losses on disposition or through taxes saved by depreciation.

Sunk costs are not the only irrelevant or nonincremental costs. A manufacturing firm's fixed costs are nonincremental with respect to the manager's decision about how many units to produce within the relevant range. At any level within that range fixed costs will be the same. If you are deciding between two competing pieces of machinery and the crews required for each are identical, then you can ignore labor costs (as long as you have decided you will purchase one of the two machines). Many people use the terms *avoidable* and *unavoidable* to describe incremental and nonincremental costs.

Opportunity Costs

An **opportunity cost** is the benefit foregone by using a resource in one way as opposed to another. For instance, one of the major costs of going to college is the salary you could earn during your time in college. Time is an important resource, as the saying, "time is money," indicates. In a decision making context, consider the following example. A company has a supply of components that are no longer used in its products. The components originally cost $12,000 and could be sold as-is for $7,000. The components could be used for a one-time special order of products. The order will sell for $23,000 and incremental costs (without considering the components) are $13,000. A manager objects to using the components this way and prepares the following analysis:

Selling price of order		$23,000
Costs of order:		
Components	$12,000	
Other	13,000	25,000
Loss		($ 2,000)

Is this analysis correct? You should see that the $12,000 original cost of the components is sunk and therefore irrelevant, but what cost, if any, is associated with the components? The correct cost is the opportunity cost of $7,000—the next best use.

Selling price of order		$23,000
Costs of order:		
Components	$ 7,000	
Other	13,000	20,000
Gain		$ 3,000

Opportunity cost is a tricky concept because it depends on viewpoint—what you are doing or contemplating doing with a resource. The opportunity cost is that of the best alternative use. Let us change our example to illustrate this important point. Suppose that the components are still being used in the company's products and that buying them now costs $15,000. (The lot on hand might have been bought a considerable time ago.) What now is the opportunity cost of using them in the special order? It is $15,000, the replacement cost, because the company must buy more if it uses them. The order is now unprofitable. Note that the historical cost is still irrelevant. Interestingly, the market resale price is also now irrelevant; selling the components is no longer the best alternative use because the company must continue to buy them.

Joint (Common) Costs

Many decisions involve segments of a firm: product lines, products, geographical areas, factories, and so on. Costs that benefit more than one segment of the firm are called **joint** or **common** to the benefited segments. Joint costs will not change as a result of decisions affecting one of the segments to which they are joint. For example, the fixed costs of producing a particular product are joint to each of the units produced. Producing more or fewer units will not affect total fixed costs, so they are not differential with respect to decisions involving the quantity of production. However, if dropping the product would eliminate the fixed costs, they are differential and relevant to the decision to drop that product.

Joint costs can be variable as well as fixed. An oil refinery produces many products. The variable costs of crude labor associated with refining are joint to all the oil and petrochemical products that ultimately result.

The principal problem with joint costs is that they frequently are allocated to units of product, product lines, departments, and other segments of a firm. These allocations are sometimes made to conform with external reporting requirements: either generally accepted accounting principles or regulatory agency requirements. If the company uses only one accounting system that does not differentiate costs needed for financial accounting from those needed for management decision making, the accountant must remove the allocated costs before using the information for making decisions. As we discussed in Chapter 4, allocated costs are irrelevant. Any cost that is joint with respect to the decision at hand is not differential.

It is not always easy to determine what costs are common or joint; it depends on the particular situation. The salary of a plant manager is common to the units produced. Therefore, it is irrelevant in determining whether to increase or decrease production. But if the decision is whether to shut the entire plant down, the salary is relevant because it would be avoided if the plant were closed. The person making a decision must carefully analyze the alternatives and the scope of the decision to ascertain which costs are relevant and which are not. It is impossible to develop general rules regarding the relevance of particular items of cost. We cannot say, for example, that all variable costs are relevant to all decisions or that all fixed costs are not relevant. We must analyze each case separately.

Of particular concern in analyzing costs is that savings can often be gained from costs that appear to be common. Suppose a factory has six manufacturing departments and several service departments such as Personnel and Accounting. People in the Personnel Department do work that relates to employees in all departments, so Personnel Department salaries are common to all departments. However, if the factory dropped one of its manufacturing departments, it would probably be possible to rearrange work so that Personnel needed fewer people. There would surely be a reduction in Personnel's workload, so there could be cost reductions even though Personnel's costs appear common to all departments. The principal question in such cases is usually the size of the discontinued department. Dropping a department with 2 percent of the workforce might not permit any reductions in Personnel Department costs. This point grows out of the idea of examining activities to determine their use of resources, as Chapter 4 discussed.

Qualitative Factors

As noted earlier, in decision making qualitative factors are often ignored. We get tied into looking at expected costs and benefits and forget the effect of nonquantitative factors on our decision. Thus, besides looking at differential costs, management needs to consider issues relating to pollution, community responsibility, safety, and the perceptions that employees, the community, and/or customers might have about various decisions. While some of these concerns will have measurable monetary effects on a company, many cannot be accurately quantified.

Many students think that the accountant's role involves just looking at "the figures" and that someone else should deal with the nonquantitative aspects of a problem. Our perspective is that we accumulate, analyze, and use information—including quantitative and qualitative information.

COMMON TACTICAL DECISIONS

The discussion so far shows that relevance is situational; what is relevant in one case might not be in another. The question to ask is what revenues and/or costs will *change* if one alternative is chosen over another? These are the relevant, incremental revenues and costs.

We illustrate the important concepts by looking at three common tactical decisions: **make or buy**, **special orders**, and **dropping a segment**.

Make or Buy?

A manager deciding whether to make a part or to buy it from an outside vendor must consider several factors besides the relevant costs. Will the vendor's product be of acceptable quality? Will the vendor meet an acceptable timetable for delivery? Will buying outside mean that workers in the firm's plant will be laid off, and, if so, what is the firm's responsibility to them and the community? Will the supplier offer a long-term pricing agreement that will reduce the impact of inflation?

Charbroil Burgers is a chain of fast food restaurants in Indianapolis. Currently it bakes its own buns at a central plant where it also makes hamburger patties. Costs for a typical month are as follows:

Hamburger meat	$10,000
Spices	500
Wheat and yeast	3,000
Electricity—bakery	500
Labor	5,000
Fixed costs (depreciation, rent, manager's salary)	5,000
	$24,000

Labor is evenly divided between the bakery and hamburger production, and output is 40,000 hamburgers and 40,000 buns. A bakery offers a contract to Charbroil to bake and deliver 40,000 buns for 18 cents each. When asked to compute costs per bun at Charbroil, a manager says that costs are $21\frac{1}{4}$ cents each. He made this calculation using these costs:

Wheat and yeast	$3,000	
Electricity—bakery	500	
Labor ($\frac{1}{2}$ total)	2,500	
Fixed costs ($\frac{1}{2}$ total)	2,500	
Total	$8,500	÷ 40,000 = $0.2125

The manager assigned fixed costs to the bakery on the basis of the relative amounts of labor cost for the hamburgers and the buns. Based on his analysis, he says Charbroil should buy buns rather than make them. What are the relevant costs in this case? The costs that *change* if Charbroil chooses to buy buns are:

Costs saved if buns bought from outside supplier:	
Wheat, yeast	$3,000
Electricity	500
Labor	2,500
Total savings	$6,000

The $6,000 total, when compared with the $7,200 contract price (40,000 at $0.18) offered by the outside supplier, indicates that Charbroil should continue making buns. To get a unit cost comparison, we can divide the $6,000 by 40,000 buns and get $0.15 per bun.

Therefore, a proper comparison is between *make* at 15 cents or *buy* at 18 cents. If the manager wanted to include the $2,500 in fixed costs in his analysis, he would have to include it under *both* alternatives because it would be the same whether Charbroil bought or made the buns. The fixed costs of $2,500 divided by 40,000 buns gives $6\frac{1}{4}$ cents. Thus, a manager could compare *make* at $21\frac{1}{4}$ cents ($0.15 + $0.0625) with *buy* at $24\frac{1}{4}$ cents ($0.18 + $0.0625). This analysis is quantitative. Qualitative factors such as quality or delivery schedules could override the 3 cents per bun operating savings.

We see that there is a 3 cents per bun difference between the two options, whether we use incremental costs only or include nondifferential costs in *both* options. This same pattern will be followed in the other examples of tactical decisions.

Special Orders

Often it is advantageous for a company to sell its products at less than normal prices. Some firms make products to be sold under the label of a chain store such as Sears. Some such arrangements are for a single order and are one-time events. Others, such as contracts that cover a year or more, can quickly become part of the company's recurring business. Accepting recurring business at less-than-normal prices raises other issues because such business can strain resources and cause a creeping up of costs required to administer the business.[2] That is, recurring special orders probably have hidden costs that true one-shot orders do not.

In January 19X9, state officials approach the manager of Hawk Table Company with an offer to buy 1,000 tables for a new government building at $65 each. Hawk expects sales of 50,000 tables in 19X9. Hawk's plant has a capacity of 70,000 tables, and management believes this order would not affect normal demand nor weaken prices. The following is the 19X8 income statement. Management expects prices and costs to be about the same throughout 19X9. Should Hawk accept the order?

HAWK TABLE COMPANY
Budgeted Income Statement
Year Ending 12/31/X8

Sales (50,000 tables)	$5,500,000
Cost of goods sold (Schedule 1)	3,000,000
Gross profit	$2,500,000
Other expenses	1,500,000
Income before taxes	$1,000,000

[2] For some good examples, see Frank Allen, "Beware the Big Contract," *The Wall Street Journal*, June 10, 1988, p. 36R.

Schedule 1

Cost of goods sold:	
Materials	$1,000,000
Direct labor	1,250,000
Factory overhead—variable	250,000
—fixed	500,000
	$3,000,000

Cost of goods sold contains some variable costs (materials, direct labor, and variable factory overhead) as well as fixed costs (fixed factory overhead). Other expenses are all fixed. A per unit analysis follows, using the totals from Hawk's income statement divided by 50,000 units.

Materials, $1,000,000/50,000	$20
Labor, $1,250,000/50,000	25
Variable overhead, $250,000/50,000	5
Total variable costs	$50

This schedule assumes that Hawk produces only one model or that the order has the same mix of products as Hawk's overall sales mix. Obviously, this is an important assumption, since a change in mix would affect average selling price and overall average costs. As in the last illustration, fixed costs are not relevant in this decision as long as they will not change. We are assuming that fixed factory overhead will not be affected by adding 1,000 tables to the production schedule. If some fixed costs would rise if Hawk accepted this order, then these additional costs would be incremental to the analysis.

Hawk has no capacity constraints, since production was planned at a 50,000-unit level in a facility designed to produce 70,000 units. Therefore, any price exceeding $50 (the average variable cost of a table) will increase profits.

The analysis changes if Hawk is producing at or near capacity and a special order means displacing current business. For example, if Hawk expected to sell 65,000 tables and the customer wanted 8,000, the only way Hawk could meet this order (since capacity is 70,000 units) is to turn away orders for 3,000 tables at $110 each from regular customers. We then have the following:

Additional contribution margin from order, 8,000 ($65 − $50)	$120,000
Lost contribution margin from lost regular sales, 3,000 ($110 − $50)	180,000
Loss on special order	($ 60,000)

Another reason for lost regular sales is that customers who would have bought through normal channels such as a company's retail store, buy from a chain instead.

Dropping a Segment

As noted, **segment** is a general term to describe a product, product line, type of customer (wholesale or retail), geographical region, or any other part of the firm that is considered for expansion or reduction. A simple case is that of a retail store operating several departments, one or more of which is being evaluated, possibly to be dropped.[3]

Another term that many businesses use for segment is **strategic business unit**. This term is often used when evaluating a segment within the structure of a strategic plan for a business, a plan that entails looking at the life cycle of a particular product line or manufacturing process.

Barbara Reed owns Reed Pharmacy, Inc., which carries full lines of drugs, cosmetics, greeting cards, and photographic equipment. Ms. Reed has examined the income statement shown below and is considering dropping the photographic equipment and increasing the size of the card department.

REED PHARMACY, INC.
Income by Department
Year Ending 9/30/X2

	Cosmetics and Drugs	*Cards*	*Photography*	*Total*
Sales	$500,000	$30,000	$150,000	$680,000
Cost of merchandise sold	250,000	10,000	100,000	360,000
Sales salaries	100,000	11,000	39,000	150,000
Rent	5,000	900	1,100	7,000
Insurance on inventory	2,500	100	1,000	3,600
General and administrative costs	14,700	900	4,400	20,000
Depreciation on fixtures	3,000	1,500	1,500	6,000
Total costs	$375,200	$24,400	$147,000	$546,600
Income by department	$124,800	$ 5,600	$ 3,000	$133,400

The first step that Reed takes is to prepare the schedule below, showing the revenues and incremental costs of the photography department. Reed knows that rent and general and administrative costs are allocated to the departments on the basis of sales and that they will be the same in total whether or not the photography department is dropped. She also eliminates the depreciation on fixtures, because that item represents the allocation of the cost

[3] As you can see from the examples, it is difficult to sharply distinguish tactical from long-term decisions. Purely tactical decisions are few. However, the point of this chapter is to become used to thinking in terms of relevant costs no matter what the time frame. Thus, this merging of tactical and longer perspectives is unimportant at this point.

of the fixtures and is sunk. Cost of goods sold is variable. Sales personnel costs are incremental. Insurance on inventory is assessed at 1 percent of cost of sales and, therefore, is also incremental.

Photography Department
Incremental Revenues and Costs

Sales	$150,000
Cost of goods sold	100,000
Sales salaries	39,000
Insurance on inventory	1,000
Total costs	140,000
Incremental profit	$ 10,000

If there were no other effects of dropping the department, income would drop by $10,000. Therefore, if the department were dropped and the card department expanded, the card department would have to produce an increase in incremental profit of at least $10,000 to make the change profitable.

Ms. Reed's next step is to prepare the pro forma income statement shown on page 530 assuming the photography department is dropped and the card department expanded. Reed has collected the following information:

1. Increasing the size of the card department would double card sales; cosmetic and drug sales would be unaffected. This is a key set of assumptions. She is saying that sales in various departments are independent of one another. Any analysis would have to test these statements.
2. The only variable costs are cost of goods sold and insurance on inventory. The latter is 1 percent of cost of sales.
3. The fixtures now used in the photography department can be used in other departments. New fixtures for the expanded card department would be provided by the card manufacturers at no cost to Reed.
4. Reed estimates that the cost of additional salespeople in the expanded card department would be $4,000, which would bring total sales personnel salaries of that department up to $15,000.
5. Rent and general and administrative expenses are allocated (common) costs that would remain the same in total under either alternative.

It is very important to spell out carefully all the estimates you make. They will be explicit and open for questioning, and you can recognize where you are making safe estimates and where you are guessing. You can identify which expectation has the greatest impact on your analysis and often can reduce your uncertainties about these estimates.

REED PHARMACY, INC.
Pro Forma Income Statement

	Cosmetics and Drugs	*Cards*	*Total*
Sales	$500,000	$60,000	$560,000
Less:			
Cost of goods sold	250,000	20,000	270,000
Sales personnel salaries	100,000	15,000	115,000
Insurance on inventory	2,500	200	2,700
Total costs	$352,500	$35,200	$387,700
Departmental incremental profit	$147,500	$24,800	$172,300
Joint and unavoidable costs:			
Rent			7,000
General and administrative costs			20,000
Depreciation			6,000
Total			$ 33,000
Income			$139,300

Ms. Reed has a projected income statement that segregates incremental revenue and cost from joint costs. This is an effective way to deal with this information, since it makes it easier for management to analyze decisions.

The move appears wise, resulting in an increase in profit of $5,900 (from $133,400 to $139,300). While $5,900 is a reasonable additional profit, remember that Reed made several assumptions. One key assumption or estimate was that drug and cosmetic sales would not be affected by the dropping of the photography department nor by the expansion of the card department.

Another important estimate is that card sales will double. How much would card sales have to rise so that total profits would be the same as if the photography department had been retained? The photography department currently is generating a $10,000 incremental profit.

	Photography Department
Sales	$150,000
Cost of sales	100,000
Sales personnel salaries	39,000
Insurance on inventory	1,000
Total costs	$140,000
Incremental profit	$ 10,000

In the card department, cost of sales is $33\frac{1}{3}$ percent and there is insurance on inventory of 1 percent of cost of sales. In addition, there are incremental personnel costs of \$4,000. Thus, using sensitivity analysis techniques from Chapter 2, we can set up the relationship that

$$\text{card profits} = X - \tfrac{1}{3}X - (0.01 \times \tfrac{1}{3}X) - \$4{,}000$$

where X = card sales in dollars. If we set card profits at the incremental profits from the photography department (\$10,000), then

$$\begin{aligned} \$10{,}000 &= X - \tfrac{1}{3}X - (0.01 \times \tfrac{1}{3}X) - \$4{,}000 \\ 0.66333X &= \$14{,}000 \\ X &= \$21{,}105 \end{aligned}$$

Reed has projected an increase of \$30,000 in card sales; an increase of \$21,105 in sales makes her financially indifferent between the two alternatives. Thus, if card sales rise from the current \$30,000 to at least \$51,105, then Reed will be no worse off for having dropped the photography department. Now let us look at one of the other important assumptions included in the analysis.

Sales in one department of a store often are affected by the presence of other departments. People come to shop for one type of item and buy others, or they patronize stores that carry all, or nearly all, the items they wish to buy on a particular shopping trip. This was the idea behind the department store and currently behind shopping malls. It is possible, then, that sales of drugs and cosmetics could be harmed by dropping the photography department. (Conversely, a bigger card department might draw in new customers who would also buy cosmetics and drugs.) How much of a drop in these sales, we now ask, would wipe out the anticipated increase in profits of \$5,900, if additional card sales will be \$30,000?

Determining the critical drop in drug and cosmetic sales requires determining the contribution margin percentage. Cost of sales is 50 percent of sales (\$250,000/\$500,000) in this department, and insurance on inventory is 1 percent of cost of sales and, therefore, half of 1 percent of sales. The variable cost percentage of sales is 50.5 percent, and the contribution margin percentage is 49.5 percent. A drop in sales of \$11,919 (\$5,900/0.495) would leave the firm in the same position whether it kept or dropped the photography department. This is only a little more than a 2 percent change in sales. The decision is therefore sensitive to the assumption that drug and cosmetic sales would not be affected by dropping the photography department. Because of the risk involved in the proposed change, Reed might continue operating all three departments.

Remember that our analyses are inherently uncertain because they are based on estimates of future results. If it seems that estimating injects too much guesswork and subjectivity into the decision-making process, note that *some decision must be made* and that *every decision involves some estimate of future results*. If Reed elects to continue all three departments, her decision is based on prediction as surely as if she elects to drop the photography department.

Spreadsheets are useful in such analyses. Reed could set up the pro forma income statement using relationships such as we developed above in our sensitivity analysis. In this way, she could test her assumptions.

Review Problem for Reed Pharmacy, Inc.

Use a spreadsheet to set up the Reed information from the pro forma income statement in algebraic form. REED.WK1 on your diskette has the data.

1. Set up the pro forma income statement as shown in the text on page 530.
2. Assume that Reed now estimates that cosmetic and drug sales will be \$488,081 while card sales will be \$60,000. Generate a new pro forma statement.
3. Now assume that drug and cosmetic sales are \$500,000 while card sales are \$51,105. Generate a new pro forma statement.
4. Finally, assume that drug and cosmetic sales are \$495,000 and that card sales are \$54,836. Generate a new pro forma statement.

While we discuss the answers and approach at the end of this chapter, you should see that the pro forma statements for both parts 2 and 3 should show an income of \$133,400 as we discussed above. (That is why we gave the sales figures to the dollar. No one is likely to project such precise numbers.) In addition, the final part also shows the same \$133,400 income figure. Here, neither department has sales that meet the original estimate, but there are sufficient sales in both departments so that income is the same as 19X2.

TACTICAL VERSUS LONG-TERM DECISIONS

We distinguished earlier between short-term (tactical) decisions and long-term (capital budgeting) decisions. The main difference is that tactical decisions have an immediate effect, with only lingering long-term effects. For example, if a firm spends an extra \$10,000 this quarter on advertising, there is an immediate effect on quarterly earnings and probably some residual effect in the near term. At the other extreme is the long-term project. Buying land and building for a new drug store as an additional outlet might entail an investment of \$1 million or more and affect the company for many years. The examples offered above illustrating *make or buy*, *dropping a segment*, and *special-order* decisions fall in a middle ground on this continuum; they are tactical decisions that probably have some long-term implications. In fact, most decisions have *some* long-term consequences.

The important thing to emphasize is how to analyze a problem—whether tactical or long term. First we define the problem. In the Reed case it was whether to drop an existing department and expand another. We then choose feasible alternatives. For Reed these were maintaining the status quo or doubling the card department while dropping photographic equipment. Other managers might have defined the problem differently or might have chosen other alternatives. We then made reasonable assumptions and estimates and analyzed the relevant (incremental) revenues and costs based on these assumptions and estimates. Finally, we considered nonquantitative issues and did some sensitivity analysis. This basic framework will hold whether we are dealing with tactical, long-term, or strategic decisions.

DECISIONS UNDER UNCERTAINTY

Barbara Reed's original analysis was based on a set of predictions. If everything turned out exactly as she expected, income would be as she projected. We saw in our sensitivity analysis that some small differences between her predictions and the actual results could reduce profits. A 2 percent drop in cosmetic and drug sales from \$500,000 to \$488,081 would reduce profit to less than \$133,400. The same would hold true if card sales were about 15 percent less than estimated [(\$60,000 − \$51,105)/\$60,000]. She predicted that the cost of sales percentage would remain constant. These estimates and predictions allow us to start our analysis by generating the pro forma income statement on page 530 (or in the preceding Review Problem). However, we must recognize that all the basic data are based on single, certain estimates.[4] Unfortunately, rarely can one be certain about much in business. Uncertainty exists about sales levels, sales prices, costs, and virtually all other factors. Therefore, we need either to reduce our uncertainty (or risk—we shall use these terms synonymously) or, lacking that, quantify this uncertainty so that we can have more helpful analyses. We shall first discuss quantifying uncertainty and then return to the point that we should also work to reduce uncertainty.

First, some probabilities are easier to quantify than others. For example, the likelihood that a flipped coin will come up heads is a lot easier to estimate than the likelihood that it will rain in three months.

Reed originally estimated card sales would expand from \$30,000 to \$60,000. If this estimate was *certain*, there is no problem. However, the \$60,000 is a *point estimate*. Reed knew that sales would be either above or below \$60,000. She believed that the probability of \$60,000 in card sales was much higher than the probability of some other figure. Possibly, \$60,000 was an average sales level based on her assessment of several sales levels and their probabilities of

[4]Certainty means that there is no chance a value will be other than expected. Thus, if we are certain that it costs \$12.50 to buy a ticket to a baseball game, there is a zero probability of the cost being other than \$12.50. Uncertainty and risk reflect the probabilities of various events when we lack certainty. Classically there is a difference between these two terms: risk describes a situation in which there is a reasonable basis for estimating the probabilities of outcomes, and uncertainty exists when there is no way to assign probabilities to outcomes. We deal with risk as thus defined.

occurrence. In any case, to come up with this estimate, Reed had to estimate unconsciously or consciously (intuitively or systematically) the likelihood of different sales levels.

Expected Value

The following discussion uses some basic statistics. Appendix 12A introduces or reviews statistics.

Although card sales could take on any dollar value, let us assume for this example that they could be \$35,000, \$50,000, or \$75,000. Reed could hire a marketing firm that would give her these estimates of sales and ideas on the likelihood that these different sales levels would occur. Suppose that Reed did that and that a market survey revealed the following:

Greeting Card Annual Sales, x_i	*Probability of Sales Level,* $p(x_i)$
\$35,000	0.10
50,000	0.44
75,000	0.46
	1.00

This is an example of a *discrete* probability distribution. In a *continuous* distribution, the events can take on any values (like the range of outside temperature readings during an average July).

Because this example uses a discrete probability distribution, there is the assumption that the probability of *any* other sales level is zero. Obviously this is not realistic because sales can take on any value from a few dollars to many thousands of dollars. A continuous distribution can take this into account; however, discrete distributions are easier to work with and can be adequate in dealing with simple risk problems. Moreover, calculations become cumbersome in realistic examples.

If there were no probabilities associated with each level of sales, we could find a simple average estimate by adding the three numbers together and dividing by three. However, we would be implicitly assuming that each level of sales was just as likely to occur as any other level. We can see from the preceding schedule that this is not true. Higher levels of sales are much more likely than lower levels. Instead of a simple average, we can get a weighted average or **expected value**. The expected value of sales is the sum of the various sales values weighted by their probabilities. Thus, the expected value of sales (noted as $\bar{x}$) is

$$\bar{x} = (\$35{,}000)(0.10) + (\$50{,}000)(0.44) + (\$75{,}000)(0.46) = \$60{,}000$$

While \$60,000 is the expected value of sales, we must remember that sales will be either \$35,000, \$50,000, or \$75,000. Therefore, if Reed chose to drop one department and expand the card department, there is a 54 percent chance that she would be making a wrong decision—that sales would be either $50,000 or $35,000 (the probabilities of these levels are 0.10 and 0.44, totaling 0.54). At either level she would earn less than she could expect if she kept the photography department.

Reed can conclude that while the expected value of sales (or **mean** of the distribution) is $60,000, there is a greater than 50 percent probability that sales will be substantially less than this figure. If Reed and her marketing consultants had estimated probabilities associated with 7, 15, or even 20 levels of sales, she would still be using a discrete distribution and would weigh each of these sales levels (x_i) by its probability of occurrence [$p(x_i)$] to get the expected value.

Suppose that Reed was not satisfied with the data showing only three sales levels; she ordered a more intensive survey, the results of which appear in Exhibit 12–1 and are graphed in Figure 12–1.

Figure 12–2 depicts a continuous-probability distribution of sales. In comparing Figures 12–1 and 12–2, we can see how a discrete distribution can be used instead of a continuous distribution (or the reverse, for which we can use a **normal approximation** of a discrete distribution).

However, as the number of sales levels increases, Reed's problem moves closer to those of the real world. As we observed earlier, you can intuitively recognize that actual sales *could* take on *any* value between $0 and some very large figure. Practically, we could restrict this range to between, say, $20,000 and $100,000, based on experience or industry averages. By establishing a range of possible sales volumes and limiting the range, we can make the following points:

1. Because the sales range is limited to $20,000 to $100,000, there is virtually zero probability that sales will be below $20,000 or above $100,000.
2. Because any level of sales between $20,000 and $100,000 has some chance of occurring, the probability distribution is now *continuous*.

EXHIBIT 12–1 Sales Levels for Greeting Cards

Greeting Card Annual Sales x_i	$p(x_i)$
$ 20,000	0.02
30,000	0.03
40,000	0.10
50,000	0.20
60,000	0.30
70,000	0.20
80,000	0.10
90,000	0.03
100,000	0.02

FIGURE 12–1 Graph of New Probability Assessment

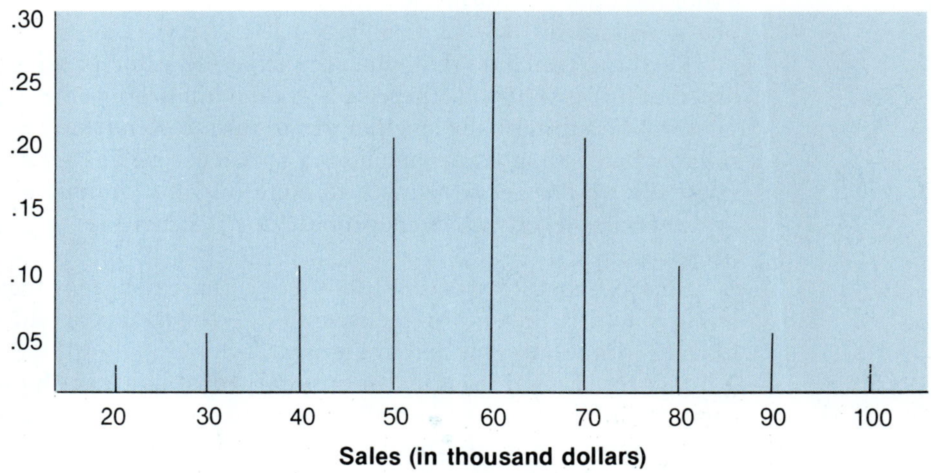

FIGURE 12–2 Continuous Distribution Approximation of Figure 12–1

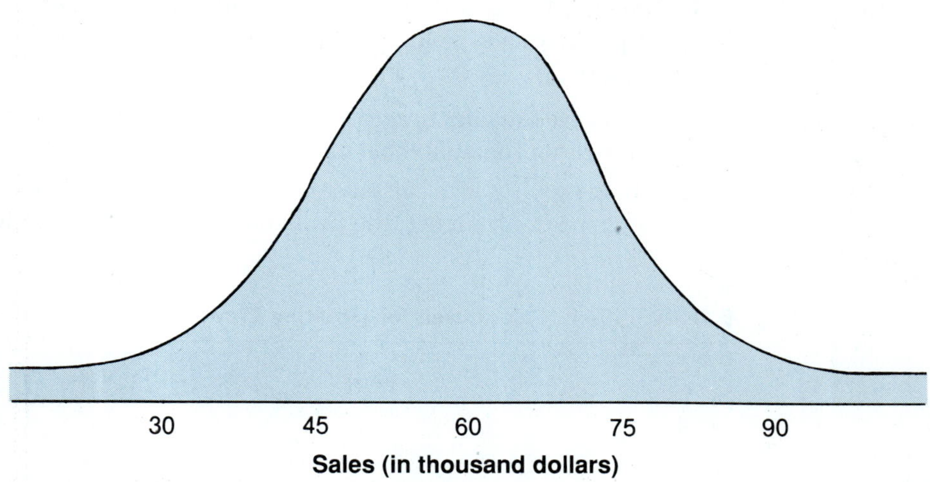

Variance and Standard Deviation

An expected value is only one measure of a probability distribution. It is the weighted average of the variable under study. Also useful is some knowledge of the dispersion of values around the mean. With the information in Exhibit 12–1 the pharmacy management can get a measure of the divergence of various sales ranges from the mean (expected value) of sales. The variance of a distribution is such a measure. The variance is the sum of the squared differences (deviations) of the values of the random variable from the expected value (mean). The square root of the variance, the **standard deviation**, is useful in our analysis. We used this measure in Chapter 3 when dealing with variation around the regression line (the standard error of the estimate). The variance for the distribution shown in Exhibit 12–1, $238,000,000, is calculated in Exhibit 12–2.

With both a mean and a standard deviation, we can make some statements to help quantify our uncertainty about sales. With a variance of $238,000,000, the standard deviation (the square root of the variance) is about $15,427. If we assume that sales are continuous and normally distributed (as in Figure 12–2), we can use the normal probability table, Table A–1 in Appendix A at the back of the book, and can say that actual sales have about a 68 percent probability of being within one standard deviation of the expected value ($60,000 ± $15,427 = $44,573 to $75,427). Managers want to know the probability that card sales will be below the indifference point of keeping the existing departments (alternative 1) and dropping one department while expanding the other (alternative 2). We stated earlier that additional sales in the card department of $21,105 would yield the same profit as the status quo. Thus, if total card sales were expected to be $51,105, management would be indifferent between expanding the card department and retaining the photography department, all other things being equal and held constant. This figure is about 0.58 ($60,000 – $51,105 divided by the standard deviation of $15,427) standard deviations below the expected value of $60,000 in sales. Using the normal probability

EXHIBIT 12–2 Calculation of Variance and Standard Deviation (in Thousands of Dollars)

(1) Sales, x_i	(2) Probability, $p(x_i)$	(3) Squared Deviation from Expected Value, $(x_i - \bar{x})^2$	(4) Col. (2) × Col. (3), $(x_i - \bar{x})^2[p(x_i)]$
$ 20	0.02	$1,600,000[a]	$ 32,000
30	0.03	900,000	27,000
40	0.10	400,000	40,000
50	0.20	100,000	20,000
60	0.30	0	0
70	0.20	100,000	20,000
80	0.10	400,000	40,000
90	0.03	900,000	27,000
100	0.02	1,600,000	32,000
		Variance, thousands	$238,000
		Standard Deviation, thousands	$ 15.427

[a]For example: ($20,000 – $60,000)^2 = $1.6 billion.

table, we see that there is about a 28 percent probability that sales will fall below this level. Reed may not be willing to take this high a risk and, therefore, may choose to keep the status quo.

Objective and Subjective Probabilities

The Reed example assumes that managers can make adequate assessments of risk. Actually, probability assessments fall along a continuum from objective to subjective. The likelihood of occurrence of some event is an **objective probability** if a group of impartial observers could agree on it. Examples are the probability of a head when flipping a fair coin or the probability of drawing an ace from a full deck of cards. Neutral bystanders would agree the former has an objective probability of 0.5 and the latter has an objective probability of 4/52. At the other end of the continuum is a **subjective probability**, one person's assessment. A person driving 65 mph in a 55-mph zone might feel that there is about a 50 percent chance of getting a speeding ticket, while another might feel that there is only about a 40 percent chance.

Most everyday business and personal probability assessments that we all make, either explicitly or implicitly, lie between these two extremes. Naturally, if a decision maker is going to compute expected values and variances, the resulting information is only as good as the original estimates of probabilities. This point cannot be taken lightly. Too often models proposed to aid decision makers are not accompanied by the "GIGO" warning: if you put garbage in, you get garbage out.

ACCOUNTANTS AND QUANTITATIVE METHODS

Accountants want to provide information in its most useful form. To accomplish this purpose, we need to be able to decide what quantitative models are cost effective, and we need to be able to interpret data so we can explain our analyses to managers. We should not ignore mathematical tools, nor should we ignore social or behavioral implications. We need to know how to use all the available cost-effective tools and information. While gathering information is one of our functions, analyzing that information and coming to logical conclusions are also important.

DECISION TREES

Multiple Decisions and Events

We look now at a decision-making aid that relies on probabilities. This approach is helpful when the decision maker confronts a multiple-decision or multiple-event task.

Carney Manufacturing Company is trying to decide whether to change the price of one of its major products. The managers have estimated the following results if they do not change the price.

Profits	*Probability*
$30,000	0.2
40,000	0.5
50,000	0.3

The expected value of profits is $41,000 based on the above. If the new pricing policy is adopted, managers must then decide whether to engage in an advertising campaign to promote the new policy or to let word of mouth carry the message. Here, we have two decisions that are tied together sequentially. First is the decision about pricing policy. Then, if the new policy is adopted, comes a decision about whether to advertise. In this type of sequential decision problem, a decision tree is a useful management tool for visualizing and solving this problem. Before showing the decision tree framework, let us look at management's estimates of profits if the new policy is followed.

The profits with advertising (including advertising cost of $50,000) are estimated to be

Profit (loss)	*Probability*
$(10,000)	0.3
50,000	0.4
90,000	0.3

The expected value is $44,000.

The profits without advertising are estimated to be

Profit	*Probability*
$ 5,000	0.3
50,000	0.4
70,000	0.3

The expected value is $42,500.

The decision is illustrated in Figure 12–3 in a **decision tree**. The problem depicted has two decisions (pricing policy and whether to advertise) and one set of events (profits that will result from the various actions). Management has assessed the outcome of each decision and the events that follow. Only one outcome can occur, however. For example, if management changes the pricing policy and engages in the advertising program, profits will be either −$10,000, $50,000, or $90,000. Using the decision tree framework, management can look at the expected values (or **expected monetary values** as they are sometimes called) and decide on the best course of action. Figure 12–3 shows the **conditional values** (profits) from each outcome of the decision tree, as well as the expected monetary values. We can see that if the new pricing policy

FIGURE 12–3 Decision Tree

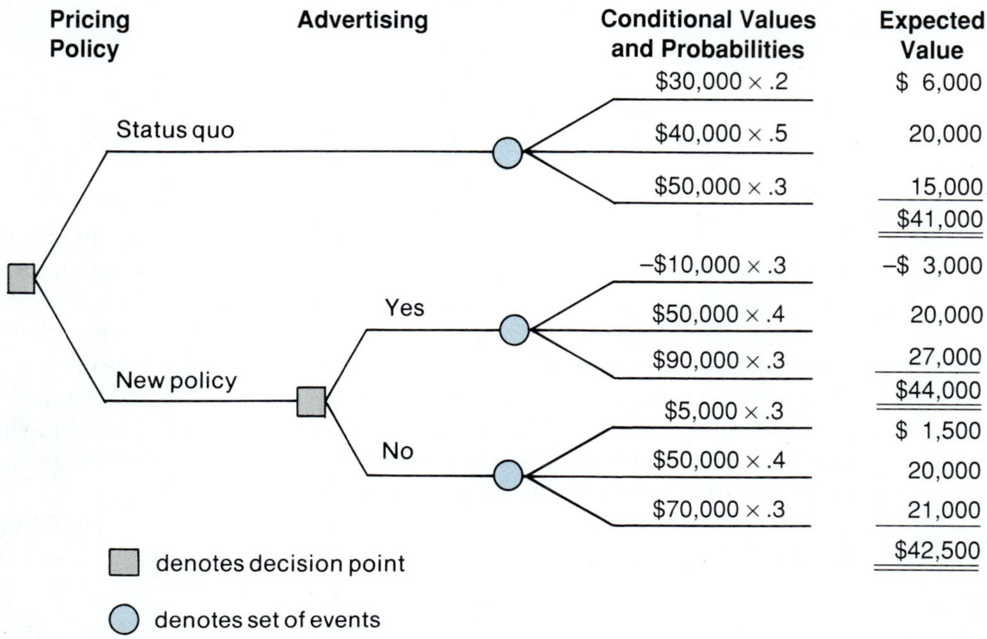

is chosen, the better decision is to spend the $50,000 for advertising, since the expected value of that action is $44,000, compared to $42,500 for not advertising. Thus, we look at the last decision first in decision tree analysis. We can now compare the $44,000 expected value of the new prices with advertising with the $41,000 expected value of keeping the current pricing. The choice is to go with the new policy.

In this example, we have two decisions and one set of events. Conditional values are predicted for the events. The criterion is to **maximize expected value**. The variance of the event is not considered. This can be a fault of the criterion used in this method, and risk should be accounted for in some way.

This analysis could be expanded into more than two decisions and more than one event. The strength of this framework is that it allows managers to visualize a multiple decision setting in which sequential decisions are needed. By solving the tree backward (last decision is decided first), management can work its way through complex decision settings.

LINEAR PROGRAMMING

In discussing tactical decisions we have looked at relevant revenues and costs and derived measures of uncertainty regarding them. In considering a special order when the firm was already at capacity, we dealt briefly with a constrained resource. In the Reed Pharmacy example, space is a constraint. Reed has a limited amount of retail space and wants to use it to achieve as great a profit as possible. Sometimes there are many constraining (or scarce) resources to deal with. Firms face shortages of such things as material, skilled workers, capacity, and funds. One way in which accountants and other managers can deal with the problem of maximizing profit, for example, given the scarcity of resources, is to use linear programming.

Our discussion here requires some prior knowledge of linear programming and the use of the simplex method. Appendix 12B discusses linear programming in more detail.

Linear programming is one of a class of mathematical techniques designed to optimize results. Scarcity of resources is a prerequisite to the use of linear programming. A firm must have limited resources such as time, money, or materials, to profit by this tool. We are also interested in the technique for its use in sensitivity analysis for tactical decisions. Sensitivity analysis allows us to deal with the issues of uncertainty we dealt with in earlier examples.

Broden Paint Company produces two products, paint and stain. The contribution margin per gallon is $4 for paint and $5.10 for stain. Because of a material shortage, only 50,000 gallons of base mix are available. A half-gallon of base mix is required for each gallon of finished paint or stain. The plant capacity is 120,000 gallons per year of paint, 90,000 gallons of stain, or any linear combination of the two. The formulation of this simple maximization problem is presented in Exhibit 12–3. Exhibit 12–4 shows the final tableau from a simplex solution. Exhibit 12–5 shows the input and output from a computer program. The formulation and solution to the problem are deterministic. No measures of risk (or dispersion) are included. In our discussion of sensitivity analysis, we will allow one item at a time to vary. This will suggest where we need to get additional data and to quantify various uncertainties.

EXHIBIT 12–3 Objective Function and Constraints

Maximize: $Z = \$4X_1 + \$5.10X_2$

Subject to:

$$\tfrac{1}{2}X_1 + \tfrac{1}{2}X_2 \leq 50{,}000 \text{ (base mix)}$$
$$\tfrac{3}{4}X_1 + X_2 \leq 90{,}000 \text{ (capacity)}$$
$$X_1, X_2 \geq 0$$

EXHIBIT 12–4 Final Tableau

				$4.00	$5.10	$0	$0
	C_j	Product Mix	Quantity	X_1	X_2	S_1	S_2
Paint	$4.00	X_1	40,000	1	0	8	−4
Stain	$5.10	X_2	60,000	0	1	−6	4
		Z_j	$466,000	$4.00	$5.10	$1.40	$4.40
		$C_j - Z_j$		0	0	−$1.40	−$4.40

EXHIBIT 12–5 Computer Input and Output

```
MAX      4 PAINT + 5.1 STAIN
ST
         .5 PAINT + .5 STAIN <=   50000
         .75 PAINT + STAIN <=    90000
END

: look
ROW:
all

MAX      4 PAINT + 5.1 STAIN
SUBJECT TO
       2)   .5 PAINT + .5 STAIN <=   50000
       3)   .75 PAINT + STAIN <=    90000
END

:go
LP OPTIMUM FOUND  AT STEP      2

         OBJECTIVE FUNCTION VALUE

 1)         466000.000

 VARIABLE        VALUE          REDUCED COST
    PAINT     40000.000000          .000000
    STAIN     60000.000000          .000000


      ROW   SLACK OR SURPLUS     DUAL PRICES
       2)          .000000         1.400000
       3)          .000000         4.400000

 NO. ITERATIONS=        2

DO RANGE(SENSITIVITY) ANALYSIS?
? y


RANGES IN WHICH THE BASIS IS UNCHANGED:

                          OBJ COEFFICIENT RANGES
VARIABLE         CURRENT         ALLOWABLE          ALLOWABLE
                  COEF           INCREASE           DECREASE
   PAINT         4.000000         1.100000            .175000
   STAIN         5.100000          .233333           1.100000

                          RIGHTHAND SIDE RANGES
    ROW          CURRENT         ALLOWABLE          ALLOWABLE
                   RHS           INCREASE           DECREASE
      2      50000.000000      10000.000000       5000.000000
      3      90000.000000      10000.000000      15000.000000
```

First we relax the condition that only 50,000 gallons of base mix can be purchased. The normal price of the base mix is $2 per gallon. Another supplier will sell Broden 10,000 gallons of product of the same quality for $3 per gallon. Is it in Broden's interest to buy more base mix? Yes. In fact, any price up to $3.40 per gallon is acceptable. The contribution margin in the optimal solution is $466,000. If Broden purchased an additional 10,000 gallons of base mix at $3.40 per gallon, as opposed to the normal price of $2 per gallon, there would be an additional expense of $14,000. The new optimal solution (Exhibit 12–6) yields an additional $14,000 before the cost of base mix. Therefore, the higher contribution margin and additional expenses cancel each other, proving that any price up to $3.40 is acceptable.

The new solution is derived by taking the matrix of values associated with the slack variables in the final tableau (Exhibit 12–4) and multiplying these values by the new constraints. In this case, only one constraint changed. The result is a new solution of 120,000 gallons of paint and zero gallons of stain. Check this solution against the constraints in Exhibit 12–3 (with the 10,000-gallon adjustment in base mix availability).

The final tableau shown in Exhibit 12–4 has a row labeled $C_j - Z_j$. The figures shown in this row are called **shadow prices** or **dual prices**. Note these same figures ($1.40 and $4.40) are shown in Exhibit 12–5. The original formulation of the linear program assumed an absolute value of the amount of available base mix. Usually, however, constraints are not as strictly fixed as the mathematical equations imply. Sometimes it is possible to expand capacity or get more raw materials. Here is where sensitivity analysis and shadow prices come into play.

A shadow price is the profit if one more unit of a constrained resource were available, everything else remaining constant. For example, if one additional gallon of base mix were available, the optimal solution would call for eight more gallons of paint (at $4 per gallon) and six fewer gallons of stain (at $5.10 per gallon). This is a net increase of $1.40.

We can use the shadow price to get changes in total contribution margin by multiplying the shadow price associated with the constraint under study by the addition to the constraint. In the present case,

$$(\$1.40)(10{,}000) = \$14{,}000$$

There is an upper limit to the number of gallons Broden can purchase without violating other constraints. Exhibit 12–5 shows this upper limit as

EXHIBIT 12–6 Sensitivity Analysis—Mix

$$\begin{pmatrix} X_1 \\ X_2 \end{pmatrix} = \begin{pmatrix} 8 & -4 \\ -6 & 4 \end{pmatrix} \begin{pmatrix} 60{,}000 \\ 90{,}000 \end{pmatrix} = \begin{Bmatrix} (8)(60{,}000) + (-4)(90{,}000) \\ (-6)(60{,}000) + (4)(90{,}000) \end{Bmatrix} \begin{matrix} = 120{,}000X_1 \\ = 0X_2 \end{matrix}$$

and

$$(120{,}000)(\$4.00) = \$480{,}000$$
$$(0)(\$5.10) = \$0$$

EXHIBIT 12–7 Sensitivity Analysis—Capacity

$$\begin{pmatrix} X_1 \\ X_2 \end{pmatrix} = \begin{pmatrix} 8 & -4 \\ -6 & 4 \end{pmatrix} \begin{pmatrix} 65{,}000 \\ 99{,}000 \end{pmatrix} = \begin{pmatrix} 124{,}000X_1 \\ 6{,}000X_2 \end{pmatrix}$$

(124,000)($4.00 cm/gal paint)	$496,000
(6,000)($5.10 cm/gal stain)	30,600
	$526,600
Less: ($1.40)(15,000 gal)	21,000
New margin	$505,600
Current margin	466,000
	$39,600

10,000 gallons (Righthand Side Ranges—Allowable Increase). If Broden purchased, say, an additional 20,000 gallons, then the only binding constraint would be capacity and an excess of 10,000 gallons of base mix would sit unused.

Now let us examine the other constraint: capacity. Suppose that an equipment manufacturer approaches Broden. The manufacturer has equipment capable of producing 9,000 gallons per year. If Broden can get an additional 15,000 gallons of base mix at $3.40 per gallon, how much would it be willing to pay the manufacturer for a one-year lease on this equipment? Exhibit 12–7 shows that Broden could offer up to $39,600 and be better off than in the current situation.

Finally, sensitivity analysis can be applied to selling price (or variable cost), since any change in selling price or variable cost affects contribution margin. The $4 and $5.10 per gallon contribution margins have been presented as givens. The solution to the original problem (Exhibits 12–4 and 12–5) calls for a fairly even production of paint and stain. The subsequent changes in raw material availability or capacity reduced stain production. What change in stain contribution margin will result in this same shift? Obviously, if the stain contribution margin is less than that for paint, the solution will call for no stain because of the capacity constraint. In fact, with the original constraints, as long as the stain contribution margin is at any value higher than the paint margin, the current optimal solution will hold. If paint's margin drops below $3.83 (and stain's margin remains at $5.10), however, the optimal solution will call for zero paint production. An analysis shows that stain production stays constant as long as its contribution margin is at least $4.01 (giving a leeway of $1.09 from the current level), while paint production is based on a contribution margin of at least $3.825 (or a leeway of $0.175). Obviously, paint is much more sensitive to changes in price or variable cost than is stain. This new information is an aid to managers. They can assess how likely it is that the paint contribution margin will drop more than $0.17 per gallon. Exhibit 12–5 shows upper and lower bounds to the contribution margins in the objective function (Obj Coefficient Ranges—Allowable Decrease). Paint shows an allowable decrease of $0.175.

Minimization Problems

Managers often face cost minimization problems. Rather than dealing with contribution margins, they deal with costs. For example, a feed company wants to minimize the cost of horse feed; however, there are several constraints: the diet needs certain percentages of protein, roughage, calcium, and phosphorus, and so on. In addition, there might be constraints on the availability of ingredients such as corn or oats. Exhibit 12–8 shows the objective function and constraints for the Lea Feed Company where the variables (corn, oats, barley) are in pounds. The first constraint shows that management does not want corn to be more than half of any feed mixture (corn ≤ 0.5). The second constraint shows that whatever combination there is of corn, oats, and barley, it must add up to 1 pound. The next constraint deals with the protein content of the grains (15% for corn, 20% for oats, and 10% for barley) and the final mix (a minimum of 14% overall). The final constraint deals with the roughage content of each grain (corn, 10%; oats, 25%; and barley, 35%) and the final mix (a minimum of 25%). The optimal solution and sensitivity analysis from a computer output are also shown in Exhibit 12–8. The final solution calls for each pound to be composed of 30 percent corn, 25 percent oats, and 45 percent barley. Each pound costs $0.4175 [(0.30 × $0.30) + (0.25 × $0.50) + (0.45 × $0.45)].

Shadow prices (*dual prices* in Exhibit 12–8) are interpreted in light of the constraints. For example, either through a nutritional analysis or from market needs, management has specified that feed must contain at least 14 percent protein. If protein requirements could be lowered to 13 percent, there would be a savings of $0.01375 per pound (0.01 × $1.375). An independent computer run will yield (as you can verify) an optimal mix of 35 percent corn, 12.5 percent oats, and 52.5 percent barley when the protein requirement is lowered to 13 percent and everything else remains constant. This solution has a cost of $0.40375 per pound [(0.35 × $0.30) + (0.125 × $0.50) + (0.525 × $0.45)].

The same kind of analysis can be performed on the last constraint. If roughage requirements are lowered from 25 to 24 percent, the cost per pound will drop by $0.00875 (0.01 × $0.875) to $0.40875. Finally, the first constraint has no opportunity cost. Changing the corn requirement from 50 percent to 49 percent will not change the optimal mix or cost. (The second constraint cannot be changed since a pound of feed must equal 1 pound!)

Sensitivity analysis shows the ranges of costs for corn, oats, and barley before the solution changes. Interestingly, as long as the constraints call for 14 percent protein, oats will be required no matter what their price. Managers might do well to investigate other grains for cost, protein, and roughage as a substitute for oats.

The *right-hand-side ranges* shown in Exhibit 12–8 also guide the manager. We have already seen the effect of lowering protein from 14 percent to 13 percent. At 12 percent (*allowable decrease* of 2%), the solution calls for zero oats. The other allowable increases and decreases give similar information for the protein, roughage, and percent of corn requirements.

EXHIBIT 12–8 Minimization Problem and Solution

```
MIN     .3 CORN + .5 OATS + .45 BARLEY
SUBJECT TO
       2)   CORN <=   .5
       3)   CORN + OATS + BARLEY =   1
       4)   .15 CORN + .2  OATS + .1  BARLEY >=   .14
       5)   .1  CORN + .25 OATS + .35 BARLEY >=   .25
END



: go
LP OPTIMUM FOUND AT STEP      4

         OBJECTIVE FUNCTION VALUE

 1)         .417500000

 VARIABLE         VALUE         REDUCED COST
     CORN          .300000          .000000
     OATS          .250000          .000000
   BARLEY          .450000          .000000

      ROW   SLACK OR SURPLUS    DUAL PRICES
       2)          .200000          .000000
       3)          .000000        -.006250
       4)          .000000       -1.375000
       5)          .000000        -.875000

NO. ITERATIONS=        4


DO RANGE(SENSITIVITY) ANALYSIS?

? y

RANGES IN WHICH THE BASIS IS UNCHANGED:

                          OBJ COEFFICIENT RANGES
VARIABLE         CURRENT        ALLOWABLE          ALLOWABLE
                  COEF          INCREASE           DECREASE
    CORN          .300000          .175000          INFINITY
    OATS          .500000         INFINITY             .110000
  BARLEY          .450000          .183333             .350000

                          RIGHTHAND SIDE RANGES
    ROW          CURRENT        ALLOWABLE          ALLOWABLE
                   RHS          INCREASE           DECREASE
       2          .500000         INFINITY             .200000
       3         1.000000          .088889             .133333
       4          .140000          .060000             .020000
       5          .250000          .060000             .040000
```

Linear programming is a quantitative technique that allows an accountant to look at possible optimal solutions when resources are scarce. We can maximize contribution margin per unit of various scarce resources. Linear programming is limited by requiring single-point estimates for contribution margin, use of constrained resources, and availability of constrained resources. We saw earlier that certainty rarely exists. Thus, sensitivity analysis becomes an important tool to direct manager's attention to prices, costs, usages, or constraints that have the greatest potential impact on profitability. This analysis also allows management to identify areas where specific probability assessments could be cost effective. Management continually asks: "What if . . . ?" Sensitivity analysis pervades the concept of quantitative and qualitative analysis.

SUMMARY

Accountants supply much of the information used in tactical (short-term) decision making. Generally, managers should take the action that they expect to produce the highest income for the company. This criterion considers only quantifiable economic factors. Many decisions present circumstances that can have economic effects but which are extremely difficult to estimate. Sometimes the best economic action is not taken because it conflicts with company policy or strategy. Qualitative factors such as these should be considered as well as the expected economic results.

In a quantitative analysis, the relevant revenues and costs are the differential revenues and costs, including opportunity costs. Costs and revenues that remain constant no matter what are irrelevant and can be ignored. Costs already incurred—historical costs—are sunk and irrelevant to decisions because they cannot be changed. Whether a cost will or will not change is a matter for determination in each case. Some fixed costs will change if certain courses are pursued. Whether or not a cost will change does not depend on whether it is variable or fixed.

Among the endless variety of tactical decisions are whether to make or buy, dropping a product or product line, and accepting a special order. Virtually all decisions have some uncertainty. Ways to deal with uncertainty include sensitivity analysis and the use of expected values and variances. Decisions where the optimal use of scarce resources is important call for linear programming.

APPENDIX 12A: BASIC CONCEPTS OF PROBABILITY AND STATISTICS

Decision making seeks a single well-defined outcome. Probability theory has the same goal, but many events are possible. In a simple case, as when you flip a coin, the only events that can occur are heads or tails. In the Reed example, the various possible sales levels are events.

When a coin is flipped, the probability of a head is one-half, or 50 percent, and the probability of a tail is also 50 percent. Generalizing from this example, the probability of occurrence of any event is greater than or equal to zero. In addition, the sum of the probabilities associated with all possible events equals one. Symbolically:

$$p(\text{event}) \geq 0 \quad [\text{or } p(x_i) \geq 0]$$

$$p[\text{sum of all the } p(x_i)] = 1 \quad \left[\text{or } \sum_{i=1}^{n} p(x_i) = 1\right]$$

Expected Value

A set of events and the probabilities of their occurrence is called a probability distribution. If events are defined as particular finite values, as was the case in Reed, then the distribution is **discrete**. If events are an indefinite number of values (perhaps an infinite number), the distribution is **continuous**.

We use two general measures to assess a probability distribution, the expected value (or mean) and the dispersion (or variance). The **expected value** is the average outcome. The **variance** is a measure of how much we can expect other values to differ from the expected outcome.

To calculate the average or expected value for a discrete distribution:

$$\bar{x} = \sum_{i=1}^{n} x_i p(x_i)$$

where

$\bar{x}$ = the expected value

x_i = an event (and there is a total of n events)

$p(x_i)$ = probability of occurrence of an event

The expected value in the Reed example was calculated as follows[5]:

x_i	$p(x_i)$	$x_i p(x_i)$
$35,000	0.10	$ 3,500
50,000	0.44	22,000
75,000	0.46	34,500
	$\sum_{i=1}^{n} p(x_i) = 1.00$	$\$60,000 = \sum_{i=1}^{n} x_i p(x_i)$

[5] With a discrete probability distribution the expected value can be an unattainable figure. Even though $\bar{x}$ = $60,000, note that there is a zero probability that sales will be $60,000.

Variance

If we are certain an event will occur, its probability is 1.0. If we are uncertain about the outcome, we can look not only at a measure of central tendency (the expected value) but also at the dispersion or spread of events around the mean. The variance is a measure of this dispersion. Dispersion refers to the amount by which other values *deviate* from the mean. Each deviation is noted as

$$(x_i - \bar{x})$$

since it is the difference between any value and the expected value. For the example above, the deviations are:

Values, x_i	Deviations from the Mean, $x_i - \bar{x}$
\$35,000	−\$25,000
50,000	− 10,000
75,000	15,000

The sum of the deviations is zero. The variance (σ^2) is the sum of the squared deviations multiplied by the probabilities.

$$\sigma^2 = \sum_{i=1}^{n} (x_i - \bar{x})^2\, p(x_i)$$

Our example shows this process:

Deviations $x_i - \bar{x}$	Deviations Squared, $(x_i - \bar{x})^2$	Probabilities, $p(x_i)$	Weighted Squared Deviation, $(x_i - \bar{x})^2\, p(x_i)$
−\$25,000	\$625,000,000	0.10	\$ 62,500,000
− 10,000	100,000,000	0.44	44,000,000
15,000	225,000,000	0.46	103,500,000
		Variance $= \Sigma\,(x_i - \bar{x})^2\, p(x_i) =$	\$210,000,000

The square root of the variance, called the **standard deviation**, is the common measure of variation.

$$\sqrt{\sigma^2} = \sigma = \sqrt{\$210{,}000{,}000} \approx \$14{,}491$$

APPENDIX 12B: LINEAR PROGRAMMING

When several constraints are present and several products can be manufactured, linear programming (LP) can be used to determine the combination of products that will maximize profits. Linear programming can also be used to find the combination of input factors that minimizes the cost of an activity. For example, a company with several factories and warehouses can determine the least-cost method of moving the required quantities of finished product from factories to warehouses.

The mathematics involved in linear programming can be complex; we do not cover their details in this book. You should be able to recognize the kinds of problems that can be solved with linear programming, understand the formulation of the problem and what is being done when the problem is solved, and interpret a typical computer output.

Using linear programming, we solve a system of simultaneous equations that includes an objective function specifying what is to be maximized (usually contribution margin) or minimized (usually cost). The other equations state the constraints.

Graphical Analysis

One way to solve LP problems is by graphical analysis. We use Hawk Table Company from the chapter. Hawk produces a round table and a square table. The contribution margin on the round table is \$20; on the square table it is \$15. If there were no limitations on capacity, Hawk could produce as many of each product as it could profitably sell. However, the process requires a cutting machine and a laminating machine, both of which have limited capacity. Exhibit 12B–1 shows the relationship in these two production processes.

The first step is to formulate the objective of maximizing contribution margin. The objective function is

$$\text{maximize: } Z = \$20x_1 + \$15x_2$$

where

Z = total contribution margin

x_1 = number of round tables produced

x_2 = number of square tables produced

The next step is to set up the constraints. Hawk has 60 hours available in the cutting department and 48 hours available in the laminating department. Our solution cannot exceed these hours. Any combination of the two products

EXHIBIT 12B–1 Manufacturing Information

	Round Tables	*Square Tables*	*Total Hours Available per Week*
Cutting time	2 hr	1 hr	60
Laminating time	1 hr	2 hr	48
Contribution margin, per unit	\$20	\$15	

must use a total of 60 hours or less in cutting, for example. We note this by the following inequalities:

$$\begin{aligned} 2x_1 + x_2 &\leq 60 \\ x_1 + 2x_2 &\leq 48 \end{aligned}$$

The first constraint states that cutting hours cannot exceed 60 per week. It takes two hours to cut a round table and one hour to cut a square table, so the production of each type of table multiplied by the required time is the total time required, which cannot exceed 60 hours. Finally, we must specify that the minimum amount we can produce is zero. We cannot produce minus 10 square tables. Therefore,

$$\begin{aligned} x_1 &\geq 0 \\ x_2 &\geq 0 \end{aligned}$$

In summary, the whole problem is formulated as

$$\text{Max Z} = \$20x_1 + \$15x_2$$

subject to the following constraints:

$$\begin{aligned} 2x_1 + x_2 &\leq 60 \\ x_1 + 2x_2 &\leq 48 \\ x_1 &\geq 0 \\ x_2 &\geq 0 \end{aligned}$$

We can portray these relationships graphically. The equation for the cutting department allows for up to 30 round tables if no square tables are produced $[(30)(2) + (0)(1) \leq (60)]$ or up to 60 square tables if no round tables are produced.

The same relationship can be drawn for laminating. Figure 12B–1 shows both production constraints. Any combination of round and square tables falling within the shaded region on Figure 12B–1 fulfills the inequalities. This area is called the **feasible region**, since it contains all the feasible solutions to the LP problem.

In linear programming an optimal solution always occurs at a corner, an intersection of two lines. (The axes are considered lines. In some cases there might be more than one optimal solution, but *one* of them will occur at an intersection.) Points A, B, C, and O are the points for our analysis, since they lie at intersections. The contribution margin for each point follows.

$$\begin{aligned} &\text{Point } O: (0, 0) = (\$20)(0) + (\$15)(0) = 0 \\ &\text{Point } A: (0, 24) = (\$20)(0) + (\$15)(24) = \$360 \\ &\text{Point } B: (24, 12) = (\$20)(24) + (\$15)(12) = \$660 \\ &\text{Point } C: (30, 0) = (\$20)(30) + (\$15)(0) = \$600 \end{aligned}$$

Point B, where the constraint lines meet, has the highest contribution margin (\$660). This is the only point in the feasible space where all the hours in both

FIGURE 12B–1 Graph Showing Both Constraints

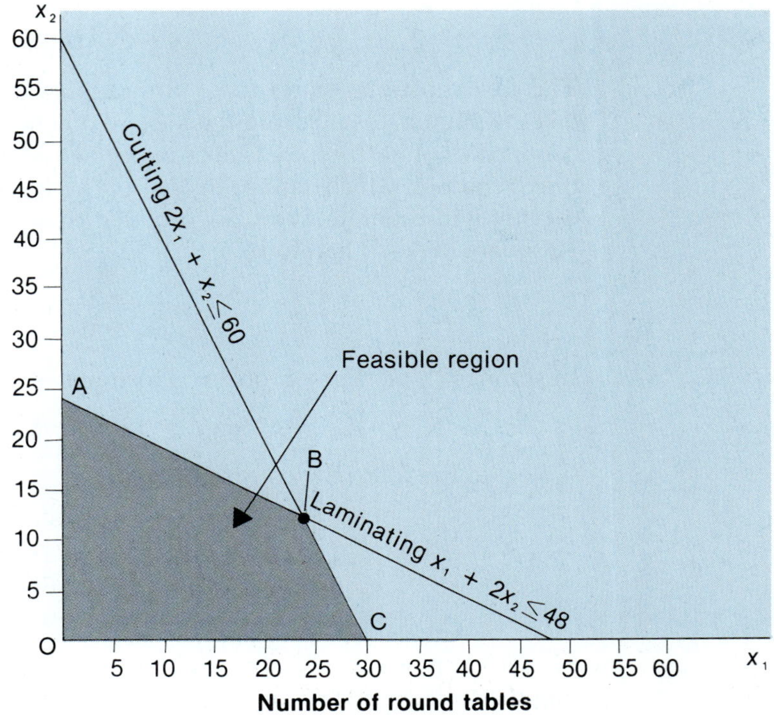

departments are used. If we plot the objective function, we can see how this is the logical maximum point. $\$20x_1 + \$15x_2$ can be drawn at any point as long as we define a total contribution margin. If we choose \$240, then $\$240 = \$20x_1 + \$15x_2$. Using the same technique for plotting as we used for the constraints, we show the objective function in Figure 12B–2. The equation $\$240 = \$20x_1 + \$15x_2$ is called an **isoprofit line**. If we choose any other total contribution margin, the new isoprofit line will be *parallel* to the one in Figure 12B–2. In fact, our optimum solution of $\$660 = \$20x_1 + \$15x_2$ is a line parallel to the original isoprofit line that touches the feasible region solely at point *B*, as shown in Figure 12B–3. Any isoprofit line greater than \$660 in total contribution margin violates one or more constraints, since it would be outside the feasible region.

Graphing is sometimes awkward. We can often find corners or intersections of constraints using simultaneous equations. Usually it is no problem to find the corners that lie on one axis or the other. Simply determine how much of each product can go through the department, machine, or whatever the constraint is, and select the smaller of the two values. Finding the intersection

FIGURE 12B–2 Graph Showing Isoprofit Line

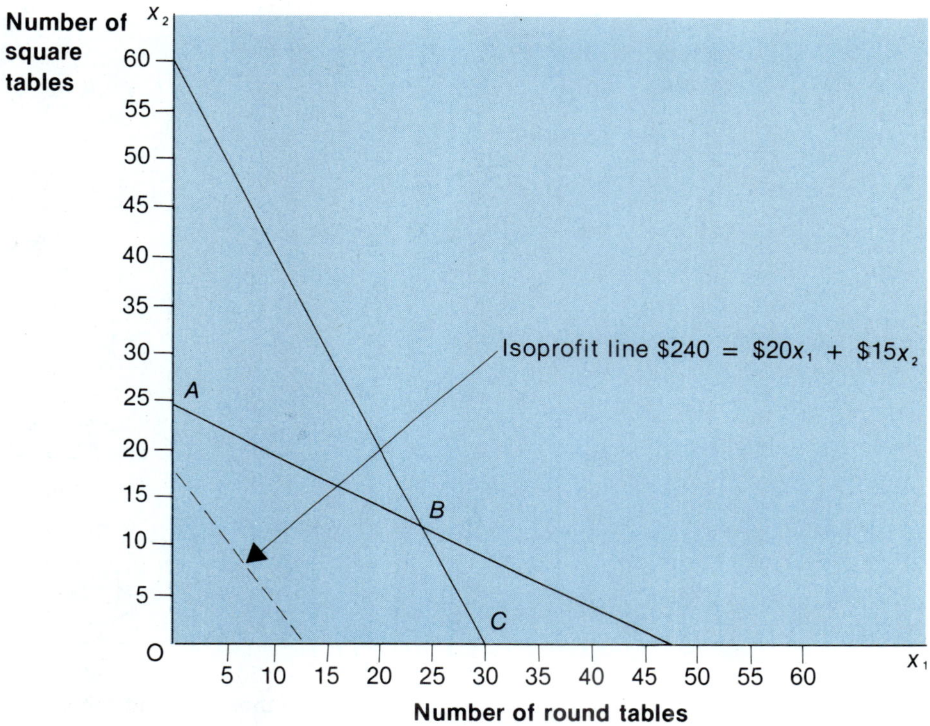

of constraints requires that we turn the inequalities into equalities and solve simultaneously.

$$2x_1 + x_2 = 60$$
$$x_1 + 2x_2 = 48$$

Multiplying the first equation by two and subtracting the second,

$$4x_1 + 2x_2 = 120$$
$$x_1 + 2x_2 = 48$$
$$3x_1 = 72$$
$$x_1 = 24$$

Substituting 24 for x_1 in the first equation,

$$2(24) + x_2 = 60$$
$$x_2 = 12$$

FIGURE 12B–3 Graphical Solution

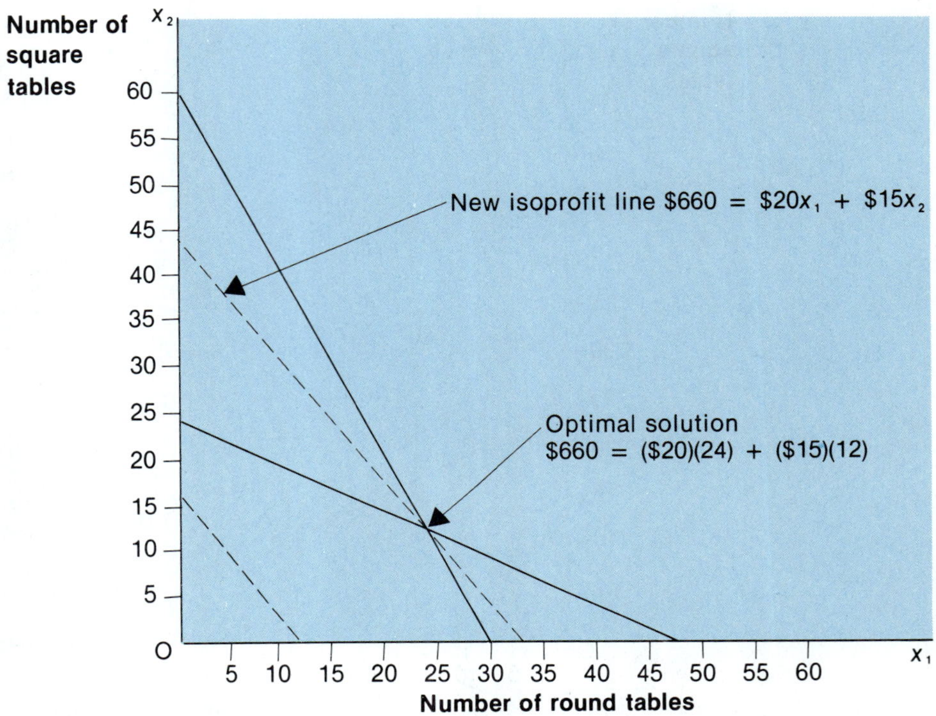

We get the same result as the graph gave us, make 24 round and 12 square tables.

ASSIGNMENTS

12–1 Special Order (AICPA Adapted) Wagner Company sells product A at $21 per unit. Wagner's cost per unit based on the full capacity of 200,000 units is as follows:

Direct materials	$ 4
Direct labor	5
Overhead (two-thirds of which is fixed)	6
	$15

A special order to buy 20,000 units was received from a foreign distributor. The only selling costs that would be incurred on this order would be $3 per unit for shipping. Wagner has sufficient existing capacity to manufacture the additional units.

REQUIRED

How much should Wagner consider as a minimum selling price when negotiating on this special order?

12–2 Special Order (AICPA Adapted) Jordan Company budgeted sales of 400,000 calculators at $40 per unit for the year. Variable manufacturing costs were budgeted at $16 per unit, and fixed manufacturing costs at $10 per unit. A special order to buy 40,000 calculators for $18 each came in March. Jordan has sufficient plant capacity to manufacture the additional quantity; however, the production would have to be done on an overtime basis at an estimated additional cost of $3 per calculator. Acceptance of the special order would not affect Jordan's normal sales, and no selling expenses would be incurred.

REQUIRED

What would be the effect on operating profit if the special order were accepted?

12–3 Make or Buy (AICPA) Kingston Company needs 10,000 units of a certain part to be used in its production cycle. The following information is available:

Cost to Kingston to make the part:	
Direct materials	$ 6
Direct labor	24
Variable overhead	12
Fixed overhead applied	15
	$57
Cost to buy the part from Utica Company	$53

If Kingston buys the part from Utica instead of making it, Kingston could not use the released facilities in another manufacturing activity. Sixty percent of the fixed overhead applied will continue regardless of what decision is made.

REQUIRED

In deciding whether to make or buy the part, the total relevant costs to make the part are

1. $342,000
2. $480,000
3. $530,000
4. $570,000

12–4 Relevant Costs Martin Company makes a number of products used by industry. Some time ago the firm bought a large supply of xylon, a chemical used in one of its major products. Subsequently the firm stopped using xylon because it found a cheaper substitute. For the past six months, the price of xylon has hovered around $2.45 per pound and the firm could buy or sell it at that price. The 3,400 pounds now in inventory cost $3.32 per pound eight months ago and are carried at that value.

The firm now has an opportunity to fill a special order that requires 2,700 pounds of xylon. The substitute could not be used for this order. Total incremental costs associated with the order are $12,540, without considering xylon, and the price is $20,500. The controller is puzzled about the cost to be used for xylon in determining whether to accept the order.

REQUIRED

1. Calculate the gain or loss Martin will show on its books if it accepts the order.
2. Determine whether Martin should accept the order.

12–5 Short-Term Decisions CLT Company makes three products. The income statement for a typical month follows:

	Product			
	C	*L*	*T*	*Total*
Sales	$300	$400	$800	$1,500
Variable costs	100	200	400	700
Contribution margin	200	200	400	800
Fixed costs:				
Direct and avoidable	80	100	120	300
Common, allocated	60	100	160	320
Total fixed costs	140	200	280	620
Profit	$ 60	$ 0	$120	$ 180

REQUIRED

Answer each of the following questions independently.

1. If product L were dropped, what would profit be?
2. CLT is considering the introduction of a new product, P, to replace C. Product P sells for $7 per unit, has variable costs of $5 per unit, and has direct avoidable fixed costs of $130. How many units of P must CLT sell to maintain its $180 income?
3. The selling price of product T is $10. A chain store has offered to buy 40 units of T per month at $8 per unit. Fixed costs in total and variable costs per unit will remain unchanged if the order is accepted. CLT can produce 110 units of T per month. If the offer is accepted, what will CLT's monthly income be?

12–6 Relevant Costs Moran Furniture Company has received an offer from a European firm that wants to buy 10,000 tables at $70 each. This offered price is well below Moran's customary price of $95. Moran currently has 25,000 tables of the type wanted by the European firm carried at the following unit costs:

Materials	$33.50
Direct labor	18.40
Variable overhead, 60% of direct labor	11.04
Total variable cost	$62.94

If the company accepts the order, it will ship tables from inventory and the customer will pay delivery charges. The tables in question are good sellers, and Moran anticipates selling 90,000 or so during the coming year. Moran has sufficient capacity to fill the order and meet all demand at regular selling prices.

The chief cost accountant for Moran expects some rapid cost increases. Specifically, she believes that materials costs will increase by 10 percent and direct labor by 15 percent within a short time. Variable overhead should continue to be 60 percent of direct labor cost.

REQUIRED

Determine whether Moran should accept the order.

12–7 Basic Make or Buy Decision (AICPA Adapted) Standard cost and other data for two component parts used by the Griffon Electronics Company appear below.

	Part A4	*Part B5*
Direct material	$0.40	$ 8.00
Direct labor	1.00	4.70
Factory overhead	4.00	2.00
Total unit standard cost	$5.40	$14.70
Units required per year	6,000	8,000
Machine hours per unit	4	2
Unit cost if purchased	$5.00	$15.00

In past years Griffon has manufactured all its requirements of A4 and B5. However, during the coming year the firm will have only 30,000 hours of machine time available for producing components. Accordingly, some of them must be purchased from outside suppliers. In producing parts, the firm applies factory overhead at $1 per machine hour. Fixed manufacturing costs, which are unaffected by the volume of machine hours, are 60 percent of the $1.

REQUIRED

1. Determine the unit costs of A4 and B5 that are relevant to the make or buy decision.
2. Determine the number of units of each component that Griffon should make during the coming year.

12–8 Temporary Shutdown The management of Kalman Company is considering shutting down for the months of October, November, and December. The firm makes food products, largely from corn, and has been experiencing very hard times. Its products sell in highly competitive markets, and selling prices have been forced down by large supplies.

The controller prepared the following income statement for the three-month period, assuming that the firm remains open.

Revenue	$4,300,000
Cost of goods sold	3,700,000
Gross margin	600,000
Operating expenses	1,450,000
Expected loss	($ 850,000)

Cost of goods sold includes about $800,000 in fixed costs, and operating expenses include about $1,100,000 fixed costs. The firm could avoid about 70 percent of total fixed costs if it shut down. However, shutting down and then reopening the firm would result in additional costs of about $90,000 for mothballing and restarting equipment, severance pay, retraining, and so on.

REQUIRED

1. Determine whether the firm should shut down.
2. Determine the level of sales that makes staying open equally attractive (or equally unattractive) as shutting down. Assume that variable costs will bear the same percentages to revenue that are reflected in the income statement above.

12–9 Trade Agreement Booker Automobile Agency sells a wide variety of cars. Recently the manager of television station KRZ-TV proposed the following arrangement to Booker's manager. If Booker would provide the station with an automobile, the station would run advertisements for the agency. In particular, the station wanted the car as part of a deal it had swung to hire John Goodlooking, a proven news anchor, who had demanded a car as part of his compensation. The car that the station wanted retails for $45,000; the cost to the dealer is $36,000.

The costs of a television station are about 90 percent fixed. Its output, the programming it does, is set at eighteen hours per day, seven days per week. Some of the costs are discretionary, but few are variable. Pricing for advertising depends on ratings: the higher the ratings, the higher the price per minute. Prices also depend on the time, with commercials shown in prime time (generally 7:30 P.M. to 11:00 P.M.) selling for about 150 percent of the price charged in nonprime time.

If the two firms were to reach an agreement, KRZ-TV would show Booker's advertisements on a space available basis; that is, they would appear during periods of commercial time for which there were no paying advertisers. Consequently, Booker could not control the timing of the showings. Since the amount of time devoted to commercials is limited by law, KRZ-TV could not easily slip in commercials for Booker unless it had unsold time.

REQUIRED

Write a formal memorandum to management, using a microcomputer and word processing program with a spreadsheet program for supporting schedules. See Appendix B for guidelines for memoranda presentation.

You have been hired by Leslie Nenn, General Manager of KRZ-TV, to analyze the situation. Write Nenn a letter in which you discuss the issues and questions that both Booker and KRZ-TV would consider in reaching a price for the car. Make a recommendation to Nenn of how much to offer, from KRZ-TV's position. However, also give her your assessment of how much you believe that Booker would offer. Support your analysis and recommendations. Deal with any questions that you believe must be resolved before a final price is reached. Use appropriate examples in your discussion.

12–10 Relevant Costs Rich Miller, Treasurer of Fairview Insurance Agency, has a problem. The president of Fairview has asked him to determine whether the firm should ask Henry Daniel, one of its agents, to leave. Fairview is a general insurance agency consisting of 20 agents, an accounting department, a data processing department, and an underwriting department. When an agent sells a policy to a client, the commission from the policy is divided 60/40 between the agent and Fairview. In addition, insurance policy writers (carriers) give Fairview a yearly commission based on total premium volume. Daniel has been generating premiums of about $650,000 per year with average commissions of $6\frac{1}{4}$ percent. The following costs have been associated with Daniel:

Secretary	$15,000
Rent	1,000
Telephone	300
Accounting services	2,000
Data processing	250
Miscellaneous	2,150
	$20,700

In analyzing this information, Miller has ascertained the following facts.

1. The secretary works only for Daniel.
2. Rent is determined on the basis of a square-foot allocation of total rent. Fairview's lease runs out at the end of this year. The offices are in a high rise downtown building, and unused space can be sublet.
3. Telephone includes direct local and long-distance costs.
4. Accounting services and data processing have been allocated on the basis of the number of billing transactions.
5. Miscellaneous expenses include $300 of direct supplies plus an $1,850 share of general expenses, including such items as the office receptionist, the underwriting department, general telephone, and supply costs.

Fairview expects to write policies with total premiums of $21,670,000 in the current year.

REQUIRED

Write a memo to Fairview's president recommending whether to fire Daniel. Include an analysis of the relevant data and appropriate calculations. See Appendix B for guidelines to memoranda presentation.

12–11 Inventory Values Arman Company bought 1,000 gallons of Ansolium, a solvent, for $8.10 per gallon several months ago. Ansolium now costs $9.70 per gallon including freight-in. Arman could sell it for only $8.80 per gallon. An order has just arrived that requires all 300 gallons left. The order price is $35,000. Incremental costs, excluding Ansolium, are $25,600.

REQUIRED

Answer each of these questions independently:

1. Arman has stopped making the product that uses Ansolium and had planned to sell it before the order arrived. Should Arman accept the order?
2. Suppose now that Arman does use Ansolium regularly so that if it accepts the order it will have to buy additional quantities for its regular production. Should Arman accept the order?

12–12 Machine Versus Labor Intensive Production (CMA Adapted) Candice Company has decided to introduce a new product. The new product can be manufactured by either a capital-intensive or a labor-intensive method. The manufacturing method will not affect the quality of the product. The estimated manufacturing cost by the two methods are as follows:

	Capital Intensive		*Labor Intensive*	
Raw materials		$5.00		$5.60
Direct labor	0.5 DLH at $12	6.00	0.8 DLH at $9	7.20
Variable overhead	0.5 DLH at $6	3.00	0.8 DLH at $6	4.80
Directly traceable incremental fixed manufacturing costs		$2,440,000		$1,320,000

Candice's market research department has recommended an introductory price of $30. Incremental selling expenses are estimated to be $500,000 annually plus $2 for each unit sold regardless of manufacturing method.

REQUIRED

1. Calculate the breakeven point in annual unit sales of the new product if Candice Company uses the
   a. capital-intensive method
   b. labor-intensive method
2. Determine the annual unit sales volume at which Candice Company is indifferent between the two methods.
3. Candice's management must decide which method to employ. One factor it must consider is operating leverage.
   a. Explain operating leverage and the relationship between operating leverage and business risk.
   b. Explain the circumstances under which Candice should employ each of the two manufacturing methods.
4. Identify the business factors other than operating leverage that Candice must consider before selecting the capital-intensive or labor-intensive manufacturing method.

12–13 Basic Decisions The controller of VRS Company has developed the following estimates of *monthly* results for the coming year:

	Total		*Per Unit*	
Sales		$100,000		$25
Variable costs	$48,000		$12	
Fixed costs	24,000	72,000	6	18
Profit before taxes		$28,000		$ 7

Variable cost consists of a $9.50 variable manufacturing cost and a 10 percent sales commission.

REQUIRED

1. A chain store has approached VRS with an offer to buy 500 units at $15 each. There will be no commission on these units. VRS's managers estimate that if

they take the order they will lose some sales at the regular price because some customers will buy from the chain instead of from VRS. How many units could VRS lose and maintain its current profit?

2. VRS has 100 units of an obsolete model on hand that were produced at a variable cost of \$9. Usually, there is no market for these units. Now, however, a potential customer is interested in buying these 100 units plus 200 units of the product that VRS now makes, a total of 300 units. There will be no sales commission on the deal. Since the information shown above was collected, material prices have increased by \$1.50 per gallon. Each unit of product requires 1 gallon of material. However, the 200 units of the current product will come from inventory already produced. Determine the total price for the 300 units that will make VRS as well off, economically, whether or not it accepts the order.

12–14 Review of Short-Term Decisions Kroll Furniture expects the following results for three of its chair styles, before considering the changes described later.

	Style		
	A–101	C–555	L–379
Selling price	\$120	\$400	\$800
Variable costs	40	160	320
Fixed costs	30	120	420
Total costs	70	280	740
Profit per unit	\$ 50	\$120	\$ 60
Annual volume	8,000	3,000	4,000

All fixed costs are direct, but unavoidable.

REQUIRED

Answer each of the following items independently of the others unless otherwise instructed.

1. What is expected total profit?
2. What will happen to profit if the company drops L-379?
3. What will happen to profit if the company drops A-101 but shifts machinery to making more L-379, so that volume of L-379 increases to 7,000 units? (Total fixed costs remain constant.)
4. The variable cost per L-379 includes \$60 for parts that the company now buys outside. Kroll could make the parts at a variable cost of \$45. It would also have to increase fixed costs by \$35,000 annually. What would happen to profit if Kroll took the proposed action?
5. Kroll has received an offer for 1,000 C-555s at \$250. There is sufficient capacity to make the additional units, and sales at the regular price would not be affected. What would happen to profit if Kroll accepts the order?
6. Repeat part 5 assuming now that the order is for 1,500 units and that capacity is limited to 4,000.

12–15 Make or Buy Vivian Company currently makes all the components for a laser compact disk player. Vivian has been approached by a company in Malaysia to supply a part for $50 each. Vivian's managers are convinced that the foreign firm can supply these parts with consistent quality and acceptable delivery schedules. An analysis of the cost records associated with this part shows the following:

Materials	$15
Labor (1 hr)	10
Overhead	40
	$65

Normal volume is 10,000 units a month. Overhead consists of $15 per hour in costs that vary directly with labor hours, $5 per hour allocated for rent on machinery used exclusively to produce this part, and $20 of allocated general factory rent, supervision, accounting, and computer costs.

REQUIRED

At 10,000 units per month, should Vivian's managers elect to make or buy this component?

12–16 Relevant Costs The following information is available about the Scallop Division of Princess Manufacturing:

Plant manager annual salary	$50,000
Supervisor annual salaries:	
Smith	35,000
Lopez	30,000
Rent for building	45,000
Depreciation on equipment:	
Product A	10,000
Product B	20,000
Product C	30,000
Hourly workers	$10 per hour
Allocated corporate costs	5 per hour
Variable plant overhead	2 per hour

Scallop Division has three product lines. Smith supervises products A and B, while Lopez supervises product C. Workers are paid for 40 hours a week, and there are 10 workers assigned to the product A line, 12 to B, and 15 to C. It takes $\frac{1}{4}$ hour to produce A, $\frac{1}{4}$ hour to produce B, and $\frac{1}{2}$ hour for C.

REQUIRED

1. Ignoring material costs, what are the fixed and variable costs common to the plant and separable to each of the three products?
2. If Scallop's managers are considering dropping product B, what are the relevant costs to consider?
3. Scallop's managers think that if product B were discontinued, Smith could be reassigned to an opening in another division and Lopez could supervise both products A and C. With this in mind, how would you amend your answer to part 2?

12–17 Special Order Johnson and Masters Sleepwear makes a complete line of men's and women's pajamas and nightgowns. Recently management has been approached by a chain of department stores to make a special order of children's pajamas carrying a movie theme.

The head of cost estimating has come up with the following figures for the special order of 50 gross requested by the store. He has followed management's policy of full pricing, which includes a fair share of selling and administrative expenses plus a 15 percent markup.

	Cost per Gross
Manufacturing costs:	
Cloth	$ 150
Buttons	16
Franchise fee	72
Direct labor	350
Overhead	280
Selling and administrative costs	80
Total costs	948
Markup	142
	$1,090

Other information that you have received is:

1. The plant is currently operating at 70 percent of capacity and is making 10,000 gross of various products per year.
2. Overhead is applied at 80 percent of direct labor dollars. Annual fixed overhead is expected to be $980,000, and total overhead is expected to be $2,800,000.
3. The franchise fee has to be paid to the movie company to use its name and characters.
4. Fixed selling and administrative expenses are $400,000 for the current year. Since variable selling and administrative costs are believed to be a function of the total number of units produced, selling and administrative costs are applied on units produced.

REQUIRED

1. If the chain store offered $41,500 for the 50 gross, should Johnson and Masters accept the order?
2. How would your answer change, if at all, if Johnson and Masters is currently operating at capacity?
3. What else should you consider in making this decision?

12–18 Evaluating a Decision The sales manager of Baker Industries recently agreed to sell significant amounts of one of the company's principal products to another company for overseas distribution. Baker does not now sell any of its products overseas. It wanted to continue the arrangement and the sales manager wanted to determine how profitable the business had been so far. At the sales manager's request, the controller prepared the income statement below related to the business for the first eight months.

Sales	$280,000
Cost of sales	217,000
Gross margin	63,000
Operating expenses	61,000
Profit	$ 2,000

The controller said that a $2,000 profit on $280,000 sales was too little to justify the bother as well as run the risk of being unable to supply regular customers. Recently the company had operated close to, but not at, capacity. The controller also provided additional data regarding the income statement.

(a)	*Cost of sales includes the following:*	
	Materials	$ 76,000
	Labor	31,000
	Overhead, 60% variable	110,000
	Total	$217,000
(b)	*Operating expenses:*	
	Sales salaries	$ 32,000
	Clerical	12,000
	Other	17,000
	Total	$ 61,000

The sales manager was confused about some items and received the following additional explanation. The sales salaries cover the time of a sales representative who devotes 75 percent of her time to this account. The $32,000 is 75 percent of her salary over the eight month period. The clerical costs are for a part-time clerk who works exclusively on this account. The bulk of the "other" category is a $14,000 administrative charge. The company charges all products 5 percent of sales to cover administrative expenses. The remaining $3,000 is incremental costs.

The sales manager sought your help in understanding the statement and evaluating the order. He was confused and wondered whether to bother discussing renewal of the arrangement.

REQUIRED

Prepare a new income statement that will assist the sales manager in evaluating the business.

12–19 Basic Decision Making Arnold Company makes a bottle-capping machine used in the soft drink industry. The following data reflect management's expectations of a typical month for the coming year:

Sales $31,000 price for 20 units		$620,000
Manufacturing costs:		
Materials	$ 80,000	
Direct labor	100,000	
Overhead	200,000	380,000
Gross profit		240,000
Selling and administrative expenses		200,000
Income		$ 40,000

All manufacturing costs are variable, except for $120,000 in fixed overhead. Variable overhead is related to direct labor hours. The direct labor rate is $10 per hour, and each machine requires 500 hours. Capacity is 25 machines per month.

Selling and administrative expenses include a $2,000 per unit variable component, with the remainder fixed.

Unless otherwise instructed, treat each situation below independently of the others.

REQUIRED

1. What is the maximum amount the firm can earn in a month?

2. Would the firm be wise to accept a contract to deliver ten machines per month to a large soft drink company at $25,000 each? The prospective customer has never bought machines from Arnold before, and the expected volume given above does not reflect any sales to it. Arnold would not incur the $2,000 variable selling and administrative expense on these units.

3. This question assumes the facts from part 2. The limit on Arnold's capacity relates to direct labor hours. Arnold cannot work its own direct laborers more than 12,500 hours per month. An outside contractor could supply suitable workers. These new workers would be as efficient as Arnold's own. Variable overhead would be incurred at the same rate per labor hour on the new workers as on the existing ones. The contractor could supply enough workers to bring Arnold's total capacity to 30 units per month. What is the maximum amount, per month, that Arnold would pay to acquire the workers?

4. The marketing manager believes that Arnold could increase prices by $2,000 per unit and lose sales of only two units per month to competitors. Variable selling and administrative expenses would increase to $2,200 per unit. Would the increase in price be wise?

5. The machine requires a part that Arnold currently makes. Data for the part, one of which is used in each machine, are as follows:

Materials	$180
Direct labor, 20 hrs at $10	200
Overhead	400
Total	$780

Variable overhead for making this part is the same per direct labor hour as in any other operation. An outside firm has offered to supply the part for $650. Should Arnold accept the offer?

6. Repeat part 5, except that Arnold is now working at capacity of 25 units per month. Arnold could sell any additional output it could make, and purchasing the part outside would free up enough labor time to make one additional unit. Would it now be wise to purchase the part?

12–20 Special Order Pricing (CMA Adapted) Framar, Inc., manufactures automation machinery to customer specifications. The company is relatively new and has grown each year. Framar operated at about 75 percent of practical capacity during the 19X7–19X8 fiscal year. Operating results for the most recent fiscal year appear below.

FRAMAR, INC.
Income Statement
For the Year Ended September 30, 19X8
(in Thousands)

Sales		$25,000
Less: Sales commissions		2,500
Net sales		$22,500
Expenses:		
Direct material		6,000
Direct labor		7,500
Manufacturing overhead—variable:		
Supplies	$ 625	
Indirect labor	1,500	
Power	125	2,250
Manufacturing overhead—fixed:		
Supervision	$ 500	
Depreciation	1,000	1,500
Corporate administration		750
Total expenses		$18,000
Net income before taxes		$ 4,500
Less: Income taxes (40%)		1,800
Net income		$ 2,700

Top management of Framar wants a more organized and formal pricing system to prepare quotes for potential customers. Therefore, it has developed the pricing formula presented below. The formula is based on the company's operating results for the 19X7–19X8 fiscal year. The relationships used in the formula are expected to continue during the 19X8–19X9 year. The company expects to operate at 75 percent of practical capacity during the upcoming fiscal year.

APA, Inc., has asked Framar to submit a bid on some custom designed machinery. Framar used the new formula to develop a price and submitted a bid of $165,000. The calculations to arrive at the bid price are given next to the pricing formula shown below.

Details of Pricing Formula		*APA Bid Calculations*
Estimated direct material cost	$XX	$ 29,200
Estimated direct labor cost	XX	56,000
Estimated manufacturing overhead calculated at 50% of direct labor	XX	28,000
Estimated corporate overhead calculated at 10% of direct labor	XX	5,600
Estimated total costs excluding sales commissions	$XX	$118,800
Add 25% for profits and taxes	XX	29,700
Suggested price (with profits) before sales commissions	$XX	$148,500
Suggested total price equals suggested price divided by 0.9 to adjust for 10% sales commission	$XX	$165,000

REQUIRED

1. Calculate the impact the order from APA, Inc., will have on Framar Inc.'s net income after taxes if Framar's bid of $165,000 were accepted.
2. Assume APA, Inc., has rejected Framar's price but is willing to pay $127,000 for the machinery. Should Framar, Inc., accept the counteroffer? Explain your answer.
3. Calculate the lowest price at which Framar Inc. can supply this machinery without reducing its net income after taxes.
4. Explain how the profit performance in 19X8–19X9 would be affected if Framar Inc. accepted all its work at prices similar to the $127,000 counter-offer described in part 2.

12–21 Expected Values Managers of Borgman Feedlots are trying to determine when to sell a batch of 100 cattle. The animals currently weigh 700 pounds each, and the selling price per pound for an animal is expected to be $0.65 throughout the next several months. The schedule below shows weight gains and associated probabilities if the animals are held for one additional month and for two additional months. The total variable cost to keep an animal on the lot for a month is $40, and Borgman has already spent an average of $250 to acquire and feed the animals. Borgman must decide now whether to sell the animals today, hold them for one more month, or hold them for two more months.

One Additional Month		*Two Additional Months*	
Weight Gain	*Probability*	*Weight Gain*	*Probability*
120 lb	0.30	170 lb	0.40
160 lb	0.70	210 lb	0.60

REQUIRED

Determine how long Borgman should hold the cattle.

12–22 Expected Value (AICPA) In planning its budget for 19X2, King Company prepared the following payoff probability distribution describing the relative likelihood of monthly sales volume levels and related contribution margins for Product A:

Monthly Sales Volume	*Contribution Margin*	*Probability*
4,000	$ 80,000	0.20
6,000	120,000	0.25
8,000	160,000	0.30
10,000	200,000	0.15
12,000	240,000	0.10

REQUIRED

What is the expected value of the monthly contribution margin for Product A?

12–23 Expected Value (AICPA) Duguid Company is considering a proposal to introduce a new product, XPL. An outside marketing consultant prepared the following payoff probability distribution describing the likelihood of monthly sales volume levels and related income (loss) for XPL:

Monthly Sales Volume	*Probability*	*Income (loss)*
3,000	0.10	$(35,000)
6,000	0.20	5,000
9,000	0.40	30,000
12,000	0.20	50,000
15,000	0.10	70,000

REQUIRED

What is the expected value of the added monthly income if Duguid decides to market XPL?

12–24 Expected Values (AICPA) During your examination of the financial statements of Benjamin Industries, the president asked your help in evaluating several financial management problems in his home appliances division; he summarized the problems in the following manner.

Management wants to determine the best sales price for a new appliance, which has a variable cost of $4 per unit. The sales manager has estimated probabilities of achieving annual sales levels for various selling prices as shown in the following chart:

Sales Level (Units)	*Selling Price* $4	$5	$6	$7
20,000	—	—	20%	80%
30,000	—	10%	40%	20%
40,000	50%	50%	20%	—
50,000	50%	40%	20%	—

REQUIRED

Prepare a schedule computing the expected incremental income for each of the sales prices proposed for the new product. The schedule should include the expected sales levels in units (weighted according to the sales manager's estimated probabilities), the expected total monetary sales, the expected variable costs, and the expected incremental income.

12–25 Uncertainty Palit Company forecasts sales of 100,000 pounds of its major product for the upcoming year. In addition, the sales manager has estimated that the probability that sales will be between 90,000 and 110,000 pounds is 75 percent.

REQUIRED

1. What is the standard deviation in units?
2. What is the probability that sales will exceed 95,000 pounds?

3. If fixed costs are $850,000, if variable costs are $10 per unit, and if selling price is $20 per unit, what is the probability of breaking even?

12–26 Product Selection—Statistics As president of Wehman Company, you make the final decisions on all products. Presently you are trying to decide which of two products to bring out next year. Capacity is not sufficient for both, so you must choose one or neither. Information about the two products appears below.

	Product 101	Product 102
Expected monthly volume, units	100,000	200,000
Expected selling price	$40	$50
Expected unit variable cost	30	37
Expected monthly fixed costs, all incremental to the product	600,000	2,000,000

REQUIRED

1. Determine which product to select, based on the information available.
2. You recognize that the expected values may not materialize and that you should perform sensitivity analysis. Determine how high or low each variable would have to go to bring each product to breakeven. Do each variable independently of the others. (Hold all but one constant at the expected value.) Determine the percentage changes from the expected value to the new one. Does this new information support the decision you made in part 1?
3. Suppose now that you are reasonably certain about all the variables except the variable cost per unit. Pilot studies, statistical analyses, and industrial engineering techniques indicate that variable cost per unit is normally distributed with means as given above and standard deviations of $1.50 and $3 for Products 101 and 102, respectively. Does this new information change your decision? Support your analysis with appropriate calculations.

12–27 Pricing and Expected Values The marketing department has developed the following estimates of volumes at four prices that you are considering for a new product. The estimated ranges of volume at each price reflect uncertainty. The marketing people do not believe that the probabilities are uniform over each range, and they do not consider it reasonable to make more explicit statements about probabilities.

Price	Expected Volume	Range of Volume
$40	10,000	7,000–13,000
35	13,000	11,000–15,000
30	16,000	15,000–17,000
25	18,000	17,000–19,000

Unit variable cost is $10, and incremental fixed costs are $250,000.

REQUIRED

Recommend a price, justifying your answer with whatever calculations you believe appropriate.

12–28 Sensitivity Analysis and Statistics Gruenwald Thread Company makes a variety of threads, including one used in residential carpeting. The firm recently employed a consultant who developed the following regression equation for this thread:

$$Y = 218{,}365 + 163.6X; \qquad r^2 = 0.602; \qquad S_e = 316{,}280$$

where

Y = monthly sales of thread, in yards

X = the number of housing starts in the geographical region that Gruenwald serves

r^2 = the coefficient of determination

S_e = the standard error of the estimate

The state commerce department has estimated that regional monthly housing starts will average about 12,400 during the coming year. The thread sells for $1.20 per yard, variable costs are $0.48 per yard, and monthly incremental fixed costs are $1,214,000.

REQUIRED

1. Determine the expected average monthly profit.

2. Determine the probability that sales will be below the breakeven point. Use the normal distribution.

3. The president of the firm wants to know the confidence interval for profits with 95 percent probability. What are the limits of the interval? Use the normal distribution.

12–29 Decision Tree Your firm is the largest manufacturer of word processing equipment, and your competitors usually price their units about $100 below yours. Your equipment is generally thought to be better than your competitors', so they must charge less to make inroads into the market.

You have good reason to believe that your competitors might price as much as $175 below you in the coming year in all-out efforts to break your dominance on the market. You have been thinking about two prices, $1,800 and $1,600. At $1,600 you believe there is only a 10 percent probability of your competitors' pricing at $175 below you, but at $1,800, a 60 percent probability.

You believe that your sales will be about 50,000 units if your price is $100 over your competitors', about 30,000 units if you are $175 higher. These unit estimates apply at either the $1,600 or $1,800 price. Variable cost is $1,000 per unit.

REQUIRED

Analyze the alternative prices, using a decision tree.

12–30 Decision Tree The managers of Elmar Products are evaluating a series of strategies associated with the possible marketing of a new product. Existing capacity is available on machinery being used for a product that may be phased out. The existing product, Pow-Add, an additive for diesel fuel, has an annual contribution margin of $30,000. Management feels that the new product, Sun-Set, a chemical medium for heat storage for solar heating systems, will prove more profitable.

If Sun-Set is introduced, market research has shown there is a 50/50 chance of demand's being either 8,000 gallons per month or 12,500 gallons per month at a price of $35 per gallon. If Elmar produces this chemical, variable costs of production are uncertain. Sun-Set must be produced in large batches. The firm's engineers think that the batch size should be 10,000, 15,000, or 20,000 gallons at a time. Estimated costs and probabilities of these costs are shown below. Once the choice of batch size has been made, it cannot be reversed.

Batch Size and Cost per Gallon

10,000 Gallons		*15,000 Gallons*		*20,000 Gallons*	
Cost	*Probability*	*Cost*	*Probability*	*Cost*	*Probability*
$25	0.1	$20	0.2	$20	0.2
30	0.2	25	0.2	25	0.1
35	0.7	30	0.6	30	0.7

In addition, Elmar has been approached by Wolff, Inc., which has offered a one-year contract to make 100,000 gallons at $2,700,000 or 150,000 gallons at $3,750,000.

REQUIRED

Assume that products unsold at year-end are worthless.

1. Model this problem using a decision tree. [*Hint*: Identify what decisions are called for and identify what occurrences are probabilistic.]
2. Using the tree in part 1, put in all conditional values and probabilities.
3. Solve the decision tree.

12–31 Decision Tree Analysis (CMA Adapted) Various quantitative business methods are referred to as operations research or management science techniques. Many of these mathematical or statistical techniques can be applied by the management accountant to aid in business analysis and decision making. Decision tree analysis is one such technique that has proved useful to the management accountant.

REQUIRED

1. Describe the environment and the circumstances for which decision tree analysis is an appropriate model.
2. For decision tree analysis:
   a. Explain what a decision tree is and include a description of its component elements.
   b. Identify the mathematical or statistical concepts employed in the model.
   c. Explain how the decision model works.

12–32 Linear Programming—Setting Up Problem ARG, Inc., operates a cattle feedlot. Providing the necessary nutrients to each animal requires 5 pounds of protein per day and 7 pounds of carbohydrates per day. A pound of corn, which costs $0.80, is 20 percent protein, 60 percent carbohydrate, and 20 percent nonessential stuff. A pound of prepared feed supplement, costing $1.20, is 40 percent protein, 50 percent carbohydrate, and 10 percent inert material. Write the equations (inequalities) needed to determine the optimal combination of feed to use per animal per day.

12–33 Linear Programming (CIA) An internal auditor developed the following data for a linear programming model for its southern plant:

	Product		
	X1	X2	X3
Selling price	35	90	20
Costs:			
Material	15	30	10
Labor	15	30	3
Variable overhead	2	5	1
Fixed overhead[a]	5	10	1
Profit/(loss) per unit	(2)	15	5

[a] Allocated to products on the basis of labor hours.

REQUIRED

Based on these data, what is the correct objective function to maximize profit from that plant?

12–34 Linear Programming Optimal Solution (CMA Adapted) A small company makes only two products with the following two production constraints representing two machines and their maximum availability:

$$2X + 3Y \leq 18$$
$$2X + Y \leq 10$$

where

X = the units of the first product
Y = the units of the second product

REQUIRED

If the profit equation is $Z = \$4X + \$2Y$, what is the maximum possible profit?

12–35 Linear Programming Constraints (AICPA) Johnson, Inc., manufactures Product X and Product Y, which are processed as follows:

	Type A Machine	Type B Machine
Product X	6 hours	4 hours
Product Y	9 hours	5 hours

Contribution margin is \$12 for Product X and \$7 for Product Y. The available time daily for processing the two products is 120 hours for machine type A and 80 hours for machine type B. How should the restriction (constraint) for machine type B be expressed?

1. $4X + 5Y$.
2. $4X + 5Y \leq 80$.
3. $6X + 9Y \leq 120$.
4. $12X + 7Y$.

12–36 Linear Programming (AICPA Adapted) Golden Hawk Manufacturing Company seeks to maximize the profits on its three products, for which the following data are available:

	Product		
	A	B	C
Contribution margin per unit	$2	$5	$4
Production requirements, hours in each department:			
Assembling	2	3	2
Painting	1	2	2
Finishing	2	3	1

Total capacities, in hours, for each department are: assembling, 30,000; painting, 38,000; finishing, 28,000.

REQUIRED

Set up the objective function and constraints for the linear programming problem that will maximize Golden Hawk's profits.

12–37 Linear Programming (AICPA) Select the best answer for each of the following parts.

1. In a linear programming maximization problem for business problem solving, the coefficients of the objective function usually are:
a. marginal contributions per unit
b. variable costs
c. profit based on allocations of overhead and all indirect costs
d. usage rates for scarce resources
e. none of the above

2. The constraints in a linear programming problem usually model:
a. profits
b. restrictions
c. dependent variables
d. goals
e. none of the above

3. If there are four activity variables and two constraints in a linear programming problem, the most products that would be included in the optimal solution would be:
a. 6
b. 4
c. 2
d. 0
e. none of the above

4. Linear programming is used most commonly to determine:
a. the mix of variables that will result in the largest quantity
b. the best use of scarce resources
c. the most advantageous prices
d. the fastest timing
e. none of the above

5. Assume the following data for the two products produced by Wagner Company:

	Product A	Product B
Raw material requirements (units):		
X	3	4
Y	7	2
Contribution margin per unit	$10	$4

If 300 units of raw material X and 400 units of raw material Y were available, the set of relationships appropriate for maximization of profit using linear programming would be

a. $3A + 4B \geq 300$
$7A + 2B \geq 400$
$10A + 4B \quad \max$

b. $3A + 7B \geq 300$
$4A + 2B \geq 400$
$10A + 4B \quad \max$

c. $3A + 7B \leq 300$
$4A + 2B \leq 400$
$10A + 4B \quad \max$

d. $3A + 4B \leq 300$
$7A + 2B \leq 400$
$10A + 4B \quad \max$

e. none of the above

6. A final tableau for a linear programming profit maximization problem is:

	X_1	X_2	X_3	S_1	S_2	
X_1	1	0	4	3	−7	50
X_2	0	1	−2	−6	2	60
	0	0	5	1	9	1,200

If X_1, X_2, X_3 represent products, S_1 refers to square feet (in thousands) of warehouse capacity, and S_2 refers to labor hours (in hundreds), the number of X_1 that should be produced to maximize profit would be

a. 60
b. 50
c. 1
d. 0
e. none of the above

7. Assuming the same facts as in part 6, the contribution to profit of an additional 100 hours of labor would be

a. 9
b. 2
c. 1
d. −7
e. none of the above

8. Assuming the same facts as in part 6, an additional 1,000 square feet of warehouse space would

a. increase X_1 by 3 units and decrease X_2 by 6 units
b. decrease X_2 by 6 units and increase X_1 by 2 units
c. decrease X_1 by 7 units and increase X_2 by 2 units
d. increase X_1 by 3 units and decrease X_2 by 7 units
e. do none of the above

9. The following is the final tableau of a linear programming profit maximization problem:

	X_1	X_2	S_1	S_2	
X_1	1	0	−5	3	125
X_2	0	1	1	−1	70
	0	0	5	7	500

The marginal contribution to profit of 5 for each added resource unit S_1 can be maintained if the added resource units do not exceed

a. 125
b. 100
c. 70
d. 25
e. none of the above

10. Assume the following per unit raw material and labor requirements for the production of Product *A* and the production of Product *B*.

	Product A	Product B
Pounds of lead	5	7
Hours of labor	3	4

Assuming that 13,400 pounds of lead and 7,800 hours of labor are available, the production of products *A* and *B* required to use all of the available lead and labor hours is shown in the following final Gaussian tableau.

$$\left[\begin{array}{cccc|c} 1 & 0 & -4 & 7 & 1{,}000 \\ 0 & 1 & 3 & -5 & 1{,}200 \end{array}\right]$$

If the available amounts were increased to 15,000 pounds of lead and 8,800 hours of labor, the matrix operation to determine the production schedule that would fully utilize these resources is:

a. $\begin{pmatrix} 5 & 7 \\ 3 & 4 \end{pmatrix}\begin{pmatrix} 15{,}000 \\ 8{,}800 \end{pmatrix}$.

b. $\begin{pmatrix} 15{,}000 \\ 8{,}800 \end{pmatrix}\begin{pmatrix} -4 & 7 \\ 3 & -5 \end{pmatrix}$.

c. $\begin{pmatrix} -4 & 7 \\ 3 & -5 \end{pmatrix}\begin{pmatrix} 1{,}000 \\ 1{,}200 \end{pmatrix}$.

d. $\begin{pmatrix} -4 & 7 \\ 3 & -5 \end{pmatrix}\begin{pmatrix} 15{,}000 \\ 8{,}800 \end{pmatrix}$.

e. none of the above

11. The following schedule provides data for Product A, which is processed through processes 1 and 2, and Product B, which is processed through process 1 only.

	Product A	*Product B*
Raw material cost per gallon	\$ 4	\$ 9
Process 1 (500-gal input capacity per hour):		
Processing cost per hour	\$60	\$60
Loss in processing	30%	20%
Process 2 (300-gal input capacity per hour):		
Processing cost per hour	\$50	
Loss in processing	10%	
Selling price per gallon	\$20	\$40

If the objective were to maximize profit per eight-hour day, the objective function of a profit-maximizing linear programming problem would be

a. $20A + 40B - 4A - 4B$

b. $20A + 40B - 4A - 4B - 60(A + B) - 50A$

c. $20(0.63A) + 40(0.80B) - 4(0.63A) - 9(0.8B)$
$$- 60\left(\frac{A + B}{500}\right) - 50\left(\frac{0.7A}{300}\right)$$

d. $20(0.63A) + 40(0.80B) - 4A - 9B$
$$- 60\left(\frac{A}{500} + \frac{B}{500}\right) - 50\left(\frac{0.7A}{300}\right)$$

e. none of the above

12. Assuming the same facts as in part 11, a constraint of the problem would be

a. $0.63A \leq 2{,}400$

b. $0.8A \leq 2{,}400$

c. $0.7A + 0.8B \leq 4{,}000$

d. $0.9A \leq 4{,}000$

e. none of the above

13. The accompanying graph shows engineering estimates of costs of various volumes. In developing the firm's cost function, the point at $x = 0$ would be

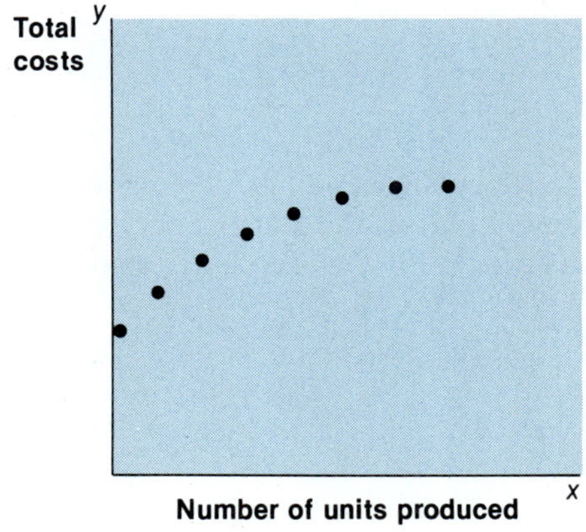

a. an estimate of variable cost
b. an estimate of fixed cost
c. the total cost of the first unit
d. the slope of the curve
e. none of the above

14. Dancy, Inc., will begin producing a new chemical cleaner by combining alcohol, peroxide, and enzyme. Each quart of the new cleaner will require $\frac{1}{2}$ quart of alcohol, 1 quart of peroxide, and $\frac{1}{3}$ quart of enzyme. The costs per quart are 40 cents for alcohol, 60 cents for peroxide, and 20 cents for enzyme. The matrix operation to determine the cost of producing one quart of new chemical cleaner is

a. $(\frac{1}{2}, 1, \frac{1}{3})\begin{pmatrix}0.40\\0.60\\0.20\end{pmatrix}$

b. $\begin{pmatrix}\frac{1}{2}\\1\\\frac{1}{3}\end{pmatrix}\begin{pmatrix}0.40\\0.60\\0.20\end{pmatrix}$

c. $(\frac{1}{2}, 1, \frac{1}{3})(0.40, 0.60, 0.20)$

d. $\begin{pmatrix}0.40\\0.60\\0.20\end{pmatrix}(\frac{1}{2}, 1, \frac{1}{3})$

e. none of the above

15. A linear programming model is used to determine the quantities of each of two products having different profitabilities per unit to produce to maximize profit over a one-year period. One component of cost is raw materials. If both products use the same amount of the same raw material
a. this cost *may* be ignored, because it is the same for each product
b. this cost *must* be ignored, because it is the same for each product
c. this cost must be included in the objective function, since it varies with the independent variables in the model
d. More information about the products and the other components of the objective function is needed to determine whether to include this cost.
e. none of the above

12–38 Expected Values (CMA Adapted) Video Recreation, Inc., (VRI) supplies video games and video equipment such as large-screen televisions and video cassette recorders. The company has recently concluded a major contract with Sunview Hotels to supply games for the hotel video lounges. Under this contract, a total of 4,000 games will be delivered to Sunview Hotels throughout the western United States, and all of the games will have a warranty period of one year for parts and labor. The number of service calls required to repair these games during the first year after installation is estimated as:

Number of Service Calls	*Probability*
400	.1
700	.3
900	.4
1,200	.2

VRI's Customer Service Department has developed three alternatives for providing the warranty service to Sunview; these three plans follow.

Plan 1 VRI would contract with local firms to perform the repair services. It is estimated that six such vendors would be needed to cover the appropriate areas and that each of these vendors would charge $15,000 annually to have personnel available and to stock the appropriate parts. In addition to the annual fee, VRI would be billed $250 for each service call and would be billed for parts used at cost plus a 10 percent surcharge.

Plan 2 VRI would allow the management of each hotel to arrange for repair service when needed and then would reimburse the hotel for the expenses incurred. It is estimated that 60 percent of the service calls would be for hotels located in urban areas where the charge for a service call would average $450. At the remaining hotels, the charge would be $350. In addition to these service charges, parts would be billed at cost.

Plan 3 VRI would hire its own personnel to perform repair services and preventive maintenance. Nine employees in the appropriate geographical areas would be required with average salaries of $24,000 annually. The fringe benefit expense for these employees would amount to 35 percent of their wages. Each employee would be scheduled to make an average of 200 preventive maintenance calls during the year; each of these calls would require $15 worth of parts. Because of this preventive maintenance, it is estimated that the number of hotel calls for repair service would decline 30 percent and the cost of parts required for each repair service call would be reduced by 20 percent.

VRI's Accounting Department has reviewed the historical data on repair costs for equipment installations similar to those proposed for Sunview Hotels and found that the cost of parts required for each repair occurred in the following proportions.

Parts Cost Per Repair	*Proportion*
$30	15%
40	15
60	45
90	25

REQUIRED

Recommend which of the three plans presented above should be adopted by VRI. Support your recommendation with appropriate calculations and analysis.

12–39 Use of Capacity (CMA Adapted) WoodCo is a wholesale distributor supplying a wide range of equipment and tools to the logging industry. About half of WoodCo's products are purchased from other companies, and the remainder WoodCo manufactures. WoodCo makes a fiberglass reinforced case used to carry long-bladed chain saws. In a normal year, WoodCo manufactures and sells 5,000 of these cases. This production makes full use of WoodCo's capacity in the Fiberglass Processing Department, which is limited by the amount of direct labor at a fixed number of work stations. WoodCo believes it could sell 7,000 cases if it had the manufacturing capacity. Below are the actual revenue and cost data for manufacturing chain saw cases.

Selling price per case		$80.00
Costs per case:		
Fiberglass and resin	$24.00	
Handle, hinges, latch	7.00	
Direct labor ($12.00/hr.)	12.00	
Manufacturing overhead	6.00	
Selling and administrative cost	16.00	65.00
Profit per case		$15.00

WoodCo has looked into the possibility of purchasing chain saw cases for distribution. The company learned that Murphy Supply could provide the cases in volume quantities at a price of $60.00 each delivered to WoodCo's facility. The maximum number of cases that Murphy could supply to WoodCo in any given year is 6,000, and the cases must be bought in increments of 1,000. Other goods supplied from Murphy in the past have been of very good quality, and WoodCo regards Murphy as reliable.

The only other product that WoodCo's Fiberglass Processing Department could make is a brightly colored hard hat. At present, WoodCo does not sell hard hats; however, a market analysis indicates there is room for another producer. The market analysis revealed that a sales price of $35.00 per hat is best; at this price, WoodCo expects to sell 9,500 hard hats annually. The data gathered indicate that the profit per hard hat is considerably less than the profit per chain saw case. The estimated manufacturing costs for the hard hats are presented below.

Selling price per hat		$35.00
Costs per hat:		
Fiberglass and resin	$12.00	
Liner, strap, rivets	5.00	
Direct labor ($12.00/hr.)	4.80	
Manufacturing overhead	2.40	
Selling and administrative cost	3.50	27.70
Profit per hat		$ 7.30

WoodCo employs departmental rates for applying manufacturing overhead to its products. Direct labor hours are the application base for the Fiberglass Processing Department. Included in manufacturing overhead for the current year is $20,000 of factory-wide fixed manufacturing overhead that has been allocated to the Fiberglass Processing Department.

In addition, $80,000 per year of company-wide fixed selling and administrative costs are allocated to the Fiberglass Processing Department using a 20 percent of sales application rate. To encourage new products, however, WoodCo's policy is to allocate company-wide fixed selling and administrative costs at 10 percent of sales rather than the usual 20 percent.

WoodCo's management is, of course, interested in increasing profitability. Therefore, company Controller David Roman has been asked to review the available data and recommend what combination of products WoodCo should manufacture and/or purchase in the future.

REQUIRED

1. In formulating this recommendation on the nature of WoodCo's future business,

a. Explain the decision rule that Roman should apply.
b. Discuss the important factors that Roman needs to identify when preparing his analysis.

2. Prepare an analysis based on the data presented, that will show which product or products WoodCo should manufacture and/or purchase in order to maximize the company's profitability. Support your answer with appropriate calculations.

12–40 Warranty Costs (CMA Adapted) Bodkin Corporation is a major producer of motorcycles in the United States. Bodkin's management is formulating a warranty policy for a new motorcycle, model BK-1250, that will be released in January 19X6. The company expects to sell 4,000 units of model BK-1250 in 19X6 at a unit price of $3,900. There are two warranty options under consideration.

Option I is a twelve-month or 3,000-mile warranty agreement that requires the company to replace all defective parts and to provide the repair labor at no cost to the customer.

Option II is a twelve-month or 3,000-mile warranty agreement that requires the corporation to replace defective parts at no cost to the customer; however, the warranty agreement for labor only extends for a 30-day period. The customer may purchase an 11-month extension on the labor warranty for $50. The probabilities for the number of 11-month labor extension warranty contracts to be sold to customers for $50 are estimated as shown below.

Number of Labor Extension Warranty Contracts to be Sold	*Estimated Probability*
3,600	.1
2,700	.2
1,800	.3
900	.4

Management believes that the parts costs under the warranty for the BK-1250 will be about eight percent greater than the warranty parts costs of the BK-1000, a similar motorcycle introduced in 19X1. The increase is attributable to the more sophisticated design of the BK-1250. The average warranty parts costs for the BK-1000 are estimated to be $150 during 19X5.

Bodkin would use company employees to do the labor under Option I. The warranty labor cost per unit sold for the BK-1000 cycle is estimated to be $20 for 19X5; the company is convinced that time involved will be similar for the BK-1250. Variable overhead related to warranty work averages 40 percent of direct labor charges.

The company has decided that if it chooses Option II, it will utilize a service agency to perform the labor. Bodkin would supply the agency with the appropriate parts. The service agency wants a contract for a guaranteed fee of $12 per unit sold to cover the labor cost for expected warranty work that would occur in the first 30 days after the sale and an additional $20 for each labor warranty extension contract Bodkin sells.

Bodkin estimates that inflation will occur at a constant rate of five percent per year in each of the next two years (i.e., 19X6 and 19X7). This will have a uniform impact on all in-house warranty costs. However, Bodkin will hold its prices stable at the amounts given for 19X6.

All sales are assumed to occur evenly throughout the year, and warranty work is incurred evenly throughout the warranty period.

REQUIRED

1. Calculate Bodkin Corporation's estimated net warranty cost that would result from the expected 19X6 sales of model BK-1250 under:
   a. Option I
   b. Option II
2. Identify any other factors Bodkin Corporation should consider before it decides which warranty option to select.

12–41 Linear Programming (AICPA) Beekley, Inc., manufactures widgets, gadgets, and trinkets and has asked for advice in determining the best production mix. Demand for the company's products is excellent, and management finds that it is unable to meet potential sales with existing plant capacity.

Each product goes through three operations: milling, grinding, and painting. The effective weekly departmental capacities in minutes are: milling, 10,000; grinding, 14,000; and painting, 10,000.

The following data are available on the products:

	Selling Price per Unit	Variable Cost per Unit	Per Unit Production Time (in minutes) Milling	Grinding	Painting
Widgets	$5.25	$4.45	4	8	4
Gadgets	5.00	3.90	10	4	2
Trinkets	4.50	3.30	4	8	2

REQUIRED

Select the single best answer to the following questions.

1. The objective function for this problem using the simplex method might be expressed
   a. $f\text{ min} = 4.45X_1 + 3.90X_2 + 3.30X_3 + 0X_4 + 0X_5 + 0X_6$
   b. $f\text{ max} = 5.25X_1 + 5.00X_2 + 4.50X_3 + X_4 + X_5 + X_6$
   c. $f\text{ max} = 0.80X_1 + 1.10X_2 + 1.20X_3 + X_4 + X_5 + X_6$
   d. $f\text{ max} = 0.80X_1 + 1.10X_2 + 1.20X_3 + 0X_4 + 0X_5 + 0X_6$
2. The requirement that total production time in the painting department may not exceed 10,000 minutes per week might be expressed
   a. $4X_1 + 2X_2 + 2X_3 \geq 10{,}000$
   b. $4X_1 + 2X_2 + 2X_3 > 10{,}000$
   c. $4X_1 + 2X_2 + 2X_3 \leq 10{,}000$
   d. $4X_1 + 2X_2 + 2X_3 < 10{,}000$
3. The variables X_4, X_5, X_6 in the answers to part 1 are referred to as
   a. artificial variables
   b. primary variables
   c. stochastic variables
   d. slack variables

4. The variables X_1, X_2, X_3 in the answers to part 1 are referred to as
   a. artificial variables
   b. primary variables
   c. stochastic variables
   d. slack variables

5. The coefficients for X_1, X_2, and X_3 in the answers to part 1 are
   a. the coefficients of the objective function in the problem
   b. the coefficients of the artificial variables in the problem
   c. the coefficients of the constraints in the problem and represent the contribution margin for each project
   d. the shadow prices of the stochastic variables in the problem

12–42 Linear Programming Results (CMA) Jenlock Mill Company produces two grades of interior plywood from fir and pine lumber. The fir and pine lumber can be sold as saw lumber or used in the plywood.

To produce the plywood, thin layers of wood are peeled from the logs in panels and the panels are glued together to form plywood sheets and then dried. The peeler can peel enough panels from logs to produce 300,000 sheets of plywood in a month. The dryer has a capacity of 1,200,000 minutes for the month. The amount of lumber used and the drying time required for each sheet of plywood by grade are shown below.

	Grade A Plywood Sheets	*Grade B Plywood Sheets*
Fir (in board feet)	18	15
Pine (in board feet)	12	15
Drying time (in minutes)	4	6

The only restriction on the production of fir and pine lumber is the capacity of the mill saws to cut the logs into boards. These saws have a capacity of 500,000 board feet per month regardless of species.

Jenlock has the following quantities of lumber available for July production:

Fir	2,700,000 board feet
Pine	3,000,000 board feet

The contribution margins for each type of output are:

Fir lumber	$0.20 per board foot
Pine lumber	$0.10 per board foot
Grade A plywood	$2.25 per sheet
Grade B plywood	$1.80 per sheet

The demand in July for plywood is expected to be a maximum of 80,000 sheets for grade A and a maximum of 100,000 sheets for grade B. There are no demand restrictions on pine and fir lumber.

Jenlock Mill Company uses a linear programming model to determine the production quantities of each product. The correct formulation of the linear programming model is below, and a summary of the solution of the model follows.

Formulation

F = board feet of fir lumber to be sold
P = board feet of pine lumber to be sold
A = number of sheets of grade A plywood to be sold
B = number of sheets of grade B plywood to be sold

Maximize: $0.20F + 0.10P + 2.25A + 1.80B$

Subject to:

Amount of fir available	F			$+$	$18A$	$+$	$15B$	$\leq$	2,700,000
Amount of pine available			P	$+$	$12A$	$+$	$15B$	$\leq$	3,000,000
Peeler capacity					A	$+$	B	$\leq$	300,000
Dryer capacity					$4A$	$+$	$6B$	$\leq$	1,200,000
Saw capacity	F	$+$	P					$\leq$	500,000
Maximum demand:									
Grade A plywood					A			$\leq$	80,000
Grade B plywood							B	$\leq$	100,000

SUMMARY OF SOLUTION

Summary of the Primal Problem

Solution Variables	*Solution Values*
Pine lumber to be sold	500,000 board feet
Grade A plywood to be sold	80,000 sheets
Grade B plywood to be sold	84,000 sheets
Slack items:	
Pine available	280,000 board feet
Peeler capacity	136,000 sheets
Dryer capacity	376,000 minutes
Demand for grade B plywood	16,000 sheets

Nonsolution Variables	*Opportunity Costs*
Fir lumber to be sold	\$.02
Constraining items:	
Fir available	\$.12
Saw capacity	\$.10
Demand for grade A plywood	\$.09

Ranges of the Restraining Values of the Constraints (in Thousands)

Constraints	*Initial Constraint Value*	*Lower Limit*	*Upper Limit*
Amount of fir available	2,700	1,440	2,940
Amount of pine available	3,000	2,720	Infinity
Peeler capacity	300	164	Infinity
Dryer capacity	1,200	824	Infinity
Saw capacity	500	0	780
Demand for plywood:			
Grade A	80	67	150
Grade B	100	84	Infinity

Ranges of Objective Function Coefficients

Objective Coefficient	Initial Value	Lower Bound	Upper Bound
Fir lumber	$0.20	Negative infinity	$0.22
Pine lumber	$0.10	$0.08	Positive infinity
Grade A plywood	$2.25	$2.16	Positive infinity
Grade B plywood	$1.80	$1.50	$1.875

REQUIRED

Refer to the *Summary of Solution* to answer each of the following requirements. The requirements are independent of each other.

1. How much fir, pine, grade A plywood, and grade B plywood should Jenlock Mill Company produce? What is the total contribution margin of this mix?
2. Will Jenlock Mill Company use all of its resources to their capacities during July if it follows the solution derived from the linear programming model? Explain your answer.
3. Two items regarding fir lumber appear under nonsolution variables: fir lumber to be sold with an opportunity cost of $0.02 and fir available as a constraining item with an opportunity cost of $0.12. Explain what these two items mean.
4. Assuming there is no change in price, should Jenlock Mill Company attempt to acquire any more fir for use during July? If so, how much should be acquired? Explain your answer.
5. Jenlock Mill Company has been asked by one of its competitors to sell it some drying time. How much, if any, drying time should Jenlock sell to its competitor? Explain your answer.
6. Jenlock Mill Company can acquire the use of additional mill saw capacity at the rate of $1,800 for an eight-hour day. The additional saw capacity can process 20,000 board feet of lumber in an eight-hour day. Should Jenlock acquire the use of extra saw capacity? If so, how much time should it acquire? Explain your answer.
7. What is the range within which the contribution of the grade B plywood can fluctuate before the optimal solution changes?

12–43 Linear Programming Mork Pharmaceuticals, Inc., is a small producer of prescription drugs. During 19X3, a scare caused by another manufacturer's drugs being tampered with resulted in the recall of many over-the-counter remedies. This in turn positively affected prescription drugs, since consumers turned to them in the short run. Mork had been operating at about 70 percent of capacity before the recall. Orders were now flooding in, especially for two items, Epaine and Nache. Both products are marketed in capsule form and are made on the same piece of machinery. Management needs to decide how much of each product to produce this month on its now limited resources. The following information comes from the company's cost records for these two products:

	Cost per 1,000 Capsules	
	Epaine	*Nache*
Materials	$1.00	$1.25
Direct labor	1.00	0.75
Overhead	2.00	1.50
Total	$4.00	$3.50

The key ingredient of both products is Esperine. Epaine uses 3 milligrams of Esperine per 1,000 capsules, while Nache uses 4 milligrams per 1,000 capsules. The current inventory of Esperine is 100,000 milligrams, and the supplier has informed management that no more will be available this month.

Labor is $10 per hour. Overhead is based on direct labor hours and is 40 percent variable and 60 percent fixed. Machine capacity is limited to 3,500 hours this month.

Epaine sells for $5.00 per 1,000 capsules, while Nache sells for $4.50 per 1,000 capsules.

REQUIRED

Write a formal memorandum to management, using a microcompter and a word processing program with a spreadsheet for supporting schedules. See Appendix B for guidelines for memoranda presentation.

You are an outside consultant hired by the managers of Mork. Write a memorandum to management (avoiding the use of jargon) in which you cover these issues:

1. If management decides to use linear programming to help in the production decision, what are appropriate objective function and constraints? Be sure to identify properly the variables.

2. Assume that a linear program has been run with the following results, where E = thousands of Epaine capsules, N = thousands of Nache capsules, S_1 refers to the materials constraint, and S_2 refers to the capacity constraint.

	E	N	S_1	S_2
33,333.333	1	1.3333	0.3333	0
166.667	0	-0.0583	0.0333	1

Fully explain these results. What is the meaning of each row? Each column?

3. Using your analysis and answers to the above, make recommendations to management in the following areas:

a. Is it worthwhile to pursue additional sources of Esperine? Why? What is the maximum price management should be willing to pay for additional material?

b. Is it worthwhile to pursue additional machine capacity? Why? What is the maximum price management should be willing to pay for additional machine capacity?

4. In your memorandum, prepare a statement for management in which you discuss the appropriate use of linear programming and its strengths and weaknesses. This discussion should include issues relating to data, the model, and output.

12–44 Expected Values (AICPA) Your firm of CPAs audits Food Products, Inc. The president of Food Products asked you for help in solving the following problem.

A Food Products plant on the coast produces a food product and ships 10,000 units per day in an airplane owned by Food Products. The area is sometimes fogbound, and shipment can then be made only by rail. The plant does not operate unless shipments are made. Extra costs of preparation for rail shipment reduce the marginal contribution of this product from $0.40 per unit to $0.18 per unit, and there is an additional fixed cost of $3,100 for modification of packaging facilities to convert to rail shipment (incurred only once per conversion).

The fog may last for several days, and Food Products normally starts shipping by rail only to meet commitments to customers.

A meteorological report reveals that during the past ten years the area has been fogbound 250 times for one day and that fog continued 100 times for a second consecutive day, 40 times for a third consecutive day, 20 times for a fourth consecutive day, and 10 times for a fifth consecutive day. Occasions and length of fog were both random. Fog never continued more than five days, and there were never two separate occurrences of fog in any six-day period.

REQUIRED

1. Prepare a schedule presenting the computation of the daily marginal contribution (ignore fixed conversion cost):
   a. when there is no fog and shipment is made by air
   b. when there is fog and shipment is made by rail

2. Prepare a schedule presenting the computation of the probabilities of the possible combinations of foggy and clear weather on the days following a fogbound day. Your schedule should show the probability that, if fog first occurs on a particular day:
   a. the next four days will be foggy
   b. the next three days will be foggy and day 5 will be clear
   c. the next two days will be foggy and days 4 and 5 will be clear
   d. the next day will be foggy and days 3, 4, and 5 will be clear
   e. the next four days will be clear

3. Assume you determine it would probably be unprofitable to start shipping by rail on the fourth or fifth consecutive foggy day. Prepare a schedule presenting the computation of the probable marginal income or loss that should be expected from rail shipments if they were started on the third consecutive foggy day and the probability that the next two days will be foggy is 0.25, the probability that the next day will be foggy and day 5 will be clear is 0.25, and the probability that the next two days will be clear is 0.50.

4. In this engagement the CPA should consider the reliability of the data on which any conclusions are based. What questions should be considered regarding:
   a. financial data reliability
   b. meteorological data reliability?

12–45 Risk and Return "It's tempting to take the sure thing, but if I do I could miss out on some healthy business," mused Joe Bardon, owner and operator of Bardon Construction Company, which specialized in road-building and earth-removing work. Bardon was tempted because Morton Industries, Inc., a large diversified company, had offered to lease some of his equipment for the coming year for $384,000. Morton was building a plant in a remote area and needed road-building and earth-moving equipment. Employees of Morton's construction subsidiary would do the work.

Bardon explained some aspects of his business:

> Nearly all of my work requires about the same mix of equipment: grader, scraper, a truck or two, and so on. Consequently, I can pretty well measure my volume by using what I call an equipment day, which is a day's work for the five or six machines that I need. I have five sets of equipment, so that I can do about 1,100 equipment days working the usual 220-day year. Naturally, I seldom do that much work because of bad weather, breakdowns, and lack of business. I average between 900 and 1,120 days per year.
>
> Morton wants what amounts to two sets, so that I'd have three sets left. They want the newest pieces, of course, so I'll be lucky to get 590 to 610 days out of the three sets even if I can get the business. I had planned to bid on two state jobs, but if I lease to Morton I could only bid on one. I think that I can get either one, and maybe both, but it's no sure thing by any means. I am committed to doing about 350 equipment days of work, and I can probably get close to 700 days if I have the equipment available. I usually charge $2,200 per equipment day, but on state jobs you have to set a total price, so I would try to get a bit more to give myself a cushion in case I can't finish in the number of days I expect.
>
> Why don't you look at the figures I've pulled together? These are my best estimates, and I'm usually fairly close, but things could change over the year.

Bardon's figures follow:

Operating Costs

Variable per equipment day:	
Fuel, oil	$ 95
Wages, fringe benefits, other	870
Total	$ 965
Fixed per year:	
Depreciation on equipment	$280,000
General and administrative	595,000

State Contracts

	Job A	*Job B*
Bardon's estimated bid	$510,000	$880,000
Expected equipment days required	210	380

REQUIRED

Analyze the alternatives, developing information that will be useful to Bardon. Be prepared to make a recommendation and to support it, based on the information available.

13

CAPITAL BUDGETING DECISIONS

Managers continually face decisions about whether to acquire or replace major capital assets. Starting with profit plans and sales budgets, managers analyze existing facilities and equipment to see if they are adequate. New and improved manufacturing processes continually become available and managers must evaluate them. The models that managers use for such evaluations are called *discounted cash flow* (DCF) models and rely on the basic principle of the *time value of money*. Appendix 13A explains the time value of money, while Tables A–3 and A–4 in Appendix A at the end of the book contain discount factors used in these models. If you need to learn or to review the time value of money, read Appendix 13A now.

CAPITAL RESOURCE ALLOCATION

Chapter 12 defined tactical decisions as those whose major economic impact comes in the short term. In contrast, capital budgeting decisions require long-term commitments of substantial resources. For example, building a new 100,000-square-foot factory and putting in new production equipment is a decision (or series of decisions) that could cost $25 million and affect the company for 20 years. The dollar amounts involved in some capital budgeting decisions make it important for managers to analyze them carefully. Of special concern is that such decisions are not easily reversed: if the company buys machinery designed specifically to produce a new product and the product fails the company will almost surely lose nearly all of its investment.

Managers can use available investment funds in many ways. They replace older equipment, modernize factories, and expand capacity. Research and development or marketing departments also propose investments. Finally, funds could be invested in securities or used to reduce outstanding indebtedness, pay dividends, or buy treasury stock. Proposals to buy new equipment and facilities are, therefore, competing with other uses of the same funds.

Although some firms will generate enough cash to meet all their needs, most companies will need to secure funds through such means as selling stock or bonds or entering into other long-term financing arrangements with banks, insurance companies, or leasing companies. Obviously, any funds obtained from an outside party have a cost in the form of interest or dividends, as does internally generated cash. While dividends are not an accounting expense, they are a cost. The company must earn enough to pay dividends or its stockholders will sell their shares. Additionally, internally generated cash has an opportunity cost; unless it is used wisely, the company's value declines and shareholders' investments are hurt.

The question is what is the best use of available cash. What investments should the company make? Usually a wide variety of investments is available, some expected to yield relatively sure but low returns, others uncertain but potentially high returns. The job of managers is to develop a suitable mix of investments.

We begin with a discussion of the role of cash flow in capital budgeting. Before we proceed, note two important points: first, capital budgeting decisions, like the tactical decisions in Chapter 12, are based on *estimates*. It does not pay to try to be too precise when working with estimates whose results are 5 to 25 years in the future. There is sometimes a false sense of precision accompanying, say, a computer printout that shows an answer down to the last penny. Resist the temptation to be unwarrantedly precise. With rare exceptions, cash flows are not certainties; trying to make them appear so is not helpful.

Second, capital budgeting models give only economic results and they depend on the information available. Managers have many reasons to make investments that appear unprofitable, or to refuse investments that appear profitable. For instance, an investment that increases product quality might appear unprofitable based on the reasonably hard estimates. However, the company might make the investment because its overriding strategy is to become the highest-quality producer in the industry. A company might also reject a profitable investment that requires moving outside its normal areas of expertise in marketing or manufacturing. We made this point in Chapter 12 and return to it throughout this chapter and the next.

CASH FLOWS

In this section we explore models that consider the time value of money (DCF models) and some that do not. Most models are based on the cash inflows and outflows, rather than the income, generated by an investment.

Cash Flow Versus Net Income

In evaluating a decision, we ask what the economic impact of each alternative will be and we make an incremental analysis of this impact. Capital budgeting decisions focus on expected incremental cash flows. Because this focus departs from the traditional accounting stress on net income, it is desirable to discuss why cash flows are the relevant data.

First, over the life of a firm, net income and net cash inflow usually will be the same.[1] However, the timing of the incomes and cash inflows might differ substantially. Because of the time value of money, it is better to receive cash now rather than later, since cash can be invested to earn more cash. You cannot invest net income, only cash. The following schedule shows incomes and cash flows expected from investing in two companies. If you could buy either company for $30,000, which would you select?

	Company A	*Company B*
First year:		
Net income	$20,000	$40,000
Cash inflow	20,000	0
Second year:		
Net income	20,000	0
Cash inflow	20,000	40,000

Company A is the correct answer, because even though both companies return the same total net income and total cash flow, company A returns cash faster. You could take the $20,000 from company A at the end of the first year and invest it at some interest rate, say 10 percent. Thus, while you would receive only $40,000 in total from firm B after two years, you would have $42,000 in total [($20,000 × 1.1) + $20,000] if you had invested in firm A.

Net income is an accounting measure based, in part, on the matching concept. Costs become expenses as they are matched against revenue. The actual timing of cash inflows and outflows is ignored. Some expenses do not even require a cash outflow. Depreciation is the best example of this type of expense. Even though depreciation is deducted from revenue, no cash is paid to

[1]Differences between net income and net cash inflow may arise when assets are acquired through the issuance of stock, but for our purposes we can ignore these differences.

anyone. Rather, the cash payment is made when the asset is bought. (Even if the company borrows the money to buy the asset, in effect, it still pays for it at delivery. The borrowing and subsequent repayment of the loan are financing flows, not investing flows. In Chapter 14 we discuss the difference between deciding to invest in a project and how to finance it. Whatever way an asset is financed, in essence, it is paid for at the beginning of the project.)

Because we are interested in cash flows, we need to consider income taxes. In addition, noncash expenses such as depreciation reduce income taxes because they reduce taxable income. We also have to consider the cash flow consequences of taxes on gains and losses from selling assets. However, since this is not a tax course, we will simplify some tax aspects for our analyses. The idea is to get a basic understanding of how taxes affect cash flows and to keep from being too tied to the current tax code, since it changes. At this juncture, the Tax Acts of 1981, 1982, and 1986 influence our analyses. The effects of these acts are explained in Appendix 13B.

Types of Cash Flows

Cash flows associated with an investment typically include investment-related flows, cash flows from operations (which include changes in working capital), and other miscellaneous flows. Remember that we do not consider financing flows such as interest payments.

In general, three types of flows are associated with buying a piece of machinery: the original investment, the tax effects of depreciation over its life, and the net after-tax inflows (or outflows) on selling or disposing of the asset when its economic life is finished. For example, Exhibit 13–1 shows data for the Dahl Corporation for a new product.

In this first example we will use straight-line depreciation as you would find it in financial accounting. We will deal with depreciation under the current law later. We ignore salvage value in computing annual depreciation. This is permitted under tax law and means that, when received, the salvage value is subject to tax. Dahl's combined state and federal marginal tax rate is 40 percent. An income statement for the incremental business from the investment is shown on the next page.

EXHIBIT 13–1 Data for New Product—Dahl Corporation

Cost of machinery	\$250,000
Useful life	5 years
Expected salvage value	\$ 20,000
Annual straight-line depreciation	\$ 50,000
Expected incremental revenues	\$500,000
Expected incremental cash costs	\$350,000

Revenue	$500,000
Expenses:	
Cash operating expenses	(350,000)
Depreciation	(50,000)
Income before taxes	$100,000
Income taxes	40,000
Net income	$ 60,000

What is the net cash inflow for this period? The $350,000 in operating expenses and taxes of $40,000 (40% of income) are outflows. Depreciation is not a cash expense and is *not* an outflow. A comparison of income and cash items follows:

	Income	*Cash Flow*
Revenue	$500,000	$500,000
Expenses:		
Operating	(350,000)	(350,000)
Depreciation	(50,000)	
Income before taxes	$100,000	
Income taxes (40%)	40,000	(40,000)
Net income	$ 60,000	
Net cash flow		$110,000

If cash receipts and revenue coincide and operating expenses and disbursements also coincide, yearly cash flows equal net income *plus* depreciation. Adding the $50,000 depreciation to the $60,000 income also gives the $110,000 cash flow.

As we shall see, it is often helpful to calculate after-tax operating flows separately from the tax savings from depreciation. Although a project may have a useful (economic) life of, say, ten years, tax laws might allow us to depreciate that asset over five years. In Dahl's case,

a. cash flows from operations:

$$\$500{,}000 - \$350{,}000 = \$150{,}000 \text{ before taxes}$$
$$\$150{,}000(1 - 40\% \text{ tax rate}) = \$90{,}000 \text{ after taxes}$$

b. savings in taxes due to depreciation:

$$\$50{,}000 \text{ depreciation} \times 40\% \text{ tax rate} = \$20{,}000$$

c. total net cash flows: $\$90{,}000 + \$20{,}000 = \$110{,}000$

In this second method, revenues and cash expenses are multiplied by *1 − tax rate* to deduct taxes and achieve a net cash flow. However, because depreciation itself has no associated cash flow, its value in a cash-related analysis stems from the *taxes saved* because depreciation can be deducted as an expense. Thus, depreciation is multiplied by the *tax rate* to get the net cash effect of depreciation. This is also called the **tax effect of depreciation** or the **tax shield from depreciation**.

Although this company expects to receive $20,000 for the machinery, it probably will receive some other amount. Predicting a salvage value five years away is obviously subject to substantial error.

In our example, we depreciated all $250,000 of the asset's cost. Thus, any amount we receive will generate a gain when the asset is sold after five years. To illustrate both gains and losses, let us look at the tax basis of the asset after four years. Here, the tax basis is $50,000 ($250,000 less 4 years' depreciation of $50,000 per year). We will now assume that the machine can be sold for $60,000, then that it can only be sold for $35,000. The analyses appear below.

Cash Flow—Gains and Losses on Salvage

	Gain	*Loss*
Tax basis of asset	$50,000	$50,000
Net selling price[a]	60,000	35,000
Gain (loss)	$10,000	($15,000)
Tax on 40% on gain (loss)	(4,000)	6,000
Net cash received:		
Selling price	$60,000	$35,000
Tax consequences	(4,000)	6,000
Net cash received	$56,000	$41,000

[a]Net selling price is cash received less any costs of removal.

As you can see, the $10,000 gain *reduced* the net cash received by the 40 percent tax ($4,000) on that gain. However, with a $15,000 loss, the company will *save* $6,000 in taxes, and net cash inflow is cash received from the sale *plus* the taxes saved because of a book loss. As with depreciation, the gains and losses are not important in themselves, only their tax consequences. Notice that the sale at a gain brings in more cash. Selling at a loss simply to get a tax deduction is usually unwise. You should be able to calculate for our original example of the asset being sold after five years for $20,000 that the net cash received is $12,000.

Timing of Depreciation Tax Shield No matter how we depreciate the machinery, total accumulated depreciation at the end of its tax life will equal the original cost and tax basis of the machine. Here is where we need to differentiate depreciation methods used in financial accounting and those used in tax accounting. While methods like sum-of-the-years'-digits and double-declining-balance depreciation are used for financial accounting, the current tax code requires using either the **Accelerated Cost Recovery System** (ACRS) or a **modified straight-line** depreciation method. As Appendix 13B illustrates, it is generally to a company's advantage to take as short a tax life as possible and to use accelerated methods rather than straight-line methods. While you will depreciate the same amount *in total*, the *timing* of the cash flows will differ.

Shorter lives and accelerated depreciation allow a company to receive the tax benefits from depreciation *sooner*. This is important because money has a time value, and this point holds with almost any accelerated method of depreciation compared with straight-line.

Cash Flows from Operations Cash flows from operations include receipts from sales and operating expense disbursements. Because the tax effect of depreciation was handled separately above, operating cash flows do not include the tax effect from depreciation. In our original example there were cash operating inflows of $500,000 and operating outflows of $350,000. Thus, net after-tax cash flows from operations were $90,000 ($150,000 less 40% taxes), as we developed before. To generalize, after-tax cash flows from operations are found by multiplying before-tax flows by "1 − tax rate." This relationship holds for net inflows and net outflows.

It is important to recognize that while cash flows from operations may change over time, the tax savings from depreciation are fixed at the time an asset is purchased as long as tax rates do not change. ACRS depreciation is often over five years, while other cash flows may go on for several more years. If we keep the tax savings from depreciation separate from cash flows from operations, we have a simpler, more adaptable planning and control tool and can use spreadsheet software to change our analyses more easily.

Working Capital Investment

We stated earlier that in the Dahl example, cash receipts equaled sales and cash disbursements equaled operating expenses, except for depreciation. That is often not the case: sales are not collected immediately, giving rise to accounts receivable; inventories often change, increasing or decreasing; and payments to suppliers might lag behind purchases. All of these differences can be handled by evaluating changes in working capital elements, current assets and current liabilities. Note as we proceed that working capital changes have no tax effects because they do not affect income.

Working capital consists of current assets and current liabilities. Many projects lead to changes in working capital. For instance, a new product usually generates higher receivables and inventories, as well as higher payables and accruals. Investments in working capital usually occur at the beginning of a project and, unlike investments in fixed assets, are typically returned at the end of the life. A company will build up inventory during the first year of a new product, then draw the inventory down at the end of the life. We usually treat working capital investment as if it took place at the beginning of the life of the project, even though the investment does not usually take place right at the beginning of the project. It is conventional to treat them as if they do, which is conservative.

Exhibit 13–2 is part of a Lotus 1-2-3 template that gives additional information about Dahl's new product venture. We incorporate that information into an analysis that considers working capital changes and complete the template.

EXHIBIT 13–2 Dahl Company Product Information

Annual unit sales:	50,000
Selling price	$10
Unit variable manufacturing cost	$ 3
Total cash fixed manufacturing costs	$150,000
Selling expenses, all fixed	$ 50,000
Other data:	
1. Cost of capital	12%
2. Collection period for sales, in days	45
3. Finished goods inventory supply, in days	30
4. Other inventories	$40,000
5. Accounts payable	$15,000

The significance of each item is explained below.

Cost of Capital Cost of capital is the opportunity cost of making investments, which we consider more closely in Chapter 14. For now, it is simply the discount rate used to determine present values of future cash flows. We include it in this exhibit for easy reference. Other terms that refer to the discount rate are the *hurdle rate*, *target rate*, and *relevant discount rate*.

Accounts Receivable Because Dahl collects its sales in 45 days, its cash flow in the first year is not the $500,000 sales from Exhibit 13–1 (50,000 units × $10), but something less. In years two through five, sales and cash collections will be the same because sales are the same in each year. Thus, the receivables at the beginning of year two (45 days' sales from year one) are collected early in year two. That amount equals the receivables of 45 days' sales at the end of year two. Thus, if sales remain constant so do receivables, and collections equal sales. However, at the beginning of the sixth year, there will be collections on sales made in year five. We could handle this by reducing the cash inflow shown for year one, and adding to the cash flow the collection in year six. We would do this in a more complicated case where sales varied from year to year. However, here we can handle the adjustment more simply by considering the initial increase in receivables to be part of the initial investment, and the recovery to be an inflow in the last year of life.

In our example, the initial increase in accounts receivable is

$$\begin{aligned}\text{accounts receivable} &= \text{collection period} \times \text{average daily sales}\\ &= 45 \times \$500{,}000/365\\ &= \$62{,}000 \text{ rounded}\end{aligned}$$

Notice also that 45 days is 1/8th of a 360 day year (it is reasonable to use a 360 day year), so receivables are expected to be about $500,000/8 = $62,500. Remember that this number is an estimate; there is no reason for precision to the last dollar.

Inventory The finished goods inventory of 30 days' sales is calculated as is accounts receivable, but the reasoning is slightly different. In year one the company must produce not only enough units to meet year one sales, but also enough to have the desired inventory at year end. In the last year, the company will stop making the product while it is still being sold, drawing down the inventory. In this example, the unit inventory is about 4,117 (30 days × 50,000/365). In year one, production needs to be about 54,117, but in year five it need be only about 45,883. The question is how much to show: the choices are the variable cost of the inventory or the absorption cost. The variable cost is correct because it is the incremental cost and incremental cash flow associated with the first year's extra production. Absorption cost includes fixed costs that we treat as part of the operating cash flows. Therefore, the cash invested in finished goods inventory should be about \$12,500.

$$\begin{aligned}\text{inventory investment} &= \text{units in inventory} \times \text{unit variable cost}\\ &= 30 \times 50{,}000/365 \times \$3\\ &= \$12{,}500 \text{ rounded}\end{aligned}$$

Again, because 30 days is 1/12th of a 360 day year, we could divide 50,000 by 12 to get the units in inventory and multiply by \$3.

Other Inventories and Payables The other inventories (materials, components, and some work in process) as well as payables could have been determined by analytical processes such as those used above. Here, we simply have those numbers as a result of someone else's analysis. The increase in payables is a negative investment: it reduces the cash outflow in the first year and is made up in the final year. The schedule below shows the working capital requirements.

DAHL COMPANY
New Product

	Working Capital Requirements
Accounts receivable	\$62,000
Finished goods inventory	12,500
Other inventories	40,000
Payables	(15,000)
Net increase in working capital	\$99,500

For all practical purposes, the increased working capital investment is \$100,000 and we shall use that number in our analyses.

If an investment is expected to decrease working capital, the treatment is not so clear. In all cases, the reduction in working capital is an inflow, usually at time zero, the time of the initial investment. The question is whether an offsetting outflow occurs at the end of the life. In some cases, such an outflow occurs. For example, a company might return to its current manufacturing methods and therefore experience an increase in inventory. The exception arises with major investments that change, probably for good, the character of the manufacturer's operations. The adoption of just-in-time manufacturing

EXHIBIT 13–3 Dahl Company Cash Flows (thousands of dollars)

Item	Year 0	1	2	3	4	5
Equipment	($250)					
Salvage value						20
Less tax on salvage						(8)
Working capital	(100)					100
Operating cash flow, net of tax		90	90	90	90	90
Depreciation shield		20	20	20	20	20
Net cash flows	($350)	$110	$110	$110	$110	$222

principles is the best example. If the implementation of JIT is the source of decreases, the reduction is treated as an inflow, but it is best not to assume an offsetting outflow at the end of the life. The reason is that a company should never return to higher levels of inventory once it has mastered JIT principles.

Let us use Dahl Company to illustrate the principal capital budgeting techniques. Exhibit 13–3 is the part of the template that outlines the cash flows. By convention, we usually treat cash flows as if they occur at the ends of years. All of these items were calculated earlier. Refer to pages 591–592 to see where they originate. We are now ready to use several capital budgeting techniques to evaluate the investment. The first three of the methods use discounted cash flows (DCF), and are conceptually sound. The last two do not use DCF and are therefore flawed, but one of these is widely used. All three of the DCF methods give the same indication for a specific investment, that is, accept it or reject it.

CAPITAL BUDGETING MODELS

Net Present Value

Perhaps the most commonly used capital budgeting technique is the net present value (NPV) method. The **net present value** method requires determining whether the present value of the future inflows exceeds that of the future outflows. The future flows are discounted at the relevant discount rate, typically cost of capital. The fundamental decision rule with the NPV method is to accept a project with a positive NPV and reject one with a negative NPV.

The template in Exhibit 13–4 shows the NPV calculations for Dahl's product at the 12 percent cost of capital. The present value factors are calculated the same as those in Table A–3 in Appendix A at the back of this book. There is really no need to show the 1.000 for year zero, because an outlay (or inflow)

EXHIBIT 13–4 DCF Analysis of Dahl Product

	Year					
	0	1	2	3	4	5
Equipment	($250)					
Salvage value						20
Less tax on salvage						(8)
Working capital	(100)					100
Operating cash flow		90	90	90	90	90
Depreciation shield		20	20	20	20	20
Net cash flows	($350.0)	$110.0	$110.0	$110.0	$110.0	$222.0
Present value factors	1.0000	0.8929	0.7972	0.7118	0.6355	0.5674
Present values	($350.0)	$98.2	$87.7	$78.3	$69.9	$126.0
Net present value	$110.1					
Internal rate of return	0.22774					

today has a present value equal to its nominal value. This is not true, of course, for flows to be received or paid in the future. The net present value of $110.1 thousand is the sum of the present values, beginning with the negative $350.0 thousand and continuing to the $126.0 thousand. The NPV is positive, so *from a financial perspective* the investment is desirable. The NPV is also large in relation to the investment, instilling even more confidence about the investment. Had the NPV been $1.5 thousand, we might decide not to go ahead because the margin for error is very small. The question of margins for error, of course, surfaced in Chapter 2 and we have reinforced it since.

Internal Rate of Return

Exhibit 13–4 also includes a figure called the internal rate of return. The **internal rate of return** (IRR) is the discount rate that equates the present values of the cash inflows and outflows. More intuitively, it is the discount rate that makes the NPV zero. You can verify this by discounting the flows in years one to five at 22.774 percent. The result will be $350 thousand (perhaps with some rounding error), the outflow at time zero. The IRR is sometimes called the **true rate of return**, or the **time-adjusted rate of return**.

The IRR is a percentage and, therefore, eliminates the size of an investment, just as calculating the current ratio in financial analysis eliminates the dollar amounts of current assets and current liabilities. As a percentage the IRR has advantages and disadvantages. One advantage is that it is easy to interpret: any manager can say that a 25 percent IRR is good and a 4 percent IRR bad (a checking account yields more than 4 percent), but it is not as easy to say that an NPV of $100,000 is good or bad. It depends partly on the amount to be invested, as we discuss shortly. We take up some other disadvantages of the IRR in Chapter 14.

The IRR and NPV have specific relationships. The discount rate is the rate used to determine the NPV. If the NPV is zero, the discount rate equals the IRR, as we stated above. If the NPV is positive, the IRR is greater than the discount rate; if the NPV is negative, the IRR is less than the discount rate. Therefore, knowing that the NPV was positive and fairly large we could tell that the IRR is greater than the 12 percent discount rate, probably a good deal greater.

Many people calculate the IRR, especially now that it can easily be done with spreadsheets. Without a spreadsheet, financial calculator, or dedicated computer program, calculations of the IRR use trial-and-error methods. Using trial-and-error methods, you pick a likely rate, say 18 percent, discount the cash flows and see whether the NPV is positive or negative. If it is positive, you move up the discount rate and try again. Within a few iterations you should have the rate fairly well nailed down. With the numbers in our example, it is enough to know that the rate exceeds 22 percent.

Using the IRR method alone, that is, not in connection with the NPV method, requires having a hurdle rate—a rate to which to compare the IRR to see if the investment is wise. In our example, the investment is wise for any hurdle rate up to 22.77 percent. Of course, if the hurdle rate were 15 percent and the IRR 15.1 percent, you would be leery of the investment and seek more information.

Present Value Index

The **present value index** (PVI) is the ratio of the present value of net cash inflows to the investment made at time zero. This ratio is also called the **benefit-cost ratio** (BCR). The idea of this ratio is to eliminate the size of investments. For instance, if two investments have \$10,000 NPVs, but one requires a \$1,000,000 investment and the other a \$100,000 investment, the second is probably more attractive because its NPV is much greater in relation to the amount invested. The PVI for Dahl's new product is

$$\begin{aligned} \text{PVI} &= \frac{\$98.2 + \$87.7 + \$78.3 + \$69.9 + \$126.0}{\$350.0} \\ &= \$460.1/\$350.0 \\ &= 1.32 \end{aligned}$$

Using PVI we accept a project if its PVI is greater than 1. This means, of course, that its NPV is positive. A PVI of 1.32, as in Dahl's case, is very good. Again, the decision rule is financial only. Notice that we can also calculate the PVI using the NPV. Because the NPV is the present value of the future flows minus the investment, adding the NPV of \$110.1 to the investment of \$350.0 gives the present value of the future flows of \$460.1, as we got by adding all of the present values of the future flows.

In summary, the project passes all three tests (if it passes any, it passes all) and is therefore a desirable investment. Another important point: the example uses a new product, which has net cash inflows. The analysis is equally applicable to a cost-saving situation, where outflows are reduced by savings in materials, labor, or other factor. Thus, the pretax operating inflows of $150 thousand (excluding the depreciation tax shield) could equally have been from savings of materials by using more efficient equipment.

Finally, many of the changes in working capital can be either positive or negative. We showed an increase in inventories, but some investments will decrease inventories. Companies moving toward just-in-time manufacturing will often make investments that, among other things, reduce inventories.

Decision Making and Present-Value Models

These three models (NPV, IRR, and PVI) all give a yes or no answer to the question: Is this a worthwhile project? To review, the decision criteria are:

Net present value:	accept if NPV > 0
Internal rate of return:	accept if IRR > relevant discount rate
Present-value index:	accept if PVI > 1.0

Realistically, however, a manager might not accept a project where the investment is, say, $600,000 and the net present value is $5. As we have discussed, and will discuss in some detail in Chapter 14, we are *estimating* economic life, cash receipts, cash disbursements, and so on. A manager therefore might feel uneasy about a large investment in which the decision is close. This is why we use IRR and PVI.

These three models, then, are the principal discounted cash flow (DCF) models. We shall discuss a few modifications as we proceed. All the models are appropriate. We tend to stress NPV as the least flawed model, but many people who want to relate returns to a percentage figure find IRR very useful.

All three models give the same answer (yes or no) to the accept/reject question: if net present value is greater than zero, then the present-value index is greater than 1.0 and the internal rate of return is greater than the relevant discount rate. Likewise if NPV is negative, the PVI is less than 1.0 and the IRR is less than the relevant discount rate. In some cases, discussed in Chapter 14, conflicts can exist in ranking projects using each of the three methods.

Quantitative analysis is one part of decision-making. Our approach has been to analyze cash flows and then, using one of the present-value models, discount the flows and make a decision. However, many factors that are not quantifiable directly might have a great effect on a decision. Qualitative factors might be important enough that a project with NPV greater than zero would be rejected while another with NPV less than zero would be accepted. We shall discuss the qualitative factors shortly.

Non-DCF Models

Two commonly used models ignore the time value of money: *payback* and *book rate of return*. We discuss these models because you might meet them in practice and because they can serve as rough screens for capital budgeting decisions. For example, as we shall show, if a project has a long payback period, it is almost certainly not desirable and, therefore, is of no value to analyze it using discounted cash flow methods.

In addition, as we shall see, payback is related to internal rate of return. It is a valuable aid in the search for an IRR. Book rate of return is closely tied to return on investment (ROI), a common measure of profitability and a ratio used in evaluating segment performance, as will be discussed in Chapter 17. The use of these models is widespread, which alone makes them a valid subject.

Payback

Using the **payback** method, we ask, How long does it take to recover the original investment? For example, a $100 investment that produces cash flows of $30 per year for ten years would have a four-year payback if funds were received at the end of each year. If funds were received continuously, we would say this project has a $3\frac{1}{3}$ year payback. This can be shown as follows:

Year 0	($100)	investment	
Year 1	30	inflow	Payback $3\frac{1}{3}$ (or 4) years
Year 2	30		
Year 3	30		
Year 4	30		
.			
.			
.			
Year 10	30		

Thus, payback merely looks at the cumulative *amount of inflow* up to the payback period and ignores timing of flows within the payback period. For example, assume that another investment of $100 produces the following inflows:

Year 0	($100)	investment	
1	$60	inflow	Payback $3\frac{1}{3}$ (or 4) years
2	15		
3	15		
4	30		
5	180		

Again, payback is four years. However, two things have changed. First, instead of even payments of $30 per year, this new investment has uneven cash flows. Second, instead of being received over ten years, the total of $300 is received over only five years. The earlier receipt of funds is seen not only in the shorter life but also in the way the first $100 (the payback) is received. While payback rates both of these projects the same (four years), either the NPV or IRR criterion would show the second opportunity to be better than the first.

Payback ignores profitability. If a project costing $90 returns $30 per year for three years, its payback is three years, but it is obviously an unwise project, since the discount cash flows yield a negative NPV at any rate of interest greater than zero.

When using the payback method, you set a maximum acceptable payback period. The length of the period differs among firms: some use four years, others three years, and so on. You accept projects with payback periods equal to or less than the cutoff period. Additionally, in ranking investment opportunities, you use their payback periods. Dahl's payback is just over three years. After year three the project will have returned \$330 thousand (\$110.0 thousand × 3), and \$440 thousand by the end of year four.

The payback method has some uses and is widely employed in industry. First, it provides a rough screen. A project with a long payback period is likely to rank low in internal rate of return and present value. In fact, payback is automatically calculated when you have equal cash flows and use the internal rate of return method: the present-value factor for an annuity is the payback period, year zero net cash flows divided by annual cash flows. For this purpose, we compute payback with fractional years. For instance, we would use $3\frac{1}{3}$ years for the project above where we expected \$30 annually from a \$100 investment.

Second, when risk is an important consideration, payback gives some guidance, because the longer the payback, the less certain you can be that the investment will turn out well. The further away the cash inflows, the less you can be sure of their amounts. Most businesspeople believe that they are safer if they can get their money out of an investment in a short period.

Payback Reciprocal Payback is the number of years needed to recapture the original investment. For even cash flows, this is

$$\text{payback} = \frac{\text{investment}}{\text{annual cash flows}}$$

We are using the term *investment* to denote all the cash flows that occur in year zero of a project. If you refer to the section on internal rate of return, you will see that IRR is the discount rate that forces the cash flows in year one through the end of a project exactly to equal cash flows in year zero. This can be shown as

$$(\text{annual cash flows})(\text{PV annuity factor}) = \text{original investment}$$

when cash flows are even. With even annual cash flows, the payback period is the same as the present value of an annuity factor found in Table A–4 in Appendix A.

As shown in Appendix 13A, the factors found in Table A–4 are all calculated from the formula

$$PV = C\frac{1 - (1 + r)^{-t}}{r}$$

Here, C is the even annual cash flow and r is the relevant discount rate. As the life of the project, t, becomes very large, the term $(1 + r)^{-t}$ becomes very small, so that the numerator approaches one. In this case

FIGURE 13–1 Payback and IRR

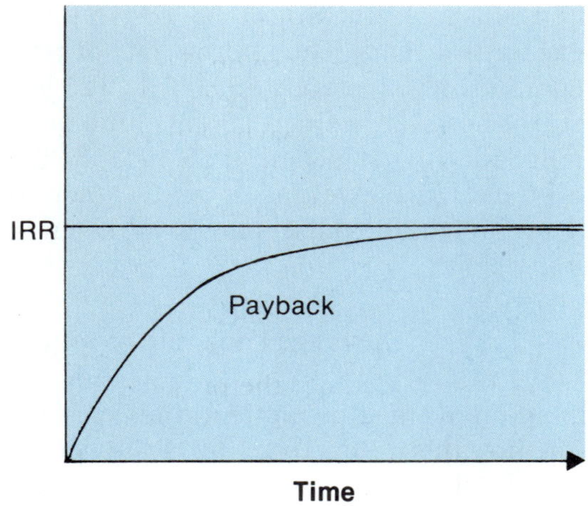

$$PV = C\frac{1}{r} \quad \text{or} \quad PV = \frac{C}{r}$$

Multiplying both sides by r and dividing both sides by PV gives

$$r = \frac{C}{PV}$$

C/PV is the payback reciprocal, since for IRR the present value (PV) of the inflow equals the investment (I). Thus, $r = C/I$. The payback reciprocal usually is a good estimator of the IRR if the economic life of a project is at least twice as long as the payback period. See Figure 13-1.

In summary, payback is not a good method because it ignores profitability and does not consider the time value of money, only the nominal value of money. It has limited advantages, but should never be used in place of DCF methods.

Book Rate of Return

The book rate of return[2] is the only model we discuss that uses book income figures, not cash flows. This model yields an accounting measure of an average income return on investment. Its most common definition is **average book rate of return** (ABRR), shown as follows:

[2]Book rate of return is also called *accounting rate of return* because it is calculated from accounting net incomes rather than cash flows.

$$\text{average book rate of return} = \frac{\text{average annual income}}{\text{average investment}}$$

Let us look at a project that costs \$100 and yields cash flows of \$58.39 per year for two years. The internal rate of return of this project is about 11 percent (\$58.39 × 1.7125 = \$99.99; 1.7125 is from Table A–4). For book rate of return, however, we need to take into account depreciation of \$50 per year straight line to get income of \$8.39 (\$58.39 − \$50). Average investment is one-half the original investment, or \$50, under the rationale that the investment is worth \$100 at the outset and \$0 at the end, or an average of \$50 over its life. This yields

$$\text{average book rate of return} = \frac{\$8.39}{\$50} = 0.168$$

Based on average investment, then, the book rate of return is 16.8 percent. Note how this differs from the IRR of 11 percent. DCF models deal with cash flows. Book rate of return, on the other hand, is an income-based measure and uses financial accounting measures.

This measure has the additional deficiencies of payback in that it ignores the timing of flows. As we pointed out, cash flows are the important measure of project desirability, since cash has alternative uses and can be reinvested, while income cannot.

Summary of Capital Budgeting Models

We have explored various useful capital budgeting models. We have identified three discounted cash flow models (NPV, IRR, and PVI), one nondiscounted cash flow model (payback), and a model that relies on income rather than on cash flows (ABRR). The DCF models yield better results.

The argument is sometimes advanced that too many assumptions must be made to use such sophisticated models as NPV. What is the life? The cash flows? The discount rate? Changes in working capital? But, as you can see, even the payback and book rate of return models require basically the same assumptions. Although any model is only as good as the data and a set of underlying assumptions, sophistication of a model is not a reason to doubt its practical usefulness.

REPLACEMENT DECISIONS

To this point, we have discussed new-asset decisions, where management has considered either expanding or introducing new equipment. Managers also decide whether to replace existing assets, especially machinery. They might replace machinery because it is old and worn out or because it is economically obsolete. They might replace machinery that no longer provides acceptable quality or is so slow that it creates bottlenecks, disrupts production, or slows deliveries to customers.

Cash Flows and Replacement

The analysis of a replacement decision parallels that of any other decision. The question is whether the incremental net cash flows from replacement justify the investment. The determination of net cash flows and investment for a replacement decision is more complicated than for the decisions considered earlier for several reasons. First, the investment is usually not just the cost of the proposed new equipment, because the old equipment might have some resale value or there may be tax effects of selling or scrapping it. Second, the net depreciation tax shield from replacement is not the depreciation on the new equipment but the difference between depreciation on the new and on the existing equipment.

Illustration: Alpedo, Inc.

Alpedo, Inc., is currently making a product using machinery bought five years ago. New machinery has just come on the market. Data for these two pieces of equipment are:

	Existing Machinery	*Proposed Machinery*
Cost	$800,000 (5 yr ago)	$1,000,000
Life	20 yr	15 yr
Depreciation	SL/20 yr	ACRS/5 yr
Current book value and tax basis	$600,000	—
Estimated salvage value now	$400,000	—
Estimated salvage value at end of life	$0	—
Cash operating costs	$340,000	$190,000
Marginal tax rate, 40%		
Discount rate, 10%		

The net investment is calculated below.

Purchase of new machinery		$1,000,000
Selling price of existing machinery		(400,000)
Tax effect of sale:		
Tax basis	$600,000	
Selling price	400,000	
Tax loss	200,000	
Tax savings at 40%		(80,000)
Net investment		$ 520,000

The present value of the future flows is calculated below. The factors in the depreciation calculation are from Table A–5 in Appendix A at the back of the book, which is explained in Appendix 13B.

Annual cash savings ($340,000 − $190,000)	$150,000
Less: tax at 40%	60,000
Net cash flow	$ 90,000
Present value factor, 15 years at 10%	7.6061
Present value of operating savings	$684,549
Present value of ACRS tax shield	
$1,000,000 × 40% × 0.774	309,600
Less: present value of existing tax shield	
$40,000 × 40% × 7.6061	(152,122)
Present value of future flows	$842,027
Less: investment	520,000
Net present value	$322,027

The new equipment has a positive net present value and therefore should be bought.

In this illustration the net book value ($600,000) is the tax basis for the old asset. However, some firms use one type of depreciation for financial reporting (straight-line, for example) with ACRS depreciation for tax purposes. In those cases, the book value and tax basis of an asset will nearly always be different. The book value of the asset is irrelevant, but the tax basis is important. It will determine the taxable gain (or loss) on disposal of old equipment and, therefore, the cash flow consequences from the saving of taxes or payment of additional taxes.

Using our example, the old machine cost $800,000 and has a book value and tax basis of $600,000. Assume the worst: the machine is now worthless. The company will receive nothing when it discards the machine and the books will show a $600,000 loss. However, the company will receive a tax deduction of $600,000 and will therefore save $240,000 ($600,000 × 40%) in income taxes. The loss itself *has no cash consequences; only the tax effect of the loss affects cash flow.*

The approach outlined above dealt with incremental cash flows. It is also possible to look at the separate cash flows associated with the current and the proposed equipment. In a restatement of the above example we determine the present value of future outflows associated with each choice. The one with the lower present value is better.

Keep Existing Equipment	
Cash operating costs ($340,000 × 60% × 7.6061)	$1,551,644
Less present value of tax shield, above	152,122
Present value of future costs	$1,399,522

Replace Equipment

Investment at time zero	$ 520,000
Cash operating costs ($190,000 × 60% × 7.6061)	867,095
Less present value of tax shield, above	(309,600)
Present value of future costs	$1,077,495

Here, the idea is to select the alternative with the lower present value of future cash flows. The difference between the present values of the future costs is $322,027 ($1,399,522 − $1,077,495), the same as the net present value of replacing that we calculated earlier. That relationship always holds. No matter how you do the analysis, you should get the same numerical result, subject to rounding errors.

CAPITAL BUDGETING AND QUALITATIVE FACTORS

Managers are now more interested in benefits that might have escaped their attention a few years ago. For instance, managers are now much more concerned with reducing inventory of materials, components, and in-process and finished goods. Investment analyses are likely to have estimates of the benefits of more rapid production, increased quality, and the like.

Even more than in short-term decisions, in capital budgeting decisions hard-to-quantify and qualitative factors influence and override quantitative analyses. Consider a project that will improve the quality of products in one product line. Such a project might show a negative NPV based only on the relatively hard data. The quantitative analysis might include estimates of the effects of increased sales of the higher quality products, but it might very well be that unless the company raises its quality, its sales will decline. The correct base against which to measure sales is not existing sales but sales expected if quality is not increased.

The monetary effects of other possible benefits such as better customer service and employee morale might be omitted altogether because they are very difficult to estimate. Other qualitative factors might include enhancing a reputation as a high-quality producer. Employees might be more productive if they can take pride in the products they make. Customers are more likely to try other of the company's products if they are satisfied with some. Such factors could be so important that the company accepts a project that fails to meet quantitative criteria.

On the other side, managers might also reject projects that show positive NPVs. For example, a company committed to producing high-quality, high-priced products might reject a proposed product that is relatively cheap. Or a company that manufactures toys might not make toy guns because of the convictions of its top managers. Where qualitative reasons support the undertaking of a project, managers should not ignore quantitative analyses because they will give them a better idea of the cost to the firm of accepting a particular qualitative objective as paramount.

INVESTMENTS TO SUPPORT STRATEGIES AND TECHNOLOGY

One important factor in capital budgeting is that companies often commit themselves to pursue particular objectives by following specific strategies, despite the short-term costs. Managers should be certain that their investment proposals are not inconsistent with their principal objectives and strategies. For instance, a company might pursue an objective of total quality control, the unwillingness to accept *any* defects. It might well be that the best productive equipment, in present value terms, unavoidably generates some defective parts. Managers should reject the equipment because it does not advance the overriding objective. The corporate objective of quality is based partly on the belief that quality will minimize long-term costs, including customer dissatisfaction and other costs not factored into routine capital budgeting analyses. Of course, production managers should understand and support the objectives and strategies used to attain such objectives.

Technological advancement is often an objective or a strategy for achieving objectives. It is sometimes difficult to justify high-technology investments for reasons we discussed earlier—that the hard quantitative data do not indicate sufficient savings to justify the investment. Here again the question might be qualitative benefits, such as being at the forefront of technology. A company thus perceived is likely to attract better scientific and managerial talent, be more favorably viewed by customers, and enjoy better supplier relations. These benefits, though real, are probably impossible to quantify. Additionally, there are benefits that are difficult, but not impossible, to quantify. Failure to invest in technology can result in lost sales as competitors use new technology to improve quality and reduce delivery times.[3]

Justifying high-technology investment can still be analytical; it should not be necessary to resort to pleas such as "to keep up with the times" or "We have to do it because everyone else is." The problem is often estimating reasonable enhancements of cash flow. There is no magic formula: accountants and other managers must be alert to the possibilities and examine each investment proposal on both its merits and how well it fits into the company's strategies.

[3] Robert S. Kaplan, "Must CIM be Justified by Faith Alone?," *Harvard Business Review*, March-April 1986, pp. 87–95.

Life Cycle

One aspect of strategic investing relates to the stage of life of a product or process. All products begin in an embryonic, or nascent, stage, where they are beginning to gain acceptance in the market. Survivors typically go through a growth stage, where their sales increase rapidly for a time. They then mature, with growth limited to, say, growth in population. Eventually they decline. Each stage lasts a different time for each product. Companies should plan their capital budgets to be consistent with strategies appropriate to the various life cycles. For instance, investments in products in the nascent stage probably look less attractive than investments in mature products: the estimates of volume of nascent products are much less certain, as are future costs and prices. But the company must support such products to remain competitive. The 3M Company, for example, expects 25 percent of its sales to come from products that it did not make five years ago. That commitment to developing new products requires a flexible, responsive capital budgeting strategy.

SUMMARY

Capital budgeting decisions commit the company to large expenditures with uncertain returns. The best ways to evaluate such decisions require discounting the associated cash flows. These cash flows are almost always estimates, not certainties. Moreover, qualitative factors can override decisions reached on purely economic grounds.

An important aspect of capital budgeting is recognizing the importance of the time value of money. The discounted cash flow methods (NPV, IRR, and PVI) recognize the time value of money, while payback and book rate of return do not. The latter two methods are therefore not suitable, although payback can be useful as a rough screening device and a measure of risk.

Managers must also recognize that strategic considerations can affect capital budgeting decisions. Modern businesses face extremely complex problems, and many factors are very difficult to quantify.

REVIEW PROBLEM

Data for a new product appear below. Set up a spreadsheet template using the skeleton shown below, or use CAPBUD.WK1 on your diskette. Determine the net present value of the investment.

Volume: 600 thousand units in year one increasing 50 thousand units each year. Year eight will then have 950 thousand units.

Selling price			$10.00			
Unit variable cost			$6.00			
Cash fixed manufacturing costs			$1,100 thousand			
Selling and administrative costs			$650 thousand			
Cost of depreciable assets			$4,500 thousand			
Useful life			8			
ACRS percentages, 5 year assets						
	0.2	0.32	0.192	0.115	0.115	0.058
Tax rate			40.00%			
Cost of capital			12.00%			

OUTPUT SECTION===

Present value analysis, thousands of dollars

	0	1	2	3
Equipment				
Operating flows, net of tax				
Depreciation shield				
	-------	-------	-------	-------
Net cash flow				
Present value factor				
	-------	-------	-------	-------
Present value of future flows				
Net present value				

	4	5	6	7	8
Equipment					
Operating flows, net of tax					
Depreciation shield					
	-------	-------	-------	-------	-------
Net cash flow					
Present value factor					
	-------	-------	-------	-------	-------
Present value of future flows					

ANSWER TO REVIEW PROBLEM

Present value analysis, thousands of dollars

	0	1	2	3
Equipment	($4,500.0)			
Operating flows, net of tax		$390.0	$510.0	$630.0
Depreciation shield		360.0	576.0	345.6
	-------	-------	-------	-------
Net cash flow	($4,500.0)	$750.0	$1,086.0	$975.6
Present value factor	1.0000	0.8929	0.7972	0.7118
	-------	-------	-------	-------
Present value of future flows	($4,500.0)	$669.6	$865.8	$694.4
Net present value	$502.5			

	4	5	6	7	8
Equipment					
Operating flows, net of tax	$750.0	$870.0	$990.0	$1,110.0	$1,230.0
Depreciation shield	207.0	207.0	104.4		
	-------	-------	-------	-------	-------
Net cash flow	$957.0	$1,077.0	$1,094.4	$1,110.0	$1,230.0
Present value factor	0.6355	0.5674	0.5066	0.4523	0.4039
	-------	-------	-------	-------	-------
Present value of future flows	$608.2	$611.1	$554.5	$502.1	$496.8

```
Sample calculations:
    Operating flows, year three = (700 units × $4 contribution - $1,750 cash fixed
costs) × 60% = $630.0
    Depreciation tax shield, year three = $4,500.0 × .192 × 40% = $345.6
```

APPENDIX 13A: TIME VALUE OF MONEY

Suppose you received a call from a radio station announcing that you had won its grand prize of \$100 in a contest, and you had the choice of getting \$100 now or \$100 in one year. You would choose the \$100 now, since you could either spend it a year earlier or put it in a bank and earn interest for a year, thereby having more than \$100 at year-end.

Now let us change the situation slightly. Assume that your choice was between \$100 now and \$109 in one year. To see which choice is better economically, you have to see what you could do with \$100 received now. This problem relates to the important concept that money has a time value. If the only possible use of \$100 received now is to put it in a savings account earning (the *value* part) 10 percent per year (*time*), you would have \$110 in a year (\$100 × 1.10). You would then prefer \$100 now to \$109 in one year.

Present and Future Values

The preceding example illustrates the time value of money. Money received now can earn some positive cash return (interest) over time. Thus, \$100 in the present (called a **present value**) is worth \$110 a year in the future (a **future value**). Since (\$100)(1.10) = \$110, we can say that, for one year

$$(\text{present value})(1 + \text{interest rate}) = (\text{future value})$$

or

$$(PV)(1 + r) = FV$$

If you could invest \$100 for *two* years at 10 percent, you would have a future value of \$121 in two years:

$$(\$100)(1.10) = \$110 \text{ at end of year one}$$
$$(\$110)(1.10) = \$121 \text{ at end of year two}$$

We could write this as one step:

$$[(\$100)(1.10)](1.10) = \$121$$

or

$$(\$100)(1.10)^2 = \$121$$

This **compound-interest formula** translates present values into future values. If t denotes the number of years until receipt this formula becomes

(13A–1) $$(PV)(1 + r)^t = FV$$

Thus, if we know a future value (a cash flow occurring in the future), we can rearrange equation 13A–1 and get

$$(13A\text{–}2) \qquad PV = \frac{FV}{(1 + r)^t} \quad \text{or} \quad PV = FV(1 + r)^{-t}$$

In words, the present value of a sum received t years in the future at r rate of interest is the PV shown in equation 13A–2. In the \$100 example:

$$\$100 = \$121\ (1 + 0.10)^{-2}$$
$$\$100 = (\$121)(0.8264)$$

The portion of the formula shown by

$$(13A\text{–}3) \qquad (1 + r)^{-t}$$

is called a **present-value factor** of receiving \$1 in t years at r rate of interest. Discount factors for present values for various periods and rates of interest are shown in Table A–3 in Appendix A at the back of the book. While an interest factor is used to move a present sum to a future sum, a present-value factor or **discount factor** is used in going from the future to the present. Equation 13A–3 can be used to find the present-value factor for any number of periods or rates of interest, even if they are not shown on a table.

Present Value of an Annuity

So far we have looked at a present value (\$100) and a future value received as a lump sum in two years (\$121). Let us assume that you could receive even payments of \$57.62 each year for two years. The receipt of even cash flows each year is called an **annuity**. What is the present value of these even cash inflows?

$$\begin{aligned} PV &= (\$57.62)(1 + 0.10)^{-1} + (\$57.62)(1 + 0.10)^{-2} \\ &= (\$57.62)(0.9091) + (\$57.62)(0.8264) \\ &= (\$57.62)(0.9091 + 0.8264) \\ &= (\$57.62)(1.7355) \\ &= \$100 \end{aligned}$$

Thus, the present value of an annuity is found by adding together all the PV factors for each year. Since this is tedious, Table A–4 shows these discount factors for receiving \$1 *per year* for t years at various discount rates. These factors are found by using the following formula:

$$(13A\text{–}4) \qquad \frac{(1 + r)^t - 1}{r(1 + r)^t} \quad \text{or alternatively,} \quad \frac{1 - (1 + r)^{-t}}{r}$$

Formula 13A–4 is found by a geometric progression summing up various years.

A two-year annuity of \$57.62 per year (received at the end of each year) has a future value at 10 percent interest of

$$(\$57.62)(1.10) + (\$57.62) = \$121$$

The concepts of present value and future value as well as the receipt of a single sum or an annuity are parts of a time continuum tied to a discount rate.

	Cash Received		
Present Value	Year 1	Year 2	Future Value
$100		$121	$121
$100	$57.62	$ 57.62	$121

The choice offered at the beginning of this discussion was between receiving $100 now or $109 in one year. While the answer, assuming a 10 percent rate of interest, is obvious, the following illustrates the choice of receiving $100 now.

	Present Value	Future Value
Alternative 1 ($100 now)	$100	$110
Alternative 2 ($109 in 1 year)	$ 99.09	$109

Thus, from either a present-value or a future-value perspective alternative 1 is superior.

As a final illustration, assume that you have $100 now and place it in a bank at 10 percent interest. You can withdraw $57.62 per year for two years, since you are earning 10 percent interest. This is illustrated as follows:

	(a) Beginning Balance	(b) 10% Earnings	(c) [(a) + (b)]	(d) Withdraw	(e) Ending Balance [(c) − (d)]
Year 1	$100	$10.00	$110.00	$57.62	$52.38
Year 2	$ 52.38	$ 5.24	$ 57.62	$57.62	0

Summary of Appendix 13A

Money can be invested; therefore, it has a time value. Present-value factors can be calculated for a single sum received in the future or for a steady stream of sums (annuity). By using compound interest we can translate present sums to future sums. By using present-value (discount) factors we can translate future sums to present sums. Since we are dealing with cash flows, the decision models based on this concept are called *discounted cash flow models* (DCF).

APPENDIX 13B: EFFECTS OF CURRENT TAX LAWS ON CAPITAL BUDGETING

The Economic Recovery Tax Act of 1981 (ERTA), the Tax Equity and Fiscal Responsibility Act of 1982 (TEFRA), and the Tax Reform Act of 1986 (TRA) changed many of the tax laws affecting ownership of personal property. We will only deal with personal property (machinery and equipment, as opposed to land and buildings) in this summary of the provisions of these tax acts that affect capital budgeting decisions.

Provisions Before 1981

Under previous law, the economic (useful) life of an asset was to be used for depreciation. Thus, if an asset was expected to have an eight-year life, an appropriate depreciation method was chosen and used over the eight years. Accelerated methods such as sum-of-the-years'-digits and double-declining-balance methods were popular because they yield a higher present value of tax savings from depreciation than does straight-line depreciation. Although the nominal amount of tax savings from depreciation is the same over the life of an asset, moving them earlier in the life of the asset (accelerating them) yields a higher present value.

Under the old law, if salvage value was expected to be greater than 10 percent of the original purchase price, you could depreciate that asset down only to its expected salvage value. (Actually, it is a bit more complicated, but this is a reasonable simplification.) If salvage value was expected to be equal to or less than 10 percent of the original purchase price, then the asset could be depreciated down to zero.

The useful lives of assets under pre-1981 law were determined by Asset Depreciation Ranges (ADR). The ADRs, set by the Internal Revenue Service, detailed virtually every available capital asset. An ADR was stated as a range of years over which a taxpayer could depreciate that type of asset. Thus, an ADR for a particular asset could have been 12 to 16 years. The ADR mid-point, the average life (14 years in the above example), became important in 1986.

From time to time before and after 1981, an Investment Tax Credit (ITC) has enabled taxpayers to deduct part of the cost of qualifying assets (not all assets were eligible) from their tax. Thus, when the credit was 10 percent, a taxpayer buying a $1 million qualifying asset reduced the tax payment by $100,000. The objective of the ITC was to stimulate capital investment by making it cheaper. The ITC is no longer available, but might return.

The 1981 and 1982 Acts

Several major provisions of the 1981 Act interest us. One is that it established six class lives to replace the thousands of ADRs. This meant that taxpayers could now put most of their assets into only a few categories, instead of the many ADRs. Another important provision is that the Act introduced the Accelerated Cost Recovery System (ACRS), which was in effect a declining balance method using the six class lives (though most companies had assets in only two or three classes). The term *depreciation* was not used, but *recovery*. The life over which an asset was depreciated was called its *recovery period*.

These provisions set the stage for the current law. The 1982 Act modified the ITC and made some other adjustments, but left intact the fundamental principles of ACRS.

The Tax Reform Act of 1986

This Act carried forward the principles of the earlier acts, but dropped the ITC. It also lowered tax rates for corporations. The Act modified ACRS, creating eight classes of ACRS lives and changing the pattern of recovery. Exhibit 13B–1 shows the ACRS periods and descriptions.

It is not as important to know the definitions as to understand that assets fall into particular categories and are depreciated according to specific methods. For the three-, five-, seven-, and 10-year assets, the depreciation method is double-declining balance, with a switch to straight line when straight-line depreciation exceeds double-declining balance depreciation. For the 15- and 20-year classes, 150 percent declining balance is used, while for the 27.5 and 31.5-year classes, straight line is required. A modified straight-line method can also be used for any asset.

Additionally, the Act required the half-year convention, which assumes that an asset is placed in service halfway through the year it is acquired. This means that the asset is depreciated over one year longer than the ACRS recovery period, a three-year asset over four years, 10-year asset over 11 years, and so on. The reason is that some tax basis is left at the end of the recovery period because only a half-year worth was taken in year one.

Exhibit 13B–2 shows the percentages of depreciation to be taken each

EXHIBIT 13B–1 ACRS Classes

Recovery Period	*Description of Assets*
Three-year	Assets with ADR midpoints of four years or less, some exclusions such as automobiles and light trucks. Examples include small tools.
Five-year	ADR midpoint more than four years, but under 10 years, also includes automobiles and light trucks, office equipment such as typewriters, computers, and copiers.
Seven-year	ADR midpoint more than 10 years, but less than 16 years, also assets without ADR lives. Examples include most manufacturing machinery, office equipment.
Ten-year	ADR midpoint more than 16 years, but less than 20 years. Specific enumerated machinery, such as railroad cars.
15-year	ADR midpoint more than 20 years, but less than 25 years. Sewage plants, certain telecommunications equipment.
20-year	ADR midpoint more than 25 years, except for real property. Includes certain electric utility equipment.
27.5-year	Residential real estate, elevators and escalators.
31.5-year	Other real estate.

EXHIBIT 13B–2 Recovery Percentages

Recovery Year	3-year Asset	5-year Asset	7-year Asset	10-year Asset	15-year Asset
1	33.3%	20.0%	14.3%	10.0 %	5.0 %
2	44.5	32.0	24.5	18.0	9.5
3	14.8	19.2	17.5	14.4	8.6
4	7.4	11.5	12.5	11.5	7.7
5		11.5	8.9	9.2	6.9
6		5.8	8.9	7.4	6.2
7			8.9	6.6	5.9
8			4.5	6.6	5.9
9				6.6	5.9
10				6.6	5.9
11				3.1	5.9
12					5.9
13					5.9
14					5.9
15					5.9
16					3.0
	100.0%	100.0%	100.0%	100.0 %	100.0 %

year, but to solidify your understanding, we shall go through the calculations for five-year assets.

The points where the percentages begin to repeat (in the five-year and up classes) are where the straight-line switch comes in. The final year is a half year, so except to get the total depreciation to 100 percent, it is half of the previous year's.

Now to the proof for the five-year class. Assume an asset of $100,000. Double-declining balance depreciation for a five-year life is 40 percent, which is $\frac{1}{5}$ multiplied by two. However, in the first year we only take a half year, or 20 percent. The schedule is:

Year	*Depreciation*	
1	$ 20,000	$100,000 × 40% × $\frac{1}{2}$
2	32,000	($100,000 − $20,000) × 40%
3	19,200	($100,000 − $20,000 − $32,000) × 40%
4	11,500	($100,000 − $20,000 − $32,000 − $19,200) × 40%
5	11,500	same as year 4
6	5,800	$11,500/2, adjusted to total $100,000
Total	$100,000	

In year four, straight-line depreciation and double-declining-balance depreciation give the same result. The asset's basis is down to $28,800, which, divided by $2\frac{1}{2}$ remaining years of life, gives \$11,500. So does 40 percent of \$28,800.

Table A–5 in Appendix A at the back of the book gives the present values of ACRS tax shields for various discount rates. You can verify any of these figures to see how the table was constructed. Find the present value of the depreciation deductions using a convenient asset cost such as \$100,000. Add them and divide by \$100,000 to get the percentage. Using the Table requires you to multiply the factor by the tax rate to determine the tax shield. The numbers in the table, in effect, represent a 100 percent tax rate. Using the figures we just calculated for 5-year assets, and a 10 percent discount rate (see Table A–3 for factors), we get the following:

\$20,000 × .9091 =	\$18,182
32,000 × .8264 =	26,445
19,200 × .7513 =	14,425
11,500 × .6830 =	7,855
11,500 × .6209 =	7,140
5,800 × .5645 =	3,274
Total	\$77,321

The value in Table A–5 is .7732, which is \$77,321/\$100,000. The present value of the shield is the tax rate multiplied by \$77,321. The rounding error is in using the present value factors from Table A–3; Table A–5 was created using a Lotus 1-2-3 spreadsheet.

ASSIGNMENTS

13–1 Sunk Costs Solidon Company has a number of old typewriters. Its office manager plans to sell some of them and replace them with newer models. The president of the firm has told the office manager to be sure to sell the ones that are fully depreciated, so that the firm will make a profit on the sale. The firm uses straight-line depreciation for tax and financial reporting purposes.

REQUIRED

Comment on the president's suggestion.

13–2 Relevant Cost Your firm has a machine that cost \$10,000 earlier this year. It is capable of producing 1,000 units of a product, after which it will collapse. It has produced 400 units so far and accumulated depreciation using the units of production method is \$4,000.

REQUIRED

Is the \$10 per unit depreciation a variable cost? An incremental cost? An opportunity cost? A relevant cost in making decisions?

13–3 Basic Cash Flows SaraSoda Company is considering expanding its product line by producing a nonalcoholic soft drink that tastes like beer.

REQUIRED

Using a format like that of Exhibit 13–2, show the timing of the effects of the following. The marginal tax rate is 40 percent.

1. Equipment that will last five years will be purchased at a cost of $300,000. Expected salvage value is $20,000. The firm uses three-year ACRS for depreciation for tax purposes.

2. Annual sales for the life of the project are expected to be $480,000. It is expected that the firm will have an average of $1\frac{1}{2}$ months' sales in receivables.

3. Cash balances of $10,000 in addition to current balances will be maintained, and $100,000 in additional inventory will have to be carried over the life of the project.

4. Operating expenses (exclusive of depreciation) are expected to be $250,000 per year, and various payables will increase by $40,000.

13–4 Working Capital Investment The managers of Trapnell Automotive Enterprises want to introduce a new wax. They anticipate volume of 500,000 cans annually for the next five years at $8 each. They expect variable costs of $3 per unit and annual cash fixed costs $1,400,000. The wax requires machinery costing $1,500,000 with a five-year life and no salvage value. Trapnell uses straight-line depreciation. Additionally, accounts receivable will increase about $600,000, inventories about $400,000. These amounts will be returned in full at the end of the five years. The tax rate is 40 percent and cost of capital is 16 percent.

REQUIRED

Determine the NPV of the investment.

13–5 Effects of Depreciation Changes Can the United States (or any other) government encourage or discourage capital investment by changing the tax rules on depreciation? How?

13–6 Discounting

1. Find the approximate IRR for each of the following investments.
   a. investment of $30,000 with annual cash flows of $5,000 for 14 years
   b. investment of $90,000 with a single return of $120,000 at the end of three years

2. Find the NPVs of the following investments at a 12 percent discount rate.
   a. annual flows of $30,000 for 10 years produced by an investment of $120,000
   b. investment of $28,000 with annual flows of $8,000 for four years

13–7 Basic Cash Flows Lamming Company is developing a projection on a proposed new product line in the microcomputer market. The marginal tax rate for Lamming is 40 percent.

REQUIRED

Using a format like that of Exhibit 13–2, show the timing of the effects of the following. Assume all cash flows occur at the end of a period.

1. Equipment that is expected to last six years will be purchased at a cost of \$240,000. Salvage value is projected to be \$15,000 at the end of its life. The firm will use 5-year ACRS depreciation for tax purposes (five-year life) and will use straight-line depreciation for financial reporting purposes.
2. The company expects to raise cash balances from \$50,000 to \$75,000 during the life of this project. Additional inventories of materials and finished goods will total \$90,000. It is expected that accounts receivable will average one month's sales from the new product.
3. Annual sales are expected to be \$360,000 and cash operating expenses (exclusive of depreciation) are expected to be \$200,000 per year. Accounts payable will increase by \$10,000.

13–8 Basic DCF Models Refer to Assignment 13–7 for the data on the Lamming Company.

REQUIRED

1. Find the net present value of the project using an 8 percent discount rate.
2. Find the net present value of the project using a 25 percent discount rate.
3. What is the internal rate of return of the project?
4. What is the present value index at 8 percent discount rate?

13–9 Questions about Cash Flows You and your fellow students are discussing capital budgeting, and the following questions arise.

REQUIRED

Respond to each statement or question.

1. "This whole thing about depreciation not being a cash flow really baffles me. I've looked at lots of cash flow statements and they take net income and add depreciation. If that's not a cash flow, what is it?"
2. "I was looking at a problem where inventory went up by \$100,000 and the project had a life of three years. In my analysis I showed an outflow of \$100,000 for each year. That's right, isn't it?"
3. "We keep hearing about after-tax cash flows. I'm confused about what to do when you buy a piece of equipment. Say you spend \$250,000 and the tax rate is 50 percent; wouldn't you show a net cost of \$125,000 after taxes?"
4. "If receipts from sales on our new project are \$100,000 per year and cash outflows from operations are \$40,000, what is the net annual cash flow with a 40 percent marginal tax rate?"
5. "If working capital increased by \$100,000 at the beginning of a project, what can I expect to recover at the end of the project with a 40 percent marginal tax rate?"

13–10 Present Values and Investment Cycle McPike Company is buying some new equipment that will cost \$200,000 and has an economic life of six years. It is expected that salvage value will be \$10,000 at the end of five years. The relevant discount rate is 12 percent. The marginal tax rate is 40 percent.

REQUIRED

Using ACRS depreciation, calculate the present value of all cash flows associated with this equipment.

13–11 NPV and IRR Portland Millworks is considering equipment that promises to save \$6,000 in cash operating costs per year. The equipment will cost \$16,800. Its estimated useful life is four years. It will have no salvage value. (Ignore taxes.)

REQUIRED

1. Compute the NPV if the minimum desired rate of return is 10 percent.
2. Determine the IRR.

13–12 Time Value of Money Answer the following questions:

1. Jack received \$6,440 from an investment made five years ago at an interest rate of 10 percent. How much did he invest?
2. An investment of \$2,000 returned a single payment of \$5,400. The interest rate was 18 percent. How many years elapsed between the investment and the return?
3. A person received seven annual payments of \$1,000 from an investment. The interest rate was 12 percent. What was the amount of the investment?
4. A \$20,000 investment made today will provide a 10 percent return. The returns will be paid in equal amounts over five years. What is the amount of the annual payment?

13–13 Cost Savings Wilson Sportswear currently makes about 200,000 pairs of Superlux jeans per year at a variable cost of \$11.50. Wilson can buy equipment for \$400,000 that will reduce unit variable cost to \$9.25, while increasing cash fixed costs by \$200,000. The equipment will have no salvage value at the end of its four-year life and will be depreciated using the straight-line method. Wilson has a 40 percent income tax rate and 12 percent cost of capital.

REQUIRED

Determine the NPV of the investment.

13–14 NPV and IRR Grone, Inc., can reduce its annual cash operating costs by \$20,000 by spending \$60,000 for equipment that has a five-year life and no salvage value. Grone uses straight-line depreciation. Cost of capital is 14 percent.

REQUIRED

1. Determine the NPV of the investment, ignoring taxes.
2. Determine the approximate IRR.

13–15 Taxes (Continuation of Assignment 13–14) Redo the previous assignment assuming a 40 percent income tax rate.

13–16 Capital Budgeting for a Hospital Plandome General Hospital does not perform X-rays, but sends patients to a nearby clinic. The hospital can acquire an X-ray machine for \$120,000. The machine should last for ten years and have no salvage value. Estimated revenue is \$85,000 per year, and estimated annual cash costs are \$63,000. The hospital uses an 8 percent discount rate for its capital budgeting decisions.

REQUIRED

Determine the NPV, payback period, and IRR.

13–17 New Product—Working Capital Martin Furniture is considering an office cabinet with the following expected results.

Annual unit volume	250,000
Selling price	$60
Unit variable cost	$25
Annual cash fixed costs	$4,500,000

Making the cabinet will require $6,000,000 in equipment that has a three-year life with no salvage value. Cost of capital is 12 percent, the income tax rate is 40 percent, and straight-line depreciation will be used. There will also be additional accounts receivable of about $3,500,000 and additional inventories of $1,200,000.

REQUIRED

Determine the NPV of the investment. Use thousands of dollars.

13–18 Retirement Options Jill Barber retires soon. Her employer has a pension plan that offers an annuity of $40,000 per year beginning the day of retirement and ending at death. Jill could live on $40,000 per year but prefers to spend $50,000 per year and be more comfortable. As an alternative, the plan offers a lump sum settlement of $350,000 to be paid on the day of retirement. Barber believes that she would earn a 10 percent return investing the lump sum payment. She has no relatives and does not care whether she leaves an estate.

If Barber chooses the lump sum payment, she will take $50,000 to live on the first year of retirement and invest the rest. She will then draw $50,000 at the beginning of every year until the money runs out.

REQUIRED

Determine how long Barber can keep spending $50,000 per year.

13–19 Donation to Charity Jack Billingsley is a wealthy man who recently suffered a heart attack. Because of the excellent care he received at Madison Memorial Hospital, he has decided to give it a substantial donation. He is considering two ways to make the gift. One is to give $10 million today, the other is to give $1.6 million per year for 10 years.

Billingsley uses a 9 percent discount factor in making decisions that involve cash flows over an extended period. The hospital does not have a formal method of evaluating such alternatives. Dr. Sym, the administrator of the hospital, believes that 8 percent is a reasonable discount rate because it is the cost of borrowing.

REQUIRED

1. Determine which alternative is better for the hospital.

2. Determine which alternative is better for Billingsley.

3. How much does Billingsley have to give per year to have a $10 million present value?

4. How much does the hospital have to receive per year to have a $10 million present value?

13–20 Expanding Production Managers of Turnbury Manufacturing Company have been considering for some time an expansion of productive capacity. Demand for their major products regularly outstrips their production ability. They have been reluctant, however, to embark on an expensive expansion program without reasonable assurance of profitability.

The production manager has determined that he could produce another $800,000 worth of goods (at selling prices) annually with new equipment that costs $900,000. The equipment has a four-year life with no salvage value, will add $200,000 to annual cash fixed operating costs, and will be depreciated using the straight-line method. Variable costs, which will be unaffected by the new equipment, are 25 percent of sales. Cost of capital is 10 percent and the tax rate is 40 percent.

REQUIRED

Determine whether Turnbury should acquire the equipment.

13–21 Basic DCF Models Sonata Company has embarked on a new project that will cost $250,000 and last eight years. Annual cash flows from operations will be $90,000, not including depreciation and taxes. The company expects no salvage value. The tax rate is 40 percent.

REQUIRED

1. If five-year ACRS depreciation is used, what is the net present value at an 18 percent discount rate?
2. Is the internal rate of return 18 percent? Higher? Lower? Why?
3. Determine the internal rate of return.
4. Determine the payback.
5. Using your results from part 1, find the benefit-cost ratio of this investment.

13–22 Present-Value Relationships Each of the following cases is independent. All projects assume a five-year life and a marginal tax rate of 40 percent.

REQUIRED

Fill in the blanks.

Investment	PV of Tax Shield ACRS Depreciation	After-tax Cash Flow from Operations Excluding Depreciation	Net Present Value	Discount Rate
1. ______	$77,320	______	$54,768	0.10
2. ______	______	$100,000	$57,840	0.18
3. $200,000	$64,904	$ 80,000	______	___

13–23 Explaining NPV You receive the following memo from your boss:

> I have been hearing about discounted cash flow models and the such for a while but never really understood them. When I went to school, all they ever talked about was book return on investment and payback.
>
> The other day you suggested we use net present value to evaluate investments. I'd like you to explain net present value to me. Please don't use any technical terms. Just use plain English. I don't want a description, I want an explanation. Also, why is this method better than the ones I learned about in college?

REQUIRED

Write a memo to your boss responding to his memo to you. Be complete.

13–24 DCF Relationships

REQUIRED

Answer each of the following cases independently.

Investment	Present-Value, Straight-Line Tax Effect of Depreciation	Annual After-Tax Cash Flows (Excluding Depreciation)	Present Value of Inflows	Life	Tax Rate	Discount Rate
1. ?	$33,158	?	$100,000	3 years	0.40	0.10
2. $250,000	$99,818	$33,000	$231,577	5 years	?	?
3. $ 20,000	?	$ 7,010	$ 30,000	?	0.45	0.09
4. $ 40,000	?	$10,000	?	4 years	0.40	0.10

13–25 IRR and Payback Reciprocal

Vino Company is contemplating a project expected to last 10 years. Annual cash flows (not including the tax effect of depreciation) are planned at $3,000, and an original investment of $9,000 is required. Vino has a marginal tax rate of 40 percent and an after-tax hurdle rate of 9 percent. Use straight-line depreciation.

REQUIRED

1. What is the net present value of the project?
2. What is the payback?
3. Using the payback reciprocal as a guide, find the internal rate of return.

13–26 Alternative Use of Funds

Geemat Company is considering two alternative investment opportunities. First, management can invest in municipal bonds that will cost $50,000 and pay a tax-free yield of $4,000 annually. The alternative investment, a new project, costs $50,000. Pretax cash flows (excluding depreciation) are expected to be $15,500 annually. Straight-line depreciation will be used, and the applicable tax rate is 40 percent. Ignore the half-year convention. Both investments will last five years. Management has only approximately $50,000 available to invest this year. The new project will require $5,000 additional in net current assets, which will be recovered at the end of the project. All cash flows take place at the end of the year.

REQUIRED

1. Which investment yields the higher return?
2. If the after-tax cost of capital for this firm is 11 percent, should management invest in the bonds or in the new project?

13–27 Investing in JIT

One of Robson Industries' several plants is moving toward JIT manufacturing. One of the first investments the plant will make is roughly $4 million to rearrange the factory into manufacturing cells. This cost is tax deductible over five years using the straight-line method. The managers expect to save about $600 thousand in annual manufacturing costs for the foreseeable future as a result of using cells. The tax rate is 40 percent and cost of capital is 10 percent.

REQUIRED

Determine the net present value of the investment. Use a 30-year period for the annual cost savings.

13–28 Manufacturing Cells, JIT Some plant managers of Carson Manufacturing Company are trying to switch to JIT manufacturing. The manager of the Cushnet Plant has developed the following data on the effects of introducing JIT, mainly from talks with managers whose plants have adopted JIT principles.

	Current Cost	*Estimated JIT Cost*
	(all amounts in thousands)	
Materials	$1,876.4	$1,692.0
Direct labor	2,845.2	2,312.0
Supervision	434.6	88.3
Maintenance	493.2	23.6*
Inspection, incoming and outgoing	256.3	32.8*
Other	673.9	569.5
Totals	$6,579.6	$4,718.2

*Most costs of maintenance and inspection will be carried out by workers in their cells, greatly reducing centrally administered amounts.

Moving to cellular manufacturing requires investments of $8 million for rearranging and for new machinery more suited to cellular manufacturing. All of these costs can be deducted for tax purposes over 10 years. None of the depreciation and amortization of these costs is included in the figures above. The company has a 40 percent tax rate and a 12 percent cost of capital. The horizon for discounting the after-tax savings in operating flows is 20 years.

REQUIRED

Determine the net present value of the proposed change.

13–29 New Product ICL Company is considering a new product whose useful life it expects to be six years. Other estimates relating to the product appear below.

Annual volume	40,000 units
Selling price	$20
Unit variable manufacturing costs	$8
Unit variable selling expenses	$1
Annual fixed cash manufacturing costs	$150,000
Annual fixed selling expenses	$100,000

The product requires machinery that costs $400,000 and should have about $30,000 salvage value at the end of six years. The firm uses five-year ACRS depreciation.

The tax rate is 40 percent, and cost of capital is 14 percent.

REQUIRED

1. Determine the net present value of the investment.
2. Determine the payback period.
3. Determine the approximate internal rate of return.

13–30 Life of Project Gullo Products was evaluating Albert Corporation's $400,000 buyout offer. When asked how this figure was derived, Albert's chief negotiator stated they had taken Gullo's last year's cash flows of $100,000 and divided those flows by Albert's cost of capital of 25 percent. Gullo's cost of capital is 16 percent.

REQUIRED

1. Explain the rationale Albert might have for the method chosen.
2. From both Gullo's and Albert's perspectives, what other things should be considered?

13–31 Basic Review (CMA Adapted) Yipann Corporation is reviewing an investment proposal. The initial cost as well as the estimate of the book value of the investment at the end of each year, the net after-tax cash flows for each year, and the net income for each year are presented in the following schedule. All cash flows are assumed to take place at the end of the year. The salvage value of the investment at the end of each year is equal to its book value. There will be no salvage value at the end of the investment's life.

Investment Proposal

Year	Initial Cost and Book Value	Annual Net After-Tax Cash Flows	Annual Net Income
0	$105,000		
1	70,000	$50,000	$15,000
2	42,000	45,000	17,000
3	21,000	40,000	19,000
4	7,000	35,000	21,000
5	0	30,000	23,000

Yipann uses a 24 percent after-tax target rate of return for new investment proposals.

REQUIRED

1. What is the traditional payback period for the investment proposal?
2. What is the accounting rate of return for the investment proposal over its life using the initial value of the investment?
3. What is the net present value for the investment proposal?
4. The payback reciprocal is often used as an approximation of an investment proposal's internal rate of return. Which one of the following is the correct reason for not being able to use the payback reciprocal to approximate the internal rate of return for this investment proposal?
   a. The life of an investment proposal must be at least twice the payback period.
   b. The life of an investment proposal must be at least ten years.
   c. The net after-tax cash flows must be constant over the life of the investment.
   d. Only straight-line depreciation can be employed when determining the net after-tax cash flows.
   e. The profitability index must be greater than one.

13–32 Present Value and Alternatives (CMA Adapted) Kravel Corporation is a diversified manufacturing company with several manufacturing plants. Kravel's Dayton plant has been supplying parts to midwestern truck manufacturers for more than 30 years. The last shipment of truck parts from the Dayton plant will be made in December 19X4. Kravel's management is studying three alternatives relating to its soon-to-be-idle plant and equipment in Dayton.

1. Wasson Industries has offered to buy the Dayton plant for $3,000,000 cash on January 1, 19X5.
2. Harr Enterprises has offered to lease the Dayton facilities for four years beginning January 1, 19X5. Harr's annual lease payments would be $500,000 plus 10 percent of the gross dollar sales of all items produced in the Dayton plant. Probabilities of Harr's annual gross dollar sales from the Dayton plant are estimated as follows:

Annual Gross Dollar Sales	*Estimated Probability*
$2,000,000	0.1
4,000,000	0.4
6,000,000	0.3
8,000,000	0.2

3. Kravel is considering the production of souvenir items to be sold in connection with a world's fair in 19X6 and the 19X8 Olympic Games. The Dayton plant would be used to produce 70,000 items per month at an annual cash outlay of $2,250,000 during 19X5, 19X6, and 19X7. Linda Yetter, Vice President of Marketing, has recommended a selling price of $5 per item and believes the items will sell uniformly throughout 19X6, 19X7, and 19X8.

The adjusted basis of the Dayton plant as of the close of business on December 31, 19X4, will be $4,200,000. Kravel has used straight-line depreciation for all capital assets at the Dayton plant. If the Dayton plant is not sold, the annual straight-line depreciation charge for the plant and equipment will be $900,000 each year for the next four years. The market value of the plant and equipment on December 31, 19X8, is estimated at $600,000.

Kravel requires an after-tax rate of return of 15 percent for capital investment decisions and is subject to corporate income tax rates of 40 percent on operating income and 20 percent on capital gains. Assume all recurring cash flows take place at the end of the year.

REQUIRED

1. Calculate the present value (at December 31, 19X4) of the expected after-tax cash flows for each of the three alternatives available to Kravel Corporation regarding the Dayton plant.
2. Discuss the additional factors, both quantitative and qualitative, Kravel Corporation should consider before a decision is made regarding the disposition or use of the idle plant and equipment at the Dayton plant.

13–33 DCF Analysis: Make or Buy (CMA Adapted) Lamb Company manufactures several lines of machine products. One unique part, a valve stem, requires specialized tools that need to be replaced. Management has decided that the only alternative to replacing these tools is to acquire the valve stem from an outside source. A supplier is willing to provide the valve stem at a unit sales price of $20 if at least 70,000 units are ordered annually.

Lamb's average use of valve stems over the past three years has been 80,000 units each year. Expectations are that this volume will remain constant over the next five years. Cost records indicate that unit manufacturing costs for the last several years have been as follows:

Direct material	$ 3.80
Direct labor	3.70
Variable overhead	1.70
Fixed overhead[a]	4.50
Total unit cost	$13.70

[a] Depreciation accounts for two-thirds of the fixed overhead. The balance is for other fixed overhead costs of the factory that require cash expenditures.

The specialized tools cost $2,500,000 and will have a disposal value of $100,000 after their expected economic life of five years. Straight-line depreciation is used for book purposes but ACRS is used for tax purposes. The specialized tools are considered three-year property for ACRS purposes. The company has a 40 percent marginal tax rate, and management requires a 12 percent after-tax return on investment.

The sales representative for the manufacturer of the new tools stated, "The new tools will allow direct labor and variable overhead to be reduced by $1.60 per unit." Data from another manufacturer using identical tools and experiencing similar operating conditions, except that annual production generally averages 110,000 units, confirms the direct labor and variable overhead savings. However, the manufacturer indicates that it experienced an increase in raw material cost due to the higher quality of material that had to be used with the new tools. The manufacturer indicated that its costs have been as follows:

Direct material	$ 4.50
Direct labor	3.00
Variable overhead	0.80
Fixed overhead	5.00
Total unit cost	$13.30

REQUIRED

1. Present a discounted cash flow analysis covering the economic life of the new specialized tools to determine whether Lamb Company should replace the old tools or purchase the valve stem from an outside supplier. Consider all typical tax implications.
2. Identify additional factors Lamb Company should consider before a decision is made to replace the tools or purchase the valve stem from an outside supplier.

13–34 Disposal Decision Hardison Manufacturing Company owns two drill presses. Because of a decline in business, the firm can get by with only one, and the managers are trying to decide which one to sell. Data on the two presses appear below.

	Press A	*Press B*
Original cost	$80,000	$100,000
Accumulated depreciation, tax and book	$80,000	$ 75,000
Estimated remaining useful life	5 years	5 years
Current market resale value	$12,000	$ 21,000
Estimated resale value at end of life	0	0

Both presses have the same operating costs, exclusive of depreciation. Press B has two years of life remaining for purposes of tax depreciation at $12,500 per year. Press A is fully depreciated because it was acquired when a special fast-writeoff provision was in the tax code.

One manager has suggested that press A be sold because it is fully depreciated and the firm will therefore show a $12,000 profit. The firm has a tax rate of 40 percent and cost of capital of 15 percent.

REQUIRED

Determine which press the firm should sell.

13–35 Working-Capital Investment Cramer Company has an opportunity to invest in a new product. Data appear below.

Required Investment:	
Plant and equipment, 10-year life	$1,000,000
Accounts receivable, 25% of annual sales	
Inventory of work in process and finished goods, 40% of annual production	
Annual Returns:	
Expected revenue, 50,000 units at $60	$3,000,000
Variable production costs	$30/unit
Fixed production costs, annual, including $100,000 depreciation	$ 800,000
Fixed selling and administrative expenses, annual	$ 140,000

Cost of capital is 15 percent. The firm uses straight-line depreciation. Ignore taxes.

REQUIRED

1. Determine the number of units the firm will produce in the first year, assuming it will reach the stated level of inventories by the end of the year.
2. Determine the cash outflows associated with manufacturing the product in the first year.
3. Determine the cash inflows expected from sales in the first year.
4. Determine the investment in working capital that the firm will carry over the life of the product.
5. Determine whether the investment is desirable.

13–36 Replacement Decision Worthington Manufacturing Company owns a machine with the following characteristics:

Current market value	$30,000
Net book value (equals tax basis)	$24,000
Remaining useful life	6 yr
Capacity in units of output	14,000
Fixed cash operating costs	$18,000/yr
Annual depreciation	$4,000

The product made on the machine sells for $5 and has variable costs of $2. The sales manager believes that he could sell 20,000 units per year at $5 if the firm had more capacity.

A new machine with a capacity of 22,000 units per year is available. Data follow.

Cost	$60,000
Fixed cash operating costs	$24,000/yr
Useful life	6 yr

Neither machine will have salvage value at the end of six years. The firm uses straight-line depreciation for the old machine but would use ACRS for the new. The tax rate is 40 percent and cost of capital is 20 percent.

REQUIRED

Determine whether the firm should replace the existing machine.

13–37 Basic Replacement Decision The controller of Tantrum Enterprises wants to know whether it is advantageous to replace a piece of machinery. The machine was purchased for $400,000 ten years ago and is expected to last another ten years. Depreciation was set up on a sixteen-year basis (straight-line) at purchase. Current operating costs for labor, material, and variable overhead are $240,000 annually. If the old machine were sold now, the firm would get $100,000. Tax basis is $150,000. It is expected that if it were sold in another ten years, it would bring $20,000.

A manufacturer has offered Tantrum new pieces of equipment costing a total of $750,000. The expected life of the new equipment is ten years and there is no expected salvage value. Operating costs are expected to be $150,000 in the first year and $100,000 per year thereafter.

The firm uses five-year ACRS depreciation and a hurdle rate of 15 percent. The tax rate is 40 percent.

REQUIRED

1. Using an incremental analysis, compare the cash flows of the new machines with those of the old.
2. Calculate the net present value of these differences and make a recommendation to management.

13–38 Replacement Decision Apple Qume Photo began business in 19X0. At that time it bought a building for $90,000 and equipment for photo processing totaling $200,000. While the building was being depreciated over thirty years, the equipment was depreciated over ten years. Straight-line depreciation was used for both book and tax purposes. In 19X2, Koduck, the manufacturer of the processing equipment, introduced a new photographic paper processor model CSL that costs $80,000. The current model

DR processor was part of the original equipment bought in 19X0, and it cost $30,000 at that time.

In 19X0, Koduck estimated the following costs for the Model DR:

	Cost per 100 Square Inches of Paper Processed
Color paper at $0.03/sq in	$3.00
Chemicals at $0.01	1.00
Direct labor at $8/hr	0.67
Variable overhead, at $4/DLH	0.33
	$5.00

At the beginning of 19X2, labor costs have risen to $10 per hour, variable overhead is $5 per DLH, color paper is $0.07 per square inch, and chemical costs are $0.02 per square inch. Costs are expected to rise $1 per DLH, $0.50 per hour variable overhead, $0.005 per square inch for chemicals, and $0.03 per inch for color paper at the beginning of 19X6.

The new model CSL would be depreciated using five-year ACRS, and is estimated to have an eight-year life. Koduck estimates that it will have no salvage value at the end of its life but will cost $300 to haul away. Operating costs are estimated to be the same for paper as the old machine, but chemicals will be 75 percent of those used for the old machine, and labor will be cut in half.

The old machine has a resale value of $5,000. If it is held until the end of its life, there will be no salvage value.

This decision is being analyzed at the beginning of 19X2, the marginal tax rate is 40 percent, and the after-tax hurdle rate is 13 percent.

Normal production is 1,360,000 square inches of paper per year.

REQUIRED

Use the net present-value method to determine whether the company should retain the model DR or buy the new model CSL.

13–39 Using Excess Capacity (CMA Adapted) Hammond Industries is a toy manufacturer that will have excess capacity at its single plant after 19X1. Hammond's management is currently studying two alternative proposals to utilize this excess capacity.

Proposal 1 Hammond has been approached by GloriToys, one of its competitors, to manufacture a partially completed doll. GloriToys, owner of the distribution rights for the doll, would finish the dolls in its plant and then market them. The GloriToy doll does not compete directly with any of Hammond's products.

GloriToys would contract to purchase 5,000 unfinished dolls each month at a price of $7.50 each for the period of 19X2 through 19X5. Hammond's estimated incremental cash outlays to manufacture the doll are $250,000 per year during the four-year contract period. In addition, this alternative requires a $400,000 investment in manufacturing equipment. The equipment will have no salvage value at the end of its useful life.

Proposal 2 Hammond is considering the production of a new stuffed toy to be added to its own product line. The new stuffed toy would be sold at $15 per unit and the expected annual sales over the estimated six-year product life (19X2–19X7) for the toy is:

Year	Unit Sales
19X2	65,000
19X3	90,000
19X4	90,000
19X5	65,000
19X6	50,000
19X7	50,000

Variable unit manufacturing and selling costs are estimated to be $6.00 and $1.00 respectively over this six-year period. The estimated annual incremental cash outlay for fixed costs is $300,000. The manufacture and sale of the new stuffed toy requires a $700,000 investment in new manufacturing equipment; this equipment will have a salvage value of $50,000 at the end of the six-year period.

Hammond Industries is subject to a 30 percent income tax rate on all income. Hammond's management assumes that annual cash flows occur at the end of the year for evaluating capital investment proposals. Hammond uses a 15 percent after-tax discount rate. Hammond uses straight-line depreciation and ignores the half-year convention.

REQUIRED

1. Calculate the net present value at December 31, 19X6, of the estimated after-tax cash flows of Hammond Industries' proposal of:
   a. manufacturing unfinished dolls for GloriToys
   b. manufacturing and selling a new stuffed toy to be added to its own product line

2. Without prejudice to the net present value calculations in part 1 and only considering the environment for Hammond Industries as described, identify other factors that increase the attractiveness of
   a. manufacturing the unfinished dolls for GloriToys
   b. manufacturing and selling a new stuffed toy

13–40 Net Income and Cash Flows Joplin Corporation has approached Pine County Bank for a loan. Mr. Scott, the president of Joplin, has presented the following income statement to the loan officer at the bank.

Income Statement, 19X0

Sales	$300,000
Cost of sales	150,000
Gross margin	$150,000
Sales and administrative expense	50,000
Income before taxes	$100,000
Taxes	40,000
Net income	$ 60,000

Scott feels that net income will grow at about 5 percent per year. In the declining economy at the time, receivables are expected to go up by 10 percent of sales yearly. For example, at the beginning of 19X0, receivables increased by $30,000. Depreciation makes up $20,000 of sales and administrative expenses. Marginal taxes are at 40 percent. The bank is offering a loan floating with prime rate for five years that is expected to average 15 percent over the life of the loan. Mr. Scott hopes to pay 50 percent of net income to investors as a dividend. Cost of sales are all variable.

REQUIRED

If you were the bank officer, what is the maximum amount you would lend Mr. Scott? The loan will be repaid at the end of 19X4.

13–41 Contrasting Methods of Capital Budgeting Jeffrey Lawrence, manufacturing director of Millbrook Enterprises, is considering some new product lines. Corporate management of Millbrook has developed several measures for evaluating projects. Projects expected to last less than five years are judged under the payback method, with a required payback of two years or less for moderately risky projects and of three years for moderately safe projects. In addition, the risky projects must show a 15 percent after-tax average book rate of return.

On longer projects, management uses net present value and internal rate of return. The estimated cost of capital for Millbrook is 12 percent. However, management has established goal-oriented rates of 18 percent for moderately risky projects and 14 percent for moderately safe projects. Millbrook uses straight-line depreciation. Taxes are 50 percent.

REQUIRED

1. One project requires $30,000 in equipment, will last an expected four to five years, and is considered relatively risky. Net income is expected to be $3,300 per year. Evaluate this project under Millbrook's criteria.
2. The other project requires $50,000 in equipment, will last about six years, and is considered moderately risky. After-tax cash flows are expected to be $14,000 per year, including the tax savings from depreciation. Evaluate this project under Millbrook's criteria.
3. Discuss the criteria that management has developed for capital budgeting decisions. What are their strengths and weaknesses? Use the examples from parts 1 and 2 to illustrate your discussion.

13–42 By-Product and Capital Budgeting Shull Company operates a combined factory/office building that it currently heats with natural gas at a cost of about $250,000 annually. The production process requires a great deal of heat, which is also supplied by natural gas at an annual cost of about $1,240,000. One of the plant engineers believes that it is economical to recycle the heat from the production process and use it to heat the building. He estimates that the move would reduce consumption of natural gas by about $200,000 in the first year alone. The saving relates to the $250,000 now spent to heat the building.

Recycling the heat requires large fans, considerable ductwork, and other equipment, with an aggregate cost of about $600,000 and a useful life of five years. The tax rate is 40 percent and cost of capital is 15 percent. The best estimates available indicate that the price of natural gas will rise at about 10 percent per year for the next five years. The firm uses straight-line depreciation for tax purposes.

REQUIRED

Determine whether the firm should install the system.

14

CAPITAL ASSET ACQUISITIONS—ADVANCED CONSIDERATIONS

Chapter 13 treated basic capital budgeting matters. This chapter looks at some refinements. We discuss the concept of cost of capital. We also examine preference rules for ranking competing investments and show how to deal with mutually exclusive investments. We illustrate the use of sensitivity analysis, and finally, examine financing decisions in the context of leases.

COST OF CAPITAL

The selection of a discount rate is an important capital budgeting matter because the net present value of an investment is extremely sensitive to the rate. Consider for a moment the net present values calculated below using 10 percent and 15 percent discount rates. Suppose we have an investment of $2,000, and equal annual net cash flows of $400 for 10 years.

	Net Present Values	
	At 10%	At 15%
Annual cash flow	$400	$400
Discount factor, Table A–4	6.1446	5.0188
Present value	$2,458	$2,007
Less investment	2,000	2,000
Net present value	$ 458	$ 7

At 10 percent, the PVI is 1.23 ($2,458/$2,000), while at 15 percent it is not significantly different from one. The project appears very profitable at 10 percent, but only marginally so at 15 percent. Thus, the selection of the discount rate is very important. Surveys have shown that companies calculate cost of capital, or establish discount rate, in several ways. The most common seems to be the weighted average cost of capital.[1]

Weighted Average Cost of Capital

The **weighted average cost of capital** is simply the cost of each component of capital multiplied (weighted) by its percentage in the capital structure. The cost of debt is relatively easy to determine. Simply calculate the interest rate implicit in the market price of the debt. If a bond is selling at face value, its effective rate equals its nominal rate. If the bond sells at some other price, you can use a bond table or computer to determine the effective rate. (The effective rate is the internal rate of return, which equates the present value of the future interest payments and repayment of principal with the current market price of the bond.) We then adjust the effective interest rate to its after-tax equivalent by multiplying it by one minus the tax rate. We do this because interest is tax deductible, so the net cost is the gross cost less the tax savings.

The stickiest point here is determining the cost of equity capital. It is not simply the dividend yield (dividends divided by market value of stock) nor the price earnings ratio (stock price divided by earnings per share). The cost of equity might be expressed in several ways; a common one is the dividend yield plus the expected growth rate in dividends. The problem is that it is difficult to determine the growth rate that investors expect. Courses in managerial finance devote considerable attention to this issue.

We then weight the costs of debt and equity to determine the weighted average cost of capital. The schedule below shows a simple example.

[1]See John J. Clark, Thomas J. Hindelang, and Robert E. Pritchard, *Capital Budgeting*, 3rd ed. (Englewood Cliffs, NJ: Prentice-Hall, 1989), p. 176.

Interest rate on debt	10%
Percentage debt in capital structure	30%
Required return to common stockholders	15%
Tax rate	40%

Weighted average cost of capital:

Element	*After-Tax Cost*	*Percentage in Capital Structure*	*Weighted Cost*
Debt	6% (10% × 60%)	30%	1.8%
Equity	15%	70%	10.5%
Weighted average cost of capital			12.3%

Opportunity Cost

Cost of capital is an opportunity cost because if there are no attractive investments, the company could contract by buying back its debt and equity. In fact, if the company cannot make investments at or above cost of capital, it should return the cash to its creditors and stockholders, for they can presumably make better use of it than the company can. Cost of capital is also an opportunity cost in the sense that the company must earn that rate of return to continue to attract investors. If the company earns less than its cost of capital, the prices of its bonds and stock will fall because the company is not earning enough to keep investors satisfied.

Target Rates

Some companies do not wish to express a cost of capital because of the difficulties of making the calculations. Instead, they establish a **target rate** or **hurdle rate**, which serves the same function as cost of capital—to discount future cash flows. In some companies, the hurdle rate is higher than cost of capital. Managers recognize that indirect costs and indirect investments often creep up as the company expands. Capital budgeting decisions focus on the separable, incremental, identifiable aspects of decisions. Some managers argue, then, that using a higher rate compensates for failing to include indirect costs and investments.

Some companies take the opposite approach, setting the target rate lower than cost of capital, at least for some types of investments. Among these are investments in technology or other areas where many benefits are difficult to quantify. Chapter 13 discussed similar issues and stated that managers might accept projects with negative NPVs because of qualitative and hard-to-quantify benefits. Reducing the target rate for such investments is another approach.

SENSITIVITY ANALYSIS

Early in this book we stressed the importance of analyzing the sensitivity of a decision. All decisions relate to the future and are therefore based on estimates, not certainties. We argued that if a decision would change as a result of a relatively small change in one variable, then it would be good to seek additional information or take other steps to guard against the unfavorable change. That principle is even more important in capital budgeting because of the amounts of money involved—when millions of dollars are riding on an investment, it is prudent to be as sure as possible that the investment will not turn sour because of a small unfavorable change in a variable.

Capital budgeting decisions are also likely to be sensitive because of multiplier effects. For example, a $1 change in annual cash flow from a project with a ten-year life where cost of capital is 15 percent yields a $5.0188 change in the present value of the future cash flows. (The present value factor for a 10-year, 15 percent annuity is 5.0188.) Similarly, a change in a per unit amount, such as the expected selling price of a product, is multiplied by unit volume, then reduced for the tax effect, and multiplied again by the present value factor. A relatively small change in a per unit amount can have enormous effects as it works through the analysis.

We shall illustrate sensitivity analysis using the example in Exhibit 14–1, a Lotus 1-2-3 template, for a new product for Tracy Company.

The investment has a positive NPV and should be accepted. However, let us look at the critical factors. We can examine any factor. In fact, calculating the IRR is essentially doing a sensitivity analysis on the discount rate. How high does the discount rate have to rise before the investment becomes undesirable? The answer in this case is to more than 23.3 percent, which is nearly double the 12 percent rate, so the decision is not sensitive to the discount rate. The particular variables that you select for analysis depend on the circumstances. How hard, or certain, are the estimates? If the estimate of $300 thousand cash fixed manufacturing costs is thought very reliable, there is probably little point in analyzing that factor. There is less of a multiplier effect with fixed costs than there is with volume related variables.

There are several approaches to sensitivity analysis. One is to use a spreadsheet or dedicated computer program for a brute force analysis, changing the value of the variable in question until the NPV approaches the desired figure, usually zero. We can also proceed analytically, by solving for the critical value of the variable as we solved for volumes or prices that yielded target profits in Chapter 2. In all cases, we hold all factors constant except the one we are testing.

Useful Life

You probably noticed the row in Exhibit 14–1 labeled *Cumulative Net Present Value*. This row is simply the cumulative total of the present value figures. This number becomes positive in year five, which means that if the investment lasts

EXHIBIT 14–1 Tracy Company Product Analysis Template

INPUT SECTION

Annual volume	100 thousand
Selling price	$10.00
Unit variable cost	$4.00
Cash fixed manufacturing costs	$300 thousand
Selling and administrative costs	$80 thousand
Cost of depreciable assets	$600 thousand
Useful life	8
ACRS life	5
Tax rate	40.00%
Cost of capital	12.00%

OUTPUT SECTION

Present value analysis, thousands of dollars

	0	1	2	3	4	5	6	7	8
Equipment	-600.0								
Operating flows, net of tax		132.0	132.0	132.0	132.0	132.0	132.0	132.0	132.0
Depreciation shield		48.0	76.8	46.1	27.6	27.6	13.9		
Net cash flow	-600.0	180.0	208.8	178.08	159.6	159.6	145.92	132.0	132.0
Present value factor	1.000	0.893	0.797	0.712	0.636	0.567	0.507	0.452	0.404
Present value, future flows	($600.0)	$160.7	$166.5	$126.8	$101.4	$90.6	$73.9	$59.7	$53.3
Cumulative net present value	($600.0)	($439.3)	($272.8)	(146.1)	($44.6)	$45.9	$119.8	$179.5	$232.9
Net present value	$232.9								
IRR	23.31%								

for five years, it will show a positive net present value. The point at which the cumulative net present value becomes positive tells us how long we must sell the product (or save costs or whatever generates the cash flows) not only to get our money back, but also to earn cost of capital on the investment.

Some people call the five year result here the **discounted payback**, which means that we not only recover the investment, as ordinary payback calculates, but also earn cost of capital. However, the five years here is slightly pessimistic. If the investment were to become worthless, we would have the equipment, which might have some resale value and at a minimum a tax basis available for write-off. The most pessimistic analysis, then, is to suppose that the equipment becomes worthless at the end of each year, determine the tax benefit of the write-off, and add that to the cumulative net present value already calculated. This is easy to do with a spreadsheet. We show below the calculation for years three and four. All other years are done the same way. This calculation gives the **discounted bailout payback**. The term *bailout* comes from the draconian alternative of abandoning the investment well before its useful life is over. The tax saving on scrapping equipment is the remaining tax shield. Thus, at the end of year three, the remaining tax shield, which will all be taken if the equipment is scrapped, is the tax shield available for years four, five, and six.

Total Years	*Cumulative NPV (see Exh. 14–1)*	*Tax Saving from Scrapping Equipment*	*Present Value*	*Total Net Present Value*
3	−$146.1	$69.1 ($27.6 + $27.6 + $13.9)	$49.2	−$96.9
4	−$44.6	$41.5 ($27.6 + $13.9)	$26.4	−$18.2

In this example, the discounted bailout payback is greater than four years but considerably less than five years. It is less than the discounted payback although both are reached in year five. Again, it appears that useful life is not a critical factor. If the investment had a working capital component, we would state our expectations about recovery and include the present value of the recovery in each year's analysis. Some working capital would surely be recovered, receivables almost certainly, and some inventory even if the product does not sell well.

Unit Volume and Contribution Margin

Let us now look at unit volume. How far can it fall before the investment becomes only marginally desirable? Look at Exhibit 14–1. If we allow unit volume to fall, the only item affected is the operating flow. Accordingly, we can solve for the value that operating flow must have to make the net present value zero or any other target amount and then determine what unit volume (or price or variable cost or any other variable) must be to satisfy the condition. In this case, the operating flow is an annuity, the same amount every year, which makes the task simpler. Exhibit 14–2 shows one way to do the calcula-

EXHIBIT 14–2 Tracy Company Sensitivity Analysis

Investment	$600
Less: present value of ACRS tax shield ($600 × .40 × 0.7381)	177
Required present value of operating flows	$423
Divided by annuity factor	4.9676
Required annual net cash operating flow	$85.2
Divided by 1—tax rate equals required pretax flow ($85.2/.60)	$142.0
Add cash fixed costs ($300 + $80)	380.0
Required contribution margin	$522.0
Divided by contribution margin per unit ($10—$4)	$6
Equals unit volume required	87.0

tions: find the present values of all flows save the one affected by the change, in this case operating flows, and then determine the value for unit volume that gives the desired result.

Annual unit volume must be about 87,000 units to make the investment just barely desirable. The decline is 13 percent, (from 100 thousand to 87 thousand). Note that the net present value of $232.9, 38.8 percent of the investment ($232.9/$600), is high, but the decline in unit volume that would wipe out the net present value is only 13 percent, a much smaller figure. Notice also that once we have calculated the required contribution margin, we can also determine the required price, or variable cost. We simply divide the $522 thousand required contribution margin by 100 thousand units to get a required unit contribution margin of $5.22. The price needed for a $5.22 contribution margin is $9.22 ($4.00 variable cost + $5.22 contribution margin), or a variable cost of $4.78 ($10.00 selling price − $5.22 contribution margin). Remember again that we are holding the other variables constant when we solve for each value. The $9.22 selling price is a drop of only 7.8 percent from the original $10 ($0.78 decline/$10). We have already mentioned that decisions are usually more sensitive to per unit amounts such as price than to almost any other factor.

An alternative calculational approach is often more convenient. It relies on the already calculated net present value and calculates the allowable decline in unit volume or contribution margin. From Exhibit 14–1 we know that the net present value is $232.9 thousand. In a variation on determining the volume required for a zero net present value, suppose that we want the unit volume that will yield a $50 thousand net present value. That figure could be the manager's desired safety margin. Thus, the net present value can decline by $182.9 thousand and we can find the figure in the following way:

Allowable decline in net present value	$182.9
Divided by annuity factor	4.9676
Equals allowable decline in net operating flow	$ 36.8
Divided by 1 − tax rate equals pretax decline	$ 61.3
Divided by contribution margin per unit	$ 6.00
Equals allowable decline in unit volume	10.2 thousand

Thus, unit volume could decline to 89.8 thousand (100 − 10.2) before net present value drops below $50 thousand. Note that if we did this analysis using the original net present value of $232.9, we would get 13.0 thousand, which corresponds to the result we obtained earlier, where the volume was 87 thousand, a decline of 13 thousand. This alternative is also useful in cases where operating flows vary from year to year, perhaps because volume varies. Trying to find the volume for each year is extremely difficult and must be done using a spreadsheet. However, the technique just illustrated allows us to find the decline in average annual volume that brings the net present value to zero. Thus, if the net present value were $182.9 thousand with volumes ranging from 60 thousand to 125 thousand, it would be very difficult to find directly the year-by-year volumes that give a zero net present value. We could still find the decline of 10.2 thousand, however. We could then subtract 10.2 thousand from each volume to determine the specific year-by-year amounts.

To find the allowable decline in unit contribution margin, we need only divide the $61.3 thousand above by the annual volume of 100 thousand to get $0.613. Subtracting $0.613 from the original $6.00 gives $5.387 for unit contribution margin, which could happen by reduced price or increased variable cost, or a combination of the two.

Sensitivity analysis is used to see how sensitive decisions are to changes in variables. If a particular variable is very critical, where a small change in it moves an investment from the accept to the reject category, we should seek more information or try to satisfy ourselves in other ways that the likelihood of such a change is not high. At the least, we should monitor such a variable closely if we make the investment.

Multiple-Variable Sensitivity Analysis

To this point, we have looked at single variables and how a change in economic life or units sold can affect net present value. In some cases, managers might want to look at ranges of changes for several variables. They might vary life, price, variable cost, and volume both one at a time and all together. Multiple-variable sensitivity analysis can really only be done effectively on a computer using a spreadsheet. If the data section of the spreadsheet has all the variables separated, then all you have to do is to change as many of these variables as you desire and see the effect on total net present value. A manager can experiment with values to see the combination of changes in several variables that would bring the net present value to zero or to some prespecified level (like a target NPV). In this way, the manager can look at margin of safety much in the same way as we did in Chapter 2 dealing with breakeven analysis.

An important point about sensitivity analysis is that many factors can affect net present value. We can ask questions such as:

1. What external factors are most critical? Are there changes in markets and technology that we should be concerned about? Some companies face what they consider to be hostile government regulators. Others operate in countries with unstable political situations.

2. Are there potential problems with input factors? For example, many companies today are concerned that the supply of skilled workers will not be sufficient because many high school students are not able to work with high technology.
3. Does the industry face severe competition from abroad, or from substitute products? Might the industry not exist in 20 years?

This kind of analysis should go into making the original estimates of each variable and such factors should be reviewed when doing sensitivity analysis.

MUTUALLY EXCLUSIVE INVESTMENTS

Mutually exclusive investments arise from alternative ways of doing the same thing or because of management policy (for instance, to bring out only one new product per year). The problem with mutually exclusive investments is that they might rank differently using each of the DCF measures. That is, project A might have the highest IRR, while project B has the highest net present value. The question is then how to rank the projects. Except under very special circumstances, NPV is preferable to either IRR or PVI for ranking competing alternatives. Let us see how the three criteria perform in an example, and then explain those special circumstances.

Below are data for two mutually exclusive investment opportunities. Cost of capital is 10 percent. Project Y has both a higher IRR and a higher PVI than project X, which ranks higher only under the NPV criterion.

	X	Y
Investment required	$50,000	$10,000
Cash flow, end of year 1	$55,991	$11,403
Net present value at 10%	$ 896	$ 365
IRR	12%	14%
PVI	1.018	1.037

Provided that the 10 percent cost of capital is the rate at which alternative investments could be made, project X should be selected. The simplest way to show this is as follows.

The company must have at least $50,000 for investment, otherwise it could not a consider project X. If project Y is accepted (outlay of $10,000), $40,000 is still available. This $40,000 will be invested (or it should be returned to debtholders and shareholders) at cost of capital, or higher. For our purposes, we assume investment at cost of capital. What cash will the firm have at the end of the year if it selects project Y and invests $40,000 at 10 percent? The cash position is summarized below.

Cash provided by investment in project Y	$11,403
Cash provided by investment at cost of capital ($40,000 × 1.10)	44,000
Total cash available at end of year	$55,403

At the end of the year, the firm has $55,403. But had the firm invested the entire $50,000 in project X, it would have had $55,991 at the end of the year. Thus, accepting project Y and using the excess funds for another project produces less cash than does accepting project X. Some analysts recommend using these *terminal values* instead of present values, to make decisions.

There is one case where the project with the higher IRR should be chosen over one with the higher net present value: if investing in the higher-IRR project enables the firm to invest the additional cash at a sufficiently high rate to provide more total cash than the project with the higher NPV does, *and* if that latter opportunity is not available if the firm chooses the higher-NPV project. Thus, in our example, suppose that investing in project Y allows us to invest also in project Z, but that we cannot invest $40,000 in project Z if we accept project X. Roughly speaking, we should choose project Y if project Z yields more than $44,588 at the end of one year ($55,991 from project X − $11,403 from project Y). This is a return of about 11.5 percent. Why might we be able to invest in project Z if we accept project Y, but refuse project X? The most likely reason is that project Y begins, or carries on, a strategy with which project X is incompatible. Step-by-step automation is an example. Project X might involve machinery that cannot be used with the machinery encompassed by project Z.

Unequal Lives

Alternative investment opportunities often have different useful lives. A conveyor should outlast a forklift truck. In such cases, we must somehow equate the lives of the investments. We shall illustrate one way to deal with this special problem, the assumption of a chain of replacements. Assume the following facts about two mutually exclusive investment opportunities, different versions of a machine essential to the firm's operation.

	Model X1	*Model X2*
Purchase price	$40,000	$70,000
Annual cash operating costs	$18,000	$16,000
Expected useful life	4 years	8 years

Neither machine has any expected salvage value at the end of its useful life. Cost of capital is 14 percent. Ignore taxes. (There is no difference in the *form* of the analysis if we include taxes.) Because the longer life is twice the shorter, we can equate the lives by implicitly replacing the X1 at the end of four years. If the lives were, say, four and six years, we would need a 12-year horizon (the least common multiple of four and six).

We estimate that an X1 will cost $44,000 at the end of four years, and that its operating costs and useful life will be the same as those of an X1 bought today. The present value of the future flows associated with acquiring the longer lived model is calculated below. Note that here, because we are dealing with outflows, we want the lower present value of future outflows.

	Model X2
Annual operating costs	$ 16,000
Present value factor, eight years, 14%	4.6389
Present value of operating costs	74,222
Investment	70,000
Total present value of future outflows	$144,222

We now do the same for the X1, assuming the replacement at the end of four years.

	Model X1
Annual operating costs, years 1–4	$ 18,000
Present value factor, 4-year annuity at 14%	2.9137
Present value of operating outflows, years 1 to 4	$ 52,447
Present value of replacement at end of year 4	
($44,000 × .5921, single payment factor, 4 years)	26,052
Present values of operating flows, years 5–8:	
Year 5 $18,000 × .5194	9,349
Year 6 $18,000 × .4556	8,201
Year 7 $18,000 × .3996	7,193
Year 8 $18,000 × .3506	6,311
Investment now	40,000
Total present value of future outflows	$149,553

Notice that the present value of the replacement X1 ($26,052) is substantially less than its actual cost ($44,000). This is to be expected because replacement will not be needed for four years.

Comparing the present values of the future outflows for each alternative, it appears that the less expensive alternative is to buy the X2. However, the two present values are not far apart ($144,222 to $149,553), and the managers will consider other factors. For example, how confident are they in the forecast of the replacement cost of the X1 in four years? What is the likelihood of a significant change in technology? These and other factors influence the final decision. Rapid changes in technology and in manufacturing methods argue for shorter commitments. Tying up money in long-lived manufacturing equipment is risky. In our example, the managers might select the shorter lived X1 partly because they expect more efficient models to develop. Of course, if they were confident that there would be new models they would use estimates about such models, not estimates about the replacement of X1.

This replacement chain technique is reasonable when both investments are relatively short-lived. It is not as useful if the lives are, say, three years and 15 years, necessitating five replacements. Where replacement chains are not useful, one plausible technique is to assume a sale or abandonment of the longer lived project at the end of the life of the shorter lived project. Using our example, and supposing that the X2 will sell for \$5,000 at the end of four years, we have the following analysis.

	Model X1
Annual operating costs, years one to four	\$18,000
Present value factor, 4-year annuity at 14%	2.9137
Present value of operating outflows, years one to four	52,447
Investment	40,000
Present value of future flows	\$92,447

	Model X2
Annual operating costs	\$ 16,000
Present value factor, four years, 14%	2.9137
Present value of operating costs	46,619
Investment	70,000
Salvage value, \$5,000 × .5921	(2,961)
Total present value of future flows	\$113,658

If there were income taxes, we would determine the net recovery including the gain or loss for tax purposes.

Multiple IRR—Another Problem

The IRR method can, as we have shown, cause problems in evaluating mutually exclusive investments. It can also cause difficulties in analyzing some non-competing investments. It is possible to have more than one IRR for a particular investment. This can happen *only* when the cash flows go from positive to negative or vice versa more than once. The typical investment that we have considered starts with a negative flow, then has all positive flows. Sometimes, however, there are negative flows in later years, perhaps for a major overhauling of equipment. The following flows demonstrate the problem.

Year	*Cash Flow*
0	−\$234,050
1	552,250
2	−324,300

Discounting these flows at both 10 and 26 percent gives virtually zero NPVs, so both IRRs are valid. What should we do? Use the net present value method, recognizing that these cases can have curious results.

CAPITAL RATIONING

Companies that do not have enough cash to make all of the investments that are economically acceptable face **capital rationing**. In theory, there should always be enough cash available because the capital markets should be willing to provide it to the company at cost of capital. However, it is not always practical to raise money in capital markets, so companies often have more investment opportunities than cash. Capital rationing can also be self-imposed. A company might simply limit its capital budget to conserve cash for the future, because the investment climate is not good, or for other reasons. There are several approaches to capital rationing.

Solutions for Capital Rationing

Managers can deal with this problem using a variety of approaches. The main idea is to find that group of projects that will best use available capital resources.

Solution by Inspection With a limited number of projects, managers can group those found acceptable when discounted at the cost of capital and pick the set of projects that maximizes present value. Assume that Rubber Tire Company is considering several projects but has only $100,000 in available funds this year. A list of projects and needed investments appears below. None of these projects is mutually exclusive.

	Cost	*Net Present Value*
1. New aligning machine	$50,000	$65,000
2. Expanded retail facilities	75,000	37,000
3. Computer for inventory, billing	25,000	24,000

As you can see, several combinations of these three projects are feasible. With unlimited funds, there are 2^n (or 8 in this example) possible combinations. However, with the capital constraint of $100,000, the only feasible combinations are as follows.[2]

	Cost	*Net Present Value*
Project 1	$ 50,000	$65,000
Project 2	75,000	37,000
Project 3	25,000	24,000
Projects 1 and 3	75,000	89,000
Projects 2 and 3	100,000	61,000

Thus, the combination of projects 1 and 3 yields the maximum present value. The $25,000 of excess funds can be invested at cost of capital. If the projects have unequal lives, this analysis becomes more complex.

[2] To be complete, we could include *no projects* as an alternative.

Mathematical Solution Techniques Our original discussion of this problem identified capital rationing as a problem of having limited resources. Therefore, it can be dealt with like other such problems using mathematical programming. Both linear and integer programming techniques are useful. We will not undertake a complete discussion of these models but will outline a single example so you can see how they fit into the general mathematical programming framework.[3]

Let us expand the Rubber Tire Company problem to include limited fund availability now plus limited funds available in one year. Assume that the company has the following four projects to consider:

Project	*Funds Needed Now*	*Funds Needed in One Year*	*NPV*
A	$20,000	−$10,000	$ 4,000
B	30,000	− 10,000	6,000
C	20,000	30,000	10,000
D	20,000	50,000	12,000

If this firm has $40,000 to invest now and $60,000 in a year, this problem can be formulated as an integer program:

$$\begin{aligned} \text{Maximize:} \quad & Z = 4{,}000X_1 + 6{,}000X_2 + 10{,}000X_3 + 12{,}000X_4 \\ \text{Subject to:} \quad & 20{,}000X_1 + 30{,}000X_2 + 20{,}000X_3 + 20{,}000X_4 \le 40{,}000 \\ & -10{,}000X_1 - 10{,}000X_2 + 30{,}000X_3 + 50{,}000X_4 \le 60{,}000 \\ & X_1, X_2, X_3, X_4 = 0 \text{ or } 1 \end{aligned}$$

We could add other constraints such as limited machine capacity, supplier availability, supervision time, and environmental concerns.

Mathematical programming rests on several assumptions. In this case, we assume (to name a few) that funds cannot be transferred between periods, that we know the cash flows with relative certainty, that the constraints and objective function are linear, and that the projects are fully independent. Some authors point out that relaxing these assumptions tends to weaken the model.[4]

Summary of Capital Rationing

In many cases, managers must select projects in the presence of constrained capital resources. In simpler situations, techniques such as raising the discount rate or selecting by inspecting all combinations of projects are appropriate. As the number of projects and the number of constraints rise, more sophisticated techniques involving various forms of mathematical programming can be used. Finally, as we relax more and more assumptions of, say, known life and cash flows, techniques such as simulation can be used to find a solution.

[3] See Clark, et. al., *op. cit.* p. 351ff.

[4] Ibid.

INVESTING DECISIONS AND FINANCING DECISIONS

So far we have not considered the way that a firm intends to finance an investment. That is, we did not specify that the company would issue debt or common stock or finance the investment with internally generated cash flows. We have not considered financing because investing decisions should be separated from financing decisions. An investment should be accepted or rejected on its operating characteristics, not its financing.

Two common mistakes occur in dealing with financing. One is to use the interest rate on debt to discount the flows from an investment to be financed with debt (or the cost of equity for investments financed with equity). It is incorrect to say that, for example, if a firm were to finance an investment with 10 percent bonds, it should use 10 percent to discount the cash flows. Similarly, if it were financing an investment with equity, which costs 14 percent, it is incorrect to use 14 percent to discount the cash flows. The second mistake is to subtract interest payments from operating cash flows.

The fallacies of these errors are subtle, but important. A company should not accept a project that it expects to return less than cost of capital; it should accept projects that it expects to return more than cost of capital. If the company issues debt to make investments that earn more than the interest rate on debt, but less than cost of capital, the debt load increases its risk of financial failure. If projects do not earn cost of capital, the company risks not meeting its interest and dividend payments. Additionally, if the company cannot earn at least cost of capital, it will be unable to meet expectations for growth in profits upon which its stock price depends. If the company earns returns above the interest rate but below cost of capital, it will be unable to raise capital. (Stockholders will sell their stock, reducing the price and thereby raising the cost of equity. Lenders will require higher interest rates, thereby raising the cost of debt capital.)

Including interest payments as a cash flow fails to recognize that discounting automatically provides for the recovery of the investment *and* for a return on the investment equal to the cost of capital. Subtracting interest payments counts interest twice, once explicitly as a cash flow, once implicitly as part of the discount rate. However, in some unusual instances, the operating and financing traits of an investment are so interwoven that they cannot be separated.

LEASING

In recent times leasing has become a major source of financing. If a firm purchases an asset, funds can come from equity investment, debt, or other sources. When leasing, funds are provided by the lessor at some cost. Thus, the cost of leasing can be compared with the cost of owning to find out the cheaper way to finance an acceptable project.

Financial Accounting Versus Capital Budgeting

As there is a difference between using, say, straight-line depreciation over ten years in financial accounting compared with ACRS over five years for capital budgeting calculations, there is a distinction between looking at leases when comparing financial accounting requirements to management decisions. We are not concerned whether a lease is considered a capital or operating lease in analyzing a financing decision. The Internal Revenue Service allows the deduction of many lease payments annually (as long as the lease meets certain criteria) regardless of how the lease is classified on the financial accounting statements.

Because leasing is a financing alternative, the cost of the lease can be expressed as an interest rate just as the cost of a loan can. Thus, the effective lease rate can be calculated and compared with other sources of funds. Several methods have been proposed to find the interest rate implicit in a lease. In most of these methods two factors are important. One is the comparison of interest rates in the lease to alternative sources of financing. The second is the comparison of depreciation under owning to implicit depreciation under a lease.[5] We will explore this subject using the basic framework of Chapters 13 and 14.

The basic difference between owning and leasing has to do with different tax consequences. A firm that owns an asset can deduct depreciation and interest expenses. However, a firm can deduct only the lease payments when leasing an asset: there is no depreciation.

Basically we set up two schedules: owning and leasing. The first schedule has the cost of the asset, the tax shield of depreciation, and the net salvage value. Under the leasing alternative, we show the annual after-tax lease payments. Any other differential cash flows such as maintenance costs incurred under owning but included in the lease should be shown as well.

As an illustration, a manager considering an investment of $50,000 for a project with a five-year life is offered a lease at $14,000 per year. The project is acceptable on NPV grounds. There are two approaches to follow. The first is to use the after-tax interest rate of the best alternate source of financing. Assume that the best alternative is a loan at 12 percent. With a marginal tax rate of 40 percent, this loan has an after-tax cost of 7.2 percent [$0.12 \times (1 - 0.4)$]. Thus, in Exhibit 14–3, both sets of cash flows are discounted at 7.2 percent. Since the effective after-tax interest rate of the lease is higher than 7.2 percent, the present value of the cost of the lease alternative is higher than the buy alternative, indicating that buying is better.

The second technique is to find the interest rate that equates the buy costs with the lease costs. This method will tell you the after-tax effective interest

---

[5] William L. Ferrara, "Capital Budgeting and Financing or Leasing Decisions," *Management Accounting*, July 1968, pp. 55–63; Clifton D. Mann, "Evaluating the Cost in a Lease Proposal," *Management Accounting*, July 1971, pp. 56–58; Lanny G. Chasteen, "Implicit Factors in the Evaluation of Lease vs. Buy Alternatives," *The Accounting Review*, 48:4, October 1973, 764–767.

EXHIBIT 14–3 Comparison of Leasing and Buying

BUY

Cost of asset					$50,000
Less: present value of ACRS tax shield at 7.2 percent					

Year	ACRS Percentage	Tax Rate	Present Value Factor	Present Value	
1	0.200	0.40	0.9328	3,731	
2	0.320	0.40	0.8702	5,569	
3	0.192	0.40	0.8117	3,117	
4	0.115	0.40	0.7572	1,745	
5	0.115	0.40	0.7064	1,628	
6	0.058	0.40	0.6589	759	
					16,549
Net cost					$33,451

LEASE

Present value of after-tax lease payments ($14,000 × 0.60 × 4.0783)	$34.258

rate of the lease. The best way to accomplish this analysis is to use a spreadsheet and vary the interest rate until the two schedules show equal present values. Here, this is accomplished when the after-tax interest rate is 7.08 percent, which equates to 13.0 percent (0.0708/0.6) before taxes. This can be compared with the alternative source of funds, a loan at 12 percent. Exhibit 14–3 highlights the differences in *net cash flows* between owning and leasing. Only differential flows are considered. For example, operating revenues and cash expenses would not change due to the ownership of the asset and, therefore, are not considered.

The preceding example assumed that lease payments occur at year-end. Many leases require payments at the beginning of each year. It is easy to shift the flows in the above analysis to accommodate this timing difference. We would get the present value of an annuity for four years and add the first lease payment to that since it would be paid in year zero.

Other Reasons for Leasing

In our discussion of cash flows, a common assumption has been that the company has enough taxable income to take advantage of the ACRS savings. However, situations exist in which firms have had a series of poor years or extraordinary events have adversely affected profits. Thus, there might not be taxable income expected in the near term, and the advantages of accelerated depreciation are virtually lost.

Before illustrating this consideration, we must discuss one of the properties of current federal income tax law. Firms that show losses on their tax returns are permitted to carry the loss *back* for three years and *forward* for five years, offsetting the loss against taxable income in those years.[6] When the loss is carried back, the firm gets a refund of prior-year taxes; when carried forward, the taxable income and, therefore, income tax are reduced.

The following example shows the effects of the carryback and carryforward. The tax rate is 40 percent in all years.

Year	*Taxable Income*	*Income Tax (refund)*
1	$ 40,000	$16,000
2	$ 30,000	$12,000
3	$ 50,000	$20,000
4	($200,000)	($48,000)
5	$ 60,000	0
6	$ 50,000	$12,000

In year four the firm gets a refund from carrying the loss back three years. Because the loss exceeded the taxable income in those years ($200,000 − $40,000 − $30,000 − $50,000 = $80,000), the firm has an $80,000 carryforward to apply against taxable income for the next five years. In year five it uses $60,000 of the carryforward and pays no tax. In year six it uses the remaining $20,000, thus paying tax on $30,000 ($50,000 taxable income − $20,000 remaining carryforward).

Now, if a firm has sustained a large loss and has carryforwards that exceed its expected taxable income for the next five years, it will pay no tax for those years. If it has been operating at near zero taxable income and expects losses for the next five years, it will also pay no tax. If we consider the example above in the context of such a firm, the analysis changes. All the tax considerations are dropped. Essentially we need to find the discount rate that equates the $14,000 yearly lease payments over five years to the $50,000 outright purchase price.

INFLATION

Inflation is rampant in many economies. The 1970s saw very high rates of inflation in the United States, spurred by many factors including energy prices. Inflation makes dollars to be received in the future less valuable than dollars

[6] The provision is known as the net operating loss carryback and carryforward. It does not apply to all losses, as you may learn in a tax course.

on hand today. In this respect, inflation is like the passage of time. A dollar to be received in the future is worth less than a dollar now because of both the time value of money and inflation. Investors realize this; therefore, cost of capital includes inflation factors. Both debt-holders and equity-holders demand higher rates when they expect significant inflation. Similarly, cash flows to be received in the future are less valuable with inflation.

Two important terms in discussing inflation are *real* and *nominal*. By *real*, we mean with the effects of inflation removed. In referring to flows, *real* means that the dollars are expressed in today's purchasing power. *Nominal* refers to cash flows and discount rates that already include the effects of inflation. Thus, if you expect to sell 10,000 units of product at a $1.21 price in two years, you project a *nominal* cash flow of $12,100 at the end of two years. If the expected rate of inflation is 10 percent, then the real flow—the amount in current dollars—is $10,000. This is $\$12{,}100/(1.10)^2$. Restating a nominal cash flow to a real cash flow is done essentially the same as is discounting.

Incorporating Inflation

There are two ways to handle inflation in capital budgeting. One is to work with real dollars and the real discount rate. The other is to use the nominal discount rate *and* nominal cash flows.

The calculation of the real discount rate is:

$$\text{real rate} = (1 + \text{nominal rate})/(1 + \text{inflation rate}) - 1$$

and the nominal rate is

$$\text{nominal rate} = (1 + \text{real rate}) \times (1 + \text{inflation rate}) - 1$$

Thus, you must adjust both cash flows and the discount rate or adjust neither. These two approaches give the same result. The following example illustrates both methods. Exhibit 14–4 gives data. The pretax cash flows are nominal, meaning that they are the actual expected amounts and therefore *include* inflation. That is why under the first method it is necessary to adjust the cash flows to their real amounts.

Notice that the net present values are the same, except for rounding differences. The present value for each year is also the same under the two methods ($40,403 and $40,406 in year one, etc.), again with rounding differences. This should not be surprising since method 1 entails multiplying the nominal cash flows by the inflation factor then by the present value factor, while method 2 requires multiplying the nominal flows by a present value factor that is the product of the real discount rate and the inflation rate. Thus, the factor .8418 for year one, method 2 equals the product of factors .9259 and .9091 from method 1.

You must be careful to understand whether you are dealing with real or nominal amounts. Some people use the terms *adjusted* and *unadjusted* to mean what we mean by real and nominal. The important point is that real amounts have the effects of inflation removed, while nominal amounts do not.

EXHIBIT 14–4 Data for Inflation Example

Investment		$90,000 three-year life, no salvage value, straight-line depreciation
Annual *nominal* pretax cash flows:		
Year 1	$ 60,000	
2	80,000	
3	120,000	
Inflation rate	8%	
Cost of capital, nominal	18.8%	
Tax rate	40%	

Method 1, find and use real cash flows and real discount rate

	Year		
	1	2	*3*
Nominal pretax flow	$60,000	$80,000	$120,000
Depreciation	30,000	30,000	30,000
Taxable income	30,000	50,000	90,000
Tax at 40%	12,000	20,000	36,000
Net income	$18,000	$30,000	$ 54,000
Plus depreciation	30,000	30,000	30,000
Nominal net cash flow	$48,000	$60,000	$ 84,000
Inflation adjustments[a]	.9259	.8573	.7938
Real cash flows	$44,443	$51,438	$ 66,679
Present value factors, 10%[b]	.9091	.8264	.7513
Present values	$40,403	$42,508	$ 50,096
Total present value	$133,007		
Less investment	90,000		
Net present value	$ 43,007		

Method 2, use nominal flows and nominal discount rate

Nominal net cash flow (above)	$48,000	$60,000	$ 84,000
Present value factors at 18.8%	.8418	.7086	.5964
Present values	$40,406	$42,516	$ 50,098
Total present value	$133,020		
Less investment	90,000		
Net present value	$ 43,020		

[a] $1/1.08$, $1/1.08^2$, $1/1.08^3$

[b] real rate $= 1.188/1.08 - 1 = .10$

BEHAVIORAL AND QUALITATIVE FACTORS

We have focused on quantitative methods for evaluating investments. As seen in earlier chapters, profitability is just one aspect of a decision. Some projects are undertaken for health, safety, or other social reasons even if an economic analysis reveals that they will not produce an adequate return. A firm might install pollution-control devices in excess of legal requirements because of a commitment to the social good. Certain health and safety investments must be made because of OSHA and other governmental agencies' regulations.

Behavioral issues can also affect the choice of alternatives. The most profitable machinery available might have adverse effects on the morale of workers. Some new-equipment alternatives might mean laying off workers. Management must consider not only the cash consequences of retraining and severance pay, but also its responsibility to find other positions for displaced workers.

Book Losses

One serious behavioral problem results from the use of book income for evaluating performance. Lower level managers are evaluated by upper level managers, and upper level managers are evaluated by stockholders and other outside parties. Book income is not the only criterion for evaluation, but it is usually important.

Selling an asset at a loss can adversely affect book income, perhaps so much that a manager is influenced against it, even if the move is wise. Although book income will rise in the future because of improved operations, a loss now could seriously affect a manager's bonus and prospects for promotion. The book value of an asset is a sunk cost, but financial reporting does not usually recognize losses until assets are sold or scrapped, so long as they continue in service. Therefore, managers have an incentive to keep assets that are productive, even if they should be replaced.

Qualitative Factors and Uncertainty

Chapter 13 discussed investing in new technology and some reasons why managers often avoid it. Investing in new technology often has qualitative and hard-to-quantify benefits that make managers reluctant to propose such investments. Some benefits do not accrue to the company, but to people in surrounding areas. Should a company install pollution-control equipment that exceeds state and federal standards when a cheaper alternative that barely meets standards is available? Should it invest in equipment that will require retraining workers, even though its managers are sure that once retrained, some workers will leave for better opportunities?

Uncertainty about benefits is one problem; frequently there is also uncertainty about costs. Investments in computer-assisted design and manufacturing often have hidden costs in the form of employee training, turnover, and temporarily lessened productivity.

Again, in such cases sensitivity analysis is useful. It is also useful to quantify as much as possible, then determine what the remaining benefit or cost must be to make the investment desirable. For instance, suppose that the difference in the present values of future costs of an investment in pollution-control equipment beyond legal requirements over one that barely meets the requirements is $2 million. Someone should be able to judge whether the increased qualitative benefits, including being a good corporate citizen, are worth $2 million. Perhaps only the president can make such decisions, but they should be brought to attention of top management.

EVALUATING DECISIONS

Control is an often overlooked area. In capital budgeting, control is the ongoing evaluation of how projects are coming along, compared both to original plans and updated information.

In variance analysis, actual costs are compared with budget (standard) and deviations are dealt with. However, as we have seen, capital budgeting projects may last several years. As each year passes, cash flows become more and more certain. After four years of a 10-year project, not only does management have in hand actual cash flows from four years, but it also should have a better estimate of what the risk will be over the final six years. Thus, the original project evaluation can be updated. Marketing and production forecasts can be refined. Managers can also re-evaluate projects in light of changes in corporate goals and strategies, the economic environment, and technology.

Abandonment

An important part of evaluation is to see whether a project should be abandoned. Is the present value of future cash flows greater than the net cash that could be realized if the capital assets were sold? That is the abandonment question.

This question can be rephrased into two parts. First, what is a project's updated NPV? If it is negative, then other options should be explored. Second, even if a project has a positive NPV, can the firm get an even higher NPV by terminating that project and beginning another? In times of capital rationing, this is an important consideration, since funds become less scarce if a project is abandoned.

SUMMARY

Chapters 13 and 14 provided an overview of the main topics of capital budgeting. Accountants must know how various models work and their strengths and weaknesses. We established the major criteria for accepting an investment project on (NPV > 0; IRR > discount rate; PVI > 1.0). Our discussion progressed to deciding how to establish the relevant discount rate needed in DCF models and to sensitivity analysis with which a manager can test estimates used in an original DCF analysis. Sensitivity analysis and a thorough qualitative analysis become the focal point of a manager's attention in the decision-making process.

Since managers can choose from several DCF models, we discussed the possible conflicts among these models. Our interest in constrained resources was expanded in the exploration of investment choices when limited capital is available. Investing decisions were clearly differentiated from financing decisions. Finally, we discussed leasing, inflation, and nonquantitative issues affecting decisions.

REVIEW PROBLEM

The following data are available for an investment.

Annual pretax flows	$100,000
Cost of equipment	$250,000
Working capital	$ 80,000
Useful life	eight years (ACRS life is 5 years)
Tax rate	40 percent
Cost of capital	12 percent

1. Find the net present value, using the format of Exhibit 14–1.

2. Determine the discounted payback period.

3. Determine the discounted bailout payback, assuming that salvage value is zero.

SOLUTION TO REVIEW PROBLEM

Spreadsheet templates of the solution appear below.

1 and 2. The net present value is $121,863, the cumulative net present value at the end of the life of the investment. The discounted payback period is over four years, as the cumulative net present value turns positive in year five.

	Year 0	Year 1	Year 2	Year 3	Year 4
Equipment	($250,000)				
Operating flows, net		60,000	60,000	60,000	60,000
Depreciation shield		20,000	32,000	19,200	11,500
	------	------	------	------	------
Net cash flow	($250,000)	$80,000	$92,000	$79,200	$71,500
Present value factor	1.0000	0.8929	0.7972	0.7118	0.6355
Present value	(250,000)	71,432	73,342	56,375	45,438
Cumulative NPV	(250,000)	(178,568)	(105,226)	(48,851)	(3,413)

	Year 5	Year 6	Year 7	Year 8
Operating flows, net	60,000	60,000	60,000	60,000
Depreciation shield	11,500	5,800		
	------	------	------	------
Net cash flow	$71,500	$65,800	$60,000	$60,000
Present value factor	0.5674	0.5066	0.4523	0.4039
Present value	40,569	33,334	27,138	24,234
Cumulative NPV	37,156	70,491	97,629	121,863

3. The discounted bailout payback is just under four years, not much different from the discounted payback period. The analysis is in thousands.

Year	*Cumulative Net Present Value (Above)*	*Loss, equals Tax Basis of Equipment*	*Tax Saving at 40%*	*Present Value*	*Total Net Present Value*
1	−$178.6	$200 ($250 − $50)	$80	$71.4	−$107.2
2	−$105.2	$120 ($200 − $80)	$48	$38.3	−$ 66.9
3	−$ 48.8	$ 72 ($120 − $48)	$28.8	$20.5	−$ 28.3
4	−$ 3.4	$ 43.25 ($72 − $28.75)	$17.3	$11.0	$ 7.6

ASSIGNMENTS

14–1 Criticism of DCF Approach George Pinches, writing in *Financial Management* (Autumn 1982), criticizes the general approach to capital budgeting. He says:

> There is . . . ample evidence that financial specialists have taken a myopic or short-sighted view of the capital budgeting process. The main failure of academicians is due to focusing too much of their attention on the selection phase to the exclusion of the identification, development, and control phases. Very little attention has been given to the interface between strategic planning and capital budgeting. Likewise, academicians have tended to ignore the information requirements and the generation of cash flows—all too often they are assumed to be given. Perhaps this is why academicians have focused on developing many different techniques for dealing with risk, but none of them has much following in practice. Finally, the role of the post audit has not received much attention in academic circles.

Robert Kaplan (*The Accounting Review*, October 1983) quotes from Pinches and says that we tend to ignore factors such as "improved product quality, increased manufacturing flexibility, reduced inventory levels, and the capacity for increased product innovations" since we "have inadequate means for quantifying their benefits."

REQUIRED

1. Critique and comment on Pinches' and Kaplan's statements.

2. In real world capital budgeting situations, how would you address the problems and issues these two authors raise?

14–2 Cost of Capital, Pretax and After-Tax Your firm has been using the net present-value method of evaluating capital investments for several years. One manager has suggested that it would simplify the calculations if the firm used pretax, rather than after-tax, data. The hurdle rate, after-tax, is 15 percent. Because the tax rate is 40 percent, the manager argues, the firm could get the same results (accept or reject an investment) if it used a 25 percent rate to discount pretax cash flows. The 25 percent is 15 percent divided by 60 percent, which is one minus the tax rate.

REQUIRED

Evaluate the manager's suggestion. Show the results you would get using the present method and the proposed method with the following hypothetical investment:

Investment required, all depreciable assets	$10.0 million
Annual pretax operating cash flows	$2.75 million
Life of investment	10 years

Use straight-line depreciation (no salvage value) to do the after-tax analysis.

14–3 Basic Sensitivity Analysis Moorman Products Company is considering a new product that will sell for $10 and have variable costs of $6. Expected volume is 20,000 units. New equipment costing $150,000 and having a five-year useful life and no salvage value is needed, and will be depreciated using the straight-line method. The machine has cash operating costs of $20,000 per year. The firm is in the 40 percent tax bracket and has cost of capital of 12 percent.

REQUIRED

1. Determine the net present value of the investment.
2. Determine how many units per year the firm must sell for the investment to earn 12 percent.
3. Suppose the 20,000 estimated volume is sound, but the price is in doubt. Determine the selling price needed to yield a 12 percent return.

14–4 Cash Flows and Discount Rate The managers of Ferris division are contemplating a new product for their line of automobile accessories—special design wheels. Equipment is available to manufacture this product at $700,000. To accommodate the new product, some warehouse space in the plant will be turned into manufacturing space. Additional warehouse space will have to be leased at $10,000 per year with rent due at the beginning of each year. Management expects that the net of accounts receivable, cash, and inventory in excess of accounts payable to increase by $125,000 immediately. They feel that after two years they will be able to reduce the working capital level by $25,000. Sales are expected to be 10,000 units the first year and 15,000 the second year. Sales are then expected to grow at 10 percent per year. The equipment, according to the manufacturer, has a life expectancy of eight years; it will then have little, if any, salvage value. Ferris's marginal tax rate is 40 percent. ACRS depreciation, five-year, will be used.

There has been a discussion regarding the appropriate discount rate. Mr. Courtenay, Vice President of Finance, estimates that current after-tax cost of capital is about

11 percent. Because of inflation, however, the prime rate has been rising, with short-term borrowing rates of 12 percent and higher expected in the next few years before rates again level off near 10 percent. Thus, a rate tied to short-term rates could be used. Mr. Carver, President and a major shareholder, has suggested to Courtenay that a goal-oriented rate be established, based on corporate goals for the next five years. This rate was set at 15 percent.

The sales department has estimated that the sales price will be $50 per wheel to begin with, but should be raised $5 per wheel per year until it reaches $70. Other manufacturing fixed costs requiring cash associated with this project are $130,000 in the first year. Fixed costs are expected to go up $10,000 per year. Variable cost of goods sold (materials, labor, variable overhead) is estimated to be $30 per unit and, owing to inflation, will rise at about 8 percent per year.

REQUIRED

1. What is the appropriate discount rate? Justify your answer.
2. What is the net present value of this project, using the discount rate you have chosen in part 1? Round units sold to the nearest hundred, and round costs to two places.
3. Evaluate your NPV analysis from part 2.

14–5 Mutually Exclusive Investments Robin Corporation is considering two new pieces of equipment to replace an existing manufacturing process. The existing process is labor intensive, and since the equipment is getting old, maintenance costs are rising and both quality and efficiency are suffering. The production manager working with the cost accounting staff has narrowed possible new equipment purchases to machines from Gray, Inc., and from Leah Company. Fred Lyon, Production Manager, has written the following memo to Walter Reid, Manufacturing Vice President, on replacement equipment.

> As we have discussed, I am sending you this memo to summarize the costs and benefits from purchasing equipment from Gray or Leah. Either piece of equipment will last about five years and will produce equally high-quality products. The net cash flows (after all tax considerations) comparing each of these pieces to our existing equipment are:

	Gray	*Leah*
Net investment	$250,000	$150,000
Annual net savings (5 years)	$ 85,000	$ 45,000
Expected net salvage value	$ 0	$ 50,000

> Not only am I indifferent between the two from a production point of view, but I also feel we are indifferent financially since both yield about a 21% internal rate of return.

REQUIRED

1. Verify that the IRR of both projects is about 21 percent.
2. If the firm has a hurdle rate of 10 percent, what is the NPV of each project? Which project would you choose and why?

14–6 NPV, IRR, Payback (AICPA Adapted) The net present-value method and the internal rate of return method are both sophisticated capital budgeting techniques.

REQUIRED

1. State the advantages that both the net present-value method and the internal rate of return method have over the payback method.
2. State the limitations of the net present-value method.
3. State the limitations of the internal rate of return method.

14–7 Internal Rate of Return Beryl Products is considering two pieces of machinery. The first machine costs $50,000 more than the second machine. During the two-year life of these two alternatives, the first machine has a $155,000 more cash flow in year one and a $110,000 less cash flow in year two than the second machine. All cash flows occur at year-end.

REQUIRED

1. Which machine should be purchased if the relevant discount rate is 8 percent? 15 percent? 125 percent?
2. Which machine should be purchased if evaluated using IRR?

14–8 Investing and Financing Doe Manufacturing has an investment opportunity to embark on a project where yearly revenues for five years are expected to be $4,000 and operating costs $1,048. The equipment costs $10,000, and straight-line depreciation will be used for book and tax purposes. No salvage value is expected at the end of the project's life. The corporation has a 40 percent marginal tax rate and a 10 percent cost of capital. The equipment manufacturer has offered a delayed payment plan of $5,605 per year at the end of the first and second years. There will be no changes in working capital.

REQUIRED

Should Doe Manufacturing invest in this project? If not, why not? If so, why—and how should this project be financed?

14–9 JIT, Inventory The Greenville Plant of Busch Industries is moving toward JIT principles. So far it has been setting up manufacturing cells and smoothing the flow of work. The next phase involves a multitude of changes related to reducing the number of vendors, ensuring the quality of the parts provided by the remaining vendors, opening walls so that trucks can make deliveries straight to the cell where the parts are used, and teaching new skills to workers.

All of these activities are estimated to cost about $4.5 million, of which $3.0 million can be expensed immediately for income tax purposes. The remaining $1.5 million is for changes in physical plant that must be depreciated over the next 10 years, using the straight-line method. The estimated annual cash savings before taxes over the next 10 years are $250 thousand. Based on conversations with other plant managers, the Greenville Plant manager expects inventory to fall to about $80 thousand from the current $3.8 million. The tax rate is 40 percent and cost of capital is 12 percent.

REQUIRED

Determine the net present value of the investment.

14–10 Investing in Quality, JIT Inc., manufactures a variety of products in a relatively old plant. Parts of the manufacturing process are very outmoded and the quality of the output is slipping. The company is coming to be viewed as a low-quality producer, which is expected to affect future sales adversely. The manufacturing managers have been looking at new machinery and equipment that would increase quality so that the company could again enjoy a favorable reputation. They have also been considering JIT principles. Outfitting the plant for the new machinery and to accommodate JIT will cost about $5.5 million. The entire investment can be depreciated over its 10-year useful life. It has no salvage value. The company uses straight-line depreciation. The new machinery will not affect variable costs, but will increase cash fixed costs by $0.8 million per year.

The managers do not expect sales to increase markedly if they fail to make the investment. Rather, they expect sales to fall by about $2 million per year if they do not make the investment. The contribution margin ratio is about 60 percent on the normal product mix. The managers also expect to reduce inventory by $4.4 million if they make the investment. The tax rate is 40 percent and cost of capital is 12 percent.

REQUIRED

Determine the NPV of the proposed investment.

14–11 Capital-Budgeting Criteria The president of Crowlton Company is considering three investment opportunities, which are summarized below (in thousands of dollars):

	A	B	C
Investment	$2,500	$9,745	$6,645
Cash inflows, net:			
Year 1	0	1,000	3,000
Year 2	0	2,000	4,000
Year 3	0	3,000	1,000
Year 4	0	7,000	1,000
Year 5	8,650	6,000	0

The firm's cost of capital is 15 percent. The IRRs of the projects are: project A, 28 percent; project B, 20 percent; project C, 17 percent.

REQUIRED

Assuming that the projects are mutually exclusive, which one do you pick? Which one is your second choice?

14–12 Alternative Uses of Facilities (AICPA) Marshall Manufacturing, Inc., has produced two products, Z and P, at its Richmond plant for several years. Management is going to drop P from the product line as of January 1, 19X3. Marshall manufactures and sells 50,000 units of Z annually, which is not expected to change. Unit material and direct labor costs are $12 and $7, respectively.

The Richmond plant is in a leased building; the lease expires December 31, 19X7. Annual rent is $75,000. The lease provides Marshall the right of sublet; all nonremovable leasehold improvements revert to the lessor. At the end of the lease, Marshall intends to close the plant and scrap all equipment.

P has been produced on two assembly lines, which occupy 25 percent of the plant. The assembly lines will have a book value of $135,000 and a remaining useful life of seven years as of January 1, 19X3. This is the only portion of the plant available for alternative uses.

Marshall uses one unit of D to produce one unit of Z. D is purchased under a contract requiring a minimum annual purchase of 5,000 units. The contract expires December 31, 19X7. A list of D unit costs follows:

Annual Purchases (units)	Unit Cost
5,000– 7,499	$2.00
7,500– 19,999	1.95
20,000– 34,999	1.80
35,000– 99,999	1.65
100,000–250,000	1.35

Alternatives are available for using the space previously used to manufacture P. Some may be used in combination. All can be implemented by January 1, 19X3. Should no action be taken, the plant is expected to operate profitably, and manufacturing overhead is not expected to differ materially from past years when P was manufactured. Following are the alternatives:

1. Sell the two P assembly lines for $70,000. The purchaser will buy only if she can acquire the equipment from both lines. The purchaser will pay all removal and transportation costs.

2. Sublet the floor space for an annual rental of $12,100. The lease will require that the equipment be removed (cost nominal) and leasehold improvements costing $38,000 be installed. Indirect costs are expected to increase $3,500 annually as a result of the sublease.

3. Convert one or both P assembly lines to produce D at a cost of $45,500 for each line. The converted lines will have remaining useful life of ten years. Each modified line can produce any number of units of D up to a maximum of 37,000 units at a unit direct material and direct labor cost of $0.10 and $0.25, respectively. Annual manufacturing overhead is expected to increase from $550,000 to $562,000 if one line is converted and to $566,000 if both lines are converted. The marginal tax rate is 40 percent. The relevant discount rate is 15 percent. Straight-line depreciation is used.

REQUIRED

Prepare a schedule to analyze the best utilization of the following alternatives for the four years ended December 31, 19X7:

1. Continue to purchase D; sell equipment; rent space.

2. Continue to purchase D; sell equipment.

3. Produce D on two assembly lines; purchase D as needed.

4. Produce D on one assembly line; purchase D as needed.

14–13 Capital Budgeting and Pricing (CMA Adapted) Wardl Industries is a manufacturer of standard and custom designed bottling equipment. Early in December 19X3 Lyan Company asked Wardl to quote a price for a custom designed bottling machine to be delivered on April 1, 19X4. Lyan intends to make a decision on the purchase of such a machine by January 1 so Wardl would have the entire first quarter of 19X4 to build the equipment.

Wardl's standard pricing policy for custom designed equipment is 50 percent markup on full cost. Lyan's specifications for the equipment have been reviewed by Wardl's Engineering and Cost Accounting Departments, and they made the following estimates for raw materials and direct labor:

Raw materials		$256,000
Direct labor	11,000 DLH at $15	165,000

Manufacturing overhead is applied on the basis of direct labor hours. Wardl normally plans to run its plant 15,000 direct labor hours per month and assigns overhead on the basis of 180,000 direct labor hours per year. The overhead application rate for 19X4 of $9.00/DLH is based on the following budgeted manufacturing overhead costs for 19X4:

Variable manufacturing overhead	$ 972,000
Fixed manufacturing overhead	648,000
Total manufacturing overhead	$1,620,000

The Wardl production schedule calls for 12,000 direct labor hours per month during the first quarter. If Wardl is awarded the contract for the Lyan equipment, production of one of its standard products will have to be reduced. This is necessary because production levels can only be increased to 15,000 direct labor hours each month on short notice. Furthermore, Wardl's employees are unwilling to work overtime.

Sales of the standard product equal to the reduced production will be lost, but there will be no permanent loss of future sales or customers. The standard product whose production schedule will be reduced has a unit sales price of $12,000 and the following cost structure.

Raw materials		$2,500
Direct labor	250 DLH at $15	3,750
Overhead	250 DLH at $ 9	2,250
Total cost		$8,500

Lyan needs the custom designed equipment to increase its bottle-making capacity so that it will not have to buy bottles from an outside supplier. Lyan Company requires 5,000,000 bottles annually. Its present equipment has a maximum capacity of 4,500,000 bottles with a directly traceable cash outlay cost of $0.15 per bottle. Thus, Lyan has had to purchase 500,000 from a supplier at $0.40 each. The new equipment would allow Lyan to manufacture its entire annual demand for bottles at a raw material cost savings of $0.01 for each bottle manufactured.

Wardl estimates that Lyan's annual bottle demand will continue to be 5,000,000 bottles over the next five years, the estimated economic life of the special purpose equipment. Wardl further estimates that Lyan has an after-tax cost of capital of 15 percent and is subject to a 40 percent marginal income tax rate, the same rates as Wardl.

REQUIRED

1. Wardl Industries plans to submit a bid to Lyan Company for the manufacture of the special purpose bottling equipment.
   a. Calculate the bid Wardl would submit if it follows its standard pricing policy for special purpose equipment.

b. Calculate the minimum bid Wardl would be willing to submit on the Lyan equipment that would result in the same profits as planned for the first quarter of 19X4.

2. Wardl Industries wants to estimate the maximum price Lyan Company would be willing to pay for the special purpose bottling equipment.

a. Calculate the present value of the after-tax savings in directly traceable cash outlays that Lyan could expect to realize from the new special purpose bottling equipment.

b. Identify the other factors Wardl would have to incorporate in its estimate of the maximum price Lyan would be willing to pay for the equipment.

c. Describe how the cost savings (part 2a) and the other factors (part 2b) would be combined to calculate the estimate of the maximum price Lyan would be willing to pay for the equipment.

14–14 Sensitivity Analysis The management of Treefeather Winery in the Napa Valley is considering expanding by adding champagne to its existing line of still table wines. Champagne is made using different equipment and aging processes than the other wines. At the beginning of 19X2 management received a bid from Chandome Manufacturing to provide the necessary stainless steel tanks, fermenting racks, and automatic bottle turning equipment for $300,000 including installation costs. In addition, an existing tank that has no tax basis would be used for this project. Otherwise the tank would be sold as surplus equipment for $20,000. All the equipment has a life expectancy of at least ten years.

Champagne requires fermentation for three years in the bottles in which it will be sold. Thus, inventory of work in process will increase annually until the product matures and is sold. As each year's lot of champagne matures in three years, it will be sold in one block to Treefeather's distributor.

Production costs that can be inventoried will be $30,000 per year for the first three years. In the fourth year, pretax cash inflows from operations (excluding depreciation and its tax effect) are expected to be $100,000. These flows are expected to grow at 10 percent per year thereafter.

Besides the increase in work-in-process inventory, other inventories and cash net of accounts payable are expected to increase $50,000 within the first month of the new project. Treefeather's marginal tax rate is 40 percent, and its after-tax relevant discount rate is 10 percent. However, if this project is accepted, it will be financed using a 12 percent bank loan.

REQUIRED

Assume for ease of computation that all changes in working capital are recovered after ten years. Assume all cash flows are at the end of a period. Assume a ten-year life in your analysis (straight-line depreciation) as appropriate. Round all computations to the nearest dollar. [*Hint*: Read all the parts of the question before attempting to answer. If you think about how you are going to answer parts 2, 3, and 4 when you are setting up your analysis for part 1, you can save yourself time. You do not need to set everything up from scratch in each part. Establish some basic relationships and do sensitivity analysis].

1. Find the net present value of this project. Show and label all cash flows clearly.

2. What is the average annual pretax cash flow from operations (excluding the tax effect of depreciation) that Treefeather must achieve in years 4 through

10 in order to at least break even on a net present value basis? (Hold all other variables constant.)

3. If the annual pretax operating flows (excluding the tax effect of depreciation) are \$167,000 for years 4 through 10, how many full years will it take to achieve discounted payback? (Hold all other variables constant.)
4. If cash flows are as originally specified in the problem, how much would the bid from Chandome have to be to drive the net present value to zero? (Hold all other variables constant.)
5. Using your analysis from parts 1, 2, 3, and 4, make a recommendation to management about this project. If there is additional information you desire or factors to consider, state them clearly.

14–15 Sensitivity Analysis The management of Stump Iron Works, a company that fabricates metal parts, was investigating a new stamping process. Jack Stump, Vice President of Production, estimated the installed cost of this new process at \$100,000. He also knew that the company will have to experiment with this equipment, and he expected to spend \$20,000, \$10,000, and \$5,000, respectively, for research in each of the first three years of the project. Stump also estimated that the net increase in cash balances, inventory, and receivables offset by expected payables would be \$30,000 immediately and \$20,000 at the end of the first year. Stump uses straight-line depreciation for financial accounting and five-year ACRS for tax purposes. The marginal tax rate is 40 percent, and Stump requires that projects earn at least 15 percent after taxes.

REQUIRED

1. If annual fixed costs are \$60,000 and the project has a six-year life, what annual total pretax contribution margin is needed to break even on a present-value basis?
2. If the pretax contribution margin is estimated to be \$130,000 annually and the fixed costs, working capital needs, original investment, and life remain as stated above, what is the annual amount of research funds that Stump could expend in years one through three and still have a positive net present value of \$10,000?
3. Discuss the use of sensitivity analysis in capital budgeting decisions. Use examples from this assignment to illustrate your points.

14–16 Discounted Payback Gene Etics, the manager of Equine Products, has decided to use sensitivity analysis coupled with discounted cash flow techniques in evaluating a new product. He plans to do market research and to estimate the probabilities of this project's lasting various lengths of time. If he knows how sensitive various factors are to the time dimension, he can use this information in making a decision about the project.

The project involves providing a new way to supply minerals to horses. The entire concept includes manufacturing a disposable mineral feeder and two different mineral blocks—one for calcium and one for phosphorus.

He expects that new manufacturing equipment totaling \$500,000 will have to be bought. The physical life of the equipment is 10 years (but IRS regulations will allow five-year ACRS depreciation). This is special-purpose machinery and will have minimal salvage value if any. There will be an initial advertising budget in the first year of \$100,000, and current plans are for \$40,000 per year thereafter. It is expected that inventories and receivables will build, which, when offset against increased payables, will result in the following changes in working capital:

Year	Change in Working Capital
0	$200,000
1	150,000

The firm has a 40 percent marginal tax rate. Because of the riskiness of this project, management wants to use an 18 percent discount rate. Annual fixed costs of production are expected to be $500,000, not including depreciation.

REQUIRED

1. What total yearly pretax contribution margin is needed to break even on a net present-value basis?
2. If operating cash flows before taxes and the tax effect of depreciation are $400,000 per year, how many full years would it take to break even on a net present-value basis?

14–17 Inflation (CMA Adapted) Catix Corporation is a divisionalized company; each division has the authority to make capital expenditures up to $200,000 without approval of corporate headquarters. The corporate controller has determined that cost of capital for Catix Corporation is 12 percent. This rate does not include an allowance for inflation, which is expected to occur at an average rate of 8 percent over the next five years. Catix pays income taxes at the rate of 40 percent.

The Electronics Division of Catix is considering the purchase of an automated assembly and soldering machine for use in the manufacture of its printed circuit boards. The machine would be placed in service in early 19X1. The divisional controller estimates that if the machine is purchased, two positions will be eliminated, yielding a cost savings for wages and employee benefits. However, the machine would require additional supplies and more power would be required to operate the machine. The cost savings and additional costs in curent prices are as follows:

Wages and employee benefits of the two positions eliminated ($25,000 each)	$50,000
Cost of additional supplies	$ 3,000
Cost of additional power	$10,000

The new machine would be purchased and installed at the end of 19X0 at a net cost of $80,000. If purchased, the machine would be depreciated on a straight-line basis for both book and tax purposes. The machine will become technologically obsolete in four years and will have no salvage value at that time.

The Electronics Division compensates for inflation in capital expenditure analyses by adjusting the expected cash flows by an estimated price level index. The adjusted after-tax cash flows are then discounted using the appropriate discount rate. The estimated year-end index values for each of the next five years are presented below.

Year	Year-End Price Index
19X0	1.00
19X1	1.08
19X2	1.17
19X3	1.26
19X4	1.36
19X5	1.47

The Plastics Division of Catix compensates for inflation in capital expenditure analyses by adding the anticipated inflation rate to the cost of capital and then using the inflation adjusted cost of capital to discount the project cash flows. The Plastics Division recently rejected a project with cash flows and economic life similar to those associated with the machine under consideration by the Electronics Division. The Plastics Division's analysis of the rejected project was as follows:

Net pretax cost savings	$37,000
Less incremental depreciation expenses	20,000
Increase in taxable income	$17,000
Increase in income taxes (40%)	6,800
Increase in after-tax income	$10,200
Add back noncash expense (depreciation)	20,000
Net after-tax annual cash inflow (unadjusted for inflation)	$30,200
Present value of net cash inflows using the sum of the cost of capital (12%) and the inflation rate (8%) or a minimum required return of 20%	$77,916
Investment required	(80,000)
Net present value	$ (2,084)

All operating revenues and expenditures occur at the end of the year.

REQUIRED

1. Using the price index provided, prepare a schedule showing the net after-tax annual cash flows adjusted for inflation for the automated assembly and soldering machine under consideration by the Electronics Division.
2. Without prejudice to your answer to part 1, assume that the net after-tax annual cash flows adjusted for inflation for the project being considered by the Electronics Division are as follows:

	19X1	19X2	19X3	19X4
Net after-tax annual cash flow adjusted for inflation	$30,000	$35,000	$37,000	$40,000

   Calculate the net present value for Electronic Division's project that will be meaningful to management.

3. Evaluate the methods used by the Plastics Division and the Electronics Division to compensate for expected inflation in capital expenditure analyses.

14–18 The Abandonment Option It has been suggested that the decision tree framework for dealing with probabilities can be used in dealing with the abandonment option. When managers assess a project, they likely have an idea about possible cash flows and the probabilities of achieving these flows. In the decision tree framework of Chapter 12, we dealt with events and cash flows occurring in the *same* time period. Let us extend this analysis to multiple time periods. We have a single decision to make: Do we invest in a project? The events are cash flows in each year of a project's life.

One new aspect is the idea of an *abandonment value*. An easy way to think of this concept is to think of a plant nursery built on land in a suburb to a city. If you abandon the nursery business, the land has a sales value. When the current net sales value is greater than the net present value of the future flows from operating the business, it may be a good idea to abandon the business and sell the land.

Assume Hiburgler Company has an opportunity to invest \$11,000 in a project expected to last three years. Cash flows and the probabilities that management thinks are associated with them appear below. The relevant discount rate is 10 percent.

NET CASH FLOWS

YEAR 1		YEAR 2		YEAR 3	
Cash Flow	Probability	Cash Flow	Probability	Cash Flow	Probability
\$2,000	0.7	\$1,000	0.2	\$600	0.6
				\$1,000	0.4
		2,000	0.5	\$3,000	0.5
				\$5,000	0.5
		4,000	0.3	\$5,000	0.4
				7,000	0.6
4,000	0.3	5,000	0.2	6,000	0.6
				8,000	0.4
		8,000	0.5	10,000	0.5
				13,000	0.5
		10,000	0.3	14,000	0.4
				18,000	0.6

REQUIRED

1. Draw these cash flows and probabilities in a decision tree framework. To do this, you need to calculate joint probabilities and conditional values discounted at 10 percent. For example, the probability that cash flows in year 1 (C_1) = \$2,000, C_2 = \$1,000, and C_3 = \$600 is 0.7 × 0.2 × 0.6 = 0.084. The conditional value (present value at 10%) associated with that same chain of cash flows is (\$2,000)(0.9091) + (\$1,000)(0.8264) + (\$600)(0.7513) = \$3,095. You need to calculate the joint probabilities and conditional values for the other 11 branches. Round all figures to the nearest dollar.
2. Using the joint probabilities and conditional values, calculate an expected net present value.
3. Without considering any abandonment values, you should have come to a few-hundred-dollar *negative* NPV in part 2. Now assume that if you abandon

the project at the *end* of year one, you can receive a net abandonment value of \$5,000. In other words, you will receive a cash flow at the end of year one of either \$2,000 or \$4,000 *and* an additional \$5,000 if the project is abandoned at that time. Use the decision tree framework and see if it is wise to abandon the project after one year. You are seeing whether the expected present value of cash flows at the *end* of year one is greater than \$5,000. Thus, you will be repeating the same method you used in parts 1 and 2 *except* you will be dealing only with a two-year time frame (years two and three), with the year one cash flow not considered. You should see that you do *not* have to do this for the whole bottom half of the tree where C_1 = \$4,000, since all the NPVs in that half are positive. Thus, just do it assuming C_1 = \$2,000.

4. In part 3, the expected PV of the cash flows will be greater than \$5,000. Thus, you would not want to abandon after one year. Now assume that the abandonment value at the end of two years is \$4,000. Look at a one-year time frame (year three) given year two cash flows of \$1,000, \$2,000, or \$4,000 and see whether the expected value of year three flows is greater or less than \$4,000.

5. In part 4, you should find out that if C_2 = \$1,000 or \$2,000, it would be better to abandon the project at the end of year two rather than continuing on into year three. Amend the decision tree in parts 1 and 2 by including this information. To redraw the tree, you will be dealing with the following cash flows:

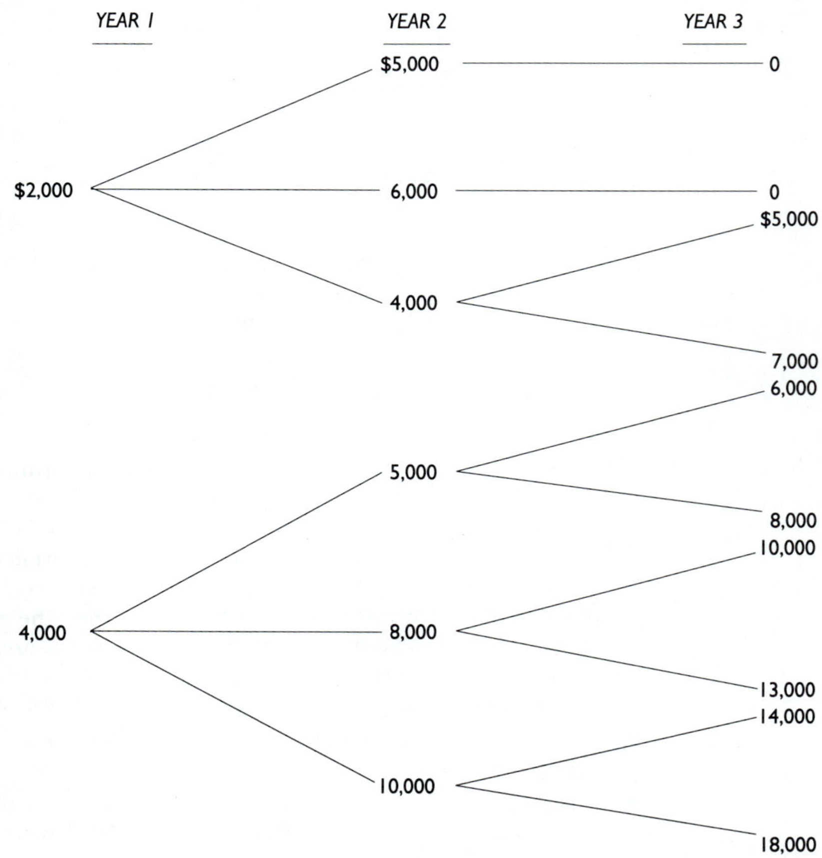

Put in the proper discounted conditional values and joint probabilities. Calculate a new expected NPV, given the inclusion of the abandonment option.

14–19 Capital Budgeting Criteria The capital budgeting manual of Turnburry Manufacturing Company contains the following statements:

> Investments will be defined in one of the following ways: new product or new market; expansion of capacity for existing products; replacement; and required by government regulation. The criteria for acceptance of investments in each category follow.
>
> *New product or market.* These investments are more speculative than the others and so must show higher returns. Any investment in this category must show an internal rate of return (IRR) of 18 percent after taxes and a payback period of no more than eight years. Cash flows to be included at the end of the eighth year for determining whether the payback criterion is met should include a 90 percent recovery of working capital investment and recovery of 50 percent of the net book value of fixed assets, adjusted for appropriate tax effects.
>
> When fixed assets have unequal lives, the useful life calculation shall be the weighted average. For example, if an investment of $400,000 has a 10-year life and another investment of $600,000 a 15-year life, the weighted average is 13 years (40% × 10) + (60% × 15).
>
> *Expansion.* These investments must show an IRR of 15 percent after taxes, along with a payback period not to exceed three-fourths of the useful life of the fixed investment.
>
> *Replacement.* Investments that replace existing facilities must earn a 12 percent after-tax IRR. There is no payback criterion.
>
> *Government-required investments.* Any investment required by governmental regulation will be made. Managers should determine the least-cost method of complying with the regulation, as measured by the present value of the total required outlay, both investment and operating costs, using an 18 percent discount rate.
>
> *Additional criteria.* The IRR and payback criteria given above assume that the investment is special purpose, so the machinery, equipment, and buildings could not be converted to general use. Where the investment is in general-purpose assets, the IRR for each category should be reduced by two percentage points and the payback period increased by two years (if applicable). These additional criteria reflect the lower risk associated with general-purpose investments.

REQUIRED

Assume that the cost of capital for the firm is about 13 percent. Discuss the criteria the firm uses, making sure to comment about the likely purpose of each criterion and whether it should accomplish the purpose. (For example, why include a payback criterion?) What problems do you see in using these criteria?

14–20 Eliciting Information and Capital Expenditure Analysis[7] Junior Executive has been asked to determine whether his company should trade in its old airplane and purchase a new one. The company manufactures and sells highly specialized, complex machinery, which often requires extensive technical selling, installation, and subsequent service. The airplane is used in the business for two purposes: (1) to transport company executives to plants of potential new customers or to bring the executives of potential customers to the company's office for sales demonstrations, and (2) to provide quick troubleshooting and repair service to customers.

The problem involves whether to replace a single-engine Arrow airplane with a

[7] Earl A. Spiller, Jr., "Capital Expenditure Analysis: An Incident Process Case," *The Accounting Review*, 56:1, January 1981, 158–165.

twin-engine Navajo model. The company is considering the larger plane for two reasons. First, its greater seating capacity will allow more people to be transported for sales demonstrations. Second, its ability to fly in adverse weather conditions will result in even faster repair service, thus enhancing the firm's reputation for reliable service. The president of the company finds it impossible to quantify the increased value of the larger airplane. Instead she has asked Junior to estimate by how much the new airplane would have to increase yearly sales to justify its purchase economically. Junior also is supposed to determine whether to lease the new airplane or to buy it outright, if the company decides to acquire it.

The company is using a four-seat Arrow purchased a year ago on January 5, 19X9, at a cost of $58,000. The airplane was flown more than 1,000 hours during the first year. It is common practice with this type of aircraft to have an extensive engine overhaul or exchange every 1,600 to 1,700 flying hours. Because the Arrow will be scheduled for this overhaul within the year, the president thinks that now is the ideal time to consider buying a larger plane.

The larger aircraft being considered is a six-seat Navajo. The dealer has offered the Navajo at a cash price of $294,500. The Arrow would be sold for $42,000 as a used airplane. Alternatively, the dealer will buy the Arrow for $50,000 and lease the Navajo to the company under a six-year noncancellable lease at a monthly rental of $5,200. The rental fee covers only the basic use of the aircraft and property taxes.

Junior has asked you to help him. He has access to all company data but has trouble deciding which data are relevant or how to formulate the decision framework. He must report to the president by January 10, 19Y0.

REQUIRED

You will be a member of a team that will consult with Junior Executive. Your instructor will give you more complete instructions. You will be meeting with and submitting questions to Junior Executive. The results of your analysis will be a written report to management recommending actions and supporting these recommendations with appropriate financial and other data.

14–21 Uncertainty Anthrax Company is considering two mutually exclusive projects. After estimating the cash flows of each and calculating the present values based on appropriate discount rates, they determined the following approximate probability distributions of net present values:

Project 1		Project 2	
Probability	*NPV*	*Probability*	*NPV*
0.3	$30,000	0.3	$ 1,000
0.4	40,000	0.4	35,000
0.3	50,000	0.3	70,000

REQUIRED

1. What is the expected NPV and the standard deviation for each project?
2. Which project is preferable and why?

14–22 Capital Rationing (CMA Adapted) Franklin Industries is composed of four divisions, each operating in a different industry. The divisions are currently preparing capital expenditure budgets for the coming year. Caledonia Division, located in the northeast United States, manufactures home appliances that it distributes nationally. The manufacturing and marketing departments of Caledonia have proposed six capital expenditure projects for next year. The Division Manager must analyze these investment proposals and select those projects to be included in the capital budget to be submitted to Franklin Industries. The proposed projects are listed below and are considered to have the same degree of risk.

Project A Redesign and modification of an existing product that is currently scheduled to be dropped. The enhanced model could be sold for six more years.

Project B Expansion of a line of cookware that has been produced on an experimental basis for the past year. The expected life of the cookware line is eight years.

Project C Reorganization of the plant's distribution center, including the installation of computerized equipment for tracking inventory. This project will benefit both administration and marketing.

Project D Addition of a new product, a combination bread and meat slicer. In addition to new manufacturing equipment, a significant amount of introductory advertising will be required. If this project is implemented, Project A will not be feasible because of limited capacity.

Project E Automation of the packaging department that will result in cost savings over the next six years.

Project F Construction of a building wing to house offices presently located in an area that could be used for manufacturing. The change will not add capacity for new lines but will alleviate crowded conditions, making it possible to improve the productivity of two existing product lines that have been unable to meet market demand.

Franklin Industries has established a hurdle rate of 12 percent for capital expenditures for all four divisions. Additional information about each of the proposed projects is presented below.

CALEDONIA DIVISION
Proposed Capital Projects

Required investment and operating after-tax cash flows by project:

	Project A	*Project B*	*Project C*	*Project D*	*Project E*	*Project F*
Capital investment	$106,000	$200,000	$140,000	$160,000	$144,000	$130,000
Operating after tax cash flows						
Year 1	$ 50,000	$ 20,000	$ 36,000	$ 20,000	$ 50,000	$ 40,000
Year 2	50,000	40,000	36,000	30,000	50,000	40,000
Year 3	40,000	50,000	36,000	40,000	50,000	40,000
Year 4	40,000	60,000	36,000	50,000	20,000	40,000
Year 5	30,000	60,000	36,000	60,000	20,000	40,000
Year 6	40,000	60,000		70,000	11,600	40,000
Year 7		40,000		80,000		40,000
Year 8		44,000		66,000		42,000
Total after tax cash flows	$250,000	$374,000	$180,000	$416,000	$201,600	$322,000

(*continued*)

Additional project information:						
Present value of operating cash flows at 12%	$175,683	$223,773	$129,772	$234,374	$150,027	$199,513
Net present value at 12%	$ 69,683	$ 23,773	$(10,228)	$ 74,374	$ 6,027	$ 69,513
Present value index (Profitability index)	1.66	1.12	.93	1.46	1.04	1.53
Internal rate of return	35%	15%	9%	22%	14%	26%
Payback period	2.2 years	4.5 years	3.9 years	4.3 years	2.9 years	3.3 years
Economic life	6 years	8 years	5 years	8 years	6 years	8 years

REQUIRED

1. If Caledonia Division has no budget restrictions for capital expenditures and has been told to maximize the value to the company, identify the capital investment projects that should be included in the Division's capital budget submitted to Franklin Industries. Explain the basis for your selection.
2. Without prejudice to your response to part 1, assume Franklin Industries has specified that Caledonia division will be restricted to a maximum of $450,000 for capital expenditures, and Caledonia should select projects that maximize the value to the company. Further, assume that any budget money not spent on the identified projects will be invested at the hurdle rate. Identify the capital investment projects Caledonia should include in its capital expenditures budget submitted to Franklin in this situation, and explain the basis for your selection.
3. Discuss the propriety of using the same hurdle rate for all four divisions of Franklin Industries.

14–23 Capital Rationing—Integer Programming Amorsh Company has the following cash constraints: it can invest $50,000 now, $40,000 in a year, and $30,000 in two years. It will not be possible to transfer funds between years. Management is evaluating four projects with the following characteristics:

			Net Cash Flows	
Project	*Net Present Value*	*Original Investment*	*Year 1*	*Year 2*
1	$4,000	$12,000	$ 6,000	$12,760
2	5,000	10,000	40,000	−25,850
3	3,000	18,000	−18,000	45,210
4	6,000	36,000	24,200	24,200

REQUIRED

Using the techniques described in Chapter 12 on linear programming, set up this rationing problem with an objective function and appropriate constraints. (Do not try to solve the problem.)

14–24 Leasing, Unequal Lives The president of Jasmin Corporation is evaluating two new projects that the director of manufacturing has proposed. Because of financial and space constraints, only one project will be accepted, if any.

One project is to produce a solar-powered water heater. Various equipment would have to be purchased to fabricate the solar panels and heater system. The total installed price quoted by the manufacturer of this equipment is $3,500,000. It is expected that completed heater systems will sell for $2,500 each for a 50-gallon model and $3,500 for a 100-gallon model. Market research has led the sales department to believe that the sales mix will be about three-fourths 50-gallon units and one-fourth 100 gallon units. They think that they will sell a total of 1,000 units the first year, 2,000 the second year, and that sales will grow by 400 units a year thereafter. Manufacturing costs are expected to be as follows:

	50-Gallon System	100-Gallon System
Materials	$ 800	$1,400
Labor	400	400
Variable overhead	300	300
	$1,500	$2,100

Fixed manufacturing overhead and additional sales costs are $500,000 (not including any depreciation) and are expected to increase by 15 percent per year.

It is expected that the technology for solar heaters will remain stable for at least seven years. Working capital requirements are estimated to be $500,000 and will be fully recovered at the end of the life of the project.

The other proposal is to make projection television sets. The price for these sets is $3,000 each. Management is proposing that almost all the sophisticated parts of the set be made internally, while the cabinet will be purchased from an outside source. This venture is expected to last 10 years. Investment in equipment will be $3 million. Costs of starting up in year one will be $300,000 (fully deductible), and $200,000 in additional working capital (fully recoverable) is expected to be needed. Variable costs of manufacturing and buying components are expected to be $1,800 per unit. Fixed manufacturing (excluding depreciation) will be $400,000 per year. Advertising and sales costs are planned at $300,000 to begin with and will increase proportionally to sales. Sales volume is expected to start at 1,500 units and increase at 10 percent per year (rounded to the nearest 50 units).

The hurdle rate that management has set is 10 percent after taxes. Prices and variable costs are to be kept stable per unit for this analysis. The marginal tax rate is 40 percent. No equipment is expected to have a salvage value. ACRS depreciation (five-year life) is used for tax purposes.

REQUIRED

1. Evaluate the water heater system.
2. Evaluate the television project.
3. Since one project is expected to last three years longer than the other, state how you will choose between them. What information would you need?
4. The management of Jasmin has been offered 8 percent financing from its major bank and has been offered a lease by the manufacturer of the equipment for the television project as follows: ten equal payments of $450,000 to be paid at the end of each year. Assuming that these are the only two viable financing alternatives open at this time, which should be chosen if management decides to invest in the television project?

Part III

BUDGETING AND CONTROL

15

COST MANAGEMENT: GENERAL AND BEHAVIORAL ASPECTS

Management accounting covers the cycle from planning to controlling. Based on a company's mission, managers set goals and objectives and develop strategies and operating plans to achieve them. This is the planning phase. As managers evaluate whether strategies and tactics are accomplishing their goals and objectives and whether to update these goals and objectives, managers are in the controlling stage. As you might expect, both goal setting and assessing performance based on goals can involve heightened feelings among managers. If a manager will be evaluated on his or her performance based on plans, the manager wants these plans to be reasonable, fair, and based on operations under his or her control, to name a few conditions. The evaluation phase, then, should include reasonable measures of success based on factors that the manager can control.

While planning and controlling have always been integral parts of management, changing competitive and manufacturing environments have increased managers' awareness of the importance of good information to support these functions. Managers must react faster to changes in the competitive environment. If a major competitor is coming out with a new product line, managers must react quickly to retain or gain market share; they want to beat the competition to the market. In the new environments, traditional measures of performance are inadequate. While traditional monetary measures of success retain their importance, the marketplace warrants new measures including quality, technological leadership, and vendor relationships. The changing environment, the need for immediate action, and the need for new measures to evaluate how managers and segments are doing are sparking a new interest in both planning and controlling.

As we discussed in earlier chapters, companies in Japan, Korea, and other places have increasingly dominated some industries. The changes in Europe in 1992 are causing companies to change their plans. Ongoing changes in Eastern Europe might open new markets to U.S. manufacturers. Manufacturing is changing as well. In Chapter 4 we discussed how some companies are incorporating computer-controlled equipment with the result of raising equipment and overhead costs, lowering direct labor, and blurring what is a direct or indirect cost in the old financial accounting framework. However, some U.S. companies have not been affected by competition from companies in other countries; some companies are still competitive using labor-based manufacturing processes.[1] Thus, when we discuss behavioral issues regarding planning and controlling, we must consider the varied nature of the service and manufacturing sectors and how they are changing.

RELATIONSHIPS WITH EARLIER AND LATER CHAPTERS

In this chapter we discuss some general concepts and behavioral issues related to planning and controlling. Virtually all the material in this book involves some part of the needs that Chapter 4 outlined:

1. cost of products for managerial decision making
2. product costs for financial accounting
3. operational control
4. special studies

This division is based on different information for different decisions. As stated in Chapter 4, our emphasis is on internal decision making. Thus in this chapter changes needed in cost of products for managerial decision making and operation control are of special importance.

Both cost of products for managerial decision making and operational control information are based on the idea of traceability of costs and control over costs. In cost-volume-profit (CVP) analysis we separated costs by behavior and discussed the artificiality of fixed-cost per unit figures since changes in quantity do not affect fixed costs within the relevant range. Chapter 4 illustrated how incorrect attribution of costs to products can lead to poor decisions

[1]These companies do not necessarily do everything by hand, but they have about the same mix of people and machinery that they have had for years. They are competitive and low-tech.

regarding pricing and assessment of product profitability. We also illustrated the difference between costs needed for financial accounting purposes and those for managerial purposes, with the latter relying on all traceable costs associated with a product. Traceable costs are those that stop if the product is dropped.[2] Such cause-and-effect attribution might also mean that specific managers have control over these costs. We also saw that whether a cost is traceable or common is a matter of the decision at hand; at some point all costs are traceable and someone has control over them.[3] Thus, in these early chapters we learned some basic tenets of management accounting:

1. *Cost behavior.* Costs are either variable or fixed. Managers must know what changes in volume (e.g., direct labor hours, machine hours, or units) or what changes in activities (e.g., setups, number of orders, or number of shipments) affect variable and step-variable costs.
2. *Activities cause costs.* All costs are tied to some activity; costs do not come into being on their own. Hiring an additional person to schedule production is the result of increased complexity and activity in the scheduling department.
3. *Traceable costs are the key to good information.* Including common costs can cause dysfunctional behavior.
4. *Cost responsibility.* All costs can be controlled in the long run. Most costs can be controlled in the short run. In all cases, some manager or group of managers is responsible for all costs (and revenues). In fact, companies should be organized into responsibility centers, a subunit under the control of a manager.

In the following chapters we explore the budgeting cycle and several topics related to evaluating the performance of business segments and their managers. In previous chapters we looked at what might appear to be discrete topics (e.g., normal costing, capital budgeting techniques, linear programming). In fact, these topics are not separate. In what follows, however, the need to integrate topics from several areas becomes clearer. For example, budgeting involves CVP relationships, use of scarce resources (linear programming), and costs based on standards. Budgets will be traced to different departments, segments, and managers. The budget is a concrete plan that shows, in monetary form, how managers expect to achieve goals and objectives and what strategies and tactics they will use. In Chapters 17, 18, and 19 we deal with segment and managerial performance evaluation. The budget is the basis for much evaluation, along with other monetary measures as well as non-monetary mea-

[2] Again, this is not literally true. Some traceable costs (e.g., setup, material-handling, finished-goods, and shipping) may not disappear immediately unless more than one product is dropped. We discuss how this problem affects behavior later in this chapter.

[3] We can dispute this statement in that some costs are common to the entire company and some are not controllable since they are fixed by long-term contracts. However, even these cases include a level of traceability, even if at the corporate level, and usually something can be done to deal with costs even those tied to a long-term arrangement.

sures. Before these topics, let us discuss some basic behavioral aspects and problems.

THE BUDGETING CYCLE

Budgets are useful in planning, coordinating, communicating, and negotiating within a company. Figure 15–1 diagrams the overall budgeting cycle. The arrows in the figure give a basic idea of the process; in reality, these arrows go back-and-forth between the activities. A considerable amount of reappraisal, redevelopment, and re-evaluation occurs at each stage. Budgeting is a continuous and dynamic process that looks to the future.

Goals and objectives are usually expressed in general terms, such as to *increase market share*, to *be the technological leader in the field*, or to *control cost*. However, managers must adopt specific plans or strategies to accomplish these goals. For example, to increase market share, managers set targets for each product line for the year. Setting these targets requires considering, among other things, planned product availability, product prices, sales incentives, physical and human resources to produce these products, financial resources to fund the required activities, research and development, and cost control to become more competitive. The budget reflects each of these targets. The budget is the prime way that operating managers know what is expected of them and what resources they have to carry out plans. Budgets put teeth into a com-

FIGURE 15–1 The Budgeting Process

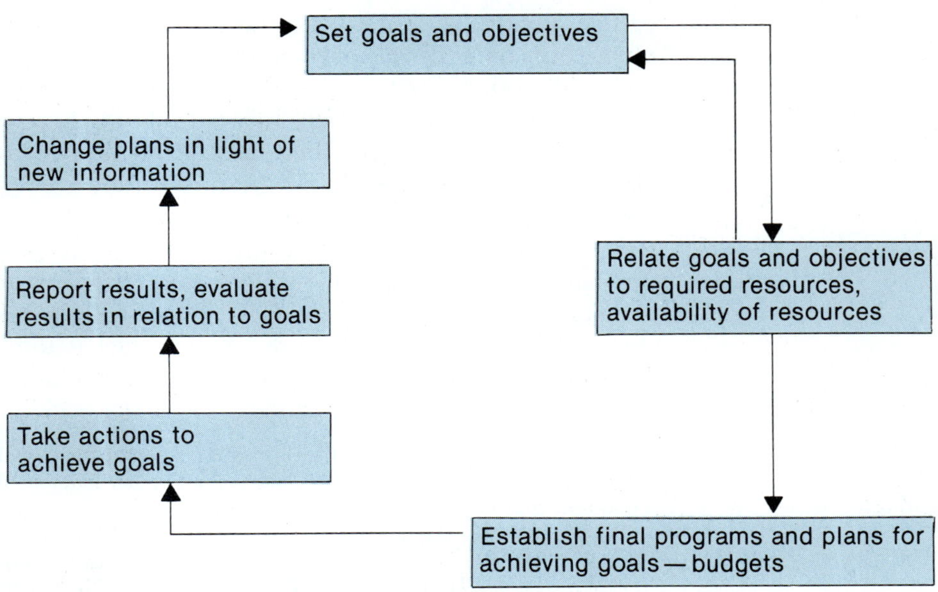

pany's plans. If upper management wants the company to be a leader in product innovation, lower level managers expect commitments to research, development, and engineering. If insufficient resources are budgeted, this is testimony that either the goal needs to be redefined or the budget adjusted.

Budgets can include both monetary and non-monetary information. For example, a budget specifies how parts and components are to be manufactured or purchased. It also reflects estimates and assumptions regarding lead time (the time it takes between placing an order and delivery), quality (not only defect rates, but also quality in the field after a product is delivered), and technology.

KEY FACTORS OF SUCCESS

In the planning process it is important to identify a few key factors (sometimes called *key result areas* or *critical success factors*),[4] which vary from industry to industry. In some industries, quality is paramount. In others, being innovative and technologically ahead is important. In industries in the mature part of their life cycle, cost (and, therefore, price) control is critical. When a product line is in a declining stage, attention focuses on when to cease operations. Managers should plan strategies that will enable the company to achieve these critical factors.

The importance of identifying critical success factors is that they enable managers to focus on a few areas, not to try to watch everything. Thus, budgets should highlight these factors. If cost control is especially important, managers want detailed estimates of direct costs and support department costs associated with certain product groups. For a product in its infancy, managers focus on development and engineering costs and capital equipment acquisition plans. Put another way, managers must analyze the means to achieve their goals and must have reasonable ideas of the effectiveness and efficiency of different ways of achieving them. This is a major role of the budget.

At the other end of the cycle, budgets are the basis for comparison. In a standard cost setting, such as that developed in Chapters 7 and 8, variances are individual and collective signals that operations differed from the budget. Many managers use actual costs as a basis for comparison; for instance, this month's costs should be better than last month's. In this case, the budget is a reflection of expected improvement over the year. Deviations from the budget mean that plans were not met or were exceeded. Therefore, the budget forms an important feedback link to managers.

[4] See J. R. Daniel, "Management Information Crisis," *Harvard Business Review*, 43:5 (September–October 1961), for an analysis of informational requirements related to success factors. Robert N. Anthony, John Dearden, and Norton M. Bedford *Management Control Systems*, 5th ed. (Homewood, Ill.: Richard D. Irwin, Inc., 1984), also consider the points in their Chapter 4.

BUDGETS AND PLANNING

A master budget consists of an interrelated coordinated group of forecasts—plans for the future. Some of the forecasts are in financial statement form. Examples are a budgeted income statement, budgeted balance sheet, and budgeted statement of changes in financial position. These statements are often called **pro forma** financial statements as well as budgeted statements. A pro forma statement is one made *for the form*, including the hypothetical transactions planned for the coming period rather than historical transactions.

Other forecasts in the budget include production quantities and costs, capital asset requirements, personnel requirements, levels of activity in various departments, and financing through short-term debt, long-term debt, and common stock.

Budgets are developed in one of two general ways. In the top-down approach, upper level managers state what they expect from their subordinate managers in regard to production, sales, costs, personnel, and other factors. Lower level managers then negotiate with upper level managers the items that they do not think reasonable. For example, if upper level management sends a budgeted sales figure of $400,000 to a district manager, he may try to have it modified on grounds that it is not realistically achievable. As another example, the data processing manager might be given a budget that requires cutting two employees. She might argue that such a cut would severely impair the service that the department provides. Whether these negotiations work out as the lower level managers hope is another matter.

The other way to develop budgets is to start at the bottom, with managers of responsibility centers proposing what they expect to accomplish and what resources (principally personnel and cash) they believe necessary to achieve their goals. Upper level managers then make revisions and suggestions, ask questions regarding the importance of various activities, and perhaps require resubmission. For example, a district sales manager might ask for six additional salespeople and an increase in her travel and entertainment budget over the previous year's figure. Her requests probably would be accompanied by an explanation of how she planned to use the salespeople and travel money, why the firm would benefit, and what unfavorable results might come from a failure to meet her requests. A good deal of discussion might take place between the district manager and upper level managers before they reached agreement. Both the top-down and the bottom-up methods usually involve negotiation and revision until a final budget is accepted.

BUDGETING AND RESPONSIBILITY ACCOUNTING

A good budgeting system is an indispensable component of a responsibility accounting system. Each **responsibility center** has budgeted objectives and resources for accomplishing them. The budget indicates what is required of each manager, and comparisons of budgeted and actual results enable managers to see whether particular centers meet their objectives and efficiently used resources.

The assignment of responsibility to centers is facilitated by a careful examination of budgets. This is especially true when budgets submitted by individual managers show clearly what the money is needed for—what the department (center) expects to accomplish. Duplication and gaps may become apparent when budget requests detail the objectives of the centers. In contrast, when budgets are simply requests for money based on prior-year amounts or on some expansion of activities, the manager evaluating the budget request has no real idea what the firm is getting for its money.

Many organizations, especially governments, follow the practice of **line budgeting**. Individual managers submit budget requests detailing the items of expenditure—salaries, supplies, travel, and so on—with no indication of the contribution that the unit should make to the goals of the organization. Indeed, it is sometimes difficult to see what the goals and objectives of the unit are by examining its budget request. In contrast, **program budgeting** focuses on objectives; it requires managers to justify their budget requests by showing what they will accomplish with the resources given them. Program budgeting also forces managers to show how the accomplishment of the departmental goals contributes to the accomplishment of the organization goals. Zero base budgeting, another technique for improving the process, is discussed in the appendix.

ADVANTAGES OF BUDGETING

Systematic Planning

Many industries face rapidly changing environments. The life cycle of many products is short; changes in the marketplace come quickly. In such cases, some managers argue that budgeting is not worthwhile; if reality is always changing, how can any set of plans be meaningful? While it is correct for managers (and companies) to remain flexible, there are good arguments for why budgeting is appropriate even in a dynamic environment.

Earlier we discussed accuracy versus precision; when dealing with the cost of a product, it is important to know that it costs about $20 per unit rather than worrying about a cost to the penny. The same thing is true with budgets. While budgets are specific, they are not expected to be followed to the last dollar. Budgets reflect the quantitative results of following a set of plans to achieve a given set of goals and objectives. As these plans need adjustment, managers are expected to adapt and adjust accordingly.

In addition, even in a dynamic environment managers must plan. Every action that a manager takes implies some expected result. Budgets make these plans explicit and subject to more objective scrutiny. Consider a company in a growing market. A cash budget is important to make sure that the company can grow and remain solvent. If an unexpected order comes in, various budgets will have to be adjusted. As a result, the chief financial officer can use an updated cash budget to explore what problems and options exist. Without an original budget, that manager may not have sufficient information to see if there is a cash problem.

Managers cannot focus their attention solely on running day-to-day operations. To do so ignores the future, which can have disastrous results. To a great extent the future is a product of the past and present, and the actions that managers now take or do not take can greatly affect the future. As explored above, the most common example is planning (or lack of it) for financing requirements given rapid growth. Paradoxically, successful, growing firms can experience cash shortages and the threat of bankruptcy.

The fact that budgets force managers to plan is important. Managers must state their premises and expectations and consider the possible consequences of their actions. A formal budgeting process provides a systematic framework for planning and control, which is more likely to be successful than a wait-and-react approach to management.

Chapter 12 emphasized systematic decision making, as opposed to the random or inspirational type.[5] Budgeting is a form of systematic decision making, because the plans that a firm makes require decisions about numbers of workers to hire, quantities of various components to make, raw materials and components to buy, and many other matters. If conditions change and the original budget no longer seems feasible, it will still have served a purpose, because it will make it easier for managers to adapt to the changed conditions. That is, managers who have a budget can adapt better to changing circumstances than managers without one. The discipline of developing the formal relationships involved in the budgeting process will help them understand how changed conditions should affect their planning and decision making in the future.

RESPONSIBILITY ACCOUNTING AND HUMAN BEHAVIOR

We can see that budgeting has behavioral components. Managers might not believe more accurate accounting information or might use such information illogically. This leads us to an examination of some basic principles of human behavior and management accounting.

Budgets are quantitative and monetary plans used as a reference point in the control process. Thus, managers have a stake in the budgeting process. In addition, accounting is not just numbers. As we explore in Chapter 17, man-

[5] See especially the quotation from Morris, *Decision Making*, on pages 519–520 in Chapter 12.

agers look to accounting to help develop not only new nonfinancial quantitative measures of success, but also nonquantitative measures.[6]

The Traditional Role of Responsibility Accounting

Originally, budgets were seen as devices to check up on operating managers. In this scenario, budgets were imposed from the top of the organization. Usually, upper management was authoritarian and workers were viewed as lazy and motivated only by money. It is a natural extension of these ideas that budgets should be used as part of close supervision to control behavior. The emphasis in such a system is on inadequate performance.

A manager who accepts such traditional assumptions is wary of relinquishing any authority. The manager does not trust subordinates and wants to keep a close watch on them. However, it is usually not possible for upper level managers to exercise such supervision. They simply do not have the time to control everything themselves.

McGregor[7] argued that authoritarian managers work out of this problem by using staff personnel such as accountants and engineers. These staff people collect information that the manager uses to control the operation. Budget information and standard cost variances are good examples. Thus, the accountant became the eyes and ears for the authoritarian manager.

Because budgets were imposed top-down, lower level managers did not participate. Thus, the budget was not only beyond the control of operating managers, but also used as a club by upper management. A result of this type of management was a focus on meeting short-term budget results no matter what the consequences. In addition, since the budget system was considered unfair, managers worked to circumvent it.[8]

Modern Behavioral Considerations

In a modern setting, management style is quite different from the old authoritarian mold. (Of course, not all companies accept modern behavioral assumptions nor employ the techniques this section describes.) Management sees people as diverse and working for many reasons, including job satisfaction. Managers and subordinates now work as a team; the entire enterprise is successful when each of its members trusts the other members. Workers are viewed as an integral part of the planning and controlling process. Quality circles are

---

[6] Examples of these measures are found in Daniel P. Keegan, Robert G. Eiler, and Charles R. Jones, "Are Your Performance Measures Obsolete?," *Management Accounting* (June 1989), pp. 45–50.

[7] Douglas McGregor, *The Human Side of Enterprise* (New York: McGraw-Hill Book Company), 1960.

[8] A classic on this topic is Chris Argyris, *The Impact of People on Budgets* (New York: Financial Executives Research Foundation), 1952.

one example of how upper management seeks workers' ideas to establish plans to meet stated objectives.

In this setting, accounting is seen as a feedback mechanism equally useful for the manager and the managed. While information is not entirely neutral,[9] budgets are not seen as pressure devices. Rather, they are a way for managers to negotiate about resources and to communicate about strategies. In the main, budgets are seen as a basis for planning rather than a fixed objective.

In addition, since people are seen as diverse and motivated by different things, there is no single best way to budget or administer responsibility accounting. In a stable, mature industry, top-down budgets may be accepted and appropriate; nothing much changes and top management has the records to generate the budget. However, in a company with considerable uncertainty and complexity, participation and a bottom-up budget might be best. Managers close to the diverse operations will know more about what might happen than will upper level managers. This is a virtue of decentralized management, as we discuss in Chapter 17.

Implementing New Cost Management Systems

Because managers are evaluated partly through budgets, the budgeting process as well as the evaluation process must take human behavior into account. One side of the budgeting process is receiving new attention from managers: the implementation of new manufacturing accounting systems based on (1) the separation of costs to serve the four needs listed early in this chapter, and (2) the introduction of activity-based cost attribution. Product costs for financial accounting affect income, a basic monetary, quantitative measure used to evaluate performance. Costs of products for managerial decision making are used when pricing, determining the resources to manufacture products, and in dealing with the best use of scarce resources. Therefore, both costs related to financial accounting and those for managerial decision making might affect budgeting and operational control.

As we illustrated in Chapter 4, a cost system can not only produce inaccurate figures, but these figures can also lead to dysfunctional decisions. We looked at the Sanibel Company, where the cost system was based on a single cost driver, direct labor hours. A study of resources and how they were used identified several other cost drivers. While the new system was more accurate, the results (product costs under the old and the new systems) were not significantly different. Thus, even if managers used inaccurate costs, they would probably make correct decisions. However, the same chapter looked at the Lighthouse Company, where the new cost system was not only more accurate than the old, but the resulting numbers were substantially different. Managers using the original, direct labor based system would make poor decisions regarding pricing and sales efforts, and incorrect evaluations of product profitability.

[9] For information to be absolutely neutral, it cannot affect or bias decision making in any way. Although difficult to accomplish, this is the objective of accounting information.

Managers (like most of us) resist change. Consider an operating manager and an accounting manager in a company that had been applying overhead using a plantwide rate based on direct labor hours. The system has worked for a long time and the company has been doing well. In this kind of a system, managerial attention is focused on controlling direct labor (labor efficiency variances, for example) for each task. Operating managers had machines arranged by type (e.g., all the grinding machines in one part of the factory) and budgeting and control followed this arrangement. It would be common in such a company for a single cost system to serve the uses of financial accounting, managerial decision making, and operational control. Lest we be too critical of this approach, it worked for this company for many years. When it was instituted, the company was labor based and had a fairly low level of complexity in the plant—it produced relatively few products.

However, in recent years, the basic competitive and manufacturing environments of this company have changed. Growth has brought with it a host of additional products, some long run and some short run. In addition, industrial engineers have rearranged the physical facilities into manufacturing cells where similar components are fabricated. This rearrangement has reduced the need for in-process inventories and material handling and storage support costs. Finally, the newest machinery is digitally controlled (also called *numerically controlled*). This machinery incorporates automatic quality checking by using a video camera where drilled holes are checked for placement and size specifications; any components that fail this test are automatically rejected from the assembly line. Workers perform more support duties than direct labor jobs. Within the manufacturing cell, workers move from task to task as the flow of the production process dictates. Rather than being in charge of one or two machines, workers are now part of a team in a mini-factory, the manufacturing cell.

As we demonstrated in Chapter 4, a change in complexity means more support department costs. In addition, labor has become virtually a fixed cost and a much smaller percentage of total manufacturing costs (less than 10 percent). The system needs to be revised to account for new cost drivers; while managers are used to volume-based drivers, new measures include activities such as number of components, setups, and shipments. In addition, the company has adopted quality as a major goal; its major competitors are known to be high quality and this company cannot afford to be viewed as having lesser quality. In this environment, managers are more interested in looking at overall measures of efficiency. The focus is on the process as a whole rather than on its parts.

These kinds of changes in how costs are accumulated and how they are used may be too much for some managers to accept. While a company has progressed technologically, its managers are lagging behind in believing in change. After all, the company has been successful using the existing system. Managers may think that nothing is really wrong with the system and that this attention to change is just a fad. In some cases, the news brought about by the new cost system may be so depressing that the changed system is rejected. In a labor based system, short-run products look relatively more profitable and long-run products look relatively less profitable when compared to an activity based system. Imagine a company where managers thought they were making lots of money on short-run items and have directed their sales force to solicit these kinds of jobs. When activity based costs are accumulated, they may reveal that these products are actually *losing* money and strategies that managers thought would improve profits are really strangling the company. This may be too much for many managers to believe. They rationalize that it's all accounting numbers anyway—the new system is no better than the old. This might lead to the death of the company.[10]

New cost systems can also lead to dysfunctional behavior even when managers believe in them. In one New England company, managers rearranged the plant into manufacturing cells and went to just-in-time inventory (JIT). The result was the virtual elimination of work in process and attendant support department costs for materials handling, moving, and storage. In fact, about 25 percent of the plant was freed up in the process. Two interesting things happened, however. First, upper management did not change how they evaluated the plant given the change in production methods. They were unable to see that the change from a traditional factory layout to cells and from workers being in charge of one machine and one task to being part of a team that manufactured entire components would be slow to take effect. Both managers and workers had to unlearn old ways as well as learn new ones. Costs might actually increase in the short run until everyone was comfortable with the new setting. Thus, upper level managers should have focused on whether the timetable for conversion to the new process was being followed, whether costs were in line with the budget during the conversion, and the effect on throughput, lead time, and employee morale.

The second problem came about from the freeing of space within the plant. Another plant owned by the same company produced a single product. After an incremental cost analysis, it was clear that it was cost effective for the other plant to be closed down and its operations and workers moved to the New England plant. About a year after the move, however, the plant controller commented, "It's interesting. The products we had here before we closed down the other plant are now more profitable while the product we brought here from the other plant is less profitable." How is this possible? An incremental cost analysis showed that it was *cheaper* to make the product in the New England plant; how could it be less profitable? The problem was that even though the company had adopted up-to-date manufacturing ideas, the cost system was still single purpose. Managers had taken plant occupancy costs and had divided them based on square footage between the existing product and the new one. Obviously the existing product had fewer costs allocated to it: 75 percent rather than 100 percent. However, the 25 percent allocation to the new product was more than the occupancy costs of the entire plant in its origi-

[10] A good discussion of this topic is in Thomas B. Lammert and Robert Ehrsam, "The Human Element: The Real Challenge in Modernizing Cost Systems," *Management Accounting* (July 1987), pp. 32–37.

nal setting. Therefore, the cost system made it *look* as if the new product were less profitable after the move. As we discussed in Chapter 10, this scenario is unreasonable and leads to poor decision making.

While this problem might seem related either to cost of products for managerial decision making or to support department allocation issues, such costs and allocations are part of corporate budgets. Thus, managers might come to incorrect conclusions about strategies to follow given this budgetary information.

DYSFUNCTIONAL BEHAVIOR

Even with modern management philosophies, the planning and controlling processes can lead to dysfunctional behavior. Managers must budget and evaluate others' performance carefully. Both the budgeting process and resulting evaluation might lead to unexpected results.

Unnecessary Spending

Sometimes budgeting can lead to behavior contrary to organizational needs. Such behavior is called a lack of *goal* or *behavior congruence*. Say a company is trying to control costs and is budgeting next year's sales expenses. The sales manager had a $20,000 travel and entertainment budget for this year. However, she has only used $12,000 of that total to date, and based on current needs does not see that she would use more than another $4,000 by year end. On one hand, this seems good; costs are lower than budget. However, the sales manager is planning next year's efforts and might be afraid that if she does not use all of this year's budget, her resources for next year will be curtailed. Thus, to protect her position in the budgeting process, she spends the $20,000 to make the point that she "needs" at least that same amount next year.

The same kind of behavior can be seen in governmental agencies. Budgets are based on line items, that is, money is appropriated for a specific use such as the purchase of computer equipment. As the year draws to a close and money is left in the computer equipment line, managers will buy equipment (even if it is not really needed) since (1) if they do not spend it this year it will not be available to spend next year, and (2) if they spend less than the budget, the budget will be cut for next year.

Budgetary Slack

Even in modern organizations, there is a push to beat last year's numbers. This might cause managers to pad their budget requests to make themselves look good as the year progresses. Revenues might be understated and costs overstated in such a situation. At a regional repertory theatre, the budget was always supposed to show no worse than a breakeven for the year. However, professional managers and the volunteer board knew that there was a certain amount of risk inherent in the season. Single ticket revenues depended on reviews by critics and were affected by competing events (e.g., baseball play offs). Costs for some plays were more uncertain than others. To allow for these uncertainties, the budget was permitted to include some slack—conservative estimates that would allow some managerial flexibility as the season progressed.

Managers in a new manufacturing setting might be prone to include budgetary slack. They have no experience to budget costs and performance. Thus, to be safe (and to look better) they will underestimate production and overestimate costs. These same managers might have been much more optimistic when they proposed the capital project for the new machinery or equipment.

Incorrect Performance Measures

One cause of dysfunctional behavior is incorrect performance measures. In Chapters 7 and 8 we developed standard cost variances. We noted that one manager could affect the performance of others, for example, by buying inferior materials that lead to unfavorable material use variances. If there is an unfavorable material use variance not linked with a favorable purchase price variance because of inferior materials, management might come to incorrect conclusions about operations. In addition, in new manufacturing environments, managerial focus on standard cost variances might be unwarranted.

Variances are based on several premises. First, there is the tendency to look at labor as the driving force and, therefore, to stress labor efficiency variances. Even in a labor based environment, this impulse might be dysfunctional. With absorption costing, a manager can affect labor use and overhead application by producing more units. In a new environment where labor is a small part of total costs and is relatively fixed, to focus on labor is to pay attention to the wrong thing. Even material use variances take on lesser meaning since a stress on vendor quality and zero defects in production makes these variances quite small.

Variances, even when they are linked one to another, still focus on individual operations in the main (e.g., departments) and, within departments, might be divided into cost classifications (materials as opposed to labor, for example). Today, many managers want to take a broader view of the entire manufacturing process. Labor efficiency in one department may be causing a line imbalance and the creation of additional work in process. The traditional cost system does not capture this information. On one hand the management accounting system shows that the manager is being efficient, while on the other hand the manager causes inefficiencies in the overall operation by creating a surplus of buffer stock between departments.

MANAGEMENT REPORTS

The next few chapters deal with different parts of management reports. Chapter 16 shows the full budget cycle and reports that go along with it. Chapters 17, 18, and 19 deal with decentralized organizations and how they are evaluated. Since reports are used by managers in both planning and controlling and since the marketplace and the plant are changing, managers should direct their attention to creating new types of useful reports.

This is the computer age. At very little cost, we are capable of creating reams of paper, data dealing with the most minute details. However, managers want us to organize these data into useful information. Having a good data base is necessary to create useful information, but the data by themselves are not useful.[11] Managers want quantitative financial, quantitative nonfinancial, and qualitative information regarding critical factors of success. Since most organizations are hierarchical, reports should also be tailored to the level of management they serve.

Controllability

A basic principle of responsibility accounting is that reports either include only controllable costs or that any allocated costs be clearly labeled and isolated in the report. In budgeting, this principle means that expectations are based on items under a manager's control. Costs such as allocated corporate expenses should not be part of a department's budget; the manager has no way to affect such costs. Including them can cause confusion and dysfunctional decisions. Say that allocated corporate costs are included in a departmental budget and that the allocation increases during the year. To make a target profit, a manager might cut preventive maintenance to meet the budget. This could have serious long-term effects.

Aggregation

Generally, the higher up in the organization a report goes, the more it is summarized and aggregated. A departmental operating budget might detail information on component production, labor crewing, separable overhead, and the like. This same information at the executive vice president level might be aggregated; the vice president can request more detailed data if needed.

Consultants are aware of the need to aggregate information. Commonly, they present their recommendations to management in an oral report with a single page outlining the major points. An executive summary often precedes the written report, to allow busy executives to see the gist of the report before reading it. Scholarly journals take this approach when they present an abstract of an article before the full article.

Aggregation loses information. For example, suppose a company has a net of $40,000 in unfavorable variances and a net of $45,000 in favorable variances. If only one figure is shown ($5,000 net favorable) information about the magnitude of the variances is lost. Even reporting a net unfavorable variance and a net favorable variance loses the details of what caused these figures.

---

[11] A good discussion of this topic is included in Robert A. Howell and Stephen R. Soucy, "Management Reporting in the New Manufacturing Environment," *Management Accounting* (February 1988), pp. 22–29.

Form, Order, Format

Too often we take decisions on the form, order, and format of information too lightly. In today's computer world, others choose how we can format our spreadsheets or word-processed reports. Since we can produce so much information, it is important to make good choices on how and what to present.

Decisions include what to present in table form or in prose. What should be presented as numbers or graphs? What is the best, most effective organization? Should recommendations be summarized before or after an explanation of the analysis? If there is good news and bad news, which should come first? These are all form, order, and format issues.

SUMMARY

The external and internal environments are changing for many companies. While responsibility accounting reports based on traditional measures have been useful in the past, needs are emerging to change the way we think about our role as accountants. Budgeting remains a prime way for managers explicitly to state their assumptions, estimates, and plans. Since budgets are used as a basis for comparison against actual results, managers are very interested in the budgeting process. However, managers want more than just financial information. As companies increasingly desire higher quality, better customer satisfaction, shorter lead times, and zero defects, managers want information that might seem non-traditional to many accountants: qualitative and non-financial quantitative information. If accountants cannot meet their needs, managers will look elsewhere in the organization for information. Thus, this is a challenging time for operating and accounting managers as we struggle with information needs in a dynamic world.

APPENDIX 15A: ZERO BASE BUDGETING

Zero base budgeting (ZBB) is the practice of requiring managers to justify budget requests by justifying the existence of the activities that they control.[12] Managers must demonstrate that the organization will benefit from granting the requests, as if the activities were being undertaken for the first time. ZBB was developed to overcome several objections to traditional budgeting methods, particularly the momentum that incremental budgeting generates. With incremental budgeting, more or less automatic increases in budget requests are granted, so that there might be little analysis of the activities themselves.

[12] For a complete description and examples, see Peter A. Phyrr, *Zero-Base Budgeting* (New York: John Wiley, 1972).

Hence the term *ZBB* conveys the idea that managers cannot expect to have activities funded without showing why the organization needs the activities and what benefits the organization can expect from its spending.

ZBB has been used in private business and government for many years. Governmental applications are better known principally because former President Jimmy Carter required it for federal agencies. Carter used ZBB when he was governor of Georgia and firmly believed in its benefits. Texas Instruments was one of the first corporations to use the technique.

ZBB usually is not applied as strictly as the name suggests. Not all managers justify all their activities every year. Rather, a manager will do a complete justification perhaps every three to four years. ZBB can be costly in the managerial time of the managers doing the budgeting and those reviewing the budgets. ZBB is not one-sided, however. Its advocates point out that managers using it can take the opportunity to propose new programs as well as to defend existing ones. This is because of the basic structure of ZBB.

1. The lowest levels for which budgets are required are called **decision units**. Managers of decision units must determine and state clearly the objectives of their units.
2. These managers must present and evaluate alternative ways of meeting their objectives. For instance, if the data processing manager is installing a new production scheduling system, she might use outside consultants or hire a qualified person to work full time.
3. Managers present budget requests in the form of **decision packages**. A decision package is a description of the objectives of the unit, a set of activities proposed to achieve them, their budgeted costs, and a discussion of alternative ways to perform the activities. Additionally, there is usually a statement of the probable consequences of not accepting a given decision package.

Decision packages are ranked so that the package related to providing a basic level of service is first, followed by those describing expanded levels of service. For example, the data processing manager could present a basic package calling for meeting the existing, nonreducible needs of the company (processing payrolls, doing routine bookkeeping, etc.). This first package typically calls for less service than the unit currently renders. The next package probably calls for providing the current level of service (status quo). The next one might support the implementation of the scheduling system mentioned above. Note that the analysis of the benefits of the scheduling system would be developed by other managers (production manager, marketing manager, etc.). Thus, ZBB forces cooperation and coordination among managers, which is one of its principal advantages. In this example, the DP manager must sell the users on the system, or else she will not have support for the request.

Although ZBB can be applied beneficially to production activities, its greatest potential advantages are perhaps most obvious with discretionary activities, which are extremely difficult to control because of the lack of a neat,

EXHIBIT 15A–1 Sample Zero Base Incremental Request

MORTON COMPANY
Zero Base Budget Request
for 19X7

Department: Data Processing and Information Systems

Manager: J. Warren **Date:** 9-28-X6

Decision Package: 2 of 5

Description/Objectives for Increment: Purchase hardware and software to permit department managers to use their existing and planned microcomputers to access a common data base management system (DBMS). The increasing complexity of the business and related problems of coordination make a DBMS necessary. Individual department managers have already been inquiring about the use of a DBMS.

Alternative Ways to Accomplish Objective:

1. Allow each department to set up its own DBMS. While initially less costly than the preferred alternative, this option would involve considerable duplication of effort, lack of standardization, inability of one department to use another's data base, and eventually greater cost.
2. Purchase a DBMS for use on the mainframe computer. This alternative is costlier, both to purchase and to maintain, requires much more learning time for the users, and is considerably less flexible.

Consequences of Not Approving Request: The departments will begin to develop their own DBMS, with attendant lack of coordination and standardization. The benefits of using a DBMS will be limited unless a common system is installed.

Cost of Request:	*19X7*	*19X8*
Personnel	$28.5	$30.8
Hardware	32.5	—
Software	12.5	8.8

One person is needed to install the networking system and the DBMS. That person will support the departments and provide continuing assistance to them.

measurable output such as a unit of product. Using ZBB does not make the output of discretionary centers measurable, but it forces their managers to provide more concrete expressions of the roles of the units, their relationships to other units, the services that they provide, and the consequences of not granting their requests. Exhibit 15A–1 is a sample request for incremental funds. The manager of the decision unit (department) would also have prepared a base level request, as well as other incremental requests. Because this request is number 2 of 5 (see the Decision Package entry), the manager considers this request very important.

ASSIGNMENTS

15–1 Why Budget? Jack Falls, president of Waters Company, a small but rapidly growing manufacturing company, told his controller: "I don't see why you keep talking about budgets. We have been doing fine without them until now. All they would do is take our people's time away from running the business, and we wouldn't follow them anyway because things are always changing."

REQUIRED

As the controller, draft a reply to the president. Use Appendix B as a guide for your response.

15–2 Budgeting—Spending and Requests Many organizations, especially governmental units, follow the practice called *incremental budgeting*. In this practice the upper levels of management approve next year's budget on the basis of the current year's *spending*. For example, if a state agency spent $300,000 out of its $320,000 budget this year, and the total state budget was to be 10 percent higher next year, the agency's budget would be $330,000 next year ($300,000 × 1.10), not $352,000 ($320,000 × 1.10).

REQUIRED

Discuss the practice. What potential dysfunctional consequences do you see?

15–3 Budgetary Slack Lee Widner, the president of Safco, Inc., recently read an article that described ways that managers introduced slack into their budget requests. He decided to begin a new policy: he would reduce each manager's budget request by 10 percent across the board. Although he had no reason to believe that his managers were padding their requests, he thought it wise not to take any chances.

REQUIRED

Comment on Widner's proposed action. Is it wise? Is it likely to reduce budgetary slack?

15–4 Line Budgeting Many organizations, especially governmental units, follow the practice called *line budgeting*. Under line budgeting, the budget for a responsibility unit, such as a department, factory, school, or entire firm, is broken down by individual categories (lines)—telephone, travel, postage, salaries, equipment purchases, overtime, part-time help, and so on. The manager of the unit is held accountable for meeting each and every line, not just the total budget. Managers are not permitted to shift expenditures from one line to another without permission. For example, the chair of an accounting department who had a budget of $800 for telephone and $1,100 for travel could not spend $900 for telephone and $1,000 for travel, even though the total spent would equal the total budgeted.

REQUIRED

Comment on the practice. Do you think it promotes the welfare of the organization? Why or why not?

15–5 Budgeting and Behavior Bill Walsh, manager of the Southeastern Sales Office of National Products, Inc., had an equipment budget of $65,000 of 19X5. About $20,000 of that amount was for microcomputers that personnel would use for word processing, data base management functions, and spreadsheet analyses. Walsh had anticipated spending the $20,000 late in 19X5 because a lot of preliminary planning was necessary before the computers arrived. In November, Walsh read about significant price reductions in microcomputers. Most authorities expected drops of 15 to 25 percent to take place early in 19X6. Walsh remembered how long and hard he had negotiated over the budget. He wondered whether he would have to go through the whole process again if he waited until January to acquire the computers.

REQUIRED

What should Walsh do, from the standpoint of the company? What will he probably do? How could the company and Walsh avoid such problems in the future?

15–6 Budgeting, Compensation, and Motivation The upper level managers of Gorb-Warren Company have not been happy with cost control in their manufacturing operations. To achieve better control, they have decided to experiment with three systems of compensation for department managers.

System A—The manager receives a $2,000 bonus during any month in which a favorable budget variance is shown.

System B—The manager receives a bonus equal to 20 percent of any favorable budget variance in a given month. There are no penalties for failing to meet the budget in a month.

System C—The manager receives a bonus of $6,000 if the budget is met over a three-month period. No attention is paid to individual months within the period.

The schedule below shows the variances of managers X, Y, and Z over a six-month period. Each was compensated according to one of the systems described above, and no two managers were compensated under the same system. Each manager is in charge of a large production department. Budgeted costs include materials, labor, and various overhead items such as repairs and maintenance, supplies, employee training, and utilities. The budgets are flexible, based on output, and average about $100,000 per month. Output fluctuates, as do the budgets. For the manager under system C, months 1, 2, and 3 are one period, months 4, 5, and 6 are another. Parentheses denote favorable variances.

	Month 1	*Month 2*	*Month 3*	*Month 4*	*Month 5*	*Month 6*
Manager X	$10,000	$6,000	$14,000	($2,000)	($1,000)	$2,000
Manager Y	28,000	(13,000)	(12,000)	24,000	(19,000)	(11,000)
Manager Z	(500)	17,000	(1,000)	(1,200)	22,000	(900)

REQUIRED

1. Determine which manager was compensated under which system. Support your answer. Assume that all three managers wished to maximize their compensation.
2. Describe some of the ways that a manager operating under each of the compensation systems could beat the system and earn bonuses though not acting in the firm's best interests.

15–7 Budgetary Pressure Grading systems used in colleges are similar to budgets in the sense that they establish standards for performance and result in rewards or punishments. Presumably, a student's principal goal in taking a course is to learn. Suppose that you enrolled for a course and read the following on the assignment sheet:

> A passing grade in this course is 90, with 93 being a C and 95 being a B. An A requires a 99. You will have a quiz every day on the material assigned for that day, and these quizzes will be 80 percent of your grade, with a final examination being 20 percent.

REQUIRED

Comment on the policies described above and relate them to the material in the chapter.

15–8 Organizational Goals and Group Norms Some workers are on piecework, which means that they are paid for their output, not for their time. A person who is reasonably talented and works hard can earn more than co-workers who are less talented or ambitious.

REQUIRED

Do you think that those who work hard to improve their incomes are popular with their fellow workers? Respected by them?

15–9 Budgets and Responsibility Bill Stasiuk, Purchasing Manager of Northcote Products, was upset about his performance report for July. The report showed that he had overspent his July budget for telephone by $250 and that he had paid $2.30/lb for 22,000 pounds of plyton, a raw material used in one of the firm's products. The standard price of plyton is $2.12/lb.

Stasiuk had been buying plyton at the standard price from two suppliers in accordance with the purchases budget approved at the beginning of the year. Early in July the sales department accepted a rush order for the product that required plyton, and the production manager agreed to make it. However, there was not enough plyton on hand, so Stasiuk had to find the additional 22,000 pounds required. Neither of the firm's regular suppliers could fill the need, so Stasiuk spent several days on the telephone trying to track down the required amount. Eventually he located the plyton and had it delivered in time to meet the production schedule.

REQUIRED

Discuss the issue and recommend a solution.

15–10 Performance Measures Listed below are jobs and measures of performance for the people in them. For each, indicate whether the measure is likely to motivate the person to act in accordance with the goals of the organization. A significant part of the employee's evaluation is whether he or she meets the budgeted results.

Job	*Measure of Performance*
Production manager	Number of units produced
Sales manager	Total dollar sales
Research and development manager	Number of patentable products or processes
Police officer	Number of arrests

15–11 Responsibility Accounting (CMA Adapted) Family Resorts, Inc. is a holding company for several vacation hotels in the northeast and mid-Atlantic states. The firm originally purchased several old inns, restored the buildings, and upgraded the recreational facilities. The inns have been well received by vacationing families as many services are provided that accommodate children and afford parents time for themselves. Since the completion of the restorations ten years ago, the company has been profitable.

Family Resorts has just concluded its annual meeting of regional and district managers. This meeting is held each November to review the results of the previous season and to help the managers prepare for the upcoming year. Before the meeting, the managers have submitted proposed budgets for their districts or regions as appropriate. These budgets have been reviewed and consolidated into an annual operating budget for the entire company. The 19X7 budget has been presented at the meeting and was accepted by the managers.

To evaluate the performance of its managers, Family Resorts uses responsibility accounting. Therefore, the preparation of the budget is given close attention at headquarters. If major changes need to be made to the budgets submitted by the managers, all affected parties are consulted before the changes are incorporated. Presented below are two pages from the budget booklet that all managers received at the meeting.

FAMILY RESORTS INC.
Responsibility Summary
($000 omitted)

Reporting unit: Family Resorts	
Responsible person: President	
Mid-Atlantic Region	$605
New England Region	365
Unallocated costs	(160)
Income before taxes	$810
Reporting unit: New England Region	
Responsible person: Regional Manager	
Vermont	$200
New Hampshire	140
Maine	105
Unallocated costs	(80)
Total contribution	$365
Reporting unit: Maine District	
Responsible person: District Manager	
Harbor Inn	$ 80
Camden Country Inn	60
Unallocated costs	(35)
Total contribution	$105
Reporting unit: Harbor Inn	
Responsible person: Innkeeper	
Revenue	$600
Controllable costs	(455)
Allocated costs	(65)
Total contribution	$ 80

FAMILY RESORTS INC.
Condensed Operating Budget—Maine District
For the Year Ending December 31, 19X7
($000 omitted)

		Region		New England District				Maine District Inns		
	Family Resorts	*Mid-Atlantic*	*New England*	*Not Allocated*[1]	*Vermont*	*New Hampshire*	*Maine*	*Not Allocated*[2]	*Harbor*	*Camden Country*
Net sales	$7,900	$4,200	$ 3,700		$ 1,400	$ 1,200	$1,100		$ 600	$ 500
Cost of sales	4,530	2,310	2,220		840	720	660		360	300
Gross margin	$3,370	$1,890	$ 1,480		$ 560	$ 480	$ 440		$ 240	$ 200
Controllable expenses										
Supervisory expense	$ 240	$ 130	$ 110		$ 35	$ 30	$ 45	$ 10	$ 20	$ 15
Training expense	160	80	80		30	25	25		15	10
Advertising expense	500	280	220	$ 50	55	60	55	15	20	20
Repairs and maintenance	480	225	255		90	85	80		40	40
Total controllable expenses	$1,380	$ 715	$ 665	$ 50	$ 210	$ 200	$ 205	$ 25	$ 95	$ 85
Controllable contribution	$1,990	$1,175	$ 815	$ (50)	$ 350	$ 280	$ 235	$ (25)	$ 145	$ 115
Expenses controlled by others										
Depreciation	$ 520	$ 300	$ 220	$ 30	$ 70	$ 60	$ 60	$ 10	$ 30	$ 20
Property taxes	200	120	80		30	30	20		10	10
Insurance	300	150	150		50	50	50		25	25
Total expenses controlled by others	$1,020	$ 570	$ 450	$ 30	$ 150	$ 140	$ 130	$ 10	$ 65	$ 55
Total contribution	$ 970	$ 605	$ 365	$ (80)	$ 200	$ 140	$ 105	$ (35)	$ 80	$ 60
Unallocated costs[3]	160									
Income before taxes	$ 810									

[1] Unallocated expenses include a regional advertising campaign and equipment used by the regional manager.

[2] Unallocated expenses include a portion of the district manager's salary, district promotion costs, district manager's car.

[3] Unallocated costs include taxes on undeveloped real estate, headquarters expense, legal fees, audit fees.

REQUIRED

1. Responsibility accounting has been used effectively by many companies, both large and small.
   a. Define responsibility accounting.
   b. Discuss the benefits that accrue to a company using responsibility accounting.
   c. Describe the advantages of responsibility accounting for the managers of a firm.
2. Family Resorts Inc.'s budget was accepted by the regional and district managers. Based on the facts presented, evaluate the budget process employed by Family Resorts by addressing the following.
   a. What features of the budget preparation are likely to result in the managers adopting and supporting the budget process?
   b. What features of the budget presentation shown above are likely to make the budget attractive to managers?
   c. What recommendations, if any, could be made to the budget preparers to improve the budget process? Explain your answer.

15–12 Implementing Change (CMA Adapted) More than 400 years ago, Machiavelli wrote in *The Prince*, "It must be considered that there is nothing more difficult to carry out, nor more doubtful of success, nor more dangerous to handle, than to initiate a new order of things." This statement is as applicable today as it was in 1520.

Implementing organizational change is one of the most demanding assignments any executive faces. It has been suggested that every change requires three steps; "unfreezing" the current situation, the change itself, and finally "refreezing" the effected change. This view, however, lacks the specific details needed by an operating manager who must effect a change.

REQUIRED

1. Identify and describe the specific steps a manager must take to implement an organizational change.
2. When an organization makes a change that affects employees directly or how they conduct their operations, discuss
   a. why employees generally resist change
   b. the ways a manager can reduce the resistance to change

15–13 Responsibility for Costs MBI Corporation, a large multinational company, runs an extensive training program for newly recruited college graduates. Each graduate spends from one to three months in each of six different departments to gain understanding of various phases of the firm's operations.

In the past, the salaries of the trainees were charged to a general administration account and would subsequently be reallocated to other departments as part of the overall allocation process. The basis for the allocation was the total costs of each department.

The controller now intends to charge the salaries directly to the departments where the trainees work. He believes that this will give a fairer picture of the costs. Some departmental managers are not happy with the proposal. A typical complaint follows:

> I don't really mind paying for the costs of trainees through the allocation. Someone has to pay it. The allocations of all costs are lumped together, anyway, as an uncontrollable cost, so that they don't affect my performance report. The problem that I see arising is that the direct charge will make us less eager to take trainees. If the cost is to be considered controllable, the departmental managers will be hurt. The trainees are really no good to us: by the time they learn something they're about to go to the next stop.

REQUIRED

Comment on the proposal and on the current system. You might wish to use the department manager's comments as a basis for yours.

15–14 Setting Sales Budgets Balston Products employs a sales manager for each of its 15 product lines. One critical element in evaluating their performance is whether they meet their sales budgets. Generally, missing the budget by a large amount (either over or under) is not as important as at least achieving the budgeted results.

The company has recently adopted the following policy for setting sales budgets for each line. The budget for a year is to be 105 percent of the quantity: prior year's budget × 0.50 + prior year's actual × 0.50. The reasoning behind this policy is: (1) the company has an overall target rate of growth of 5 percent; (2) there should be some consideration of actual results in setting future budgets (which is why the budget is not simply 105 percent of the prior year's budget); (3) the sales managers should not get lower or higher budgets just because of their actual results (which is why the budget is not simply 105 percent of the prior year's actual sales).

REQUIRED

Discuss the strong and weak points of the policy and make any recommendations you think desirable.

15–15 Responsibility The budget director of a medium-sized manufacturing company recently told you his troubles:

> My purchasing manager is responsible for buying materials and components at standard prices, and that is how we evaluate his performance. The production manager is responsible for meeting budgeted production goals at budgeted costs. The system does not seem to be working out.
>
> The production manager keeps telling me that the purchasing manager is so intent on getting goods at prices below standard that he buys inferior goods and uses unreliable suppliers. He claims that his costs are higher because of these actions and that he sometimes fails to meet his production budget because he doesn't have an adequate supply of a material or component.
>
> He also tells me that the purchasing manager often buys in huge lots to get a good price. He is then responsible for storing and safeguarding the goods, which also adds to his costs. He says that it's always feast or famine; either he has a huge oversupply or an inadequate supply.
>
> When I talk to the purchasing manager, he says that he is doing just what he is expected to do and won't change so long as he is evaluated by whether or not he gets materials and components at standard prices. I'm telling you, it's a real mess.

REQUIRED

What suggestions can you make?

15–16 Budgeting and Goal Congruence (CMA Adapted) In late 19X1 Mr. Sootsman, the official in charge of the State Department of Automobile Regulation, established a system of performance measurement for the department's branch offices. He was convinced that management by objectives could help the department reach its objective of better citizen service at a lower cost. The first step was to define the activities of the

BARRY COUNTY BRANCH PERFORMANCE REPORT

	19X2		*19X3*		*19X4*	
	Budget	*Actual*	*Budget*	*Actual*	*Budget*	*Actual*
Population served	38,000		38,500		38,700	
Number of employees:						
Administrative	1	1	1	1	1	1
Professional	1	1	1	1	1	1
Clerical	3	3	2	3	$1\frac{1}{2}$	3
Budgeted Performance Points[a]						
1. services	19,500		16,000		15,500	
2. citizen comments	500		600		700	
	20,000		16,600		16,200	
Actual Performance Points[a]						
1. services	14,500		14,600		15,600	
2. citizen comments	200		900		200	
	14,700		15,500		15,800	
Detail of Actual Performance[a]						
1. new drivers licenses						
a. examination and road tests (3 pt)	3,000		3,150		3,030	
b. road tests repeat—failed prior test (2 pt)	600		750		1,650	
2. renew drivers licenses (1 pt)	3,000		3,120		3,060	
3. issue license plates (0.5 pt)	4,200		4,150		4,100	
4. issue titles						
a. dealer transactions (0.5 pt)	2,000		1,900		2,100	
b. individual transaction (1 pt)	1,700		1,530		1,660	
	14,500		14,600		15,600	
5. citizen comments						
a. favorable (+0.5 pt)	300		1,100		800	
b. unfavorable (−0.5 pt)	100		200		600	
	200		900		200	

[a]The budget performance points for services are calculated using 3 points per available hour. The administrative employee devotes half time to administration and half time to regular services. The calculations for the services point budget are as follows:

19X2: $4\frac{1}{2}$ people × 8 hours × 240 days × 3 pts × 75% productive time = 19,440 rounded to 19,500
19X3: $3\frac{1}{2}$ people × 8 hours × 240 days × 3 pts × 80% productive time = 16,128 rounded to 16,000
19X4: 3 people × 8 hours × 240 days × 3 pts × 90% productive time = 15,552 rounded to 15,500

The comments targets are based on rough estimates by department officials. The actual point totals for the branch are calculated by multiplying the weights shown in the report in parentheses by the number of such services performed or comments received.

branch offices, to assign point values to the services performed, and to establish performance targets. Point values, rather than revenue targets, were employed because the department was a regulatory agency, not a revenue-producing agency. Further, the specific revenue for a service did not adequately reflect the differences in effort required. The analysis was compiled at the state office, and the results were distributed to the branch offices.

The system has been in operation since 19X2. The performance targets for the branches have been revised each year by the state office. The revisions were designed to encourage better performance by increasing the target or reducing resources to achieve targets. The revisions incorporated noncontrollable events, such as population shifts, new branches, and changes in procedures.

The Barry County branch is typical of many branch offices. A summary displaying the budgeted and actual performance for three years follows.

Mr. Sootsman has been disappointed in the performance of branch offices because they have not met performance targets or budgets. He is especially concerned because the points earned from citizens' comments are declining.

REQUIRED

1. Does the method of performance measurement encourage goal congruence? Why or why not?
2. The Barry County branch came closer to its budgeted points in 19X4 than in either previous year. Does this mean that it improved its performance in 19X4? Why or why not?

15–17 Time Frames for Comparisons The vice president for sales of Wiggins Company is considering a change in budgeting procedures. The company now budgets sales by region for the entire year. There are no sales budgets for months or quarters within the year. The vice president tracks sales during the year to see whether it is likely that the region will meet its annual budget.

The change she proposes is to develop monthly sales budgets for each region as well as the annual budget. She would hold each regional manager responsible for meeting the monthly budgets. Her rationale is that since she is now doing mental calculations to see whether each region seems to be on target for the year, she might as well formalize the process. She also believes that monthly budgets would keep the regional managers on their toes, so that they would not be able to let things slide in the hope of making it up later in the year.

REQUIRED

Comment on the good and bad points of the vice president's proposal.

15–18 Responsibility Acton Company has adopted a policy of approving budgets in total, rather than by specific items. Its managers believe that those responsible for carrying out the tasks should be free to spend money as they see fit within the limit of the total budget. For instance, a production supervisor should be allowed to meet peak production requirements by hiring temporary workers or by putting regular employees on overtime. In some companies the supervisor would have to use overtime if he had already spent up to the limit on temporary help or vice versa.

The general categories of cost that Acton's production managers are responsible for are materials; direct labor; manufacturing overhead items such as indirect labor, utilities, and supplies; quality control; and employee training.

REQUIRED

Discuss the strong and weak points of Acton's policy, as opposed to a policy that requires managers to adhere to each specific item in a budget.

15–19 Setting Standards RST Company uses industrial engineering techniques to set standards. The most recent project was to establish standards for a new product that requires very close machining operations. A summary of data that the industrial engineering department collected appears below. The industrial engineering department observed workers performing the operations.

Worker	*Number of Units per Day*
A	65
B	70
C	70
D	80
E	80
F	85
Total	450
Average	75

The industrial engineering department wants the standard to be 85 units, contending that it is achievable with good performance. The production manager prefers the average of 75 units, while the supervisor of the machining operation wants 70 units. The supervisor argues that setting the standard any higher would mean that only half, or fewer, of the workers could meet the standard.

REQUIRED

You are a consultant hired by RST's president. Using the guidelines in Appendix B, write her a memo in which you comment on each position and make a recommendation with an appropriate rationale.

15–20 Behavior and Budgeting Policy (CMA) Marshall Electronics, a division of Kramer Industries, manufactures microchips for a wide variety of applications. Four months ago, Kramer sent a team from their Internal Audit Department to Marshall Electronics to perform a routine review of operations. A portion of the audit report presented to Kramer on the operations of Marshall Electronics is presented below.

Before making the Preliminary Management Response proposed in the audit report, the president and the controller of Marshall Electronics announced to the departmental managers that the company was planning to accept the audit recommendation to implement a departmental budgeting system. The managers were asked for suggestions on implementation procedures and were encouraged to raise any questions they might have about the budget system.

Observation Departmental budgets are not being utilized at Marshall Electronics. Currently, the division does not have the automated systems capability to produce budget analyses at the departmental level. Traditionally, the plant has been controlled through a total plant concept rather than a departmental approach to cost control. Given present business conditions, this approach may no longer be the optimum control process. Increased competition in the marketplace, declining profits, deteriorating margins, and increased costs have combined to necessitate an aggressive approach to cost reduction. Based on experience at other Kramer plants, we believe Marshall Electronics would benefit from the development and use of departmental budgets for all functions.

Recommendation We recommend that Marshall Electronics establish a management objective to develop and utilize flexible departmental expense budgets for all departments. Resources and systems development efforts should be devoted to this objective as they become available. We suggest, as an interim step, that operating budgets be employed on a monthly basis. Operating targets for both direct labor and indirect labor expense should be established for each manufacturing department monthly. Departmental managers should track performance and explain deviations from targets as part of the regular agenda at the weekly production meetings.

Preliminary Management Response The Marshall Electronics plant will develop and utilize a flexible departmental budget system. In the interim, work has begun to establish daily, month-to-date, and annual targets for direct and indirect labor for the manufacturing departments. These targets include efficiency objectives, overtime objectives, and indirect labor staffing objectives based on volume and product mix.

REQUIRED

1. Describe the benefits, other than better cost control, that are likely to accrue to Marshall Electronics from the implementation of departmental budgeting.

2. Discuss the behavioral impact the introduction of departmental budgeting is likely to have on Marshall's
   a. departmental managers
   b. production workers

3. Discuss the managerial mistakes that Marshall Electronics must avoid to gain acceptance of this change in operating procedure.

15–21 Budgeting and Responsibility Accounting (CMA Adapted) Argon County Hospital is located in a well-known resort area. The county population doubles in the May–August period and hospital activity more than doubles during these months because of vacation-related accidents and ills. The hospital is organized into several departments and, despite its small size, has attracted a competent staff.

The hospital hired an administrator a year ago to improve the business aspects of its operation. Among the new ideas he introduced was responsibility accounting. He announced the program in a quarterly cost report supplied to each department head. In the past, department heads had received cost reports infrequently and at irregular intervals. Excerpts from the announcement and the report to the head of the laundry department appear below.

> The hospital has adopted a *responsibility accounting system*. From now on you will receive quarterly reports comparing the costs of operating your department with budgeted costs. The reports will highlight the differences (variations) so you can zero in on the departure from budgeted costs. (This is called management by exception.) Responsibility accounting means you are accountable for keeping the costs in your department within the budget. The variations from the budget will help you identify what costs are out of line, and the size of the variation will indicate which ones are the most important. Your first such report accompanies this announcement.

ARGON COUNTY HOSPITAL
Performance Report—Laundry Department
July–September 19X3

	Budget	Actual	(Over) Under Budget	Percent (Over) Under Budget
Patient days	9,500	11,900	(2,400)	(25)
Pounds processed—laundry	125,000	156,000	(31,000)	(25)
Costs:				
Laundry labor	$ 9,000	$ 12,500	$ (3,500)	(39)
Supplies	1,100	1,875	(775)	(70)
Water, water heating and softening	1,700	2,500	(800)	(47
Maintenance	1,400	2,200	(800)	(57)
Supervisor's salary	3,150	3,750	(600)	(19)
Allocated administration costs	4,000	5,000	(1,000)	(25)
Equipment depreciation	1,200	1,250	(50)	(4)
	$ 21,550	$ 29,075	$ (7,525)	(35)

Administrator's comments: Costs are significantly above budget for the quarter. Particular attention needs to be paid to labor, supplies, and maintenance.

The annual budget for 19X3 was constructed by the new administrator. Quarterly budgets were computed as one-fourth of the annual budget. The administrator compiled the budget from analysis of the prior three years' costs. The analysis showed that all costs increased each year, with more rapid increases between the second and third year. He considered establishing the budget at an average of the previous three years' costs, hoping that the installation of the system would reduce costs to this level. However, in view of the rapidly increasing prices he finally chose 19X2 costs less 3 percent for the 19X3 budget. The activity level measured by patient days and pounds of laundry processed was set at 19X2 volume, which approximately equalled the volume of each of the past three years.

REQUIRED

1. Comment on the method used to prepare the budget.
2. Does the report effectively communicate the level of efficiency of the laundry department? Why or why not?

15–22 Compensation Plans and Goal Congruence (CMA) Parsons Co. compensates its field sales force on a commission and year-end bonus basis. The commission is 20 percent of standard gross margin (planned selling price less standard cost of goods sold on a full absorption basis), contingent on collection of the account. Customer's credit is approved by the company's credit department. Price concessions are granted on occasion by the top sales management, but sales commissions are not reduced by the discount. A year-end bonus of 15 percent of commissions earned is paid to salespeople who equal or exceed their annual sales target. The annual sales target is usually established by applying approximately a 5 percent increase to the previous year's sales.

REQUIRED

1. What features of this compensation plan would seem to be effective in motivating the salespeople to accomplish company goals of higher profits and return on investment? Explain why.
2. What features of this compensation plan would seem to be countereffective in motivating the salespeople to accomplish the company goals of higher profits and return on investment? Explain why.

15–23 Budgetary Slack (CMA Adapted) Noton Company has operated a comprehensive budgeting system for many years. This system is a major component of the company's program to control operations and costs at its widely scattered plants. Periodically the plants' general managers gather to discuss the overall company control system with the top management.

At this year's meeting one of the most senior plant managers severely criticized the budgetary system. He said that the system discriminated unfairly against the older, well-run, established plants in favor of the newer plants. The impact was lower year-end bonuses and poor performance ratings. In addition, there were psychological consequences in the form of lower employee morale. In his judgment, revisions in the system were needed to make it more effective. The basic factors of Noton's budget include

1. Announcement of an annual improvement percentage target established by top management.
2. Plant submission of budgets implementing the annual improvement target.
3. Management review and revision of the proposed budget.
4. Establishment and distribution of the final budget.

The target percentage for improvement is the same for all plants, which policy was one of the matters that most concerned the plant manager. In support of his arguments, he compared the budget revisions and performance results. The older plants were expected to achieve the improvement target but often were unable to meet it. On the other hand, the newer plants were often excused from meeting a portion of this target in their budgets. However, their performance was usually better than the final budget.

He further argued that the company did not recognize the operating differences that made attainment of the annual improvement factor difficult, if not impossible for older plants. His plant had been producing essentially the same product for its twenty years. The machinery and equipment, which had undergone many modifications in the first five years, had had no major changes in recent years. Because they were old, repair and maintenance costs had increased each year and the machines were less reliable. The plant management team had been together for the last ten years and worked well together. The labor force was mature, with many of the employees having the highest seniority in the company. In his judgment, the significant improvements had been wrung out of the plant over the years so that merely keeping even was difficult.

For comparison he noted that one plant opened within the past four years would have an easier time meeting the company's expectations. The plant was new and contained modern equipment that was in some cases still experimental. Major modifications in equipment and operating systems had been made each year as the plant management obtained a better understanding of the operations. The plant's management, although experienced, had been together only since its opening. The plant was located in an area that had previously had very little industry, and the work force was relatively inexperienced.

REQUIRED

1. Evaluate the views of the manufacturing manager.
2. Discuss how managers of both old and new plants could incorporate slack into their budgets.

15–24 Budgetary Slack (CMA Adapted) Bob Bingham is the controller of Atlantis Laboratories, a manufacturer and distributor of generic prescription pharmaceuticals. He is currently in the process of preparing the annual budget and reviewing the current business plan. The business unit managers of Atlantis prepare and assemble the detailed operating budgets, with technical assistance from the corporate accounting staff. The final budgets are then presented by the business unit managers to the corporate executive committee for approval. The corporate accounting staff reviews the budgets for adherence to corporate accounting policies, but does not do detailed review for reasonableness of the line items within the budget.

Bingham is aware that the upcoming year for Atlantis may be a difficult one because of the expiration of a major patent and the loss of a licensing agreement for another product line. He also knows that during the budgeting process, budgetary slack is created in varying degrees throughout the organization. Bingham believes this slack has a negative effect on the overall business objectives of Atlantis Laboratories and should be eliminated.

REQUIRED

1. Define "budgetary slack."
2. Explain the advantages and disadvantages of "budgetary slack" from the point of view of
   a. the business unit manager who must achieve the budget
   b. corporate management
3. Bob Bingham is considering implementing zero-based budgeting at Atlantis Laboratories.
   a. Define zero-based budgeting.
   b. Describe how zero-based budgeting could be advantageous to Atlantis Laboratories in controlling budgetary slack.
   c. Discuss the disadvantages Atlantis Laboratories might encounter from using zero-based budgeting.

15–25 Conflicting Goals William Jacobs founded WMJ Company 15 years ago, after leaving his job as chief engineer of Ramsey Industries. He believed he could make industrial measuring devices that were vastly superior to those available, and events proved him right. WMJ Company flourished and now employs 2,500 people.

The company maintains a large engineering department that constantly works to improve the product line, and Jacobs spends nearly half his time either supervising or working with that department. The firm's products are well known for quality and are priced somewhat above those of its competitors.

In recent years the firm has lost business to competitors who make less accurate devices. Some customers do not need devices of the quality of WMJ's for some applications and accordingly seek out cheaper ones. Jacobs has refused to make less-accurate devices and considers his firm to be the standard of quality of the industry. The manufacturing superintendents have complained that the engineers require such low tolerances that nearly 10 percent of the units fail to pass final inspection.

The firm's financial vice president, Allen Rose, has become distressed during the two years that he has been with the firm. Rose has often commented to Jacobs that the firm keeps unreasonably high inventories and accounts receivable. One reason for the high inventories is that Jacobs insists on being able to supply a customer's needs quickly. The high receivables are due in part to Jacob's unwillingness to pressure old and valued customers for prompt payment. The current level of interest rates encourages customers to withhold payments as long as they can.

Rose believes that the company is headed for trouble. The high investment in current assets has been financed largely with bank loans at very high interest rates.

The firm uses only the most up-to-date manufacturing equipment, and Rose has never known Jacobs to deny a request from the engineering department for personnel, instruments, or other equipment. Rose has prepared budgets, but Jacobs has dismissed them with the comment that he didn't build the firm with budgets. In fact, Jacobs recently told Rose to keep to his own area and not to meddle in the operations of the business.

REQUIRED

What are the probable reasons for the situation, and what would you suggest be done?

15–26 Effect of Tight Budget (CMA Adapted) Tom Emory and Jim Morris strolled back to their plant from the administrative offices of Ferguson & Son Mfg. Company. Tom was manager of the machine shop in the company's factory; Jim was manager of the equipment maintenance department. The men had just attended the monthly performance evaluation meeting for plant department heads.

"Boy, I hate those meetings!" Tom exclaimed. "I never know whether my department's accounting reports will show good or bad performance. I'm beginning to expect the worst."

Tom has just received his worst evaluation ever in his long career with Ferguson & Son. He had been promoted from machinist to machine shop supervisor when the company expanded and moved to its present location. The president, Robert Ferguson, Sr., had often stated that the company's success was due to the high quality of the work of machinists like Emory. As supervisor, Tom stressed the importance of skilled craft-work.

When Robert Ferguson, Jr., became plant manager, he directed that monthly performance comparisons be made between actual and budgeted costs for each department. The departmental budgets were intended to encourage the supervisors to reduce inefficiencies and to seek cost reduction opportunities. The company controller was instructed to have his staff tighten the budget slightly whenever a department attained its budget in a given month, to reinforce the plant supervisor's desire to reduce costs.

Tom Emory remarked to Jim Morris:

> I really don't understand. We've worked so hard to get up to budget, and the minute we make it they tighten the budget on us. We can't work any faster and still maintain quality. I think my people are ready to quit trying. Besides, those reports don't tell the whole story. We always seem to be interrupting the big jobs for all those small rush orders. All that setup and machine adjustment time is killing us.
>
> The accountants seem to know everything that's happening in my department,

sometimes even before I do. I thought all that budget and accounting stuff was supposed to help, but it just gets me into trouble.

Tom Emory's performance report for the month in question is reproduced below. Actual production volume for the month was at the budgeted level.

Machine Shop—October 19X8
T. Emory, Supervisor

	Budget	*Actual*	*Variances*
Direct labor	$ 39,600	$ 39,850	$ 250U
Direct materials	231,000	231,075	75U
Depreciation—equipment	3,000	3,000	0
Depreciation—buildings	6,000	6,000	0
Power	900	860	40F
Maintenance	400	410	10U
Supervision	1,500	1,500	0
Idle time	0	1,800	1,800U
Set up labor	680	2,432	1,752U
Miscellaneous	2,900	3,300	400U
	$285,980	$290,227	$4,247U

REQUIRED

1. Identify the problems in Ferguson & Son Mfg. Company's budgetary control system and explain how they may reduce the system's effectiveness.
2. Explain how the budgetary control system could be revised to improve its effectiveness.

15–27 Participation, Standards, Overhead Allocation (CMA Adapted) Kelly Company, founded 20 years ago, has achieved a moderate degree of success. The company manufactures and sells pottery items. All manufacturing takes place in one plant, which has four departments. Each manufacturing department produces only one product. The four products of Kelly Company are plaques, cups, vases, and plates. Sam Kelly, the president and founder, attributes the company's success to the well-designed quality products and an effective cost control system. The system was installed early in the firm's existence to improve cost control and to serve as a basis for planning.

The company establishes standard costs for material and labor with the participation of plant management. Each year top management invites the plant manager, department heads, and time-study engineers to recommend changes in the standards for the next year. Top management reviews these recommendations and the records of actual performance for the current year before setting the new standards. As a rule, top management sets tight standards representing very efficient performance, so that no inefficiency or slack will be included in cost goals. The plant manager and department heads are charged with cost control responsibility, and the variances from standard costs are used to measure their performance.

No standards are set for factory overhead because management believes it is too difficult to predict overhead and relate it to output. The actual factory overhead for the departments and the plant is accumulated in a single pool. The actual overhead is then allocated to the departments on the basis of departmental output. The schedule below is a three-year summary of overhead allocation among the departments.

19X5

Department	Units Produced	Allocated[a] Overhead
Plaques	300,000	$120,000
Cups	250,000	100,000
Vases	200,000	80,000
Plates	250,000	100,000
Total	1,000,000	$400,000

19X6

Department	Units Produced	Allocated[a] Overhead
Plaques	330,000	$126,000
Cups	270,000	103,091
Vases	220,000	84,000
Plates	280,000	106,909
Total	1,100,000	$420,000

19X7

Department	Units Produced	Allocated[a] Overhead
Plaques	180,000	$ 60,000
Cups	360,000	120,000
Vases	300,000	100,000
Plates	360,000	120,000
Total	1,200,000	$400,000

[a] Dollar amounts are rounded to the nearest dollar.

The company's executives are convinced that they can control costs more effectively. A review of cost performance for recent years disclosed several factors that led them to this conclusion.

1. Unfavorable variances were the norm rather than the exception, although the size of the variances was uniform.
2. Department managers took steps that, while benefiting their own departments, were detrimental to overall company performance.
3. Employee motivation, especially among first-line supervisors, appeared low.

REQUIRED

1. What are the probable effects, if any, on the motivation of the plant managers and departmental heads from
   a. the participative standard cost system?
   b. the use of tight standards?
   Explain the reasons for your conclusions.

2. What effect, if any, will the practice of applying actual overhead costs on the basis of actual units produced have on the motivation of the department heads to control the overhead costs? Explain your answer.

15–28 Allocations and Transfer Prices National Electronics Company is a large, decentralized firm. One centralized activity is research and development (R&D). Managers of operating divisions suggest projects for R&D, and the individual section heads in R&D (for example, fiber optics, lasers, solid state physics) also authorize and carry out projects that they believe desirable. The head of R&D makes the final decisions on project selection, as there are always more requests (both from operating divisions and from section heads) than time and money. The ability of section heads to gain approval for their projects often determines which projects will survive.

The president of the firm is not satisfied with the current arrangements. R&D is a cost center, so the operating managers are not billed for work that they request. The president also believes that R&D people spend too much time on projects that interest them but are of little economic promise. He believes that the scientists who run R&D are more interested in their fields of expertise than in the firm. A number of the scientists are internationally known for their research, but a good deal of their research has not borne fruit for the firm.

The president is now considering two plans. One is to allocate both the costs and investment of R&D (about $26 million and $65 million, respectively) to the operating divisions on the basis of sales or total divisional investment. The other is to make R&D into a profit center. R&D would have to sell its services to the operating divisions and to convince the operating managers that they should pay to support particular research projects.

REQUIRED

Discuss the merits and disadvantages of each proposed plan, as well as the current situation.

15–29 Advertising and Promotional Budgets Hampton Corporation makes and markets a wide variety of household products including dishwashing liquids, detergents, floor care products, and furniture polishes and waxes. The firm is organized into several divisions, each concentrating on a single line of products. A regional manager is in charge of operations of each division in each of the geographical areas that the division serves. Each division has from four to eight regional managers. Both divisional and regional managers are responsible for profits.

Advertising and promotion (newspaper coupons are the major promotional cost) are extremely important in the markets that Hampton serves. A great deal of effort is involved in the budgeting of these expenses.

Each regional manager submits a budget for the coming year. The divisional manager reviews them, frequently asking for justification and revision. After approval at the divisional level, the budgets go to the corporate budget committee, which also frequently request additional justification and revisions.

During the year, regional managers make many requests for supplemental amounts to meet changing circumstances, such as heavier promotion by competitors. These requests go through the divisional manager, and if she concurs, to the budget committee. The committee meets monthly and grants about half the requests by number, about one-third by dollar amount.

The system satisfies very few managers. The regional and divisional managers complain that they cannot get quick enough action from the budget committee. Too often, by the time the request for additional funds has been granted, it is too late. Sales have been lost to competitors who have been more aggressive. One of the regional managers related a typical case:

> I was faced by an increase in advertising of a competitor's liquid detergent. Its sales were increasing rapidly, and we were doing nothing about it. I asked for a 20 percent increase in my budget to go for advertising and newspaper coupons giving 10 cents off the regular price. The request was eventually granted, but it took five weeks from the time I decided to take the action and initiate the request. By then we had lost two percentage points of market share in my geographical area and smaller, but significant, amounts in others.

Members of the budget committee were equally unhappy. Their feelings were expressed by the treasurer of the firm:

> These guys just won't try to understand that we cannot approve changes instantly. First, all of us have jobs to do besides looking at these requests. We could spend half our time in meetings going over these requests, and that seems to be what the regional managers want. I have recommended that we give the divisional managers the authority to shift funds around among their regions. Right now, a divisional manager can't reduce spending in one area to increase it in another. Some of the members of the committee are against it because they feel that the regional managers will all be clamoring for money and the one with the loudest voice will get it. Still, it's obvious that we have to do something soon.

The president of the firm was well aware of the situation and had asked a management consultant to make confidential recommendations. The president had not discussed these recommendations with anyone because she wanted to give them careful consideration.

In essence, the consultant recommended two major changes. One was to give the divisional managers the authority to reallocate funds from region to region, as the treasurer had recommended. The second was to set formulas for governing the total advertising and promotional budget for each division. These formulas would permit the divisional manager to spend an amount equal to some specified percentage of sales. The budget would then be flexible, not static. The percentages used would be negotiated by the divisional managers and the budget committee, but the consultant expected that historical ratios of advertising and promotion to sales dollars would be the bases.

The sales figures to be used would be quarterly. Each quarter, the budget would be the specified percentage of the sales of the previous quarter. Quarterly sales figures were usually available by the second week of the subsequent quarter. The consultant had stated that it was important to keep the budget current, so that basing the current year's budget on the prior year's sales was unwise. However, he also said that using monthly sales figures to determine the following month's budget would cause confusion and be difficult to implement.

The consultant argued that the proposed changes would have a number of benefits. The budget committee would no longer be involved in the continual evaluation of supplemental requests. Only in rare cases would divisional managers request changes during the year. The firm's regional managers could respond more quickly to competitive pressures, because they could go straight to the divisional manager with supplemental requests. The time in the budget committee review would be eliminated, so actions could be taken when they would still be effective.

The continual updating of the budgets would keep them more current and in line with current requirements. The divisional managers would also understand that they had to earn their budgets. Higher sales would lead to higher budgets and lower sales to lower budgets. Total budgets would be in line with the firm's ability to pay.

REQUIRED

Evaluate the consultant's recommendations. Make your own recommendations to supplement those of the consultant or to replace those that you do not agree with.

15–30 Responsibility Accounting (AICPA Adapted) For some years Avey Company has used a standard cost system for production costs, and its managers have been happy with the results. However, distribution expenses have risen rapidly, and the managers are not able to determine whether or not they are under control. They have decided to give each local manager an income statement for his or her territory showing monthly and year-to-date results for the current and prior year. Each territory is assigned to a single manager, who is responsible for sales and distribution expenses. The local managers forward sales orders to the main office. A central warehouse ships the goods. The main office also handles billing and collection.

The managers at the main office have decided to classify costs by function, then allocate them to each territory in the following ways:

Function	*Allocation Basis*
Sales salaries	Actual
Other selling expenses	Relative sales dollars
Warehousing	Relative sales dollars
Packing and shipping	Weight of package
Billing and collection	Number of billings
General administration	Equally

REQUIRED

1. What objectives are the managers of Avey trying to achieve by the territorial income statements? Will the comparative income statements serve their needs?
2. Discuss the allocation bases that the managers have proposed.

16

BUDGETING: ANALYTICAL AND TECHNICAL ASPECTS

Chapter 15 dealt with general aspects of budgeting and concentrated on behavioral considerations; this chapter deals with analytical and technical aspects. We consider the problem of forecasting and budgeting sales, from which all other budgets flow. A principal goal is to see how the budgeting process explicitly relates means and ends, resources and goals. The development of cash budgets is of special importance: firms, especially fast-growing ones, get into more difficulty from running short of cash than from anything else.

Managers of economic organizations spend much time preparing budgets. One reason is that modern, complex organizations have many interrelated activities, most of which must be considered in developing budgets. Thus, there may be many intermediate steps between a sales forecast and a cash budget.

Electronic spreadsheets are especially useful for preparing budgets. The various pieces of the master budget can be linked to a basic set of data. This common database and set of budgets allow managers to use sensitivity analysis to change one or more of their assumptions or estimates and see the effects on the different parts of the budget.

COMPONENTS OF THE MASTER BUDGET

The set of budgets that the managers of a firm prepare is collectively called the **master budget** or **comprehensive budget**. Different firms prepare different individual budgets, but the following list is representative:

budgeted income statement, or pro forma income statement, showing the income expected for the budget period

sales budget, perhaps by product, territory, class of customer (such as government, commercial) or other segment of interest

production budget, by product, by plant

purchases budget, by type of raw material

labor budget, by type of worker required, in hours or in number of workers

production cost budget, by product, by plant

budgets for other expenses, by category depending on the relative importance of various types of expenses (selling, general, administrative, research and development, and so on)

cash receipts budget

cash disbursements budget

cash budget, summarizing receipts and disbursements, indicating financing requirements

budgeted balance sheet, or pro forma balance sheet, showing the balance sheet expected at the end of the budget period

This set of budgets also includes unit cost budgets (standard costs as discussed in Chapter 7) as supporting schedules as well as a budget for capital expenditures (capital budgeting, which is discussed in Chapters 13 and 14). The order of these budgets is logical, not the only order that companies use; but, as we will see, there is an interrelationship among budgets.

Time Frames of Budgets

Budgets are almost always prepared for a year. Some firms also budget two to five years in advance. Most firms, especially those with seasonal operations, also budget for shorter periods. Depending on the sharpness of the seasonal patterns of business, a firm might budget quarterly, monthly, or even weekly for some important factors. Cash is one item that a firm might budget for very short periods.

Some companies use **continuous budgeting**. Each month the managers add an additional month to the budget, thus keeping a 12-month budget always available. At the end of January, for example, the firm has budgets through the end of the following January, and so on. Continuous budgeting keeps the firm's plans ahead. If the firm prepares only annual budgets, its plans will be formalized only through the end of the current year. Toward the end of each year it will have to prepare a new budget for the coming year. The budgeting process involves a great deal of work, and continuous budgeting spreads it throughout the year instead of concentrating it.

Some budgets are oriented not to time but to events. This is typical of project budgets and capital budgets. A **project budget** relates to a large job, such as the construction of a new plant. A **capital budget**, discussed in Chapters 13 and 14, relates to the firm's spending for new assets.

Relationships Among Budgets

Chapter 15 discussed and diagrammed the overall process of budgeting. This chapter works with the budgets themselves. Figure 16–1 diagrams the relationships among various budgets as well as various policies and assumptions regarding inventory and cash receipts and disbursements. The figure is simplified: the relationships and interrelationships are very complex. For instance, managers developing production budgets from the sales budgets might find that they cannot produce the required amounts because of shortages of labor, materials, or machinery. The process would have to restart, and the firm might change its strategies regarding particular products. Because it could not

FIGURE 16–1 Relationships Among Budgets

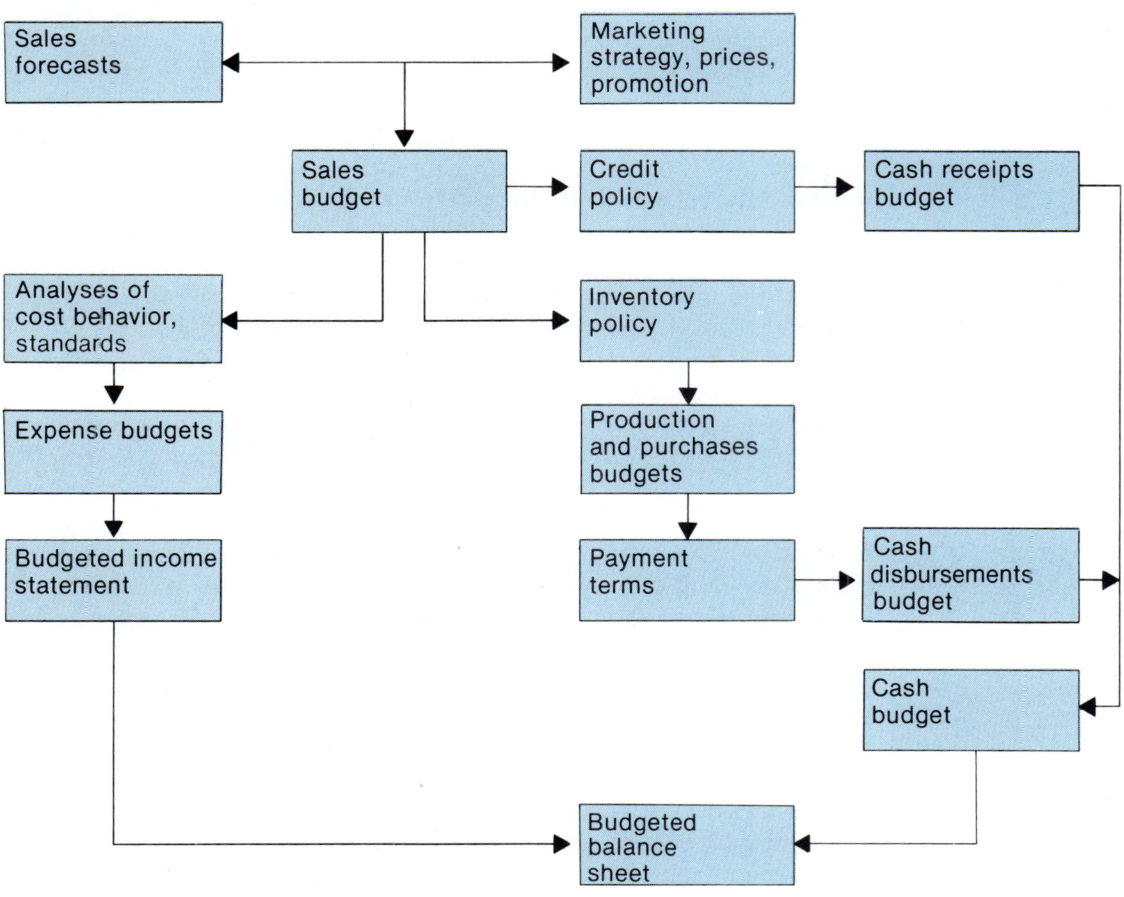

make all the units originally called for, it might raise prices or lower promotional expenses.

There could be similar to-and-fro movement between sales budgets and credit policy, and virtually all other budgets and policies. A completed first run at a master budget is like a smooth pond: a stone tossed into it will send ripples in all directions for considerable distances. Changing credit terms from a 60- to 30-day payment in an effort to collect cash more rapidly could adversely affect sales and profits, as could reducing the quantity of inventory of finished goods to save interest expense.

SALES BUDGETING

The sales budget is the starting point in developing the master budget. From it flow the production budget and flexible-expense budgets for costs that vary with sales and production. Sales budgeting usually begins with forecasts of sales of individual products. These forecasts can be by region, class of customer, or some other important breakdown. Sales forecasts are based on many assumptions, some explicitly stated, some implicit. Examples are the prices charged by the firm and its competitors, economic activity in the geographical areas the firm serves, number of salespeople, and advertising and promotional expenditures.

Because different managers use different assumptions about critical factors, there might be several forecasts of sales for each product or product line. Also, different forecasts might result from different forecasting techniques. As we shall describe, managerial judgment, historical trend analysis, and statistical techniques can all be used in developing forecasts. Therefore, a sales forecast is not a sales budget. The budget reflects, sometimes implicitly, one particular set of assumptions about prices, competitors' actions, and other critical factors. Managers must use forecasts to make decisions about the critical factors under their control such as prices, sales force, advertising, and geographical coverage.

Upper level managers might decide to de-emphasize one product or product line because of poor long-range potential. They might decide that serving a particular geographical market is unwise because of high transportation costs. A host of decisions must be made before sales forecasts become sales budgets.

The distinction between sales forecasting and sales budgeting comes down to passive versus active management. Managers who accept forecasts are acting passively. Those who attempt to influence the environment by altering policies and strategies are active, making decisions and taking actions to improve the firm's position.

In the interplay of forecasting and budgeting, the accountant plays an important role. Some sales managers are conscious of only a few factors, such as total volume and market share. They might not analyze the benefits and costs of changing strategies. The accountant might be involved in determining whether, for example, an increase in sales volume obtained by reducing prices and increasing advertising expenditures would be more profitable than the original strategy. Sensitivity analysis, the use of the basic principles of CVP analysis, and examining incremental costs and benefits are important tools that the accountant can bring to bear in this process. Because they are the principal providers of much of the information used in forecasting, accountants might also be involved in the development of forecasts. The following sections describe some common techniques of forecasting.

Statistical Approaches

Statistical approaches to the forecasting of sales come in two general types, time series analysis and indicator analysis. **Time series analysis** uses the techniques of regression analysis (and scatter diagrams) to predict sales based on patterns of historical sales. In general, the dependent variable in the regression equation is sales and the independent variable is time. We have seen that the past is not necessarily an accurate guide to the future; time series analysis is therefore unreliable in a changing environment.

When no major changes in the basic environmental conditions are expected, time series analysis may be valuable for forecasting sales. However, time series analysis is useful only for forecasting, not necessarily for budgeting, because it fails to consider whether management action in the past was good, bad, or indifferent. This criticism parallels the one in Chapter 7 regarding the use of historical performance for setting standard costs. The observed fact that unit sales have risen at a four percent annual rate says nothing about the effectiveness of managerial action: the market for the product might have been rising at a six percent rate and the company might have been lax in not achieving a higher rate of growth. Time series analysis can be extremely valuable in forecasting industry sales, and if the firm has been able, or expects to be able, to capture a specific percentage of the market, a good forecast of company sales might be obtainable. Such a forecast could be a starting point for developing a sales budget.

The major tools of **indicator analysis** are regression analysis and scatter diagrams. The independent variable is the **indicator**, the variable that is closely correlated with the sales of the firm or the industry. Indicators that firms find valuable range from the Gross National Product to the number of marriages, the number of building permits, and the sales of another product. Like time series analysis, indicator analysis can be most helpful in forecasting industry sales, from which the managers of a particular firm will have to develop budgets for their own firm based on an expected market share.

Indicators vary in value. The best indicator is one that *leads* the firm's sales. That is, the indicator rises before sales of the firm rise and falls before sales of the firm fall. If the indicator rises and falls along with sales, it is of little value for forecasting, because its signals come too late for management to take any action. For example, a manufacturer of cement used largely for building foundations could not use building starts as an indicator. By the time the number of building starts was published, the demand for the cement would already have materialized, because foundations are poured early in building. However, the cement manufacturer might be able to use building permits as an indicator because they are issued several months before actual building begins. As building permits rose or fell, the manufacturer could adjust production to meet the changing demand.

Indicators are also valuable if they are predictable, even if their rises and falls accompany those of the firm's sales. The Gross National Product is usually predictable within fairly narrow limits, and firms whose sales closely follow GNP are often able to predict sales quite well. Some firms use complex econometric models that include a great number of variables. Others buy the services of universities or companies that develop models of the economy and use them in their own sales forecasting and overall business planning.

Judgmental Approaches

Sales budgets are often set through consultations of salespeople, sales managers, and top management. Individual salespeople might submit budgets that are reviewed by district sales managers. The revised budgets go to upper levels of sales management (such as the vice president for sales) and finally to the chief executive officer. She, in turn, might make some revisions, consult with the sales vice president, and send the budgets back down the line. Another round or two of this process might ensue before the budget is finally adopted.

The major disadvantage of this process is that it lacks analytical content. People setting budgets are motivated by many factors, and the lack of some objective standard by which to judge the reasonableness of the budget makes the process iffy. On the plus side, the consultation and adjustment that take place involve the people responsible for carrying out the plans and meeting the goals. To the extent that participation is desirable, such consultation is desirable. Additionally, the method relies on the experienced judgment of people who should have a reasonably good idea of market conditions. At times, the judgment of experienced salespeople and sales managers might validly modify or override a budget based on a statistical forecast.

DEVELOPING THE MASTER BUDGET

Once the sales budget and the relationships among sales and the other critical variables are known or estimated, the actual development of the budgets is primarily a matter of technical analysis.

The mechanics of budgeting, the actual calculations of budgeted results, are now done largely by computer, whether by a program written to the company's specifications, a financial modeling package, or a microcomputer spreadsheet. Doing a budget by computer does not guarantee that it will be correct. First, the formulation could be logically incorrect. The person setting up the relationships might state that cash receipts from customers will be 40 percent of current month sales plus 70 percent of the previous month sales, which means that the company would collect 110 percent of its sales—an impossibility.

Second, the formulation could be logically correct, but the relationships could be misstated. For instance, if the company's customers pay 60 days after the sale, they pay in the second month after the sale (March sales paid in May, April's in June, etc.). The person doing the budget might misinterpret the facts as meaning that sales are collected in the month after the sale. Finally, the relationships might be correct in that they reflect the best available information, but things might not come about as budgeted. Sales might not materialize as budgeted, customers might take longer than expected to pay their bills, costs might be higher or lower than budgeted, and so on.

Generally speaking, the sales budget is done first because it is the basis for the budgeted income statement and budgets of purchases or production. From these budgets flow those for purchasing or manufacturing costs, selling and administrative expenses, cash receipts and disbursements, and finally, the budgeted, or pro forma, balance sheet. However, on occasion it is not possible to achieve the budgeted sales because of, for example, insufficient capacity. That is, the production budget required to meet the sales budget might not be achievable, so managers would have to revise the sales budget. Additionally, the sales budget is often developed in conjunction with budgets for some types of selling expenses, such as advertising, promotion, and sales salaries (and the number of salespeople to be employed). Thus, the budgets interact rather than flow in a straight line from the sales budget through the rest of the budgets in the package.

Illustration: Comprehensive Budget for the Enco Company

We shall use the data in Exhibit 16–1 to prepare the comprehensive budget for the Enco Company for March and April.[1] As you read the data, you will see that some of the existing facts (balances) do not agree with company policies. For example, the policy is to have finished goods inventory equal to 150 percent of the coming month's budgeted sales. Thus, as of 2/28/X0, finished goods should equal 13,500 (1.50 × 9,000 units budgeted for March), but they are only 11,800.

The inventory of raw materials is also lower than expected, but this is not

---

[1] You can use the electronic spreadsheet template BUDGET1.WK1 (shown in Exhibit 16–5) to help you use the information in Exhibit 16–1 and the budgets in Exhibit 16–2. In addition, a review problem relies on this template; thus, using it as you go through the example (to verify the results shown in Exhibit 16–2) will prepare you for the review problem as well.

obvious from the balance sheet because we do not yet know budgeted production for March, which would determine how much raw material Enco would budget to have on hand.

The reason for the shortfall in finished goods inventory could be that February sales were higher than budgeted, with February production based on the lower budgeted figure. It could also result from a problem in the produc-

EXHIBIT 16–1 Data for Comprehensive Budget—Enco Company

Product Data

Selling price		$25
Costs (at standard)		
Raw materials (4 lb at $0.50)	$ 2	
Direct labor ($\frac{1}{2}$ hr at $6)	3	
Variable overhead (at $8 per DLH)	4	
Fixed overhead	5[a]	
Total manufacturing cost	$14	
Selling and administrative costs		
Variable (commissions)		$2 per unit
Fixed		$35,000 per month

Sales Budget

March, 9,000 units; April, 12,000 units; May, 11,000 units; June, 10,000 units; July, 12,000 units.

Other Data

1. *Cash collections.* About 20 percent of sales are collected in the month of sale, another 78 percent in the month after sale, with about 2 percent becoming bad debts.
2. *Inventories.* Finished goods inventory is generally kept at about 150 percent of the coming month's budgeted sales requirements. Raw material inventory is held about equal to 80 percent of the coming month's budgeted production requirements.
3. *Cash disbursements.*
   a. Purchases of raw materials are paid, on average, 60 percent in the month of purchase, 40 percent in the month after purchase.
   b. All other production costs requiring cash disbursements are paid 80 percent in the month of production, 20 percent in the following month. All production costs require cash disbursement except the $15,000 monthly depreciation.
   c. Fixed selling and administrative expenses all require cash and are paid in the month incurred. Variable selling expenses (commissions) are paid in the month after they are earned.
   d. Enco expects to declare and pay a $5,000 cash dividend in April.
4. *Income taxes.* The income tax rate is 40 percent. The taxes payable on the February 28 balance sheet will be paid in April. Taxes accrued on income for March and April will be paid in July.

(continued)

(EXHIBIT 16–1 continued)

Balance Sheet as of February 28, 19X0

Assets		*Equities*	
Cash	$ 52,000	Accounts payable	
Accounts receivable, net	154,000	(raw materials)	$ 6,600
Inventories:		Taxes payable	15,000
Finished goods, 11,800		Commissions payable	16,000
units at $14	165,200	Accrued expenses	
Raw materials, 35,200 lb		(production costs)	22,000
at $0.50	17,600		
Plant and equipment:		Common stock	1,700,000
Cost	2,460,000		
Accumulated			
depreciation	(940,000)	Retained earnings	149,200
Totals	$1,908,800		$1,908,800

[a]Based on budgeted fixed costs of $60,000 per month and normal activity of 12,000 units per month. Depreciation is $15,000 per month.

tion process and/or from deliberate management action. The policies stated for Enco are simplified. Firms adopt different policies for different conditions. For example, a firm might wish to keep its inventory of finished goods at 80 percent of the coming month's budgeted sales during its slow selling season, and at 200 percent during the busy season. We shall see why shortly. The point here is that budgets are based on expectations. We do not expect actual results to reflect budgeted results precisely. Hence, the budgets to be prepared should be regarded as plans, not as commitments to be met regardless of future conditions.

As we go through individual components of the master budget, first attempt to determine how each budget would appear, then check your answers in the appropriate schedule in Exhibit 16–2. Be sure that you understand each schedule thoroughly before proceeding to the next, because the results are cumulative.[2] Most of the schedules depend on prior schedules.

Cash Receipts Budget

The pattern of collection of sales depends on credit policies and customers' behavior. Some firms offer discounts for payment within a specified period such as 10 days. Firms offer 30 days, 60 days, or some other period for payment without a discount, depending on trade practice and the creditworthiness of customers.

All things being equal, a firm would prefer that its customers pay immediately on receipt of the goods or in advance of delivery. Collection would be

[2]Again, we encourage you to use the template BUDGET1.WK1.

EXHIBIT 16–2 Comprehensive Budget for March and April—Enco Company

Schedule A—Cash Receipts Budget

	March	April
Collections of current month's sales, 20%	$ 45,000	$ 60,000
Collections from prior month, 78%	154,000[a]	175,500
Total budgeted receipts	$199,000	$235,500
Net accounts receivable at month end, 78% of month's budgeted sales	$175,500	$234,000

[a]Accounts receivable balance from February 28 balance sheet. All net receivables at end of a month are collected in the following month.

Schedule B—Production Budget

	March	April	May[b]
Desired ending inventory[a]	18,000	16,500	15,000
Budgeted sales	9,000	12,000	11,000
Total requirements	27,000	28,500	26,000
Beginning inventory	11,800[c]	18,000	16,500
Production	15,200	10,500	9,500

[a]150% of following month's budgeted sales—for example, March ending inventory = 12,000 × 150%.
[b]May production figures are needed to find April purchases.
[c]From balance sheet for February 28.

Schedule C—Purchases Budget—Pounds

	March	April
Desired ending inventory[a]	33,600	30,400
Used in production[b]	60,800	42,000
Total requirements	94,400	72,400
Beginning inventory	35,200[c]	33,600
Purchases budgeted	59,200	38,800
Dollar purchases at $0.50/lb	$29,600	$19,400

[a]80% × coming month's budgeted production × 4 lb.
[b]Current month's budgeted production × 4 lb.
[c]From balance sheet for February 28.

Schedule D—Production Cost Budget

	March	April
Direct labor at $3 per unit	$ 45,600	$ 31,500
Variable overhead at $4 per unit	60,800	42,000
Fixed overhead	60,000	60,000
Total production costs	$166,400	$133,500
Less depreciation	15,000	15,000
Production costs requiring cash payments	$151,400	$118,500

(continued)

(EXHIBIT 16–2 continued)

Schedule E—Cash Disbursements Budget

	March	April
Materials purchases—		
prior month (40%)	$ 6,600[a]	$ 11,840
current month (60%)	17,760	11,640
Production costs—prior month (20%)	22,000[a]	30,280
current month (80%)	121,120	94,800
Commissions, $2 × prior month's sales	16,000[a]	18,000
Fixed selling and administrative expenses	35,000	35,000
Taxes	—	15,000[a]
Dividends	—	5,000
Total	$218,480	$221,560

[a]From February 28 balance sheet.

Schedule F—Cash Budget

	March	April
Beginning balance	$ 52,000[a]	$ 32,520
Receipts (from receipts budget)	199,000	235,500
Total available cash	251,000	268,020
Disbursements (from disbursements budget)	218,480	221,560
Ending balance	$ 32,520	$ 46,460

[a]From February 28 balance sheet.

Schedule G—Budgeted Income Statement
March and April, 19X0

Sales $25 × (9,000 + 12,000)		$525,000
Standard cost of sales $14 × 21,000		294,000
Standard gross margin		231,000
Volume (application) variance[a]		8,500F
Actual gross margin		239,500
Selling and administrative expenses:		
Variable, 21,000 × $2	$42,000	
Fixed	70,000	
Bad debts, 2% × $525,000	10,500	122,500
Income before taxes		117,000
Income taxes at 40%		46,800
Net income		$ 70,200

[a]Production of 25,700 units for the two months minus 24,000 units normal activity, multiplied by $5 standard fixed cost per unit.

(continued)

(EXHIBIT 16–2 continued)

Schedule H—Pro Forma Balance Sheet as of April 30, 19X0

Assets		Equities	
Cash (from cash budget)	$ 46,460	Accounts payable[e] (materials)	$ 7,760
Accounts receivable, net[a]	234,000	Taxes payable[f]	46,800
Inventories:		Commissions payable[g]	24,000
Finished goods, 16,500[b] × $14	231,000	Accrued production costs[h]	23,700
Raw materials, 30,400[c] × $0.50	15,200	Common stock	1,700,000
Plant and equipment	2,460,000		
Accumulated depreciation[d]	(970,000)	Retained earnings[i]	214,400
Total	$2,016,660		$2,016,660

Each of the balance sheet figures can also be determined using standard financial accounting analysis. For example, accounts receivable at the end of April are equal to the beginning balance of $154,000 plus sales of $525,000 minus collections of $434,500 ($199,000 + $235,500) and bad debts of $10,500. Similar analyses may be used for inventories and liabilities.

[a] 78% × April budgeted sales of $300,000.

[b] From production budget, Schedule B = 1.5 × budgeted May sales of 11,000 units.

[c] From purchases budget, Schedule C = 0.80 × budgeted May production of 9,500 units × 4 lb per unit.

[d] $940,000 beginning balance plus $30,000 depreciation for March and April.

[e] 40% of April purchases of $19,400, from purchases budget, Schedule C.

[f] From income statement.

[g] $2 × April budgeted sales of 12,000 units.

[h] 20% × April budgeted production costs requiring cash, from production cost budget, Schedule D.

[i] Beginning balance of $149,200 plus net income of $70,200 minus dividend of $5,000.

certain, and the firm would not have to finance the investment in accounts receivable. A firm with receivables must obtain cash to pay current bills while awaiting the receipt of cash from credit customers. Securing these funds has at least an opportunity cost to the firm, since they are tied up. This idea was developed in Chapter 13 on capital budgeting. However, a requirement for immediate cash payment would severely reduce sales for many firms, because their customers would patronize more accommodating firms. Some firms prefer that their customers take plenty of time to pay, because they can charge high interest rates. For example, the interest rate on some retail stores' charge accounts may run to 18 percent or more, which is a good return on the investment in receivables.

Enco's cash receipts budget appears in Schedule A of Exhibit 16–2. March receipts are budgeted at 20 percent of March sales plus receivables at the end of February. April receipts are equal to 20 percent of April budgeted sales plus 78 percent of March budgeted sales. Net accounts receivable at month-end (accounts receivable less allowance for doubtful accounts) equal 78 percent of the monthly sales. We do not distinguish between gross accounts receivable and the allowance for doubtful accounts. The balance in the allowance account depends on how soon the firm writes off the individual bad debts as they become known.

This is a good time to point out that the balance sheet becomes a starting point for various parts of these schedules. In the cash receipts budget, accounts receivable is one such starting point; the balance coupled with the expectation that it will be collected in March (and that it is net of bad debts) is incorporated in the budget. This same point holds true for the production budget (beginning inventory of finished goods in March), the purchases budget (beginning inventory of materials in March), the cash disbursements budget (payables at the beginning of March and assumptions about when they will be paid), and the cash budget (beginning cash balance).

Production and Purchases Budgets

The firm's inventory policy governs production levels and levels of purchases. Inventory of finished goods is typically held equal to some budgeted sales requirements, such as twice the coming month's budgeted unit sales. This is done to meet extraordinary demands and as a hedge against short-term breakdowns or work stoppage. Inventory of raw materials is generally kept at a desired amount based on budgeted production for coming periods. For example, Enco Company keeps its raw materials at 80 percent of the budgeted requirements for the coming month's production.

A number of factors govern inventory policy. It is costly to hold inventory: insurance, taxes, cost of the capital invested (opportunity cost), obsolescence, and pilferage can amount to 20 to 25 percent of the cost of inventory over a year. However, carrying very little inventory of finished goods may result in lower sales; carrying small quantities of raw materials may result in stoppages in production. Inventory is also bought as a hedge against price increases.

Wide swings in production may be very costly. A firm that produces at 50 percent of capacity one month and 85 percent the next month may lose good workers, who get tired of being laid off in slack months. Overtime pay during high production periods may also be costly. Such companies might decide to downplay inventory levels and keep production at a more-or-less level rate throughout the year. Inventory would then rise rapidly in months of low sales and decline as sales pick up. The trend to a just-in-time (JIT) inventory and manufacturing philosophy results in extremely small inventories of materials, work in process, and finished goods.[3] JIT and models for determining

[3]Small inventories in finished goods may also require a flexible manufacturing system (FMS).

the optimal amount of inventory to carry and to buy or produce are presented in Chapter 20.

From a technical standpoint, the determination of required production or purchases in units is based on the familiar relationship

$$\text{beginning inventory} + \text{production} - \text{ending inventory} = \text{units sold}$$

Rearranging the equation gives

$$\text{production} = \text{ending inventory} + \text{units sold} - \text{beginning inventory}$$

Purchases of raw materials for a manufacturer will be expressed as:

$$\text{units purchased} = \text{ending inventory} + \text{units used in production} - \text{beginning inventory}$$

The two equations have the same general form, the difference being that material purchases are based on production, not sales, and are expressed in units of material (pounds, gallons, and so on), not of finished product.

A merchandising firm may express its required purchases of merchandise using the first formula expressed in dollars of cost:

$$\text{purchases in dollars} = \text{cost of ending inventory} + \text{cost of goods sold} - \text{cost of beginning inventory}$$

In general, a manufacturing firm must solve for production in units, rather than cost, because of fixed manufacturing costs. Raw material purchases may be solved for in terms of either units or cost. Enco's production and purchases budgets appear in Schedules B and C of Exhibit 16–2. Its budget for production costs is shown in Schedule D.

Cash Disbursements Budget

The cash disbursements budget relies on the patterns of payments for materials, other production costs, and selling and administrative expenses. In general, firms do not pay for raw material purchases in cash at delivery, but in 10 days, 30 days, or some other time depending on the supplier of the particular material. Workers are not paid as soon as they work, but perhaps a week later. Thus, we would not expect cash disbursements to match costs incurred in the same period. Costs incurred but not paid show up as accounts payable and accruals in the current liability section of the balance sheet. The cash disbursements budget also contains sporadic items such as dividends, insurance premiums, property taxes, quarterly payments of estimated income taxes, and purchases of plant and equipment. Schedule E of Exhibit 16–2 presents Enco's cash disbursements budget.

It is important to separate cash receipts and disbursements from sales and incurrence of costs or expenses. While an income statement for an interim period (such as March and April) will only show one-sixth of annual expenses such as insurance, the cash disbursement budget reflects the entire insurance premium in the month it is paid. In addition, some items appear on the cash disbursements budget that are not explicitly shown in the income statement and/or the balance sheet. Examples include payments for dividends, principal on loans, and capital asset acquisitions.

Cash Budget

This budget is an extremely important part of planning. Firms are severely embarrassed and may go bankrupt if they run out of cash or allow it to get so low that emergency financing is required. A banker considering whether to lend to a firm is more favorably disposed if the firm can show why it needs cash and how soon it can expect to repay the loan. If the treasurer of the firm rushed into the bank just as cash was about to run out, the banker would be reluctant to grant a loan because the firm's performance would indicate poor planning. Anticipating cash requirements and seeking financing well in advance of the need would give the company a much better chance of obtaining the loan and would probably help to ensure a lower rate of interest than would a distress loan.

The other side of the coin is excess cash. Cash on deposit in a checking account does not (generally) earn interest. A company that expects a surplus of cash above its normal desired balance would try to invest it in income-producing securities. A surplus that is expected to last for three months might be invested in 90-day government notes or other securities due within the three-month period. Schedule F gives Enco's cash budget.

Budgeted (Pro Forma) Income Statement

Schedule G shows the budgeted income statement for the two-month period. We could prepare this statement earlier in the process, but sometimes the cash budget will show that the firm needs to borrow money and will then have interest expense to be reflected in the budgeted income statement. We shall show the effects of financing shortly.

The budgeted income statement is important to the managers: they want to know whether budgeted operations will produce a satisfactory profit, and if not, what they might do to increase profits. Here again, the interplay of budgets is important. The managers might decide to raise prices, offer more-generous credit terms, or increase advertising and promotional expenses. They would then redo the set of budgets to see what would result if their expectations were borne out.

Additionally, the budgeted income statement shows the budgeted income taxes for the period, which the firm will have to pay in July (see item 4 of Other Data in Exhibit 16–1). This piece of information is needed for the budgeted balance sheet, as is the budgeted net income, which we shall add to retained earnings at February 28 in determining the April 30 balance of retained earnings.

Budgeted (Pro Forma) Balance Sheet

The treasurer is extremely interested in the cash budget, because obtaining financing and investing surplus cash are among his duties. The budgeted balance sheet is also helpful to the treasurer, because it shows some sources and uses of cash in the period after its date. In our example, the treasurer would see from the pro forma balance sheet (Schedule H) that the firm should expect to collect about $234,000 from outstanding receivables. He would also see that cash requirements for accounts payable and other current liabilities are already in place. The pro forma balance sheet does not indicate all sources and uses of cash for the coming period. Cash will be collected from sales in the coming period and paid for purchases and production in the coming period.

Additionally, the pro forma balance sheet might be part of a package of budgeted statements prepared for an application for a bank loan, or published for stockholders and other external parties (especially if dated at the end of a fiscal year). Some firms have loans requiring that a certain working capital (current assets minus current liabilities) or a certain current ratio (current assets divided by current liabilities) be maintained. If these requirements are not met, the loan might fall due immediately. In such cases the treasurer would want to see whether the company is in default on any of these provisions and, if so, take some corrective action. He might arrange to sell additional common stock, postpone purchases of plant and equipment, or seek to reduce production to conserve cash.

Finally, the pro forma balance sheet provides an estimate of the assets that the firm needs to achieve the sales, production, purchases, and cash budgets as well as projected income. When listing current and fixed assets, managers might find that the assets exceed the current estimate of available equities and that ready and/or affordable sources to balance assets and equities are not available. This discovery would cause a restructuring of the asset side of the balance sheet and a reworking of the other budgets with the pro forma balance sheet as a limitation. This additional example of the interrelationships among the budgets is illustrated in the next section.

In practice, many more schedules make up the comprehensive budget. Labor hours by department, overhead costs in itemized form, several products, and several raw materials probably are reflected in the budgets of a real company. Increased complexity does not require any changes in the basic procedures already illustrated: there would simply be more budgets of each type.

Cash Shortages and Financing

A serious problem arises if the cash budget shows a negative balance, or even a positive balance below the required minimum. No large firm would attempt to operate with $50 budgeted cash. Errors in estimating the flows of cash could easily turn such a low amount into a sizable deficit. Remember that we are dealing with expectations, so we cannot be sure that budgeted results and actual results will be the same.

Dealing with an expected cash shortage requires additional steps in the cash budget. Let us illustrate, using Enco Company and assuming that it has a minimum required cash balance of $40,000, that it can borrow at 1 percent interest per month, and that it borrows and repays in multiples of $10,000 (the last assumption is for simplicity). The cash budget from Exhibit 16–2 follows, along with the financing plan to cover the temporary shortage for March.

Revised Cash Budget—Enco Company

	March	April
Beginning balance	$ 52,000	$ 42,520
Receipts	199,000	235,500
Total available	251,000	278,020
Disbursements	218,480	221,560
Indicated balance	32,520	56,460
Minimum desired balance	40,000	40,000
Excess (deficiency)	(7,480)	16,460
Borrow (repay)	10,000	(10,000)
Interest	—	(200)[a]
Balance (equals indicated balance plus borrowing minus repayment and interest)	$ 42,520	$ 46,260

[a]$10,000 × 1% × 2 months.

If Enco followed the policy of keeping cash above $40,000, it would borrow at the beginning of March and repay at the end of April. The cost would be $200 interest expense, but it might be worthwhile to borrow rather than risk running out of cash.

OTHER BUDGETING TECHNIQUES

Pro Forma Balance Sheets

Cash budgeting sometimes uses pro forma balance sheets, especially when a manager wants to know how much cash is likely to be available at a future date to meet a specific obligation. For example, a bond issue might fall due in six months, a payment on a large plant expansion come due in one year, or a target dividend fall due in eight months. The treasurer wants to know whether sufficient cash will be available, and if not, what steps might be taken.

The analytical method used in such problems varies according to the circumstances and preferences of the managers. One method is to determine total asset requirements other than cash and total available equities. Cash is then a plug figure, which may be positive or negative, and is compared with the minimum balance that the firm wishes to keep on hand. To illustrate, we use the data in Exhibit 16–3. They relate to Beach Company, a retailing firm.

EXHIBIT 16–3 Data for Beach Company

Balance Sheet as of December 31, 19X4

Cash	$ 168,000	Accounts payable	$ 81,000
Accounts receivable	374,000	Other current liabilities	145,000
Inventory	244,000	$9\frac{1}{2}$% Bonds payable, due December 31, 19X5	450,000
Net fixed assets	1,210,000	Common stock	1,260,000
		Retained earnings	60,000
Total	$1,996,000		$1,996,000

Budgeted Income Statement for 19X5

Sales	$2,400,000
Cost of sales	960,000
Gross margin	1,440,000
Selling, general, and administrative expenses[a]	1,100,000
Income before taxes	340,000
Income taxes	167,000
Net income	$ 173,000

Other Data

1. Sales are expected to be evenly spread throughout the year.
2. Accounts receivable are collected in 60 days, on the average. Thus, receivables generally approximate sales for the prior two months.
3. The firm generally carries about a three-month supply of inventory. Sales in the first quarter of 19X6 are expected to be about $660,000 with the same cost of sales percentage as 19X5.
4. Purchases of fixed assets will be about $440,000 in 19X5.
5. Purchases are paid for about 30 days after purchase.
6. At the end of 19X5 *other current liabilities* are expected to be about $153,000.
7. The firm's treasurer hopes to pay a $75,000 dividend in 19X5.

[a] Includes $240,000 depreciation and $42,750 interest on $9\frac{1}{2}$% bonds.

Its treasurer is determining whether the firm will be able to pay its 9.5 percent debt due on December 31, 19X5.

A pro forma statement of required assets and available equities appears in Exhibit 16–4. It shows that if the firm does pay off the $9\frac{1}{2}$ percent bonds, it will have a negative cash balance of $415,000. Its assets needed to operate will be $2,074,000 exclusive of cash, while its available equities will be only $1,659,000. A negative cash balance is generally not possible; Beach will have to raise additional cash to bring the budgeted balance above zero, with a corresponding increase in equities.

EXHIBIT 16–4 Budgeted Required Assets and Available Equities—Beach Company, December 31, 19X5

Assets Required		Available Equities	
Accounts receivable[a]	$ 400,000	Accounts payable[d]	$ 88,000
Inventory[b]	264,000	Other current liabilities[e]	153,000
Net fixed assets[c]	1,410,000	Common stock	1,260,000
		Retained earnings[f]	158,000
Total	$2,074,000		$1,659,000

Indicated cash balance = ($415,000) = $1,659,000 − $2,074,000

[a] From other data items 1 and 2. Sales of $2,400,000 evenly spread gives average monthly sales of $200,000 ($2,400,000/12). Two months sales will be uncollected at year end.

[b] From other data item 3, sales in the first quarter of 19X6 are expected to be $660,000. Cost of goods sold is 40% of sales ($960,000/$2,400,000 from 19X5 budgeted income statement). The inventory of a three-month supply is then $660,000 × 40%.

[c] Beginning balance of $1,210,000 plus purchases of $440,000, from other data item 4, minus depreciation for the year of $240,000 from the note to the 19X5 budgeted income statement.

[d] December purchases of $88,000. With a three-month supply of inventory, purchases are made three months before sale. December purchases equal March cost of sales ($660,000/3 × 40%).

[e] Given in other data item 6.

[f] Beginning balance of $60,000 plus net income budgeted at $173,000 minus dividends budgeted at $75,000.

This method has some advantages over preparing a cash budget. It is much quicker, because preparing a cash budget requires determining the year-end balances of some of the balance sheet items anyway, and many more calculations. Variations of the method are used for making rough estimates of long-term financing requirements.

Budget Simulations

Many companies use computer programs to develop budgets under various assumed conditions. Once the firm has a program that does the calculations, it is relatively easy to test a large number of alternatives. For instance, the managers might be uncertain about the total market for its products during the coming year, but they might have in mind a range that seemed reasonable and achievable. They could run the simulation several times, using different levels of sales, to get some idea of the ranges of important variables such as income and cash flow.

In some cases a budget simulation could use regression analysis. The managers might put historical data into the computer, from which the program would develop estimates of relationships such as accounts receivable to sales, inventory levels of cost of sales, and so on. The program would then use these regression results along with the managers' forecasts of sales to develop budgeted income statements, balance sheets, and cash flow statements. Some commercial programs have these capabilities.

Firms might also develop simulation models of parts of their operations, perhaps using linear or other forms of mathematical programming to locate optimal actions. Some models allow the manager to simulate the behavior of competitors. For instance, the manager could see what would happen if the firm raised prices and competitors raised their prices by a lesser amount. Such a model requires estimates of the effects on volume of changes in prices and in the relative prices that all the firms charge.

Simulation models are costly to develop but relatively cheap to run. The programming effort can be huge, requiring the services of many people over a long period. Commercially available models are likely to be cheaper but are also likely to require modification to fit the firm's particular circumstances. Nevertheless, firms will probably continue to develop models of varying size and complexity to help them to simplify the enormous complexity of modern business operations.

Most microcomputer spreadsheets offer little formal simulation, although they allow extensive "what if" analysis because the user can change estimates, policies, and assumptions one or many at a time and see a new set of budgets quickly. The review problem uses such a spreadsheet and illustrates how sensitivity analysis is useful in the budgeting process.

SUMMARY

This chapter focused on the development of budgets. We saw that a large array of budgets may be necessary to get a fairly accurate portrayal of the firm's operations and its requirements for resources, especially cash.

The sales forecast is the beginning step in the development of budgets. Sales forecasts, along with assumptions derived from experience or specified by company policy, are the foundation on which the remaining budgets are built.

Budgets for manufacturing operations are developed with the aid of techniques described in earlier chapters, including standard costing. The cash budget is especially important because running out of cash is serious. Although managers cannot expect everything to go according to plan, they have a much better basis for making decisions when they use budgets.

REVIEW PROBLEM

Before starting the review problem, use the template BUDGET1.WK1 (supplied with the text) to verify the results in Exhibit 16–2. A copy of this template is shown in Exhibit 16–5. When using the template, link all parts of the Solution Section (the various pieces of the budget) to the Data Section at the

EXHIBIT 16–5 BUDGET1.WK1—Enco Company

```
 1     B       C       D       E         F         G        H        I        J        K
 2 Exhibit 16-5
 3 BUDGET1.WK1
 4 Enco Company
 5
 6 DATA SECTION (From Exhibit 16-1)
 7                                       cost/              cost/
 8 Product Data                 inputs   input      total    unit
 9  Selling price                                          $25.00
10  Costs (at standard)
11   Raw materials   (pounds)        4   $0.50       2.00
12   Direct labor     (hours)      0.5    6.00       3.00
13   Variable overhead             0.5    8.00       4.00
14   Fixed overhead                                  5.00  $14.00
15
16 Total fixed overhead
17  Depreciation               $15,000
18  Other (cash)                45,000
19   Total                     $60,000 per month
20
21 Normal activity              12,000 units
22 Fixed overhead per unit       $5.00
23
24 Selling and administrative costs
25  Variable (commissions)                                  $2.00
26  Fixed                      $35,000
27
28 Sales Budget                          March     April      May     June     July
29  Units                                9,000    12,000   11,000   10,000   12,000
30
31 Collections
32  Month of sale                   20%
33  Month after sale                78%
34  Uncollected                      2%
35                                ----
36         Total                   100%
37
38  Inventories
39   Finished goods                150% of next month's sales
40   Raw materials                  80% of next month's production requirements
41
42 Cash Disbursements
43  Purchases
44   Paid in month of purchase      60%
45   Paid in month after purch      40%
46
47  Other production costs
48   Paid in month of incurred      80%
49   Paid in month after incur      20%
50
51  Fixed selling/admin costs
```

(continued)

(EXHIBIT 16–5 continued)

```
  Paid in month of incurred     100%
  Paid in month after incur       0%

 Variable selling costs
  Paid in month of incurred       0%
  Paid in month after incur     100%

 Other cash disbursements
  Dividends                           $5,000 April

Income taxes
 Rate                                   40%
 Paid                             Current taxes payable paid in April
                                  April and May taxes paid in July

Balance Sheet as of February 28, 19X0
         Assets                                            Equities
 Cash                                      $52,000  Accounts payable
 Accounts Receivable, net                  154,000   (raw materials)              $6,600
 Inventories                                        Taxes payable                 15,000
  Finished goods                                    Commissions payable           16,000
         11,800 units at   $14.00          165,200  Accrued expenses
  Raw materials                                      (production costs)           22,000
         35,200 lbs. at     $0.50           17,600
 Plant and equipment                                Common stock               1,700,000
  Cost                                   2,460,000  Retained earnings            149,200
  Accumulated depreciation                (940,000)

                                        -----------                          -----------
                                        $1,908,800                            $1,908,800

SOLUTION SECTION (Based on Exhibit 16-2)

A.  Cash Receipts Budget
                                            March      April
Collections of current month's sales
Collections from prior months
                                           -------    -------
  Total budgeted receipts                       $0         $0

Net accounts receivable-month end

B.  Production Budget (Units)
                                            March      April       May
Desired ending inventory
Budgeted sales
                                           -------    -------    -------
  Total requirements                             0          0          0
Beginning inventory
                                           -------    -------    -------
Production                                       0          0          0
```

(continued)

(EXHIBIT 16–5 continued)

```
103
104 C.  Purchases Budget (Pounds)
105                                                March     April
106 Desired ending inventory
107 Used in production
108                                              -------   -------
109  Total requirements                                0         0
110 Beginning inventory
111                                              -------   -------
112 Purchases budgeted                                 0         0
113 Dollar purchases @                               $0        $0
114
115 D.  Production Cost Budget
116                                                March     April
117 Direct labor @    $       per unit
118 Variable OH @     $
119 Fixed overhead
120                                              -------   -------
121  Total production costs                            0         0
122 Less: depreciation
123                                              -------   -------
124 Production costs requiring cash                  $0        $0
125
126 E.  Cash Disbursements Budget
127                                                March     April
128 Materials purchases
129  prior month
130  current month
131 Production costs
132  prior month
133  current month
134 Commissions
135 Fixed selling and administrative
136 Taxes
137 Dividends
138                                              -------   -------
139  Total                                           $0        $0
140
141 F.  Cash Budget
142                                                March     April
143 Beginning balance
144 Receipts
145                                              -------   -------
146 Total available cash                               0         0
147 Disbursements
148                                              -------   -------
149 Ending balance                                   $0        $0
150
151 G.  Budgeted (Pro Forma) Income Statement
152     March and April, 19X0
153
```

(continued)

(EXHIBIT 16–5 continued)

```
154 Sales
155 Standard cost of sales
156                                              ---------
157 Standard gross margin
158 Application variance
159                                              ---------
160 Actual gross margin                                  0
161 Selling and administrative expenses
162  Variable
163  Fixed
164  Bad debts                                           0
165                                       ------ ---------
166 Income before taxes                                  0
167 Taxes
168                                              ---------
169 Net income                                          $0
170                                              =========
171
172 H.   Pro Forma Balance Sheet as of April 30, 19X0
173
174          Assets                                                 Equities
175  Cash                                               Accounts payable
176  Accounts Receivable, net                            (raw materials)
177  Inventories                                        Taxes payable
178   Finished goods                                    Commissions payable
179                 units at $                          Accrued expenses
180   Raw materials                                      (production costs)
181                 lbs. at  $
182  Plant and equipment                                Common stock
183   Cost                                              Retained earnings
184   Accumulated depreciation
185
186                                             -----------                           -----------
187                                                     $0                                     $0
```

top of the template. This will allow you to change estimates or assumptions in the data section and have them fully reflected through the master budget.

After verifying the results in Exhibit 16–2, change the appropriate data to reflect the following:

1. The sales manager of Enco (chapter illustration) has just informed you of a major development—a strike at a competitor's plant. She has also informed the president, who wants a new set of budgets for March and April based on these new sales projections: March, 12,000; April, 15,000; May, 16,000; June, 13,000; and July, 15,000. Change this information in the data section of BUDGET1.WK1 and print out all the schedules.
2. As you should verify, income increases to $141,300. However, the president was disturbed by the projected negative cash balance of

$9,240 at the end of March. Rather than the company going to the bank, the president has asked you to look at the possibility of changing the payment patterns for various expenses for March and April only.

a. What is the effect of changing the payments of Other Production Costs in the month incurred to 70 percent from 80 percent with the balance paid in the next month?

b. Independent of the above, what is the effect of changing the payments of Other Production Costs in the month incurred to 75 percent and the payment of Material Purchases to 55 percent (from 60 percent) with the balance paid the next month?

Results from part 1 are shown below. We have noted that income has gone up but that cash balances are down. These changes are results of the leads (purchase inventory in advance of sale) and lags (collect sales after sale is made).

In part 2a, if Other Production Costs are now paid on a 70%/30% pattern instead of 80%/20%, ending cash balances are:

March	$11,150
April	30,950

In part 2b, if Other Production Costs are paid on a 75%/25% basis and Material Purchases are paid based on 55%/45%, ending cash balances would be:

March	$ 3,665
April	24,175

Obviously, other combinations are possible, as you might discover in experimenting.

ANSWERS TO REVIEW PROBLEM—PART I

	March	*April*
Cash receipts budget:		
Current month	$ 60,000	$ 75,000
Prior month	154,000	234,000
Total	$214,000	$309,000
Production budget:		
Desired ending inventory	22,500	24,000
Sales	12,000	15,000
Total	34,500	39,000
Beginning inventory	11,800	22,500
Production	22,700	16,500
Purchases budget, lb:		
Desired ending inventory	52,800	36,800
Used	90,800	66,000
Total	143,600	102,800
Beginning inventory	35,200	52,800
Purchases	108,400	50,000
Dollar purchases	$ 54,200	$ 25,000

		March	*April*
Production cost budget:			
Direct labor		$ 68,100	$ 49,500
Variable overhead		90,800	66,000
Fixed overhead		60,000	60,000
Total costs		218,900	175,500
Less depreciation		15,000	15,000
Cash production costs		$203,900	$160,500
Cash disbursements budget:			
Materials—current month		$ 32,520	$ 15,000
—prior month		6,600	21,680
Production costs—current		163,120	128,400
—prior		22,000	40,780
Commissions		16,000	24,000
Fixed S, G, & A		35,000	35,000
Taxes			15,000
Dividends			5,000
Total		$275,240	$284,860
Cash budget:			
Beginning balance		$ 52,000	($ 9,240)
Receipts		214,000	309,000
Disbursements		(275,240)	(284,860)
Indicated balance		($9,240)	$ 14,900
Budgeted income statement, March–April:			
Sales			$675,000
Standard cost of sales			378,000
Standard gross margin			297,000
Volume variance			76,000
Actual gross margin			373,000
Commissions		$ 54,000	
Bad debts		13,500	
Fixed S, G, & A		70,000	137,500
Income before taxes			235,500
Income taxes	40%		94,200
Net income			$141,300

ASSIGNMENTS

16–1 Cash Receipts Budget Thurston Company, a retailer, collects its sales 30 percent in the month of sale and 70 percent in the following month. It has the following sales budget for the first few months of 19X6: January, $100,000; February, $120,000; March, $110,000; April, $130,000; May, $120,000. Receivables at December 31, 19X5, are $60,000.

REQUIRED

Prepare cash receipts budgets for January, February, and March and for the three months as a whole.

16–2 Purchases Budget (Continuation of Assignment 16–1) Thurston's cost of sales is 65 percent. It keeps inventory equal to the budgeted sales requirements for the next two months. Inventory at December 31, 19X5, is $95,000.

REQUIRED

Prepare purchases budgets for January, February, and March and for the three months as a whole.

16–3 Cash Budget (Continuation of Assignment 16–2) Thurston pays for its purchases in the month after purchase. It has $10,000 monthly fixed costs, of which $4,000 is depreciation. Its only other cash cost is a 7 percent commission on sales that it pays in the month after it is earned. The beginning accounts payable for merchandise are $55,000, and the beginning accrual for sales commissions is $7,000. Beginning cash is $20,000.

REQUIRED

Prepare cash budgets for January, February, and March and for the three months as a whole.

16–4 Budgeted Income Statement and Pro Forma Balance Sheet (Continuation of Assignment 16–3) Thurston's balance sheet at the beginning of January appears below.

THURSTON COMPANY
Balance Sheet
December 31, 19X5

Cash	$ 20,000	Payables	$ 55,000
Receivables	60,000	Accruals	7,000
Inventory	95,000	Common stock	220,000
Fixed assets	250,000	Retained earnings	143,000
Total	$425,000		$425,000

REQUIRED

Prepare a budgeted income statement for the first three months of 19X6 (total only, not by month) and a pro forma balance sheet as of March 31, 19X6.

16–5 Cash Flow Businesspeople often use the term *cash flow* to mean net income plus depreciation. This definition refers only to operating cash flows, not to borrowings, issues of stock, purchases of plant assets, and other short-term and long-term sources and uses of cash.

REQUIRED

What is wrong with the definition? Does it leave anything out? Does it include too much?

16–6 Cash Receipts Analysis The data below reflect the sales, receivables, and cash receipts for Allen Company for the past five months.

	March	*April*	*May*	*June*	*July*
Sales	$64,000	$ 81,000	$ 75,000	$ 92,000	$114,000
Receivables, end of month	89,000	113,000	115,500	129,500	160,000
Cash collections	90,000	57,000	72,500	78,000	83,500

REQUIRED

Determine the pattern of collection of sales. (For example, sales are collected in 30 days.)

16–7 Cash Disbursements Budget Farnsworth Manufacturing Company makes a number of products. The firm uses normal costing, charging direct labor and materials at actual cost and applying overhead at a rate of $4.80 per direct labor hour. Variable overhead is about $3 per direct labor hour, and fixed overhead is budgeted at $54,000 per month, including $6,500 depreciation.

Both direct labor and variable overhead are paid for 75 percent in the month incurred, 25 percent in the following month. Fixed overhead requiring cash is paid in the month incurred. All direct laborers earn $8 per hour. An assistant to the controller has prepared the following budgets of production cost. Material purchases are budgeted separately.

	April	*May*	*June*	*July*
Direct labor	$226,500	$284,200	$310,100	$295,600
Overhead at $4.80/DLH	135,900	170,520	186,060	177,300

The assistant has used these figures in budgeting cost of goods manufactured but is unsure how to use them in budgeting cash disbursements.

REQUIRED

Prepare cash disbursements budgets for May, June, and July for direct labor and overhead.

16–8 Master Budget (CMA Adapted) SecCo manufactures and sells security systems. The company started by installing photoelectric security systems in existing offices and has expanded into the private home market. SecCo has a basic security system of three standard products, each of which can be upgraded to meet the needs of customers. SecCo's manufacturing operation is moderate in size as the bulk of the component manufacturing is completed by independent contractors. The security systems are approximately 85 percent complete when received from contractors and require only final assembly in SecCo's plant. Each product passes through at least one of three assembly operations. SecCo employs a standard cost system in its manufacturing operation to promote cost and inventory control.

SecCo operates in a flourishing community. There is evidence that a great deal of new commercial construction will take place soon, and SecCo's management has decided to pursue this new market. To be competitive, SecCo will have to expand its operations.

In view of the expected increase in business, Sandra Becker, SecCo's Controller, believes that SecCo should implement a master budget system. Becker has decided to make a formal presentation to SecCo's president explaining the benefits of a master budget system and outlining the budget schedules and reports that would be required.

REQUIRED

1. Explain the benefits that can be derived from implementing a master budget system.
2. If Sandra Becker is going to develop a master budget system for SecCo:
   - ***a.*** identify, in order, the schedules and/or statements that will have to be prepared

b. identify the subsequent schedules and/or statements that would be derived from the schedules and statements identified in part 1.

16–9 Basic Comprehensive Budget The following data pertain to Newhall Company, which operates a wholesale business:

Sales Forecasts—19X6

January	$ 80,000
February	100,000
March	120,000
April	110,000
May	100,000

Balance Sheet, December 31, 19X5

Cash	$ 20,000	Accounts payable	$ 27,000
Accounts receivable, net	70,000	Accrued commissions	9,000
Inventory	115,000	Common stock	220,000
Net fixed assets	190,000	Retained earnings	139,000
Total	$395,000		$395,000

Other data:

1. All sales are on credit. About 40 percent of sales are collected in the month of sale, 58 percent in the month after sale, with 2 percent bad debts.
2. Cost of sales runs about 60 percent of sales.
3. A 7 percent commission on sales is the only variable cost besides cost of sales. The commissions are paid in the month after they are earned.
4. The firm keeps inventory about equal to a two-month supply.
5. The firm pays for its merchandise in the month after purchase.
6. Fixed operating costs are $12,000 per month, including $4,000 depreciation.

REQUIRED

1. Prepare a budgeted income statement for the quarter ending March 31. Do not break it down by month.
2. Prepare a cash budget and all necessary supporting schedules for each of the first three months of 19X6.
3. Prepare a pro forma balance sheet as of March 31, 19X6.

16–10 Cash Budget Lyman Company is a wholesaler of school supplies. The firm's busy season is July through September, when sales trail off. In June 19X7 the controller was preparing a cash budget to determine whether he would have to use the firm's line of credit at a local bank. He had amassed the following information:

Sales forecast. June, $217,500; July, $325,600; August, $337,200; September, $296,400; October, $243,100; November, $211,300.

Cost of sales averages 60 percent of sales. Operating expenses are $37,400 per month plus 10 percent of sales, all paid during the month incurred except for $2,800 in depreciation. The firm tries to keep a two-month supply of inventory on hand and pays for its purchases in 30 days. Its customers pay, on average, in 60 days.

The controller would like to keep a cash balance of at least $30,000 and was therefore not happy at the projected balance of $28,750 at the end of June (see below). Balance sheet data expected at June 30 appear below.

Cash	$ 28,750
Accounts receivable	416,300 ($198,800 from May, $217,500 from June)
Inventory	367,200
Accounts payable	198,240 (anticipated from expected purchases in June)

REQUIRED

Prepare a cash budget by month from July through September and supporting schedules showing whether the firm will need to use its line of credit and when it can pay off any loans. Assume that borrowings against the line of credit, if needed, are made in multiples of $10,000. Ignore interest.

16–11 Cash Budgets (CMA) Riley Instruments, a rapidly expanding electronic parts distributor, is formulating plans for 19X8. Bill Stockton, the firm's Director of Marketing, has completed his 19X8 forecast and is confident that sales estimates will be met or exceeded. The following sales figures show the growth expected and will provide the planning basis for other corporate departments.

Month	*Forecasted Sales*	*Month*	*Forecasted Sales*
January	$1,800,000	July	$3,000,000
February	2,000,000	August	3,000,000
March	1,800,000	September	3,200,000
April	2,200,000	October	3,200,000
May	2,500,000	November	3,000,000
June	2,800,000	December	3,400,000

Samantha Carlson, Assistant Controller, has been given the responsibility of formulating the cash flow projection, a critical element during a period of rapid expansion. The following information will be used in preparing the cash analysis.

Riley has experienced an excellent record in accounts receivable collection and expects this trend to continue. Sixty percent of billings are collected in the month after the sale and 40 percent in the second month after the sale. Uncollectible accounts are nominal and will not be considered in the analysis.

The purchase of electronic parts is Riley's largest expenditure; the cost of these items is equal to 50 percent of sales. Sixty percent of the parts are received by Riley one month prior to sale and 40 percent are received during the month of sale.

Historically, 80 percent of accounts payable have been cleared by Riley one month after receipt of purchased parts and the remaining 20 percent have been cleared two months after receipt.

Hourly wages, including fringe benefits, are a factor of sales volume and are equal to 20 percent of the current month's sales. These wages are paid in the month incurred.

General and administrative expenses are projected at $2,640,000 for 19X8. The composition of these expenses is given below. All of these expenses are incurred uniformly throughout the year except property taxes. Property taxes are paid in four equal installments in the last month of each quarter.

Salaries	$ 480,000
Promotion	660,000
Property taxes	240,000
Insurance	360,000
Utilities	300,000
Depreciation	600,000
	$2,640,000

Income tax payments are made by Riley in the first month of each quarter based on the income for the prior quarter. Riley is subject to an effective income tax rate of 40 percent. Riley's net income for the first quarter of 19X8 is projected to be $612,000.

Riley has a corporate policy of maintaining an end-of-month cash balance of $100,000. Cash is invested or borrowed monthly, as necessary, to maintain this balance.

Riley uses a calendar year reporting period.

REQUIRED

1. Prepare a pro forma schedule of cash receipts and disbursements for Riley Instruments by month for the second quarter of 19X8. Be sure that all receipts, disbursements, and borrowing/investing are presented on a monthly basis. Ignore the interest expense and/or income associated with borrowing/investing.
2. Discuss why cash budgeting is particularly important for a rapidly expanding company such as Riley Instruments.

16–12 Basic Budgets for Production and Purchases Morlin Company makes a single product. Data appear below.

Raw materials, 2 pounds at $3/lb.

Inventory requirements, two-month supply of finished goods, one-month supply of raw materials (based on production needs).

Sales forecasts (in units): January, 1,000; February, 1,200; March, 1,300; April, 1,500; May, 1,400; June, 1,600.

The firm began January with 1,800 units of finished goods; 2,300 pounds of raw materials.

REQUIRED

1. Prepare production budgets for months January through April.
2. Prepare budgets of purchases of raw materials, both in pounds and in dollars, for as many months as you can. Explain why you had to stop where you did.

16–13 Cash Budget—Manufacturer The treasurer of Malta Manufacturing Company has been developing information to prepare a cash budget for the period August–October. He has amassed the following:

Sales forecast. August, 68,000 units; September, 82,000 units; October, 70,000 units; November, 64,000 units; December, 61,000 units.
Price and cost data. The selling price is $10 per unit. Material cost is $2 per unit, direct labor and variable manufacturing overhead are $4 per unit. Fixed factory overhead is $120,000 per month, including $15,000 depreciation. Selling and administrative expenses are $42,500 per month (all cash costs), plus $0.80 per unit sold (commission).
Inventory policy. The firm tries to keep finished goods inventory at $1\frac{1}{2}$ times the coming month's budgeted sales. It keeps raw material inventory at twice the coming month's budgeted production. It makes purchases evenly over a month.
Collection of sales. Sales are collected about 40 percent in the month of sale, 58 percent in the following month, with 2 percent bad debts. Bad debts are not included in the cost data given above.
Cash disbursements. The firm pays for two-thirds of its materials in the month after purchase, one-third in the second month after purchase. Selling and administrative expenses are paid in the month incurred, except that the $0.80 commission is paid in the month after sale. Manufacturing costs, other than for materials, are paid in the month incurred.
Balance sheet data. At the end of July the firm should have about $78,000 in cash, $348,000 in net accounts receivable, 95,000 units of finished product, and $288,000 in raw material inventory. Accounts payable due in August from July purchases are $126,000, from June purchases are $67,000. Another $63,000 is due in September from July purchases. Sales commissions payable in August are $48,000 from July sales.

REQUIRED

Prepare a cash budget by month for the August–October period. Keep cash at least at $50,000 for borrowing and repaying in $10,000 multiples. Ignore interest.

16–14 Balance Sheet Data (Continuation of Assignment 16–13)

REQUIRED

Use your solution to assignment 16–13 to develop as many items as you can that would appear on Malta Manufacturing's balance sheet as of the end of September. Assume that the firm uses variable costing for its finished-goods inventory.

16–15 Cash Budget—One Month Burlington Dry Goods Company makes all its purchases on credit, paying in 10 days to obtain the 2 percent discount offered by its suppliers. The firm records its inventory net of the discount and tries to keep inventory at gross cost about equal to the sales requirements budgeted for the next two months. The firm sells on credit, with 40 percent of its customers paying within 20 days to take advantage of the 1 percent discount that Burlington offers for prompt payment. The remainder pay in 60 days. Cost of sales (gross) averages 47 percent of sales.

The following additional information is available:

Sales:	
August (actual)	$340,000
September (actual)	404,000
October (budgeted)	385,000
November (budgeted)	410,000
December (budgeted)	390,000
Inventory at September 30	365,500
Purchases in September (net of discount)	176,000
Operating expenses budgeted for October	144,000 + 6% of sales
Cash at September 30	53,500

The 6 percent variable operating expenses is for sales commissions. Depreciation included in the $144,000 is $12,500. All operating expenses requiring cash are paid in the month incurred. Sales and purchases are made evenly throughout each month. Assume that each month has 30 days.

REQUIRED

Prepare a cash budget for October.

16–16 Selected Budgeting Results Borner Company has the following sales forecast, in units: January, 12,000; February, 11,000; March, 13,000; April, 14,000; May, 16,000; June, 17,000; July, 18,000; August, 15,000. The company sells its product for $12. Variable manufacturing costs are $8, including $3 for materials. Monthly fixed manufacturing costs are $60,000, including $5,000 depreciation. The company collects its sales in 15 days. It maintains finished goods inventory at double the coming month budgeted sales and keeps a two-month supply of materials inventory.

REQUIRED

1. Determine budgeted cash collections for April.
2. Determine budgeted production for March.
3. Determine budgeted purchases of materials for February.
4. The company pays all of its costs, including material purchases, immediately. Determine budgeted cash disbursements for February.

16–17 Changes in Estimates (CMA) WestWood Corporation is a woodstove manufacturer located in southern Oregon. WestWood manufactures three models—small stoves for heating a single room, medium-sized units for use in mobile homes and to supplement central heating systems, and large stoves with the capacity to provide central heating.

The manufacturing process consists of shearing and shaping steel, fabricating, welding, painting, and finishing. Molded doors are custom built at an outside foundry in the state, brass plated at a plater, and fitted with custom etched glass during assembly at WestWood's plant. The finished stoves are delivered to dealers either directly or through regional warehouses located throughout the western United States. WestWood owns the three tractor trailers and one large truck used to ship stoves to dealers and warehouses.

The budget for the year ending February 28, 19X6, was finalized in January of 19X5 and was based upon an assumption of the continuation of the 10 percent annual growth rate that WestWood had experienced since 19X0.

Stove sales are seasonal, and the first quarter of WestWood's fiscal year is usually a slack period. As a consequence, inventory levels were down at the start of the current fiscal year on March 1, 19X5.

WestWood's sales orders for the first quarter ended May 31, 19X5, were up 54 percent from the same period last year and 40 percent above the first quarter budget. Unfortunately, not all of the sales orders could be filled because of reduced inventory levels at the beginning of the quarter. WestWood's plant was able to increase production over budgeted levels, but not in sufficient quantity to compensate for the large increase in orders. Therefore, there is a large backlog of orders. Furthermore, preliminary orders for the busy fall season are 60 percent above the budget and the projections for the winter of 19X5–X6 indicate no decrease in demand. WestWood's president attributes the increase to effective advertising, the products' good reputation, the increased number of installations of woodstoves in new houses, and the bankruptcy of WestWood's principal competitor.

REQUIRED

1. WestWood Corporation's sales for the remainder of the 19X5–X6 fiscal year will be much greater than were predicted five months ago. Explain the effect this increase will have on the operations in the following functional areas of WestWood.
   a. production
   b. finance and accounting
   c. marketing
   d. personnel
2. Some companies follow the practice of preparing a continuous budget.
   a. Explain what a continuous budget is.
   b. Explain how WestWood Corporation could benefit by the preparation of a continuous budget.

16–18 Pro Forma Balance Sheet Amcom Company had the following balance sheet at December 31, 19X3.

Cash	$ 20	Current liabilities	$ 80
Accounts receivable	100		
Inventory	60		
Plant & Equipment (net)	400	Stockholders' equity	500
Total	$580		$580

The budgeted income statement for 19X4 shows:

Sales	$800
Cost of sales	480
Gross margin	320
Operating expenses (includes $30 depreciation)	250
Net income	$ 70

Amcom expects to pay a $50 dividend in mid-19X4. It collects its sales in 90 days and maintains a two-month supply of inventory. Current liabilities are expected to be $80 at the end of 19X4, and sales in 19X5 are expected to be 10 percent higher than in 19X4, with cost of sales remaining at 60 percent of sales. Amcom does not plan to buy any plant assets in 19X4.

REQUIRED

Determine the amount of cash, or the financing gap, that the company should have at the end of 19X4.

16–19 Sales Forecasting, Regression Analysis The sales manager of Bramon Cement Company has collected the following data to get an idea of the relationship, if any, between the firm's sales and total dollars spent on construction in the area that Bramon serves. All dollar amounts are in millions.

Year	Total Construction	Sales of Bramon
19X1	$3,200	$27
19X2	3,600	30
19X3	2,400	22
19X4	3,100	24
19X5	3,900	35
19X6	3,800	32

REQUIRED

1. Develop a regression equation that relates Bramon's sales to total construction spending. Find the standard error of the estimate and of the b coefficient, and the value of r^2.
2. The sales manager has read a series of forecasts of construction spending in 19X7. They range from \$3,500 to \$3,700 (in millions). What would you forecast for Bramon's sales for 19X7, and how much confidence would you have in your forecast?

16–20 Pro Forma Balance Sheet Whittaker Company is a wholesaler of dry goods. The firm has a \$200,000 line of credit with a local bank that the company's treasurer expects to use during the coming period. In fact, she is not sure whether the firm will be able to get by with only \$200,000 and has decided to prepare a pro forma balance sheet as of the end of April 19X7. She has assembled the following information.

Month	Sales Forecast	Purchases Forecast
January	$280,000	$210,000
February	315,000	382,000
March	476,000	302,000
April	490,000	156,000
May	375,000	138,000

Other data are:

1. Cost of sales averages 60 percent of sales.
2. All sales are on credit, with payments made in 60 days.
3. The firm generally maintains an inventory of about twice the coming month's budgeted sales requirements. The purchases forecasted above reflect this policy.
4. The firm pays for its purchases in 30 days.
5. Operating expenses, all fixed, are \$130,000 per month. They are paid as incurred, except for depreciation, which is \$10,000 per month.
6. The dividend payable shown below will be paid in April.

The expected balance sheet at December 31, 19X6, is given below.

Balance Sheet (Expected), December 31, 19X6—Whittaker Company

Cash	$ 80,000	Accounts payable (merchandise)	$ 165,000
Accounts receivable	650,000	Dividend payable	40,000
Inventory	328,000	Long-term debt	400,000
Plant and equipment (net)	920,000	Stockholder equity	1,373,000
Totals	$1,978,000		$1,978,000

The treasurer believes that $70,000 is the minimum balance of cash that the firm needs to operate.

REQUIRED

Determine whether the firm will need more than $200,000 at the end of April by preparing a pro forma balance sheet as of April 30, 19X7. You need not prepare cash budgets for each month to make the determination.

16–21 Sales Forecasting Multitronics, Inc., is a large manufacturer of various high-technology products. The budget director of the firm has been working on sales budgets for each major line and has run into a problem with the semiconductor segment of the business.

The firm generally captures about 15 percent of the total semiconductor market; 13 percent was the lowest share in recent years and 16.5 percent was the highest. A recent article in a trade journal forecast a 20 percent increase in semiconductor sales for the coming year, assuming that economic conditions did not deteriorate. A mild recession, the article stated, would drop the increase to about 12 percent, while a severe recession would reduce it to 4 percent. Total industry sales for the current year should be about $68 million.

The sales manager has told the budget director that he expects Multitronics to sell about $14 million worth of semiconductors in the coming year.

Reports from government agencies and private economic consulting firms indicate that the probability of a mild recession is about 25 percent, of a severe recession, 15 percent.

REQUIRED

Develop an optimistic forecast for Multitronics, a pessimistic one, and one that you would use for budgeting production, labor supply, and other items for the coming year. Be prepared to defend the figure you use for budgeting.

16–22 Cash Collection Patterns The following independent situations describe the cash collection experiences of various firms:

1. A firm makes 20 percent of its sales for cash. Its credit sales, except for bad debts equaling 2 percent of credit sales, come in 30 days after sale.
2. A firm's records show that its accounts receivable equal sales for the current month plus 40 percent of sales for the prior month.
3. A firm's accounts receivable turnover (sales/accounts receivable) is four times per year.
4. A firm offers a 2 percent discount for customers who pay within 10 days after sale. Customers accounting for 80 percent of total sales pay within the discount period; the remainder pay in 60 days.

5. A firm makes 10 percent of its sales for cash. It makes available a 1 percent discount to the customers who pay within 20 days, and the cash customers get that discount. Of the credit sales, about 1 percent become bad debts, 40 percent of the total credit sales are paid within the discount period, and the remainder are collected in 60 days.

REQUIRED

Assuming that sales are made evenly throughout each month, and that each month has 30 days, write an equation to determine cash collections for each firm. Use the notation C_t = cash collections in month t, S_t = sales in month t, S_{t-1} = sales in the prior month, and so on.

16–23 Cash Management (CMA) Royal Container, a privately held firm founded in 19X2, specializes in the packaging of toys and games. The company's administrative offices are in Chicago, and the regional packaging plants are located in Seattle, Little Rock, Nashville, and Hartford. Royal Container expects 19X6 sales to exceed $25 million, and the company is forecasting its first profitable year.

Because of its rapid growth, Royal Container has had ongoing requirements for additional working capital. The bank that participated in the initial financing of the company has arranged for additional long-term loans and extended a $3 million line of credit to the company. However, the bank is now reluctant to enter into a new loan agreement and has declined to increase the company's line of credit.

The Board of Directors of Royal Container is concerned about the company's working capital position and has recently hired Jim Wilson as Treasurer of the company. Wilson has been directed to improve the company's working capital position. Since joining Royal Container, Wilson has gathered the following information about the company's operations.

Based on sales data received from the regional plants, all invoices are prepared at the Chicago office during the last week of each month. All sales are made on a credit basis, and payment terms are net 30 days.

Customers' checks are sent to the Chicago office for processing and are deposited in the bank at 3:00 p.m. each afternoon. Approximately one and one-half days are required to process and deposit a check once it is received at the Chicago office.

The collection effort on past due accounts is haphazard and consists entirely of phone calls made by the controller when time allows. The company does not charge interest on past-due accounts.

Royal Container has a strict credit policy, but it is not applied evenly. Because sales are made from all five locations, credit is often granted by the individual making the sale.

Each of Royal Container's regional plants has its own bank account for disbursements for payroll, inventory purchases, and repair and maintenance of equipment. These accounts are replenished by wire transfer of funds from the Chicago office.

Because each plant controls its own disbursements, payment procedures are not standardized. Some locations take advantage of vendor discounts while others pay in 30 days.

Royal Container has yet to develop inventory policies and procedures. Each plant does its own purchasing and maintains its own inventory records. New toys and games are continually being developed to keep up with changing tastes and Royal Container must keep pace. Therefore, new items are frequently being added to inventories.

Royal Container's board is concerned about the company's working capital position; however, it does not wish to make a public offering to raise cash unless it becomes absolutely necessary.

REQUIRED

1. Discuss how Jim Wilson could improve Royal Container's working capital position by addressing the following areas of cash management.
   a. acceleration of cash receipts
   b. deceleration of cash disbursements
   c. generation of cash
2. Describe how Royal Container's cash management might differ between a period of high interest rates and a period of low interest rates.

16–24 Maintaining a Cash Balance (CMA) Lektron Corporation, a small but rapidly growing electronic components manufacturer with an industrial clientele, was founded in 19X3 by Barbara Siebert, and quickly gained a reputation as a low cost, high quality producer with an innovative product line. As a result, sales have been growing and reached $18 million for the fiscal year ended November 30, 19X8.

Although there are no requirements for Lektron to maintain compensating balances, it has been Siebert's policy to maintain an average cash balance of $100,000 in the corporate checking account. However, over the last several months, the cash needs have increased, with the cash balance recently falling below $30,000. Siebert has become concerned about the decreasing liquidity of her company. In the past, she has noticed that periods of rapid growth have reduced the cash balance. A new product line is scheduled to be introduced in two months that should result in another rapid sales expansion. To avoid a liquidity problem, Rich Simon, an experienced cash manager, has been hired to oversee the credit approval and collection procedures.

After review, Simon has proposed the following changes to the current procedures to improve cash management at Lektron. Neither proposal will affect gross sales.

Proposal 1—Improve collection efforts Simon has recommended a more concentrated credit and collection management system that should reduce the average collection period to 32 days, and should reduce the bad debt to one-half percent of sales. Currently all sales are on a credit basis with terms of net 30 days; the company has an average collection period of 42 days. The provision for bad debts equals one percent of sales; this amount is similar to the actual experience with accounts receivable write-offs. Siebert has previously approved all credit sales, and a clerk has handled the collection process, both of them performing these functions in addition to their regular duties. The proposed system will require more personnel and a more extensive use of outside credit reports and agencies. Simon has estimated that current procedures for credit and collections have cost the company $20,000 annually, while the new system would require total annual expenditures of $130,000.

Proposal 2—Offer cash discount Simon has also recommended an early payment cash discount of one percent that would change the credit terms to 1/10, net 30 days. It is estimated that 25 percent of the customers will take advantage of the discount and that the average collection period for all the accounts will be further reduced by an additional eight days.

For the purpose of any calculations, assume a 360-day year and use a pretax opportunity cost of 12 percent, simple interest.

REQUIRED

1. Barbara Siebert has been attempting to maintain a large cash balance in the firm's checking account.
   a. Identify and explain three motives for a company to maintain a substantial cash balance.
   b. Describe two alternatives to maintaining a large cash balance that Rich Simon could implement at Lektron Corporation, and explain how the company would benefit from these alternatives.
2. If only the proposed credit and collection procedures, Proposal 1, had been implemented at the beginning of the fiscal year ended November 30, 19X8,
   a. Determine the change to Lektron's cash position due to payments of accounts receivable.
   b. Determine the change to the annual pretax profit.
3. If only the early payment cash discount on sales proposal, Proposal 2, had been implemented at the beginning of the fiscal year ended November 30, 19X8,
   a. Determine the change in Lektron's cash position due to the reduction in the average days of collections and the effect of the discount.
   b. Determine the change in the annual pretax profit.

16–25 Cash Budget—Two Months Craven Company is a wholesaler in the dry goods business. The firm is growing rapidly, and its owner is wondering whether she will need short-term financing over the next two months. She has amassed the following information for you to develop a cash budget for the next two months (July and August):

Sales forecast. July, $100,000; August, $140,000; September, $160,000.

Cost of sales is 40 percent of sales.

The firm keeps inventory at 150 percent of the following month's forecasted sales requirements.

Collections of sales are as follows: month of sale, 30 percent; month after sale, 68 percent; bad debts, 2 percent.

Monthly expenses, other than cost of sales and bad debts, are 10 percent of sales for commissions and other variable costs, and $40,000 fixed, including $5,000 depreciation.

The firm pays for its purchases of merchandise (goods) in 30 days and for operating expenses as incurred.

The balance sheet at June 30 is expected to be as follows. Inventory is lower than the firm's policy would indicate, because June sales were higher than expected.

Cash	$ 18,000	Accounts payable (merchandise)	$ 43,000
Accounts receivable, net	85,000	Taxes payable, due July 15	28,000
Inventory	35,000	Common stock	100,000
Furniture and fixtures, net	110,000	Retained earnings	77,000
Total	$248,000		$248,000

REQUIRED

Prepare cash budgets for July and August. If you determine that cash will go below $15,000, which is the minimum balance that the owner considers acceptable, assume that the firm borrows enough to bring the balance up to $15,000.

16–26 Cash Budget CLT Company has the following sales forecast, in units: January, 10,000; February, 12,000; March, 14,000; April, 13,000; May, 15,000; June, 16,000. The company sells its product for $20. Variable manufacturing costs are $6, including $2 for materials. Monthly fixed manufacturing costs are $60,000, including $5,000 depreciation. Monthly selling and administrative expenses are $30,000, all requiring cash disbursement. The company collects its sales in 45 days. Collections of December receivables are budgeted at $60,000 in February. Cash at January 31 is expected to be $48,000. CLT maintains a two-month supply of finished goods inventory and keeps its materials inventory equal to double the coming month budgeted production needs. It pays for purchases on delivery. It pays all cash costs as incurred.

REQUIRED

Prepare a cash budget and all necessary supporting schedules for the months of February and March.

16–27 Budgeting (AICPA Adapted) Helpat Corporation, a retail store, had the following balance sheet at January 31, 19X7:

Cash	$ 8,000	Accounts payable, merchandise	$ 61,875
Accounts receivable, net of $2,000 allowance for doubtful accounts	38,000		
Inventory	16,000	Common stock	50,000
Fixed assets, net	40,000	Retained earnings (deficit)	(9,875)
Totals	$102,000		$102,000

Sales budgets are $110,000 for February and $120,000 for March. The firm collects 60 percent of its sales in the month of sale, 38 percent in the following month; 2 percent are uncollectible. Gross margin is 25 percent of sales. Purchases are 75 percent of the following month's budgeted sales requirements (at cost). Accounts payable are paid in 30 days. Other expenses are $21,500 per month, including $5,000 depreciation.

REQUIRED

1. Prepare a budgeted income statement for February.
2. Determine budgeted cash collections for February.
3. Determine budgeted accounts payable at the end of February.
4. Determine sales for January.
5. Determine cash disbursements for February.

16–28 Receipts and Disbursements (AICPA Adapted) The controller of Patsy Corporation has estimated the following activity for December 19X1.

Sales	$350,000
Gross profit percentage of sales	30%
Increase in gross accounts receivable during month	$ 10,000

Increase in inventory during month	$ 5,000
Variable selling and administrative expenses, as a percentage of sales, including 1% estimated bad debts	15%
Fixed selling and administrative expenses	$ 35,500
Depreciation, included in fixed S&A expenses	$ 20,000
Change in accounts payable during month	$ 0

REQUIRED

1. Determine the estimated cash receipts for December.
2. Determine the estimated cash disbursements in December.

16–29 Sales Budgeting, Regression Analysis The manager of Cleanhair Products, Inc., has asked you to help him understand the results of regression analyses that one of his assistants has developed. The notation used is Y = monthly sales of Glowbright, one of the firm's products, X_1 = dollars spent on advertising Glowbright in magazines, and X_2 = dollars spent on advertising Glowbright on television. Standard errors of the coefficients are in parentheses.

$$Y = \$467{,}000 + \underset{(\$1.73)}{\$3.98X_1}, \qquad r^2 = 0.47,\ S_e = \$64{,}320$$

$$Y = \$381{,}000 + \underset{(\$1.86)}{\$4.23X_2}, \qquad r^2 = 0.53,\ S_e = \$54{,}060$$

$$Y = \$752{,}300 + \underset{(\$0.79)}{\$0.87X_1} + \underset{(\$0.99)}{\$0.91X_2}, \ r^2 = 0.876,\ S_e = \$34{,}210$$

"What does all of this mean, should I advertise or not, and where? I don't get it."

REQUIRED

Comment on the results.

16–30 Pro Forma Balance Sheet One of your first duties after taking over as controller of Clete Products Company, a small manufacturer of camping equipment, was to determine whether the firm could meet two goals set by Howard Clete, the president. Clete wanted to buy $140,000 in new equipment and to pay a $40,000 dividend without having to borrow or sell additional common stock. He wanted to buy the equipment and pay the dividend before March 31, 19X6, the end of the firm's current fiscal and tax year.

You began your task in late September 19X5 and collected the following information:

1. Sales forecasts, October 19X5 through January 19X6, $130,000 per month; February 19X6, $180,000; March 19X6, $200,000; April through July, $150,000 per month. The firm collects receivables in 45 days.
2. Variable manufacturing cost is 45 percent of sales, and there is a 5 percent sales commission on all sales in the month after earned. Raw materials are about 70 percent of variable manufacturing costs.
3. The firm generally keeps a three-month supply of finished goods and a one-month supply of raw materials. It uses variable costing for finished goods inventory.
4. Fixed manufacturing costs, including depreciation of $13,000, are about

$35,000 per month. Fixed selling and administrative expenses are about $20,000 per month, including $2,000 in depreciation.

5. The firm pays for its purchases of raw materials in 30 days. Except for commissions and taxes (below), all expenses requiring cash are paid as incurred.
6. Clete has told you that the firm will make a payment on estimated income taxes in December. The payment will cover taxes due for income for the first half of the 19X6 tax year (April 1, 19X5, to September 30, 19X5). The firm will not pay any estimated amount on income for the last half of the tax year. In other words, the liability at March 31, 19X6, will be equal to taxes on income from October 1, 19X5, to March 31, 19X6. The tax rate is 40 percent.
7. At September 30, 19X5, the firm will have about $750,000 in net plant and equipment and about $1,050,000 in stockholder equity.

REQUIRED

Prepare a pro forma balance sheet as of March 31, 19X6, to see whether Clete will be able to buy the equipment and pay the dividend without borrowing money.

16–31 Pro Forma Balance Sheet, Ratio Analyses The controller of Towson Company has been planning the firm's cash requirements for the coming year, 19X6. Before going into a detailed month-by-month cash budget, he wants to get a first cut at the end-of-year results to get some idea of the firm's financing needs. He has gathered the following information.

1. Sales in 19X6 should be about $2 million, cost of sales about $1.4 million, and operating expenses $250,000. The income tax rate is 40 percent.
2. Sales in 19X7 should be about 10 percent higher than in the coming year, and cost of sales should remain constant as a percentage of sales. Sales are fairly even throughout each year.
3. The firm generally has about 60 days' sales in accounts receivable, 90 days in inventory.
4. The minimum required cash balance is $80,000.
5. Under the terms of agreements related to long-term debt, current liabilities must be no more than 50 percent of current assets. The long-term debt is $450,000, and no payments are planned for the coming year (except interest, which is included in operating expenses above).
6. At year end, according to budgeted purchases and depreciation, net fixed assets will be about $950,000.
7. Stockholder equity at the beginning of the year is $640,000, and the firm plans a dividend of 60 percent of its income after taxes.

REQUIRED

Prepare a pro forma balance sheet as of December 31, 19X6, to determine whether or not Towson Company will need additional financing, and if so how much. Make any assumptions you think are reasonable.

16–32 Budgeting and Regression Analysis The president of Holton Industries has asked for your assistance. The firm has recently begun to use statistical analyses in developing its budgets, and the president believes that some managers will not be receptive to the idea. He wants you to give a seminar on the use of regression analysis in budgeting, concentrating on sales forecasting and cost estimation. He gives you the following regression equations that one of his staff developed for use as examples (standard errors are in parentheses):

$$\text{sales} = \$2{,}367{,}000 + \$4.723\ (\text{advertising expenditures})$$
$$(\$2.560)$$
$$r^2 = 0.57, \qquad S_e = \$489{,}345$$
$$\text{factory overhead cost} = \$1{,}096{,}356 + \$3.77\ (\text{direct labor hours})$$
$$(\$1.58)$$
$$r^2 = 0.71, \qquad S_e = \$104{,}234$$

REQUIRED

Prepare a set of comments as the basis for the presentation.

16–33 Budgeting and Linear Programming Hooper Chair Company makes many different chairs in two basic models, modern and traditional. The materials and labor requirements for all modern chairs are about the same, and the materials and labor requirements are about the same for all traditional chairs. Accordingly, the managers of the firm consider that they have two products.

The sales manager has estimated the maximum amounts of each model that the firm could sell as 60,000 modern, 50,000 traditional. The production manager knows that he cannot produce all the chairs that the firm could sell and decides to use a linear program to determine the optimal mix. The schedule below gives the times that each chair requires in the two departments and the total available times in them.

	Required Times, Hours		*Total Available*
	Modern	*Traditional*	*Time*
Cutting	0.80	1.50	70,000
Assembly	1.60	0.50	100,000

The direct labor rate is $10 per hour in both departments. The variable overhead rates are $4 per hour in cutting, $6 in assembly. Contribution margins on each chair are as follows:

	Modern	*Traditional*
Selling price	$64.00	$73.00
Material cost	15.20	24.00
Direct labor	24.00	20.00
Variable overhead	12.80	9.00
Total variable costs	52.00	53.00
Contribution margin	$12.00	$20.00

Total fixed manufacturing costs are $410,000, and selling, general, and administrative expenses are $145,000.

REQUIRED

1. Find the optimal production mix, solving graphically the linear programming problem.
2. Determine the total profit that the firm will be earning at the optimal mix.
3. Would you recommend that the firm stick to the original mix or change to the one you determined in part 2?

16–34 Budgeting, Linear Programming, and Sensitivity Analysis The president of Hooper Chair Company (see assignment 16–33) looked at the production schedule that the managers developed. She wondered about the overhead rates, especially in the assembly department. The rates came from regression equations, and the standard errors of the coefficients (the variable overhead rates) were $0.65 in the cutting department and $2 in the assembly department.

"Let us suppose," the president said, "the true rate in the assembly department is $8, which is one standard error above what the mean is. Will this hurt us badly if we stick to the mix of 57,500 modern chairs and 16,000 traditional chairs? What will the optimal schedule be if the rate is $8?"

REQUIRED

1. Determine the effects on the contribution margin of modern and traditional chairs if the variable overhead rate in the assembly department were $8 per labor hour.
2. Determine the optimal product mix under the new circumstances. You need only find the contributions at each of the mixes you analyzed in assignment 16–33. The corner points remain the same.

16–35 Cash Budget: Not-for-Profit (CMA Adapted) United Business Education, Inc., (UBE) is a nonprofit organization that sponsors a wide variety of management seminars throughout the United States. In addition, it is heavily involved in research into improved methods of educating and motivating business executives. The seminar activity is supported largely by fees and the research program from member dues.

UBE operates on a calendar-year basis and is finalizing its budget for 19X9. The following information has been taken from approved plans, which are still tentative.

In the seminar program, UBE expects $12 million in revenue for the year. Programs totaling $1,440,000 will be offered in each of the first five months of the year; the remaining revenue will be split evenly through the months of September, October, and November. No programs are offered in the other four months of the year. Revenue is collected in the month a program is given. All programs are budgeted to produce the same amount of revenue.

Seminar expenses consist of instructors' fees, facility fees, and promotional costs. Instructors' fees are paid at the rate of 70 percent of the seminar revenue in the month following the seminar. Facilities are $5.6 million annually and are paid in the month a program is given. Promotional costs are $1.2 million annually, spent equally in each month.

The research program has a large number of projects nearing completion. The other main research activity this year includes feasibility studies for new projects to be started in 19Y0. As a result, the total grant expense of $3 million for 19X9 is expected to be paid out at the rate of $500,000 per month during the first six months of the year.

UBE expenses include the following:

Office lease—annual amount of $240,000 paid monthly at the beginning of the month.

General administrative expenses (telephone, supplies, postage, and so on)—$1,500,000 annually, or $125,000 a month.

Depreciation expense—$240,000 a year.

General UBE promotion—annual cost of $600,000 paid monthly.

Salaries and Benefits

Number of Employees	Annual Salary Paid Monthly	Total Annual Salaries
1	$50,000	$ 50,000
3	40,000	120,000
4	30,000	120,000
15	25,000	375,000
5	15,000	75,000
22	10,000	220,000
50		$960,000

Other information:

Membership income—UBE has 100,000 members, each of whom pays an annual fee of $100. The fee for the calendar year is invoiced in late June. The collection schedule for the organization is:

July	60%
August	30%
September	5%
October	5%
	100%

Capital expenditures—The capital expenditures program calls for a total of $510,000 in cash payments to be spread evenly over the first five months of 19X9.

Cash and temporary investments at January 1, 19X9, are estimated at $750,000.

REQUIRED

1. Prepare a budget of the annual cash receipts and disbursements for UBE, Inc., for 19X9.
2. Prepare a cash budget for UBE, Inc., for the first six months of 19X9.
3. Using the information you developed in parts 1 and 2, identify two important operating problems of UBE, Inc.

16–36 Budgeting and Receivables (CMA) Weldon's Bike Shop has been in business for five years. The shop buys medium-quality to high-quality bicycles and related bike accessories for resale to customers.

The bike shop has shown profits for the past four years. The projected results for the current year are presented below.

WELDON'S BIKE SHOP
Projected Statement of Income
for the Year Ended December 31, 19X8

	Dollars (in Thousands)	*Percent*
Sales revenue	$300	100%
Cost of goods sold	180	60
Gross margin	$120	40%
Operating expenses:		
Sales commissions	$ 15	5%
Fixed expenses:		
Advertising	9	3
Salaries	21	7
Rent	18	6
General administration	12	4
Total operating expenses	$ 75	25%
Net income before taxes	$ 45	15%
Income taxes (40%)	18	6
Net income	$ 27	9%

The sales figure results from strict cash sales. No personal checks are accepted, nor are credit or credit card sales made. Ann Weldon, the owner, is deciding whether to accept these payment methods:

Personal checks only.
Bank credit cards only.
Both personal checks and bank credit cards.

Ann believes that sales will increase if she accepts other payment methods in addition to cash. She also realizes that some cash customers will change to a different method of payment if alternative methods are available. The schedule below presents Weldon's estimates of how sales will increase under each of the proposed three payment methods and how total sales will be collected:

		Percentage of Total Sales Paid By		
Alternatives	*Percentage Increase in Sales*	*Cash*	*Check*	*Credit Card*
Payment by check	10%	60%	40%	—
Payment by bank credit card	20%	50%	—	50%
Payment by check and bank credit card	25%	20%	40%	40%

If checks are accepted as a method of payment, approximately 10 percent of all check sales can be expected to be returned for nonsufficient funds (NSF). Half of the NSF checks (5 percent of total sales) will be collectible through a collection agency at a cost of 25 percent of the amount collected. The remaining half of the NSF checks will never be collected. In addition, the merchandise paid for by NSF checks will not be recovered.

Bank credit card sales can be deposited daily as if they were cash. However, the bank charges a 4 percent discount fee when credit card sales are deposited.

The cost behavior patterns of the existing costs and expenses are expected not to change regardless of the payment method.

REQUIRED

Prepare an analysis that shows the effect of each of the proposed payment methods Weldon is considering on the shop's net income. Based upon your analysis, explain whether Weldon's should accept any of the proposed payment methods in addition to strict cash, and if so, identify the method.

16–37 Master Budget—Manufacturer "It looks as if we are in good shape," said Roland Eustis, president of the E&W Manufacturing Company. Eustis was looking at the budgeted income statement for the first two months of 19X6.

E&W MANUFACTURING COMPANY
Budgeted Income Statement—
January–February, 19X6

Sales		$9,300,000
Cost of sales:		
Materials	$ 600,000	
Labor and variable overhead	2,736,000	
Fixed overhead	1,700,000	5,036,000
Gross margin		4,264,000
Selling and administrative expenses		2,830,000
Income before taxes		$1,434,000

E&W makes two models of the same basic product: regular and deluxe. Additional data appear below.

	Regular Model	*Deluxe Model*
Unit selling price	$200	$250
Materials, in pounds	2	4
Direct labor hours	3	4
Sales collection period, in days	30	60
Material cost per pound	$ 5	
Direct labor cost per hour	$10	
Variable overhead per direct labor hour	$ 9	
Sales commissions, percentage of sales	10%	
Monthly fixed manufacturing overhead	$850,000	(including $100,000 depreciation)
Monthly fixed selling and administrative expenses	$950,000	(no depreciation)

The firm tries to keep finished inventories at 200 percent of budgeted sales for the coming month and raw material inventories at production requirements budgeted for the coming month. Sales budgets by month and product are, in units

	Regular Model	*Deluxe Model*
January	10,000	7,000
February	14,000	11,000
March	18,000	9,000
April	17,000	11,000

Selected balance sheet information, as of December 31, 19X5, is

Cash	$ 648,000
Accounts receivable:	
Regular model	2,800,000
Deluxe model	3,750,000
Accounts payable, materials	143,000
Accrued payroll, direct labor	240,000
Accrued commissions	330,000

Of the receivables for the deluxe model, 40 percent are from sales in December, 60 percent from November. The firm expects to have 17,000 units of the regular model on hand at December 31, 19X5, 12,000 units of the deluxe model, and 90,000 pounds of materials.

The firm pays for materials in 15 days. It pays sales commissions in the month after they are earned. It pays 80 percent of direct labor cost in the month incurred, 20 percent in the following month. It pays all other expenses requiring cash in the month incurred. The firm makes sales and purchases evenly during each month.

Mr. Eustis was happy with the budgeted income statement, but he also wanted to see how much his cash position would improve as a result of the profitable operations.

REQUIRED

Prepare the following budgets for January, February, for the two-month period as a whole:

1. cash receipts budget

2. production budget, by product

3. material purchases budget

4. budgets of direct labor and variable overhead cost

5. cash disbursements budget

6. cash budget

16–38 Cash Flow and Income (Continuation of assignment 16–37) You have prepared and submitted the budgets to E&W. Eustis's response follows:

> You can't be serious! We expect to earn over $1,400,000 in January and February, and you tell me that we'll run out of cash? Show me why, and you'd better make it good.

REQUIRED

Show Eustis why the firm will run out of cash, even if all goes according to budget. Make it good.

16–39 Cash Budgeting Model (CMA Adapted) Over the past several years, Programme

Corporation has encountered difficulties estimating its cash flows. The result has been a strained relationship with its banker.

Programme's controller would like to develop a means to forecast the firm's monthly operating cash flows. The following data were gathered to facilitate the development of such a forecast:

1. Sales have been and are expected to increase at 0.5 percent each month.
2. Thirty percent of each month's sales are for cash; the other 70 percent are on open account.
3. Of the credit sales, 80 percent are collected in the first month following the sale and the remaining 20 percent are collected in the second month. There are no bad debts.
4. Gross margin on sales averages 25 percent.
5. Programme purchases enough inventory each month to cover the following month's sales.
6. All inventory purchases are paid for in the month of purchase.
7. Monthly expenses are: payroll, $1,500; rent, $400; depreciation, $120; other cash expenses, 1 percent of that month's sales. There are no accruals.
8. Ignore the effects of corporate income taxes, dividends, and equipment acquisitions.

REQUIRED

The controller asks you to develop mathematical expressions of the following elements of cash flow using the following notation: S = sales in current month, t = number of months in the future the forecast is desired.

1. sales t months from now
2. cash collections t months from now
3. purchases t months from now
4. cash disbursements t months from now

16–40 Budget Formulas (CMA) SunVu Company manufactures deck chairs. Because of the seasonality of the business, SunVu's managers prepare detailed annual budgets. SunVu's Controller, Barbara Webster, is particularly concerned with cash flow, as plans must be made to provide for the company's cash needs during the off-season. Webster has been developing models to assist her in forecasting various elements of the cash flow. The information presented below will be used to develop a model to predict the cash requirements for quarterly dividends. Dividends payable is based on 30 percent of quarterly earnings available for dividends on common stock.

SunVu manufactures its deck chairs only to order, that is, one month's production is equivalent to the next month's shipments. Therefore, the detailed operating budgets are developed in terms of units to be produced, 450,000 units for the upcoming year. SunVu's deck chairs sell for $60 each.

Variable manufacturing costs for the deck chairs are:

Raw materials	$11 per unit
Direct labor	$10 per unit
Variable overhead	150% of direct labor dollars

Fixed manufacturing overhead is projected to be \$3,600,000 for the year, applied on the basis of units produced.

Fixed administrative and selling costs are budgeted at \$540,000, to be expended evenly throughout the year. Variable selling expense is \$1.50 per unit.

SunVu uses the straight-line method to depreciate its machinery and equipment. At January 1, the beginning of the budget year, monthly depreciation expense will total \$44,000. Acquisitions of new equipment are planned for May 1 (\$60,000—5 year life, no salvage value) and August 1 (\$96,000—5 year life, no salvage value). SunVu begins depreciating assets in the month of acquisition.

SunVu has a license agreement with ClearPlus, Inc., for the use of a finishing process that is patented by ClearPlus. Under the agreement, SunVu must pay ClearPlus a fee of \$.20 per unit produced; these payments are made at the end of the month.

SunVu has a long-term note with its primary bank that requires monthly interest payments and a principal payment on December 31 of each year. On January 1 of the budget year, the outstanding balance of the note will be \$1,200,000; the annual interest rate is 9 percent, and the annual principal payment is \$200,000.

SunVu will have 500,000 shares of common stock issued and outstanding on January 1 and does not plan additional equity issues during the year. The company plans to pay quarterly cash dividends equal to 30 percent of earnings available for dividends on common stock for each quarter.

SunVu uses the calendar year as its fiscal year. Income taxes are expected to be negligible due to loss carryforwards and for this reason are not considered in the budgeting process.

Webster wants to develop a model that will help her predict the cash requirements for quarterly dividends. The model is to be stated in terms of units produced using the following notation:

$$P = \text{units produced in a month}$$
$$t = \text{time}$$

For example, P_t would stand for production during the month t, for example, if earnings in month t are dependent upon production activity in the second prior month, the appropriate notation would be P_{t-2}.

REQUIRED

1. For each of the items listed below, develop the appropriate notation for use in Webster's model. This version of the model will be used to calculate SunVu's earnings available for dividends on common stock for the quarter ending June 30, that is, $t = 6$. The notation should be stated in terms of P and t where appropriate.

a. revenue
b. variable manufacturing cost of sales
c. total selling and administrative expense
d. depreciation expense
e. licensing fees
f. interest expense

2. Describe how Barbara Webster's model would change if SunVu abandoned its policy of manufacturing only to order and began to maintain an inventory of items ready for immediate shipment.

3. Describe the change(s) that must be made to the model to calculate earnings available for dividends on common stock should SunVu decide to issue preferred stock.

16–41 Budget Spreadsheet Errors (CMA Adapted) Brian Haggerty, manager of budgeting and analysis for Fiber Products, Inc., is preparing to issue the first quarter's income statement in spreadsheet format. Haggerty has used the reporting format already developed in the spreadsheet software on his microcomputer, and is reviewing the spreadsheet report shown as (D) with Fiber Products' controller before presentation at the quarterly management meeting. Upon review, Haggerty and the controller have found errors in the report. Actual income before income taxes for March was $10,000, while the income before income taxes reported on the spreadsheet report is $13,000.

(A) BUDGET FILE

BUDGX8 4/10/X8	JAN	FEB	MAR
Budget			
Revenues:			
Sales	24	27	28
Other revenue	0	0	0
Total revenue	24	27	28
Cost of goods sold	10	11	11
Bad debt expense	2	2	2
Total direct expenses	12	13	13
Fixed expenses	5	5	5
Income before income taxes	7	9	10
* * * *	*	*	*
Revised Budget			
Revenues:			
Sales	25	27	29
Other revenue	2	2	2
Total revenue	27	29	31
Cost of goods sold	10	11	11
Bad debt expense	2	2	2
Total direct expenses	12	13	13
Fixed expenses	5	5	5
Income before income taxes	10	11	13

(B) ACTUAL FILE

ACTX8	4/10/X8	JAN	FEB	MAR
Revenues:				
Sales		25	26	29
Other revenue		1	3	2
Total revenue		26	29	31
Cost of goods sold		9	12	11
Bad debt expense		2	2	2
Total direct expenses		11	14	13
Fixed expenses		5	6	5
Income before income taxes		10	9	13

#1

(C) ACTUAL FILE
(printed when Haggerty updated the March actuals)

ACTX8	4/4/X8	JAN	FEB	MAR
Revenues:				
Sales		25	26	30
Other revenue		1	3	1
Total revenue		26	29	31
Cost of goods sold		9	12	12
Bad debt expense		2	2	3
Total direct expenses		11	14	15
Fixed expenses		5	6	6
Income before income taxes		10	9	10

This is the first time that Haggerty has prepared and issued these reports. Joan Michaels, the financial analyst who prepared these management reports for the quarterly meeting, terminated her employment on March 25. Before leaving, she gave Haggerty a brief lesson on issuing this report from the spreadsheet package. Although Michaels had not developed any specific directions for using this spreadsheet model, she believed that Haggerty was proficient enough to produce the report.

The quarterly report is formatted by compiling information from a budget spreadsheet file and an actual spreadsheet file onto a third new spreadsheet. The saved budget spreadsheet file is called BUDGX8, shown as (A), and has provisions for both the original budget and the revised budget. The saved actual spreadsheet file is named ACTX8 and is shown as (B). This was initially developed by copying the revised budget file and is updated monthly with actual information. Before merging the information from BUDGX8 and ACTX8 into the quarterly report, Haggerty had entered the March actuals into ACTX8 on April 4, 19X8, and printed the updated actual file for the first quarter, (C). The reported actuals for both January and February were correctly reported.

The first quarter's management report comparing the first quarter's actuals to the revised budget is presented as (D). Six of the errors that the controller and Haggerty observed are indicated in all files (#1–#6).

(D) MANAGEMENT REPORT PRODUCED

April 10, 19X8

FIBER PRODUCTS INC.
Income Statement Compared
to the Revised Budget
March 31, 19X8
($000)

Desired contribution (as a percent of sales revenue) 60%
Effective tax rate 40%

	JAN	FEB	MAR	First Quarter Actual	First Quarter Revised Budget	Actual Better/ (Worse) Revised Budget
Revenues:						
Sales	$25	$26	$29	$80	$79	$ 1
Other revenue	1	3	2	6	0	6
Total revenue	$26	$29	$31	$86	$79	$ 7
Cost of goods sold	9	12	11	21 ← #2	32	(11)
Bad debt expense	2	2	2	6	6	--
Total direct expenses	11	14	13	38	38	--
Contribution	15	15	18	48	41	7
Contribution %	60%	58%	58%	56% ← #3	52%	
Fixed expenses	5	6	5	16	15	1 ← #6
Income before income taxes	$10	$ 9	$13	$32	$26	$ 6
Income tax (calculated and rounded)	4	4	8 ← #4	16	10	6
Net income	$6	$ 5	$5	$16	$16	$ --

#5 (the whole column) [First Quarter Revised Budget]

REQUIRED

Describe the six errors identified on Fiber Products, Inc.,'s spreadsheets and explain why each computer spreadsheet error occurred.

Part IV

DIVISIONAL PERFORMANCE EVALUATION

17

DECENTRALIZATION: OPERATIONAL CONTROL

In Chapter 4 we introduced the idea of different information systems to meet different management needs. This chapter begins a series of chapters that deals with issues of operational control, one type of information system. Earlier chapters have introduced this area. Chapters 7 and 8 dealt with operational control at the departmental level in production cost centers, through the use of standard costs and standard cost variance analysis. Chapter 11 discussed some aspects of operational control regarding how to charge support department services. Chapters 15 and 16 included overall plans (budgets) and the behavioral issues associated with budgets, since managers compare budgets with actual performance.

This chapter continues the themes of responsibility, operational control, and performance evaluation, paying particular attention to performance evaluation. While this and the following chapters build on earlier material, the discussion focuses on managers and on units of a company responsible for revenues, costs, and investment. Managers of such units have broader responsibility than those responsible only for costs.

Recall that a cost center is a unit that controls only cost. It does not sell products or services; hence it does not earn revenue. A **profit center** is a unit that controls both revenues and costs. An **investment center** controls revenues, costs, and investment. There are very few pure profit centers: almost any unit that controls revenues and costs requires assets ranging from receivables through plant and equipment. Units that sell services, such as consulting or law firms, usually have relatively little investment, but most profit-seeking activities require capital investment. In practice, the term *profit center* often describes both profit centers and investment centers. No harm arises from this usage as long as people know what type of center they mean.

Generally, profit centers and investment centers are relatively large units of companies. Most are called divisions, although some companies use other titles. With the rise of strategic planning by major corporations, one increasingly popular title is strategic business unit (SBU). An SBU might be a single division or a collection of divisions that operate in the same markets. Whatever the title, the principles are the same.

CENTRALIZATION AND DECENTRALIZATION

An important framework in evaluating profit and investment centers is the basic nature of decision making within the organization: is the firm centralized or decentralized? Centralization exists when few managers have authority to make important decisions. Decentralization exists when the authority to make decisions is spread to lower levels in an organization. In fact, the concepts apply also to nations. For example, the United States is relatively decentralized, with many vital decisions made locally, rather than by the federal (central) government. Education in the United States traditionally has been governed by local school districts and states, rather than by the federal government. Furthermore, in recent years discussion and changes in the political structure of Central and Eastern Europe have dealt with issues of centralization and decentralization.

In a decentralized company, managers at relatively low levels make decisions that their counterparts in centralized companies do not. For instance, in one company a particular manager might be authorized to set prices for products and to decide from whom to buy materials and components. Her counterpart in a more centralized company might have to get permission from a higher level to change a price or supplier. Of course, pure centralization and pure decentralization are extremes unknown in the real world: virtually all organizations give managers *some* decision-making authority; virtually none give managers complete freedom. Nevertheless, it is usually possible to judge the extent of decentralization by seeing what managers are permitted to do without permission from higher levels. Moreover, central corporate managers act differently in the two types of companies. In a centralized company, corporate level managers make many operating decisions: what products to make, what prices to set, what suppliers to use. In a decentralized company, those managers will not make such decisions but will review the performance of managers who do.

While not a perfect indicator, widespread use of profit and investment centers usually suggests decentralization. The reason is that profit and return on investment are critical, and if lower level managers have such responsibility, then corporate management is delegating very important authority to lower levels. If a company is organized functionally, with managers responsible for production and marketing rather than for profit, it is likely that the company is relatively centralized. A company with many profit and investment centers can be highly centralized, with its managers unable to, say, change a supplier without going to corporate headquarters for permission. Likewise, a company with relatively few profit centers can permit managers wide latitude in making decisions. Still, it is a good bet that managers in a company with many profit centers have more authority than those in companies with few profit centers.

Let us consider an example. Figure 17–1 shows partial, simplified organization charts of two hypothetical steel companies. Notice that both firms are vertically integrated, controlling virtually the entire process from the mining of iron ore and coal through the making of various types of steel through the marketing to customers.

FIGURE 17–1 Alternative Organizational Structures

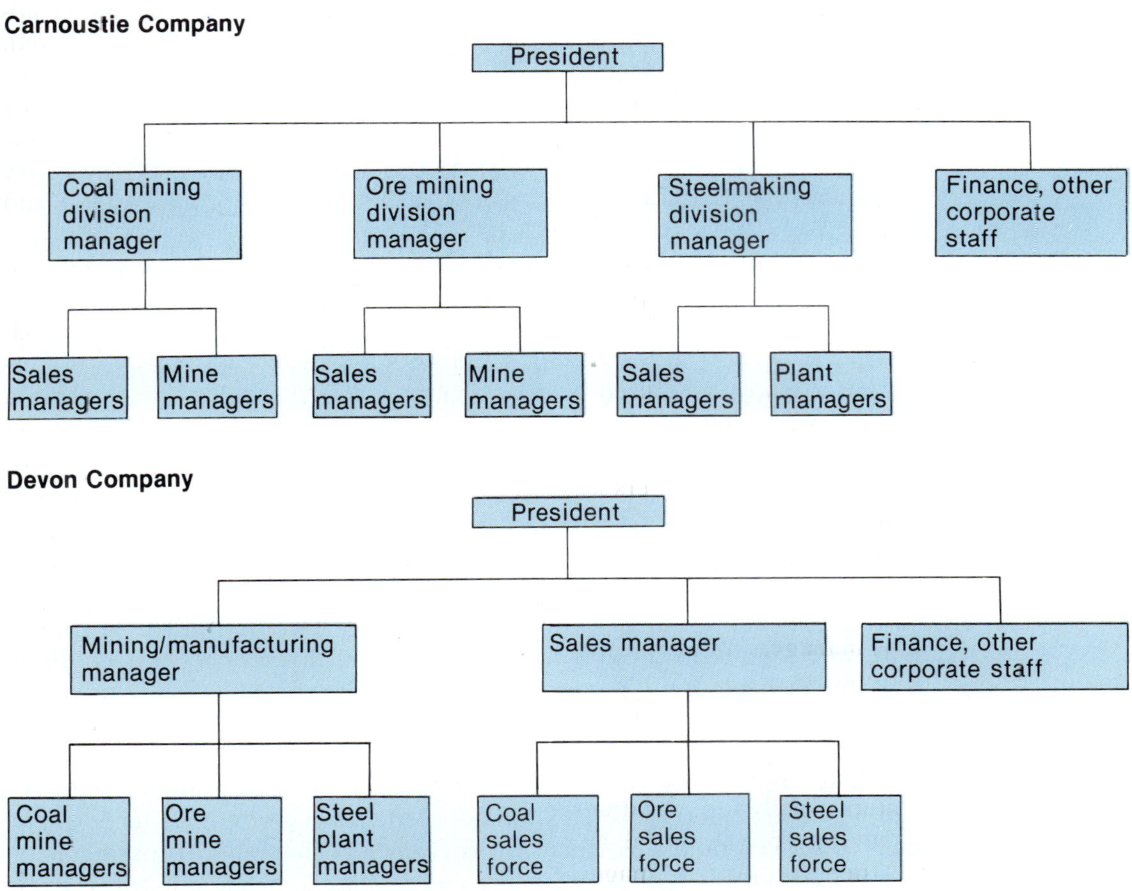

The charts in Figure 17–1 show that both firms are organized into divisions and that each division has subunits, individual mines, plants, and sales offices. The organizations differ in the degree of autonomy of the managers of the divisions and subunits within them, although the charts do not necessarily show it. The division managers of Carnoustie Company are free to deal as they like. The managers of the mining operations may sell ore to the steelmaking division or to outside firms. The managers of the steelmaking division are free to set prices, determine product mix, select suppliers (that is, buy from the firm's mining divisions or from mines owned by other companies), and to a degree, operate as if they were separate companies.

The degrees of autonomy may vary within the divisions of Carnoustie. The mining division may give much autonomy to the manager of each mine, while the steelmaking division might give little autonomy to plant managers. The opposite could also be true. The point is that a firm can make varying uses of decentralization at different levels or in different divisions at about the same level.

The general level of autonomy at Carnoustie can be compared to Devon Company, where the managers are not so autonomous. Central headquarters dictates whether the steelmaking division may buy from outsiders and whether the mines can sell to outsiders. Prices, product mix, and other factors are also determined by central management. Thus, the role of a division manager in Devon Company is to carry out the orders of central headquarters. Carnoustie Company is highly decentralized, while Devon Company is highly centralized.

One way to express the difference between the two firms is to say that the divisional managers of the Carnoustie Company, and some managers of subunits within divisions, have **profit responsibility**. They are responsible for generating revenues, controlling costs, and earning a satisfactory return on the capital invested in their operations. The managers of Devon Company do not have profit responsibility. The steel fabricating plant manager has no control over sources of supply, mix, or selling prices. All these responsibilities have been assumed by corporate top management.

Evaluation should be based on the notion of controllability: managers should be held responsible only for what they can control. Thus, for our purposes, decentralization or centralization is the structure that companies use to set policies regarding how low (or high) decisions can be made in an organization. Highly autonomous segments and their managers are evaluated much as is an independent company. Important measures used in evaluation include short- and long-term profitability and return on investment. On the other hand, highly centralized segments and their managers might be evaluated on costs (including comparison with budgets and standard cost variance analysis), throughput, quality, and production goals.

There are benefits to both centralization and decentralization. However, even in the most decentralized company, certain decisions and functions are reserved for central management. In virtually all companies, corporate management controls long-term financing and major capital expenditures. Even where divisions issue long-term debt or common stock (if they are separate corporations), the decisions to do so come from top management as a part of overall corporate financing strategies.

BENEFITS OF DECENTRALIZATION

Proponents of decentralization point to a number of advantages, not all of which can be achieved by all firms, since the degree of benefit depends on the operating characteristics of the firm. Benefits seem to be substantial, because in recent years the trend has been to greater decentralization.[1]

Environmental Complexity

Firms face both an internal and an external environment. If the firm has a relatively simple internal structure (i.e., few products and divisions), centralization might be reasonable. However, as the internal environment becomes more complex, decentralization becomes more beneficial. Many different lines of business, segments, and products mean that more decisions have to be made. Principles of span of control suggest that as the internal structure becomes more complex, it becomes increasingly necessary for local managers to make decisions; corporate management cannot track everything, nor have the requisite expertise to deal with all problems.

The external environment can also become complex. Companies might deal with several outside vendors on a daily basis for materials and purchased components. Competition, now worldwide in many industries, causes managers to become more concerned with local customs, exchange rates, and their competitors' cost structure and products. These same concerns are also evident in dealing with worldwide customers. Some divisions are dynamic, with technology changing at an ever increasing rate. In other areas, prices might fluctuate on active world markets. As the external environment becomes more complex, decentralization is a reasonable response. Local managers are closer to the issues and have more experience with them.

Spreading the authority to make decisions throughout the firm is likely to lead to better and quicker decisions. Managers of the individual divisions are closer to the situation and are in a much better position to evaluate circumstances and act quickly. If, for example, a division manager had to obtain permission to make a price concession to secure a large order, he might not receive permission until the customer had gone elsewhere and the sale had been lost. Whether accepting the sale at a reduced price was wise is important, but the presumption must be that the division manager is in the best position to make that determination.

---

[1] McGregor, cited in Chapter 15, and many others, have argued for greater decentralization as a better way to manage.

Cost of Information

Information can be costly to create and transmit. This issue ties in with ideas of timeliness and local expertise. If a decision is to be made by upper management, lower level managers must provide sufficient background information for upper management to make an informed decision. The cost of informing (training) upper management might be prohibitive. These costs include not only the direct cost in managerial time to prepare the information, but the cost to the firm of not acting in time because of the need to transmit information upward and wait for a decision.

Motivation

Behavioral research indicates that workers and managers tend to have higher morale and productivity when their tasks are broadened. Workers who perform simple repetitive chores such as those done on assembly lines tend to be dissatisfied. The term **job enlargement** describes the broadening of responsibility and authority. In the same way, managers who are nearly autonomous are likely to be better motivated than those whose actions are severely constrained.[2]

The broad responsibility that accompanies decentralization provides good training for future corporate managers, since managers who have been responsible for profit, rather than just revenues or costs, have acquired a more comprehensive outlook. Divisional managers with high degrees of autonomy provide a good pool of talent for the top slots in a firm.

Segment Performance Evaluation

Another positive aspect of decentralization is the aid it offers in evaluating divisions and their managers. In a centralized company, it is often difficult to assess how well each part of the firm is performing. For example, if two plants with entirely different products and operating characteristics were combined so that only one set of information existed to use in managerial and segment evaluation, it would be difficult for top management to evaluate the efficiency, cost characteristics, and profitability of each plant or the two managers separately. Combined information makes it difficult for managers to give specific feedback regarding performance and to decide where to take corrective actions.

Decentralization brings advantages in evaluating the performance of managers and, to a greater degree, in evaluating the divisions themselves. Many companies not only evaluate the current performance of segments, but periodically review their progress in relation to the overall strategic plans of the company. Such reviews are usually of strategic business units, which, as we mentioned, can consist of several divisions.

---

[2]Two theories of motivation, expectancy theory and the need hierarchy theory, support the position that decentralization provides greater motivation to managers.

Service Centers

In some firms, service centers such as maintenance, data processing, and legal services are either profit or investment centers. Service department costs are not allocated to user divisions and departments. Instead, the service department charges a price for the service. The user is charged with the price of services received, and the providing department is credited with revenue.

Making service centers into profit centers helps to spot poorly run service centers. If operating managers do not use the firm's data processing facilities because they can buy the services elsewhere more cheaply, it might be a sign that the data processing department is not well run. Measures of performance of service departments that do not act as profit centers are limited, as a rule, to measures of work done, not the value of work done. The data processing department manager might argue that he is performing well because his department processed 30 million transactions in the past month. The unanswered questions are whether all of those transactions should have been processed and at what cost. If the department charged users for the service and showed a reasonable profit at prices approximating market prices for the same service, it would indicate that the department was operating reasonably well.

PROBLEMS WITH DECENTRALIZATION

Decentralization is not a cure-all. It requires a great many competent managers whom central management can trust. Decentralization is not always feasible or cost effective. Some activities and services can be performed more efficiently if they are centralized. Most firms centralize research and development, legal services, and cash management. Financial functions relating to long-term debt and common stock are administered centrally. To the extent that the first activities are decentralized, the autonomy of the division increases, but the cost could well be higher than if they were centralized. Duplication of effort can be very costly.

In any organization, whether business or not-for-profit, no matter how centralized or decentralized, each manager acts in effect as an agent of his or her superior. (The president of a company acts as an agent for the board of directors and stockholders.) We hope that our agents act in our best interests. This brings up the chief problem of decentralization: motivation for managers to act in the company's best interests. When managers do so, we say that there is *goal* or *behavior congruence*, as defined in Chapter 15.

How does central management ensure that division managers work in the best interests of the firm? When managers are evaluated on the basis of performance of their own operations, they naturally take actions that benefit themselves. Under some circumstances the actions that divisional managers take to benefit their divisions also benefit the firm. Sometimes, however, the action of one divisional manager benefits his division but harms the firm as a whole. When managers act in ways that benefit themselves while harming the firm, they are said to be acting in a *suboptimal* or *dysfunctional* way. The literature is replete with references to such behavior, and we shall see some examples.

Central management might inadvertently promote dysfunctional behavior by the measures it chooses to evaluate segments and segment managers. In addition, since many measures of performance are designed to promote goal and behavior congruence, lower level managers can see such measures as manipulations by central management and a decreasing of the autonomy of divisional managers.

If divisions of a particular firm are highly interdependent, dealing primarily with one another, it is very difficult to decentralize profit responsibility. If, for reasons of technological dependence or management strategy, the divisions are not free to deal with outsiders, they probably should not be profit centers. The reason is that the essence of profit centers is independence: if the manager is not free to operate reasonably independently, it is not possible to evaluate performance by looking at profit. The manager does not have profit responsibility, because he does not have autonomy and freedom to deal with other firms.

Finally, some companies will not decentralize simply because the top executives are uncomfortable delegating authority. They might believe that autonomous divisional managers would not act appropriately. For example, the top executives might be unwilling for the company to take on a high level of risk. They might further believe that divisional managers would be likely to take unacceptable risks. Thus they would not delegate authority.

There is a considerable body of literature on agency theory, the relationships between principal and agent such as corporate management and divisional managers. Some managers and accountants believe that such research will help to guide the development of control systems. A major concern of agency theory is the extent to which superior and subordinate managers share attitudes about risk. For instance, a divisional manager might reject risky investments that central management would accept. Central management might encourage the divisional manager to accept such investments by seeing to it that accepting them would not adversely affect the divisional manager's reported performance. One way to do this is to charge some of the costs to central headquarters instead of to the division.

BASES FOR DECENTRALIZING

Even when upper level management decides to decentralize, it faces choices. Firms can decentralize in various ways, and the best way is not always obvious. Most modern firms are also in a more or less constant process of changing. Old markets dry up, new markets open, technological changes occur, and governmental regulations evolve. For example, a firm in a high technology business that has been dealing primarily with the government might enter the consumer field with a set of new products. It might separate its governmental products and business from those designed for the general public. The company might hire managers who have experience with consumer goods to lend specific expertise to the new division, and these managers might be offered extensive autonomy as an inducement to join the company.

There are several ways firms can logically decentralize. Selecting a basis for decentralizing depends on the characteristics of the firm, the attitudes of upper level managers, and a host of other factors. A given company might use more than one basis. Some of the more common bases are discussed below.

Product Lines

The product line basis is usually best where the products are diverse and require different skills and experience. Managers dealing with consumer products such as toothpaste require different skills and knowledge from those who deal with structural steel or bulk chemicals. Both technological and marketing differences are involved in these examples.

Product line decentralization is not usually possible when a single plant makes several different products and product lines. The large amount of common costs makes it difficult to evaluate each product or product line separately. Unless it is reasonably easy to make such evaluations, it is not advisable to decentralize, because pinpointing responsibility for profit is crucial to evaluating decentralized operations.

Type of Customer

In firms that use classes of customers to assign profit responsibility, one investment center might deal exclusively with governmental work, another with commercial work, a third with colleges and universities. This type of classification will most often be used when different customers have special needs, so that salespeople, engineers, product designers, and other personnel need expertise of a particular sort to compete with other firms.

Geographical Areas

Most multinational companies decentralize by geographical area as well as by, perhaps, product line. Domestic companies might decentralize by region, putting regional managers in charge of all products made and sold in their areas. In some industries, each plant is an investment center serving a limited area. This occurs when shipping costs are extremely high or other factors limit the market to a fairly small geographical area.

Technological Similarity

Some investment centers produce different products but use the same basic production process for all of them. An example is industries where joint products are prevalent. Many chemical processes provide gases used in other industries. A chemical division would therefore also produce and market gases that have no similarity to its chemicals except that they arise from the same process.

A slightly different type of example develops when a production process can be used to make quite different products. Tires, vinyl wallpaper, plastic cards, and several other products are all made using the same basic process. Here the division takes advantage of technical expertise to broaden its markets.

MEASURES OF DIVISIONAL PERFORMANCE

Evaluating the performance of a division is not the same as evaluating the performance of its manager. Different measures and different standards should be applied in these two types of evaluation. We shall return to this point after discussing some of the techniques most commonly used and misused for both types of evaluation. Let us point out that the major considerations in selecting measures of performance of managers are behavioral. Will the measures encourage managers to act in the best interests of the firm (goal congruence), and will they provide a fair and equitable assessment of how well the managers have performed their jobs? If either question is answered negatively, the evaluation system could work against the firm.

From the standpoint of measuring the performance of the division itself, the major question is whether a measure gives corporate management a good basis for determining how well the division is meeting corporate goals. Corporate management is also interested in whether or not the division should be expanded, let alone, or phased out.

Measures of divisional performance can be divided into measures related to financial accounting, other monetary measures, and nonmonetary measures. As you shall see, short-term financial accounting measures are the most popular. However, with an increasing awareness of long-term viability, a new emphasis on quality, new manufacturing methods, and worldwide competition, other measures are being added to those related to financial accounting.

Measures Based on Financial Accounting

Accounting (book) income by itself is a prime measure and is often used as part of other measures such as return on investment and residual income. We begin by discussing return on investment and residual income and return to a discussion of income as a measure by itself and as a component of these other measures.

Return on investment (ROI) is the most commonly used measure of divisional performance.[3] It is defined as income divided by investment. The two

[3] See John S. Mauriel and Robert N. Anthony, "Misevaluation of Investment Center Performance," *Harvard Business Review*, 48:3 (March–April 1966) and James S. Reece and William R. Cool, "Measuring Investment Performance," *Harvard Business Review*, 56:3 (May–June 1978).

terms, *income* and *investment,* are measured in a variety of ways that we consider later.[4] For now, we point out that ROI is a ratio. The use of ratios in analyzing performance has the advantage and disadvantage of eliminating the effects of size. Thus, if a firm has two divisions, A and B, with data as shown below, division B is better than division A using the ROI criterion.

	Division A	*Division B*
Annual divisional income	\$1,200,000	\$ 300,000
Divisional investment	6,000,000	1,000,000
ROI	20%	30%

Notice that although division B has a much higher ROI than division A, it contributes far less dollar profit to the firm, and dollars, as well as ratios, are important. In contrast to ROI, **residual income** (RI) focuses on dollars of profit after a charge is assessed for the cost of the investment in the division. RI is given by the formula

$$\text{RI} = \text{divisional income} - (\text{divisional investment} \times \text{required ROI})$$

The required rate of return in this calculation is, theoretically, cost of capital. In most cases, it is a cutoff rate based on the firm's overall strategy and objectives. The excess of the divisional income over this charge for the use of capital is the *residual* that the division returns to the firm. For the two divisions in the above example, we obtain the following RIs, assuming that the minimum required return is 15 percent.

	Division A	*Division B*
Incomes	\$1,200,000	\$300,000
Less: Required return:		
\$6,000,000 × 0.15	900,000	
\$1,000,000 × 0.15		150,000
Residual incomes	\$ 300,000	\$150,000

We see that the picture has changed: using the RI criterion, division A is better than division B because it returns a higher amount to the firm after allowing for the cost of funds invested in the divisions. It is not universally true that it is easier to earn higher rates of return by investing smaller amounts, but it tends to be true. As divisions grow, it frequently becomes more difficult to find investments that have ROIs in excess of the current rate. In addition, in older divisions investments were made in many earlier periods when the firm may have had different profitability objectives. The use of RI specifically addresses the problem that increasing both size and ROI are often incompatible objectives.

---

[4]Different ways of measuring investment have given rise to various terms describing return on investment. Among the most common are *return on assets* (ROA), *return on capital employed* (ROCE), and *return on net assets* (RONA).

The purpose of using RI is to focus attention on the dollar contribution that a division makes to the firm. Using terms from capital budgeting, RI may be viewed as *similar* to net present value, while ROI may be viewed as *similar* to the internal rate of return. We say similar because book values are most frequently used to calculate ROI and RI, and book values are not compatible with discounted cash flow measures. But, as a policy of maximizing the internal rate of return is generally inferior to one of maximizing net-present value, a policy of evaluating divisions and managers based on ROI is usually inferior to one based on RI. The major reasons are behavioral, as the following illustration shows.

Illustration of ROI and RI

Two divisional managers in the same firm are considering investment proposals. The firm has cost of capital of 15 percent and uses ROI to evaluate performance.

One manager is considering a project that would add $100,000 to divisional income and increase divisional investment by $500,000. Thus, the project has a book ROI of 20 percent. The division manager expects to earn ROI of 26 percent without the investment and so would probably reject it. Acceptance would reduce ROI below the 26 percent expected level—to the detriment of the manager's perceived performance.

The other manager is considering a $500,000 project that would increase divisional profit by $40,000, giving an 8 percent ROI, which is very low. He expects the division to show an ROI of 4 percent without considering the investment, and so he would probably accept it. Divisional ROI would increase, even though the project is unwise. The internal rate of return could not be greater than 8 percent, even if the project had an unlimited life.

Where the life of a project is very long, the book ROI and internal rate of return approach one another. Suppose that that is the case with both investments described above. The first investment is desirable and the second is not, but the first would be rejected and the second accepted. If RI were used to evaluate the divisions and managers, the picture would change. At a minimum required rate of 15 percent, the first investment would be acceptable to both managers and the second unacceptable.

Thus, RI overcomes some of the objections to ROI. This technique focuses on a hurdle rate in the same way that the net present value does. While it is not a discounted cash flow method, it tends to encourage wise projects and discourage unwise ones more consistently than does ROI.

Other Problems

A related but slightly different problem arises when we consider more typical investments: ones with shorter lives. Book ROI and internal rate of return rarely coincide in such cases, as we know from Chapter 13. Moreover, if the investment has low cash flows in the early years, high flows in later years, it might reduce both ROI and RI for some time. Suppose that the manager of the division currently earning a 26 percent ROI can invest $500,000 now and obtain cash flows of $200,000 in the first year, $480,000 in the second year. The project has an internal rate of return of about 20 percent, but the book results for the first year would be disappointing, as the data below show.

	Year 1	*Year 2*
Cash flow	$200,000	$480,000
Depreciation, straight line	250,000	250,000
Income (loss)	($50,000)	$230,000

Obviously, both ROI and RI in the first year would be lower than they would have been if the investment had not been accepted. They would also both be higher in the second year. The two-year life was used to minimize calculations. However, a more realistic example would be likely to show the same result: lower ROI and RI in the early years of the life of a project. It is easy to say that a manager should be patient, but it is not so easy when it is *your* performance that is being evaluated. Later in this chapter we show how to overcome this problem using compound-interest depreciation.

The problem of managers' accepting unwise projects can be alleviated by requiring that capital investments be justifiable using discounted cash flow analysis. If ROI or RI would be lowered in the early years of the life of a desirable project, the managers could be evaluated on the basis of whether they achieve budgeted results rather than the values of ROI or RI. So long as actual results were close to budgeted results, the manager and the division would be considered to be performing adequately. Budgeting for declines in ROI and RI might take discipline and patience. Most managers and investors are used to comparing current performance against the prior period. With the emphasis today on growth in profits, managers might find it hard to explain to their superiors that they have started projects they expect to lower current earnings but to increase future earnings. Encouraging managers to take the best long-term action, even at the expense of the short term, is a difficult behavioral problem. Some companies exclude new investment from the base until it has had time to become productive.

There is an inherent, and generally true, assumption here: managers are evaluated on short-term measures related to income. Bonuses, salary adjustments, and promotions are based on a record of accomplishment over a long time period. However, that record might be viewed on a year-to-year basis. Especially in critical times (e.g., when the company is experiencing short-term financial pressures or when a promotion is possible), managers might be much more motivated to act for short-run results since they are being evaluated by annual ROIs or RIs.

The use of RI does not eliminate all problems of undesirable behavior. Both ROI and RI are short-term measures, and managers can improve them by taking actions that could hurt the firm in the long run. Reducing or postponing expenses such as maintenance, research and development, employee training, and engineering will improve short-run results, including both ROI and RI. However, the long-term effects could be harmful. Both measures are also subject to criticism because of their reliance on book figures, and we now turn to such problems.

MEASURING INCOME AND INVESTMENT

Several interrelated questions are involved in selecting methods for determining both income and investment for calculating ROI or RI. Two basic types of questions must be answered: what items are to be included, and how are they to be measured? There is reasonable agreement among accountants and other managers that income should be based on controllable items and that investment should be limited to the assets (and perhaps liabilities) that a divisional manager can use to generate income.

Income

Determining the revenues and expenses that a divisional manager can control is not simple. There is certainly reason to exclude allocated costs such as the costs of central headquarters on the grounds that the manager cannot control them. Some managers, however, feel that allocating such costs is desirable because it alerts divisional managers to the need to cover all costs, not just the costs direct to the division.

The divisional income or divisional profit figure used in calculating ROI and RI does not usually provide for income taxes. Taxes on income are determined by tax law and do not reflect the operating performance of divisions. Income taxes are considered in making capital budgeting decisions, but they are rarely included as expenses in a divisional income statement.

Similarly, it is rare to find interest expense on corporate debt allocated to divisions, because divisional managers do not control the issuance of debt and common stock. However, it is not uncommon to see an imputed cost of the capital employed in the division charged to it. In fact, that is exactly what is done to calculate residual income. Other variations of this type of imputation of opportunity cost can be found in the practice of charging interest based on the divisional investment in receivables and inventory. Such interest charges are not controllable in the usual sense of the term, but the amount of investment in receivables and inventory is, within limits, controllable by many divisions. Interest on corporate debt, however, especially long-term debt, is not controllable at the divisional level.

Most firms have all divisions use the same accounting methods for greater comparability. Thus, all divisions generally use either FIFO or LIFO for inventory, and straight-line, sum-of-the-years'-digits, or double-declining-balance depreciation, and so on. Exceptions will arise. A firm might have 10 divisions using LIFO, but one or two using FIFO, average cost, or specific identification, because they cannot use LIFO. An obvious example is a division that does mainly job order work. It could use LIFO for materials but would have to use specific identification for finished goods and work in process.

Cash Flow

One way to avoid some problems of accounting measurements of income is to use cash flow as the numerator in ROI and RI calculations. Cash flow can be roughly defined as income plus depreciation, or it can also include changes in current assets and current liabilities. For example, an increase in accounts receivable means that cash collections from customers were less than sales. An increase in accrued wages means that payments were less than wages expense.

The appeal of the crude form of cash flow, income plus depreciation, is that it eliminates the problems of useful life, salvage value, and depreciation method from the analysis. The more refined version of cash flow, which includes all operating cash flows, has the further advantage of providing a measure that indicates what the division is releasing to the firm for reinvestment. Recall from the capital budgeting chapters that reinvestment of cash flows is an important part of the investment decision. The firm cannot invest accounts receivable and inventories: it needs cash to invest.

Although some firms do use cash flow rather than income, most probably do not. Managers are leery of return figures that do not include depreciation. Upper level corporate managers might not be comfortable with cash flow figures and may prefer to evaluate their divisional managers and divisions using the more common income measures. The rapid inflation of the late 1970s, however, generated considerable interest in cash flow because of the distortions in income that arise during inflation.

Yuji Ijiri has proposed an interesting variation of cash flow measurement, which he calls the corporate recovery rate (CRR).[5] The rate is a ratio, the numerator is cash flow (including changes in working capital and proceeds from sales of fixed assets), while the denominator is total assets, with fixed assets included at gross book value. Ijiri's proposal was specifically intended to evaluate historical performance.

Investment

Determining the elements of investment and measuring those elements presents some extremely difficult problems. First we consider the question of the elements of investment; then we examine some alternative measurement bases.

Some firms consider investment to be the total assets employed by a division, with no consideration of liabilities. Others subtract current liabilities such as trade accounts payable and accrued expenses from total assets employed to

---

[5] Ijiri, Yuji, "Recovery Rate and Cash Flow Accounting," *The Financial Executive*, March 1980.

determine investment. The concept of leverage and various definitions of investment in a context of financial statement analysis might be familiar from courses in accounting and finance. The example below shows the effects of leverage of ROI and RI under different definitions of investment.

The Bergen Division of Semtrol, Inc., has the following data for 19X5:

Divisional income	$ 2,500,000
Assets employed by division	16,000,000
Current liabilities of division	1,800,000
Minimum required ROI	12%

The schedule below shows ROI and RI when current liabilities are included and excluded in determining investment. As the example shows, both ROI and RI are increased by including current liabilities in determining net investment. This seems justified, since current liabilities of various divisions relate to ordinary operating matters.

	Include Current Liabilities	*Exclude Current Liabilities*
Income	$ 2,500,000	$ 2,500,000
Investment	14,200,000	16,000,000
ROI	17.6%	15.6%
RI at 12% required return	$ 796,000	$ 580,000

Accounts payable and accrued expenses for payroll and utilities are liabilities arising out of normal divisional operations.

Long-term liabilities are not usually considered, because divisions typically do not issue long-term debt. Moreover, divisions are usually viewed as operating units, and to deduct interest expense on long-term debt from divisional income as well as deducting long-term debt from divisional investment, would blend measures of operating effectiveness with measures of financial effectiveness. Leveraging or trading on the equity is not usually considered part of the responsibility of operating (divisional) management.

Another significant issue in divisional performance evaluation is whether to allocate assets to divisions. Should divisions be allocated a portion of the investment in central research and development and central headquarters? For the most part, accountants and other managers would answer no. Investment in centrally directed activities is not controllable by divisional managers and should not be part of their responsibility. However, in many cases it is reasonable to impute investment, as well as costs, to divisions. For example, in some firms central headquarters handles nearly all cash disbursements. Often it is best for the firm as a whole to centralize cash management. Divisions then carry very little cash, only enough to cover minor disbursements made locally, such as freight charges. It is then reasonable to impute some cash to each division in calculating ROI and RI. The amount allocated to each division is based on some idea of how much cash each division would have to carry if central headquarters did not handle its disbursements. The idea is that the divisions benefit from the central disbursing activity and should pay for it in the form of having to earn a return on their share.

Leases

Before the issuance of Financial Accounting Standard No. 13, long-term noncancellable leases were not usually capitalized.[6] The annual lease payments were shown on the income statement as expenses, but no asset (right to use leased property) or liability for the present value of the future payments was recognized. Presumably, divisions followed the same practices as the consolidated firm, so managers of divisions could increase ROI and RI by leasing assets rather than buying them. That option is no longer available if the lease meets certain requirements of Standard No. 13. However, the potential subterfuge is still alive and well.

Consider the following situation. A division leases a computer on a 10-year noncancellable lease for $300,000 per year. The machinery is likely to have negligible salvage value at the end of 10 years, so the lease would be capitalized under Standard No. 13. Assuming a 9 percent interest rate, the present value of the future payments is $1,925,400 ($300,000 × 6.418). Capitalizing the lease would give the following journal entry at the inception of the lease:

Capital Lease (asset)	$1,925,400	
Liability under Capital Lease		$1,925,400

That is, the lease would be treated somewhat the same as a purchase of the machinery. Presumably, the cash price of the machinery would approximate $1,925,400, so that an asset and liability result from the signing of the lease. Before Standard No. 13, the lease might have been treated as a simple rental, with a $300,000 debit to Lease Expense and credit to Cash each year.

Suppose further that the machinery provides operating savings of $370,000 per year. Under the old method, the division would show $70,000 higher income each year, with no additional investment, thereby increasing its ROI and RI. However, if the lease is capitalized, the payment is treated as part interest, part repayment of principal, and the asset is amortized. If the division uses straight-line amortization for the asset, as prescribed by Standard No. 13, it would show the following results in the first year:

Expense	
Amortization, $1,925,400/10	$192,540
Interest, $1,925,400 × 0.09	173,286
Total	$365,826

[6] Financial Accounting Standards Board, *Statement No. 13, Accounting for Leases* (Stamford, Ct.: FASB, 1976).

The increase in income from the savings in operating costs would give a net saving of only $4,174 ($370,000 − $365,826). The ROI in the first year, based on the beginning-of-year investment of $1,925,400, is only 0.002, which would help the ROI of very few divisions and would harm the RI of nearly any division. The internal rate of return on the investment is about 14 percent, so the investment is wise if the target rate is less than 14 percent. Again, the wise decision might not be made if corporate management emphasized short-term ROI.

Suppose now that the division could lease the same machinery on a year-to-year basis for $320,000. The extra $20,000 rental would compensate the lessor for the risk that the division might cancel at any time. Such a lease would not qualify as a capital lease under Standard No. 13 and would probably be treated as an operating lease for purposes of analyzing divisional performance. An operating lease is accounted for by treating the payment as an expense, and there is no capitalization of the liability and asset. The division would then increase its income by $50,000 per year ($370,000 − $320,000), with no increase in investment, again boosting its ROI and RI, but the decision to lease year-to-year might be inferior to the 10-year lease. If the divisional manager expects to continue leasing the same machinery for 10 years at $320,000, the decision to accept the noncancellable 10-year lease is clearly superior, but the book results could point the manager in the wrong direction.

Bases for Determining Investment and Income

Historical Costs Very few firms use bases other than historical cost for evaluating divisional performance. The principal questions are whether to use gross or net book values for fixed assets and whether to subtract liabilities from assets to determine investment. The use of gross book values (original costs with no accumulated depreciation) is sometimes recommended on grounds that net book values reflect estimated useful lives and different depreciation methods, making it difficult to compare divisions.

An additional argument for using gross book values is that ROI and RI based on net book values tend to increase with time. We saw an example of this problem earlier, but an extended example will make the difficulty clearer. The example uses uniform cash flows. In practice, we would be much more likely to find cash flows increasing for some part of the life of the investment. The increasing ROI and RI would be even more evident with increasing cash flows. If cash flows decrease during the latter part of the investment's life, the phenomenon of increasing ROI and RI could still occur. It would depend on whether the decline in cash flows was more rapid than the decline in the investment.

Illustration Suppose a division increases its plant and equipment by $1 million, expecting to obtain annual net cash flows of $350,265 for four years. (We use this figure to obtain a 15 percent internal rate of return.) If the division uses straight-line depreciation, it will show the following results, assuming the use of beginning-of-year book values for calculating ROI and RI. The division is evaluated on both ROI and RI, with a minimum required return of 15 percent.

Year	Cash Flow	Depreciation	Income	Net Book Value of Investment	ROI	RI at 15%
1	$350,265	$250,000	$100,265	$1,000,000	10.0%	($49,735)
2	350,265	250,000	100,265	750,000	13.4	(12,235)
3	350,265	250,000	100,265	500,000	20.1	25,265
4	350,265	250,000	100,265	250,000	40.1	62,765

The implication of these results is that the manager will appear to be doing well if he keeps new investment to a minimum. The ROI and RI on the existing investment will rise, and the lack of new investment will not penalize performance. It is also worth noting that if an accelerated depreciation method, such as SYD, were used, the problem would be worse. ROI and RI would start out very low and then increase enormously.

The use of original cost (gross book value) eliminates the problem of rising ROI and RI for investments that have equal annual cash flows. However, we expect some decreases in cash flows toward the end of the life of a project, which would then penalize divisions with older assets. DuPont is one of the most prominent firms to use gross book values. One reason is the rising ROI. Another is its managers' belief that because they maintain assets in top shape throughout their lives, the manager should be responsible for earning a satisfactory return on gross book value.[7] The theoretical solution to the problem of rising ROI and RI is the use of compound-interest depreciation.

Compound-Interest Depreciation While using the gross value of assets allows ROI to remain constant, managers can argue that they expect an asset to depreciate in terms of its worth to the company. The speed of recent technological change renders some equipment obsolete. Compound-interest depreciation is appealing in that (1) it is tied to the discounted cash flow analysis of a project, (2) it reflects a decreasing value of the asset over time (although the rate of this decrease is an issue with this method), and (3) ROI remains constant.

Compound-interest depreciation is calculated using the internal rate of return. That rate is applied to the investment at the beginning of the period to determine income for the period. Depreciation is the difference between cash flow and income. Depreciation represents the recovery of capital portion of cash flow. The process is illustrated in Exhibit 17–1.

Exhibit 17–1 shows that the compound-interest method provides a con-

[7]Frank R. Rayburn and Michael M. Brown, "Measuring and Using Return on Investment Information," in Homer A. Black and James Don Edwards, eds., *The Managerial and Cost Accountants Handbook* (Homewood, Ill.: Dow Jones-Irwin, 1979), p. 331.

EXHIBIT 17–1 Compound-Interest Depreciation

Year	(a) [prior value − (d)] Investment at Beginning of Year	(b) Cash Flow	(c) [(a) × 0.15] Income at 15%	(d) [(b) − (c)] Depreciation Expense
1	$1,000,000	$ 350,265	$150,000	$ 200,265
2	799,735	350,265	119,960	230,305
3	569,430	350,265	85,414	264,851
4	304,579	350,265	45,686	304,579
Total		$1,401,060	$401,060	$1,000,000

stant book ROI that also equals IRR. The method thereby overcomes two objections to the use of net book value in calculating ROI: the low ROI in the early life and the rising ROI in the later life of an investment. If the minimum required return were less than 15 percent, RI would be positive.

If expected cash flows do not materialize, the schedule of depreciation would have to be modified to reflect the different internal rate of return. It would then be obvious that things were not going according to plan. ROI would drop below the originally calculated internal rate of return, and residual income would be negative.

Compound-interest depreciation is rarely if ever found in practice. One reason is that it usually gives a rising amount of depreciation expense, which many managers think unconservative and inappropriate. If cash flows fall markedly from period to period, compound-interest depreciation gives straight-line or even decreasing depreciation expense, but the fall has to be quite rapid. The apparent complexity of the method as well as the problems involved in estimating cash flows has probably also contributed to its disuse.

Finally, some investments are not made on economic (discounted cash flow) grounds. Firms must invest in pollution-control equipment, safety devices, and other types of equipment because of regulations of state and federal governments and as matters of company policy regarding social responsibility and corporate citizenship. Investments that do not increase cash flows cannot be depreciated using the compound-interest method because their rates of return are negative.

Additional Decision-Making Problems We have already seen that the use of ROI and RI can discourage managers from making sound acquisition decisions. Capital budgeting also encompasses disposal decisions, and here again ROI and RI based on book data can be dysfunctional. This is especially likely where gross book values are used to determine the investment base. Consider the following data for two divisions, one evaluated using gross book value, the other using net book value.

	Gross Division	Net Division
Divisional profit	$ 250,000	$ 200,000
Divisional investment	$2,500,000	$1,200,000
ROI	10.0%	16.67%

Both divisions have machinery that originally cost \$500,000 and now has a net book value of \$100,000. The remaining useful life is five years, and annual straight-line depreciation is \$20,000. The machinery could now be sold for its net book value, but selling it would result in increased cash operating costs of \$34,000 for additional labor and associated variable overhead. First, assume that cost of capital is 18 percent. Then the \$34,000 cash savings has a present value of \$106,318 (\$34,000 × 3.127), so the machinery should be kept. The calculations below show that the divisional managers would be tempted to sell the machinery because of the boost in their ROIs. Notice that the income of Gross Division is reduced by the full cash saving, while the income of the Net Division is reduced by the cash flow lost minus the depreciation on the machinery. If the Gross Division income included depreciation, which is inconsistent with using gross book value, the increase in its ROI would be even greater, because the reduction in income would be lower.

$$\text{gross division ROI} = \frac{\$250{,}000 - \$34{,}000}{\$2{,}500{,}000 - \$500{,}000} = \frac{\$216{,}000}{\$2{,}000{,}000} = 10.8\%$$

$$\text{net division ROI} = \frac{\$200{,}000 - \$34{,}000 + \$20{,}000}{\$1{,}200{,}000 - \$100{,}000} = \frac{\$186{,}000}{\$1{,}100{,}000} = 16.9\%$$

The Net Division ROI will be lower in later years if it sells the machinery than if it keeps it, but the one-period increase in ROI might be tempting to the manager. Generally, the use of net book value is much less likely to encourage dysfunctional decisions than is the use of gross book value, especially when fully depreciated assets are involved.

Suppose that the two divisions have fully depreciated machinery with an original cost of \$300,000. The machinery is expected to save \$10,000 per year in cash operating costs for the next three years. Its salvage value is zero. Starting from the original ROI data for the two divisions, and assuming the scrapping of the machinery, we would obtain the following results:

$$\text{gross division ROI} = \frac{\$250{,}000 - \$10{,}000}{\$2{,}500{,}000 - \$300{,}000} = \frac{\$240{,}000}{\$2{,}200{,}000} = 10.9\%$$

$$\text{net division ROI} = \frac{\$200{,}000 - \$10{,}000}{\$1{,}200{,}000 - 0} = \frac{\$190{,}000}{\$1{,}200{,}000} = 15.8\%$$

In this case the use of net book value does not encourage the manager to scrap the machine, because there is no reduction in the investment base. The

Gross Division manager would be inclined to scrap the machinery, but the decision would be unwise.[8]

Problems in Interpretation The use of historical costs, either gross or net, suffers from a defect widely noted in connection with financial reporting—the problem of price changes. An old plant might have been bought at prices much lower than those currently prevailing, which would tend to make its ROI and RI higher than that of a newer plant doing the same work. However, older plant is likely to be considerably less efficient than newer plant and probably requires much higher maintenance costs. These factors tend to offset the lower historical cost, so it is not possible to generalize about the net effects of having older plant. The lower cost and consequent lower investment and depreciation might be much more significant than the increased maintenance and lower efficiency, or vice versa; it depends on the particular circumstances.

The following sections describe some alternatives to historical cost that have been recommended in the literature; these may become more popular as inflation makes comparisons of plant acquired at different times an extremely difficult job.

Present Values

The use of present values of future cash flows for asset valuation is often argued to be the theoretically best method. But there are several problems with attempting to value assets in that manner. One is that interest rates, the cost of equity capital, and, therefore, the weighted-average cost of capital are subject to change. If we attempted to value assets at present values based on cost of capital, we would have a good deal of disagreement determining what cost of capital was at any given time.

Additionally, it is usually not possible to value individual assets on the basis of future cash flows, but only collections of assets. This is the interaction problem: a single asset that does not produce any cash flows by itself is essential to the production of cash flows. A factory building without machinery will not produce cash flows, nor will machinery that is not installed inside a building. Hence we would have to determine present values for batches of assets not just individual items.

An estimate of the present value of future cash flows (after tax) is needed if management is considering the sale of a division. The present value is com-

---

[8] Reece and Cool studied the practices of 620 firms, 96 percent of which used profit or investment centers. They found that 65 percent used only ROI, 2 percent used only RI, and 28 percent used both ROI and RI for evaluation. About 85 percent of firms used net book values for plant assets, 14 percent used gross cost, and 2 percent used replacement costs. About 51 percent included current payables in the investment base, 49 percent did not allocate corporate costs, and 84 percent did not allocate corporate assets.

An earlier study by Mauriel and Anthony found 52 percent using only ROI, 6 percent using only RI, and 41 percent using both. They also found 18 percent using gross book value, 73 percent using net book value, and 3 percent using replacement costs. The percentages above do not total 100 percent because of "other" and "no answer" responses in both studies.

pared to the best price offered to determine whether the sale should take place. This, of course, is a capital budgeting decision. Sales of individual assets would be considered at the divisional level using standard capital budgeting techniques.

Market Resale Prices

For some purposes, the individual assets of a division should be valued at current resale prices. The most common case is when the divisional manager is considering the sale of one or more specific assets. (Estimates of present values are also needed.) In some cases, the company plans to dispose of a division and the only question is whether to sell it as a whole or sell its assets piecemeal. The question then is whether the price offered for the entire division is greater than the expected selling prices of the individual assets.

If ROI based on current selling prices is low, and is expected to remain low, the assets should probably be sold and the funds invested elsewhere. The key point is whether the low ROI is expected to continue. A low current ROI is obviously not something to be happy about, but if corporate management expects improvements, the division might be kept. We see, then, that market resale prices are valuable primarily in determining whether to dispose of a division or some of its assets, or to continue operating. ROI based on market resale values is not particularly useful for evaluating the performance of divisional managers. Many divisional assets, such as specialized machinery, have very low selling prices, and ROI will appear quite high if it is based on selling prices of such assets.

Replacement Costs

Some accountants advocate using replacement costs in evaluating the performance of divisions and their managers. **Replacement costs** are the amounts estimated as needed to replace the existing inventory and fixed assets. Replacement costs are often expressed as those necessary to replace productive capacity, not necessarily to replace the existing assets with physically similar ones because the company would not now buy the same types of assets. For instance, a company that has a great deal of hand-fed machinery might express its replacement cost as the cost of automatically fed machinery because it would not now buy more of the hand-fed type. The cost is not the current price of the automatic machinery, but that price less depreciation reflecting the remaining useful life of the hand-fed machinery.

Advocates of using replacement costs for divisional performance evaluation point out that a manager is given the responsibility of using the assets prudently and profitably. The monetary measure of those assets is replacement cost, not historical cost, because replacement cost represents the amount needed to provide the existing capacity. It is that cost, not historical cost, on which managers should be required to earn an adequate ROI.

Using replacement costs also eliminates many of the problems in interpreting historical-cost results that we discussed earlier. Managers would all be put on the same cost basis, so that those with old assets would not have the advantage of a low investment in calculating ROI and residual income. Each division and manager is evaluated as if it had just begun operations. Depreciation expense based on replacement cost also better reflects the current costs of operating the division than does historical-cost based depreciation.

Despite the arguments of advocates of replacement costing, it is not widely used in practice.

Price-Level Adjustments

There is an unfortunate tendency to lump together replacement-cost accounting and price-level accounting. The two methods are quite different, although they sometimes use similar techniques. **Price-level accounting** emphasizes changes in the general purchasing power of money. Price-level adjusted valuations of assets represent the current purchasing power invested in the asset, not the replacement cost. Changes in the general price level are reflected in changes in broad indexes of prices, such as the Gross National Product Implicit Price Deflator. Such an index averages the prices of a whole host of goods and services; it tells you nothing about the changes in prices of specific items.

An illustration should clarify the difference between the two techniques. Assume that land was bought for $100,000, when the general price-level index was 80. The general price-level index has advanced to 120, a 50 percent increase [(120 − 80)/80]. A specific price index for land of the same type is now at 180 and was 100 when the land was bought. The specific price index will often be used to estimate the replacement cost, as shown below, along with the general price-level adjusted cost.

Replacement cost	$100,000 × 180/100	$180,000
General price-level adjusted cost	$100,000 × 120/80	$150,000

The general price-level adjusted cost represents the current purchasing power invested in the land. The general purchasing power of the dollar has declined, so $1.50 is needed now to buy the same goods and services that cost $1 when the land was bought. But that $1.50 represents the average prices of many goods and services, not necessarily land or any other specific item. Because general price-level adjustments do not reflect the current costs of a division's assets, such adjustments are of doubtful value in evaluating divisional performance.

ANALYZING ROI

The basic equation for ROI can be expanded into two (or more) components, depending on how detailed the accountant wishes to make the analysis. We can look at ROI as composed of investment turnover and return on sales:

$$\text{ROI} = \frac{\text{sales}}{\text{investment}} \times \frac{\text{income}}{\text{sales}}$$

This expansion enables the accountant to look at the relative performance of a division in regard to two components rather than one. A division might have a high turnover (sales/investment) but a low return on sales (income/sales). The result could be a high or low ROI, depending on the relative magnitudes of the components. Comparisons of each component with those of firms in the same industry or with divisions within the same firm can highlight areas of possible improvement. Additionally, firms in different industries, or firms in the same industry using different strategies, frequently depend on either a high turnover (with low return on sales) or high return on sales (with low turnover) to achieve satisfactory ROIs. Discount stores are the classic case of dependence on turnover. The profit margin (return on sales) of a discount record, drug, or department store is usually considerably lower than that of a conventional operation. The high turnover of the discount store often makes up for the lower profit margin.

Consider the two divisions for which data are given below. They both earn a 20 percent ROI, but in quite different ways. The jewelry chain has a high profit margin and low turnover, the chain of food stores the reverse.

	Jewelry Chain	*Food Chain*
Sales	$22,000,000	$560,000,000
Income	2,200,000	11,200,000
Investment	11,000,000	56,000,000
Turnover, sales/investment	2 times	10 times
Return on sales, income/sales	10%	2%
Return on investment	20%	20%

Analyzing return on investment using its components has several advantages. It allows managers to focus on the key result area, which for most firms is one component or the other. That is, many companies rely on keeping one measure relatively high, and managers watch that component closely.

Consider some steps that managers might take to increase ROI. One is to reduce investment while holding other values constant. Another is to increase income without increasing investment. Notice that an increase in sales, with both income and investment remaining constant, has no effect on ROI, because the increase in turnover cancels the decrease in profit margin. Inventory and receivables are two elements of investment subject to a reasonable degree of managerial discretion. Receivables can be reduced by tightening credit terms, inventory by stocking less. The problem is that changes in one variable might not be easily made in a vacuum: reducing inventory might also lead to reduced sales and income. Tightening credit terms might have the same effect. Accountants and other managers must always be alert to the possible interactions involved in decisions, especially undesirable side effects.

OTHER MEASURES OF PERFORMANCE

Besides measures related to accounting book income, other measures that may be used are related to strategic planning and the life-cycle of products.

Cash Flow as a Measure of Performance

Long-term asset acquisition is based on discounted cash flow analysis. It seems natural to evaluate the asset during its life based partly on the cash flows it generates. Discounted cash flow (DCF) analysis acts as a long-term cash budget that can be compared with actual performance.

Defining cash flow as a measure of performance can be as complex as defining income. At the simplest level, it can be historical accounting income plus depreciation, a measure often used in DCF analysis. Changes in working capital should also be included. Questions arise about what charges to assess a particular project for corporate services, interest expense, cash management, and so on. There are the same issues regarding controllability and separability that exist when using accounting income as a measure of success.

There is also a more complex issue of separability. Projects are originally evaluated (somewhat naively at times) as independent. Theoretically, all interdependencies and jointness of costs and benefits should be included. However, from a practical standpoint, this inclusion is often not possible. As a project becomes part of an ongoing business segment, its individuality becomes obscured. Therefore, comparing cash flows generated by projects with original DCF analysis becomes difficult.

On the positive side, cash flow is one of the most important measures of long-term viability and the ability to pay a return to investors. Income and increases in retained earnings do not necessarily mean that *cash* is available to pay dividends to investors.[9] In addition, changes in cash can be accurately measured over time. Cash is by definition valued at its current worth, compared with accounting income and balance sheet values, which include historical costs.

Life-Cycle Issues and Performance Evaluation

Segments and their products are usually at different points of their life cycles. There are four parts to a life cycle: embryonic, growth, mature, and aging. Segments that are at different stages might best be evaluated using different measures. Thus, revenues should build over the first two stages and peak as

[9]See Yuji Ijiri, "Recovery Rate and Cash Flow Accounting," *The Financial Executive*, March 1980.

the segment reaches its mature stage.[10] Net income starts as a loss and grows to its maximum during the mature stage. Net cash flows are also negative during the embryonic stage but should turn positive during the growth period and reach their highest point as the segment moves into its aging stage. Based on these expected patterns, ROI by itself may not be a useful measure in the beginning or ending stages.

Thus, other measures besides ROI should be used. During the embryonic stage, management should measure the achievement of specific technological milestones, market share goals, expected project cost, and budgeted cash outflows. In the growth stage, market share, profit margins (and contribution margins), ROI, cash flow, and improvements in productivity are important. Profit margins, ROI, cash flow, and improvements in productivity are also important in the mature, steady-state stage as is an emphasis on controlling production costs. Finally, in the aging stage, when a company is looking at when to cease operating or to sell a segment, cash inflows, profit margins, and operating costs are good measures.

Strategic Planning and Performance Evaluation

Many companies use formal strategic planning. Managers develop a mission statement, set goals and objectives to achieve over a three- to five-year period, and propose specific strategies for the near term. This same process can be employed at the divisional level. An in-depth analysis precedes the formal statements outlined above. This analysis includes assessing the competitive environment, looking at the strengths and weaknesses of the organization, looking at changes in technology, and establishing critical factors for success. Such companies would logically use their goals and objectives and the critical factors of success as measures to see if the strategic plan is being met and if the plan should be modified.[11]

DIVISIONAL AND MANAGERIAL PERFORMANCE

Both divisions and their managers are evaluated. A division might be dropped or enlarged. Its manager's requests for capital expenditures might be turned down or approved. Evaluation of the division revolves around the best alternative uses of funds and the importance of the division to the firm. Evaluating

[10] See Allen H. Seed, III, "Using Cash Flows to Measure Business Unit Performance," *Corporate Accounting*, Summer 1983, pp. 14–19.

[11] Classics in the field are Igor H. Ansoff, *Corporate Strategy: An Analytical Approach to Business Policy for Growth and Expansion* (McGraw-Hill Book Company, 1965) and Michael E. Porter, *Competitive Strategy: Techniques for Analyzing Industries and Competitors* (The Free Press: New York, 1980).

the manager of a division is a separate matter. One example is that of a highly competent manager being put in charge of a poorly performing division to straighten it out. The manager might be doing a superb job in raising its ROI from 2 to 5 percent.

At the other extreme, the most profitable division might be managed by an incompetent. Such a division might be capable of earning an ROI of 35 percent or so, with corresponding high RI, but might actually earn 25 percent. In evaluating managers, it is not their actual results that matter, but whether those results are as good as they could be given what the manager has to work with. Therefore, companies should look beyond whether a division is doing well or poorly. In the case of the above, the company might benefit more if attention were directed at improving already profitable divisions than by concentrating on less profitable ones.

Performance Report

Exhibit 17–2 gives an income statement format and calculation of investment bases that reflect, however imperfectly, the differences between the performance of the manager and that of the division. In making this distinction, we want to concentrate on the factors that the manager currently in charge of the division can control, as opposed to those to which previous managers have committed the division through their decisions. Distinctions between what the

EXHIBIT 17–2 Sample Report of Managerial and Divisional Performance (Millions of Dollars)

	Budget	*Actual*	*Variance*
Sales	$46.5	$47.3	$0.8
Variable costs	28.2	28.7	(0.5)
Contribution margin	18.3	18.6	0.3
Controllable fixed costs	6.2	6.1	0.1
Controllable profit	12.1	12.5	0.4
Noncontrollable costs	5.0	5.0	0.0
Divisional profit	$ 7.1	$ 7.5	$0.4
Current assets less current liabilities	$18.2	$18.4	$0.2
Controllable fixed assets	17.9	17.6	(0.3)
Controllable investment	36.1	36.0	(0.1)
Noncontrollable investment	10.2	10.2	0.0
Total divisional investment	$46.3	$46.2	($0.1)
ROI on controllable investment ($12.1/$36.1, $12.5/$36)	33.5%	34.7%	
RI on controllable investment, 12% minimum	$ 7.8	$ 8.2	
ROI on total investment ($7.1/$46.3, $7.5/$46.2)	15.3%	16.2	
RI on total investment	$ 1.5	$ 2.0	

incumbent manager can and cannot control are bound to be imprecise, but much can be done.

The controllable profit and investment relate to the manager, while the noncontrollable items (costs and investment) relate to the division. Noncontrollable items include allocated corporate expenses and assets.

Standards for Comparison

The use of any measure of performance presupposes an idea of good performance. Is 15 percent a satisfactory ROI? Is $23,500,000 a satisfactory RI? The level achieved on a performance measure must be related to some standard or norm. A 15 percent ROI is, other things equal, better than one of 8 percent. However, other things are rarely equal. In general, managers evaluate divisions in several ways. They compare ROI and RI figures for each division within the firm. They probably compare ROIs of particular divisions with those of independent firms in the same industry. Thus, if a division is exclusively engaged in packaging, upper level management might compare its ROI with that of one or more companies in the packaging business. Some industry associations publish data showing averages of various operating characteristics of firms in the industry. If such statistics are not available, upper level management might turn to annual reports of firms comparable to the division.

Corporate management might also compare current-period ROI and RI with those of prior periods, looking for improvement or deterioration. Corporate management is also interested in whether the division earned its budgeted ROI or RI. Budgeted results are in fact probably the most common basis for comparison, and they have some advantages over other bases. Budgeted results represent management's best judgment of what a division should do. Comparisons of divisions with others within the firm suffer from the defect that divisions operating in different industries should be expected to have different ROIs. For example, ROIs in consumer goods industries are generally higher than those in producers' goods industries such as industrial equipment.

Comparisons with independent firms operating in the same industry as a division are not always possible. It might be difficult to find a firm with a business approximating that of your division. There could be so few such firms that comparisons are not reliable guides. Additionally, a division should have higher ROI and RI than an independent firm of about the same size, because the division benefits from centrally provided services. The division does not have to provide a staff for finance, legal services, and other such activities. The charges that the company might make for such services are probably less than the cost to an independent company.

Comparing actual current-period results with those of prior periods does not indicate whether performance is good or bad, only its direction. The problem is the same as in using historical results to set standard costs.

Even granting the subjectivity in budgeted ROI and RI, comparisons of actual and budgeted results might be the best of the comparisons we have mentioned. The problem of comparing historical and current-period results extends to comparing divisions within the firm and comparing divisions with independent companies outside the firm. There is no guarantee that the standards used for comparison constitute good performance.

RISK, ROI, AND RI

The previous discussion assumed that the risks involved in all divisions were the same, which is not likely to be true in practice. Where divisions engage in lines of business of different risk, their ROIs should be different. A division in a high-risk business should earn a higher ROI than one in a low-risk business. The high-risk division should also earn RI based on a higher minimum required return. In fact, it could be argued that different types of investment should earn different ROIs.

Some companies use a technique that recognizes the relative riskiness of different types of investment.[12] The Burlington system employs a Use of Capital Charge (UOCC) based on corporate management's estimates of the cost of capital and the proportions of total investment in three classes. The classes, from least risky to most risky, are: accounts receivable, net of accounts payable; inventories; and plant and equipment. The corporation charges each division a dollar amount based on the amounts of assets in each class and the applicable rates.

For example, the following schedule shows the calculation of the UOCC using hypothetical data:

Assets	*Amount*	*Required ROI*	*UOCC*
Receivables less payables	$ 2,300	7%	$ 161
Inventories	8,400	12%	1,008
Plant and equipment	18,600	22%	4,092
Total	$29,300		$5,261

Weighted average UOCC = 18% ($5,261/$29,300)

This technique recognizes the relative riskiness of investing in different types of assets. The risk rises as the investment is committed for longer periods and is accordingly less liquid.

The use of different required returns for different divisions on the basis of relative riskiness is not prevalent in practice. However, managers recognize different degrees of riskiness by informally requiring higher ROIs for riskier divisions. A corporate manager expects a division in a high technology, rapidly

[12] See Donald R. Hughes, "Burlington Industries, Inc.," in Thomas J. Burns, ed., *The Behavioral Aspects of Accounting Data for Performance Evaluation* (Columbus, Ohio: College of Administrative Science, The Ohio State University, 1968), pp. 49–65.

changing, and therefore risky field such as lasers to earn a higher ROI than one in a relatively stable field such as food processing.

SUMMARY

Divisional performance evaluation is a constant problem for accountants and other managers. Much depends on these evaluations, because they are used for determining which managers should receive praise (and rewards), which should be penalized. They are also used to determine if the firm should remain in a particular line of business, expand the line, or drop it.

ROI is the criterion most frequently used for evaluating performance of both divisions and their managers, but it is generally inferior to residual income. Problems of determining how income and investment should be defined for the purpose of calculating ROI and RI are serious. There are no easy solutions. Accountants and managers advocate many different ways to make the required measurements and controversy abounds.

REVIEW PROBLEM

Cannon Industries operates several divisions. Budgeted results for the Barcomb Division appear below. The minimum required ROI is 20 percent.

Sales, 100,000 units at $10	$1,000,000
Variable costs, 100,000 at $4	400,000
Contribution margin	600,000
Fixed costs	400,000
Income	$ 200,000
Investment	$ 800,000

REQUIRED

1. Determine ROI.
2. Determine RI.
3. The manager of the division has the opportunity to invest another $300,000 and expects annual income to increase by $66,000. Would the manager be likely to accept the investment if the basis for evaluation were ROI? What if it were RI?

ANSWERS TO REVIEW PROBLEM

1. 25%; $200,000/$800,000
2. $40,000; $200,000 − 20% × $800,000
3. The manager would not accept the investment if ROI were the basis

because it yields 22 percent ($66,000/$300,000), which is less than the 25 percent now earned. If RI were the basis, the manager would accept the investment because it would increase RI by $6,000 ($66,000 − 20% × $300,000).

ASSIGNMENTS

17–1 Investment Bases At a recent seminar, several presidents of decentralized companies were discussing the asset bases that they used to calculate ROI and RI. Summaries of their comments appear below. All the firms use historical costs.

> PRESIDENT SMITH: We use total assets with no reduction for liabilities or for accumulated depreciation. Our belief is that operating managers are just that—operating managers—and don't have anything to do with financing the business. Further, using gross book value for fixed assets allows us to overcome the problems of different useful lives and different depreciation methods.
>
> PRESIDENT JONES: We use net book value for fixed assets. We also use working capital, instead of total current assets. We think that our managers should get the benefit of short-term liabilities' being included in the base because they are really related to operations, not to financing.
>
> PRESIDENT BROWN: We use net book value for fixed assets. We also allocate corporate debt to the divisions, so that their net investment amounts added together equal the stockholder equity of the firm. This way, the weighted average ROI for the divisions equals the return on stockholder equity for the firm as a whole. We allocate income taxes and interest to the divisions as well.

REQUIRED

Comment on each method, citing both strong and weak points.

17–2 Allocated Assets Ponta Mona Company is a decentralized firm with 11 operating divisions. Each division keeps a small amount of petty cash (from $10,000 to $60,000 depending on the size of the division) while paying for materials, labor, and other cash costs directly from the company bank account.

In determining the ROI of each division, the controller of the company allocates cash to each division in the amount of 30 days' average cash disbursements. The company bank account generally contains about 30 days' requirements, with any excess invested in short-term securities. Naturally, the division managers are not happy with this allocation.

REQUIRED

Present arguments for and against the firm's policy on allocating cash. What would you do if you were the president of the company?

17–3 ROI and RI The operating data for the three divisions of IML Industries appear below, in millions of dollars.

	Automotive Parts	Consumer Products	Industrial Equipment
Income	4.5	14.6	6.1
Investment	17.8	43.6	40.7

REQUIRED

1. Determine ROI for each division.
2. Determine RI for each division at a minimum required return of (a) 15 percent and (b) 20 percent.

17–4 Compound-Interest Depreciation Glen Company is considering the acquisition of machinery that will have a five-year life and produce after-tax cash flows of $33,435 per year. The machinery will cost $100,000 and have no salvage value.

REQUIRED

Prepare a schedule of depreciation for the equipment, using the compound-interest method.

17–5 ROI and RI Relationships

REQUIRED

Fill in the blanks in the schedule below. Each case is independent of the others. In all cases, the minimum required ROI is 20 percent.

	Case			
	A	B	C	D
Sales	$200	$___	$400	$800
Income	$___	$___	$___	$___
Investment	$___	$600	$200	$___
Margin	15%	8%	___	5%
Turnover	___	3	___	___
ROI	30%	___	___	___
RI	___	___	$ 10	$ 20

17–6 Behavior of ROI and RI The general manager of the Rebach division of Continental Products, Inc., has the opportunity to invest $2 million in plant and equipment that will have a useful life of four years. The investment should add income before depreciation of $700,000 annually. The proposed investment meets the firm's capital budgeting criterion of a 15 percent internal rate of return.

Because the general manager is evaluated on the basis of a combination of ROI and RI, he wants to know the likely effects of the investment on these two results. The division now earns an ROI of 20 percent, and the minimum required ROI is 15 percent. The firm uses straight-line depreciation on all assets and calculates ROI using end-of-year amounts of net assets (cost less accumulated depreciation).

REQUIRED

Prepare a schedule showing the ROI and RI on the proposed investment in each year.

17–7 Analyzing Results—Budget Versus Actual Bourque division of Stanton Company had the following budgeted and actual results for 19X4, in thousands of dollars:

	Budget	*Actual*
Sales	$355.3	$371.8
Expenses	325.1	338.6
Profit	$ 30.2	$ 33.2
Investment	$146.0	$178.2
ROI	20.7%	18.6%

REQUIRED

Use the margin times turnover breakdown of ROI to explain the difference between budgeted and actual ROI.

17–8 ROI and Decisions The general manager of the Warren division of MNI, Inc., is trying to decide about several matters. She has projected the divisional income for the coming year at $2 million and divisional investment at $10 million without considering the effects of taking the following possible courses of action:

1. The division has old equipment that is fully depreciated but is still in service. Replacement equipment costing $100,000 and having a 10-year life is available. That equipment would provide savings of $25,000 per year. The division uses straight-line depreciation. At the firm's cost of capital, the investment would be desirable using discounted cash flow methods.
2. The division also has equipment with a book value of $200,000 and annual depreciation of $40,000. It could be sold at book value, with the proceeds returned to corporate headquarters and therefore not included in the division's investment. If the equipment were sold, labor costs would rise by $70,000. The sale would not be desirable using discounted cash flow techniques.

REQUIRED

Considering each case independently, determine whether the manager would be likely to make a decision that is bad from the standpoint of the firm. The manager is evaluated on the basis of book ROI.

17–9 ROI, RI, and Investment Decisions The general manager of the Wyner division of General Industries, Inc., expects income of $250,000 on an investment of $1 million without considering the opportunities listed below.

Investment Opportunity	*Income*	*Investment*
A	$40,000	$ 80,000
B	60,000	300,000
C	40,000	250,000
D	25,000	98,000

REQUIRED

1. Assuming that the manager is evaluated on the basis of ROI, which investment opportunities would she accept?
2. Assuming that the manager is evaluated on the basis of RI with a minimum required return of 20 percent, which investments would she accept?

17–10 Improving ROI George Petty, president of the Wycomb division of QMC Group, Inc., received the following budgeted data from his controller. The information relates to 19X6.

Sales	$8,000,000
Cost of sales, 60% variable	6,000,000
Gross profit	2,000,000
Selling and administrative expenses, all fixed	1,200,000
Divisional profit	$ 800,000
Investment:	
Cash, 5% of sales	$ 400,000
Receivables, 25% of sales	2,000,000
Inventories, 40% of cost of sales	2,400,000
Plant, net	5,000,000
Total investment	$9,800,000

Petty was not happy with the expected ROI and wanted to improve it. He expected that cash and receivables would maintain their percentage relationships to sales, inventories would maintain the percentage relationship to cost of sales, and plant and equipment would remain at $5 million, unless otherwise specified.

REQUIRED

Treating each of the following actions independently of the others, determine the ROI that the division would earn if the action produced the stated effects.

1. An increase in selling expenses of $80,000 coupled with a 10 percent increase in selling prices would reduce unit volume by 10 percent.
2. Increased selling expenses of $300,000 would increase unit volume by 12 percent.
3. Customers now pay their bills, on average, in 90 days. Allowing them more time to pay would increase unit volume by 5 percent and increase the percentage of accounts receivable to sales to 40 percent.

17–11 Analyzing Divisional Performance Horner Industries is a large conglomerate with highly decentralized divisions. The Parker division is in the cosmetics business and had been growing very slowly until Phillipa Bates became its manager early in 19X4. Bates had been a marketing vice president for many years and undertook aggressive campaigns to increase the division's sales.

Selected results for the first three years of her tenure appear below, in millions of dollars.

	19X4	19X5	19X6
Sales	$10.0	$12.0	$15.0
Income	2.0	2.5	3.2
Investment:			
Receivables	1.0	1.9	3.0
Inventory	2.0	2.7	4.4
Net fixed assets	4.0	4.6	5.4
Total investment	$ 7.0	$ 9.2	$12.8

The divisions do not keep cash. Corporate headquarters pays all bills directly. In 19X3, the year before Bates took over the division, it had earned $1.2 million on sales of $8.7 million. ROI was 29.4 percent.

REQUIRED

1. Appraise the performance of the Parker division during Bates' tenure.
2. The assignment states that Bates acted to increase sales. Do any of the results shown above suggest what some of her actions might have been?

17–12 Value of Division to Firm York Company has eight divisions. Data on three of them appear below (in millions of dollars).

	Division		
	Wellington	*Heathcliff*	*Nelson*
Sales	$160	$225	$600
Income	16	20	45
Investment	80	120	300
Depreciation, included in determining income	10	15	40

The three divisions are all relatively mature. Their current assets and liabilities remain fairly constant from year to year. The firm has a minimum required ROI of 10 percent. The other five divisions are all growing rapidly, and their invested capital increases commensurately.

REQUIRED

Write a formal memorandum to management, using a microcomputer and a word processing program, with a spreadsheet program for supporting schedules. See Appendix B for guidelines for memoranda presentation.

You are a consultant hired by Willard York, the President of the company. Write York a memorandum in which you rank the three divisions in order of their contribution to the firm. York wants you to use at least three methods for ranking. However, after you rank and explain your ranking by these criteria, he wants an overall appraisal of the divisions and a justification of why you chose one of the ranking methods. Make sure to include both quantitative and qualitative issues in your discussion.

17–13 Choice of Performance Measures (CMA) Lawton Industries has manufactured prefabricated houses for more than 20 years. The houses are constructed in sections to be assembled on customers' lots.

Lawton expanded into the pre-cut housing market in 1980 when it acquired Presser Company, one of its suppliers. In this market, various types of lumber are pre-cut into the appropriate lengths, banded into packages, and shipped to customers' lots for assembly. Lawton decided to maintain Presser's separate identity and, thus, established the Presser Division as an investment center of Lawton.

Lawton uses return on average investment (ROI) as a performance measure with investment defined as operating assets employed. Management bonuses are based in part on ROI. All investments in operating assets are expected to earn a minimum return of 15 percent before income taxes.

Presser's ROI has ranged from 19.3 to 22.1 percent since it was acquired in 19X0. Presser had an investment opportunity in 19X5 that had an estimated ROI of 18 percent. Presser's management decided against the investment because it believed the investment would decrease the division's overall ROI.

The 19X5 operating statement for Presser Division is presented below. The division's operating assets employed were $12,600,000 at the end of 19X5, a five percent increase over the 19X4 year-end balance.

PRESSER DIVISION
Operating Statement
For The Year Ended December 31, 19X5
($000 omitted)

Sales revenue		$24,000
Cost of goods sold		15,800
Gross profit		$ 8,200
Operating expenses:		
Administrative	$2,140	
Selling	3,600	5,740
Income from operations before income taxes		$ 2,460

REQUIRED

1. Calculate the following performance measures for 19X5 for the Presser Division of Lawton Enterprises.
   a. return on average investment in operating assets employed (ROI)
   b. residual income calculated on the basis of average operating assets employed

2. Would the management of Presser Division have been more likely to accept the investment opportunity it had in 19X5 if residual income were used as a performance measure instead of ROI? Explain your answer.

3. The Presser Division is a separate investment center within Lawton Industries. Identify the items Presser must control if it is to be evaluated fairly by either the ROI or residual income performance measures.

17–14 ROI and Internal Rate of Return The manager of the Knute division of Montauk, Inc., has been considering an investment in new fixed assets. He expects the investment to yield annual net cash flows of $386,250 for its four-year life. The cost is $1 million. The firm has a minimum required rate of return on investment of 15 percent. The calculation of the minimum required dollar return is based on net assets (cost less accumulated depreciation) at the beginning of each year. The firm uses straight-line depreciation. Ignore taxes.

REQUIRED

1. Determine the internal rate of return of the investment.
2. Prepare a schedule showing the residual income (or loss) that the investment would give in each of the four years of its life.
3. Suggest a way to reconcile the conflict.

17–15 ROI and Investment Carpenter Company operates a number of divisions, including the Drake division, which manufactures automotive ignition parts. The division has been having a great deal of difficulty in recent years because of its inability to produce electronic parts, which have been taking over the market.

Three years ago, Georgia Maxwell became the division manager at Drake. The division then showed income of $80,000 on an investment (book value) of $3 million. The division is now earning about $350,000 on an investment of $2 million at book value. Maxwell cut expenses and working capital but has gone about as far as she can. There have been almost no replacements of fixed assets in the past five years. Annual depreciation is about $200,000.

The one bright note is that the division is located in an area where real estate values have been increasing. The land that the division occupies is currently worth about $6,000,000, although the building and equipment are nearly valueless.

REQUIRED

As president of the firm, what would you do?

17–16 ROI, RI, and Decisions M-Tronics Company operates several divisions that specialize in various types of electronic components. Budgeted data for two divisions appear below.

	Z-Tron Division	*Excelsior Division*
Divisional profit	$ 1,300,000	$1,600,000
Divisional investment	$13,200,000	$6,800,000

There is an investment opportunity that either division could take. Its expected profit is $300,000 on an expected investment of $1,600,000.

REQUIRED

1. Suppose that the division managers are evaluated on ROI. Would either divisional manager accept the project?
2. Suppose that the managers are evaluated on residual income. The minimum required return is 15 percent. Would either manager accept the project?
3. If a 15 percent return reflects cost of capital, would it be in the firm's interest for one of the divisions to accept the project?

17–17 DuPont ROI Analysis The diagram on the next page depicts the DuPont method of analyzing the components of ROI. The method expands the basic margin times turnover model by building up the individual elements so that the manager can look more closely at them to see where he might make improvements.

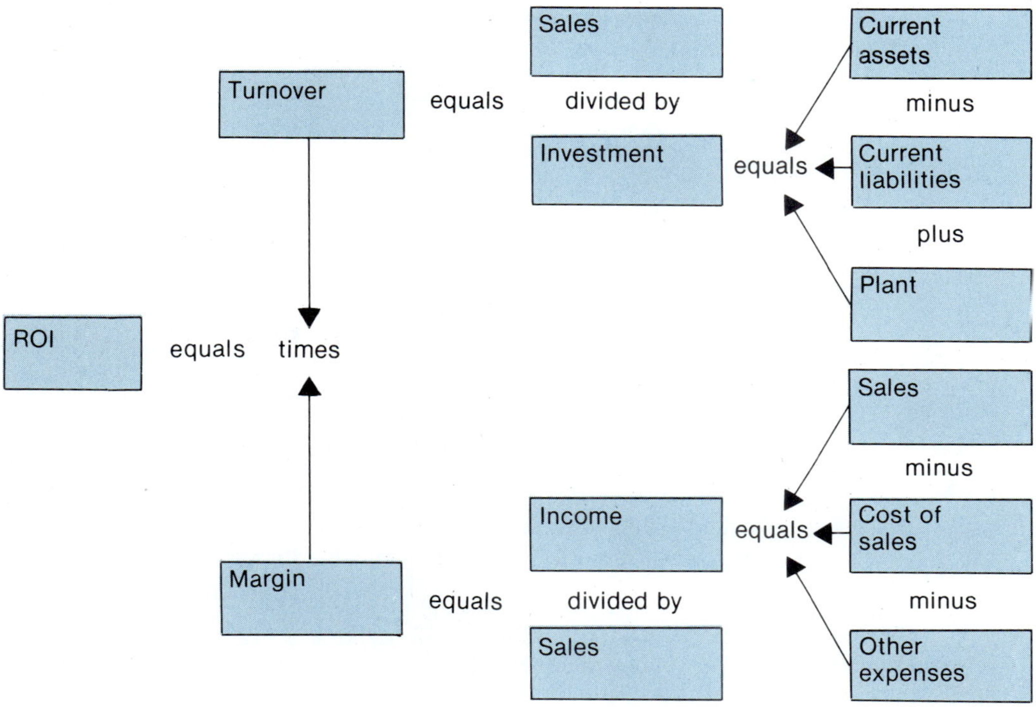

Abington Company operates a number of divisions. Data for the Kraftone division appear below, along with other data that reflect averages for the construction supplies industry, which is where Kraftone operates (all data in millions):

	Kraftone	*Industry Average*
Sales	$121.7	$100.0
Cost of sales	(86.3)	(64.2)
Other expenses	(21.4)	(20.0)
Income	$ 14.0	$ 15.8
Current assets	$ 27.7	$ 31.6
Current liabilities	18.6	15.6
Plant and equipment, net	54.4	55.8

REQUIRED

1. Analyze the industry and the Kraftone division, using the DuPont model.
2. Comment on the significant differences between Kraftone and the industry and suggest some possible reasons for the differences. For example, does Kraftone perhaps charge higher prices, require faster payment of receivables, hold lower inventories? You cannot be sure of any suggestion, but you should be able to support your reasoning.

17–18 ROI, CVP Analysis, and Variable Investment The manager of the Anderson division of General Industries, Inc., expects the following results in 19X7, dollar amounts in millions:

Sales		$49.60
Variable costs, 60% of sales		29.76
Contribution margin		19.84
Fixed costs		12.00
Profit		$ 7.84
Investment:		
Plant and equipment	$19.51	
Working capital	14.88	$34.39
ROI, $7.84/$34.39		22.80%

The division has a target ROI of 30 percent, and the manager has asked you to determine how much sales volume the division would need to reach that. He states that the sales mix is relatively constant so variable costs should be close to 60 percent of sales, fixed costs and plant and equipment should remain constant, and working capital (cash, receivables, and inventories) should vary closely with sales in the percentage reflected above.

REQUIRED

Determine the sales volume that the division needs to reach the 30 percent ROI target.

17–19 Corporate Charges and Behavior Like many other corporations, Borthwick Industries charges its divisions a management fee. Borthwick levies the fee on total invested capital at a rate of 5 percent. It defines total invested capital as assets under divisional control less current liabilities associated with divisional operations (mostly trade payables and accruals). The charge usually approximates the costs of operating corporate headquarters, including interest on corporate debt. About 95 percent of total assets for the firm are controlled by divisions; about 75 percent of the firm's current liabilities are associated with divisional operations.

The manager of the Gregson division is considering a promotional campaign designed to increase sales over the next few years. His staffpeople have developed the following estimates, in millions of dollars, of the incremental effects of the campaign:

Sales	$4.9
Cost of sales	2.8
Gross margin	2.1
Operating expenses, including promotion	1.3
Income	$0.8

The division's receivables typically run about 30 percent of sales and its inventories about 25 percent of cost of sales. Trade payables average 50 percent of inventory and accruals are negligible. The division would also need about $0.8 million in additional equipment.

The firm evaluates divisions and their managers using ROI. The manager of Gregson expects ROI to be in the 28 to 30 percent range without considering the promotion. The effects of the corporate charge on invested capital are not reflected in the information given above.

REQUIRED

Determine whether or not the manager would undertake the campaign, based on his own best interests. Is it likely that his decision is not in the best interests of the firm? Why or why not?

17–20 Corporate Charges and Behavior Assume the same facts as in Assignment 17–19 except that the corporate charge is 2 percent of revenue instead of 5 percent of investment.

REQUIRED

1. Determine whether the division manager would undertake the campaign, based on his own best interests.
2. Will his decision be in the firm's best interests? Why or why not?

17–21 Return on Assets (CMA) The Motor Works division of Roland Industries is located in Fort Wayne, Indiana. A major expansion of the division's only plant was completed in April, 19X4. The expansion consisted of an addition to the existing building, new equipment, and the replacement of obsolete and fully depreciated equipment that was no longer efficient or cost effective.

Donald Futak became Division Manager of the Motor Works division effective May 1, 19X4. Futak had a brief meeting with John Poskey, Vice-President of Operations for Roland Industries, when he assumed the division manager position. Poskey told Futak that the company employed return on gross assets (ROA) for measuring performance of divisions and division managers. Futak asked whether any other performance measures were ever used in place of or in conjunction with ROA. Poskey replied, "Roland's top management prefers to use a single performance measure. There is no conflict when there is only one measure. Motor Works should do well this year now that it has expanded and replaced all of that old equipment. You should have no problem exceeding the division's historical rate. I'll check back with you at the end of each quarter to see how you are doing."

Poskey called Futak after first quarter results were complete because the Motor Works' ROA was considerably below the historical rate for the division. Futak told Poskey at that time that he did not believe that ROA was a valid performance measure for the Motor Works Division. Poskey indicated that he would get back to Futak. Futak received perfunctory memorandums after the second and third quarters, but there was no further discussion on the use of ROA. Now Futak has received the memorandum that follows.

May 24, 19X5

TO: Donald Futak, Manager—Motor Works Division
FROM: John Poskey, Vice-President of Operations
SUBJECT: Division Performance

The operating results for the fourth quarter and for our fiscal year ended on April 30 are now complete. Your fourth quarter return on gross assets was only nine percent, resulting in a return for the year of slightly under 11 percent. I recall discussing your low return after the first quarter and reminding you after the second and third quarters that this level of return is not considered adequate for the Motor Works Division.

The return on gross assets at Motor Works has ranged from 15 percent to 18 percent for the past five years. An 11 percent return may be acceptable at some of Roland's other divisions, but not at a proven winner like Motor Works—especially in light of your recently improved facility.

I would like to meet with you at your office on Monday, June 3, to discuss ways to restore Motor Works' return on gross assets to its former level. Please let me know if this date is acceptable.

Futak is looking forward to meeting with Poskey. He knows the division's ROA is below the historical rate but the dollar profits for the year are greater than prior years. He plans to explain to Poskey why he believes return on gross assets is not an appropriate performance measure for the Motor Works Division. He also plans to recommend that ROA be replaced with three measures—dollar profit, receivables turnover, and inventory turnover. These three measures would constitute multiple criteria to evaluate performance.

REQUIRED

1. On the basis of the relationship between John Poskey and Donald Futak as well as the memorandum from Poskey, identify apparent weaknesses in the performance evaluation process of Roland Industries. Do not include in your answer any discussion on the use of return on assets (ROA) as a performance measure.
2. From the information presented, identify a possible explanation of why Motor Works Division's ROA declined in the fiscal year ended April 30, 19X5.
3. Identify criteria that should be used in selecting performance measures to evaluate operating managers.
4. If Poskey agrees to use multiple criteria for evaluating the performance of the Motor Works Division as Futak suggests, discuss whether the multiple criteria of dollar profit, receivables turnover, and inventory turnover would be appropriate.

17–22 Multiple Required Rates of Return One difficulty with using residual income is that a single rate of return fails to consider the relative riskiness of different types of assets under divisional control. Requiring an ROI of, say, 20 percent on plant and equipment might be reasonable, but it is less likely to be reasonable for accounts receivable. A lower rate would better reflect the lower risk in receivables.

One way to circumvent this problem is to use different ROIs for different assets. The following data relate to two divisions of Walton Company, in millions of dollars:

	SCC Division	Trutone Division
Cash and receivables	$ 18.6	$ 9.4
Inventories	37.2	17.9
Net plant and equipment	63.5	97.0
Total	$119.3	$124.3
Profit	$ 27.5	$ 33.5

REQUIRED

1. Calculate the RI for each division, assuming that the firm uses a 20 percent minimum required ROI on all assets.
2. Calculate the RI for each division, assuming that the firm uses the following minimum ROIs: cash and receivables, 12 percent; inventories, 15 percent; plant and equipment, 24 percent.

3. Comment on the differences between the results in parts 1 and 2. Does the idea of using different minimum required ROIs seem reasonable to you? Why or why not?

17–23 ROI, RI, and Decisions Penn Division of Houston Products expects the following results for 19X3:

Unit sales	70,000
Unit price	$10
Unit variable cost	$ 4
Total fixed costs	$300,000
Total investment	$500,000

The minimum required ROI is 15 percent, and divisions and their managers are evaluated on RI.

REQUIRED

1. What is expected ROI? Expected RI?
2. A foreign customer has approached Penn's manager with an offer to buy 10,000 units at $7 each. If Penn accepts the order, it would not lose any of the 70,000 units at the regular price. Accepting the order would increase fixed costs by $10,000 and investment by $40,000. Show whether Penn should accept the order.
3. What is the minimum price that Penn could accept for the order and still maintain its expected RI?
4. Redo parts 2 and 3 assuming that Penn has capacity of 75,000 units. The foreign customer will not accept fewer than 10,000 units.

17–24 Bases for ROI Fulmer Company operates three divisions and has been calculating ROI for each division using controllable profit and controllable investment. Recently, the president of the firm decided to allocate corporate assets, debt, and expenses to each division so that divisional ROIs would more closely reflect the return that the firm earns on its stockholder equity.

Controllable profit for the divisions does not include any allocated corporate expenses and is pretax. Controllable investment includes only the assets under the control of the divisions, with no liabilities, either corporate or related to the divisional operations, included. The following data relate to divisional operations for the current year (in millions):

	Cooper Division	*Dalmas Division*	*Brockton Division*
Controllable profit	$160	$150	$ 300
Controllable investment	400	600	1,000

Total corporate expenses, largely for interest on long-term debt, are $150 million. Corporate assets not controlled by divisions total $200 million, mostly investments in long-term securities. Income on securities is netted against expenses. Corporate debt is $880 million. The tax rate is 40 percent, and no income taxes are reflected above.

The president wants you to calculate the return on equity of each division and the firm as a whole. He asks you to allocate corporate expenses to divisions on the basis of their relative controllable investments, then determine after-tax income for each division. He also wants corporate assets and liabilities allocated on the basis of relative controllable investments. Thus, the equity figures computed for each division should add up to the firm's total stockholder equity of $1,320 million.

REQUIRED

1. Calculate the ROI for each division, using controllable profit and controllable investment.
2. Calculate the return on equity for each division in accordance with the president's instructions.
3. Does the president's method seem reasonable to you? Why or why not?

17–25 Lease-Buy Decision The manager of the CCM division expects income of $50,000 on an investment of $200,000 for the next 10 years without considering some new machinery that she will acquire. The machinery costs $20,000, has a 10-year life with no salvage value, and would save $9,000 in pretax cash operating costs each year. The firm uses straight-line depreciation for tax and book purposes, and the tax rate is 40 percent. Capital budgeting techniques show that the investment is desirable.

The machinery is also available on a year-to-year lease, cancellable by both lessor and lessee, for $5,000 per year, paid at year end. The manager wonders whether it might be better to lease instead of buy, especially since her performance is judged by book ROI. The income figure used for ROI is pretax, and investment is net book value of assets at the beginning of the year. The relevant discount rate for deciding whether to lease or buy is 10 percent. The lease is an operating lease, so it would not affect investment.

REQUIRED

1. Evaluate the lease or buy decision by comparing (1) the present value of the after-tax lease payments and (2) the purchase price less the present value of the depreciation tax shield. The smaller present value indicates the better choice.
2. Determine the effects on book ROI of buying versus leasing for the first three years.

17–26 ROI, Special Order The manager of the Granger division of Mildyne Industries is considering an offer from the Meers Company, a large retail chain. Granger makes a line of high-quality appliances that it markets through independent dealers, and Meers wants to buy 250,000 units of various appliances during the coming year, to be sold under its own label. The average price per unit that Meers has offered is $23, and the mix of appliances is about the same as that reflected in the following budgeted data (dollar values in thousands):

Sales, 1,000,000 units at average price of $38	$38,000
Cost of sales	22,000
Gross margin	16,000
Selling and administrative expenses	5,500
Divisional profit	$10,500
Required cash, 5% of sales	$ 1,900
Receivables	6,800
Inventories, at variable production cost	4,400
Net plant and equipment	16,200
Total investment	$29,300

Cost of sales includes $5,000,000 in fixed manufacturing costs. Selling and administrative expenses include a charge of 5 percent of sales levied by the parent company and are otherwise fixed. The charge is for centrally provided services such as data processing, research and development, and finance.

The manager of the Granger division expects sales at regular prices to fall by 5 percent if he accepts the offer from Meers. He anticipates that cash requirements would remain at 5 percent of sales and that inventories would change proportionately with the net change in volume ensuing from accepting the offer. He also expects that Meers will follow its usual practice of paying for its purchases in 120 days.

Corporate management at Mildyne evaluates divisional managers based on ROI.

REQUIRED

Determine whether the manager of the Granger division should accept the offer, both from his standpoint and from the standpoint of the firm. Make whatever assumptions you feel you need and be prepared to justify them.

17–27 Corporate Resources and Growth "I've done a good job with this division over the past eight years, and the people at corporate headquarters have told me so, but they turn around and cut my requests for capital expenditures by nearly two-thirds." John Bolinski, the general manager of the heavy equipment division of General Industries, was lamenting that the firm seemed to view his division as a cash cow, a generator of funds for use in other, faster growing divisions.

He went on: "They say that they want to put the money where it will do the most good. My equipment is getting out of date and we ought to be replacing it a lot faster than they are allowing. All of my proposals show internal rates of return of 15 percent or so, which ought to make them satisfactory, but I only get money for replacements that just have to be made. I generated over $14 million in cash flow last year, including $5.2 million in depreciation, yet my replacements are running at only $3.2 million. My ROI is 22 percent, which is better than some of the divisions where they are pouring in the money. It is awfully discouraging."

REQUIRED

Comment on the issues: Does the behavior of the corporate headquarters seem reasonable? Why or why not?

17–28 Strategic Planning (CMA) Western Corporation is a holding company with three subsidiaries—an electric utility, a natural resource development company, and an electronics manufacturer. Western is regarded as a utility because the utility subsidiary accounts for more than 65 percent of revenues and net income. Virtually all of Western's officers and top executives have risen through the utility. The presence of the other subsidiaries is unusual for a utility. The diversification plus perceptive management have served Western well. The recent hard times for utilities had some impact on Western, but the company emerged in sound condition.

Western's diversification is a coincidence arising from its policy of acquiring other electric utilities. One acquisition included a coal deposit, and from that beginning, other deposits and development activities were added to form the natural resource subsidiary. Similarly, another acquisition included a telephone company that provided the basis for the electronics manufacturing subsidiary.

The acquisition of other electric utilities no longer presents the growth opportunities it did in the past. Western has already acquired virtually all of the smaller utilities in its region that make a reasonable fit with Western. A proposed merger with another large utility would face strong opposition from state and federal regulators. Future economic expansion within Western's territory is now the main growth opportunity for the electric utility. However, the region's economy has been depressed, and the five-year forecast is not optimistic.

Western's strategy for expanding the other two subsidiaries has been to respond to offers initiated by sellers rather than to seek acquisitions actively. This strategy has resulted in the expansion and profitability of the electronics subsidiary. However, the natural resource subsidiary is another matter. Heavily dependent on coal, it has closely tracked the coal market's recent boom and bust. The coal market's future is uncertain. As the result of top management's dismay over the depressed coal market, Western has completed its initial strategic-planning exercise. The following statements of strategy for each subsidiary were developed to formulate the basis for the master plan.

Electric Utility The key variables for this subsidiary are efficient operations and effective relations with regulators. Maximum generation of cash for use in further diversification by the corporation's other subsidiaries is the principal objective for the electric utility.

Natural Resources An orderly divestiture of low potential assets is the initial objective. Once the divestitures are accomplished, formulating an acceptable profit and growth strategy for the remaining units is the main objective of the natural resource subsidiary.

Electronics The corporation's discretionary resources are to be employed to support the growth and diversification of this subsidiary. The future officers of Western are to be developed here.

These strategy statements were part of the strategic plan presented to Western's Board of Directors. The Directors' only debate was whether Western should sell the entire natural resource subsidiary rather than parts of it. In the end, the statements, as presented, received the Board's approval. Following the Board's action, all three statements were circulated to managers throughout the three units and described as the corporation's "new marching orders."

REQUIRED

1. Identify corporate practices or policies that must be present within Western Corporation for the strategic plan to be effective.
2. Several important characteristics differentiate Western Corporation's three subsidiaries.
   a. Identify these distinguishing characteristics.
   b. Describe how these characteristics influenced the formation of a different strategy for each subsidiary.
3. Discuss the likely effects of the three strategy statements on the behavior of both the top management and the middle management of the electric utility subsidiary of Western Corporation.

17–29 Personnel Evaluation (CMA) Mywrite Corporation designs and builds sophisticated machinery for manufacturers of microcircuitry. The rapidity of technological advancement in this industry creates a continuing demand for highly complex, well-developed production equipment. Competition has grown in intensity in the struggle to meet market demands. Mywrite has managed to attract many bright engineers and always seems to be looking for talented people for all of its departments.

Ted Raull, Cost Accounting Manager, has been with Mywrite for six months. He had been with a competitor, but that company had failed to receive sufficient contracts to stay in business. He considered himself fortunate that Mywrite happened to be looking for cost accountants a few months before his old company was dissolved. Raull's initial impression of Mywrite's costing procedures was that they were not as good as those used by his former employer. Thus, he thought he could contribute to improving the costing system.

Mark Philips, Human Resource Manager, has asked Raull to interview a job applicant for a position in Mywrite's finance area. Philips indicated that the employee who usually conducts such interviews is attending an out-of-town convention. "This applicant is an excellent prospect. You're in a better position to evaluate the candidate anyway, Ted. Who knows, you may get some good information that will help us out. He's currently employed by Vestron, our biggest competitor," said Philips.

Raull was flattered at first that he was asked to conduct the interview, but he then realized that there was no opening in the finance area. Raull asked a friend in the Human Resource Department why Mywrite had advertised for a position that did not exist. His friend said, "We do it all the time. The ads attract people from our competitors, and in the course of the employment interview, they spill all kinds of useful information trying to impress us with their capabilities. We just listen and encourage them. Sometimes we even hire one. It sure keeps us informed and keeps us abreast of the competition. Vestron apparently has a financing arrangement that we'd like to know about."

Raull's reaction was that perhaps he and others at his old company had been used. In fact, he thinks that Mywrite's actions are unethical.

REQUIRED

1. Explain why Mywrite Corporation's practice of interviewing people for nonexistent positions to obtain information is unethical.
2. Raull is trying to decide what action he should take with regard to the request of Philips to conduct the interview of the Vestron employee.
   a. Identify the alternatives that would be appropriate for Raull to take in this situation.
   b. Recommend the alternative that you identified in part 1 that you believe Raull should take and explain why.
3. Discuss the responsibility, if any, that Raull has to eliminate the practice of Mywrite's Human Resource Management Department of interviewing people for nonexistent positions.

17–30 Compensation System Porter & Campbell was a large diversified company making industrial parts and some consumer goods. The firm was organized into 14 divisions that were nearly autonomous. Each division concentrated on a line of products, and there was almost no overlap among them. For some years the divisional managers had been paid salaries that were determined largely by the sizes of their respective divisions. Although there was no explicit formula, a manager of a division twice the size of another (measured by total investment) would receive about 50 percent more pay. There were also bonuses for divisional managers, based on the firm's profits and the managers' salaries. Each manager's bonus was the same percentage of salary, so a manager earning 30 percent more salary than another would receive a 30 percent larger bonus. Bonuses had averaged about $22,000 in recent years.

Albert Hodges, president of the firm, was not satisfied with the compensation system and requested a proposal for changing it so that it recognized merits of the individual managers. The proposal, prepared by Bill Morris, an assistant to the president, was as follows.

Each manager would receive a salary at his or her current level. The bonus would be calculated in two parts. The first part of the bonus, which could not exceed \$20,000, was 2 percent of the difference between the division's current-year profits and 110 percent of the average profit of the division over the past three years. Morris called this part of the bonus the profit-growth portion and supported it by appealing to the firm's goal of steadily increasing profits.

The second part of the bonus, which could not exceed \$15,000 (so that the maximum possible bonus was \$35,000), was based on return on investment. Each division had the same target ROI, which was 105 percent of the firmwide average ROI over the past three years. The ROI portion of the bonus was to be calculated as:

$$\text{ROI bonus} = 0.02 \times \left\{ \begin{pmatrix}\text{divisional}\\ \text{profit}\end{pmatrix} - \left[\begin{pmatrix}\text{target}\\ \text{ROI}\end{pmatrix} \times \begin{pmatrix}\text{divisional}\\ \text{investment}\end{pmatrix} \right] \right\}$$

In words, the ROI portion of the bonus was to be 2 percent of the excess of divisional profit over a target profit based on a target ROI. The justification for this portion of the bonus was that ROI was also an extremely important factor that divisional managers should be concerned with, and therefore it should be a factor in their compensation. The firm's ROI had averaged 12 percent in the past three years.

Failure to meet either criterion would not carry a penalty. That is, there would not be a negative value for one portion offset against the other. Thus, if profits were lower than 110 percent of the prior three-year average, there would be no bonus for increasing profits, but there could be one for meeting the ROI target.

REQUIRED

Evaluate the proposed system.

17–31 Decentralization—Or Is It? (CMA Adapted) Edwin Hall, Chair of the board and President of Arrow Works Products Company, founded the company in the mid-1970s. He is a talented and creative engineer. Arrow Works was started with one of his inventions, an intricate diecast item that required a minimum of finish work. The item was manufactured for Arrow Works by a Gary, Indiana, foundry. The product sold well in a wide market.

The company issued common stock in 19X2 to finance the purchase of the Gary foundry. Additional shares were issued in 19X5, when Arrow purchased a fabricating plant in Cleveland to meet the capacity requirement of a defense contract.

The company now consists of five divisions. Each division is headed by a manager who reports to Hall. The Chicago division contains the product development and engineering department and the finishing (assembly) operation for the basic products. The Gary plant and Cleveland plant are the other two divisions engaged in manufacturing operations. All products manufactured are sold through two selling divisions. The eastern sales division is located in Pittsburgh and covers Chicago to the east coast. The western sales division, which covers the rest of the country, is located in Denver. The western sales division is the newest operation, established eight months ago.

Hall, who still owns 53 percent of the outstanding stock, actively participates in the management of the company. He travels frequently and regularly to all of the company's plants and offices. He says, "Having a business with locations in five different cities spread over half the country requires all my time." Despite his regular and frequent visits he believes the company is decentralized, with the managers having complete autonomy. "They make all the decisions and run their own shops. Of course they don't understand the total business as I do, so I have to straighten them out once in a while. My managers are all good people, but they can't be expected to handle everything alone. I try to help all I can."

The last two months have been a period of considerable stress for Hall. During this period, John Staple, manager of the fabricating plant, was advised by his physician to request a six-month sick leave to relieve the work pressures that had made him nervous and tense. This request came three days after a phone call in which Hall had directly and bluntly blamed Staple for the lagging production output and increased rework and scrap of the fabricating plant. Hall made no allowances for the pressures created by the operation of the plant at volumes in excess of normal and close to its maximum rated capacity for the previous nine months.

Hall thought he and Staple had had a long and good relationship before this event. Hall attributed his loss of temper in this case to his frustration with several other management problems that had arisen in the past two months. The sales manager of the Denver office had resigned shortly after a visit from Hall. The letter of resignation stated he was seeking a position with greater responsibility. The sales manager in Pittsburgh asked to be reassigned to a sales position in the field; he did not feel that he could cope with the pressure of management.

REQUIRED

Using the guidelines in Appendix B, present a memo to Hall covering these points:

1. How do centralized and decentralized management differ?
2. Analyze whether Arrow Works Products Company is as decentralized as Edwin Hall believes. Explain your answer.
3. Advise Hall, on the basis of the facts presented in the problem, whether the events that have occurred over the past two months in Arrow Works Products Company should have been expected. Explain your conclusion in a useful way.

17–32 Performance Evaluation (CMA Adapted) George Johnson was hired as assistant general manager of the Botel division of Staple, Inc., on July 1, 19X2. It was understood that he would be promoted to general manager of the division on January 1, 19X4, when the then general manager retired. This was duly done. In addition to familiarizing himself with the division and with the duties of the general manager, Johnson was specifically charged with developing the budgets for 19X3 and 19X4. As general manager in 19X4 he was, of course, responsible for the 19X5 budget.

The company is a highly decentralized, multiproduct firm where the divisions are very autonomous. The corporation staff approves operating budgets prepared by the divisions, seldom making changes. The corporate staff is active in decisions involving capital expenditures and makes the final decisions. Divisional management is responsible for carrying out the capital-investment program. Divisional managers are evaluated principally on Contribution Return on Division Net Investment. The following budgets and actual results are available. The budget for 19X5 will not be revised, even though 19X4 results departed from the approved budget.

BOTEL DIVISION
(in Thousands of Dollars)

	Actual			Budget	
Accounts	*19X2*	*19X3*	*19X4*	*19X4*	*19X5*
Sales	1,000	1,500	1,800	2,000	2,400
Less: Division variable costs:					
Material and labor	250	375	450	500	600
Repairs	50	75	50	100	120
Supplies	20	30	36	40	48
Less: Division managed costs:					
Employee training	30	35	25	40	45
Maintenance	50	55	40	60	70
Less: Division committed costs:					
Depreciation	120	160	160	200	200
Rent	80	100	110	140	140
Total	600	830	871	1,080	1,223
Division net contribution	400	670	929	920	1,177
Division investment:					
Accounts receivable	100	150	180	200	240
Inventory	200	300	270	400	480
Fixed assets	1,590	2,565	2,800	3,380	4,000
Less: Accounts and wages payable	(150)	(225)	(350)	(300)	(360)
Net investment	1,740	2,790	2,900	3,680	4,360
Contribution return on net investment	23%	24%	32%	25%	27%

REQUIRED

Write a formal memorandum to management, using a microcomputer and a word-processing program, with a spreadsheet program for supporting schedules. See Appendix B for guidelines for memoranda presentation.

You are a consultant hired by George Johnson's immediate superior, Hubbel Scope. Write a memorandum to Scope in which you:

1. Describe and identify Johnson's responsibilities under the management and measurement program described above.
2. Appraise the performance of Johnson in 19X4.
3. On the basis of your analysis, recommend to Scope any changes in the responsibilities assigned to managers or in the measurement methods used to evaluate division management. Make sure to include in your discussion issues and concerns generated by the new manufacturing and competitive environments. Discuss and/or use appropriate statistics and evaluation models discussed in the current literature.

17–33 Evaluating Divisional Managers (CMA Adapted) The divisional managers of Texon Company are responsible for all components of ROI, revenue, expenses, and acquiring and financing assets. Two such managers are now under consideration for the vice presidency for general operations, which will become vacant shortly. Both managers took over their divisions in late 19X5. Data related to their performances since then appear below (in thousands):

	Division A			Division F		
	19X6	19X7	19X8	19X6	19X7	19X8
Estimated industry sales —market area	$10,000	$12,000	$13,000	$5,000	$6,000	$6,500
Division sales	$ 1,000	$ 1,100	$ 1,210	$ 450	$ 600	$ 750
Variable costs	$ 300	$ 320	$ 345	$ 135	$ 175	$ 210
Managed costs	400	405	420	170	200	230
Committed costs	275	325	350	140	200	250
Total costs	$ 975	$ 1,050	$ 1,115	$ 445	$ 575	$ 690
Net income	$ 25	$ 50	$ 95	$ 5	$ 25	$ 60
Assets employed	$ 330	$ 340	$ 360	$ 170	$ 240	$ 300
Liabilities incurred	103	105	115	47	100	130
Net investment	227	235	245	123	140	170
Return on investment	11%	21%	39%	4%	18%	35%

The divisions serve different geographical regions. The manager of division A served as assistant manager for five years before being appointed manager. The manager of division F served as assistant manager of division B before being promoted to manager of division F. Division F is relatively new, having been formed in 19X4, while division A is in its fifteenth year of operation.

REQUIRED

On the basis of the financial information available, which manager would you promote to the vice presidency? What other information would you seek before deciding?

17–34 Not-for-Profit Segment Evaluation (CMA) Center Hospital is an acute care facility that provides a wide range of services. The hospital has 450 beds for inpatients, outpatient facilities including an emergency room, and the necessary support services.

Center Hospital's Administrator has installed a direct cost system for management control purposes. Each revenue producing department is held responsible for both its revenue and direct expenses. Direct expenses include variable costs and traceable fixed costs. Thus, a contribution can be calculated for each revenue producing department.

Departments that do not generate any revenue are considered expense centers. These departments are only held accountable for their expenses, none of which are allocated to revenue producing departments.

The condensed forecast for Center Hospital for the three-year period 19X5–19X7 follows. Only expense center costs are adjusted for inflation. The revenues and expenses of the revenue producing departments are not adjusted for inflation. The Administrator assumes that if the costs of the revenue producing departments increase because of inflation, the fees charged for services will be increased proportionately to offset the cost increases.

CENTER HOSPITAL
Three-Year Forecast
Years Ending December 31, 19X5, 19X6, 19X7
($000 omitted)

	19X5 Proposed Budget	*Forecast for Year Ending 12/31/X6*	*Forecast for Year Ending 12/31/X7*
Revenue Producing Departments			
Nursing Service:			
Revenues	$ 3,457	$ 3,632	$ 3,814
Expenses	2,456	2,622	2,889
Excess revenues (expenses)	$ 1,001	$ 1,010	$ 925
Intensive Care Unit:			
Revenues	$ 987	$ 1,008	$ 1,152
Expenses	825	806	845
Excess revenues (expenses)	$ 162	$ 202	$ 307
Operating Room:			
Revenues	$ 1,960	$ 2,387	$ 2,764
Expenses	1,347	1,659	1,775
Excess revenues (expenses)	$ 613	$ 728	$ 989
Emergency Room:			
Revenues	$ 1,082	$ 1,176	$ 1,283
Expenses	1,441	1,727	1,882
Excess revenues (expenses)	$(359)	$(551)	$(599)
Laboratories and Radiology:			
Revenues	$ 1,979	$ 2,737	$ 3,168
Expenses	1,305	2,337	2,171
Excess revenues (expenses)	$ 674	$ 400	$ 997
Pharmacy:			
Revenues	$ 1,007	$ 1,266	$ 1,477
Expenses	542	602	701
Excess revenues (expenses)	$ 465	$ 664	$ 776
Physical/Occupational Therapy:			
Revenues	$ 482	$ 501	$ 576
Expenses	510	517	560
Excess revenues (expenses)	$(28)	$(16)	$ 16
Total of excess revenues (expenses)	$ 2,528	$ 2,437	$ 3,411
Other revenue:			
Interest revenue	$ 18	$ 20	$ 10
Grant revenue	52	75	62
Auxiliary revenue	15	15	15
Cafeteria/Gift Store	35	40	45
Total other revenue	$ 120	$ 150	$ 132

Excess revenues (expenses) before expense centers	$ 2,648	$ 2,587	$ 3,543
Expense Centers			
Administrative Office	$ 927	$ 982	$ 1,091
Food Service	522	528	619
Laundry	416	489	472
Business Office	185	215	228
Data Center	225	376	428
Finance Office	210	286	301
Total expense centers	$ 2,485	$ 2,876	$ 3,139
Inflation factor (5% annual)	—	144	322
Adjusted total indirect expense	$ 2,485	$ 3,020	$ 3,461
Excess revenues (expenses)	$ 163	$(433)	$ 82

REQUIRED

1. Center Hospital uses a contribution reporting approach that determines a contribution for each revenue producing department and does not allocate the costs of the expense centers to the revenue producing departments. Explain whether this is an appropriate reporting technique to evaluate the performance of the revenue producing departments.
2. Discuss the impact of inflation on the preparation of budgets and forecasts.
3. Only the costs of the expense centers have been adjusted for inflation in the last two years of the three-year forecast for Center Hospital. Discuss the appropriateness of the method used to recognize and incorporate inflation in Center Hospital's forecast.

17–35 Behavior and Performance Evaluation (CMA Adapted) CenPointe Device Inc. is a manufacturer of continuous fluid metering devices for use in laboratories, chemical and pharmaceutical manufacturing operations, and nuclear power plants. The company distinguished itself from the competition by the high precision and extended reliability records of its equipment. In the last few years, however, foreign competition has made inroads into CenPointe's market by offering better prices and delivery times as well as high quality products. CenPointe responded to this intensified competition by retooling its manufacturing operations to achieve lower production costs, to improve quality, and to shorten delivery times. This allowed the company to sell at a more competitive price and emphasize very short delivery time, even for equipment designed specifically for a new application.

The company is organized along functional lines. Manufacturing operations are the responsibility of the Vice-President of Production. Mary Rafferty, Director of Manufacturing Operations, reports to the Vice-President of Production, and all of the Production Supervisors of CenPointe's various product lines report to her. Josh Gibson, Director of Quality Control, also reports to the Vice-President of Production, and he supervises the quality control personnel working on each product line.

The Production Supervisors of each product line have, in the past, received a listing of the orders to be filled during the month and measured their performance by how many orders they were able to fill. High quality was always stressed, and the Production Supervisors cooperated even if it meant some unfilled or reworked orders at the end of the month. The Production Supervisors were proud of their work.

The production data received from the floor was primarily used for accounting, financial reports, product pricing, and materials purchasing. Management reports went only to top management and the Quality Control Director for scrap performance.

To improve its competitive edge, CenPointe decided to develop a productivity measure for its manufacturing operations. For each product line, the company established goals for the quantity of material used in production, the amount of scrap, and the number of good units completed. The performance for each month was to be discussed at a monthly meeting that included Rafferty, Gibson, all Production Supervisors, and a representative from the Accounting Department. The production supervisors' initial reaction to this system was positive because they saw an opportunity to participate and make suggestions.

Four months after the productivity measuring system and monthly meetings were implemented, the following conversation took place among three production supervisors. The conversation was among Roger Grier, Dana Berch, and Neil Bass.

GRIER: "I really dislike these monthly meetings. The accounting people present data on last month's production that we have never seen before and Rafferty expects us to have answers."

BERCH: "It's like an ambush by the enemy. When the accounting people have finished with us, Gibson hits us with his data."

GRIER: "Where do the standards for material cost usage come from anyway?"

BERCH: "I'm not sure. I think the Bill of Materials has something to do with it."

GRIER: "But the data they present is in dollars and the Bill of Materials is in units. And how does the scrap rate data Gibson hits us with affect the accounting data?"

BERCH: "I don't know."

GRIER: "Let's talk to Rafferty about how all this information is assembled."

BERCH: "Do you really want to talk about anything to the boss right now after she just criticized us in the meeting?"

GRIER: "But she criticizes us every month. All the departments are always at least 20 percent below the financial standards. In fact, I consider it a good month when my department performs at 75 percent of standard."

BERCH: "Let's just forget it. At next month's meeting, we can look amazed at the results again, apologize, and say that we will do better next month. That's what we have been doing for the last four months."

GRIER: "I'm tired of looking bad at every monthly meeting. I'm going to find a way to look good at next month's meeting. Here comes Neil. I wonder what he thinks?"

BASS: "After the meeting, Rafferty gave me the production schedule requirements for my department for the rest of the month. I told her the schedule far exceeded the capability of my department. She told me that she was sure that I could find a way to meet the schedule. I told her that the product specifications had not yet been received from Quality Control for many of the orders that the Sales Department had committed to ship before the end of the month. She just smiled and walked away."

REQUIRED

1. Based on the conversation among the three Production Supervisors of CenPointe Device Inc., discuss the likely motivation and behavior during the coming months of

  a. the Production Supervisors

  b. the employees who work for the Production Supervisors

2. Based upon the conversation,

  a. identify and explain the weaknesses of CenPointe's productivity measurement system and monthly meetings

  b. present a recommendation for correcting each identified weakness.

17–36 Employee Evaluation System (CMA) Boston Design Group is an architectural firm specializing in the planning and development of shopping malls and office complexes. The company has a staff of 150, approximately half of whom are professional employees including architects, engineers and technical writers. The remaining staff supports the professional group with drafting services, financial analysis for bid preparation, and secretarial and clerical skills.

Mark Olson, President of Boston Design, recently approved a new performance review system that applies to all employees. The system evaluates employees in categories such as accuracy, cooperativeness, ability to follow instructions, attendance and loyalty, and it rates performance on a five point scale from unsatisfactory to exceptional. Olson believes the new system reviews the employee attributes that are essential to the efficient operation of the firm.

The company's Vice-President of Design, Alan Reese, objects to the use of the same performance evaluation procedure for all employees. Reese argues that the qualities he believes are essential to the performance of his professional staff are given little or no consideration under the new system, and that the system does not fulfill the needs of his professional employees.

Reese approached Olson with the suggestion that Boston Design implement a separate performance review system for its professional employees. "Your people are only seeking an additional pat on the head," replied Olson. "What is good enough for the rest of the staff is good enough for your professionals."

REQUIRED

1. According to Maslow's Hierarchy of Needs, humans share a concern for five levels of need satisfaction: physiological, safety, social, esteem (ego), and self-actualization.
   a. Describe the five basic need categories associated with Maslow's theory of motivation.
   b. Identify the need category or categories most closely associated with professional employees, and explain why each category identified applies to professional employees.

2. Recommend changes to Boston Design Group's evaluation system that might fulfill the needs of the professional employees under Alan Reese's supervision.

3. Mark Olson believes that Boston Design's new evaluation system "reviews the employee attributes that are essential to the efficient operation of the firm." Identify other aspects of an employee evaluation system that should concern Mark Olson and explain why.

17–37 Life Cycle Issues (CMA) Burke Company manufactures various electronic assemblies that it sells primarily to computer manufacturers. Burke's reputation has been built on quality, timely delivery, and products that are consistently on the cutting edge of technology. Burke's business is fast-paced. The typical product has a short life; the product is in development for about a year and in the growth stage, with sometimes spectacular growth, for about a year. Each product then experiences a rapid decline in sales as new products become available.

Burke has just hired a new Vice President of Finance, Devin Ward. Shortly after reporting for work at Burke, Ward had a conversation with Andrew Newhouse, Burke's President. A portion of the conversation follows.

NEWHOUSE: "The thing that fascinates me about this business is that change is its central ingredient. We knew when we started out that a reliable stream of new products was one of our key variables—in fact, the only way to cope with the threat of product obsolescence. You see, our products go through only the first half of the traditional product life cycle—the development stage and then the growth stage. Our products never reach the traditional mature product stage or the declining product stage. Toward the end of the growth stage, products die as new ones are introduced."

WARD: "I suppose your other key variables would be cost control and efficient production scheduling?"

NEWHOUSE: "Getting the product to market on schedule, whether efficiently or not, is important. Some firms in this business announce a new product in March to be delivered in June, and they make the first shipment in October, or a year from March, or sometimes, never. Our reputation for delivering on schedule may account for our success as much as anything."

WARD: "Where I previously worked, we also recognized the importance of on-time deliveries. Our absorption cost system set 93 percent on-time as a standard."

NEWHOUSE: "The key variable that is your responsibility is cash management. It took us a while to recognize that. At first, we thought that profit was the key and that cash would naturally follow. But now we know that cash is the key and that profits naturally follow. Still, we don't do cash management well. Improving our cash management is the main thing we expect from you."

REQUIRED

1. Discuss the cash generating and cash usage characteristics of products in general in each of the four stages of the product life cycle—development, growth, maturity, and decline.
2. Describe the cash management problems confronting the Burke Company.
3. Suggest techniques that Devin Ward might implement to cope with Burke Company's cash management problems.

18

TRANSFER PRICING

Transfer prices are the prices that one segment of a firm pays to another for goods or services. This chapter deals mainly with goods, raw materials, or components that are used to create a final product to be sold on the outside market. In Chapter 11 we discussed services such as maintenance and computer services. Most of the issues and solutions offered in this chapter apply equally well to support department prices. In decentralized companies, transfer prices are extremely important because they affect the revenues of the selling division and the costs of the buying division.

As we discussed in Chapter 17, book income, ROI, and RI are still the most important indicators used to evaluate segment managers although newer measures such as throughput and quality are also used. If a manager has the option of buying a component from another division of the same company or purchasing it from an outside vendor, the decision could raise accounting measures of profitability for the division but lower such measures for the company as a whole.

If a segment chooses to buy a component from another segment of the same company, however, the transfer price itself has no effect on overall firm income. Because the revenue to the selling division is cost to the buying division, they cancel each other out. If a transfer price increases, the selling division earns more revenue, but the buying division has higher costs. So long as the divisions transfer the same quantities of product as they had in the past, there is no effect on income for the firm, only for the divisions.[1] However, if a change in a transfer price induces a manager to increase or decrease the

[1] A special problem arises when goods transferred internally are in the inventory of the buying division at the end of an accounting period. For financial reporting and tax purposes, the accountant eliminates the profit on the transferred goods so that all inventories are shown at cost to the firm. Courses in advanced accounting cover this problem in depth.

quantity bought from or sold to another division, it may affect the income of the firm. A common example is when a division begins to buy products from outside suppliers that it had previously bought inside. Another example is when increased orders from another division cause the selling division to turn away outside buyers.

PROBLEMS OF TRANSFER PRICING

The ways in which transfer prices are set, the mechanisms for resolving disputes among divisional managers, and the policies regarding the amounts of autonomy that divisional managers exercise have important behavioral consequences. It is critical that the system work in the best interests of both the divisional managers and the firm, that the divisional managers perceive it as fair, and that it is easily understood. No one system can always guarantee success, but any system should provide an atmosphere that is relatively conducive to success.

Because transfer prices are revenues to selling divisions and costs to buying divisions, divisional managers regard them much as they would external market prices. They use transfer prices to decide whether to make a component or buy it from another division, whether to use existing capacity to supply another division or outside customers, whether to increase productive capacity, and so on through the range of decisions that managers customarily make.

From the standpoint of the firm as a whole, the critical question is whether the transfer should take place, not what the price is. If one division transfers components to another that uses them in the assembly of a finished product, the question is whether the selling division can make the components for less than the buying division could acquire them from an outside supplier. From the standpoint of the firm, the decision is whether to make or buy.[2] Of course, it is necessary to consider all costs, including opportunity costs of using scarce resources and the cost of capital on increased investment.

Accordingly, corporate management wants the transfer price to encourage the divisional managers to act in the best way for the firm as a whole. Naturally, divisional managers want to take the actions that are best for their divisions. If the transfer price signals the divisional managers to take the best action for the firm as well as for their divisions it is doing its job, promoting goal and behavior congruence.

Chapter 11 (on cost allocation) described how transfer prices might be used to motivate managers to demand more or less of a service provided internally. Corporate management can encourage the use of some service such as

[2] We could also look at the decision of one of further processing. The question could be put: should the firm sell the components in their current state of completion or process them into other products?

data processing or engineering by charging a very low transfer price. Conversely, if demand for a service is greater than corporate management desires, the price may be raised. Thus, transfer prices have the motivational impact of encouraging or discouraging the use of internally provided goods or services.

Research into the problems of transfer pricing shows that it is not possible to make general statements. Whether a particular transfer price fosters goal congruence depends on factors such as the type of market, the strategies adopted by the firm regarding internal and external sales, how transfer pricing policies are administered, and the cost structure that the divisions encounter. Like other generalizations, those made about transfer pricing are subject to exceptions because of the range and complexity of the topic. Obviously, many factors affect goal congruence (and motivation). Transfer pricing is an important one, since divisional managers are judged on what transfer prices affect: profit, return on investment, and residual income.

Both theoretical research and surveys of corporate practice identify several bases for transfer prices. The main categories are market based, cost based, negotiated, and programmed transfer prices. Of these, market based (which may include some elements of negotiation) seem to be the most popular with business.[3]

MARKET PRICES

Eccles states that the first thing to determine with internal sales is the strategy that a firm employs regarding such sales.[4] The first question is whether a policy of vertical integration exists: must divisions buy internally if a source exists within the company? If the answer is no, then divisional managers are truly autonomous in buying and sales decisions.[5] If autonomy is present to this extent, and if there are outside markets for the goods, then a transfer price will often approximate market price. If the selling division is operating at capacity and can sell its output to outside customers at, say, \$10 per unit, it will not accept less than \$10 from an inside customer because doing so would reduce divisional profits, and could reduce corporate profits. (In practice, the actual transfer price could be less than \$10, because the selling division might have lower costs on inside sales than on outside sales. Shipping, commissions, and other costs could be significantly less on inside sales.) If the selling division is operating at capacity, it should charge another division the market price (less

[3] For example, see Daniel P. Keegan and Patrick D. Howard, "Transfer Pricing for Fun and Profit," *Review*, Number 3, 1986, Price Waterhouse, pp. 37–45.

[4] Robert G. Eccles, "Analyzing Your Company's Transfer Pricing Practices," *Journal of Cost Management for the Manufacturing Industry*, Summer 1987, pp. 21–33.

[5] Eccles says that even if a policy exists for vertical integration, if a selling division is seen as a distinct business on both internal and external sales, then market prices are appropriate. In other circumstances market prices are appropriate regardless of a firm's attitude toward internal sales.

any costs avoided by inside dealing). The market price is the opportunity cost of the goods—the amount that the firm as well as the division can get by selling them outside.

If the selling division is not operating at capacity, it will probably accept a lower price for sales to another division. Consider the following example. Shaw division of IMC Company makes a variety of pumps, fans, and other equipment used in heating and air-conditioning equipment. The divisional manager expects the following results for model 3405 blower:

Sales, 2,000 units at $100 per unit	$200,000
Variable costs at $40	$ 80,000
Contribution margin	120,000
Separate fixed costs	70,000
Profit	$ 50,000

Lakehart division of IMC makes equipment that could use the model 3405 blower. Its manager asks the manager of Shaw to give him a price.

First, it should be obvious that if Shaw could produce only 2,000 blowers, it could charge Lakehart the full $100 (less any savings from dealing internally). Any reduction in price to Lakehart would reduce overall profits because sales at $100 would be lost. However, suppose that Shaw has the capacity to produce 2,500 units without having to reduce production of other products. Lakehart division's managers might know that Shaw has excess capacity and they would know the market price for the blower. They want a price lower than $100. Shaw would like to get $100 per blower but knows that anything it receives above $40 would increase short-term profits. Thus, with the market price as both a starting point and an upper bound, and with incremental cost ($40) as the lower bound, the stage is set for negotiation between the managers of the two divisions.

When the selling division operates below capacity, the ideal transfer price equals incremental cost because the buyer then uses incremental cost to make a decision. However, the selling division will not be happy selling a product at its incremental cost. If an internal sale is to be made, negotiation between buyer and seller will lead to a transfer price that is greater than incremental cost but less than market price. In this case, any transfer price that falls between the incremental cost and the market price (the lower and upper bounds discussed above) and that promotes the sale of these blowers is ideal. As we mentioned earlier, this is because the question to the firm is whether the transfer should take place, not what the transfer price is.

Advantages of Market Prices

There is much to recommend market prices as transfer prices. If a division is operating at capacity, a market price is the opportunity cost of the goods. It is also the incremental cost to the buying division, because that division would have to buy the goods in the market if it could not get them from another division.

Using market prices as transfer prices also makes it possible to evaluate divisions as if they were independent companies. A division that cannot succeed by selling its products at market prices to other divisions presumably could not succeed as an independent firm. Market prices discipline managers to act as if they were managing independent companies. In fact, any attempt by corporate managers to impose transfer prices that are significantly different from market prices will meet the justified criticism that they are tampering with the autonomy of the divisional managers. Thus, market prices best fit the goals of decentralization, autonomy, and responsibility accounting.

Limitations of Market Prices

Market prices can be obtained in a variety of ways, depending on the type of product. Very active markets exist for many raw materials, especially agricultural commodities, with quotations easy to get. It is also a simple matter to get reliable prices for a variety of manufactured products, especially ones made by several companies that are relatively standard, such as sheet steel or paper. Prices for such goods can be obtained directly from the companies and are likely to be reliable.

A problem exists when divisions sell products exclusively to other divisions. An outside market might not exist for the products, and therefore, no opportunity might arise to test the market. The same problem exists when it is the firm's policy that components be bought internally if possible. If a division transfers a significant portion of its output internally or if a policy mandates transfer of goods internally, selling (and perhaps buying) divisions are not independent autonomous units regarding internal sales. If much capacity is devoted to internal sales, to a great extent the selling division is a captive of the divisions it supplies. Because success is tied to products marketed by the buying divisions, there is a question whether such selling divisions should be treated as profit or investment centers.

The firm might try to determine what a reasonable market value would be by seeking quotations from outside suppliers. Unfortunately, outside firms might not give quotations that reflect the market. If the outside firm does not really expect to get the business, it will not be likely to spend much time working up a quotation. It might quote a price much higher than reasonable. The reverse could also be true: an outside firm might quote a very low price for a limited quantity of the product to use excess capacity. The outside firm might have lower variable costs, and higher fixed costs, than the internal supplier, and it might be willing to quote a low price to get the business. It might be fine in the short run for the buying division to accept a price below the variable cost of the selling division. However, the selling division might reduce its capacity or take other measures that impair its ability to supply the buying division in the longer run. If the outside supplier later raised the price, the firm could suffer considerably.

Often the firm will neither buy nor sell outside certain products or components for strategic reasons such as ensuring a steady, reliable source of supply, quality control, protection of trade secrets, and encouraging technological progress. Market prices do not help here, even when the amounts of product involved are relatively low in relation to the selling division's total business, nor are quotations from potential suppliers useful, because the firm has no intention of going outside for business.

However, in some cases it might be possible to refer to external markets to develop transfer prices. If the selling division could operate at capacity without the internal business, it should not have to lose profits because it serves the other division. It would be reasonable for the transfer price to be high enough to keep the total profit of the selling division where it would have been if it had kept the external business.

Finally, there are circumstances in which market prices induce managers to take actions that are unwise from the standpoint of the firm.[6] To show how this can happen, we shall present some economic analyses of transfer pricing, dealing with three different situations. The analyses will show that managers may make unwise decisions (from the firm's point of view) in two common situations. Then we turn to cost-based transfer prices, which can give satisfactory, if not optimal, results.

TRANSFER PRICING AND ECONOMIC ANALYSIS

A substantial body of literature deals with the economics of transfer pricing, some of which we cover in the appendix. Here, we briefly introduce the question. The principal conclusion we reach is that market prices are ideal transfer prices in two cases: where there is perfect competition for the intermediate product, or where the selling division is operating at capacity (as we covered earlier). In fact, these two cases are really equivalent. The crux of the analysis is that each division, in seeking to maximize its profits, will try to equate its marginal revenue and marginal cost (the basic principle of microeconomic behavior). The appendix to this chapter provides graphical and mathematical analyses of the points covered here.

Perfectly Competitive Market for Intermediate Product

Economists define perfect competition strictly. The major point for our analysis is that under perfect competition for the intermediate product, the selling division can sell all it wishes to at the same price. The price that the selling

[6] It would not be an exaggeration to say that 90 percent or more of the literature on transfer pricing deals with the reconciliation of goal congruence and autonomy. The principal objective of most transfer-pricing proposals is to achieve both.

division charges its outside customers does not change as it offers more or fewer units. Therefore, its marginal revenue equals its selling price. This means that the selling division maximizes its profits when its marginal cost equals the selling price, because selling price is marginal revenue. Accordingly, the selling division might not operate at capacity, because if its marginal cost curve is rising, its marginal revenue and marginal costs might be equal before it reaches capacity. In other words, the selling division's total cost curve does not rise linearly, but rises at an increasing rate reflecting increases in per unit variable cost. These increases can arise because of overtime premium, hiring less experienced (and less efficient) workers, and other inefficiencies that crop up when a producer begins to approach capacity.

We pointed out earlier that from the standpoint of the company the question is not the transfer price, but whether the transfer should take place. We also pointed out that the incremental (marginal) cost was the ideal transfer price from the company's standpoint when the selling division was operating below capacity. With perfect competition for the intermediate product, market price is the incremental (marginal) cost to the buying division. The opportunity cost of a unit of the intermediate product is its selling price because the selling division can sell the unit at the market price. Moreover, the selling price of the intermediate product is also its marginal cost to the selling division because that division will offer units for sale until the selling price (which is also marginal revenue) equals marginal cost. Under these fairly restrictive conditions market price is the ideal transfer price precisely because it is equal to both the opportunity cost of a unit and the marginal cost of a unit.

No Intermediate Market

The extreme case is where the selling division cannot sell any units outside because there is no market for the intermediate product. In such cases, the selling division is a captive of the buying division.

A numerical example illustrates the point. Suppose that Lakehart division makes a component for Shaw division and is the sole source of supply. For ease of calculation, assume that Lakehart would buy either 10,000 or 12,000 components and, therefore, Shaw would make either 10,000 or 12,000. Data from the firm's perspective for the component and the final product appear below. Because these data are shown from the company's perspective, no transfer price is included.

	Incremental Cost				
Quantity	*Lakehart*	*Shaw*	*Firm*	*Revenue to Shaw*	*Profit to Firm*
10,000	$100,000	$50,000	$150,000	$200,000	$50,000
12,000	122,000	60,000	182,000	235,000	53,000

The firm as a whole makes a higher profit at 12,000 units than it does at 10,000 units. Suppose now that the manager of Lakehart decides to set the transfer price at $13. The manager of Shaw will see the following data:

		Total Costs		
Quantity	*Revenue*	*Transfer Price*	*Additional Costs*	*Profit*
10,000	$200,000	$130,000	$50,000	$20,000
12,000	235,000	156,000	60,000	19,000

Thus, the manager of Shaw will probably take only 10,000 units because his division's profit is higher at that volume. If the price were the marginal cost of $11 per unit, he would make the best decision from the standpoint of the firm. The marginal cost of $11 is the difference between the total cost that Lakehart incurs at 12,000 units and at 10,000 units ($122,000 − $100,000 = $22,000) divided by 2,000 units (12,000 − 10,000). Of course, the manager of Lakehart would not accept that price because he could earn more selling 10,000 units at $13 than he could selling 12,000 units at $11. In the following section we show that the two managers might be able to work out an arrangement that benefits both of them as well as the firm.

The case of the captive division indicates that when a division exists primarily to serve another, there is considerable doubt that the captive should be a profit center. The reason is that from the standpoint of the firm the ideal transfer price is marginal cost, which might be reasonably close to variable cost for most firms. However, the manager of the captive division would certainly balk at selling at marginal cost because her profits would be less than at a higher price and lower output. Because goal congruence is incompatible with divisional autonomy in this extremely simple case of perfectly straight revenue and cost functions, it is difficult to see how the two features would be compatible in a more realistic situation.

Imperfect Competition

We deal with one final case in this section. The producing division faces a declining price curve (demand curve) for its product. Selling price no longer equals marginal revenue. The division that buys the intermediate product, processes it further and then sells it, also faces a declining demand curve.[7] Again, we see that the selling division shows its highest profit producing below the amount that is optimal for the firm. Here, we shall again use IMC.,

Lakehart division makes a particular model that has variable costs of $300, not including the transfer price of a component made by the Shaw division. The market research staff of Lakehart estimates that it could sell 13,000 units at $900 or 17,000 units at $800. The variable cost of the component that Shaw

[7] We could also assume that it faced rising marginal costs and drop the assumption of a declining demand curve. The assumption that we use is simpler to employ in developing the numerical example that follows.

supplies is $100. Shaw's managers expect that they could sell 7,000 units on the open market at $250 or 10,000 units at $200.[8]

The following schedules show that the optimal actions for the firm are to sell 7,000 units of the component to outsiders at $250 and to sell 17,000 units of the finished product at $800. The analysis for the finished product includes the variable cost to both Lakehart and Shaw, totaling $400. The market prices that Shaw could obtain are relevant only for determining how many units of the component to sell outside. Because Shaw does not operate in a perfectly competitive market, it cannot sell all that it wishes to at a given, constant price. Similarly, Lakehart cannot buy all the components it wishes to at a given price from outside suppliers. If the transfer price were set at the $100 variable cost, the schedules below would also reflect the results of each division. The 17,000 units of the component that Shaw would make and transfer to Lakehart would bring no additional contribution margin to Shaw, because the price would equal variable cost.

Finished Product (Lakehart)

Price	*Unit Contribution Margin (Price − $400)*	*Volume*	*Total Contribution Margin*
$900	$500	13,000	$6,500,000
800	400	17,000	6,800,000

Outside Sales of Component (Shaw)

Price	*Unit Contribution Margin (Price − $100)*	*Volume*	*Total Contribution Margin*
$250	$150	7,000	$1,050,000
200	100	10,000	1,000,000

Now let us look at the situation from the standpoint of the manager of Shaw. Begin by supposing that he refuses to sell to Lakehart at any price below the $250 that he can obtain on the market. At that transfer price, the manager of Lakehart would restrict his output to 13,000 units, as shown below.

Price	*Unit Contribution Margin (Price − $300 − $250)*	*Volume*	*Total Contribution Margin*
$900	$350	13,000	$4,550,000
800	250	17,000	4,250,000

[8]We limit the choices to make the calculations more straightforward. The point of the example is valid if we allow additional levels of volume at different prices.

The $250 transfer price induces the manager of Lakehart to make fewer units of the finished product. While this is a good decision from his point of view, it is bad from the point of view of the firm. IMC would have earned $7,850,000 contribution margin if Lakehart had made 17,000 units (the sum of $6,800,000 from outside sales of the finished product and $1,050,000 from outside sales of the component). At the $250 transfer price, and 13,000 units for Lakehart, the divisions show the following results:

	Lakehart	*Shaw*
Sales:		
Finished product, 13,000 at $900	$11,700,000	
Component, 20,000 at $250		$5,000,000
Variable costs—at $550 ($300 + $250)	7,150,000	
—at $100		2,000,000
Contribution margin	$ 4,550,000	$3,000,000

Total contribution margin for the firm is $7,550,000 ($4,550,000 + $3,000,000), which is $300,000 below the level that would have been achieved if Lakehart had produced 17,000 units. Notice that we could also work simply with the contribution margin on sales to outsiders. The finished product would show total contribution margin of $6,500,000 from the first schedule and the outside sales of the component $1,050,000. The distribution of the $6,500,000 would be $4,550,000 to Lakehart and $1,950,000 to Shaw. (The $1,950,000 is $150 multiplied by 13,000.) While the transfer price is irrelevant for determining the total profit of the firm (because it washes out as revenue to one division, expense to the other), a bad transfer price can affect the actions of a manager and thus the total profit of the firm.

The manager of Shaw would show total contribution of $3,000,000 if he insisted on the $250 price, which is $1,950,000 greater than he would show if he altruistically made the transfer at $100. Let us make one final check to see whether the two managers could reach a solution optimal for both of them and for the firm. Suppose that corporate management were aware of the market research study performed by Lakehart and had asked the divisional managers to come up with a transfer price that would encourage optimal decisions.

The transfer price would have to result in both divisions' preferring the transfer of 17,000 units. It is possible to make the managers of both divisions better off by transferring 17,000 units, because the total profit to the firm is higher and that additional profit can be shared by the divisions.

The problem is that the two managers must agree on both a transfer price and an amount to be transferred. Simple agreement on price will not necessarily work to the advantage of the firm.

Let us begin by determining the minimum transfer price that the manager of Shaw would accept if he were to transfer 17,000 units to Lakehart. The manager knows that he can transfer 13,000 units at $250, which will provide a contribution margin of $1,950,000. He would therefore be willing to transfer

17,000 units at a price that would give total contribution margin of $1,950,000 or more. Accordingly, the minimum acceptable price is $214.70 using basic CVP relationships. The calculations are as follows:

$$\begin{aligned}
\text{required price} &= \frac{\text{total required contribution margin}}{\text{unit volume}} + \text{variable cost per unit} \\
&= \frac{\$1{,}950{,}000}{17{,}000} + \$100 \\
&= \$114.70 + \$100 \\
&= \$214.70
\end{aligned}$$

The manager of Lakehart can earn a contribution margin of $4,550,000 if he buys 13,000 units at $250, as calculated above. He must obtain a transfer price for 17,000 units that would give at least $4,550,000 in contribution margin to induce him to make 17,000 units. Here, we need to solve for the maximum variable cost that would give that contribution margin. The selling price for 17,000 units of the final product is $800. Again using CVP relationships:

$$\begin{aligned}
\text{maximum variable cost} &= \text{selling price} - \frac{\text{total contribution margin}}{\text{unit volume}} \\
&= \$800 - \frac{\$4{,}550{,}000}{17{,}000} \\
&= \$800 - \$267.65 \\
&= \$532.35
\end{aligned}$$

Lakehart incurs $300 variable costs of its own, so that the maximum allowable transfer price is $232.35 ($532.35 − $300).[9]

Lakehart's maximum is above Shaw's minimum, so the two managers should be able to come to an agreement somewhere in the middle. However, they might not, for various reasons. The manager of Shaw might refuse to lower the price, however unwisely. Corporate management might have to intervene to force the managers to make decisions that are optimal from the

---

[9] If the managers or corporate management consider only the transfer price, not both the transfer price and the quantity to be transferred, the above analysis is derailed. The manager of Lakehart is better off selling (and buying from Shaw) only 13,000 units so long as the transfer price is greater than $175. If the manager of Shaw offers to sell any quantity at a price above $175, the manager of Lakehart will take 13,000 units. Let X = the contribution margin per unit at sales of 13,000 units. Then $X - \$100$ is contribution margin per unit at sales of 17,000, because the price at which Lakehart could sell 17,000 units is $800, compared with $900 at 13,000 units. The indifference contribution margin, X, is

$$\begin{aligned}
13{,}000X &= 17{,}000(X - \$100) \\
4{,}000X &= \$1{,}700{,}000 \\
X &= \$425
\end{aligned}$$

For a contribution margin of $425 at 13,000 units, $325 at 17,000 units (both of which would yield $5,525,000 total contribution), total variable costs must be $475 ($900 − $425 or $800 − $325). Subtracting the $300 leaves $175 for the component from Shaw.

firm's standpoint. Please notice especially that the *market price* of the component does not *provide the information needed for optimal decisions*. Negotiation and compromise are required.

Other Assumptions

The previous analysis requires that the divisions be independent in the sense that the actions of one do not affect the results of the other. If the assumption does not hold, the divisions are interdependent and the analysis becomes complex. Two types of independence are of special importance: revenue and cost. Taking revenue first, the divisions are independent if the price that one charges does not affect the demand for the product of the other. In this respect, the divisions of a large automobile manufacturer are not independent. An increase in the price of Oldsmobiles, for example, will probably result in higher demand for Chevrolets.

Cost independence requires that the output of one division not affect the level of costs of the other. If two divisions compete for resources, their costs are likely to be interdependent. For example, if two divisions require highly skilled labor, the more that one division demands, the higher the wages both divisions will have to pay.

If divisions are significantly interdependent, it is extremely difficult to evaluate them as if they were separate, autonomous units. An extreme example is the division that makes a product without an intermediate market and can set the output of the final product by setting the output of the intermediate product. As already seen (no intermediate market), it is useless to treat the divisions as separate profit centers.

Conclusion

This discussion of economic analyses is useful in many ways. It not only illustrated when market prices are appropriate transfer prices, but it also introduced the ideas of cost-based transfer prices and negotiated transfer prices, topics we shall cover next.

The most disturbing conclusion of the economic analyses is that market prices serve as good transfer prices only in perfectly competitive markets for intermediate products, or if the selling division is at capacity. Even then, revenue and cost interdependencies are possible. If they exist, market prices might not be ideal transfer prices. In the real world, we do not expect to find many perfectly competitive markets. Markets for agricultural products are about as close as we could come. In most other markets, including those for raw materials such as metals, some very large buyers or sellers affect the market price.

Accordingly, it does not seem possible to achieve both goal congruence and autonomy in practice. Of course, if intrafirm transfers are relatively small, the loss of some autonomy or profits from suboptimal decisions might not be worth worrying about. However, there is an additional point to consider. The economic analysis assumes that managers have perfect knowledge of demand

and cost curves. (More precisely, it assumes that they have single-point expectations regarding these curves, rather than ranges of expectations.) The question is whether managers operating in practice tend to make more goal-congruent decisions than ones in economic analyses.

In the absence of perfect knowledge, managers are likely to be more cautious. Most notably, they would probably set prices based on costs and competition (which need not mean perfectly competitive markets), then strive to sell a budgeted quantity. In dealing with sister divisions, they might act as if they were dealing with another customer, using their selling prices to outsiders as the basis for negotiating transfer prices. In short, they might very well make decisions that do not provide the greatest profit to the firm.

The gloom is not unrelieved. Very few managerial situations (or any others, for that matter) present clear-cut choices of all good or bad consequences. It might be that losses in profits resulting from suboptimal decisions are more than offset by higher profits resulting from dealings with outside firms. Suboptimal decisions involving intrafirm transfers might be a small price to pay for decentralization. Corporate management simply cannot respond as quickly as divisional management when circumstances change and opportunities arise.

An interesting and instructive parallel is given by centrally controlled economies, such as those of socialist countries.[10] Central planners make decisions regarding prices and quantities in such countries. Their records are not unblemished. Newspapers and magazines provide numerous accounts of shortages of some products, gluts of others. Black-market activities are notoriously common when prices are centrally controlled. Economic dislocations are prevalent. The press in 1991 was filled with stories about possible changes in such practices in the Soviet Union and Eastern Europe. We are not taking a position here on the role of government. We simply point out that central planners must possess knowledge that is exceedingly difficult to develop. Decentralization in national economies seems to work much better than centralization.

COST-BASED TRANSFER PRICES

Marginal cost is the lower bound of a transfer price. The ideal transfer price is when the selling division operates below capacity; it is the opportunity cost to the firm much as when the selling division is operating at capacity the market price is the ideal transfer price. In dealing with marginal cost (or any other cost-based transfer price), several issues come into play. First, based on recent

[10] Much of the theory of transfer pricing owes an intellectual debt to researchers who were trying to develop optimal methods of allocating resources in centralized economies. The use of mathematical programming techniques, described briefly later in this chapter, directly descends from such research.

surveys showing the prevalence of market-based transfer prices, some authors argue that cost-based transfer prices have no relevance in the real world.[11]

A firm may decide that a policy that mandates internal purchases of components is in its best interests. For example, for a long time General Motors had such a policy; they believed that it would promote the lowest cost, highest quality components for the firm as a whole. However, recently General Motors reversed itself and announced that vertical integration was no longer a company policy. Vertical integration might be based on the notion that "we can do it better and cheaper," or may have other bases. For example, a division that makes patented components used by another division might be required to sell only to that division and to refuse offers from outside. Other strategic considerations such as ensuring a reliable long-run supply might make it sensible to require internal purchase and sale. In such situations, the rule that one division should be able to treat another division like any other customer or supplier does not prevail. If vertical integration is a policy, the buying and selling divisions are really not independent of one another. Internal sales might not be evaluated from a profitability standpoint, but on costs.

If vertical integration is a company policy (or if no intermediate market exists), transfer prices are an allocation of the profit received from the sale of the final product. If the selling division charges only incremental costs, the entire profit is allocated to the buying division. At any transfer price above incremental costs, the selling division is allocated some profit. This allocation is no different from the allocations discussed in Chapters 4 and 11. With this basis, let us discuss different ways that cost can be employed in setting a transfer price.

Actual Costs

Perhaps the worst basis for setting transfer prices is actual cost, either absorption or variable cost. The reason is that actual cost does not encourage the manager of the selling division to control costs: someone else will pay them. Actual cost can even encourage the manager of the selling division to allow costs to rise deliberately. This can occur when a margin for profit is included in the pricing formula.

Consider an example. Suppose that the manager of Lakehart division orders 1,000 fans from Shaw division. The transfer price is to be actual full cost (with fixed overhead applied) plus a 10 percent allowance for profit.[12] The fan usually requires 2 labor hours, and total variable costs should be $20 per

[11] See Keegan and Howard, *op. cit.* In addition, Eccles states that the use of market-based prices or cost-based prices is really a matter of strategy decisions on sourcing (are internal sales/purchases mandated or optional?) and on pricing (is the selling division seen as an independent business for both internal and external sales?). In addition we have seen that negotiation may be part of any final transfer price; costs play a part in such negotiation.

[12] The price is based on normal cost because of the application of fixed overhead. We consider the "pure" actual cost case shortly.

fan. Shaw applies fixed overhead at a rate of $4 per direct labor hour. The transfer price is $30.80 per fan, calculated as follows:

Total variable cost	$20.00
Applied fixed overhead	8.00
Total cost	28.00
Allowance for profit (0.10 × $28)	2.80
Price	$30.80

Suppose that through inefficiency, total labor time per unit increased to 2.5 hours and total variable costs increased to $25. Fixed overhead is then $10 ($4 × 2.5), total cost $35, and the transfer price $38.50 ($35 + $3.50). The manager of Lakehart is charged with the inefficiency of Shaw, and in fact pays even more because both fixed overhead and the profit margin are affected by actual labor hours.

The situation would be worse if actual fixed costs rather than normal fixed costs were used. First, fixed overhead budget variances are incorporated into the transfer price. Second, the activity of the period affects the rate per direct labor hour, which in turn affects the overhead cost allocated to the fans, and the transfer price. The manager of Shaw could be tempted to schedule the production of the fans in periods of low volume, when the rate is higher, with a corresponding increase in the transfer price.

The use of actual variable cost rather than actual absorption cost relieves one problem: the level of activity during the period does not affect the transfer price. However, assuming that the transfer price is set at some multiple of variable cost to allow for recovery of some fixed costs, the objection that the manager has no incentive to control costs still holds.

Standard or Budgeted Costs

In some cases, variable cost approximates marginal cost, making variable cost an excellent transfer price as long as it represents efficient operation. Standard variable costs should fulfill that requirement: they should be representative of efficient operation; therefore, they overcome the problem of failing to motivate the manager to control costs.

If standard variable costs do serve as transfer prices, with no allowance for recovery of fixed costs and contribution to profit, the manager of the selling division is penalized. She is expected to produce goods for another division in an efficient manner and show no increase in total profit. Obviously, managers of selling divisions will not be delighted with this. The only chance of showing any profit on transfers is to make the goods at less than standard variable cost. Accordingly, there is an incentive to cut corners and otherwise try to reduce costs. This tendency might be beneficial, but it could also be harmful if quality suffers. Some alternatives might prove satisfactory, and we next consider a few of these.

Standard Absorption Cost One possibility is to use standard absorption cost, with or without a markup. This overcomes the problems associated with using actual costs, but does not provide a transfer price that reflects the marginal cost of the transferred goods, and so it could lead to poor decisions.

Suppose that there is no market for the fans that Shaw is to make for Lakehart division. Assume further that the $20 variable cost is standard and that the transfer price is $30.80 as calculated above. Now, the manager of Lakehart might solicit bids from outside firms for the fans. Suppose that an outside firm offers to supply them at $26 per unit. If the manager of Shaw does not meet that price, the manager of Lakehart will buy from the outside firm.

Buying the fans outside would reduce profits for the firm. The incremental (marginal) cost of production internally is $20 per unit, which is less than the $26 outside price. As we noted earlier, this is a make-or-buy decision from the standpoint of the firm. The manager of Shaw should be willing to meet the price because it provides $6 per unit in contribution margin and increased profit. However, the standard full cost transfer price does not encourage optimal action. Notice that this case does not conform to the market situation. It might be argued that the $26 outside bid is a market price, but it is not a price that could be used for decisions stretching beyond the single sale. If Lakehart needed 1,000 fans per year for several years, it should not use the $26 price for a single year's supply as the basis for making the long-run decision. The supplier could turn out to be unreliable or could raise the price after the first year.

The main advantage of using standard absorption costing with a markup is that it might reflect the price that would prevail if there were a market for the goods. The reasoning is that if other firms were making the same product, they would probably base their prices on absorption cost plus a markup. If their cost structures and markup policies were similar to those of the internal division, their prices would approximate the transfer price. There is some evidence that firms sometimes set transfer prices by building up costs and markups based on what an outside firm would do if it were going to market the product.

Standard Variable Cost Plus Lump Sum Using standard variable cost plus lump sum as a basis for transfer pricing has distinct advantages. As an allocation method, it works as follows. The user is charged a flat amount per period based on expected long-run use of the service and a variable amount that depends on actual use in each period. In a transfer-pricing context, the selling division charges the buying division some flat amount per month or per year. It also charges an amount approximating variable cost per unit for the number of units actually transferred during a given period. This is similar to the issues raised in Chapter 11 about charging for capacity versus charging current operating costs for support departments.

For example, Shaw division might charge Lakehart division $30,000 per year for the fans, plus $20 per fan. The $30,000 could be determined in a number of ways. It could represent a share of fixed costs based on the expected share of direct labor hours that the fans would require over a three-year period. It could also include some margin for profit. It could also be a figure negotiated by the two managers, without much attempt to analyze fixed costs.

The major advantage of this method is that it results in the individual units' being transferred at an amount that approximates marginal cost. The buying division incurs the flat fee no matter how many units it buys—it is a sunk cost and is irrelevant in deciding how many units to buy from the inside supplier. Because the individual units are transferred at variable cost, make-or-buy decisions are simplified. If an outside supplier is willing to provide the units at less than the internal variable cost, it should be welcome to do so. (Of course, this conclusion assumes that the supplier is able to meet delivery schedules, quality standards, and so on.)

Dual Pricing

A method that offers the best of both worlds is to charge the buying division with the marginal cost of the transferred goods and to credit the selling division with a higher amount. The higher amount could be a market price or a figure based on standard absorption costs with an allowance for profit. This method is not widely used, at least partly because revenue to the selling division is greater than cost to the buying division, which strikes many managers and accountants as extremely artificial. The different amounts are reported only on internal statements and are not recorded in company accounts.

The major advantage of the system is that both divisions benefit. The managers are likely to make goal-congruent decisions because each is working with a relevant value. The manager of the buying division is confronted with a make-or-buy or a further processing decision, and the marginal cost of the goods is a critical datum. The manager of the selling division is not penalized for dealing internally and, therefore, does not care where the goods go.

Besides its strangeness, the method has another drawback. The manager of the selling division is not motivated to keep costs down unless the transfer price is a market price. If a cost-plus formula is used, the manager of the selling division may become complacent because he has a near-captive customer. The manager of the buying division is unlikely to find an outside supplier whose prices are less than the marginal costs of producing internally, and so he is almost certain to be bound to the selling division.

Gaming and Misinformation

One of the problems of using cost-based transfer prices is that they may encourage misestimations of costs. Consider the following example. Division A makes a number of products in a single factory. It sells them all to outside customers except for product X, which it sells exclusively to division B, which makes it into another product. Corporate management as well as the manager of division B wants the transfer price of product X to approximate its variable cost.[13] Corporate management wants variable cost as the transfer price, because the principal decision is whether to process product X beyond the point to which division A brings it.[14]

The manager of division A has a different view. Even if she decides to supply the needs of division B at variable cost, there is still room to maneuver. The manager of division A will likely try to build some cushion into the variable cost figure by overstating costs. It is rarely possible to estimate variable costs with certainty, and the estimates of the manager of division A might be significantly higher than actual costs. The problems here are obvious. The firm would not be using valid data for deciding on the various matters related to product X (whether to process it further, whether to seek an outside supplier, and so on).

The manager of division A is clearly in a better position than corporate management and the manager of division B to determine variable cost. It is, therefore, likely that she would be able to get a price somewhat above variable cost. In fact, if the manager of division A is not in a better position to develop and interpret information regarding the operations of division A, there is no need to decentralize. Recall that one principal benefit of decentralization is that people who are close to the information needed to make decisions are the ones who make the decisions.

SURVEYS OF CURRENT PRACTICE

We have looked at economic theory, market-based prices, and cost-based prices. There seems to be no integrated theory nor any pat answers. Before dealing with negotiated transfer prices and those set using mathematical programming, let us look at current practice as reflected in two studies to see how transfer pricing works. Vancil's 1979 study[15] generally classified current practice as either market based or cost based. A little under half of the companies surveyed (46.8 percent) used cost-based transfer pricing, most of whom used full cost and cost plus. Only 4.6 percent of the respondents used some form

---

[13] For variable cost, we could substitute marginal cost. We assume for simplicity that variable cost equals marginal cost.

[14] There might be outside sources of product X, so division B and the firm as a whole could also be looking at a make-or-buy decision. However, if other firms made product X, it is likely that division A could sell the product to someone else. Other firms would not be likely to make a product that had no market. Of course, other firms might make product X to process it further into product Y. Such a firm would be interested in serving division B.

[15] Richard F. Vancil, *Decentralization: Managerial Ambiguity by Design* (Homewood, IL, Dow Jones-Irwin: Financial Executives Research Foundation, 1979), p. 180, Exhibit B–10.

of variable costs as a basis. Over half of the firms used market-based prices (53.2 percent). Vancil separates this number into 31 percent that use market price or competitor's price and 22.2 percent that use negotiated prices. Presumably, the negotiated prices are based on some measure of market prices to be classified as such in the survey.

It is interesting that the idea of marginal cost (which usually translates into variable cost) is not used in practice. If one combines cost plus pricing[16] with the market-based companies, almost 70 percent of the companies use something akin to market prices as the basis for transfer pricing policies. Possibly, managers see full costs as the opportunity costs for their divisions. As we pointed out in Chapter 4, managers may be so conditioned by financial accounting that they confuse product costs for financial accounting with cost of products for managerial decision making.

Keegan and Howard use a 1984 Price Waterhouse study that shows that 31 percent of companies use cost-based transfer prices and 69 percent use market-based prices. If we reclassify the results from Vancil then these two studies show remarkably similar results. In addition, 72 percent of the companies reported that negotiation was part of the transfer pricing process. Thus, based on these two studies, it seems that managers generally agree that some form of market-based transfer prices form the basis for negotiating a price.

Eccles might provide the unifying concept in the framework we presented earlier. He sees transfer pricing as a natural extension of the basic strategic planning process of a company. He divides strategic questions into the source question and the price question that we explained. He proposes that without a policy that divisions must buy internally (the source question), the selling division should deal with the buying division in the same way it would with any external company seeking goods. If there is a policy for vertical integration (i.e., divisions must buy internally), the next question is whether the selling division is seen as a distinct business for external and internal sales (the pricing decision). If the answer is yes, the selling division should be mandated to use market prices as a basis for transfer pricing. If the answer is no, the selling division should use full costs with no margin for profit for internal sales. While Keegan and Howard propose that only market-based prices are relevant, their position really does not conflict with that of Eccles. Eccles only proposes cost-based prices when (1) there is a policy that components must be bought internally if possible and (2) the selling division is not considered an independent division insofar as internal sales are concerned. This is a restrictive case where decisions are not decentralized and divisions not autonomous.

These survey results and the basic strategic policy questions posed by

---

[16] If no market exists, some companies try to approximate market prices by building up costs, including allocations, then adding a profit margin. The idea is that the result should be close to market price.

Eccles flow from the earlier discussion of market-based prices and economic analysis: what managers perceive as the opportunity cost is the lower bound; market price (or some surrogate for this price) is the upper bound; and negotiation is the key to agreeing on price and whether an internal transfer will take place.

NEGOTIATED TRANSFER PRICES

Negotiation is a possible solution to the transfer-pricing problem. Managers are left to deal with one another much as they would with an external supplier or customer; central management intervenes only if an impasse arises. There is much to recommend negotiation. Divisional managers negotiate such matters as delivery schedules, specifications, and quantities on interdivisional transfers, so it seems reasonable to allow them to negotiate prices as well.[17]

The usual objection to negotiated transfer prices is that the performance of a divisional manager is affected by his or her skill as a negotiator as well as by efficiency and effectiveness in operating the division. The counter to this objection is that negotiating ability is part of the package of talents that a manager needs. Divisional managers negotiate with their peers within the firm and with outsiders on many of the same kinds of matters as well as others.

In addition, some authors argue that in most negotiation situations it is unusual to find both parties with equal power.[18] Larger divisions dominate smaller ones; divisions that need a component quickly may be taken advantage of by selling divisions; buying divisions that know the loss of their business would be a severe blow to a selling division may exert unusual influence. If the source decision does not require vertical integration, then dealing with buying divisions is no different from dealing with any other company. Power and influence are part of the negotiation process. If, however, there is mandated vertical integration, then issues of power should be included in how transfer prices are administered by central management.

A transfer-pricing system that allows negotiation requires some provision for appeal to a higher level. The corporation might have a board or a single arbitrator who steps in when divisional managers cannot agree and something must be done. Appeal to a higher authority does lessen the degree of autonomy, but it might be necessary if the well-being of the firm is at stake. For example, the manager of the buying division might dispute the cost data that the manager of the selling division is providing to support his claim for a particular price. If the transfer is clearly in the interests of the firm, it is reasonable for corporate management to intervene and set a price.

[17] For example, see Arthur L. Thomas, *A Behavioural Analysis of Joint-Cost Allocation and Transfer Pricing* (Stipes Publishing Company, 1980).

[18] See David J. H. Watson and John V. Baumler, "Transfer Pricing: A Behavioral Context," *The Accounting Review*, 50:3 (July 1975), pp. 466–474.

PROGRAMMED PRICES

We have seen that when the selling division is operating at capacity it should transfer goods at the outside market price (less any costs avoided by dealing inside) because the market price is the opportunity cost of the goods. Linear programming provides opportunity costs of using scarce resources—the shadow prices on the constraints. Moreover, a large firm that does extensive inside transferring could use linear programming to determine the best overall mix of dealing inside and outside.

The idea is that transfer prices should be the variable costs of a division, including any transfer prices it has paid, plus the opportunity costs (shadow prices) of the scarce resources that the division uses in making the product. The central headquarters of the firm determines the optimal overall mix, and the divisional managers implement it. Unfortunately, as several writers have pointed out, there can be very sticky questions and potentially dysfunctional behavior on the part of divisional managers.[19]

We consider a simple example. To the extent that problems arise in a simple case, we can expect worse difficulties in a more realistic one.

ILLUSTRATION OF PROGRAMMED PRICES

ABC Company operates three divisions, A, B, and C. Division A makes a product that it can sell only to division B. In turn, division B can sell outside or to division C, which sells only to outsiders. We assume for simplicity that all costs are fixed, so that selling price equals contribution margin. The work that each division does requires one unit of capacity for each unit of product. No other firm makes the product. The following schedule shows the selling prices that each division can obtain, along with its capacity.

Division	*Selling Price*	*Capacity*
A	none	100
B	\$15	110
C	20	60

Letting A, B, and C denote the quantities sold outside by the respective divisions, we have the following linear programming problem.

Maximize: $\$0A + \$15B + \$20C$

Subject to:

$$A + B + C \leq 100 \quad \text{(division A constraint)}$$

$$B + C \leq 110 \quad \text{(division B constraint)}$$

$$C \leq 60 \quad \text{(division C constraint)}$$

$$A, B, C \geq 0$$

[19]Thomas, *op. cit.*, provides an extensive discussion and a comprehensive bibliography.

The optimal solution is $40B$ and $60C$, which uses all the capacity of divisions A and C, while leaving 10 units of division B capacity idle. The shadow price on division A capacity is \$15. Because any additional units that division A could make should go through division B and then be sold at \$15, the shadow price exceeds the market price of units sold outside after division A has processed them. The shadow price on division B capacity is zero, because the division cannot work at capacity. Thus, division B would sell to division C at the transfer price that division B pays division A (which is division B's variable cost).

If we interpret the opportunity costs strictly, division A would charge division B \$15 per unit. Division B would then earn zero contribution margin because it would pay \$15 and sell for \$15, both outside and to division C. Market prices would be fine as transfer prices here if we had a market price for units made by division A.

Of course, it might be possible to work out acceptable arrangements among the divisions, but the corporation would be imposing its will on the divisional managers if it developed a product mix program and set the transfer prices. Thus, one of the salient objections to the use of linear programming is that it destroys, or at least seriously impairs, divisional autonomy.

Lest we assume that mathematical programming has no place in transfer pricing, let us point out that it is useful as the economic model is useful. Any transfer price should be based on a notion of cost and optimality. Even if managers decide to follow different criteria for decisions on product mix, quantity, and transfer prices, accountants will want to provide incremental cost, marginal cost, and programmed solutions as information to be used in various decisions.

TRANSFER PRICING AND MULTINATIONAL COMPANIES

Multinational companies might face special problems with transferring goods and services among and between divisions. Each division operates using the currency of its own country. In addition, different nations have distinct tax laws. Finally, most multinational companies want to aggregate information regarding divisions (and certainly the firm) into the currency of the country where headquarters is located. Thus, there are unique problems associated with both transfers between countries and evaluations of divisions in several different nations.

Some problems arise because of changes in exchange rates, which vary in respect to the U.S. dollar. Say a company has a division in France. The division will do business using francs and the results (income and investment, for example) will be stated in that currency. However, the multinational firm would probably want to look at results from all divisions in denominations of U.S. dollars. With fluctuating exchange rates, the performance of a divisional manager might be affected by factors outside her control. If, say, one unit of a foreign currency is worth $2.00 and income is 200,000 units of that currency, the translation would be $400,000 ($2 × 200,000). However, if exchange rates dropped so that one unit of that currency is now worth $1.80, then income would be $360,000, a significant change not related to controllable operations.

Other difficulties emanate from differences in tax rates. Not only can these differences cause problems in evaluating divisions, but they can affect whether a transfer will be made at all. From the corporate perspective, divisions in lower tax countries should have higher profits than those in higher tax countries; this will maximize overall profits. If transfers are made, they might affect total profits through transfer prices. Assume that division X buys a component from division Y. Both divisions are in Europe and use a common currency, denoted as β. Data regarding these divisions appear below.

Selling price of division X's product	β200
Variable cost, excluding transfer price	40
Tax rate in division X's country	25%
Variable cost of division Y's product	β 80
Tax rate in division Y's country	60%

Suppose that managers are contemplating transferring 1,000 units of division X's component at either β80 or β120. Income statements below reflect the different results under each option.

	Transfer at β80	
	Division X	Division Y
Sales (1,000 × β200)	200,000	
(1,000 × β80)		80,000
Variable cost (40 + 80)	120,000	
		80,000
Contribution margin	80,000	0
Taxes	20,000	

	Transfer at β120	
	Division X	Division Y
Sales (1,000 × β200)	200,000	
(1,000 × β120)		120,000
Variable cost (40 + 120)	160,000	
		80,000
Contribution margin	40,000	40,000
Taxes	10,000	24,000

As you can see, total taxes are only β20,000 at the lower price compared to β34,000 at the higher. To maximize corporate profits, division Y should sell its component to division X at its variable cost. This would not make sense to managers of division Y if they were being evaluated as a profit or investment center. A requirement to transfer at incremental cost would cause some problems in how transfer pricing policies are administered, a subject that we cover next.

Many countries have import or export duties based on value. These tariffs can affect interdivisional transfers in the same way that difference in tax rates do. Perhaps movements within Europe will minimize some of these problems, but they will still exist on a worldwide basis after 1992.

Management fees and allocations of corporate costs are another area where income can be shifted. While this shifting is not involved with transfer pricing directly, it affects reported profitability and the evaluation of divisions and managers, a strong element of the transfer-pricing problem. While some fees might be traceable to a foreign subsidiary, most assignments of fees and corporate costs are allocations of common costs. It would be to the interest of the parent company to allocate as many of these costs to divisions in high tax countries and as few as possible to those in low tax countries. As with any allocated cost, inclusion in divisional reports will distort performance, and such costs are not controllable by operating managers. As we have pointed out, when managers feel that they are being treated unfairly (e.g., their evaluations include noncontrollable costs), they tend to try to get around the system. Finally, taxing authorities review such allocations to make sure that they are reasonable.

ADMINISTERING TRANSFER PRICES

Decentralization and the desire for goal congruence might conflict. On one hand, central management wants segment managers to act independently for all the reasons cited in Chapter 17. On the other hand, central management also wants segment managers to make decisions congruent with overall corporate goals. To promote goal congruence, central management usually restricts the independence of its lower managers. Transfer pricing policies and administration are areas where such interference can arise.

Perhaps the best place to start is with the basic goals and organization of a company. As we have pointed out, there are many good, general reasons why a firm is centralized or chooses vertical integration. There are other reasons for full decentralization and total independence in source decisions. It is important, therefore, to make sure that any policies within the company are consistent with these organizational and strategic decisions.

Whatever policies are adopted, a clear method should be proposed for administering the policies. Administration should also be in concert with the general strategic decisions. For example, if the choice whether to sell or buy internally or externally is open and if basic policies show that divisions are being evaluated as if they were independent companies, it would be inconsistent for upper management to interfere in the source or price decisions of segment managers. However, even in this case, administration procedures could allow central management to act as arbitrators among divisions if asked to do so by the divisional managers.

Administration also involves the sharing of information. Will all divisions know the costs and sales of other divisions or will this information only come out in negotiation? In addition, there should be a mechanism to change transfer prices. Most transfer prices are short term. Will they change as market prices change? That is an administrative policy as well.

SUMMARY

Transfer pricing is a complex and difficult topic. If it is difficult to promote both goal congruence and divisional autonomy even in simple situations, we can see why so much effort has been expended dealing with this problem. If a transfer takes place, there is no effect on corporate profits no matter what the transfer price. Thus, we are dealing with a behavioral issue. Practice shows that full costs are often used as a floor and market prices as a ceiling in the negotiations leading to a transfer price.

REVIEW PROBLEM

Hughes Company operates several divisions. Budgeted results for Ransom division, all anticipated from sales outside the company, appear below.

Sales, 100,000 units at $10	$1,000,000
Variable costs, 100,000 at $3	300,000
Contribution margin	700,000
Fixed costs	300,000
Income	$ 400,000

The manager of Mirco division has approached Ransom's manager about buying some of its product for use in a new product that Mirco is considering. Mirco expects to sell 20,000 units at $18 per unit and to incur variable costs of $9 in addition to the transfer price it would pay Ransom.

REQUIRED

1. Suppose that Ransom is operating at capacity. If the transfer of 20,000 units were to take place at a price of $8 per unit, what would happen to the profits of Ransom, Mirco, and the company as a whole?

2. Redo part 1 assuming that Ransom is operating well below capacity.
3. Assuming that Ransom is operating well below capacity, what is the lowest price it would accept for the units?
4. What is the highest price that Mirco would pay for the units?

ANSWERS TO REVIEW PROBLEM

1. Ransom's profits would fall by \$40,000 because it would lose sales at \$10 to make them at \$8. The \$2 drop in revenue for 20,000 units is \$40,000. Mirco's profits would rise by \$20,000, and the company's would fall by \$20,000.

Mirco: 20,000 × (\$18 − \$9 − \$8)	\$20,000
Company:	
Revenue from Mirco, 20,000 × \$18	\$360,000
Lost revenue of Ransom, 20,000 × \$10	200,000
Net gain in revenue	160,000
Less: Mirco variable costs, 20,000 × \$9	180,000
Net loss	\$ 20,000

Or Mirco gains \$20,000, while Ransom loses \$40,000, giving a loss to the company of \$20,000. Or the company loses a contribution margin of \$140,000 by failing to sell 20,000 units outside (20,000 units × Ransom's \$7 (\$10 − \$3) unit contribution margin). It gains only \$120,000 on the new product, 20,000 units times the contribution margin of \$6 (\$18 − \$9 Mirco variable cost − \$3 Ransom variable cost).

Of course, the manager of Ransom would not willingly sell for \$8 units that he sells for \$10. The manager of Mirco would not pay \$10 (market price) because he would then lose \$1 per unit (\$18 − \$9 − \$10 = −\$1). Here, the market price is appropriate because it guides both managers to the correct decision.

2. Mirco still gains \$20,000, Ransom gains \$100,000 [20,000 × (\$8 − \$3)], and the company gains \$120,000, the sum of the division's changes.

Company:		
Revenue from Mirco		\$360,000
Variable costs:		
Mirco, 20,000 × \$9	\$180,000	
Ransom, 20,000 × \$3	60,000	240,000
Increase in profit		\$120,000

3. \$3, its variable cost per unit.
4. \$9, because at any higher price it would show a negative contribution margin.

APPENDIX 18A: SOME ECONOMIC ASPECTS OF TRANSFER PRICING

Economists and management scientists devote much attention to the problems of transfer pricing.[20] This appendix gives graphical and mathematical analyses of the problem.

For the following examples, we shall use a firm that has two divisions, A and B. Division A makes product A. Division B buys product A and performs additional work to convert it into product B. We shall consider several combinations of different market conditions. Before we begin, we reiterate that market price is the ideal transfer price when the selling division is operating at capacity. All the analyses that follow assume excess capacity.

Perfectly Competitive Market for Intermediate Product

Figure 18A–1 depicts three possible situations. The price of the intermediate product, A, is *P*(A). The marginal revenue line for product A is straight and horizontal, reflecting the assumption that product A is sold in a perfectly competitive market. Division A will not accept a price less than *P*(A) from division B because to do so would reduce its profits. Accordingly, division A will produce up to the point where its marginal cost curve, denoted *MC*(A), meets its marginal revenue curve, *P*(A). To simplify the graphs, we have used only one line to denote division B's activities. The line labeled *NMR*(B) represents the marginal revenue of division B less the marginal cost that division B incurs in further processing product A. Thus, *NMR*(B) is net marginal revenue to division B and does not include the transfer price that division B would pay to division A. Accordingly, it represents the change in profit that division B experiences at a given volume, excluding the transfer price. The line slopes down to the right, which could reflect a falling price per unit as volume rises, increasing marginal costs of making product A into product B, or a combination of the two. Division B maximizes its profits where its net marginal revenue equals the transfer price. The transfer price is a marginal cost to division B.

Graph (a) of Figure 18A–1 shows that production of A, *Q*(A), equals that of B, *Q*(B). In other words, division A sells all its output to division B, which converts it into product B and sells it to outside firms. Graph (b) shows that when the profit-maximizing output for product A is greater than that of product B, division A will sell some of its output in the external market. Finally, graph (c) shows the case where the profit-maximizing output for product B is

[20] Jack Hirshleifer did much of the early work in this area and this section draws on that work. See Jack Hirshleifer, "On the Economics of Transfer Pricing," *Journal of Business*, 29:3 (July 1956), pp. 172–184.

FIGURE 18A–1 Profit-Maximizing Outputs—Perfect Competition for Intermediate Product

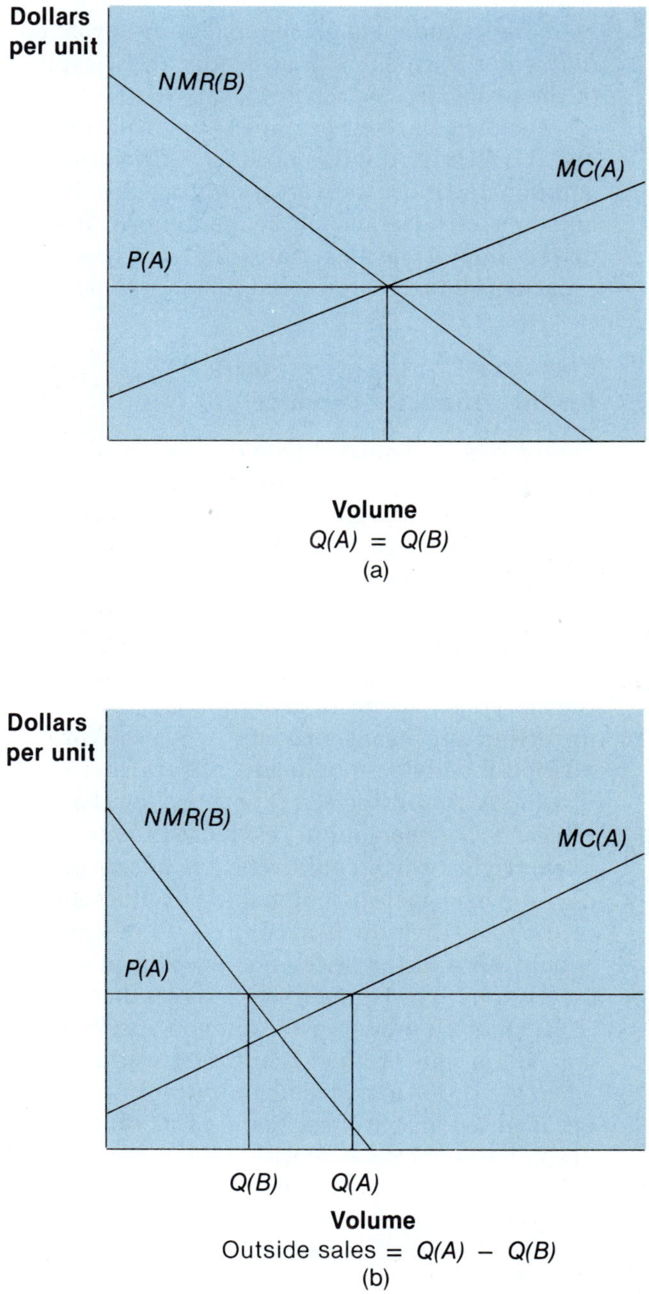

FIGURE 18A–1 (continued)

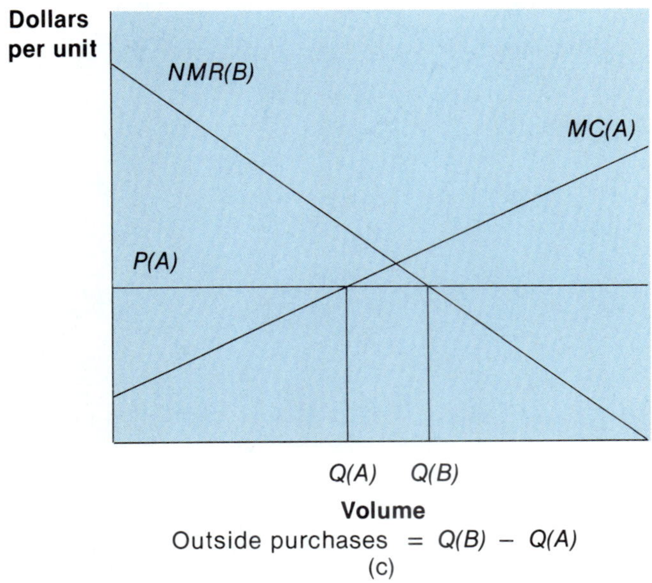

greater than that for product A. Here, division B will buy additional units of product A from the outside market, while still taking all of division A's output.

We see from Figure 18A–1 that the market price of product A is a good transfer price in that it encourages both managers to maximize not only the profits of their divisions, but also the profits of the firm. The manager of division A will sell units of product A to whoever wants them until marginal revenue equals marginal cost. The manager of division B will determine the profit-maximizing output of product B and will buy as many units of product A as she needs, either from division A or from outside firms.

No Intermediate Market

Assume that product A can be used only by division B, so no external market exists for this intermediate product. Further, assume that, at least in the short run, no other firm makes product A, so that division A is division B's sole supplier. In this situation, the ideal transfer price is the marginal cost of product A.

The profit-maximizing output of the firm is simply the point where the net marginal revenue of division B (which is the NMR of product B) equals the marginal cost of product A. Figure 18A–2 shows that this output is 96 units. The figure also shows that the manager of division A would earn higher profits by restricting output to 62 units. At that point division A maximizes its profits. The reason is that net marginal revenues of division B are also the average revenue of division A. Division B will pay an amount up to the NMR of prod-

FIGURE 18A–2 Profit-Maximizing Outputs— No Intermediate Market

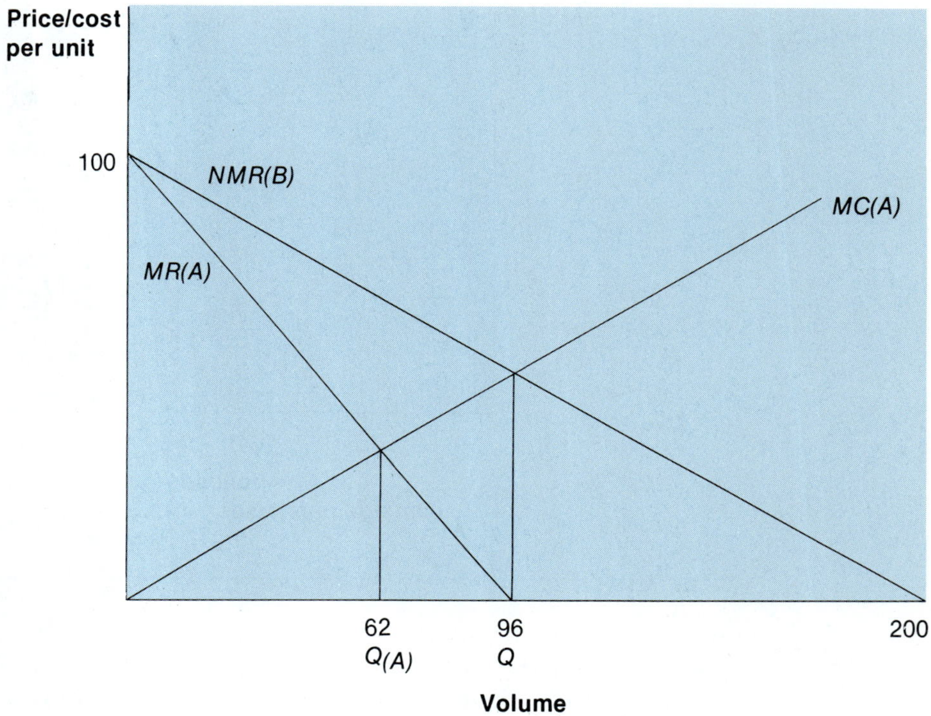

uct B to obtain product A. This is true because the transfer price of product A is the marginal cost to division B.

The line labeled *MR*(A) is the marginal revenue curve for division A and is derived from the demand curve for product A (the NMR curve of division B). The manager of division A would seek to equate marginal revenue and marginal cost, which occurs at 62 units and a price of \$68. This level of output is below the 96 units that are optimal output from the standpoint of the firm. Similarly, the manager of division B would like to obtain additional units of product A until the price equals the net marginal revenue of product B. The extreme case is that the manager of division B would like to acquire 200 units of product A at a price of zero. It is at that point that the net marginal revenue of product B is zero, which is the point of profit maximization for division B.

Mathematical Analysis

This part of the appendix gives a mathematical solution to the transfer-pricing problem in Figure 18A–2. The figure shows net marginal revenue from sales of product B, marginal cost of product A, and marginal revenue of product A derived from net marginal revenue of product B. We provide here a more complete treatment that should help you understand how such functions are developed. We begin with the net marginal revenue curve of product B, which is given by

$$NMR(\mathrm{B}) = 100 - 0.50Q \tag{18A–1}$$

where

$NMR(\mathrm{B})$ = net marginal revenue of product B
Q = the number of units of product B sold

Because product B requires product A, and because division A is the only supplier of product A and division B is the only buyer of product A, the quantities of products A and B must be equal. (We ignore inventories.) Therefore, Q equals the number of units of product A and of product B sold during the period.

Net marginal revenue is the marginal revenue less the marginal cost of product B, without considering the transfer price that division B pays to division A. Accordingly, net marginal revenue is the change in profit resulting from a change in quantity of product sold and, therefore, is the first derivative of the profit function of product B (again, excluding the transfer price, which is a cost to division B). We can write the equation that depicts the profit of division B before the transfer price:

$$NR(\mathrm{B}) = 100Q - 0.25Q^2 - F \tag{18A–2}$$

where

$NR(\mathrm{B})$ = profit for division B before transfer price
F = fixed costs of division B

Fixed costs would disappear in determining the first derivative of $NR(\mathrm{B})$, and we shall assume that they are zero to reduce calculations and notation. Including fixed costs would have no effect on the results of our analysis.

We now turn our attention to division A. The total costs of division A are assumed to be:

$$TC(\mathrm{A}) = F + 4Q + 0.25Q^2 \tag{18A–3}$$

where

$TC(\mathrm{A})$ = total costs of division A
F = fixed costs of division A

Again, we assume that fixed costs are zero, without diminishing the significance of the results. Division A's marginal cost, $MC(\mathrm{A})$, is the first derivative of total cost:

$$MC(\mathrm{A}) = 4 + 0.50Q \tag{18A–4}$$

The profit-maximizing output for the firm occurs where the net marginal revenue from product B equals the marginal cost to produce product A. Using equations 18A–1 and 18A–4, we get

$$100 - 0.50Q = 4 + 0.50Q$$
$$Q = 96$$

At an output of 96 units of product B, the marginal cost of product A will be \$52, which is the optimal transfer price ($52 = 4 + 0.50Q$). The net revenue, or profit excluding the transfer price, from product B is \$7,296, determined by equation 18A–2:

$$\begin{aligned} NR(\text{B}) &= 100Q - 0.25Q^2 \\ &= 100(96) - 0.25(96)^2 \\ &= \$7{,}296 \end{aligned}$$

The total costs of division A are \$2,688, from equation 18A–3:

$$\begin{aligned} TC(\text{A}) &= 4(96) + 0.25(96)^2 \\ &= \$2{,}688 \end{aligned}$$

Total profits for the firm are \$4,608. Using the \$52 transfer price, profits for division A are \$2,304 [\$52(96) – \$2,688] and for division B are also \$2,304 [\$7,296 – \$52(96)]. The equality of profits is coincidental.

A couple of other points should be mentioned here. At a transfer price of \$52, division B maximizes its profits by taking 96 units of product A and changing them into product B. This is because the transfer price is a marginal cost to division B, and it maximizes its profits when its net marginal revenue equals its marginal cost. Thus, if its marginal cost is \$52, it maximizes profits at 96 units. Using equation 18A–1:

$$100 - 0.50Q = 52$$
$$Q = 96$$

Division A also maximizes its profits, again given the transfer price of \$52, at an output of 96 units. The \$52 is marginal revenue to division A and so it will produce until its marginal cost equals \$52, which is at 96 units. Unfortunately, as we show in the next section, both divisions could do better (although not both at the same time) by acting suboptimally.

Divisional Standpoints

Let us begin with division B. It would naturally like the lowest possible transfer price. In fact, it would like a transfer price of zero. At that price, division B would take 200 units and earn total profits of \$10,000. A transfer price of zero gives the manager of division B a marginal cost of zero. Therefore, he would take units until his net marginal revenue became zero. Using equation 18A–1, we find:

$$100 - 0.50Q = 0$$
$$Q = 200$$

Total profits will be given by equation 18A–2:

$$NR(\mathrm{B}) = 100(200) - 0.25(200)^2$$
$$= \$10{,}000$$

However, the firm as a whole will show a loss of \$800 because division A will incur costs of \$10,800, as given by equation 18A–3:

$$TC(\mathrm{A}) = 4(200) + 0.25(200)^2$$
$$= \$10{,}800$$

Would it be possible for the manager of division B to somehow get 200 units of A at a transfer price of zero? Probably not, but he or she certainly has inducement to persuade corporate management that the transfer price should be lower than its current level and that division A should supply all of division B's needs. The manager of division B might argue that the manager of division A is not controlling costs well, or is overstating costs to get a higher transfer price. The manager of division B wants the lowest transfer price obtainable and has a good deal of inducement to seek that objective.

The manager of division A can also act unwisely, perhaps more easily than the manager of division B. We saw above that the manager of division B must somehow get the transfer price lowered and get as many units of product A as he needs to maximize profits. The manager of division A, if he is able to act autonomously, can increase his divisional profit by reducing the supply of product A and charging a higher price. The net-marginal-revenue curve of division B is the demand curve, or price curve, for division A. This is because division B's manager will pay an amount up to net marginal revenue to get a given number of units of product A. Division B's manager would prefer to pay less, but he will pay up to net marginal revenue if forced. The following analysis shows why.

The price curve facing division A is equation 18A–1. Therefore, the total revenue curve facing division A is equation 18A–1 multiplied by Q. Thus, total revenue to division A from sales to division B are given by equation 18A–5:

(18A–5) $$TR(\mathrm{A}) = 100Q - 0.50Q^2$$

Therefore, marginal revenue to division A is the first derivative of equation 18A–5, given by equation 18A–6:

(18A–6) $$MR(\mathrm{A}) = 100 - Q$$

The manager of division A maximizes profits where marginal revenue equals marginal cost:

$$100 - Q = 4 + 0.50Q$$
$$96 = 1.5Q$$
$$Q = 64$$

The manager of division A will charge \$68 per unit, relying on equation 18A–1:

$$\begin{aligned} NMR(\text{B}) &= 100 - 0.50(64) \\ &= \$68 \end{aligned}$$

And the manager of division B would take 64 units at the $68 price. The manager of division A would increase profits to $3,072, given by equation 18A–5 minus equation 18A–3:

$$\begin{aligned} \text{profit} &= 100(64) - 0.50(64)^2 - [4(64) + 0.25(64)^2] \\ &= 6{,}400 - 2{,}048 - 256 - 1{,}024 \\ &= \$3{,}072 \end{aligned}$$

The income of the firm will fall to $4,096. Division B will show a profit of $1,024, from equation 18A–2 and the transfer price:

$$\begin{aligned} \text{profit} &= 100(64) - 0.25(64)^2 - 68(64) \\ &= 6{,}400 - 1{,}024 - 4{,}352 \\ &= \$1{,}024 \end{aligned}$$

What is to prevent the manager of division A from restricting output to obtain a higher transfer price? Either altruism or a directive from corporate headquarters. It is unlikely that a manager would be motivated by altruism if she were evaluated on the basis of profits (or ROI, or RI, both of which depend on profits). And if corporate headquarters imposes a solution, the autonomy of the divisions is lost. The answer in the limited case considered here was given in the text: make division A a cost center instead of a profit center. The lack of an outside market makes it unwise to evaluate managers on the basis of profits.

ASSIGNMENTS

18–1 Market Price and Variable Cost Gorman Company has several operating divisions expected to act autonomously. The firm maintains a central data processing department that recently became a profit center and began to charge divisions for its work at market prices. Market prices for data processing services are easy to obtain, so the prices are reliable indicators of what the divisions would have to pay to acquire the services outside.

The manager of one operating division has data processing requirements that would cost $12,500 if bought either outside or from the internal department. He could develop the required information using clerical labor at a cost of $9,500. The variable cost to provide the services through the internal data processing department is about $2,800.

REQUIRED

Discuss the issues and problems involved in the situation.

18–2 Transfer Pricing Dispute Industrial Products Division (IPD) of Chemco, Inc., has been leasing warehouse space from Consumer Products Division (CPD) for several years. The agreement provides that CPD will reserve 20 percent of its available space in each of five warehouses for IPD at a rent of $90,000 per year.

Until recently, IPD has used all of its allotment, but demand for some of its products has fallen and it will not use more than about 60 percent of its allotted space in the coming year. The manager of IPD informed the manager of CPD, who was able to find customers for the space that IPD would not use. The aggregate rentals from the space are $37,000 for the year. The manager of IPD has asked for a reduction in his rental payment to $53,000. He argues that CPD will not be losing money, as its total rentals will still be $90,000 for the space.

The manager of CPD retorts that he will not accept any reduction because he was willing to provide the space, had IPD needed it. He further points out that he has gotten the additional $37,000 through his own efforts and has no intention of giving it up.

REQUIRED

Discuss the issues and make a recommendation.

18–3 Transfer Pricing—Data Processing Services The manager of the billing department of Conway Industries received the following charges for computer use:

	March	*April*
Central processing unit:		
5,890 minutes at $0.984	$ 5,795.76	
6,102 minutes at $0.783		$ 4,777.87
Storage:		
597 units at $33.47	19,981.59	
537 units at $37.23		19,992.51
Other	1,203.67	1,451.32
Total	$26,981.02	$26,221.70

The manager is held responsible for data processing costs and has consistently been over budget during the past six months. His inquiries to the data processing manager have brought the following information.

Data processing costs are largely fixed. Each department that uses data processing services receives charges based on actual use for the period. The controller's office has prescribed allocations of data processing costs into central processing unit, storage, and other, based on formulas published in trade journals. Accordingly, each user is charged with a proportionate share of the cost of each of the three basic components of use.

REQUIRED

Comment on the system that the firm uses to charge for data processing costs. Would you recommend any changes?

18–4 Transfer Prices and Decisions Tourny division sells its one product to outsiders and to Crayton division, which is also part of National Products Company. Crayton uses the product as a component of one of its products. The income statement on the next page gives budgeted results for Tourny division for the coming year.

	Total	Outside Sales	Sales to Crayton Division
Sales	$350,000	$200,000	$150,000
Variable costs	160,000	80,000	80,000
Contribution margin	190,000	$120,000	$ 70,000
Fixed costs	120,000		
Income	$ 70,000		
Assets employed	$280,000		

The selling price to outside customers is $20, to Crayton division $15. Divisional managers are evaluated on ROI.

REQUIRED

1. The manager of Crayton division receives an offer from an outside firm to supply the product at $11. If the manager of Tourny division will not meet the price, she will take the business outside. Tourny cannot increase its sales to outsiders. It will save $20,000 in fixed costs and reduce its assets employed by $40,000 if it loses Crayton's business. From the standpoint of Tourny division, should its manager reduce the transfer price?
2. Suppose now that if Crayton division went outside for the product, Tourny division could increase its outside sales by 4,000 units. Its fixed costs would be $120,000 and its assets employed would be $260,000. From the standpoint of Tourny division, what action should its manager take? Assume also that Tourny cannot increase its outside sales unless it drops the Crayton business because of capacity limitations. Further, the outside supplier will not supply fewer than 10,000 units at the $11 price, so that Tourny supplies either 10,000 units or none to Crayton.
3. Answer parts 1 and 2 from the standpoint of the firm.

18–5 Transfer Pricing (AICPA Adapted) Mar Company operates two decentralized divisions, X and Y. Division X has been buying a component from division Y at a price of $75 per unit. Because division Y plans to increase the price to $100, division X has found an outside supplier who will furnish the component at $75 per unit. Division Y incurs the following costs:

Variable cost per unit of component	$70
Annual fixed costs	$15,000
Annual production of component	1,000 units

If division X does buy from an outside supplier, the facilities that division Y devotes to producing the component would be idled.

REQUIRED

Select the *best* answer to the following question: What would be the effect of Mar Company's enforcing a transfer price of $100 and requiring division X to buy from division Y?

1. It would be suboptimization for the firm, because X should buy from an outside supplier at $75 per unit.

2. It would provide lower overall company profit than a transfer price of $75.
3. It would provide higher overall company profit than a transfer price of $75.
4. It would be more profitable for the company than allowing X to buy from an outside supplier at $75 per unit.

18–6 Prices and Market Conditions Oliver Company has several divisions that deal in different types of electronic products. Nason division makes integrated circuits, selling about 90 percent of its output to outside firms. The division is operating well below capacity because of oversupply of the type of circuit that it makes.

Recently, Frith division, which makes consumer products, developed an electronic bridge game that could use the circuit made by Nason division. The manager of the Nason division quoted a price of $72 per circuit, which would provide a $41 contribution margin. The price is somewhat below the current market price of the circuit.

The controller of the Frith division developed the following estimates of costs for the bridge game.

Materials, including $72 for one circuit from Nason	$157
Direct labor	22
Factory overhead	80
Selling and administrative expenses	14
Total cost	$273

Factory overhead is about 50 percent fixed, and selling and administrative expenses contain $4 variable cost, with the remainder fixed.

Frith division's head of marketing submitted the following estimates of volumes at different selling prices.

Price	*Volume*
$400	4,000 units
350	6,000
300	9,000
250	13,000

Nason has enough capacity to meet the 13,000 maximum volume that Frith could obtain. Divisional managers are evaluated on ROI, and total investment would be the same for any of the volumes that Frith may sell.

REQUIRED

1. As the manager of Frith division, what price would you charge for the bridge game?
2. As the president of the firm, what price would you like Frith division to charge for the game?
3. If your answers to parts 1 and 2 conflict, suggest a way to achieve goal congruence, while maintaining the autonomy of the divisional managers.

18–7 Prices and Market Conditions Refer to assignment 18–6. Suppose that Nason division has no excess capacity even without the business from Frith division. The market price of the circuit that Nason could supply to Frith is $72.

REQUIRED

1. What is the optimal price of the bridge game from the standpoint of the firm?
2. If Nason charges Frith \$72 per circuit, what is the optimal price of the bridge game from the standpoint of the Frith division?
3. What is the optimal transfer price, or the range of optimal transfer prices to foster goal congruence and maintain autonomy?

18–8 International Transfers RSE Company operates divisions in several nations. Moore division operates in country A, Bowton division in country B. Bowton division wants to buy a component from Moore division for \$100, while Moore wants the price to be \$150. Variable cost to Moore is \$40. Bowton incurs an additional \$50 cost per unit and sells the finished item for \$250.

The tax rate in country A is 42 percent, in country B, 46 percent. Additionally, country B levies a duty of 12 percent of the price of any goods imported into it. (Bowton would pay the duty.) The duty is tax deductible.

REQUIRED

Determine which transfer price would be better from the standpoint of RSE Company.

18–9 No Intermediate Market (Appendix) SP Company has two divisions. Division P manufactures a single product and transfers it to division S, which sells it with no further processing. The revenue and cost functions appear below.

$$NMR(\text{S}) = \$350 - \$3Q \quad \text{(the net marginal revenue for division S)}$$
$$\text{profit(S)} = \$350Q - \$1.5Q^2$$
$$TC(\text{P}) = \$1{,}000 + \$10Q + \$0.20Q^2$$

REQUIRED

1. Determine the output that will maximize the profits of the firm.
2. Determine the output that division S would select to maximize its profits.

18–10 Make or Buy (AICPA) Blade division of Dana Company produces hardened steel blades. One-third of the division's output is sold to Lawn Products division of Dana, and the remainder is sold to outside customers. Blade division's budgeted results for the coming year appear below.

	Lawn Products	*Outsiders*
Sales	\$15,000	\$40,000
Variable costs	(10,000)	(20,000)
Fixed costs	(3,000)	(6,000)
Profit	\$ 2,000	\$14,000
Unit sales	10,000	20,000

The fixed costs are allocated based on a per unit basis and are all unavoidable. Lawn Products division has the opportunity to buy 10,000 blades of identical quality at \$1.25 per unit. Blade division cannot increase its outside sales.

REQUIRED

1. Determine whether it is in Dana Company's best interest for Lawn Products division to buy blades outside.

2. Determine whether it is in the best interest of Blade division to meet the $1.25 outside price.

18–11 Ranges of Transfer Prices The budgeted income statement for Calcom Division of Travis, Inc., appears below. Calcom sells the same product both to outsiders and to the Varan Division.

	Varan Division	*Outsiders*
Sales—10,000 units	$100,000	
20,000 units		$280,000
Variable costs	60,000	120,000
Contribution margin	40,000	160,000
Fixed costs, unavoidable	30,000	60,000
Profit	$ 10,000	$100,000

Investment is $400,000, and the minimum required ROI is 20 percent. The company evaluates divisions and managers on RI.

REQUIRED

Consider each item independently unless otherwise told.

1. Varan Division has been approached by an outside supplier with a great deal of excess capacity. The supplier has offered to fill Varan's needs at $8 per unit. If Varan goes outside, Calcom will be able to reduce its investment by $60,000. Calcom cannot increase its outside sales. If Calcom meets the $8 price and Varan continues to buy from Calcom, what will happen to the RI of the company as a whole?
2. If Varan goes outside, what will happen to the RI for the company as a whole?
3. Should the manager of Calcom meet the price? Show clearly why or why not from the standpoint of the division.

18–12 Transfers and Transfer Prices (AICPA) Ajax division of Carlyle Corporation produces electric motors, 20 percent of which it sells to Bradley division of Carlyle and the remainder to outside customers. Carlyle treats its divisions as investment centers and allows divisional managers to choose their customers and sources of supply. Corporate policy is that interdivisional transfers be priced at variable cost. Ajax's estimates of results for the coming year appear below. Ajax expects to operate at its full capacity of 100,000 units.

	Bradley	*Outsiders*
Sales	$900,000	$8,000,000
Variable costs	(900,000)	(3,600,000)
Fixed costs	(300,000)	(1,200,000)
Profit (Loss)	($300,000)	$3,200,000
Unit sales	20,000	80,000

Ajax has the opportunity to sell 20,000 units to an outside customer at $75 per unit during the coming year. This special sale would not affect Ajax's sales to its other outside customers. Bradley could purchase its requirements from an outside supplier at $85 per unit.

REQUIRED

1. Determine whether the manager of Ajax should sell the 20,000 units outside or continue selling them to Bradley, from the standpoint of the manager of Ajax.
2. Determine whether it is in the best interest of Carlyle Corporation for Ajax to sell the 20,000 units outside.
3. Suppose now that Carlyle allows divisional managers to negotiate transfer prices. Would they be likely to set a price that would keep Ajax supplying Bradley? Within what limits would the price have to fall?

18–13 Interdependence Priam division of Chester Company requires an electric motor for a new lawn mower that it intends to market next summer. The purchasing manager of the division has secured three bids from outside firms and one from the Jay division of Chester. Jay bid \$60 for the motor and would incur variable costs of \$47. Jay has excess capacity, and making the motors would not bring the division up to capacity operations.

The bids submitted by the outside firms are summarized below. Norton Motors bid \$54. Jasper Electric bid \$57, but would buy parts for the motor from the Monroe division of Chester for \$22. The \$22 is market value for the parts, and Monroe earns about 60 percent contribution margin. Monroe would operate at capacity whether or not it sold parts to Jasper Electric, and its manager has assured Jasper that it would meet its needs, after being informed that the motor was for Priam division. Coulton, Inc., bid \$58 for the motor and would buy parts from Allen division of Chester for \$28. Allen division has excess capacity and would incur variable costs of \$15.

REQUIRED

You have been hired by Jake Messing, Manager of Priam, as a consultant. Use a word processing program and the guidelines for memorandum presentation in Appendix B. Write a memorandum to Mr. Messing in which you discuss what he would do to act in his own best interests, what he should do in the firm's best interests, and, if these two perspectives conflict, your recommendation on how to resolve the problem. Support your arguments with appropriate rationales.

18–14 Transfer Prices and Profit Centers PS Company has been centralized for some years. The sales manager orders units from the production manager, who is obligated to supply as many as are ordered. The sales manager is evaluated on total revenue, the production manager on unit cost. Recently the president of the firm decided it might be worthwhile to set up the sales and production functions as profit centers, evaluated on the basis of profits. The two managers would negotiate the transfer price.

The following schedule shows the possible selling prices of the product on the outside market, the volume associated with each price, and the total production cost for that level of output. The selling division has no costs. The production manager cannot sell directly to the market: his only customer is the sales manager.

Selling Price	*Volume*	*Total Production Costs*
\$10	100,000	\$ 880,000
9	120,000	930,000
8	150,000	1,026,000
7	180,000	1,131,000
6	200,000	1,203,000

These relationships have held in the past and are expected to continue. Under the proposed setup, the transfer price must be an even dollar amount.

REQUIRED

1. Determine the number of units that the sales manager would have been ordering under the old arrangement, where he was evaluated based on total revenue.
2. What is the optimal outside price/volume combination for the firm?
3. Suppose that the production manager sets a transfer price and the sales manager decides how many units to take at that price. How many units will the sales manager buy at transfer prices of $9, $8, $7, and $6?
4. At what transfer price would the sales manager be indifferent between (a) selling 100,000 units at $10 and 120,000 at $9 and (b) selling 120,000 units at $9 and 150,000 at $8?
5. What suggestions would you make to the president, who has asked your advice in helping him decide whether to decentralize?

18–15 Prices and Actions (CMA Adapted) The manager of Frigidwind division of National Industries, Inc., believes that he can increase sales of his air conditioners if he reduces the selling price by $20. A budgeted income statement for the coming year, without considering the proposed reduction, is given below.

Sales, 4,000 units at $400	$1,600,000
Variable costs at $200 per unit	800,000
Contribution margin	800,000
Fixed costs	420,000
Profit before taxes	$ 380,000

The proposed price reduction would increase volume by 500 units, according to a market research study in which the manager has a great deal of confidence. Part of the variable cost of the product is a compressor that the division now buys for $70 from an outside supplier. The manager approaches the manager of the compressor division of National Industries and offers to pay $50 per unit for a compressor that the division currently makes and sells exclusively to outside firms. The manager of Frigidwind will not accept fewer than 4,500 units.

Data for the compressor division are given below.

Budgeted sales, 17,000 units at $100		$1,700,000
Variable costs:		
Production	$510,000	
Selling	102,000	612,000
Contribution margin		$1,088,000

The compressor division has the capacity to produce 20,000 units per year. The division would not incur the variable selling costs on units sold to Frigidwind.

REQUIRED

1. Determine whether the compressor division should supply the 4,500 units to Frigidwind. The managers of divisions are evaluated on the basis of profit earned.

2. Determine whether it would be in the best interests of the firm for the compressor division to supply the units to Frigidwind division.

3. Determine the lowest price that the compressor division could accept for the units without reducing profits below what they would be if none were sold to Frigidwind.

18–16 Opportunity Costs and Transfer Prices Morton division of United Industries, Inc., has in the past sold its products only to outsiders. Recently, Morton was approached by Crago division, which needed a component for one of its products. Morton does not now make the component for outsiders, but it could produce it by making extensive modifications and combining several of the products it now makes. The component would be unique, and no market price is available to guide the setting of a transfer price. Data related to the component appear below.

Material cost	$ 7.50
Direct labor ($\frac{1}{2}$ hr)	4.50
Overhead at $11/labor hour	5.50
Total estimated cost	$17.50

Variable overhead is about $7 per direct labor hour, fixed overhead about $4 at normal activity. Morton's budgeted income statement for the coming year is as follows:

Sales	$21,500,000
Cost of sales	13,400,000
Gross margin	8,100,000
Selling and administrative expenses	6,300,000
Profit	$ 1,800,000

The division's inventories will be about the same at the beginning and end of the year. Materials included in cost of sales are about $5,400,000, and direct labor is about $3,600,000. All direct laborers receive very close to the same hourly wage. Selling and administrative expenses are virtually all fixed. Morton's investment would be unaffected by doing the work for Crago.

REQUIRED

1. Suppose that the Morton division has excess capacity and could easily accommodate Crago division's needs. What is the minimum transfer price that Morton division's manager would accept, acting in his own best interests? (He is held responsible for ROI.)

2. Suppose now that Morton expects to work at full capacity (measured by labor hours) without considering the component for Crago. On the basis of the information that you have available, estimate the transfer price that Morton would demand. Make your assumptions clear.

18–17 Transfer Price, Personnel Ron Goode, manager of ITM division, approached Earl Robinson, manager of Fleeton division, with a proposal to buy some labor time. Goode offered to pay the workers' usual hourly wage plus fringe benefits to employ them on a project that he expected to begin soon. The factories of the two divisions are adjacent, so that no travel or lodging costs would be involved.

Robinson was reluctant to accept the proposal because he was running the division at full capacity. He collected the following data:

Wage rate	$12/hr
Total budgeted labor hours	120,000 hr
Total budgeted contribution margin	$2,400,000
Variable overhead rate per direct labor hour	$8/hr

Robinson could not replace the hours that Goode would use, because the workers have special skills and it is impossible to hire and train others on short notice.

REQUIRED

1. What would you, acting in Robinson's place, charge Goode for each hour of labor time that you sell him?
2. Assuming that Robinson has excess capacity, and that fringe benefits are $2 per hour out of total variable overhead of $8 per hour, how much should he charge Goode? Robinson would continue to pay their wages and fringe benefits. All variable overhead except fringe benefits relates to hours worked, not hours paid.

18–18 Transfer Pricing and ROI The divisional managers of Argive Company are evaluated on ROI. Recently, the manager of Selmon division offered to buy 4,000 units per month of a particular component from Franklin division at a price of $44. The chief cost accountant of Franklin division estimated the variable cost of the component at $40. He also determined that the division would not need to add to its plant and equipment to service Selmon, but it would require increased investment in working capital, which he estimated as follows:

Raw materials inventory	$45,000
Inventory of finished components	2 months' supply
Accounts receivable	1 month's sales

The firm values inventories at variable cost. It also provides for one month's credit on intracompany business, so that the selling division will have a receivable and the buying division a payable in the same amounts. In calculating total investment for a division, the firm includes current liabilities.

Franklin is currently earning a 30 percent ROI, and its manager wants to know whether the $44 price will maintain it.

REQUIRED

1. Determine whether Franklin would earn a 30 percent ROI on the business with Selmon.
2. Comment on the firm's policy of recognizing intracompany receivables and payables in determining the investment base. Would it lead to goal congruence or hinder it?

18–19 Transfer-Pricing Dispute, Linear Programming BCH Company operates several divisions. The manager of Compto division is planning to bring out a new product, a desktop computer that will sell for about $350. He has approached the manager of the electronics division with a proposal that electronics make a component for the computer. Satisfactory components are available from outside firms at $47 each. The manager of the electronics division developed the following data and quoted a price of $53. The electronics division does not now make the component.

Materials cost	$14
Direct labor cost	12
Overhead at 150% of direct labor	18
Total cost	44
Allowance for profit at 20% of cost, rounded	9
Quoted price	$53

The manager of Compto division was unhappy with the quotation, citing the market price as an upper limit. He said, "I know that your overhead is only about 40 percent variable, so you are really trying to get rich on me." The manager of the electronics division replied that he was operating at capacity and would have to forego other business if he made the component for Compto. He said, "My operations research people tell me that the shadow price for direct labor time is $22 per hour. The component requires one hour, which would reduce my profits if I didn't charge you based on my usual formula."

REQUIRED

If you were the manager of the electronics division, what price would you have quoted?

18–20 Profit on Transfers Sacramento division of CalNev Industries purchases components from the Las Vegas division. Determining the transfer price has become an annual ordeal, and the president of CalNev has proposed instituting the policy of pricing transfers at standard absorption cost plus a 10 percent margin for profit. The manager of Sacramento division was not thrilled at the prospect. She argued that Las Vegas division would be making more than her division did on the final product, without the effort of selling it to the ultimate customer.

She showed the group the following example of a high-volume component:

	Unit Costs
Direct materials	$12.00
Direct labor	22.50
Overhead at 150% of direct labor (one-third variable)	33.75
Total standard cost	$68.25
Plus: 10% margin	6.83
Transfer price	$75.08

The manager of Las Vegas division asked what was wrong with a 10 percent margin. "After all," he said, "we make about a 17 percent gross margin on the products we sell outside, so why should you be unhappy with 10 percent?"

REQUIRED

As an impartial observer, comment on the profitability of the $75.08 price to the Las Vegas division.

18–21 Transfer Prices and Decisions SRS division of MultiCo, Inc., expects the following results in 19X2, all from sales to outsiders:

Sales, 10,000 units at $50	$500,000
Variable costs	200,000
Contribution margin	300,000
Fixed costs, unavoidable	100,000
Profit	$200,000

SRS has a 12,000-unit capacity. BW division of MultiCo is introducing a new product. Its general manager expects to sell 3,000 units at $80. The product requires a unit of SRS's product, which BW would modify at a variable cost of $45. BW division would not take fewer than 3,000 units.

REQUIRED

1. Is it in the company's best interest for the transfer to take place? Show clearly why or why not.
2. If BW bought 3,000 units from SRS at $25, what would happen to the profit of the company? What if BW paid $30 each for the 3,000 units?
3. What is the minimum price that SRS would accept for the 3,000 units, the price that would keep its profit the same as it currently expects?
4. What is the maximum price that BW would be willing to pay for the 3,000 units?
5. What would your answers to parts 1 and 4 be if SRS had a 15,000-unit capacity?

18–22 Promotion Decisions and Transfer Prices Marchmont division of ICC Industries supplies Cooper division with 100,000 units per month of an LED (light-emitting diode) that Cooper uses in a calculator that it makes and sells. The transfer price of the LED is $8, which is the market price. However, Marchmont does not operate anywhere near capacity.

The variable cost to Marchmont of the LED is $4.80, while Cooper incurs variable costs (excluding the transfer price) of $12 for each calculator. Cooper's selling price is $32.

Cooper's manager has been considering a promotional campaign. The market research department of the division has developed the following estimates of additional monthly volume associated with additional monthly promotional expenses.

Additional Monthly Promotional Expenses	*Additional Monthly Volume*
$ 80,000	10,000 units
120,000	15,000
160,000	18,000

REQUIRED

1. As the manager of Cooper division, which level of additional promotional expenses would you select?
2. As the president of the firm, which level would you like Cooper division to select?
3. If your answers to parts 1 and 2 are different, make a recommendation to resolve the problem.

18–23 Perspective of Selling Division (CMA Adapted) MBR, Inc., consists of three divisions that have operated as if they were independent companies. Each division has its own sales force and production facilities. Each division management is responsible for sales, cost of operations, acquisition and financing of divisional assets, and working capital management. The corporate management of MBR evaluates the performance of the divisions and division managements on the basis of return on investment.

Mitchell division has just been awarded a contract for a product that uses a component manufactured by the Roach division as well as by outside suppliers. In preparing its bid for the new product, Mitchell used a cost figure of $3.80 for the component manufactured by Roach. This cost figure was supplied by Roach in response to Mitchell's request for the average variable cost of the component and represents the standard variable manufacturing cost and variable selling and distribution expense.

Assume that Roach's regular selling price for this component is $6.50. The two divisions are at an impasse. Roach has offered to sell the component to Mitchell for $6.50 less variable selling and distribution expenses. Mitchell's management has countered with an offer to pay the standard variable manufacturing cost plus 20 percent. A corporate vice president has suggested a compromise of standard full manufacturing cost plus a 15 percent markup. Both divisions have rejected this suggestion.

The unit cost structure for the Roach component and the three suggested prices are shown below:

Regular selling price	$6.50
Standard variable manufacturing cost	$3.20
Standard fixed manufacturing cost	1.20
Variable selling and distribution expenses	0.60
	$5.00
Regular selling price less variable selling and distribution expenses ($6.50 − 0.60)	$5.90
Variable manufacturing plus 20 percent ($3.20 × 1.20)	$3.84
Standard full manufacturing cost plus 15 percent ($4.40 × 1.15)	$5.06

REQUIRED

1. How would Roach's management rank each of these three proposed prices in relationship to how Roach itself is evaluated?
2. What is the role of negotiation and of corporate management in this case?

18–24 Transfer Pricing Morgan Company operates 22 divisions in various industries. The divisions are relatively decentralized, and the managers are responsible for earning a satisfactory ROI. A large percentage of their compensation comes from bonuses related to ROI. The ROI calculation has been based on the direct profit earned by the division. Corporate overhead is allocated to divisions, but is "below the line" and does not reduce the profit figure used to determine ROI.

The treasurer of the firm wants to develop a transfer pricing scheme for legal services performed for the divisions. The workload of the legal department and its costs have been rising rapidly in the face of increased governmental regulation and costly litigation ranging from suits over product liability to charges of discrimination in hiring and promoting practices.

The treasurer believes that making the department into a profit center and billing its services to divisions would make sense because the divisions are the beneficiaries of the services, even of those performed on general corporate work such as bond issues. He has decided that standard hourly rates be developed for all the lawyers and paraprofessionals in the department, but he is still open on the question whether the rates should be set to cover costs or to provide a profit.

There is no question about the growing demand for legal services from the divisions. Much of the demand is forced by directives from corporate headquarters. For example, any new-product proposal must be submitted to the legal department for review regarding potential liability. Divisions must also submit capital investment proposals to the department for review for conformity with various governmental regulations.

The treasurer anticipated objections from the divisional managers and was concerned with developing rebuttals. He was convinced that the size of the cost make it imperative to charge the divisions, and he wanted to be well prepared for the objections that were certain to come.

REQUIRED

1. As a divisional manager, prepare arguments against the proposed system.

2. As the treasurer, rebut the arguments you developed in part 1.

3. Make any recommendations that you think would help to make the system more palatable to the divisional managers.

18–25 Role of Arbitration (CMA Adapted) Lorax Electric Company is organized into several autonomous divisions. Corporate management is pleased with the results of decentralization and evaluates divisions on profits and return on investment.

The devices division, currently operating at capacity, has been asked by the systems division to supply a large quantity of integrated circuit IC378. Devices currently sells this circuit to its regular customers at $40 per hundred.

The systems division, which is operating at about 60 percent of capacity, wants this particular component for a digital clock system. It has an opportunity to supply large quantities of these digital clock systems to Centonic Electric, a major producer of clock radios and other popular electronic home entertainment equipment. This is the first opportunity any of the Lorax divisions have had to do business with Centonic Electric. Centonic Electric has offered to pay $7.50 per clock system.

The systems division prepared an analysis of the probable costs to produce the clock systems. The amount that could be paid to the devices division for the integrated circuits was determined by working backward from the selling price. The cost estimates employed by the division reflected the highest per unit cost the systems division could incur for each cost component and still leave a sufficient margin so that the division's income statement could show reasonable improvement. The cost estimates are summarized below.

Proposed selling price		$7.50
Costs excluding required integrated circuits (IC378):		
Components purchased from outside suppliers	$2.75	
Circuit board etching—labor and variable overhead	0.40	
Assembly, testing, packaging—labor and variable overhead	1.35	
Fixed overhead allocations	1.50	
Profit margin	0.50	6.50
Amount that can be paid for integrated circuits IC378 (5 at $20 per hundred)		$1.00

As a result of this analysis, the systems division offered the devices division a price of $20 per hundred for the integrated circuit. The bid was refused by the manager of the devices division, because he felt the systems division should at least meet the price of $40 per hundred that regular customers paid. When the systems division found that it could not obtain a comparable integrated circuit from outside vendors, the situation was brought to an arbitration committee, set up to review such problems.

The arbitration committee's analysis showed that $0.15 would cover variable costs of producing the integrated circuit, $0.28 would cover the full cost including fixed overhead, and $0.35 would provide a gross margin equal to the average gross margin on all the products sold by the devices division. The manager of the systems division responded: "They could sell us that integrated circuit for $0.20 and still earn a positive contribution toward profit. In fact, they should be required to sell at their variable cost of $0.15 and not be allowed to take advantage of us."

Lou Belcher, manager of devices, countered: "It doesn't make sense to sell to the systems division at $20 per hundred when we get $40 per hundred outside on all we can produce. In fact, systems could pay us up to almost $60 per hundred and still have a positive contribution to profit."

The recommendation of the committee, to set the price at $0.35 per unit ($35 per hundred), so that devices could earn a fair gross margin, was rejected by both division managers. Consequently the problem was brought to the attention of the vice president of operations.

REQUIRED

1. What would be the immediate economic effect on Lorax Company as a whole if the devices division were required to supply IC378 to the systems division at $0.35 per unit—the price recommended by the arbitration committee? Explain your answer.
2. Discuss the advisability of intervention by top management as a solution to transfer pricing disputes between division managers such as the one experienced by Lorax Electric Company.
3. Suppose Lorax adopted a policy requiring that the price paid in all internal transfers by the buying division equal the variable costs per unit of the selling division for that product and that the supplying division be required to sell if the buying division decided to buy the item. Discuss the consequences of adopting such a policy as a way to avoid the need for the arbitration committee or for intervention by the vice president.

18–26 Market Prices and Transfers Allied Company operates a number of decentralized divisions, some of which deal extensively among themselves. IMC division currently makes a type of cathode ray tube (CRT) that Balkan division could use in a new product that it has just developed. The new product is a device for measuring the viscosity of liquids, and the CRT would allow the operator to monitor the viscosity continuously, which is important in some manufacturing processes.

IMC expects to produce and sell 20,000 of the CRTs during the coming year. The expected price is $300 and the variable cost $150. The division has sufficient capacity to produce 25,000 units, but it would have to drop its price to about $240 to sell 25,000.

Balkan division's manager has estimated the following with regard to the new product, excluding the transfer price for the CRT.

	Selling Price	
	$800	$750
Expected variable costs:		
Materials and purchased components	$75	$75
Direct labor and variable overhead	200	200
Expected volume	4,000 units	4,800 units

The manager of IMC division has quoted the market price of $300 as the transfer price to Balkan division. One CRT is needed for each measuring device. The manager of Balkan division believes that the transfer price should be the variable cost of $150 and has approached you, the president of Allied, to intercede.

REQUIRED

As the president of the firm, what would you do? Prepare any analyses that you believe are relevant.

18–27 Transfer Pricing Formulas The controller of Inverness Company has been concerned for several years about the firm's transfer pricing policies. There were often prolonged and acrimonious discussions between divisional managers, with subsequent hard feelings. The controller thought it would be possible to develop a formula, or set of formulas, to use for all products that did not have competitive market prices. He decided that the transfer price should consist of the following components:

1. Standard variable production cost.
2. A fair share of fixed production costs, measured by standard cost per direct labor hour or machine hour.
3. A satisfactory return on investment on the plant and equipment and inventories associated with the output to be transferred.

The firm did not record accounts receivable or payable on interdivisional business, so there was no need to include a provision for return on receivables. The investment in inventories would be calculated as the standard absorption cost divided by the normal inventory turnover. Investment in plant and equipment was to be based on a measure of capacity such as direct labor hours or machine hours. Thus, the controller would compute a figure called investment per labor hour (or machine hour) and use it to determine the component of the transfer price that would give the ROI on this investment. The firm used ROI to evaluate divisional managers.

The controller decided to test his ideas by working out the transfer price of a gear box that Sharp division was to make for another division. He gathered the following data regarding Sharp division and the gear box:

	Sharp Division
Normal activity in direct labor hours	200,000
Plant and equipment (net)	$2,000,000
Inventory turnover	5 times
Standard fixed production cost per direct labor hour (based on normal activity)	$8
Target ROI	20%

(*continued*)

	Gear Box
Standard variable cost per unit	$22.00
Standard fixed cost (4 standard hours)	32.00
Total standard cost	54.00
ROI component:	
Plant ($2,000,000/200,000 × 4 × 0.20)	8.00
Inventory ($54/5 × 0.20)	2.16
Transfer price	$64.16

REQUIRED

1. Suppose that Sharp division expects the following results without the internal business (in thousands):

Sales	$7,600
Standard cost of sales	4,100
Standard gross margin	3,500
Underabsorbed overhead	240
Actual gross margin	3,260
Selling and administrative expenses	2,173
Income	$1,087
Accounts receivable	$3,080
Inventory	815
Plant and equipment	2,000
Total investment	$5,895

These results are based on 85 percent utilization of normal capacity. Determine the income and investment that the division would have after the internal business at the transfer price that the controller calculated. The internal business will not affect selling and administrative expenses.

2. Calculate a new transfer price, using practical capacity of 250,000 direct labor hours to determine the standard fixed production cost and the investment per labor hour figure.

3. Comment on the general approach taken by the controller. What problems do you foresee?

18–28 ROI, RI, and Transfer Prices Walton division of GRK Industries supplies a component to Belton division as well as to outside customers. Walton's budgeted data for the coming year follow, in thousands. GRK has set a minimum required ROI of 14 percent.

	Belton	Outsiders	Total
Sales	$225.7	$1,435.6	$1,661.3
Variable costs	183.4	933.2	1,116.6
Contribution margin	42.3	502.4	544.7
Avoidable fixed costs	8.6	139.2	147.8
Incremental profit	$ 33.7	$ 363.2	$ 396.9
Unavoidable fixed costs allocated	18.5	94.0	112.5
Profit	$ 15.2	$ 269.2	$ 284.4

Investment:			
Receivables	$ —	$ 324.9	$ 324.9
Inventories	87.6	443.9	531.5
Plant	149.4	752.0	901.4
Total investment	$237.0	$1,520.8	$1,757.8
ROI	6.4%	17.7%	16.2%

Cal Hopper, manager of Walton, was unhappy at the transfer price he was receiving. He believed that the price did not provide a fair return on the investment he had to maintain to supply Belton. Hopper's controller calculated the investment for the division by estimating the actual amount of each class of investment that was dedicated to Belton and to outsiders and allocating any remaining amounts not specifically traceable to either. Admittedly, he pointed out, the allocations of plant assets were arbitrary. However, the inventory related to the Belton business was, he said, about the amount that inventory would drop if the Belton business were dropped. If the Belton business were dropped, he estimated that plant assets would fall about $25.4 thousand. Company policy is that receivables on intracompany business are not recorded.

REQUIRED

You have been hired as a consultant by Cal Hopper. Use a word processing program and the guidelines for memorandum presentation in Appendix B. Write a memorandum to Mr. Hopper in which you discuss the above situation and make a recommendation. In your memorandum, state clearly which items you would need more information about before making your conclusions firmer. Present any supporting calculations and schedules you believe important. Use a spreadsheet program for all supporting schedules and present all material in an appropriate form.

18–29 Multinational Companies (CMA) Almost all major United States companies have production facilities and marketing outlets throughout the world, and the pace of multinationalism has accelerated in recent years. By the early 1970s, United States multinationals conducted one-quarter of the world's merchandise export trade. United States direct investment abroad grew from $12 billion in 1950 to $221 billion in 1982. In aggregate terms, roughly 400 multinational enterprises produce perhaps as much as one-third of the free world's industrial output.

Multinational corporations have wholly owned foreign subsidiaries, partially owned foreign joint ventures, and/or patent and trademark licensing agreements abroad. Some of the more sophisticated corporations have foreign research and development activities and multinational management organizations.

REQUIRED

1. Describe the reasons why firms decide to become multinational.

2. Identify and describe both the advantages and disadvantages of multinational corporations from the point of view of the
   a. home country
   b. host country

18–30 Goal Congruence (CMA Adapted) Robert Products, Inc., consists of three decentralized divisions, Bayside, Cole, and Diamond. The president of Robert Products has given the managers of the three divisions the authority to decide whether or not to sell outside the company, or among themselves at a transfer price determined by the division managers. Market conditions are such that sales made internally or externally will not affect market or transfer prices. Intermediate markets will always be available for Bayside, Cole, and Diamond to purchase their manufacturing needs or sell their product. Each division manager attempts to maximize his contribution margin at the current level of operating assets for the division.

The manager of the Cole division is currently considering the two alternative orders presented below.

1. Diamond division needs 3,000 units of a motor that can be supplied by Cole division. To manufacture these motors, Cole would purchase components from Bayside division at a transfer price of $600 per unit; Bayside's variable cost for these components is $300 per unit. Cole division will further process these components at a variable cost of $500 per unit.

   If Diamond division cannot obtain the motors from Cole division, it will purchase the motors from London Company, which has offered to supply the same motors to Diamond division at a price of $1,500 per unit. London Company would also purchase 3,000 components from Bayside division at a price of $400 for each of these motors; Bayside's variable cost for these components is $200 per unit.

2. Wales Company wants to place an order with Cole division for 3,500 similar motors at a price of $1,250 per unit. Cole would again purchase components from Bayside division at a transfer price of $500 per unit; Bayside's variable cost for these components is $250 per unit. Cole division will further process these components at a variable cost of $400 per unit.

Cole division's plant capacity is limited, and the company can accept the Wales contract or the Diamond order, but not both. The president of Robert Products and the manager of Cole division agree that it would not be beneficial in the short or long run to increase capacity.

REQUIRED

1. If the manager of Cole division wants to maximize short-run contribution margin, determine whether Cole division should
   a. sell motors to Diamond division at the prevailing market price, or
   b. accept the Wales Company contract.
   Support your answer with appropriate calculations.
2. Without prejudice to your answer to part 1 assume that Cole division decides to accept the Wales Company contract. Determine if this decision is in the best interest of Robert Products, Inc. Support your answer with appropriate calculations.

19

PERFORMANCE ANALYSIS

This chapter integrates some of the questions about allocations we addressed in Chapter 10 with segment reporting as explored in Chapter 17. In addition, it extends performance analysis to the marketing function by incorporating the concept of variances as introduced in Chapter 7. The question is whether a company has met its overall goals. These goals are evidenced in the budget, which spells out resource, human, and capital needs as well as the planning horizon for these needs. How have marketing, production, and other managers done in light of these goals? We must also investigate whether these goals are realistic expectations given, for example, existing economic, market, and international monetary considerations. We also consider performance evaluation in advanced manufacturing environments.

RELATIONSHIPS AMONG FACTORS AFFECTING FINANCIAL PERFORMANCE

The basic measures of corporate or segment performance include income, return on investment, residual income, and cash flow. We set up a standard by which to judge all of these measures in the budget. Too often managers look at those measures abstractly and do not see how they relate to other areas of planning and control. For example, a manager may develop a discounted cash flow analysis of a proposed investment and not see how that project affects assets.

TIERED CONTRIBUTION ANALYSIS

Earlier chapters developed the ideas of contribution margin and contribution-margin reporting (variable costing income). We have also discussed the concept of controllability as a primary concern for segment performance reports.

We have also shown product margins and other measures where fixed costs were important. These analyses, using the idea of costs of product (vis á vis product costs for financial reporting) form the basis of tiered contribution analysis. **Tiered contribution analysis** is a formal way of showing several measures of performance, each with its own definition and uses. Basically, a tiered contribution analysis uses separable revenues and separable costs and shows profitability tiered by manufacturing and by marketing contribution.

In this analysis we use the word *contribution* in a broader context than before. While *variable manufacturing contribution* is revenue less variable manufacturing costs, *total manufacturing contribution* is akin to gross margin in that it is variable manufacturing contribution less separable fixed manufacturing costs.

As Figure 19–1 shows a breakdown of factors that affect financial performance, we will break down our analysis first into segments (such as operating divisions) and then into products or lines within the segment. (We could also use other segment definitions such as geographical areas where we would first define a region, Europe, for example, and break that down by countries and areas within countries.)

Exhibit 19–1 shows the tiered contribution analysis for the KSH Division of Melding Company. There are two product groups: videotape recorders and laser disc players. The Division Total column includes all revenues and costs traceable to the division. A cost that is not traceable to a product group is placed in the Corporate/Nonallocated column. For example, $2,800 of discounts to customers were given by the divisional office and are not ascribed to either product group. Selling and distribution common costs total $88,200. All general and administrative expenses are common. Some of these costs are common to the groups, while others are common to the divisions of the corporation.

Thus, managers can see a Variable Manufacturing Contribution (product group net revenues less variable manufacturing costs) and Total Manufacturing Contribution (much like gross margin on an income statement). Separable marketing and distribution costs are subtracted to yield Marketing Contribution. At this point, we can view the separable margins: the videotape recorders have a Marketing Contribution of $144,600 (36.3 percent) and the laser disc players, $525,300 (60.0 percent). We see a significant difference between these two margins, principally from the relatively higher fixed manufacturing costs (44.3 percent to 21.4 percent).

The *Unallocated/Corporate* column is for costs (and possibly revenues) that are not traceable and, therefore, should not be assigned to divisions or products. These costs are finally allocated to groups at the bottom of the statement, and clearly shown as allocated. In this case, the allocation is based on relative direct segment margins, which is arbitrary, but perhaps better than sales as a basis. Chapters 11 and 17 contain rationales for and against allocating common costs and we shall not repeat those arguments.

Remember that these exhibits are only one way to report. There are many other possibilities. One common format is to subtract all variable costs first, as we do in Chapter 2, to show contribution margin. Here, we wanted to show manufacturing and marketing contributions, which precludes showing

FIGURE 19–1 Relationships Among Factors Affecting Financial Performance

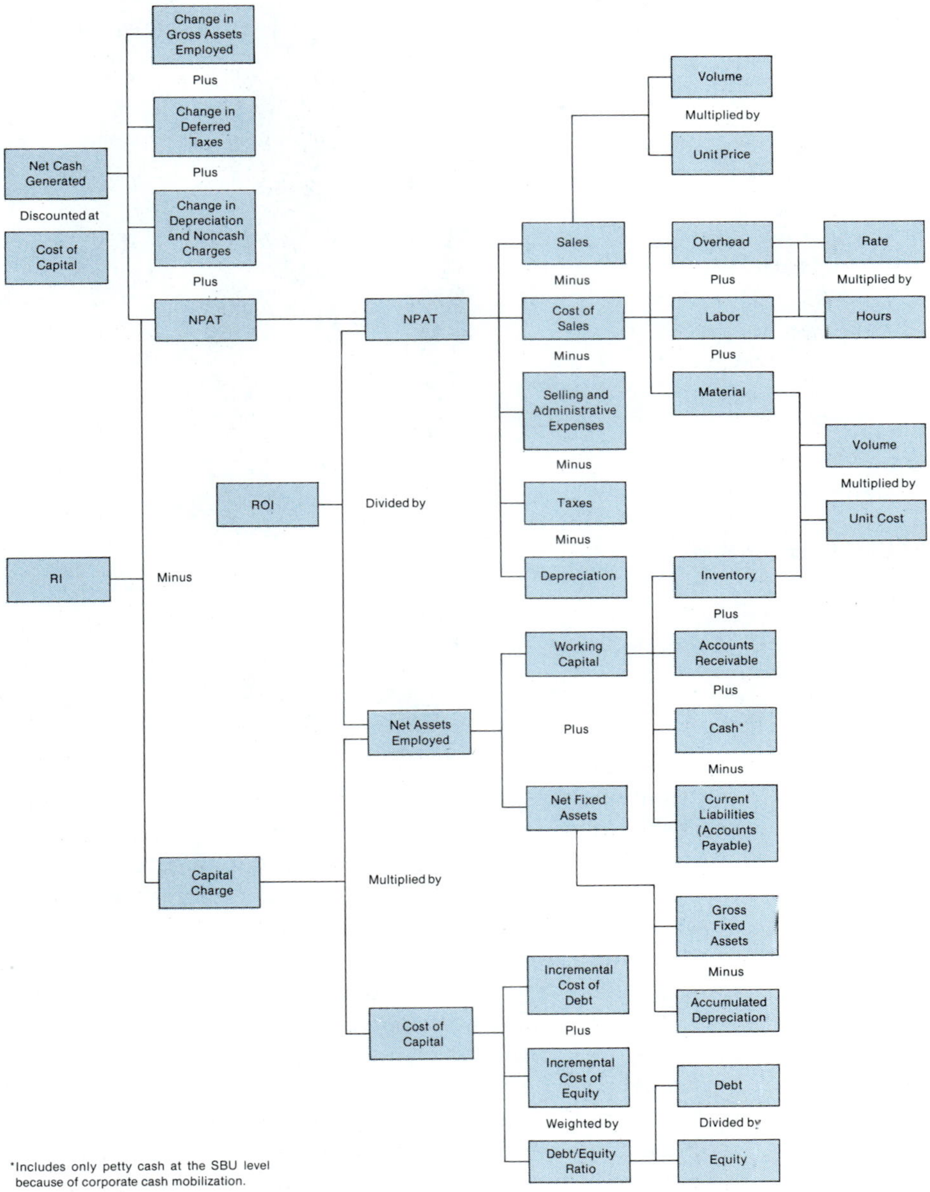

*Includes only petty cash at the SBU level because of corporate cash mobilization.

EXHIBIT 19–1 Template to Analyze Melding Company, KHS Division

	Recorders		CD Players		Unallocated Corporate	Total	
Gross sales	$398.3	100.0%	$876.0	100.0%	$0.0	$1,274.3	100.0%
Discounts and allowances	11.2	2.8%	9.1	1.0%	2.8	$23.1	1.8%
Net sales	387.1	97.2%	866.9	99.0%	(2.8)	$1,251.2	98.2%
Variable manufacturing costs	34.6	8.7%	113.2	12.9%	0.0	$147.8	11.6%
Variable manufacturing margin	352.5	88.5%	753.7	86.0%	(2.8)	$1,103.4	86.6%
Direct fixed manufacturing costs	176.3	44.3%	187.4	21.4%	43.8	$407.5	32.0%
Direct manufacturing margin	176.2	44.2%	566.3	64.6%	(46.6)	$695.9	54.6%
Direct selling/distribution costs:							
Variable	19.3	4.8%	29.2	3.3%	0.0	$48.5	3.8%
Fixed	12.3	3.1%	11.8	1.3%	88.2	$112.3	8.8%
Total	31.6	.7.9%	41.0	4.7%	88.2	$160.8	12.6%
Direct marketing contribution	144.6	36.3%	525.3	60.0%	(134.8)	$535.1	42.0%
Direct administrative expenses	13.8	3.5%	19.2	2.2%	145.2	$178.2	14.0%
Direct segment margin	130.8	32.8%	506.1	57.8%	(280.0)	$356.9	28.0%
Allocated by segment margin	57.5	14.4%	222.5	25.4%	(280.0)	$0.0	0.0%
Income	$73.3	18.4%	$283.6	32.4%	$0.0	$356.9	28.0%

contribution margin on the same statement. The needs and preferences of the users should govern the form and content of such reports.

In analyzing this report, we cannot state that, for example, fixed manufacturing costs are too high, because we do not know enough about the business. However, the relevant managers should be able to evaluate costs and revenues to help in improving operations. As Chapter 17 noted, we cannot be sure that the manager of the group is not doing as well as the manager of CD players, because we do not know the potential of either product group. We do see, however, that the recorder group earns significantly less profit than CD players.

In preparing these statements, we must be especially careful with fixed costs. Determining how much fixed cost can be considered direct to a segment is difficult. Some costs are clearly direct, such as salaries of people whose time is spent exclusively on one segment. In other cases, as we have noted, some costs appear to be common to several segments, but have some characteristics of avoidability and can therefore be treated as direct. As an example, if the payroll department's employees serve all segments, their salaries are common to those segments. But if dropping a particular segment would allow the transfer of three people out of payroll, then even though those people work for all segments, it is legitimate to treat their salaries as direct to that segment.

In other words, it might be possible to estimate the requirements of the payroll department (or whatever other support department is involved) given that segment A is dropped, then segment B, and so on. The reduction from the current level to the estimated level is then reasonably treated as a direct cost. This argument parallels our treatment of the subject in Chapter 12.

In advanced manufacturing environments, the problems associated with tracing fixed cost are not as severe as in conventional environments. Manufacturing cells are more self-contained; the workers do much of their own maintenance, inspection, materials handling and other activities that are often centrally managed in a conventional factory. Such costs are therefore clearly traceable to cells and their products. In conventional factories, centrally managed costs are much harder to trace to products.

Exhibit 19–2 shows the same type of analysis for recorders, dividing that group into two sub-groups. The format is the same as in Exhibit 19–1 except for the lines beginning *Allocated from corporate*, which bring the $57.5 thousand allocated to recorders in Exhibit 19–1 into the picture. This allocation makes the individual amounts add up to the totals. That is, the $73.3 thousand total

EXHIBIT 19–2 Template to Analyze KHS Division, Recorders Group

	Standard		*Deluxe*		*Unallocated Division*	*Total*	
Gross sales	$101.0	100.0%	$297.3	100.0%	$0.0	$398.3	100.0%
Discounts and allowances	5.9	5.8%	4.7	1.6%	0.6	11.2	2.8%
Net sales	95.1	94.2%	292.6	98.4%	(0.6)	387.1	97.2%
Variable manufacturing costs	15.4	15.2%	19.2	6.5%	0.0	34.6	8.7%
Variable manufacturing margin	79.7	78.9%	273.4	92.0%	(0.6)	352.5	88.5%
Direct fixed manufacturing costs	56.6	56.0%	79.1	26.6%	40.6	176.3	44.3%
Direct manufacturing margin	23.1	22.9%	194.3	65.4%	(41.2)	176.2	44.2%
Direct selling/distribution costs:							
Variable	7.0	6.9%	12.3	4.1%	0.0	19.3	4.8%
Fixed	3.8	3.8%	5.4	1.8%	3.1	12.3	3.1%
Total	10.8	10.7%	17.7	6.0%	3.1	31.6	7.9%
Direct marketing contribution	12.3	12.2%	176.6	59.4%	(44.3)	144.6	36.3%
Direct administrative expenses	6.6	6.5%	3.4	1.1%	3.8	13.8	3.5%
Direct segment margin	5.7	5.6%	173.2	58.3%	(48.1)	130.8	32.8%
Allocated from corporate					57.5	57.5	
Total to allocate					105.6		
Allocated by segment margin	(3.4)	−3.3%	(102.2)	−34.4%	(105.6)		0.0%
Income	$9.1	9.0%	$275.4	92.6%	$0.0	$73.3	18.4%

for the two sub-groups equals the total for recorders in Exhibit 19–1. Some reports would not reallocate the $57.5, so that the total income for the sub-groups is $130.8 ($73.3 + $57.5), the direct segment margin.

The direct segment margin of only $5.7 thousand in Exhibit 19–2 indicates that standard recorders are only marginally profitable and the division should probably do something about them. We cannot know what the division should do, but some possibilities are to drop them, raise their prices, or try to increase their volume through additional promotion. However, increasing volume of standard recorders could reduce the volume of deluxe recorders, which is certainly not helpful. The purpose of such reporting is to highlight areas where knowledgeable managers can make sensible decisions to correct problems. The numbers by themselves do not *tell* managers what to do.

MARKETING VARIANCES

Chapter 7 introduced the concept of variances and showed how they can be incorporated into performance appraisal of manufacturing managers. We expand on the analysis of such variances and variance reporting in Chapter 20. Managers are also interested in evaluating performance by marketing and sales managers. We use the same basic format for marketing variances that we use for standard cost variances.

Although the principal use of the technique is to analyze differences between planned and actual margin, it is applicable to other comparisons. One common use is to analyze differences between time periods, say last month to this month, or the third quarter of 19X0 to the same quarter of 19X1. Another possibility is to analyze the differences between territories, such as the southwest and northeast.

We can perform the analysis on either gross margin or contribution margin. The choice between contribution margin and gross margin depends on how the company reports its income statements. If the statements use the CVP format, the variances should be based on contribution margin, but if the income statements use the financial accounting format, with cost of goods sold including both fixed and variable costs, the variances are usually based on gross margin. The important point is that the analyses are consistent and they help the managers to determine desirable actions. We believe that contribution margin is the better choice because it better portrays the economic results of changes in volume. Gross margin, however, depends not only on sales but also on production.

BASIC VARIANCE FRAMEWORK

We begin with the two basic variances—price and volume. The simplest reasons for profits to differ from budget are that unit sales or selling prices dif-

EXHIBIT 19–3 Data for Example

	Budgeted Results	Actual Results
Selling price	$20.00	$21.00
Variable cost	11.40	11.40
Contribution margin	$ 8.60	$ 9.60
Volume	200,000	190,000
Total contribution margin	$1,720,000	$1,824,000

fered from budget (remember that we are holding unit costs constant). Exhibit 19–3 includes data for an example.

We can see that the actual selling price was higher than budgeted, while actual volume was lower than budgeted. The net result is that contribution margin is $104,000 higher than budgeted. (Remember that we could also use gross margin.) Our task is to determine how much of the difference related to selling price and how much to unit volume. We can find out using the same type of format that we introduced in Chapter 7. Note that actual total contribution margin is the product of actual unit contribution margin and actual unit volume, while budgeted total contribution margin is the product of budgeted unit contribution margin and budgeted unit volume. We use standard production costs in the analyses (or at least hold unit production costs constant) because we follow the fundamental principal of variance analysis—hold all factors constant except the one you are analyzing. We want to determine how the marketing function performed, which necessitates holding production costs constant. We analyze differences between standard and actual costs elsewhere, so we do not ignore them. We can compare each of those to the product of actual unit volume and budgeted unit contribution margin to isolate the variances, as done below. Therefore, even if actual unit variable cost were different from budget, say $11.20, we should still use the budgeted cost.

Actual Results	*Actual Volume × Budgeted Unit Contribution Margin*	*Budgeted Results*
190,000 × $9.60	190,000 × $8.60	200,000 × $8.60
$1,824,000	$1,634,000	$1,720,000

$190,000 F — Sales price variance

$86,000 U — Sales volume variance

$104,000 F — Total marketing variance

Note that the sales price variance is also the difference between budgeted and actual contribution margin per unit ($9.60 − $8.60 = $1) times actual volume of 190,000 units. Volume is constant at 190,000 units, and the effect on total contribution margin of the change in selling price is isolated. Similarly, the sales volume variance is budgeted unit contribution margin times the difference between actual and budgeted unit volume, or \$8.60 × 10,000 units (200,000 − 190,000). The middle term, then, represents total contribution margin (or gross margin) given the actual unit sales, but at the budgeted selling price. In equation form,

$$\text{sales price variance} = (\text{actual contribution margin} - \text{budgeted contribution margin}) \times \text{actual volume}$$

$$\text{sales volume variance} = (\text{actual unit volume} - \text{budgeted unit volume}) \times \text{actual contribution margin}$$

A word of caution: an unfavorable variance, either sales price or sales volume, is not necessarily a bad outcome. A marketing manager might deliberately reduce a price to sell more units. The total variance is usually more important than either variance taken separately.

Multiple-Product Companies

The previous example used a single product. Firms that sell many products can calculate variances related to each product and can add a new dimension: a variance caused by changes in the sales mix. We explored weighted-average contribution margins in Chapter 2 and saw how profits could be affected by changing the sales mix. Let us use an example with two products.

	Planned	*Actual*
Product A:		
Sales price per unit	\$30	\$26
Production cost per unit	17	
Sales volume	100,000 units	114,000 units
Production B:		
Sales price per unit	\$10	\$14
Production cost per unit	3	
Sales volume	100,000 units	76,000 units

We can see that the expected mix of the 200,000 units of planned sales volume was 50 percent each for products A and B. The actual mix of A and B is 60/40 (114,000/190,000 = 0.60). Thus, a higher than budgeted percentage of product A with a contribution margin of \$13 (\$30 − \$17) was sold in comparison to a lower than budgeted proportion of B with a contribution margin of \$7 (\$10 − \$3). This means that profits should have risen.

Sales Price Variance Actual margin is \$1,862,000.

$$114{,}000(\$26 - \$17) + 76{,}000(\$14 - \$3) = \$1{,}862{,}000$$

The actual quantities at standard (budgeted) prices yield

$$114{,}000(\$30 - \$17) + 76{,}000(\$10 - \$3) = \$2{,}014{,}000$$

Therefore, the sales price variance is \$152,000U (\$1,862,000 − \$2,014,000). How do we explain this? The company got \$4 more on only 76,000 units of product B, while it got \$4 less on 114,000 units of product A.

Sales Mix Variance When you calculate a sales mix variance, you are also recalculating the sales volume variance. If we simply calculated the one-product sales volume variances for products A and B, we get the following.

Product A	\$13 × (114,000 − 100,000) =	\$182,000 F
Product B	\$7 × (76,000 − 100,000) =	168,000 U
Total sales volume variances		\$ 14,000 F

The total of the sales mix variance and new sales volume variance will be \$14,000 favorable. Whenever you refine a variance, you usually split an existing variance into two or more constituent parts.

Now, we will determine the effects of two events: selling a total of 190,000 units instead of 200,000, and selling a mix of 60/40, instead of 50/50. Exhibit 19–4 shows the variances. The right-hand column is simply budgeted results, as you are familiar with. We wish to isolate the difference in contribution margin that results from a change in *total* unit volume from 200,000 to 190,000, so

EXHIBIT 19–4 Two-Product Case Sales Variances

Actual Volume *Actual Price* *Actual Mix* *Budgeted Cost*	*Actual Volume* *Budgeted Price* *Actual Mix* *Budgeted Cost*	*Actual Volume* *Budgeted Price* *Budgeted Mix* *Budgeted Cost*	*Budgeted Volume* *Budgeted Price* *Budgeted Mix* *Budgeted Cost*
114,000(\$26 − \$17) + 76,000(\$14 − \$3) = \$1,862,000	114,000(\$30 − \$17) + 76,000(\$10 − \$3) = \$2,014,000	95,000(\$30 − \$17) + 95,000(\$10 − \$3) = \$1,900,000	100,000(\$30 − \$17) + 100,000(\$10 − \$3) = \$2,000,000

Sales Price Variance	Sales Mix Variance	Sales Volume Variance
\$152,000 U	\$114,000 F	\$100,000 U

Total Sales Variance

\$138,000 U

we find what the contribution margin would have been if the company had sold 190,000 at the expected 50/50 mix. This is the \$1,900,000. Comparing that result with the original budget of \$2,000,000 gives the \$100,000 unfavorable sales volume variance. Comparing that same \$1,900,000 with the contribution margin at the actual volumes of 114,000 and 76,000 gives the \$114,000 favorable sales mix variance and the two total \$14,000 favorable.

Should a multiproduct company always calculate sales mix variances? The answer depends on the relationship of the products. A sales mix variance makes sense for a group of competing products, such as models of personal computers. With such products, it is desirable not only to sell more, but to sell relatively more of the high-margin products—to enrich the product mix. If products do not compete with each other, such as personal computers and mainframe computers, there is no reason to calculate mix variances. A separate analysis of each product makes more sense because no one can convince someone looking for a \$1,200 personal computer to buy a \$1 million mainframe computer. Essentially, then, the question is whether customers might substitute one product for another. If so, a mix variance can be helpful information.

Other Sales Variances

Other analyses of sales performance are possible. For example, a company could look at its actual market share as compared with its expected market share. External factors could be included, such as how the economic climate affected sales. Remember that we want to use variances to analyze results and find out what we can do to improve future results. In addition, we want to evaluate managers on controllable factors. Thus, our variances should be disaggregated on whatever basis or dimensions that will serve these purposes. A sales market share variance or a variance reflecting noncontrollable market forces can advance these objectives.

Market Size and Market Share Variances

If the general economy is good and the market for a product is rising (or if the market is falling or the economy is poor), management should differentiate between sales volume increases or decreases related to external factors and those related to internal factors. Thus, if sales are budgeted to be 100,000 units, but the market for the industry grows by 10 percent, management should expect sales to increase by 10 percent. That expected growth yields a market size variance. This variance is related to external factors: market growth or decline. Thus, the **market size variance** is the actual total market for the product less the budgeted total market times a budgeted market share and times the budgeted contribution margin per unit.

$$\text{market size variance} = (ATM - BTM)(BMS)(BM)$$

where

ATM = actual total market volume
BTM = budgeted total market volume
BMS = budgeted market share
BM = budgeted contribution margin

Marketing managers cannot usually control market expansion or contraction. However, they can affect the share of the market the company obtains. Thus, the other segment of the sales volume variance is the market share variance. The **market share variance** is the difference between actual market share and budgeted market share times the actual total market and times budgeted contribution margin.

$$\text{market share variance} = (AMS - BMS)(ATM)(BM)$$

Let us extend the first example, using the data from Exhibit 19–3. Additionally, suppose the expected market was 2,000,000 units, the actual 1,750,000. The company therefore budgeted a 10 percent market share (200,000/2,000,000) and actually had a 10.857 percent share (190,000/1,750,000). The market declined and the company increased its share, though not enough to meet its original budgeted unit volume. Using the formulas we get the following results.

$$\begin{aligned} \text{Market size variance} &= (1{,}750{,}000 - 2{,}000{,}000) \times 10\% \times \$8.60 \\ &= \$215{,}000 \text{ unfavorable} \\ \text{Market share variance} &= (.10857 - .10) \times 1{,}750{,}000 \times \$8.60 \\ &= \$129{,}000 \text{ favorable (rounded)} \\ \text{Total volume variance} &= \$215{,}000 - \$129{,}000 = \$86{,}000 \text{ unfavorable} \end{aligned}$$

Notice that the market size and market share variance simply partition the originally calculated volume variance (page 885) of $86,000. We are refining the volume variance into its two constituent elements, market size and market share, as we previously did for sales price and sales volume.

We can lay out these variances in columnar form. We calculate the total contribution margin that we should have earned had we kept our share at 10 percent of the actual market and compare it with actual contribution margin (at budgeted selling price) and with the original budget.

Actual Volume × Budgeted Unit Contribution Margin	*Budgeted Market Share × Actual Market × Budgeted Contribution Margin*	*Budgeted Results*
190,000 × $8.60	.10 × 1,750,000 × $8.60	200,000 × $8.60
$1,634,000	$1,505,000	$1,720,000

$129,000 F — Market share variance
$215,000 U — Market size variance

$86,000 U
Total volume variance

The significance and interpretation of the size and share variances depends on circumstances. The market size variance at first glance appears to be noncontrollable. A few industry giants such as General Motors or IBM can influence the total size of a market by, say, changing prices. But even such companies cannot control the total market size. However, the point is that there can be high costs of misforecasting the market. Many managers make plans from the forecasts—sales budgets, production budgets, hiring employees, financing budgets—these and more are set in motion by the market forecast. Accordingly, the persons responsible for forecasting the market should be held responsible for their forecasts and should have incentives to be accurate. Of course, the market size might change because of external factors. The economy might make an unexpected move up or down, new products might affect the demand for the company's product, or an industry leader might make a move such as changing prices.

The market share variance, of course, is principally the responsibility of the marketing and sales departments. They are charged with selling the products. Here again, external and internal factors could affect this variance, so it might not be solely the responsibility of the marketing and sales managers. For example, a strike at a competitor's plant might boost the company's share, though clearly not through the skills and talents of the managers. Or if production did not keep pace with demand, the lost sales should be the responsibility of production. Or the company might have tightened or loosened its credit terms after setting the original budget. The interpretation of marketing variances is subject to the same kinds of caveats we stated about production variances. Managers might take actions that directly affect one variance while indirectly affecting another. For instance, a manager might reduce prices because competitors are reducing theirs and failing to respond might result in a severe drop in volume.

Variances often arise because conditions were not as expected when the original plans were developed. For instance, suppose the planned volume was based on forecasts of rapid growth for the industry and that growth failed to materialize. The company probably could not meet its planned volume, but the managers are not at fault because they cannot control industry sales. (The managers are responsible for accepting the inaccurate forecast, however.)

An important consideration in analyzing variances is whether the marketing people are adhering to the company's strategies for each product, or group of products.[1] For example, a company that is investing in a particular product, trying to increase its acceptance in the market, should not increase its price because doing so will reduce its volume *below what it would have been*. So even if volume is above budget, it could have been higher. This action violates the strategy because the company wants the highest possible market penetration for that product.

---

[1] Vijay Govindarajan and John K. Shank, "Profit Variance Analysis: A Strategic Focus," *Issues in Accounting Education*, Fall 1989, pp. 396–410.

PERFORMANCE MEASURES IN AN ADVANCED MANUFACTURING ENVIRONMENT

Managers control traditional manufacturing operations with standard costs and budgets. The costs of the components of manufacturing cost—materials, labor, and overhead—provide a basis for evaluating individual responsibility centers. However, in newer environments, such as JIT manufacturing, computer-assisted manufacturing, and flexible manufacturing systems, the emphasis is on the entire operation, not on its components.

Even in the more traditional setting there are problems with looking at variances one at a time and failing to recognize interdependencies, as we noted in Chapter 7. Chapter 7 used the example of a purchasing manager who bought sub-standard materials or components, and thereby showed a favorable material price variance. However, the effects of using the materials—unfavorable variances for material use, labor efficiency, and variable overhead efficiency—could far outweigh the lower cost. This point is even more critical in advanced manufacturing environments.

Advanced manufacturers emphasize 100 percent quality and zero defects. There is no buffer inventory available if problems develop. Therefore, when a defective unit comes down the line, the line shuts down and idles the workers. Labor efficiency variances then do not necessarily tell us about efficiency, but about a mixture of efficiency and availability of work.

Some argue that traditional variances are virtually useless in advanced environments. The objectives of improving quality, productivity, and cost are retarded by using standards because they are viewed as ideals, and therefore not improvable. Advocates of this position argue that current actual results should be compared with previous actual results. These comparisons show whether improvements are being made. Thus standard costs are not used in such settings, as Chapter 7 pointed out.

How then do advanced companies measure performance? For one thing, there is more emphasis on non-financial measures. Of course, companies have used non-financial measures for years. Some of the measures discussed below are not new, but their applications have perhaps been less widespread or their relative importance might not have been as great as it is now. One aspect of performance measurement in an advanced environment is that multiple measures are used, rather than just one (again, something that many companies have done for years). This brings up the question of the relative importance of the measures in evaluating performance, a knotty issue under any conditions.

A measure of the achievement of the zero inventory objective is the *throughput ratio*, or *manufacturing efficiency ratio* calculated below.

$$\text{throughput ratio} = \text{process time/throughput time}$$

Throughput time, or cycle time, is the total time it takes a product to go through the manufacturing process, while process time is the time actually spent working on it. Throughput time can be analyzed into various components. One common breakdown is:

throughput time = process time + wait time + move time + inspection time

The point of looking at these individual components is that they show that all costs are not equal. Only process time adds value. Inspection should be done during the process, not tacked on. Ideally, products should never wait and should move very short distances.

The ideal value for the ratio is, of course, one. In that ideal case, there is no wasted time: a unit is always being worked on, always having value added to it. The ratio is important because it highlights the extent to which the company has achieved the objective, and how far it has to go to achieve it. This ratio does not directly measure cost, but it is a **key result area** or **critical success factor**—a concept introduced in Chapter 15, which shows how well the company is doing with respect to an extremely important aspect of its success. Many managers have decided that measuring such critical success factors gives them better insights into progress and performance than do strictly financial measures. We believe that one must eventually have financial measures of performance, because, after all, a business must be profitable to survive.

Other performance measures relate to quality, meeting customer needs, operating efficiency, and cost. For example, a leading manufacturer of electronic systems, equipment, and components uses the following measures in its ASIC plant, which makes Applications Specific Integrated Circuits. As suggested by its name, the plant manufactures many different circuits. Diversity, of course, complicates manufacturing operations compared with a simple case where a single product is made. Actual results are evaluated not against standard costs, but against theoretical perfection—the best that can be done.[2]

Unit cost: the actual cost is evaluated against theoretical perfection, determined by dividing budgeted cost for each manufacturing cell by the maximum possible output of the cell.

Cycle time: total time spent in process, with a target of three days for the ASIC plant.

On-time delivery percentage: how often the plant meets delivery schedules, with 100 percent as the goal.

Quality: measured as the percentage of defective parts. The target is 100 percent, or zero defects.

Linearity of production: measures how closely the plant hews to level output, avoiding costly peaks and valleys.

---

[2] C. J. McNair, William Mosconi, and Thomas Norris, *Meeting the Technology Challenge: Cost Accounting in a JIT Environment* (Montvale, NJ: National Association of Accountants, 1988) pp. 180–182.

Inventory: determined by cycle time. A three-day supply of inventory means that inventory turns over about 120 times per year (365/3).

Scrap loss: The target is zero. This relates to quality—how many units are scrapped as opposed to how many meet the quality test.

These measures are used for manufacturing cells or teams, and form the basis for bonuses to groups. The company does not pay piece rates, nor does it give bonuses to individual workers, only to teams. This accords with the view that total performance, rather than individual performance, is the important factor.

The area of performance measures in advanced environments is relatively new and much study needs to be done on it. Some of what we say here will likely be obsolete soon; something only hinted at here may be widely used soon.

SUMMARY

Tiered contribution analysis helps managers see what areas might be improved and what segments might need attention. The analysis should assist managers in understanding the overall profitability or lack of it.

The same type of variance analysis that we did for manufacturing costs can help us to understand marketing results. Various types of analyses are possible, from a simple two-factor case to more complicated and, it is hoped, more informative multifactor analyses. Again, interpretation of variances is critical, for the "obvious" explanation is not always correct.

Advanced manufacturing environments create problems in evaluating performance because they do not run in the same ways as conventional operations. Moreover, the emphasis on total performance goes against the grain of historical performance measurement, which has always been concerned with isolating responsibility. Nonetheless, new measures are appearing and the future should see better applications of these and other measures.

REVIEW PROBLEM

Calculate and explain all sales variances obtained from the following data. The answer appears below and in Exhibit 19–5.

	Product I	*Product J*	*Product K*
Actual sales price	$12	$20	$8
Actual volume (units)	100,000	100,000	100,000
Planned sales price	$13	$19	$9
Planned volume	125,000	62,500	62,500
Unit cost	$5	$10	$6

EXHIBIT 19–5 Answer to Review Problem

	Actual Volume Actual Price Actual Mix	*Actual Volume Budgeted Price Actual Mix*	*Actual Volume Budgeted Price Budgeted Mix*	*Budgeted Volume Budgeted Price Budgeted Mix*
Product I	100,000 (\$12 − \$5)	100,000 (\$13 − \$5)	150,000 (\$13 − \$5)	125,000 (\$13 − \$5)
Product J	100,000 (\$20 − \$10)	100,000 (\$19 − \$10)	75,000 (\$19 − \$10)	62,500 (\$19 − \$10)
Product K	100,000 (\$8 − \$6)	100,000 (\$9 − \$6)	75,000 (\$9 − \$6)	62,500 (\$9 − \$6)
	\$1,900,000	\$2,000,000	\$2,100,000	\$1,750,000

\$100,000U price variance | \$100,000U mix variance | \$350,000F volume variance

Total Sales Variance = \$150,000F

1. The company sold 300,000 units instead of the 250,000 planned. Therefore, there is a favorable volume variance.
2. The mix was one-third each instead of one-half, one-fourth, one-fourth as planned. This means that proportionately more of products J and K were sold and less of product I.
3. Prices were lower by \$1 for both I and K and higher by \$1 for J.

ASSIGNMENTS

19–1 Gross Margin Variances Apple Products uses a standard costing system. It recently had a sales price variance of \$4,000F and a sales volume variance of \$5,500U. Apple has only a single product. Actual gross margin (actual sales less actual costs) was \$137,000, which includes \$2,000 of favorable production variances.

REQUIRED

Compute total budgeted gross margin.

19–2 Marketing Variances The marketing manager of Triloff Company believes that she could increase unit volume of the firm's major product, a dishwashing liquid, if she decreased the price. The budget for the coming year shows the following:

Sales	100,000 cases
Contribution margin per case	\$ 7
Budgeted contribution margin	\$700,000

She is considering a \$0.20 reduction per case, which she expects to increase unit volume by 20,000 cases.

REQUIRED

Suppose that the manager reduces the price and gains the additional volume as she expects. What will the sales price variance and sales volume variance be?

19–3 Gross Margin Analysis (AICPA) Garfield Company, which sells a single product, provided the following data from its income statements for the calendar years 19X4 and 19X3:

	19X4
Sales (150,000 units)	$750,000
Cost of goods sold	525,000
Gross profit	$225,000

	19X3 (base year)
Sales (180,000 units)	$720,000
Cost of goods sold	575,000
Gross profit	$145,000

REQUIRED

In an analysis of variation in gross profit between the two years, what were the effects of changes in sales price and sales volume?

19–4 Evaluating the Marketing Department (CMA) Kane Corporation has practical production capacity of one million units. The current year's master budget was based on the production and sales of 700,000 units. Actual production for the year was 720,000 units, while actual sales amounted to only 600,000 units. The units are sold for $20 each, and the contribution margin ratio is 30 percent.

REQUIRED

What is the dollar amount that best quantifies the marketing department's failure to achieve budgeted performance for the current year?

19–5 Standards and Variances (From a Problem Prepared by Professor Jack R. Blann) At the end of 1923 Al Kapon, vice president of the Chicago Syndicate, Inc., stared out of the window of his posh West Side office in dismay. His expectations for a highly profitable year were dashed. The disappointing results appear below.

	Plan	*Actual*	*Variance*
Sales	$500,000	$456,000	$44,000
Direct materials	50,000	48,000	(2,000)
Direct labor	200,000	201,000	1,000
Variable overhead	100,000	92,000	(8,000)
Total variable costs	350,000	341,000	(9,000)
Contribution margin	150,000	115,000	35,000
Fixed costs	100,000	98,000	(2,000)
Syndicate profit	$ 50,000	$ 17,000	$33,000

Kapon realized that because sales were down, expenses too should fall, such that profit should be somewhat more than $17,000. His organization, which made only one product (the identity of which cannot be disclosed), incorporated the following data in its plans:

Standard Cost and Contribution Margin

Selling price		$10/unit
Direct materials (2 quarts at $0.50)	$1	
Direct labor (0.80 hr at $5)	4	
Variable overhead ($2.50/labor hour)	2	7
Standard contribution margin		$ 3

The firm planned sales of 50,000 units, but sold only 48,000 at an average price of $9.50 per unit. Materials averaged $0.48 per quart for the 100,000 quarts bought and used. Direct labor hours were 40,000. Production was 48,000 units.

Kapon made you an offer that you could not refuse, so you accepted the assignment below.

REQUIRED

1. Prepare an income statement at standard. That is, given that sales were 48,000 units at $9.50, and assuming that variable costs were incurred at standard (prices and quantities), and that fixed costs were incurred as budgeted, determine the income that the organization would have earned.
2. Calculate the marketing variances. Their sum should equal the difference between the income you determined in part 1 and the $50,000 that the firm planned.
3. Calculate the price and quantity variances for variable costs. Does the sum of those variances equal the difference between the actual income ($17,000) and the income you computed in part 1? If not, what is missing? What do you call this variance?
4. Prepare a memo to Kapon explaining what possible causes gave him his difficulties. Be sure that he will understand your explanation, as he becomes violent (occasionally) when business is bad.

19–6 Comprehensive Variance Analysis Gorton Company makes a device that returns soccer balls kicked into it. The device has been very successful over the past few years, and therefore the managers of the firm were not especially happy when they saw the following results for 19X6, in thousands.

	Budget	*Actual*
Sales	$854.0	$830.0
Standard cost of sales	550.0	495.0
Standard gross margin	304.0	335.0
Production variances (favorable):		
Materials		12.4
Direct labor		8.1
Overhead		(3.4)
Actual gross margin		317.9
Selling and administrative costs	140.0	162.0
Income before taxes	$164.0	$155.9

Other information given with the report was that unit volume was 10 percent below budget, but that increased prices had softened the potential blow. Higher advertising expense also helped, in the view of the sales manager. The average labor time to make a unit was 0.60 hour, which was above the 0.55 hour used in budgeting. The direct labor rate is $7 per hour, and variable overhead is $6 per direct labor hour. During the year the firm produced 20,000 units and sold 18,000. Budgeted sales and production were both 20,000 units. The firm uses budgeted production to set its standard fixed overhead costs.

Materials prices from suppliers rose about 4 percent over standard for the year. Materials cost per unit of product is $12.

REQUIRED

Identify as many variances as you can, so that you can tell the managers why profits were below budget. You will not be able to find all the variances.

19–7 Basic Marketing Variances Gibbon Company budgeted 1,000,000 cases of Kleerup, its best-selling skin care product. It actually sold 970,000. The budgeted selling price was $50.70 per case, the actual price $49.30. Per case variable cost is $12.35.

REQUIRED

Compute the sales price and sales volume variances.

19–8 Market Size and Share Variances (Continuation of Assignment 19–7) Gibbon budgeted the 1,000,000 cases based on a 20 percent share of the expected market. The actual market was 5,200,000 cases.

REQUIRED

Compute the market size and market share variances.

19–9 Sales Mix Variance The president of Corham Company was discussing the performance of the marketing manager, using the data given below. The president was pleased at the favorable quantity variances but was critical of the unfavorable mix variance.

	Product		
	Regular	*Deluxe*	*Super*
Budgeted volume	10,000	6,000	4,000
Actual volume	12,000	7,000	4,500
Budgeted and actual contribution margin	$3	$5	$8

The marketing manager thought it was unreasonable to say that there was an unfavorable mix variance. "After all, my job is to get as much volume as we can at favorable prices, and I did just that. To criticize me for not increasing sales of all products at the same rates is unfair and does not present a true picture of my performance."

REQUIRED

1. Calculate the sales quantity and sales mix variances.
2. Comment on the position taken by the marketing manager.

19–10 Gross Margin Variances The income statement for Franklin, Inc., is presented below. Franklin makes men's shirts.

FRANKLIN, INC.
Income Statement
19X3

Sales	$646,800
Cost of sales	374,600
Gross profit	272,200
Sales expenses	50,000
Administrative expenses	45,000
Income before taxes	$177,200

Sales consist of 12,000 units divided as follows: 40 percent deluxe designer shirts, 30 percent western style shirts, and 30 percent dress shirts. The average prices were $30 for the dress shirts, $35 for the western shirts, and $86 for the designer shirts. Plans for the period called for sales of 5,250 designer shirts, 4,500 western shirts, and 5,250 dress shirts.

Cost of sales includes $5,000 unfavorable variable cost variances. Standard costs of sales for designer shirts are $44 and for dress and western shirts $22 each. Budgeted prices for the line call for $80 designer, $40 western, and $30 dress shirts.

REQUIRED

1. Calculate the gross margin price, volume, mix, and total variances.
2. Explain these variances.

19–11 Marketing Variances in a Service Firm Jan McMinn, managing partner of McMinn & Co., consulting engineers, gave you the following data regarding budgeted and actual revenue for 19X8.

	Budgeted	*Actual*
Chargeable hours	65,000	65,470
Total revenue	$1,885,200	$1,870,600

Virtually all costs are fixed, so that revenue is the critical determinant of profit. McMinn wants you to analyze the figures to give him an idea why there was a shortfall in revenue.

REQUIRED

Give McMinn an appropriate analysis.

19–12 Marketing Variances in a Service Firm (Continuation of Assignment 19–11) McMinn later gave you the following data that show actual and budgeted results by category of engineer that the firm employs:

	Budgeted		Actual	
	Chargeable Hours	Average Rate	Chargeable Hours	Average Rate
Junior engineer	45,700	$21.75	47,100	$21.60
Senior engineer	13,300	35.20	12,650	35.30
Partner	6,000	70.50	5,720	71.10

REQUIRED

Determine the sales mix, sales price, and sales volume variances. Round your calculations of values for revenues to the nearest $100.

19–13 Interpretation of Variances (Continuation of Assignment 19–12) McMinn looked at the analysis that you prepared for assignment 19–12 and made the following comments:

> I see what you mean about the mix of engineers changing from the budgeted one, but wasn't my real problem the shortfalls in chargeable hours for seniors and partners? Granted, the ratio of juniors increased over the budget, but that was because I was able to use juniors more than I had originally planned. Look, why don't you do a price and volume analysis for each category, treating them individually, and drop the mix variance. That might help me more.

REQUIRED

Do as McMinn suggests. Compare the results with those you obtained in the preceding assignment and comment on the differences, especially with regard to the information that they give McMinn.

19–14 Gross Margin Variances (CMA) The year-end income statement of Duo, Inc., is presented below (000s omitted).

REQUIRED

1. What is the net effect on profit of the unit sales volume variance of product AR-10?
2. What is the net effect on profit of the sales price variance for product ZR-7?

	Product AR-10		Product ZR-7		Total	
	Budget	Actual	Budget	Actual	Budget	Actual
Unit sales	2,000	2,800	6,000	5,600	8,000	8,400
Sales	$6,000	$7,560	$12,000	$11,760	$18,000	$19,320
Cost of goods sold	$2,400	$2,800	$ 6,000	$ 5,880	$ 8,400	$ 8,680
Fixed costs	1,800	1,900	2,400	2,400	4,200	4,300
Total costs	$4,200	$4,700	$ 8,400	$ 8,280	$12,600	$12,980
Net profit	$1,800	$2,860	$ 3,600	$ 3,480	$ 5,400	$ 6,340

3. What is the net effect on profit from the change in the unit cost of goods sold of product ZR-7?

4. If products AR-10 and ZR-7 are substitutes for each other, a sales mix and sales volume variation for the combined products can be calculated. If this combination is calculated, what is the net effect on profit of the change in the unit sales mix?

5. What sales volume variance calculation would complement the variance calculated in the previous question?

19–15 Sales Variances (CMA) Handler Company distributes two home use power tools to hardware stores—a heavy duty ½″ hand drill and a table saw. The tools are purchased from a manufacturer that attaches the Handler private label on the tools. The wholesale selling prices to the hardware stores are $60 each for the drill and $120 each for the table saw.

The 19X2 budget and actual results are presented below.

HANDLER COMPANY
Income Statement
for the Year Ended December 31, 19X2
(000s omitted)

	Hand Drill		*Table Saw*		*Total*		
	Budgeted	*Actual*	*Budgeted*	*Actual*	*Budgeted*	*Actual*	*Variance*
Sales in units	120	86	80	74	200	160	40
Revenue	$7,200	$5,074	$9,600	$8,510	$16,800	$13,584	$(3,216)
Cost of goods sold	6,000	4,300	6,400	6,068	12,400	10,368	2,032
Gross margin	$1,200	$ 774	$3,200	$2,442	$ 4,400	$ 3,216	$(1,184)
Unallocated costs:							
Selling					$ 1,000	$ 1,000	$ —
Advertising					1,000	1,060	(60)
Administration					400	406	(6)
Income taxes (45%)					900	338	562
Total unallocated costs					$ 3,300	$ 2,804	$ 496
Net income					$ 1,100	$ 412	$ (688)

The budget was adopted in late 19X1 and was based on Handler's estimated share of the market for the two tools.

During the first quarter of 19X2, Handler's management estimated that the total market for these tools would actually be 10 percent below its original estimates. To prevent Handler's unit sales from declining as much as industry projections, management developed and implemented a revised marketing program; included in the program were dealer discounts and increased direct advertising. The table saw line was emphasized in this program.

REQUIRED

1. Analyze the unfavorable gross margin variance of $1,184,000 in terms of
   a. sales price variance
   b. cost variance
   c. volume variance

2. Discuss the apparent effect of Handler Company's special marketing program (i.e., dealer discounts and additional advertising) on 19X2 operating results. Support your comments with numerical data where appropriate.

19–16 Sales Variances (CMA)

XERBERT COMPANY
Budgeted and Actual Income Statements
For the Year Ended December 31, 19X2
(000s omitted)

	Budgeted			*Actual*		
	Xenox	*Xeon*	*Total*	*Xenox*	*Xeon*	*Total*
Unit sales	150	100	250	130	130	260
Net dollar sales	$900	$1,000	$1,900	$780	$1,235	$2,015
Variable expenses	450	750	1,200	390	975	1,365
Contribution margin	$450	$ 250	$ 700	$390	$ 260	$ 650
Fixed expenses:						
Manufacturing			$ 200			$ 190
Marketing			153			140
Administration			95			90
Total fixed expenses			$ 448			$ 420
Income before taxes			$ 252			$ 230

REQUIRED

1. The variance of actual contribution margin from budgeted contribution attributable to unit variable cost changes is
   - *a.* $165,000 unfavorable
   - *b.* $165,000 favorable
   - *c.* $137,000 favorable
   - *d.* $137,000 unfavorable
   - *e.* zero because actual unit variable costs were the same as budgeted unit variable costs

Xerbert Company considers Xenox and Xeon substitutes for each other. Therefore, it separates the portion of the variance in contribution margin due to changes in volume into a mix variance (part 2) and a quantity variance (part 3). These two variances are based on budgeted unit contribution margins.

2. The variance in contribution margin from budgeted contribution margin attributed to a change in mix is
   - *a.* $13,000 unfavorable
   - *b.* $78,000 unfavorable
   - *c.* $15,000 favorable
   - *d.* $28,000 favorable
   - *e.* zero because equal quantities of each product were sold
3. The variance in contribution margin from budgeted contribution attributed to a change in quantity is
   - *a.* $13,000 unfavorable

b. $78,000 unfavorable
c. $15,000 favorable
d. $28,000 favorable
e. $50,000 unfavorable

4. The variance of actual contribution margin from budgeted contribution margin attributable to sales price is
a. $ 50,000 unfavorable
b. $115,000 unfavorable
c. $115,000 favorable
d. $ 65,000 favorable
e. $ 65,000 unfavorable

19–17 Performance Evaluation in a JIT Environment TRS Millworks had begun moving to JIT principles by setting up manufacturing cells, involving workers more in inspection and maintenance, and working with suppliers to increase quality. The program to convert to JIT was well along and Bev Wilkins, the controller, was concerned that the performance measures used in the past were not as relevant.

TRS had used a typical standard costing system and calculated the usual variances. After the move toward JIT had begun, Wilkins began to develop other data, such as the following for two recent months.

	March	*May*
Average process time, hours	31	29
Average cycle time, hours	87	83
Production, units	4,800	5,550
On-time delivery percentage	89.2%	91.3%
Defective units	52	54
Inventory of materials, days supply	6	3
Inventory of work in process, days supply	7	8
Inventory of finished goods, days supply	3	2

REQUIRED

Use the data above to describe where TRS is improving and where it is not.

19–18 Product Analysis in a JIT Environment JIT environments typically use manufacturing cells that concentrate on a single product. Each cell has all the machinery needed to make the product. Conventional manufacturers ordinarily group similar machines in departments devoted to performing particular operations. How might you expect the analysis of products to differ in the two environments? What differences might you expect in segmented income statements in the two environments?

19–19 Analyzing Results—Sales and Cost Variances Managers of Reed Blanket Company were disappointed at the shortfalls in profit for 19X7, as shown in the income statements on the next page, in millions.

REQUIRED

The president wants an analysis showing why profit fell short of budget. He wants you to determine the effects of the difference between budgeted and actual unit volume, budgeted and actual selling prices, and budgeted and actual costs for the volume achieved. Production equalled sales. Prepare such an analysis and be sure that it fully accounts for the difference between budgeted and actual profit.

	Budgeted	*Actual*
Unit sales	10.0	10.8
Sales	$120.0	$122.1
Variable manufacturing costs:		
Materials	20.0	21.8
Direct labor	15.0	17.0
Variable overhead	5.0	5.2
Total variable costs	40.0	44.0
Contribution margin	80.0	78.1
Fixed costs:		
Manufacturing	50.0	50.8
Selling and administrative	20.0	19.9
Total fixed costs	70.0	70.7
Profit before taxes	$ 10.0	$ 7.4

19–20 Comprehensive Analysis (CMA Adapted) Allglow Company is a cosmetics manufacturer specializing in stage makeup. The company's best selling product is SkinKlear, a protective cream used under stage makeup to protect the skin from frequent use of makeup. SkinKlear is packaged in three sizes—eight ounces, one pound, and three pounds—and regularly sells for $21.00 per pound. The standard cost per pound of SkinKlear, based on Allglow's normal monthly production of 8,000 pounds, is as follows.

Cost Item	*Quantity*	*Standard Cost*	*Total Cost*	
Direct materials:				
Cream base	9.0 oz.	$ .05/oz.	$ .45	
Moisturizer	6.5 oz.	.10/oz.	.65	
Fragrance	.5 oz.	1.00/oz.	.50	
				$ 1.60
*Direct labor:**				
Mixing	.5 hr.	$4.00/hr.	$2.00	
Compounding	1.0 hr.	5.00/hr.	5.00	
				7.00
Variable overhead**	1.5 hr.	$2.10/hr.		3.15
Total standard cost per pound				$11.75

*Direct labor dollars include employee benefits.
**Applied on the basis of direct labor hours.

Based on these standard costs, Allglow prepares monthly budgets. Presented on the following page are the budgeted performance and the actual performance for May 19X6 when the company produced and sold 9,000 pounds of SkinKlear.

Contribution Report for SkinKlear
May 19X6

	Budget	Actual	Variance
Units	8,000	9,000	1,000 F
Revenue	$168,000	$180,000	$12,000 F
Direct material	12,800	16,200	3,400U
Direct labor	56,000	62,500	6,500U
Variable overhead	25,200	30,900	5,700U
Total variable costs	$ 94,000	$109,600	$15,600U
Contribution margin	$ 74,000	$ 70,400	$ 3,600U

Barbara Simmons, Allglow's President, was not pleased with these results; despite a sizeable increase in the sales of SkinKlear, there was a decrease in the product's contribution to the overall profitability of the firm. Simmons has asked Allglow's Cost Accountant, Brian Jackson, to prepare a report that identifies the reasons why the contribution margin for SkinKlear has decreased. Jackson gathered the information below to help prepare the report.

May 19X6 Use Report for SkinKlear

Cost Item	Quantity	Actual Cost
Direct materials:		
Cream base	84,000 oz.	$ 4,200
Moisturizer	60,000 oz.	7,200
Fragrance	4,800 oz.	4,800
Direct labor:		
Mixing	4,500 hr.	18,000
Compounding—manual	5,300 hr.	26,500
Compounding—mechanized	2,700 hr.	13,500
Compounding—idle	900 hr.	4,500
Variable overhead		30,900
Total variable cost		$109,600

While doing research, Jackson discovered that the Manufacturing Department had mechanized one of the manual operations in the compounding process on an experimental basis. The mechanized operation replaced manual operations that represented 40 percent of the compounding process.

The workers' inexperience with the mechanized operation caused increased use of both the cream base and the moisturizer; however, Jackson believed these inefficiencies would be negligible if mechanization became permanent and the workers' skills were improved. The idle time in compounding was traceable to having fewer workers for the mechanized process. During this experimental period, idle time was charged to direct labor rather than overhead. The excess workers could either be reassigned or laid off in the future. Jackson was also able to determine that all of the variable manufacturing overhead costs over standard could be traced directly to the mechanization process.

REQUIRED

1. Prepare an explanation of the $3,600 unfavorable variance between the budgeted and actual contribution margin for SkinKlear during May 19X6 by calculating the following variances.
   a. sales price variance
   b. material price variance
   c. material quantity variance
   d. labor efficiency variance
   e. variable overhead efficiency variance
   f. variable overhead spending variance
   g. contribution margin volume variance
2. Allglow Company must decide whether the compounding operation in the SkinKlear manufacturing process that was mechanized on an experimental basis should continue to be mechanized. Calculate the variable cost savings that can be expected to arise in the future from the mechanization. Explain your answer.

19–21 Contribution Statement (CMA Adapted) Music Teachers, Inc., is an educational association for music teachers that had 20,000 members during 19X5. The association operates from a central headquarters but has local membership chapters throughout the United States. Monthly meetings are held by the local chapters to discuss recent developments in topics of interest to music teachers. The association's journal, *Teachers' Forum*, is issued monthly with features about recent developments in the field. The association publishes books and reports and sponsors professional courses that qualify for continuing professional education credit. The Statement of Revenues and Expenses for the current year is presented below.

MUSIC TEACHERS, INC.
Statement of Revenues and Expenses
For the Year Ended November 30, 19X5
($000 omitted)

Revenues	$3,275
Expenses:	
Salaries	$ 920
Personnel costs	230
Occupancy costs	280
Reimbursement to local chapters	600
Other membership services	500
Printing and paper	320
Postage and shipping	176
Instructors fees	80
General and administrative	38
Total expenses	$3,144
Excess of revenues over expenses	$ 131

The Board of Directors has requested that a segmented statement of operations be prepared showing the contribution of each revenue center (i.e., Membership, Magazine Subscriptions, Books and Reports, Continuing Education). Mike Doyle has been assigned this responsibility and has gathered the following data prior to statement preparation.

Membership dues are $100 per year, of which $20 is considered to cover a one-year subscription to the journal. Other benefits include membership in the association and chapter affiliation. The portion of the dues covering the magazine subscription ($20) should be assigned to the Magazine Subscriptions revenue center.

One-year subscriptions to *Teachers' Forum* were sold to non-members and libraries at $30 each. A total of 2,500 of these subscriptions were sold. In addition to subscriptions, the magazine generated $100,000 in advertising revenue. The costs per magazine subscription were $7 for printing and paper and $4 for postage and shipping.

A total of 28,000 technical reports and professional texts were sold by the Books and Reports Department at an average unit selling price of $25. Average costs per publication were as follows.

Printing and paper	$4
Postage and shipping	$2

The association offers a variety of continuing education courses to both members and non-members. The one-day courses cost $75 each and were attended by 2,400 students in 19X5. A total of 1,760 students took two-day courses at a cost of $125 for each course. Outside instructors were paid to teach some courses.

Salary and occupancy data are as follows.

	Salaries	*Square Footage*
Membership	$210,000	2,000
Magazine Subscriptions	150,000	2,000
Books and Reports	300,000	3,000
Continuing Education	180,000	2,000
Corporate staff	80,000	1,000
	$920,000	10,000

The Books and Reports Department also rents warehouse space at an annual cost of $50,000. Personnel costs are 25 percent of salaries. Printing and paper costs other than for magazine subscriptions and books and reports relate to the Continuing Education Department. General and administrative expenses include all other costs incurred by the corporate staff to operate the association.

Doyle has decided he will assign all revenues and expenses to the revenue centers that can be traced directly to a revenue center or allocated on a reasonable and logical basis to a revenue center.

The expenses that can be traced or assigned to corporate staff as well as any other expenses that cannot be assigned to revenue centers will be grouped with the general and administrative expenses and not allocated to the revenue centers. Doyle believes that allocations often tend to be arbitrary and are not useful for management reporting and analysis. He believes that any further allocation of the general and administrative expenses associated with the operation and administration of the association would be arbitrary.

REQUIRED

1. Prepare a segmented Statement of Revenues and Expenses that presents the contribution of each revenue center and includes the common costs of the organization that are not allocated to the revenue centers.
2. If segmented reporting is adopted by the association, in what ways can the information provided by the report be utilized by the association?
3. Mike Doyle decided not to allocate some indirect or nontraceable expenses to revenue centers because he believes that allocations tend to be arbitrary.
   a. Beside the arbitrariness argument, what reasons are often presented for not allocating indirect or nontraceable expenses to revenue centers?
   b. Under what circumstances might the allocation of indirect or nontraceable expenses to revenue centers be acceptable?

19–22 Isolating Variances Plimsoll Company had the following budgeted and actual results in a recent month.

	Budget	*Actual*
Selling price	$8.50	$8.75
Variable cost	3.20	3.40
Contribution margin	$5.30	$5.35
Unit volume	32,000	31,700

REQUIRED

Compute the sales price and sales volume variances.

19–23 Analyzing Monthly Results Bronson Company had the following results in two recent months.

	August	*September*
Selling price	$6.30	$6.75
Variable cost	3.10	3.10
Contribution margin	$3.20	$3.65
Unit volume	30,000	29,200
Total contribution margin	$96,000	$106,580

The president has asked you to help analyze the month-to-month differences.

REQUIRED

Explain why the results of September differed from those of August, using appropriate calculations.

Part V

KEY AREAS FOR FURTHER STUDY

20

OPERATIONAL CONTROL—INVENTORIES

Inventories of manufacturing firms usually include raw materials and purchased components, work in process, and finished goods.[1] Maintaining and managing inventory has costs; the central theme of inventory management is to control inventory-related costs given the constraints of the purchasing, manufacturing, and sales environments. Changes are now taking place in the external environment (more competition within the United States as well as worldwide) and the internal environment (how manufacturing processes are organized, more use of robotics, and the number and variety of products that are offered) that affect operational control of inventories. Therefore, inventory management techniques and philosophies such as manufacturing process planning (MPP), manufacturing resource planning (MRP-II), and just-in-time (JIT) are popular topics among managers and academics. In this chapter, we discuss the basics of inventory management as well as how efforts to reduce inventory through JIT coupled with manufacturing cells, computer integrated manufacturing (CIM), or flexible manufacturing systems (FMS) affect these basics.

[1] Although this discussion focuses on manufacturing companies, the same issues are relevant for merchandising companies.

BASIC ISSUES

Inventory policy is complex. Consider a firm that makes several hundred products using 40 or so types of material and hundreds of purchased components. On one hand, the managers who deal with purchasing, production scheduling, and inventory control must make sure that enough finished units are available to meet demand. On the other hand, to be competitive in the world marketplace, they must keep down inventory costs (including holding costs, opportunity costs associated with space used for inventories, and support department costs).

This chapter examines the basic inventory questions (how much to make or buy at a time, and at what level to replenish inventory) as well as the changes in management thinking brought on by an emerging worldwide competitive environment in many industries and changes that are taking place in how products are made.

Holding inventory is costly. Money tied up in inventory has an opportunity cost, as we discussed in Chapter 13. If a company has, say, \$250,000 of raw materials inventory and the relevant after-tax interest rate is 9 percent, annual holding costs for *interest alone* (actual or imputed) are \$22,500 (0.09 × \$250,000). Additionally, there are costs associated with, for example, the space that the inventory uses, the people who manage inventory, and losses through spoilage, obsolescence, and pilferage. Space taken up by inventory might have an opportunity cost.[2] Perhaps a company rents space for warehousing that could be given up if inventories were cut. In other cases, a company might be able to use the space to manufacture more goods, thereby creating additional profits. Some practitioners argue that the real cost of holding inventory exceeds 30 percent.

Both the complexity of the inventory (number of items) and its type affect support department costs. First, if there is a single inventory item, ordering, storing, and moving are simpler than they are for a company with hundreds of different items in inventory. Second, dealing with a significant inventory of an easily traded commodity (gold or silver, for example) will usually cause higher support department costs (e.g., record keeping, security, storage costs) than having the same dollar amount of inventory in large, heavy industrial machine components. Since holding inventory can be costly (including opportunity costs), it is in management's best interest to reduce inventory.

However, there are good reasons for holding inventory.[3] Inventory levels might be related to aspects of the marketplace for raw materials and pur-

[2] In our discussion of linear programming in Chapter 12, space was mentioned as a binding constraint with an opportunity cost. One way to achieve more space is to reduce inventory.

[3] Some authors argue that many reasons proposed by management are really incorrect. As we discuss later, inventory buildup may be a symptom of other problems.

chased components, the production process, and the marketplace for finished product. In the first instance, some goods are available only at certain times of the year. This is especially true with agricultural products. For example, a firm making apple products will often acquire its entire annual supply of apples during the fall harvest. In other cases, a source of supply might be interrupted. Say that management predicts a strike at a major supplier. Managers might stock up on a particularly scarce resource as a hedge against the strike. The newspapers are filled with stories of supermarkets being bought out of certain items after adverse weather predictions or other factors. If significant price increases are anticipated, a company might increase its short-term buying. Companies offer quantity discounts to induce the purchase of larger quantities at one time. Other companies may offer year-end sale prices. These are examples why a company might maintain a sizable inventory. However, this is just one part of the puzzle.

The area causing the most current controversy is the level of in-process inventory. Some reasons for keeping in-process inventories relate to the manufacturing process. Perhaps the nature of the product causes large work in process. This is true in winemaking, for example, where the fermentation process takes years. In other industries, parts of the manufacturing cycle are accomplished in large batches, other parts in small batches. Work in process from a large batch may be kept to feed the small-batch process. Finally, some processes have significant setup costs; to reduce these costs, large amounts are produced at once.

In the past, another major reason for work in process has been the need for a buffer between work stations. Managers wanted to make sure that each station was busy. A buffer allows subsequent stations to keep working even if a prior operation is temporarily shut down. Another reason to keep buffers is to make sure enough components are available to accommodate changes in demand. This rationale and the cost of setups are drawing the most attention today.

Finally, the external marketplace gives reasons to maintain inventory. For companies that make a seasonal good such as children's toys, inventory of finished goods is built up to meet the needs at the peak selling season. It is often less costly to build up inventory in these cases than to have the capacity to meet seasonal demands. In some companies, fluctuating demand as well as the desire to keep down *lead time* (the time between the placing of an order and its delivery) are proposed as good reasons to maintain not only finished goods inventory, but also appropriate levels of purchased and manufactured components. There is often an opportunity cost to being out of stock when an order is placed. Therefore, there are legitimate reasons for companies to maintain certain levels of inventory. When we couple these reasons with the desire to use as much as possible of the plant for productive purposes and to keep the costs of inventory down, managers are faced with difficult questions.

We can take the costs associated with inventory and break them down into three basic types: the cost of having inventory (called *holding costs* or *carrying costs*), the costs of setting up a production run or of placing a purchase order (called *setup costs* or *ordering costs*), and the costs of being out of inventory (*stockout costs*). Examples of these costs appear in Exhibit 20–1.

The costs relevant to determining inventory policies are the incremental costs of setup, carrying, and stockout. Some of these costs are difficult to measure because they are opportunity costs and are not recorded in the accounts. The opportunity cost of money tied up in inventories, costs associated with internal complexity, and lost sales because of stockouts are examples of such costs.

Some of the costs in Exhibit 20–1 are likely to be step-variable. If there is a purchasing department, at least one person will purchase raw materials and components. As additional types of material and components are needed, more people will be hired. While such costs do not go up linearly, at some point a second and then a third person will be needed. The same can be said for costs in other support departments that deal with setups, storing, and managing inventory. Thus, it is difficult at times to see the incremental costs associated with any one single action (e.g., redesigning a product so that it uses more components). As with most parts of relevant information for managerial

EXHIBIT 20–1 Inventory-Related Costs

Set up (Ordering) Costs

1. contribution margin of production lost during changeover, if operations at capacity
2. initial scrap, if any
3. unloading and inspecting incoming materials and components*
4. support department costs of ordering, data processing, scheduling, making changeovers, and expediting associated with each order or production run

Carrying (Holding) Costs

1. opportunity cost of investment in inventory
2. opportunity cost of space used for inventory
3. support department costs associated with maintaining inventory
4. insurance, personal property taxes
5. obsolescence, spoilage, deterioration

Stockout Costs

1. opportunity cost of lost sales
   a. contribution margin on lost sales during stockout period
   b. contribution margin on lost future sales (customer ill will)
2. idle time of workers (assuming sales are not lost because of stockout)
3. disruptions and changeovers in production schedules
4. costs of expediting including support department costs and higher costs of transportation (air freight versus surface transportation)

*This assumes some fixed portion of unloading is associated with each order or inbound vehicle.

decision making, the accountant must rely on sound analysis based on reasonable assumptions and estimates.

ECONOMIC ORDER QUANTITY

Economic order quantity (EOQ), also called *economic lot size* or *economic production quantity* (EPQ), is a basic inventory management model. EOQ is the optimal amount of product to be made in a single production run (or ordered in a single order). At the optimal quantity, expected setup costs are balanced with expected holding costs and each of these cost elements is minimized. We will consider stockout costs later when we discuss when to reorder or replenish stock.

Total setup and carrying costs for a period can be expressed as follows:

$$\begin{aligned} \text{total cost} &= \text{period carrying cost} + \text{period setup cost} \\ TC &= (Q/2 \times h) + (D/Q \times k) \end{aligned}$$

where

TC = total holding cost plus setup cost

Q = quantity produced on each run (or purchased)

h = holding cost per unit per period

D = expected demand for the period

k = setup cost for each run (or purchase)

The term $Q/2$ reflects average inventory and is the amount on which the firm incurs holding costs. The term D/Q gives the number of runs of each product or component during the period.

This expression of total costs assumes that demand for the product, material, or component is reasonably uniform throughout the period. Otherwise, $Q/2$ does not reflect the average inventory. We are also assuming that reasonable estimates can be made for k and h.[4] We will explore sensitivity analysis later in the chapter regarding these variables.

We can determine the optimal value for Q, which we call Q^*, the EOQ, by differentiating the equation for total cost with respect to Q and setting the derivative equal to zero.[5]

[4] Let us reaffirm that a reasonable estimate may be quite rough. It is more important to know that setup costs are around \$500 than to try to pin them down at \$437 or \$542. Accuracy is more important than precision.

[5] The derivative of the total cost equation is

$$\frac{dTC}{dQ} = \frac{h}{2} - \frac{kD}{Q^2}$$

Setting the derivative equal to zero gives $h/2 = kD/Q^2$. Solving for Q:

$$Q^* = \sqrt{\frac{2kD}{h}}$$

$$Q^* = \sqrt{\frac{2kD}{h}}$$

To illustrate the EOQ, assume the following data:

Setup cost	\$250 per run
Carrying cost	\$12 per unit per year
Expected annual demand	25,000 units

The EOQ is about 1,021 units:

$$\begin{aligned} Q^* &= \sqrt{\frac{2 \times \$250 \times 25{,}000}{\$12}} \\ &= \sqrt{1{,}041{,}667} \\ &\cong 1{,}021 \end{aligned}$$

The optimal policy is to produce 1,021 units at a time, which means that there will be about 24.5 production runs per year (25,000/1,021). Obviously, this figure is an average because fractional runs are impossible. As a practical matter, the firm will probably make 1,000 units each run.

Using the EOQ, carrying costs equal setup costs, except when quantity discounts apply, as we will illustrate. At the EOQ, total costs are about \$12,248, calculated as follows:

Carrying costs = (1,021/2) × \$12	\$ 6,126
Setup costs = (25,000/1,021) × \$250	6,122
Total costs	\$12,248

Total cost does not change much near the EOQ. You should verify the following using a spreadsheet.

(a)	Runs per year	20	22	24	25	26
(b)	Setup cost = (a) × \$250	\$ 5,000	\$ 5,500	\$ 6,000	\$ 6,250	\$ 6,500
(c)	Units per run = 25,000/(a)	1,250	1,136	1,042	1,000	962
(d)	Average inventory = (c)/2	625	568	521	500	481
(e)	Carrying costs = (d) × \$12	\$ 7,500	\$ 6,816	\$ 6,252	\$ 6,000	\$ 5,772
(f)	Total costs = (b) + (e)	\$12,500	\$12,316	\$12,252	\$12,250	\$12,272

Figure 20–1 confirms the relative insensitivity of total costs to the quantity produced (or, equivalently, to the number of runs per period), by depicting the behavior of costs for the illustration we have been using. Notice the relatively long range over which the total cost curve is fairly flat.

FIGURE 20–1 Cost of Inventory Policy

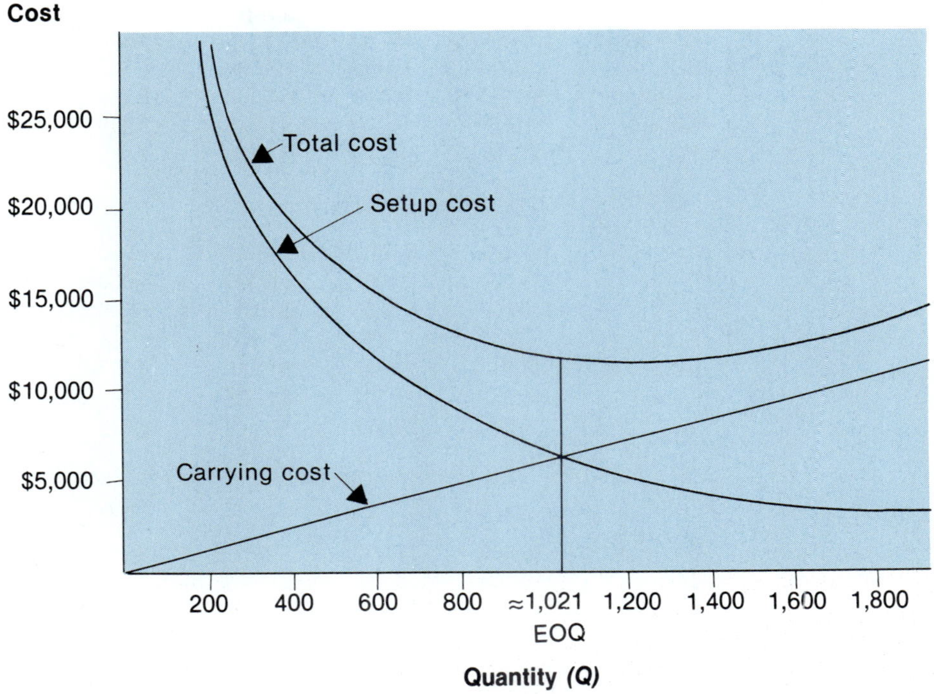

Sensitivity Analysis: Effects of Changes in *h* and *k*

As we shall discuss, managers place considerable emphasis on reducing setup costs. With a heightened awareness of the opportunity costs associated with holding inventory, managers are also raising their estimates of holding costs. Let us look at the effect of changes in holding costs, setup costs, and a combination of the two. Exhibit 20–2 was created using a spreadsheet. You might use a format such as Exhibit 20–2 to vary h and k to other levels to see the effects.

EXHIBIT 20–2 Sensitivity Analysis— Holding and Setup Costs

BASIC DATA		
Holding cost per unit per period	*h*	$12
Expected demand for the period	D	25,000
Setup cost for each run	*k*	$250
Computed total cost	TC	$12,247
Computed EOQ:	EOQ	1,021

SENSITIVITY ANALYSIS: Effect of change in holding cost

h	$12.00	$6.00	$1.00	$25.00	$50.00	$100.00
D	25,000	25,000	25,000	25,000	25,000	25,000
k	$250.00	$250.00	$250.00	$250.00	$250.00	$250.00
EOQ	1,021	1,443	3,536	707	500	354
Holding $	$6,124	$4,330	$1,768	$8,839	$12,500	$17,678
Setup $	$6,124	$4,330	$1,768	$8,839	$12,500	$17,678
TC	$12,247	$8,660	$3,536	$17,678	$25,000	$35,355

SENSITIVITY ANALYSIS: Effect of change in setup cost

h	$12.00	$12.00	$12.00	$12.00	$12.00
D	25,000	25,000	25,000	25,000	25,000
k	$100.00	$50.00	$10.00	$1.00	$0.25
EOQ	645	456	204	65	32
Holding $	$3,873	$2,739	$1,225	$387	$194
Setup $	$3,873	$2,739	$1,225	$387	$194
TC	$7,746	$5,477	$2,449	$775	$387

SENSITIVITY ANALYSIS: Effect of changes in both holding and setup costs

h	$100.00	$100.00
D	25,000	25,000
k	$1.00	$0.25
EOQ	22	11
Holding $	$1,118	$559
Setup $	$1,118	$559
TC	$2,236	$1,118

The base case is the illustration we have been using. As holding costs fall, EOQ rises and total costs fall. As holding costs rise, EOQ falls and total costs rise. As setup costs fall, EOQ falls and total costs fall. Finally, if holding costs rise and setup costs fall, EOQ falls and total costs fall.

There are many reasons that managers want to lower the EOQ. The basic reason is that a low EOQ increases the flexibility of a company to meet current customer needs with a variety of products that can be made in small production runs.

Some practitioners state that unless setup costs are reduced more than 70 to 75 percent, only minor adjustments occur to the EOQ model. Note that when *k* goes from $100 to $50, a 50 percent reduction, EOQ and total costs go down about 29 percent. However, when *k* falls to $10, a 90 percent reduction, EOQ and total costs are down by 68 percent. This kind of a change is a completely different way of thinking. If you are just trying to reduce costs, any reduction in the setup costs helps. However, if you are really trying to change the way you do business, drastic cuts in setup costs are necessary.

Sensitivity Analysis: Cost Estimation

Figure 20–1 shows that total costs do not differ significantly from those at the optimal level as long as the order quantity is reasonably close to the computed EOQ. What happens if the firm bases inventory decisions on the EOQ model but misestimates the costs of setting up and carrying inventory? This is different from the analysis above, where we looked at the effects of real changes in these costs. Now we are dealing with estimation errors and their costs.

Let us assume that the firm incorrectly estimates setup costs at \$500, which is double the original figure of \$250. The cost of making this error is the difference in total cost given the error less the total cost of using the correct EOQ of 1,021 units.

Using the incorrect \$500 setup cost, the firm would set the EOQ at 1,443 units:

$$Q = \sqrt{\frac{2 \times \$500 \times 25{,}000}{\$12}}$$
$$\cong 1{,}443$$

The order quantity of 1,443 units would yield total costs as follows:

Carrying costs, 1,443/2 × \$12	\$ 8,658
Setup costs, 25,000/1,443 × \$250	4,331
Total costs	\$12,989
Cost at correct EOQ	12,248
Difference	\$ 741

The \$741 difference is about 6 percent of the cost of following the EOQ. Thus, a 100 percent error in the estimate of setup costs results in increased costs of about 6 percent. Suppose now that the carrying costs are incorrectly estimated at \$24, rather than \$12, and that setup costs are correctly estimated at \$250. The calculated order quantity would be about 722 units:

$$Q = \sqrt{\frac{2 \times \$250 \times 25{,}000}{\$24}}$$
$$\cong 722$$

At an order quantity of 722, total costs are

Carrying costs, 722/2 × \$12	\$ 4,332
Setup costs, 25,000/722 × \$250	8,657
Total	\$12,989

The cost is the same as for an order quantity of 1,443 units, so it also is about 6 percent over the lowest obtainable cost. Thus, we see that the total cost in this case is not very sensitive to estimation errors of either cost factor. However, in many cases the cost of misestimating could be very high. Incidentally, if the estimation errors were 50 percent low (\$125 for setup, \$6 for carrying) the results would be the same as shown above. That is, halving setup costs has the same effect on the EOQ as doubling carrying costs and vice versa.

Quantity Discounts

Purchased products, materials, and components are often subject to discounts on individual orders exceeding certain specified quantities. For example, the unit price of a component might be $2 for orders under 1,000 units, $1.97 for orders from 1,000 units through 1,999 units, and $1.93 for orders of 2,000 or more. The EOQ model does not consider quantity discounts. They must be worked in ad hoc. Quantity discounts create an additional problem. Part of the carrying cost of an item depends on the cost of the item: carrying costs are not constant amounts per unit. The opportunity cost of funds invested in inventory depends on the cost per unit, as does insurance based on cost, and personal property taxes levied on inventories.[6] Other costs, such as storage, depend on units, not on cost per unit. Thus, some carrying costs will change if the cost of a unit changes, and these changes also must be worked into the analysis.

Suppose the product that we have been dealing with is purchased, not made. The $250 setup cost is now the incremental cost of placing and handling a single order. Suppose further that the price per unit is $100 for orders up to 5,000 units, $99 for orders of 5,000 through 12,499 units, and $98 for orders of 12,500 or more units. Finally, assume that $2 of annual per unit carrying costs are constant per unit, and that the remaining $10 consists of interest, insurance, and other costs that are 10 percent of the purchase price. Thus, carrying costs will drop to $11.90 if the firm pays $99 for each unit [$2 + (0.10 × $99)] and to $11.80 if the price is $98 [$2 + (0.10 × $98)].

We already know that the EOQ without considering quantity discounts is 1,021 units. We also know the cost of following this policy. All we need to do to determine the new EOQ is to test the costs, including the quantity discounts, of following policies of buying 5,000 units at a time and 12,500 units at a time to see which is the least expensive overall. The schedule below shows the costs of each policy.

(a)	Order size	1,020	5,000	12,500
(b)	Number of orders per year = 25,000/(a)	24.5	5	2
(c)	Order cost = $250 × (b)	$ 6,125	$ 1,250	$ 500

[6] For manufactured goods, the opportunity cost of funds tied up in inventory depends on incremental production costs. Allocated fixed costs that are not incremental are irrelevant because they are incurred at any level of production within the relevant range. However, if taxes and insurance or other carrying costs are based on absorption costs, the allocated fixed costs must be considered, because they affect the amounts of relevant costs. The situation is analogous to the role of depreciation in capital budgeting; it does not affect cash flows per se but affects income taxes that are cash flows.

(d) Average inventory			
= (a)/2	510	2,500	6,250
(e) Carrying costs			
= $12 × (d)	$ 6,120		
= $11.90 × (d)		$29,750	
= $11.80 × (d)			$73,750
(f) Quantity discount			
= $1 × 25,000		($25,000)	
= $2 × 25,000			($50,000)
(g) Total costs			
= (c) + (e) − (f)	$12,245	$ 6,000	$24,250

The results show that buying 5,000 units five times per year is the least-cost policy. The additional $25,000 quantity discount that could be obtained by ordering 12,500 units twice a year is more than offset by increased carrying costs. In some cases there may be savings in manufacturing large quantities at one time, rather than making smaller quantities more often. The analysis shown here can be applied to those situations. We illustrated the analysis using quantity discounts on purchased items because that is a more prevalent source of savings.

REPLENISHMENT POINT

We have considered the effects of set up and carrying costs to this point. The third set of costs, those associated with stockouts, raises the question when to replenish inventory stocks. The *replenishment point*, often called the *reorder point*, is the level of inventory at which an order is placed. For the finished product of a manufacturer it is the level of finished goods that triggers a production order. At individual work stations, the replenishment point is the level of in-process inventory that triggers additional production. For materials, purchased components, and merchandise, it is the point at which a purchase requisition is initiated, and an order sent to a supplier.

Some companies have standing orders from ongoing customers to deliver goods. They have fairly level production on a daily basis and, barring equipment breakdown, need a steady flow of materials. Other companies generate purchase orders on a more sporadic basis as a reorder point is reached. In both cases, managers need to be aware of the lead time for an order. *Lead time* is the period, usually measured in days, required from initiating an order to receiving the goods. As with setup costs, managers try to reduce lead times to remain competitive with other manufacturers, both domestic and foreign.

Because units are being withdrawn during the lead time, it is necessary to place an order before inventory goes to zero. In addition, the demand for units during the lead time might be greater than normal, or the lead time might be longer than usual. Both factors argue for the use of safety stock. **Safety stock** is the amount of inventory carried in excess of the expected use

FIGURE 20–2, PART (a) Inventory Behavior under Certainty*

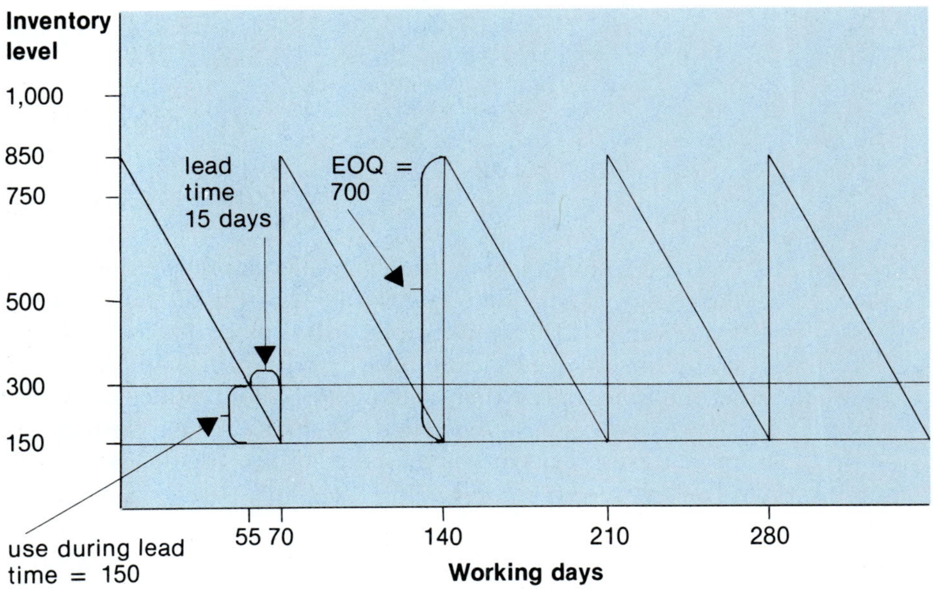

*Assumptions: EOQ = 700; lead time = 15 days; average use = 10 units per day; replenishment point = 300 units; safety stock = 150 units.

during the lead time to provide a cushion and guard against stockouts. Thus, the replenishment point is the sum of the expected use during the lead time and the safety stock. In equation form

$$RP = (\text{average daily use} \times \text{lead time in days}) + \text{safety stock}$$

where

RP = the replenishment point

It is possible to express the lead time and average use in weeks or months. For some items the lead time might be quite long. In most cases, lead times are short enough to use days, usually working days rather than calendar days. The average daily use is simply the expected demand for the period divided by the number of working days in the period.

The behavior of the level of inventory under certainty is shown in Figure 20–2, Part (a). Notice that there is no need to have safety stock under certainty because the use during the lead time is always equal to 150 units, the daily use of 15 units multiplied by the lead time of 10 days. Figure 20–2, Part (b) shows the behavior under uncertainty. The declines in inventory are not always the same each day, and the lead time is not always the same. Even with safety stock, there is some probability of running out, as occurs on the third cycle in Figure 20–2, Part (b).

FIGURE 20–2, PART (b) Inventory Behavior under Uncertainty*

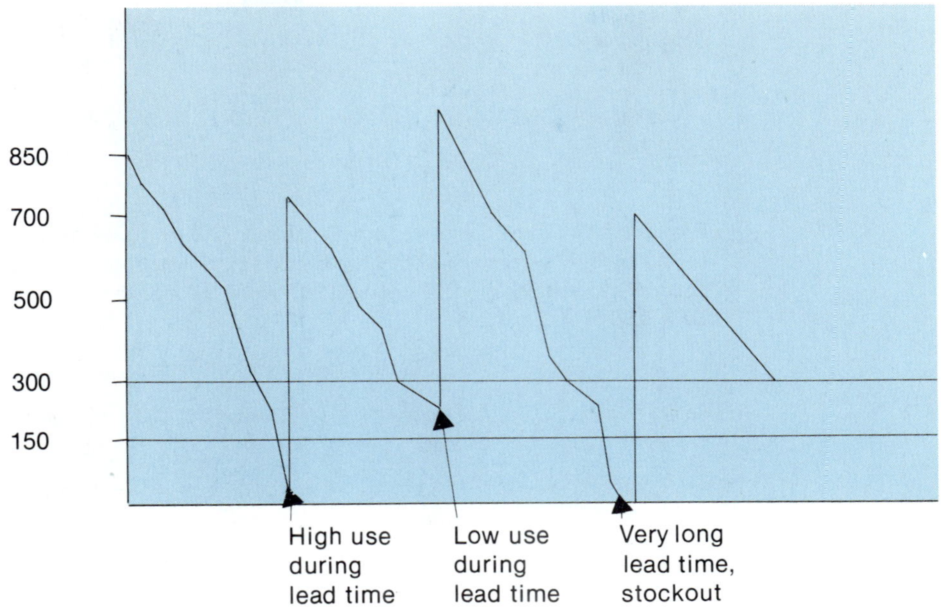

*Assumptions: Same as for Figure 20–2, Part (a) but daily demand and lead time are uncertain.

Determining the replenishment point under uncertainty could involve some very sophisticated methods. We shall illustrate two fairly straightforward ones. Our objective in determining the replenishment point is to minimize the sum of the carrying costs on safety stock and the costs of stockouts. Recall that the basic EOQ model does not consider the cost of carrying safety stock. The EOQ is independent of the replenishment point, and the costs of holding safety stock are not incremental to the EOQ but only to the quantity of safety stock carried.

Setting the amount of safety stock requires the use of expected values. Assume the following data from historical records.

The number of orders placed per year (determined using EOQ) is 20.

Use During Lead Time	*Probability*
1,000	0.30
1,100	0.60
1,200	0.10

Estimated stockout cost per unit (excess of air freight over trucking and other expediting costs)	$2
Estimated carrying cost per unit per year	$6

EXHIBIT 20–3 Replenishment Point

Expected Stockouts per Year

Replenishment Point	Use During Lead Time 1,000	1,100	1,200	Stockouts
1,000	0	1,200	400	1,600
1,100	0	0	200	200
1,200	0	0	0	0

Each calculation is the number of orders per year (20) multiplied by the probability of use during the lead time multiplied by the number of units short. For example, for a policy of replenishing at 1,000 units and use during the lead time of 1,100, we have 20 × 0.60 × 100 = 1,200.

Costs of Replenishment Policies

Replenishment Point	Safety Stock	Stockout Costs	Carrying Costs	Total Costs
1,000	0	$3,200	$6,000	$9,200
1,100	100	400	6,600	7,000
1,200	200	0	7,200	7,200

The firm could adopt any number of replenishment points, including ones that would virtually guarantee stockouts, such as any point substantially less than 1,000 units. It might be economical to allow stockouts if stockout costs are near zero. That is not the case for the firm in our example, as can be seen in Exhibit 20–3. The expected stockouts when the replenishment point is set at each of the possible values of use during the lead time appear there, along with the costs of following each policy. For example, if the replenishment point is 1,100 units, the firm has 100 units of safety stock above the minimum expected demand, giving carrying costs of $600 (100 × $6), while it would expect stockouts of 100 units twice a year (20 orders × 0.10 probability of demand's being 1,200 units), giving expected stockout costs of $400.

The policy of ordering when inventory is 1,100 units provides the lowest total cost. This policy gives safety stock of 100 units above the minimum expected use during the lead time.

In this example the uncertainty was not specifically identified with either the lead time or the average daily use. It could be that the lead time is known to be 10 days and that average daily demand is either 100, 110, or 120 units. Or it could be that the average daily demand is always 100 units, but the lead time could be 10, 11, or 12 days. Either situation gives the same total use figures. In practice, there are likely to be uncertainties regarding both factors, and then the joint probabilities must be calculated. An example appears in Exhibit 20–4. Appendix 20A contains a review of marginal, conditional, and

EXHIBIT 20–4 Sample Calculations of Probabilities of Use During Lead Time

Data

Lead Time in Days	*Probability*	*Average Daily Use*	*Probability*
8	0.20	80	0.10
9	0.50	110	0.70
10	0.30	130	0.20

Uses and Joint Probabilities

Lead Time	*Average Daily Use*	*Total Use*	*Joint Probability*
8	80	640	0.02
9	80	720	0.05
10	80	800	0.03
8	110	880	0.14
9	110	990	0.35
10	110	1,100	0.21
8	130	1,040	0.04
9	130	1,170	0.10
10	130	1,300	0.06
Total probabilities			1.00

Each joint probability is the product of the probabilities of each of the two events, lead time and daily use. For example, the joint probability of a lead time of eight days combined with daily use of 80 units is $0.20 \times 0.10 = 0.02$.

joint probabilities. Obviously, in real situations there are many possible levels of use during the lead time.

Service Levels

When the probability distribution of use during the lead time is continuous, or contains so many possible values that calculation by hand is awkward, managers might simply set the safety stock at a level that provides for stockouts less than some specified percentage of the time, say five or 10 percent. For example, suppose that demand during lead time is normally distributed with mean of 1,000 units and standard deviation of 150 units. The firm's managers have set a policy of replenishing inventory soon enough to keep stockouts from occurring more than 10 percent of the time. Thus, we wish to find the number of standard deviations that corresponds to a 10 percent level of probability of being exceeded just in one tail. We use a one-tail test because we are concerned only with cases where demand is high during the lead time, not where it is low.

Using Table A–1 in Appendix A at the back of the book, we find that the probability of 10 percent in one tail corresponds to about 1.28 standard deviations. We are searching for the standard deviation such that 40 percent of the area above the mean is included within the range z to the mean. Using this information, the managers will set the replenishment point at

$$1{,}000 + (150 \times 1.28) = 1{,}192$$

This approach to determining the replenishment point does not involve explicit consideration of the costs of safety stock and of stockouts. It is simply a policy that the company adopts without explicitly considering costs. Of course, the percentage limit is set with some regard for costs. A manager does not want to be stocked out of a high-use item that goes into many products because stocking out could shut down the whole line. A manager is more willing to stockout of a little-used component.

THE NEW COMPETITIVE AND MANUFACTURING ENVIRONMENT

In recent years, foreign companies have competed successfully in U.S. markets. In the automobile industry, not only have U.S. companies lost market share to Japanese companies, but also the Big Three auto makers import cars made by other manufacturers in other countries. For example, a Chrysler product might have been made by Mitsubishi in Japan. Among other things, this is a sign that U.S. costs are higher than those in Japan. In the television and electronics industries, the combination of quality and price has all but eliminated U.S. production;[7] the market is dominated by Japanese and Korean companies. Their lower costs of production (and higher quality) are related not only to wage rate and cultural differences, but also to different philosophies of management. This difference can be seen in the several Japanese owned plants in the United States.

Toyota was one of the pioneers in changing basic management philosophy in Japan. Just-in-time inventory, Kanban, and a flexible work force helped Toyota reach its goals: the right quantity of defect-free goods, at the right time, at low cost.

Just-in-Time

Just-in-time (JIT) inventory and production is not a new concept. It is based on having inventory available only when needed. Take a local bottler of soft drinks, for example. Empty bottles take up space, have little value, and are

[7] As of 1989, no U.S. producer made television picture tubes in the United States.

costly to store. It has been the norm for years that bottle suppliers deliver bottles as they are needed on the production line. The recent emphasis on JIT involves more than delivery of goods to a purchaser so that they are used immediately instead of stockpiled; the philosophy now involves all aspects of purchasing and manufacturing. Chapter 1 introduced some principles of advanced manufacturing; we elaborate some of these in the following sections.

Let us take a company with a single product that goes through five departments before it gets to the shipping department. As goods in the shipping department reach a specific level (reorder point), finished goods are produced by Department 5. As components in Department 5 fall below a certain level, Department 4 works to replenish them. This same backwards set of signals goes all the way to the purchasing function. This is called a *pull* system; nothing is done until needed by the next department.

Part of this concept is to reduce all support department costs and in-process inventories as much as possible. Proponents of JIT argue that many companies keep large buffers of work in process to even out scheduling and to adjust for parts that will be rejected during inspection. Thus, if a company attacks its scheduling problems and has higher quality, it can substantially reduce or eliminate work-in-process inventories.

Work flow and scheduling have at least two dimensions. First, many companies organize their productive facilities by machine type. This means that in-process goods must travel from department to department as they require machines of different kinds. While in some firms this system makes sense, in others such a layout causes high inventories. It takes time to store goods, remove them from storage, and move them around the plant. Second, the focus on cost centers and individual worker performance and responsibility can contribute to uneven and inflexible scheduling.

The manufacturing cell helps managers eliminate work in process. A cell is a mini-factory within the plant. It consists of all the machinery and people needed to manufacture a specific group of components. Rather than moving a component back and forth to different machine areas, all the machinery for one or more types of component is brought to one place. As part of this change, workers typically are part of a cell production team. This is the flexibility referred to about Toyota. No longer is one person responsible for one type of machine while another is responsible for another type. Now, all the workers within a manufacturing cell work on all positions within the cell. Thus, idle time is reduced and work in process is virtually eliminated. In one midwestern plant making parts for the replacement automotive market, the change to cells freed up almost one-third of the plant and allowed the parent company to move a whole other production line to that plant.

Kanban

A technique for managing JIT is Kanban, a regular signal that tells managers when to produce and how much to produce. Briefly, a *Kanban* is a tag attached to the containers or racks on which components are kept. Let us again use the example of a company with a single product and five producing departments.

As parts in a container in department 3 are being used, a worker takes the Kanban and places it in a box with other Kanban for that component. As with other techniques for a reorder point, managers set a number of Kanban as a signal to replenish. Empty containers and the same number of Kanban are taken to the prior department, department 2. An equal number of full containers are withdrawn from department 2. Each of these new containers has a production Kanban attached to it. The worker who is withdrawing these containers takes the production Kanban and the Kanban she has brought with her (withdrawal Kanban) and places them in a box in department 2. These are accumulated in department 2 until a predetermined level is reached, which signals production of the component. Production of these components is kept in department 2 until department 3 withdraws them as described above. This same process flows from the shipping area to the purchasing function.

Management wants to minimize inventory costs using Kanban as a control technique. Besides deciding on the replenishment point, managers can calculate the total number of Kanban (containers of components) needed for the system to operate. Exhibit 20–5 shows the formula for determining this amount and sensitivity analysis to see how different variables affect the system. This exhibit is presented in terms of days. The formulas can be adjusted to show everything in terms of an hour. The objective is to have a low number of containers (Kanban) in the system. If waiting time can be reduced, inventory

EXHIBIT 20–5 Determining Kanban

Basic Kanban Formula

$$n = \frac{Q(T_w + T_p)(1 + r)}{c}$$

Where

n = total number of Kanban in the system

Q = average demand, quantity per day

T_w = waiting time along the production lines (days)

T_p = time needed for processing and withdrawal of parts (days)

r = indicator of inefficiency at the shop

c = container capacity

Base Case

Q	5,000	5,000	5,000	5,000	5,000	5,000
T_w	1	0.5	0.125	0.125	0.125	0.125
T_p	0.0625	0.0625	0.0625	0.03125	0.03125	0.03125
r	0.25	0.25	0.25	0.25	0.5	0.1
c	250	250	250	250	250	250
n	26.56	14.06	4.69	3.91	4.69	3.44
n rounded	27	14	5	4	5	3
Total parts	6,750	3,500	1,250	1,000	1,250	750

levels are reduced. The same is true for processing and withdrawal of parts. The term r is used as a safety mechanism given uncertainties in the other factors as well as uncertainties about the efficiency of a particular department. In the short run, Kanban are not expanded even if average demand rises. Managers try to cut back on waiting and processing times. Under steady demand, if waiting or processing times increase, the number of Kanban increase and managers have to explain why inventory is growing.

Push Versus Pull Inventories

JIT and Kanban *pull* inventory through production. In the strictest sense, the only department that knows a production schedule is the shipping department. All other departments produce based on inventory being pulled from the end of the production line. This is contrasted to a *push* system where goods are manufactured for inventory. The production schedule is known throughout the plant. Manufacturing in all departments is geared toward a daily output figure.

Advocates of the pull system claim to have better line balancing; there is less buffer inventory and better utilization of capacity. This causes dual savings. Not only are there savings in raw material, work in process, and finished goods inventories (and their attendant space and support costs), but also a more balanced line means that less overall capacity is needed and a lower investment in capital and human resources. Part and parcel of this process is worker flexibility. Workers have to be able to move from one area to another (even outside their cells) to go where they are needed.

Summary—The New Environment

Managers are increasingly sensitive about support-department costs. Some managers categorize all support-department costs as *non-value added*. These are compared to *value-added* costs of material, direct labor, and the cost of productive assets, for example. To become more competitive, managers are looking for new ways to arrange production equipment (e.g., manufacturing cells) and to reduce inventory costs. Inventory has been targeted because it is a significant cost to most companies. There are opportunity costs associated with holding inventory; relying on large production runs limits a company's ability to adjust rapidly to needs in the market. Therefore, JIT, Kanban, and other methods are employed to lower costs while raising quality.

Some behavioral implications are associated with JIT. As stated earlier, JIT is more of a philosophy than a specific technique. Philosophies only work if everyone from the factory workers to the president believes they can work and makes an effort to make them work. Successful implementation of JIT can also mean changes in basic management style such as including workers in many production decisions.[8]

---

[8] For example, many U.S. companies have adopted Japanese style quality control circles.

OTHER TECHNIQUES

The use of EOQ and various models for setting the replenishment point can be very costly. We have already mentioned that firms may have a manager whose principal job is inventory control, which indicates its importance. However, inventory control is not equally important for all products, components, and materials. A low-volume product that is not essential to the sales of other products does not require constant attention. Managers do not need to watch a material or component with low value that can be stored outside as carefully as a high-value item.

ABC Method Managers recognize the benefits and costs of various levels of control by using the ABC method. Inventoried items are classified A, B, or C depending on their value. High-value products are classified as A's and are watched carefully; low-value products are classified as C's and given little attention. Those classified as B's fall in the middle. In some firms, the percentages of products are inversely related to their total dollar volume. For instance, 10 percent of the products might account for 65 percent of sales, while 70 percent of them contribute only 20 percent of sales. Formal models could be used in the A's and eyeballing techniques used for the C's. The items classified as B's might receive more regular review and analysis than the C's but less than the A's.

In general, the ABC method works best with finished products. Low-value materials and components might be essential in the production process, and shortages could cause high stockout costs. A way to deal with these items is to keep them in two bins. When one bin is empty, an order is placed and the contents of the other bin are used. The order will usually be received before that bin is empty. Variations on this method include placing tags in stacks of items. When the unit just above the tag is removed, the tag is sent to the purchasing department, which will order another batch. The height at which the tag is placed indicates the relative value of the item: the higher in the stack, the higher the replenishment point. In some senses, this is a crude Kanban application.

Perpetual Inventory Methods Firms that keep perpetual inventory records frequently set a replenishment point that triggers an order. This method relies on the records, not on a physical count as do the two-bin method and its variations. Its accuracy, therefore, depends on the accuracy of the perpetual inventory records. The elaborate cash registers now in use in many stores not only record the sales, but also update perpetual inventory records through computer linkages.

Managers may receive printouts daily that show the quantities of each product on hand as well as information on sales. The data help managers to determine which products are moving rapidly or slowly and can be used as the basis for replenishing. Sales personnel also use these data to make tactical decisions on special prices or special promotion on slow-moving items.

PERISHABLE PRODUCTS

A special problem arises when a firm deals in perishable products. The term *perishable* refers to economic life, not necessarily to physical life. Thus, fresh fruits and vegetables are physically and economically perishable. Newspapers, magazines, and programs for athletic and cultural events are economically perishable even though physically they might last for years. Very few day-old newspapers or month-old magazines are sold. The general problem is determining the quantity to order or make when unsold units must be disposed of at a loss. Again, the problem involves expected values and risk-return trade-offs.

Illustration of Perishable Products

Ascot Company makes a variety of products, including fad items. It has developed a toy that managers think could be a big seller at Christmas but will have almost no sales afterward. The managers must decide now how many units to produce, because the firm will not be able to produce more and get them into the department stores once the selling season starts. The firm will charge retailers \$20 for each toy, but it will also agree to take back any unsold units by January 10 of the coming year. The variable cost of production is \$7, and returned toys can be sold for \$2 each in bulk lots. Based on previous sales of similar items and other analyses, the sales manager has made the following forecasts and estimated probabilities. To make the calculations tractable, we have limited to four the values that demand can take on. We shall consider more realistic continuous distributions in the next section.

Demand	*Probability*
10,000	0.10
12,000	0.40
14,000	0.30
16,000	0.20
Total	1.00

Managers often use payoff tables to solve problems of this sort. Payoff tables are similar to decision trees and easier to work with when several actions are possible. We assume for now the firm can produce, or the manager has decided to produce, one of the quantities given above. That is, the firm will not produce 13,000 units, or 12,400 units, but one of the estimated levels of demand.

The payoff table appears in Exhibit 20–6. Each entry is the profit that the firm expects to earn, given the demand and the quantity produced. The figures are conditional values because they depend on the action (production) and the event (demand). The table at the bottom of Exhibit 20–6 shows the

EXHIBIT 20–6 Payoff Table for Production Strategies—Ascot Company

Profit—Conditional Values

	Strategy (Production)				
Demand	*10,000*	*12,000*	*14,000*	*16,000*	*Probability*
10,000	$130,000	$120,000	$110,000	$100,000	0.10
12,000	130,000	156,000	146,000	136,000	0.40
14,000	130,000	156,000	182,000	172,000	0.30
16,000	130,000	156,000	182,000	208,000	0.20

The quantity sold is the lesser of demand or production. If demand is equal to or greater than production, profit is simply production × $13. If production exceeds demand, the calculations are: (demand × $13) − [(production − demand) × $5] or (demand × $20) − (production × $7) + [(production − demand) × $2]. For example, if 14,000 units are produced and 12,000 sold, (12,000 × $13) − (2,000 × $5) = $146,000.

Expected Values of Profit (Conditional Values × Probabilities)

		Production			
Demand	*Probability*	*10,000*	*12,000*	*14,000*	*16,000*
10,000	0.10	$ 13,000	$ 12,000	$ 11,000	$ 10,000
12,000	0.40	52,000	62,400	58,400	54,400
14,000	0.30	39,000	46,800	54,600	51,600
16,000	0.20	26,000	31,200	36,400	41,600
Total	1.00	$130,000	$152,400	$160,400	$157,600

Note: When the conditional values for several levels of demand are the same, you can simply add the probabilities of the equal conditional values and multiply the sum by the conditional value. For example, the expected value of the strategy of producing 12,000 units is ($120,000 × 0.10) + ($156,000 × 0.90) = $152,400.

expected values of profit for each production strategy. Using the expected-value criterion, the firm would produce 14,000 units.[9]

If demand is greater than production, then the company will be able to sell all of the units it produced. In fact, if demand exceeds production, it does not matter by how much, because sales are limited to the number of units produced. However, if demand is less than production, the company will be

[9] Notice that the expected value of profits under each action, except producing 10,000 units, is not equal to any one of the profit figures that could occur. For example, the expected profit of $160,400 from producing 14,000 units cannot be realized under our assumptions: it does not correspond to the conditional profit for any level of demand. This occurs because of the assumption that demand can take on only one of four values.

able to sell only the quantity demanded at the \$20 price and will have to sell the remaining units at the \$2 return price.

Selecting the action with the greatest expected value is only one possible decision rule. The expected-value criterion for selection depends on the law of large numbers. It assumes that the decision recurs often enough so that the events will occur in proportion to their assessed probabilities. However, Ascot Company faces this decision only once. Consider an analogy in a different setting. Suppose that someone offered you the opportunity to toss a fair coin, heads you win \$20,000, tails you lose \$5,000. The expected value of the game is \$7,500 [\$20,000(0.50) − \$5,000(0.50)]. You probably would not play the game if you had only one chance, because you could lose \$5,000. But if you could play it 1,000 or so times, you probably would, because the number of heads would be fairly close to half of the tosses. Playing the game only once, or even six to eight times, does not give the laws of probability enough time to operate in your favor.

Earlier we introduced the concept of variance and its role in decision making. It is obvious from Exhibit 20–6 that the variance of profit increases as production increases. The strategy of producing 10,000 units has a zero variance, with all values equal to the expected value of \$130,000. This strategy is the safest. Every other has some probability of showing profits below \$130,000. A very risk-averse manager might select 10,000 units for that reason.

A venturesome manager might decide to produce 16,000 units because of the possibility of a \$208,000 profit. Managers using the same information may arrive at different decisions because they have different attitudes about risk and return, a point that we have made many times.

Value of Information

Suppose now that the example we have been using is for daily or weekly activity, so the expected value of profit becomes a stronger decision criterion than it is under the assumption of a unique event. How much would a manager be willing to pay to forecast demand accurately and thereby know in advance how many units to produce? While it is rare that a manager could obtain perfect information, it is also rare that he could not obtain *some* information that would narrow down the possible events or improve probability estimates. Let us first look at the value of perfect information, which is the extreme case but nonetheless instructive. First, if our example were for a firm that made production decisions weekly, the firm would probably make 14,000 units per week because that would give the highest expected profit over a good number of weeks. The value of perfect information is the difference between expected profits with perfect information and the expected profits given the optimal strategy without perfect information.

If the managers of Ascot Company knew demand in advance, they would produce the quantity to be demanded. The expected value of profit is then the sum of the elements on the main diagonal (upper left to lower right) of the payoff table that shows expected values of profit—that is, \$13,000 + \$62,400 + \$54,600 + \$41,600 = \$171,600. The expected value of perfect information is then \$11,200 (\$171,600 − \$160,400). Look at it slightly differently. Out of each 10 weeks the firm would sell 10,000 units once (0.10), 12,000 units four times (0.40), and so on. Thus, because they would produce exactly what was demanded, the firm would show profits of \$130,000 once, \$156,000 four times, \$182,000 three times, and \$208,000 twice. Total profits for the 10 weeks would then be \$1,716,000. (The \$1,716,000 is also \$171,600 multiplied by 10.) If the firm produced 14,000 units each week it would expect to earn \$110,000 once, \$146,000 four times, and \$182,000 five times, for total profits of \$1,604,000, which is \$112,000 less than \$1,716,000. Hence the value of perfect information for each of the 10 weeks is \$11,200 (\$112,000/10).

Obviously, perfect information is hard to come by. However, sample information is usually available. Market research surveys and test marketing are methods of acquiring additional information and perhaps of narrowing the range of the probability distribution.

A General Approach

The perishable-products problem can be approached more generally than by using payoff tables. The analytical method that we describe here can be used for both discrete and continuous probability distributions and has some characteristics that make it adaptable to practical use.

First, to maximize profits the firm must set production or purchases so that the expected value of selling an additional unit equals the expected value of the loss of making or buying the unit but not selling it. The expected value of selling the unit is the contribution margin multiplied by the probability of selling the unit, and the expected value of the loss is the variable cost minus salvage value multiplied by the probability of not selling the unit. The probability of not selling the unit is $(1 - p)$, where p is the probability of selling the unit. In equation form, the expected value of profit is maximized when

$$cp = h(1 - p)$$

where c = contribution margin per unit

h = the loss sustained if a unit is not sold, which is variable cost per unit less salvage value per unit, if any

$$cp = h - hp$$

$$p = \frac{h}{c + h}$$

In words, the critical value of p is the ratio of the loss on unsold units to the sum of the contribution margin and loss. The firm that seeks to maximize the expected value of profits will produce up to the critical value of p. In the Ascot Company case, the values are as follows: $c = \$13$, $h = \$5$. Solving for p:

$$p = \frac{\$5}{\$13 + \$5} = .278$$

Ascot Company should produce to the point where the probability of selling at least one additional unit is 0.278. This is another way of saying that it should produce up to the point where the cumulative probability of demand's being less than production is 0.722, which is 1 − 0.278. Let us look at the probability distribution for Ascot.

Demand	*Probability*	*Cumulative Probability*
10,000	0.10	0.10
12,000	0.40	0.50
14,000	0.30	0.80
16,000	0.20	1.00

The cumulative probability column shows the total probability that demand will be equal to or less than each level of demand. Thus, there is an 80 percent probability that demand will be equal to or less than 14,000 units. The critical ratio, 0.278, is greater than the probability of demand's being 16,000 units. It is also greater than the probability of demand's exceeding 14,000 units, because the only level of demand above 14,000 units is 16,000 units. The ratio indicates that the optimal level of production is somewhat below 14,000 units, but because this example is limited to four discrete levels of demand, 14,000 units is the optimal production quantity. At production of 12,000 units there is a 50 percent probability that demand will exceed production, which is considerably greater than the 27.8 percent value that we seek.

The critical value of p is easier to interpret when demand is more realistically assumed to take on a continuous probability distribution. Obviously, most firms will not find demand limited to four values. The problem with using continuous probability distributions is that calculating expected profits from following a strategy requires a computer and a great many calculations. Suppose that a manager believes that demand is reasonably well described as normally distributed with mean of 10,000 and standard deviation of 1,800. To calculate expected profits with production of 11,000 units requires a separate calculation for each possible level of demand. Each calculation is the profit at that level of demand, given production of 11,000 units, multiplied by the probability of occurrence of that level of demand. Even though it would be reasonable to use, say, intervals of five or 10 units instead of one unit, the calculations would be overwhelming if done by hand.

However, determining the optimal production level is straightforward. Assume that a firm faces the demand distribution just stated, mean of 10,000 and standard deviation of 1,800, and that the critical value for p is 0.278. The optimal level of production is shown visually in Figure 20–3. The objective is to find the number of standard deviations from the mean that corresponds to

FIGURE 20–3 Probability Distribution of Demand

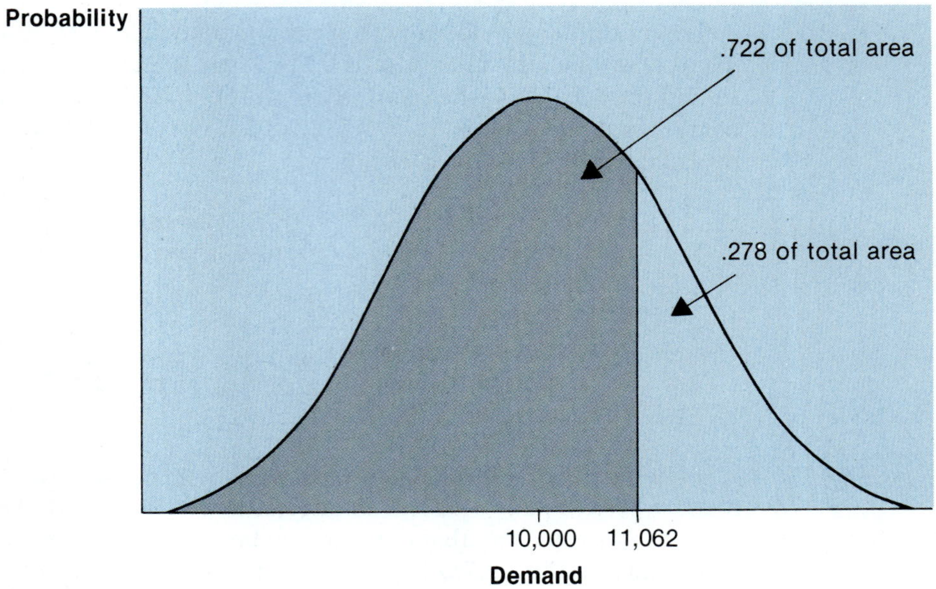

0.278 of the area under the curve falling to the right. From Table A–1 we find that the z value for the standard deviation is about 0.59. (We are looking for the z value where 22.2 percent of the area lies between the mean and z. The 22.2% is $1 - 0.50 - 0.278$. Therefore, we look for the value closest to 0.222, which is at 0.59 standard deviations.) Optimal production is then 11,062 units, which is $10,000 + 0.59(1,800)$.

This method does not require a complete specification of the probability distribution of demand. It only requires an estimate of the demand level corresponding to (or reasonably close to) the critical value of the probability of selling an additional unit.

In some cases, a manager may be willing to make statements about the probability that demand will be greater than some particular amount, even though she is unwilling to make estimates about means, standard deviations, or the shape of the probability distribution of demand. For instance, a sales manager may be willing to say that there is about 30 percent probability of demand's being greater than 20,000 units, a 50 percent probability of its exceeding 17,000 units. In a situation such as this, the data developed by the cost accountant could be very helpful. Suppose that the accountant has estimated contribution margin at \$12 and the loss on unsold units at \$2. The critical value for the probability of selling an additional unit is 0.143, which is \$2/\$14. Thus, the optimal policy is to produce the quantity that gives a 0.143 probability that demand will exceed production. The sales manager may have no idea what the demand is, but if she is confident that the probability of demand's being greater than 20,000 is about 0.30, then a level of production somewhat above 20,000 units is likely to be a reasonable level. If the critical ratio were 0.45, then somewhere around 17,000 units would be indicated.

Practical Considerations

We mentioned earlier that illustrating the concept of expected value requires unrealistic data. Few firms would face only four levels of demand. The calculations required for a more realistic probability distribution are easy to handle on a computer. However, the question of the value of probabilistic techniques remains. The essential question is whether managers can make reasonably accurate estimates of the probability distributions of demand.

Some firms can probably do so with reasonable success. Publishers of newspapers and magazines amass a great deal of experience in estimating newsstand sales. Bakeries and other perishable food producers also gain a good deal of experience in estimating probable levels of demand. One of the points made in Chapter 15 on budgeting can be fruitfully repeated here. Managers must make decisions. They must, for example, decide on levels of output. A manager's subjective judgment or feel is one basis for deciding, but it is haphazard and likely to be inconsistent.

Market research techniques offer ways to elicit probabilistic statements regarding demand. Firms will frequently test-market a product in a relatively small geographic area to see how well it does before committing themselves to major marketing efforts. Test marketing is one way to obtain sample information. Perfect information is rarely obtainable, no matter what the cost. Over a reasonable period, it is likely that such sample information will help managers to make better decisions.

The Accountant's Role

Managers need information for decision making. Inventory-related costs are part of product costs for financial accounting, cost of products for managerial decision making, operational control, and special studies. Accountants are faced with a new array of methods to capture data and new challenges to quantify opportunity costs associated with inventories. While accountants might not be charged with determining an EOQ or the proper number of Kanban, they will help develop relevant information for the technical and operating personnel who will make these decisions.

The accountant will increasingly take on a role beyond providing just financial data—costs. He or she will be the focal point for all quantitative and qualitative information that managers need.

SUMMARY

Inventory control is important because the cost of inventory is significant. Managers are becoming more aware of opportunity costs associated with high inventory levels. Accountants can help operating managers accumulate and analyze information and present their conclusions to other managers. Accountants can help maintain existing inventory systems such as EOQ, and can aid in the success of new ways of dealing with inventory, like JIT. Finally, since accountants may be more at ease with numerical information, they can explain payoff tables and other ways of dealing with uncertainty to other managers.

REVIEW PROBLEM[10]

Bolton Company has the following expected results for one of its major components:

Annual use	250,000 units
Incremental order cost	$250
Purchase price	$24 per unit
Holding cost	26.5% of purchase price

REQUIRED

1. Determine the EOQ and the annual ordering cost, holding cost, and total cost when this policy is followed. Use BOLTON.WK1 to calculate the EOQ and total costs. This template is illustrated in Exhibit 20–7, with instructions for use.
2. View and print out the graph named EOQ. Change the increment from 20 to 5 and view and print out the graph named EOQ. Leaving the increment at 5, view and print out the graph named TCSENS. As a result of these graphs and the figures generated on the template, discuss the costs of ordering at figures different than the EOQ.

ANSWERS TO REVIEW PROBLEM

1. The EOQ is about 4,433 with a total cost of $28,196 as shown in Exhibit 20–8. Row 26 of that exhibit shows annual ordering costs, holding costs, and total costs at the EOQ.

[10]The format for this problem comes from James E. Hopson, Donald R. Gibson, and Steven M. Zimmerman, "Simplifying the Use of the Economic Order Quantity Formula to Control Inventory Cost," *Journal of Cost Management for the Manufacturing Industry*, Winter 1990, pp. 8–12.

EXHIBIT 20–7 Bolton Company

```
                          BOLTON.WK1
 1      B          C        D         E         F         G         H
 2 Exhibit 20-7
 3 Bolton Company
 4
 5 DATA SECTION
 6
 7 Annual demand                   250,000 units
 8 Incremental ordering cost       $250.00
 9 Purchase price                    $24.00 per unit
10 Annual carrying cost               26.50% of purchase price
11
12 SOLUTION SECTION
13
14 EOQ                                                  Increment       20
15 EOQ rounded
16
17 EOQ Graph
18                                                                Percent
19  Percent     Order     Order   Holding     Total                Change
20   of EOQ      Size      Cost      Cost      Cost            Total Cost
21
22       20      0.00                            $0
23       40      0.00                             0
24       60      0.00                             0
25       80      0.00                             0
26      100      0.00                             0
27      120      0.00                             0
28      140      0.00                             0
29      160      0.00                             0
30      180      0.00                             0
```

Instructions for BOLTON.WK1

1. Fill in the EOQ formula in cell E14. Cells C22 through C30 should then show the EOQ plus or minus the percents shown in column B.
2. Fill in the annual ordering cost formula in cell D22 and the annual holding cost formula in cell E22. Cell F22 should then show the total annual costs. Copy cells D22 and E22 so that the rest of the table is filled in.
3. Note that the table will identify the minimum cost as well as percentage deviations from the minimum cost.
4. Viewing graphs is accomplished by /GNU command in Lotus 1-2-3. Graphs should be saved and printed.

EXHIBIT 20–8 Bolton Company— Solution of Review Problem

```
1        B          C          D         E          F          G          H
2 Exhibit 20-8
3 Bolton Company
4
5 DATA SECTION
6
7 Annual demand                      250,000 units
8 Incremental ordering cost          $250.00
9 Purchase price                      $24.00 per unit
10 Annual carrying cost                26.50% of purchase price
11
12 SOLUTION SECTION
13
14 EOQ                               4433.293             Increment          20
15 EOQ rounded                           4433
16
17 EOQ Graph
18                                                                      Percent
19  Percent      Order      Order  Holding      Total                  Change
20   of EOQ       Size       Cost     Cost       Cost               Total Cost
21
22       20     886.66    $70,489   $2,820    $73,309                   160.00
23       40    1773.32     35,245    5,639     40,884                    45.00
24       60    2659.98     23,496    8,459     31,955                    13.33
25       80    3546.63     17,622   11,278     28,901                     2.50
26      100    4433.29     14,098   14,098     28,196 Minimum             0.00
27      120    5319.95     11,748   16,917     28,666                     1.67
28      140    6206.61     10,070   19,737     29,807                     5.71
29      160    7093.27      8,811   22,557     31,368                    11.25
30      180    7979.93      7,832   25,376     33,208                    17.78
```

2. Figures 20–4, 20–5, and 20–6 show the graphs requested. In Figure 20–4, with the interval set at 20 (20 percent change around the EOQ), changes around the EOQ seem costly. By changing the range to an increment of 5 percent (Figure 20–5), the total cost curve is almost flat. An increment of five percent allows a closer look of the range EOQ±20%. Total costs only change by 2.5 percent if 80 percent of the EOQ is ordered on a regular basis and by about 1.7 percent if 120 percent of the EOQ is ordered. This is graphed in Figure 20–6. Thus, deviating from the EOQ by 20 percent either way is not very costly.

FIGURE 20–4 Order Cost, Holding Cost, Total Cost

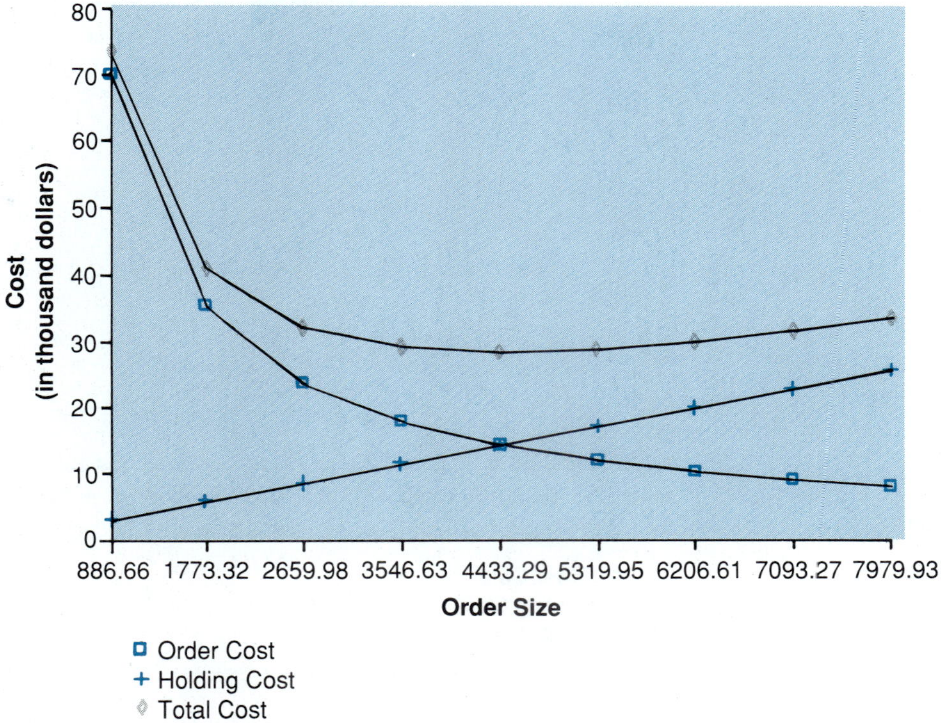

REVIEW PROBLEM: PAYOFF TABLE

Coleman Company sells fresh fruits and vegetables by the case. Data per case appear below.

Selling price	$12.00
Variable cost	4.00
Salvage value of unsold units	0.80

Demand	*Probability*
40,000	0.1
50,000	0.4
60,000	0.3
75,000	0.2

FIGURE 20–5 **Order Cost, Holding Cost, Total Cost**

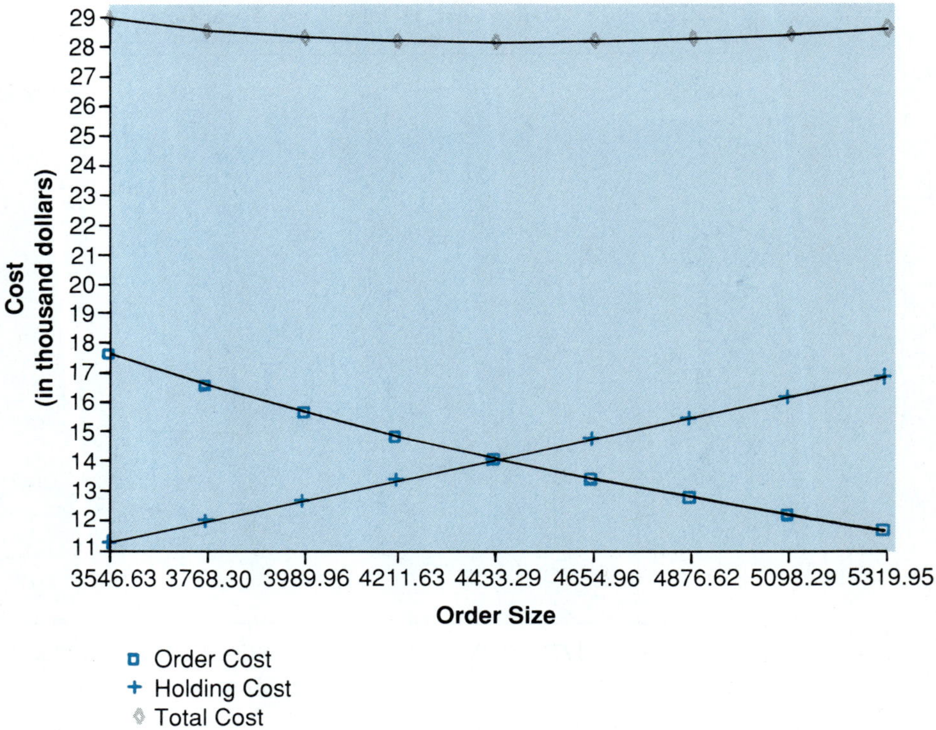

FIGURE 20–6 **Sensitivity Analysis, Total Costs**

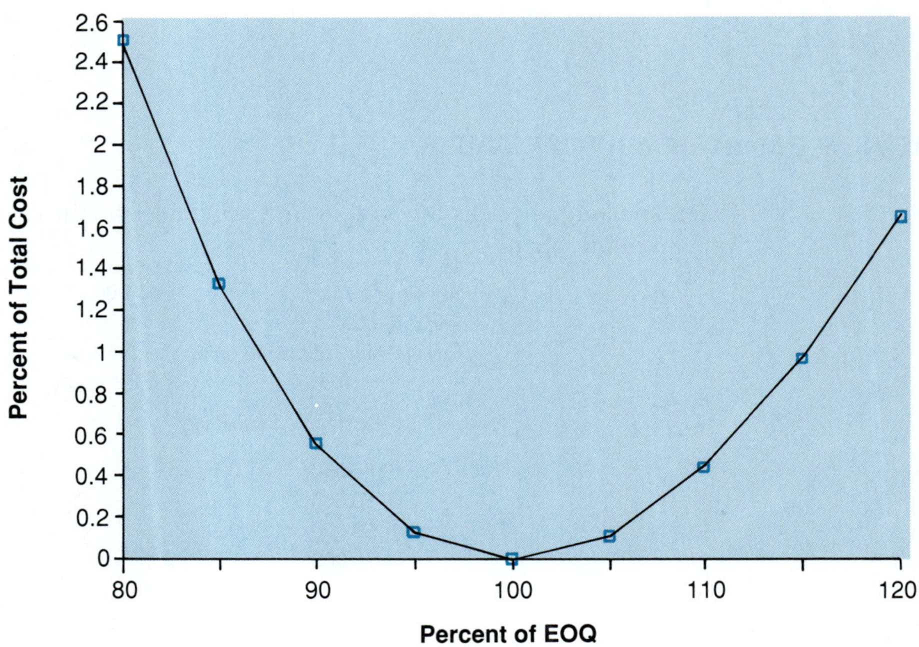

REQUIRED

Prepare a payoff table to determine the optimal number of cases to order.

ANSWERS TO REVIEW PROBLEM

Conditional values:

	Strategy—Purchases			
Demand	*40,000*	*50,000*	*60,000*	*75,000*
40,000	$320,000	$288,000	$256,000	$208,000
50,000	320,000	400,000	368,000	320,000
60,000	320,000	400,000	480,000	432,000
75,000	320,000	400,000	480,000	600,000

If purchases exceed demand, all conditional values are (demand × price) − (purchases × variable cost) + [(purchases − demand) × salvage]. If demand equals or exceeds purchases, the conditional value is demand × (price − variable cost). For example, when 60,000 cases are purchased and 50,000 are demanded,

$$\begin{aligned} \text{profit} &= (50{,}000 \times \$12.00) - (60{,}000 \times \$4.00) + [(60{,}000 - 50{,}000) \times \$0.80] \\ &= \$600{,}000 - \$240{,}000 + \$8{,}000 = \$368{,}000 \end{aligned}$$

Expected values:

	Strategy—Purchases			
Demand	*40,000*	*50,000*	*60,000*	*75,000*
40,000	$ 32,000	$ 28,800	$ 25,600	$ 20,800
50,000	128,000	160,000	147,200	128,000
60,000	96,000	120,000	144,000	129,600
75,000	64,000	80,000	96,000	120,000
Expected value	$320,000	$388,800	$412,800	$398,400

All expected values are the conditional values multiplied by the probability of occurrence.

APPENDIX 20A: JOINT PROBABILITY DISTRIBUTIONS

Often a manager wants to deal with more than one random variable. Perhaps there are probability distributions associated with sales of various products, and the manager wants to know the mean and variance of total sales. Assume, for example, a company sells lawn mowers and chain saws. The probabilities associated with various levels of sales of these products are presented below.

Lawn Mower Sales, x_i	$p(x_i)$	Chain Saw Sales, y_i	$p(y_i)$
$3,000	0.30	$1,000	0.20
4,000	0.30	1,500	0.40
5,000	0.40	2,000	0.15
		2,500	0.25

The probabilities associated with one set of events (such as lawn mower sales) are called **marginal probabilities**; the distribution, then, is a marginal distribution. If the marginal distribution for lawn mower sales is not affected by the level of chain saw sales (and vice versa), then we can look at these two distributions together. The **joint probability** of $3,000 in lawn mower sales *and* $1,000 in chain saw sales is calculated by multiplying the two independent marginal probabilities:

$$\begin{array}{rr} & p(L = \$3{,}000) = 0.30 \\ \times & p(C = \$1{,}000) = 0.20 \\ \hline & p(L = \$3{,}000 \text{ and } C = \$1{,}000) = 0.06 \end{array}$$

where

L = lawn mower sales

C = chain saw sales

We have already defined $p(x_i)$ as the probability that an event will occur. We can now say $p(x_i)$ is a marginal probability. A joint probability can then be noted as $p(x_i, y_i)$ and:

$$p(x_i, y_i) = p(x_i) \times p(y_i)$$

or, more simply,

$$p(A, B) = p(A) \times p(B)$$

when events are independent. If the company added a line of lawn mower accessories (leaf sweepers, mulchers, and so on), this line might have sales dependent on lawn mower sales. For dependent probabilities we want to know the probability that an event will occur *given* that another event *has occurred*. For example, we would want to know the probability that accessory sales (A) would be $500 *given that* lawn mower sales are $4,000. This is called a **conditional probability** and is expressed as:

$$p(A = \$500 \text{ if } L = \$4{,}000) \quad \text{or} \quad p(A = \$500 \mid L = \$4{,}000)$$

More generally this is

$$p(z_i \mid x_i) \quad \text{or} \quad p(B \mid A)$$

We have seen that $p(A, B) = p(A) \times p(B)$ when there is independence. When two distributions are dependent, the basic probability relationship is

$$\text{joint probability} = (\text{marginal probability}) \times (\text{conditional probability})$$
$$p(A, B) = p(A) \times p(B \mid A)$$

We can see that if A and B are independent, then $p(B) = p(B \mid A)$, since the level of A does not affect the probability of occurrence of any event B.

ASSIGNMENTS

20–1 Assumption of Level Demand The chapter states that the EOQ model is correct only if demand is level throughout the period. Thus, if annual demand were 12,000 units, with alternate months showing demands of 1,000 and 3,000 units, the EOQ based on annual data would not be correct.

REQUIRED

Can you reason out why the assumption of level demand is necessary?

20–2 Basic EOQ and Replenishment Point Braintree Wholesale Company experiences relatively constant demand of 24,000 units per year for one of its products. The product, an electric mixer, costs the firm $30. Placing an order costs about $200, and annual carrying costs are about $2 per unit. The firm works 200 days per year and desires a safety stock of 300 units. The lead time for an order is 15 working days.

REQUIRED

1. Determine the economic order quantity and the costs (ordering and carrying) associated with it.
2. Determine the replenishment point.

20–3 EOQ (AICPA) Barclay Company sells 20,000 pocket calculators evenly through the year. The cost of carrying one unit in inventory for one year is $2, and the order cost is $72 per order.

REQUIRED

Determine the EOQ.

20–4 Quantity Discounts Ramsey Company requires 10,000 subassemblies per year that it buys from a single supplier. The supplier recently published the following new price list keyed to the quantity ordered at a time:

Price	*Quantity*
$10.00	up to 999 units
9.90	1,000 to 1,999 units
9.80	2,000 and up

Ramsey's chief accountant has estimated incremental ordering costs at $50 per order. He also estimates incremental carrying costs at $1 per unit, plus 20 percent of purchase price for the required return on investment.

REQUIRED

Determine the optimal number of units that Ramsey should order at a time.

20–5 Economic Lot Size (AICPA) Pierce Incorporated must manufacture 10,000 blades for its electric lawn mower division. The blades will be used evenly over the year. The setup cost to manufacture a batch of blades is $80, and the cost to carry a blade in inventory is $0.40 per year.

REQUIRED

Determine the number of production runs of blades that Pierce should make.

20–6 Sensitivity Analysis Burgoyne Furniture Company uses about 200,000 yards of a particular fabric each year. The fabric costs $2.50 per yard. The current policy is to order the fabric four times per year. Incremental ordering costs are about $200 per order, and incremental carrying costs are about $0.75 per yard, much of which represents the opportunity cost of the funds tied up in inventory.

REQUIRED

1. Determine the total annual costs of following the current policy.
2. Determine the EOQ and the total annual costs associated with it.

20–7 Relevant Costs Warren Company uses 30,000 pounds of strip steel per year in making its own products. The firm manufactures and uses steel evenly over the year. The following data relate to the purchase and use of steel:

Cost per pound	$0.80
Carrying costs:	
Annual warehousing costs, salaries, and rent	$64,000
Insurance	$ 0.20/lb
Taxes, levied on the basis of average inventory	$ 0.08/lb
Return on investment, at cost of capital	15%
Ordering cost:	
Clerical salaries, annual total	$43,000
Forms, postage, telephone	$ 1.50/order
Freight	$ 1,000/order
Receiving and handling	$23,000 annually plus $40 variable cost per order for extra help

REQUIRED

Determine the EOQ. Be prepared to explain why you included or excluded individual items of cost.

20–8 Basic Safety Stock Newman Company orders one of its raw materials 10 times per year using the EOQ model. The firm's cost accountants have estimated that annual carrying costs for the material are $2 per pound. Stockout costs seem to be about $3 per pound, as best the accountants can estimate them.

Recent records show the following amounts of use of the material during the lead time and the associated probabilities:

Use During Lead Time (pounds)	Probability
800	0.40
900	0.40
1,000	0.20

REQUIRED

Determine the optimal replenishment point.

20–9 Relationships Each of the following situations is independent of the others.

Case	EOQ	Ordering Costs	Carrying Cost per Unit, per Year	Annual Demand
a	1,000	$ 50	———	10,000
b	2,000	———	$2	50,000
c	2,000	$100	$5	———

REQUIRED

Fill in the blanks.

20–10 Finding Annual Demand (AICPA Adapted) Garmar, Inc., has determined the following for a given year:

EOQ	5,000 units
Total cost to place orders for year	$10,000
Cost to place one order	$50
Cost to carry one unit for one year	$4

REQUIRED

Determine the annual use.

20–11 Payoff Table Horton Publishing Company generally has a press run of 100,000 copies of *Daily*, a newsmagazine that comes out weekly. The managers have been wondering whether this run is optimal and have amassed the following information about demand, which they believe should hold true in the future:

Demand	Probability
60,000	0.20
80,000	0.30
100,000	0.30
120,000	0.20

The magazine sells for $1, and variable cost to print is $0.30. Unsold magazines are given to a recycling plant.

REQUIRED

Set up a payoff table to determine the optimal strategy and determine the value of perfect information.

20–12 Service Level (AICPA Adapted) Helms, Inc., operates a number of sales offices. The manager of one such office has developed the following probability distribution of daily sales of a perishable product. The office restocks the product each morning.

X (units sold)	p(sales = X)
100	0.20
150	0.50
200	0.20
250	0.10

REQUIRED

The firm desires a 90 percent service level in satisfying sales demand. What should the initial stock balance be for each day?

20–13 Probabilities *The Eastern News-Leader* is a daily newspaper with wide circulation throughout several small towns in New England. The paper is plagued with returns of unsold copies, for which it gives dealers full credit. That is, the company buys back the papers at the wholesale price of $0.09. The variable cost of printing a copy is about $0.03, and the unsold copies bring about $0.005 as waste paper.

The publisher has been trying to determine how many copies to print per day. Information available from records indicates that sales are uniformly distributed between 5,000 and 7,000 copies per day. Any value between 5,000 and 7,000 is equally likely, or so close as not to matter. For example, there is a 50 percent probability that sales will be greater than 6,000 copies, a 25 percent probability that they will exceed 6,500 copies, and so on.

REQUIRED

Determine the number of copies that the paper should produce each day.

20–14 Find Set up Cost (AICPA) Metro, Inc., makes dolls. The cost of carrying one doll in inventory is $0.60 per year. Annual volume is 6,000 units and is evenly distributed over the year.

REQUIRED

If Metro's EOQ is 200 units, what are its set up costs?

20–15 EOQ (AICPA) Brady Sporting Goods buys baseballs at $20 per dozen. Brady sells 36,000 dozen per year, evenly distributed. Brady requires a 10 percent return on investment. Insurance, taxes, and other carrying costs average $0.40 per dozen balls per year. The ordering cost is $10 per order.

REQUIRED

1. Determine the EOQ.
2. If Brady were to order 800 dozen at a time, what would the total inventory-associated costs be for the year?

20–16 Advance Purchases The controller of RST Industries has just been informed that a major supplier will raise its price from $4.50 per pound to $4.70 per pound in the next few weeks. He estimates that RST will use 15,000 pounds of the product in each month of the coming year. Cost of capital is 15 percent, and other carrying costs are estimated at $0.25 per pound per year. Ordering costs are about $600 per order. RST has an inventory of 12,000 pounds. The reorder point is 10,000 pounds.

REQUIRED

Make a recommendation to the controller regarding the number of pounds to buy now.

20–17 EOQ and Relevant Costs The Wininger Company makes a number of products. Data for model M-2203 appear below.

Cost of production:	
Variable	$10/unit
Fixed, based on 12,000 units	$4/unit
Cost to set up production run	$1,000
Carrying costs:	
Storage	$2/unit
Insurance	$4/unit

Storage cost is allocated based on square footage normally occupied by each product. The firm has ample storage space, and the space has no alternative use. The firm also requires a 15 percent return on investment. The 12,000 units normally demanded during a year are spread evenly throughout the year. Insurance costs are variable with the number of units that are in inventory.

REQUIRED

1. Determine the economic lot size.
2. Determine the total annual costs associated with the answer to part 1.
3. Determine the total annual costs associated with producing *double* the economic lot size.

20–18 Sensitivity Analysis Jordan Jeans orders one of its major products 20 times a year. Carrying costs on the product are about $2 per unit annually, and the sales manager and treasurer have been arguing about the stockout costs for some time. The sales manager believes it desirable that the firm never run out, while the treasurer would like to keep a relatively low amount of safety stock to minimize carrying costs. The treasurer is on record as having said: "He [the sales manager] would keep the place full to bursting just to make sure he doesn't lose $5 in sales." The sales manager holds an equally complimentary view of the treasurer.

As the new controller, you have landed smack in the middle, and both parties have appealed to you to support their positions. You have gathered some information about the use during lead time of the product and associated probabilities, but are not yet sure whether you have a handle on stockout costs.

Use During Lead Time	*Probability*
1,000	0.20
1,200	0.30
1,500	0.45
1,800	0.05

The product has a contribution margin of $4, and the sales manager is sure that anyone coming in to buy the product who cannot get it will go elsewhere. The treasurer is equally sure that a good many customers do wait until Jordan has the product in stock. He believes that no more than 25 percent of stockouts result in lost sales.

REQUIRED

Make a recommendation on the replenishment point.

20–19 Replenishment Point United Millwork Corporation uses 12,000 pounds of a particular raw material each year. The EOQ is 1,200 pounds, so the firm orders it 10 times per year. Carrying costs are $2 per unit, stockout costs $6 per unit. The following schedule shows both lead times and average daily use with their associated probabilities:

Lead Time	*Probability*	*Average Daily Use*	*Probability*
10 days	0.30	40 units	0.20
12 days	0.70	60 units	0.60
		80 units	0.20

REQUIRED

Determine the optimal replenishment point.

20–20 Cost Analysis The treasurer of Delmar Company has insisted on ordering very small quantities of materials and components with the objective of keeping the inventories at a minimum. As a consequence, the workload of the purchasing, receiving, and bookkeeping departments has grown rapidly.

The president of the firm has asked you to serve as a consultant on inventory policy. As you begin your study, you pick out one high-volume component, part M-302. The firm uses about 120,000 units of the part per year and currently orders it from its suppliers twice a month. You have satisfied yourself that $0.20 per unit per year is a reasonable estimate of the carrying cost of the part. However, you are unable to make a good determination of the incremental ordering costs because the part is only one of many that the firm uses. Nevertheless, you believe that the twice-a-month ordering policy is unsound.

REQUIRED

Prepare whatever analysis you believe appropriate to support the position that ordering twice a month is too often. You need not determine the optimal order quantity, only make a plausible argument that the current policy is unsound.

20–21 Finding Setup Costs (CMA Adapted) Pointer Furniture Company manufactures and sells office furniture. In Pointer's line of desks each model is unique. Thus, a changeover (setup) is required on the manufacturing equipment whenever a batch of each model is put into production.

One model (JE 40) is a junior executive desk. The accounting department has been asked to determine the setup costs for this model.

The equipment maintenance department consists of 10 employees who are paid $9 an hour plus employee benefits of 20 percent of wage costs. This department is responsible for changeover adjustments on the production line. Other costs in the maintenance department are $50,000 per year, which includes items such as supervision, depreciation, and insurance.

Two workers are required to make the change on the desk line for model JE 40. They are expected to spend three hours on machinery changes, one hour on testing, and one hour readjusting the machinery. The manufacturing line requires five workers who must be present during changeover. However, they are idle 40 percent of the time during changeover.

Production workers are paid $7.50 per hour. Overhead for these workers is applied as follows:

	Based on Direct Labor Hours	*Based on Machine Hours*
Variable	$2.75	$ 5.00
Fixed	2.25	15.00
	$5.00	$20.00

These rates are based on an expected activity of 10,000 direct labor hours and 1,500 machine hours. Other setup costs include $200 in direct materials. However, $50 is recovered through salvage of these materials.

REQUIRED

Estimate the setup cost for model JE 40. For each cost item you identify, justify the amount and the reason for including this cost item in your estimate. Also explain the reason for excluding any cost item.

20–22 Safety Stock (AICPA Adapted) Polly Company management wants to determine the amount of safety stock that it should maintain to minimize the costs of product D. The following information is available:

Carrying cost	$2 per unit per year
Number of orders	5/year

Units of Safety Stock	*Probability of Stockout*
10	50%
20	40%
30	30%
40	20%
50	10%
55	5%

If the firm runs out of product D, it must fly in units at a cost of $80, no matter how many units it requires. There are no other stockout costs.

REQUIRED

Determine the safety stock that the firm should carry.

20–23 Relevant Costs In response to your request for information bearing on the EOQ and replenishment point for one of your firm's major products, your assistant gave you the following data:

Annual demand	20,000 units
Selling price per unit	$100

(continued)

Purchase price per unit	$60
Freight in by railroad	$1.50/unit plus $500/shipment
Delivery to customer	$0.90/unit plus $100 per delivery to each customer
Insurance	$0.80/unit
Storage	$2.50/unit ($0.60/unit variable)
Pilferage and shrinkage	2% of inventory
Postage, forms, and other incremental ordering costs	$90/order
Annual clerical salaries and other costs of purchasing department	$87,000
Opportunity cost of funds	20%
Sales commissions	$10/unit

The firm can rush order units at some additional cost. Air freight is $7 per unit plus $1,200 per shipment. The firm also incurs the $90 ordering cost if it places special orders.

REQUIRED

1. Determine the ordering costs and carrying costs needed to determine the EOQ.
2. Determine the stockout costs needed to determine the replenishment point, assuming that:
   a. the firm can fill all sales by using air freight to obtain the units
   b. the firm cannot fill sales using air freight and so loses sales when it stocks out

20–24 Stockpiling and Price Changes The purchasing manager of Westcott Industries recently approached the treasurer and asked if she could buy 200,000 pounds of glycol, a raw material that the firm uses in great quantities. She wanted to make the purchase now because she expected the price to rise from the current $2.90 per pound to $3.15 within a few weeks.

The treasurer promised to look into the matter and get back within a day. He then assembled the following information:

EOQ in current use	13,100 lb
Annual carrying cost per unit, including 20% required return on investment of $2.90	$0.70
Incremental ordering cost	$300/order

Annual demand is about 200,000 pounds, so that the purchasing manager in effect wants to buy an entire year's supply.

REQUIRED

Evaluate the purchasing manager's proposal.

20–25 Just-in-Time Inventory Analysis The management of Boray Company is considering the just-in-time inventory technique. Various managers have analyzed different aspects of the question and have come up with the following information:

	Current	*Just-in-Time*
Average investment in materials	$6,900,000	$1,380,000
Annual freight charges	$ 475,000	$1,615,000
Ordering costs	$ 37,000	$ 96,000

The increases in freight and ordering costs result from the need for more frequent orders and shipments. The managers expect shipments every several days, rather than every several weeks. The best estimate of carrying costs is 22 percent of cost.

REQUIRED

1. Recommend whether Boray should adopt the just-in-time policy.
2. Suppose that the managers are not sure of the level to which they can reduce materials inventories. Determine how low inventories must fall to make the costs of the two policies equal.

20–26 Just-in-Time Inventory (CMA Adapted) Margro Corporation is an automotive supplier that uses automatic screw machines to manufacture precision parts from steel bars. Margro's inventory of raw steel averages $600,000 with a turnover rate of four times per year.

John Oates, President of Margro, is concerned about the costs of carrying inventory. He is considering the adoption of the just-in-time inventory control method to eliminate the need to carry raw steel inventory. Oates has asked Helen Gorman, Margro's Controller, to evaluate the feasibility of just-in-time for the corporation. Gorman identified the following effects of adopting just-in-time.

Without scheduling any overtime, lost sales due to stockouts would increase by 35,000 units per year. However, by incurring overtime premiums of $40,000 per year, the increase in lost sales could be reduced to 20,000 units. This would be the maximum amount of overtime that would be feasible for Margro.

Two warehouses presently used for steel-bar storage would no longer be needed. Margro rents one warehouse from another company at an annual cost of $60,000. The other warehouse is owned by Margro and contains 12,000 square feet. Three-fourths of the space in the owned warehouse could be rented for $1.50 per square foot per year.

Insurance and property tax costs totaling $14,000 per year would be eliminated.

Margro's projected operating results for the 19X6 calendar year follow. Long-term capital investments by Margro are expected to produce a rate of return of 12 percent after income taxes. Margro is subject to an effective income tax rate of 40 percent.

MARGRO CORPORATION
Pro Forma Income Statement
For the Year Ending December 31, 19X6
($000 omitted)

Sales (900,000 units)		$10,800
Cost of goods sold:		
Variable	$4,050	
Fixed	1,450	5,500
Gross profit		$ 5,300
Selling and administrative expenses:		
Variable	$ 900	
Fixed	1,500	2,400
Income before interest and income taxes		$ 2,900
Interest		900
Income before income taxes		$ 2,000
Income taxes		800
Net income		$ 1,200

REQUIRED

1. Calculate the estimated dollar savings (loss) for Margro Corporation that would result in 19X6 from the adoption of the just-in-time inventory control method.
2. Identify and explain the conditions that should exist for a company to successfully install just-in-time.

20–27 Quantity Discounts, Supplier's Viewpoint CZM Company supplies Morgan Company with 45,000 units of part A-506 per year. Morgan uses an EOQ model with estimated order costs of $200 and estimated carrying costs of $2 per unit to determine that it should order 3,000 units 15 times per year.

CZM sets up and runs the component each time Morgan orders it, incurring setup costs of $2,000 each time. It is not possible for CZM to carry an inventory of part A-506 because of space limitations, and its managers have thought of offering Morgan quantity discounts to order larger amounts less frequently. CZM ships the finished parts quickly and has no carrying costs.

REQUIRED

1. The managers of CZM have asked you to determine the largest quantity discount that they could offer Morgan to buy only twice a year. That is, they want the upper limit, where CZM would earn the same income that it does now.
2. Determine whether or not the discount you calculated in part 1 would be enough to induce Morgan to buy only twice per year.
3. Repeat parts 1 and 2, assuming that CZM wants to induce Morgan to order once per year. Treat this part independently of parts 1 and 2. That is, assume that CZM and Morgan have not agreed on a discount that would reduce the number of orders to two per year.

20–28 Payoff Table Wycomb Company makes corsages that it sells through salespeople on the streets. Each sells for $2 and has variable production costs of $0.80. The salespeople receive a $0.50 commission on each corsage they sell, and the company must spend $0.05 to get rid of each unsold corsage. The corsages last for only one week and cannot be carried in inventory.

The managers of the firm have estimated demand per week and associated probabilities as follows:

Demand	*Probability*
100,000	0.20
120,000	0.20
140,000	0.30
160,000	0.30

REQUIRED

Determine the optimal weekly production of the corsage and the value of perfect information.

20–29 Inventory, Expected Value, and Information (CMA Adapted) Jessica Company has decided to use the expected-value model in a small department to see if this model will help in decision making. This department buys and resells a perishable product. A large purchase at the beginning of each month provides a lower cost than more frequent purchases and also ensures that Jessica Company can buy all of the item it wants. Unfortunately, if too much is purchased, the product unsold at the end of the month is worthless and must be discarded.

If an inadequate quantity is purchased, additional quantities probably cannot be purchased. If any should be available, they would probably be of poor quality and be overpriced. Jessica chooses to lose the potential sales rather than furnish poor-quality product. The standard purchase arrangement is $50,000 plus $0.50 for each unit purchased for orders of 100,000 units or more. Jessica is paid $1.25 per unit by its customers.

The needs of Jessica's customers limit the possible sales volumes to only four quantities per month—100,000, 120,000, 140,000, or 180,000 units. However, the total quantity needed for a given month cannot be determined before the date Jessica must make its purchases. The sales managers are willing to place a probability estimate on each of the four possible sales volumes each month. They note that the probabilities for the four sales volumes change from month to month because of the seasonal nature of the customers' business. Their probability estimates for December 19X8 sales units are 10 percent for 100,000, 30 percent for 120,000, 40 percent for 140,000, and 20 percent for 180,000.

The following schedule shows the quantity purchased each month, based on the expected-value decision model. The actual units sold and the product discarded or sales lost are shown also.

	Quantity (in units)			*Sales Units*
	Purchased	*Sold*	*Discarded*	*Lost*
January	100,000	100,000	—	20,000
February	120,000	100,000	20,000	—
March	180,000	140,000	40,000	—
April	100,000	100,000	—	80,000
May	100,000	100,000	—	—
June	140,000	140,000	—	—
July	140,000	100,000	40,000	—
August	140,000	120,000	20,000	—
September	120,000	100,000	20,000	—
October	120,000	120,000	—	20,000
November	180,000	140,000	40,000	—

REQUIRED

1. What quantity should be ordered for December 19X8 if the expected-value decision model is used?

2. Suppose Jessica could ascertain its customers' needs before placing its purchase order rather than relying on the expected-value decision model. How much would it pay to obtain this information for December?

3. The model did not result in purchases equal to potential sales except during two months. Is the expected-value model unsuitable in this case, or is this a characteristic of the model? Explain your answer.

20–30 Payoff Table, Alternative Strategies Robert Jablonski, the owner of a large produce market, has been trying to work out a strategy for purchasing merchandise. The average crate of produce costs him $6, and he sells it for $10. He must order in advance for each week and must discard all produce unsold at the end of the week. He has developed the following probability distribution of demand:

Demand in Crates	*Probability*
10,000	0.10
14,000	0.20
18,000	0.20
22,000	0.50

He asks you to determine the strategy with the highest expected value of profit. Also he wants to know, for each possible strategy, the probability that profits will equal or exceed each of the following targets: $40,000, $50,000, and $60,000. That is, for each strategy, what percentage of the time should profit equal or exceed each of the targets?

REQUIRED

Do the analyses that Jablonski has asked for and recommend a strategy.

20–31 Order Strategy Boston Flower Shop sells corsages. It must order them in advance, at the beginning of each week, and cannot obtain more once the week begins. The purchase price is $1.50, the selling price $4. Any unsold corsages are discarded. An examination of demand in previous weeks indicates that demand is approximately normally distributed, with a mean of 5,000 and standard deviation of 1,200. The owner of the shop wants to maximize the expected value of profits.

REQUIRED

1. Determine the optimal number of corsages to order each week.
2. Without making any additional calculations, answer the following questions:
   a. What would be the effect on the optimal order quantity if the purchase price increased, with the selling price held constant?
   b. What would be the effect on the optimal order quantity if the standard deviation of demand were greater than 1,200 units?

20–32 Relevant Costs for EOQ and Reorder Point Gilbert Company manufactures a variety of products that use some of the same components. Gilbert buys one particular component, BZ-44, from a single supplier for $80 per unit. Annual use of the component is 120,000 units, spread more or less evenly over each month. However, daily use fluctuates considerably, as will be shown. Sandy Hart, Gilbert's controller, has estimated the annual carrying cost per unit at $15. The vendor ships the component by rail, unless otherwise instructed by Gilbert. Rail shipment takes 10 days from the time Gilbert places an order, and each shipment costs $1,200 plus $0.90 per unit. Air freight takes only one day, but it costs $3,000 plus $1.50 per unit. Gilbert uses air freight only when it stocks out. Incremental costs for postage and other such ordering costs are $70 per normal (rail) order and $90 for orders to cover stockouts (air freight).

Gilbert hires people from an employment service to unload each incoming shipment (rail or air). The reason for hiring outsiders is that some special equipment is needed, which Gilbert must rent from the service. The service charges $500 per day plus $20 per hour of each unloader's time. Each unloader takes off about 50 units per hour. The unloading is always done in one day.

Gilbert's own employees supervise unloading and inspect a sample of the shipment. BZ-44 is stored in a warehouse, along with other components, that Gilbert rents for $27,000 per year. BZ-44 occupies about 20 percent of the space. The warehouse manager has said that loading BZ-44 on the shelves and removing it when a requisition arrives takes about 25 percent of his time. (He is the only employee in the highly automated warehouse.) His annual salary is $24,000.

Gilbert's current policy is to place an order when inventory falls below 6,000 units. Average use during the lead time is 4,800 units. However, about 30 percent of the time only 3,600 units are needed, while another 30 percent of the time 6,000 are needed. The remaining 40 percent of the time 4,800 are needed.

REQUIRED

Determine the EOQ and reorder point. State clearly any assumptions that you believe you must make.

20–33 EOQ and Safety Stock (CMA) Clyde Peterson, General Manager of Adam Desk Company, is exasperated because the company exhausted its finished goods inventory of Style 103—Modern Desk twice during the previous month. This led to customer complaints and disrupted the normal flow of operations.

"We ought to be able to plan better," declared Peterson. "Our annual sales demand is 18,000 units for this model or an average of 75 desks per day based upon our 240-day work year. Unfortunately, the sales pattern is not this uniform. Our daily demand on that model varies considerably. If we do not have the units on hand when a customer places an order, 35 percent of the time we lose the sale, 40 percent of the time we pay an extra charge of $24.00 per unit to expedite shipping when the unit becomes available, and 25 percent of the time the customer will accept a back order at no out-of-pocket cost to us.

"When we run out of units, we cannot convert immediately because we would disrupt the production of our other products and cause cost increases. The set up process for this model results in the destruction of 12 finished desks, leaving no salvageable materials. Once we get the line up, we can produce 200 units per day. I would prefer to have several planned runs of a uniform quantity rather than short unplanned runs often required to meet unfilled customer orders."

The manager of the cost accounting department has suggested that an EOQ model be adopted to determine optimum production runs and then establish a safety stock to guard against stockouts. The cost data for the Modern Desk that sells for $110.00 is available from the accounting records. The manufacturing costs are:

Direct materials	$30.00
Direct labor (2 DLH @ $7.00)	14.00
Manufacturing overhead	
Variable (2 DLH @ $3.00)	6.00
Fixed (2 DLH @ $5.00)	10.00
Total manufacturing cost	$60.00

Cost Accounting estimates that the company's carrying costs are 19.2 percent of the incremental out-of-pocket manufacturing costs. This percentage can be broken down into a 10.8 percent variable rate and an 8.4 percent fixed rate.

The EOQ formula referred to by the cost accounting manager is as follows.

$$EOQ = \sqrt{\frac{2DC}{K}}$$

where

D = annual demand in units
C = cost of placing an order
K = annual unit cost of carrying inventory

REQUIRED

1. Adam Desk Company can solve part of its production scheduling problems by adapting the EOQ model to determine the optimum production run.
   a. Explain what costs the company would be attempting to balance when it adapts the EOQ model to production runs.
   b. Calculate the optimum quantity that Adam Desk Company should manufacture in each production run of Style 103—Modern Desk.
   c. Calculate the number of production runs of Modern Desks that Adam Desk Company would schedule during the year based upon the optimum quantity calculated in part 1b.

2. Adam Desk Company should establish a safety stock level to guard against stockouts.
   a. Explain what factors affect the desired size of the safety stock for any inventory item.
   b. Calculate the minimum safety stock level that Adam Desk Company could afford to maintain for the Style 103—Modern Desk and not be worse off than if it were unable to fill orders equal to an average day's demand.

20–34 Kanban Bute Manufacturing uses Kanban to help manage work flows through its factory. This idea is new to them, and Jade Bute, the company president, is seeking information about the effects of changing various variables associated with Kanban. Initially, production managers suggest that the following variables apply to a particular component Bute makes:

Average demand per hours (Q)	100
Waiting time along production line (hours) (T_w)	1
Time needed to process and withdraw parts (hours) (T_p)	0.25
Indicator of inefficiency at the shop (r)	0.25
Container capacity (c)	50

REQUIRED

Ms. Bute has hired you as an outside consultant to write her a report in which you:

1. Determine the total number of Kanban in the system (n) given the original estimates.

2. Determine the effect on n of changing container capacity from 50 to 75 and from 50 to 100.

3. Determine the effect on n of changing the waiting time along the production line. In even tenths of an hour, holding everything else at the original estimates, how low would T_w have to go before the value for n found in part 1 is reduced by one? How far would T_w have to be reduced before n is reduced by two?

4. Determine the effects on n of changing the time needed for processing and withdrawal of parts. Holding all other values at their original estimates, how far would T_p have to drop in order to reduce the value of n found in part 1 by 1? How far would it have to rise for n to go up by 1?
5. Analyze your results and make recommendations to Bute regarding the areas where her company might profit most in seeing how different variables could change.

Refer to Appendix B regarding the form and format of memorandum preparation and presentation.

20–35 Inventory Control in the New Manufacturing Environment Respond to the questions below.

1. What is meant by a system that pulls inventory?
2. What is meant by a system that pushes inventory?
3. What is the basic idea of just-in-time inventory (JIT)?
4. What is the basic idea of Kanban?
5. How are JIT and Kanban compatible or different?

21

VARIANCE INVESTIGATION AND REPORTING

Chapters 7 and 8 discussed and illustrated identifying variances, assigning responsibility for them, and recording them in standard costing systems. As various illustrations have shown, variances might be fairly small or quite large. In addition, while it may be easy to classify a variance, it is more difficult to determine its cause.

For example, while an unfavorable material use variance may mean that the production department used too much material, it does not give evidence of the cause, which could be poor-quality material (not the responsibility of production), sloppy construction, faulty production equipment, or some other cause. Thus, it is not enough to know the dollar amount of a specific variance. Was a variance a random event or a sign that something serious is happening with the production process? Can anything be done to eliminate a variance and, if so, at what cost? These matters relate to investigating variances.

We also discuss variance reporting. Even though calculating variances is fairly routine, managers need to decide which variances to report and how to report them. The subjects of variance reporting and variance investigation are tied together since the results of an investigation might be part of how we choose to report variances, or, what we report may trigger the investigation process. We begin by looking at variance investigation.

TWO CONCERNS OF INVESTIGATION

Managers have two distinct concerns about variances. First, because a variance has economic consequences, managers want to see what corrective actions are warranted and possible. Identifying the causes of variances might show a manager that unfavorable variances in one area were caused by favorable variances in another. (For instance, low quality material—favorable price variance—could result in higher labor time—unfavorable efficiency variance.) It is not enough to know that a variance occurred. We also need to know why and how it relates to other variances. If the changes reflected by a variance are more or less permanent, then managers need to make appropriate changes in standard costs and, perhaps, in product mix or production methods to reflect this new reality.

Second, an important reason for identifying variances is to assign responsibility. Therefore, managers need a system not only to calculate variances but also to assess their importance. Normal or expected deviations from standards should be differentiated from major or unexpected deviations.

WHY VARIANCES OCCUR

There are many reasons why actual results differ from standards. A simple yet often overlooked cause is the accuracy of the data. A second cause is that production conditions, and therefore costs, have changed so that new standards are needed. Third, variances can be caused by random happenings (remember that standards are estimates). Finally, variances can result from especially efficient or inefficient operations.

Inaccurate Data

If actual results differ from standard costs, it might be wise to check the source data. Were costs recorded properly? Was labor use accurately calculated?

The data that an accountant obtains result from many steps and many people. Products go through several departments. Multiple-shift operations mean that different people handle a product within the same department. In many three-shift operations, there are fewer supervisory personnel on the 11 P.M. to 7 A.M. shift than on the others. For these and many more reasons, recorded data can be inaccurate. A good managerial accounting system includes ways to check incoming data for accuracy and reasonableness. In this way, errors can be detected before they are used in the financial or cost system of the firm.

There are other reasons. Production supervisors may intentionally report inaccurate data. For example, say one job was produced efficiently, another inefficiently. By switching some hours from the inefficient job to the efficient one, a manager manipulates the data and dampens both variances, hoping that neither will be noticed. Alternatively, supervisors might simply report incorrect production data.

Out-of-Date Standards

Standard costs might be outdated. Inflation can make it difficult for standard prices to be realistic over periods of six months or even less. Therefore, persistent price variances may mean that standard prices need to be adjusted.

Perhaps new machinery has replaced older equipment, or crews are now more experienced than originally contemplated. If such efficiencies persist, then standards can be revised. However, as we have discussed, tightening standards too much with each new indication of efficiency can have serious behavioral repercussions, as can too lax standards.

Sometimes when a job was bid standards were set based on an expected set of routing and operations on the shop floor. Because of various constraints on productive capacity or a reengineering of the product, the manufacturing process has been revised. Thus, standards should be revised to reflect this change.

Many companies now have much greater worker participation than in the past. Advanced manufacturers are always striving to improve, and worker involvement is one important aspect. Many workers now make recommendations that are incorporated into the production process. Some of these are not large enough to warrant separate adjustment of standards, but taken cumulatively, a few weeks or months' worth of such incremental changes might well render standards out-of-date. Variances in such situations can signal that improvements are having a significant effect on costs.

Random Happenings

Standards are the product of managers' estimates, engineering studies, behavioral considerations, and other factors. The standard cost of a product includes many separate standards for price and use of materials and conversion costs. In essence, each standard is an expected value. Managers *expect* costs to fluctuate around the standard cost within some limits, even under ideal working conditions. The statistical model we will discuss later in this chapter identifies a reasonable band of costs around the standard cost. Thus, any result falling within these control limits can be considered random and not cause for concern.

Out-of-Control Operations

There is always the possibility that something is wrong with the process. A bearing might be wearing out, making a motor increasingly inefficient, or a pump might be adding an improper mix or consistency of materials. The process is changing from the efficiency level used in establishing the standards. Statistical techniques can be used to identify trends and to assess the cost and benefit of investigating and trying to cure the cause of the inefficiency. It is especially important to catch these problems.

WHEN TO INVESTIGATE

As we have seen, there are many reasons for variances. Managers need to decide whether to spend resources in investigating the causes of variances so that appropriate corrective action can be taken. Many companies use arbitrary policies. For example, management could state that any variance of at least $1,000 or greater than ±10 percent of standard will be reviewed. Other companies rely on statistical methods such as control charts, as we discuss shortly. We want to investigate and correct variances caused by problems in production, and not to investigate those caused by random factors. The problem, of course, is that we do not know why the variance occurred without investigating.

Management by Exception

Obtaining information is costly. If every variance from standard were investigated or reviewed, investigation costs might exceed variances. Additionally, managers would be swamped with reports, which would soon lose any sense or meaning. Therefore, from both cost and human information-processing perspectives, it is reasonable to set guidelines for variance investigation. Managers will see only the exceptions.

Several inventory accounting computer software packages allow management to specify a minimum variance amount and a minimum variance percentage. If either of these minimums is exceeded, a variance will be shown on a variance report printout. Otherwise, the variance is not reported.

Cost Versus Benefit

Investigating a material price variance might require a couple of hours on the phone with the purchasing department and suppliers. However, a material use or labor use variance might be much more complex and costly to investigate. Investigation might be in vain; the cause of the variance might not be identifiable or, if identifiable, not correctable. Finally, even a large variance can occur randomly, and if nothing is done it will disappear. Therefore, a manager needs to estimate both the expected costs and the expected benefits of investigation.

Perhaps the major cost of investigating variances is the opportunity cost of using valuable managerial or supervisory time. Of course, the more variances investigated, the more managers and supervisors the company must have. Given a fixed supply of managerial and supervisory time, the question is the best use of that time; investigating variances is one competing use.

Some costs of not investigating variances are also opportunity costs. While one of the major costs of failing to investigate and correct a variance can be a simple continuation of the variance, it could also be that the variance is accompanied by a decline in the quality of the product, resulting in lost future sales. Or, a variance in a bottleneck resource such as a group of highly skilled workers might result in lost production and therefore lost sales.

Expected Value and Investigation

Payoff tables and expected value (EV) can be used to help in investigation decisions. As with many models, it is reasonable to start off with simple assumptions and relax them later. A simple decision rule is to investigate if the expected benefit is greater than the expected cost.

Suppose a $600 variance has occurred. The data below summarize the situation.

Expected cost to investigate	$ 500
Expected cost if problem exists and is not corrected	$2,000
Probability of variance being random	20%
If variance caused by problem, probability that variance can be corrected	60%

The probability of there being a problem causing the variance is 100 percent less the probability that the variance is random. That is, there are only two possibilities: the variance is random or it is not. Similarly, *given that the variance was caused by a problem*, the probability of correcting the problem is 60 percent, so the probability of not being able to correct it is 40 percent (100 percent − 60 percent). These percentages relate to the 80 percent probability that there is a problem (the variance is not random). Exhibit 21–1 summarizes the analysis.

Exhibit 21–1 shows that the expected cost to investigate is less than the expected cost not to investigate. The company should therefore investigate. Expected value analysis assumes that the laws of large numbers have a chance to work—that is, the same choices must occur many times. Expected-value analysis is less valuable in one-shot cases or in those that occur relatively few times.

As usual, we should perform sensitivity analyses. For instance, we could compute the cost of the variance that would make us indifferent between investigating and not investigating, or the probability that the variance is random that would make us indifferent. The objective, as always with sensitivity analysis, is to determine whether a small change in a variable would change our decision. If so, we might wish to get more information about that variable. Suppose we want to know the indifference point for the probability that the variance is random. Let P = the probability that the variance is *not* random. Then we set up an equation representing the respective costs. Each term in the equation representing the cost of investigating is the analogue of the line entry in Exhibit 21–1.

$$\begin{aligned}
\textit{Cost of investigating} \quad & \quad \textit{Cost of not investigating} \\
\$500(1 - P) + \$500(.60)P + \$2{,}500(.40)P &= \$2{,}000P \\
\$500 - \$500P + \$300P + \$1{,}000P &= \$2{,}000P \\
\$500 &= \$1{,}200P \\
P &= 0.4166, \text{ or } 41.7\%
\end{aligned}$$

The probability that the variance is random is 100 percent minus 41.7 percent, or about 58.3 percent, which is much higher than the 20 percent original value. We can conclude that the decision is not sensitive to that estimate. We

EXHIBIT 21–1 Expected Costs of Investigating and Not Investigating

Choice I: Do Not Investigate

Event	Conditional Value	Probability	Expected Value
Variance is random, will stop	$0	.20	$ 0
Variance will continue	$2,000	.80	1,600
Totals		1.00	$1,600

Choice II: Investigate

Event	Conditional Value*	Probability**	Expected Value
Variance is random, will stop	$ 500	.20	$ 100
Variance has correctable cause	500	.48	240
Variance has uncorrectable cause	$2,500	.32	800
Totals		1.00	$1,140

*The $500 cost of investigating for the first two events, the $500 plus the $2,000 expected cost if the cause is not correctable for the last.
**The 20 percent probability of a random cause for the first, then 80 percent × 60 percent for the second (probability of problem times probability of correctable cause), then 80 percent × 40 percent for the third (probability of problem times probability of noncorrectable cause).

could do similar analyses with the probability of being able to correct the variance and with any of the costs. The key is simply setting up the equation that describes the indifference point.

STATISTICS AND VARIANCES

Because a standard is an expected value, the framework for investigating variances should use this expected value and its standard deviation.[1] First we establish normal bounds for costs. Then we deal with investigation costs and probable benefits.

Sample Statistics

We discussed confidence intervals and sampling in Chapter 3. In variance analysis, observations are made daily, weekly, or monthly. As each week (day,

[1]We have a wording problem in this section. We are dealing with operating *variances* and statistical *variance*. Where practicable, we shall deal with a standard deviation for statistical purposes and save the use of the word *variance* to refer to operating variances.

month) passes, production results can be observed and a mean and standard deviation of costs calculated. This sample mean ($\bar{x}_i$) is an estimate of the true cost of production (μ).

As time goes by, we accumulate more samples. If we average the sample means of several periods, the result is the grand mean denoted as $\overline{\overline{X}}$ (read as X double-bar). As we have noted before, the larger the sample, the more confident we can be that $\overline{\overline{X}}$ is a good estimator of the true cost, μ.

We shall assume initially that observations of actual cost are normally distributed. If a manager is fairly confident that the observations are normally distributed but wants to use fewer than 30 observations, he can then use a t distribution.[2] The variance of the distribution of sample means is denoted as $\sigma_{\bar{x}}^2$ and is calculated by dividing the true variance of costs by the sample size. Thus

$$\sigma_{\bar{x}}^2 = \frac{\sigma_{\bar{x}}^2}{n}$$

and $\sigma_{\bar{x}}^2$ decreases as n increases. It is usual that μ is unknown. Thus, we estimate μ by $\overline{\overline{X}}$. In the same way, $\sigma_{\bar{x}}^2$ is also unknown and we estimate it by s^2. We calculate s, the sample standard deviation, by

$$s = \sqrt{\frac{\Sigma(x_i - \bar{x})^2}{n - 1}}$$

and s is an unbiased estimator of the standard deviation.

Illustration of Calculations

Labrea Carpet makes an industrial carpet. At standard, each square yard of carpet takes 1.5 pounds of newlon fiber, at a standard price of \$1.10 per pound. The standard material cost for newlon is \$1.65 per yard of carpet. The \$1.65 is not the true cost, μ, but is the best estimate of the true cost, given that the process is operating at normal efficiency. The estimate is based on engineering studies and actual observations made under close supervision to ensure that they reflect operations under normal efficiency.

Naturally, some of the observations were different from \$1.65 despite the close supervision. Suppose that the standard deviation of the sample means was \$0.06, holding constant the \$1.10 standard price per pound. (Remember that we are interested in the material use variance separate from the material price variance.) The managers of Labrea can now make the same kinds of statements about whether future observed values are within certain limits as

---

[2] Actually, the use of a t distribution is warranted when the variance, $\sigma_{\bar{x}}^2$, is unknown. However, as the number of observations increases, the values of the t distribution approach the values for a normal distribution (a Z table). Finally, even if the underlying variable has an unknown distribution, the distribution of sample means is normal.

we did when looking at the standard error of a regression equation or at the slope of the regression line.

We shall be testing the hypothesis that actual observations come from a distribution with a mean of \$1.65 and standard deviation of \$0.06. Therefore, we denote $\overline{\overline{X}}$ as \$1.65 and $\sigma_{\bar{x}}$ as \$0.06.

Suppose that in April actual use of newlon is 247,500 pounds and production is 150,000 square yards. At the standard price of \$1.10 per pound, the cost is \$1.815 per yard of finished goods. A mean of \$1.815 is 2.75 standard deviations above the grand mean, where, for a normal distribution

$$Z = \frac{1.815 - 1.65}{0.06} = 2.75$$

Therefore, as you can see from Table A–1 in Appendix A at the back of the book, there is only a 0.003 probability that an observation of \$1.815 or above is from a distribution with a mean of \$1.65 and a standard deviation of \$0.06. It is extremely likely that this observation comes from another distribution and that material use for this period has shifted upward. In other words, it is very unlikely that the observation comes from a distribution that reflects normal efficiency, with a mean of \$1.65 and a standard deviation of \$0.06. The observation of \$1.815 is too far above the expected cost of \$1.65 to be ignored. If we looked at a 95 percent confidence interval of costs, the upper limit is \$1.7676 [\$1.65 + (1.96 × \$0.06)].

CHOOSING CONTROL LIMITS

Whatever statistical technique (or nonstatistical technique) is used, the manager must set limits beyond which to investigate. The limit could be the 99 percent range, 95 percent range, or any other. Observations outside the selected range are investigated; observations within it are not.

In deciding whether to investigate a variance, we take one of two risks. If we investigate and find that the process is in control (variance caused by some random factors), we have accepted a false hypothesis (that investigation was called for) and have wasted time and effort in the investigation. If we do not investigate, and later find that the process was out of control and the variance continues, we have rejected a true hypothesis (that investigation was called for) and have borne the extra costs of variances that we might have been able to avoid by taking corrective action.[3] In statistics these are called Type I and Type II errors, respectively.

In a later section we develop some explicit rules for investigating. At this point we offer some basic suggestions. First, suppose we have decided to use a

[3] Notice that we say "might have been able to avoid." A variance may be caused by some factor that we cannot correct, and so it would continue even if we investigated it. We will return to this important point shortly.

99 percent confidence interval and, therefore, investigate only when an observed cost has a $\frac{1}{2}$ percent or lower probability.[4] If we lower the interval to, say, 85 percent, we increase the likelihood that we will incorrectly judge a sample mean falling outside this range to be a candidate for corrective action. However, we also increase the likelihood of catching out-of-control operations and reducing future variances. There is a cost-benefit trade-off.

Because investigation is costly, managers want to investigate only when there is clear reason to do so or when the consequences of failing to investigate could be very costly. Managers therefore set relatively narrow control limits for high-cost factors and wide limits for low-cost factors. If direct labor is 75 percent of total cost, an uncorrected problem can do a great deal more damage than if labor were 15 percent of total cost.

CONTROL CHARTS

We can calculate limits for each element of price and quantity that goes into standard costs. Much as we can graph CVP relationships, we can also graph charts for various levels of production. Returning to the Labrea example, Figure 21–1 shows such a chart for newlon material use. Managers can easily check costs to see if they are within the normal range for that level of production.

Statistical Control Charts

If managers at Labrea have a fairly large sample to draw on, they can establish a 99 percent control range of $\overline{\overline{X}} \pm 2.57\sigma_{\bar{x}}$ or \$1.8042 to \$1.4958. These control limits are shown graphically in Figure 21–2. The top line is called the **upper control limit** (UCL) and the bottom line the **lower control limit** (LCL). The middle line is the standard cost. As sample data become available, they are plotted on this chart. Note that Figure 21–2 is based on per unit cost data, while Figure 21–1 deals with total cost and volume. Figure 21–2 also allows trends to be observed over time, as the mean of each sample is plotted weekly or monthly.

Control Chart for Range

As we have pointed out, a mean–standard deviation relationship underlies this statistical analysis. As a way to deal with the standard deviation, we examine the data to find the *range* of values in each sample. As we calculated control limits and drew a control chart for $\bar{x}$, the sample mean, we can do the same thing for the range (which is usually denoted as R). Charts are available for different sample sizes for $\bar{x}$ and R control charts. Statistically there is a reason

[4] We are dealing with both tails of the distribution.

FIGURE 21–1 Newlon Material Use

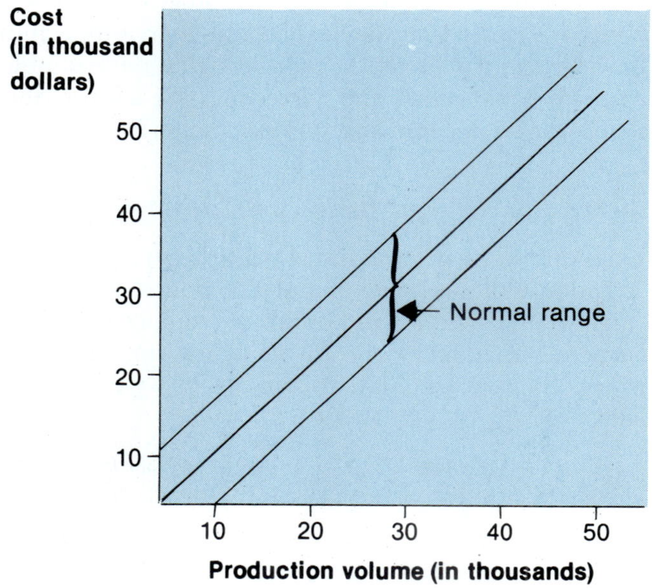

FIGURE 21–2 $\bar{x}$ Control Chart

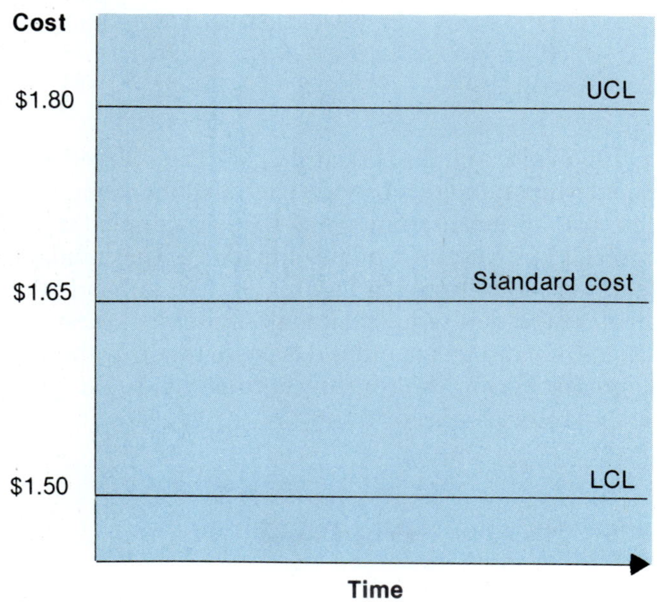

to investigate results when either the UCL or LCL is violated on *either* control chart.

If managers see a trend developing, they investigate well before control limits are crossed. As quality becomes increasingly important, managers lower (tighten) control limits. They believe that the cost of lower quality exceeds the costs of investigating and correcting. We address the cost-benefit part of an investigation decision later in this chapter.

Illustration: Weight Range for Carpeting

Each yard of carpet that has gone through the weaving process should contain 1.5 pounds of newlon fiber and 0.25 pound of backing. Thus, carpeting at this stage should weigh 1.75 pounds per square yard. During January samples of carpeting that had gone through just the weaving process were inspected every other working day. For simplicity, we use samples of five yards. The results are:

Day	Sample No.	Weight per Square Yard Measured					$\bar{x}$	R
Jan. 2	1	1.76	1.70	1.72	1.74	1.73	1.73	0.06
4	2	1.80	1.79	1.81	1.78	1.71	1.78	0.10
8	3	1.83	1.82	1.83	1.85	1.84	1.83	0.03
10	4	1.60	1.69	1.67	1.70	1.73	1.68	0.13
12	5	1.75	1.71	1.80	1.76	1.77	1.76	0.09
16	6	1.70	1.76	1.68	1.73	1.72	1.72	0.08
18	7	1.70	1.74	1.74	1.73	1.75	1.73	0.05
22	8	1.88	1.89	1.86	1.87	1.92	1.88	0.06
24	9	1.82	1.72	1.78	1.78	1.76	1.77	0.10
26	10	1.82	1.82	1.89	1.83	1.82	1.84	0.07

Figures 21–3, Part (a), and 21–3, Part (b), reflect the control limits (established when standard costs were set) that management established for $\bar{x}$ and R. The overall mean from these 10 new samples is 1.77 (rounded), and $\bar{R}$ is 0.077. These results can be compared to the standard of 1.75 and 0.075, respectively, as reflected in Figures 20, Part (a), and 20, Part (b). Thus, not only do all of the new sample data fall inside the preestablished control limits, but also the overall mean and the average range of these new samples are close to standard. Finally, the control charts show the fairly random fluctuations with no apparent pattern or trend.

BAYESIAN REVISIONS AND INVESTIGATION

The analysis of probabilities is not limited to the current sample. We can also incorporate information from the past. For instance, managers often believe that a process is in control with some specific probability, based on their expe-

FIGURE 21–3, PART (a) $\bar{x}$ **Chart**

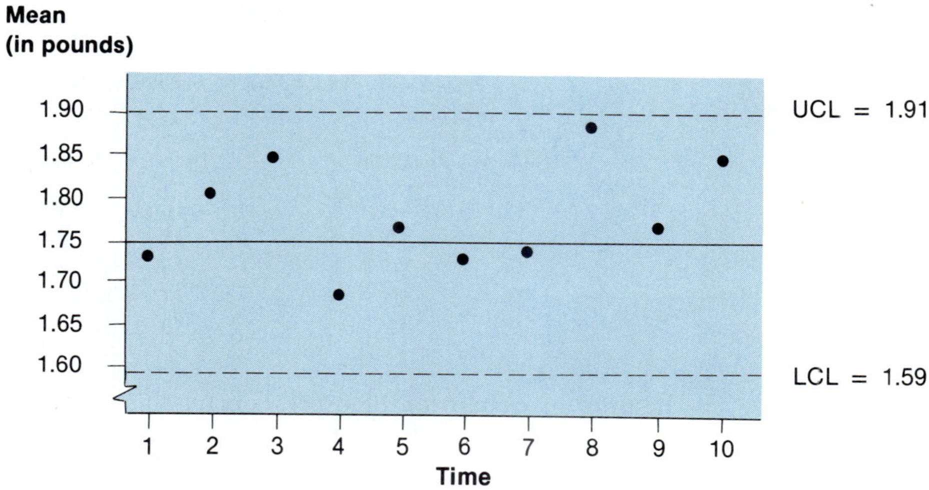

FIGURE 21–3, PART (b) ***R*** **Chart**

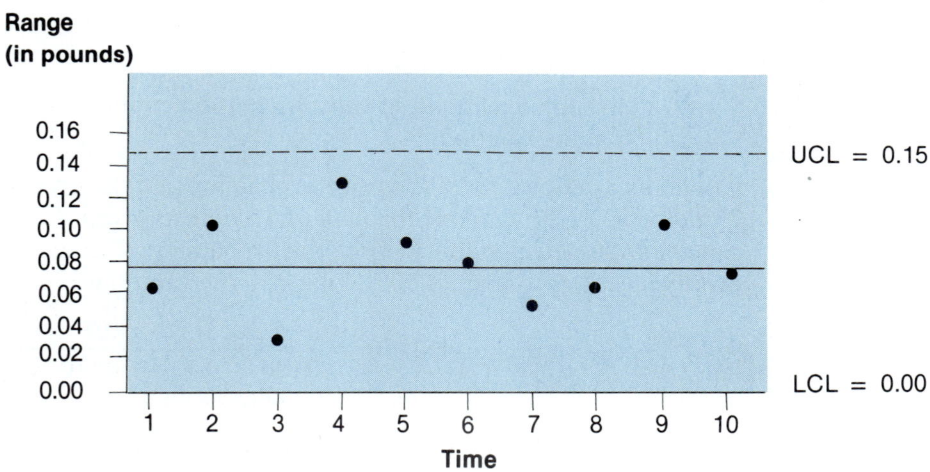

rience. We can also use historical results to estimate such probabilities. A probability that is based on historical results or judgment is called a **prior probability**. A prior probability can incorporate various pieces of information that we already have. We can use this prior probability in conjunction with information from the sample to calculate a **posterior probability**. A posterior probability is calculated using Bayes Theorem and reflects both the prior probability and the information from the current sample. The idea, then, is not to rely solely on the current sample, but also on past information.

An example should help. The data below have been collected from an operating department over a period of many weeks. The question is whether the process is operating under control. If it is not, machine parts will wear, causing waste to increase, which increases costs.

Process in Control		*Process Not in Control*	
Defects	*Probability*	*Defects*	*Probability*
12	.10	14	.20
13	.40	15	.30
14	.30	16	.30
15	.20	17	.10
16	.10	18	.10

The prior probability of the process's being in control is 75 percent. During the most recent week, there were 15 defects. Bayes' Theorem for the posterior probability is:

$$\frac{p(B|A) \cdot p(A)}{p(B|A) \cdot p(A) + p(B|\bar{A}) \cdot [1 - p(A)]}$$

where

$p(B|A)$ = the conditional probability (called a likelihood) of B *given* A

$p(A)$ = the prior probability of A

$p(B|\bar{A})$ = the likelihood of our observation coming from an *out-of-control* distribution.

Using our example, $P(A)$, the prior probability that the process is in control, is 75 percent, $P(B|A)$, the probability of 15 defects given that the process is in control, is 20 percent, and $P(B|\bar{A})$, the probability of 15 defects given that the process is not in control, is 30%. Filling in the values, we have:

$$\text{Posterior probability} = \frac{0.20 \times 0.75}{(0.20 \times 0.75) + (0.30 \times 0.25)}$$
$$= 0.6666, \text{ or } 66.7\%$$

We see that the probability of the process being in control is 66.7 percent, which is less than the prior probability. Whether it is low enough to warrant investigation depends on the cost/benefit characteristics. The cost/benefit analysis should consider whether the process is crucial and the number of defects a cause for serious concern. If so, the acceptable lower limit for the posterior probability might be quite high.

Of course, we must recognize that virtually all of the data we work with are estimates, not certainties. Even the number of defects actually observed could have some variation. We need to develop estimates for guidance, rather than seek precision. This point was introduced in Chapter 4 and has been repeated throughout. Accuracy to the fourth decimal place is rarely desirable.

Bayesian analysis permits the manager to incorporate information not only from current operating conditions, but also from past conditions. Thus, by not relying solely on one sample (current performance), it can give managers more confidence in their judgment.

INVESTIGATION AND DECISION MAKING

We have emphasized standard costs for product costing as well as for planning and control. Since much attention has been devoted to variances, it is easy to assume that control, responsibility, and evaluation of managers are more important than planning. This is not so. In fact, variances and variance investigation, while occurring at the control stage, are keys to planning for upcoming periods.

Setting New Standards

Variance analysis can indicate that current standards are inadequate and that new standards should be established. This opens the door to decisions on product mix, quality, prices, and so on. For example, if standard prices on a material such as a certain grade of plastic have changed, a television and radio manufacturer might analyze other materials available to do the same job at a lower price. If labor costs for a handmade product are rising rapidly, managers need to examine alternative methods of production.

Decision Models

Companies use quantitative models to make decisions. If the parameters of these models have changed, the models should be solved again for a new optimal solution. For example, assume that a linear programming model was employed to find an optimal product mix. Statistical variance investigation could show that one of the production processes was out of control and that the cause was too costly to correct. Thus, the basic CVP relationships for that process would change, and the old optimal linear programming solution should be revised.

Reasons for Investigating Favorable Variances

Unfavorable variances that continue from period to period cost money; obviously, at some point they should receive attention. It is not so obvious that favorable variances require attention. With management by exception, it seems reasonable to be concerned when things are going poorly and unconcerned when they are going well. There are several reasons why favorable variances should be investigated, provided that they are large enough.

In some cases, favorable variances might be caused by poor work, by cutting corners. Line managers might feel pressure to show favorable variances and might pressure workers to speed output. The resulting decline in quality could have disastrous effects, such as recalls of products and lawsuits brought by people injured by faulty performance of the products. Such behavior is most likely to occur when management over-emphasizes cost reduction.

Failing to investigate favorable variances might also result in failing to spot improved methods of operation. It is not uncommon for workers to be able to beat standards. A host of material in the organizational behavior literature testifies that workers can keep standards at low levels. Remember that standards are often set by industrial engineers who observe workers in action. The standards developed in this way may be quite loose, because the workers may be able to produce more than they show when they are observed.

There are extremely tough behavioral problems in attempting to encourage workers to increase output. Courses and textbooks in organization behavior show how subtle and intractable these problems can be, and accountants need to be aware of these difficulties.

Practical Use of Statistics

The examples regarding probabilities and variance investigation assume that a manager can adequately estimate various probabilities. Ideas such as Bayesian revisions may sound nice as academic theory but look impractical in the business world. How do managers determine probability distribution characteristics? Can they estimate the parameters of in-control and out-of-control operations? The simple decision rule for investigation assumes certain costs and benefits. Can we really know these costs with reasonable certainty? What has all this statistical material to do with accounting? Should we leave this field to the engineers, line managers, or quality control people?

The emphasis throughout this book is on useful information for managerial decision making. In this chapter we examined decisions to investigate and decisions *not* to investigate. Statistical data can help managers make these decisions. Although it is possible to make such decisions without statistical data, a systematic approach to the problem will usually yield better decisions. Therefore, even if estimates of probability distributions are inaccurate, they can still provide a framework that assists managers to direct their effort in a profitable way.

It is true that first-line supervisors, the people who observe daily operations firsthand, are in a position to determine whether operations are going relatively well or poorly. However, problems can remain undetected without proper analysis. In addition, higher level managers cannot personally observe the production process. They must rely on reports and must have a working knowledge of an acceptable range of costs. Accountants provide all levels of management with information about production, thereby calling attention to items in need of investigation.

Consider an example. If you own a car, you may keep track of gas mileage and use that information to decide whether to take the car to a garage for an inspection to see whether something is wrong. For example, you might take the car in for a checkup and possible action (tune-up, repairs) if gas mileage drops below a particular level. You realize that mileage is lower than normal when you do a good deal more city driving than usual, so low mileage after a period of high city driving would not cause you as much concern as after a period of average city-highway driving. Accordingly, you make decisions based on available information such as mileage and performance. Your decision rule could be fairly simple, such as take the car in every six months or 8,000 miles unless something is obviously wrong. However, if you operated a fleet of cars, you would probably adopt a more sophisticated decision rule, such as one derived from the statistical analysis we have illustrated. Although the cost of taking your one car to a garage might be significant, it is not likely to be so great as to require a control chart and Bayesian analysis. If you operated 150 cars, however, you might be well advised to use such analysis.

Investigation in Advanced Manufacturing Environments

Earlier chapters noted that advanced manufacturing companies often use actual costs rather than standard costs. The principles elaborated here may still be relevant to such companies.

In just-in-time and other advanced environments, investigation of variances and defects becomes both more and less important. More important because it is essential in such environments to know why variances occur: the processes are often so much more precise than traditional processes that variances are not expected. Thus, if a variance occurs, it is important to understand why. Investigation as a topic becomes less important because variances are much less likely to occur, defects are spotted much earlier, and the line is shut down until the reason for the defect is determined. Some advanced companies do not use standards at all, but rolling actual averages.

Some Japanese companies hold that a defect or other evidence of a problem is a jewel to be treasured because it enables the company to learn more about the process and to defeat further problems before they arise. Similar comments can be made about variances; they offer the opportunity to find out about problems, perhaps before they have occurred, and to avoid them in the future.

One more point about variances in advanced environments is relevant. One characteristic of such environments is a concern with the operation as a whole, not with its individual parts. Variance analysis was developed partly because of the need to evaluate the performance of individual departments and their managers. Critics of cost accounting argue that calculating variances is dysfunctional because it fosters the idea that the parts of the operation are more important than the whole. Concentrating on individual variances in individual department not only obscures the more important question of how well the entire operation is doing, but also makes it more difficult to manage the operation. This concern may or may not be valid in specific circumstances. It is clearly necessary to analyze and evaluate parts of an overall operation as well as the operation itself. Moreover, calculating variances does not imply a lack of concern with the overall operation.

VARIANCE REPORTS

We have discussed the mathematics of variance identification and the statistics surrounding possible investigation. Chapter 7 dealt with a key use of variances—as a way to assess responsibility and evaluate various managers. This section deals with the timing, format, and use of variance reports. Naturally, it discusses behavioral problems as we lend our own perceptions to reports we prepare and use.

Timing of Reports

A formal variance report must await the collection of data over a week or month, and a report form typed or generated by data-processing equipment. As timely as reports can be, they are still after the fact. They summarize events that took place last week or last month, while people are already dealing with new problems.

There is a trade-off between timeliness and accuracy. Certain tentative interim information can be fed back to line personnel hourly or daily. Managers in advanced environments, especially where processes are computer monitored, can obtain much information in real-time, as it happens. The ability to know immediately that something is wrong is extremely helpful, but there still need to be periodic reports to summarize activities per day, week, or month. Immediate feedback is excellent for monitoring and taking corrective action, while a formal report describes a relatively long period. The feedback allows for ongoing monitoring and corrective action, while the formal variance report is a summary of a whole week or month.

Variance reports are not always useful for making some operating decisions because they are too late. Managers in some situations can act knowledgeably far in advance of receiving a report. However, variance reports can be extremely useful in some areas of control.

Consider the use of control charts. A manager may look at the trends developing or may even use a computer-based forecasting model to predict future trends. A slowly deteriorating process can be identified and alternatives formulated. It is also possible that variance reports will verify seat of the pants information (also called *heuristic* information) with hard data.

Some people argue that variance reporting is too little too late and that we should not even bother with it. (As we stated earlier, some believe that even calculating variances is unwise because it focuses on small areas, not the whole.) Discontinuing variance reporting could be a sensible move for many companies, but others will probably find that the reports are beneficial. Real-time monitoring allows immediate corrective action, but, as we said above, variance reports show how a whole period looks. It is difficult to get a handle on an entire period by real-time monitoring. Some managers, therefore, will benefit from variance reporting.

Basic Reports

Exhibit 21–2 shows a basic variance report. All variances are reported on one form, and it is assumed that analysis has revealed that the variances are independent. This example is offered as a basis for discussion rather than as an illustration of a suggested report format, and all figures are assumed.

This report is a monthly summary. It simply lists variances by responsibility area. There are relatively few breakdowns of gross figures. There are no editorial or descriptive comments. The order is that in which we calculated variances in our previous discussion. We list these characteristics as starting points for discussing the form and format of these reports.

Form and Format of Variance Reports

There is no single standard type of report. Rather, managers must address the reasons for the reports and how they are perceived before they can create a useful set of reports. Many managers state that they just want to understand variances and that they do not want to wade through supporting explanations to see what the variances are all about.

Responsibility An important consideration is responsibility. If a variance is listed as part of production operations, the assumption is that the variance is indeed attributable to that department and controllable by its manager. For example, Exhibit 21–2 shows a $500 favorable variable overhead price variance under the heading of production operations. If this variance was caused by a change in supply costs not contemplated at the beginning of 19X1, the

EXHIBIT 21–2 Summary of Variances, March 19X1

Purchasing department:		
Price		$3,400F
Production scheduling:		
Labor rate		400U
Production operations:		
Material use	$1,300U	
Labor efficiency	510F	
Variable overhead price	500F	
Variable overhead efficiency	135F	
Net		155U
Capacity:		
Application		1,155U
March total		$1.690F

production manager cannot be held responsible (or given credit) for it. For this reason, a variance report should carefully distinguish between controllable and uncontrollable variances to yield a fair view of each manager.

Exhibit 21–2 lists variances with no way to compare them. This makes interpretation difficult. Is the material use variance 2 percent over standard or 20 percent over? Is it about the same as it was January or February? Unless users have a common frame of reference when looking at these figures, their perception of the value, materiality, and effect of the variances is left open, allowing for possible misinterpretation.

As part of a frame of reference, variances that are material should be highlighted and differentiated from those that are minor. Variances that violate control limits could be listed separately from those that do not.

Order and Aggregation Research has shown that the order in which variances are presented can affect user perception of how efficient the manager in question is.[5] Will the listing of all unfavorable variances first have a different effect on user perception than the listing of all favorable ones first instead? Level of aggregation is another question to be dealt with. How much should information be summarized (aggregated), and how much should it be presented in detail (disaggregated)?[6] Will the level of aggregation affect the usefulness or perception of the report? These order, format, and aggregation questions are still to be answered. The answers may vary with specific firms and specific managers.

Global Versus Local Perspective Listing each variance separately and reporting by area of responsibility (usually departments) emphasizes local operations. Managers and workers are evaluated and rewarded partly on the basis of local unit performance. Some managers believe that a global perspective is better. In some cases rewards for individual managers and workers are based on how well the entire plant performs with regard to productivity, quality, cycle time, and other measures. In such an environment, local unit variance reporting loses a great deal of value.

Exception Reports Managers are often deluged with reports and other paperwork. Certainly, to increase the usefulness of variance reports the idea of exception reporting should be employed. The number and detail of variances reported would be less for the plant manager than for a line supervisor. The plant manager is not interested in the details of every variance. She is interested in a report that draws her attention to key problem areas that warrant her attention. Therefore, the question of materiality is not just one of size of a variance, but also of who will see that variance.

---

[5] L. D. Bourne, *Order Effects in Accounting Variance Reports: A Laboratory Experiment* (unpublished Ph.D. dissertation, Washington University, 1976).

[6] J. Ronen, "Nonaggregation Versus Disaggregation of Variances," *The Accounting Review*, 49:1 (January 1974), 50–60.

Computer Screen Design Managers are becoming increasingly aware of form, order, and format issues as they help to design displays (often called screens) for computer terminals. New productivity-aid tools allow managers to design both screens and computer-generated reports with little or no help from professional programmers. Although these new programs have certain rules, the user can choose how much information to present and where to present it on each screen. The next time you look at a microcomputer screen showing, say, a menu for a program or some instructions, think of all the choices that were made regarding form, order, and format.

Verbal Analysis

Accounting reports that consist merely of a set of numbers are usually incomplete. If causes are known or if corrective action has been taken, it is good to communicate this to the user in the form of remarks.

It is important in a report such as this to distinguish facts from opinions, inferences, and assumptions. Facts are the result of unbiased procedures, such as statistical analysis of the figures. Other facts might include establishing that a worn part was the cause of a specific variance. The opinions or judgments derived from an investigation of the facts should be listed as such, along with evidence to support these interpretations of the results.

Too often variance reports can be used to fix blame. We have said that variances should be isolated by managerial responsibility. However, a verbal analysis of variances can show respect for line managers. Favorable variances that were caused by efficient operations can be praised. If a manager has taken steps to correct an unfavorable situation, that can be pointed out. Variance analysis as a cost management tool includes adaptive, corrective action. Management should be more concerned with problem solving for future periods than it is with blame fixing for the past. As a motivational footnote, repeated blaming (for failure) of a person who is not high in achievement motivation can increase that person's internal acceptance of failure and increase the tendency to *avoid* accepting the challenge of taking corrective action.

Cost-Benefit and Reporting

As can be seen from the preceding discussion, there are many behavioral dimensions to variance reporting. The discussion of standard setting in Chapter 7 pointed out how sensitive managers are about standards, because tight standards will likely produce unfavorable variances—a negative connotation, to be sure. Our analysis of the costs and benefits of collecting data and preparing variance reports is colored by these many behavioral considerations.

Computer Reports Variance reports can be generated economically as a by-product of the gathering of data in a financial accounting system that employs standard costs. With data processing equipment, variances can be identified and easily printed out. While this one report has a relatively low monetary cost, care must be given when assessing the true cost. A carelessly prepared report just listing variances can be costly in human terms for reasons discussed above.

Beyond the Computer It is important to deal specifically with issues of form and format, cost, and the benefits derived. Overt decisions in this area allow management to deal with raw variance data generated by any system—computer or human.

Reporting can be an iterative process in two ways. First, each new report can improve as a result of learning from past reports. As managers receive and use reports, they can feed back information designed to increase the effectiveness and efficiency of the reports. This feedback coupled with a cost-benefit analysis can be used to determine the form and content of reports for the next period. Obviously, as a situation becomes relatively static, the reports will become fairly routine and consistent in form.

Second, reports can be designed so that each level of management is able to add numerical, analytical, or descriptive data as a report moves from the production supervisors through the general superintendent to the plant manager and beyond. These new data can be additional facts about such things as material tolerances or the cost to replace or adjust faulty parts. They can include any corrective action that has taken place. At higher levels, specific appraisals of performance can be included. The object is to design reports that are optimal at each level of use.

SUMMARY

This chapter, along with Chapters 7 and 8, covered the idea of standards and variances, how to record standard costs in the accounting system, and statistical methods for analyzing variances. Our approach combined on-the-job experience and analysis of the cost recording system with various statistical techniques. These statistical tools are not an answer in and of themselves. However, with computers available to handle the mechanics of such methods, we can effectively use statistics to aid us and to help management save money. This is the goal of all the models from control charts through Bayesian revision. Finally, since variances from standard can be used as part of performance evaluation, we must be continually aware of how we transmit variance information so that managers will use it creatively to enhance motivation.

ASSIGNMENTS

21–1 Questions About Variances Respond to the questions below.

1. A friend has just read some material on variances and says to you, "I would think you would want to really look at all variances and find out why they happened no matter what their size. Oh, I might overlook a $10 variance, but anything that is bigger should be investigated."

2. "It would seem to me," another student says, "that if the production variances are bad, then the person in charge of that production facility should be held responsible for the poor performance."

3. A friend has done a problem where she had to find a critical value for the probability of success in investigating a variance. She tells you, "So I solved the problem and found the answer to be 58 percent. How am I ever going to know in a practical setting whether the probability of success is 58 percent?"

21–2 High Productivity Through Statistical Analysis An article in an issue of *People* magazine (September 8, 1980) discussed Dr. W. Edwards Deming and his work in Japan and the United States regarding statistical analysis. The article reminds us that "Made in Japan" used to be a joke and a synonym for shoddiness. Today Japanese products are highly regarded for their quality. Dr. Deming was instrumental in working with industry in Japan and is currently working with industry in the United States to increase quality and productivity.

Asked why American industry has not adopted his methods, Dr. Deming criticized it for not being willing to commit to a long training program for all workers. He added: "And, to my horror, I have discovered that most American companies think they already have statistical control of quality. What they have is lots of printouts full of irrelevant and out-of-date information."

Dr. Deming asserted that management has much more responsibility in declining productivity than do the workers. As an example, he discussed the purchase of inferior material that caused unfavorable efficiency variances in the production line. Management had not directed its attention to the correlation between material quality and production efficiency. Asked what could be done about ineffective management, he said:

> For one thing, our business schools have to change. Their graduates get good economics, law, finance—overall a good education. But they don't teach statistical methods in research and production. For instance, they don't teach the connection between what people need, the cost of materials and what can be produced economically.

He recommends using statistical methods to improve quality. He criticized final inspection of products or inspection at major assembly points as being inefficient and ineffective. Instead, he said, we must rely more on the statistical methods available to us for quality control.

REQUIRED

Comment on the philosophy espoused by Dr. Deming in light of the material presented in this chapter.

21–3 Control Chart Portland Carpet Company maintains a standard costing system and a set of control charts like the one that follows on the next page, which relates to direct labor cost per unit of a particular model carpet. The firm investigates a variance when the actual unit cost goes outside the limits drawn on the chart.

REQUIRED

1. Using the firm's criterion for investigating a variance, when will it first investigate direct labor cost for carpet model 397?

2. Do you have any suggestions for the firm?

Assignment 21–3 Control Chart—Direct Labor, Model 397

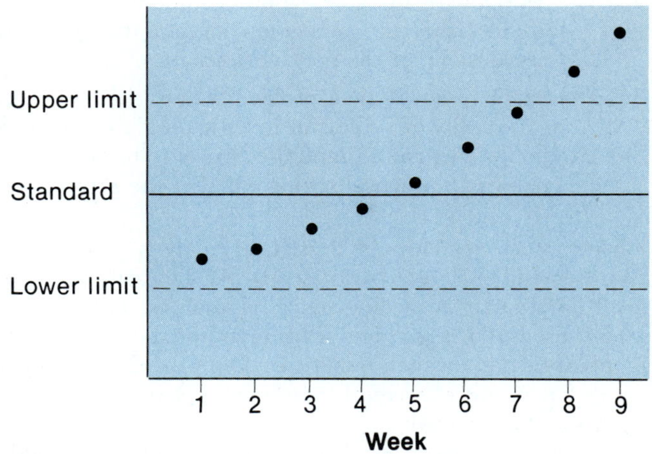

21–4 Purpose of Variance Reports (AICPA) Meyer Company's cost accounting department has prepared a factory overhead variance analysis report using the two-variance method. The plant manager of Meyer Company is interested in understanding the managerial usefulness of this report.

REQUIRED

1. What are the purposes of a factory overhead variance analysis report?
2. Identify and explain the underlying assumptions associated with the two-variance method. Discuss the significance of each variance.

21–5 Variance Investigation Porter Corporation's controller has determined that it costs \$300 to investigate a variance and that in one out of five cases investigated corrective action is possible. An unfavorable variance of \$1,000 has just been reported. Because of a major overhaul of equipment scheduled for a month from now, any savings would last only a month if corrective action could be taken.

REQUIRED

Should the variance be investigated?

21–6 Variance Investigation: Expected Values Blake, Inc., has experienced a \$2,500 unfavorable variance. The production manager believes there is a 30 percent chance that the variance is a unique occurrence. She believes that if an investigation is made, the chance of correcting the variance is 40 percent (therefore, the chance of not correcting it is 60 percent). It costs \$700 to investigate a variance. It is expected that the most that will be lost if the variance continues is \$3,000.

REQUIRED

1. Calculate the expected costs of investigating and not investigating the variance.
2. Should an investigation be made?

21–7 Variance Investigation: Expected Values (AICPA) Bilco Oil Company sells three grades of gasoline: regular, premium, and regular plus, which is a mixture of regular and premium. Regular plus is advertised as "at least 50 percent premium." Although any mixture containing 50 percent or more premium gas could be sold as regular plus, it is less costly to use exactly 50 percent. The percentage of premium gas in the mixture is determined by one valve in the blending machine. If the valve is properly adjusted, the machine provides a mixture that is 50 percent premium and 50 percent regular. If the valve is out of adjustment the machine provides a mixture that is 60 percent premium and 40 percent regular.

Once the machine is started it must continue until 100,000 gallons of regular plus have been mixed. The following cost data are available:

Cost per gallon—premium	$ 0.32
—regular	$ 0.30
Cost of checking the valve	$80.00
Cost of adjusting the valve	$40.00

Subjective estimates of the probabilities of the valve's condition are estimated to be

Event	*Probability*
Valve in adjustment	0.7
Valve out of adjustment	0.3

REQUIRED

1. What is the expected cost of checking the valve and adjusting it if necessary?
2. What is the conditional cost of not checking the valve when it is out of adjustment?
3. What is the critical probability for investigations?

21–8 Variance Investigation: Expected Values Current variance reports from Schlechter Company show an unfavorable $2,000 variance this month. The production supervisor has analyzed past data and estimates that about 30 percent of the time a variance of this size is experienced there is nothing wrong with the process and the variance stops. When there is a problem with the process, about 60 percent of the time the variance continues for two additional months (at $2,000 per month) and 40 percent of the time it continues at $2,000 per month for three months.

Just investigating the variance will cost Schlechter $800. A correctable problem usually occurs about 40 percent of the time (for either two-month or three-month variances). If a correctable cause is found, it is estimated that another $600 would be spent to solve the problem.

REQUIRED

Determine the expected costs of investigating and of not investigating.

21–9 Decision to Investigate Standard costs for Crawford Frozen Foods Company include the following for one of its largest-selling products:

Standard Material Costs
Chinese Beef and Asparagus Dinner
per 8-oz Package

Choice grade sirloin strips, 8 oz uncooked weight at \$3/lb	\$1.50
California select thin asparagus, 3 oz uncooked weight at \$1.50/lb	0.28
Secret blend of herbs and spices, $\frac{1}{2}$ oz	0.20

Production starts in the food preparation department, where all raw foodstuffs are cut. From there, the raw foods go to the cooking department, where workers combine the ingredients according to Crawford's recipes. Portion control is very important from the standpoint of cost as well as of quality and consistency. Foods shrink when cooked; it is expected that the net weight of a package after shrinkage is eight ounces. Management has set up control limits as follows, using a three-sigma range for the finished product:

$\bar{X}$: 7.92 to 8.16 oz
R: 0 to 0.12 oz

Crawford is limited by federal government rules to providing packages that weigh no less than 99 percent of the stated weight. Thus, while the upper control limit is three sigmas, the lower limit is truncated for $\bar{X}$.

During February the following samples were taken at random over a one-week period:

		Sample Packages			
Sample	*Work Shift*	*1*	*2*	*3*	*4*
1	1	7.95	8.09	8.06	8.03
2	2	8.16	8.13	8.18	8.11
3	2	8.14	8.19	8.12	8.15
4	1	8.05	7.93	8.07	8.05
5	1	8.05	8.03	8.02	8.15
6	2	8.12	8.20	8.15	8.17

REQUIRED

1. Plot the data on $\bar{X}$ and R charts.
2. On the basis of these data, what recommendations would you make to the managers of Crawford?

21–10 Developing Control Charts Rather than calculating control limits for $\bar{\bar{X}}$ (and $\bar{R}$) by using $\bar{\bar{X}}$ and σ_x, tables are available to use just $\bar{\bar{X}}$ and $\bar{R}$ in the calculations. Under this method, control limits for $\bar{\bar{X}}$ are $\bar{\bar{X}} \pm F\bar{R}$.

where F is a factor (Exhibit 21–3) for 3 standard deviations (a confidence interval of 99.73 percent using the normal distribution). Limits for $\bar{R}$ are

upper limit: $U\bar{R}$
lower limit: $L\bar{R}$

EXHIBIT 21–3 Control-Limit Factor for $\overline{\overline{X}}$ Charts, F

n	F
2	1.880
3	1.023
4	0.729
5	0.577
6	0.483
7	0.419
8	0.373
9	0.337
12	0.266
14	0.235
16	0.212

EXHIBIT 21–4 Control-Limit Factors for R Charts, U and L

n	U	L
2	3.268	0.000
3	2.574	0.000
4	2.282	0.000
5	2.114	0.000
6	2.004	0.000
7	1.924	0.076
8	1.864	0.136
9	1.816	0.184
12	1.716	0.284
14	1.671	0.329
16	1.636	0.364

where U and L (Exhibit 21–4) also are 3 standard deviations from the mean, $\bar{R}$. In both cases, n refers to the number of items in each sample.

Tercela Company produces a chemical called Plake that is delivered to customers in five-pound buckets. As part of cost control it is important to check that the net weight of each bucket of Plake is within reasonable limits of 5 pounds. On January 28 management sampled production runs over an eight-hour shift. The weights found in Exhibit 21–5 were recorded for samples taken at random during each hour.

REQUIRED

1. Using the techniques described above, establish upper and lower control limits for $\overline{\overline{X}}$ and $\bar{R}$.
2. Use the techniques in the chapter to confirm a 3-standard-deviation UCL and LCL calculated for $\overline{\overline{X}}$ and $\bar{R}$ in part 1.

EXHIBIT 21–5 Tercela Company Production Runs

	Samples (in Pounds)					
Hour	*1*	*2*	*3*	*4*	*5*	*6*
1	5.22	5.06	4.97	5.11	5.02	5.03
2	4.95	5.18	5.08	5.00	5.06	5.12
3	5.11	5.09	5.06	5.13	5.10	5.01
4	4.98	5.00	5.06	4.96	5.07	5.10
5	5.05	5.18	5.01	5.15	5.01	5.09
6	5.11	5.04	5.06	5.10	5.18	5.20
7	5.07	5.11	5.08	4.99	5.00	5.02
8	5.13	5.02	5.09	5.08	5.15	5.10

21–11 When to Investigate Frank Strout, Manager of Midcourse, Inc., has been accumulating data over several years concerning the costs, benefits, and probability of success when seemingly excessive variances have been investigated. These data show that about 90 percent of the time that material use is higher than $2\frac{1}{2}$ standard deviations from standard, the process can be considered out of control. Past records also show that use under $2\frac{1}{2}$ standard deviations from standard means that there is an 85 percent chance the process is in control.

REQUIRED

1. What is the probability that the process is in control given each of the following situations?

a.

	Standard Cost per Unit	σ
Material	3 lb at $4	$1
Actual use	1,000 units produced using $15,000 of materials at standard prices	

b.

	Standard Cost per Unit	σ
Material	4 gal at $5	0.2 gal
Actual use	1,000 units produced using 4,400 gal	

2. If we assume that the cost to investigate variances is $1,500 and the expected savings are $2,000 in part 1a, what is the breakeven point for investigation? Would you investigate in this case? What about part 1b?

21–12 Investigation Decisions Studies by the industrial engineering staff indicate that the direct labor time on product 804 should average 12.6 hours. The distribution should be about normal, with a standard deviation of 1.4 hours. You have established 95 percent confidence limits of 9.8 and 15.4 hours for deciding whether or not to investigate labor efficiency variances.

Results for the past seven weeks appear below.

Week Number	Average Labor Time
1	12.4
2	12.9
3	12.7
4	13.4
5	13.6
6	14.0
7	14.3

Week 7 is the most recent week for which you have data. You have not investigated any variances during the seven-week period because labor time has remained well within the 95 percent confidence limits.

REQUIRED

Discuss whether you would investigate the labor efficiency variance even though labor time is within the 95 percent confidence limits. Would your answer be different if the product were a high-volume item with a contribution margin of $28 per unit when labor time was 12.6 hours, and if total labor and variable overhead was $9.50 per labor hour?

21–13 Linear Programming and Variance Investigation Many companies use linear programming in resource allocation. The constraint on labor time, for example, includes standard times for each different unit produced. If actual times vary either favorably or unfavorably beyond some point, the company would be better off to produce a different mix than the mix of products called for using a linear programming solution.

Assume that cost data for Egrad Company are as follows:

	Product 1	Product 2
Sales price	$20.00	$21.00
Materials at $1/lb	3.00	5.00
Labor at $2/hr	5.00	4.00
Overhead	6.00	4.80
Margin	$ 6.00	$ 7.20

Constraints are as follows:

Materials	200 lb
Labor	100 hr

The final tableau of a simplex solution to the linear programming problem appears below.

Final Tableau

			$6	$7.20	$0	$0
C_j	Product Mix	Quantity	X_1	X_2	S_1	S_2
$7.20	X_2	30.769	0	1	.3846	−.4615
$6	X_1	15.385	1	0	−.3077	.7692
	Z_j	$313.85	$6	$7.20	$.9229	$1.2924
	$C_j - Z_j$		0	0	−$.9229	−$1.2924

REQUIRED

1. What level of labor is required to change the solution? [*Hint*: Use sensitivity analysis developed in Chapter 12.]
2. During the current month, variances on product 1 for 1,000 units were as follows:

Material use variance	$ 600U
Labor efficiency variance	$1,200U

If these variances are investigated and found permanent, should the production schedule be changed or kept the same? If it is change, what is the new solution?

21–14 Variance Reports Doonsberry division of Zonker Enterprises produces footballs, basketballs, and soccer balls for home, school, and professional use. The following is a variance report issued on January 11, 19X1, for production during November 19X0:

Variance Report, Footballs—Model H25

Sales variances	$1,200F
Production variances:	
Material use variance	$ 300U
Labor rate variance	200U
Labor efficiency variance	800U
Variable overhead efficiency variance	600U
Material price variance	400F
Variable overhead rate variance	100F
Fixed overhead spending variance	1,000F
Fixed overhead application variance	400F

REQUIRED

Comment on this report and offer suggestions for improvement.

21–15 Bayesian Revision Harris Stowe, the production manager of Redeye Manufacturers, has been developing data on one of the main pieces of manufacturing equipment. As a cost accountant, you have been using these data to look beyond simple variance calculations. The main forming machine usually produces parts that are within standard tolerances. For example, the standards for a #80-H shaft include a diameter of 2.5 cm and an acceptable variance of 0.01 cm. However, internal parts of the machine are subject to wear. Past experience indicates that when average diameter is 2.9 cm and the variance is 0.09 cm, the process is out of control and repairs are called for costing $38,000 at current prices. During December, production data combined with standard costs showed $8,000 in unfavorable variances associated with the production of #80-H shafts. You have been asked to give Stowe information to help him decide whether to order the $38,000 overhaul. December production reports show an average diameter for #80-H shafts of 2.75 cm.

REQUIRED

If management is 90 percent confident that a variance of 10 percent or less means that the production process is within normal ranges of tolerance, calculate an updated probability estimate for Stowe, given the current production information. (A table of selected exact probabilities, also called ordinates, follows.)

$\frac{X - \mu}{\sigma}$	*Ordinate*
0.25	0.38667
0.50	0.35207
0.75	0.30114
1.00	0.24197
1.25	0.18265
1.50	0.12952
1.75	0.08628
2.00	0.05399
2.25	0.03174
2.50	0.01753
2.75	0.00909
3.00	0.00443

21–16 Investigation Decision In Assignment 21–15 you were asked to calculate the posterior probability that the forming process was in control. Assume Redeye management thinks that if $38,000 is spent on an overhaul, there is only an 80 percent chance that they can solve an out-of-control situation. Also assume that if the process is out of control, abnormal variances will be $90,000 per year.

REQUIRED

Using a one-year time frame, should management order an overhaul? (Use the information you calculated in the previous assignment.)

21–17 Variances and Make-or-Buy Decision Richards Company has been making an electronic subassembly that it uses in several products. The manufacturing process for the subassembly is very precise, and machine settings are critical. The following data regarding production times under two sets of conditions attest to the problem.

	Correct Setting	*Incorrect Setting*
Average labor time, hours per unit	10	14
Standard deviation of labor time	1	3

The times, under both the correct setting and the incorrect setting, are normally distributed about their respective means. Incorrect settings occur about 30 percent of the time. The total variable cost per labor hour, including labor cost and variable overhead, is $22.

New machinery on the market is less sensitive to settings. However, Richards does not make enough of the subassemblies to warrant buying the machinery. Another firm that has bought the machinery and has some excess capacity has offered to do the work in the subassemblies for $250 each. Richards would supply the material.

REQUIRED

Make a recommendation supported by whatever calculations you deem relevant.

21–18 Variances—A Chance to Review Standards The standards for overhead in Kermit Glove Company were set using linear regression and correlation analysis. Based on this analysis, variable overhead was set at $1.10 per direct labor hour. After the first six months of operations, the plant manager has pointed to the following variable overhead variances and has asked that they be investigated:

Variable Overhead Spending Variance, January–June, 19X1

	Production Level	*Variance*
January	3,000 units	$ 500F
February	3,500	1,000U
March	4,000	100U
April	4,200	500F
May	3,800	500U
June	3,300	100U

The production manager states that the last six months are typical of good production and he does not understand this big swing in variances. Further investigation reveals that the data used for the standards are as follows:

Direct Labor Hours	*Overhead Costs*
7,200	$11,982
6,600	10,721
5,800	9,552
6,300	10,004
8,030	12,017
6,850	11,325
7,500	12,031
6,700	11,197
6,500	10,578
7,850	12,040
7,000	11,930
8,120	12,006
5,500	9,505

It takes two labor hours to produce one unit based on standard costs. The efficiency variances have been fairly minimal over the last six months.

REQUIRED

1. The production manager says that the stated variances do not seem reasonable. Check the standards for variable overhead by calculating a regression equation by hand, calculator, or computer. What reply do you make to the production manager?
2. Plot the original data. Does this change your thinking? Explain.

21–19 Variances and Decisions Carlton Company makes two models of high-quality radios, model X and model Y. Data on each model appear below.

		Model X		*Model Y*
Selling price		$150		$230
Standard material cost	$25		$30	
Standard labor cost:				
Department I	10		20	
Department II	15		20	
Standard variable overhead at 200% of direct labor	50	100	80	150
Contribution margin		$ 50		$ 80

All direct laborers earn $10 per hour, and the variable overhead rate of 200 percent of direct labor cost applies to both departments. Department I does the basic assembling operations on the chassis, while department II does the final assembling. The firm has 500 direct labor hours available per week in department I, 600 hours in department II. The firm operates at capacity because it can sell all of either model that it can make.

The managers of the firm have used the data to develop the following weekly production plan: model X, 200 units; model Y, 150 units. This plan is the result of solving the linear programming problem:

$$\begin{aligned} \text{Maximize:}\quad & \$50X + \$80Y \\ \text{Subject to:}\quad & X + 2Y \leq 500 \\ & 1.5X + 2Y \leq 600 \\ & X, Y \geq 0 \end{aligned}$$

After a time, the managers have observed that it takes $2\frac{1}{2}$ hours to do a unit of model Y in department I about half the time. The department begins each week working on model Y, then uses the remaining available hours to work on model X. The reason has to do with the technology of the process. In addition, the managers must decide on the production schedule before the week starts: it is very costly to change it during the week.

Accordingly, when it does take $2\frac{1}{2}$ hours to get a unit of model Y through department I, the firm can make 150 units of Y, but only 125 units of model X. (Subtracting 2.5×150 from the available hours in department I, 500, gives 125 hours for making model X.) Additionally, the contribution margin on model Y falls by $15 because the combined labor and variable overhead per hour is $30.

REQUIRED

Analyze the alternatives and make a recommendation.

21–20 Bayesian Revisions—Two Periods Fondar Corporation has established probability distributions for the production process being in control and out of control as follows:

In Control		*Out of Control*	
Waste Percentage	*Probability*	*Waste Percentage*	*Probability*
0.10	0.05	0.13	0.05
0.09	0.10	0.12	0.05
0.08	0.20	0.11	0.15
0.07	0.30	0.10	0.35
0.06	0.20	0.09	0.20
0.05	0.10	0.08	0.10
0.04	0.05	0.07	0.10

In March 19X0, the prior probability of being in control is 0.80. If the probability of being in control falls below 40 percent, then the company will investigate the situation.

REQUIRED

1. During April, a sample revealed 10 percent waste. Should the company investigate?
2. During May, a sample revealed 8 percent waste. Should the company investigate? (Use the probability developed in part 1 as your new prior probability.)

21–21 Variance Investigation (Extension of Assignment 8–20) Refer to Assignment 8–20 for the basic data for this problem (relating to Northland division of Blann, Inc.).

REQUIRED

1. When standard costs for labor and materials were developed, standard deviations from standard costs were also developed as follows:

	Standard Cost	Standard Deviation of Standard Cost
Materials	$6.40	$0.23
Labor	2.15	0.06

Overhead standards were developed from a regression and correlation analysis, where

$$\text{overhead costs} = \$7{,}980 + \$2.963/\text{labor hour}$$

where

$r^2 = 0.9476$

$S_e = 753.07$

$S_b = 0.06$

Management has decided to accept as normal any variances falling within a 95 percent confidence interval of standard costs. Evaluate the results obtained and list for management the variances that might be investigated.

2. Assume that management is deciding whether to investigate the labor efficiency variance (and the variable overhead efficiency variance, since it is tied to labor hours worked). If it investigates this variance, it is estimated that costs will be $1,500. If a correctable problem is found, another $4,200 is expected to be spent. Experience has shown that management can expect to find a correctable cause of a labor efficiency variance about 40 percent of the time. In most cases this variance is a random event that will not recur. Even if a correctable cause is found, management estimates that ongoing savings should be based on the limits of the confidence interval calculated in part 1. Should management investigate these variances? Assume a relevant time period is three years and the relevant interest rate is 10 percent.

21–22 New Variance System—A Case (CMA) Maidwell Company manufactures washers and dryers on a single assembly line in its main factory. The market has deteriorated over the last five years, and competition has made cost control very important. Management has been concerned about the materials cost of both washers and dryers. There have been no model changes in the past two years, and economic conditions have allowed the company to negotiate price reductions in many key parts.

Maidwell uses a standard cost system in accounting for materials. Purchases are charged to inventory at a standard price with purchase discounts considered an administrative cost reduction. Production is charged at the standard price of the materials used. Thus, the price variance is isolated at time of purchase as the difference between gross contract price and standard price multiplied by the quantity purchased. When a substitute part is used in production, a price variance equal to the difference in the standard prices of the materials is recognized at the time of substitution. The quantity variance is the actual quantity used compared with the standard quantity allowed, with the difference multiplied by the standard price.

The materials variances for several of the parts Maidwell uses are unfavorable. Part no. 4121 is one of the items that has an unfavorable variance. Maidwell knows that some of these parts will be defective and fail. The failure is discovered during production. The normal defective rate is 5 percent of normal input. The original contract price of this part was $0.285 per unit; thus, Maidwell set the standard unit price at $0.285. The unit contract purchase price of part no. 4121 was increased $0.04 to $0.325 from the original $0.285 due to a parts specification change. Maidwell chose not to change the standard, but to treat the increase in price as a price variance. In addition, the contract terms were changed from n/30 to 4/10, n/30 as a consequence of negotiations resulting from changes in the economy.

Data regarding the usage of part no. 4121 during December are:

Purchases of part no. 4121	150,000 units
Unit price paid for purchases of part no. 4121	$0.325
Requisitions of part no. 4121 from stores for use in products	134,000 units
Substitution of part no. 5125 for part no. 4121 to use obsolete stock (standard unit price of part no. 5125 is $0.35)	24,000 units
Units of part no. 4121 and its substitute (part no. 5125) identified as defective	9,565 units
Standard allowed usage (including normal defective units) of part no. 4121 and its substitute based on output for the month	153 300 units

Maidwell's material variances related to part no. 4121 for December were reported as:

Price variance	$7,560.00U
Quantity variance	1,339.50U
Total material variances for part no. 4121	$8,899.50U

Bob Speck, Purchasing Director, claims the unfavorable price variance is misleading. Speck says that his department has worked hard to obtain price concessions and purchase discounts from suppliers. In addition, Speck has indicated that engineering changes have been made in several parts, increasing their price, even though the part identification has not changed. These price increases are not his department's responsibility. Speck declares that price variance simply no longer measures the Purchasing Department's performance.

Jim Buddle, Manufacturing Manager, thinks that responsibility for the quantity variance should be shared. Buddle states that manufacturing cannot control quality arising from less expensive parts, substitutions of material to use up otherwise obsolete stock, or engineering changes that increase the quantity of materials used.

The Accounting Manager, Mike Kohl, has suggested changing computation of variances to identify variations from standard with the causes and functional areas responsible for the variances. The following system of material variances and the method of computation for each was recommended by Kohl:

Variance	*Method of Calculation*
Economics variance	Quantity purchased times the changes made after setting standards that were the result of negotiations based on changes in the general economy.

(*continued*)

Variance	Method of Calculation
Engineering change variance	Quantity purchased times change in price due to part specifications changes.
Purchase price variance	Quantity purchased times change in contract price because of changes other than parts specifications or the general economy.
Substitutions variance	Quantity substituted times the difference in standard price between parts substituted.
Excess usage variance	Standard price times the difference between the standard quantity allowed for production minus actual parts used (reduced for abnormal scrap).
Abnormal failure rate variance	Abnormal scrap times standard price.

REQUIRED

1. Discuss the appropriateness of Maidwell Company's current method of variance analysis for materials and indicate whether the claims of Bob Speck and Jim Buddle are valid.
2. Compute the materials variances for part no. 4121 for December using the system recommended by Mike Kohl.
3. Indicate who would be responsible for each of the variances in Mike Kohl's system of variance analysis for materials.

21–23 Cost and Variance Reports (CMA) Denny Daniels is production manager of Alumalloy division of WRT, Inc. Alumalloy has limited contact with outside customers and has no sales staff. Most of its customers are other divisions of WRT. All sales and purchases with outside customers are handled by other corporate divisions. Therefore, Alumalloy is treated as a cost center for reporting and evaluation purposes rather than as a revenue or profit center.

Daniels perceives the accounting department as a historical number generating process that provides little useful information for conducting his job. Consequently, the entire accounting process is perceived as a negative motivational device that does not reflect how hard or effectively he works. Daniels tried to discuss these perceptions and concerns with Jan Scott, controller for the Alumalloy division. Daniels told Scott:

> I think the cost report is misleading. I know I've had better production over a number of operating periods, but the cost report still says I have excessive costs. Look, I'm not an accountant, I'm a production manager. I know how to get a good quality product out. Over a number of years, I've even cut the raw materials used to do it. But the cost report doesn't show any of this. Basically, it's always negative, no matter what I do. There's no way you can win with accounting or the people at corporate who use those reports.

Scott gave Daniels little consolation. Scott stated that the accounting system and cost reports generated by headquarters are just part of the corporate game and almost impossible for an individual to change. "Although these accounting reports are pretty much the basis for evaluating the efficiency of your division and the means corporate uses to determine whether you have done the job they want, you shouldn't worry too much. You haven't been fired yet! Besides, these cost reports have been used by WRT for the last 25 years."

Daniels perceived from talking to the production manager of the Zinc division that most of what Scott said was probably true. However, some minor cost reporting changes for Zinc had been agreed to by corporate headquarters. Daniels also knew from the trade grapevine that the turnover of production managers was considered high at WRT, although relatively few were fired. Most seemed to end up quitting, usually in disgust, because they believed that they were not being evaluated fairly. Typical comments of production managers who have left WRT are

> Corporate headquarters doesn't really listen to us. All they consider are those misleading cost reports. They don't want them changed, and they don't want any supplemental information.
>
> The accountants may be quick with numbers, but they don't know anything about production. As it was, I either had to ignore the cost reports entirely or pretend they were important, even though they didn't tell how good a job I had done. No matter what they say about not firing people, negative reports mean negative evaluations. I'm better off working for another company.

A recent copy of the cost report prepared by corporate headquarters for the Alumalloy division is shown below. Daniels does not like this report because he believes it fails to properly reflect the division's operations, thereby resulting in an unfair evaluation of performance.

ALUMALLOY DIVISION
Cost Report
for the Month of April 19X0
(in thousands of dollars)

	Master Budget	Actual Cost	Excess Cost
Aluminum	$ 400	$ 437	$37
Labor	560	540	(20)
Overhead	100	134	34
Total	$1,060	$1,111	$51

REQUIRED

1. Comment on Denny Daniels' perception of
   a. Jan Scott, the Controller
   b. corporate headquarters
   c. the cost report
   d. himself as a production manager

   Discuss how Daniels' perception affects his behavior and probable performance as a production manager and employee of WRT.

2. Identify and explain three changes that could be made in the cost information presented to the production managers that would make the information more meaningful and less threatening to them.

21–24 Variance Reports World's Fair Printing Company, located in a large midwestern city with plants throughout Ohio and Indiana, is a large printer of books and catalogs. The company was founded in the 1920s with a plant in Dayton. Over the years several suburban and rural plants have been built. Currently the company has $200 million in sales annually. The corporate headquarters are in Dayton. The general organizational structure is mostly decentralized with respect to all functions except finance and sales. These functions are carried out and coordinated by the corporate headquarters.

The Troy, Ohio, plant primarily prints catalogs for stores and mail-order companies. The plant consists of a preparatory department where plates for the offset presses are made, a pressroom containing 15 offset presses, a bindery where the sections of each catalog are collected, bound, and made ready for shipment, and a shipping department where orders are staged and shipped by truck and rail.

Purchasing consists of paper, ink, and preparatory, binding, and shipping supplies. Paper contracts are negotiated companywide at corporate headquarters by a committee consisting of the various plant managers under the direction of the vice president of production. Paper contracts tend to be long-term insofar as supply commitments are concerned, but prices vary with the market. Several mills supply paper to the Troy plant. Ink contracts for both price and quantity are negotiated by each plant manager. In some plants there are various suppliers; in other plants an ink company has installed an in-house plant for producing ink next to the production facility. This is the case at Troy. The purchasing department at each plant is responsible for the various supplies that are bought. Aluminum of a certain weight and thickness as well as various supplies and chemicals are needed for the preparatory department. Photographic materials also must be purchased, although they usually come from a major supplier such as Kodak. Wire, glue, and other supplies must be purchased for binding and shipping. Contracting for boxes and bags is handled separately from that for paper for printing. In the case of boxes and bags, the local purchasing department makes the necessary contacts.

The operations of the preparatory department are as follows: material is sent in from various customers in what is called camera-ready form. This means that all type has been set, sized, and pasted down onto thin sheets of cardboard, so that only one photo is needed per page of type. Photographs are provided loose, showing any necessary cropping and sizing. Thus, each photograph will require one photo. This camera-ready art work is taken to the camera room, where large horizontal cameras take pictures of both the type and the photographs needed for each page. Film is processed through an automatic film-processing machine and is given to a worker at a light table (a large table with a piece of glass on top and fluorescent lights underneath) to put together into eight-page groupings. The presses are set up so that each part of a catalog that is printed is basically a 16-page section. There are eight pages on each side of this section. Depending on the size of the press used, 16, 32, or 48 pages may be printed at one time. After the worker has assembled eight pages using special paper and tape, a contact print of the finished sheet (sometimes called an eight-page flat) is made on another large piece of film.

In another part of the preparatory department, thin sheets of aluminum are coated with a special chemical substance that is heat and light sensitive. The full eight-page negatives are placed on top of the aluminum plates. This sandwich is exposed to high-intensity light, which hardens all the material on the aluminum exposed through clear areas in the film. The printing plate is put through a chemical process by which the soft areas (those areas that were black on the negative) are washed away. A caustic substance is used to etch into the plate, and a copper solution is introduced into this area. When this process is completed, the remaining treated area of the plate is removed. As a result, all areas that will print have been filled with a copper substance, and all areas that will not print remain aluminum. The plate is treated with a preservative and sent to the press room. Given the number of presses at the Troy plant and the average length of production runs, an average of 50 to 60 plates are produced in each eight-hour shift. The plant generally runs three shifts a day.

The general cost accounting system for the Troy plant, as most of the other plants in the company, is basically job order costing. The costs are accumulated by each catalog for analysis by both the production department and the sales department.

REQUIRED

Plant management has just instituted a standard cost system in the preparatory department. Expected costs have been developed for the various aspects of the production process in this department. You have been asked to prepare a recommendation for variance reports reflecting the performance of the preparatory department. The variance reports will be used as appropriate by various levels of management. Part of your recommendation should include the audience and format of your reports. State all assumptions you have made. If you have questions that need to be answered before final recommendations are made, make sure to list these questions.

22

THE LEARNING EFFECT

A basic tenet of management accounting information is the division of costs into fixed and variable components. In earlier chapters we saw how some traditionally variable costs (e.g., direct labor) are becoming fixed, how to predict variable costs through techniques such as simple linear regression, and how to adjust variable costs for external forces such as inflation. Mainly, we estimate and use variable costs as if they are *constant per unit* of activity. However, variable costs can decline if workers can learn to improve productivity.

EFFECT OF LEARNING ON PRODUCTIVITY

Experience shows that the time required to produce a unit of product declines as workers learn. This phenomenon is called the **learning effect** or the **learning curve** (or similar names).[1] Managers who know about the effect of learning can make better decisions on a variety of planning and control applications including production scheduling, budgeting, setting standard costs and analyzing variances, pricing, and a host of special decisions.

LEARNING EFFECT MODELS

The basic concept of a learning effect is that the time it takes to do a particular task decreases predictably. The learning curve can be expressed in different ways. One common statement is that as cumulative production doubles, cu-

[1] Other terms include *progress curves*, *improvement curves*, and *manufacturing efficiency curve*.

mulative average time required to make a unit or a batch declines by a certain percentage. The percentage varies from situation to situation. Early studies of the learning curve in the aircraft industry showed a 20 percent decline.[2] As a rule, the learning effect is expressed by reference to the value *to* which the cumulative average declines, not the value *by* which it declines. Thus, a decline of 20 percent would bring the new value to 80 percent of the former and we would say that the learning effect was 80 percent. Similarly, if cumulative average time decreased by 15 percent, there is an 85 percent learning curve.

There are many forms of the learning curve. The two most popular are the marginal time model and the cumulative average model. Both are used in practice; the principle behind these and other forms of the learning effect is the same, only the mathematical representation differs. The main idea is to find a form that best represents the pattern of learning in a particular situation. In the discussion that follows, we focus on *time* rather than *cost* since it is time that is declining.

Marginal Time Model

In the marginal time model (or marginal model), *marginal* time goes down by a set percentage (the learning effect) each time production doubles. Consider Gordon Company, a producer of small industrial products. The purchasing manager of Morehead Industries has approached Gordon for a bid on 32 batches of components that Morehead needs for one of its products. Other firms will also bid on the job. To bid on this job, managers of Gordon must estimate the total cost to produce the components, and one part of that cost is direct labor. Industrial engineers at Gordon estimate that the first batch should take about 100 hours and that the firm should experience an 80 percent learning curve throughout the production run. Estimated times using the marginal model and an 80 percent learning curve are shown in Exhibit 22–1.

Under the marginal time model, the time for the second batch (a doubling point) is 80 hours if the first batch takes 100 hours. The next doubling point is four batches; the marginal time for the *fourth* batch is 80 percent of the second batch, or 64 hours (0.80×80). This same process applies at all the doubling points.

This model focuses attention on marginal time; we also need a formula to find cumulative time. While it is easy to see that the cumulative time for two batches is 180 hours, we cannot find cumulative time for, say, four batches. As we move to 8, 16, or 32 batches, this problem increases.

Without formulas we are also limited to looking at learning only at doubling points. We cannot find the marginal time for the third batch or the

[2] An early example is T. P. Wright, "Factors Affecting the Cost of Airplanes," *Journal of Aeronautical Science* (February 1936), 122–128.

EXHIBIT 22–1 Marginal Time Model—Gordon Company

Batches	Marginal Time	Cumulative Time
1	100 hours	100 hours
2	80 (100 × 0.80)	180
4	64 (80 × 0.80)	
8	51.2 (64 × 0.80)	
16	40.96 (51.2 × 0.80)	
32	32.768 (40.96 × 0.80)	

seventh batch. Thus we need basic formulas for a general approach to the learning problem. These formulas are shown in Exhibit 22–2. Appendix 22A contains an explanation of the derivation of the learning exponent, b. Using the basic marginal time formula, the marginal times and cumulative times for the first four batches are as follows (again assuming an 80 percent learning curve):

First, the learning exponent is $b = \ln 0.80/\ln 2 = -0.3219$.

Then calculate marginal (and cumulative) times using the formula.

Batch	Marginal Time	Cumulative Time
1	$y = (100)(1^{-0.3219}) = 100$	100
2	$y = (100)(2^{-0.3219}) = 80$	180
3	$y = (100)(3^{-0.3219}) = 70.21$	250.21
4	$y = (100)(4^{-0.3219}) = 64$	314.21

We find cumulative times by adding the marginal times. To get the cumulative time for 32 batches, we would have to calculate the marginal times for each batch and add them or use another formula that captures cumulative time in the marginal model. As a review problem, use an electronic spreadsheet and verify that the *cumulative time* for 32 batches under the marginal time model

EXHIBIT 22–2 Marginal Time Learning Effect Model

Marginal time: $y = ax^b$

where
y = marginal time for the xth batch (or unit)
a = time for first batch (or unit)
x = number of batches (or units)—e.g., first, second, third, etc.
b = the learning exponent

the learning exponent:

$$b = \frac{\ln \text{learning curve}}{\ln 2}$$

The term ln denotes natural logarithms. You can use log base 10 (log) and the results will be the same although the intermediate figures will be different.

is 1,467.86 hours. This is considerably less than the 3,200 hours (100 × 32 batches) if there were no learning present.

Cumulative Average Time Model

Lightfoot Company has found its learning is described by the cumulative average model. In the cumulative average time model (or cumulative average model), *cumulative average time* goes down by the learning percentage. Thus, in our example, if the first batch takes 100 hours, the *cumulative average time* for two batches is 80 hours (0.80 × 100). This means that *total time* for two batches is 160 hours (2 × 80 hour average time) and that the marginal time for the second batch is 60 hours (160 − 100). Exhibit 22–3 shows the cumulative average time and the total cumulative time for the 32 batches at the doubling points.

Let us compare these two models of learning. Exhibit 22–4 shows marginal times and cumulative times for each model. You can see that the cumulative average model shows lower marginal times (and, therefore, lower total cumulative times) than the marginal model *using the same learning percentage*. Each model is based on a different premise about learning patterns. Which one is appropriate depends on the situation; experience dictates which is useful.

As with the marginal time model, we need formulas to go beyond the limitations of looking at learning at doubling points. Exhibit 22–5 shows the formulas for the cumulative average time model. While the basic formula has the same symbols, y now means cumulative average time instead of marginal time (as in Exhibit 22–2). In addition, we introduce a formula for total cumulative time. Thus, with the marginal time model, it is difficult to obtain cumulative total time using the basic formula but easy, obviously, to get marginal times. With the cumulative average time model, marginal times are harder to come by. To find the marginal time for the twenty-fifth batch, we have to solve for total time for 25 batches and 24 batches and subtract. However, it is easy to get

EXHIBIT 22–3 Cumulative Average Model—Lightfoot Company

Batches	Cumulative Average Time		Total Time[a]
1	100 hr		100 hr
2	80	(100 × 0.80)	160
4	64	(80 × 0.80)	256
8	51.2	(64 × 0.80)	409.6
16	40.96	(51.2 × 0.80)	655.36
32	32.768	(40.96 × 0.80)	1,048.576

[a] Equals the product of the number of batches and cumulative average time through that number of batches. For example, for four batches, 256 = 4 × 64.

EXHIBIT 22–4 Comparison of Marginal and Cumulative Models

	Marginal Time		Cumulative Time	
Batches	Marginal Model	Cumulative Model[a]	Marginal Model	Cumulative Model
1	100.00	100.00	100.00	100.00
2	80.00	60.00	180.00	160.00
4	64.00	45.37	314.21	256.00
8	51.20	35.46	534.59	409.60
16	40.96	28.06	892.01	655.36
32	32.77	22.33	1467.86	1048.58

[a] Marginal time for the cumulative model is found by computing total time for *n* batches and for *n* − *1* batches and then subtracting. For example, total time for 2 batches is 160 hours and for 1 batch 100 hours. Thus, marginal time for the second batch is 60 hours.

directly to the concern that Lightfoot's managers have with this model—what is the estimated time to make all 32 batches? As Exhibit 22–4 shows, it is 1,048.58 hours. Remember that whichever model is used, the times are only estimates. Learning may not occur exactly as predicted; other factors might speed up or slow down production; and, as we will explore later, learning might cease.

There is a fair amount of controversy about which model to use (marginal or cumulative average). Companies employ both models. In the discussion

EXHIBIT 22–5 Cumulative Average Time Learning Effect Model

Cumulative average time: $y = ax^b$

where
y = cumulative average time for x batches (or units)
a = time for first batch (or unit)
x = cumulative batches (units) produced
b = the learning exponent

the learning exponent:

$$b = \frac{\ln \text{learning curve}}{\ln 2}$$

total cumulative time:

Total cumulative time is (average time) × (cumulative production). This is:

$$xy = (x)(ax^b)$$

This is the same as

$$xy = ax^{b+1}$$

that follows, we will generally use the cumulative average model; this is not because we believe it superior to the marginal model, but because it is easier to use and the points made in the discussion of one model are equally applicable in the main to the other.[3]

Lightfoot's managers believe that the cumulative average model best describes their learning effect. Operating managers estimate that total incremental costs other than labor and labor-related costs for the entire job are $85,000. Learning is related mostly to labor. While there might be some savings in materials as workers waste less material, these savings will not be as great as those in labor. Labor, fringe benefits, and labor-related variable overhead cost $12 per direct labor hour. Thus, the estimated total costs for the job both ignoring and incorporating learning are:

	No Learning Effect	*80 Percent Learning Effect*
Total hours	3,200	1,050 (rounded)
Rate per hour	$12	$12
Total labor and labor-related costs	$ 38,400	$12,600
Other costs	85,000	85,000
Totals	$123,400	$97,600

The difference is significant. Should Lightfoot's managers base their bid on the assumption of an 80 percent learning curve, no learning, or something in between? Clearly, if competing firms have similar cost structures and profit goals, and they incorporate some kind of learning in their bids, Lightfoot will not get the job if it assumes no learning in setting its bid. A bid based on an assumption of no learning would be higher and, therefore, safer than one based on an 80 percent learning curve, but it would likely result in someone else getting the job.

At the other end, if managers base the bid on an 80 percent learning curve and do not achieve it (say, labor hours are 1,300 or so), the firm will make less profit than expected. One factor in making the decision is the confidence that the learning curve model chosen is correct and that the estimates of 100 hours for the first batch and an 80 percent learning curve are good estimates. Sensitivity analysis can be used to see how changes in either estimate affect the total hours for 32 batches.

Batches and Units

The term x in either the marginal time model or the cumulative time model can be batches or units. The main thing to remember is that if it is batches, then a must be the time for the first *batch*, not the first unit. If x is units, then a is the time for the first *unit*. In many cases, it is impractical to determine

[3]There are other models as well; we are not limited to just these two. For example, with the *asymptotic* model, marginal time decreases at a decreasing rate rather than at a constant rate.

the time for the very first unit. To smooth out early production and to get a good basis for use in estimating time for many units, time for the first batch is often used.

FINDING THE LEARNING RATE

In the discussion that follows, we use the cumulative average model. The basic formula for cumulative average time is $y = ax^b$ (see Exhibit 22–5). Using the data from the Lightfoot example, we can graph cumulative average time as shown in the top part of Figure 22–1. In the bottom half of that figure, the same data are plotted on a logarithmic scale. The logarithmic form is linear; the ordinary form is not. In formula form, the logarithmic representation of the learning effect is

$$\ln y = \ln a + (b \cdot \ln x)$$

Total time is $xy = ax^{b+1}$ which is the following in logarithmic form:

$$\ln xy = \ln a + (b + 1)(\ln x)$$

Either of these forms allows managers to use the same techniques illustrated in Chapter 3 (scatter diagrams, the high-low method, and linear regression) to estimate the time for the first unit (batch) and the learning percentage.

It is possible to determine total output of any product as of a given date. It is also likely that the records show the total number of hours, or total cost, expended to produce that quantity. In some cases it might be necessary to go back through records to determine total output of a product, because the cumulative total might not be routinely reported. Once data are available, both scatter diagram and regression techniques will help to determine parameters of interest, cost to produce the first unit (a), and learning-curve exponent b.

We shall use the following data to illustrate each method. Such data would be collected during the early stages of production of a new product.

Total Number of Units		*Average Hours per Unit*	
X	ln X	Y	ln Y
2	0.6932	8.9	2.1861
3	1.0986	7.2	1.9741
5	1.6094	7.0	1.9459
8	2.0794	5.7	1.7405
15	2.7081	5.4	1.6864

High-Low Method

A simple first effort is to make the calculation using the high-low, or two-point, method from Chapter 3. We simply divide the difference in the logarithms of

FIGURE 22–1 Ordinary and Log-Log Plots of Cumulative Average Time

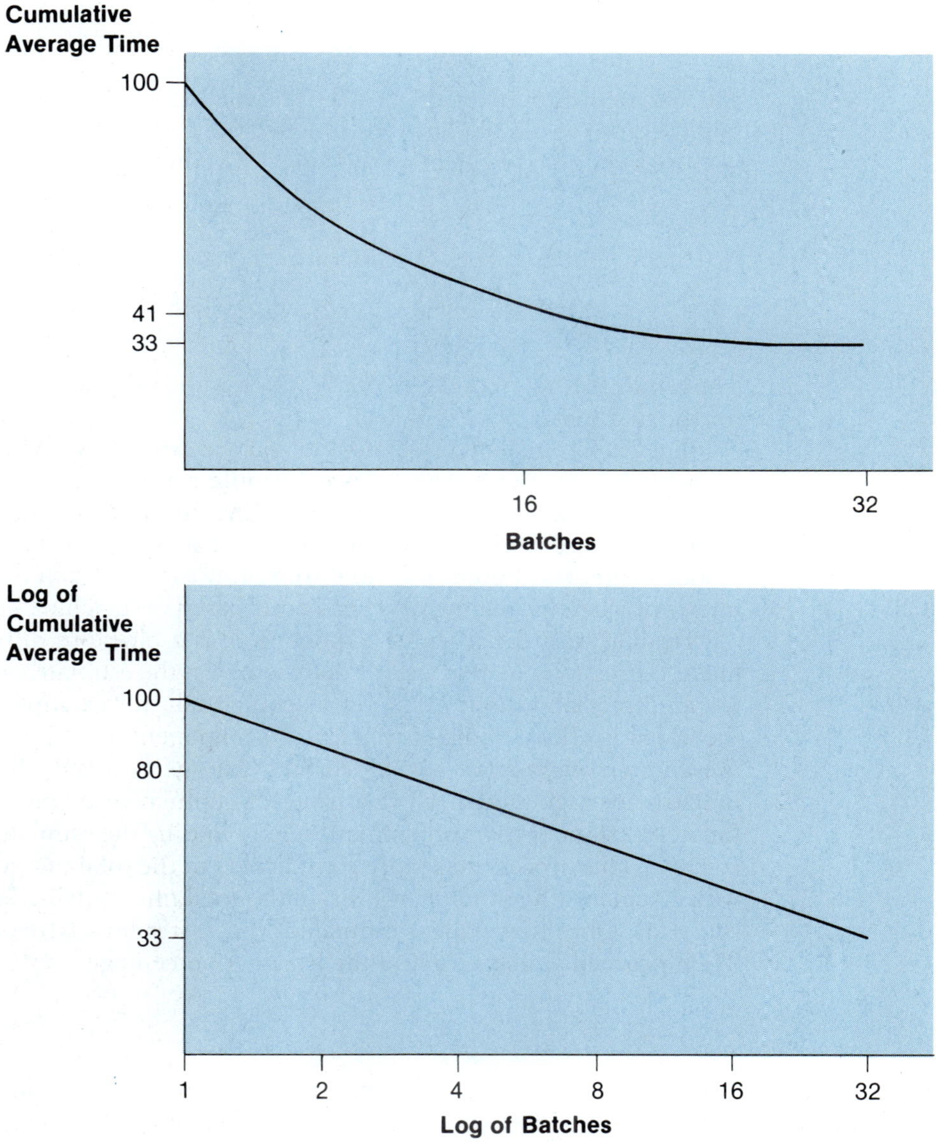

cumulative average time by the difference in the logarithms of output to find the exponent, b.

$$b = \frac{1.6864 - 2.1861}{2.7081 - 0.6932}$$

$$b = -0.248$$

Because b equals the logarithm of the learning rate divided by the log of 2, we also have

$$-0.248 = \text{log learning rate/log } 2$$
$$-0.248 = \text{log learning rate}/0.6932$$
$$\text{log learning rate} = -0.1719$$

The antilogarithm of -0.1719 is 0.842, which gives an 84.2 percent learning rate. Because we do not have the time for the first unit, we must calculate a in the same manner we calculate the fixed component of a mixed cost.

$$\log Y = \log a + b\,(\log X)$$

At 15 units, the numbers we know are

$$1.6864 = \log a + (-0.248)(2.7081)$$
$$\log a = 2.358$$

The antilogarithm of 2.358 is 10.57, which is the calculated value for the time for the first unit.

The trick is to keep track of what you are estimating. While you are dealing with logarithms and there is a formula for the learning exponent, the basics are the same as those explored in Chapter 3. 10.57 is our estimate of a, the time for the first unit. Even though we had to go through a log transformation to get this figure, it is no different in concept from finding the linear intercept when estimating overhead costs based on machine hours.

Dealing with the learning exponent, b, is a bit more difficult. In simple linear regression, the regression coefficient, b, is the estimate you are seeking—$4 per direct labor hour or $3 per machine hour, for example. However, with the learning effect, finding b, the learning exponent, is a step in estimating the *learning percentage* since $b = \ln(\text{learning exponent})/\ln(2)$. Thus, with the cumulative average model, when solving for cumulative average time (y), we estimate the slope (b) as a preliminary step to finding the estimated learning percentage. This process gets more complicated in the total time version. Dealing with a remains the same. However, in the total time (solving for xy), the slope is $(b + 1)$. Once that slope is estimated, you first subtract 1 from the estimate. Then proceed as above to find the learning percentage.

Scatter Diagram

The scatter-diagram method may be used in two ways. One is to plot logarithms of cumulative production (X) and resultant average production time (Y) on ordinary graph paper. The other is to use log-log paper for a plot of the data. The intercept and slope of such a plot are estimates of the time for the first unit (a) and learning curve (b or $b + 1$). Figure 22–2 is a plot of the logarithms, from the schedule on page 1004. The line fitted to the points shows the intercept and slope estimated visually. The individual points fall very close to the line, indicating a good fit. The result should be suitable for planning, so long as there are no major changes in operating techniques.

FIGURE 22–2 Plot of Logarithms

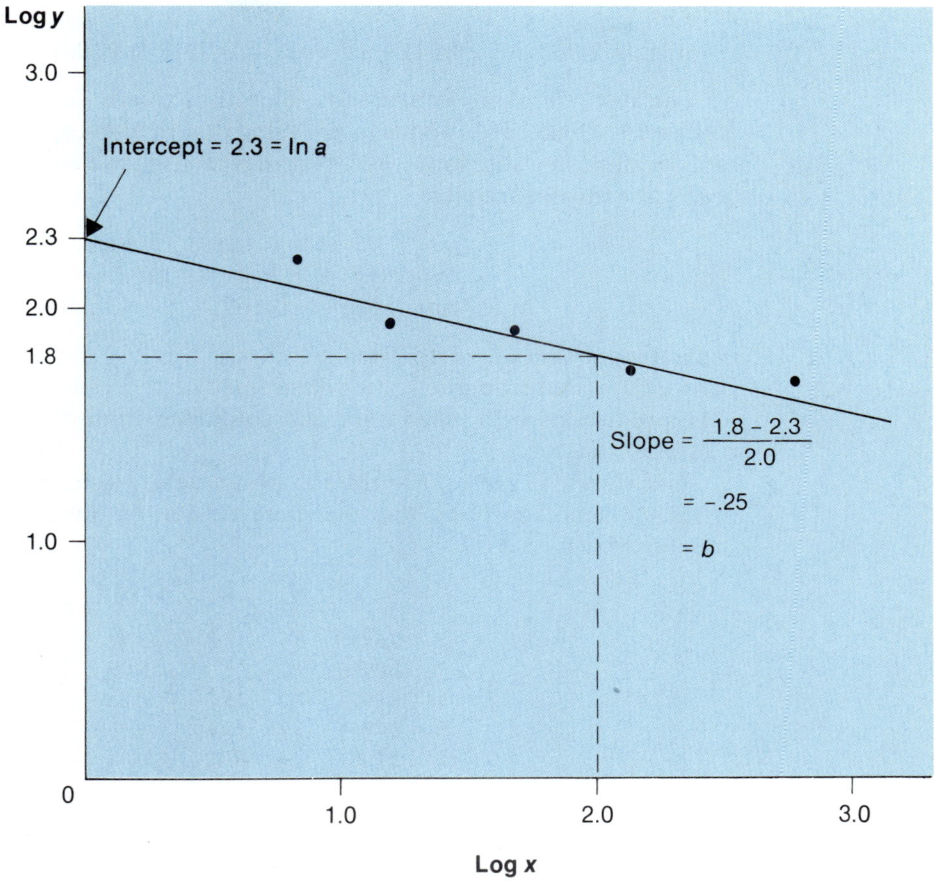

The estimates of the intercept and slope appear in Figure 22–2. The intercept of 2.3 gives a calculated value for *a* of 9.97 (antilogarithm of 2.3). The slope of −0.25 multiplied by the logarithm of 2 (0.6932) gives −0.1733, which is the logarithm of the learning rate. The antilogarithm of −0.1733 is 0.84, which is fairly close to the one we calculated using the high-low method.

Regression Analysis

The scatter diagram is helpful, but it gives only a rough look at the closeness of fit. Regression analysis would enable us to make more precise determinations. The same points that held true in Chapter 3 hold here. In using regression analysis, we first convert the *X* and *Y* values to logarithms, then use the logarithms to perform the regression. This is done to retain a linear format of

$Y = a + bx$. Regressing the natural logarithms of production and cumulative average time gives the following equation and measures, which you should verify:

$$\ln Y = 2.303 + (-0.2418) \ln X;\ r^2 = 0.921;\ S_e = 0.065;\ S_b = 0.041$$

The next step is to convert the logarithm values. The antilogarithm of 2.303 is 10, which corresponds to the value that we determined using the scatter diagram. The value for b, -0.2418, may be used to determine the learning rate as already illustrated.

$$b = \ln \text{learning rate}/\ln 2$$
$$-0.2418 = \ln \text{learning rate}/0.6931$$
$$\ln \text{learning rate} = -0.1676$$

The antilogarithm of -0.1676 is 0.8457, which is just about the value of 0.84 that we estimated from the scatter diagram. The regression results allow us to make predictions with more rigor and confidence than those obtained from the scatter diagram.

As a review problem, use the following data to estimate both a and the learning percentage using the total time version of the cumulative average time model.

x	$\ln x$	y	xy	$\ln xy$
2	0.6931	8.9	17.8	2.8792
3	1.0986	7.2	21.6	3.0727
5	1.6094	7.0	35.0	3.5553
8	2.0794	5.7	45.6	3.8199
15	2.7081	5.4	81.0	4.3944

Use either a linear regression package or an electronic spreadsheet such as Lotus 1-2-3 to calculate the intercept and slope. The results are shown in Exhibit 22–6. Note that the estimates of both a and the learning percentage are the same using either formula of the cumulative average time model.

SENSITIVITY ANALYSIS

In their roles as providers of information for planning and control, accountants estimate future costs of new products or contracts in which the learning curve is assumed. The accuracy of the estimate of the learning curve can be extremely important, especially when large quantities of product are concerned. The accountant would be well advised to analyze the sensitivity of total costs and profits to changes in the assumed learning curve.

The following schedule shows that relatively small changes in the learning curve can have significant impacts on total costs subject to the learning curve.

EXHIBIT 22–6 Cumulative Average Time—Total Time Formula

Regression analysis using Lotus 1-2-3:

```
        Regression Output:

Constant                      2.302671 ln a
Std Err of Y Est              0.064869
R Squared                     0.991374
No. of Observations                  5
Degrees of Freedom                   3

X Coefficient(s) 0.758148          (b+1)
Std Err of Coef. 0.040828

Therefore, the estimate of a is       10.00

The estimate of (b+1) is              0.7581
Therefore, b is                      -0.2419
and the learning percentage is        84.57%
```

We assume that the first unit requires 50 hours and that labor and labor-related costs are $15 per hour.

Total Labor and Labor-Related Learning Effect

Quantity Produced	Learning Percentage			
	90%	85%	82.5%	80%
25	$ 11,495	$ 8,815	$ 7,674	$ 6,652
50	20,691	14,986	12,662	10,643
100	37,244	25,476	20,893	17,030
200	67,039	43,309	34,473	27,247
400	120,670	73,626	56,880	43,596

The impact of a misestimation of even $2\frac{1}{2}$ percentage points (82.5 from 85 percent, or 80 from 82.5 percent) can be significant, especially at high levels of output.

CONDITIONS FOR LEARNING

The learning effect is not an automatic natural phenomenon. Not all processes will show increased efficiency. Among those that do, the differences in learning rates and the length of time over which learning takes place can be substantial. In addition, manufacturing techniques are changing and might limit the amount of learning that is possible.

The traditional learning effect was based on labor-intensive manufacturing operations. In general, the higher the labor content, the more opportunity for learning. Today, many plants are highly automated and machine paced. In an assembly department, for example, there might be a good deal of hand work. Workers take various components and assemble them into a final product. The pace of this assembly is based on the speed of the workers. However, in a manufacturing line using robotics, where the worker feeds materials or components into one end of the process and the robots and machines set the pace, the worker affects production time less. Thus, in a mostly labor-based environment with repetitive tasks, there can be substantial learning. In machine-driven operations, learning might still occur, but will not be as great as in the labor-intensive process.

A different kind of consideration involves the amount of planning done before a new product is manufactured or new contract begun. Suppose that the managers of the firm spend much time and effort to develop production techniques, such as the flow of materials and product through the plant, the scheduling of different operations, and the assignment of personnel. Then the labor time on the first batches will be lowered and the apparent learning effect reduced. The more preliminary work done, the lower the initial time is likely to be, with a correspondingly lower learning rate. In contrast, if a product is put into mass production with little advance planning, its early production time will be high, but improvement will be rapid. It is wise, then, before projecting results into the future, to determine whether early data are from a process that had been pretty well ironed out. A high rate of learning (say, a 70 percent or so learning curve) might not be sustainable for very long because it partly reflects rushing into production and getting some of the bugs out as well as the learning effect. That is, the improvement occurs partly through learning and partly through other factors.

LEARNING AND THE NEW MANUFACTURING ENVIRONMENT

Managers usually think of the learning effect as relating only to improvements in the time it takes workers to perform an operation. Improvements due to changes in machinery, materials, or the sequence of processing have not traditionally been thought of as part of the learning effect. As companies adopt more computer-integrated-manufacturing (CIM) and flexible manufacturing systems (FMS), some authors are re-examining this premise. We can see the beginning of the idea of looking beyond labor time in the discussion above;

learning can be affected by planning. Pattison and Teplitz[4] report on a study at General Dynamics where direct labor and supervision contributed 24.5 percent of total cost reductions gained from additional output while engineering improvement was 30 percent, tooling 25 percent, and material, production control, industrial engineering, and miscellaneous factors the final 20.5 percent. While others may label improvements in these non-labor items as different from the traditional learning effect, General Dynamics treated them as part of learning. The study the company conducted compared existing production (which experiences a learning effect) with a new flexible manufacturing system (which also experiences learning); all savings were viewed as part of that package.

Pattison and Teplitz offer the following example to illustrate how to compare an older system with a new FMS. They define the following:

$$Rate_{new} = Rate_{old} + [(1 - Rate_{old}) \times L \times R]$$

where

$Rate_{new}$ = learning percentage of new FMS
$Rate_{old}$ = learning percentage of old, conventional system
L = proportion of learning attributed solely to direct labor
R = proportion of direct labor being replaced

Assume that direct labor is being completely replaced in the new system. Thus, $R = 1.0$. Using the General Dynamics figures above, $L = 25$ percent (rounded). Also assume that the company experienced an 80 percent learning curve in its current operations. Thus, $Rate_{new} = 0.80 + [(1 - 0.80) \times 0.25 \times 1.0] = 0.85$. Because less learning was attributable to labor savings, the learning curve is flatter with the new equipment. This is an extreme case, where all labor is eliminated; obviously, if there were no labor, there would be no learning. In most situations, this will not happen and this illustration is meant as a bound to the formula. As you should verify, if the proportion of labor being replaced is 50 percent, the revised learning percentage is 82.5 percent.

In the new manufacturing and competitive environment, learning takes on a new meaning. We use the learning percentage (such as an 80 percent learning curve) to bid on work. However, one of the features of new trends in management is to improve results consistently. Standard costs and standard cost variances are being replaced by some managers with actual costs and the goal to continually improve on those costs. In the same vein, managers might not be satisfied just to estimate a learning percentage. They might want to improve it continually. Therefore, if production now reflects an 82 percent learning effect, the goal might be 81 or 80 percent or even better for tomorrow.

[4] Diane D. Pattison and Charles J. Teplitz, "Are Learning Curves Still Relevant?," *Management Accounting*, February 1989, pp. 37–40.

While learning because of labor might be a much smaller part of overall learning, the idea of improvement (or learning) is very important in today's competitive environment.

CESSATION OF LEARNING

It is not usually reasonable to expect learning to continue forever. At some point workers will reach maximum efficiency and will not continue to improve performance. The term **steady state** is often used to describe this situation. Naturally, the question of when the steady state arrives is of utmost importance to managers. For example, if they expect that learning will continue throughout the duration of a contract and find that it ceases halfway through, they will show lower profits than anticipated.

Determining where learning stops is an empirical matter. Managers might observe different points on different types of products and production processes. In some cases, workers approach some theoretical limit imposed by constraints on machinery or on the human body. For example, a worker using a power saw cannot go any faster than the saw will allow. Constraints on the human body vary among individuals. Some people can work faster than others, and even the fastest usually reach a limit.

In other cases learning per se might not stop, but improvement might stop because of externally imposed constraints. Union regulations frequently provide for maximum outputs. An example is the speed of an assembly line. In the automobile industry, managers often plan for a period of learning in the early part of a new model year. The assembly line runs slower during that period, gradually increases, and finally reaches a maximum that is negotiated between the management and the union. It is possible that workers could improve further, but they do not because of the negotiated regulation.

If managers had reasonably good information about where learning stops, they would incorporate it into decisions. They would assume that the learning effect on a new product or contract would continue over a given period of time or amount of production, then stop. If the learning effect lasted longer than expected, costs would be lower than expected, and vice versa.

To say that learning stops means that incremental time stabilizes, not that cumulative average time stabilizes. Incremental time is less than cumulative average time. For cumulative average time to stabilize, incremental time would have to increase. That is, unlearning would have to occur. The schedule below shows that cumulative average time continues to fall after learning stops. The assumptions in the schedule are that the first batch requires 100 hours, the learning effect is 90 percent, and learning stops after the fourth batch. The incremental time per batch stabilizes at 70 hours.[5] Accordingly, the cumulative

[5]The incremental time for the fourth batch is about 70 hours, the difference between total time for four batches and total time for three batches. The theoretical incremental time, assuming

average times and total times after the fourth batch are determined from the incremental time, instead of vice versa.

Number of Batches, X	Cumulative Average Time, Y	Total Time, XY	Incremental Time per Batch
1	100	100	100
2	90	180	80
4	81	324	72
8	75.5 (604/8)	604 [324 + 70(4)]	70
16	72.75 (1,164/16)	1,164 [604 + 70(8)]	70
32	71.375 (2,284/32)	2,284 [1,164 + 70(16)]	70

Contrast these results with what we would get if learning continued through the 32nd batch. Cumulative average time for eight batches would be 72.9 hours (81 × 0.90), through 16 batches, 65.61 hours (72.9 × 0.90), and through 32 batches, 59.049 hours (65.61 × 0.90). Total time for 32 batches would be about 1,889 (59.049 × 32), a good many fewer than the 2,284 shown above. If managers anticipate that learning will stop, they must plan for it to develop reasonable estimates of cost.

Managers might develop estimates of learning curves from a regression analysis. They should watch out for the problem of a learning curve applying for a while, then stopping. Regression results can be misleading if some of the data come from periods after learning has stopped. The learning curve will be misestimated, and the correlation and standard error of the estimate and of the *b* coefficient will also be off. Again, the scatter diagram is helpful in such cases because managers will be able to see the behavior of cumulative average time.

ADDITIONAL APPLICATIONS OF THE LEARNING CURVE

The learning curve is clearly relevant for planning costs and is therefore important in bidding on contracts, as illustrated briefly in the Gordon Company example. The learning curve is also important in pricing decisions involving new products. Managers frequently have a range of choices in setting prices, with each price likely to lead to a different volume. In general, the lower the price, the more volume. Applying the learning curve could well indicate that the managers would be wise in setting a relatively low price to gain high

perfectly continuous learning throughout each unit as well as each batch, is the first derivative of the function for total time. Thus $XY = aX^{b+1}$ and $dXY/dX = a(b + 1)X^b$. In the example above, the result is 68.69, which is not significantly different from 70, when we consider that we are dealing with estimates.

volumes. The following example illustrates the point. We ignore the time value of money for simplicity. Incorporating it would only require determining the expected cash flows by year and discounting them.

	$10 Price	*$13 Price*
Total volume, 5-year life	500,000	350,000
Total variable costs, first 10,000 units	$90,000	$90,000

The learning curve is estimated at 80 percent, and we assume for simplicity that all variable costs are subject to the learning curve.

Without the learning curve, the $13 price is better. Contribution margin would be $4 per unit ($13 − $9) for a total of $1,400,000 ($4 × 350,000). The $10 price gives contribution margin per unit of $1 ($10 − $9) and total contribution margin of $500,000. However, when we incorporate the learning curve, the picture changes. Given that the first batch is 10,000 units, we have 50 batches (500,000/10,000) to produce at the $10 price and 35 batches at the $13 price. The exponent, $b + 1$, for an 80 percent learning curve is 0.67807 (1 − 0.32193), so we have the following results:

	$10 Price	*$13 Price*
Total revenue:		
500,000 × $10	$5,000,000	
350,000 × $13		$4,550,000
Total variable costs:		
$90,000 × $50^{0.67807}$	1,277,212	
$90,000 × $35^{0.67807}$		1,002,833
Total contribution margin	$3,722,788	$3,547,167

The analysis indicates that the firm is better off at the $10 price. Of course, the values used for volume and the learning curve are estimates and might prove wrong. Because the difference in total contribution margin is not overwhelmingly in favor of the $10 price, the managers might decide to set a $13 price on grounds that it would be safer. As we have pointed out several times, decision making relates to the future, which is uncertain, and accounting data are estimates, not known quantities.

Production Planning

Decisions involving quantities of output usually have a time horizon. A decision to accept a special order usually requires that the firm produce and deliver the goods within a specified time. Contracts usually state delivery dates, and the seller can be penalized for failing to meet the agreed schedule.

In determining whether the firm will be able to produce some specified quantities by given dates, a manager considers many factors. One factor might be the learning curve. Consider the following example.

Cipolla Company makes industrial equipment. A skilled crew is currently working on an order of 20 large machines. The first machine required 1.5 weeks, and the firm usually experiences an 85 percent learning curve. The order must be completed within six months. The firm also has the opportunity to bid on another contract that must be completed within six months and that would require five weeks of the time of the same skilled crew.

For the firm to accept the new contract, it must be able to complete the existing order in 21 weeks (the 26 weeks in six months minus five weeks for the new contract). The expected total time to complete the existing order is given by the following equation (the exponent, $b + 1$, for an 85 percent learning curve is 0.76553):

$$XY = 1.5 \times 20^{0.76553} = 14.86 \text{ weeks}$$

The firm should have plenty of time available to work on the new contract, if the 85 percent learning curve holds for the existing contract. In fact, the firm will have time to produce both orders unless the learning effect is greater than 92 percent, since $XY = 21$ when the learning curve is at this level. When we wish to find the learning rate that will allow us to achieve an objective, such as being able to fill the new contract in this example, we must solve for the exponent, b. In the Cipolla example, we need to solve

$$\begin{aligned} 21 &= 1.5 \times 20^{(b+1)} \\ \ln 21 &= \ln 1.5 + (b + 1) \ln 20 \\ 3.044 &= 0.405 + (b + 1)(2.996) \\ b + 1 &= 0.881 \\ b &= -0.119 \\ b &= \frac{\ln \text{learning rate}}{\ln 2} \end{aligned}$$

$\ln$ learning rate $= -0.083$

The antilogarithm is 0.921, for a 92 percent rate.

In Japan, the learning curve is used widely to aid in scheduling.[6] Managers schedule production on the assumption that there will be an improvement (learning) each day; this improvement can be modeled using the learning curve.

Standard Costs and Budgets

While some managers use actual cost as a base for comparison, many others rely on standard costs and standard cost variances. When there is a learning effect, the accountant must make some adjustments to standard cost information and budgets. Because we expect labor time and cost to decline as production increases, we cannot compare actual costs against a predetermined

[6] See Richard J. Schonberger, *Japanese Manufacturing Techniques*, (NY: Free Press, 1982).

average unit cost based on the life of a product or contract. An example should make the point clear.

Royal Aircraft has begun production of its new model 477 long-range private plane. The firm's engineers and accountants expect an 80 percent learning effect over the first 1,000 planes, at which time learning will cease. The total labor time on the first 10 planes should be about 10,000 hours. The standard wage rate is $9.50 per hour.

We can calculate the expected hours to complete the first 1,000 planes and the average hours per plane. Because a batch is 10 planes, there will be 100 batches. Total time, XY, is given by the following equation, where 0.67807 is the coefficient, $b + 1$, of an 80 percent learning curve:

$$\begin{aligned} \ln XY &= \ln 10{,}000 + (0.67807 \times \ln 100) \\ &= 9.2103 + (0.67807 \times 4.6052) \\ &= 12.3329 \end{aligned}$$

The antilogarithm is about 227,040, giving an average standard labor time of 227.04 hours per plane over the first 1,000.

We cannot use the 227.04 hours to determine whether production is going as expected until the first 1,000 planes are completed. At any point, we must compute the expected time based on actual production to date to see whether operations seem to be in line with expectations.

Suppose that in the last quarter of 19X6 the firm began production and finished 54 planes using 33,790 direct labor hours. Any labor rate variance would be calculated in the usual way. The labor efficiency variance must be calculated based on the expected time to complete 54 planes, not by using the 227 hours per plane expected over the entire 1,000 units. Working with total time, XY, we calculate the expected time for 5.4 batches (54/10):

$$\begin{aligned} \ln XY &= \ln 10{,}000 + (0.67807 \times \ln 5.4) \\ &= 9.2103 + 1.1435 \\ &= 10.3538 \end{aligned}$$

The antilogarithm is about 31,376. The labor efficiency variance is $22,933 unfavorable, calculated as follows:

$$\begin{aligned} \text{labor efficiency variance} &= \$9.50 \times (33{,}790 - 31{,}376) \\ &= \$22{,}933\text{U} \end{aligned}$$

Inventory Valuation and Reporting

One important aspect of learning curves is that costs in the early stages of production are considerably higher than those in the later stages. Unit costs of early batches could exceed selling prices. That would give rise to a serious problem in valuing inventory and reporting inventory and cost of goods sold. Earlier chapters showed that actual cost is the usual basis for inventory valuation. However, the lower of cost or market rule states that inventory should not be shown at an amount greater than net realizable value (selling price minus cost to complete and sell).[7] Accordingly, if cost exceeds net realizable value, the difference must appear on the current period income statement as a loss or as part of cost of sales. The following example illustrates the problem. Epco Company has a contract to produce and deliver 16,000 components. The data below summarize operations over a two-year period.

	19X6	19X7
Units produced	2,000	14,000
Units delivered	1,000	15,000
Price per unit	$14	$14
Cost of production	$40,000	$123,840

The cost of production figures reflect an 80 percent learning curve on all production costs (assumed for computational ease). The average cost of production in 19X6 was $20 per unit ($40,000/2,000), which is higher than the $14 selling price. The maximum valuation of the ending inventory for 19X6 is $14,000. The following partial income statements show results for the two years:

	19X6	19X7
Sales at $14	$14,000	$210,000
Beginning inventory	0	$ 14,000
Production costs	40,000	123,840
Ending inventory, at net realizable value	14,000	0
Cost of sales	26,000	137,840
Gross profit (Loss)	($12,000)	$ 72,160

The income statements for both years are misleading in that they do not reflect the economics of the situation. The circumstances were not as bad as depicted by the 19X6 statement, nor as good as shown in the 19X7 statement.

Some writers have argued that inventory and cost of sales should be shown at the expected cumulative average cost, not the actual cost.[8] The difference between actual costs and expected cumulative average costs would appear in

[7] *Market* is defined as replacement cost with a ceiling of net realizable value and a floor of net realizable value less a normal profit margin. In situations in which the learning curve exists, replacement cost will be lower than actual cost (barring increases in material prices, labor rates, and prices of other inputs). If actual cost exceeds net realizable value, it is likely that replacement cost also will exceed net realizable value, so that "market" usually will be net realizable value.

[8] For example, see Wayne J. Morse, "Reporting Costs that Follow the Learning Curve Phenomenon," *The Accounting Review*, 47:4 (October 1972), 761–773.

two places. First, any variances such as we described in the previous section would be expensed in the period incurred (actual cost minus standard cost for the cumulative output). Second, expected variances would be deferred as an asset on the balance sheet. In our example, cumulative average cost for the entire lot of 16,000 units is $10.24 ($40,000 + $123,840)/16,000. Cost of sales and inventory for 19X6 would be shown at $10.24, with deferred production costs of $19,520 calculated as follows:

19X6 cost of sales	$10,240	(1,000 × $10.24)
19X6 ending inventory	10,240	(1,000 × $10.24)
Total	20,480	
Actual costs	40,000	
Deferred production costs	$19,520	

The $19,520 would appear as an expense on the 19X7 income statement. Gross profit in total for the two years would be the same, but now 19X6 would show $3,760 ($14,000 − $10,240) and 19X7 would show $56,400 ($210,000 − $10,240 beginning inventory − $123,840 production costs − $19,520 deferred production costs).

SUMMARY

The learning phenomenon is important to accountants because it affects total costs and, therefore, profits. Accountants must be alert to the possibility of a learning effect to develop reliable estimates of costs for pricing, bidding on contracts, production planning, and the development of standards and budgets. Estimates of cost are often very sensitive to the estimated value of the learning curve, so that it is a very critical variable.

The general form of the learning curve is that as cumulative output doubles, cumulative average cost falls to a percentage of its previous level. The learning curve is a function that contains an exponent, and it can be put into a linear form using logarithms.

Learning curves are most often found by examining data from past experience. In some companies, the learning effect can be estimated by industrial engineers, while in others it may be found using linear regression with data from previous jobs. Some companies find that they experience a plant-wide learning rate with each new product rather than specific rates. Learning is associated with labor. Thus, the most learning can be expected in labor-intensive operations such as assembly. While learning can occur in more machine-driven environments, it will be less than those primarily using labor. Finally, learning still has a place in new manufacturing environments and managing philosophies where doing better (learning) is expected.

REVIEW PROBLEM

Gnon Company manufactures large engines. The company is now negotiating with a customer on a contract for 60 engines. The best available estimates follow.

Material cost per engine	$8,000
Direct labor time for first batch (5 engines)	1,500 hr
Direct labor cost per hour	$12
Variable overhead per DLH	$8
Learning rate	85.00%

1. Determine the total cost for the 60 engines.
2. Determine the learning rate that would allow costs to total $650,000.

ANSWERS TO REVIEW PROBLEM (solved using electronic spreadsheet)

1.

Materials, 60 × $8,000		$480,000
Direct labor @ $12	10,052 hrs	120,621
Variable overhead @ $8		80,414
		$681,035

Direct labor time:

$b = \ln 0.85 / \ln 2 = -0.23446$

total time $= 1500 \times 12^{0.76553}$

$= 10{,}052$

Calculations above not rounded.

2.

Learning percent	81.12%
Learning exponent	−0.30187
Total time	8,502 hours

Materials	$480,000
Direct labor @ $12	102,019
Variable overhead @ $8	68,013
	$650,032

You can solve for this algebraically or use an electronic spreadsheet and "plug" for the percentage that drives total cost to about $650,000..

APPENDIX 22A: DETERMINING THE LEARNING EXPONENT

This appendix shows why the exponent, b, is the logarithm of the learning rate divided by the log of 2. Using natural logs,

$$b = \frac{\ln \text{learning percentage}}{\ln 2}$$

We can show why b is determined in this way by looking at the logarithmic form of the equation. Suppose that we calculated the value of Y at two values for X, one of which is double the other.

(22–A1) $\ln Y_2 = a + b \ln 2X$

(22–A2) $\ln Y_1 = a + b \ln X$

where

Y_2 = cumulative average time at the output level $2X$, which is double output X

Y_1 = cumulative average time at output X

Subtracting Equation 22–A2 from 22–A1 gives the following:

$$\ln Y_2 - \ln Y_1 = b(\ln 2X - \ln X)$$

$$b = \frac{\ln Y_2 - \ln Y_1}{\ln 2X - \ln X}$$

$$b = \frac{\ln (Y_2/Y_1)}{\ln 2}$$

The ratio Y_2/Y_1 is the learning percentage when Y_2 is determined at the value of X that is double the value where Y_1 was determined. In the first example in the chapter, at $X = 2$, $Y = 80$ and at $X = 4$, $Y = 64$, so that we get $64/80 = 0.80$. (Also, at $X = 1$, $Y = 100$, and at $X = 2$, $Y = 80$; $80/100 = 0.80$. Thus, any values of X and, therefore, $2X$ will yield the 80 percent learning curve. To prove this, try it with $X = 8$ batches from Exhibit 22–1.) In fact, any matched values of X's and Y's will work. They need not be doubling points.

ASSIGNMENTS

22–1 Basic Learning Curves Wilkes Company manufactures large grape presses. The firm generally experiences a learning effect on new models, at least through the first 75 or so units. Data on a new press appear below.

Labor time for first unit	800 hr
Labor rate	$10/hr
Variable overhead	$8/labor hour
Materials	$6,000/press

The manager of the firm wants to know the expected total cost of making the first 32 units, assuming a learning effect on labor of 80 percent and of 85 percent.

REQUIRED

1. Prepare schedules showing the cumulative average times for all doubling points up through 32 units for an 80 percent learning rate.
2. Repeat part 1 for an 85 percent rate.
3. Determine the total costs for the first 32 units estimated under each assumption.

22–2 Learning Curves and Volume The managers of MZT Computer Company expect that the desk-top model they are about to introduce will sell 100,000 units in the next two years if it is priced at $800 and 75,000 units if it is priced at $1,000. The main reasons for the differences are that potential competitors will be more likely to bring out their own models if MZT's price is high.

Cost estimates for the first 10,000 units are, per unit:

Materials	$400
Direct labor and variable overhead	300

Direct labor and variable overhead are expected to drop, reflecting an 80 percent learning curve, which is what the firm has experienced on its new products.

REQUIRED

Determine which price you would charge and justify your answer.

22–3 Cumulative Costs (AICPA) Green Company's new process has an expected learning rate of 80 percent. Costs subject to the learning curve for the first batch of product were $10,000.

REQUIRED

Determine the cumulative average cost for the first 16 batches.

22–4 Bidding and Target Contribution Margin Icarus Aircraft Company is preparing to bid on 16 amphibious airliners of a type that it has never made before. The potential buyer is West Pacific Airlines, which plans to use the airliners to service small islands that do not have landing fields. The managers of Icarus believe that their major competitor, Birch Airplane Company, will bid $6 million per plane.

The managers of Icarus want to earn an average contribution margin of $800,000 on the planes. They have developed the following estimates:

Materials and purchased parts, per plane	$2,800,000
Labor and variable overhead for first plane	3,800,000
Learning curve on labor and variable overhead	85%

REQUIRED

1. Determine whether or not Icarus can meet the $6 million bid and still earn its target contribution margin.

2. Determine the learning curve that will make Icarus just meet the target contribution margin at a price of $6 million per plane.

22–5 Production Scheduling Rockland Manufacturing Company has received an order for 25 machines of a type that it has not previously made. The customer wants all 25 delivered by the end of 19X5, and the production manager of Rockland is not certain that he can make it. He has summary information from several sources.

Total labor time available until year-end	14,000 hr
Labor time committed on existing orders	8,800 hr
Estimated time for first machine	500 hr
Estimated learning rate	80%

The production manager does not want to disrupt any of the existing orders. He wants to know whether he can finish the new order in 5,200 labor hours.

REQUIRED

Determine whether the firm will be able to finish the order by year-end.

22–6 Standard Costs and Learning Curves (CMA Adapted) Horace Company uses a standard cost system. In developing standard costs the firm builds in an 80 percent learning effect for direct labor based on its past experience.

The firm is planning for an automobile electrical timing device that requires assembling purchased components. Each production lot will have five units, and the firm expects the learning effect to disappear after the eighth lot. The first lot required 90 direct labor hours. The standard wage rate is $6 per hour.

REQUIRED

1. Determine the standard amount that the firm should establish for total direct labor cost for the first eight lots.
2. Discuss the factors that the managers of the firm should consider in establishing the direct labor requirements for each unit produced beyond the eighth lot.

22–7 Learning Curve Relationships

REQUIRED

Fill in the blanks for each of the following independent cases.

Case	*Time for First Batch*	*Number of Batches*	*Cumulative Average Time*	*Learning Rate*
(a)	______	8	20 hr	80%
(b)	70 hr	15	40 hr	____
(c)	1,000 hr	___	685 hr	90%

22–8 Learning Curve in a Service Function The manager of the claims department of Midwest Insurance Company has studied the productivity of the workers who do basic operations in processing forms, such as making sure that all of the lines are filled out, that the policy number is correct, and so on, before the claims forms go to adjusters who examine them more closely. The manager is especially interested in the apparent improvement in productivity because the turnover of these employees is very high. The findings appear below.

Total Claims Processed	Total Time to Process (in Hours)
1,000	200
2,000	320
3,000	420
4,000	520

The data are cumulative. Thus, a worker who has processed 2,000 claims forms usually requires about 120 hours to process the second 1,000 (320 − 200), and so on.

REQUIRED

1. Estimate the learning curve.
2. Suppose that the learning curve will continue until the worker has processed 16,000 forms. How long will it take the worker to do all 16,000?

22–9 Learning Curves, Regression Analysis The general manager of the components department of Chicago Machine Works has known for some time that workers become more efficient as they produce more of a particular component, but he is unsure how much more efficient they become. He has collected the following data and wants you to analyze them and tell him how rapidly the workers improve so that he can use the information in planning.

Number of Batches	Total Time (in Hours)
1	200
2	330
3	420
4	520
5	590

REQUIRED

Determine the learning rate using regression analysis.

22–10 Variance Analysis and Learning Effects Jepson Company makes industrial products used by a wide variety of firms. Nearly all its business is done on contracts ranging from one to three years, over which Jepson delivers the products according to a schedule set by the contract. In determining a price per unit for each contract, Frances Miller, the controller, incorporates a 90 percent learning effect for labor and variable overhead.

The firm uses job order costing and Miller makes periodic comparisons of actual and budgeted costs. She has recently been working on a special project for the president and has asked you to analyze two jobs to see whether or not they are going smoothly. Data on the jobs appear on the following page.

	Job	
	XZ-456	*UH-040*
Total number of units to be delivered	12,000	6,000
Number completed to date	7,000	2,000
Labor and variable overhead costs to date	$162,180	$ 78,300
Cost of first 100 units = budget	$ 3,800	
Total budgeted cost for entire order		$192,000

The cost of the first 100 units is not available for job UH-040 because of clerical oversight. Miller has mislaid the estimated cost to produce the entire order of job XZ-456.

REQUIRED

Determine the costs that should be accumulated for each job at its current state of completion.

22–11 Make-or-Buy Decision Warner Company has been buying a number of components from ICC Company for several years. One of them, called part #65-198, has cost the Warner Company $34.50 for the past several years. A representative of ICC has notified Warner that the price will rise to $39 for the coming year, with prices in future years likely to rise as well. However, ICC is willing to negotiate a five-year contract to supply the part at $42.

On learning of the price increase, managers of Warner Company began to explore making the part internally. The firm has sufficient capacity but lacks some of the sophisticated machinery that ICC uses. There is considerable lead time on acquiring this machinery, so if Warner decided to make the part, it would have to use much more hand labor than ICC. The best available estimates appear below.

The fixed costs included in the cost to make the part are all incremental. The production manager believes that the firm would experience a learning effect in making the part and that the effect would be confined to direct labor time. The best estimate of the learning effect is 85 percent, but that is a very rough estimate. Whatever the learning effect turns out to be, the best estimate is that the direct labor time below will be the average for the first 14,000 units. In other words, the first year's output is the first batch.

	Cost to Make Part #65-198
Direct labor hours	2.50
Direct labor and variable overhead per hour	$ 10.50
Direct labor and variable overhead per unit	$ 26.25
Materials cost per unit	8.65
Total variable cost per unit	$ 34.90
Annual requirements, in units	14,000
Total annual variable cost	$488,600
Additional fixed costs per year	175,000
Total annual cost	$663,600
Cost to buy, 14,000 × $42	588,000
Advantage to buying	$ 75,600

REQUIRED

Ignore the time value of money.

1. Determine the total cost of making part #65-198 over the next five years, with a learning effect of (a) 85 percent, (b) 80 percent.
2. Determine the learning effect that would make the total cost of making the part the same as the total cost of buying it under the five-year contract.
3. What advantages might there be to buying the part under a one-year arrangement at $39? What disadvantages?
4. What added information would you like before making a decision?

22–12 Make or Buy and Learning Curves Philip Riccardi, Production Manager of Brison Company, has asked for your assistance. The firm has obtained a contract to supply radar systems to a major aircraft manufacturer over the next three years. The managers of Brison had expected to subcontract one assembly of the system to Holt Electronic Company at a cost of $500 each. Riccardi has since learned that he can purchase machinery costing $180,000 that can be used to make the assembly internally. The machinery has an estimated useful life of six years, but it probably would not be suitable for use after the contract expired and would be sold for about $30,000.

Riccardi developed the following estimates related to internal production. His estimates were based on similar types of work that the firm had been doing for several years, so that he was reasonably confident of their validity.

Materials cost per unit	$ 100
Direct labor hours, per unit in first year	10 hr
Direct labor rate in first year	$ 12/hr
Variable overhead rate in first year	$ 8/labor hour
Total annual fixed overhead	$65,000

Riccardi believes that the only incremental fixed overhead would be $50,000 in depreciation expense, based on the cost less estimated salvage value of the machinery. He anticipates a 10 percent increase in the direct labor rate and a 5 percent increase in the variable overhead rate to take effect at the beginning of the second year. He believes that both rates will increase an additional 4 percent at the beginning of the third year.

The order will be filled in three batches; 300 units at the ends of each of the first two years and 600 units at the end of the third year. Riccardi is confident that the firm will experience an 80 percent learning effect on the labor time. He states that the firm uses a 16 percent cutoff rate of return and is subject to a 40 percent tax rate.

REQUIRED

Determine what course of action Brison Company should follow. Be prepared to discuss the significance of the learning curve for the decision.

22–13 Scatter Diagram The accompanying figure shows cumulative output and cumulative average time on a log-log plot.

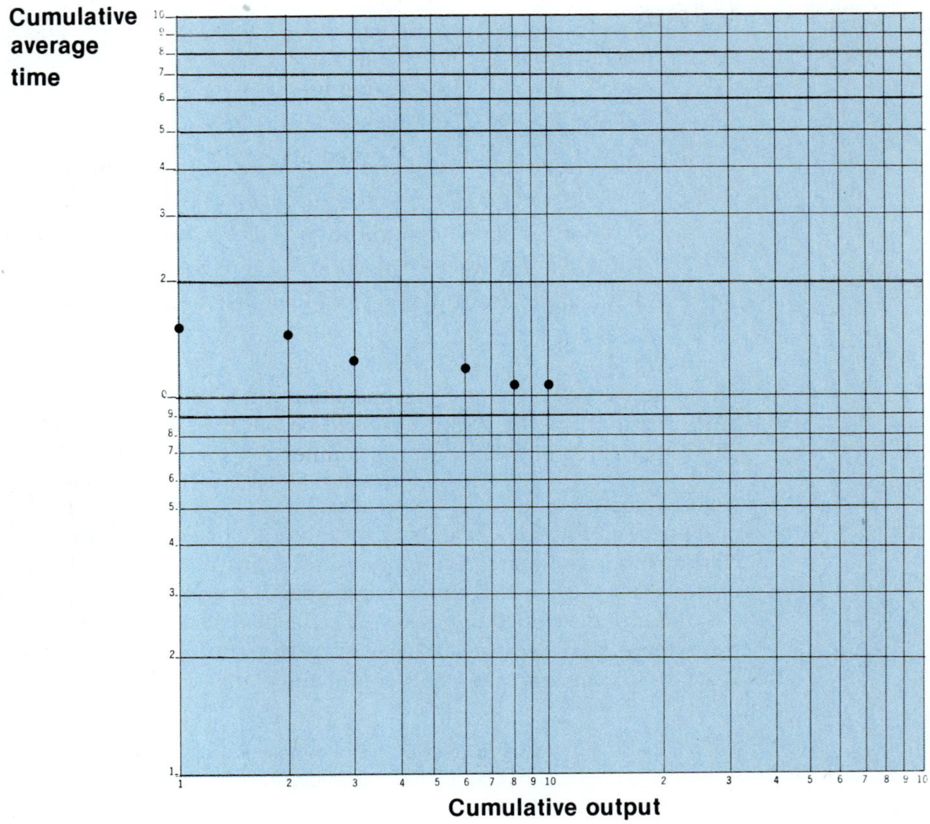

REQUIRED

Use the plot to determine the values that you would need for predicting times in the future.

22–14 Make-or-Buy Decision ACX Company buys a component for $90 and is considering making it. Estimated data for the first batch of 500 units appear below.

	Total for First 500 Units	*Per Unit*
Materials	$20,000	$ 40
Direct labor	30,000	60
Variable overhead (varies with direct labor hours)	10,000	20
Fixed overhead	10,000	20
Total cost	$70,000	$140

The company usually experiences an 85 percent learning effect. Fixed overhead is allocated to all activities based on labor dollars.

REQUIRED

1. Determine how many units the company must make to benefit from making the component than buying it—that is, the total volume at which total costs under the alternatives will be equal.
2. The managers are concerned about the estimate of an 85 percent learning effect. Determine the learning rate that the company would have to achieve to break even over the first 2,000 units. That is, determine what learning rate would make the cost of making the first 2,000 units equal to the cost of buying them.

22–15 Service Business MicroWare, Inc., designs custom software. Its managers have been negotiating a contract for a set of programs that they estimate will run to 30,000 lines of computer code. The potential customer wants the package in six months. Because of other commitments, MicroWare would be able to use only three programmers on the job. Experience shows that a programmer working on a new project produces about 120 lines of usable code in the first week, with a learning effect of about 85 percent. They assume that each programmer will work 26 weeks during the six months.

REQUIRED

1. Determine whether three programmers should be able to finish the job in six months.
2. Determine the learning rate at which it would take three programmers just 26 weeks to finish the job.

22–16 Service Function, Employee Requirements A large state operates a program that gives college students rebates on tuition at the state university. The department manager in charge of processing the applications hires workers for a six-week period, during which she must get all the work done. The applications must be in by the first of June, and the applicants must be notified of the amount of the rebate by July 15.

The manager expects about 20,000 applications in 19X6. From experience, she is confident that the average worker will start out slowly and improve over the period. The pattern has been that the average worker takes 20 hours to do the first 10 applications and improves at an 80 percent rate. The total working time for the six-week period is 240 hours per worker.

REQUIRED

Determine how many workers the manager should hire for the period.

22–17 Learning Effects and Income Statements In August 19X5, Moore Company began work on a contract to make 30 printing presses for the Wynnant Newspaper chain. Results for 19X5 and 19X6 showed the following:

	19X5	*19X6*
Presses completed and shipped	12	18
Materials used	$120,000	$180,000
Direct labor cost	500,000	400,000
Variable overhead cost	250,000	200,000
Fixed overhead applied	60,000	90,000

The selling price was $70,000 per press. There were no inventories of in-process or finished goods at the end of 19X5. All costs were incurred as budgeted.

REQUIRED

1. Prepare conventional income statements for each of the two years, down to gross margin.
2. Prepare income statements using the format on page 1017, with cost of sales based on the expected cumulative average unit cost over the life of the contract.
3. Comment on the usefulness of the two sets of statements for internal reporting and for reporting to shareholders.

22–18 Job Orders, Learning Curves, and Cost Analysis Lahti Company produces high-quality gear assemblies used in several types of industrial machinery. Although each order is custom built, it usually includes many standard parts combined with specially made components. Late in 19X8 the firm received an invitation to bid on 300 assemblies of a type it had not made before. The invitation was from Brockton Tool and Die Company, which had never done business with Lahti.

Jon Miller, Lahti's Sales Manager, hoped that he could submit a good bid because he thought there was considerable opportunity for future business from Brockton. He had learned that a competitor was prepared to bid about $61 per unit for the assemblies.

The estimating department developed the analysis of costs that follows. Miller was unhappy with the $81.80 price, because he was sure that Brockton would not accept it. He then asked George DiLello, Production Superintendent, whether the estimates looked reasonable.

DiLello told Miller that the estimates had been based in part on observations of workers asked to perform a couple of the required operations. He said that the firm usually experienced a learning effect somewhere in the range of 85 to 90 percent on fairly large orders of new assemblies and that this effect should be considered when a final bid was determined.

Miller then went to Tod McMaster, the firm's controller, to ask about the incremental components of the cost estimate. McMaster said that materials, purchased parts, and labor were variable, along with 70 percent of overhead. Overhead generally varied closely with labor cost. The allowance for selling and administrative expenses was not itself variable: it was based on total expected expenses for the year. McMaster believed that selling and administrative expenses tended to vary with sales dollars, at a rate of about 2 percent.

	Analysis of Costs
Materials	$13.55
Purchased parts	17.80
Assembly labor	14.50
Overhead at 150% of labor	21.75
Total manufacturing costs	67.60
Allowance for selling and administrative expenses at 10%	6.76
Total cost	74.36
Allowance for profit at 10%	7.44
Price	$81.80

Miller felt strongly that the firm should underbid the competition so long as it did not take an incremental loss. He knew that Brockton Tool and Die could be a source of a good deal of business. However, he did not want to bid so low that Brockton would expect unreasonably low prices on future business.

REQUIRED

Make a recommendation, supporting it with whatever analyses you believe relevant.

22–19 New Product RST Company is beginning production of a new product. Estimated data for the first batch of 1,000 units appear below.

	Total for First 1,000 Units
Materials	$ 30,000
Direct labor	50,000
Variable overhead	40,000
Fixed overhead	20,000
Total cost	$140,000

Each *unit* sells for $120. The company usually experiences an 85 percent learning effect. Fixed overhead is allocated to all products based on labor dollars. Variable overhead varies closely with labor time.

REQUIRED

1. Determine the incremental profit or loss that the company should earn for the first 7,000 units.

2. Determine the number of units that the company must make and sell to achieve a $40 contribution margin *per unit*.

3. Total direct labor cost for the first 5,000 units turned out to be $190,000. Determine the actual learning rate.

4. The learning rate is 85 percent, but learning typically stops after the first 5,000 units. Determine the total variable cost to produce units 5,001 through 6,000—that is, the *next* 1,000 units.

22–20 Contract Modification (CMA) Simon Corporation has been a supplier to the ORION Project since the program's inception. Two years ago Simon received a contract to provide 960 telecommunication devices to be used in space exploration. Funding for the ORION Project has been curtailed, and Simon has received a contract modification decreasing the quantity of devices to be delivered to 240 units, the minimum permissible under the existing contract.

The telecommunication device engineered and manufactured by Simon incorporates highly sophisticated technology, and each ORION satellite carries 18 of these devices. The direct material cost for each device is $60,000 per unit. Direct labor is subject to a 90 percent learning curve. The average direct labor cost was estimated at $40,000 per unit for the first lot of 30 units. This average direct labor cost figure and the 90 percent learning curve were used to develop Simon's original bid. Variable manufacturing overhead was estimated at 60 percent of direct labor cost. In calculating the original bid price, Simon added its regular markup of 25 percent on all variable manufacturing costs.

The learning curve of 90 percent has proven to be accurate over the first 60 units. Maximum efficiency is expected to be achieved with the production of 240 units.

REQUIRED

1. Describe the theory underlying the use of learning curves.
2. Determine Simon Corporation's cumulative average unit cost of labor for production of 240 units supplied to the ORION Project.
3. If Simon Corporation should be asked to produce any additional telecommunication devices beyond the 240 units covered by the amended contract, calculate the unit price Simon should bid employing the same markup used in the original bid.

22–21 Make or Buy (CMA Adapted) Hauser Company, a family owned business, engineers and manufactures a line of mopeds and dirt bikes under the tradename Trailite. The company has been in business for almost 20 years and has maintained a profitable share of the recreational vehicle market because of its reputation for high quality products. In addition, Hauser's engineering department has kept the company in the forefront through the incorporation of the latest technology in the Trailite bikes. Most subassembly work for the bikes is subcontracted to reliable vendors. However, the final assembly and inspection of all products occurs at Hauser's plant.

Hauser recently developed a new braking system for the Trailite Model-500 dirt bike. Because of the current availability of production capacity at Hauser, Jim Walsh, Production Manager, recommended that the first lot of the new braking system be manufactured in-house rather than subcontracted. This 80-unit production run has now been completed. The cumulative average labor hours per unit for the braking system was 60 hours. Hauser's experience with similar products indicates that a learning curve of 80 percent would be applicable and that the learning factor could be expected to extend through the fourth production run. Hauser's direct labor cost is $14.50 per direct labor hour.

Hauser's management must decide whether to continue producing the braking system in its own plant or to subcontract the subassembly work. Joyce Lane, Hauser's Purchasing Agent, has received a proposal from MACO, a company specializing in component assembly. MACO has done work in the past for Hauser and has proved to be efficient and reliable. The terms of MACO's proposal follow.

Hauser must supply all materials required for the braking system.

The first 80 units produced by MACO will require direct labor input at the rate of 56 hours per unit. Current direct labor cost is $15.00 per hour. The direct labor cost charged to Hauser will be the hourly rate in effect at the time the work is performed.

A learning curve factor of 75 percent will be applied through the fourth production run, and all benefits derived from the learning factor will accrue to Hauser.

Hauser Company must pay for all labor incurred plus a five percent margin based on actual labor cost.

The only uncertainty associated with the MACO proposal is that MACO's current labor contract with the union is about to expire. The union is requesting wage and benefit changes that would increase direct labor costs six percent. However, MACO's management believes that other issues such as job security are more important to the union and that the actual settlement will not increase direct labor costs.

REQUIRED

1. Hauser Company has an immediate requirement for total of 1,000 units of the braking system. Determine Hauser's future out-of-pocket costs for the completion of the required braking system units if the units are:
   a. manufactured in-house by Hauser
   b. subcontracted to MACO and MACO's direct labor cost increases six percent
   c. subcontracted to MACO and MACO's direct labor cost remains at $15.00 per direct labor hour
2. The learning curve model is a power function expressed as $y = ax^b$.
   a. Discuss the implications of a 75 percent learning curve as opposed to an 80 percent learning curve.
   b. What conditions would minimize the effects of a learning curve in a manufacturing setting?

Appendix A TABLES

TABLE A–1 Area under the Normal Curve Between the Mean and Successive Values of z

Example: If z = 1.87, the area between the mean and 1.87 standard deviations is .46926 and the area to the right of z is .03074 (.50000 − .46926).

z	.00	.01	.02	.03	.04	.05	.06	.07	.08	.09
.0	.00000	.00399	.00798	.01197	.01595	.01994	.02392	.02790	.03188	.03586
.1	.03983	.04380	.04776	.05172	.05567	.05962	.06356	.06749	.07142	.07535
.2	.07926	.08317	.08706	.09095	.09483	.09871	.10257	.10642	.11026	.11409
.3	.11791	.12172	.12552	.12930	.13307	.13683	.14058	.14431	.14803	.15173
.4	.15542	.15910	.16276	.16640	.17003	.17364	.17724	.18082	.18439	.18793
.5	.19146	.19497	.19847	.20194	.20540	.20884	.21226	.21566	.21904	.22240
.6	.22575	.22907	.23237	.23565	.23891	.24215	.24537	.24857	.25175	.25490
.7	.25804	.26115	.26424	.26730	.27035	.27337	.27637	.27935	.28230	.28524
.8	.28814	.29103	.29389	.29673	.29955	.30234	.30511	.30785	.31057	.31327
.9	.31594	.31859	.32121	.32381	.32639	.32894	.33147	.33398	.33646	.33891
1.0	.34134	.34375	.34614	.34849	.35083	.35314	.35543	.35769	.35993	.36214
1.1	.36433	.36650	.36864	.37076	.37286	.37493	.37698	.37900	.38100	.38298
1.2	.38493	.38686	.38877	.39065	.39251	.39435	.39617	.39796	.39973	.40147
1.3	.40320	.40490	.40658	.40824	.40988	.41149	.41309	.41466	.41621	.41774
1.4	.41924	.42073	.42220	.42364	.42507	.42647	.42785	.42922	.43056	.43189
1.5	.43319	.43448	.43574	.43699	.43822	.43943	.44062	.44179	.44295	.44408
1.6	.44520	.44630	.44738	.44845	.44950	.45053	.45154	.45254	.45352	.45449
1.7	.45543	.45637	.45728	.45818	.45907	.45994	.46080	.46164	.46246	.46327
1.8	.46407	.46485	.46562	.46638	.46712	.46784	.46856	.46926	.46995	.47062
1.9	.47128	.47193	.47257	.47320	.47381	.47441	.47500	.47558	.47615	.47670
2.0	.47725	.47778	.47831	.47882	.47932	.47982	.48030	.48077	.48124	.48169
2.1	.48214	.48257	.48300	.48341	.48382	.48422	.48461	.48500	.48537	.48574
2.2	.48610	.48645	.48679	.48713	.48745	.48778	.48809	.48840	.48870	.48899
2.3	.48928	.48956	.48983	.49010	.49036	.49061	.49086	.49111	.49134	.49158
2.4	.49180	.49202	.49224	.49245	.49266	.49286	.49305	.49324	.49343	.49361
2.5	.49379	.49396	.49413	.49430	.49446	.49461	.49477	.49492	.49506	.49520
2.6	.49534	.49547	.49560	.49573	.49585	.49598	.49609	.49621	.49632	.49643
2.7	.49653	.49664	.49674	.49683	.49693	.49702	.49711	.49720	.49728	.49736
2.8	.49744	.49752	.49760	.49767	.49774	.49781	.49788	.49795	.49801	.49807
2.9	.49813	.49819	.49825	.49831	.49836	.49841	.49846	.49851	.49856	.49861
3.0	.49865									
4.0	.49997									

Courtesy of Professor Lyn Pankoff, Washington University

TABLE A–2 Critical Values of Student's *t* Statistic

Degrees of Freedom	Levels of Significance for One-Tailed Test .10	.05	.025	.005	Degrees of Freedom	Levels of Significance for One-Tailed Test .10	.05	.025	.005
1	3.078	6.314	12.706	63.657	16	1.337	1.746	2.120	2.921
2	1.886	2.920	4.303	9.925	17	1.333	1.740	2.110	2.898
3	1.638	2.353	3.182	5.841	18	1.330	1.734	2.101	2.878
4	1.533	2.132	2.776	4.604	19	1.328	1.729	2.093	2.861
5	1.476	2.015	2.571	4.032	20	1.325	1.725	2.086	2.845
6	1.440	1.943	2.447	3.707	21	1.323	1.721	2.080	2.831
7	1.415	1.895	2.365	4.499	22	1.321	1.717	2.074	2.819
8	1.397	1.860	2.306	3.355	23	1.319	1.714	2.069	2.807
9	1.383	1.833	2.262	3.250	24	1.318	1.711	2.064	2.797
10	1.372	1.812	2.228	3.169	25	1.316	1.708	2.060	2.787
11	1.363	1.796	2.201	3.106	26	1.315	1.706	2.056	2.779
12	1.356	1.782	2.179	3.055	27	1.314	1.703	2.052	2.771
13	1.350	1.771	2.160	3.012	28	1.313	1.701	2.048	2.763
14	1.345	1.761	2.145	2.977	29	1.311	1.699	2.045	2.756
15	1.341	1.753	2.131	2.947	30	1.310	1.697	2.042	2.750
					∞	1.282	1.645	1.960	2.576

To find the critical value for a two-tailed test, simply multiply the levels of significance by 2. That is, the values for the one-tailed test with significance of .10 are also those for a two-tailed test with .20 significance, and so on.

Courtesy of Jeannine A. Myer, Southern Illinois University at Edwardsville

GRAPH FOR TABLE A–1

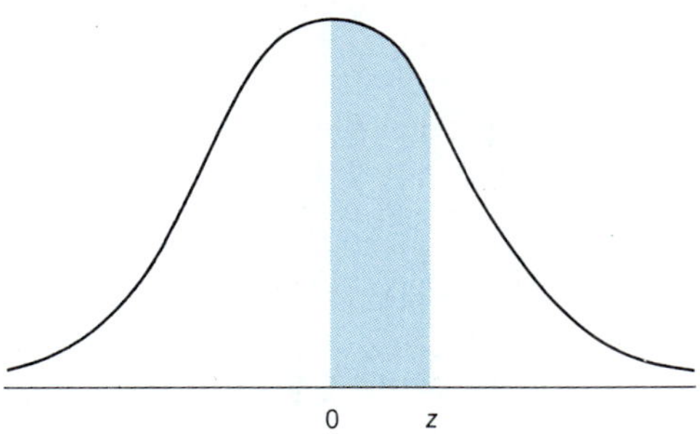

GRAPH FOR TABLE A–2

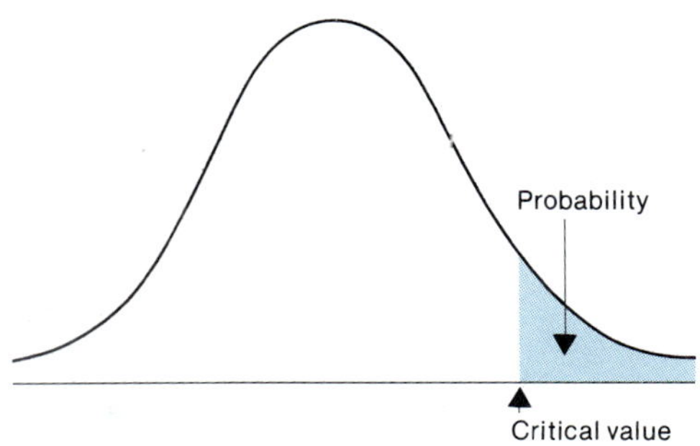

TABLE A–3 Present Value of $1

$$\frac{1}{(1+r)^t}$$

t/r	4%	5%	6%	7%	8%	9%	10%	11%	12%	13%	14%	15%	16%	17%	18%	19%
1	.9615	.9524	.9434	.9346	.9259	.9174	.9091	.9009	.8929	.8850	.8772	.8696	.8621	.8547	.8475	.8403
2	.9246	.9070	.8900	.8734	.8573	.8417	.8264	.8116	.7972	.7831	.7695	.7561	.7432	.7305	.7182	.7062
3	.8890	.8638	.8396	.8163	.7938	.7722	.7513	.7312	.7118	.6931	.6750	.6575	.6407	.6244	.6086	.5934
4	.8548	.8227	.7921	.7629	.7350	.7084	.6830	.6587	.6355	.6133	.5921	.5718	.5523	.5337	.5158	.4987
5	.8219	.7835	.7473	.7130	.6806	.6499	.6209	.5935	.5674	.5428	.5194	.4972	.4761	.4561	.4371	.4190
6	.7903	.7462	.7050	.6663	.6302	.5963	.5645	.5346	.5066	.4803	.4556	.4324	.4104	.3898	.3704	.3521
7	.7599	.7107	.6651	.6227	.5835	.5470	.5132	.4817	.4523	.4251	.3996	.3759	.3538	.3332	.3139	.2959
8	.7307	.6768	.6274	.5820	.5403	.5019	.4665	.4339	.4039	.3762	.3506	.3269	.3050	.2848	.2660	.2487
9	.7026	.6446	.5919	.5439	.5002	.4604	.4241	.3909	.3606	.3329	.3075	.2843	.2630	.2434	.2255	.2090
10	.6756	.6139	.5584	.5083	.4632	.4224	.3855	.3522	.3220	.2946	.2697	.2472	.2267	.2080	.1911	.1756
11	.6496	.5847	.5268	.4751	.4289	.3875	.3505	.3173	.2875	.2607	.2366	.2149	.1954	.1778	.1619	.1476
12	.6246	.5568	.4970	.4440	.3971	.3555	.3186	.2858	.2567	.2307	.2076	.1869	.1685	.1520	.1372	.1240
13	.6006	.5303	.4688	.4150	.3677	.3262	.2897	.2575	.2292	.2042	.1821	.1625	.1452	.1299	.1163	.1042
14	.5775	.5051	.4423	.3873	.3405	.2992	.2633	.2320	.2046	.1807	.1597	.1413	.1252	.1110	.0985	.0876
15	.5553	.4810	.4173	.3624	.3152	.2745	.2394	.2090	.1827	.1599	.1401	.1229	.1079	.0949	.0835	.0736
16	.5339	.4581	.3936	.3387	.2919	.2519	.2176	.1883	.1631	.1415	.1229	.1069	.0930	.0811	.0708	.0618
17	.5134	.4363	.3714	.3166	.2703	.2311	.1978	.1696	.1456	.1252	.1078	.0929	.0802	.0693	.0600	.0520
18	.4936	.4155	.3503	.2959	.2502	.2120	.1799	.1528	.1300	.1108	.0946	.0808	.0691	.0592	.0508	.0437
19	.4746	.3957	.3305	.2765	.2317	.1945	.1635	.1377	.1161	.0981	.0829	.0703	.0596	.0506	.0431	.0367
20	.4564	.3769	.3118	.2584	.2145	.1784	.1486	.1240	.1037	.0868	.0728	.0611	.0514	.0433	.0365	.0308
21	.4388	.3589	.2942	.2415	.1987	.1637	.1351	.1117	.0926	.0768	.0638	.0531	.0443	.0370	.0309	.0259
22	.4220	.3418	.2775	.2257	.1839	.1502	.1228	.1007	.0826	.0680	.0560	.0462	.0382	.0316	.0262	.0218
23	.4057	.3256	.2618	.2109	.1703	.1378	.1117	.0907	.0738	.0601	.0491	.0402	.0329	.0270	.0222	.0183
24	.3901	.3101	.2470	.1971	.1577	.1264	.1015	.0817	.0659	.0532	.0431	.0349	.0284	.0231	.0188	.0154
25	.3751	.2953	.2330	.1842	.1460	.1160	.0923	.0736	.0588	.0471	.0378	.0304	.0245	.0197	.0160	.0129
30	.3083	.2314	.1741	.1314	.0994	.0754	.0573	.0437	.0334	.0256	.0196	.0151	.0116	.0090	.0070	.0054
35	.2534	.1813	.1301	.0937	.0676	.0490	.0356	.0259	.0189	.0139	.0102	.0075	.0055	.0041	.0030	.0023
40	.2083	.1420	.0972	.0668	.0460	.0318	.0221	.0154	.0107	.0075	.0053	.0037	.0026	.0019	.0013	.0010
45	.1712	.1113	.0727	.0476	.0313	.0207	.0137	.0091	.0061	.0041	.0027	.0019	.0013	.0009	.0006	.0004
50	.1407	.0872	.0543	.0339	.0213	.0134	.0085	.0054	.0035	.0022	.0014	.0009	.0006	.0004	.0003	.0002

(continued)

(TABLE A–3 continued)

t/r	20%	21%	22%	23%	24%	25%	26%	28%	30%	32%	34%	36%	38%	40%	45%	50%
1	.8333	.8264	.8197	.8130	.8065	.8000	.7937	.7813	.7692	.7576	.7463	.7353	.7246	.7143	.6897	.6667
2	.6944	.6830	.6719	.6610	.6504	.6400	.6299	.6104	.5917	.5739	.5569	.5409	.5251	.5102	.4756	.4444
3	.5787	.5645	.5507	.5374	.5245	.5120	.4999	.4768	.4552	.4348	.4156	.3975	.3805	.3644	.3280	.2963
4	.4823	.4665	.4514	.4369	.4230	.4069	.3968	.3725	.3501	.3294	.3102	.2923	.2757	.2603	.2262	.1975
5	.4019	.3855	.3700	.3552	.3411	.3277	.3149	.2910	.2693	.2495	.2315	.2149	.1998	.1859	.1560	.1317
6	.3349	.3186	.3033	.2888	.2751	.2621	.2499	.2274	.2072	.1890	.1727	.1580	.1448	.1328	.1076	.0878
7	.2791	.2633	.2486	.2348	.2218	.2097	.1983	.1776	.1594	.1432	.1289	.1162	.1049	.0949	.0742	.0585
8	.2326	.2176	.2038	.1909	.1789	.1678	.1574	.1388	.1226	.1085	.0962	.0854	.0760	.0678	.0512	.0390
9	.1938	.1799	.1670	.1552	.1443	.1342	.1249	.1084	.0943	.0822	.0718	.0628	.0551	.0484	.0353	.0260
10	.1615	.1486	.1369	.1262	.1164	.1074	.0992	.0847	.0725	.0623	.0536	.0462	.0399	.0346	.0243	.0173
11	.1346	.1228	.1122	.1026	.0938	.0859	.0787	.0662	.0558	.0472	.0400	.0340	.0289	.0247	.0168	.0116
12	.1122	.1015	.0920	.0834	.0757	.0687	.0625	.0517	.0429	.0357	.0298	.0250	.0210	.0176	.0116	.0077
13	.0935	.0839	.0754	.0678	.0610	.0550	.0496	.0404	.0330	.0271	.0223	.0184	.0152	.0126	.0080	.0051
14	.0779	.0693	.0618	.0551	.0492	.0440	.0393	.0316	.0254	.0205	.0166	.0135	.0110	.0090	.0055	.0034
15	.0649	.0573	.0507	.0448	.0397	.0352	.0312	.0247	.0195	.0155	.0124	.0099	.0080	.0064	.0038	.0023
16	.0541	.0474	.0415	.0364	.0320	.0281	.0248	.0193	.0150	.0118	.0093	.0073	.0058	.0046	.0026	.0015
17	.0451	.0391	.0340	.0296	.0258	.0225	.0197	.0150	.0116	.0089	.0069	.0054	.0042	.0033	.0018	.0010
18	.0376	.0323	.0279	.0241	.0208	.0180	.0156	.0118	.0089	.0068	.0052	.0039	.0030	.0023	.0012	.0007
19	.0313	.0267	.0229	.0196	.0168	.0144	.0124	.0092	.0068	.0051	.0038	.0029	.0022	.0017	.0009	.0005
20	.0261	.0221	.0187	.0159	.0135	.0115	.0098	.0072	.0053	.0039	.0029	.0021	.0016	.0012	.0006	.0003
21	.0217	.0183	.0154	.0129	.0109	.0092	.0078	.0056	.0040	.0029	.0021	.0016	.0012	.0009	.0004	.0002
22	.0181	.0151	.0126	.0105	.0088	.0074	.0062	.0044	.0031	.0022	.0016	.0012	.0008	.0006	.0003	.0001
23	.0151	.0125	.0103	.0086	.0071	.0059	.0049	.0034	.0024	.0017	.0012	.0008	.0006	.0004	.0002	.0001
24	.0126	.0103	.0085	.0070	.0057	.0047	.0039	.0027	.0018	.0013	.0009	.0006	.0004	.0003	.0001	.0001
25	.0105	.0085	.0069	.0057	.0046	.0038	.0031	.0021	.0014	.0010	.0007	.0005	.0003	.0002	.0001	.0000
30	.0042	.0033	.0026	.0020	.0016	.0012	.0010	.0006	.0004	.0002	.0002	.0001	.0001	.0000	.0000	
.35	.0017	.0013	.0009	.0007	.0005	.0004	.0003	.0002	.0001	.0001	.0000	.0000	.0000	.0000	.0000	
40	.0007	.0005	.0004	.0003	.0002	.0001	.0001	.0001	.0000	.0000						
45	.0003	.0002	.0001	.0001	.0001	.0000	.0000	.0000								
50	.0001	.0001	.0000	.0000	.0000											

TABLE A–4 Present Value of an Annuity of $1

$$\frac{1 - \frac{1}{(1 + r)^t}}{r}$$

t/r	4%	5%	6%	7%	8%	9%	10%	11%	12%	13%	14%	15%	16%	17%	18%	19%
1	.9615	.9524	.9434	.9346	.9259	.9174	.9091	.9009	.8929	.8850	.8772	.8696	.8621	.8547	.8475	.8403
2	1.8861	1.8594	1.8334	1.8080	1.7833	1.7591	1.7355	1.7125	1.6901	1.6681	1.6467	1.6257	1.6052	1.5852	1.5656	1.5465
3	2.7751	2.7232	2.6730	2.6243	2.5771	2.5313	2.4869	2.4437	2.4018	2.3612	2.3216	2.2832	2.2459	2.2096	2.1743	2.1399
4	3.6299	3.5460	3.4651	3.3872	3.3121	3.2397	3.1699	3.1024	3.0373	2.9745	2.9137	2.8550	2.7982	2.7432	2.6901	2.6386
5	4.4518	4.3295	4.2124	4.1002	3.9927	3.8897	3.7908	3.6959	3.6048	3.5172	3.4331	3.3522	3.2743	3.1993	3.1272	3.0576
6	5.2421	5.0757	4.9173	4.7665	4.6229	4.4859	4.3553	4.2305	4.1114	3.9975	3.8887	3.7845	3.6847	3.5892	3.4976	3.4098
7	6.0021	5.7864	5.5824	5.3893	5.2064	5.0330	4.8684	4.7122	4.5638	4.4226	4.2883	4.1604	4.0386	3.9224	3.8115	3.7057
8	6.7327	6.4632	6.2098	5.9713	5.7465	5.5348	5.3349	5.1461	4.9676	4.7988	4.6389	4.4873	4.3436	4.2072	4.0776	3.9544
9	7.4353	7.1078	6.8017	6.5152	6.2469	5.9952	5.7590	5.5370	5.3282	5.1317	4.9464	4.7716	4.6065	4.4506	4.3030	4.1633
10	8.1109	7.7217	7.3601	7.0236	6.7101	6.4177	6.1446	5.8892	5.6502	5.4262	5.2161	5.0188	4.8332	4.6586	4.4941	4.3389
11	8.7605	8.3064	7.8869	7.4987	7.1390	6.8052	6.4951	6.2065	5.9377	5.6869	5.4527	5.2337	5.0286	4.8364	4.6560	4.4865
12	9.3851	8.8633	8.3838	7.9427	7.5361	7.1607	6.8137	6.4924	6.1944	5.9176	5.6603	5.4206	5.1971	4.9884	4.7932	4.6105
13	9.9856	9.3936	8.8527	8.3577	7.9038	7.4869	7.1034	6.7499	6.4235	6.1218	5.8424	5.5831	5.3423	5.1183	4.0095	4.7147
14	10.5631	9.8986	9.2950	8.7455	8.2442	7.7862	7.3667	6.9819	6.6282	6.3025	6.0021	5.7245	5.4675	5.2293	5.0081	4.8023
15	11.1184	10.3797	9.7122	9.1079	8.5595	8.0607	7.6061	7.1909	6.8109	6.4624	6.1422	5.8474	5.5755	5.3242	5.0916	4.8759
16	11.6523	10.8378	10.1059	9.4466	8.8514	8.3126	7.8237	7.3792	6.9740	6.6039	6.2651	5.9542	5.6685	5.4053	5.1624	4.9377
17	12.1657	11.2741	10.4773	9.7632	9.1216	8.5436	8.0216	7.5488	7.1196	6.7291	6.3729	6.0472	5.7487	5.4746	5.2223	4.9897
18	12.6593	11.6896	10.8276	10.0591	9.3719	8.7556	8.2014	7.7016	7.2497	6.8399	6.4674	6.1280	5.8178	5.5339	5.2732	5.0333
19	13.1339	12.0853	11.1581	10.3356	9.6036	8.9501	8.3649	7.8393	7.3658	6.9380	6.5504	6.1982	5.8775	5.5845	5.3162	5.0700
20	13.5903	12.4622	11.4699	10.5940	9.8181	9.1285	8.5136	7.9633	7.4694	7.0248	6.6231	6.2593	5.9288	5.6278	5.3527	5.1009
21	14.0292	12.8212	11.7641	10.8355	10.0168	9.2922	8.6487	8.0751	7.5620	7.1016	6.6870	6.3125	5.9731	5.6648	5.3837	5.1268
22	14.4511	13.1630	12.0416	11.0612	10.2007	9.4424	8.7715	8.1757	7.6446	7.1695	6.7429	6.3587	6.0113	5.6964	5.4099	5.1486
23	14.8568	13.4886	12.3034	11.2722	10.3711	9.5802	8.8832	8.2664	7.7184	7.2297	6.7921	6.3988	6.0442	5.7234	5.4321	5.1668
24	15.2470	13.7906	12.5504	11.4693	10.5288	9.7066	8.9847	8.3481	7.7843	7.2829	6.8351	6.4338	6.0726	5.7465	5.4509	5.1822
25	15.6221	14.0939	12.7834	11.6536	10.6748	9.8226	9.0770	8.4217	7.8431	7.3300	6.8729	6.4641	6.0971	5.7662	5.4669	5.1951
30	17.2920	15.3725	13.7648	12.4090	11.2578	10.2737	9.4269	8.6938	8.0552	7.4957	7.0027	6.5660	6.1772	5.8294	5.5168	5.2347
35	18.6646	16.3742	14.4982	12.9477	11.6546	10.5668	9.6442	8.8552	8.1755	7.5856	7.0700	6.6166	6.2153	5.8582	5.5306	5.2512
40	19.7928	17.1591	15.0463	13.3317	11.9246	10.7574	9.7791	8.9511	8.2438	7.6344	7.1050	6.6418	6.2335	5.8713	5.5482	5.2582
45	20.7200	17.7741	15.4558	13.6055	12.1084	10.8812	9.8628	9.0079	8.2825	7.6609	7.1232	6.6543	6.2421	5.8773	5.5523	5.2611
50	21.4822	18.2559	15.7619	13.8007	12.2335	10.9617	9.9148	9.0417	8.3045	7.6752	7.1327	6.6605	6.2463	5.8801	5.5541	5.2623

(continued)

(TABLE A–4 *continued*)

t/r	20%	21%	22%	23%	24%	25%	26%	28%	30%	32%	34%	36%	38%	40%	45%	50%
1	.8333	.8264	.8197	.8130	.8065	.8000	.7937	.7812	.7692	.7576	.7463	.7353	.7246	.7143	.6897	.6667
2	1.5278	1.5095	1.4915	1.4740	1.4568	1.4400	1.4235	1.3916	1.3609	1.3315	1.3032	1.2760	1.2497	1.2245	1.1653	1.1111
3	2.1065	2.0739	2.0422	2.0114	1.9813	1.9520	1.9234	1.8684	1.8161	1.7663	1.7188	1.6735	1.6302	1.5889	1.4933	1.4074
4	2.5887	2.5404	2.4936	2.4483	2.4043	2.3616	2.3203	2.2410	2.1662	2.0957	2.0290	1.9658	1.9060	1.8492	1.7195	1.6049
5	2.9906	2.9260	2.8636	2.8035	2.7454	2.6893	2.6351	2.5320	2.4356	2.3452	2.2604	2.1807	2.1058	2.0352	1.8755	1.7366
6	3.3255	3.2446	3.1669	3.0923	3.0205	2.9514	2.8850	2.7594	2.6427	2.5342	2.4331	2.3388	2.2506	2.1680	1.9831	1.8244
7	3.6046	3.5079	3.4155	3.3270	3.2423	3.1611	3.0833	2.9370	2.8021	2.6775	2.5620	2.4550	2.3555	2.2628	2.0573	1.8829
8	3.8372	3.7256	3.6193	3.5179	3.4212	3.3289	3.2407	3.0758	2.9247	2.7860	2.6582	2.5404	2.4315	2.3306	2.1085	1.9220
9	4.0310	3.9054	3.7863	3.6731	3.5655	3.4631	3.3657	3.1842	3.0190	2.8681	2.7300	2.6033	2.4866	2.3790	2.1438	1.9480
10	4.1925	4.0541	3.9232	3.7993	3.6819	3.5705	3.4648	3.2689	3.0915	2.9304	2.7836	2.6495	2.5265	2.4136	2.1681	1.9653
11	4.3271	4.1769	4.0354	3.9018	3.7757	3.6564	3.5435	3.3351	3.1473	2.9776	2.8236	2.6834	2.5555	2.4383	2.1849	1.9769
12	4.4392	4.2784	4.1274	3.9852	3.8514	3.7251	3.6059	3.3868	3.1903	3.0133	2.8534	2.7084	2.5764	2.4559	2.1965	1.9846
13	4.5327	4.3624	4.2028	4.0530	3.9124	3.7801	3.6555	3.4272	3.2233	3.0404	2.8757	2.7268	2.5916	2.4685	2.2045	1.9897
14	4.6106	4.4317	4.2646	4.1082	3.9616	3.8241	3.6949	3.4587	3.2487	3.0609	2.8923	2.7403	2.6026	2.4775	2.2100	1.9931
15	4.6755	4.4890	4.3152	4.1530	4.0013	3.8593	3.7261	3.4834	3.2682	3.0764	2.9047	2.7502	2.6106	2.4839	2.2138	1.9954
16	4.7296	4.5364	4.3567	4.1894	4.0333	3.8874	3.7509	3.5026	3.2832	3.0882	2.9140	2.7575	2.6164	2.4885	2.2164	1.9970
17	4.7746	4.5755	4.3908	4.2190	4.0591	3.9099	3.7705	3.5177	3.2948	3.0971	2.9209	2.7629	2.6206	2.4918	2.2182	1.9980
18	4.8122	4.6079	4.4187	4.2431	4.0799	3.9279	3.7861	3.5294	3.3037	3.1039	2.9260	2.7668	2.6236	2.4941	2.2195	1.9986
19	4.8435	4.6346	4.4415	4.2627	4.0967	3.9424	3.7985	3.5386	3.3105	3.1090	2.9299	2.7697	2.6258	2.4958	2.2203	1.9991
20	4.8696	4.6567	4.4603	4.2786	4.1103	3.9539	3.8083	3.5458	3.3158	3.1129	2.9327	2.7718	2.6274	2.4970	2.2209	1.9994
21	4.8913	4.6750	4.4756	4.2916	4.1212	3.9631	3.8161	3.5514	3.3198	3.1158	2.9349	2.7734	2.6285	2.4979	2.2213	1.9996
22	4.9094	4.6900	4.4882	4.3021	4.1300	3.9705	3.8223	3.5558	3.3230	3.1180	2.9365	2.7746	2.6294	2.4985	2.2216	1.9997
23	4.9245	4.7025	4.4985	4.3106	4.1371	3.9764	3.8273	3.5592	3.3254	3.1197	2.9377	2.7754	2.6300	2.4989	2.2218	1.9998
24	4.9371	4.7128	4.5070	4.3176	4.1428	3.9811	3.8312	3.5619	3.3272	3.1210	2.9386	2.7760	2.6304	2.4992	2.2219	1.9999
25	4.9476	4.7213	4.5139	4.3232	4.1474	3.9849	3.8342	3.5640	3.3286	3.1220	2.9392	2.7765	2.6307	2.4994	2.2220	1.9999
30	4.9789	4.7463	4.5338	4.3391	4.1601	3.9950	3.8424	3.5693	3.3321	3.1242	2.9407	2.7775	2.6314	2.4999	2.2222	2.0000
35	4.9915	4.7559	4.5411	4.3447	4.1644	3.9984	3.8450	3.5708	3.3330	3.1248	2.9411	2.7777	2.6315	2.5000	2.2222	2.0000
40	4.9966	4.7596	4.5439	4.3467	4.1659	3.9995	3.8458	3.5712	3.3332	3.1250	2.9412	2.7778	2.6316	2.5000	2.2222	2.0000
45	4.9986	4.7610	4.5449	4.3474	4.1664	3.9998	3.8460	3.5714	3.3333	3.1250	2.9412	2.7778	2.6316	2.5000	2.2222	2.0000
50	4.9995	4.7616	4.5452	4.3477	4.1666	3.9999	3.8461	3.5714	3.3333	3.1250	2.9412	2.7778	2.6316	2.5000	2.2222	2.0000

TABLE A–5 Present Value of ACRS Tax Shield

Discount Rate	*Five-Year Assets*	*Seven-Year Assets*
.08	.8113	.7662
.10	.7732	.7215
.12	.7381	.6810
.13	.7215	.6622
.14	.7055	.6442
.15	.6901	.6270
.16	.6753	.6106
.18	.6472	.5799
.20	.6211	.5517
.22	.5967	.5258
.25	.5631	.4907

Using Table A–5. Find the factor for the appropriate ACRS life and discount rate. Multiply that factor by the cost of the asset multiplied by the income tax rate. For example, for a \$500,000 asset that qualifies for five-year treatment, 35 percent tax rate, and 12 percent discount rate, \$500,000 × .35 × .7381 gives \$129,168. Table A–5 gives the sums of the ACRS percentages multiplied by the present value factors for each year during which depreciation is taken. Thus, the five-year factor at 10 percent is (rounded): (.20 × .9091) + (.32 × .8264) + (.192 × .7513) + (.115 × .6830) + (.115 × .6209) + (.058 × .5645).

Appendix B

GUIDELINES FOR CASE AND MEMORANDUM PREPARATION

INTRODUCTION

Cases and expanded problems are a way to include more real-world issues and problems in a course. They can be broad and include general, strategic issues, or they can be focused and deal with a specific problem at hand. When we discuss these cases or expanded problems, we can develop and integrate the ideas that are introduced in the text and/or other readings. Oral analysis in class, coupled with written presentation, helps develop analytical thinking skills and oral and written communication skills.

These guidelines deal with two types of written assignments: a classic written case presentation and a shorter memorandum to management. These two differ in format and possibly in perspective.

Cases

Cases deal with one or more issues, usually contain several pages of information, and require you to present an in-depth analysis several pages long. You may be asked to respond to a case as a neutral third party (i.e., a student) writing to another neutral third party (i.e., your instructor), or you may be asked to assume the role of a consultant or a member of management writing to a particular audience in the company (e.g., the president, the plant manager, and so on). Assignments will specify your role and your audience.

Memoranda

Shorter assignments (e.g., textbook problems) provide an opportunity to develop skills in communicating with management in mostly single-issue settings. The background material is usually shorter than case material. You will write memoranda from the perspective of either a consultant or a member of management writing to a particular audience in the company (as explained above). Assignments will specify your role and your audience.

Various instructors have specific requirements for case analysis and presentation or memorandum formats; this is a general guideline. If your instructor wants to deviate from this guideline, he or she will tell you so.

BASIC REQUIREMENTS

Microcomputers and Word Processing

You are expected to be familiar with microcomputers and at least one word processing package. Microcomputers give you the ability to draft, redraft, and edit your material. You are required to use microcomputers for all cases and memoranda.

Writing Skills

What you present and how you present it are intertwined. This is how you are evaluated in the workplace. You are expected to possess basic English skills. You must write and think clearly, present your information in an organized format, keep your audience's needs firmly in mind, use correct grammar, spelling, sentence and paragraph structure, reference citation, and so on. You might purchase the most recent edition of a style book such as the *Harbrace College Handbook* with MLA documentation style. You might also use the writing laboratories on campus.

Background Knowledge

You are expected to possess basic knowledge about American business in general. You should regularly read *The Wall Street Journal*, a major business magazine, and a national news magazine. If appropriate, use the library to gain background information about a particular company and/or industry.

Definition of Purpose

Make certain that you understand your purpose for each writing task. Clarify your role and clarify your audience. If you are uncertain of the purpose behind writing a case or memo, ask your instructor for clarification.

Audience Analysis

No writing assignment can be successfully completed without defining and analyzing your audience. Ask yourself these questions: Who will be reading this? What is my relationship with the reader(s)? What do my readers know about the subject? Do my readers have strong feelings about this subject? By answering these questions, you will gain an audience profile that will help shape what you say and how you say it.

Analysis versus Restatement

Many students confuse analysis with restatement. Restatement is a summary of the facts in a situation. An analysis involves critical thinking and requires that you go beyond the facts to answer the following questions: What is the ramification of this information? How does this information affect the present or future situation? What impact does this information have on my audience? By answering these questions, you are performing an analysis. All memoranda and cases require analysis; mere restatement is insufficient.

Names and Abbreviations

Names of individuals and companies should first be stated in full. Do not substitute "Co." for "Company," "Incorporated" for "Inc.," or make any change in the name of a company. Define your abbreviations. For example, you could state, "In 1989, the situation at Federal Paper, Inc. (Federal) involved . . ." From that point, you could refer to the company as Federal. Once you have defined an abbreviation, use it consistently. The first time that names are used they should be stated in full. If you want to abbreviate an individual's name, use the last name (e.g., Smith for Robin Smith) or use Ms. Smith. Your perspective will dictate how formal or informal to be with names.

Supporting Schedules

All supporting schedules, exhibits, graphs, and tables must be properly labeled and referred to in your analysis. Supporting materials that include numbers can be called exhibits or tables. Graphic material should be referred to as figures. Exhibits and/or figures should be numbered in the order that they are referred to in the paper. When you refer to a specific exhibit, refer to it as "Exhibit 1," not "exhibit 1." All exhibits, tables, or figures must have a heading that describes their content as well as an exhibit, table, or figure number identifying order of presentation.

You are encouraged to generate material that would be useful for exhibits and/or figures by using programs such as Lotus 1-2-3, graphics packages, a regression package, or a linear programming package. However, be selective in what you include in an exhibit or figure. Consider your audience, role, and task; carefully format your exhibits, make sure they are properly titled, and provide appropriate references to sources. Finally, make sure all abbreviations are defined.

Use of Jargon

Make sure you get specific instructions from your instructor regarding the use of jargon (topic- or industry-specific terminology) and the inclusion of background information. You should be able to present your analyses without jargon, buzz words, or cliches.

Environmental Constraints

Each set of problems has some constraints imposed by the internal and external environments of the situation. You should clearly state these constraints. They may limit how you present your analysis, what problems you are supposed to address, and what information is available, to name a few.

CASES

A case is a glimpse of a real-world situation where you are limited in what you know by the information contained in a few pages. Sometimes the case issues are clear, and sometimes they are not. However, you can see what problems are emerging and the kinds of decisions needed to solve these problems. The lack of complete information is not an excuse for avoiding dealing with the case issues.

Reading the Case

First, read and reread the case. Get an overall understanding of the situation and supporting facts. When you reread the case, take notes about key facts, assumptions, and issues. Outline appropriate analytical techniques to help you gain additional information (e.g., net present value analysis, simple or multiple linear regression, and linear programming). Look at existing quantitative information to see if it is accurate, consistent, and well presented. Look at the case questions (if any), and formulate an idea about how to approach your analysis.

In reading the case, avoid rushing to a conclusion. If you do, you might overlook important information or distort information to fit a preconceived idea. Second, be sure that you fully understand the case before you try to work on appropriate numerical analysis. Third, differentiate between facts, estimates, and assumptions or suppositions.

As you read, ask yourself a broad range of questions: What are the problems and opportunities here? What information given will aid you in solving these problems? What information is lacking? What is going on here? Why are these problems still unsolved? What is happening among the people in this company? When you use an appropriate analytical technique, what will you learn? How sensitive is your analysis to changes? How probable are these changes? What assumptions and/or estimates do you have to make?

You should be very careful not to confuse the basic problem with its symptoms. For example, a decline in sales is probably a symptom of a problem and not the problem per se. Make sure you understand what background information is called for. Depending on the case, you might have to discuss factors inside the organization (management team, marketing issues, finances, etc.) and outside the organization (industry makeup, foreign competition, economic conditions, government regulations, etc.). The more a problem is related to strategic planning issues, the more it will be important to identify the strengths and weaknesses of a firm in relation to its internal and external environment.

In analyzing and planning how to respond to a case, do not be limited by the specific questions asked. Do not feel bound to address specific questions in a lockstep manner. Remember that a case should be used as a springboard for any relevant issues that can usefully be brought into the analysis. Also remember that you will be writing this response after having done all the supporting analysis. Thus, there should be a feeling of integration about your presentation. For example, if there are four sequential parts to a case, your answers to part 1 should not be presented as if you had not read and solved parts 2, 3, and 4.

Since a case extends the text in many instances, do not expect that you can always find specific text references or techniques for your analysis or solution. You might have to integrate ideas and/or techniques from several sources.

Form and Format Guidelines

Perspective of Writer and Reader Make your perspective clear and consistent. Are you writing a formal paper with all references in the third person? Is your approach from the perspective of a member of management or as a consultant? Who is your audience? Is it your instructor, as a neutral third person, or a specific member of the management of a company involved in the case?

If you are writing a formal paper (sometimes referred to as a classic case presentation), take the detached role of a person observing the information and problem(s) who is analyzing and commenting on appropriate issues. Your audience is another person who is detached from the situation. Instructions should be clear about how much information your audience requires (how much is known background information and how much you should explain and/or summarize).

If you are writing from the perspective of an outside consultant hired by the company or a member of management of a company, you are working with management to deal with appropriate issues. The case instructions or specific instructions from your instructor will let you know what perspective to take and your audience. Knowing your audience should help you decide how much background information or explanation is appropriate.

Headings Headings help to form transitions between sections and help the reader know where you are going. In addition, they provide a good framework for your analysis and can help you write a more organized paper. You are expected to use appropriate headings.

General Writing Guidelines

The following guidelines for case presentation should be amended depending on your assigned perspective (neutral, consultant, member of management) and instructions from your instructor.

Executive Summary Some instructors want a paper to start with an executive summary in which, in about one page, you summarize your recommendation(s), basic findings (problems and pertinent information), and necessary explanations. This section should be brief and to the point. A statement of the problem and identification of alternate courses of action can follow this summary.

Beginning/Introduction The introduction to your analysis should include a statement of the problem(s) you have identified. You should state how you have approached the analysis and solution to the case problems and what you have identified as alternate courses of action. If you employ quantitative techniques, justify their use. List the decisions you need to make and whether they are dependent and/or sequential. If you have made assumptions and/or estimates, state them clearly and justify them. If there is information that you deem relevant, call attention to that fact. Finally, include a brief summary of the conclusions you have reached (including actions recommended). Make sure that you demonstrate the specific evidence in the case to support your position. In addition, some instructors want you to summarize relevant background information, while others want you to assume that the reader is familiar with the case material.

The introduction sets the tone for what follows. Make sure that you build a sufficient foundation regarding the problems or issues, the facts, your approaches, and so on. Make sure it is clear to the reader what you are doing and why.

Middle/Analysis This is the heart of the paper, where you present your analysis and how you formed conclusions. What criteria are you using to select a course of action? What are the results of your analysis? Make sure to support your analysis. Do not make assertions without evidence or argument to support them. Here is where you need to spend the greatest amount of time and space. Your conclusions and recommendations should be clear and logically follow your analysis. Finally, there must be a way to measure the consequences of your recommendations. Therefore, this section should do the following:

1. Identify and explain viable courses of action open to the organization or the individual in the case. Not all such courses of action may be explicitly delineated in the case.
2. Clearly explain the criteria that will be used to select the final course of action. If criteria are mentioned in the case, you should evaluate them and justify their use. If no criteria are presented, you should develop realistic and applicable criteria through your analysis of case information and examination of secondary sources.
3. Select a course of action and identify step-by-step how it will be implemented. If it is appropriate, assign detailed duties and responsibilities to specific individuals. Establish a time table. Be as complete as possible with your plan.
4. Discuss means to measure the consequences of your recommendation(s). Establish standards by which the success or failure of your proposed course of action should be judged. If realistic in terms of the case, establish a system of rewards (positive and negative) for named individuals or officials based upon the standards and objectives you set.

You should build a logical presentation, integrating several ideas and issues within this section. Organization and the use of headings is very important. Everything should flow in a logical order; it should be clear how you have come to your conclusions and why you have made particular choices.

End/Conclusion Your ending section should summarize the solutions to the problems you defined in the introduction. If there are unanswered problems, name them and what you would do to resolve them. Give whatever recommendations you have. This final section should bring everything together in a natural end to the paper. There should be no surprises or new material; everything should continue logically from the previous sections and must be fully supported by discussion and facts presented prior to the conclusion.

MEMORANDA TO MANAGEMENT

Some assignments require you to write a memorandum to management about a specific problem. In most instances, such memoranda will be shorter and more focused than case analyses and presentations. The general guidelines above regarding names, headings, supporting schedules, jargon, and environmental constraints also apply to memoranda. In addition, other things to consider include:

1. Use proper memo format, including a heading, to whom the memo is addressed, who wrote the memo, the date, and the subject. Make sure to align names (see below). Also see that your name appears on the

memo so you can receive credit! See the illustration of memorandum format that follows.

2. Be direct and to the point. Do not use fancy words, and avoid jargon as much as possible. Define your audience and make sure that you provide information in an understandable way. If you were the person you are addressing, how would you want information presented to you?
3. Make your purpose clear. Executives are busy. If you do not grab their attention and hold it, they will scan your report with little interest or throw it away. Make it clear what response you would like from the reader.
4. Use opening of memo to establish a link between what you have been asked to do and your report (memo). At the end of the memo, tie things together and end in a way that the reader feels good about your work and knows you are available to answer additional questions. Set the stage for future work/assignments.

Illustration of Memorandum Format

MEMORANDUM

To: John Jones, Sales Manager
From: Mary Smith, XYZ Consulting Company
Date: January 19, 1991
Subject: Analysis of Current Planning Issues

John, this memo is in response to your request for us to analyze your current performance evaluation procedures. We believe you will be pleased with the results of our work. First of all, we see the following issues to resolve: . . . .

Appendix C

SELECTED REFERENCES

In addition to the books and articles referenced in the relevant chapters, the following sources might provide more extensive treatment of particular topics.

ANTHONY, ROBERT N., John Dearden, and Norton M. Bedford, *Management Control Systems*, 5th edition, (Homewood, IL: Richard D. Irwin, Inc., 1984)

ANTHONY, ROBERT N., *The Management Control Function* (Boston: Harvard Business School Press, 1988.)

BENNETT, ROBERT E., James A. Hendricks, David E. Keys, and Edward J. Rudnicki, *Cost Accounting for Factory Automation* (Montvale, NJ: National Association of Accountants, 1987.)

BERLINER, CALLIE, and James A. Brimson, eds, *Cost Management for Today's Advanced Manufacturing: The CAM-I Conceptual Design* (Boston: Harvard Business School Press, 1988.)

CAPETTINI, ROBERT and Donald K. Clancy, Editors, *Cost Accounting, Robotics, and the New Manufacturing Environment* (Sarasota: American Accounting Association, 1987.)

CLARK, JOHN C., Thomas J. Hindelang, and Robert E. Pritchard, *Capital Budgeting*, 3rd edition (Englewood Cliffs, NJ: Prentice-Hall, Inc., 1989)

GOLDRATT, ELIYAHU M., and Robert E. Fox, *The Race* (Croton-on-Hudson, NY: North River Press, 1986)

GOLDRATT, ELIYAHU M., and Jeff Cox, *The Goal: A Process of Ongoing Improvement* (Croton-on-Hudson, NY: North River Press, 1986)

HOWELL, ROBERT A., James D. Brown, Stephen R. Soucy, and Allen H. Seed, III, *Management Accounting in the New Manufacturing Environment* (Montvale, NJ: National Association of Accountants, 1987.)

JOHNSON, H. THOMAS, and Robert S. Kaplan, *Relevance Lost: The Rise and Fall of Management Accounting* (Boston: Harvard Business School Press, 1987.)

LEE, JOHN Y., *Managerial Accounting Changes for the 1990s* (Artesia, CA: McKay Business Systems, 1987.)

MCNAIR, CAROL J., William Mosconi, and Thomas Norris, *Meeting the Technology Challenge: Cost Accounting in a JIT Environment* (Montvale, NJ: National Association of Accountants, 1988.)

MERCHANT, KENNETH A., *Rewarding Results: Motivating Profit Center Managers* (Boston, Harvard Business School Press, 1989.)

NATIONAL ASSOCIATION OF ACCOUNTANTS, *Cost Accounting for the '90s: The Challenge of Technological Change—Conference Proceedings* (Montvale, NJ: National Association of Accountants, 1986.)

SHANK, JOHN K., and Vijay Govindarajan, *Strategic Cost Analysis: The Evolution from Managerial to Strategic Accounting* (Homewood, Illinois, Richard D. Irwin, Inc., 1989.)

Index

A

D

K

L

S

T

W

Y

Z